Child Development

Risk and Opportunity

Murray Krantz
Florida State University

Wadsworth Publishing Company

Belmont, California
A Division of Wadsworth, Inc.

Development Editor: John Boykin
Editorial Assistant: Kate Peltier
Production Editor: Karen Garrison
Managing Designer: Ann Butler
Print Buyer: Barbara Britton
Art Editor: Kelly Murphy
Permissions Editor: Jeanne Bosschart
Designer: Design Office/Peter Martin
Copy Editor: Jennifer Gordon
Photo Researcher: Christine Pullo
Technical Illustrator: Lotus Art
Illustrators: Barbara Barnett and Diana Thewlis
Compositor: Thompson Type
Cover: Design Office/Peter Martin
Cover Photography: © Jennifer L. Sauer
Signing Representative: Mark Francisco
Printer: Rand McNally/Taunton

International Thomson Publishing
The trademark ITP is used under license.

Printed in the United States of America

1 2 3 4 5 6 7 8 9 10 — 98 97 96 95 94

Library of Congress Cataloging-in-Publication Data

Krantz, Murray, 1943–
     Child development : risk and opportunity / Murray Krantz.
          p.   cm.
     Includes bibliographical references and index.
     ISBN 0-534-13170-0
     1. Child development.   I. Title.
HQ767.9.K73   1993
     305.23'1—dc20   93-30939

BRIEF CONTENTS

Part One Foundations 1

Chapter 1 Introduction 2
Chapter 2 Theories of Child Development 13
Chapter 3 Research in Child Development 41

Part Two Pregnancy and Birth 63

Chapter 4 Prenatal Development and Genetics 65
Chapter 5 Birth and the Newborn 103

Part Three Infancy 137

Chapter 6 Perceptual and Physical Development in Infancy 138
Chapter 7 Cognitive and Language Development in Infancy 176
Chapter 8 Emotional and Social Development in Infancy 209

Part Four Early Childhood 253

Chapter 9 Physical and Motor Development in Early Childhood 254
Chapter 10 Cognitive and Language Development in Early Childhood 288
Chapter 11 Social and Emotional Development in Early Childhood 329

Part Five Middle Childhood 369

Chapter 12 Physical Development and Disability in Middle Childhood 370
Chapter 13 Cognitive Development and Schooling in Middle Childhood 395
Chapter 14 Social and Emotional Development in Middle Childhood 436

Part Six Adolescence 471

Chapter 15 Physical and Cognitive Development in Adolescence 472
Chapter 16 Social and Emotional Development in Adolescence 506

Glossary 540
References 554
Author Index 589
Subject Index 600

PART ONE

Foundations

Chapter 1 Introduction   2

The Concept of Development   3

Development Is Gradual   3

Development Is Cumulative   3

Developmental Change Is Relatively Permanent   4

Development Is Transactional   4

Development Takes Place in an Ecosystem   5

Risk and Opportunity   6

Coping with Risk   8

Facilitating Development   9

The Uniqueness of Child Development   10

Key Terms   12

Chapter 2 Theories of Child Development   13

The Role of Theory in Understanding Child Development   14

Issues in the Study of Development   16

Psychoanalytic Theory   18

Freud's Psychoanalytic Theory   19

Erikson's Psychosocial Theory of Development   21

Critique of Psychoanalytic Theory   23

Learning Theory   23

Operant Learning   25

BOX 2.1 Operant Learning in Practical Settings: A Critique   26

Social Cognitive Theory   27

Critique of Social Cognitive Theory   28

Piaget's Cognitive-Developmental Theory   **29**

The Active Nature of the Child   **30**

Mental Structures and Adaptation   **30**

Stages of Cognitive Development   **31**

Critique of Cognitive-Developmental Theory   **33**

Information Processing Theory   **34**

Components of an Information Processing System   **35**

The Development of Information Processing   **36**

Critique of Information Processing Theory   **36**

Ethological Theory   **37**

Critique of Ethological Theory   **39**

The Theories in Perspective   **40**

Key Terms   **40**

Chapter 3   Research in Child Development   **41**

The Scientific Study of Child Development   **42**

The Scientific Method   **42**

The Research Process: A Simulation   **43**

The Research Topic: Third-Party Entry   **44**

CAREERS: The Research Scientist   **45**

Formulating the Research Problem   **46**

Gathering Evidence   **48**

BOX 3.1   Data-Gathering Methods with Children   **49**

Design of the Study   **51**

BOX 3.2   Reading Published Research: Consumer Beware!   **55**

Reporting Research Findings   **56**

Access to Scholarly Research on Children   **57**

Ethical Considerations in Research with Children   **58**

Looking Back   **60**

Chapter Review   **60**

Key Terms   **61**

PART TWO

Pregnancy and Birth

Chapter 4 Prenatal Development and Genetics   65

Conception   66

The Woman's Reproductive System   66

The Man's Reproductive System   67

Infertility   67

Prenatal Development   70

The Period of the Zygote   70

The Period of the Embryo   71

The Period of the Fetus   72

Environmental Influences on Prenatal Development   74

Teratogens   74

Maternal Diseases as Teratogens   80

Maternal Stress During Pregnancy   82

Maternal Nutrition and Exercise   83

Genetic Influences on Development   85

The Mechanisms of Heredity   85

Sex Chromosomes and Sex Determination   88

Genetic Transmission   89

Dominant-Recessive Inheritance   89

Sex-Linked Inheritance   93

Chromosomal Abnormalities   93

Detecting and Controlling Genetic Disorders   95

Genetic Screening and Genetic Counseling   95

CAREERS: The Genetic Counselor   96

Prenatal Diagnosis   97

Ethical Issues Concerning Prenatal Development   100

Looking Back   101

Chapter Review   101

Key Terms   102

Chapter 5 Birth and the Newborn   103

Preparing for Childbirth   104

When Will the Birth Take Place?   **105**

BOX 5.1 The Birth Plan   **106**

Who Will Facilitate the Birth?   **107**

Where Will the Baby Be Born?   **107**

CAREERS: The Certified Nurse-Midwife   **108**

How Do You Prepare?   **110**

Labor and Childbirth   113

The Stages of Labor   **113**

Medicated Labor   **115**

Monitoring the Baby During Labor   **117**

Dealing with Labor Complications   **119**

BOX 5.2 Resilience and the Birth Process   **121**

The Newborn   122

Evaluating the Newborn's Condition   **123**

Low Birth-Weight Babies   **126**

BOX 5.3 The Resilience of the High-Risk Infant   **129**

CAREERS: The Developmental Specialist   **131**

States and State Regulation in the Neonate   **133**

Infant Sleep and Sleep Cycles   **134**

Looking Back   135

Chapter Review   135

Key Terms   136

PART THREE

Infancy

Chapter 6 Perceptual and Physical Development in Infancy 138

Physical Growth in the First Two Years 140
Changes in Height and Weight 140
Changes in Body Proportion 141
Nutrition in Infancy 142

Development of the Brain 143
The Building Blocks: Neurons and Their Function 143
Structures of the Brain 145
Brain Development and Experience 146
BOX 6.1 Patterning the Human Infant 148

Sensory and Perceptual Development in Infancy 149
How Infant Perception Is Studied 149

The Development of Vision 149
BOX 6.2 The Scientific Study of Infant Perception 150
The Eye 152
Tracking Moving Objects in Space 152
Object Perception 152
Depth Perception: Objects in Three-Dimensional Space 156
BOX 6.3 The Visual Cliff 157

Auditory Perception 158
Early Detection and Discrimination of Sounds 158
Locating Sound Sources 158
BOX 6.4 Talking to the Fetus: Wasted Breath? 159
Perception of Speech Sounds 159

Other Sensory Developments 160
Taste and Smell 160
Touch and Pain 161

Motor Control Development   **161**

    Reflex Behaviors   **161**

    Early Spontaneous Movement   **164**

    Voluntary Control of Movement   **164**

    Motor Control in Transactional Perspective   **169**

    Facilitating Motor Control in Infants   **170**

    BOX 6.5 Facilitating Visually Directed Reaching   **172**

Looking Back   **173**

Chapter Review   **174**

Key Terms   **175**

Chapter 7 Cognitive and Language Development in Infancy   176

Infant Learning   **178**

    Habituation   **178**

    Conditioning   **180**

    Observational Learning   **182**

Early Development of Memory   **184**

    Do Newborns Remember Their Experiences?   **185**

    When Does Long-Term Memory Develop?   **185**

Piaget's View of Infant Cognitive Development   **186**

Substages of the Sensorimotor Period   **188**

    Substage I: The Use of Reflexes (Birth–1 Month)   **188**

    Substage II: Primary Circular Reactions (1–4 Months)   **189**

    Substage III: Secondary Circular Reactions (4–8 Months)   **189**

    Substage IV: The Coordination of Secondary Schemas (8–12 Months)   **192**

    Substage V: Tertiary Circular Reactions (12–18 Months)   **193**

    Substage VI: Inventing New Means Through Mental Combinations (18 Months and Up)   **193**

Language Development in Infancy   **196**

    The Study of Early Language Development   **196**

Theories of Language Development   **197**

    The Learning Explanation of Language Acquisition   **198**

    The Nativist Explanation of Language Acquisition   **200**

The Course of Infant Language Development   **201**

    Prespeech (Birth–10 Months)   **201**

    Naming: The First Word and Beyond (10–18 Months)   **203**

    First Word Combinations (18–22 Months)   **204**

Facilitating Early Language Development   204

Looking Back   206

Chapter Review   206

Key Terms   207

Chapter 8 Emotional and Social Development in Infancy   209

Emotional Development in Infancy   210

Theories of Emotional Development   212

Discrete Emotions Theory   212

Cognitive Emotions Theory   212

Do Infants Feel What We Think They Feel?   214

Emotional Transactions Between Infants and Caregivers   216

Temperament   222

Dimensions of Temperament: The New York Longitudinal Study   223

Temperament and Infant-Parent Relationships: Goodness-of-Fit   225

Culture and Temperament   226

The Development of the Concept of Self   226

Social Development   227

Parents and Newborns: The Bonding Controversy   228

The Development of Attachment Relationships   230

Perspectives on Attachment   231

Phases in the Development of Attachment   234

Variations in Attachment Patterns   236

BOX 8.1 The Strange Situation   237

Explaining Differences in Attachment Patterns   238

BOX 8.2 Strange Behavior in the Strange Situation   239

The Consequences of Attachment Status   241

Attachment and Culture   242

Attachment to the Father   243

Day Care, Attachment, and Emotional Development   246

BOX 8.3 The Business of Infant Day Care   247

CAREERS: The Infant Care Director   249

Looking Back   250

Chapter Review   251

Key Terms   252

PART FOUR

Early Childhood

Chapter 9 Physical and Motor Development in Early Childhood   **254**

Physical Growth During the Preschool Years   256

The Development of Motor Skills   257

Walking, Stair Climbing, and Running   **257**

Jumping and Hopping   **258**

Self-Help: Grooming and Feeding   **259**

Self-Help: Toilet Training   **260**

BOX 9.1 Early Toilet Training: The Digo of East Africa   **260**

Construction Skills   **262**

Physical Fitness   262

Obesity in Preschool Children   **263**

Physical Fitness and Cardiovascular Disease   **265**

Physical Fitness in the Preschool   **265**

BOX 9.2 Promoting Motor Skill Development in Preschoolers   **266**

Minor Childhood Illness   267

Negative Effects of Childhood Illness   **267**

Positive Effects of Childhood Illness   **268**

BOX 9.3 Day Care and Infectious Disease   **269**

Accidental Injury   270

Car Accidents and Restraints   **270**

Children's Psychological Characteristics and Injury   **271**

BOX 9.4 Promoting the Use of Safety Belts by Young Children   **271**

CAREERS: The Child Life Specialist   **272**

Injuries on Playgrounds   **274**

BOX 9.5 Building Developmentally Appropriate Playgrounds   **275**

Stress   275

Maltreatment   277

Causes of Maltreatment   **279**

Maltreated Children   **280**

Maltreating Parents   **281**

The Parent-Child Relationship   **283**

BOX 9.6 The Maternal Deprivation Syndrome   **284**

The Maltreating Family in the Community   **285**

Maltreatment and Culture   **285**

Looking Back   286

Chapter Review   286

Key Terms   287

Chapter 10 Cognitive and Language Development in Early Childhood   288

Cognitive Development in the Preschool Years   290

Piaget's Preoperational Stage   **290**

BOX 10.1 Piaget's Egocentrism: An Opposing View   **295**

Reasoning in Specific Content Domains   **296**

BOX 10.2 Phases of Classification   **299**

BOX 10.3 Five Principles of a Counting System   **302**

Explaining Cognitive Development   **304**

BOX 10.4 Appearance and Reality   **304**

The Information Processing Perspective   **306**

Developing a Theory of Mind   **309**

Language Development in the Preschool Years   311

The Growth of Vocabulary   **312**

Learning the Rules of Grammar   **312**

Communicating with Others   **313**

Private Speech   **315**

Cognitive and Language Development in Social Context   **316**

Risk and Opportunity in the Home Environment   **317**

BOX 10.5 The HOME Scale   **318**

The Influence of the Nursery School   **320**

Risk and Opportunity in Day Care   **321**

CAREERS: The Corporate Day Care Director   **322**

Compensatory Preschools   **323**

BOX 10.6 Project Head Start: Past, Present, and Future   **324**

CAREERS: The Head Start Teacher   **325**

Looking Back **327**

Chapter Review **327**

Key Terms **328**

Chapter 11 Social and Emotional Development in Early Childhood **329**

The Development of Social Play **332**
Social Play **332**

Social Pretend Play **333**

Promoting Social Pretense **335**

Relating to Peers **336**
Social Preference **336**

Friendships **337**

BOX 11.1 Measuring Social Preferences and Social Status **337**

Conflicts **339**

Aggression **341**

Dominance **345**

BOX 11.2 The Medieval Kingdom Model of Dominance Relations **347**

The Parents' Role in Promoting Social Competence **348**
Indirect Influences on Social Competence **348**

Direct Influences on Social Competence **350**

BOX 11.3 A Closer Look at Parenting Styles **351**

The Development of Prosocial Behavior **353**

The Development of Gender Roles **355**
Learning Gender Roles: Theoretical Approaches **355**

Parental Influence on Gender Role Learning **358**

BOX 11.4 Raising Nonsexist Children in a Sexist Society **359**

Learning Gender Roles in the Same-Sex Peer Group **360**

Emotional Development During the Preschool Years **363**
Sending Masking Emotional Signals **363**

Reading Emotional Signals **365**

Looking Back **366**

Chapter Review **367**

Key Terms **368**

PART FIVE

Middle Childhood

Chapter 12 Physical Development and Disability in Middle Childhood   **370**

Physical Development in Middle Childhood   **373**

Changes in Body Proportion, Body Type, and Body Image   **373**

Gender Differences in Play-Game Skills   **375**

Physical Fitness in Middle Childhood   **377**

Children with Special Needs   **381**

Mental Retardation   **381**

CAREERS: The School Psychologist   **382**

Hyperactivity   **383**

Children with Multiple Handicaps   **386**

Educating Children with Special Needs   **386**

Parenting Children with Disabilities   **389**

Behavior Problems in Children with Disabilities   **392**

Looking Back   **393**

Chapter Review   **393**

Key Terms   **394**

Chapter 13 Cognitive Development and Schooling in Middle Childhood   **395**

Cognitive Development in Middle Childhood   **396**

Piaget's Concrete Operations   **397**

BOX 13.1 Training Conservation in Young Children   **401**

The Information Processing View   **407**

The Schooling of Our Children   **412**

What Makes a School Good?   **413**

Schooling and Minorities   **413**

CAREERS: The Elementary School Principal   **414**

Parents and Schooling   **415**

CAREERS: The Inner-City Teacher   **416**

BOX 13.2 The Learning Gap: A Cross-Cultural Comparison   **419**

The Motivation to Learn and Achieve   **420**

Learning to Read   **421**

BOX 13.3 The Problem of Overachievement: Type A Behavior **422**

BOX 13.4 Reading Problems: Whole-Word Readers and Decoders **426**

Learning Mathematics **427**

Schooling the Intellectually Gifted and Talented **431**

Looking Back **432**

Chapter Review **433**

Key Terms **435**

Chapter 14 Social and Emotional Development in Middle Childhood **436**

Friendship in Middle Childhood **438**

Making Friends **439**

Keeping Friends **441**

Social Status and Behavior **442**

Social Information Processing and Social Competence **445**

Interpreting Social Cues and Events **446**

Generating Responses **448**

Evaluating and Selecting the Optimal Response **449**

Enacting the Response **450**

Integrating the Components of Information Processing **451**

Rejection and Loneliness **452**

Peer Rejection and Later Adjustment **455**

Short-Term Effects of Rejection **455**

Long-Term Effects of Rejection **456**

Social Cognition and Social Competence **456**

The Development of Prosocial Behavior **458**

Prosocial Moral Reasoning and Prosocial Behavior **459**

Empathy, Sympathy, and Prosocial Behavior **460**

Divorce and Children's Social Adjustment **461**

CAREERS: The Marriage and Family Therapist **463**

Working, Parenting, and Children's Social Adjustment **465**

BOX 14.1 Latchkey Children **466**

Looking Back **468**

Chapter Review **468**

Key Terms **469**

PART SIX

Adolescence

Chapter 15 Physical and Cognitive Development in Adolescence   472

Physical Development in Adolescence   473

The Experience of Puberty   473
The Surge of Hormones   474
The Growth Spurt   474
Achieving Sexual Maturity   476
The Timing of Puberty   477

Wellness in Adolescence   481
Leisure Time and Sports   481
Dieting and Eating Disorders   483
Sexually Transmitted Diseases and the Risk of AIDS   487

Cognitive Development in Adolescence   491
Formal Operational Thought   492
Adolescent Egocentrism   494
Achieving in School   497
CAREERS: The High School Teacher   498
Moral Reasoning in Adolescence   500
BOX 15.1 To Cheat or Not to Cheat?   502

Looking Back   503

Chapter Review   504

Key Terms   505

Chapter 16 Social and Emotional Development in Adolescence   506

Friendship and Peer Relations   507
The Increasing Influence of Peers   508
Cliques and Crowds   509
BOX 16.1 Hanging Out in Junior High School: The Development of Crowd Behavior   510
Peer Pressure and Conformity   512
Adolescent Friendships   513
Social Acceptance and Rejection   514

Dating and Sexual Relationships   516

BOX 16.2 Teenagers and Contraception   **517**

Biological Influences   **518**

Parents and Peer Influences   **519**

Cultural Influences   **520**

Searching for Identity   521

BOX 16.3 The Search for Identity in Minority Teenagers   **526**

Adjustment Problems in Adolescence   528

Adolescent Substance Abuse   **528**

CAREERS: The Prevention Counselor   **532**

Adolescent Suicide   **533**

Juvenile Delinquency   **534**

Looking Back   537

Chapter Review   538

Key Terms   539

Glossary   **540**

References   **554**

Photo Credits   **588**

Author Index   **589**

Subject Index   **600**

For the Instructor

I wrote this book because I want students to learn that what they do and how well they do it can make a significant difference in the outcome of their children's development. Naturally, I want the book to cover what is scientifically known about children. But more important, I want to inspire and encourage students to get creatively involved in children's lives. I want to present the cutting edge of theory and research, but to do so in a context of practical application.

This book grows out of five beliefs that I have formed over the 20-plus years I have been working with and studying children:

- I believe that every child is born with an enormous potential for development that goes well beyond the expectations of even the most optimistic or idealistic parent or teacher. Each child could be the next Einstein, Gandhi, Da Vinci, Picasso, Freud, Darwin, Mother Teresa, Marie Curie, or Martin Luther King.

- I believe that most children—perhaps all children—fail to realize more than a fraction of their full developmental potential. Some children do better than others, of course, but most of the potential of most children remains unfulfilled.

- Despite recent evidence of potent genetic effects on children's behavior and development, I believe that parents and professionals who deal with children can create optimal environmental conditions to promote their children's development. However, few parents or practitioners take full advantage of this opportunity, sacrificing their children's potential with no sense of loss or disappointment.

- I believe that the science of child development can teach us a great deal about how to help children realize their developmental potential. We have identified many of the forces that place development at risk, and we know more than ever about how to minimize or eliminate those risks. We are learning how to design optimal environments for physical, cognitive, social, and emotional development.

- Finally, I believe that studying child development and its application can change how students think about children and how competently they interact with children. These goals can be accomplished more effectively when instructors use a text that is designed for these purposes.

These ideas have prompted me to write a text that is firmly based in contemporary scholarly research and theory but designed to address the applied needs of people who will deal with children on a daily basis. My goal is to thoroughly explore what researchers know about the development of children and then to show how caregivers can apply that knowledge to facilitate competence in all children. I believe that even the most complex scholarly knowledge can be presented meaningfully and applied to child service professionals' daily process of decision making.

While, as a scholar, I report facts and findings objectively, I believe the care and development of the next generation is too critical for us to stop there. I believe that there is an optimal set of decisions that caregivers can make to maximize the realization of each child's potential. I intend this book to equip caregivers to make those decisions. At the end of each discussion, I give practical recommendations of how caregivers can apply the research findings just covered in their day-to-day dealings with children. My purpose is not to give the right or only course of action, but to illustrate how the findings might be effectively applied to reduce the risks and make the most of the opportunities.

The reader will leave each section of this text keenly aware of what an essential natural resource our children are and what an enormous cost we pay when developmental potential is wasted. I explicitly intend that my readers make noticeable progress toward becoming more sensitive and committed parents to the next generation.

I have studied children with the objectivity of the scientific method and the subjectivity of the roles of father and stepfather. I have observed children through one-way mirrors and raced them to the tops of jungle gyms (and lost!). I have worked with the rich and the very poor, with "normal" children and ones who are "atypical." So in writing this book I felt no need to portray the development of children as a benign and inexorable sequence of stages and experiences that inevitably turn out happily. That common cheery perspective rings false with many students because it fails to reflect the childhood experience they remember.

Instead, I make a point of balancing treatment of risks and opportunities to realistically reflect the problematic nature of development in contemporary society. I use the research base to facilitate rational discussion of such controversial issues as child abuse and neglect, inadequate prenatal care, divorce, substitute childrearing, dual careers, and family dysfunction.

The research base also anchors subjective consideration of the emotional and moral aspects of such issues. I intend the text to affect students' social conscience and to spark conflict and argument—informed by research and theory—among them. I want them to struggle with the moral dilemmas inherent in professional and parental involvement with children who are essentially at risk from the moment of their conception.

In short, I am not content to simply add to the readers' knowledge; I want to change how they think and act in their dealings with children.

I approached this task by following a consistent format in each chapter: I introduce what we know from research about various aspects of children's behavior and development, use examples and case studies to show these tendencies at work in real children's everyday lives, and translate what we know into applied recommendations for parents and practitioners who interact with children and influence their lives.

Acknowledgments

I would like to thank the many students who, over the years, showed me—through their interest, confusion, and insight—what they wanted and needed in a child development textbook. I believe that this text honors their contributions.

I am indebted to the many children I have observed and come to know throughout my career. They have taught me most of what I know about risk and opportunity in development. I most especially wish to thank Heather, Carlos, and Leshonda.

I thank my wife, Sharon, and my children, Lisa, Brad, and Julie, who have supported my efforts with their patience, tolerance, encouragement, and faith in my ability.

Special thanks to the many students at Florida State University who helped with computer searches, locating articles, and duplication. I owe them a great deal.

I thank my mentor, Vladimir de Lissovoy, Professor Emeritus at Pennsylvania State University, who showed me how to be a scholar and a caring individual simultaneously. Val is truly a professor's professor.

I am grateful to the highly competent team at Wadsworth Publishing Company. Editor Suzanna Brabant, in particular, believed in my ideas and supported my every effort. Developmental Editor John Boykin contributed greatly to the integrity and flow of the manuscript. Production Editors Karen Garrison and Cathy Linberg, Managing Designer Ann Butler, and Art Editor Kelly Murphy were most competent.

Finally, I would like to thank my colleagues around the country who reviewed various drafts of the book and provided their helpful comments and suggestions. They include:

Reviewers

Polly Applefield, *University of North Carolina at Wilmington*

Thomas L. Bennett, *Bowling Green State University, Ohio*

George R. Bieger, *Indiana University of Pennsylvania*

Kathryn Norcross Black, *Purdue University*

Edward Brady, *Belleville Area College*

Toni Campbell, *San Jose State University*

Alice S. Carter, *Yale University*

Frederick Clemens, *Radford University*

Susan Coady, *Ohio State University*

Kaaren C. Day, *University of North Texas*

Sheridan DeWolf, *Grossmont College*

Victoria Jean Dimidjian, *Miami-Dade Community College*

Beth Doll, *University of Colorado at Denver*

Dianne Eyer, *Cañada College*

William Fisk, *Clemson University*

David Geary, *University of Missouri at Columbia*

Margaret Stanley-Hagan, *University of North Carolina at Charlotte*

Lorraine Harner, *City University of New York, Brooklyn College*

David Hill, *Millersville University*

Richard Ida, *Diablo Valley College*

Janice Johnson, *University of Central Oklahoma*

Kay Johnston, *Colgate University*

Barbara Kane, *Indiana State University*

Simi Linton, *City University of New York, Hunter College*

Ruth Lyell, *San Jose State University*

Susan Mantyla, *Santa Barbara City College*

Mary Ann McLaughlin, *Clarion University of Pennsylvania*

Melanie Moore, *University of Louisville*

June Gustafson Munro, *Thomas Nelson Community College*

Edward Nelson, *Arizona State University*

Evelyn Oka, *Michigan State University*

Richard Passman, *University of Wisconsin at Milwaukee*

Joseph H. Pearl, *Oklahoma State University*

Phyllis Povell, *Long Island University, C. W. Post Center*

Lis Reboy, *University of Kansas*

Toni E. Santmire, *University of Nebraska at Lincoln*

Edythe Schwartz, *California State University, Sacramento*

Gabrielle Sweidel, *Kutztown University*

Joan S. Timm, *University of Wisconsin at Oshkosh*

Ignatius Toner, *University of North Carolina at Charlotte*

Irma J. Van Scoy, *University of South Carolina*

I assume that you are taking this course because you know that children will be an important part of your life, as a parent and/or as a professional teacher, therapist, child life specialist, social worker, pediatric nurse, or pediatrician. In any case, you will be intimately involved in children's lives and responsible for their well-being. That is why, throughout this book, I refer to them as *your* children.

How well you perform will affect your children's development profoundly. You'll need energy, sensitivity, tolerance, patience, persistence, reliability, love, firmness combined with flexibility, and much more. But, as you will discover in this book, you will also need knowledge and skills. I have developed and refined this book to help you learn certain necessary tradeoffs: protecting children while encouraging exploration, making demands while promoting autonomy, disciplining while fostering self-control, loving without spoiling, to name a few.

You must, in short, learn to balance risks and opportunities. This is a continuing theme in the book. Your success in balancing the risks and opportunities, based on each child's unique needs and potential, can result in optimal growth and development. I believe this text offers you an important first step toward realistic preparation for this challenging task. On the following pages, you will find examples of some techniques I use to translate an immense body of research and methods into a form you can readily learn and apply in your everyday experiences with children. I hope they will help you translate "text-book learning" into effective interaction with your children and their development.

—*Murray Krantz*

A Student's Visual Guide Through This Book

Child Development
Risk and Opportunity

Murray Krantz

Risk and Opportunity Theme

I believe that every event in a child's life involves both an opportunity for growth and the risk of sacrificing that potential. As you read about research into the factors that place children at risk, consider how to minimize or eliminate those factors and how to design optimal environments for physical, cognitive, social, and emotional growth.

Academics and Applications

I translate theory and research into practical recommendations for dealing directly with children. Following objective presentation of theory and a wide range of research, the **application sections** offer suggestions of ways you, as a caregiver, *might* apply what researchers have learned. Use them as a starting point to consider what you believe.

BOX 6.5   172   PART THREE   INFANCY

Facilitating the Visually Directed Reaching

Burton White and Richard Held (1966) studied infants living in an orphanage under conditions of moderate stimulus deprivation. They wanted to know how experience affects the development of visually directed reaching in one- to four-month-old infants.

They divided the infants into three groups. The first group, called the massive enrichment group, had patterned sheets and crib bumpers (the bumpers were periodically removed to vary their visual experience). These infants experienced plenty of extra handling by caregivers and were given improved mattresses to facilitate spontaneous movement and a large complex stabile (a nonmoving mobile).

The second group, the so-called moderate enrichment group, had two pacifiers attached to the sides of the crib, one with a patterned disk and one an unpatterned disk. The control group received no special treatment.

The results were somewhat surprising. In both the massive and moderate enrichment groups, visually directed reaching was accelerated by one month, so that these infants were able to successfully grasp an object by 3½ months on average. However, the moderate enrichment group actually showed earlier swiping and reaching than the massive enrichment group. Contrary to expectation, massive enrichment seemed to overwhelm the infants during the first two months, as they indicated with excessive crying and looking away from stimulus materials. By 2½ months, however, the massive experience infants were better able to cope with the stimulation and rapidly developed the visually directed reach.

The results support the facilitating effects of enrichment with infants who are developing under less than optimally stimulating conditions. It is not clear, however, whether enrichment would accelerate the development of normal infants in the typical ecology of a family home. In any case, White and Held's early research has had enormous influence on the design and sale of stimulating nursery materials. Patterned sheets and bumpers, elaborate mobiles with visual and auditory stimulation, and an endless variety of crib toys are standard fare for the newborns of the nineties.

The typical middle-class American baby is very likely to be reared in an environment even more stimulating than White and Held's massive enrichment condition. Parents need to recognize the limitations of their young infants' emerging perceptual and motor capabilities. The possibility that massive enrichment may overwhelm very young infants should be kept in mind for those who are tempted to create their own special effects and training regimens to enrich their babies. The natural ecology of the average home nursery undoubtedly pushes the limits of the perceptual processing capacity of young infants.

Moderate enrichment group

Massive enrichment gr[...]

A second developmental progression is the spatial accuracy of hand placement. Grasping would be of little adaptive value if infants could not visually direct their arms and hands to the location of the object they wish to hold. Again, spatial placement of the hand follows a predictable sequence. Newborns start off with **visually initiated reaching**, a primitive form of swiping in the general direction of objects. Such prereaching movements are rarely successful in contacting the object because the neonate is still unable to make use of vision to direct the arm and hand to the object (von Hofsten, 1984). This prereaching behavior drops out in the second month of life.

By three months infants begin to show some accuracy in **visually directed reaching**—that is, reaching for objects on the same side as the hand that does the reaching. And by 4½ months they can grasp objects with considerable accuracy straight in front of them or even on the opposite side of the reaching hand (Bushnell, 1985). Toward the end of the first year, infants depend less on visual information to guide their arm and hand movements (Bushnell, 1985). Once the infant has visually located an interesting object, she can use her arm and hand to find the object while using her eyes to look for new challenges.

The third developmental progression in manual control is the achievement of self-help skills such as drinking from a cup, putting on clothing, and washing hands. Although infants in the second year can perform certain self-help skills, cognitive and perceptual limitations slow development in this area, much to the dismay of caregivers.

A P P L I C A T I O N

Promoting Your Toddler's Self-Help Skills

Your toddler's self-help skills (such as washing his hands or dressing himself) are limited by three factors: the slow development of manual control, the even slower development of coordinated movements, and the child's lack of motivation to change. The following suggestions may be helpful.

■ Recognize that every self-help skill is made up of many components. For example, washing one's hands involves turning the faucet, wetting the hands, grasping and rubbing the soap, scrubbing, rinsing, and drying the hands, and hanging the towel. Focus first on teaching subcomponents, then on coordination.

■ To motivate your child to learn, reinforce any noticeable progress and avoid punishing for lack of improvement. Modeling the skills—particularly by older siblings—may be more effective than direct instruction.

Bottom Line: Be patient. With persistence, parents who encourage the development of self-help skills can expect their children to dress in simple garments, eat with utensils, and wash and dry their hands by the end of the second year.

Motor Control in Transactional Perspective

The development of motor control can be understood as a transactional process within an ecological context (Keogh & Sugden, 1985). In this perspective, the central nervous system affects and is affected by the infant's movements and the consequences of those movements. For example, as infants improve their control of head and eye movements and reaching and grasping movements, they not only find it easier to explore objects manually but also become better able to perceive increasingly complex features of objects. These perceptions, in turn, provide more complex stimulation to the central nervous system, thereby altering its neuronal structure. This altered structure enables the infant to explore even more efficiently and perceptively.

traordinary levels of achievement that distinguish them from other less proficient children. They approach motor tasks with great confidence and consistently perform with efficiency, competence, and grace. Are these children our future athletes and ballet dancers? Although research has had little to say about the long-term effects, it seems likely that such children will maintain their advantage into later childhood and beyond if their skills are encouraged.

Self-Help: Grooming and Feeding

Parents and other caregivers tend dutifully to the grooming, feeding, and elimination needs of children through the first two years of life. The novelty of these caregiving tasks wears off quickly, and most parents look forward to the day when their children will be able to perform these tasks independently. Late in the second year, children's increasing strivings for autonomy and advances in fine and gross motor control allow the development of many self-help skills, including washing, brushing teeth, dressing, and self-feeding. To the frustration of parents, these skills emerge rather slowly. Consider Carlos at 30 months.

This child's fluid running motion on an irregular, declining surface shows the preschool child's potential for coordinated gross motor skill. Her expression suggests that she is not only skilled for her age, but that she has growing confidence in her ability. Each new level of sophistication in physical skills builds on skills mastered earlier.

> *Carlos decides that he is going to put his jeans on by himself for the first time. The jeans lie in a shapeless clump on the floor. As he lifts the jeans, he looks at them as if he were seeing them for the first time. He doesn't know the top from the bottom, the front from the back, or the inside from the outside. He remembers vaguely that his mother starts by putting his foot in a hole, but his first attempt only gets his foot stuck in a pocket. After some maneuvering, he gets his right leg into the left pant leg and falls over, twisting his body to get his left leg into the right leg of the pants.*
>
> *After several more tries, he runs triumphantly to his parents' room. Carlos stands proudly before Maria and Emilio with his jeans on backwards and inside out. As he turns to run back to his room, his bare bottom, protruding through the unzipped fly, signals that it will still be some time before he perfects the act of putting on jeans.*

Although Carlos is motivated to dress himself, he lacks the conceptual and motor skills to accomplish the task. In the next 12 to 18 months he will learn to dress by first reshaping the jeans into a recognizable form, orienting the jeans in space to match the orientation of his body, balancing his body to facilitate control of dressing movements, and zipping, snapping, or buckling to keep the jeans from falling down. Conceptually, Carlos must develop a schema of the relevant body parts and a matching schema of the garment that covers those body parts; then he must integrate those schemas to coordinate the relevant fine and gross motor skills involved in dressing. This should be accomplished for most garments—including putting on and lacing shoes—during the second half of the fourth year (Knobloch & Pasamanick, 1974).

Self-help skills at the dinner table also develop quite slowly. Although most children have learned to feed themselves with a cup and spoon by 24 months, some food continues to find its way to the floor well into the third year. With coaching from parents, competent handling of eating utensils improves significantly during the third and fourth years.

CAREERS

The Developmental Specialist

Dr. Jean Lowe is a developmental specialist and certified diagnostician in the Department of Pediatrics at the University of New Mexico School of Medicine. She has an undergraduate major in elementary education, and a Master's degree and Ph.D. in special education, with a minor in neuropsychology.

Jean is a member of a developmental team—including a physician, nurse-practitioner, social worker, pediatric occupational therapist, and speech therapist—that cares for low birth-weight and critically ill newborns through the first months of their lives. As the developmental specialist, Jean assesses the infant's behavioral capabilities, identifies specific disabilities, and recommends interventions.

What is it like to work with low birth-weight babies?
The challenge is enormous. All of these babies are at risk because they are born too early and/or at low birth weight, but many are also critically ill due to disease or drug exposure. About 10 percent of our babies test positive for drugs such as cocaine or heroin. Some of our babies weigh less than 1,500 grams, and many of them suffer from intraventricular hemorrhage (bleeding in the brain).

When they first come to us, every minute is a life and death struggle. But keeping the baby alive is only half the battle; the challenge is to create an environment—both in and out of the

hospital—that will promote the child's optimal development over time.

What do you do to help these babies develop normally?
We begin with an initial comprehensive assessment and develop an individualized care plan for each baby. Each member of the team plays an essential role in implementing that care. I use the Neonatal Behavioral Assessment Scale (the Brazelton) and other tests to determine the baby's adaptive capability and to guide our interventions. We use massage to deal with a baby's stiffness and irritability. Because these babies can be passive and unresponsive, we train parents to actively engage their babies and to be sensitive to their needs. These babies stand a much better chance if we can train the parents to continue our interventions at home. We videotape parents interacting with their babies to show them how they affect their baby's mood and behavior. We also do home visits to follow up on the babies and their parents.

Is there a lot of stress?
This work is very stressful. The number of critical care babies increases each year, and we fight for every one. But sometimes our best is just not good enough. We try to accept our limitations, but dealing with permanent disability or the death of a baby is always very difficult. The members of the developmental team are your main source of emotional support.

What is the most exciting part of your work?
The best part is seeing a baby overcome tremendous odds and survive. Even better, I enjoy seeing a mother grow along with her baby. Some of our mothers feel helpless; they don't know how to care for their critically ill babies. But, with time and our best efforts, many mothers bond with their babies and come to care deeply about them. That's very rewarding.

What is the career path to becoming a developmental specialist?
Begin by volunteering in the newborn nursery as a cuddler. Spend enough time in the hospital to understand the pressures, the politics, and the rewards. If it seems right for you, pursue an undergraduate degree in early childhood special education, with an emphasis in family and child development. Continue on to graduate study and seek out training in specialized techniques like the Brazelton. The Ph.D. is important if you hope to be effective in the hospital environment.

For more information, write to: Association for the Care of Children's Health, 7910 Woodmont Avenue, Suite 300, Bethesda, Maryland 20814-3015.

Three Continuing Case Studies

Throughout the book, you will follow the development of Carlos, Leshonda, and Heather. These **case studies**, based on my observations of real children I have known and worked with, are designed to help you gain insight into the complexity and diversity of child development. They can also anchor your grasp of theory and research to reality as you trace these children's development from the prenatal period through infancy, early and middle childhood, to adolescence.

Guidance on the Career Track

I have included a number of **careers inserts** to demonstrate the exciting possibilities for anyone who wishes to work with children. Based on interviews I have conducted with professionals throughout the country, these boxed sections provide information on how various specialties serve children, along with practical and specific advice on opportunities for employment, the type and extent of training required for entry-level jobs, and the possibilities for career advancement.

Features to Help You Learn

Each chapter opens with a **Looking Ahead** section that previews the major concepts and questions explored in the chapter. Each chapter concludes with a **Looking Back** section that capsulizes the chapter's main ideas and a brief point-by-point **Chapter Review**.

Also, I translate scholarly research into everyday language and illustrate points with concrete examples. Key terms are shown in **boldface** type when they first appear. They are defined within the text and in the **Glossary** at the end of the book. **Charts, photographs, and captions** are integral parts of the text, chosen largely to reinforce the text's main ideas.

My twin goals with this book are to present what researchers have learned about child development and to suggest ways you can apply that knowledge in your dealings with children. The result, I hope, is that you will be equipped to balance risks and opportunities in helping your children reach their full potential.

6

Perceptual and Physical Development in Infancy

Looking Ahead

- Infants grow rapidly in weight and height and their body proportion changes dramatically during the first two years. What are these changes?
- Rapid growth in infancy, particularly in the first four to six months, creates unique nutritional requirements. What are these requirements and how are they met? Is breast milk better for the baby than formula?

- The development of the central nervous system affects all aspects of development. What is the relationship between the development of the central nervous system and experience?
- The infant's visual perception changes rapidly during the first months. What does the newborn see? How does the infant come to perceive the world of objects in three-dimensional space?

- The infant's ability to hear is well developed at birth. When does the infant learn to discriminate sounds, particularly those associated with speech?
- The infant's ability to control movement evolves quickly in the first months, from simple reflexes to the complex movements involved in sitting up, creeping, walking, and using the hands. What specific changes take place? Can the rate of motor development be facilitated?

This text advocates facilitating the optimal expression of naturally inherited potential. From this perspective, the concept of *repairing* broken genes sounds rather promising, but the concept of *replacing* them raises a large red flag. Those who deal with children must begin to discuss these issues and seek answers to these questions. If our values are to be clarified before this seductive technology becomes a reality, time is growing short.

Looking Back

From the moment of conception, the developing embryo and fetus walk a fine line between risk and opportunity. Genetic predisposition to disease, chromosomal abnormalities, teratogens, and inadequate prenatal care threaten prenatal development; benign genetic traits and high-quality prenatal care promote optimal development. Advances in our understanding of prenatal development have created numerous opportunities to prevent certain problems and to detect and intervene with others to lessen their effects. However, it is clear that only well-informed parents will be in a position to minimize risk and maximize opportunity for their offspring's prenatal development.

CHAPTER REVIEW

FEMALE REPRODUCTIVE SYSTEM The functioning of the female reproductive system is orchestrated by a complex series of hormonal secretions, the timing of which is known as the menstrual cycle. The system is uniquely designed to produce an egg (or ovum), and facilitate fertilization in the fallopian tubes and implantation in the uterus.

MALE REPRODUCTIVE SYSTEM The male reproductive system is designed to produce large numbers of healthy sperm and to deposit those sperm in the female vagina. The large numbers are necessary to overcome the hazardous journey from the cervix to the fallopian tubes.

INFERTILITY Approximately one couple in six is infertile; infertility increases with age, particularly in males in the late thirties. Female infertility typically results from failure to ovulate, cervical hostility, or blockage of the fallopian tubes. Male infertility results from failure to produce healthy sperm in sufficient numbers and problems with erection and ejaculation.

TIMING INTERCOURSE The brief viability of sperm and ova create a window

of opportunity for fertilization of about three days. Chances of achieving conception can be improved by estimating the time of ovulation and coordinating it with intercourse.

PRENATAL DEVELOPMENT Prenatal development is divided into three periods. During the period of the zygote (two weeks), the fertilized egg (zygote) moves to the uterus and is implanted in the uterine wall (endometrium); the placenta is formed. During the period of the embryo (the third through the eighth week), the structures of all the major organ systems are formed (except the genitals) in a process called organogenesis. During the period of the fetus (the ninth week to birth), the organ systems continue to grow and begin to function. By about 26 weeks — the age of viability — the fetus is likely to survive if born prematurely.

TERATOGENS Certain diseases, drugs, and other potentially harmful chemicals, collectively called teratogens, can cross the placenta and devastate the developing embryo and fetus. The damage depends on dosage, timing, protective

factors in the mother, and the resilience of the fetus. The most vulnerable time is the critical period for each organ's development.

MATERNAL NUTRITION AND EXERCISE The mother's health during pregnancy has significant effects on her fertility and on her pregnancy. Mothers must change their eating patterns and exercise in moderation.

HEREDITY Each human cell contains 23 matched pairs of chromosomes, with one member of each pair inherited from the father and the other from the mother. Each chromosome is made up of two threads of DNA, with each thread organized into thousands of genes. The blend of genetic material at birth is the genotype; the observable expression of genetic potential is the phenotype.

MITOSIS AND MEIOSIS The duplication of body cells is called mitosis; the duplication of sex cells is meiosis. The division of chromosomes in meiosis ensures genetic diversity through crossing over, the exchange of genetic material from the individual's mother and father.

Foundations

1

Introduction

The purposes of this book are to describe what we presently know about child and adolescent development and to help you apply that information in your interactions with children. We will begin working toward these goals by introducing several key concepts that are used throughout the book. First, we describe what we mean by the term *development*. We then introduce the idea that the course of development and its outcomes vary significantly among children, depending on each child's unique experience of risk and opportunity. Finally, we describe the different ways that children respond to risk and opportunity, and how those who deal with children—parents, caregivers, and other practitioners—can facilitate development by minimizing children's exposure to risk and maximizing their exposure to opportunity.

The Concept of Development

Development obviously refers to change, but humans go through many types of change, only some of which are considered developmental. For example, suppose a three-year-old girl wants a toy that her four-year-old brother is playing with. If she begins to nag him for the toy, saying "Gimmee, gimmee, gimmee," and then escalates to whining and crying, the change in her behavior is not typically considered developmental. However, when she eventually abandons whining and for the first time offers her brother a cookie to encourage him to share, the change from whining to the more sophisticated strategy *is* considered developmental. Likewise, when the brother shows awareness of his sister's feelings for the first time and responds empathically by sharing, the change in his behavior is also considered developmental.

Such examples illustrate development, but we still need to define it. We need a general definition that identifies all changes that are developmental. **Developmentalists**—researchers and practitioners who study the development process—have defined **development** as the gradual accumulation of relatively permanent, age-related changes through transactions with the environment. Let's look more closely at each component of that definition.

Development Is Gradual

Though the specific events described above are considered developmental, development itself does not take place right before our eyes. Rather, it is observed or measured over periods of months or years. This is evident when a visiting relative comments, "My, how much she has grown!" to the surprise of the parents. Relatives see the children less frequently than parents, so they are more likely to notice developmental changes. The gradual nature of developmental change has important practical implications: To facilitate your children's development you must be both persistent and consistent in your efforts over extended periods of time.

Development Is Cumulative

Developmental changes build upon one another. A child's features at one point in time combine with new additions to form more complex features. For example, the infant's creeping movements combine with advances in strength and balance toward the end of the first year to produce walking and climbing. These features, in turn, anticipate even newer additions that continue to accumulate over time. This implies that no change in a child's behavior should be considered trivial; virtually every change is a potentially important advance in some skill or ability, even if the final form of the ability remains unclear. From a practical perspective, caregivers and practitioners can better facilitate a child's development when they understand the sequence of developmental changes that leads to a particular skill or ability. For example, teachers can be more effective in reading instruction if they understand the sequence of cognitive, perceptual, and linguistic skills that children must acquire to learn to read.

Developmental Change Is Relatively Permanent

Developmental change is typically irreversible. For instance, when a toddler first learns to put words together to approximate adult sentences, she makes that skill part of her repertoire, and she will never revert to exclusive use of single-word utterances to convey her meaning. When preschool-age children discover that appearances do not always reflect reality, they are permanently transformed into more skeptical and more inquiring human beings. Unfortunately, some less favorable developmental changes may also become relatively permanent. Children who are maltreated or who fail to develop close emotional relationships with caregivers in their early years may have lasting difficulties in forming social relationships. Likewise, children who develop in unstimulating or chaotic home environments may suffer permanent reduction of their intellectual potential.

Although irreversibility is the rule, there are some extraordinary circumstances that can reverse a child's developmental advances. For instance, when a new baby arrives, an older sibling may *regress* to infantile behaviors to gain attention. The stress of moving into a new neighborhood and school may cause a child to achieve well below her potential. Fortunately, such reversals in development tend to right themselves over time, as children adapt to their new circumstances. More serious reversals in development—for example, those brought about by illness, injury, deprivation, abuse, or severe trauma—may be turned around by specialized interventions. For instance, children who have suffered intellectual deficits early in life may be helped by educational programs that compensate for certain forms of deprivation.

Development Is Transactional

Those who deal with children every day often try to explain children's behavior and development. For example, a kindergarten teacher speculates that a child's highly aggressive behavior may have been *caused* by a frustrating experience, a conflict in the child's family, aggressive role-modeling by older siblings, or the family's low-income status. Each of her explanations points to a single cause that clearly preceded the problem behavior in time.

However, developmentalists have come to recognize that single-direction, cause-and-effect explanations of behavior and development are overly simplistic (Bell, 1979; Sameroff & Chandler, 1975). Arnold Sameroff and Richard Chandler (1975) have argued that children influence their environment as much as their environment influences them. In the above example, while the teacher believes that conflict in the child's family may have caused him to be aggressive, his aggression may be the major source of the family's conflict. Similarly, while younger children often imitate the aggressive behavior of older siblings, older children's behavior frequently regresses to the less mature level of their younger brothers and sisters.

Thus, simple cause-and-effect explanations do not capture the complexity of children's interactions with the people around them. In practical terms, every action you direct toward your child has some important reaction in the child. Regardless of your original intention, you will find yourself reacting to the child's reaction to your original action. You have not done something *to* your child; you and your child have entered into a *transaction*. Over time, the sequence of transactions between your child and his or her social and physical environments forms a unique pathway through development. Later in this book, you will see how viewing development as transactional helps to explain many aspects of children's lives, including their experience of maltreatment (deLissovoy, 1979) and their experience of divorce (Hetherington, 1989).

Development Takes Place in an Ecosystem

Ecology is the study of the relationships between living organisms and their environments. According to Urie Bronfenbrenner (1979, 1986), a developmental psychologist, the *ecology of human development* refers to the study of the transactions "between an active growing human being . . . and the settings in which the developing person lives." (1979, p. 21). From the ecological perspective, we conceive of children developing within an **ecosystem**, interacting with nested levels of environmental influences (see Figure 1.1). The ecosystem has the four following levels.

In the *microsystem*, children interact with family, peers, and services such as day care and the public school. The family system is typically the dominant force in the microsystem. Dramatic changes in recent years in the structure and function of the family as a system—particularly with respect to divorce, remarriage, stepfamilies, and dual careers—have had extensive effects on the organization and influence of the microsystem as context for child development.

The *mesosystem* describes relationships among elements of the microsystem. The relationship between the family and the day care center is an important example. Day care centers that promote parent involvement in their activities and parents who actively seek such involvement are more likely to develop a common perspective on children's care and to work together to promote continuity of care between home and the center. Open communication between parents and caregivers concerning children's moods, likes and dislikes, and health status facilitates children's daily transitions between the home and the center. Lack of communication promotes distrust between parents and caregivers and compartmentalizes children's life experiences.

The *exosystem* identifies social supports available to the family in the community. For instance, while some employers offer day care services and flextime to employees, other employers show no concern for the family's ability to provide care for its children during working hours. The availability of social support for families in the community such as neighbors and social services can make the difference between "hard times" and "crisis."

The outermost layer, the *macrosystem*, deals with the cultural context of development—societal values reflected in social policies toward children. A convincing argument has been made in recent years that public policy toward children has had devastating effects on the family's ability to fulfill the developmental potential of their children, particular children who live in poverty (Edelman, 1991). Unfortunately, public policy is most often formulated by politicians and bureaucrats, far removed from the lives of children and families they allegedly represent. With millions of children living in poverty and families under increasing stress, support for social and educational services plays a critical role in the welfare of our children in our society. We must come to understand the nested levels of environmental effects on developmental process and

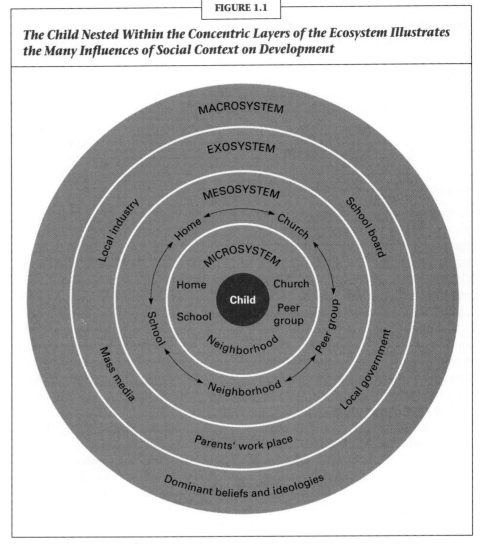

FIGURE 1.1

The Child Nested Within the Concentric Layers of the Ecosystem Illustrates the Many Influences of Social Context on Development

SOURCE: *Reprinted by permission of the publishers from* The Ecology of Human Development: Experiments by Nature and Design *by Urie Bronfenbrenner, Cambridge, Mass.: Harvard University Press, Copyright © 1979 by the President and Fellows of Harvard College.*

outcome if we are to design and implement strategies that increase opportunity and reduce risk at each level of the ecosystem.

Risk and Opportunity

Each child's development is a unique journey through a series of events that no one has ever experienced in that precise form and sequence. Except for identical twins, each child begins the journey genetically different from every other child, with a unique potential for growth and development. Each child's pathway is paved with risk and opportunity that determine how much of that potential he or she will fulfill. **Risk** threatens to undermine development and sacrifice the child's potential; **opportunity** supports development and promotes the realization of that potential.

Most childhood experiences involve *both* risk and opportunity. For example, when a toddler attempts to climb stairs for the first time, the opportunity to improve his motor skills and expand his range of exploration is balanced against the risk of physical injury. When a preschooler tries to enter the ongoing play of her peers, the opportunity for acceptance is balanced against the risk of rejection. Each time a child gets a new teacher in elementary school, his or her opportunity for intellectual growth may be threatened by the risk of incompetent instruction. We can facilitate our children's development if we understand the delicate, shifting balance of risk and opportunity in every aspect of their lives.

For some children — particularly those who are economically advantaged — the opportunities for development far outweigh the risks, virtually assuring them of optimal development. They have healthy genes and mothers and fathers who are physically and emotionally prepared for the responsibilities of parenthood. They get excellent prenatal care, their births are uneventful, and their parents welcome them with unconditional love and responsive care. They are raised in environments that consistently provide every possible opportunity for healthy physical and psychological development from birth to maturity. These children can anticipate productive careers, financial well-being, and healthy social and psychological adjustment throughout their lives.

But being born into an economically advantaged family does not guarantee a child's optimal physical and psychological development. Children often fall prey to risks that are unique to middle- and upper-class families. Some parents simply do too much for their children. They try to solve their children's every problem and cater to their every whim, undermining their children's motivation and sense of initiative. David Elkind, an expert in child development, believes that the contemporary yuppie family's approach to childrearing promotes a child's sense of helplessness (Elkind, 1981).

While some parents do too much *for* their children, others do too much *to* their children. These parents view childrearing as a competitive activity in which the goal is to produce Superchild, a child who outperforms all other children on every known measure of human development. These parents confuse rapid development with optimal development. They relentlessly stimulate their children's learning in the belief that they will gain some advantage by learning faster than their peers. These parents often have unrealistic expectations for their children's progress that doom their children to repeated experiences of failure.

Still other parents do too little for their children. Overwhelmed by their upwardly mobile lifestyle, these parents find little time to be with their children. They make excessive use of substitute child care (nannies, daycare, babysitters), provide inadequate supervision for their children before and after school, and find little time to interact with them directly. Although some of these parents reserve some "quality time" for their children on weekends, their children's development is clearly not a priority.

Not surprisingly, the pressures on children growing up in middle- and upper-class families often result in various forms of rebellion and antisocial behavior, including substance abuse, delinquency, suicide, and school failure.

While advantaged children are at risk of less than optimal development, less advantaged children face risks that dramatically reduce their potential for development from the moment of conception. While still in their mothers' wombs, they are bathed in drugs and alcohol, which diminishes their chance for survival and permanently reduces their potential for growth and development. They receive little or no prenatal care, increasing their susceptibility to disease problems at birth. They receive inadequate stimulation during their first few years, slowing cognitive development and reducing their ability to learn. Their family life often involves a relationship with an intensely dis-

How can we explain the conflict between this mother and her child? Does the boy simply want something the mother does not want him to have, or did the mother say something the boy does not like? Many developmentalists reject the idea that complex human behavior can be explained in simple cause-and-effect terms. The conflict here may have resulted from countless transactions between the mother and child over a period of hours, days, or even weeks. Describing and explaining children's behavior in transactional perspective is a major challenge in the study of child development.

tressed and depressed mother who is overwhelmed by the responsibilities of raising her children. The absence of traditional sources of social support from extended family, neighbors, and community deepens the mother's sense of isolation and further undermines her ability to care for her children.

And the risks faced by these children extend beyond their homes and families into the community. Many children grow up afraid to walk the streets of their own neighborhoods, severely limiting the quality of their social experience. Their peer groups are training grounds for crime, drugs, and violence. They attend schools that are typically unprepared to deal with their differences or their deficits. Under these conditions, their potential for development is progressively and often irreversibly sacrificed with each passing stage of development. Not surprisingly, these children are typically less prepared than more advantaged children for the challenges of adult life. Most of them will live their lives in poverty and will have children who will, in turn, live their lives in poverty.

Coping with Risk

While all children are exposed to risk in varying degrees, they show wide individual differences in their ability to cope with threats to their development (Rutter, 1984). While some children succumb to relatively mild difficulties and problems, others overcome even the most severe threats to their development. We refer to the tendency to overcome risk as **resilience**; the tendency to fall prey to risk is **vulnerability**. Individual differences in resilience and vulnerability have critical effects on a child's developmental outcome (Horowitz, 1987). For instance, children vary greatly in their reaction to divorce: One child, after some initial difficulty, adapts to the situation and shows normal developmental progress; another child becomes chronically depressed, noncompliant, and does poorly in school (Hetherington, 1989). Similarly, while some abused children suffer its consequences throughout their lives, others transcend the experience and manage to live free of difficulty. One of the great challenges of the study of child development is to identify the factors that influence resilience and vulnerability.

Facilitating Development

Every hour of every day brings with it potential hazards that may rob the child of some developmental achievement and even, in extreme cases, of the potential for further developmental achievement. But every hour also brings with it opportunity to realize the child's potential. Few of us passively observe our children's growth and development. We tend to actively intervene to **facilitate** development by minimizing risk and maximizing opportunity: We childproof our homes, warn our children about talking to strangers, buy them educational toys, help them with their homework, and provide advantages we never had when we were children. While not all opportunity can be seized and not all risk can be avoided, some approaches to children's development are far more effective than others.

Facilitating development is an extraordinarily complicated task that requires dedication and persistence. Parents and practitioners must learn to identify and deal proactively with the risks and opportunities inherent in their children's daily activities. Clearly, this can only be accomplished by adults who are actively and intimately involved in those activities. Risks often appear without warning or are hidden in seemingly benign experiences. While more conscientious parents anticipate risk—for example, the dangers inherent in infant walkers and on playgrounds—less involved parents fail to see the dangers and to protect their children.

Parents and practitioners also vary in their ability to see and take advantage of opportunities for their children's development. Many opportunities are short-lived and only apparent to those adults who are waiting and watching for them to appear. For example, two parents read stories to their children in very different ways. While one drones on mechanically from page to page, the other uses her voice and emotions to highlight and emphasize aspects of the story that make it more interesting and meaningful to her child. More conscientious parents select experiences for their children—such as toys, games, and TV programs—that provide unique opportunities for learning. Good teachers recognize the potential for learning in their curriculum and anticipate teachable moments that make children's learning virtually irresistible.

One of the challenges adults face is deciding how to promote their children's development. Some parents and teachers believe that their children's development is totally dependent on what they do. They dominate their children's lives by manipulating their environment and regulating their behavior. This approach assumes an essentially passive child who is infinitely pliable and changeable. In contrast, other parents believe that development is a natural process that is predetermined by forces operating solely within the child. They feel justified in doing very little. Unfortunately, both of these approaches are supported by the pap that parents find in mall bookstores: *Teach Your Toddler to Read, Toilet Train in Less than a Day, Respect the Inner Child*, and so on.

Those who believe that developmental change can be promoted simply by doing something *to* a child or by sitting back and waiting for nature to take its course are dangerously naive. Doing nothing borders on neglect; overdoing it borders on abuse. What should we do? We must learn to approach children based on what we know about development. We have defined development as the gradual accumulation of relatively permanent, age-related changes through transactions with the environment. Knowing that development is gradual suggests that we must take our time and be patient. Knowing that it is cumulative and irreversible suggests that every experience is important. Knowing that development is transactional suggests that developmental change does not result from doing something to a child or from simply sitting back and passively observing. We can promote favorable developmental outcomes only by entering into transactions with our children—encouraging change as we experience change in ourselves. Those who seek to promote children's optimal development must be prepared to grow with their children.

A steadily increasing percentage of the children in our society are failing to fulfill their genetic potential. There are ominous signs that poverty, abuse, neglect, disease, and widespread indifference to the welfare of children have gained the upper hand. While most Americans find this situation intolerable, few of us do very much to improve our ability to facilitate children's development. You can use the knowledge of development and applied recommendations presented in this text to do your part to help reverse this trend, but only if you are deeply committed to improving the lives of children and are willing to do the hard work necessary to accomplish this purpose.

The Uniqueness of Child Development

The purpose of this book is to present what we have come to know about the forces that influence development and to show how you can apply this knowledge to promote your children's optimal development. Regrettably, most of our knowledge of child development and practice is expressed in general terms and principles that describe the behavior of groups of children at various ages. For example, we will frequently refer to the average performance of children at various ages in various domains: By the end of the first year, most children will take their first independent step and utter their first intelligible word; by age seven, most children acquire the ability to understand another individual's perspective; by age 15 or 16, most adolescents have reached sexual maturity.

While these norms are helpful in understanding development, they do not express the *uniqueness* of an individual child's experience. As we have suggested earlier, no two children experience development in exactly the same way. To help you appreciate the uniqueness of child development, we will follow the progress of three individual children: Leshonda Martin, Heather Allen, and Carlos Rodriguez. We will show how their very different experiences of risk and opportunity have affected the course of their lives and the various ways they and their caregivers have coped with risk and taken advantage of opportunity. Before we begin tracing their development from conception through adolescence, let's put that development in perspective by meeting them first at age 16.

Since her birth, Leshonda Martin has lived with her mother and father in an infamous neighborhood in Brooklyn, New York, named after two city streets that form its geographic borders: Bedford and Stuyvesant Avenues. "Bed-Stuy" is a predominantly African American, poor, and exceedingly hazardous context for child and adolescent development: Stray bullets have penetrated Leshonda's front door, drugs are sold 24 hours a day at her curb, and rats and cats battle for scraps of food in piles of garbage behind her apartment building. The extremes of excitement and terror, love and hate, and hope and despair that characterize daily life in this community make survival itself an accomplishment. Leshonda and her friends have ensured their own survival by learning to be streetwise.

At age 16, Leshonda is lean, muscular, and striking in appearance; the boys say she is "fine." In many ways she is like the other students in her high school. She loves to dance, has a boyfriend, and dresses in a mixture of designer fashions and Goodwill castoffs that both defies and begs for imitation.

But Leshonda is also very different from most of her peers. She enjoys school immensely, studies intensely, and excels in all her subjects. Her unpretentious style allows her to be simultaneously favored by her teachers and respected by her peers—an accomplishment in any high school, but a triumph in Bed-Stuy. She is bidialectical: She speaks fluent black English and fluent standard English, depending on the situation. Leshonda is also socially skilled. She initiates relationships easily and shares an intimacy with several best friends. She maintains a consistently positive mood, sustained by a sense of humor that helps her and those around her to cope. Leshonda at 16 is truly unique, particularly in this part of the world.

Heather Allen lives in a predominantly white, working-class neighborhood in Milwaukee with her depressed, alcoholic mother. Heather never knew her father. Her relationship with her mother is a perpetual cycle of mutual physical and verbal abuse. Heather does not remember a time when it was otherwise. The chaos of her home has forced her to seek asylum in the streets, where she spends her time hanging out with young people very much like herself. The streets have offered her acceptance and a sense of control. From an adult's perspective, Heather is impulsive, angry, unpredictable, rebellious, and manipulative. She is unmanageable in school and has been expelled several times. She has been drinking since she was 10, taking drugs since she was 12, and having sex since she was 13. She looks much older than her 16 years.

Heather's friends have a very different, much more positive perspective. They know Heather as clever, assertive, dependable, persistent, and loyal. They like her and frequently defer to her judgment. And there are other positive signs. Although Heather has experimented with drugs, she is not addicted. Although she has had sex with many different boys, she has avoided both pregnancy and disease. Most important, she seems to have avoided her mother's depression. Although her present lifestyle seems self-destructive, she is a survivor. The glint in Heather's eye suggests that she will emerge from adolescence uniquely prepared to cope with the many challenges of adult life.

Carlos Rodriguez lives with his mother and father in a middle-class suburb of Los Angeles. At 16, he is shy, socially incompetent, and has no close friends. He has always been "the fat kid," and no one wants to be friends with the fat kid. His obesity has taken its toll emotionally, a fact that he admits to no one. He has been lonely and depressed for as long as he can remember. Having no one to play with, he gets no exercise, so neither his weight problem nor his social and emotional consequences seem likely to change.

Carlos might be described as a nerd. He is intensely bright and creative. He is enrolled in honors classes in every subject and has already selected a college that he hopes to attend. He is also compulsively dedicated to several hobbies, including reading, chemistry, and collecting just about anything that can be collected: baseball cards, comic books, coins, stamps.

These brief descriptions of Leshonda's, Heather's, and Carlos's present lives raise many interesting questions. How did their striking differences in personality and life-style come about? Could inborn differences in genetic potential have predetermined them? To what extent were the differences caused by differences in their environments? Did the differences result from the random occurrence of significant events at critical times in their respective lives? Such questions have challenged the intellect and creativity of developmental theorists, researchers, and practitioners throughout this century. Their efforts have provided not only answers to these questions, but the foundation for a scientific study of child and adolescent development. The next two chapters will introduce you to the theoretical and research foundations of this science.

Key Terms

developmentalists	opportunity
development	resilience
ecosystem	vulnerability
risk	facilitate

2

Theories of Child Development

T hose who deal with children ask seemingly endless questions about why children do the things they do, about how what they do changes over time, and about how caregivers and practitioners can best influence those changes. Consider the questions generated by Heather's behavior in day care.

> *Soon after her second birthday, Heather graduated from the infant room to the toddler room at her day-care center. Within hours of the transition, her behavior begins to degenerate: She cries, sucks her thumb, and refuses to comply with caregivers' requests. Within a few days her negative behavior intensifies: She begins to hit children and caregivers, and on two occasions, she bites through the skin of another child. When caregivers intervene, she goes into intense tantrums that last 30 to 40 minutes.*
>
> *Most upsetting to the caregivers is a new behavior pattern that Heather displays daily at naptime: After an extended period of disrupting other children, she rolls over onto her stomach, sucks her thumb, and masturbates with the other hand. After seeing Heather's naptime performance, one caregiver comments, "So what? All my kids did that when they were that age." Another caregiver comments insensitively, "I never saw anything like that before in my life! That's one sick baby in there! We need to get her out of here." A social worker (who has not actually observed Heather) implies in a telephone consultation that Heather's behavior suggests the possibility of sexual abuse.*

Those who witness Heather's behavior desperately need an explanation. Why is she behaving so differently from the other children? Is the overt expression of sexual or aggressive behavior abnormal at her age? Not surprisingly, Heather's caregivers turn to their own past experiences for answers. While the first caregiver interprets the behavior as normal and sees no reason to respond, the second caregiver views the behavior as abnormal, implies that it might be harmful to others, and recommends a drastic course of action. Although the relative merit of the caregivers' interpretations is unclear, obviously personal experience is inadequate as the *sole* basis for explaining child behavior and development.

Clearly, we must transcend personal experience and opinion in our search for explanations of child behavior and development. In science, this role is accomplished by *theory*. A **theory** is a set of interrelated ideas intended to *explain* the workings of highly complex events. It answers the how and why questions that people ask when trying to understand those events. Fortunately, several decades of theory construction in the science of child development have provided some reasonable explanations for many of the whys and hows. This chapter presents several of the most useful theories.

The Role of Theory in Understanding Child Development

The major theories of child development offer very different perspectives on children's behavior and development. Consider, for example, how differently two of the most influential theories of child development, *psychoanalytic theory* and *learning theory*, would explain Heather's behavior in the day-care center. From the psychoanalytic perspective, sexual and aggressive behavior in children is not considered abnormal; it is a natural expression of instinct at any age. However, the developmental timing of Heather's behaviors would be of some concern. While biting would be considered normal in infancy, biting by a three-year-old would suggest psychological disturbance. Thus, if Heather continues to bite over the next year, her behavior should be looked at more closely. On the other hand, masturbation would not be unusual in children later in childhood but seems precocious in a toddler. Consistent with the social worker's speculation and Freud's early writings, sexual abuse would certainly be considered as a possible cause of Heather's behavior.

In contrast, learning theory would suggest that Heather's sexual and aggressive behaviors probably began quite innocently but were inadvertently reinforced when the caregivers overreacted. Heather learned that she could get all the attention she wanted simply by engaging in inappropriate behaviors. Had the caregivers ignored the behaviors, they would have eventually disappeared.

It is important to recognize that both of these theories help to organize our thinking with respect to behavior and development. But what constitutes a good theory? For a theory to be acceptable from a scientific point of view, it must be presented in a formal way that allows researchers to study the theory and its usefulness in providing explanations. A good theory must meet all of the following criteria:

- A theory must *communicate* meaning that can be shared among people. Theories use jargon, but they must also provide definitions that will ensure consistent interpretation. For instance, a psychoanalyst might use the term *oral-sadistic* to describe Heather's biting behavior—a term that could easily be misinterpreted. Would Heather's mother, the staff of the center, and other professionals all get the same meaning from that term? Similarly, would they all interpret the term *reinforcement* in the same way? In general, theorists are more likely to communicate the same meaning to all people by grounding their terms in people's everyday experience and by consistently referring to observable aspects of children's behavior.

- A theory must be *verifiable*. That is, the major concepts and principles of a theory must be presented so that they can be tested by the scientific method. For example, we can test experimentally the prediction that reinforcing aggression will result in more aggression: Reinforce aggressive acts in some children and withhold reinforcement from others. Such research may result in the acceptance, refinement, or outright rejection of all or part of the theory. The function of research in the study of development is presented in Chapter 3.

- Theories must be *generalizable*, that is, their explanations and predictions must apply across varied populations of children and environmental settings. For example, no single case could prove the psychoanalytic notion that sexual abuse *causes* precocious sexual behavior in children. Scientists must demonstrate that a theory can be applied as a general principle rather than limited to particular children in unique circumstances.

- A good theory does not simply explain; it should have *applied* value in dealing with children in practical situations. Some scientists would disagree with this as a general criterion for the evaluation of theory. This text, however, has been written with the express purpose of serving the practical needs of those who deal with children. The greater a theory's potential for application, the more this text will draw on it.

The theories to be presented in this chapter all meet the above criteria within acceptable limits. Some are clearly more testable than others, and some are more generalizable.

However, all have had enormous impact on both the science and practice of child development. Our primary concern is with *developmental* changes and the process of *facilitating* such changes. These theories have all commented extensively on development and have dealt, either implicitly or explicitly, with the process of facilitation and the associated concepts of risk and opportunity.

The theories have evolved over many years, derived from the observations of many scientists and scholars. Each theory has a logic and an integrity of its own. Its principles are highly interrelated, defining a unique system of knowledge. Once you understand the system, it will help you to think about children and organize your behavior with respect to children in practical settings; theories come alive and gain meaning in applied contexts.

Issues in the Study of Development

Child development theories vary widely in scope and content. Psychoanalytic theory focuses on the emotional and motivational aspects of development. Learning theory is concerned generally with the effects of the environment on behavior and, more specifically, with how those who deal with children can control their behavior. Piaget's theory focuses on the development of intellectual functioning: adaptive problem solving, reasoning, and concept formation. Information processing theory is concerned primarily with children's attention, memory, and problem-solving abilities. Ethological theory explores the effects of evolution on children's adaptive behavior.

But the theories do not just differ in content; they take very different positions on certain fundamental issues about the nature of development. Are children an active force in their own development? Is development continuous or discontinuous? Are there critical periods in development? Is development the product of nature or nurture?

Are Children an Active Force in Their Own Development? Some theories portray children as essentially passive with respect to developmental change. In this view, children do not initiate behavior or spontaneously act upon the environment; they merely *re*act to stimuli from the environment. Thus, some theorists see development as the accumulation of learned associations between environmental stimuli and responses (Bijou, 1989; Bijou & Baer, 1961; 1957).

Other theories portray children as active agents in their own development. In this perspective, children selectively and spontaneously involve themselves with specific aspects of the environment and alter the environment in ways that affect the nature of their experiences. For example, a child who develops an interest and aptitude for motor skills may begin to select activities — such as joining a team and practicing — that further develop these motor skills. Thus from the moment of conception, each individual must be understood as an *active* force in development, affecting the environment as much as he or she is influenced by that environment (Lerner & Busch-Rossnagel, 1981). This view promotes a sense of humility among those who seek to steer children's development by external interventions. To enhance development, we must understand what children bring to a situation, what they want and need, and whether they will spontaneously cooperate with our efforts.

There is no simple resolution to the differences between the passive and active views. Both seem valid. Children do appear to actively affect some developmental changes, such as acquiring language and social skills. Other changes, such as physical growth and changes in certain infant reflexes, seem to occur with less or perhaps no active participation of the child. Thus the complexity of development can be best explained by theories that encompass both passive and active involvement of the child in developmental change.

Is Development Continuous or Discontinuous? Many developmentalists believe that the accumulation of developmental change is not a matter of adding one new skill after another. Instead, they believe that developmental change causes "the rules of the system to change" (Green, 1989, p. 17) or to *reorganize*. For example, when a 13-month-old suddenly discovers that he can let go of furniture and toddle across the living room, the rules for the system of movement in space change irreversibly. At a more advanced level of development, when a five-year-old discovers that a few cookies can be called one, two, and three, her mental system for conceptualizing quantity is completely reorganized. She can now count cookies and tell whether her brother has more or fewer than she has.

The controversy of continuity versus discontinuity is this: Some theorists say that children go through various developmental stages defined by reorganizing changes while other theorists reject the notion of stages. A **developmental stage** refers to the time elapsing between any two sequential developmental changes that reorganize the system. Sigmund Freud (1940/1964) proposed that personality emerges in a sequence of five developmental stages organized around qualitatively different aspects of sexual functioning. Jean Piaget (1983) theorized that cognitive development occurs in a series of four sequential stages characterized by distinct forms of thinking and problem solving. Theorists who accept the concept of stages view development as **discontinuous**.

Other theorists—such as social learning theorists (Bandura, 1989) and information processing theorists (Bjorklund, 1987; Klahr, 1989)—explain development without reference to the stage concept. They view development as a gradual accumulation of minute changes and see no basis for arbitrarily dividing development into stages. Developmentalists who reject the concept of stages view development as **continuous**.

Are There Critical Periods in Development? Some developmentalists believe that children go through *critical periods* or *sensitive phases* during which certain forms of experience have very specific effects on development. If the experience occurs either before or after but not during the critical period, those effects will not take place. Thus, the notion of critical periods suggests that timing is everything.

The idea of critical periods has been used to describe both risks and opportunities for development. For example, *ethological theory* has suggested that the first two years of life provide a unique opportunity for the development of relationships to caregivers (Bowlby, 1988). Parents who provide sensitive, responsive caregiving will foster healthy attachment relationships with their toddlers. In contrast, psychoanalytic theory proposes that traumatic experiences in early childhood will have devastating effects on the development of personality.

Other developmentalists—including learning theorists and information processing theorists—find little evidence of critical periods in human development.

Is Development the Product of Nature or Nurture? The individual's genetic inheritance is permanently established at the moment of conception. While developmentalists agree that inheritance certainly determines physical features such as eye color, they disagree about the effects of genetics on behavior and development. We typically use the term *nature* to refer to genetic effects and *nurture* to refer to environmental effects on development.

Proponents of the nature perspective say that biological factors have a greater effect on behavior and development than environmental factors. Arnold Gesell (1929) proposed an extreme form of this perspective earlier in this century. He believed that all developmental change is predetermined by an inherited biological plan for the gradual unfolding of individual growth. He called this plan **maturation**. He attributed individual differences in growth and behavior to variations in inherited predispositions and believed that children progress through a series of maturational stages that are largely unaffected by environmental stimulation.

From a practical perspective, the nature view suggests that parents and other caregivers have little influence on the course of their children's development. Parents must simply be prepared to cope with (but not influence) the terrible twos, the conforming threes, and the inquisitive fours. This view is not very encouraging to those who would prefer to believe that caregivers have substantial influence over developmental outcomes. The nature perspective continues to be well represented in the popular child-rearing literature (Ames, Gillespie, Haines, & Ilg, 1978).

In contrast to the nature view, the nurture perspective emphasizes the environmental effects on behavior and development. At about the same time Gesell was formulating his theory, John B. Watson (1930) presented a theory that totally contradicted Gesell's. Watson believed that development reflected no more than the accumulation of learned behaviors and that learning resulted from the way caregivers manipulate the child's environment. Watson vividly expressed his view on nurture and developmental outcome:

> Give me a dozen healthy infants, well formed and my own special world to bring them up in, and I'll guarantee to take anyone at random and train him to become any type of specialist I might select—Doctor, lawyer, artist, merchantchief, and yes, even beggar and thief, regardless of his talents, penchants, tendencies, abilities, vocations and race of his ancestors. (p. 104)

Do we really have that much power over our children's developmental outcome? Although Watson vastly overstated the potential effects of training, his view has had pervasive influence on the study of child and adolescent development. From a practical perspective, the nurture approach promises a great deal to those who seek to influence children's development. The question is whether it promises more than it delivers.

Despite a long history of extreme positions taken by various theorists in the nurture/nature controversy, most contemporary developmentalists have come to accept that nature and nurture are both essential considerations in the formulation of developmental theory. It is generally understood that all developmental change results from the *interaction* of genetic potential and the child's experiences (Horowitz, 1987; Sameroff & Chandler, 1975). A child can realize his or her genetic potential within a facilitating environmental context, and even the most supportive environment will have no effect without the genetic foundation for a particular developmental change.

Psychoanalytic Theory

Psychoanalytic theory is the oldest and most controversial of the theories of development. The controversy stems from the provocative ideas of its originator, the Viennese neurologist Sigmund Freud (1856–1939). Despite the controversy, Freud's ideas have had identifiable impact on the life of virtually every individual born in Western culture in this century. Although many scholars have contributed to the development of psychoanalytic theory, we will limit our discussion to Freud's theory and the important elaboration and extension of his work by Erik Erikson.

Freud's Psychoanalytic Theory

Freud was born in Freiberg, Moravia, in 1856 and lived most of his life in Vienna, Austria. He died in England in 1939, two years after fleeing the German occupation. Trained as a neurologist, Freud became interested in patients who were suffering from mental disorders. At the time, scientists knew very little about the causes of mental illness, and treatment was largely a matter of forced confinement. Consistent with his medical training, Freud hoped to identify brain abnormalities that would account for his patients' disturbed behavior; but many of their symptoms—physical pain, paralysis, and loss of motor control and memory—had no identifiable physiological base. Freud's success using hypnosis to relieve some of his patients' symptoms convinced him that *psychological* processes rather than *physiological* processes were the cause of mental illness (Breuer & Freud, 1895). Moreover, he speculated that the basis of mental illness could be found in the early development of the child—particularly during the first five years of life.

Sigmund Freud and his father. Freud would go on to develop his highly controversial psychosexual theory of personality development. This theory revolutionized the way we think about children, sensitizing us to the critical effects of early experience on the development of personality and mental illness.

The Structure of Personality Freud (1923/1960) proposed that, from birth, individuals are endowed with biologically based sexual and aggressive *instincts* that unconsciously motivate everything humans think, say, or do throughout their lives. The instincts are expressed in the form of **libido**—a form of energy that drives all thinking and behavior. Libido is stored in the **id**, a place in the mind that Freud called the "reservoir of libido" (p. 53). (See Figure 2.1.) The id may be thought of as a storage battery that has a relentless need to discharge its energy from the moment of birth. Investments of libidinal energy are discharged through activities and objects that afford pleasure by reducing tension. We may invest libido in reality or in fantasy; thus dreams can be a source of great pleasure. All of the activities of the id are unconscious; thus we are all unaware of our instincts and their profound and virtually irresistible effects on our behavior.

The process of investment undergoes important developmental change. Infants invest libido according to the **pleasure principle**, an approach that demands instant gratification. Infants find this gratification at their mothers' breast. However, parents soon begin

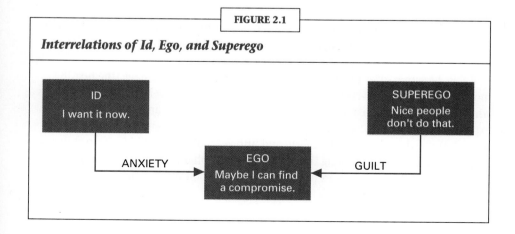

FIGURE 2.1

Interrelations of Id, Ego, and Superego

ID
I want it now.

SUPEREGO
Nice people
don't do that.

ANXIETY

EGO
Maybe I can find
a compromise.

GUILT

to socialize their infants to delay gratification, tolerate frustration, and seek pleasure in more socially competent ways. Freud believed that these demands promote the development of the **ego**, the component of personality that uses conscious perception and intelligence to find pleasure in a world where needs are not typically met on demand. Because the ego recognizes the frustrations inherent in living in the real world, it is said to function on the basis of the **reality principle**.

The third and final component of the personality, the *superego*, emerges rather suddenly during the fifth or sixth year of life. The **superego** is the seat of morality. It has two distinct components: The *conscience* is a collection of beliefs, attitudes, and rules for behavior that functions as an internal standard for the appropriateness of behavior; the *ego ideal* is an internalized image of distinctly human form that the child (and later the adult) unconsciously strives to become. The problem is that there is nothing necessarily ideal about the ego ideal; its features may be positive or negative or both.

The beliefs, rules, and images that constitute the superego are not taught to the child, nor are they learned as one would memorize a list of rules at school. The superego is formed by **identification**, a special form of learning in which the characteristics of significant persons—in this case, the same-sex parent and to a lesser extent the opposite-sex parent—are incorporated into the child's personality (Freud, 1923/1960).

Psychodynamics Freud suggested that the id, ego, and superego interact in a dynamic system. When the ego attempts to satisfy the id's insatiable needs, it is destined to fail due to the difficulty of finding love and hate objects in civilized society. The ego's failure results in *unconscious anxiety*, which undermines the ego's ability to function. Conversely, if the ego does its job too well, rules or ideals in the superego are violated, resulting in *unconscious guilt*. Guilt, like anxiety, impairs the functioning of the ego. The ego, therefore, exists between a rock and a hard place, in a persistent state of internal stress and conflict.

Freud suggested that while the ego is vulnerable to the ravages of guilt and anxiety, it can fight back with **defense mechanisms**, unconscious mental strategies that provide *temporary* relief from anxiety and guilt. He described several defense mechanisms and their effects: *Repression* forces libido back into the id, stifling all desire for an object; *denial* conveniently wipes out memories of traumatic events; *rationalization* reduces the desire for an object by depreciating its value (the proverbial sour grapes). While an individual may temporarily avoid turmoil by using defense mechanisms, there is danger in their *overuse*. For instance, while denial can fend off anxiety or guilt, persistent denial distorts a person's view of reality, laying the foundation for mental illness.

Psychosexual Development Freud believed that personality emerges gradually over the first five to six years of life in a progression of **psychosexual stages** of development. Each stage is defined by the presence of libido in a particular part (or zone) of the body. Libido's presence creates an **erogenous zone** that is highly sensitive to sexual stimulation and a focus of pleasure.

Table 2.1 summarizes the psychosexual stages. During the **oral stage** (the first 18 months of life), pleasure is derived from variations on sucking behavior. The stage ends when the infant is weaned from sucking to sipping. During the **anal stage**, the child experiences pleasure in the act of defecation. The stage ends when the child is toilet trained. Somewhere between the fourth and fifth years of life, the libido again shifts location to the genitals, marking the beginning of the **phallic stage**. Freud believed that the child selects the opposite-sex parent as a love object during this stage—a choice that

TABLE 2.1		
Freud's Stages of Psychosexual Development		
Stage	Age	Source of Pleasure
Oral	0–18 mos.	Nursing, sucking, biting
Anal	18 mos.–3 yrs.	Elimination and retention of feces; toilet play
Phallic	3–6 yrs.	Genital play; erotic fantasy regarding opposite-sex parent
Latency	6–11 yrs.	Sexual drives repressed; temporary loss of sexual interest
Genital	Puberty and adolescence	Resurgence of sexual strivings from early childhood

creates considerable emotional conflict within the child and within the family. This so-called **Oedipal conflict** is resolved when the child relinquishes his desire for the parent and takes on a superego.

Freud believed that emotional upheavals of the phallic stage are followed by massive repression of sexual and aggressive drives during middle childhood, a stage he called **latency**. In the final stage, the **genital stage**, the young adolescent experiences a rebirth of sexual and aggressive strivings and the return of unresolved conflicts from earlier stages. The genital stage begins in adolescence and extends through adulthood.

Freud speculated that **trauma**—extreme experiences of anxiety during the first five years of life—may cause the individual to be permanently vulnerable to psychological maladjustment. In fact, he traced particular forms of disturbance directly to specific traumatic events during the oral, anal, and phallic stages. For example, infants who are weaned too abruptly may remain dependent on others throughout their lives and are prone to develop eating disorders in adolescence. Toddlers who are either physically punished or overindulged by their parents during toilet training may become rigid, compulsive adults. Children who fail to resolve the intense emotional conflicts during the phallic stage may have permanent problems relating to others.

Erikson's Psychosocial Theory of Development

Erik Erikson was born in 1902 in Frankfurt, Germany. He studied psychoanalysis in Vienna with some of the most reknown psychoanalysts, including Freud and his daughter Anna. Like Freud, Erikson left Vienna to escape the Nazis, immigrating to the United States. Several years after Freud's death, Erikson presented an interpretation of Freud's theory that has had significant impact on the study and practice of child development.

Erikson argued that classical Freudian theory had several serious limitations: It did not adequately describe the powerful effects of family and culture on the development of the personality; it greatly underestimated the ego's role in psychological adjustment; and it did not account for the continued development of the ego beyond the childhood years. To compensate for these shortcomings, Erikson formulated his **psychosocial theory** of development, a theory that traced the development of the ego throughout the lifespan.

Erikson described the development of the ego through a series of eight stages. The stages are presented in Table 2.2. Each stage represents a specific form of developmental change, resulting from the resolution of an intense conflict known as a **psychosocial**

Erik Erikson. Erikson revised and expanded Freud's theory, accepting the notions of unconscious mental states and the structure of personality, but rejecting Freud's exclusive emphasis on sexuality. Erikson recognized the effects of family and culture on the development of personality and mental illness.

TABLE 2.2

Erikson's Stages of Psychosocial Development

Psychosocial Crisis	Critical Events	Positive Resolution	Negative Resolution
Trust vs. mistrust (0–1½ yrs.)	Mutual regulation in care and feeding	Positive, optimistic outlook on life; "I feel safe and secure"	Negative outlook on life; "I am afraid"
Autonomy vs. shame (1½–3 yrs.)	Power conflicts with caregivers over toilet training and exploration	"I can make decisions, conform, and compromise when I need to"	"I must have it my way" or "I must conform"
Initiative vs. guilt (4–6 yrs.)	Conflicts in taking the initiative	"I can make things happen" and "I can set goals and persist"	"I feel helpless"
Industry vs. inferiority (6–12 yrs.)	Struggle to learn the skills of the culture: the value of *work*	"I am competent" and "I take pleasure in work"	"I feel inadequate" or "I am lazy"
Identity vs. role confusion (adolescence)	Conflict between the roles and responsibilities of child vs. adult	"I know who I am and what I intend to do with my life"	"I don't know who I am or where I am going"
Intimacy vs. isolation (young adult)	Forming intimate relationships	"I can love and care for others"	"I am only capable of superficial relationships"
Generativity vs. stagnation (middle age)	Marriage, parenthood, balancing work and family	"I will have children and be a competent parent"	"I have no interest in children"
Integrity vs. despair (old age)	The meaning of one's life and accepting death	"My life has been meaningful and I can accept death"	"I fear death for my life has had no meaning"

SOURCE: *Adapted from Erikson, 1963.*

crisis. Resolution of each crisis causes permanent change in the ego's sense of the world. For example, during the oral stage, infants experience a crisis of *trust versus mistrust* as they endure cycles of pleasure and frustration in their parents' care. A healthy resolution of the crisis fosters a **sense of trust**—a belief in the world as a potentially satisfying but sometimes frustrating context for development. During the anal stage, toddlers experience a crisis of *autonomy versus shame* as they struggle with their parents over control. A healthy resolution fosters a **sense of autonomy**, the ability to deal effectively with power and decision making in relationships.

Erikson emphasized that each successive crisis can only be resolved when families engage in **mutual regulation**—that is, sensitive, reciprocal caring and emotional sharing between parent and child. In Erikson's words,

> We distort the situation if we abstract it in such a way that we consider the parent as "having" such and such a personality when the child is born and then, remaining static, impinging upon a poor little thing. For this weak and changing being moves the whole family along. Babies control and bring up their families as much as they are controlled by them; in fact, we may say that the family brings up a baby by being brought up by him. Whatever reaction patterns are given biologically and whatever schedule is predetermined developmentally must be considered to be a series of *potentialities for changing patterns of mutual regulation.* (1950/1963, p. 69)

In Erikson's view mutual regulation between children and their caregivers is the key to healthy psychological development.

Critique of Psychoanalytic Theory

By the criteria presented earlier in this chapter, psychoanalytic theory falls far short of good theory. The principles are steeped in jargon that are only occasionally grounded in observable aspects of children's behavior. The concepts and relationships defy verification by the scientific method, and its exclusive reliance on individual case studies limits generalizability. Freud's view that only trained psychoanalysts are qualified to gather data or to deal directly with children's emotional problems severely limits both the theory's testability and its practical application. On the other hand, psychoanalytic theory fares better as developmental theory. Both Freud and Erikson conceive of development as a gradual accumulation of relatively permanent changes through transactions with the environment. This said, we will briefly consider the broader strengths and weaknesses of the theory.

The great value of psychoanalytic theory is its emphasis on the importance of early experience in personality development. While Freud's portrayal of early development as a time of extreme emotional vulnerability may be overly foreboding, his work has sensitized several generations of parents and practitioners to the risks and opportunities for social and emotional development in infancy and early childhood. The psychoanalytic notions of the unconscious mind, trauma, and the importance of sexuality in early development have greatly expanded our perspective on child development.

The weaknesses of psychoanalytic theory—beyond its limitations as theory—lie in its overly negative view of development and its overemphasis on the importance of early sexuality in personality development. Freud's view of children as emotionally vulnerable fails to recognize their resilience in the face of risk. His notion of the long-term effects of early trauma on emotional development has gained little support through research. While Freud helped us to recognize young children's sexual responsiveness, his belief in the critical importance of early sexual experience for personality development seems greatly exaggerated.

Learning Theory

Earlier in this century, many psychologists in the United States searched for a more scientifically objective discipline of child study than psychoanalytic theory. The most famous pioneer in this search was the American psychologist John B. Watson (1878–1958), who declared that the purpose of psychology was not to speculate about the existence of unconscious states but to uncover principles that would allow for the prediction and control of human behavior. For Watson, prediction and control of behavior was the equivalent of explanation; thus he referred to this exclusive focus on behavior as the science of **behaviorism**.

Watson was influenced by the earlier work of the Russian physiologist Ivan Pavlov (1849–1936), whose studies of salivating reflexes in dogs led to his discovery of a type of learning known as **classical conditioning**. Pavlov would strap a dog into a harness and repeatedly present food to elicit the salivating response. This response was innate or natural; no learning was involved. Dogs simply salivate when food is presented. A stimulus such as the food in Pavlov's experiment that naturally elicits a response is referred to as the **unconditioned stimulus** (or UCS); an unlearned response, such as the salivating, is known as the **unconditioned response** (or UCR).

In the course of his experiments, Pavlov noticed that his dogs began to salivate even *before* food was presented, as when other cues (such as the sound of the trainer's approaching footsteps) told them that food would be delivered soon. To investigate this phenomenon, Pavlov changed the design of his research. Just before presenting food, he presented another stimulus—a ringing bell. After just a few such pairings, the bell alone was able to elicit the salivation response. In other words, the dogs had learned something. The new stimulus, the ringing of the bell, was the **conditioned stimulus** (or CS). The learned response to this conditioned stimulus was known as the **conditioned response** (or CR). This form of learning is referred to as **classical conditioning**. Another example of classical conditioning is when an infant learns to suck (conditioned response) at the sight of the mother entering the infant's room (conditioned stimulus). The infant's prior association of the mother's breast (unconditioned stimulus) and the sucking reflex (unconditioned response) establishes the foundation for this classically conditioned response.

Watson tried to show that classical conditioning could be applied to children. His most famous experiment involved a toddler named Little Albert (Watson & Rayner, 1920; see Figure 2.2). At 11 months, Albert was a normal, healthy youngster who showed no natural fear of a white rat. Watson aimed to condition a new response to the previously neutral stimulus (the rat) by pairing it with an aversive or unpleasant stimulus. Whenever Albert reached for the rat, the experimenter struck a metal bar with a hammer, creating a sudden loud sound (the UCS), which frightened Albert and caused him to cry (the UCR). After several repetitions, Albert began to show fear and to cry in response to the appearance of the rat alone. He had learned to show a fear response (the CR) to the rat (the CS).

Watson recognized that manipulating the environment enough to condition a child is much easier in a laboratory setting than under natural conditions. However, he believed that the goal of controlling children's behavior could be accomplished by an objective approach to childrearing, as summarized in this quote from Watson's child-care manual, *Psychological Care of Infant and Child* (1928):

> There is a sensible way of treating children. Treat them as though they were young adults. Dress them, bathe them with care and circumspection. Let your behavior always be objective and kindly firm. Never hug and kiss them, never let them sit in your lap. If you must, kiss them once on the forehead when they say goodnight. Shake hands with them in the morning. Give them a pat on the head if they have made an extraordinary good job of a difficult task. Try it out. In a week's time you will find how easy it is to be perfectly objective with your child and at the same time kindly. You will be utterly ashamed of the mawkish, sentimental way you have been handling it. (pp. 81–82)

Fortunately, Watson had much more effect on his fellow psychologists over the next few years than on parents of young children. Watson's recommendations for child care were generally recognized as overly restrictive and potentially harmful. However, Watson's classical conditioning procedure established the laboratory study of learning as a primary emphasis in the field of psychology.

FIGURE 2.2

Watson's Classical Conditioning Experiment on Little Albert

Operant Learning

Watson's focus on classical conditioning was eventually transcended by new and more powerful insights into learning, stimulated largely by the work of B. F. Skinner (1904–1990). Skinner (1953) formalized the principles of **operant conditioning**, a form of learning in which spontaneous behaviors, which he called *operants*, are altered by the consequences they yield. An **operant** is simply a behavior that exists in an individual's repertoire: physical behaviors such as climbing and running, perceptual behaviors such as visual gaze and explorative touch, and social behaviors such as hitting and sharing.

Extensive research has demonstrated that when certain behaviors consistently result in certain types of consequences, these behaviors will be modified in predictable ways. Here is how each type of consequence works:

- **Reinforcements** are consequences that increase the frequency of a behavior. This may include naturally occurring events such as finding a lost toy or specific rewards such as praising a child for behaving appropriately. If a child experiences a *reinforcement* immediately after doing something, he or she is likely to do the same behavior more often. For instance, reinforcement has been shown to increase such diverse behaviors as sucking in newborns (Siqueland, 1968) and the use of seat belts in preschool children (Sowers-Hoag, Thyer, & Bailey, 1987).

- **Punishments** are consequences that decrease the frequency of those same behaviors. If a child experiences a punishment immediately after performing some operant, he or she is unlikely to do that behavior as often. Thus consistent use of punishment has been shown to effectively reduce aggression (Parke & Deur, 1972).

- **Extinction** is a process that decreases the frequency of a behavior simply by *ignoring* its occurrence.

These principles assume that the behavior to be modified is already in the child's repertoire but at unacceptably low or high frequency. How are *new* behaviors created?

One answer is Skinner's (1953) *shaping procedure*. **Shaping** simply assumes that all complex behavior can be broken down into simpler subcomponents and that each behavior can be individually and systematically reinforced to approximate a desired behavior. For example, sharing—a valued but elusive behavior in young children—can be broken down into the following sequence of components: playing with a toy, playing with the toy near a peer, showing the toy to the peer, allowing the peer to touch the toy

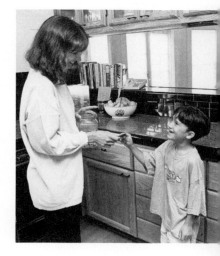

Parents often try to control their children's behavior by reinforcing positive behaviors and by punishing negative behaviors. Here a mother combines a smile and a cookie to reward her son for helping with the chores. If she does this consistently over time, her child is likely to continue to do his chores. Unfortunately, many children come to perceive chores as punishments, significantly reducing the effect of their parents' reinforcement.

BOX 2.1

Operant Learning in Practical Settings: A Critique

Behavior modification sounds almost too good to be true: All one needs are reinforcements, punishments, and the ability to ignore, and you are in a position to modify children's behavior. The problem is that the principles of behavior modification are based on certain assumptions, not all of which are realistic.

First, operant conditioning principles assume that the behavior (or a component of it) is *reasonably frequent* in the child's repertoire, that an observer can see it happen, and that the child is *reasonably accessible* to be reinforced immediately. In practical terms, these assumptions require that a highly observant adult, armed with the appropriate reinforcement, be able to focus attention on and stay close to a child over extended periods of time so that he or she can reinforce the desired behavior the moment it occurs. Realistically, that hardly ever happens. Even the most vigilant caregiver may occasionally be distracted by interruptions such as household tasks. In group situations such as day care or school such close monitoring is almost impossible to achieve.

Second, operant conditioning assumes that the facilitator will have effective reinforcements and punishments available. Unfortunately, something that works one day will often fail to work the following day. Children tend to *satiate* on reinforcers and on punishments, so that they lose their effect. For instance, after getting candy or treats as rewards a few times, children may become bored. Likewise, children who have been frequently spanked may reach a point where they appear to feel no pain, rendering the punishment ineffective. Even the ubiquitous advice to use social praise tends to ignore the fact that many children simply do not respond consistently to praise as reinforcement. In all, children are complex individuals, and numerous personality and social relationship issues influence the effectiveness of reinforcement and punishment from one child to another and even from one moment to the next. Until the effects of reinforcement and punishment are studied and understood in the context of complex human relationships, the use of these techniques will fall short of its full potential.

Operant conditioning also assumes that the facilitator will ignore inappropriate behavior. Again, this assumption is unreasonable. People who deal with children can ignore only up to a point. If the child's behavior becomes harmful to the child or to others, ignoring becomes neglecting; additionally, other children's inappropriate behavior is disinhibited, and the situation rapidly degenerates to chaos.

Although a vast body of scientific literature has documented the effects of behavior modification with young children, most of this research has been performed in highly controlled environments, typically in university-based laboratory settings. Such demonstrations have also used highly trained personnel, unusually high staff-to-child ratios, and plentiful and varied reinforcers. The critical issue, however, is not how effective behavior modification can be in a laboratory, but how effective it can be in the real world of local day-care centers or public schools. In summary, operant learning theory, when packaged as a behavior modification technique, may promise more than it can realistically deliver.

A final concern is the failure of operant theory to encompass a developmental perspective. In its quest for universal principles, operant theory tends to generalize across age, gender, socioeconomic status, and even species. It provides little guidance for working with specific children in particular stages of development and within particular social contexts. These can be serious shortcomings. Modifying a toddler's behavior is simply not the same as modifying a 10-year-old's behavior, just as techniques that work with one child at home may be ineffective on a busy playground. Most important, older children interpret their parents' reinforcements and punishments very differently than younger children do. For example, older children are much more likely to interpret reinforcement as a bribe, or to see the hypocrisy when their parents punish behaviors that they themselves engage in.

Using behavior modification techniques to influence children's behavior can be very difficult in large open spaces such as this playground. The large number of children, their high activity level, and extraneous stimulation makes it difficult for an adult to deliver reinforcements and punishments effectively.

briefly, and finally giving the toy to the peer with no effort to take it back. Shaping begins by reinforcing the first behavior in the sequence to increase its frequency. Then when the next step approximating sharing occurs, only that new behavior is reinforced. This process continues until the child actually shares.

Those who deal with children tend to take considerable interest in techniques that promise to increase appropriate behaviors and decrease inappropriate behaviors. They have therefore welcomed the field of **behavior modification** — the system of applied operant techniques — that has emerged in recent years. Behavior modification strategies are typically presented in user-friendly manuals that are designed for application in specific settings, such as day-care centers and public schools. A critique of the widespread use of behavior modification with children in natural settings is presented in Box 2.1.

Social Cognitive Theory

If all learning had to depend on reinforcement coming as soon as a child accidentally approximated a competent skill, learning even rudimentary skills such as eating with a fork might take a lifetime. As it is, children often learn highly complex behaviors without identifiable sources of reinforcement. Learning theorists had to explain how. The solution has come in the form of **social cognitive theory** (Bandura, 1977, 1989), an advanced theory of learning that not only accounts for the fundamental issue of the efficiency of learning, but now aspires to the status of a developmental theory.

Observational Learning   Social cognitive theory is built around a central concept of **observational learning**, the idea that children can learn simply by observing the behavior of a model (for example, a friend or an older sibling) and the consequences of the model's behavior. Observational learning has two components: *acquisition* and *performance*. In acquisition the child merely observes a model's behavior and learns which of the model's behaviors lead to which consequences in which situations. During acquisition, the model is the one who gets reinforced or punished, not the child. The child then stores these expectations in memory for future reference. By observing the model over time, the child may solidify, nullify, or modify his or her expectations.

Performance, the second component of observational learning, refers to whether the child will eventually do the same things he or she has seen the model do. Whether the child does depends on both the observed consequences to the model and the similarity of the child's situation and the model's. For instance, the child may think, "My brother got to stay up late when he ignored my father. Maybe I can too." If the model had not been reinforced or the situation was dissimilar, the child would be less likely to imitate the modeled behavior.

Learning and the Self   Social cognitive theory departs significantly from operant learning theory by crediting the child with a *self* (Bandura, 1989). The social cognitive view of the self is, however, very different from the dynamic Freudian ego. In the learning perspective, the self is merely a way of addressing certain critical cognitive functions that affect the learning process. One such function is the effect of a child's perception of his or her competencies on the likelihood that he or she will imitate modeled behaviors. For example, consider a child who is tempted to imitate a new dance step that she has seen her older sister perform. If she believes that she has the necessary skill, she will probably give it a try; if she doubts her ability, she is unlikely to attempt it. Thus, the child's *self-perceived competency* influences the likelihood of imitative response.

Learning in Transactional Perspective   In social cognitive theory, the passive learner is replaced by a child who is an active influence in learning situations, selecting problems to solve and deciding among solutions to those problems. Criticizing earlier approaches to behavior modification, Bandura states unequivocally, "One-sided developmental analyses of how parents influence their children have given way to transactional analyses of how parents and children influence each other" (1989, p. 4). This new portrayal of the child as an active learner in transactional perspective is an important step in the emergence of social cognitive theory as a theory of development.

Critique of Social Cognitive Theory

Social cognitive theory does quite well on the criteria of good theory, but not as well as a developmental theory. Bandura's concepts are well grounded in children's observable behavior and easily communicated to researchers and practitioners. While Bandura's ideas are somewhat more difficult to research than traditional learning theory, they are far more testable than Freud's or Piaget's concepts. For example, whether or not a child imitates a model's behavior can be readily tested in laboratory or natural settings. The concepts have generalized across various populations of children, and the theory has been shown to have great practical value. However, social cognitive theory's failure to deal effectively with age-related changes in children's ability to learn earns it low marks as developmental theory.

The great strength of social cognitive theory is its acceptance of cognitive influences on children's learning. In contrast to traditional learning theory, Bandura recognized that children's thought processes have powerful effects on their learning. Unfortunately, social cognitive theory has a long way to go before it fully integrates what we presently know about children's cognitive development into the theory. As you will see in the following sections on Piaget's theory and information processing theory, this will be no easy task.

Piaget's Cognitive-Developmental Theory

Jean Piaget (1896–1980) was one of the great creative intellects of this century. His theory has had massive impact on the thinking and behavior of all those who deal with children, including researchers, parents, teachers, day-care workers, therapists, and those who design products and services for children. His theory has inspired thousands of

Jean Piaget interacting with preschoolers. Piaget viewed children as active learners, constantly searching for problems to be solved. His detailed observations of children's behavior and provocative theory of cognitive development have broadly influenced the study of children's intellectual abilities.

research studies, innovations in curriculum and instruction, and new parental approaches to the intellectual development of children. These effects show every sign of continuing into the next century. Although his theory is familiar to many, it is not always well understood.

Unlike the perspectives discussed earlier in this chapter, Piaget's theory focuses almost exclusively on cognitive development. It explains how children develop knowledge of their world, how they think and solve problems, and how these cognitive processes change in a stage-by-stage progression from birth to maturity. Thinking is an extraordinarily complicated process, and Piaget developed an extraordinarily complicated theory to explain the process. Fully understanding this theory demands years of study, a task well beyond our scope here. The next few paragraphs are intended merely to provide an initial overview.

The Active Nature of the Child

Piaget portrayed children as innately and irrepressibly active, acting upon their environment rather than simply reacting to it. Action is, therefore, assumed as a spontaneous and universal quality central to the cognitive development of all children. Children are by nature curious and explorative, persistently seeking novelty and trying to incorporate that novelty into their understanding of the world. Infants express the active nature of their cognitive system by exploring every object within their reach. Older children express this active quality in persistence in problem solving and intellectual curiosity.

Piaget assumed that children do not passively wait for other people to present problems to them; they actively seek problems to solve. It is just in their nature to be curious, inquisitive, and interested in novelty. In practical terms, those who deal with children should assume that, irrespective of age or stage, *all* children are *intrinsically motivated* to improve their understanding of the world around them. Optimal cognitive development requires a rich environment that can be actively explored for novelty and challenge. In this view, rigidity of thought, passivity, and lack of curiosity are considered abnormal states that require explanation. Unfortunately, Piaget's theory offers little explanation for children who appear intellectually unmotivated and slow to learn.

Mental Structures and Adaptation

The central focus of Piaget's theory is the concept of *structure*. He used the term *structure* in two ways. First, he suggests that all aspects of the real world are structured entities. In the world of an infant, for example, individual objects such as rattles, blankets, and mother's face have structure. In the expanded world of the preschool child, the arrangement of toys on a shelf, friendships with peers, and problems encountered in preschool have structure. Still later in development, children must solve structured math problems in school and engage in structured social relationships. In this use of the term, *structure* refers to the complexity of some aspect of the environment.

Piaget's second use of the term *structure* refers to **cognitive structures** — the mental units that children use to represent reality, to think about the objects, events, and relationships in their experience, and the strategies they use to solve problems. Put simply, cognitive structures are the way the child *knows* the world. A child knows the world to the extent that he or she has cognitive structures that match the structure of objects and events in the real world. Piaget's theory is an explanation of the development of cognitive structures from infancy through adolescence and how cognitive structures facilitate adaptation to the environment.

Adaptation is the process by which cognitive structures are applied to and are modified by the child's experiences. Piaget defined two distinct processes by which adaptation occurs: *assimilation* and *accommodation*. In **assimilation**, a child uses an existing cognitive structure to interpret some experience. For instance, when a familiar rattle is presented to an infant, she shows that she knows the rattle by grasping it and shaking it to make a rattling sound. Piaget would say that the infant has assimilated the rattle to the cognitive structure of "things that shake and make noise." However, the infant may subsequently grasp a pacifier, assimilate it to the same cognitive structure, and shake it in anticipation of the sound. The new object has been interpreted as if it were an instance of "rattle." Thus assimilation interprets the new in terms of the old.

In **accommodation**, the child modifies an existing cognitive structure to conform to some new aspect of reality. For instance, for young infants a rattle is at first just one more object to be grasped and all objects are assimilated to the cognitive structure for grasping. After repeated experience with rattles and other objects, though, the infant modifies the cognitive structure and begins to distinguish between rattles and non-rattles. Thus accommodation represents developmental change in cognitive structures— an integration of the new into the old.

Piaget viewed the mind as never completely satisfied with its current level of understanding of objects, events, or relationships. Every act of assimilation implies some degree of accommodation to some previously unnoticed feature of reality. The result is an improved adaptation to that reality. Thus cognitive structures are always moving slowly but steadily toward ever-improving approximations of reality.

Stages of Cognitive Development

Piaget described cognitive development as a series of qualitative changes in the way children think and solve problems from infancy through adolescence. He identified four stages of cognitive development, each with a unique form of cognitive structure. Each new structural form derives from the previous form, but with new and more sophisticated capabilities. Piaget believed that all children in all cultures progress through these stages in exactly the same sequence and that no one ever skips a stage. However, some children progress through the stages more quickly than others, and those who progress more slowly may never reach the final stage.

Piaget's four stages are described briefly below; they are also summarized in Table 2.3. As with the theories of Freud and Erikson, more detailed accounts of development within each stage will be provided in appropriate chapters later in the text.

Sensorimotor Stage (0–24 months) The **sensorimotor stage** is characterized by action-oriented problem solving. At the beginning of this stage, the newborn's cognitive organization is limited to an elaborate set of "wired-in" reflexes such as startling in response to a loud noise or turning the head toward a stroke on the cheek. However, as newborns actively touch, taste, and visually scan the world around them, they develop what Piaget called sensorimotor **schemas**—simple cognitive structures that regulate the infant's body movements and the effects of those movements on objects. For example, the grasping schema organizes the infant's voluntary opening and closing of his or her hands and the grasping and manipulation of objects. In time, they accommodate these primitive schemas into more sophisticated schemas that enable them to influence their environment in increasingly complex ways. For instance, they accommodate their aimless arm and hand movements in the first three or four months into movements that manipulate the environment—pushing, squeezing, banging, tearing, lifting, and crush-

TABLE 2.3		
Piaget's Stages of Cognitive Development		
Stage	Mental Structure	Description of Cognitive Functioning
Sensorimotor (0–24 mos.)	Schemas	Knowledge is constructed by active exploration of objects; objects become permanent; schemas can be sequenced to solve problems
Preoperational (2–6 yrs.)	Preconcepts	Symbolic reasoning used for the first time but centration and irreversibility constrain logical thought processes
Concrete operations (7–11 yrs.)	Concrete operations	Logical systems of thought now possible but thinking and problem solving limited to physically present objects
Formal operations (12 yrs. and beyond)	Formal operations	Abstract reasoning about hypothetical events now possible

ing—by six to eight months. By the end of the first year they use their arms and hands to manipulate simple instruments such as a fork or spoon, a milestone of sensorimotor intelligence.

Preoperational Stage (2–6 years) The action-oriented problem solving of the sensorimotor stage is gradually replaced by thought that is mediated by words and images. Piaget called this thought **symbolic reasoning**. Children engage in increasingly complex forms of symbolic reasoning as they develop from childhood to adolescence. Piaget named each of the remaining stages after the form of symbolic reasoning that characterizes each stage: In the *preoperational stage*, preschoolers reason with preoperations (or preconcepts); in the concrete operational stage school-age children reason with *concrete operations*; and in the formal operational stage, adolescents reason with *formal operations*.

During the **preoperational stage**, children no longer are limited to thinking about the objects in their immediate perceivable environment. They can now organize mental images of events and objects both present and absent into primitive concepts (or preoperations) that they can use to solve simple problems. For example, preschoolers know what toys they own and where they are at all times, and they use that knowledge to organize their play.

Although preoperational thought represents a quantum leap from earlier sensorimotor thought, it has many limitations. One is a tendency to focus on isolated parts of an event rather than seeing the whole picture. Piaget called this **centration**. For instance, after meeting the new teacher at day care, a preschooler may be unable to remember what she looks like but remembers her earrings in great detail. Another limitation of preoperational thought is that it is often illogical. Parents and practitioners are alternately frustrated and entertained by the preschooler's confused concepts of time, space, classification, and quantitative relationships. For example, when preschool children are asked to retell a story read to them, they tend to reverse sequences of events, confuse cause and effect, and mistake appearance for reality.

Perhaps the most serious limitation of preoperational thought, however, is its *irreversibility*. Preschool children can literally think their way into a problem but are unable to

Although Piaget described preschoolers as immensely curious, he also noted the limitations of their thinking. This three-year-old is able to take the object apart, but will be unable to think through the actions needed to put it back together. Piaget believed that young children cannot reverse their thinking, severely limiting their ability to adapt to the environment.

reverse their thought process. For instance, when a three-year-old boy who has a brother is asked if he has a brother, he will say yes. However, when asked if his brother has a brother, he will say no. Thus, while preoperational thought represents a great step forward from sensorimotor thought, it fails to provide a logical, systematic way of adapting to the world.

Concrete Operations (7–11 years)   During the **concrete operations stage**, children's thinking becomes increasingly logical. The new form of cognitive structure, the **concrete operation**, organizes thoughts into *logical systems*. For example, children gradually come to understand that adding, subtracting, multiplying, and dividing are interrelated mathematical operations and that classes are composed of subclasses. They also begin to understand logical relationships. For instance, if three sticks of different length are displayed, a child will reason that if the first stick is longer than the second stick, and the second is longer than the third, then the first stick must be longer than the third stick. Concrete operational thought is *reversible*, allowing the child to think his or her way into problems and back out. For example, an eight-year-old is much more likely than a five-year-old to think about how he is going to put something back together before he takes it apart.

The child does well with such problems because they involve concrete items that are familiar to the child. If, however, the problem involves abstract concepts or objects with which the child is not familiar, the child does poorly. For example, if a child is told (with no objects present) that A is greater than B, and that B is greater than C, the child is unlikely to conclude that A must be greater than C. At this stage the child can deal only with real objects that can be seen and touched. Abstract concepts of hypothetical events and outcomes are still beyond the child's capability.

Formal Operations (12 years and beyond)   The hallmark of the **formal operations stage** is the ability to consider general propositions and principles and to think about hypothetical events. For the first time, the individual can reason about phenomena that do not exist in reality, such as abstract concepts of morality, science, and mathematics. Once individuals enter the formal operations stage, they are also able to think about thinking—both their own thinking and other people's. This capability is an enormous advantage in communication and social relationships. For instance, when a formal operational teenage boy wants to meet a certain teenage girl, he can think about what she might be thinking about him and plan his behavior accordingly.

Although Piaget proposed four stages, he noted that not everyone reaches the stage of formal operations. At each stage of development, children must have access to appropriately challenging experiences. Children who are deprived of these experiences will develop more slowly than other children and are unlikely to fulfill their full intellectual potential.

Critique of Cognitive-Developmental Theory

Piaget's theory satisfies some criteria of good theory better than others. Despite his use of highly abstract terms and concepts, Piaget's detailed descriptions of children's behavior have helped communicate the meaning of his concepts to researchers and practitioners. While Piaget and other researchers have had little difficulty testing the theory in thousands of studies, his more abstract concepts have proven difficult to research. Significant questions remain concerning the generalizability of his concepts. For example, it is unclear whether his descriptions of stages hold up across children in different cultures and socioeconomic status. More positively, Piaget's theory is good developmental theory. Piaget's detailed descriptions of the gradual accumulation of age-related changes in specific content areas are exemplary.

The great strength of Piaget's theory lies in its broad view of cognitive development. Piaget presented both general principles that integrate all cognitive functioning and detailed descriptions of development in numerous content domains, such as logic, language, morality, causality, time, space, number, seriation, and classification, to name just a few. His theory has stimulated thousands of research studies over the last 30 years, and it has spawned several spin-offs, including the provocative work of Robbie Case (1985) and Kurt Fischer (1980).

Piaget's theory has also had significant impact on the practice of child development. His detailed accounts of development in specific content areas have helped educators create curriculum and approaches to instruction at all age levels. His concept of the child as an active learner has encouraged teachers to gear instruction to children's intrinsic motivation and natural curiosity.

But Piaget's work has significant weaknesses. Some of his concepts — such as assimilation and accommodation — are highly abstract and difficult to tie directly to children's behavior. How do we know when a child is accommodating in a learning situation? What criteria should we use to determine when a cognitive structure has changed? Other concepts — particularly some of his notions of formal operational reasoning — have not been verified by research.

Despite its shortcomings, Piaget's theory has transformed our understanding of child development and will continue to influence researchers and practitioners well into the next century.

Information Processing Theory

Piaget's use of highly abstract concepts, his disdain for traditional experimental methods of studying children, and the slow translation of his writings into English delayed the acceptance of his work in the United States in the 1940s and 1950s (Flavell, 1985). Although his theory became much more widely studied and accepted by American developmentalists in the 1960s and 1970s, many researchers sought more objective approaches to cognitive theory and research — approaches that would provide more precise descriptions of the mechanisms by which humans think, reason, and solve problems.

One source of inspiration for an alternative approach grew out of the boom in high-speed computers in the 1960s and 1970s. Theorists recognized that the human mind could be thought of as a computer — that is, as a device that accepts information as *input*, transforms it by internal processes to accomplish some goal, and generates an *output* that reflects the effects of those internal processes. They came to view the human mind as a series of components that manage the flow of information in human thinking, reasoning, attention, memory, and problem solving. They referred to this sequence of components as an **information processing system**. Thus **information processing theory** describes and explains cognitive functioning as the distinctly human capacity to derive information from the environment, to interpret that information, and to organize behavior on the basis of such interpretation.

Unlike the theories of Freud and Piaget, information processing is not a single theory developed primarily by an individual theorist. Instead, it represents a general perspective of a large number of researchers who have studied the way in which the cognitive system operates during memory, attention, and problem-solving processes (Case, 1985; Klahr, 1989; Shiffrin & Atkinson, 1969; Siegler, 1983). The similarities among these perspectives far outweigh the differences, suggesting that they be referred to as a distinct theory. As you will see, the theory provides a highly logical perspective on the nature of cognitive process.

Components of an Information Processing System

Shiffrin and Atkinson's (1969) model of the role of memory in an information processing system illustrates this perspective. Their model represented the cognitive system in the form of a *flowchart*, a diagram that expresses the relationships among the components of a system (Figure 2.3).

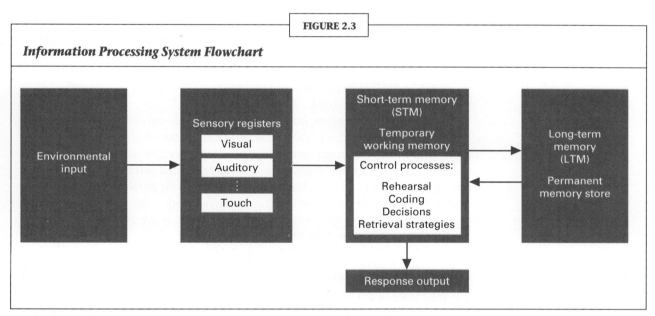

FIGURE 2.3

Information Processing System Flowchart

SOURCE: *Based on Atkinson & Shiffrin, 1969.*

The flowchart describes the step-by-step movement of information through the cognitive system. While in the system, information can be maintained in one of three **memory stores**, or sites for storing and processing information. The first store, the *sensory register*, is where information is first perceived. There are separate registers for each sense, and each can hold information for only a split second. A second system, the *short-term store*, selects information from a register and holds it for slightly longer, perhaps up to one minute. The short-term store—also referred to as *working memory*—is where information is processed: interpreting, thinking, reasoning, and problem solving.

Some information moves from short-term store to *long-term store*, a permanent memory of unlimited capacity. If a child deliberately tries to memorize something, such as a telephone number, he might try the strategy of repeating the information over and over. This strategy is called *rehearsal*. A second strategy is to organize multiple bits of information into groups that one can more easily remember. For example, if a child is asked to memorize a series of numbers such as 873685229, she can recall the information much better if she breaks that long string of numbers into smaller groups of numbers: 873 – 685 – 229. This strategy is called *chunking*.

The Development of Information Processing

It is generally accepted that children improve at processing information as they improve at applying strategies with increasing age. In a classic study of children's use of rehearsal, John Flavell and his colleagues (1966) studied 5-, 7-, and 10-year-olds' ability to recall the order of pictures the researchers presented to them. If the children moved their lips between the time they saw the pictures and the time they were asked to recall the order, that was interpreted as an indication of rehearsal. In general, 5-year-olds used no rehearsal, whereas approximately half of the 7-year-olds and virtually all of the 10-year-olds rehearsed. Not surprisingly, rehearsal was associated with superior performance. In a subsequent experiment (Keeney, Cannizzo, & Flavell, 1967) nonrehearsers improved their performance when they were instructed to rehearse. Thus in general, preschool children are unable to use strategy at all, school-age children use strategies when prompted, and still older children tend to develop sophisticated strategies and apply them spontaneously as needed.

Like social cognitive theory, information processing theory portrays developmental change as a continuous process, emphasizing age differences in children's ability to apply various strategies to improve attention, memory, and problem-solving abilities. Children tested and trained in a laboratory do improve their performance in problem solving when researchers teach them a strategy suited to the problem. In most of these studies the child is the passive recipient of an intervention. There has been little study of changes in the cognitive system resulting from children's active exploration of the environment, the primary emphasis in Piagetian theory.

Critique of Information Processing Theory

The great value of the information processing theory is its ability to account for the enormous complexity of children's cognitive development in extremely precise terms. This precision enables researchers to design rigorous experimental tests of the theory. For example, a researcher can compare children at different ages in their ability to remember the content of stories. Differences in their recall at different ages can provide precise estimates of developmental improvements in memory capacity. Thus, information processing theory communicates the meaning of its terms unambiguously, its propositions are highly verifiable, and the results of research are generalizable.

Information processing theory has sensitized those who deal with children to the enormous complexity of everyday tasks that children try to learn. Placing pegs in pegboards, for example, requires that the child understand the demands of the task, compare the relative sizes and shapes of pegs and holes, remember which peg placements did and did not work before, coordinate eye, arm, and hand, and generate cognitive rules such as square pegs do not fit in round holes. If placing pegs in pegboards requires all this, consider the task demands of learning to use the potty, dressing oneself, having conversations, making friends, riding a bike, and learning to read. Thus, by revealing the complexity of everyday tasks, describing ideal solution strategies, and demonstrating when and where training interventions can be effective, information processing theory provides the foundation for applications in all aspects of children's lives.

Information processing theory also has important limitations, particularly as a developmental theory. When researchers show that children's information processing strategies advance with age, that does not explain *how* they change. Even when researchers demonstrate that training can enhance children's use of strategies, that does not necessarily prove that children learn strategies by being trained in real life. Similarly, when researchers write computer programs that can come up with the same answers to problems as children do, that does not necessarily mean that children's minds go through the same steps as the computer does. At best, the functioning of a computer can provide only a loose model of the workings of the human mind, and its usefulness as a model of cognitive development has not yet been demonstrated.

Ethological Theory

When we observe children in natural settings, we are impressed by the diversity of their physical size and shape and the vast individual differences in their behavior. Charles Darwin (1809–1882), an English naturalist, studied various species of plants and animals in different parts of the world and concluded that diversity was a universal characteristic of all species of plants and animals, including humans. Darwin came to believe that the variation among the members of a species is essential to survival of the species in natural environments.

In *The Origin of Species* (1859/1958), Darwin presented the theory of **evolution**—a theory with profound implications for the study of child development. Darwin viewed each species of living things in a "struggle for survival" within its natural environment. He understood the natural environment in terms of risk and opportunity for survival: Predators, disease, and natural disasters threaten survival; the availability of food, shelter, and favorable climate promote survival. Darwin proposed that only those members of a species with the most adaptive traits would be likely to live long enough to reproduce and pass these traits on to successive generations. Greater diversity in traits among members of a species increases the likelihood that adaptive traits will be available to overcome any risk to survival. Adaptive traits are thus *selected* into the species across generations. Darwin proposed that a species' survival is dependent on this process, which he called **natural selection**.

Darwin's theory implies that the course of development has evolved as a solution to the problem of survival of the species. Moreover, the development of each individual may be thought of as a unique experiment in survival: a unique combination of genetic traits confronting the ongoing process of natural selection. **Ethology** is the scientific study of behavior and development in evolutionary perspective. Its purpose is to identify behavior patterns that have had, and may continue to have, significant impact on the survival of a species.

The study of ethology as a distinct discipline derives from the work of Niko Tinbergen and Konrad Lorenz in the 1930s. Lorenz (1937) proposed that certain behavior patterns are inherited, much as physical structures are inherited. Innate behaviors appear in the form of reflexes and fixed action patterns. **Reflexes** are wired-in responses to specific forms of stimulation. Infants, for example, will grasp your finger when you press it into their palm. **Fixed action patterns** are more complex behaviors that are necessary for survival, such as foraging for food, searching for mates, and attacking or running.

Important ethological contributions to the study of child development have come from studies of animals in their natural environment. Lorenz (1952) observed that in a certain species of birds, there is a brief **critical period** of time during which the newborn is particularly sensitive to certain forms of learning. For instance, if geese are exposed to their mother shortly after birth, they learn to recognize their mother and to follow her. Exposure after the end of the second day will be ineffective. Lorenz called this biological readiness for learning **imprinting**. Lorenz soon discovered that geese's predisposition to imprint was so powerful that they would imprint on virtually any moving form (including Lorenz himself) that he exposed them to during that critical period.

John Bowlby (1969, 1988) incorporated aspects of the ethological view into his theory of how the human infant develops emotional ties to its mother. Bowlby believed that

Konrad Lorenz demonstrated that some animal species have a critical period for learning early in their development. Baby geese, for example, learn to follow their mother during the first hours after birth. In this demonstration, Lorenz substituted himself for the mother during the critical period, causing the baby geese to imprint on his form. Here they instinctively follow him through a field.

infants and their caregivers are biologically predisposed to form an emotional relationship that promotes staying close together. Consistent with ethological principles, staying close together would serve to protect the infant from threats to survival such as predators and accidental injury. Bowlby's important contribution to our understanding of early emotional development will be revisited in later chapters.

Ethological theory contradicts learning theory by suggesting that behavior is not always learned through conditioning. Some forms of behavior, particularly behavior that promotes survival, may be built into the species and elicited only under special environmental circumstances. Aggression, for example, may be expressed when the individual is threatened, regardless of prior learning experiences. Similarly, some forms of learning may not be controlled by the principles of classical or operant conditioning. Ethologists suggest that humans may be predisposed to certain forms of learning during critical periods of development.

In practical terms, it would seem prudent to consider all aspects of behavior and development in evolutionary perspective. For instance, some infants in the first few weeks of life experience *colic* — prolonged bouts of crying, intestinal upset, and an inability to be soothed. Scientists have failed to find a physiological or environmental cause for colic. In ethological perspective, colic may be a genetic holdover from a much earlier period in evolution when intense crying was needed to elicit caregiving from mothers who were less responsive to their offspring.

Ethological theory also suggests that the degree of risk or opportunity raised by a developmental event may depend on when the event happens. For example, whereas a staircase may place a six-month-old at risk of injury, it is a challenging opportunity for a toddler to develop his or her motor skills. This perspective also suggests that certain forms of learning can take place only if a certain *quality* of experience is provided. For instance, infants raised in institutions typically show deficits in motor and language development (Dennis, 1973) and in social and emotional development (Spitz, 1945, 1946). Is it possible that the rapidly emerging trend toward substitute care for infants in our society will have similar effects? Ethological theory provides an important perspective for studying many of the critical issues in child development. This perspective will appear repeatedly throughout the chapters of this text.

Critique of Ethological Theory

As theory, ethology suffers from serious problems of verifiability. For example, what types of data can prove that a particular behavior ensures survival of the species? There is also some question about generalizing from behavior patterns observed in animals to human behavior. Moreover, while ethologists have provided many new concepts to the study of behavior and development, many of the terms — for example, critical periods and instincts — are not well defined and are difficult to measure.

Ethological theory has helped expand the way we think about the causes of human behavior. While other theories cited in this chapter have emphasized either the immediate causes of behavior or the effects of early experience on later development, ethological theory finds explanation of development in the evolution of the species. These explanations help us to understand why certain behaviors are universal and why other behaviors vary enormously from one social context to another. It also helps us to accept that there may be limits to our ability to change certain aspects of human behavior. Finally, it has heightened our awareness of the concept of readiness, warning us that while timing may not be everything in development, it often influences the magnitude of our effects on children's behavior and development.

The Theories in Perspective

The theories presented in this chapter have had profound effects on the study and practice of child development. They have accomplished what theories are supposed to accomplish: They have stimulated a broad range of research and have been refined and elaborated by the results of that research. The theories have also been used by parents and practitioners to improve the lives of children and to facilitate their development. The names of some theorists—such as Freud, Erikson, and Piaget—have become household terms.

While the theories have proven useful, they have also shown limitations. All of the theories are less than adequate as theory and as developmental theory. The theories use terms that are difficult to define and measure, slowing researchers' efforts to test the theories and practitioners' efforts to apply the theories. All of the theories are far better at describing developmental change than at explaining how that change occurs. Perhaps the greatest difficulty is the fact that each theory has tried to explain only one aspect of child development while ignoring all other aspects. Freud and Erikson focused on emotional development and virtually ignored the effects of cognition. Piaget studied cognitive development and omitted the effects of emotions. Thus, the search for universal principles of child development has proven elusive.

Key Terms

theory	trauma	cognitive structures
developmental stage	psychosocial theory	adaptation
discontinuous	psychosocial crisis	assimilation
continuous	sense of trust	accommodation
maturation	sense of autonomy	sensorimotor stage
psychoanalytic theory	mutual regulation	schemas
libido	behaviorism	symbolic reasoning
id	classical conditioning	preoperational stage
pleasure principle	unconditioned stimulus (UCS)	centration
ego	unconditioned response (UCR)	concrete operations stage
reality principle	conditioned stimulus (CS)	concrete operation
superego	conditioned response (CR)	formal operations stage
identification	classical conditioning	information processing system
defense mechanisms	operant conditioning	information processing theory
psychosexual stages	operant	memory stores
erogenous zone	reinforcements	evolution
oral stage	punishments	natural selection
anal stage	extinction	ethology
phallic stage	shaping	reflexes
Oedipal conflict	behavior modification	fixed action patterns
latency	social cognitive theory	critical period
genital stage	observational learning	imprinting

Research in Child Development

Looking Ahead

■ Most everyone has opinions about what causes children to do the things they do, but we need more than conjecture. How do developmentalists develop factual knowledge of children's behavior and development?

■ Researchers systematically approach the study of children by formulating the research problem, gathering

evidence, and reporting their results. What is involved in each of these steps and how do the procedures ensure objectivity?

■ Researchers report their research in professional journals. How can practitioners gain access to this knowledge?

■ Studying children involves certain forms of risk. How do researchers ensure that children are not negatively affected by their research studies?

■ The scientific method is a way of thinking and behaving that ensures objectivity. How can practitioners apply the scientific method in their everyday dealings with children?

The Scientific Study of Child Development

T hose who deal with children—parents, teachers, day-care workers, child life specialists, therapists, psychologists, doctors, social workers, and, in some instances, politicians—have a desperate need to understand what makes children do the things they do. They often *sound* as though they understand, as when

- A social worker claims that Heather's "erotic" behavior in the day-care center (Chapter 2) indicates possible sexual abuse.
- A school administrator questions whether a decrease in the achievement levels of first graders might be related to the increasing number of crack babies entering the school system.
- A caregiver recommends that Heather be removed from the day-care center, since her behavior might begin to have a negative impact on the behavior and development of other children.
- A politician says, "The only way to reduce the number of high school dropouts is to invest more in early childhood education."

In each of these cases, the speaker is making a **causal inference**—a belief that one factor is (or was or will be) the cause of something else. But typically such statements are merely *conjecture*—inferences based on inconclusive or incomplete evidence. When those who deal with children accept conjecture as fact, the lives of children are immediately affected, sometimes with unfortunate consequences. For instance, the time-worn expression "Spare the rod and spoil the child" has been used to justify corporal punishment for thousands of years, even though there is little evidence to support it.

For as long as you work with children, you will be bombarded with supposed facts and notions about why children do what they do. But to do an effective job of navigating among the risks and opportunities facing your children, you need to base your efforts on more than conjecture. You need the most reliable information available. How do you judge whether information is reliable? The better you understand how ideas and facts are tested scientifically, the more critically you can evaluate the things you hear.

The Scientific Method

When a research scientist suspects that one factor may be related to another, he or she plans specific efforts to confirm or disconfirm the relationship. These efforts will be based on the **scientific method**—a systematic approach to develop factual knowledge based on observation of phenomena in the real world. The most important characteristic of the scientific method is **objectivity**—a requirement that researchers agree on what is observed or what is to be done or has been done in research (Kerlinger, 1979). In the study of child development, objectivity is promoted in the following ways:

1. *Researchers gather evidence directly from the study of children.* Various methods may be used—including observations, tests, and interviews—but all information derives from a common focus on the children as subjects of research. For example, Jacquelyn Mize and Gary Ladd (1990) studied whether unpopular preschool children could be trained to learn social skills that would make them better accepted

by their peers. The researchers observed the children's social behaviors and interviewed children to determine their popularity among their peers before and after training.

2. *Researchers communicate detailed descriptions of all methods they use to gather evidence.* When reporting their results, they provide detailed descriptions of the observers, the observational method, the children, and the context of the observations. Such communication ensures that other researchers can *replicate* or repeat the study to confirm its results. In the social skills training study, the researchers listed 10 distinct social behaviors—for example, making positive suggestions and reinforcing peers—that would be observed, and then they described the conditions in which the children would be observed.

3. *Researchers demonstrate the **reliability** of their observations.* That is, they provide evidence that their observations are not biased or distorted. For instance, a researcher might be required to demonstrate *interobserver reliability:* Two observers, viewing the same child from two different vantage points, would record the same information. In the social skills training study, the researchers reported that their observers agreed on their observations more than 90 percent of the time (Mize & Ladd, 1990). Similarly, if a test were used to gather data, it would be necessary to demonstrate *test-retest reliability:* The same results would be obtained if the test were given twice.

4. *Researchers establish the **validity** of their observations.* That is, they demonstrate that their evidence is a true reflection of reality. For instance, in the social skills training study, the researchers used observational techniques that are firmly grounded in the children's behaviors, leaving little doubt that they are measuring what they say they are measuring. Validity can also be determined by comparing the techniques to be used with other techniques of known validity.

5. *Researchers state their expectations of what results they expect* prior to *gathering evidence.* Their expectations are presented as *hypotheses*, formal statements of the anticipated relationship between factors. For instance, in the social skills study, the researchers hypothesized at the outset that they expected that children who would be trained would improve their social skills and become more accepted by their peers than children who would not be trained (Mize & Ladd, 1990). This ensures that the researchers' expectations are not revised after the fact to fit the results obtained from the research.

Research scientists believe that hypotheses confirmed by the scientific method are more reliable and valid than someone's well-intentioned but not necessarily well-informed conjecture or opinion. We now examine the application of the scientific method to a particular research problem in child development research.

The Research Process: A Simulation

The scientific study of children is not a series of esoteric activities conducted by scientists hidden away in laboratories. It is a way of *thinking* and *behaving* that anyone who deals with children can use in virtually any setting. It offers all who seek to facilitate development a way of operating rationally and systematically. To explore this helpful way of thinking, we will walk through a typical research project. By seeing how a researcher

Researchers have studied the variation in children's ability to enter the ongoing play of other children. What causes some children to be more accepted and others more rejected as third-party entrants? Do social skills make a difference? Is it more difficult for a child to join the play of other children who happen to be best friends? These and other questions can be answered by correlational and experimental research studies.

proceeds at each step and why, we can understand the research process from an insider's perspective. You may gain additional insight into the research process by meeting Kenneth Dodge in "Careers: The Research Scientist."

The Research Topic: Third-Party Entry

Child development research typically begins when a researcher observes an important behavior in the natural experience of children. "Important" here means that the behavior has some demonstrable effect on development and can be of practical significance to those who deal with children. A prime example of such behavior is *third-party entry behavior* (Corsaro, 1981; Putallaz & Wasserman, 1989). Third-party entry is a social situation in which two (or more) children are involved in play and a third child attempts to join their activity. For instance, consider Carlos's first day at day care.

> *His family has just moved to the neighborhood and he knows no one—not one child, not one caregiver. Carlos enters with his dad and, after a tearful separation, he is led to a room already filled with 25 other 4-year-olds who are 5 minutes into a free play period, having already chosen their toys and social partners. Carlos walks in somewhat tentatively and avoids the crowd by veering toward an alcove just off the main room. The alcove is empty except for two boys who are actively engaged in cooperative play with a set of toy animals and associated props. Carlos finds the toys attractive and would like to join the two boys.*

Carlos is in a common third-party entry situation. The other boys may accept him or may reject him. Repeated social rejection in third-party entry situations can have significant negative impact on long-term social adjustment (Parker & Asher, 1987), so it is important for caregivers to help make third-party entry easier.

The Research Scientist

Kenneth Dodge is a professor of clinical and developmental psychology at Vanderbilt University in Nashville, Tennessee. He and his longtime colleague and mentor, John Coie (Duke University), have made an outstanding contribution to our understanding of children's peer relationships (see summaries of their work in later chapters). In particular, they have described the powerful, long-term negative effects of peer rejection on children's personality and social development in early and middle childhood. They have shown how aggression frequently leads to peer rejection, and they have begun to explore how we may intervene to reduce the long-term consequences of peer rejection.

I interviewed Kenneth Dodge at his office at Vanderbilt University.

How did you first become interested in research with children?

When I was in high school, I worked with children in a day camp, and in college I did quite a bit of babysitting. I knew then that I would enjoy a professional career that involved children. As a student in psychology, I was inspired by two of my undergraduate professors — Sharon Guwirtz and B. J. Underwood — who showed me how exciting research could be. I remember when Professor Underwood told us one day that he had given up his career coaching basketball to become an experimental psychologist. When someone asked him why, he said, "Coaching was boring, but psychological research,

that's always exciting!" I was most impressed. He helped me see the perpetual challenge in research — that answering one research question always opens a host of new questions that no one knew to ask. I somehow believed that the most interesting questions — at least for me — would be in the study of child development.

How did you become involved in the study of peer relationships?

When I began my graduate work at Duke University, I studied with Professor John Coie, who had just begun a longitudinal study of children's social development. I guess I was in the right place at the right time. Our early work was highly productive and it opened our eyes to a whole new way of thinking about children's social behavior. We have worked together for over 14 years, and we are now involved in the most exciting and important work of our careers: trying to understand how children become violent and what we can do to prevent that from occurring.

How can a student pursue a career as a research scientist?

Begin with an undergraduate major in psychology and child development and get involved in a professor's research as soon as possible. Volunteer for the dirty work: observing and testing children and processing and analyzing data. Get to know every phase of the research process. If the experience excites you, look for a graduate program that provides immediate opportunity as a research assistant. Before too

long you'll be asking your own research questions and conducting your own research. Ask professors to recommend graduate schools that have outstanding research programs and look them up in your university library. Use a reference book called *Graduate Programs in Psychology* published by the American Psychological Association.

But how? To know how, we must know something about why children accept or reject third-party entrants. That is the kind of everyday question developmental researchers set out to answer—not by conjecture, but by scholarly research. We will use this example to simulate a research project.

Formulating the Research Problem

The first and most important challenge faced by the researcher is to formulate the research problem (Figure 3.1). The **research problem** identifies the specific aspect of behavior or development that the researcher seeks to explain, the theoretical perspective that will be applied in providing that explanation, and a formal statement of the relationships that the research seeks to confirm.

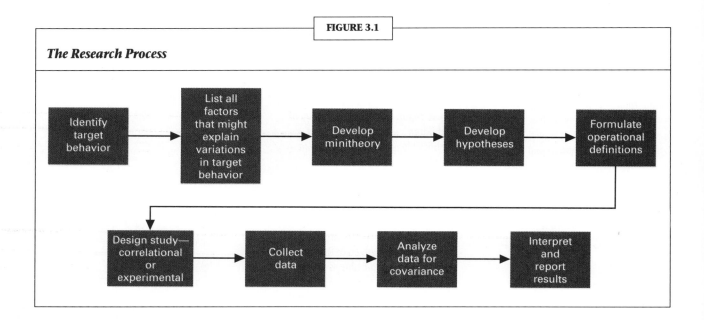

FIGURE 3.1

The Research Process

Identifying the Target Behavior The researcher begins by identifying the *target* of the research—the specific aspect of behavior or development that the research seeks to explain—such as variations in children's attitudes, beliefs, thought processes, perceptions, motivations, emotions, or skills. The challenge is to identify the target as specifically as possible and to do so in behavioral terms. For example, in Carlos's situation in the day-care center, the target behavior is the attempt to enter into the play of other children—an observable behavior whose success or failure can be determined objectively. For instance, successful entry may be specified in terms of a minimum period of toy sharing and conversation between Carlos and the boys at play.

Developing a Minitheory Once the target behavior has been specified, the researcher establishes a theoretical perspective for explaining the variation in the target behavior. Unfortunately, the major theories of child development presented in Chapter 2 leave significant gaps with respect to explaining the enormous variation in children's behavior. The third-party entry situation is an excellent case in point. Although some aspects of each of the major theories might be useful, none of these theories deals explicitly with the particular elements of third-party entry. So it falls to the individual researcher to develop a theoretical frame of reference encompassing the relevant factors and their respective relationships to the target behavior. This theoretical frame of reference is known as a **minitheory**. The minitheory is the researcher's best guess—based on past research, existing theory, and the scientist's intuition—as to the factors that may affect variation in the target behavior. In this case, that means factors that influence different children's success or failure in joining play.

Developing the minitheory begins with making an *exhaustive list* of factors that may explain variations in the target behavior. In the third-party entry situation, for example, significant factors may include Carlos's age, gender, years of previous day-care experience, previous social experience in other settings, physical attractiveness, social skills such as sharing and helping, social cognitive skills such as knowledge of social strategies and interpersonal relationships, experience with the toys the other children are using, and ability to anticipate the possible outcomes of various strategies for gaining entrance. Significant factors may also include the length of time the other two boys have been playing, the degree of satisfaction each boy is experiencing at the moment Carlos arrives, their individual attitudes about letting another child join them, and the nature of their existing relationship. For instance, if the two boys have had a long-term, relatively exclusive friendship, Carlos's chances for successful entry may be decreased.

In analyzing the children, the task, and related behaviors to identify all possible relevant factors, the investigator must, of course, use some discretion. Many aspects of the situation are irrelevant to variations in the target behavior. For instance, the color of the alcove walls, the age of the caregivers, and the nutritional status of the children seem unlikely to affect the outcome of entry attempts, as long as they remain within normal limits. Thus these factors would not be included.

An example of a minitheory of third-party entry behavior is presented in Figure 3.2. In this instance, the researcher has limited the scope of the minitheory to three of the

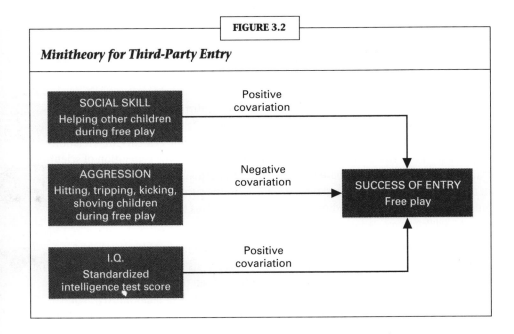

FIGURE 3.2

Minitheory for Third-Party Entry

SOCIAL SKILL
Helping other children during free play

Positive covariation

AGGRESSION
Hitting, tripping, kicking, shoving children during free play

Negative covariation

I.Q.
Standardized intelligence test score

Positive covariation

SUCCESS OF ENTRY
Free play

Figure portrays the hypothetical relationships between the third-party entrant's characteristics and success of entry. Arrows indicate type of covariation that is anticipated (positive or negative).

entrant's personal characteristics (social skill, aggression, and IQ). Each of these factors bears a logical relationship to the target behavior: successful entry into the boys' play.

The value of the minitheory is its ability to organize the thinking and activities of the researcher. The minitheory should not, however, be confused with fact; it merely provides a logical but speculative explanation of the variation in the target behavior. The results of the study alone will determine how well the proposed factors in the minitheory account for this variation.

Developing Hypotheses   The minitheory poses a series of research questions that the research study will address. In the third-party entry situation, for example, the minitheory asks: "Is there a relationship between the prospective entrant's social skills and the likelihood of successful entry?" "Is the entrant's aggressive behavior related to acceptance as a third-party entrant?" and "Is the entrant's IQ related to acceptance as a third-party entrant?" Each research question is restated in the form of a **hypothesis**—a formal statement that alleges the possibility of a relationship between two factors. The hypothesis is *not* a statement of fact; it is a best guess, based on the existing knowledge on the topic. For instance, the three research questions presented above would be restated as:

> *Hypothesis I*   Children with greater social skill will experience *more* success as third-party entrants than children with less social skill.
> *Hypothesis II*   Children who are more aggressive will experience *less* success as third-party entrants than less aggressive children.
> *Hypothesis III*   Children who have higher IQ will experience *more* success as third-party entrants than entrants with lower IQ.

Note that the researcher states hypotheses *before* gathering evidence. This is a critical aspect of the scientific method because it ensures objectivity in the confirmation or disconfirmation of the theory underlying the study. Without this provision, hypotheses could easily be revised after the fact to conform to the obtained results, completely compromising the role of theory in scientific inquiry. Put simply, the scientific method requires that you place your bets (hypotheses) before the game is played.

Once hypotheses have been formally stated, the research moves to its next critical phase: gathering evidence.

Gathering Evidence

The scientific method requires that relationships be confirmed by evidence gathered directly from the study of behavior, rather than by appeals to authority, common sense, or reason (Kerlinger, 1979). But how does the scientist provide evidence that relationships exist? Although there are many different approaches to the generation of scientific evidence, all approaches are based on the concept of explaining individual differences in a target behavior—in this instance, variations in the success of children's third-party entry behavior. Explaining individual differences involves three interrelated concepts: *operational definition, variance,* and *covariance.*

Operational Definitions   If individual differences in a target behavior are to be explained, the researcher must describe that behavior and its variations precisely in an **operational definition**. Unlike a dictionary definition, an operational definition describes the factors in ways that can be measured *qualitatively* or *quantitatively*. For example, with respect to third-party entry, children can be categorized by qualitatively different approaches to entry, such as active or passive, or they can be described quantitatively by observing how often they succeed in joining the play of other children in a given period of time. In our simulated study, the operational definitions of the target behavior and related factors are as follows:

Success of entry is defined as the number of times a child joins the play of other children without being rejected for a minimum of two minutes during one hour of observation of free play.

Social skill is defined as the number of times a child offers help to other children during one hour of free play.

Aggression is defined as the number of times a child hits, kicks, trips, or shoves other children during two hours of observation of free play.

IQ is defined as the child's score on a standardized intelligence test.

Some of the commonly used methods for generating both qualitative and quantitative data on children are summarized in Box 3.1.

BOX 3.1

Data-Gathering Methods with Children

A key element in planning a research study with children is deciding on operational definitions of the factors involved in the study. Each of the following methods offers the researcher a unique view of children's behavior.

Naturalistic Observation

Some behaviors—like aggression, dependency, and motor skills—can be observed in natural settings such as the home, classroom, or playground. Researchers can record and tabulate how often the behaviors occur and aspects of the context in which they occur. The researcher may choose among several different approaches to naturalistic observation, each of which offers certain advantages for certain types of behavior.

Event Sampling is the method of choice to observe behaviors that occur infrequently but are relatively easy to spot when they do occur. For example, a researcher might be interested in documenting how often children engage in arguments, conversations, or spontaneous games of tag. The observer scans groups of children, recording instances of the event and the context in which they occur. Event sampling is most useful in the early hypothesis-generating stage of research.

Time Sampling is the method of choice when the researcher wants to compare how often different children engage in behaviors that occur frequently, such as dependency or aggression. Observations may be sampled over extended periods of time and across diverse situations to provide data that are representative of true differences among children. Observations are conducted in brief periods known as *time samples*. The frequencies of the recorded behaviors are then summed across time samples, generating quantitative variables. The variables of social skill, aggression, and success of third-party entry included in our simulation could be operationalized using a time-sampling observational method.

Structured Observations

Although observing behavior in its natural context offers certain advantages, it has disadvantages as well. For instance, some behaviors are difficult to observe in the natural environment due to their infrequent occurrence. Toddlers' spontaneous sharing of toys, for example, is an infrequent but developmentally significant behavior. Researchers also have difficulty controlling the stimulation that children experience in the natural environment. There are two (continued)

BOX 3.1

Data-Gathering Methods with Children (continued)

commonly used approaches to these problems.

Analogues Researchers can work more efficiently by creating *analogues*—contrived situations designed to simulate conditions that promote or "pull for" target behaviors. Researchers frequently make analogues more realistic for the subjects by employing *confederates*, individuals trained to act out certain roles. For instance, confederates have been used to portray individuals in distress to elicit prosocial helping behavior from children (Schenk & Grusec, 1987).

By using analogues, the researcher can also control the factors that may influence the target behavior. For instance, in third-party entry, a researcher could create a situation in which two children are allowed to play for several minutes. The researcher could then control the friendship status of the two children, the novelty of the toys, and the duration of their playtime. Potential third-party entrants could then be observed in the analogue situation under varied conditions.

Experimental Tasks Researchers often design laboratory tasks that offer precise control over the stimulation experienced by the child. For example, in studies of memory, researchers must carefully regulate the timing and duration of children's exposure to test materials and the children's exposure to distracting stimulation. These goals can be accomplished by designing tasks that limit the child's exposure to a viewing screen and isolate the child from sources of extraneous stimulation.

Structured Interviews

When the target of the research is not a behavior but a mental attitude, perception, belief, opinion, feeling, or strategy, the researcher may ask children (or adults) a standard set of questions in face-to-face interviews. Some interviews are highly structured, only giving children specific options for their answers, while others are more open-ended, allowing the child free expression of ideas. For instance, a child might be asked a series of open-ended questions about what she would do if she were playing with her best friend and a third child tried to join their play. Children's responses to the questions can be scored to produce quantitative or qualitative variables. Structured interview questions may be presented in the form of a written *questionnaire* to children or adolescents who have sufficient reading skill.

Clinical Interviews

The standard interview places the child in a passive role: No matter what the child answers, the researcher goes on to the next question on the list. Pia-get recognized that more could be learned by interviewing in a give-and-take format—that is, having each question play off the child's previous answer. A clinical interview with Carlos illustrates Piaget's clinical approach.

INTERVIEWER:
 What happened?

CARLOS:
 They won't play with me.

INTERVIEWER:
 Why won't they play with you?

CARLOS:
 They're best friends, that's why!

INTERVIEWER:
 Best friends don't play with other children?

CARLOS:
 No, never. I hate them.

INTERVIEWER:
 Do you think *some* friends would be nice and let you play with them?

CARLOS:
 No, friends are mean. They're never nice.

INTERVIEWER:
 Do you think they like making you feel bad?

CARLOS:
 Yes, because they were laughing and teasing!

Note that each of Carlos's responses formed the basis for the interviewer's next question. The clinical interview enables the researcher to probe the child's thinking in a way that would be difficult by any other method. The clinical interview is most useful in the early stages of research, rather than as a source of quantitative data.

Variance and Covariance   Once factors have been operationally defined, the researcher proceeds to measure the relevant factors and target behavior, generating distributions of scores for the factors included in the study. Table 3.1 provides a simulated set of scores for the target behavior (success of entry) and our operationally defined factors (social skill, aggression, and IQ). The data were gathered on a group of 10 4-year-old boys in a preschool classroom. Column 1 identifies each boy; columns 2, 3, and 4 represent the boys' scores on social skills, aggression, and intelligence (IQ), respectively; and column 5 presents success of entry scores. The differences among children's scores on each factor are called **variance**.

The purpose of the study is to explain the variance in the third-party entry scores. Our first hypothesis suggests that the variance in social skill is related to the variance in third-party entry success. When the variance on one factor is related to the variance on another factor, the factors are said to *covary*. **Covariance** is the tendency of two factors to vary systematically with respect to each other. Scholars accept demonstrated covariance between factors as evidence of a relationship between those factors.

TABLE 3.1

Simulated Data for Target Behavior and Related Variables in Correlational Study

Name	Social Skill	Aggression	IQ	Success of Entry
Ted	2	34	130	0
Tim	7	38	95	1
Tom	16	15	135	7
Terrell	14	12	100	8
Taylor	4	50	125	2
Tyrone	22	8	99	10
Travis	0	44	105	2
Troy	10	24	110	5
Tory	18	3	124	9
Todd	3	0	102	9

Design of the Study

The researcher's strategy to demonstrate covariation between factors is referred to as the **design** of the study. The research design organizes how the researcher collects and analyzes data to confirm or disconfirm the hypotheses. Researchers use two general designs to study covariation: the *correlational design* and the *experimental design*.

The Correlational Design   Researchers use the **correlational design** to demonstrate covariation among factors in natural settings where the researcher has made no effort to influence the variation. This design can be explained most easily by examining our simulated data in Table 3.1. Focus your attention for a moment on the scores for social skills. A simple code has been applied to the scores: Scores that have a circle around them are the relatively low scores *within* the variable; scores that have a square around them are the relatively high scores within that variable. Now skip over to the success of entry scores and observe that the code has also been applied to identify the relatively high and low scores *within* that variable. Next compare the pattern of circles (low scores) and squares (high scores) *across* the two variables. It should be obvious that there is a strong tendency for high scores for social skills to go with, or covary with, high scores for success of entry and, similarly, for low scores to covary with low scores. This is an example of *positive covariation*.

It is important to note that scientists do not work with circles and squares to demonstrate covariation; they demonstrate covariation by applying statistical formulas to data to derive best estimates of the strength of the relationship between variables. In this instance, the name of the statistic is the *correlation*. This explains why the design used in this study is called the correlational design.

The demonstration of positive covariation (or positive correlation) is interpreted as evidence that the hypothesis has been confirmed: Boys who were more socially skilled were more likely to enter groups successfully than boys with less social skill.

Now look again at the data in Table 3.1. Column 3 is a measure of physical aggression operationally defined as the number of times each subject hit another child during two hours of observation of freeplay. The code has again been applied to indicate relatively high and relatively low scores for aggression. The pattern of codes is very different for this combination of variables; high scores go with low scores in a pattern that we refer to as *negative covariation* or *negative correlation*. Thus our second hypothesis was also confirmed: More aggressive boys were less successful as third-party entrants than were less aggressive boys.

Column 4 of Table 3.1 displays data for a measure of children's IQ. You will note that there is *no* consistent tendency for the square and circle codes to go together. We conclude that there is no evidence of covariation in these data. Thus, Hypothesis III is not confirmed; children's intelligence appears to be unrelated to success of third-party entry.

Although the correlational design is most useful in identifying the covariation of factors in the natural environment, it does have one serious limitation: It tells us only that there is a *relationship* between the variables, not that the variation in one variable necessarily *caused* the variation in the other (see Figure 3.3). In our example above, the positive covariation between social skills and success of entry does not necessarily mean that social skills *cause* successful entry. The relationship may be due to the fact that both

---

FIGURE 3.3

Research Reveals Correlations But Not Necessarily Causation. Further Research is Needed to Determine What Causes What.

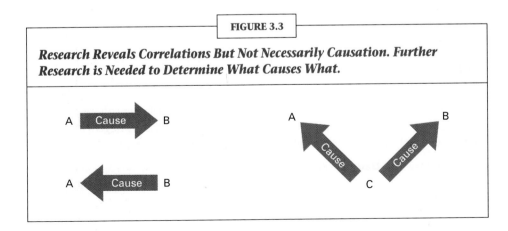

variables covary with yet a third factor that was not measured in this study. To find out what causes what, the researcher now proceeds to the experimental design.

The Experimental Design   In the **experimental design**, the investigator manipulates one factor in order to study its effect on the variation of a second factor, the target behavior. The manipulated factor is called the **independent variable**. The second factor, whose variation is hypothesized to depend upon variation of the independent variable, is called the **dependent variable**.

In the experimental design, the researcher *controls* all known factors that may affect the target behavior and varies them one at a time. In our simulation, for instance, the researcher may create two levels of social skill by training one group of children to help others during play, while withholding training from a second group. The first group is called the *experimental group* and the second group the *control group*. The research must ensure that the experimental and control groups differ only on the factor chosen as the independent variable. For example, if the average age of the children in the experimental group were significantly greater than the age of the children in the control group, their older age might account for third-party entry success. *Random assignment* of subjects to groups is typically used to control such differences.

Once the children have been assigned to experimental and control groups, the experimenter initiates the training intervention. After the intervention has been completed, the researcher observes children from both groups in multiple third-party entry situations. Table 3.2 presents simulated results the experimenter might obtain. You will note that the children in the experimental group had an average of 6.4 successes while the children in the control group averaged 2.3 successes. After appropriate statistical tests are applied, the researcher could conclude that social skills training *caused* an increase in success in third-party entry.

TABLE 3.2

Simulated Data for Success of Entry for Experimental and Control Groups

Control Group		Experimental Group	
Name	Success of Entry	Name	Success of Entry
Susan	3	Betty	5
Sally	0	Bess	4
Sharonda	2	Beth	8
Suzanna	4	Bonnie	6
Sherry	1	Brittany	6
Sophie	2	Barbara	7
Sadie	5	Bethany	8
Sonia	0	Brenda	3
Sissy	2	Belinda	9
Selina	4	Bonita	8
Mean =	2.3	Mean =	6.4

Designs for Studying Development   Although the results of the experimental study (and the correlational study) provide insight into the behavior of particular age groups, these studies do not shed light on the *development* of third-party entry behavior. For instance, the researcher might ask whether five-year-olds are more successful at third-party entry than three-year-olds. Such questions are of interest in all areas of development.

To study developmental change, the researcher must make observations across age or stage periods. Researchers may select among various designs for collecting developmental data, each suited to a particular set of circumstances. In the **longitudinal design**, the researcher observes the same group of children at predetermined intervals over time. In the **cross-sectional design**, various age groups of children are studied at a single point in time. Thus, developmental change is reflected in the differences in the average performances of *different* groups of children across age periods.

Each design has its advantages and disadvantages. The designs can be compared by extending our simulated study of third-party entry. Suppose a researcher was interested in describing the development of third-party entry behavior during the elementary school years. Let's assume that two researchers in two different universities decided to conduct such a study, one using the longitudinal design and the other the cross-sectional design.

The longitudinal study would begin with the selection of several classrooms of kindergarten children, representative of the overall population of five-year-olds. All of the children would be tested each year for six years. The advantage of this longitudinal approach is that developmental changes in the children's third-party entry skills could be described in detail. The disadvantages are that (1) the overall effort would take a minimum of six years and (2) by the last year of testing, a large percentage of the original sample might have dropped out. This dropoff is called *attrition*. If the majority of children who dropped out of the study were unique in some way — for instance, all from highly mobile yuppie families — the remaining group would no longer be representative of the overall population and the results would therefore not be generalizable.

In the cross-sectional study, attrition would not be a problem, but the results of the study would be based on differences among groups of 5-, 6-, 7-, 8-, 9-, and 10-year-old children. What if these groups had additional differences besides age that the researcher had not intended? For instance, suppose the 9- and 10-year-olds had lived through a time of great prosperity and security for their families during their first 2 to 3 years, resulting in very secure personalities. Suppose further that this secure period in the economy was followed by several years of hard times: The six- and seven-year-olds in our study would have spent their first two to three years in very adverse circumstances, resulting in insecure personalities. If the 9- and 10-year-olds outperformed the 6- and 7-year-olds, would the researcher be justified in concluding that third-party entry skills improve with age? No. The results are confounded by the fact that the older children had a more secure infancy than the younger children. The researcher has no way of separating the historical trends from the developmental changes in the children.

One solution to this problem is the **cross-sequential design** in which children are tested more than once but less frequently than in the longitudinal design. For instance, in our study of third-party entry, groups of kindergarteners, second graders, and fourth graders would be selected and tested, then retested one year later. Thus six years of development would be described with only one year between testings. This approach allows the researcher to separate the evidence of true developmental change from the unique experiences of different age groups of children in the study.

*Reading
Published
Research:
Consumer
Beware!*

Although scientists have adopted and adhered to strict ethical standards, consumers of information on child development face other problems. First, even though the vast majority of research reported in scientific journals is credible, there are some concerns. It is rare, for instance, for research to be *replicated*. Put simply, if a study is performed only once, how certain are we that the same results would be obtained if it were conducted again under the same circumstances? Replication is so rare in child development that it would not be inaccurate to describe child development as a science of, as yet, unreplicated results. That is not to say that results *could not* be replicated — only that, for the most part, they *have not* been replicated. Our scientific knowledge is, therefore, somewhat tentative.

A second very disturbing fact is that research findings are generally reported only if the results of the study are positive (that is, if they came out as predicted). If the anticipated results are not confirmed, journals simply are unlikely to publish the results. Thus, we could conclude that the research literature in child development is a collection of predictions that were confirmed. This state of the literature poses a serious problem. If a study does not confirm a result predicted by theory, it suggests that the theory that generated the research questions may not be *valid*. A theory that does not explain predicted phenomenon may need to be revised or abandoned. However, if disconfirming results are not published, their significance will be lost and an invalid theory retains an unblemished reputation. This can be illustrated by a hypothetical case. Imagine that 10 research projects at 10 different universities are conducted to study a predicted positive relationship between TV violence and aggression in children. Further imagine that 9 out of these 10 studies show *no* positive results, but 1 study does confirm the expected relationship. Since the 1 study with positive results is far more likely to get published than the 9 studies with negative results, the published findings will tend to confirm the theory, although the collective result of the 10 studies was disconfirming.

A third problem is that a great deal of the most accessible information on child development is falsely presented as grounded in scientific research. The last 10 years have witnessed a proliferation of popular media that mix scientific study and "expert opinion" in equal measure. TV and radio talk shows and syndicated advice columns in newspapers and magazines provide self-proclaimed authorities who address the questions and concerns of parents and professionals on child-related issues. Although some make an effort to base their advice on research published in journals, others do not bother. Trying to discern who and what are worthy of consideration can be a difficult task, in part because these "experts" communicate in jargon that sounds authoritative even though their message may have little or no scientific merit. An educated consumer of scientific information can learn to trace the scientific basis of these opinions. Those who deal with children must accept this responsibility as a moral imperative.

Reporting Research Findings

After the researcher has collected, analyzed, and interpreted the results of the study and made the appropriate revisions in the minitheory, the next step is to report the results and conclusions to the scientific community. This is not a simple process. It begins with the preparation of the research report. Fortunately, all scholars in the child development field have accepted the *Publication Manual of the American Psychological Association* (APA, 1983) as the standard reporting format for research publications. The manual provides highly specific guidelines that ensure total comparability of research reports in the journals. It is particularly useful for new researchers who are in training and/or reporting their first studies.

The typical research report includes the following sections:

1. *Introduction*   This section provides the *rationale* for the study—that is, it explains why this research is the next logical step in the progression of knowledge

---

FIGURE 3.4

Major Journals for Research in Child and Adolescent Development

Child Development

Child Study Journal

Cognitive Development

Development and Psychopathology

Developmental Psychology

Developmental Review

Genetic Psychology Monographs

Journal of Abnormal Child Psychology

Journal of Adolescence

Journal of Applied Developmental Psychology

Journal of Child Language

Journal of Child Psychology and Psychiatry

Journal of Experimental Child Psychology

Journal of Genetic Psychology

Journal of Infant Behavior and Development

Journal of Pediatrics

Journal of Research on Adolescence

Journal of the American Academy of Child and Adolescent Psychiatry

Journal of Youth and Adolescence

Merrill-Palmer Quarterly

Monographs of the Society for Research in Child Development

Pediatrics

on the particular topic. The rationale is typically stated as a minitheory, using existing theory and research to justify the inclusion of relevant factors. The introduction generally ends with a formal statement of the hypotheses.

2. *Methods*   This section includes a detailed description of the subjects of the study, operational definitions for factors, a statement of the design, and a description of the procedures used in processing data. This section gives other researchers the information they need to replicate the study.

3. *Results*   Results are reported as the end product of statistical analyses that indicate the degree of confidence that the reader may have in the findings.

4. *Discussion*   The discussion usually begins with a brief review of the most important findings, typically in nonstatistical terms. The discussion allows the investigator to interpret the results by exploring their implications for the theory, previous research on the topic, future research, and, occasionally, practical implications for those who deal with children.

The vast majority of studies are reported in research *journals*, publications devoted solely to reports of research. The child development field is served by a wide variety of journals across several disciplines, but a number of journals are devoted exclusively to research on child behavior and development. Figure 3.4 lists the most significant of these journals. They are available in most university or state library collections.

After the article is written, the researcher submits it to a journal for review for possible publication. This is a very elaborate process in which the manuscript is examined and critiqued by other scholars. The journal editor makes the final decision about which reports to publish. The review process has become rather sophisticated in recent years. As a result, some journals reject over 80 percent of submissions so the quality of research that does get published is very high. Nonetheless, there are certain weaknesses in the system that you, as a consumer of scholarly information, should know about (see Box 3.2, page 55).

Access to Scholarly Research on Children

Those who deal with children have a persistent need for information on highly specific topics: hyperactivity, noncompliance, discipline, learning disabilities, cognitive stimulation, frustration tolerance, delay of gratification, learned helplessness, and so on. How do you find reports of research on these and other topics?

The best place to start is with a comprehensive text such as the one you are now reading. The *subject index* in this text will direct you to specific locations within chapters where those topics are treated. Within the chapter, citations of the research will be identified by the investigator and by the date of the publication (e.g., Ladd, 1983). You can then locate the full citation in the References section in the back of the text. The reference librarian in your college or university library can help you locate the journal. Each journal article will list further references.

If your search in the text does not meet your needs, a more comprehensive source is available. The Society for Research in Child Development publishes the *Child Development Abstracts and Bibliography* for your convenience. The *Abstracts* have been published several times per year since the 1930s. Each issue provides brief summaries of all research related to children published within any given year. The *Abstracts* have both an author index and a subject index. Thus, if you have identified an investigator well known for accomplishments on your topic, or you have a key word (or short phrase) that uniquely defines your topic, your search will be highly productive. You should begin with the most recent issue and work your way systematically back through time.

You may be overwhelmed at first by the enormous volume of information available on most topics. Your reference librarian can teach you strategies to narrow your search and thereby save you a great deal of time. Ask the librarian about getting access to computer-based data banks (such as the PSYCLIT Database, American Psychological Association, 1989), which are frequently available in university libraries.

Ethical Considerations in Research with Children

Conducting psychological research presents some risks to the children being studied. Several of these risks can be illustrated in our study of third-party entry.

Imagine that Carlos has been selected as a subject for the study because of his tendency to be rejected in such situations. Imagine further that Carlos has been assigned to the experimental group that receives social skills training, which requires that he be taken out of his regular classroom part of each day for several weeks. At the end of the training, the researchers stage a third-party entry situation to test the progress of the children in both groups.

Although these procedures may seem benign, there are several possible problems. First, in order to select Carlos for the study, the researchers had to observe Carlos's repeated rejection by his peers without intervening in any way. Were the observers justified in not intervening at that time? Second, when Carlos is taken from the room each day, he is teased by the other children. Does Carlos (and the other children being trained) suffer from the stigma associated with their special treatment? Third, at the end of the training period, Carlos is tested in a third-party entry situation that has previously caused him great anxiety. Are researchers justified in subjecting children to testing that may be psychologically damaging? Finally, what if Carlos had been assigned to the control group where efforts to improve his social skills would have been severely restricted to control extraneous influences on the outcome of the study? Is it possible that this placement may have compounded Carlos's problem? Is withholding training from at-risk children any different from withholding treatment in medical experiments on the effectiveness of potentially life-sustaining drugs?

Such questions are applicable to a wide range of psychological research studies with children. Developmentalists have become highly sensitive to these issues in recent years and have agreed on certain *Ethical Standards for Research with Children* (SRCD, 1990), which are summarized in Figure 3.5.

In addition to the ethical standards regarding working with children as subjects, there are other standards that apply to the investigator. It is understood that no efforts will be made to tamper with the research findings. We must be able to assume the researcher's integrity in reporting results. Hypotheses cannot be altered after the fact to fit the data, and data cannot be altered to fit the hypotheses. Investigators must also credit all those who contribute significantly to a study in the publication and avoid taking credit for the work of others. These ethical principles have been adopted by the vast majority of researchers in the field of child development.

FIGURE 3.5

Ethical Standards for Research with Children

1. All proposed research should be submitted to peer review (scrutiny by a committee of objective scientists) prior to the use of children as subjects. The rights of the child supercede the rights of the investigator.

2. The child should be informed of the nature of his/her participation in the study and given an opportunity to choose to participate or not to participate.

3. The *informed consent* of parents should be obtained in writing. The parents should be provided with information concerning the nature of the child's involvement and given an opportunity to refuse participation of their child without penalty.

4. The investigator must avoid the use of any procedures which may cause the child psychological or physical harm.

5. Any concealment or deception employed by the investigator necessary to the conduct of the study must be thoroughly reviewed and approved by a scientific review committee prior to implementation in the study.

6. The investigator must maintain the *confidentiality* of all information gathered with respect to the children in the study.

7. The investigator must assume the responsibility of *debriefing* child subjects with respect to misconceptions which may have resulted from participation in the study.

SOURCE: *Society for Research in Child Development, 1990*

A P P L I C A T I O N

The Scientific Method and the Practitioner

Although you may never conduct a research study, you can apply the principles of the scientific method in both your dealings with children and your evaluation of advice from so-called experts.

- *Do not accept simple explanations of child behavior and development that identify single factors as causes.* No target behavior is ever caused by one factor alone. Similarly, no single cure is likely to solve a general problem.

- *Always demand that experts provide their sources of information or evidence for their causal inferences.* Ask for documentation! When someone says, "Research supports the fact that . . . ," ask for specific references. Be skeptical if you do not get a very specific answer. Be even more skeptical if the expert suggests that you may not be competent to retrieve or interpret those references. Many so-called experts have learned to feign scientific grounding for the advice they are peddling.

- *When you try a new technique in your work with children, exercise as much control over the process as possible.* You can study the effects of your interventions with children by isolating and altering one variable today, a different one tomorrow, and another next week. More specifically, you can compare your present efforts (interventions) with your previous efforts in similar situations by carefully altering only one aspect of your approach at a time. You can then see how effective your intervention was by correlating it with changes in outcomes. You can also compare your efforts with co-workers' efforts by varying one factor at a time.

- *Insist on operational definitions in your work and in your criteria for accepting and applying the work of others.* We live in a sea of jargon, and it is easy to drown in vague references and imprecise use of terms. For example, early childhood educators suggest that their programs promote children's social-emotional and intellectual development. What do they mean by those terms? How can these effects be measured?

Measurement of our "effects" keeps us accountable—in our homes, our schools, our clinics, as well as in the research laboratory. The next time someone in authority uses a term that you do not fully understand, or suggests that their program has a specific effect, ask him or her how it is measured. Don't be surprised if the answer is less than satisfactory.

■ *Be aware that it is unlikely that a topic has gone unresearched.* The scope of research in child development is so vast that it would be difficult to find a topic that has not been studied in considerable detail. This chapter has shown you how to find this information and how to interpret original research. Now that you have access to this valuable information, there is no excuse for not taking advantage of it in your work with children.

Looking Back

We have shown the critical role that research plays in the theory and practice of child development. Research allows us to test, revise, and elaborate our existing theories of children's behavior and development. Principles of child development that have been validated through research take us from a world of conjecture and opinion to a world of facts.

We have also taken the mystery out of the research process. Research is a highly organized and logical sequence of activities: Select a target behavior, develop a minitheory that may account for its variance, formulate hypotheses, operationalize your factors, choose an appropriate design, test the children, and analyze and interpret the results with respect to the minitheory. Once you understand the process, you are well on your way to reading the research literature and applying it in your daily work with children.

Finally, we have shown that the scientific method is more than something that scientists do in their laboratories; it is a way of thinking that can be of value to all those who deal with children. A commitment to precise use of terms helps us to describe children's behavior and development and to communicate our expectations and concerns. The notion of control helps us evaluate our efforts to facilitate development. Above all, thinking like a scientist helps us to be skeptical when we deal with peoples' opinions and conjecture about our children.

C H A P T E R   R E V I E W

SCIENTIFIC METHOD   Those who deal with children need to understand what makes children do the things they do. When we accept conjecture as fact, the lives of children may be at risk. The scientific method provides an objective, systematic approach to developing factual knowledge based on observations in the real world.

OBJECTIVITY   Researchers ensure objectivity by gathering evidence directly from children, describing their methods, demonstrating reliability and validity of methods, and formulating hypotheses before gathering data.

RESEARCH PROBLEM   The research problem identifies the behavior the researcher

seeks to explain, the theory that will provide explanation, and the relationships that the research seeks to confirm.

MINITHEORY   The minitheory is the theoretical frame of reference for a particular study. It identifies the target behavior and the factors that the researcher believes explain that behavior. The minitheory is based on existing theory and research and the researcher's intuition.

HYPOTHESIS The hypothesis is a formal statement that alleges the possibility of a relationship between two factors. It is the researcher's best guess, not a statement of fact. The scientific method requires that hypotheses be formulated and stated before data are gathered.

OPERATIONAL DEFINITION Researchers must define the factors in their studies with operational definitions that state how the factors will be measured. The definitions must be sufficiently detailed so that other researchers are able to replicate the study.

VARIANCE AND COVARIANCE Variance refers to the individual differences among children on a given factor. Covariance is the tendency of two factors to vary systematically with respect to each other. Scholars accept demonstrated covariance between factors as evidence of a relationship between those factors.

DESIGN The researcher's strategy to demonstrate covariation between factors is referred to as the design of the study. It organizes how the researcher collects and analyzes data to confirm or disconfirm the hypotheses. Researchers use two general designs to study covariation: The correlational design identifies covariation in naturally occurring factors, and the experimental design studies covariation between the independent variable and the dependent variable. Only the experimental design allows the researcher to say that one factor causes the variation in another.

STUDYING DEVELOPMENT To study developmental change, the researcher makes observations across age or stage periods. In the longitudinal design, the researcher repeatedly observes the same group of children at predetermined intervals over time. In the cross-sectional design, various age groups of children are studied at a single point in time. The cross-sequential design allows the researcher to separate the evidence of true developmental change from the unique experiences of different age groups of children by testing children more than once but less frequently than in the longitudinal design.

REPORTING RESEARCH Researchers report the results of their studies in professional journals. The reports are prepared according to the specifications in the *Publication Manual of the American Psychological Association*.

ETHICS IN RESEARCH Researchers follow a specific code of ethics to avoid placing children at risk in research studies. Researchers ask other scholars to review their procedures prior to testing, they obtain informed consent of parents, they avoid dangerous procedures, they maintain confidentiality of data, and they debrief children after participation.

PRACTITIONERS Practitioners can apply the scientific method by being skeptical of simple explanations of children's behaviors, by demanding that experts document their sources, by operationally defining the terms they use in practice, and by seeking out research studies on the problems they encounter with children.

Key Terms

causal inference	hypothesis	experimental design
scientific method	operational definition	independent variable
objectivity	variance	dependent variable
reliability	covariance	longitudinal design
validity	design	cross-sectional design
research problem	correlational design	cross-sequential design
minitheory		

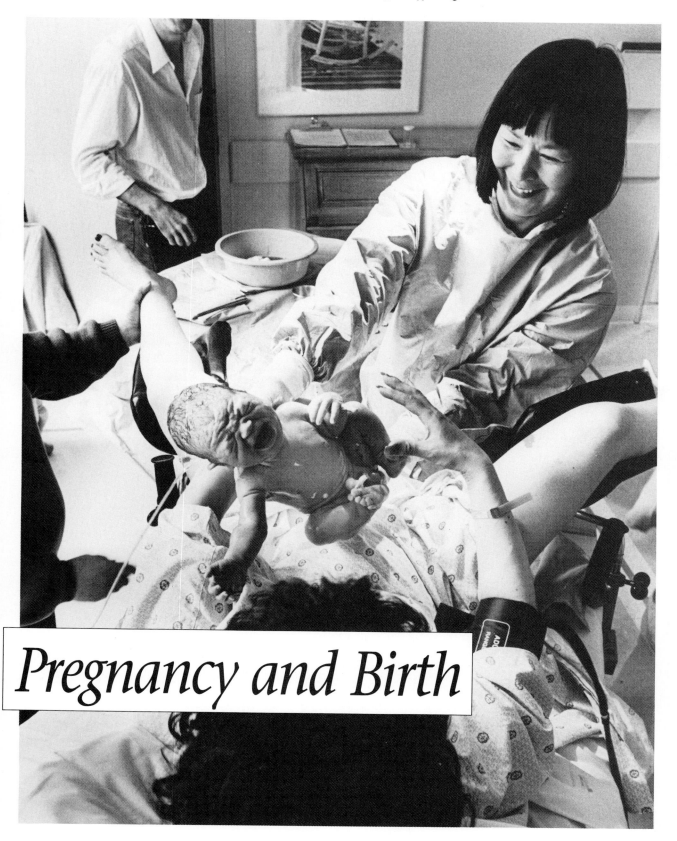

PART TWO

Pregnancy and Birth

4

Prenatal Development and Genetics

Looking Ahead

- The woman's reproductive system is uniquely and magnificently designed to facilitate the process of conception. How does this system work and how does this system fail?

- The man's reproductive system is designed to complement the woman's system to facilitate conception. How does this system work and what causes this system to malfunction?

- Many couples find that getting pregnant is not as easy as they thought it would be. What can they do to improve their chances?

- The time from conception to birth is about 266 days. How does the baby develop during this period and how is the baby sustained by the mother?

- While in the womb, the baby is highly vulnerable to certain environmental influences that may undermine development. What are these environmental factors and how can their effects be prevented?

- The health of the mother affects her fertility and the outcome of her pregnancy. How does pregnancy affect a mother's nutritional needs? Is it safe to exercise during pregnancy?

- Advances in our understanding of heredity have given us new insight into the risks and opportunities for children's development. How are traits transmitted from parents to their offspring? What are the risks?

- Scientists have developed techniques to detect, control, and prevent genetic abnormalities. What are these techniques and what do they tell us about the development of the baby before birth?

- Improvements in our understanding of genetics and prenatal testing have created opportunities to influence the genetic makeup of the child. How do we deal with the ethical issues involved in repairing or replacing human genes?

Conception

T he explanation of conception has been one of the great mysteries throughout recorded history.

> The ancient Hindus believed that there were three basic components needed for the creation of a baby: first, the father provided the white semen to form the child's bones; then the mother contributed the red semen to produce the skin, the hair and the iris of the eyes. However, it was left to God to provide the expression of the face and the child's sight, hearing, speech, and movements. (Lauersen, 1983, p. 117)

Hippocrates, the alleged father of modern medicine, not only accepted the male and female semen theory, but believed that the menstrual blood formed the flesh of a new child (Lauersen, 1983). This was not really such a bad theory, considering that Hippocrates proposed it in 400 B.C. It might even be considered advanced thinking compared to the homunculus theory of the late 1600s: A number of scientists who first viewed sperm cells under the newly discovered microscope believed that they could make out a miniature man (a homunculus) within the head of the sperm, which, by simple logic, would eventually grow into a much larger adult. Women were no more than incubators for these preformed diminutive beings. The homunculus theory was quite popular in the medical literature of that time.

It wasn't until 1843 that Dr. Martin Barrie came to the scientific conclusion that sperm and egg must unite to form a fetus. In the next few pages we will explore the female and male reproductive systems and what happens when they do not function properly.

The Woman's Reproductive System

The female reproductive system is presented in Figure 4.1. This system is uniquely and magnificently designed to facilitate the process of conception. Its functioning is orchestrated by a complex series of hormonal secretions. The timing of these secretions and the processes they regulate are known as the **menstrual cycle**. Although the following description of these events is based on a 28-day cycle, its timing and duration vary considerably from one woman to another.

The cycle begins with the onset of the *menstrual period* (or menses), typically four to five days of bleeding from the vagina. Toward the end of the menstrual period, a hormonal secretion from the pituitary gland stimulates the growth of immature eggs in one of the two ovaries. Several eggs may respond by starting to develop, but only one egg normally ripens in each cycle. If two ripen, there is a possibility that both will be fertilized and fraternal (nonidentical) twins will result.

As the egg matures, the ovary sends out a hormone of its own known as *estrogen*, which stimulates the *endometrium*, the lining of the uterus, to prepare for the arrival of the fertilized egg. The mature egg works its way to the surface of the ovary and, approximately 14 days after the first day of the cycle, the egg breaks through the ovary wall in a process called **ovulation**. The egg is transported toward the uterus by hairlike appendages within the lining of the fallopian tube. **Fertilization**, the penetration of the egg by sperm, takes place in the fallopian tube. The fertilized egg, or **zygote**, continues its journey to the uterus where it lodges itself in the wall of the uterus in a process called

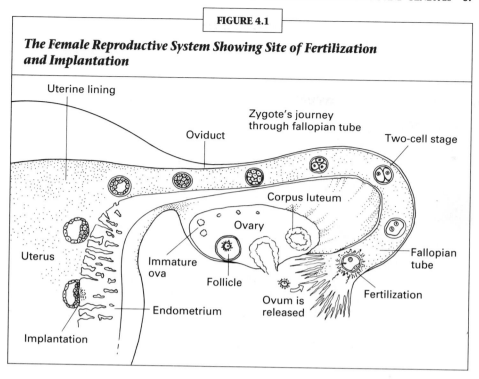

FIGURE 4.1

The Female Reproductive System Showing Site of Fertilization and Implantation

Uterine lining

Zygote's journey through fallopian tube

Oviduct

Two-cell stage

Corpus luteum

Ovary

Uterus

Immature ova

Fallopian tube

Follicle

Fertilization

Endometrium

Ovum is released

Implantation

The ovaries, a pair of oval bodies located on opposite sides of the pelvis, are the source of monthly egg, or ovum, and a critical source of enzymes necessary for pregnancy to unfold. The fallopian tubes transport the ovum to the uterus; they are also the site where a sperm cell penetrates the egg. The uterus—an expandable muscular organ about the size of an adult fist—is the womb in which the fetus grows. The muscles of the uterus provide the force required to expel the baby at its birth. The endometrium, the interior lining of the uterus, is the site of implantation.

implantation. If fertilization does not take place, the unfertilized egg and excess endometrial tissue is washed from the system in the next menstrual period.

This cycle repeats itself throughout a woman's fertile years until her late forties or early fifties. The end of the repeating menstrual cycles is known as *menopause*.

The Man's Reproductive System

The male reproductive system is presented in Figure 4.2. Sperm are produced in the testes, two oval-shaped glands about two inches long suspended in the *scrotum* just below the *penis*.

Male fertility is not tied to a particular schedule comparable to the female menstrual cycle. Barring extraordinary circumstances, a mature male should be capable of producing viable sperm on any given day of the month during his fertile years.

Any one ejaculation, or expulsion of semen, normally contains between 200 and 400 million sperm. That number seems enormous, but just a tiny fraction of them manage to traverse the four to five inches from the *cervix* through the uterus to the fallopian tubes. The trip takes only about 30 minutes, but it is a hazardous journey. Even under favorable circumstances, about a million sperm enter the uterus, and perhaps a few hundred to a few thousand manage to arrive in the fallopian tube, where the egg awaits penetration. The surviving sperm will begin to chemically eat away the protective coating of the egg to allow penetration. If a sperm penetrates the egg, a chemical reaction on the surface of the egg prevents other sperm from entering. **Prenatal development** has begun.

Infertility

Although we have been discussing the normal course of events leading to conception, this sequence does not always occur. About 75 percent of women fail to become preg-

Suspended outside the abdomen, the scrotum is uniquely designed to maintain the testes at an optimal temperature (somewhat cooler than body temperature) for the production of sperm. The sperm cells are tadpole shaped, capable of propelling themselves by rhythmic movements of their tails. The semen — the fluid that carries the sperm — is produced by the prostate gland *and the* seminal vesicles.

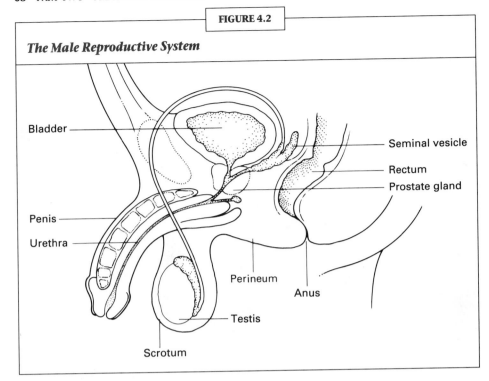

FIGURE 4.2

The Male Reproductive System

nant after one month of unprotected intercourse, 37 percent after six months, and 20 percent after one year. Approximately one couple in six is *infertile*, unable to conceive after one year of sexual relations without contraception, or unable to carry the fetus to term (Hotchner, 1984). Whereas female fertility drops gradually with increasing age, male fertility increases up to 25 years, levels off from 26 through 36, and begins to drop off dramatically in the late thirties (Schwartz et al., 1983). Younger couples who wish to conceive but have not been successful after one year should seek medical consultation, older couples after six months.

Causes of Infertility in Women Even careful timing of intercourse may not ensure conception because either the woman or the man may be at least temporarily infertile. In women, failure to ovulate is one of the most common sources of infertility. Failure to ovulate can have many causes, including severe weight loss, excessive physical exercise, obesity, thyroid disease, and various hormonal problems. Most of these conditions can be readily treated (Frisch, 1988; Green, Weiss, & Darling, 1988; Lauersen, 1983). In extreme cases, failure to ovulate can be treated with so-called *fertility drugs* that prompt ovulation. However, fertility drugs increase the likelihood of multiple simultaneous ovulations and multiple births.

One frequent cause of infertility is a condition called *cervical hostility*. Normally, the mucous plug in the cervix thins out at ovulation to permit passage of sperm; failure to thin out is cervical hostility. Since the thickness of the mucus is regulated by hormones, the condition can be treated through hormone therapy.

Another leading cause of infertility is *blockage of the fallopian tubes*. These tubes are delicate structures that can be damaged or blocked as a side effect of venereal disease or abdominal surgery such as for appendicitis. In approximately 20 percent of infertility cases in women, endometrial tissue that should have been expelled from the uterus during menstruation moves instead into the fallopian tubes, where it eventually causes blockage. The likelihood of this condition—*endometriosis*—increases with age. Drug therapy and surgery are effective for some women, but others remain infertile. Early diagnosis of the condition improves the chances of successful treatment.

Causes of Infertility in Men   Male infertility can result from failure of the testes to produce adequate numbers of healthy sperm. This condition may have numerous causes, including injury, undescended testicles, insufficient blood supply to the testes, mumps, and the presence of the XXY chromosomal abnormality (discussed on page 94).

Recent evidence suggests that some behavioral factors may also be related to infertility. The use of marijuana, wearing overly tight underwear, or taking frequent hot baths or saunas may reduce sperm count. A *semen analysis* can be readily and painlessly conducted in a physician's office to determine the number and quality of sperm in the ejaculate. A sperm count of 60 million sperm per cubic centimeter is normal; under 20 million is considered abnormally low (Lauersen, 1983). Sperm are microscopically observed for *motility* (ability to move directionally) and for abnormal structure.

Male infertility can also be due to failure to achieve and maintain erection during intercourse, *premature ejaculation*, or *failure to ejaculate* during intercourse. These problems can typically be treated successfully by a sex therapist.

Fertility and Timing of Sexual Intercourse   A couple who wants a baby can improve their chances by timing intercourse optimally. At best, sperm can survive for 48 to 72 hours after ejaculation, whereas an ovum is viable for only about 12 to 24 hours after breaking loose from the ovary. Thus the window for possible fertilization extends from about 2 days before ovulation to about 1 after ovulation, or just 3 days of the 28-day menstrual cycle (Silber, 1991). Identifying the specific timing of ovulation, therefore, can be quite useful for couples who are trying to facilitate conception.

How can this be done? A woman on a normal 28-day cycle should ovulate around the fourteenth day following the start of her period, but this may vary. A more exact way of ascertaining ovulation—for women who are regular in their cycles—is to measure *basal body temperature* (*BBT*). She must take her BBT each morning upon waking, prior to any activity. She then plots the daily reading over a period of several weeks or months. Normal temperature during and just after menstruation is about 97.5 degrees Fahrenheit. Body temperature rises about 1 degree, to 98.5, immediately after ovulation and remains at that level until returning to normal when menstruation begins (see Figure 4.3). This rise in temperature is a reasonably reliable indication of ovulation and can be helpful in timing intercourse for the most fertile point in the cycle. The BBT can also alert women to irregularities or the failure to ovulate, which should be brought to the attention of a physician. Estimating the time of ovulation can be further improved by a simple at-home hormone test available at pharmacies.

APPLICATION

Trying to Get Pregnant

Much to their surprise, many couples find that conceiving a child is not as easy as they assumed it would be and that planning for a particular date of birth is almost impossible. However, there are some strategies that can improve your chances of getting pregnant:

- Estimate the time of ovulation with the help of your physician, and time intercourse to slightly precede or to coincide with ovulation.

- Keep sex as spontaneous as possible.

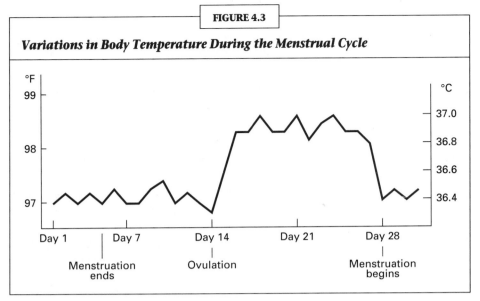

FIGURE 4.3

Variations in Body Temperature During the Menstrual Cycle

SOURCE: *John T. Queenan,* A New Life: Pregnancy, Birth & Your Child, *Van-Nostrand Reinhold, 1979. Reprinted by permission.*

- Stay in top physical and emotional health: Avoid drugs and alcohol, maintain optimal body weight for height with moderate exercise and good nutrition, and minimize stress.
- Women should not smoke or breathe anyone else's smoke.
- Men should avoid prolonged use of hot tubs, saunas, extremely tight underwear, or any other behavior that might elevate the temperature of the testicles.

- Check with your physician after 6 to 12 months of trying to conceive or when one or both partners begin to show some anxiety about the process.

   Bottom Line: Be persistent and patient but don't try too hard. Good timing and enjoyable sex are the keys to conception.

Prenatal Development

Assuming that both partners are fertile and that they have intercourse at the optimal point in the woman's monthly cycle, the chances are excellent that the woman will become pregnant. Approximately 266 days, or 38 weeks, elapse from the date of fertilization to the birth of the baby. This period of time is referred to as **prenatal stage of development**. Although growth during this time is highly continuous, scientists have divided prenatal development into three time periods: *period of the zygote* (or germinal period), *period of the embryo*, and *period of the fetus*. An alternative approach divides this time into three successive *trimesters* or three-month periods.

The Period of the Zygote

The first two weeks following fertilization are the **period of the zygote** (zī gote). For about the first three days of this period, the zygote (fertilized egg) will remain in the fallopian tube. The original cell divides into two cells at 36 hours, followed by several more divisions: By 72 hours it has developed into a ball of cells, which is transported along the fallopian tube toward the uterus. The ball of cells will continue to enlarge as it approaches and enters the uterus, where it will continue to grow while it floats for another three to four days.

By the beginning of the second week, the hollow, fluid-filled ball of cells is referred to as the *blastocyst*. Seven to nine days after fertilization, the blastocyst embeds itself into the endometrial lining of the uterus in a process called *implantation*. This is a risky procedure: By one estimate, it has a 50 percent failure rate (Roberts & Lowe, 1975). Failure to implant may result from several causes, including inadequate hormonal preparation of the endometrium or abnormal development of the blastocyst. Once the blastocyst is embedded in the endometrium, the placenta rapidly begins to form. The **placenta** is an organ that sustains the fetus by allowing oxygen and nutrients from the mother's blood to cross a semipermeable membrane to the fetus and by returning waste products from the fetus to the mother. The two blood supplies do not actually mix. The placenta is attached to the fetus by the *umbilical cord*, a tube containing two arteries and one vein that is pressurized to prevent tangling.

The Period of the Embryo

By the fourteenth day, the growing ball of cells begins to differentiate into three distinct layers of cells, each of which is destined to form specific organ systems. The outermost layer, called the *ectoderm*, develops into the brain, the spinal cord, the nerves, and the skin. The intermediate layer, the *mesoderm*, forms the skeletal system, muscles, heart, and kidneys. The innermost layer, or *endoderm*, becomes the digestive tract, the respiratory system, pancreas, and liver. The developing organism is now referred to as an *embryo*.

The **period of the embryo** extends from the beginning of the third week to the end of the eighth week of pregnancy. During these critical six weeks, the structure of all the major organ systems (except the genitals) is established, a process known as *organogenesis*. Each organ begins and completes its development according to a specific, genetically determined timetable. The time when an organ is developing most rapidly is its **critical period**. The critical period for selected organ systems is illustrated in Figure 4.4. The heart, for example, begins to emerge in the middle of the third week and is structurally complete by the end of the eighth week. By the end of the embryonic period, the organism takes on a distinctly human form and many of its systems have begun to function.

Organogenesis proceeds at a truly astonishing rate during this period. By the end of the fourth week, the ectoderm has folded over to form the neural tube (rudimentary brain/spinal cord), and a primitive heart begins to beat and circulate blood through a crude but functional circulatory system. By the end of the eighth week, the nervous system, heart, kidneys, and liver have begun to function. All of this has been accomplished in an organism that is approximately one-inch long and weighs about one-seventh of an ounce.

Two principles have been used to describe physical development during the period of the embryo. First, the **cephalocaudal principle** describes a growth trend from head to toe with growth of the head proceeding more rapidly than the lower parts of the body. This is reflected in the disproportionately large size of the head early in this period. The **proximodistal principle** describes a second trend in which development proceeds from the center (or proximal) regions of the body out toward the extremities (or distal parts). Thus, arm buds and leg buds appear early in this period, followed progressively by the upper arms and upper legs and finally by the development of the forearm and lower legs. Webbed fingers and toes appear toward the sixth week.

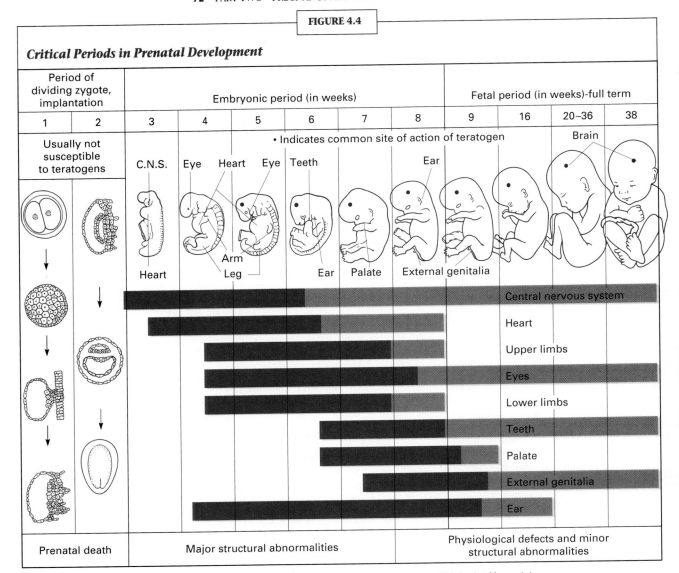

FIGURE 4.4

Critical Periods in Prenatal Development

SOURCE: *Keith L. Moore,* Before We Are Born: Basic Embryology & Birth Defects, *3rd ed., W.B. Saunders Company, 1989. Reprinted by permission.*

The Period of the Fetus

The final and longest stage of prenatal development, the **period of the fetus**, extends from the beginning of the ninth week to birth (about seven months' duration). The major organ systems continue to develop in size and function throughout this period, and the fetus's size is multiplied by a factor of 10. Table 4.1 summarizes the major physical changes during the period of the fetus. Body movements increase steadily in both intensity and variety between 10 and 16 weeks, and by 16 weeks the mother can usually begin to feel the *quickening*, the sensation of the fetus kicking against her abdomen. By 18 weeks, this movement slows as a result of advances in the regulatory functions of the higher centers of the fetal brain.

By 26 weeks, the fetus has reached the **age of viability**, the age at which it would have a reasonable chance of survival if born prematurely. Despite modern advances in medi-

TABLE 4.1

Major Development During the Fetal Period

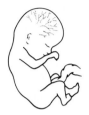

12 Weeks
The fetus weighs about 1 ounce and measures about 3 inches. The head is still quite large in relation to the body. The eyes have formed but they remain fused shut. The ovaries and testes have formed within the body, but the external genitalia are still indistinguishable. The fetus is quite active in the roomy environment of the uterus: kicking, clenching its fists, and making facial expressions. The fetus swallows amniotic fluid and excretes it.

16 Weeks
At 4 ounces and 6 inches in length, the fetus now takes on a distinctly human form. The face has been formed with the eyes large in relation to other features such as the chin. The fingers and toes are completely separated and the fetus's sex can be determined by external features. The body is now covered with downy hair, or *lanugo*. The mother may detect the first movements.

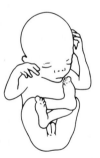

20 Weeks
The fetus now weighs 8 ounces and is 10 inches long. All of the nerve cells that the individual will have throughout life are now formed and the "insulating" of nerve fibers begins—a process that will take several years to complete. The fetus now shows many reflex reactions and can suck its thumb.

24 Weeks
Now 1 pound and 13 inches long, the wrinkled skin is covered with *vernix*, a waxy coating that protects the skin in the liquid environment. The fetus reacts to loud sounds and music. The immature lungs, kidneys, and liver cannot yet sustain life outside the womb. If born, some infants may survive but only with the best of intensive care.

28 Weeks
At 2 pounds, fatty deposits beneath the skin begin to smooth out the skin. The fetus begins to produce *surfactant*, a substance that prevents the collapse of the lungs between breaths. Babies born prematurely have 60–70% chance of survival. Fetal movements can be seen through the mother's abdomen as the uterine environment becomes crowded. The eyes open for the first time and the fetus may hiccup as it swallows amniotic fluid. The surface of the brain begins to show some wrinkling as it continues to differentiate.

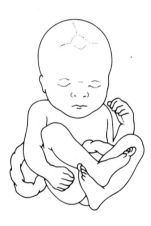

32 Weeks
At 4 pounds, 3 ounces and 16 inches in length, the lungs produce enough surfactant to give the fetus an excellent chance of survival if born prematurely. The fetus's movements can be quite vigorous, sometimes causing the mother to gasp for breath. The brain develops deep folds in its surface.

36 Weeks
The lungs are now mature, and the kidneys and liver are beginning to process waste products. Most fetuses (96%) will turn head down and many will "engage" the head into the mother's pelvis during the last prenatal month.

SOURCE: *Hotchner, 1984; Kitzinger, 1989; Queenan, 1979.*

cal care, survival with an earlier birth date is impossible because of the immaturity of the lungs and nervous system prior to week 24 or 25. Development from the period of the embryo through the period of the fetus is illustrated in Table 4.1.

Environmental Influences on Prenatal Development

In the first half of this century, it was commonly believed that the uterus and the tissues surrounding the embryo and fetus offered more than adequate protection to prenatal development. It was believed that the placenta provided an impenetrable barrier to the invasion of harmful substances.

Now, however, scientists know that some diseases, drugs, and other potentially harmful chemicals can be transmitted from the mother to the embryo. At best, the placenta may play a role in slowing down the transfer of some harmful substances and slightly reducing their concentration. The rapid development of organ systems during the period of the embryo makes the organism highly vulnerable to environmental influences. The period of the fetus is also a vulnerable period, however, with less dramatic but still significant risks for fetal development.

Teratogens

Recall from our earlier discussion that the placenta provides a semipermeable membrane for the exchange of substances between mother and embryo and fetus. As such, it can restrict some substances in the maternal blood supply (for instance, larger proteins and the mother's blood cells) from entering the blood supply of the embryo. This has some benefits: The mother's antibodies, which protect against disease, are transmitted to the embryo and provide some degree of immunity to certain forms of infection. However, many other substances—including chemical agents, viruses, and bacteria—are capable of crossing the placenta and entering the embryo and fetus. Agents that enter into the biological system of the embryo and fetus and negatively influence development are called **teratogens**, a term from the Greek word *teras,* or monster. As implied, the effects of teratogens can be devastating.

The key elements determining the effects of teratogens are dosage, timing in relation to organ development, the embryo's own resilience, and protective factors in the mother. Fetal resilience and maternal protective factors are not well understood at this time. However, our knowledge of teratogens is growing rapidly, and the following paragraphs summarize some of the most important findings.

Medications In the early 1960s, some 7,000 babies were born with severe physical deformities, most notably small, flipperlike appendages in place of arms or legs. The birth defects were traced to the mothers' use of the over-the-counter sedative thalidomide (Lenz, 1966). Although thalidomide was apparently highly effective in reducing a pregnant mother's insomnia and nausea, its effects on the embryo were devastating. The effects depended on when it was taken. If the ears were in their critical period, the baby was born without ears. If the alimentary tract was in its critical period, severe deformity resulted in various locations along the tract. Defects of the heart, liver, and kidneys were not uncommon.

Although thalidomide is no longer prescribed for women who may be pregnant, other drugs and medications that may harm a developing embryo and fetus are still on the market. One example is the synthetic sex hormones (estrogen and progestin) com-

Mothers who unknowingly took thalidomide gave birth to thousands of babies with severe limb deformities and other defects. This mother's tender care for her son will help him cope with his disabilities. Significant improvements in drug testing and labelling in recent years have decreased but not eliminated the risk of over-the-counter and prescription drugs to pregnant mothers.

monly used in birth control pills. The pill works by suppressing ovulation and by artificially creating cervical hostility—but it is not always successful (that is, conception may occur anyway). In cases where a woman is unaware of the pill's failure, she will continue using the pill through the early weeks of her pregnancy, exposing the embryo to abnormally high levels of sex hormones. This may result in abnormalities of the baby's genitalia.

Synthetic hormones have also been prescribed to correct hormone imbalances that might otherwise result in miscarriage. Between 1948 and 1969, for instance, the synthetic estrogen *diethylstilbestrol (DES)* was routinely prescribed to prevent miscarriages in up to 2 million pregnant women. (In the mid-1960s, scientists realized that DES was, in fact, ineffective in preventing miscarriage.) DES babies appeared normal at birth, but at adolescence, some girls developed a rare form of vaginal cancer. Although the worst estimates are that 1 in 500 DES daughters have developed vaginal cancer, approximately 59 percent show abnormalities of vaginal tissue and/or the cervix (Elliott, 1979). One study (Johnson, Driscoll, Hertig, Cole, & Nickerson, 1979) showed that 70 percent of female neonates whose mothers took DES displayed abnormal vaginal cells compared to 4 percent of unexposed babies. Moreover, when DES babies grow to adulthood and become pregnant, they are more likely to miscarry than other women. Male offspring, although less severely affected by DES, have been shown to have genital abnormalities and an increased risk of testicular cancer (Stillman, 1982).

The DES example illustrates that some of the negative effects of apparently safe drugs introduced today may not show up for many years. We know almost nothing about possible long-term teratogenic effects of thousands of drugs that are commonly prescribed by physicians and many others sold over-the-counter.

An added warning comes from the drug *Accutane*, which is the treatment for an extreme form of cystic acne. Even small doses of Accutane are extremely teratogenic; therefore, its prescription is accompanied by appropriate warnings against use by pregnant women. Despite these precautions, however, many babies have been born with severe birth defects (of the brain, heart, and face) in instances where the woman either was unaware she was pregnant or borrowed the drug from someone else and therefore did not know its potential effects (Milunsky, 1989).

A P P L I C A T I O N

Taking Medication During Pregnancy

*I*n our society adults take medication for virtually every ailment, discomfort, or irregularity. Many women continue this behavior into their pregnancy, placing the embryo and fetus at risk. The following advice may help to prevent devastating consequences to your unborn child:

- If you are sexually active, use drugs only when absolutely necessary and when prescribed by a physician who is aware that you might become pregnant.

- If you must take a drug, consult a physician *and* a pharmacist for possible teratogenic effects. Table 4.2 lists common drugs with known teratogenic effects.

- Don't borrow drugs from friends.

- Don't mix your drugs. We know very little about the teratogenic effects of most drugs and even less about their effects when mixed with one another.

Bottom Line: If there is any chance you might become pregnant, take medications—over-the-counter and prescribed—only when absolutely necessary.

TABLE 4.2

Selected Medications and Birth Defects

Medication	Use	Birth Defect
Anticonvulsants	Epilepsy	Mental retardation, spina bifida
Anticancer drugs	Cancer	Fetal death
Sex hormones	Birth control	Genital deformities
Antibiotics	Infections	
tetracycline		Discoloration of teeth, underdeveloped enamel
streptomycin		Deafness
Thalidomide	Nausea during pregnancy	Limb deformities, multiple defects

SOURCE: *Adapted from Milunsky, 1989*

Smoking Approximately one out of four women who smoke cigarettes continue to smoke throughout their pregnancy (Milunsky, 1989). These mothers and their babies pay a high price for this indulgence. Babies born of mothers who smoke weigh six to seven ounces less at birth than babies of nonsmoking mothers (Nieberg, Marks, McLaren, & Remington, 1985). That's if they live. Smoking during pregnancy is also associated with a significant increase in the rate of miscarriages, stillbirths, and death of babies soon after birth (Naeye, 1978).

The reason for these effects seems to be the reduced oxygen supply to the fetus (Quigley, Sheehan, Wildes, & Yen, 1979). Fetal oxygen deprivation is associated with abnormalities of both the brain (Naeye, 1978) and the heart. The damage to the fetus is directly correlated with the number of cigarettes smoked per day; it also seems to be associated with the period of pregnancy when the mother smokes. Some evidence suggests that cutting down to four or five cigarettes daily by the fourth month of pregnancy can prevent the expected growth retardation (Butler, Goldstein, & Ross, 1972).

Alcohol Women who drink heavily during pregnancy have a high risk of giving birth to a baby with *fetal alcohol syndrome (FAS)*. FAS is characterized by mental retardation as well as a combination of deformities of the face, brain, heart, genitals, bones and joints, and growth retardation. The head may be abnormally small with inadequate development of the brain. Alcohol ranks third after Down syndrome and fragile X chromosome abnormality as a cause of mental retardation (Milunsky, 1989).

The face of the FAS baby is characterized by widely spaced eyes, a flat nose, and an underdeveloped jaw. A related pattern resulting from a lower level of alcohol consumption is referred to as *fetal alcohol effects* (Hoyseth & Jones, 1989).

Although the common perception is that FAS affects only babies of *alcoholic* mothers, research suggests that even social drinking poses dangers. One study has shown some evidence of FAS in 16 percent of the offspring of women who drank only one or two ounces of alcohol daily early in the embryonic period (Hansen, Streissguth, & Smith, 1978). There is also some evidence that occasional binges early in the embryonic period may inflict fetal damage (Hoyseth & Jones, 1989). Although estimates vary, research suggests that three to five drinks per day create a 30 to 44 percent chance of producing an affected child.

The period of greatest vulnerability to alcohol is in the first trimester (the first three months of pregnancy). The critical period is when the head is forming, during the third and fourth weeks of gestation. At this stage the mother is unlikely to know that she is pregnant and is unlikely to take precautions, particularly if she is an alcoholic. While

FAS child

decreased consumption before the third trimester may lessen the degree of growth retardation, even elimination of alcohol after the third month is unlikely to erase the probability of certain FAS symptoms (Rosett, Weiner, Lee, Zuckerman, Dooling, & Oppenheimer, 1983).

Prenatal growth retardation and damage to the fetal brain have enduring effects on a child. The child's growth remains stunted (Kyllerman, Aronson, Sabel, Karlberg, Sandin, & Olegard, 1985). IQ and attention deficits have been identified at age four for children of mothers who averaged one-and-one-half ounces of alcohol per day during their pregnancy when compared to children of abstinent mothers (Streissguth, Barr, Sampson, Darby, & Martin, 1989). Hyperactivity, distractibility, short attention span, and delay in perceptual and emotional development persist into childhood for children of alcoholic mothers (Aronson et al., 1985; Janzen & Nanson, 1993).

We know of no safe level of alcohol consumption for pregnant women. Even moderate use of alcohol appears to place the embryo and fetus at risk.

Narcotics and Other Street Drugs

When a pregnant mother takes a psychoactive drug, the drug crosses the placenta and enters the fetus's bloodstream within minutes. The fetus cannot metabolize drugs as efficiently as the mother can, so the effects of drugs stay with the fetus long after they have worn off for the mother.

When a mother who is addicted to *heroin* or *methadone* (a potent narcotic used in drug rehabilitation) gives birth, her baby too will be addicted to the drug and will soon experience withdrawal. The withdrawal symptoms are severe, including tremors, vomiting, and fever. The newborn may die if not given the drug immediately. The addiction can be eliminated by gradual reduction of the drug.

Infants of narcotic-addicted mothers are very likely to be born preterm and at low birth weight. Although malformations are usually not present, addicted newborns are highly irritable and engage in a characteristic high-pitched cry that cannot be soothed, even by the mother. Although the infant can be treated successfully for the addiction, this highly irritable behavior pattern typically presents an overwhelming challenge, especially for a mother who is still addicted and is likely to have limited coping strategies. Consequently, such mothers and their children remain in an intense state of risk.

Cocaine poses an even greater threat than heroin, in both its powder and smokable form, *crack*. Cocaine is a highly addictive drug with pervasive teratogenic effects. Its widespread use by young women greatly expands its risk level. For example, in a study of women in prenatal care at Boston City Hospital, 18 percent of women tested positive for cocaine (Frank et al., 1988). By conservative estimate, hundreds of thousands of pregnant women are placing their children at risk each year.

Research has shown that pregnant mothers who use cocaine significantly increase the likelihood of spontaneous abortion and stillbirth. Babies who do survive are likely to be born preterm, at lower birth weight, and with abnormally small head circumference and other malformations (Bingol, Fuchs, Diaz, Stone, & Gromisch, 1987; Chasnoff, Burns, Schnorr, & Burns, 1985; Chasnoff, Griffith, MacGregor, Dirkes, & Burns, 1989a; Petitti & Coleman, 1990). Cocaine-exposed newborns are irritable, easily overstimulated, and disorganized in their interaction with caregivers (Hume, O'Donnell, Stanger, Killam, & Gingras, 1989).

One positive finding is that a mother who stops using cocaine early in her pregnancy substantially reduces her baby's risk of preterm delivery and low birth weight (Chasnoff, Hunt, Kletter, & Kaplan, 1989b). Another study (Chasnoff, Griffith, Freier, & Murray, 1992) has shown that cocaine-addicted mothers who volunteered for high-quality prenatal and postnatal care helped their babies overcome the negative effects of prenatal exposure to cocaine. With such care, these babies quickly made up for their retarded growth. However, their reduced head circumference—an indication of inadequate brain development—did not catch up. When cocaine babies were followed up at age two, they were not significantly different from children who had not been exposed to cocaine on tests of infant development. However, other research has suggested that, even with improved care, cocaine-exposed children will continue to have learning and cognitive difficulties into the preschool years (Ahl, 1993; Howard, Beckwith, Rodning, & Kropenske, 1989).

While prenatal exposure to cocaine has multiple negative effects on children's development, the problem is often exacerbated by the mother's continued involvement in a drug-related lifestyle after the child is born. One study (Hawley, 1993) indicated that 60 percent of cocaine-addicted mothers admitted to emotional neglect and/or physical neglect of their infants and preschool children. One mother vividly described how cocaine affected her interaction with her baby.

> I was like "I got stuff I got to do, this is what I'm gonna do, I'm gonna feed you, change you, get you all back to sleep." So it was okay, you know, for me, at the time, but now I know it wasn't. 'Cause really, you know, it wasn't their Momma feeding them, it was like a zombie up there with a bottle in their mouth trying to get them, you know, there wasn't no feeling in it as if I were sober. Like, "Come on baby." Just stick the bottle in their mouth whether they want it or not. It's like, "Shut up, shut up." (Hawley, 1993, p. 2)

Addicted mothers described their home environment as chaotic and felt that they were generally unable to provide for their children's needs. In comparison to nonaddicted mothers, they viewed their children as lower in overall development and less likely to succeed. Thus, children who are born to cocaine-addicted mothers will be exposed to multiple forms of risk to their development.

The large number of pregnant women who use cocaine has created a problem of epidemic proportions that calls for a comprehensive response by health professionals, educators, community leaders, and government officials. Unfortunately, that response has yet to materialize for hundreds of thousands of children, and the problem seems to be growing faster than the solution.

A P P L I C A T I O N

Using Street Drugs During Pregnancy

You are more likely to have sex, less likely to use birth control, and thus more likely to become pregnant when you are high on alcohol or drugs. Before you even know you are pregnant, you will be bathing your baby in these substances. They enter your baby's bloodstream just a few minutes after they enter yours. So when you get high, your baby gets high; when you crash, your baby crashes. Your baby's liver and kidneys are immature and far less efficient than your organs are at breaking down the chemicals and cleansing the bloodstream. So your baby suffers more and is in much greater peril than you are.

Bottom Line: Say no to alcohol and drugs. If you can't or won't, say no to sex. If you must do both, use multiple forms of birth control simultaneously. If you do become pregnant, stop using all drugs immediately, and ask a physician to estimate the damage you have already done to your baby.

Maternal Diseases as Teratogens

Unfortunately, the placental barrier is only slightly better at blocking the transfer of bacteria and viruses to the fetus than it is at the transfer of drugs. Several of the most common diseases that have teratogenic effects on the fetus are described below.

Fetal Rubella Syndrome Rubella (or German measles) is an infection that causes mild cold symptoms and a rash in adults. If a mother contracts rubella during the first trimester of her pregnancy, the fetus is likely to be affected. *Fetal rubella syndrome* may result in spontaneous abortion or stillbirth; if the fetus survives, its problems may include mental retardation as well as deafness or malformation of the eyes, ears, and/or heart, depending on the period of pregnancy during which the disease is contracted. The rate of malformation is approximately 50 percent for mothers infected during the first trimester with reduced likelihood of effects from second- and third-trimester illness. Approximately 10 to 20 percent of infected infants die before age one (Bergsma, 1979).

A P P L I C A T I O N

Rubella and Pregnancy

Although the vaccine for rubella has been available for 25 years, approximately 1 in 4 women of childbearing age are not immune to the disease. Thus women who intend to become pregnant should have their immune status checked and updated at least six months before trying to conceive. (The vaccine itself is teratogenic within that period.)

Herpes Virus Two forms of herpes virus are epidemic in the United States, and both have severe effects on the fetus. *Herpes simplex 2* (*HSV*) is a very common sexually transmitted disease that causes painful genital sores in adults. HSV is transmissible only when sores are present. If the mother has HSV, the fetus is most likely to contract it at delivery through exposure to maternal secretions. There is a 50-percent infection rate for vaginal deliveries. Although this form of infection can often be avoided by cesarean section, at least one study provides evidence that the fetus can be infected before birth, as indicated by severe congenital brain abnormalities and presence of the virus in the infant's blood at birth (Hutto et al., 1987). Regardless of the mode of infection, the effects on the fetus are catastrophic. Most infected babies die within the first few months of life.

A P P L I C A T I O N

Herpes and Pregnancy

If you have been infected by herpes at any time in your life, you are still infected, even if you show no symptoms. The following precautions must be taken to avoid damaging the baby:

- If you are not yet pregnant but are sexually active, keep in mind that the only effective drug for the control of herpes (acyclovir) is a suspected teratogen. Discuss this with your physician.
- When you do become pregnant, inform your obstetrician immediately. Your pregnancy must be monitored closely. A cesarean delivery will be required to prevent possible infection of your baby during vaginal delivery.

A second common form of herpes virus, *cytomegalovirus* or *CMV*, is a highly infectious disease with symptoms resembling a mild cold. Unfortunately, the virus is not always accompanied by symptoms, and CMV can hide in the mother's system for some time and affect the fetus when the mother becomes pregnant. CMV may be present in 6 percent of women of childbearing age and infects perhaps 1 to 2 percent of newborns. Fortunately, 90 percent of infected infants show no effects of the disease; 7 percent, however, suffer mental retardation and blindness (Milunsky, 1989). Blood tests are available to determine the mother's vulnerability to the disease. Since no vaccine or cure is presently available for CMV, pregnant women — particularly those who have daily contact with young children — should avoid exposure to others with the disease.

Acquired Immunodeficiency Syndrome (AIDS) AIDS is a progressive weakening of the immune system by the *human immunodeficiency virus* (*HIV*). In infected adults, the weakened immune system creates extreme vulnerability to infection and certain types of cancer. AIDS has existed in the United States since the late 1970s. Over 300,000 people now have the active form of the disease; several times that number are infected but not yet showing symptoms. Most, perhaps all, of these people will die from the disease.

Children get AIDS in a variety of ways but the primary mode of transmission is from an infected mother to the fetus in utero or at birth. A few newborns have been infected from their mothers' breast milk, and about 17 percent of known cases in children resulted from receiving whole blood or blood products prior to 1985, when the test to screen blood became available (March of Dimes, 1987).

Infected infants suffer from frequent infection and diarrhea. They fail to thrive or gain weight. Brain damage is typical. In contrast to adults' susceptibility to opportunistic infections — including cancer and pneumonia — infants fall prey to common bacterial infections such as strep (March of Dimes, 1987). The prognosis for these infants is almost certain death within a few months. There is no cure for AIDS at any age. AZT, a drug that has extended the lives of some adults with AIDS, is presently being tested with children, but the results are not yet available.

A P P L I C A T I O N

HIV Infection and Pregnancy

*T*he only way to prevent transmission of HIV to the fetus is for infected women to avoid pregnancy. The risk of an HIV-positive mother infecting her fetus is approximately 30 to 40 percent. There is simply no safe way for an infected woman to bear a child. If you do give birth and your baby does not test positive, don't breastfeed. The virus can be transmitted to your baby by your breast milk.

Toxoplasmosis *Toxoplasmosis* is an infection caused by a parasite found in the intestines of infected cats and birds and in some raw meats. The infected animal will excrete the parasite into the litter box or onto the ground, where it can live for an extended period and find its way into the mother's system through physical contact. She can also get infected by eating extremely rare or uncooked meat.

If a pregnant woman becomes infected with toxoplasmosis, the result is likely to be miscarriage, stillbirth, or death of the baby soon after birth. If the baby survives, he or she will appear normal but may eventually develop heart disease, mental retardation, and blindness (March of Dimes, 1989). Approximately 1 out of every 1,000 newborns have toxoplasmosis, but fewer than 20 percent show any symptoms of the disease (Milunsky, 1989).

A P P L I C A T I O N

Preventing Toxoplasmosis

Pregnant mothers or those planning a pregnancy who have placed themselves at risk for toxoplasmosis should have their blood screened for toxoplasma antibodies. If you are immune, the baby is safe. If you are not immune and you become infected during your pregnancy, there is no effective treatment. Take the following precautions:

- Don't eat raw or undercooked meat, especially lamb or pork.
- After handling raw meat, wash your hands before touching anything that you might put in or near your mouth.
- Clean fresh fruits and fresh vegetables thoroughly.
- Don't feed your cat raw or undercooked meat.

- Don't empty or clean the litter box or bird cage. Have someone else do this daily, and tell them to wear gloves that can be discarded or washed immediately after use.
- Since outdoor soil may be infected by cats, wear gloves when working in the garden.
- Avoid close contact with outdoor cats or strays.
- If you have a cat, have it tested for toxoplasmosis. If the test is positive, avoid contact with it until you are assured that you are immune. If you are not immune, try living without the cat.

SOURCE:
The March of Dimes, 1989, Public Health Education Information Sheet, 09-408-00

Maternal Stress During Pregnancy

> *When Barbara (Heather's mother) misses her second consecutive period and morning sickness has become routine, she reluctantly accepts the fact that she is pregnant. This is neither the time nor the place to have a baby. She knows that the man she is currently living with is not the father of the baby. His physical and emotional abuse keep her in a constant state of terror. Every time she hears his footsteps coming up the stairs, she trembles and her nausea becomes unbearable. Late in her pregnancy, she notices that when she hears his footsteps, the baby kicks. She fantasizes that the baby is just as frightened as she is and is trying to protect itself. Barbara copes by taking enough drugs and alcohol to calm her and her baby.*

Although pregnancy can be a very happy time, it can also be a traumatic experience. Even in the best of situations, the physical stress of pregnancy promotes increased vulnerability to taxing life events. Some mothers find themselves less able to cope with marital conflict, family illness, and financial problems to name just a few. Stress increases heart rate, blood pressure, respiration, and muscle tension.

There are two compelling reasons to expect that maternal stress would have a negative impact on the fetus and/or on the birth process. First, stress hormones released into the bloodstream increase blood flow to the muscles and brain and decrease blood flow to the uterus, reducing the supply of oxygen to the fetus. Second, the mother's anxiety may increase her use of alcohol, drugs, and cigarettes, all of which have been shown to harm the fetus.

However, despite the widespread belief that maternal stress causes birth complications, studies have provided only marginal support (Norbeck & Tilden, 1983) or no support at all (Smilkstein, Helspaer-Lucas, Ashworth, Montano, & Pagel, 1984) for a direct relationship. A critical review of the studies in this area states that there is no conclusive evidence that maternal stress or anxiety has any negative effects on birth outcome or on the physical well-being of the neonate (Istvan, 1986).

Does this mean that a pregnant mother's stress and anxiety should not be taken seriously? To the contrary, stress can have negative effects on the mother's approach to prenatal care, diet, and exercise and may promote substance abuse. The stress that Barbara experienced from an abusive relationship and a disorganized lifestyle promoted her use of alcohol and drugs. Chronic maternal anxiety sends a signal that the mother may be coping inadequately with pregnancy; those who deal with pregnant mothers should take notice.

Maternal Nutrition and Exercise

The likelihood of conception, the quality of prenatal development, and the outcome of pregnancy are highly dependent on the health of the mother. The approach she and professionals take to ensure her well-being and the fetus's well-being during pregnancy is referred to as *prenatal care*. The advantages to adequate prenatal care are illustrated in Figure 4.5. Low-income mothers frequently obtain little or no prenatal care, resulting in far greater incidence of birth complications. One study showed that the pregnancies of low-income mothers who received adequate care were far less problematic than low-income mothers who received no prenatal care (Moore, Origel, Key, & Resnick, 1986). In recent years, we have become increasingly aware of the importance of maternal nutrition and exercise in a comprehensive approach to prenatal care.

Maternal Nutritional Needs During Pregnancy
The first weeks of pregnancy are critical for the formation of the embryo, but this growth does not involve large increases in mass; the mother's weight gain is typically no more than 3 pounds in the first trimester. The rate then increases to a steady gain of nearly 1 pound per week during the second and third trimesters, for a total increase of 24 to 27 pounds at term. Approximately 10 to 11 pounds of the added weight is due to the fetus, amniotic fluid, and fetal membranes; the remainder is fat deposits in the mother. Too little or too much weight gain during pregnancy can create risk to the mother and to the fetus (McWilliams, 1986).

Although there is some truth to the old saying that the pregnant mother eats for two, this does not mean that she should simply double her normal intake of food. Her *pattern* of nutritional need changes. For example, although the mother's energy requirements increase only 15 percent, her need for protein increases 60 percent and her need for iron may increase up to 300 percent. Individual women differ, so each woman should consult with a certified dietitian as an essential aspect of prenatal care.

Unfortunately, many low-income mothers cannot afford to maintain adequate nutrition during their pregnancy, increasing the likelihood of having their babies preterm and at low birth weight. Several studies have documented the success of short-term, supplementary feeding programs for pregnant mothers, such as the U.S. government's

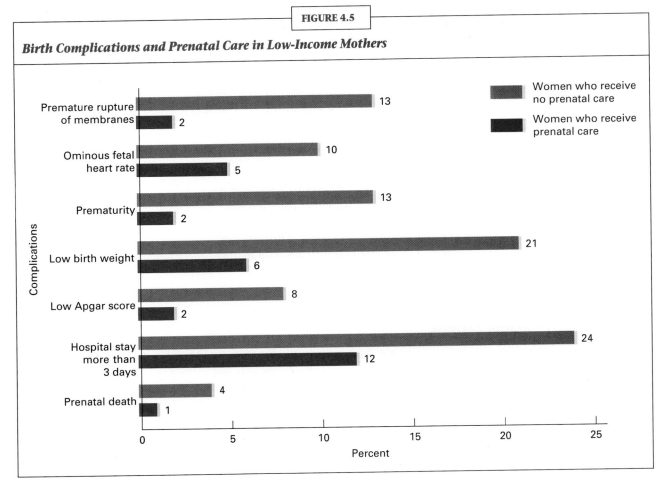

FIGURE 4.5

Birth Complications and Prenatal Care in Low-Income Mothers

SOURCE: *Moore, Origel, Key, & Resnick, 1986*

Women, Infants, and Children (WIC). One study showed that mothers who received supplements had a reduced rate of low birth weight compared to mothers without supplements (Kennedy et al., 1982). A second study of the WIC program identified higher intellectual performance of six- and seven-year-olds whose mothers had received supplemental food during the third trimester — a critical period for brain development (Hicks, Langham, & Takenaka, 1982).

Exercise During Pregnancy Many women who are concerned about physical fitness ask whether they can continue to exercise during their pregnancy. What effects does the mother's exercise have on the pregnancy and on the fetus? Unfortunately, there has been very little research on the effects of exercise on pregnancy. In one study, vigorous exercise by physically fit, first-trimester mothers had no adverse effects on the developing fetus (Clapp, 1989). A second study examined the effects of vigorous bicycle pedaling on fetal heart rate in the second trimester. Fetal heart rate declined only when mothers exhausted themselves; it then returned to normal within a half hour after the exercise was terminated (Carpenter et al., 1988). Clearly, more research is needed on this important aspect of prenatal care.

A P P L I C A T I O N

Exercise During Pregnancy

*T*he limited research available suggests that physically fit women in low-risk pregnancies may continue moderate exercise into the first and second trimesters, but only under the guidance of a physician. However, pregnancy is not the time for you to *begin* to get in shape, nor is it the time for you to take on new challenges even if you are already in good shape. The following guidelines will protect you and your baby:

- Moderate exercise includes activities that do not cause the mother's heart rate to exceed 140 beats per minute. All activities that in-

volve physical contact or falling should be avoided.

- Women should engage in little or no exercise in high-risk pregnancies or where there are signs of premature labor or possible miscarriage (Lauersen, 1987).

- There are a variety of nonstrenuous exercises that promote fitness, reduce stress, and relieve many of the physical discomforts of pregnancy and delivery (Kitzinger, 1989).

 Bottom Line: Consult with your obstetrician about *all* forms of exercise *throughout* your pregnancy.

Genetic Influences on Development

> *When Carlos's father Emilio looks into the face of his newborn son for the first time, he notices how much his son resembles a baby picture of himself that was taken soon after his own birth nearly 30 years earlier. He wonders how many of his physical traits will be passed on to his son. Will Carlos inherit his ability to fix things, his sense of humor, or his patience? Will Carlos have to struggle throughout his life to resist gaining weight? Will he have trouble with his back, a problem that Emilio has had all of his adult life?*

These thoughts are very typical of new parents and reflect their curiosity about their child's **heredity**—the genetic transmission of characteristics from parent to offspring. Our understanding of the mechanisms of heredity has progressed rapidly in recent years and has provided insight into the risks and opportunities of child development. We turn now to a discussion of the mechanisms of heredity.

The Mechanisms of Heredity

Your body is composed of billions of biological units called *cells*. The essential mechanisms of heredity are contained in the cell *nucleus*, which contains rodlike structures known as **chromosomes**. Each human cell contains 23 matched pairs of chromosomes, for a total of 46. One member of each pair is inherited from the father and the other from the mother.

Each chromosome is made up of two long molecular threads of **deoxyribonucleic acid,** or **DNA**, arranged in a ladderlike twisted spiral called a *double helix* (the upper portion of Figure 4.6). Each DNA thread in turn is organized into a sequence of smaller units called **genes** (see Color Plate 1). Any one chromosome may contain as many as 20,000 genes. Thus, genes provide the blueprints for the biological expression of all of

*The lower portion of the fig-
ure depicts the replication
process, as the two strands
of the double helix split
and then pair with the appropriate bases, which
are present in the cell
cytoplasm.*

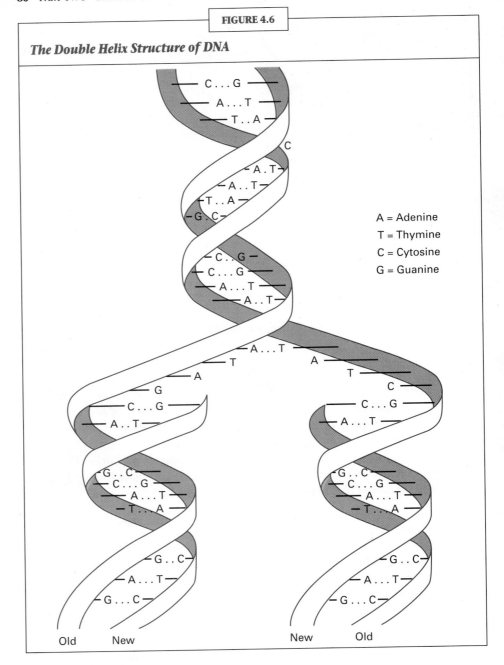

FIGURE 4.6

The Double Helix Structure of DNA

A = Adenine
T = Thymine
C = Cytosine
G = Guanine

Old   New   New   Old

our physical traits such as the structure of our bodies, the color of our hair, eyes, and
skin, and even our susceptibility to disease.

At conception, genetic material from the mother blends with genetic material from
the father to create the first living cell of a unique human being. We refer to this blended
genetic material as the **genotype**. The genotype can be thought of as a blueprint with
varying degrees of specification for the expression of physical and psychological traits of
the individual throughout development. The observable expression of these traits is the
phenotype.

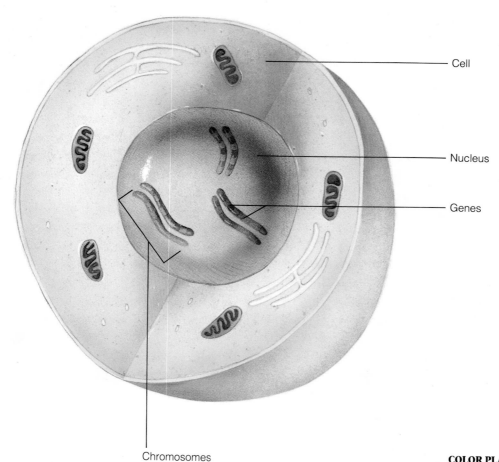

Cell

Nucleus

Genes

Chromosomes

COLOR PLATE 1

Chromosomes are located in the nuclei of cells. Each chromosome is made up of a sequence of genes that determine — individually and in combination — the transfer of traits from parents to their offspring.

SOURCES: *Color Plates 1 and 4 from* Introduction to Psychology, *3rd Edition, by James W. Kalat, Brooks/Cole Publishing Company. © 1993 Wadsworth, Inc. Color Plates 2 and 3 adapted from* Biology: The Unity and Diversity of Life, *6th Edition, by Cecie Starr and Ralph Taggart, Wadsworth Publishing Company. © 1992 Wadsworth, Inc.*

COLOR PLATE 2: THE PHASES OF MITOSIS

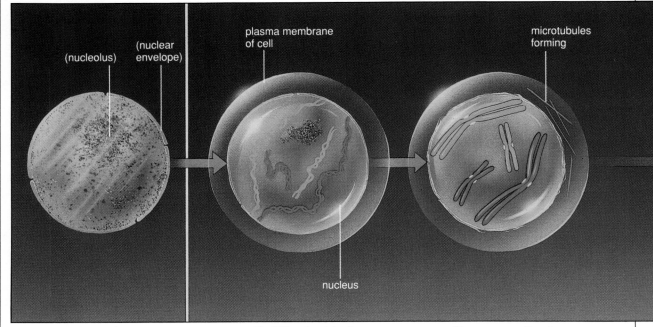

Mitosis begins when a germ cell duplicates its DNA, then the cell prepares for division.

The DNA and associated proteins start condensing into threadlike form. Two chromosomes from the male parent are shown in green; their homologues from the female are in pink.

Chromosomes continue to condense. A spindle begins to form, which will help chromosomes and their duplicates to separate prior to cell division.

COLOR PLATE 3a: THE PHASES OF MEIOSIS IN MALES

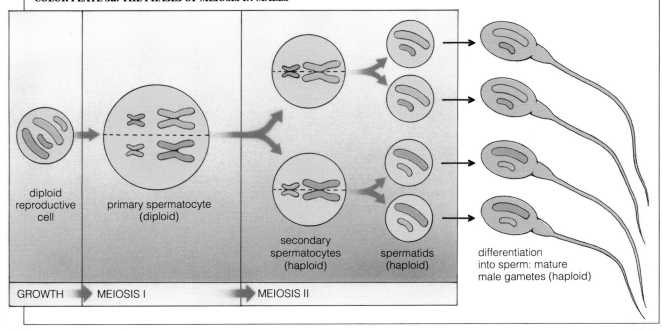

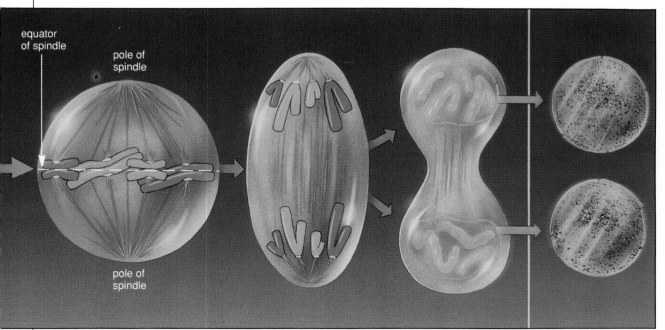

All chromosomes line up on the spindle equator.

Chromosomes separate from their duplicates, moving to opposite poles of the cell.

The cell begins to divide as two separate nuclear membranes begin to form.

The cell divides into two daughter cells, each with 23 pairs of homologous chromosomes.

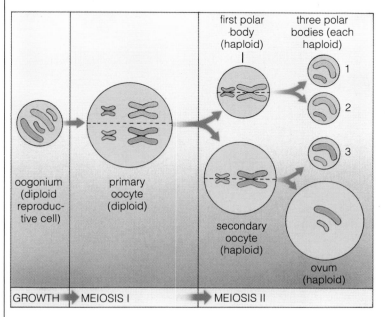

first polar body (haploid)

three polar bodies (each haploid)

1

2

3

oogonium (diploid reproductive cell)

primary oocyte (diploid)

secondary oocyte (haploid)

ovum (haploid)

GROWTH ➡ MEIOSIS I ➡ MEIOSIS II

COLOR PLATE 3b:
THE PHASES OF MEIOSIS IN FEMALES

Meiosis is the process by which the parental DNA is divided and distributed to sperm and eggs for reproduction. Although the process unfolds somewhat differently in the male production of sperm (Color Plate 3a) than in the female production of eggs or ova (Color Plate 3b), the purpose of meiosis is to reduce the number of chromosomes from 46 (the diploid number) to 23 (the haploid number) in each gamete. In the male, each reproductive cell differentiates into 4 sperm cells, each with 23 chromosomes; in the female, the reproductive cell produces only one viable ovum also containing 23 chromosomes. At fertilization, the gametes join to produce the diploid number, or 46 chromosomes in the zygote.

Mother	Father		Mother	Father
	Each parent has two genes for each trait (such as eye color or ability to digest milk), one for each chromosome in the pair.			
	Their offspring receives one chromosome of the pair from each parent.			
If the gene for a trait is identical on each chromosome of a pair, the pair is called **homozygous.**			If the gene for a trait on one chromosome is different from that gene on the other chromosome of a pair, the pair is called **heterozygous.**	

COLOR PLATE 4

When the corresponding genes on homologous pairs of chromosomes are identical for a given trait, we call them homozygous for that trait; when the corresponding genes are different, we refer to them as heterozygous. According to the dominant-recessive principle, when a trait is determined by a single gene and that gene is dominant for a given individual—for example, curly hair—the trait will be expressed in both the homozygous and heterozygous conditions. The result is illustrated by the curly haired children in the photograph below.

The genetic blueprint for the design of a human being is similar to the blueprint for the design of a physical structure. The blueprint for a house, for example, specifies precise dimensions and locations of all components; the final observable product does not vary from the original specifications. The genetic blueprint for some human traits are that precise: Heather will have blue eyes and blond hair; Carlos and Leshonda both will have brown eyes and dark hair. The phenotype for eye and hair color are completely specified in the genotype.

The vast majority of human traits, however, are merely outlined in the genotype, establishing a **reaction range** of potential phenotypic expressions. If a child is to attain the upper end of the range, he or she requires an optimally facilitating environment. For example, Heather's genotype provided the potential for a mature height of 5 feet, 7 inches, but her mother's smoking, use of drugs and alcohol, and inadequate diet during pregnancy retarded Heather's growth and limited her mature height to 5 feet, 5 inches. In contrast, Leshonda's more favorable prenatal and postnatal environment helped her reach her full genetic potential for a height of 5 feet, 6 inches. Thus, Leshonda eventually grew taller than Heather, despite Heather's initial genetic advantage. The interaction of nature and nurture determines phenotypic expression for virtually all physical and psychological characteristics.

Human life is sustained—within the individual and across generations—by the unique ability of human cells to duplicate. There are two distinct processes for accomplishing duplication. **Mitosis** is the process whereby body cells duplicate themselves; **meiosis** is the process whereby sex cells are produced.

Mitosis: The Duplication of Body Cells   When a cell duplicates itself, the DNA double helix unravels into two separate threads. The sequence of genes on each thread then functions as a *template* or model for the duplication of the DNA. Each of the unraveled threads reproduces its own DNA structure, resulting in two double helixes or chromosomes (as shown in the lower portion of Figure 4.6).

All of the 46 chromosomes of the cell duplicate simultaneously into exact copies and line up at the center of the cell; the respective copies migrate to two opposite sides of the cell. The cell then divides into two separate cells, each with identical sets of chromosomes with identical genetic messages (Color Plate 2). Each resulting cell in turn is then capable of repeating the process. This process of cell duplication (*mitosis*) generates all of the cells of the body except for the **gametes** or sex cells (sperm and ova).

Meiosis: The Production of Sex Cells   If sex cells—sperm in males and ova in females—were produced by mitosis, each would have a full set of 46 chromosomes. When the two cells join at fertilization, the resulting zygote would contain 92 chromosomes—double the normal number. The body prevents that from happening by using a different process (*meiosis*) for generating sex cells (see Color Plate 3). Meiosis takes place in two phases. In the first phase, the chromosomes duplicate and divide to produce two copies, as in mitosis. However, in the next phase, a second division takes place without duplication, producing gametes with 23 chromosomes each.

Genetic Variation Through Crossing Over   The division of chromosomes in the first phase of meiosis includes a process that ensures genetic diversity. As the first phase begins, the pairs of chromosomes line up side by side with the genetic material for particular traits. Through a process called **crossing over**, segments of genetic material may be exchanged between chromosomes (see Figure 4.7). Because the site and extent of the exchanges are random, the genetic variations resulting from crossing over number in the

FIGURE 4.7

Crossing Over

STEP 1
Chromosome pairs align
with homologous genes
side by side. (The letters
stand for different genes.)

STEP 2
Segments cross over
and connect at a
random location.

STEP 3
Segments separate after
genetic material is exchanged.

millions, thus ensuring that members of the same family, both within and across generations, will be genetically dissimilar. This diversity is further ensured when the genetically dissimilar gametes from each parent are joined at conception.

Sex Chromosomes and Sex Determination

The question of how the sex of the baby is determined has a long history, punctuated by some unscientific but creative thoughts:

> . . . In ancient Greece, philosophers believed that both men and women produced semen, and the sex of the child would be determined by the strengths of the male and female semen: strong paternal semen would result in a boy, strong female semen would produce a girl. The Talmud declared: "If a woman emits her seed first, she bears a male child, and if a man emits his seed first, she bears a female child." (Lauersen, 1983, p. 66)

FIGURE 4.8

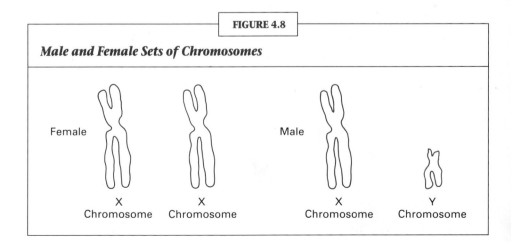

Male and Female Sets of Chromosomes

Female

X
Chromosome

X
Chromosome

Male

X
Chromosome

Y
Chromosome

Scientists now recognize that for each sex the twenty-third of the 23 pairs of chromosomes carries the genetic message that determines the sex of the offspring. In females both chromosomes in the twenty-third pair contain components called X (XX). The corresponding chromosome pair in males contains one X component and one component called Y (XY). (See Figure 4.8.) The meiotic division of the XY chromosome in the father results in either sperm carrying an X chromosome (known as a *gynosperm*) or sperm carrying a Y chromosome (an *andosperm*). In other words, the mother always contributes only X chromosomes, while the father may contribute either an X (leading to a girl) or a Y (leading to a boy). Thus, in a strictly biological sense, the father determines the sex of the offspring: a boy if the ovum (always X-carrying) is penetrated by a Y-carrying andosperm and a girl if the ovum is penetrated by an X-carrying gynosperm.

Genetic Transmission

With the exception of the XY chromosome in males, all other chromosomes are arranged in **homologous** pairs (that is, corresponding members of each pair are matched according to size, shape, and the precise sequence of genes). Thus, the maternal gene for a particular trait and the paternal gene for that trait exist side by side on their respective chromosomes. These paired genes are referred to as **alleles**. The maternal gene and the paternal gene provide different genetic blueprints for the phenotypic expression of a particular trait. For instance, a boy who inherits genes for blue eyes from both his mother and father will display the trait of blue eyes. But what if a girl inherits different alleles for eye color — say, a blue-eye gene from her mother and a brown-eye gene from her father?

Dominant-Recessive Inheritance

A genetic blueprint on a single chromosome does not guarantee its phenotypic expression as a trait in the offspring. The maternal and paternal genes for a particular trait compete for phenotypic expression. If the two genes are of identical form — as in the case of the boy with two blue-eye genes — the person is described as **homozygous** for that trait. If, however, the genes are not the same, the person is described as **heterozygous** (see Color Plate 4).

These two relationships between competing genes have very specific influence on the expression of any particular trait. When the individual is homozygous for a trait that is controlled by a single gene such as eye color, he or she will always manifest that trait. But when the child is heterozygous for that trait, the outcome will conform to the **dominant-recessive principle**.

Genes can be classified as *dominant* or *recessive* with respect to a given trait. A **dominant gene** will always win the competition when paired with a recessive gene for that trait. A **recessive gene** will achieve complete expression only when paired with a similar recessive gene. If a recessive gene is paired with a dominant gene, it does not go away: The recessive blueprint for the trait will be masked, and the individual will be a *carrier* of the recessive gene, which may be passed on to the next generation.

The inheritance of curly hair illustrates the dominant-recessive principle. The gene for curly hair is dominant, and the gene for straight hair is recessive. Regardless of

TABLE 4.3

Dominant and Recessive Features and Diseases

Dominant	Recessive
Dark hair	Blond hair
	Red hair
	Baldness in men
Curly hair	Straight hair
Facial dimples	
Farsightedness	Nearsightedness
	Congenital eye cataracts
	Red-green color blindness
	Albinism
Type A or type B blood	Type O blood
Rh positive blood	Rh negative blood
	Hemophilia
	Sickle-cell anemia
	Cystic fibrosis
	Phenylketonuria (PKU)
	Tay-Sachs disease
Huntington disease	

SOURCES: *Adapted from Behrman & Kliegman, 1990; McKusick, 1986; Stanbury, Wyngaarden, & Fredrickson, 1983*

whether the individual inherits a homozygous pair of genes for curly hair or a heterozygous pair of genes, the hair will be curly due to the dominance of the curly hair gene. Straight hair can result only if the individual inherits the recessive straight hair gene from both parents.

The dominant-recessive relationship is of great significance in the inheritance of certain diseases. Table 4.3 lists some of the most common inherited characteristics and diseases or conditions where the dominant-recessive principle applies. We will discuss several particularly notable inherited diseases.

Phenylketonuria (PKU)   One of the more frequent and potentially tragic examples of inherited disease is **phenylketonuria**, or **PKU**. PKU is a metabolic disorder in which the child fails to produce the enzyme that is needed to convert a potentially destructive amino acid called *phenylalanine* into a harmless substance. Without enough of that enzyme, phenylalanine rapidly builds up and begins to destroy the central nervous system. The infant will be listless and irritable by the fourth month of life; without treatment, he or she will be irreversibly retarded by the end of the first year. If parents are heterozygous carriers, their offspring has a 25 percent chance of inheriting the disease, a 25 percent chance of not having the disease, and a 50 percent chance of becoming a carrier of the recessive gene for the disease.

Fortunately, PKU can be successfully treated in most instances if diagnosed early. Tests administered shortly after birth can detect the disorder, and strict diet (little or no milk products, meat, and eggs or other foods that contain phenylalanine) can be highly effective in preventing the severe symptoms of the disease. The dietary restrictions can be eased in some instances in the early elementary school years, but only with appropriate medical consultation.

When female PKU babies grow to adulthood and become pregnant, the high levels of phenylalanine in their blood can cross the placenta, causing severe congenital brain damage even if the infant has not inherited the disorder. If the mother returns to the diet before her pregnancy and maintains it until the birth of her baby, there should be no negative effects (Levy, Kaplan, & Erickson, 1982).

Tay-Sachs Disease   In Tay-Sachs disease, the child is unable to produce the enzyme necessary for fat metabolism, causing fatty acids to build up in the brain, liver, and spleen. The disease can be diagnosed prenatally, but the characteristic symptoms—increasing paralysis, blindness, and retardation—will not be evident until the middle of the first year, after approximately six months of normal development. The disease is found usually among Ashkenazi Jews of eastern European descent (which includes the vast majority of American Jews). One in 25 to 30 American Jews carries the recessive gene, and 1 in 625 to 900 Jewish couples are at risk. Such couples run a 25 percent chance that each of their children will inherit the disease. Genetic screening and the resulting warnings to at-risk couples have resulted in dramatic reductions in the incidence of the disease over the last 20 years.

Sickle-Cell Anemia

As a child, Keisha never liked her cousin Darnell because he was always tired and not much fun to play with. When Keisha was 12 years old, her mother told her that Darnell was very sick and would probably not live much longer. Terribly frightened, she asked her mother if she might catch the disease. "Don't fret, baby," her mother said. "You don't catch the sickle cell. Some folks have it and some folks don't. That's the way it is." When Keisha asked if she might have it, her mother just shrugged and told her that God would watch out for her if she were a good little girl. Keisha was well behaved from that day on.

Haunted for many years by the memory of Darnell and stories of other similar-sounding illnesses and deaths in distant relatives, Keisha went to a community health center for screening for the disease that killed Darnell, sickle-cell anemia. She would never forget the pain on the face of the nurse who told her that the test has shown that she is a carrier of the sickle-cell trait. The nurse told her that if she has children with a man who also has the trait, each of their children would have a 25-percent chance of having the disease, a 50-percent chance of carrying the trait, and only a 25-percent chance of being completely free of both the disease and the trait. She wonders why she has bothered to be so well behaved for so many years.

Before long, Keisha meets Marcus and within two years they are married. But she never finds the courage to tell him that she carries the sickle-cell trait. When Keisha becomes pregnant, she silently fears for her unborn baby. After a few weeks she confides in her physician who recommends that her husband be tested. When the test shows that Marcus too is a carrier, the physician recommends a prenatal test called amniocentesis, which can tell if the baby is affected by the disease. At the sixteenth week of Keisha's pregnancy, the test is performed. Two weeks later Keisha and Marcus are told that their baby has beat the odds: She does not have sickle-cell disease and she will not carry the trait to her children. Keisha and Marcus decide not to tempt fate; Leshonda will be an only child.

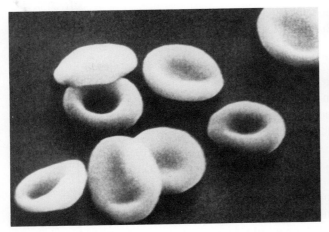

Magnified view of normal blood cells (left), and abnormal sickle cells (right).

A variant of the dominant-recessive principle is illustrated by **sickle-cell anemia**, a disease afflicting 1 out of every 650 African Americans. Paired recessive alleles produce an abnormal form of hemoglobin, which distorts the disklike shape of a normal blood cell into a sickle shape. This causes them to clog blood vessels and deprive the kidneys, brain, liver, spleen, and muscles of the high levels of blood-borne oxygen they require. The child usually dies prior to age 20 though longer survival is possible.

Sickle-cell disease is also expressed through an unusual variation on the dominant-recessive pattern. Individuals who inherit both the dominant gene for normal hemoglobin and the recessive gene for sickle cell will not suffer from the disease under normal environmental conditions. However, if the individual becomes oxygen deprived (from intense physical effort or simply breathing at high altitudes), the recessive allele will be expressed in the form of fatigue and swelling of joints and muscles.

TABLE 4.4

Chances of Genetic Disorders for Various Ethnic Groups

If you are	The chance is	that you are a carrier of	The chance that your child might inherit the disease is
African American	1 in 12	Sickle-cell anemia	1 in 650
White	1 in 25	Cystic fibrosis	1 in 2,500
	1 in 80	Phenylketonuria (PKU)	1 in 25,000
Jewish (Ashkenazic)	1 in 30	Tay-Sachs disease	1 in 3,600
Armenian or Jewish (Sephardic)	1 in 45	Familial Mediterranean fever	1 in 8,000

SOURCE: *Aubrey Milunsky*, Choices, Not Chances: An Essential Guide to Your Heredity and Health. *Copyright © 1989 Aubrey Milunsky, M.D. Reprinted by permission of Little, Brown and Company.*

The prevalence of sickle-cell anemia in African Americans and Tay-Sachs disease in certain Jews is a natural result of the inbreeding within groups that are geographically and/or socially isolated from other groups. Other genetic disorders that are affected by racial or ethnic origin are presented in Table 4.4.

Sex-Linked Inheritance

We saw earlier that the twenty-third chromosome pair in males is made up of an X and a Y chromosome, whereas in females these chromosomes are both X's. This difference makes males more vulnerable to certain conditions. When a recessive gene appears on the male's X chromosome, his Y chromosome may be missing the dominant gene that would counterbalance its effects; therefore the trait must be expressed. In the female a disadvantageous recessive trait on one X can be counterbalanced by a dominant gene on the other chromosome, thereby avoiding the expression of the trait. However, the female is a carrier of the undesirable trait and *may* pass it on to her children.

Sex-linked inheritance, therefore, refers to the genetic transmission of traits and disease by the mechanism of the twenty-third pair of chromosomes, particularly the X chromosome in males. In practical terms, the incidence of sex-linked traits is much higher in males than in females, but sex-linked traits are never directly transmitted from fathers to sons. Rather, the traits are passed from an affected male to his daughter, and from her to half of her sons. Indeed, the trait may be passed "silently" through several generations of carrier females before manifesting itself in affected males.

Although many of the traits expressed on the male X chromosome are benign (such as color blindness), hemophilia is a sex-linked trait that is particularly maladaptive. **Hemophilia** is a disease characterized by inability of the blood to clot, so cuts do not stop bleeding. It rarely occurs in females and occurs in approximately 1 in 4,000 to 7,000 male births. The disease can be diagnosed soon after birth, but it may not be discovered until later in development. Internal bleeding, the most serious symptom, may result in deformity or even death. A male hemophiliac who marries a female without the recessive gene will have sons who do not have the disease.

Chromosomal Abnormalities

We have seen that meiotic divisions, which produce the sex cells, allow the chromosomes to break at various locations and to recombine segments. Crossing over, the benign version of the balanced exchange of genetic material, is a critical process in establishing genetic variation. The meiotic splits, however, can sometimes result in less desirable outcomes.

In some instances, the sperm or ovum may receive either too many or too few sex chromosomes. In other instances, a segment of one chromosome moves over to another. Because of their extensive genetic messages, the effects of chromosomal mishaps are pervasive in the offspring. Intellectual functioning is almost always affected in some manner, as in Down syndrome. The following paragraphs look briefly at this and several other chromosomal abnormalities.

Down Syndrome The most common form of chromosomal abnormality, **Down syndrome**, occurs when the twenty-first pair of chromosomes does not separate, resulting in an offspring with 47 chromosomes. In some instances only part of the extra chromosome is present. The fetus will be affected to the extent that extra chromosomal material is present.

Down syndrome is expressed in a cluster of physical and intellectual traits. Affected individuals have a broad, flat facial structure with slanted eyes and an elongated fold of the eyelid over the inner corner of the eyes. Heart defects and intestinal tract disturbances are common, but recent medical innovations have dramatically increased life expectancy to middle age for many individuals. Down syndrome children show varying degrees of mental retardation with IQ typically less than 50 (the average IQ for the general population is 100). The syndrome also includes slow motor development and impaired speech, with all symptoms tending to increase in severity with age (Kopp, 1983). Premature aging adds to the difficulty of lifetime care that these individuals require.

The later in life a woman becomes pregnant, the greater the likelihood that her baby will have Down syndrome: 1 in 3,000 babies born to mothers under 30, 1 in 600 to mothers between 30 and 34, 1 in 280 to mothers from 35 to 39, and 1 in 80 to mothers between 40 and 44. This effect may result from the prolonged exposure of the eggs in the ovaries to negative environmental influences such as radiation, drugs, and physical trauma. Although the probability of Down syndrome increases with the age of the mother, 80 percent of these babies are born to women under age 35 — during the more productive childbearing years when the overwhelming majority of children are born.

Klinefelter's Syndrome   A second chromosomal abnormality is caused by the failure of the XY pair of chromosomes in the male to separate during meiosis, so that the sperm cell contains both X and Y chromosomes (instead of one or the other). If this sperm fertilizes a normal X-bearing egg, the result is an XXY zygote, a male with **Klinefelter's syndrome**. These so-called XXY males are usually not identified until puberty when their secondary sex characteristics emerge. Adolescents with Klinefelter's syndrome tend to be tall, overweight, nonmuscular, and feminine in appearance. Their testicles and penis are underdeveloped, they lack facial and body hair, and they are frequently mentally

The unique facial features associated with Down syndrome — a flat facial structure and skinfold over the inner corner of the eyes — are particularly apparent in this child. Children with Down syndrome show varying degrees of mental retardation, depending on the extent of the chromosomal abnormality.

retarded. Hormone treatment at adolescence may increase the genitals to normal size, but most of them remain infertile. Their combination of mental retardation and unusual appearance often results in social rejection and poor social adjustment.

Turner Syndrome   In rare instances (1 birth in 5,000), the XX chromosome pattern necessary for normal development of the female is left incomplete, a condition known as **Turner syndrome.** In these instances, all or part of one of the X chromosomes is missing, resulting in inadequate prenatal development of the ovaries and reduced levels of sex hormones. Secondary sex characteristics therefore fail to develop at puberty. Hormonal therapy is of some value, but these girls will be sterile throughout their lives. Girls with Turner syndrome are short in stature and have a 25 percent chance of heart abnormalities. Their intellectual performance is slightly impaired, and their social relationships are problematic (McCauley, Ito, & Kay, 1986). They also frequently have perceptual problems that negatively affect their handwriting and drawing skills (Pennington, Bender, Puck, Salbenblatt, & Borinson, 1982).

Fragile X Syndrome   **Fragile X syndrome** results from breaks or tears toward the outer limits of the long arms of the X chromosome. Males are much more often and more severely affected than females, since females have a second X chromosome that may be normal and thus may prevent the most severe effects of the disorder. In 1 out of 1,000 births, the male will develop abnormally large testicles, prominent chin, large ears, and varying degrees of mental retardation. Fragile X is second only to Down syndrome as a cause of mental retardation. 25 percent of mental retardation in males and 10 percent in females is attributable to fragile X syndrome (Milunsky, 1989).

Triple X Syndrome   Approximately 1 female in 1,000 inherits a third X chromosome in the **triple** X (or "superfemale") **syndrome.** The appearance of these girls is normal, but they do show signs of mild mental retardation, with particularly severe deficits in verbal skills and in short-term memory (Rovet & Netley, 1983). Women with triple X syndrome show normal sexual development and can bear children.

Detecting and Controlling Genetic Disorders

Almost by definition, genetic risks such as those just discussed seem beyond our control. While this has certainly been true throughout most of human history, recent advances in chromosomal analysis, prenatal screening, genetic counseling, medical intervention before and after birth, and educational intervention have created opportunities to prevent, detect, and control genetic abnormalities. We will look at three areas in which new insights have provided would-be parents with a growing measure of control over chromosomal abnormalities. These include genetic screening and **genetic counseling** to identify *prior to conception* whether either parent is a carrier of defective genetic material, prenatal diagnosis of disorders in the fetus, and genetic analysis and genetic therapy.

Genetic Screening and Genetic Counseling

Approximately 7 percent of American babies are born with genetic or congenital disorders (March of Dimes, 1987), perhaps 3 percent with major defects. Many of these disorders are detectable and preventable if parents have access to and take advantage of existing technology and services. Unfortunately, most couples think about problems of

The Genetic Counselor

Ellen Bloch is a genetic counselor at Children's Hospital in Oakland, California.

Why does a couple come to see a genetic counselor?

Couples come to us for a variety of reasons. Some parents have a child with a birth defect and want to know whether another child would be at risk of having a similar disorder. Some couples have had several miscarriages and want to know if there might be a genetic explanation. Others come in for testing during pregnancy because the woman is over 35 and therefore at increased risk for age-related chromosomal abnormalities, such as Down syndrome. Others may know or suspect that a close relative has been affected by a disease or disorder and they want to know how likely they or their children are to be affected. Some of our most anxious patients are those who have had prenatal testing and have been told that their fetus is at increased risk of a specific disorder.

Bad news from a test may come as a complete shock to some patients, so we explain to them that the first test indicates only increased *risk*. We then help them get follow-up testing to see if the disorder is actually there. Usually it's not. In any case, we explain in layman's terms how genetic disorders work and the probabilities involved. In the unfortunate instances where an abnormality is confirmed, we help them cope with their grief, anger, depression, and to adjust to the fact that, if the pregnancy goes to term, they won't have the normal child they expected.

How did you first become interested in genetic counseling?

I was a science and math major in college but my experience in a public health program in the Peace Corps convinced me that I needed to work directly with people. Genetic counseling let me combine my interests in science, math, and helping people.

How does one become a genetic counselor?

There are about 15 training programs around the country. Most are two-year, Master's-level programs that combine a science component — including physiology, biochemistry, and genetics — with a psychology and counseling component.

Becoming a competent genetic counselor requires a very good grasp of science and mathematics. You can't begin to explain a concept in everyday language unless you understand the concept yourself. You are always under pressure to keep up with the expanding knowledge in the field. You also have to be able to empathize with couples and understand what they're going through, whether it's grief or anger or confusion. You deal over and over with families in crisis, and that can be draining. You must be involved with your clients, but you compromise your effectiveness and risk burnout if you don't maintain some distance. Finally, you have to be able to work with a team of professionals — including physicians,

nurses, lab people, and other counselors — to deal with every facet of a patient's situation.

What's a typical day like for you?

I spend about half my time counseling couples. The rest of my time is spent answering telephone inquiries, handling administrative tasks, doing obligatory paperwork, and trying to keep up with the rapid growth of knowledge in my field. Each day seems to bring with it a new test for yet another disorder and families who will be referred for these new indications. I have also spent time coordinating a screening program and educating physicians and patients about the services available at the hospital. Some genetic counselors work in settings that enable them to be involved in research and to contribute new knowledge to this rapidly expanding field.

For more information, write to National Society of Genetic Counselors, 233 Canterbury Drive, Wallingford, Pennsylvania 19086. You can also contact the medical genetics or pediatrics department of a major hospital near you.

genetic origin only after the birth of an affected child. This doesn't necessarily mean that every couple wishing to have a baby should seek counseling. But in cases where there is some reason to suspect genetic defect, couples should ask their physician for referral to a **genetic counselor**—a professional who is specifically trained in genetics and in counseling techniques necessary for the sensitive and emotional nature of the decisions that may be required. After consultation with the genetic counselor, the couple can then weigh their chances of having an affected child and can consider alternatives. See "Careers: The Genetic Counselor" for a closer look at genetic counseling.

A P P L I C A T I O N

Consulting a Genetic Counselor

*F*or most couples, the decision to have a baby raises many questions concerning conception, prenatal care, birth, and the resources that will be required to care for the baby. Although these questions are certainly of great importance, there is one question that you must answer before all others: What are the chances that the baby we conceive will be free from genetic abnormalities? The search for an answer begins by assessing the following risk factors:

■ Either partner has a family history of a hereditary disease or of mental retardation of unknown origin.

■ The woman is over age 35.

■ Either partner has a previous child with a chromosomal or other genetic disorder or any birth defects.

■ The woman has had three or more miscarriages or a stillbirth.

■ The woman has had X-ray or other forms of exposure to radiation early in her pregnancy.

■ Either partner is in a high-risk racial or ethnic group (see Table 4.4).

■ The woman has taken a dangerous drug or experienced a severe bodily infection early in her pregnancy.

If any of these risk factors for genetic disorder are present, consultation with a genetic counselor is strongly recommended for the couple intending to have a baby.

SOURCES:
Adapted from Feinbloom & Forman, 1987; Lauersen, 1983

Prenatal Diagnosis

Some couples become aware of the risk of genetic abnormalities some time after conception. Others know the risk in advance, but choose to take their chances. Still others become aware of nongenetic problems during their pregnancy that may affect the viability of the fetus. In each instance, the couple needs information on the status of the fetus. Prenatal testing can now provide such information, just weeks after conception. The next few paragraphs will review the major techniques and their applications.

Ultrasound Ultrasound makes use of very high-frequency sound waves to form an electronic picture of the fetus (a *sonogram*). The sound waves are produced by a device applied to the mother's abdomen. The sound waves penetrate her abdomen, reaching down into the tissues of the fetus; they are then echoed back to a receiving unit that creates electronic images on a video monitor. Several types of images can be projected, including the contours of the body surface and cross-sectional "slices" through the fetus, revealing internal structures. Movement such as thumb sucking and even heartbeat can be readily detected.

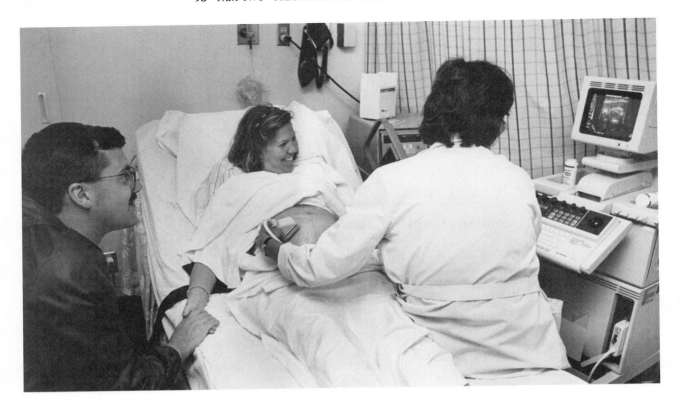

Ultrasound allows the physician to study the fetus's physical structure and movements throughout pregnancy. The outline of the fetus (sonogram) can be seen on the monitor. The parent's shared excitement at seeing the image of their baby is evident.

A P P L I C A T I O N

The Uses of Ultrasound

Advances in the technology of ultrasound have rapidly expanded in recent years. Its uses now include:

- Identifying an embryo in order to diagnose pregnancy
- Monitoring the growth of the fetus
- Determining whether a fetus has or has not been aborted
- Determining a tubal (ectopic) pregnancy
- Identifying multiple pregnancies and fetal position
- Identifying fetal abnormalities, such as neural tube defects or limb defects
- Locating the placenta and determining placental abnormalities
- Measuring the amniotic fluid
- Guiding needle insertion in amniocentesis and tube insertion in chorionic villus sampling
- Measuring the fetal heart rate during prenatal visits, stress and nonstress tests, and labor
- Treating the fetus before birth (fetal surgery)

SOURCE:
Feinbloom & Forman, 1987

How safe is ultrasound for the fetus and the mother? This question has aroused some controversy. Although no studies give clear indication of negative effects, there is a remote possibility that the technique could have some long-term effects on fetal tissues or on the mother. The National Institutes of Health recommend that the technique be applied only when there is a specific medical reason to do so and advise against its use for routine screening (NIH, 1984, as cited in Feinbloom & Forman, 1987).

Amniocentesis   A second prenatal diagnostic technique is **amniocentesis** — a procedure that is typically performed at 15 to 18 weeks following conception (Hanson, Tennant, Hune, & Brookhyser, 1992). A long hollow needle is inserted through the abdominal wall of the mother, through the uterus, and into the amniotic sac. (Ultrasound is used to guide the placement of the needle to protect the fetus.) A sample of fluid is then extracted from the amniotic sac.

This fluid is a valuable source of information because it contains cells that have been shed by the fetus. Laboratory analysis of the fluid typically takes two to three weeks, delaying any necessary medical intervention until the eighteenth to nineteenth week of pregnancy. Amniocentesis can detect the presence of over 100 disorders including Tay-Sachs disease, sickle-cell anemia, muscular dystrophy, and neural tube defects. The procedure also identifies the sex of the fetus for those parents who wish to know.

Amniocentesis is an invasive procedure and does entail some risk: Minor complications occur in 1 percent of cases, including uterine cramping, vaginal bleeding from the uterus, and scratching of the fetus. One in 400 amniocentesis procedures is followed by miscarriage, although it is unclear whether this is a direct result of the procedure. Despite the risks, the information provided by amniocentesis is so valuable that it can be worth the small chance of complications. Some experts have concluded that "for women over thirty-five, the risk of the fetus's carrying a chromosomal abnormality is between two to five times the highest estimated risk of pregnancy loss as a result of amniocentesis" (Feinbloom & Forman, 1987, p. 131).

Chorionic Villus Sampling   In **chorionic villus sampling** (CVS), a hollow tube is inserted through the vagina into the uterus and guided with ultrasound to the *chorion*, a tissue layer surrounding the embryo in the early weeks of gestation. Chorionic villi — projections from the tissue that transfer nutrients and waste between the embryonic and maternal blood supplies — are painlessly suctioned through the tube and analyzed. The safest window for performing the procedure is between the eighth and twelfth week of pregnancy (Rhoads et al., 1989).

CVS offers some advantages over amniocentesis. Because the procedure takes place earlier and analysis is much more rapid than in amniocentesis, relatively safe, first-trimester abortions are possible when serious defects are found. The scope of testing in CVS is more limited than in amniocentesis, but the value of early assessment is immense. Some health professionals have expressed concern about the risk of infection using CVS, prompting ongoing study of its safety. CVS is not used after 12 weeks, nor is it used if the mother has a history of vaginal infection or bleeding or if she has already had an unsuccessful CVS. Recent study of *early amniocentesis* (performed at 12 weeks) may offer a safe alternative to CVS that can be used early in pregnancy (Hanson et al., 1992).

Alpha Fetoprotein Testing   *Alpha fetoprotein* (*AFP*) is a substance normally produced in the fetus's liver that is secreted into the amniotic fluid in small, gradually increasing amounts throughout the prenatal period. AFP eventually crosses into the mother's blood supply.

The amount of AFP in the mother's blood is the basis for still another prenatal screening procedure — the **maternal serum alpha-fetoprotein test**, or **MSAFP**. Alpha-fetoprotein testing is conducted between the fifteenth and eighteenth weeks of pregnancy and is used to detect two conditions: *spina bifida* (exposed spine) and *anencephaly* (a condition in which the skull fails to fuse, leaving the brain exposed and underdeveloped). Both of these conditions result from a similar flaw in prenatal development. Normally, the neural tube begins to fold over early in pregnancy, eventually forming the brain and spinal column. In approximately 1 in 1,000 births, however, the neural tube fails to fuse. The result is either spina bifida or anencephaly. The open brain or tube will allow AFP to leak in abnormally high amounts into the amniotic fluid and then into the mother's blood.

A high MSAFP level in the mother's blood may mean any of several things. If her MSAFP level is high at the first testing, a second blood test is conducted two weeks later. If it remains high, ultrasound and/or amniocentesis is used to provide definite diagnosis.

Some experts advise MSAFP screening for all pregnancies and consider it mandatory when there is a family history of neural tube defect (Milunsky, 1989). About 3 to 5 percent of screenings will show raised MSAFP levels, but of these only 6 percent will actually indicate serious neural tube defect. Rates are somewhat higher for insulin-dependent diabetic women. Abnormally low levels of AFP may indicate Down syndrome or other chromosome defects.

Ethical Issues Concerning Prenatal Development

There was a time, easily within the memory of many reading this text, that we knew little more about the status of a particular embryo or fetus than the physician's stethoscope could tell us, and that was not very much. Now it is possible to learn a great deal through advanced testing techniques. Our rapidly expanding knowledge of genes allows us to predict specific abnormalities even before conception, and such predictions are becoming more and more accurate as we expand our maps of human chromosomes.

But we have not been satisfied just to know and to foresee outcomes. We have begun to intervene. We advise against pregnancy in certain instances and terminate it in others. If the fetus is stressed, we have learned to intervene directly into the womb to relieve that stress. We medicate, we operate, we induce labor, and we perform cesarean sections, all to provide optimal conditions for the fetus and mother. If the thought of some of these interventions has made you uncomfortable, you are not alone. But there is more to come.

We are entering an age in which *genetic therapy* is an available option for use at conception and during prenatal development (Milunsky, 1989). A great deal of the technology for genetic manipulation in humans is already known, and far more will be discovered in the next few years.

All of this raises many ethical questions. For example, if a gene is broken, do we fix it? Are all genes amenable to such fixing? If we don't like the form of a particular gene, do we replace it? Who will decide when to fix and when to replace? Even more problematic, if we can replace genes is it acceptable to construct genetic makeup by design? Who will do the designing? What would a society of designer babies look like?

Will we be satisfied to foster the optimal expression of naturally inherited potential? Or will we be tempted to improve potential through repair or replacement of defective genes or, perhaps, to construct inherited potential by some design that might produce a kind of human being more to our liking?

Some would argue that the technology is many years away. Others believe that governmental regulation of scientific funding will prevent the development of such technology. Yet, considering human nature, it seems highly likely that our insatiable need to know and our irresistible need to apply what we know may well overcome such obstacles before the end of this century. Consequently, the questions above are of immediate concern to all who deal with children.

This text advocates facilitating the optimal expression of naturally inherited potential. From this perspective, the concept of *repairing* broken genes sounds rather promising, but the concept of *replacing* them raises a large red flag. Those who deal with children must begin to discuss these issues and seek answers to these questions. If our values are to be clarified before this seductive technology becomes a reality, time is growing short.

Looking Back

From the moment of conception, the developing embryo and fetus walk a fine line between risk and opportunity. Genetic predisposition to disease, chromosomal abnormalities, teratogens, and inadequate prenatal care threaten prenatal development; benign genetic traits and high-quality prenatal care promote optimal development. Advances in our understanding of prenatal development have created numerous opportunities to prevent certain problems and to detect and intervene with others to lessen their effects. However, it is clear that only well-informed parents will be in a position to minimize risk and maximize opportunity for their offspring's prenatal development.

CHAPTER REVIEW

FEMALE REPRODUCTIVE SYSTEM The functioning of the female reproductive system is orchestrated by a complex series of hormonal secretions, the timing of which is known as the menstrual cycle. The system is uniquely designed to produce an egg (or ovum), and facilitate fertilization in the fallopian tubes and implantation in the uterus.

MALE REPRODUCTIVE SYSTEM The male reproductive system is designed to produce large numbers of healthy sperm and to deposit those sperm in the female vagina. The large numbers are necessary to overcome the hazardous journey from the cervix to the fallopian tubes.

INFERTILITY Approximately one couple in six is infertile; infertility increases with age, particularly in males in the late thirties. Female infertility typically results from failure to ovulate, cervical hostility, or blockage of the fallopian tubes. Male infertility results from failure to produce healthy sperm in sufficient numbers and problems with erection and ejaculation.

TIMING INTERCOURSE The brief viability of sperm and ova create a window

of opportunity for fertilization of about three days. Chances of achieving conception can be improved by estimating the time of ovulation and coordinating it with intercourse.

PRENATAL DEVELOPMENT Prenatal development is divided into three periods. During the period of the zygote (two weeks), the fertilized egg (zygote) moves to the uterus and is implanted in the uterine wall (endometrium); the placenta is formed. During the period of the embryo (the third through the eighth week), the structures of all the major organ systems are formed (except the genitals) in a process called organogenesis. During the period of the fetus (the ninth week to birth), the organ systems continue to grow and begin to function. By about 26 weeks—the age of viability—the fetus is likely to survive if born prematurely.

TERATOGENS Certain diseases, drugs, and other potentially harmful chemicals, collectively called teratogens, can cross the placenta and devastate the developing embryo and fetus. The damage depends on dosage, timing, protective

factors in the mother, and the resilience of the fetus. The most vulnerable time is the critical period for each organ's development.

MATERNAL NUTRITION AND EXERCISE The mother's health during pregnancy has significant effects on her fertility and on her pregnancy. Mothers must change their eating patterns and exercise in moderation.

HEREDITY Each human cell contains 23 matched pairs of chromosomes, with one member of each pair inherited from the father and the other from the mother. Each chromosome is made up of two threads of DNA, with each thread organized into thousands of genes. The blend of genetic material at birth is the genotype; the observable expression of genetic potential is the phenotype.

MITOSIS AND MEIOSIS The duplication of body cells is called mitosis; the duplication of sex cells is meiosis. The division of chromosomes in meiosis ensures genetic diversity through crossing over, the exchange of genetic material from the individual's mother and father.

GENETIC TRANSMISSION With the exception of the XY chromosome in males, all other chromosomes are arranged in homologous pairs. The corresponding genes on paired chromosomes compete for expression. According to the dominant-recessive principle, when the corresponding genes for a trait are dissimilar, the dominant gene will be expressed. A recessive gene is fully expressed only when paired with another recessive gene for that trait.

INHERITED DISEASE All humans carry genes for genetic diseases. Diseases such as PKU, Tay-Sachs, and sickle-cell anemia are expressed by the dominant-recessive principle.

CHROMOSOMAL ABNORMALITIES When errors occur during meiosis, the individual may inherit too many or too few chromosomes. These chromosomal abnormalities result in abnormal physical and psychological traits in affected children. Down syndrome and fragile X syndrome are the most common of these, accounting for a large percentage of those born retarded.

DETECTING GENETIC DISORDERS Recent advances in chromosomal analysis, prenatal screening, genetic counseling, and medical intervention allow us to detect, prevent, and control genetic abnormalities. Genetic abnormalities can be detected prenatally through combinations of ultrasound, amniocentesis, chorionic villus sampling, and MSAFP.

ETHICAL ISSUES Genetic screening and new advances in gene repair and replacement raise difficult ethical issues. If a gene is broken, do we fix it? If we don't like a particular trait, should we be allowed to replace it with one more to our liking? These issues demand immediate discussion.

Key Terms

menstrual cycle	chromosomes	phenylketonuria (PKU)
ovulation	deoxyribonucleic acid (DNA)	Tay-Sachs disease
fertilization	genes	sickle-cell anemia
zygote	genotype	Sex-linked inheritance
implantation	phenotype	hemophilia
prenatal development	reaction range	Down syndrome
prenatal stage of development	mitosis	Klinefelter's syndrome
period of the zygote	meiosis	Turner syndrome
placenta	gametes	fragile X syndrome
period of the embryo	crossing over	triple X syndrome
critical period	homologous	genetic counseling
cephalocaudal principle	alleles	genetic counselor
proximodistal principle	homozygous	ultrasound
period of the fetus	heterozygous	amniocentesis
age of viability	dominant-recessive principle	chorionic villus sampling (CVS)
teratogens	dominant gene	maternal serum alpha-fetoprotein test (MSAFP)
heredity	recessive gene	

5

Birth and the Newborn

Looking Ahead

■ Parents must choose among many childbirth options involving who will facilitate the birth and where the birth will take place. What are these options and how do they affect the health and well-being of the baby and the parents?

■ Parents can prepare for the pain and stress of childbirth without medication. What options are available and what benefits do they offer?

■ Approximately 266 days after conception, the mother will give birth. How does the birth process unfold?

■ A variety of medications are available to ease the pain of childbirth. What are these medications, and what effects do they have on the mother, the birth process, and the baby?

■ The baby experiences great physical stress during childbirth. How can the baby's condition be monitored during childbirth?

■ In some circumstances, the birth process does not begin on time or it progresses too slowly after it has begun. How can medical personnel control the timing and pace of delivery?

■ The newborn baby has a distinct appearance that reflects life in the uterus. What does the newborn look like?

■ When the umbilical cord is severed, the baby must begin to function independently. How do medical personnel know that the baby is functioning satisfactorily?

■ Some babies are born too soon and at low birth weight. Why are babies born early and what effect does this have on their ability to survive? What are the long-term effects?

■ Babies sleep a great deal, but they wake without regard to the clock. How does the sleep pattern change over time?

hildbirth poses a highly complex array of alternatives for the preparation and participation of parents, other members of the family, and the medical community. Many of the decisions have irreversible effects on the well-being of the mother and infant. This chapter provides a broad perspective on the risks and opportunities associated with these choices. Although we will emphasize approaches to childbirth in contemporary Western society, we must be mindful of the broad variations of the childbirth process, historically and cross-culturally. We begin with a brief look at childbirth in two cultures very different from our own.

When a Toda woman of Southern India marries, she becomes a wife not only to her husband, but to all of his brothers. Sexual privileges are rotated among the brothers on a monthly basis. When a child is conceived, there is no effort to determine the biological father. After five months, the woman and all of her husbands retire to an isolated hut for ritual celebration. She remains secluded for one month during which time the eldest brother is ceremonially designated as the legal father.

Childbirth takes place in the home, assisted by women experienced in childbirth. During delivery, the Toda woman kneels with her head on her husband's chest. If complications arise, prayers are offered. After the birth of the baby, the mother and infant return to seclusion for one month to cleanse themselves from what the Todas believe to be the impure process of childbirth. Until this century, a large proportion of female newborns were smothered and buried unceremoniously, immediately after birth. One twin, regardless of sex, was also sacrificed (Queen & Habenstein, 1967).

A hundred years ago, men of the Baganda tribe of central Africa typically had more than one wife. There were fewer males than females, because males were often killed at birth, in war, or as a sacrifice. Wives were inherited, captured in war, or, most commonly, purchased for a number of cows and goats.

The wife was expected to show signs of pregnancy within a few weeks of the marriage. Medicine men handled fertility problems and prenatal care by prescribing a strict diet and a number of drugs. When the birth seemed imminent, the woman was placed in the care of an elderly attendant, who massaged her with butter to facilitate the birth.

> The wife gives birth to the child in the garden, hanging onto a plantain tree and supported by one of the women. The other receives the child, lays it on a plantain leaf, cuts the umbilical cord with a sharp reed, and assists the child in starting to breathe by blowing up its nose. A medicine man will be called in only to assist in difficult cases. In such a contingency not only will the wife have to suffer from his primitive obstetrics, but because of the difficulty she is considered to have been guilty of adultery. (Queen & Habenstein, 1967, p. 83)

Preparing for Childbirth

Although the actual birth of a baby usually takes less than 24 hours, preparing to competently deal with that 24 hours and with the critical days and weeks following the birth requires a great deal of planning. If you are well informed about possible options, plan-

Preparing the home environment for the arrival of the newborn requires considerable planning and effort. A safe, efficient room design can save energy and improve the quality of your care. But esthetics are also important; make certain that the room is stimulating to you and your baby. These parents have ensured that their baby will not be deprived of adequate stimulation.

ning can give you a sense of personal control over the birth process that can help you and your partner manage the stress of pregnancy and childbirth (Entwisle & Doering, 1981). This control derives more from understanding the options and from participating in the decision-making process than from any particular decision that might be made.

Planning should begin well before the earliest possible date of delivery and should include answers to the following questions: *When* will the birth take place? *Where* will the birth take place? *Who* will be involved in the birthing process? *How* will the baby be delivered? *What* should be done in the case of a difficult birthing process? Each of these questions has an extensive range of possible answers, any of which could have important effects on the quality of the parents' experience and the health of their baby. The planning should involve all of the individuals who will affect or be affected by the event: mother and father, siblings, extended family, trainers, and medical personnel. At least one expert recommends that answers to these questions be recorded in a comprehensive **birth plan** (Simkin, 1989). The essential elements of a birth plan are described in Box 5.1.

When Will the Birth Take Place?

Since planning and preparing for the birth take considerable time and effort, it is important to anticipate *when* the birth will take place. Although there is no way to predict precisely when labor will begin, medical personnel can project an approximate *due date* by counting 280 days from the first day of the woman's last menstrual period. During the course of pregnancy, a physician can refine the estimate of the fetus's gestational age, which should improve prediction of the birth date. It should be noted, however, that this prediction is a best guess that may still be off by days or even weeks. Since a baby can live outside the womb after 25 to 26 weeks, it is never too early to develop a birth plan.

BOX 5.1

The Birth Plan

According to Penny Simkin (1989), a birth plan allows the mother to inform everyone concerned with her labor and delivery what options are important to her, what her priorities are, and how she wishes to be cared for under a variety of circumstances. The plan should be thought of as a guide, flexible enough to deal with most contingencies.

The first and most important option is where to have the baby: in a conventional hospital delivery room, in a homelike birthing room available in some hospitals, in an alternative birthing center, or at home. This decision influences other decisions: the person who will deliver the baby (obstetrician or certified nurse-midwife), the availability of emergency equipment and assistance, and the people who may attend the birth (father, other family members, friends).

The birth plan would also include:

Labor Options

Activity Does the mother want the freedom to change positions and get out of bed?

Food and drink Does the mother want to be able to eat and drink if the circumstances allow, or to be given intravenous fluids?

Fetal monitoring Assuming the fetus is not distressed, how does the mother feel about electronic fetal monitoring?

Birth Options

Positions for the second stage of labor Sitting, squatting, lying on the back or the side are among many options available.

Pushing techniques Spontaneous, nondirected bearing down or directed pushing?

Episiotomy If the vaginal opening is insufficient to pass the infant, does the mother prefer to risk a tear or agree to a surgical incision if recommended by the physician?

After Birth Options

Immediate care of the baby
Eye medications, blood tests?

Contact with the baby
Continuous or intermittent?

Feeding of the baby Breast or bottle?

Circumcision?

The Unexpected

Difficult labor Does the mother want to be consulted before special procedures are applied such as induction or speeding up labor?

Cesarean delivery If it is required, does the mother have preferences for sedation and does she want to hold the baby immediately after?

Stillbirth If the baby should not survive the birth, do the parents want private time with the baby, help from a therapist, memorial service, autopsy?

SOURCE:
Adapted from Simkin, 1989

A P P L I C A T I O N

Who Should Make the Childbirth Decisions?

Some argue that it is the *mother* who is pregnant, not the *physician*; therefore, the mother should make the important decisions about the birth of her baby. However, there is more to be considered than the rights of the mother. First, in high-risk births, the parents must defer completely to the expertise and authority of the physician. For example, if the fetus is in severe distress, the physician must decide on the necessity of certain medical procedures to save the life of the baby; it is not open to debate.

However, the vast majority of births are low risk and offer many options. The choices should evolve from discussions between the mother and the physician. The physician is an expert on the physical condition of the mother, the state of the fetus, and the logistics of the delivery. On the other hand, the mother has a unique vantage point: *She* is the expert on her own body, what she is willing to have done to it, and how she prefers to deal with pain. Since physicians tend to be authoritative, parents may have to assert themselves to gain some control over the process.

Bottom Line: To feel in control, study your options and discuss them with your physician early in your pregnancy.

Who Will Facilitate the Birth?

Most of the maternity care in the United States is provided by an **obstetrician**, a physician who specializes in the safe and efficient delivery of babies typically within the confines of a hospital. Obstetricians are trained to deal with routine deliveries and with a range of complications that may arise during pregnancy and birth for the mother and for the baby. Unfortunately, while the vast majority of obstetricians are competent and caring professionals, some provide less time and emotional support than some pregnant mothers desire.

One possible alternative is the use of a **midwife**, a nonphysician who is expert in the birthing of babies. There are *lay midwives*, whose expertise derives from informal experience, and *certified nurse-midwives*, registered nurses who have had one or two years of formal training beyond their nursing training and are approved by the American College of Nurse-Midwives. The nurse-midwife typically works in collaboration with a physician and may practice in a variety of settings. Nurse-midwives do not care for women with complications of pregnancy, and they are trained to know when to defer to a physician. The lesser training of the lay midwife may not provide this safeguard.

There are several potential benefits associated with selecting a certified nurse-midwife. She typically limits the number of clients she accepts to ensure that she can provide highly individualized care and develop a personal relationship with each mother; additionally, she charges less for her services, which typically include prenatal and postnatal care for the mother and baby. For a personal view of the field of midwifery see "Careers: The Certified Nurse-Midwife."

Where Will the Baby Be Born?

Most of us have come to accept and expect that when labor begins, mother is transported to a hospital—*the* place where babies are born. Ninety-nine percent of babies born in the United States are delivered in hospitals (Wegman, 1987).

However, many people view hospitals—particularly large regional medical centers—as impersonal institutions where the mother is controlled by the rules and the whims of typically male-dominated medical personnel. Institutional care can be highly insensitive to individual needs. Some believe that in an uncomplicated pregnancy—where no problems are known or anticipated for the mother or baby—the birth can take place in a variety of settings. These beliefs have stimulated the development of alternatives to the traditional hospital delivery. The choices described below create a delicate balance of risk and opportunity with respect to labor and delivery.

Home Births   Parents who seek alternatives to a hospital delivery typically seek an environment they consider more suitable for the intensely emotional experience of the birth of a child. Some people believe that only the home can provide such an intimate context.

Is a home birth a safe alternative for the mother and baby? The American College of Obstetricians and Gynecologists and the American Academy of Pediatrics consider home

The Certified Nurse-Midwife

Deanne Williams is a certified nurse-midwife. She had been in clinical practice for 13 years, and she is now the Director of Professional Services and Support for the American College of Nurse-Midwives.

How did you become interested in nurse midwifery?

Although I was a nurse for 10 years, I had had little experience with maternity. After taking time out to have a baby, I returned to nursing in obstetrics. I enjoyed the work immensely. Some time later, I began teaching in a nursing program and developed an interest in women's health care. I began to search for a way to combine clinical practice, teaching, and a commitment to women's health care. One day I realized that midwifery was an excellent way to fulfill those goals.

What does a certified nurse-midwife do, and how does it differ from the role of an obstetrician?

A certified nurse-midwife manages every aspect of a woman's care throughout her pregnancy, including the actual delivery of the baby. We begin with an initial examination that assesses the woman's health status and identifies actual and potential risks to the mother or fetus. In some states, we can prescribe medications for common problems, such as infection and postpartum bleeding. However, we are trained to recognize our limita-

tions and refer the mother to an obstetrician when certain risks are present. In some instances, we work in direct collaboration with the obstetrician to provide care and treatment throughout the pregnancy.

Management of the pregnancy is the great challenge. We try to keep the mother and baby as healthy as possible, consistently monitoring for complications. Our goal is to bring the pregnancy as close as possible to full-term. I help the mother to understand the choices she has with respect to pain medication, exercise, breastfeeding, positions during childbirth, and birth partner. My aim is to make the birth itself as natural as possible, minimizing — but not necessarily eliminating — pain medication. Interestingly, assisting the actual delivery is usually the easiest part of my job. That's where the mother does most of the work. I can also provide well-baby care immediately after the birth and provide well-woman and family planning services to women of all ages.

Where does a nurse-midwife practice?

Of the 3,500 practicing nurse-midwives in the United States, approximately 92 percent work in hospitals and 8 percent work in out-of-hospital settings, such as alternative birthing centers. Some deliver babies in the family home.

What training is required to become a certified nurse-midwife?

Training begins with a degree in nursing, followed by some years

of practical nursing experience. You then enter either a professional training program or a Master's degree program in midwifery. There are 35 such programs in the United States, with training averaging about two years. You must pass the national certification exam and meet state licensing requirements before you can practice.

How are the job prospects?

The field is rapidly expanding and the opportunities for employment are excellent. A certified nurse-midwife can expect to earn over $55,000 a year.

How can a student learn more about the profession?

Contact The American College of Nurse-Midwives, 1522 K Street N.W., Suite 1000, Washington, DC 20005, or call (202) 289-0171.

births to present unnecessary hazard during and after birth (Lesko & Lesko, 1984). Although the likelihood is low that an emergency will occur—perhaps 1 in 1,000—the tragic prospect of an unnecessarily handicapped baby or of the death of the baby and/or mother must be weighed heavily by those who consider home birth.

Alternative Birthing Centers A contemporary alternative midway between traditional birth in a hospital and birth at home is the **alternative birthing center** (or **ABC**). The privately operated (or free-standing) ABC provides a simulated home environment with limited equipment for emergency care (resuscitation and oxygen). It is typically located within a short drive to a major hospital to facilitate reasonably rapid access to emergency medical services, if required. The ABC is usually managed by a certified nurse-midwife who assumes primary responsibility for the birth. The nurse-midwife can be expected to take a highly personal approach to the mother before, during, and after the delivery. A physician may or may not be available at the center. A survey of free-standing ABCs showed that 24 percent were operated by a physician and 76 percent by certified midwives and/or lay midwives (Rooks, Weatherby, Ernst, Stapleton, Rosen, & Rosenfeld, 1989).

Is the ABC a safe alternative? Many physicians believe that although ABCs are less hazardous than a home birth, they still present an unacceptable risk in the event of an emergency. Put simply, the time required to transport a mother to the hospital and access emergency services substantially increases the risk to mother and child (Lesko & Lesko, 1984). Are physicians justified in this conclusion? One study (Rooks et al., 1989) of nearly 12,000 births in ABCs concluded that, for low-risk pregnancies, birthing centers offer a safe and acceptable alternative to hospital confinement with lower cost, a lower rate of cesarean section, and less use of anesthesia and analgesia as compared to low-risk births in hospitals. However, it is interesting to note that in this study, one woman in six had to be transferred to a hospital during labor. A commentary on this study (Lieberman & Ryan, 1989) noted that 8 percent of the mothers in the Rooks sample had a severe complication that required immediate medical attention, and that half of these women were too advanced in labor to be transported. Those who consider the ABC as an alternative must weigh the potential risks and benefits carefully before making a decision.

Hospital Birthing Rooms To encourage mothers to choose hospital delivery, many hospitals have now made special birthing rooms available to low-risk mothers that provide a less sterile and more intimate environment for the birth. The room is often carpeted and is furnished and decorated to simulate a home environment. There is no routine prepping (shaving the mother and use of IVs and enemas), pain medication, or fetal monitoring, although these procedures may be elected by the mother or recommended by the physician or nurse-midwife at any time. The close proximity of emergency care makes birthing rooms a safe alternative to the traditional or ABC delivery.

A P P L I C A T I O N

Choosing the Birthplace and Facilitator

*U*ltimately, the choice of birthplace and the choice of birth facilitator should be made by the parents, with appropriate consideration and consultation regarding medical, financial, and psychological matters.

Before making a decision,
- Gather information on the alternatives for birthplace and birth facilitator in your area. Talk directly to the people who offer the service rather than relying on rumor. Visit the

facilities, and seek the opinion of others who have used the service.

- Compare the relative cost and insurance coverage with respect to each alternative. Although a midwife-attended birth at home or in an ABC is typically less costly than a hospital birth, insurance coverage may be limited to hospital deliveries.

- Ask the nurse-midwife for a detailed account of how she deals with emergencies. Ask about prenatal and postnatal care.

   Bottom Line: Ultimately, the risk factors with respect to the health of the mother and the baby must take priority over all other factors in choosing a birthplace and a birth facilitator.

How Do You Prepare?

Vaginal delivery is perhaps *the* most stressful, painful, and exhausting event in human experience. Because of the extraordinary nature of the process, physicians have developed a variety of ways to minimize the pain and stress and maximize the likelihood of favorable outcomes for mother and child. While medication is the surest way to reduce the pain, as we will see later in the chapter, it entails certain risks. Many expecting parents seek alternatives to medication to reduce stress and pain. These approaches are collectively referred to as **prepared childbirth**. In general, prepared childbirth techniques provide for a *birth partner*—typically the father or a close relative or friend—who offers emotional support to the mother and assists her in behavioral/psychological techniques to lessen the pain.

   There are several contemporary approaches to prepared childbirth, all of which prescribe the behavior of participants in virtually every aspect of labor and delivery. All require a great deal of hard work and commitment from the mother and her partner. Underlying these approaches is the notion of childbirth without fear.

Childbirth Without Fear   In the 1920s and early 1930s, a British physician named Grantly Dick Read observed that women who had not acquired a fear of labor appeared to avoid the experience of intense pain during their labor. He reasoned that fear of labor engenders physical tension, which increases muscle pain, which in turn further increases fear. The result is a vicious cycle. Read attempted to break the cycle by educating the mother about the facts of childbirth and teaching her simple breathing techniques for relaxation. He also emphasized a low-key approach to labor, making certain that the mother was not left alone. Read's early work is the basis for today's popular Lamaze and Bradley methods.

The Lamaze Method   The **Lamaze method** requires the active involvement of both parents, with the father (or an appropriate substitute) serving as a coach. Training is initiated two to three months prior to the anticipated due date, beginning with detailed instruction concerning the normal process of pregnancy, labor, and delivery. The couple learns complex sequences of breathing and relaxation techniques, which require sustained attention by the mother, as well as considerable interaction between the coach and the mother. This involvement both distracts the mother from her pain and provides a source of constant emotional support. The goal is to reduce the degree of medication, not necessarily to eliminate its use entirely (Lauersen, 1983).

The Bradley Method   The **Bradley method** involves total relaxation along with normal, rhythmic, abdominal breathing during contractions. This method gives the father a more central role in directing the experience, rather than just supporting it, as in Lamaze. The mother's focus is on her body and the natural process of childbirth. Immediate breastfeeding of the newborn is encouraged, and the newborn remains with the mother at all times. The Bradley method emphasizes an *unmedicated* delivery, in contrast to Lamaze.

Do prepared childbirth techniques really work? Researchers who have tried to answer this question have been hampered by practical and ethical difficulties in the scientific comparison of prepared and nonprepared mothers. An experimental study would involve assigning pregnant mothers at random to treatment and control groups, an approach that would be unacceptable to most women. Despite problems, the research has been informative. In one large-scale study, Lamaze-trained mothers had one-fourth the number of cesarean deliveries, one-fifth the amount of fetal distress, and less postpartum (after-birth) infection than mothers without training (Hughey, McElin, & Young, 1978). Another study indicated that training appears to give the mother a sense of control over her delivery with an increased sense of self-esteem (Dooker, 1980). Although conclusive scientific evidence is not available, the fact that childbirth classes are offered at virtually all hospitals and birthing centers suggests considerable consensus on the merits of these approaches.

The Leboyer Technique Whereas the Lamaze and Bradley approaches emphasize the experience of the parents, Dr. Frederick Leboyer (1975), a French physician, emphasizes the experience of the infant. Leboyer believes that the bright lights, loud sounds, and rough handling of the conventional delivery should be replaced by *gentle birth*—delivering the infant in a dimly lit and quiet room, providing immediate skin-to-skin contact with the mother accompanied by massage, severing the umbilical cord only after it has stopped pulsating, and bathing the infant in warm water to simulate the experience within the womb. Although very few doctors have adopted these techniques, Leboyer successfully sensitized the medical community to the sensory experience of the newborn.

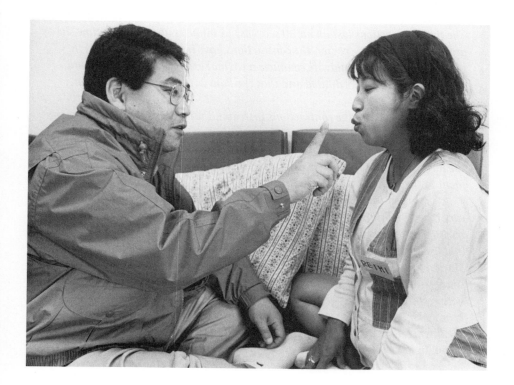

Parents' involvement in prepared childbirth classes can be a highly enjoyable experience that brings them closer together and increases their sense of control. These parents are practicing one of the basic Lamaze breathing exercises that will help the mother to cope with the pain and reduce her need for medication during labor.

A P P L I C A T I O N

Choosing an Approach to Prepared Childbirth

*I*ntuitively, being prepared for one of the most stressful, painful, and potentially rewarding of life's experiences would seem like an excellent idea. Although the benefits of prepared childbirth typically outweigh the drawbacks, pregnant women should consider the following factors when deciding whether to engage in prepared childbirth:

■ Make certain that you have a potential birth partner who is fully committed to completing the course of training and who is prepared to cope with the emotionally charged context of the delivery room or ABC.

■ Consider the quality of your relationship with the potential birth partner. The delivery room is no place to work out the problems of a troubled relationship!

■ If you choose prepared childbirth, practice the techniques to proficiency. Confusion about what to do or when to do it can do more harm than good when you are in labor.

Bottom Line: Keep in mind that the techniques are designed to reduce the mother's pain and to improve the quality of the emotional experience for the parents. Although performing the techniques may be helpful, *not* performing them does not mean that the birth experience will be diminished.

Maria and Emilio plan every aspect of the birth of their baby. Maria's uncomplicated pregnancy permits the choice of a free-standing alternative birthing center located within minutes of a university medical center. They choose a certified nurse-midwife to facilitate the birth. Maria and Emilio work closely with the midwife for several weeks to learn the Lamaze procedure. They develop a close rapport with the midwife, which eases their tension and enhances their sense of control of the process.

An abdominal pain very much like a menstrual cramp wakes Maria at 5A.M. The first contractions last about 30 seconds, 15 minutes apart. By the time she arrives at the birthing center, the contractions have intensified and she is in some discomfort. The midwife conducts a vaginal exam and determines that she is three centimeters dilated and that the baby is positioned perfectly for delivery.

As the intensity of the contractions increases, Emilio massages Maria's back and coaches her through the breathing patterns they have learned in Lamaze. Several members of the family begin to arrive, expanding the social aspect of the birth. There is soft conversation, laughing, smiling, and endless encouragement to the mother and father.

At eight centimeters, Maria's bag of waters breaks, providing some temporary relief. The fluid gives no indication of problems, and the midwife smiles reassuringly at Maria. The physician arrives, determines that she is not needed, and leaves. After another hour, the contractions are extremely painful and Maria is quite irritable, despite the dedicated efforts of her coach and the encouragement from family and friends. The midwife begins to be more directive with respect to the massage and breathing, helping Maria to resist the urge to bear down before it is time. Finally, Carlos's head begins to descend. Despite the intense pain, Maria feels great relief when she is finally permitted to bear down. In less than an hour the crown of Carlos's head appears, and everyone — except Maria — cheers. His final descent goes more quickly than anticipated and Maria's vaginal opening does not tear. Only 15 minutes after the top of his head appears, Carlos is all the way out. The midwife immediately hands him to Maria, who takes him to her breast.

Labor and Childbirth

Early in the last month of pregnancy, the head of the baby typically turns down toward the mother's pelvis and the uterus descends into the pelvic cavity. The ideal position for the baby is head down and facing the mother's back. This position allows the baby to move most easily through the cervix and birth canal.

The Stages of Labor

Labor is the process by which a woman gives birth to her baby. Labor unfolds in a series of three well-defined stages (Figure 5.1). The *first stage* begins spontaneously approximately 266 days after conception with a series of contractions that **dilate** or open the cervix to allow the baby to pass through. In the *second stage* the baby moves through the birth canal and is ejected from the mother. In the *third stage*, the placenta and membranes are pushed out by an additional series of contractions. These stages are described below.

The First Stage: Dilation   The purpose of the *first stage* is to dilate the cervix to allow passage of the baby to the birth canal. The process begins with a series of **contractions** of the muscular walls of the uterus, which push the baby against the cervix. This is typically a very slow and painful process, particularly for the first pregnancy. As the contractions gradually become longer, stronger, and closer together, the cervix thins from approximately 1½ inches thick to a paper-thin membrane. The first contractions are relatively painless, with gradually intensifying pain as dilation increases. As the cervix approaches its widest aperture, the pain can reach extraordinary levels of intensity. Complete dilation to 10 centimeters (about 4 inches) may take anywhere from 2 to 20 hours for the first pregnancy. The first stage is divided into three phases.

The *early phase* lasts until dilation reaches four centimeters, roughly the width of two fingers. The so-called bag of waters or amniotic sac may break, releasing a trickle or possibly a gush of liquid through the vagina.

The *active phase* of labor lasts from two to six hours for first-time mothers. In a low-risk pregnancy, the mother should be at the hospital or alternative birthing center by this phase. In a hospital delivery, varying degrees of *fetal monitoring* may be applied during this phase to assess reactions of the baby's heart rate to the contractions and to medications that may have been given to the mother.

The *transition phase* is marked by the dilation of the cervix from 8 to 10 centimeters. Although this phase typically lasts about 1 hour, the stress of 60- to 90-second contractions every 2 to 3 minutes may cause emotional reactions such as panic, hostility, short temper, and bewilderment (Lesko & Lesko, 1984).

When dilation is completed, the baby's head moves through the cervix and begins its descent into the vagina, or birth canal. Contractions have grown to maximum intensity, lasting about two minutes each and occurring in rapid succession, often without a lapse between them. In a conventional hospital delivery, the mother now is moved into the delivery room, where special equipment is available to assist in the actual birth.

FIGURE 5.1

Stages of Labor

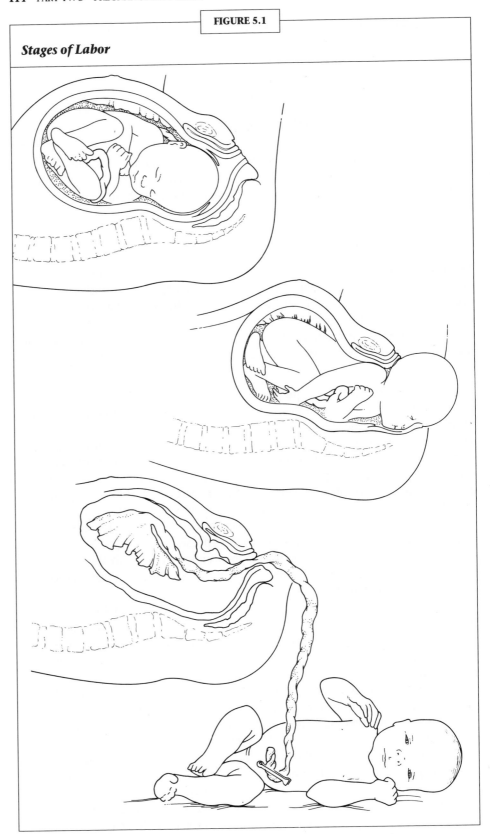

SOURCE: *Susan McCutcheon-Rosegg and Peter Rosegg,* Natural Childbirth the Bradley Way. *Copyright © 1985 Susan McCutcheon-Rosegg and Peter Rosegg. Used by permission of Dutton, an imprint of New American Library, a division of Penguin Books USA Inc.*

The Second Stage: Descent and Birth The *second stage* of labor begins when the cervix is fully dilated and ends when the baby is born. The descent of the baby can take from a few minutes up to three hours, depending on the relative size of baby, the resistance of the vagina, and the strength of the contractions. The descent is gradual and intermittent: two steps forward (as the mother bears down with each contraction) and one step back (as the mother rests).

When the top of the baby's head appears through the vaginal opening, the opening of the vagina is stretched to its limit. If the opening is not adequate to accommodate the size of the head, the physician may administer a local anesthetic and perform an **episiotomy**, a surgical incision that widens the opening to allow the head to pass. The episiotomy is performed *only* to reduce risk to the baby and to prevent the pain and injury that would result from a tear of the skin between the vagina and the anus. When the head first emerges, mucus is suctioned out of the baby's mouth to clear the passageway.

In the final minutes of descent, the last few contractions force the baby out. When the baby has emerged completely, the mouth and throat are again suctioned, and the baby soon begins to breathe on its own without the traditional (and unnecessary) slap on the buttocks. When the baby is breathing regularly, the umbilical cord is clamped and severed. After the mother is given a brief time with her baby, the nurse takes the baby for routine care as the mother enters the third stage.

The Third Stage: Delivery of the Placenta The *third stage* of labor takes place within a half-hour, as the placenta detaches itself from the uterus and is expelled along with the now-useless fetal membranes.

Medicated Labor

Physicians have developed a variety of medications to relieve mothers' pain during various stages of the birth process. According to one estimate, some form of pain medication is used in more than 9 out of 10 deliveries in the United States (Brackbill, 1979). While the prudent use of medication can reduce the mother's pain and enhance her ability to cooperate, virtually all medications carry the risk of potentially serious side effects for both mother and child.

Some pain relievers, such as the frequently used *epidural block* (pain relief from the waist down), tend to reduce the strength of contractions and the woman's urge to bear down during the second stage of labor. This slows labor and may require the use of mechanical means to assist the delivery. Medically stimulated contractions can be especially painful, and the drugs used may cause the mother's blood pressure to drop, which, in turn, reduces fetal heart rate (Poore & Foster, 1985).

Moreover, *all* medications taken by the mother cross the placenta within minutes, affecting the baby both during labor and after birth. In general, medication affects the newborn in proportion to the size of the dosage; low levels of obstetric medication appear to have few lasting effects on the behavior of otherwise healthy babies (Brazelton, Nugent, & Lester, 1987). However, when pain medications are used repeatedly over several hours and at high dosages, the baby is subjected to prolonged exposure to highly potent chemicals. Under these circumstances, the consequences for newborns are predictable: Medicated babies are born in a depressed state that may last for several days. In one study, babies of mothers who had received an epidural were described as "floppy but alert," with weaker muscle strength and tone as compared to babies of mothers who had not had the epidural (Scanlon, Brown, Weiss, & Alper, 1974). Babies of mothers who receive relatively large doses of medication tend to be sluggish, inattentive, and irritable

A physician prepares a woman for an epidural, the most frequently used form of regional anesthetic for relief of the pain of labor. Medication is injected into the space surrounding the spinal cord, eliminating all sensation from the point of injection downward.

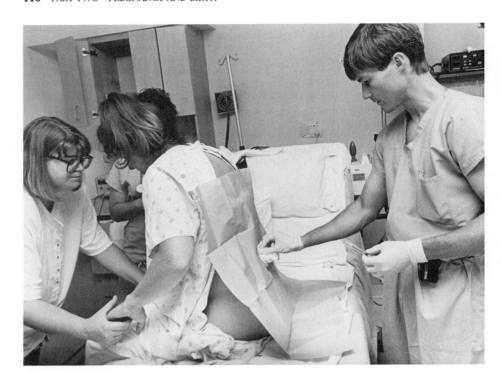

when awake and difficult to feed or pacify during the first few weeks of life (Brackbill, McManus, & Woodward, 1985).

Not surprisingly, a mother's initial transactions with a "drugged" and disorganized baby tend to be very different than those with a nonmedicated baby. One study showed that medicated mothers touched and smiled at their newborn babies less than mothers who had not received medication (Hollenbeck, Gewirtz, & Sebris, 1984). Another study showed that although physical differences between medicated and nonmedicated babies disappeared by one month, nonmedicated mothers continued to be more responsive to their baby's cries and described their babies as more sociable, rewarding, and easy to care for (Murray, Dolby, Nation, & Thomas, 1981). Thus, if a heavily medicated mother perceives her baby as unresponsive and irritable, her interaction with her baby may be suppressed well beyond the time of the drug's observable effects on the newborn's behavior (Murray et al., 1981).

A P P L I C A T I O N

Using Medication During Childbirth

*T*he opportunity to reduce pain during childbirth must be balanced against the risks to the baby and the mother. The following suggestions may be helpful.

- Study alternative medications—their timing and their effects.

- Ask your physician about his or her general approach to medication and, more specifically, how he or she anticipates using medica-

tion during your delivery. Discuss these issues with the physician well in advance of labor, and assert your right to have some say in the process. In most instances, you will find that you and your physician share the intent to minimize medication.

- If the circumstances require heavy medication, be aware that your newborn may be somewhat more irritable, passive, and difficult to feed and pacify than other babies for the first few days or weeks. These effects will pass more quickly if you maintain a positive attitude toward your baby.

Bottom Line: You can minimize the use of medications by learning their effects, discussing the issue with your physician, and using prepared childbirth.

Monitoring the Baby During Labor

Thus far we have emphasized the protracted physical and psychological stress experienced by the mother in labor. The experience of the baby during labor is also highly stressful, even under the best of conditions. Throughout all phases of labor the baby remains dependent upon supplies of oxygen from the umbilical cord, which, like the baby, is being subjected to enormous pressure. The cord must maintain this oxygen supply as it trails alongside the infant through the birth canal. The baby can safely withstand temporary interruptions in the oxygen supply (for example, during contractions), but prolonged deprivation of oxygen will result in a state of **fetal distress**. Prolonged fetal distress can cause varying degrees of damage to the central nervous system and, in extreme cases, death of the baby.

Barbara looks forward to Heather's birth only as relief from the misery of pregnancy. She pays as little attention as possible to her pregnancy and never sees a doctor. She keeps up her usual pattern of frequent alcoholic binges and occasional use of cocaine during the pregnancy.

She does not know when the baby is due, but she senses that it won't be for another month or two. Then suddenly she feels the first contractions. Her fear and intense pain force her to a hospital emergency room. The doctor guesses that she is only about 35 to 36 weeks pregnant, but it appears that labor has begun. He tries to delay the labor, but he is not very hopeful. The good news is that tests show the baby holding its own, at least for the moment. The bad news is that Barbara has alcohol on her breath and a defensive attitude. That tells the doctor everything he needs to know: This baby is at risk; the situation could degenerate quickly.

Despite efforts to delay the labor, Barbara continues to dilate, although very slowly. So the doctor changes strategy and decides to speed up the labor by breaking Barbara's bag of waters. That does not work either. He gives her a drug by IV drip that strengthens the contractions, but they soon become extraordinarily painful. He withholds pain medication, due to the alcohol content of Barbara's blood and her generally weak physical condition.

After 15 hours in labor, Barbara is fully dilated and Heather begins to descend, but very slowly. Then the doctor's worst fears materialize: Barbara's contractions are excruciating, the IV drip is slowed, the contractions have weakened, Heather has stopped her descent, and Heather's heartbeat has slowed dramatically. The doctor tells Barbara that he is concerned about the baby's pulse and that he will have to do some things to get the baby out quickly. "Whatever," Barbara snaps. "Just knock me out and get it over with."

Struggling to hold back his anger, the doctor decides that the situation requires the use of forceps. An epidural is administered, an episiotomy performed, and the blades of the forceps are inserted and locked. Heather is then gently but firmly pulled from her mother's uterus. She weighs just over five pounds.

Heather's heartbeat is slow and irregular, her body is blue, and she is hav-ing difficulty breathing. She is rushed to the intensive care unit where emer-gency measures are taken to assist her breathing. Within a few hours a nurse comes in to tell Barbara that Heather's heartbeat has become normal and that she is finally breathing on her own. Barbara shows no response to the good news and expresses no desire to see her baby in the intensive care nursery.

Causes of Fetal Distress There are many sources of fetal distress. Rather than move into the usual head-down position for birth, 1 in 30 babies will assume the **breech posi-tion**, with the head up and the buttocks or feet or both down against the cervix. If the baby is in a breech position or has not "dropped" when the bag of waters breaks, a portion of the umbilical cord may enter the vagina before the baby. When the baby begins to descend through the vagina, it will pinch the cord, thus stopping the flow of oxygen. This situation is a serious medical emergency that requires rapid intervention. An insufficient supply of oxygen can also result from the decreased efficiency of the placenta late in pregnancy, or from premature detachment of the placenta during labor.

Fetal distress can also result from Rh blood incompatibility or **Rh disease**. The *Rh factor* is a substance in the blood cells of 85 percent of men and women. Those with the substance are Rh positive and those without it are Rh negative. Incompatibility results when an Rh-negative woman and an Rh-positive man conceive an Rh-positive baby. Antigens from the baby's blood may enter the mother's blood supply during delivery, causing the mother's immune system to react to the foreign substance by producing antibodies. Although the first baby is unaffected, the antibodies in the mother's blood will damage any future Rh-positive babies that the mother conceives. This can be pre-vented by testing and treating the mother after each Rh-positive birth.

In all of the above circumstances, it is critical to identify fetal distress as early as possible to intervene appropriately. The need for information on the status of the baby has led to a variety of monitoring techniques for use during the perinatal period, includ-ing electronic fetal monitoring and fetal blood sampling.

Electronic Fetal Monitoring Electronic fetal monitoring (EFM) includes the use of both external and internal devices to monitor the fetal heart rate. The response of the fetal heart rate to contractions can be used to identify fetal distress.

If the amniotic sac has ruptured (spontaneously or by mechanical means), extremely sensitive internal monitoring techniques can be applied directly through the vagina into the uterus. EFM is recommended whenever the mother or the baby is believed to be at risk, for example when the baby is of low birth weight or labor is prolonged. One study has indicated that fetal monitoring may be credited with saving the life of the baby in 1 of every 10 births that involved serious complications (Neutra et al., 1978).

As invaluable as EFM is, these procedures also carry some risks of their own. Internal monitoring may require breaking the fetal membrane (if it is not already broken), which results in increased likelihood of infection to both the mother and the baby. This is of particular concern if the mother has an active vaginal infection such as herpes. The monitoring devices are also intrusive and/or confining and may have negative psycho-logical effects on the mother. Finally, clear-cut criteria for medical intervention have not been established due to the highly complex nature of EFM data.

Fetal Blood Sampling A second technique for monitoring the baby's condition is **fetal blood sampling**. Here, a sample of blood is taken from a small cut in the baby's scalp and analyzed for oxygen and carbon dioxide levels and other indexes of distress. The procedure provides a more accurate diagnosis of fetal distress than EFM does, and it is most valuable in determining if a cesarean section is required.

Dealing with Labor Complications

The natural process of labor is subject to a number of problems, some of which place the mother and/or the infant at risk. When serious problems arise, medical interventions are necessary to reduce the risk to mother and infant. Commonly used procedures are described below.

Inducing and Speeding Up Labor　A variety of medical circumstances may recommend that labor be initiated artificially in a process called **induction**. If the pregnancy is at or beyond the forty-second week, induction is recommended. If the amniotic sac has not yet ruptured, the physician can induce labor by purposely breaking the amniotic sac. This procedure is called the **artificial rupture of membranes (AROM)**. If AROM fails, a hormone can be given intravenously to induce or speed up labor. The dose can be varied to regulate the rate and intensity of contractions throughout labor (Lauersen, 1987). If it is medically advisable for the labor to be induced and the procedure fails, a cesarean delivery is the only reasonable alternative (Simkin, 1989).

Although inducing and speeding up labor may greatly reduce medical risk under some circumstances, these procedures also entail a number of their own risks. Artificially induced labor can cause very strong and painful contractions, thereby increasing the need for pain medication. The equipment necessary to administer the drug restricts the mother's movement, adding to her discomfort. Finally, if the due date has been significantly underestimated, induction will inadvertently result in a premature birth.

Assisting Delivery Through Mechanical Means　In some instances, after the baby's head has passed into the vagina, the contractions weaken and the baby stops or dramatically slows its descent. If procedures to induce or speed up labor have failed or are inappropriate, one remaining option is to assist the descent by mechanical means. The first procedure involves the use of **forceps**, a tonglike instrument that is inserted into the vagina around the baby's head as shown in the upper portion of Figure 5.2. The two blades of the forceps are inserted one at a time and then locked together to protect the skull from damage. The physician pulls as the mother pushes with each contraction. Forceps typically require the use of anesthesia and an episiotomy. Although techniques for the use of forceps have improved in recent years, there remains the risk of injury both to the mother and the baby.

A second mechanical procedure for assisting the descent of the baby is **vacuum extraction**, shown in the lower portion of Figure 5.2. A plastic suction cup, connected by a tube to a vacuum device, is placed on the top of the baby's head. Handles on the tube allow the physician to pull on the head as the mother pushes with each contraction. Compared to the use of forceps, vacuum extraction is less likely to damage the vagina, and can be applied higher in the birth canal.

Cesarean Delivery　If the baby or mother are thought to be at risk and other techniques are either unsuccessful or inappropriate, the baby may be delivered surgically by **cesarean section**. In this procedure, anesthesia is administered (epidural or general anesthesia), an incision is made in the abdomen and uterus, and the baby is removed through the incision. Modern techniques promote very rapid healing and a virtually invisible scar (the "bikini cut").

FIGURE 5.2

Use of Forceps (Top) and Vacuum Extraction (Bottom)

The rate of cesarean deliveries has increased substantially in recent years, accounting for 23 percent of births nationally (Placek, 1986). This increase has prompted a great deal of controversy. Proponents argue that the procedure has reduced maternal and neonatal mortality rates (Bodner, Benjamin, McLean, & Usher, 1986), while opponents emphasize the increased convenience and financial incentive for the physician (less effort, higher fees for the surgical procedure, and reduced risk of malpractice suits). Others have cited the overzealous interpretation of EFM data in the diagnosis of fetal distress as a major cause of the increase in the procedure. The controversy is likely to continue.

Even when a cesarean is clearly indicated, there are risks. There is a higher rate of postpartum infection and a prolonged period of healing in the mother. Mothers who have invested physically and psychologically in prepared childbirth may be severely disappointed and depressed by the necessity of a cesarean. Some scientists believe that babies born surgically, bypassing the stress of vaginal delivery, experience a deficiency of hormones needed for survival outside of the womb (Lagercrantz & Slotkin, 1986) (see Box 5.2). Supporters of this theory point out that some cesarean delivery babies have difficulty breathing. Finally, there is some indication that mothers of infants delivered by cesarean interact less positively with their babies than mothers who have delivered vaginally (Pedersen, Zaslow, Cain, & Anderson, 1981).

BOX 5.2

Resilience and the Birth Process

Although the baby is placed under enormous stress during birth, it is exquisitely designed to withstand that stress. Hugo Lagercrantz and Theodore A. Slotkin (1986) found that the extreme pressure of uterine contractions and the resulting oxygen deprivation apparently stimulate a surge in the baby's production of stress hormones or *catecholamines*.

Lagercrantz and Slotkin have demonstrated that these high stress hormone concentrations work in a number of ways to help the baby withstand the stresses of labor and birth. First, they decrease blood flow to the extremities and increase the blood shunted to the heart, brain, adrenal glands, and placenta. Blood pressure increases and the heart rate slows, decreasing the need for oxygen. These changes help to sustain normal babies and offer particular advantages to newborns with respiratory difficulties.

Second, the sustained increase in stress hormone levels in the hours immediately preceding birth helps clear liquid out of the newborn's lungs and releases surfactant to promote breathing in the hours following birth. The predisposition to respiratory problems in babies born by cesarean delivery may be due, at least in part, to the absence of increased levels of stress hormones.

Third, heightened hormone levels prior to birth act to increase metabolic rate at birth, which helps nourish body cells after the umbilical cord is severed. And finally, Lagercrantz and Slotkin speculate that the hormone surge may increase the arousal level of the newborn, thereby facilitating the process of parent–infant bonding. An aroused newborn will be more interactive and responsive to the social initiatives of the parents.

All in all, the stress on the baby may be understood as a natural and necessary element in the grand design of preparing the baby for survival in the outside world.

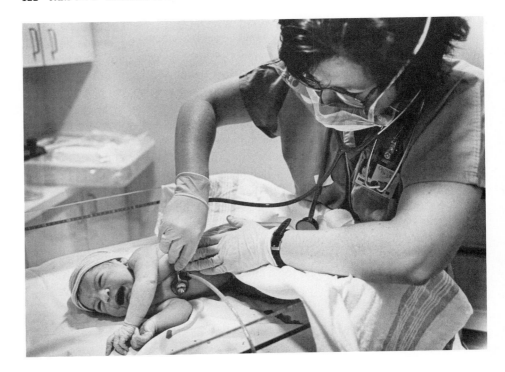

The Newborn

The average newborn weighs about 7½ pounds, although the range from 5½ to 10 pounds is considered normal. The length of the baby is typically between 18 and 22 inches. The head is disproportionately large (approximately one-quarter of the total body length) and somewhat misshapen or molded due to the pressure of vaginal delivery. Within a week to 10 days, however, the head assumes its normal shape.

Although each newborn's facial features are unique, there are certain commonalities in appearance: eyes that seem to gaze everywhere and nowhere with no coordination, a flat nose, pudgy cheeks, and a recessed chin. At the top of the baby's head are **fontanels**, soft spots where the bones of the skull have not yet fused. The fontanels allow the bones of the head to compress during delivery. Although these soft spots alarm many new parents, who think the brain is vulnerable to injury, they are actually covered by a tough membrane to protect the underlying tissues and require no special handling.

The newborn's hands and feet may be initially bluish-purple due to poor circulation at the extremities. All babies are born relatively light-skinned. Skin pigments only begin to appear several days after birth. The thin pale skin barely hides the weaving of capillaries just below the surface. Depending on the length of gestation, the body may still be covered with the remains of *lanugo*, a fine, downy hair that covers the fetus during later gestation and disappears within the first month. The baby may retain much of the waxy coating that protected the fetus from the liquid environment of the uterus. The genitals appear rather large and may cause some concern to parents who were not expecting this particular endowment.

In short, the newborn's first appearance may be something of a shock. "A face only a mother could love" may have originated from the first postpartum view of a newborn.

Evaluating the Newborn's Condition

Although for most parents there is no greater thrill than the first view of their child, the excitement is often tempered by the unspoken fear that something might be wrong. Despite great advances in fetal monitoring, there is still a great deal we do not know at the moment of birth. The baby's head and upper body have been subjected to enormous physical stress throughout the second stage of labor, periodically depriving the baby of oxygen. At the moment of birth, therefore, babies will show varying degrees of oxygen deprivation.

Once the umbilical cord is severed, this state of deprivation can be relieved only by the infant's own as-yet-untested respiratory and circulatory systems. The fetus and infant depend on very different systems for a supply of oxygen, and the transition from one system to the next provides yet another set of risks to survival.

From early in pregnancy until the instant that the umbilical cord is severed, the fetal heart circulates blood directly to and from the placenta to maintain a supply of oxygen. The as-yet-unexpanded and nonfunctioning lungs only receive enough blood to support tissue growth. When the umbilical cord is severed and the baby takes its first full breath, the blood flow in the infant changes dramatically, establishing the mature pattern of circulation. The safe window for this transition is measured in minutes and seconds. Prolonged periods of oxygen deprivation—a condition called **anoxia**—will damage the central nervous system and threaten the infant's survival.

Immediate Medical Evaluation: The Apgar Scale   It is critical that the physician immediately assess the state of the newborn. Virtually all physicians do so using the **Apgar scale** at one minute and at five minutes after birth. The Apgar provides a preliminary assessment of how well the baby's systems have developed and have coped with the birth process and the sudden demand for independent functioning.

The scale is named after its creator, Dr. Virginia Apgar (1953), whose name also provides a convenient acronym for the five subscales: *A*ppearance (color), *P*ulse (heart rate), *G*rimace (reflex irritability), *A*ctivity (muscle tone), and *R*espiration (effort and rate of breathing). The newborn receives a score of 0, 1, or 2 for each sign, so that the total score varies from 0 to 10. The criteria for allocation of points for each sign are detailed in Table 5.1. A score of 7 or above indicates a healthy baby; a score of 4 or below signifies

---

TABLE 5.1

The Apgar Scale

Sign	0	1	2
Appearance (color)	Blue	Body pink, extremities blue	All pink
Pulse (heart rate)	Absent	Slow (<100)	Rapid (100–140)
Grimace (reflex irritability)	No response	Grimace or movement	Cough, sneeze, cry
Activity (muscle tone)	Limp	Weak, inactive	Strong, active
Respiration (effortful breathing)	Absent	Irregular, shallow, slow	Regular with lusty crying

that the infant is in critical condition and requires emergency care. A low Apgar score can result from many potentially overlapping causes — including oxygen deprivation, maternal anesthesia, preterm or low birth weight, and a variety of heart, lung, or nervous system problems.

Although the Apgar provides critical information about the need for emergency care, its relationship to later neurological or motor abnormalities has not been clearly established (Francis, Self, & Horowitz, 1987). While the Apgar can tell us that the baby's heart and lungs are up to the task of short-term survival, the scale tells us very little about the infant's long-term ability to cope with life outside the uterus. Scientists have become increasingly convinced that prediction can be vastly improved by observing the infant's behavior during the first 28 days of life, the so-called neonatal period of development.

Neonatal Assessment: The Brazelton Scale   The most commonly used neonatal assessment method is the **Neonatal Behavioral Assessment Scale (NBAS)** (Brazelton, 1984; Francis et al., 1987). The Brazelton is "a test of the infant's capacities to manage his or her physiological system in response to external manipulation" (Brazelton, 1984, p. 3). The items require that the tester interact extensively with the baby to elicit the infant's "best" rather than "average" performance.

The Brazelton is made up of 28 behavioral items, each scored on a 9-point scale. The assessment of each item requires that the **neonate** (the term used for the infant during the first four weeks) be in a specified state (deep sleep, light sleep, drowsy, wide awake alert, fussy alert, or crying) so that regulation of state can be assessed. The first four items on the scale assess the baby's ability to "self-quiet" in response to repetitive presentations of aversive stimuli (light, sound, and tactile stimulation) while in a sleeping state. Healthy and physically mature infants will be able to maintain the sleep state by adjusting to the stimulation. As one part of the body is stimulated repeatedly, the neonate responds less and less with each repetition. For example, as the tester repeatedly pricks the sole of the baby's foot, the intensity of the baby's response decreases over time. Such responses reflect a well-developing nervous system that can adaptively regulate state. Item 15, the baby's "cuddliness", is assessed by holding the alert baby to the examiner's shoulder and observing if the baby actively molds and relaxes. Item 17, "consolability," rates the crying baby's ability to be soothed by a series of standard "consoling maneuvers," such as talking, restraint, holding, and rocking.

Table 5.2 presents a listing of the behavioral items with the recommended testing states designated by the numbers in parentheses. Additional items (not in the table) are used to test high-risk infants. The test also includes 18 items (not in the table) to assess the neonate's neurological responses for the identification of gross neurological abnormalities. The entire test is administered three times on day 2 or 3, on day 7 to 10, and on day 14 or day 28. The test takes about 30 minutes.

The Brazelton scale has been used for a variety of purposes: cross-cultural comparisons, the study of high-risk infants, the examination of effects of obstetric medication and maternal substance abuse, and to teach parents to interact with their high-risk babies (Brazelton et al., 1987). Using an early version of the scale, one study showed that Chinese American neonates are better at self-quieting, less perturbable, and more easily soothed or pacified than Caucasian American babies (Freedman & Freedman, 1969). Behavioral deficits have been demonstrated in babies born to diabetic mothers (Yogman, Cole, Als, & Lester, 1982) and to teenage mothers (Thompson, Cappelman, & Zeitschel, 1979). The scale is also sensitive to the effects of the medical treatment of infants — for example, the effects of phototherapy on jaundiced babies (Nelson & Horowitz, 1982).

TABLE 5.2

Behavioral Items from the Neonatal Behavioral Assessment Scale

1. Decreasing startle to repeated flashes of light (1,2,3)
2. Decreasing startle to repeated shaking of a rattle (1,2,3)
3. Decreasing startle to repeated ringing of a bell (1,2,3)
4. Decreasing foot withdrawal to repeated pricking (1,2,3)
5. Visual following of moving ball (4,5)
6. Head turning to a rattle that the infant cannot see (4,5)
7. Head turning to a rattle that the infant can see (4,5)
8. Attending to examiner's voice, face, cuddling, and rocking (4,5)
9. Attending to examiner speaking softly into baby's ear (4,5)
10. Attending to examiner speech in full view of baby (4,5)
11. Alertness (4,5)
12. Resistance of baby's body to passive movements (4,5)
13. Motor maturity (smooth arm and leg movements) (4,5)
14. Pull-to-sit (4,5)
15. Cuddliness (4,5)
16. Defensive movements to having eyes covered (3,4,5)
17. Consolability (6 to 5,4,3, or 2)
18. Peak of excitement (all states)
19. Rapidity of buildup (all states)
20. Irritability (fussing) (all states)
21. Activity (all states)
22. Presence of tremors (all states)
23. Spontaneous startles (3,4,5,6)
24. Changes in skin color (from 1 to 6)
25. Frequency of state changes (all states)
26. Self-quieting activity (6 to 4,3,2,1)
27. Hand-to-mouth facility (all states)
28. Smiles

Numbers in parentheses refer to optimal state for assessment:

1 = deep sleep;
2 = light sleep;
3 = drowsy
4 = wide awake alert
5 = fussy alert
6 = crying

SOURCE: *Adapted from Brazelton, 1984; Brazelton et al., 1987*

By making multiple assessments in the first month, users of the scale are able to detect patterns of change, identify the effects of interventions, and predict long-range behavioral outcomes much more accurately than they would with only a single assessment (Brazelton et al., 1987, p. 801).

Although the Brazelton was developed as a test, it has been increasingly applied to enhance parents' understanding of their babies' competencies. Research has demonstrated that mothers who simply observed the use of the scale with their babies were significantly more responsive to their babies in face-to-face interaction (Anderson &

Sawin, 1983) and spent more time playing with and talking to their babies (Liptak, Keller, Feldman, & Chamberlain, 1983). One study found that mothers who were taught to administer the scale themselves were even more responsive to their babies than mothers who simply observed the testing or than mothers who had no experience with the test (Worobey & Belsky, 1982). Brazelton's own assessment of the use of the scale to promote development is noteworthy:

> The studies suggest that the NBAS can be effective in helping sensitize parents to the competencies of their newborns and can facilitate early parent–infant interactions. We are convinced that the demonstration of the scale is not in itself an intervention. However, if the newborn's behavior is used as a way of enlisting the mother and father's responsiveness to the baby, either by active participation or by sharing their concerns and questions with the examiner, we think that the kind of relationship with a supportive caregiver may be enhanced. . . . (Brazelton et al., 1987, p. 802)

Low Birth-Weight Babies

Under the most favorable circumstances, babies will be born between week 38 and week 42 following conception and weigh 5½ to 9½ pounds. Most babies born within this time period and within this weight range are at minimal risk of complications, are healthy, and require little medical attention. However, 7 percent of babies are born **preterm** or *premature*, prior to week 38. An additional 7 percent are born *postmature*, after week 42. Postmature babies are considered at increased risk because the placenta becomes less and less efficient at providing adequate oxygen and nutrition. In most of these instances, labor is induced or a cesarean delivery is performed to eliminate that risk.

Preterm Babies   Preterm babies typically weigh less than 5½ pounds (2,500 grams). As suggested by the low birth weight, their body systems are not fully developed and cannot sustain normal physiological functioning. To varying degrees, all low birth-weight babies are at risk and must struggle for survival. In general, the risk to the baby is higher as the period of gestation and the birth weight decreases. Newborns weighing less than 3 pounds account for two-thirds of infant deaths within the first month (USDHHS, 1980). However, modern advances in neonatal intensive care have dramatically improved the survival rate for infants born as early as week 24 and weighing as little as 1¾ pounds (800 grams) (Buckwald, Zorn, & Egan, 1984).

Most people viewing a preterm baby for the first time are dismayed by its appearance. A fetus normally gains a pound per week in the ninth month of gestation; thus babies who have not had the benefit of that last month are characteristically thin and wrinkled. Preterm babies will continue to lack the robust, rounded appearance of full-term babies for several weeks.

The causes of premature birth are not well understood. In some instances, problems with the placenta or the cervix that threaten the viability of the fetus are associated with the preterm birth. In other instances, *toxemia* or *pre-eclampsia*—a third-trimester condition in the mother (characterized by water retention, high blood pressure, and protein in the urine)—is associated with premature birth. But by one estimate, the reason is unknown in half the cases (Harrison, 1983).

Small-For-Date Babies   Not all low birth-weight babies are preterm. Newborns are also classified as low birth weight if they weigh less than 90 percent of babies of a given gestational age, even if they are born at full term. These babies are referred to as **small-for-date** or *small-for-gestational age*.

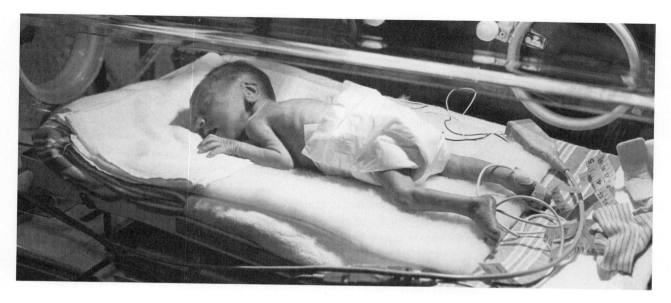

The low birth weight of small-for-date babies results from growth retardation in the womb and involves risks similar to those of a preterm baby (March of Dimes, 1986). Growth retardation early in pregnancy typically results from chromosomal abnormalities; fetal infection such as herpes, rubella, cytomegalovirus, toxoplasmosis; malnutrition; and the abuse of alcohol and drugs. Growth retardation later in pregnancy (after the twenty-fourth week) may result from other causes such as fetal heart, kidney, or lung problems; toxemia; hypertension; or sickle-cell anemia (Harrison, 1983). Cigarette smoking by the mother may also contribute to growth retardation, not only because cigarette smoke contains toxic substances, but also because carbon monoxide displaces oxygen in the maternal and fetal blood, thus depriving the fetus of oxygen (Harrison, 1983).

Put simply, the small-for-date condition results from disease, genetic defect, or destructive habits of the mother.

Helping High-Risk Babies Survive The differences between a preterm and a full-term infant are more than just appearance. A preterm infant's immature body systems cannot take over the functions that the mother provided during pregnancy (Korner, 1987). The lungs of the preterm infant may not be capable of breathing independently because they are not yet able to produce *surfactant*, a fatty substance that normally keeps tiny air sacs in the lungs expanded. When the preterm baby breathes out, the sacs collapse, resulting in *apnea*, spells during which breathing stops for more than 15 seconds. This condition is known as **respiratory distress syndrome (RDS)**. Prior to the development of modern intensive care techniques, most babies with RDS did not survive. Today, better than 85 percent of the 30,000 to 60,000 babies born with RDS each year survive. However, RDS is still a major cause of death in preterm infants (Harrison, 1983).

When physicians know that a preterm birth is imminent, they may try to delay labor by giving the mother drugs so that the lungs have more time to develop (Harrison, 1983). Another technique is a newly developed artificial substitute for surfactant that has shown excellent results. Ultimately, there is no cure for RDS other than to assist the baby's breathing artificially until its lungs begin to produce enough surfactant. In severe cases, this process can be very slow (Harrison, 1983).

The preterm's immature body systems also pose a number of other risks. The absence of fat cells, which are normally deposited during the last month of pregnancy, leaves the

The preterm baby's lack of body fat and immature body features are apparent in this photo in the intensive care nursery. Dramatic improvements in medical technology have substantially increased the chances of survival for babies born as early as the twenty-fourth week. Mothers who have access to high-quality prenatal care beginning early in pregnancy are much less likely to have their babies born before full term.

preterm infant incapable of regulating its own body temperature. The gastrointestinal tract may not be ready to absorb nutrients. The preterm infant is also highly vulnerable to bleeding in the brain, a condition that afflicts 40 percent of infants below 1,500 grams (3.3 pounds). This condition may result in brain damage or death (March of Dimes, 1986).

In the short run, even with the best of modern medical treatment, very low birth-weight babies are lucky to survive; 50 percent of infants who weigh less than 1,000 grams (2.2 pounds) will die soon after birth (Paneth, Kiely, Wallenstein, Marcus, Pakter, & Susser, 1982). A few extra ounces can make a very big difference in viability: While only half of the babies under 2 pounds survive, 90 percent of babies over 3½ pounds survive.

The *neonatal intensive care unit* has become one of the most advanced centers for medical intervention in modern medicine. Highly specialized life-saving equipment is available to sustain low birth-weight babies who would not have survived earlier (Buckwald et al., 1984; March of Dimes, 1986).

Ironically, the very interventions that can save a preterm's life may also place the infant at risk (Korner, 1987). For example, oxygen is given to help respiration, but too much oxygen in the bloodstream can result in serious eye disease. Very tiny preterms are most seriously affected, with up to 11 percent blinded by the disease. Unfortunately, as the technology for saving younger and younger preterms improves, greater percentages of babies are afflicted with the disease. Although there is no way to prevent or cure it, experimental treatments appear to lessen its severity (Harrison, 1983).

The medical staff must constantly weigh the positive and negative effects of treatments in their overall effort to ensure survival. Too much oxygen and pressure in the lungs resulting from a week or more on a respirator can cause *chronic lung disease*. Deafness can be caused by certain antibiotics given to prevent infection. The noise, bright lights, and sterile environment of the isolette and the intensive care nursery may have a negative impact on the preterm infant's ability to achieve a steady state (Korner, 1987).

Interestingly, some simple techniques for caring for preterms have proven effective. For example, if a pacifier is used along with a feeding tube, the results are fewer tube feedings, earlier transfer to bottle feeding, more rapid weight gain, and earlier discharge from the hospital (Field et al., 1982a). Placing the infant on sheepskin rather than ordinary bedding speeds up weight gain (Scott & Richards, 1979). Simply turning the baby over from time to time improves the depth of sleep and oxygen levels in the blood (Martin, Herrell, Rubin, & Farnoff, 1979). Stroking the baby's body is highly effective in improving the weight gain of very small, preterm neonates and in shortening length of the hospital stay (Field, 1986; Schanberg & Field, 1987). Dimming the lights at night and reducing noise in the NICU increases weight gain and decreases the length of stay in the hospital for high-risk, low birth-weight babies (Miller, O'Callaghan, Whitman, & White, 1993; Zahr, 1993).

Low Birth Weight: Long-Term Effects

Low Birth Weight: Long-Term Effects Although progress has been made in improving the survival rate of low birth-weight babies, a critical question remains: What are the long-term effects of being born at low birth weight? Arnold Sameroff and Michael Chandler (1975) suggest that the child's vulnerability is defined not simply by the degree of injury or defect sustained early in life, but by the child's subsequent transactions with the caregiving environment. High-risk infants who receive optimal care and stimulation from parents and teachers tend to overcome their disabilities, while those who grow in unstimulating environments will remain at risk. One can gauge how a preterm child will

The Resilience of the High-Risk Infant

Sameroff and Chandler (1975) suggest that children show self-righting forces that can potentially overcome the effects of early trauma, a quality that we have referred to as *resilience*. A longitudinal study of 670 newborns of Kauai, Hawaii, provided evidence that resilience may only be expressed in highly facilitating environments (Werner, Bierman, & French, 1971; Werner & Smith, 1982).

The newborn subjects were rated by their degree of birth complication: mild, moderate, and severe. A 10-year followup of these children found that children who had had *mild to moderate* complications at birth were doing almost as well as a matched control group of children with uncomplicated births. The most interesting finding was that, for these children, the quality of their caregiving environment was the best predictor of later difficulties. Homes rated low in family stability and educational stimulation fostered behavioral, emotional, and learning problems; homes rated more positively appeared to progressively compensate for difficulties experienced at birth.

This study provided support for the concept of resilience, but only in instances where the early complications of birth were mild to moderate and where the environment was stable and enriching. Less favorable environments led to long-term negative outcomes.

We should also point out that children who were severely affected at birth were much more likely than other children to suffer both physical and mental handicaps. Although a favorable environment can facilitate development, it cannot completely overcome birth complications.

turn out only by considering both the severity of the child's problems at birth and the quality of his or her later transactions with the environment (see Box 5.3).

Unfortunately, many factors interfere with the normal pattern of transactions between parents and their newborn preterm infants. The most obvious problem is that parents cannot hug and play with a baby confined in a climate-controlled chamber. The delay of days and sometimes weeks between birth and the first extended contact with parents is certainly not what nature intended.

Even when normal contact is possible, preterm infants lack the innate clinging, sucking, and smiling responses that typically facilitate the first social interactions. Many preterm babies remain generally unresponsive to their parents' efforts to initiate interaction throughout the first year. These one-way social contacts are less positive and less satisfying to parents than the mutual interactions typical of full-term infants and their parents (Crnic, Ragozin, Greenberg, Robinson, & Basham, 1983).

Preterm infants also cry more and are harder to soothe than full-term infants for the first several months (Field, 1979; Friedman, Jacobs, & Werthmann, 1982; Goldberg, 1979). Although these differences tend to disappear by the end of the first year, the parents' frustration may continue to affect their approach to their baby well into the second year—which in turn affects the way the baby behaves. In one study, each mother was paired with another mother's *full-term* infant. Some mothers were told that the baby they were to interact with was full term, and others were told that the infant was premature. The two groups of mothers showed very different perceptions of and behavior toward the infants in their care. The mothers touched the "premature" infants less, gave

Preterm and low birthweight babies tend to be more passive, irritable, and difficult to soothe than babies born at full term. Parents can overcome these difficulties by initiating contact and stimulation, and by tolerating their baby's crying and short temper. Parents who provide high quality care and maintain a positive outlook can ensure their preterm baby's optimal development.

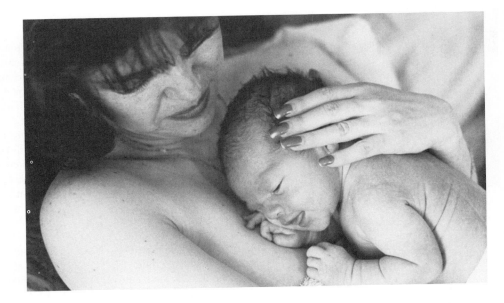

them less challenging toys to play with, perceived them as smaller and less cute, and liked them less than "full-term" infants. Further, the "premature" infants responded to this differential care by being less active than the "full-term" infants (Stern & Hilderbrandt, 1986). Simply *believing* that an infant is premature is sufficient to alter the caregiver's behavior, which negatively affects the infant's behavior. Another study showed a similar effect when mothers learned that their preterm babies had been diagnosed as "developmentally delayed" during the first year (Minde, Perrotta, & Hellmann, 1988). Fortunately, research has shown that parents can be taught to interact successfully with their preterm babies to enhance their development (Barerra, Rosenblum, & Cunningham, 1986; Field, Widmayer, Stringer, & Ignatoff, 1980). We take a look at those who work with preterm babies in "Careers: The Developmental Specialist."

A P P L I C A T I O N

Intervening with Preterm Infants

Although infants of low birth weight tend to be more passive and less responsive than infants of normal birth weight, they are capable of response when stimulated properly. Moreover, the long-term outlook for most of these children is no different than for other children if parents provide optimal stimulation throughout their children's early development. This strategy includes:

■ Being sensitive to your baby's state: Drowsy babies must be gently stimulated to an alert state, and alert preterm babies reach their limit quite easily. Avoid overstimulating your baby.

■ Learning to respond sensitively to your baby's initiatives and to respond to your baby's responses. *Sustaining interaction* is the key to overcoming your preterm infant's passivity.

■ Creating a moderately stimulating physical environment that includes variation in color, sound, and texture in your baby's clothing, blankets, sheets, and crib toys.

■ Moving your baby to different settings rather than keeping him in one position in the crib. The movement itself and the change in view arouses your baby and stimulates curiosity and exploration.

Bottom Line: The outlook for your preterm baby is excellent with sensitive, responsive care throughout his early development.

The Developmental Specialist

Dr. Jean Lowe is a developmental specialist and certified diagnostician in the Department of Pediatrics at the University of New Mexico School of Medicine. She has an undergraduate major in elementary education, and a Master's degree and Ph.D. in special education, with a minor in neuropsychology.

Jean is a member of a developmental team — including a physician, nurse-practitioner, social worker, pediatric occupational therapist, and speech therapist — that cares for low birth-weight and critically ill newborns through the first months of their lives. As the developmental specialist, Jean assesses the infant's behavioral capabilities, identifies specific disabilities, and recommends interventions.

What is it like to work with low birth-weight babies?

The challenge is enormous. All of these babies are at risk because they are born too early and/or at low birth weight, but many are also critically ill due to disease or drug exposure. About 10 percent of our babies test positive for drugs such as cocaine or heroin. Some of our babies weigh less than 1,500 grams, and many of them suffer from intraventricular hemorrhage (bleeding in the brain).

When they first come to us, every minute is a life and death struggle. But keeping the baby alive is only half the battle; the challenge is to create an environment — both in and out of the hospital — that will promote the child's optimal development over time.

What do you do to help these babies develop normally?

We begin with an initial comprehensive assessment and develop an individualized care plan for each baby. Each member of the team plays an essential role in implementing that care. I use the Neonatal Behavioral Assessment Scale (the Brazelton) and other tests to determine the baby's adaptive capability and to guide our interventions. We use massage to deal with a baby's stiffness and irritability. Because these babies can be passive and unresponsive, we train parents to actively engage their babies and to be sensitive to their needs. These babies stand a much better chance if we can train the parents to continue our interventions at home. We videotape parents interacting with their babies to show them how they affect their baby's mood and behavior. We also do home visits to follow up on the babies and their parents.

Is there a lot of stress?

This work is very stressful. The number of critical care babies increases each year, and we fight for every one. But sometimes our best is just not good enough. We try to accept our limitations, but dealing with permanent disability or the death of a baby is always very difficult. The members of the developmental team are your main source of emotional support.

What is the most exciting part of your work?

The best part is seeing a baby overcome tremendous odds and survive. Even better, I enjoy seeing a mother grow along with her baby. Some of our mothers feel helpless; they don't know how to care for their critically ill babies. But, with time and our best efforts, many mothers bond with their babies and come to care deeply about them. That's very rewarding.

What is the career path to becoming a developmental specialist?

Begin by volunteering in the newborn nursery as a cuddler. Spend enough time in the hospital to understand the pressures, the politics, and the rewards. If it seems right for you, pursue an undergraduate degree in early childhood special education, with an emphasis in family and child development. Continue on to graduate study and seek out training in specialized techniques like the Brazelton. The Ph.D. is important if you hope to be effective in the hospital environment.

For more information, write to: Association for the Care of Children's Health, 7910 Woodmont Avenue, Suite 300, Bethesda, Maryland 20814-3015.

Preventing Low Birth Weight   Despite the complex biological and medical issues that have dominated the discussion thus far, it is important to state that preterm birth and low birth weight are often preventable outcomes. The major maternal risk factors associated with low birth weight are presented in Table 5.3.

Teenage pregnancy, poor nutrition before and during pregnancy, substance abuse (including smoking, alcohol, and drugs), and inadequate prenatal care account for a

---

TABLE 5.3

Maternal Risk Factors that Increase Risk of Low Birth Weight

1. *Demographic risks*

    Younger than 17; older than 34

    Black

    Low socioeconomic status

    Unmarried

    Low level of education

2. *Medical risks predating pregnancy*

    Zero or more than 4 previous births

    Low weight for height

    Genital or urinary problems/surgery

    Diabetes or hypertension

    No immunity to selected infections (e.g., rubella)

    Poor obstetric history: previous low birth weight, multiple spontaneous abortions

3. *Medical risks in current pregnancy*

    Multiple pregnancy

    Poor weight gain

    Short time since previous pregnancy

    Hypotension/hypertension/pre-eclampsia/toxemia

    Infections, such as cytomegalovirus

    Bleeding in first or second trimester

    Placental problems

    Anemia

    Incompetent cervix

    Spontaneous premature rupture of amniotic sac

4. *Behavioral and environmental risks*

    Smoking, alcohol, and other substance abuse

    Poor nutrition

    Exposure to other teratogens

    High altitude

5. *Inadequate prenatal health care*

SOURCE: *Adapted from Brown, 1985*

significant percentage of preterm and low birth-weight babies. Mothers who receive no prenatal care are three times more likely to have low birth-weight babies than mothers who begin care in the first trimester (Brown, 1985). This indicates a great risk for the 1 in 5 white mothers and 2 in 5 black mothers who receive *no* first-trimester prenatal care, and the 1 in 20 white mothers and 1 in 10 black mothers who get either no prenatal care at all or too little, too late. This situation appears to be worsening rather than improving in most states (Wegman, 1987).

As a society, we have focused more on keeping low birth-weight babies alive than on making sure that babies are born at full term and at normal birth weight (Brown, 1985). Although neonatal mortality declined 55 percent from 1965 to 1983, the number of babies born at low birth weight declined less than 1 percent in that same period (Brown, 1985). Thus, while we have had some success in reducing infant mortality, hospital-based management of high-risk pregnancies and neonatal intensive care have accounted for virtually all of our progress.

A P P L I C A T I O N

A Commitment to Preventing Low Birth Weight

*I*f we are to facilitate the uncomplicated birth of full-term, normal birth-weight infants, we must implement a national strategy that identifies and reduces risk prior to pregnancy and ensures universal access to high-quality, first-trimester prenatal care, particularly in high-risk populations. Such a commitment would prevent the sacrifice of human potential associated with preterm delivery, low birth weight, and infant mortality. Even those who are not moved by the suffering of low birth-weight babies and their families can find financial incentive for change. We spend over $1.5 billion per year on neonatal intensive care. It is estimated that for every dollar spent on *pre*natal care we can save three dollars in *post*natal intensive care (Brown, 1985).

Bottom Line: We must make a national commitment to the prevention of preterm birth.

States and State Regulation in the Neonate

Contrary to the common perception of the neonate as passive, helpless, disorganized, and random in its behavior in the first weeks of life, developmentalists now recognize that the newborn is preadapted to cope with stimulation from the environment. The amount of stimulation that the infant receives depends on its *state*, or level of arousal. The range of infant states is presented in Table 5.4. Within the first month of life, the infant becomes an active agent in regulating its state and thus the amount of stimulation that it receives. When the baby wants to be stimulated, it can elicit sights and sounds by gazing directly at its caregivers. The baby can maintain that stimulation by staying alert and by continuing to interact. When the baby has had enough, it can actively avoid stimulation by turning away, crying, or by falling asleep (Brazelton et al., 1987).

An infant's developing ability to actively regulate its state of arousal reflects the maturing of the nervous system and related improvements in its ability to control its perception and movement. The infant's ability to self-regulate is also influenced by its interactions with caregivers. Caregivers who respond to their infant's rapidly changing states in a sensitive and timely manner help their baby to learn to regulate its level of arousal. Caregivers who consistently over- or understimulate their infant frustrate the infant's attempts to regulate the stimulation it receives. Preterm babies and full-term babies in highly medicated deliveries are less able to enter into such transactions with caregivers and thus develop more slowly.

TABLE 5.4	
States of Arousal in Infancy	
State	Description
Regular sleep (quiet sleep)	Full rest, regular breathing, baby lying still and passive with no reaction to mild stimulation or slight change in stimulation.
Irregular sleep (active sleep)	Breathing irregular, eyes may move or twitch, increased muscle tone, some reaction to mild stimulation.
Drowsiness	Transition between sleep and wakefulness, eyes open and close, regular breathing and slightly more activity.
Alert inactivity	Breathing regular but more rapid, eyes open and alert, some body movements.
Active alert	Irregular breathing with frequent and vigorous body movements.
Crying	Vigorous kicking and flailing arm movements with agitated crying.

SOURCE: *Adapted from Wolffe, 1966*

Infant Sleep and Sleep Cycles

There is good news and bad news for parents about the sleeping behavior of newborns and young infants. The good news is that they sleep a great deal. Although there is great variability, a newborn can be expected to sleep 16 to 17 hours a day, and some may sleep up to 20 hours. The bad news is that the young infant sleeps and wakes without regard to daytime and nighttime hours (Parmelee, Wenner, & Schultz, 1964). In practical terms, this means that a newborn will wake up every two to three hours, making no secret of unmet needs at one end or the other of the gastrointestinal tract. For parents who are exhausted after childbirth, caring for the newborn around the clock dramatically diminishes in the quantity and quality of their own sleep.

While asleep, the infant alternates between two distinct sleep states: irregular (or active) and regular (or quiet) sleep. Table 5.4 describes the two states. These infant states appear to be precursors of the adult patterns of **rapid eye movement (REM) sleep** and **nonrapid eye movement (NREM) sleep**, respectively. REM and NREM sleep in the adult alternate in approximately 90 minute cycles, with each cycle beginning in NREM and ending in REM. The cycles in the neonate are shorter and differently organized than in the adult. Neonates begin their cycles in REM and spend approximately equal amounts of time in REM and NREM in 50- to 60-minute cycles throughout each of their 6 to 8 episodes of sleep (Roffwarg, Muzio, & Dement, 1966). Over the first five or six weeks of life there is a rapid increase in quiet sleep at night and a decrease in active sleep during daytime naps (Coons & Guilleminault, 1982).

The circadian pattern of sleep—that is, a sleep–wake cycle based on a 24-hour clock—begins to emerge at 5 to 6 weeks, with more wakefulness during the day and more sleep during the night. Although infants vary greatly in the speed with which they adapt to the circadian rhythm, the pattern is usually well established by 12 to 16 weeks (Berg & Berg, 1987). This change is typically a welcome respite for parents, who desperately long to return to their own sleeping cycles.

Looking Back

We have described how parents may control the balance of risk and opportunity associated with labor and delivery. Parents who are well informed and assertive can reduce risk by seeking the best prenatal care and by choosing among the alternatives for prepared childbirth, the birthplace, and the birth facilitator. We have also described the risks associated with every aspect of the birth process and the broad range of medical interventions available to cope with those risks. The magnificent design of the mother's system for delivery and her ability to cope with the pain and stress of childbirth are impressive. There have been significant advances in our ability to facilitate the birth of healthy babies, even when the mother's system performs less than perfectly. Finally, we must appreciate the enormous resilience of the baby in coping with the difficulties and risks associated with the birth process. We will continue to see evidence of this resilience throughout development.

C H A P T E R R E V I E W

PREPARING FOR CHILDBIRTH Parents can make important choices about the birth of their baby by planning where the birth will take place, who will be involved in the birthing process, how the baby will be delivered, and what should be done in the event of complications. Although most parents choose an obstetrician to facilitate birth, certified nurse-midwives offer a safe alternative in low-risk pregnancies. Parents may also choose among several options for where to have their baby: Traditional delivery rooms or more casual birthing rooms are available in most hospitals, and the relaxed atmosphere of an alternative birthing center is available for low-risk pregnancies in most communities.

PREPARED CHILDBIRTH A variety of methods have been developed to prepare parents to deal with the pain and stress of delivery and to facilitate the birth process. The Lamaze method involves both parents in breathing and relaxation techniques, with the birth partner serving as coach. The Bradley method places the partner in a more directive role and attempts to eliminate all medication. Use of these techniques appears to reduce the complications of labor and delivery.

LABOR Labor, the process of giving birth, unfolds in three distinct stages. The first stage begins with mild contractions that intensify until the cervix is fully dilated. During the second stage, the baby descends through the birth canal and is born. The movement of the baby may be assisted by an episiotomy to widen the vaginal opening. The placenta and fetal membranes are expelled during the third stage.

MEDICATION The intense pain of childbirth can be relieved with a variety of pain medications. The popular epidural block causes loss of sensation from the waist down but sometimes weakens the mother's contractions. All medications cross the placenta and affect the baby both during labor and after birth. While low dosages have little effect on the baby, high dosages over long periods can make the newborn sluggish, inattentive, and irritable, and may continue to affect the interaction of mother and baby for some time.

MONITORING THE BABY The baby's ability to cope with the stress of labor and delivery can be assessed through fetal monitoring. Fetal monitoring is routine in high-risk births. External and internal devices measure fetal heart rate and the strength of contractions. Blood samples can be taken from the baby's scalp during delivery for accurate diagnosis of fetal distress.

INDUCTION If labor does not begin on time, it can be initiated by induction. The physician may break the amniotic sac or use hormones to stimulate the onset of labor. If contractions slow or weaken during labor, chemicals can be used to intensify the contractions and speed up labor.

ASSISTING THE DELIVERY If contractions weaken and the baby's descent slows or stops, the physician may have to assist the delivery by mechanical means. The physician may grasp the baby's head with forceps or use vacuum extraction to pull the baby out as the mother bears down during contractions.

CESAREAN SECTION When a vaginal delivery will place the mother or baby at unacceptable risk, the baby can be born by cesarean section. In this procedure, anesthesia is administered to the mother, an incision is made through the abdomen and uterus, and the baby is removed through the incision.

THE NEWBORN The average newborn weighs 7½ pounds and measures 20 inches. The unique features of the newborn include soft spots or fontanels on the baby's head, lack of skin pigmentation, fine hair called lanugo, and the remains of a waxy coating.

EVALUATING THE NEWBORN After the baby is born, the physician must evaluate the baby's ability to function independently of the mother. The Apgar scale provides immediate assessment of how well the fetal systems have developed and have coped with the birth process. The Neonatal Behavioral Assessment Scale or Brazelton provides a more comprehensive test of the infant's ability to cope with the outside world. The tester interacts with the neonate to determine the maturity of the nervous system and the baby's ability to regulate state. The scale has been used extensively in research and is useful in helping parents to become responsive to their high-risk babies.

LOW BIRTH WEIGHT Babies born before week 38 are typically born at low birth weight, less than 5½ pounds. All of these babies are at risk, and some will struggle to survive. Preterm birth may be caused by physical problems in the mother or disease, but often the cause is unknown. Some low birth-weight babies are born at full term, but weigh less than 90 percent of babies of a given gestational age. These small-for-date babies have been growth-retarded in the womb from chromosomal abnormalities, teratogens taken by the mother, or other physical problems in the fetus.

HIGH-RISK BABIES A preterm baby's immature body systems cannot take over the functions provided by the mother during pregnancy. The lungs may not produce enough surfactant to support breathing, a condition known as respiratory distress syndrome. These babies can be helped to survive by delaying the birth itself and by assisting the newborn's breathing by mechanical means. While only half of the babies born under 2 pounds survive, 90 percent of babies over 3½ pounds survive. Physicians must weigh the positive and negative effects of procedures to help high-risk babies. The long-term outlook for high-risk babies is dramatically improved by optimal care and teaching during infancy and early childhood. Low birth weight can be prevented in most instances by high-quality prenatal care that begins early in pregnancy.

STATE AND STATE REGULATION Developmentalists now recognize the neonate as capable of regulating its state in response to environmental stimulation. The neonate's ability to regulate state reflects the maturity of the nervous system and the quality of its interactions with caregivers.

INFANT SLEEP While newborns typically sleep up to 17 hours a day, they wake periodically without regard to daytime and nighttime hours. Infants alternate between REM and NREM sleep, similar to the pattern in adults, but with different duration and timing. The circadian pattern—based on a 24-hour clock—begins to emerge at 5 to 6 weeks for most babies, with sleep increasingly concentrated at night.

Key Terms

birth plan
obstetrician
midwife
alternative birthing center (ABC)
prepared childbirth
Lamaze method
Bradley method
labor
dilate
contractions
episiotomy

fetal distress
breech position
Rh disease
electronic fetal monitoring (EFM)
fetal blood sampling
induction
artificial rupture of membranes (AROM)
forceps
vacuum extraction
cesarean section
fontanels

anoxia
Apgar scale
Neonatal Behavioral Assessment Scale (NBAS)
neonate
preterm
small-for-date
respiratory distress syndrome (RDS)
rapid eye movement (REM) sleep
nonrapid eye movement (NREM) sleep
circadian pattern

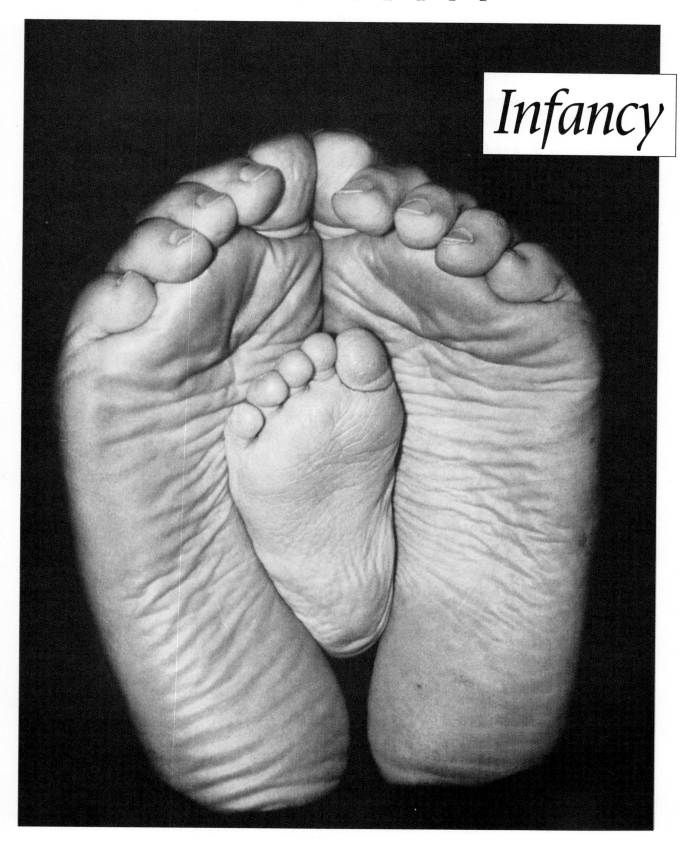

PART THREE

Infancy

6

Perceptual and Physical Development in Infancy

Looking Ahead

- Infants grow rapidly in weight and height and their body proportion changes dramatically during the first two years. What are these changes?

- Rapid growth in infancy, particularly in the first four to six months, creates unique nutritional requirements. What are these requirements and how are they met? Is breast milk better for the baby than formula?

- The development of the central nervous system affects all aspects of development. What is the relationship between the development of the central nervous system and experience?

- The infant's visual perception changes rapidly during the first months. What does the newborn see? How does the infant come to perceive the world of objects in three-dimensional space?

- The infant's ability to hear is well developed at birth. When does the infant learn to discriminate sounds, particularly those associated with speech?

- The infant's ability to control movement evolves quickly in the first months, from simple reflexes to the complex movements involved in sitting up, creeping, walking, and using the hands. What specific changes take place? Can the rate of motor development be facilitated?

This chapter will focus on the physical and perceptual development of children in **infancy**—the period from birth to the end of the second year of life. During infancy, more than any other period in development, caregivers deal with children as physical beings. In any given day, a caregiver holds, caresses, hugs, tugs, jostles, lifts, turns, bends, carries, supports, suspends, swings—and with the advent of locomotion—chases, corrals, grabs, disarms, and otherwise facilitates or inhibits an infant's free physical movement. Parents must learn to adjust their physical caregiving to the rapidly changing physical characteristics and abilities of their infants.

From the moment of first human contact, the newborn begins to sense the physical presence of caregivers and to react physically to caregiving behaviors. Although the newborn's perception and control of movement are limited, these abilities emerge rapidly within the first weeks and months of life. As they do, parents and their young infants gradually come to know each other by touching and being touched, by scanning and being scanned, and by making sounds and being heard. The world of physical objects becomes increasingly accessible as infants learn to fixate and track objects in space and to control the movements necessary for retrieving those objects. The seemingly infinite transactions between infants and caregivers and between infants and objects are what help infants develop physically (Keogh & Sugden, 1985; Sameroff & Chandler, 1975). These transactions are exemplified in Keisha's experience in feeding Leshonda through the first year:

At first it is easy: A natural and reliable reflex within her breasts "lets down" milk and Leshonda's rooting and sucking reflexes do the rest. Keisha has to learn to position herself, her breast, and her nipple to facilitate feeding, and Leshonda has to learn to search for the nipple and maintain her position. But they both make these simple adjustments with little effort in just a few days. Breastfeeding is a relaxed and sensual experience for mother and daughter.

When Keisha begins to supplement breastfeeding with cereal at four months, the experience changes. Her first efforts to spoon cereal into Leshonda's mouth are frustrating. Whatever goes in is reflexively spit out. Leshonda obviously does not appreciate the taste or texture of cereal. To make matters worse, Leshonda soon learns to intercept the approaching spoon, adding considerably to the mess; the battle of the spoon has begun! It takes several weeks and a great deal of patience before Keisha is convinced that more food was going in Leshonda than is coming back out.

By Leshonda's sixth month, though, Keisha has turned feeding into a ritualized series of simple games and songs, which sets a rhythmic routine. It is fun for both mother and baby—and it works most of the time.

At eight months Leshonda can pick up pieces of solid food and take them to her mouth (or to her eyes, nose, ears, or hair). Food now becomes both a source of nutrition and an artistic medium for Leshonda, who enjoys smearing and squooshing more than tasting and swallowing. Keisha is reassured by a magazine article she reads that suggests that this playing with food will improve her infant's eye-hand-mouth coordination. At the end of a particularly exhausting meal, Keisha will sometimes think back nostalgically to the restful days of breastfeeding.

In this chapter we trace the infant's development from the simple reflexes that allow the baby to find her mother's breast and nurse to the complex integrations of perceptual and motor behaviors that enable her to stand up and walk independently. We also examine how the quality of the transactions between infants and their caregivers affects the quality of perceptual and motor development.

Physical Growth in the First Two Years

No matter how knowledgeable we may be about the growth rate of infants, it can be astonishing to witness personally. Perceptive individuals who have not seen a particular infant for two to three weeks are often amazed by the changes during this brief period. The extraordinary rate of growth in height and weight and changes in body proportion during the first two years can be appreciated by an examination of some of the vital statistics.

Changes in Height and Weight

The average newborn weighs 7½ pounds and measures about 20 inches from head to toe. In the next two years, the infant will grow faster than during any later period, including adolescence. Figure 6.1 shows a graphic representation of height and weight gains. Birth weight typically doubles by 5 months (to 15 pounds) and triples by the first birthday (to 22 pounds). The baby gains only five to six pounds in the second year, and four to five pounds in the third year. Height increases by about half in the first year (to

FIGURE 6.1

Development of Height and Weight in the First Three Years

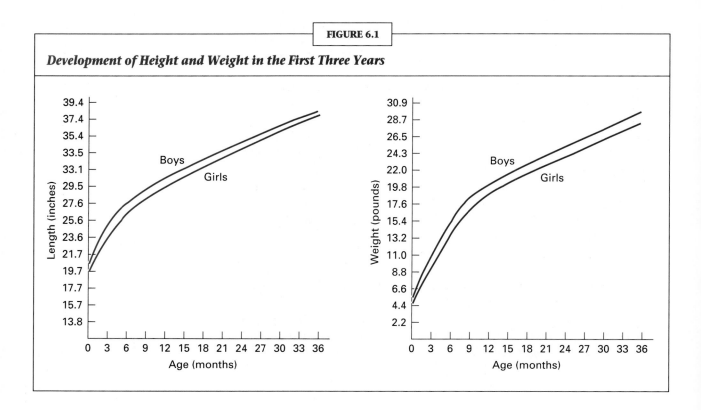

30 inches) and by an additional 5 to 6 inches in the second year. Despite the overall rapid growth during the first two years, the *rate* of growth tapers off from the first to the second year.

This growth is a challenge to the physical strength of caregivers, particularly parents. The five-month-old weighs about as much as an average bag of groceries. That may not seem like much of a burden until you consider what it would be like to add about four to five ounces to that bag each week, especially if you must carry the bag with you wherever you go. Parents must gain in muscle strength with the increasing weight of the baby; some parents suffer from the physical strain. A small industry has emerged in recent years for the manufacture of devices such as slings, backpacks, and infant seats to assist parents in transporting their increasingly heavy babies.

Changes in Body Proportion

The body proportions of the newborn and infant are dramatically different from the proportions of an adult. Figure 6.2 provides an artist's representation of the changes in body proportions from the fetal period to adulthood. These changes progress according to the two fundamental principles of physical growth that were introduced in Chapter 4. First, by the *cephalocaudal* (Latin for head to tail) *principle*—growth of the head and upper body precede growth in the lower body. Eight weeks after conception, the head is half of the fetus's length; at birth the head is only 25 percent of the body length but still roughly the length of the legs. By adulthood, the head accounts for only 12 percent of body length, whereas the legs account for about 50 percent.

Second, by the *proximodistal* (near to far) principle, the body grows from the center outward. Prenatally as well as during early childhood, the torso develops prior to the arms and legs, and the arms and legs develop prior to the hands and feet. This principle reverses just before puberty when the hands and feet grow rapidly to mature size before other parts of the body (Tanner, 1978).

FIGURE 6.2

Changing Body Proportions from the Fetal Period to Adulthood

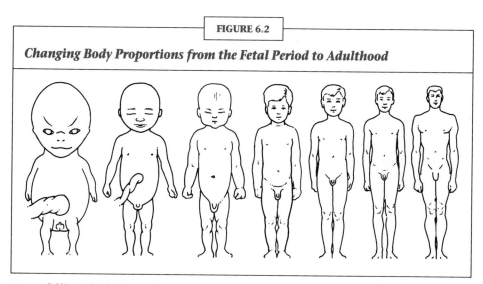

SOURCE: *Robbins, et al. (eds.), Growth (New Haven: Yale University Press), 1929. Reprinted by permission of the publisher.*

Nutrition in Infancy

Rapid growth in infancy, particularly in the first four to six months, creates unique nutritional requirements. The mother's breast milk is exactly suited to provide the infant with essential nutrients, without supplementation, through the first four to six months. Although most healthy women are physically capable of breastfeeding their newborns, many choose to bottle-feed using *formula*—cow's milk modified to approximate the nutritive content of breast milk. Approximately one quart of human milk or formula per day meets the infant's total nutritional requirements until the infant reaches about 14 pounds (McWilliams, 1986).

Is breast milk better for the baby than formula? The breast milk of a healthy, well-nourished mother contains all of the required nutrients in perfect proportion to the infant's needs during the first three to four months of life, but formulas made of modified cow's milk are also nutritionally complete. The infant's need for fats, protein, carbohydrates, minerals, and vitamins is adequately met by both human milk and formula.

However, breast milk offers one important health advantage over formula. The infant's immune system is not fully effective until the middle of the first year, leaving the infant vulnerable to infection. Immunological protection can be transmitted to the infant in the *colostrum*, a thin, yellowish fluid secreted by the breast for several days before milk is produced. Colostrum contains antibodies that cannot be duplicated in infant formula. This advantage is supported by evidence that breastfed babies are hospitalized less than bottle-fed babies during the first 18 months of life (Chen, Yu, & Li, 1988; Fallot, Boyd, & Oski, 1980). Thus, experts agree that breastfeeding provides a slight health advantage over bottle-feeding (Lozoff, 1989).

A P P L I C A T I O N

Feeding by Breast or Bottle?

Deciding whether to feed your baby by breast or by bottle involves a number of important considerations:

- Although breast milk provides your baby with immunity to some diseases, it also transmits medications, alcohol, and certain diseases that are in your body. Ask your physician whether, in your particular case, the benefits to your baby outweigh the risks.

- If you must return to work soon after your baby is born, you may find it difficult or impossible to breastfeed around working schedules. Ask your employer about flextime, which may allow you to nurse your baby during the workday.

- The immunological advantage for your infant can be achieved by breastfeeding during the brief period that colostrum is secreted (the first few days after birth).

- Beware of organized groups and overzealous individuals who pressure you to breastfeed. They tend to distort the facts and generate guilt.

- Although it is unlikely, you may be biologically incapable of producing sufficient milk to meet your baby's nutritional needs. Your ability to produce milk has nothing to do with your ability to be a good mother! (Note that the size of a woman's breasts has nothing to do with the amount of milk produced.)

- While breastfeeding may have some short-term health advantages for your infant, research has shown no *long-term* positive or negative effects on a child's physical or psychological development.

Bottom Line: Select an approach to feeding well in advance of the birth so that you may become familiar with the techniques involved. Make your own choice consistent with your personal beliefs and circumstances.

Oral reflexes in the young infant are designed to obtain food by sucking and to reject solid foods placed at the end of the tongue. After about four months, though, the infant's increasing voluntary control of its tongue, mouth, and hands changes feeding dramatically. The tongue stops rejecting solids and becomes capable of transfering food from the front to the back of the mouth for swallowing. Solid foods can then be gradually introduced into the infant's diet. Lip closure, chewing, and hand-to-mouth grasping movements all facilitate the transition to solid foods, after about six months. The development of these new skills is well timed to meet the infant's increasing need for nutrients beyond those contained in human milk or formula.

Parents should not rely on their own intuition or on unreliable sources in establishing good nutrition for their infants. In particular, parents should avoid feeding their infants as they feed themselves. In one study, infants were identified who had been inadvertently malnourished by their overzealous, health-conscious parents. These parents placed their infants on low-fat, low-calorie diets in the mistaken belief that what is good for the parent is necessarily good for the infant (Lifshitz, Pugliese, Moses, & Weyman-Daum, 1987). Follow your pediatrician's advice on meeting your infant's changing nutritional needs.

Development of the Brain

The brain, spinal cord, and a vast network of nerves connecting all parts of the body make up the *nervous system*. The mature nervous system can be thought of as an integrated communication network that enables the transport of electrochemical messages throughout the body. The sight of the mother's face, the sound of her voice, and the smell of her body signal the mother's presence to her baby's brain, and the brain signals the baby's face to smile. The brain serves as the central switchboard and as an information processing center.

The central nervous system (CNS)—of which the brain is a part—constitutes the most complicated physical structure in the body (Nowakowski, 1987). All aspects of development—everything from thinking and making friends to walking and tying shoes—are mediated either directly or indirectly by central nervous system activity. Consequently, there is no greater risk to development than those forces that endanger central nervous system development and no greater opportunity than those forces that facilitate its development. An understanding of risk and opportunity in this context requires an understanding of the development of the structure and function of the nervous system and its relation to behavior.

The Building Blocks: Neurons and Their Function

Information moves through the nervous system by means of billions of densely packed nerve cells called **neurons**, which pass along electrical impulses to one another. Each neuron has short fibers (**dendrites**) to receive impulses from neighboring neurons, and a single relatively long fiber (an **axon**) to send the impulse on to the next neuron (see Figure 6.3). A microscopic gap separates the axon of one neuron from the dendrite of the next neuron. This gap is called a *synapse*. Various chemicals known as *neurotransmitters* carry signals across the synapse from one neuron to the other.

Neural messages are received by dendrites, passed to the cell body, and forwarded through the axon. Terminal buttons at the end of the axon produce neurotransmitters that conduct messages across the synapse to the dendrites of the next neuron.

FIGURE 6.3

Schematic Illustration of a Neuron

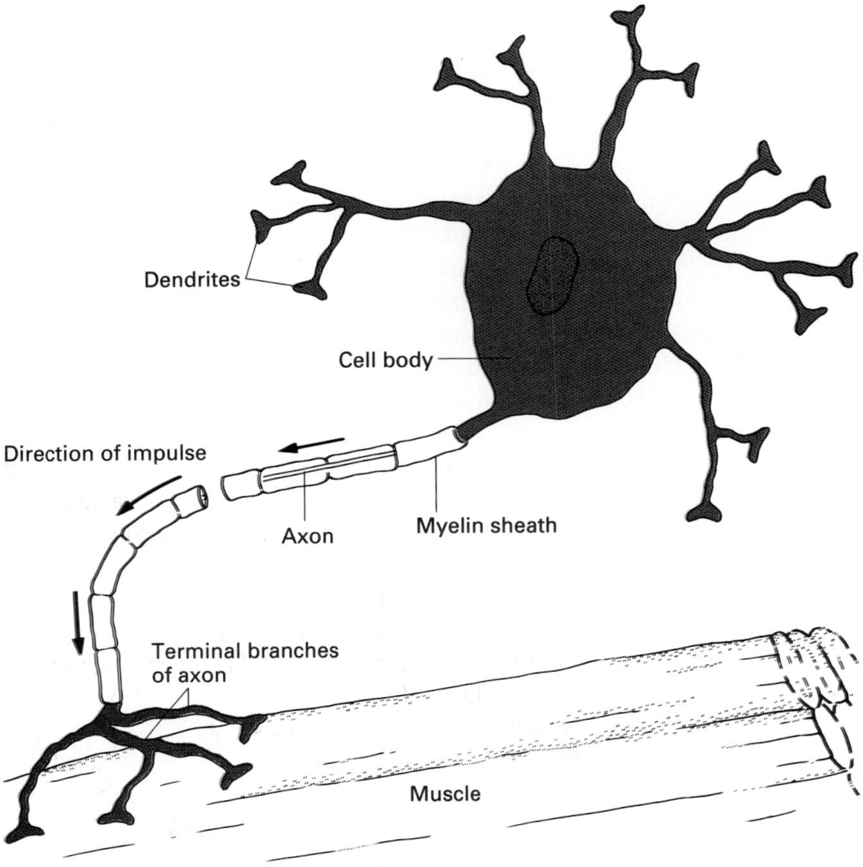

Dendrites

Cell body

Direction of impulse

Axon

Myelin sheath

Terminal branches of axon

Muscle

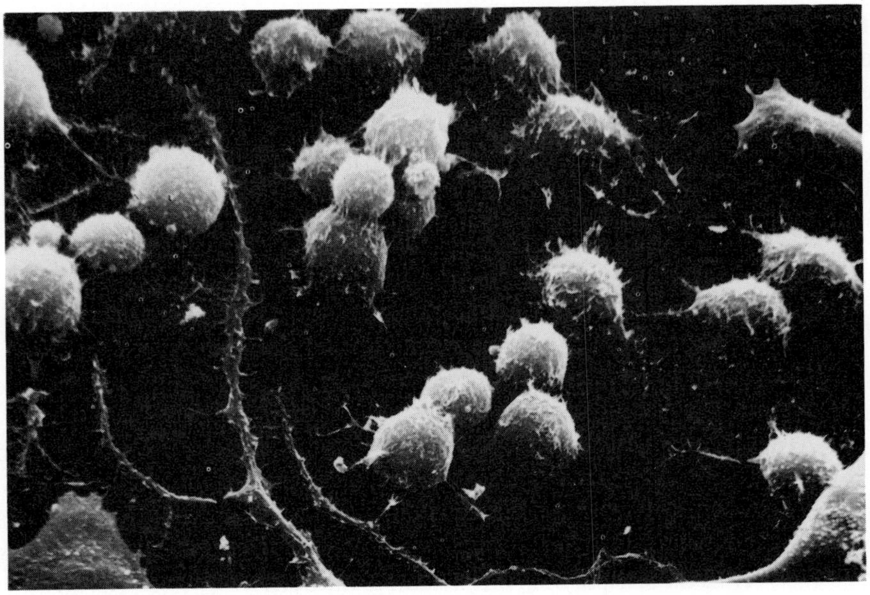

A microscopic view of the intricate connections among nerve cells in humans.

Axons are covered with a fatty coating of cells. This coating, called a **myelin sheath**, insulates the axon and helps it transmit electrical impulses faster and more efficiently. The process by which the myelin sheath forms is called *myelinization*. It starts in the fourth month of prenatal development and continues rapidly through the second year of life. When myelinization occurs in certain regions of the brain, the child gains specific forms of motor skill and muscle control that are associated with those regions. So the timing of an infant's milestones—the visually directed grasp, rolling over, sitting up, standing, and walking—is directly related to developments in that child's nervous system.

Anything that interferes with myelinization places the infant's motor development at risk. Prenatal exposure to certain teratogens, severe malnutrition (particularly deprivation of dietary fat), and exposure to lead prenatally and in the first four years of life (Lampert & Schochet, 1968) may irreversibly damage the nervous system and impair its motor functions.

Structures of the Brain

Although different regions of the brain develop at different rates before and after birth, the sequence of their development is invariable. The infant's capabilities emerge according to both the sequence and the rate that pertinent brain regions develop. The regions of the brain are illustrated in Figure 6.4.

The *motor regions*, which control gross body movements, develop first. Next are the *sensory regions*, which receive information from the sense organs (nose, eyes, ears, mouth, and skin). These are the only areas of the brain that function at birth, thus restricting the newborn primarily to reflexive behavior. The sensory and motor regions continue to mature up until the eighth month of life. The *association regions*, which mediate thought, are the last to develop and their growth continues well into adulthood (Suomi, 1982). The sequence for the development of regions of the brain and their effects on behavior in the first two years of life are presented in Table 6.1.

FIGURE 6.4

Regions of the Human Brain

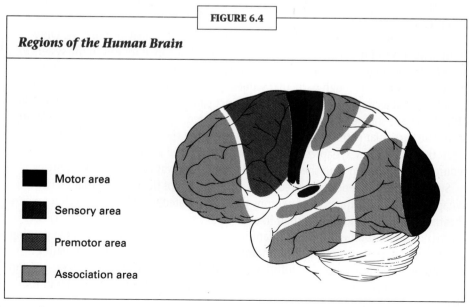

Motor area

Sensory area

Premotor area

Association area

SOURCE: *Tanner, 1978*

TABLE 6.1		

Behavioral and Cortical Development in Human Infants Over the First Two Years of Life

Age	Cortical Areas Functioning	Characteristic Behaviors
Birth to 1 month	Initial functioning of motor and primary sensory areas	Generalized actions; no reflex inhibition; no goal direction; little or no flexibility of action patterns
1 to 4 months	Initial functioning of motor, premotor, and other areas	Reflex inhibition; more visual attention paid to compound stimuli than to isolated stimuli
4 to 8 months	Initial functioning of sensory association and frontal association areas	Beginning differentiation of motor patterns; perception of sequential relationships; accidental goal direction
8 to 12 months	Initial functioning of additional association areas	Goal direction; anticipation; imitation of facial movements; incomplete body orientation in space; inability to inhibit past sensations and responses
12 to 18 months	All cortical areas functioning, but functioning of association areas is primitive	Trial-and-error search for new information and problem solution; incomplete perception of body as separate object in space
18 to 24 months	All cortical areas functioning at mature level, but interconnections between cortical areas are incomplete	Internalized mental images of goals; spatial and sequential concepts; perception of own body as a separate object from rest of environment

SOURCE: *Stephen J. Suomi from Kopp/Keakow,* The Child. © *1982 Addison-Wesley Publishing Company, Inc. Reprinted by permission of the publisher.*

Brain Development and Experience

Humans are born with all of the neurons they will ever have. In fact, we are born with far more neurons than we need for adequate "wiring" of the system (Greenough, Black, & Wallace, 1987). This oversupply means that nerve cells compete for a functional place in the system. As a result, approximately half of the neurons originally produced die (Janowsky & Finlay, 1986). If a neuron fails to link with another neuron and form a synapse, it will die.

Even if a synapse is created, the two participating neurons may not survive. Only those sequences of neurons that are repeatedly stimulated by impulses in the system will survive. As the infant experiences distinct patterns of sensation, distinct patterns of impulse are generated through particular sequences of neurons. For example, when the infant looks at a circle, the eyes generate distinct patterns of sensory impulse; when the child looks at a square, a different pattern is generated. These particular sensory patterns stimulate particular pathways in the nervous system. If the infant looks at squares more often than circles, the synapses along pathways associated with squares receive more redundant stimulation than the synapses along the pathways associated with circles.

Synapses that are repeatedly fired ensure the survival of the neurons that form the synapse. Moreover, sequences of neurons that are repeatedly stimulated develop myelin sheaths, which further increase their likelihood of survival. Thus, from a practical perspective, the environment that the infant is exposed to has direct impact on the development of the infant's nervous system. Infants who are exposed to a rich, stimulating environment can be expected to fulfill more of their potential than infants who develop in unstimulating or chaotic environments. We will expand on this notion later in the chapter.

Neural Plasticity and Resilience Why are we born with so many more neurons than we need? The surplus enables the young brain to adjust to and recover from injury. Several studies have demonstrated the remarkable recovery of children who are brain damaged very early in life (Huttenlocher, 1984). The ability of the brain to recover declines with age. For example, adults who suffer damage to the language areas of the brain typically recover only very limited language function. If, however, the same injury is sustained by infants or young children, the initial loss of language function is typically followed by much greater recovery than in the adult (Lenneberg, 1967). Apparently, damage to one part of the immature nervous system in the young child can be compensated by revisions in the circuitry. The ability of the brain to reprogram itself is called **plasticity**.

Plasticity in the physical development of the brain presents one of the most striking examples of resilience in the developmental process. It is as if evolution has provided the developing brain with a margin of error that gives the child an edge in the face of traumatic injury.

How Important Are the Timing and Type of Experience? Our discussion of the effects of experience on the organization and structure of the central nervous system raises some interesting questions. First, does the timing of exposure to experience affect the extent of modification? And second, which forms of experience are most effective in facilitating brain development?

With respect to timing, the closely related theoretical concepts of *critical period* and *sensitive phase* (see Chapter 2) have been used to explain the way in which the immature brain is modified by experience. According to this theory, the brain is especially susceptible to modification by certain forms of stimulation during particular developmental periods (Greenough et al., 1987; Suomi, 1982). Support for the concept of critical periods comes primarily from ethological studies of animal behavior. There have been no definitive demonstrations of imprinting in human development.

Most of what we know concerning the effect of the type of experience on the development of the brain comes from studies of **sensory deprivation** or **sensory enrichment**. For example, in one sensory deprivation study, groups of kittens—presumably during a time of rapid brain growth—were fitted with special goggles that allowed them to see either vertical lines *or* horizontal lines, but not both. When full grown, the cats with vertical line experience were not able to perceive horizontal lines and bumped into horizontal obstacles, whereas mature cats with horizontal line experience bumped into vertical columns (Hirsch & Spinelli, 1970). This research demonstrates that both the type and the timing of the deprivation experience are critical to the effect on perception.

Other studies of sensory enrichment contrasted the brain development of rats reared in an enriched environment—with plenty of stimulating activities such as toys—with that of rats reared in isolation in dimly lit cages with no toys. The "enriched" rats developed heavier and more differentiated brains than did the "impoverished" rats (Greenough, 1976; Rosenzweig, 1966). Such studies suggest that enrichment programs, for rats at least, can have a measurable impact on the physical development of the brain.

What are the implications of such findings for humans? Clearly, ethical issues prevent the use of experimental deprivation studies of human infants. The animal model, however, has been used to justify programs to stimulate the neurological development of severely handicapped infants (see Box 6.1). Such claims are yet to be scientifically validated. The influences of deprivation and enrichment on development will be revisited later in this chapter.

BOX 6.1

Patterning the Human Infant

Suppose for a moment that your newborn showed signs of retardation, probably from lack of oxygen (anoxia) during the birth process. The physicians have told you the condition is irreversible. Your sense of guilt, despair, and helplessness are overwhelming. But suddenly a friend tells you there is a cure! Your friend says that a group of scientists in Philadelphia, at the Institute for the Study of Human Potential, has developed a procedure called *patterning* that reverses the damage brought on by anoxia and restores the infant to normal intellectual development. You are astounded. You grab your credit card and run for the phone to order the treatment.

You have joined the ranks of thousands of parents, desperate for solutions, who are willing to do anything, at any cost, that offers hope for the future development of their children.

The theory of patterning was developed by Doman and Delacato (Doman, Spitz, & Zucman, 1960) as a treatment for brain-damaged infants. Although it wasn't based on any formal theory or research, their idea did follow a certain logic consistent with some known facts about how the brain develops. Put simply, patterning is based on two of the concepts presented in this text: the ability of the very young brain to recover from damage (plasticity) and the effects of patterned experience on the differentiation of brain function. The procedure assumes that infants are born with far more brain cells than they need—an assumption consistent with contemporary theory. Therefore, the loss of some of these cells to anoxia should not be an impossible problem. All we need is a way to stimulate the damaged brain to rally the surviving cells to compensate for lost cells.

One serious obstacle is that much of the stimulation needed to pattern the brain comes from the active explorative movements of infants in the natural environment—movements that are beyond the capability of infants with brain damage. "No problem," say the patterning experts. These movements can be simulated by passive manipulation of an infant's limbs by a team of four to six adults, working for six to eight hours per day, every day, through the first several years of life. You simply bring your team to the institute, have them trained at a nominal cost of several thousand dollars, and then return home and pattern the infant as a full-time preoccupation of every member of the family and every neighbor within walking distance of your home. This may sound difficult, but isn't the restoration and realization of the infant's intellectual potential worth any sacrifice?

The trouble with patterning is that it doesn't seem to work (Zigler, 1981). Despite the claims of its developers (Doman et al., 1960), research has consistently failed to document the gains promised by the procedure (Zigler & Seitz, 1975). The underlying theory is flawed: The plasticity of the brain offers a thin buffer against trauma, a buffer that is most likely overwhelmed by anoxia. Further, passive movements of an infant's limbs can provide, at best, only a small fraction of the quality and quantity of stimulation to the infant's nervous system provided by the infant's own movements exploring the natural environment. Put simply, thousands of hours of patterning by dozens of volunteers over several years of the child's life would be unlikely to affect the organization of the brain or the behavior it controls.

Fortunately, there is hope for parents of brain-damaged infants in the form of interventions that promise less but deliver more. Special education programs, such as those used by United Cerebral Palsy and similar agencies, help fulfill these infants' potential. Parents can think optimistically about the developmental prospects for many severely handicapped children; at the same time, they should be highly skeptical of miracle cures.

Sensory and Perceptual Development in Infancy

When a two-month-old looks up at his mother's face, does he perceive each part of her face as familiar and does he interpret these parts as the integrated components of a complete face? Exactly what sensory and perceptual abilities does a newborn have? How do these initial abilities change over the first months of life?

Since infants cannot describe their internal experiences to us, researchers have devised a variety of ingenious techniques for assessing infants' sensory and perceptual abilities (Aslin, 1987; Haith, 1986). This research has allowed an emerging understanding of exactly what an infant can see, hear, taste, smell, and feel. This information is of great significance to those who care for infants because it provides a detailed account of the infant's growing capability to interact with the world.

How Infant Perception Is Studied

Sensation refers to the ability to register information concerning internal and external events, and to transmit that information to the central nervous system. **Perception** is the processing of sensory information by the brain. All of the techniques for learning about infant sensation and perception take advantage of the infant's natural responses to stimuli. These provide some indication of what the infant perceives. For example, in the study of infant visual perception, we can learn a great deal simply by observing what the infant looks at or **fixates**. *Fixation time*—the length of time a particular stimulus (such as a square or a pattern of dots) is observed—is interpreted as a measure of the infant's interest in the stimulus. Looking longer at one stimulus (a red square) than another (red circle) is interpreted as a preference for squares. Most important, the infant's preference for one stimulus over another indicates that the infant has **discriminated** between the stimuli, that is, perceived them as different.

Although most researchers accept that an infant's preference (as indicated by greater fixation time) for one stimulus over another indicates that the infant has discriminated the two stimuli, the absence of preference does not necessarily indicate that the infant has failed to discriminate. Scientists have used a variety of approaches to study this problem, as described in Box 6.2.

Development of Vision

When Maria first brings Carlos home from the hospital, she is concerned that something is wrong with his eyes. He does not seem to be able to focus on anything for more than a few seconds, and at times his eyes seem to be looking in two separate directions. She is particularly disturbed by his jerky eye movements when an object crosses his field of vision. It seems as if his eyes are overwhelmed by the movement.

She expresses her concern when she takes Carlos to the pediatrician for his first checkup at two weeks. He grins and assures her that this is quite normal. The eye, he explains, can be thought of as a camera: Carlos must learn to aim and focus the camera by coordinating a complex set of muscles within and

The Scientific Study of Infant Perception

Developmentalists have developed a variety of laboratory methods for studying infant perception. The first technique, the *visual preference method*, was developed by Robert Fantz (1963), the father of the scientific study of infant perception. Fantz developed the *looking chamber*, a device that exposes the infant to visual stimuli in a controlled environment. The device allows the researcher to present pairs of stimuli with complete control over the duration and timing of exposure. The infant is placed in the chamber on its back, looking up toward the stimulus display. The researcher observes the infant

from a hidden vantage point between the two stimuli, detects which stimulus the infant is looking at by the reflection of the fixated stimulus on the pupil of the infant's eye, and records fixation time and any changes in fixation.

Using this procedure, Fantz (1963) demonstrated that two-day-old infants could discriminate among visual stimuli and preferred patterned stimuli such as faces and concentric circles to disorganized arrays of lines. Technical advances in

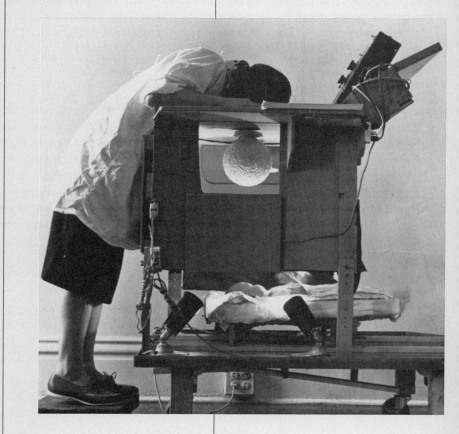

Infant in Fantz's looking chamber

around the eye. He predicts that Carlos will develop this control over the next several weeks.

When Maria returns with Carlos at 13 weeks, her concerns about her son's perception have disappeared. Maria's face has become the center of her son's universe. When she looks into his eyes, he gazes back immediately. When she moves around the room, his eyes follow her with a smooth, coordinated movement. He also seems to be attending to objects at greater distances, particularly when he is propped up in his infant seat to improve his view. The pediatrician shows her that Carlos can now track the movements of objects with consider-the recording and timing of infant response have added precision to this research area in recent years (Haith, 1986).

A second technique capitalizes on the fact that perceived stimuli generate unique patterns of electrical activity in the brain. These brain waves can be detected by placing harmless electrodes on the surface of the scalp near the region of the brain responsible for the particular sensory capability. For example, the brain's responses to sounds can be detected by placing sensors just above the brain region that processes sound. Differences in brain wave patterns evoked by different stimuli indicate that the infant has sensed that the stimuli are not the same. This is called the *method of evoked potentials.*

Still another technique, the *habituation procedure*, is based on the way we react to new stimuli or to changes in familiar stimuli. Changes in sound, smell, taste, or visual display elicit our attention: We turn our heads and move our eyes toward the stimulus. We may show external behavior such as blinking, ducking, reaching, or blushing and/or internal

behavior such as measurable physiological changes in heart rate and respiration. As the stimulus is repeated over and over at the same intensity, the individual *habituates* to the stimulus—the intensity of the responses steadily decreases. In the *habituation procedure*, the researcher lets the infant get used to a particular stimulus, then introduces some subtle change in the stimulus and records any change in the infant's responses. Failure to respond indicates that the infant does not sense the change in stimulation; a change in response indicates that the child has discriminated the change in the stimulus. The tendency for infants to readily habituate to sight, sound, touch, smell, and taste has made this a very useful and frequently used technique.

Perhaps the most clever research technique is the use of *high-amplitude sucking* (Siqueland & Delucia, 1969). The technique uses a special pacifier with an internal sensing device that emits an electrical impulse when the infant's rate or intensity of sucking increases. When the infant's sucking increases, the electrical

impulse is triggered, which in turn activates a visual or auditory stimulus. If the infant likes the stimulus, it can maintain the stimulus by continuing to suck vigorously. Once high-amplitude sucking is established, the technique can be used to demonstrate preference. In one study infants increased sucking intensity to maintain a recording of their mothers' voices but did not increase sucking to maintain a recording of a stranger's voice (DeCasper & Fifer, 1980).

High-amplitude sucking can also be combined with the habituation procedure to demonstrate discrimination between stimuli. As in the previous application, vigorous sucking is established to maintain some stimulus. With habituation, the intensity of sucking eventually decreases, causing the stimulus to cease. When the stimulus is altered, the return of high-amplitude sucking indicates that the change in stimulus has been discriminated. This approach was used to demonstrate the ability of four-month-old infants to discriminate subtle changes in a visual stimulus (Milewski, 1976).

able skill and coordination. He points out that the jerky eye movements have been replaced by the ability to jump from object to object.

Although the pediatrician is having great fun showing off Carlos's newfound competencies, it ends abruptly when Carlos falls asleep.

The interaction between Maria, Carlos, and the pediatrician illustrates that a newborn's eyes are relatively unprepared for the complex purposes they must serve—considerably less prepared, in fact, than all of the infant's other senses. A brief summary of how the eye works will illustrate the situation.

The Eye

As Figure 6.5 illustrates, light waves reflected off objects enter the eye through the lens and land on the *retina*, a complex layered tissue on the back surface of the eye made up of light-sensitive cells and nerve cells. The retina transforms visual information into neural impulses. The optic nerve carries the impulses to the brain for interpretation.

Images that land off-center on the retina are blurred and of little use. Only the **fovea**—a densely packed set of highly sensitive cells at the center of the retina—can discriminate the detail necessary to perceive objects. Since the retina and the fovea are not mature at birth, infants' visual **acuity**, or sharpness of vision, is quite low. Estimates of the visual acuity of the newborn vary, with 20/500 representing a "best guess" (Aslin & Dumais, 1980). In other words, a newborn can see at 20 feet approximately what an individual with perfect vision could see at 500 feet. Acuity improves dramatically during the first few months of life; adultlike levels are achieved by six months (Rose & Ruff, 1987).

The eye must also learn to use its ciliary muscles to bend (or focus) light waves—reflected off objects at varying distances—toward the fovea. Control of those muscles develops gradually; mature ability to make out objects at varying distances is not achieved until the infant is three months old (Banks & Salapatek, 1983).

Tracking Moving Objects in Space

The visual system must also be able to locate objects and track them as they move, in the same way that a videocamera must track its subject. Even simply locating one stationary object and then a second object is a problem for the eyes during the first two months. The young infant's efforts to switch visual focus result in the series of jerky eye movements that concerned Carlos's mother. Although newborns show some ability to jump their eyes from one object to another (Aslin & Salapatek, 1975), infants cannot perform this reliably until the end of the second month, and they do not become efficient at it until three to four months. During the same period, infants develop **smooth pursuit movements** that enable them to track the movement of objects in space (Aslin, 1987).

Thus, by the end of the fourth month, infants' eyes can locate objects in the visual field, focus on individual objects at varying distances, move from object to object, and track their motion through space. Visual acuity at four months is sufficiently developed to discriminate considerable detail: The "camera" is now ready to take moving pictures of moving objects and to discriminate detail.

While the question of how infants use their eyes is well understood, we are just beginning to learn how infants know what to look at. Newborns have no knowledge of objects. They don't know a cup is a thing to drink from or that a face is a part of the human body. They do not know the boundaries of their own body or that their body is an object among objects. The question that we now consider is how the young infant applies sensory capabilities to the task of perceiving objects in the natural environment.

Object Perception

An infant's difficulty in perceiving objects is like an eight-year-old's difficulty in solving a hidden-objects puzzle. The artist has concealed various familiar objects within the normal contours of a scene, and the child must study the contours and discriminate the objects. The difference is that the child has the advantage of past experience with the

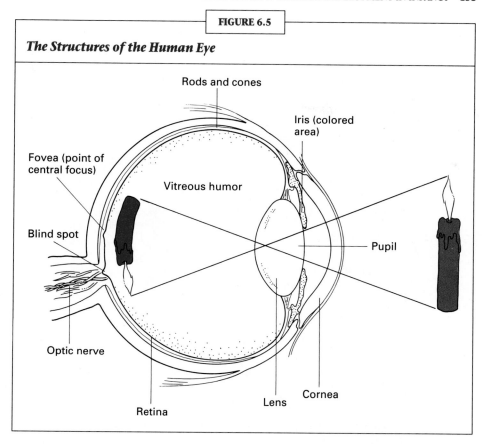

FIGURE 6.5

The Structures of the Human Eye

hidden images; the young infant has no familiarity with the vast majority of images that come into view. The very young infant sees various shapes, virtually all of which are unfamiliar. Consider what the young infant sees when he looks at his mother holding a rattle. How does he learn to identify where the rattle ends and the hand holding it begins? And how does he come to understand that this is Mommy's hand, not Daddy's?

Scanning Object Contours   Neonates are attracted to the external contours of objects, fixate almost exclusively on the external contour of a complex patterned stimulus and usually ignore interior detail (Salapatek, 1975). This tendency is illustrated in the tracing of a one-month-old's scanning of a female face in Figure 6.6. One-month-olds (but not newborns) can be enticed to scan internal features, but only if the attention value of the interior is increased by movement or complexity (Bushnell, 1979; Ganon & Swartz, 1980). By the end of the second month, however, infants switch to scanning mostly internal features (Maura & Salapatek, 1976).

Separating Figure from Ground   Once the infant has learned to explore the external contours and internal features of objects, the next task is learning to differentiate objects as separate entities. Historically, psychologists have referred to this as the problem of separating the figure from the ground (or the object from its background). Elizabeth Spelke and her colleagues (1985) believe that infants are born with an innate ability to perceive objects as unitary and bounded. Spelke suggests that this is a general ability; the

The 1-month-old focuses predominantly on the chin and hairline while the 2-month-old focuses on the internal features of the face.

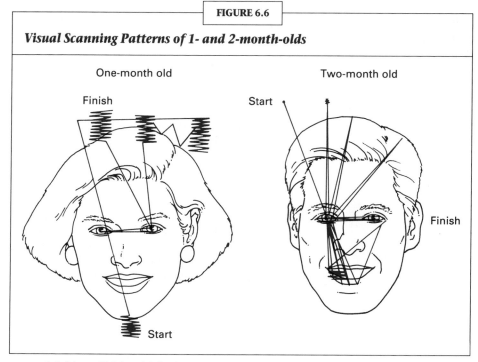

SOURCE: *L. B. Cohen and P. Salapatek,* Infant Perception: From Sensation to Cognition, *Vol. I, 1975. Reprinted by permission of Academic Press, Inc.*

young infant is merely getting started in separating the pieces of the object puzzle. She has attempted to show that it is easier for infants to separate objects in the visual field if the objects are moving in relation to one another.

In the first phase of one of her experiments, four-month-olds were shown two stationary objects: a block partially covering a stick (see Figure 6.7). Once they habituated or lost interest in it, the researcher presented two alternative test displays: a solid stick, and two stick segments separated by a space. Spelke assumed that, if the infants perceived the original stick as a unitary object (as adults would), they would show greater interest in (or be surprised by) the separated stick segments. However, contrary to the prediction, the infants did not show greater interest in the broken stick. But when Spelke

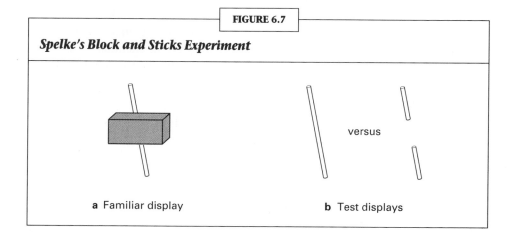

presented the stick in motion behind the block, the infants showed greater interest in the broken stick than in the solid stick (Kellman & Spelke, 1983). Thus, four-month-old infants are capable of discriminating figure from ground, but only if they see the figure and ground move with respect to one another.

In a second study (von Hofsten & Spelke, 1985), researchers showed five-month-olds two boxes, either in touching or separated positions. Only when the boxes were further separated and/or moved in different directions did infants respond to them as separate objects. When they touched or were moved in the same direction at the same speed, infants viewed them as one object.

To summarize, infants are best able to make out objects that move in relation to other objects and background. Such objects should take on special significance. No object fits this description as well as the face of the primary caregiver.

The Face as a Preferred Object   The most significant and frequent visual image an infant sees is the caregiver's face. That face is typically correlated with positive reinforcement and the reduction of aversive stimuli such as hunger or pain. From an ethological perspective, one might expect infants to develop an instinctive preference for the human face, compared to other patterned stimuli.

As expected, scientists have confirmed that the human face takes on special significance for the young infant (Aslin, 1987), but this preference for faces does not appear to be innate—some learning is involved. In one study (Maurer & Berrera, 1981), one-month-olds showed very little fixation of faces and limited their fixations only to the periphery. Two-month-olds showed considerable interest in faces and were particularly interested in the eyes. Three-month-olds discriminated among facial expressions (Barrera & Maurer, 1981). Once the infant has discriminated and shown preference for the caregiver's face, that face will express emotion, give permission, encourage, reinforce, punish, cajole, tease, sympathize, and arouse in an infinite series of transactions with the infant's emerging facial expressions.

A P P L I C A T I O N

Facilitating Your Infant's Visual Perception

Your infant's task in learning to use its eyes is similar to an adult's first attempts to use a videocamera—one without automatic settings. Locating objects, focusing in on them, following their movement, and moving from object to object require a great deal of practice. What the infant needs is something to look at consistently that is naturally interesting, different from its background, and frequently moving.

■ What better subject could the infant have than the face of its primary caregiver! Your face is almost constantly in your baby's field of vision as you tend to his or her needs throughout the day. Your facial features and constantly changing expressions are naturally interesting to the baby, and your almost con-

tinuous movement offers an ideal target for your baby's locating, tracking, and focusing.

■ You can also challenge your baby's emerging visual skills by creating an interesting environment in the crib or other places where your baby spends long periods of time. Select colorful sheets and a bumper with interesting patterns, and suspend a mobile over the infant. (Make sure that the mobile offers a more interesting sight to the infant on her back than to her parent standing next to the crib!)

■ Take your baby with you as you change locations and make sure that she is in a position that offers an interesting view in each location. Babies learn very little from staring at ceilings.

Depth Perception: Objects in Three-Dimensional Space

Although our world is composed of three-dimensional objects at varying distances from our eyes, each object registers on the retina of the eye as a two-dimensional image. How then do we perceive a three-dimensional world from a two-dimensional representation?

The answer has to do with our ability to process three types of visual information. The first type, *binocular information*, derives from the different placement of the eyes in the head. Each eye views nearby objects from a slightly different angle, thus producing two slightly different retinal images. The mature visual system is able to blend these discrepant views into a single image and to simultaneously estimate the distance of the object based on the discrepancy in images. The infant's ability to interpret binocular cues is reasonably well developed by about four months (Fox, Aslin, Shea, & Dumais, 1980).

A second type of visual information is *kinetic information*. When the infant's head moves from side to side, the image of a near object moves more rapidly across the retinal surface than the image of a more distant object. The infant's ability to detect and interpret this difference emerges slowly during the first months of life.

A great deal of what we have learned about kinetic cues and depth perception has come from studies of infants' responses to the **visual cliff**: an experimental device that provides kinetic depth cues to the infant in a controlled laboratory setting (Gibson & Walk, 1960; Walk & Gibson, 1961). A discussion of the infant's reactions to the visual cliff is presented in Box 6.3.

In general, visual cliff studies have shown that infants who are capable of crawling show depth perception after six months. Importantly, even precrawling infants show depth perception, if they have had extensive experience in self-produced movement with walkers (Bertenthal et al., 1984). Thus, the infant's ability to generate and interpret kinetic cues depends, at least in part, on the infant's ability to move its own body through the environment.

Finally, distance cues are also provided by *pictorial information*. Photographs, though they are flat, give various pictorial cues that create the impression of three dimensionality. These cues include *perspective* (objects of equal size are judged closer or farther away by their relative size in a picture) and *superimposition* (objects that block out the view of other objects are judged to be closer). Albert Yonas and his colleagues studied infants' ability to perceive relative size as an indication of physical distance (Yonas, Petterson, & Granrud, 1982). They showed five- and seven-month-old infants paired cutout photographs of their mothers—one larger and one smaller than life-size—at a distance just beyond their reach. In one condition, the infants viewed the cutouts with both eyes and in the second condition, one of the infant's eyes was covered with a blindfold to eliminate binocular distance cues. With one eye blindfolded, the seven-month-olds—but not the five-month-olds—reached more often toward the larger face, indicating that they perceived the larger face to be closer than the smaller face. With both eyes open—that is, with binocular cues available—the infants showed no preference. Other research by Yonas and his colleagues has shown that infants become sensitive to a variety of pictorial depth cues—including size, linear perspective, and texture gradients—between five and seven months (Yonas & Owsley, 1987; Yonas, Tilton, & Arterberry, 1993).

In summary, the visual system must process binocular, kinetic, and pictorial information in order to form three-dimensional perceptions. Although infants have some ability to perceive depth in the first six months, depth perception that allows infants to be adaptively mobile in a three-dimensional world of objects emerges only after the sixth month.

BOX 6.3

The Visual Cliff

The earliest studies of depth perception were conducted by observing infants' movement across the *visual cliff* (Gibson & Walk, 1960; Walk & Gibson, 1961). The visual cliff was designed to test depth perception in infants who are capable of crawling (approximately six to seven months). A sheet of plate glass covers the surface of a platform and extends out beyond the platform to create the illusion of a dropoff. A checkerboard pattern covers the platform's surface and the floor below the dropoff.

The infant is initially placed on the platform adjacent to the dropoff; the infant's mother stands at the other end of the glass just beyond the dropoff. The mother alternately encourages the infant to crawl to her across the shallow and deep sides. In the original Gibson and Walk study, all 27 infants tested crawled to the shallow side but only 3 ventured out on the dropoff. Clearly, infants who are capable of crawling are sensitive to the visual kinetic depth cues. But is it possible that infants can respond to this information earlier than six months, before they are capable of crawling?

To test this possibility, other researchers placed precrawling six-week-olds to three-month-olds face down on the dropoff side of the visual cliff, anticipating that the babies would exhibit fear responses (increases in heart rate). Although discrimination of the depth cues was indicated, the infants' heart rate slowed in response to the dropoff, indicating no fear of falling (Campos, Langer, & Krowitz, 1970). Apparently, the younger infants were capable of sensing the depth cues but perceived them differently than older infants.

Why would the younger infants respond without fear? Perhaps because the older infants are capable of active movement, practical meaning is added to the kinetic cues available on the edge of the cliff. Put simply, crawlers have experience falling and getting hurt, leading to the avoidance of dropoffs. Even precrawlers with extensive experience on walkers (a seat on wheels that precrawlers can use to move about) showed fear responses to the dropoff (Bertenthal, Campos, & Barrett, 1984). A recent summary of these and other studies suggests that natural crawling and walker training facilitate the infant's development of depth perception (Bertenthal & Campos, 1987).

APPLICATION

Promoting Your Infant's Depth Perception

Your routine handling of your baby and the natural environment are all that is required to develop your baby's depth perception. Before your baby learns to crawl, provide a consistent view of an environment rich in interesting contrasts, contours, and colors. Simple games that draw your infant's attention to objects may be helpful.

After your infant begins to crawl and then creep, she needs access to a safe environment that facilitates free movement and exploration of objects. Moving an infant passively through the three-dimensional world of objects is no substitute for the infant's active exploration in

facilitating depth perception. Simple obstacles—such as floor pillows, furniture, and steps—will provide opportunity for the crawling infant to deal with depth, but also entail some risk. The same walkers that researchers claim promote depth perception in precrawling infants place infants at considerable risk of physical injury, particularly in homes with stairs. Walkers should be avoided for *all* infants, regardless of age.

Although infants beyond six months respond to depth cues, you should not assume that they will react appropriately to dropoffs such as stairs or open windows.

Auditory Perception

Many mothers begin to talk, sing, and even play music to their babies early in their pregnancies. After the baby is born the talking and singing continue while they take care of the baby. Can fetuses hear? Are newborns too young to respond to their mothers' voices? More practically, does all this talking do any good? We will examine the research evidence.

Early Detection and Discrimination of Sounds

Unlike the eye, the ear is well developed several weeks before birth (Aslin, Pisoni, & Jusczyk, 1983), and there is convincing evidence that fetuses react to sound. In one study, researchers introduced a pulsating sound through the mother's abdomen near the ears of 24- to 28-week fetuses. The fetuses were observed to blink their eyes and startle (Birnholz & Benacerraf, 1983). Other research has shown that fetuses respond to sound with changes in their heart rate and brain wave activity (Aslin, 1987). If the fetus reacts to sound, might prenatal development be affected by the sound of the mother's voice? This question is explored in Box 6.4.

Although fluid in newborns' ears may diminish hearing for a few days after birth, neonates do discriminate among sounds of different loudness, pitch, and duration (Leventhal & Lipsitt, 1964). By six months of age, the auditory system's ability to detect different intensities of sound and variations in pitch is highly mature (Aslin, 1987).

Locating Sound Sources

Simply detecting and discriminating sounds, even the sounds of the human voice, is not in itself very useful. To deal with sounds in a meaningful way, the infant needs to be able to determine where they are coming from. She can then look in that direction to search for additional information. This ability develops in a surprising way. Newborns can locate the sound of a rattle to the left or to the right of the head (Muir & Field, 1979), but that ability *declines* over the next two months. Then, by four months, it comes back (Aslin, 1987).

Talking to the Fetus: Wasted Breath?

If the fetus can hear, does this sensory experience have an effect on development? The answer appears to be yes if the sounds are made by the human voice. Three-day-old infants preferred their own mothers' voices over the voices of unfamiliar females (DeCasper & Fifer, 1980).

They also prefer female voices (which can be heard more often and more distinctly in the womb) to male voices (DeCasper & Prescott, 1984). These effects may go beyond just the sound of the voice. In one study, newborns showed a preference for a story that had been read to them prenatally (*The Cat in the Hat*) over a new story (DeCasper & Spence, 1986). A second study showed that newborns preferred a song sung by the mother during pregnancy over a new song (Panneton, 1985).

These results indicate quite convincingly that what fetuses hear in the womb affects their auditory preferences in the days following birth (Aslin, 1987). Thus, if pregnant mothers want to read, to sing, or to simply talk to their unborn child, this can be a good way to get a headstart on the relationship—as long as the mothers avoid yelling or using electronic devices.

Keep in mind, however, that these effects are subtle. Prenatal auditory experience is unlikely to result in superior musical talent, precocious sociability, or even a special responsiveness to the sound of the mother's voice. It may, however, bring the mother somewhat closer to her baby and give her a sense of communicating.

How can this be explained? Apparently, the newborn's response to sounds is a reflex. Like other early reflexes (discussed later in this chapter), this reflex weakens over the first weeks of life and is eventually transcended by a more voluntary response. Infants become able to intentionally orient to sound as the regions of the brain that perceive sound mature (Aslin, 1987).

Perception of Speech Sounds

The rapidity with which young children develop language after 12 months suggests that a great deal of perceptual groundwork must be accomplished during infancy. Researchers who study language development now believe that newborns possess innate perceptual mechanisms that facilitate the development of language (Eimas, Siqueland, Jusczyk, & Vigorito, 1971; Eimas, 1985). In particular, researchers have shown that newborns are particularly sensitive to the sounds of the human voice.

In one study (Eimas et al., 1971), neonates heard the sound "pah"; this novel stimulus increased the rate of their sucking on a pacifier. As they habituated to "pah," their sucking slowed down. Then a slightly different sound, "bah," was introduced. They responded by again sucking faster—thus demonstrating that they had noticed the difference between the two sounds.

A number of studies have confirmed that young infants can distinguish virtually every phonetic contrast to which they have been exposed (Aslin et al., 1983). Moreover, they respond as well to the slight differences in the pronunciation of a particular sound by different speakers. Peter Eimas (1985) has proposed that this ability is an innate species-specific perceptual system that prepares humans to learn language. The function of perception of speech sounds in the early development of language will be revisited in Chapter 7.

Sucking responses of infants to phonemic changes, such as "bah" to "pah," as compared to acoustic changes. The infant watches Raggedy Ann as the sounds are played on a loudspeaker. Infants increased their rate of sucking to changes in consonants but not to acoustic changes within consonants.
SOURCE: *Eimas, 1985*

A P P L I C A T I O N

Facilitating Sound Localization and the Perception of Speech Sounds

After four months, you can promote your baby's ability to localize sound by providing an environment that is rich in sounds from easily identifiable sources—such as the human voice, a radio, toys that make sounds, and typical household sounds. Place your baby in a position that enables him to orient to the source of a sound. A babyseat that adjusts to various angles provides the necessary postural support to enable him to turn his head to the source of a sound. Toys that make sounds (rattles, rubber duckies) become increasingly interesting after

four months and help the infant connect the sound with its source.

As with vision, the most interesting and varied sounds come from humans. You can help your baby to discriminate the sounds of your language by talking and singing to your baby frequently, varying the tone and pitch of your voice for emphasis. Fortunately, most parents do this spontaneously, so just do what comes naturally. Imitate your baby's spontaneous vocal sounds, and encourage your baby's imitations of the sounds you make.

Other Sensory Developments

Keisha's attempts to feed solid foods to Leshonda were an intense sensory experience for both mother and daughter. Leshonda could see the approaching spoon and cereal and hear her mother's rhythmic song, but what determined whether she ate or not had more to do, in this instance, with Leshonda's senses of taste, smell, and touch. How well developed are these other sensory mechanisms in infancy?

Taste and Smell

There is considerable evidence that sensitivity to taste is present soon after birth (Haith, 1986). Newborns suck harder and longer to obtain sweetened liquids than clear water (Crook, 1978; Crook & Lipsitt, 1976). An interpretation from the ethological perspective would suggest that the innate preference for the sweet taste attracts the infant to breast milk, thereby promoting the bond between mother and child.

The sense of taste develops quite rapidly during the first month. It's easy to tell which tastes infants prefer by observing their facial expressions: Neonates display a slight smile and sucking movements to sweet substances; they purse the lips, wrinkle the nose, and blink to sour substances; and they spit up and choke on bitter substances (Steiner, 1977, 1979).

Infants continue to enjoy sweet substances and, after four months, show interest in salty liquids (Beauchamp & Cowart, 1985). There is some evidence that infants' preferences and parents' approaches to food selection may have long-term effects on food preferences later in childhood. For example, infants who had been regularly fed sugar water in the first year showed stronger preference for sweet liquids at age two than infants who had not had sugar water (Beauchamp & Moran, 1985). Moreover, infants who experienced a greater variety of foods developed more diverse food preferences than infants who experienced less variety (Frietas, 1984).

The sense of smell is present in the newborn and develops rapidly during the neonatal period. Newborns, like adults, turn away from strong pungent odors (Rieser, Yonas, & Wikner, 1976), smile when exposed to the smell of bananas, and wrinkle up their faces to the smell of rotten eggs (Steiner, 1977). The sense of smell may also play an important role in bonding breastfeeding mothers and their newborns. Jennifer Cernoch and Richard Porter (1985) demonstrated that two-week-old breastfeeding babies recognized (showed preference for) the underarm smell of their mothers as compared to the smell of their fathers or the smell of unfamiliar lactating mothers. Bottle-fed infants did not show this preference. And the mother's sense of smell is also important. A second study showed that mothers recognized the smell of their one- to two-day-old babies (Porter, Cernoch, & McLaughlin, 1983). Apparently, the mutual experience of smell contributes to the unique bond between some mothers—and perhaps some fathers—and their newborns.

Touch and Pain

Researchers have shown comparatively little interest in infants' sense of touch. We know that infants respond to pressure on the skin by certain reflex behaviors: If you press their palm with your finger, they will respond by grasping it, and if you stroke the sole of their foot, they curl their toes outward. These responses are so reliable that they have been incorporated into standard neurological testing of neonates such as the Brazelton scale (Brazelton, 1984) discussed in Chapter 5. The mouth shows considerable touch sensitivity in early infancy (Kisilevsky & Muir, 1984), followed later in the first year by increasing sensitivity in the extremities (arms, hands, and legs).

We also know that infants feel pain. During the neonatal period babies respond to injections and to circumcision by fussing and crying (Anders & Chalemian, 1974). There is no evidence, however, that the experience of short-term pain in early infancy has any long-term effects on physical or emotional development.

Motor Control Development

As the brain and perceptual systems develop, infants attain greater control of motor behavior. The remainder of this chapter describes their progress from involuntary reflexes to voluntary control of the movements involved in posture, locomotion, and use of the hands.

Fetal movements become quite distinct in the last trimester of pregnancy. The fetus kicks and squirms, periodically reminding the mother of its presence and providing a preview of upcoming events. Some of these movements are clearly reflexes and some appear to be spontaneous movements that serve no obvious purpose. There is some evidence that the fetus's activity level in utero may be related to its activity level later in infancy (Walters, 1965). In one early study, active fetuses were shown to develop more rapidly during the first nine months of life. Moreover, the frequency of fetal movement in the last trimester was moderately correlated with the frequency of total body movement four, six, and nine months after birth (Walters, 1965).

Reflex Behaviors

The only organized behaviors observable in the newborn are **reflexes**, involuntary stimulus–response patterns. A reflex is a congenital wired-in circuit in the nervous system that provides for a specific behavioral response to a fairly specific form of stimulation. For instance, a puff of air into an infant's (or an adult's) open eye elicits an involuntary blink, and placing the baby in water elicits a primitive swimming motion. Human infants are born with an extensive repertoire of reflexes, several of which are described and illustrated in Table 6.2.

Reflexes, because they are involuntary behaviors, are not controlled by the brain's information processing center, the cerebral cortex. Although the cortex becomes more and more important in organizing infant behavior through the first few months of life, this structure has very little effect on the behavior of the newborn. Instead, reflexes are controlled by clusters of cells within the *brain stem*, located at the upper end of the spinal cord, just below the cortex. Although the brain stem is the most highly developed component of the central nervous system at birth, its purpose is simply to receive impulses from sensory receptors and to transmit a second impulse to the musculature for a specific motor response. Little or no processing is involved.

Although by central nervous system standards, the neurological mechanism of the reflex is simple, its role in development is of considerable significance and complexity. Note in Table 6.2 that, although virtually all of the reflex patterns are functional at birth (and before birth in some instances), some of these reflexes disappear in a predictable sequence during the first few days, weeks, or months of life. The involuntary grasping reflex is replaced by voluntary control of the grasp. The stepping reflex, elicited by touching the newborn's feet on a flat surface, is replaced by voluntary control of the legs in locomotion. The disappearance of these and other so-called primitive reflexes illustrates the increasing role of the cerebral cortex in organizing and controlling the behavior of the infant over time. Several other reflex patterns that serve critical roles in survival (including breathing, coughing, sneezing, sucking, and blinking) have a permanent place in the nervous system and in the individual's repertoire of behavior.

Although reflexes may seem relatively uncomplicated from a neurological perspective, they play a significant role in development. First, the ethological perspective assumes that all reflexes must have aided survival at some point in human evolution. Some reflexes, such as sucking and breathing, have obviously maintained their survival value while the survival value of others has all but disappeared. For example, ethologists speculate that the Moro (or startle) reflex and the grasping reflex once provided valuable "clinging-to-the-mother" behaviors in dangerous situations. Such reflexes would have helped to ensure proximity to the mother, thus increasing the infant's chances of survival (Suomi, 1982).

Second, involuntary reflexes that are present at birth may be directly related to their voluntary counterparts in later development. For example, the stepping reflex, which allows the newborn to take primitive steps when their feet contact a hard surface, may be related to crawling, creeping, and walking.

Reasoning that the stepping reflex is related to later walking and that it disappears only from disuse, one research team tried to maintain the reflex by stimulating it in infants every day from the second through the eighth weeks of life (Zelazo, Zelazo, & Kolb, 1972). A control group of infants received passive exercise or no exercise of the reflex pattern. Infants in the active exercise group showed marked increase in walking behavior and walked independently one month earlier than the control group. Although the implications of this experiment for other reflex patterns are not completely clear, such findings do suggest that at least some forms of motor development may be facilitated through early training of reflex patterns.

Third, the fact that reflexes depend on precise "circuitry" through the central nervous system enables pediatricians to use these involuntary behaviors to assess the infant's neurological status. If a particular reflex can be elicited during its expected period of

TABLE 6.2

Reflexes in Human Infants

Primitive Reflexes (disappear during the first few months)

Reflex	Response Pattern	Developmental Pattern	Developmental Significance
Rooting	Turns head, opens mouth and sucks when cheek is stroked	Disappears by 3 weeks	Facilitates nursing and bonding
Stepping	Steps when feet contact surface	Disappears by 8 weeks without training	May be a precursor of walking; helps turn fetus in uterus
Moro	Sudden arching of the back and "grasping" motions of arms to loud noise or loss of support	Disappears by 6 months	May facilitate bonding
Babinski	Toes fan out and foot curls when sole of foot is stroked	Disappears by 8–12 months	Important neurological sign
Grasping	Grasp in response to pressure in palm	Disappears by 3–4 months	Important neurological sign, precursor of voluntary grasp
Tonic neck	Head to one side and body in "fencer" position when supine	Disappears by end of 4 months	Bad neurological sign if it persists

Permanent Reflexes (persistent survival value)

Reflex	Response Pattern	Developmental Pattern	Developmental Significance
Sucking	Sucking to oral stimulation	Permanent	Facilitates nursing, may affect personality development (per Freud)
Eyeblink	Rapid closing of eye to sudden sound, light, or air puff	Permanent	Protects eye; diagnostic sign for vision or auditory problems

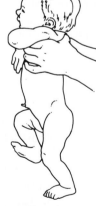

Moro reflex (Fogel)

Rooting (Rathus)

Stepping

Babinski

Grasping

operation, it indicates that that portion of the nervous system is functioning properly. A reflex that fails to appear or persists past its time may indicate a neurological problem. Reflex items form an important component of neurological screening tests such as the Dubowitz Neurological Assessment (Dubowitz & Dubowitz, 1981).

Finally, as will become clear in Chapter 7, Piaget (1936/1953) has postulated that reflexes form the basic building blocks of cognitive development. They are the first repetitive forms of organized behavior and contact with the outside world.

To summarize, reflexes provide perspective on our evolutionary history. In addition, they may be related to later voluntary behaviors, they help us to assess the integrity of the nervous system through the first months of life, and they form the basis of future advances in cognitive development.

Early Spontaneous Movement

In addition to reflexes, alert young infants show considerable movement that can only be described as general and diffuse (Keogh & Sugden, 1985). They wave their arms, kick their legs, and open and close their hands. Although some of these movements show the rigid features associated with reflexes, most of this behavior seems to be spontaneous and aimless.

Among these seemingly random movements, however, are some observable patterns: repetitions of specific movements at regular, brief intervals. For example, infants bang their arms against surfaces, kick their legs, and rock their bodies forward and backward in the creeping position. Esther Thelen (1979) observed that these patterned movements emerge gradually over the first four months and, once formed, become routinized between the fifth and eleventh months. She referred to these repetitious movement patterns as **rhythmical movement stereotypies**. Nine of the most frequently observed stereotypies are illustrated in Figure 6.8. These movement patterns are quite familiar to those who deal with young infants. Although the adaptive purpose of stereotypies is less clear than that of many reflexes, it may be that infants are simply learning to control their body parts, one by one. It seems logical that infants might need to repetitively go through the motions as a prelude to more purposive, functional use of the movements later. For example, the stereotypy of waving their arms while holding an object may prepare the infant for the act of throwing. As we will see in Chapter 7, stereotypies are very similar to Piaget's (1936/1953) descriptions of the first organized aspects of sensorimotor intelligence.

Voluntary Control of Movement

Most children achieve developmental milestones at a reasonably predictable rate and sequence. To convey an idea of the normative progression, we will explore three representative sequences: postural control, locomotion, and manual control. This discussion represents a synthesis of norms from two of the most widely used developmental assessment scales; the Bayley Scales of Infant Development (Bayley, 1969) and the Denver Developmental Screening Test (Frankenberg & Dodds, 1967), as compiled and illustrated by Jack Keogh and David Sugden (1985).

Before beginning, we must make a few qualifications. First, the descriptions should be understood as attempts to illustrate, but not explain, the normal progression of development. And second, as the ranges imply, children display wide individual differences in

FIGURE 6.8

Rhythmical Movement Stereotypies

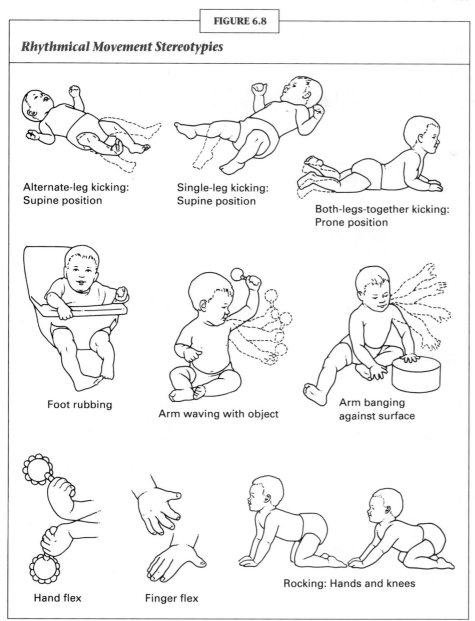

Alternate-leg kicking: Supine position

Single-leg kicking: Supine position

Both-legs-together kicking: Prone position

Foot rubbing

Arm waving with object

Arm banging against surface

Hand flex

Finger flex

Rocking: Hands and knees

SOURCE: *Thelen, 1979*

the ages at which they achieve milestones. These variations are normal. Falling outside the range is not necessarily a cause for concern. However, a child who fails to achieve these behaviors by the upper limit of the normal range should be seen by a professional for evaluation.

Postural Control   Keogh and Sugden (1985) have identified the progression of landmark achievements in postural control:

holding the head steady while moving (at 2 months)
sitting without support (at 5 months)

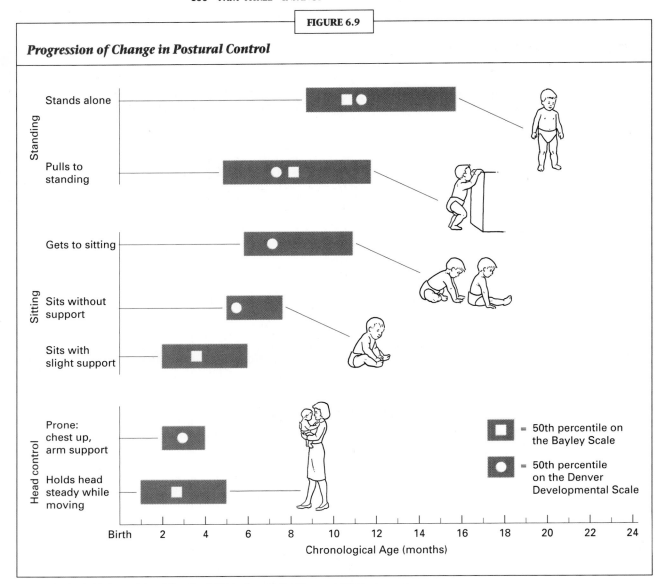

FIGURE 6.9

Progression of Change in Postural Control

SOURCE: *Reprinted with the permission of Macmillan Publishing Company from* Movement Skill Development *by Jack Keogh and David Sugden. Copyright © 1985 Macmillan Publishing Company.*

getting into a sitting position (by 7 months)
pulling to standing (by 7–8 months)
standing alone (by 11 months)

Figure 6.9 illustrates that progression. Each behavior is presented with the range of months within which that behavior typically appears. The month in which 50 percent of the studied children achieved competence in that behavior is marked with a circle and/or a square, depending on which developmental scale provided the norm.

Locomotion Although there are many significant improvements in movement control during the first six months, the infant remains immobile. The progression to **locomotion** — the ability to move one's self from one place to another — begins with rolling

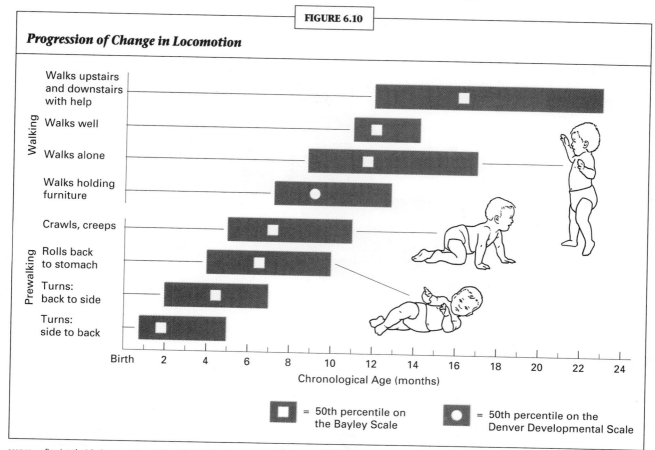

FIGURE 6.10

Progression of Change in Locomotion

□ = 50th percentile on the Bayley Scale

● = 50th percentile on the Denver Developmental Scale

SOURCE: *Reprinted with the permission of Macmillan Publishing Company from* Movement Skill Development *by Jack Keogh and David Sugden. Copyright © 1985 Macmillan Publishing Company.*

from the supine (back-down) to the prone (front-down) position. By seven months many infants can pull with their arms and push with their legs to drag their body forward in a *crawl*. **Creeping**, in which the stomach is off the floor, usually follows about a month later. Most babies are walking by their first birthday and refine their walking skill throughout the second year. The progression to walking is presented in Figure 6.10.

Manual Control   Keogh and Sugden (1985) describe three interrelated developmental progressions toward **manual control**, the self-regulation of arm and hand movements in order to manipulate objects (Keogh & Sugden, 1985). These progressions are illustrated in Figure 6.11.

The first progression is the development of the hand control necessary for grasping, holding, handling, and releasing objects. By three to four months most infants are capable of picking up a cube and holding it in their palm. By five to six months they are using their thumb to help grasp and hold the cube. By 9 to 10 months, infants can hold a small object such as a raisin in the *neat pincer grasp*, using the thumb and a single finger. This ability marks the beginning of precise finger control of objects. The development of **dexterity**, the coordinated manipulation of objects with the fingers, continues through infancy and into the preschool years. Dexterity is essential for the young child to explore the world of objects.

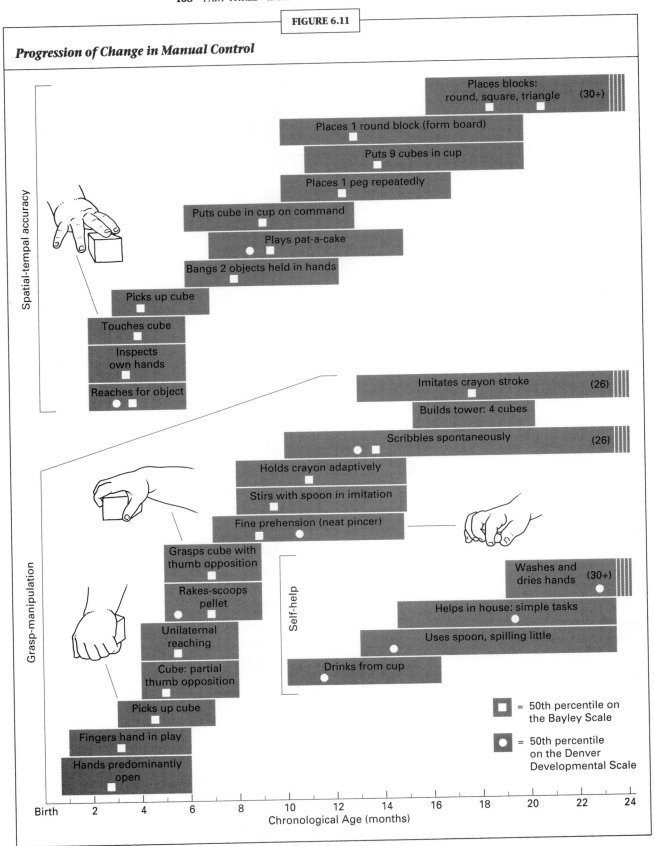

FIGURE 6.11

Progression of Change in Manual Control

Spatial-temporal accuracy

Places blocks: round, square, triangle (30+)

Places 1 round block (form board)

Puts 9 cubes in cup

Places 1 peg repeatedly

Puts cube in cup on command

Plays pat-a-cake

Bangs 2 objects held in hands

Picks up cube

Touches cube

Inspects own hands

Reaches for object

Grasp-manipulation

Imitates crayon stroke (26)

Builds tower: 4 cubes

Scribbles spontaneously (26)

Holds crayon adaptively

Stirs with spoon in imitation

Fine prehension (neat pincer)

Grasps cube with thumb opposition

Rakes-scoops pellet

Unilateral reaching

Cube: partial thumb opposition

Picks up cube

Fingers hand in play

Hands predominantly open

Self-help

Washes and dries hands (30+)

Helps in house: simple tasks

Uses spoon, spilling little

Drinks from cup

☐ = 50th percentile on the Bayley Scale

⬤ = 50th percentile on the Denver Developmental Scale

Birth 2 4 6 8 10 12 14 16 18 20 22 24
Chronological Age (months)

SOURCE: *Reprinted with the permission of Macmillan Publishing Company from* Movement Skill Development *by Jack Keogh and David Sugden. Copyright © 1985 Macmillan Publishing Company.*

A second developmental progression is the spatial accuracy of hand placement. Grasping would be of little adaptive value if infants could not visually direct their arms and hands to the location of the object they wish to hold. Again, spatial placement of the hand follows a predictable sequence. Newborns start off with **visually initiated reaching**, a primitive form of swiping in the general direction of objects. Such prereaching movements are rarely successful in contacting the object because the neonate is still unable to make use of vision to direct the arm and hand to the object (von Hofsten, 1984). This prereaching behavior drops out in the second month of life.

By three months infants begin to show some accuracy in **visually directed reaching**—that is, reaching for objects on the same side as the hand that does the reaching. And by 4½ months they can grasp objects with considerable accuracy straight in front of them or even on the opposite side of the reaching hand (Bushnell, 1985). Toward the end of the first year, infants depend less on visual information to guide their arm and hand movements (Bushnell, 1985). Once the infant has visually located an interesting object, she can use her arm and hand to find the object while using her eyes to look for new challenges.

The third developmental progression in manual control is the achievement of self-help skills such as drinking from a cup, putting on clothing, and washing hands. Although infants in the second year can perform certain self-help skills, cognitive and perceptual limitations slow development in this area, much to the dismay of caregivers.

A P P L I C A T I O N

Promoting Your Toddler's Self-Help Skills

Your toddler's self-help skills (such as washing his hands or dressing himself) are limited by three factors: the slow development of manual control, the even slower development of coordinated movements, and the child's lack of motivation to change. The following suggestions may be helpful.

■ Recognize that every self-help skill is made up of many components. For example, washing one's hands involves turning the faucet, wetting the hands, grasping and rubbing the soap, scrubbing, rinsing, and drying the hands, and hanging the towel. Focus first on teaching subcomponents, then on coordination.

■ To motivate your child to learn, reinforce any noticeable progress and avoid punishing for lack of improvement. Modeling the skills—particularly by older siblings—may be more effective than direct instruction.

Bottom Line: Be patient. With persistence, parents who encourage the development of self-help skills can expect their children to dress in simple garments, eat with utensils, and wash and dry their hands by the end of the second year.

Motor Control in Transactional Perspective

The development of motor control can be understood as a transactional process within an ecological context (Keogh & Sugden, 1985). In this perspective, the central nervous system affects and is affected by the infant's movements and the consequences of those movements. For example, as infants improve their control of head and eye movements and reaching and grasping movements, they not only find it easier to explore objects manually but also become better able to perceive increasingly complex features of objects. These perceptions, in turn, provide more complex stimulation to the central nervous system, thereby altering its neuronal structure. This altered structure enables the infant to explore even more efficiently and perceptively.

Environments that provide the necessary complexity, novelty, and diversity of stimulation facilitate these developmental processes; those which do not may inhibit or retard development.

Wayne Dennis (1960) documented such retarding effects in his study of one- to four-year-olds who had been raised under conditions of extreme deprivation of physical and psychological stimulation in two orphanages. The motor development of these children was very retarded. They were all at least one year behind schedule for sitting up independently, crawling, creeping, and walking. In one institution only 15 percent of the four- to five-year-olds could walk independently. The deprivation not only affected their rate of development but also its form. Because many of the children had been limited to lying on their backs for months at a time through infancy, their initial attempts at locomotion involved scooting along on their buttocks and pulling themselves by their legs.

Although Dennis blamed the motor retardation on the staff's failure to place children in the prone position, the transactional perspective (Keogh & Sugden, 1985) offers a more complex analysis: Unstimulated babies are unstimulating to caregivers, and unstimulated caregivers are less motivated to stimulate babies. The virtual absence of developmentally appropriate transactions between these orphans and their supposed caregivers systematically retarded their motor control development.

The transactional perspective can also help us design programs to compensate for such delay. Selma Fraiberg's (1977) work with blind children illustrates how. Blind infants typically do not creep on average until 13 months (compared to 7 months for infants with normal vision), and do not walk until late in the second year. Whereas sighted children reach for objects at about the fourth month, a blind child won't know that an object is within reach unless the object makes a sound—and few objects make noise in the absence of contact. Most blind children do not "reach on sound" until the end of the first year.

As a result, blind infants seem to lack curiosity. Their passivity discourages their parents' responsiveness, decreasing the likelihood that they will provide the stimulation that their children require. Thus a vicious cycle can easily begin.

To combat this pattern, Fraiberg (1977) developed an intervention program. Her strategy was to focus primarily on the parents' role in facilitating "reaching on sound" transactions between the infant and objects. For example, she encouraged parents to put many sound-producing objects in their infant's environment to promote reaching and touching. Blind children who received the interventions achieved movement milestones earlier than those who did not receive intervention.

Facilitating Motor Control in Infants

Although most people accept that the rate at which an adult masters a new motor skill (such as tennis or a new dance step) is highly dependent on the quality of teaching, practice, and training equipment, many have been reluctant to consider the role of training and practice in infants' development of motor control. A small group of research studies offers some insight.

Charles Super (1976) observed that a Kenyan tribe (the Kipsigi) train their very young infants to sit and to walk. Beginning at one month, mothers play with their babies by bouncing them in their laps, prompting the stepping reflex. Consequently, the stepping reflex does not disappear as it does with infants in other cultures. Beginning at six months, Kipsigi mothers prop their infants into sitting positions to encourage sitting. Kipsigi infants were observed to sit, stand, and walk approximately one month earlier than American babies. Might Kipsigi children have some genetic advantage not shared by other cultures? Apparently not: The Kipsigi babies show early acquisition of skills that are trained in the culture but not of skills that are not trained (Super, 1976).

These cross-cultural findings are highly consistent with the results of Zelazo's experiment stimulating infants' stepping reflex (Zelazo et al., 1972) discussed earlier in this chapter. Recall that Zelazo's trained infants walked at 10 months, fully 2 months earlier than untrained infants and typical expectations. Esther Thelen (1986; Thelen & Ulrich, 1991) has suggested that infants may have "hidden skills" that can only be elicited under special environmental conditions. In one study (Thelen, 1986), she demonstrated that seven-month-old infants were able to step in a walkinglike pattern when supported over a treadmill. Box 6.5 explores yet another example of the laboratory facilitation of motor control in infants.

Further insights into the effects of experience on motor development come from the pioneering work of Myrtle McGraw (1935/1975). McGraw conducted a longitudinal study of newborn fraternal twins named Johnny and Jimmy. She provided Johnny with extensive training, including skills in riding a tricycle, roller skating, climbing, and swimming. Her approach included stepwise increases in physical challenge, built into equipment that she designed specifically for the training of these skills. For example, she trained Johnny to crawl along a plank, gradually increasing the angle of incline. Before Johnny reached his second birthday, he was able to shimmy up that plank at a 70-degree incline to the top of a 7-foot-high pedestal and jump off into the researcher's arms!

Johnny's twin, Jimmy, was provided similar training after Johnny had reached proficiency in each skill. Jimmy apparently caught up quickly with Johnny's achievements, leading McGraw to conclude initially that the training had not been particularly effective. However, in a much later summary of her work, including unpublished follow-up assessments of the twins in adolescence and young adulthood, McGraw was impressed

---

FIGURE 6.12

McGraw's Motor Training

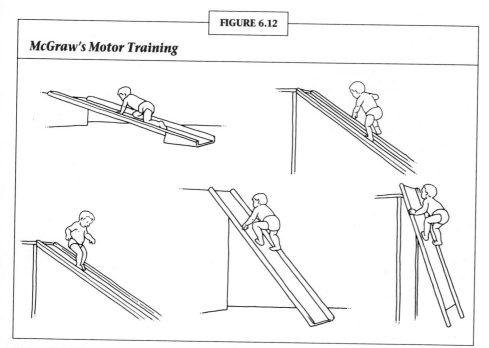

By gradually increasing the angle of incline over a period of months, McGraw helped Johnny learn to climb to the top of a seven foot pedestal. Although the rationale for teaching this particular skill is unclear, the fact that it can be done informs us of the great potential for motor learning in young children.

SOURCE: *M. B. McGraw, Growth: A Study of Johnny and Jimmy (New York: Arno Press), 1935/1975. Reprinted by permission of the publisher.*

Facilitating Visually Directed Reaching

Burton White and Richard Held (1966) studied infants living in an orphanage under conditions of moderate stimulus deprivation. They wanted to know how experience affects the development of visually directed reaching in one- to four-month-old infants.

They divided the infants into three groups. The first group, called the massive enrichment group, had patterned sheets and crib bumpers (the bumpers were periodically removed to vary their visual experience). These infants experienced plenty of extra handling by caregivers and were given improved mattresses to facilitate spontaneous movement and a large complex stabile (a nonmoving mobile). The second group, the so-called moderate enrichment group, had two pacifiers attached to the sides of the crib, one with a patterned disk and one an unpatterned disk. The control group received no special treatment.

The results were somewhat surprising. In both the massive and moderate enrichment groups, visually directed reaching was accelerated by one month, so that these infants were able to successfully grasp an object by 3½ months on average. However, the moderate enrichment group actually showed earlier swiping and reaching than the massive enrichment group. Contrary to expectation, massive enrichment seemed to overwhelm the infants during the first two months, as they indicated with excessive crying and looking away from stimulus materials. By 2½ months, however, the massive experience infants were better able to cope with the stimulation and rapidly developed the visually directed reach.

The results support the facilitating effects of enrichment with infants who are developing under less than optimally stimulating conditions. It is not clear, however, whether enrichment would accelerate the development of normal infants in the typical ecology of a family home. In any case, White and Held's early research has had enormous influence on the design and sale of stimulating nursery materials. Patterned sheets and bumpers, elaborate mobiles with visual and auditory stimulation, and an endless variety of crib toys are standard fare for the newborns of the nineties.

The typical middle-class American baby is very likely to be reared in an environment even more stimulating than White and Held's massive enrichment condition. Parents need to recognize the limitations of their young infants' emerging perceptual and motor capabilities. The possibility that massive enrichment may overwhelm very young infants should be kept in mind for those who are tempted to create their own special effects and training regimens to enrich their babies. The natural ecology of the average home nursery undoubtedly pushes the limits of the perceptual processing capacity of young infants.

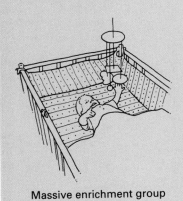

Massive enrichment group

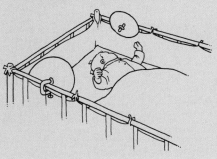

Moderate enrichment group

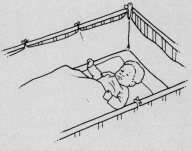

Control group

SOURCE: *White & Held, 1966*

by Johnny's continued superiority in motor skills and physical fitness as compared to Jimmy (McGraw, 1977). Perhaps the early training is what gave Johnny this superiority by enhancing his motivation and his confidence in his physical abilities. Or, the differences may have resulted from genetic differences between the fraternal twins. Our understanding of the effects of practice would be enormously expanded by a modern replication and extension of McGraw's early work.

Does training facilitate infants' motor development? Although developmentalists are unable to conclude that training regimens (similar to those used by McGraw), enhance motor development beyond what would normally be expected, experience plays a critical role in all aspects of infant motor development. Parents and other caregivers are encouraged to create physical environments for their infants that combine safety and challenging opportunities for movement experience.

A P P L I C A T I O N

Are Enrichment Strategies Worthwhile?

Although there is some evidence to support the idea that an infant's motor control can be accelerated through training, one critical question must be considered: Is there sufficient rationale for such extraordinary effort to accelerate motor control? The answer to the question depends on the circumstances.

- In situations where infants show developmental deficits in acquiring movement control — particularly where that delay is clearly attributable to stimulus deprivation or other risk factors — the answer is certainly yes. Trying to accelerate skills seems more than justified in such cases.

- But what about instances when overzealous parents use training techniques to promote *super*development of particular skills at the risk of creating imbalances in overall develop-

ment? For example, a father who wants his son to be a great distance runner might initiate an early training regimen that could actually hinder normal skeletal development. In these instances, the answer is an equally clear no.

- For the majority of cases, however, the answer is maybe. In a society where both work and leisure activities are likely to be sedentary, parents are challenged to find ways to encourage their children to realize their potential for physical and motor development. Stimulation techniques and training programs that are developmentally appropriate and sensitive to each child's genetic limitations and motivational idiosyncrasies should be considered.

Looking Back

The rapid physical changes in size, proportion, and motor skill in infancy and dramatic improvements in perceptual ability profoundly affect the infant's transactions with its environment. The infant changes from a passive, reflexive newborn to an active, explorative toddler. As the infant explores and manipulates the environment, the environment changes the infant's central nervous system, which in turn further enhances the infant's ability to perceive and affect the environment. We have shown the important mediating role of caregivers in these transactions.

We will now examine how these changes in the infant's physical and perceptual ability are paralleled by equally rapid development of the infant's cognitive and language abilities.

HEIGHT AND WEIGHT The average newborn weighs 7½ pounds and measures about 20 inches. Birth weight doubles by five months and triples by one year. Height increases by about half in the first year and by five to six inches in the second year. The overall growth rate slows from the first to the second year.

BODY PROPORTION By the cephalocaudal principle, growth of the head and upper body precede growth in the lower body; by the proximodistal principle, the torso develops before the arms and legs, which develop before the hands and feet.

NUTRITION The mother's breast milk is uniquely suited to the infant's nutritional requirements through the first four to six months. Some mothers choose to bottle-feed using formula. Both meet the infant's nutritional needs until the infant reaches 14 pounds. Breast milk offers some health advantages over formula by providing immunological protection of the infant through the first six months, until the infant's own immune system begins to function.

BRAIN The central nervous system is the most complicated physical structure in the body, affecting all functioning. The greatest risks and opportunities for development are those that affect the central nervous system.

NEURONS Information is transmitted through the nervous system by electrical impulses carried by neurons. Each neuron has short fibers called dendrites to receive impulses and a long fiber called an axon to send impulses to other neurons. The gap between neurons is called the synapse. Neurotransmitters carry signals across the synapse.

MYELINIZATION The process by which axons are covered by the myelin sheath is called myelinization. The myelin sheath insulates axons and helps them transmit electrical impulses faster and more efficiently. Rapid myelinization in certain regions of the brain is associated with gains in specific motor skills controlled by those regions.

REGIONS Different regions of the brain develop at different rates—but in an invariable sequence—before and after birth. The motor regions develop first, the sensory regions second, followed by the association regions that mediate thought.

BRAIN AND EXPERIENCE Humans are born with all the neurons they will ever have and far more than they will ever need. Nerve cells compete for survival. Neurons survive by forming synapses with other neurons and by being repeatedly fired. The child's experiences determine which pathways are fired.

PLASTICITY AND RESILIENCE The surplus of neurons enables the young brain to recover from injury by reprogramming itself—a capacity known as plasticity. Plasticity is nature's margin of error against traumatic injury.

TIMING OF EXPERIENCE According to theory, the brain is more susceptible to modification by certain forms of stimulation during critical (or sensitive) periods of development. Support for this theory comes from studies of sensory deprivation and sensory enrichment of animals.

SENSATION AND PERCEPTION Sensation refers to the ability to register information and to transmit that information to the central nervous system. Perception refers to the processing of sensory information by the brain. Visual perception has been studied by observing infants' fixation time as a measure of discrimination.

THE EYE Only images that are focused on the light-sensitive cells of the fovea can be discriminated clearly. Although immaturity of the fovea at birth makes acuity, or sharpness of vision, quite low, acuity improves dramatically during the first few months of life.

TRACKING The young infant's eyes can locate or track an object only with imprecise, jerky movements. By three to four months they develop smooth pursuit movements that enable them to track the movement of objects in space.

OBJECT PERCEPTION Infants learn to perceive objects by first scanning object contours, then internal features of objects, and finally by separating figure from ground. By four months, infants discriminate figure from ground, but only if they see the figure and ground move with respect to one another.

FACE PERCEPTION Scientists have confirmed that the human face takes on special significance for the young infant. By three months, infants can discriminate among facial expressions.

DEPTH PERCEPTION Infants learn to perceive in three dimensions by responding to binocular, kinetic, and pictorial information. Although infants have some ability to perceive depth in the first six months, depth perception that allows the infant to be adaptively mobile emerges only after the sixth month.

AUDITORY PERCEPTION The ear is well developed several weeks before birth and fetuses react to sound stimulation. Neonates discriminate sounds of different loudness, pitch, and duration. By six months, auditory perception is highly mature.

SPEECH SOUNDS Newborns possess innate perceptual mechanisms that facilitate the development of language. Young infants can distinguish virtually every phonetic contrast and respond to slight differences in the pronunciation of a particular speech sound by different speakers.

TASTE AND SMELL Sensitivity to taste and smell is present soon after birth and develops quite rapidly during the first month. Early taste sensitivity may relate to later food preferences, and early smell sensitivity may be important in breastfeeding.

MOTOR CONTROL The only organized behaviors in the newborn are reflexes: involuntary stimulus–response patterns. Reflexes are controlled by the brain stem, not the cerebral cortex. Reflexes provide perspective on our evolutionary history; they may be related to later voluntary behaviors, and they help us to assess the integrity of the nervous system.

STEREOTYPIES Among the infant's random movements are rhythmical movement stereotypies: repetitions of specific movements at regular, brief intervals. Although their adaptive purpose is not clear, they may help the infant to learn to use its body parts.

VOLUNTARY CONTROL Infants develop voluntary posture, locomotion, and manual control in fixed sequences but with variation in the rate of development.

Crawling precedes creeping, which precedes walking at about one year. Visually initiated reaching in newborns is replaced by visually directed reaching by four months.

TRANSACTIONAL PERSPECTIVE The central nervous system affects and is affected by the infant's movements and the consequences of those movements. Improved perception sends increasingly complex stimulation to the central nervous system, which in turn enhances the infant's ability to explore even more effi-ciently and perceptively. This theory helps explain retardation of institutionalized infants and facilitates the design of intervention programs to reverse developmental delay.

FACILITATION Cross-cultural research and laboratory research suggests that infant motor development may be enhanced by training and that long-term effects on motor functioning are possible. More research is needed.

Key Terms

infancy	sensation	reflexes
neurons	perception	rhythmical movement stereotypies
dendrites	fixates	locomotion
axon	discriminated	creeping
myelin sheath	fovea	manual control
plasticity	acuity	dexterity
sensory deprivation	smooth pursuit movements	visually initiated reaching
sensory enrichment	visual cliff	visually directed reaching

Cognitive and Language Development in Infancy

Looking Ahead

- Infants' capacity for learning increases rapidly over the first few months. How do infants learn and what effects does this have on their behavior?

- Infants' ability to imitate gestures and facial expressions grows gradually through the first two years. How does their ability to imitate affect their interaction with caregivers?

- Infants show an increasing ability to remember aspects of their experience in the first few months. What kinds of things do they remember?

- Infants come into the world with no understanding of physical objects. How do they learn to think about and manipulate objects to solve simple problems?

- By one view, infants' ability to adapt develops in a series of qualitative stages. What are these stages and how can we promote their progression through the stages?

- Some scientists have used learning principles to explain the development of language. Do these principles adequately account for the dramatic advances in the infant's ability to comprehend and produce language?

- Infants' language ability advances in a series of distinct phases during the first two years. What happens during these phases?

- Parents are often concerned about their infant's language development. How do parents try to promote their infant's language development? Are these measures effective?

A s far as we know, infants do not come into the world with *knowledge* as we commonly use the term. They do not know anything about objects, what can be done with them, or what they are called. Newborn infants do not know their mothers, they don't know what rattles are for, nor do they know the purpose of the mobiles suspended over their cribs. However, by the end of the period we call infancy, they become masters of action-oriented problem solving in the world of objects. Moreover, they are beginning to use language to further their mastery of that world. We can see the extraordinary nature of these changes by comparing two observations of Leshonda; first when she is 3-months-old and second when she is 21-months-old.

Keisha and Marcus have just fallen asleep after a long evening of feeding, bathing, and taking turns playing with three-month-old Leshonda. A series of loud banging sounds startles them and sends them racing into Leshonda's room. There she is, in her crib, grinning ear to ear, cooing softly, her foot entangled in the strings and dangling parts of a mobile that, earlier in the evening, had been suspended safely above the crib.

Apparently, a flaw in the design of the mobile has allowed it to descend into the crib, just a few inches from her left leg. Her leg became entangled in the strings and, each time she moves her leg, the mobile crashes against the side of the crib. The more she kicks the more it crashes; the more it crashes, the more she kicks. Although it is late, and their hearts are still beating rapidly, the two proud parents cannot get over how Leshonda has learned to make the noise, over and over and over again.

Eighteen months later, we see dramatic improvement in Leshonda's ability to solve problems and the beginnings of her use of language.

Leshonda, now 21-months-old, is standing in the middle of the living room, holding a grape in her hand. She is surrounded by an assortment of toys, pots and pans, and several of her father's size 12 shoes that she has dragged from his closet. She looks sheepishly toward her father as she raises her hand over her head. "Fo, fo, fo," she says, as she waves her arm in a throwing (or "fo-ing") motion, but without letting it go. Having decided that the look on his face is not one of disapproval, she hurls the grape across the room. It bounces off the coffee table and lands in one of her father's shoes. She yells "gape, gape, gape" as she toddles to the shoe to retrieve the grape.

Even though the grape is not visible, her repeating the word gape as she looks into the shoe is proof that she knows it has to be in there someplace. She reaches in but does not find it. She then picks up the shoe and turns it over, but the grape does not come out. "Gape allgone!" she says, as she looks up at her father.

Frustrated but determined, she turns the shoe over once again, but this time at a slightly different angle, and adds a slight shaking movement. It still does not come. She looks at her father, then back at the shoe. She turns it over once

> *more, adjusting the angle again and shakes it just a bit harder. The grape comes tumbling out, much to her delight. This time it goes directly into her mouth! "More gape, more gape," as she again reaches for her father's shoe.*

In both of the preceding vignettes, Leshonda uses knowledge of her environment and of her ability to affect environment to solve problems. Although such knowledge is not innate, we are born with the capacity to adapt to our world by acquiring this knowledge, and once acquired, to apply it to solve problems. By three months, Leshonda's perceptual and cognitive systems are ready to solve the problem of the partially descended mobile. She knows how to kick her leg and, when kicking it causes a crashing sound, she quickly learns to repeat the behavior over and over for the desired effect. Language is not a part of her repertoire and thus plays no role in her problem solving. By 21 months, her efforts to solve problems have become highly flexible and systematic; she is obviously experimenting with her knowledge, adapting it to the requirements of the grape-in-the-shoe problem. She has just begun to use words to help her solve the problem of the grape, an approach that will grow rapidly in the coming months.

Infant Learning

Learning is any relatively permanent change in behavior or knowledge resulting from experience or practice. Infants obviously learn; the question caregivers and researchers ask is, How do they learn? The answer to this question has great practical value. Learning theory does not simply explain the causes of behavior change after the fact; it offers the opportunity to gain control over the direction of behavior change. If Heather's mother wanted to improve her daughter's ability to use eating utensils, these principles might empower her to do so. If Carlos's parents would like their son to learn to avoid reaching toward the top of the kitchen stove, these principles might help them to establish that restraint. The implications for parenting are truly profound.

In each of the following sections we will review what is presently known about specific aspects of infant learning and try to answer two questions: Do the principles that account for change in adult behavior explain changes in infant behavior? If they do, what are the practical implications?

Habituation

The concept of *habituation* was presented in Chapter 6 as the infant's tendency to respond less and less to a stimulus as the infant becomes accustomed to (or learns about) it. From a practical perspective, habituation provides a key element in infants' everyday learning. Infants explore the world of objects in search of novelty; when they habituate to the novelty in one object, they resume their explorations. Habituation is also highly adaptive (Rovee-Collier, 1987). The complexity and intensity of stimulation in natural settings such as homes, day-care centers, and supermarkets can be overwhelming. Habituation is the key to making the stimulation manageable: It enables infants to adapt to the diversity and intensity of stimulation and to "shut down" when they become overloaded.

Full-term newborns habituate to auditory (Field, Dempsey, Hatch, Ting, & Clifton, 1979), visual (Slater, Morison, & Rose, 1984), and tactile stimulation (Field et al., 1979; Kisilevsky & Muir, 1984). But young infants show relatively stable individual differences

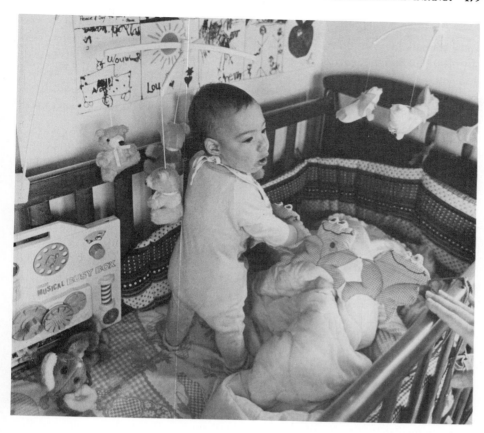

Like many infants today, this baby lives in a world rich in stimulation. Habituation helps the baby to avoid being overwhelmed and allows him to focus his attention on particular stimuli as he explores his world.

in the rate of habituation (Bornstein & Benasich, 1986) that are related to their cognitive abilities later in childhood. Higher rates of habituation in infancy are associated with higher intellectual performance in the preschool years (Bornstein & Sigman, 1986). Infants who rapidly habituate to visual stimulation at four months tend to have greater expressive vocabulary at one year and higher scores on standardized intelligence tests at age four (Bornstein, 1985). A review of similar research concludes that infants' ability to process information in the first half-year of life is associated with their cognitive competencies later in childhood (Bornstein & Sigman, 1986).

A P P L I C A T I O N

Optimal Stimulation for Babies

Parents and caregivers frequently ask, How much stimulation is good for my baby? Although infants show wide individual differences in their ability to tolerate and profit from stimulation, most babies cope well with the normal range of stimulation in a typical home. Provide an enriched environment with lots of sights, sounds, tastes, smells, and textures, but take care not to overwhelm your baby. Fortunately, she will tell you when she has had too much or too little:

- When stimulation is adequate, she will be perceptually active and alert.
- When she is overstimulated, she will fuss and withdraw.
- When she is understimulated, she will either sleep or seek attention.

Bottom Line: Your baby will show and tell you how much stimulation is optimal. Just pay attention to your baby's behavior.

Conditioning

Like habituation, other forms of learning help infants to respond adaptively to the diversity of stimulation they encounter. As indicated in Chapter 2, conditioning refers to two different forms of learning: classical conditioning (in which stimuli are manipulated *before* the response to induce learning) and operant conditioning (in which stimuli are manipulated *after* the response to induce learning). We will now consider whether these forms can be demonstrated with infants.

Classical Conditioning   In classical conditioning, the diversity of stimulation perceived by infants becomes less confusing when they learn to respond to different stimuli as if they were equivalent. Classical conditioning begins with a natural tendency for a certain stimulus (the unconditioned stimulus) to elicit an appropriate response (the unconditioned response). For example, the mother's nipple in the infant's mouth naturally elicits sucking movements in the newborn. This natural association between the stimulus and response can be the basis for organizing the young infant's response to other stimuli. If the sight and smell of the mother are always associated with the flow of milk, the infant may come to respond to the appearance of the mother as the psychological equivalent of the nipple; that is, when the mother enters the room, the infant begins to suck.

Researchers have shown that newborns, just hours after birth, can be classically conditioned (Blass, Ganchrow, & Steiner, 1984). These researchers selected stroking of the infant's forehead as the CS (conditioned stimulus), an acceptable choice since it is known that it will not elicit sucking responses. The UCS (unconditioned stimulus) was a sucrose solution delivered directly into the mouth. The experimental group received the UCS immediately after the CS; that is, a nipple containing the sweet solution was presented immediately after the infant's forehead was stroked. Two control groups had different experiences. In the first, infants received the CS after a long variable delay (which would render it ineffective), whereas the second control group received no exposure to the CS. Conditioning of sucking behavior was demonstrated in the experimental but not in the control groups. Interestingly, when the experimenters attempted to *extinguish* (or eliminate) the association between the CS and the UCS by presenting the CS repeatedly without the UCS, the infants first showed facial expressions of surprise, followed by a frowning or angry face. These reactions suggest that the conditioned infants had come to expect a taste of sucrose after being stroked and cried because their expectation was violated (Rovee-Collier, 1987).

Although somewhat limited in the neonate, classical conditionability increases rapidly in the first months of life, helping the infant to find predictability in its sensory experience. Knowing what seems to come before what engenders a sense of orderliness and sequence in the massive flow of sensory experience and enables infants to anticipate (Boswell, Garner, & Berger, 1993). This form of learning unfolds quite naturally in the course of routine caregiving: The squeak of the door comes to predict the appearance of the caregiver; the sight of the caregiver predicts relief from discomfort. Order and routine in caregiving promote this form of learning; chaos and unpredictability render it ineffective.

Operant Conditioning   In classical conditioning, responses are controlled by stimuli that *precede* the response. In operant conditioning, control is achieved by stimuli (or consequences) that *follow* the response. When the infant likes the consequences of some behavior, he or she is more likely to repeat the behavior to get those consequences again. For example, if sucking on a bottle gives the infant a sweet liquid, the infant will suck more. Consequences that increase the likelihood of the behavior (in this case, getting a sweet liquid) are called *reinforcers*. Conversely, if sucking on a bottle has the consequence of giving the infant a sour liquid, the infant will stop sucking. Consequences that decrease the likelihood of response are called *punishers*.

Can newborns and young infants be operantly conditioned? To a certain extent, yes. Infants in one study increased their rate of sucking to keep recordings of their mothers' voices playing. They did not, however, do the same to hear their fathers' voices (DeCasper & Prescott, 1984). The fact that only the mother's voice is reinforcing within hours of birth suggests that these effects may have been established prenatally, perhaps as a consequence of the presence of the sound of the mother's voice in the womb (DeCasper & Sigafoos, 1983).

In another study (Siqueland, 1968), researchers tried to condition infants to turn their heads 10 degrees or more to either side in order to get a pacifier. Within just 25 trials, the infants' normal rate of head-turning had tripled. For comparison, a control group was reinforced with the pacifier for remaining still. Those infants *decreased* their head-turning when reinforced for *in*activity.

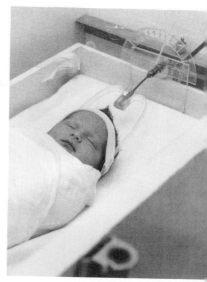

Operant conditioning of an infant's head-turning

SOURCE: *Courtesy of Einar Siqueland, Brown University.*

A P P L I C A T I O N

Operant Conditioning and Your Baby

From a theoretical perspective, you might assume that applying the principles of operant conditioning enables you to gain control of your infant's behavior. You could simply shape your infant's behavior into whatever form pleases you at the moment. However, infants' behaviors do not condition easily in natural settings, and what changes do occur come about over very long periods of time—weeks and months rather than hours and days. Most parents cannot afford the time and effort required to systematically shape all of their baby's behaviors. So of what practical use is operant conditioning with infants?

Operant conditioning is your way of telling your baby—day in and day out—what you want

him to do and not to do. Although he doesn't always listen, he will get the general idea if you are persistent and consistent in your efforts over time.

You are likely to be more effective by focusing your change efforts on one of your infant's behaviors at a time. Once you gain some control over that behavior, move on to another.

Finally, don't think that you have to do all the reinforcing and punishing. Infants get plenty of feedback from other family members and from the physical environment. For example, babies often learn not to tease the cat when the cat decides it has had enough. Some pets understand operant principles better than their owners!

Operant conditioning is usually discussed as a means by which adults train or control someone else's behavior. But one practical implication of operant learning has less to do with control of the infant by caregivers than control of outcomes by the infant. When their behaviors result in predictable outcomes, infants develop a primitive sense of control or mastery over those outcomes. For example, when Leshonda accidentally tangled her foot in the strings of her mobile and caused it to shake, she probably felt like master of the mobile. Presumably, if such experiences were to accumulate over extended periods of time, a more generalized sense of mastery might evolve. In contrast, infants who experience environments where nothing they do seems to have any effect may develop a sense of *helplessness* (Ciccheti & Aber, 1986). Although there have been no studies of the relationship between learning in infancy and later personality development, the possibility of such a relationship is intriguing. Heather's experience of an unresponsive environment and her resulting sense of helplessness are illustrated clearly at 4½ months:

> *Heather has been crying for more than 30 minutes when Barbara finally comes into her room. By that time Heather is so distraught that she barely notices her mother's presence. As her diaper is being changed, though, she quiets. She looks up at her mother's face and smiles, but Barbara just keeps scowling and quickly averts her glance to the tape on the side of the diaper. Heather stops smiling. As Barbara lowers her back into the crib, Heather waves her arms and legs, but Barbara makes no response. She leaves the room without a sound. Heather bangs her hand against the side of the crib, but that makes no sound this time: Barbara has draped a blanket over the side to stop Heather's noise. Heather picks up rubber duck and squeezes it, but again there is no sound: The sound button has fallen out, eliminating its reinforcing "quack." She begins to cry again, and again there is no response.*

Although Heather's experience is not typical of most babies, it does sensitize us to the delicate balance of risk and opportunity involved in our routine care of our babies. While routine care is not particularly interesting for parents, it presents recurring opportunities for parents to encourage their baby's sense of mastery.

Observational Learning

Social learning theory places great emphasis on the potent effects of still another form of learning, **observational learning**. If children observe the behavior of a model and the consequences of that behavior to the model, they learn not only how to perform the behavior but also what is likely to happen if they do. For example, three-year-old Darnell sees his friend Luis share candy with his brother and then be praised by his father for the kindness. Darnell then shares his candy, expecting to be praised. Although we know that preschoolers imitate the behavior of older children and adults, there is considerable disagreement as to when in development children begin to imitate behaviors that have adaptive significance. Even the principal theorist of social learning theory, Albert Bandura (1989), fails to specify the point at which observational learning begins to play a significant role.

When does observational learning develop? The most comprehensive treatment of this question was provided by Jean Piaget (1936/1953) as a major component of his description and explanation of cognitive development during the first two years of life. Piaget observed:

- a very primitive and imprecise imitation from 1–4 months
- a more precise but still limited imitation of *familiar* behaviors that the infant can see itself perform from 4–8 months
- imitation of simple unfamiliar behaviors of the model from 8–12 months
- imitation of more complex unfamiliar modeled behaviors by the first half of the second year.

Deferred imitation—that is, imitation of previously modeled behavior—is not observed until late in the second year. A detailed account of Piaget's description of the development of imitation will be presented later in this chapter.

However, some researchers believe that Piaget's account is, at best, too conservative, or, at worst, inaccurate. According to Meltzoff and Moore (1977), imitative behavior can be demonstrated even in very young infants, thus calling Piaget's view into question. Meltzoff and Moore (1977) provided the first evidence of neonatal imitation. An adult modeled sticking out the tongue, opening the mouth, and finger movements for 12- to 20-day-old infants. The investigators claimed that their neonates imitated these behaviors, two of which the infants could not see themselves perform.

When imitative behavior begins has practical significance. Once infants can plan for action sequences simply by observing a model, they can expand their array of skills much more rapidly and efficiently. Deferred imitation, in which the infant observes the model's behavior and imitates it later without the model present, is particularly useful. The earlier imitation can be demonstrated, the earlier it can be recommended to caregivers as an appropriate strategy in the socialization of self-help skills and the facilitation of fine and gross motor skills.

From a practical perspective, any form of imitation can be a potent force in the interaction of infants and their caregivers. When parents interact with their newborns, they superimpose their own organized patterns of action on their infant's disorganized patterns of action. For example, parents of young infants try to provoke smiles and other facial expressions by displaying exaggerated versions with appropriate sounds for emphasis. To a certain extent, then, the rhythm of the interaction is driven by the parents in the early weeks of life, as they eagerly watch for and try to provoke imitation from their

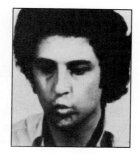

Neonates imitating adult's facial expressions.
SOURCE: *From A. N. Meltzoff & M. K. Moore,* Science, *1977. © 1977 by the American Association for the Advancement of Science. Reprinted by permission of AAAS and M. K. Moore.*

infants. The baby's inadvertent and imprecise imitations—for example, the first imitative smile at about two months—are the first indications of patterned reactions beyond simple reflex behaviors. These imitations charm the observant parent (imitation is the sincerest form of flattery!), the parent reinforces the infant's imitations, and the cycle repeats.

From an ethological perspective, young infants' primitive ability to imitate may have evolved as a way of *intermittently* reinforcing parents' modeling behavior (Bates, 1975). If the newborn were capable of exact imitation, there would be little incentive for parents to persist in their efforts to model. The very imprecision of infants' attempts to imitate requires parents to repeat their modeling over and over, as their infants get better at imitating them. Such exchanges are essential ingredients in the developing "dance" between parent and infant (Papousek & Papousek, 1975; Stern, 1977).

A P P L I C A T I O N

Modeling for Your Baby

At any age, imitating modeled behavior is easier if you observe the model closely and you systematically memorize what you observe for later reference. It also helps if you already have the behavior in your repertoire—that is, when you try to imitate, you are not performing the behavior for the first time. Finally, you will have greater incentive to imitate if you see the model get reinforced for performing the behavior.

Unfortunately, infants' attention to models is short-lived, their memory is short term, at best, and their repertoires are extremely limited. So, how do you promote an infant's imitation?

- Use movement and sound to get and maintain the baby's attention and keep the modeling as brief as possible. Repeat if the baby's attention allows.
- Model behaviors that are slight variations on behaviors the infant can already perform.
- Reinforce yourself after you have modeled the behavior.
- Model in a game format in which you imitate your baby's imitations of you, and so on. As long as you keep it fun, your baby will be learning; when you force it, learning will stop.

Early Development of Memory

The foundation of intellect is the ability to remember selected aspects of experience after that experience has been completed. For that ability to be adaptive, we must remember how we are stimulated by the environment, how we react to that stimulation, and how our reactions change the nature of environment. **Memory** records the results of our learning and stores it as knowledge.

Memory involves two related processes. **Encoding** is the process by which we store learned information, and **retrieval** is the process by which we call up memories for present use. We retrieve memories by *recognition* or by *recall*. In **recognition**, we retrieve the information in response to a cue, such as the context of the original learning. **Recall** is retrieval of stored information without the help of cues. For instance, when Keisha asks Leshonda what her babysitter's name is, Leshonda cannot *recall* the name; however, when the babysitter walks into the room, Leshonda runs to her saying her name over and over; the babysitter's appearance prompts *recognition*. As one might expect, recall develops later than recognition.

As described in Chapter 2, a mature information processing system includes both short-term memory (STM) and long-term memory (LTM) capability. We know that adults remember and can recall vast arrays of knowledge. But what is the nature of memory in infancy? Do newborns remember their experiences? And when does long-term memory develop?

Do Newborns Remember Their Experiences?

As we have seen, there is substantial evidence that neonates learn by habituating, by classical and operant conditioning, and possibly by imitating simple body movements and facial expressions. When a newborn habituates to repetitions of a particular stimulus and then reacts when presented with a modified stimulus, we assume that the initial stimulus must have been maintained in short-term memory long enough for the infant to notice that the stored perception is somehow different than the new, modified stimulus. Similarly, when an infant learns to start sucking in response to a conditioned stimulus such as having its forehead stroked, we conclude that the infant remembers the association between stroking and feeding. And if the stroking were still able to elicit the sucking response after days or weeks had passed, this could be interpreted as evidence of long-term memory capability.

However, efforts to demonstrate such carryover from one day's conditioning to the next in newborns have not been successful (Sameroff, 1968). Neonatal memory seems to be limited to minutes rather than hours or days, although that is an important beginning (Rosenblith, 1992; Zelazo, Weiss, Randolph, Swain, & Moore, 1987).

When Does Long-Term Memory Develop?

There is some evidence that long-term memory begins to emerge toward the end of the first month (Ungerer, Brody, & Zelazo, 1978) and develops rapidly during the second and third months of life (Rovee-Collier, 1987). One group of researchers (Ungerer et al., 1978) asked mothers to repeat a single word over and over for 13 days (60 times each day) to their 2- to 4-week-old infants. Then, the mothers were asked to refrain from uttering the word until 15 and 42 hours after the training. When the word was reintroduced the infants showed that they recognized it by body movements and/or widening their eyes.

Carolyn Rovee-Collier and her colleagues (1980) reasoned that, since two- to three-month-old infants can learn by operant conditioning, their ability to maintain that learning over time would reflect their recognition memory. The researchers used a task that was naturally interesting (or reinforcing) to young infants: the movement of a mobile suspended above their crib. In the first phase of the study, the researchers trained two- to three-month-old infants to shake a mobile suspended above their crib. They attached one end of a ribbon to one of the infant's legs and the other end to the mobile. The infants soon learned that by shaking their leg, they could initiate and maintain the movement of the mobile. Two weeks later—without additional training—the infants were reattached to the mobile to see if they remembered how to shake the mobile. The infants' responses were inconsistent, suggesting that they had no memory of the task.

The researchers reasoned that perhaps infants needed something to jog their memory. They tried a *reactivation procedure*. On the day prior to testing, the infants were placed in the crib but were *not* attached to the mobile. The experimenter (without being seen) simply shook the mobile by pulling the ribbon. When the infants were reattached to the mobile on the following day, they showed a high level of response, suggesting that they remembered after all.

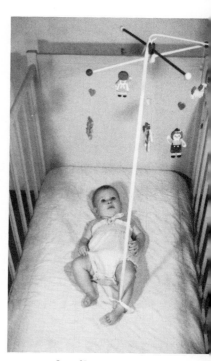

One of Rovee-Collier's infants learning to shake a mobile

Rovee-Collier concluded that two- to three-month-old infants were capable of recognition memory, but only with the assistance of a reactivation procedure. Another study showed that, if the infants were tested only one week after training, they remembered to kick their legs, even without reactivation (Sullivan, Rovee-Collier, & Tynes, 1979).

Rovee-Collier and her colleagues also investigated whether two- to four-month-old infants' memory would be sensitive to changes in the mobile's appearance from the time of training to testing. As in previous studies, the infants were trained to shake the mobile. The researchers then systematically altered the number or color of the dangling objects at testing. The infants showed reduced leg-kicking for up to three days, demonstrating that they remembered the original mobile and noticed the difference (Fagen, 1984; Mast, Fagen, Rovee-Collier, & Sullivan, 1980).

The researchers went one step further with another group of infants by changing one aspect of the appearance of the mobile every day of training. When the researchers then displayed the mobile without changing it two days in a row, the infants decreased their leg-kicking, suggesting that they had learned to expect daily change (Fagen, Morrongiello, Rovee-Collier, & Gekoski, 1984). Thus, the infants did not simply remember how to make an interesting sight last; they remembered expectations for *inconsistency* in the stimulus.

Rovee-Collier interpreted these findings as convincing evidence of long-term memory in two- to four-month-old babies. These advances in recognition memory are the first true signs of information processing in the infant, setting the stage for the broad range of adaptive learning in infancy.

A P P L I C A T I O N

Promoting Your Baby's Memory

By the second or third month, your baby has developed the ability to remember stimuli for several days. She remembers words she hears frequently, complex patterns she sees repeatedly (such as your face and its expressions), and interesting changes in what she sees and hears, particularly changes that she herself brings about. Thus, your routine but responsive caregiving provides all the stimulation that your baby needs to practice her memory skills.

Piaget's View of Infant Cognitive Development

Studies of infant learning generally portray infants passively. This perspective is reflected in the methods of study: Infants are stimulated, cued, reinforced, punished, and ignored to see what changes in behavior result. As we have seen, the principles that explain learning in infancy are essentially the same as those that explain learning at later ages.

Swiss psychologist Jean Piaget rejected this passive concept of cognitive development in infancy (or at any other stage for that matter). Instead, Piaget portrayed infants as persistently *active* by nature, requiring no stimulation to become active nor reinforcement to remain active. Instead, the impetus to action comes from within the infant. The infant is naturally curious and explorative, constantly seeking stimulation.

From the moment of birth, the infant's persistent movements bring it into direct contact with objects in the environment. But the infant comes into the world with no knowledge of objects, that is, what purpose they serve and how to manipulate them.

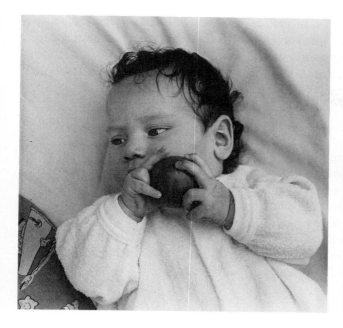 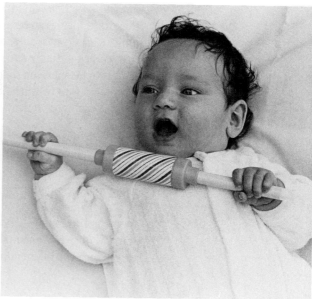

On the left, the infant's hands accommodate to an unusually shaped object. With each new accommodation, the infant's schemas grow and can be used to solve increasingly difficult problems. On the right, the infant coordinates schemas that direct the eyes, hands, arms, and mouth into a single purposeful activity.

Thus, every new object encountered by the baby is a mystery, a problem to be solved. The infant's attempt to come to terms with the ever-expanding world of physical objects—everything from crib toys and mobiles to parents and rubber duckies—is the process of **adaptation**, the purpose of cognitive development. For Piaget there is no other pursuit or purpose, at this stage or at any subsequent stage. Thus, Piaget's explanation of cognitive development in infancy accounts for how infants deal with physical objects and how they manipulate objects and use them for adaptive purposes. Knowledge of objects is acquired very gradually through the first two years of life, Piaget's **sensorimotor stage** of cognitive development.

If infants are to manage objects, they must begin by learning to control the motions of their bodies—particularly their eyes and hands—so that they can grasp objects and manipulate them. Even though infants innately perform a reflex grasp soon after birth, they do not know how to control their hands. They cannot voluntarily open and shut their hands, much less use them to pick up a toy or hold a bottle. What infants need are plans for directing the adaptive use of their hands. According to Piaget, these plans develop in the form of *schemas*, mental plans for the movement of body parts.

A **schema** is both a plan for action and the action itself. An example may help explain this. After a brief period of reflex grasping, Carlos gradually learned to voluntarily open and close his hands. Just after he was four months old, he closed his hands on a crib toy and lifted it off the surface of the mattress for the first time. Within just a few days, he was able to repeat this grasping and holding whenever he wanted. Piaget would say that Carlos had developed a *grasping schema*. The grasping schema emerges very gradually throughout the sensorimotor stage. Like all schemas, the grasping schema encompasses a *set* of action plans for using the hands, including grabbing, holding, twisting, pulling, bending, and squeezing objects. In addition to the grasping schema, infants must develop a sucking schema, a visual scanning schema, postural schemas, and numerous other schemas to regulate the actions of various parts of the body.

The schema organizes the infant's actions with respect to the object; it also constitutes the infant's knowledge of the object. You may recall from Chapter 2 that, according to Piaget, knowledge can be used adaptively either by assimilating objects or by accommodating to them. An infant can adapt to an object (or find it meaningful) only to the extent that it can be assimilated or accommodated to one or more schemas. By six months, Carlos was able to grasp several familiar crib toys with a fluid, efficient motion that worked virtually every time. Piaget would say that Carlos was able to assimilate objects to his grasping schema. He also brought every object to his mouth, assimilating those objects to his sucking schema. As the infant learns to assimilate individual objects to more and more schemas, he comes to know the object as a permanent part of his world.

Infants can expand schemas by modifying or *accommodating* their action plans to include new objects. For instance, when Carlos tried to hold a ball for the first time, he had to accommodate the grasping schema he had previously used to hold a rattle, because the movements required in holding a ball are slightly different from those already in the schema. Infants can only accommodate schemas to new objects that are within their cognitive range. Once the infant has accommodated a schema, the infant "knows" the new object. As the infant accommodates the schema to better fit the contours of the new object, the infant comes to better know the object.

A   P   P   L   I   C   A   T   I   O   N

Promoting the Development of Schemas

Your infant's schemas grow best under conditions that encourage his active exploration. His searching eyes and hands need objects that vary in size, shape, weight, color, and texture. He needs objects that he can touch and that react to his touch. He needs an environment that offers stability (the same objects are consistently available) and change (novel objects appear periodically). You should be the most responsive part of your infant's environment, acting and reacting to his initiatives with varied movement, sound, and emotion.

Substages of the Sensorimotor Period

Piaget (1936/1953) refers to the first two years of development as the *sensorimotor period*. The term was originally designed to express the idea that infants know their world only by the actions they take with respect to the objects in it. But knowing the world of objects does not come easy, nor does it occur all at once. Piaget described a series of six substages through which the infant's knowledge emerges in an invariant sequence over the first two years. Piaget's descriptions of the infant's cognitive development through the substages focuses on advances in their ability to understand objects, solve problems, and imitate modeled behavior.

Substage I: The Use of Reflexes (Birth–1 Month)

As we saw in Chapter 6, infants are born with an elaborate set of reflexes, with each reflex providing a rigid response to a narrow range of stimulation. Despite their primitive *reactive* nature, reflexes observably order the otherwise disorganized squirmings and thrashings of newborns. Although Piaget did not recognize reflexes as intelligence, he did view them as the *building blocks* of intelligence, the raw materials for the emergence of schemas.

Substage II: Primary Circular Reactions (1–4 Months)

In Substage II, infants build upon the behaviors they performed reflexively during the first month by learning to perform them spontaneously. Infants discover, quite by accident, that they can repeat certain behaviors without the recurrence of the stimulus. For example, they discover that they can open and close their hands without being stimulated by pressure in their palm. With this realization, infants begin to repeat the movement over and over in a rhythmic cycle, just for the sake of doing it. Piaget refers to these accommodated reflexes as **primary circular reactions** (PCRs), the first form of true schema.

Primary circular reactions merely create movement for the sake of movement. Infants learn to rhythmically open and close their hands, to suck with or without the presence of an object, to wave their arms and to kick their legs. As PCRs are practiced (assimilated) repeatedly, the actions become smoother and less effortful. Parents learn to anticipate these repetitive movements, recognizing them as the first signs that their baby is gaining some control over his own behavior. This control increases toward the end of this substage as infants begin to coordinate schemas: They find their own fingers to suck and visually direct their hands to grasp objects.

Despite these behavioral advances, objects are of no special significance to infants during this substage. They grasp objects but do not explore them; when they drop an object, they do not search for it, as if it no longer existed. Infants begin to display primitive imitation: If a parent models a behavior, the infant may attempt a crude approximation of it. However, the infant will make no effort to improve the imitation, even if the parent repeats the behavior.

Substage III: Secondary Circular Reactions (4–8 Months)

While practicing the primary circular reaction of swinging her arm back and forth across the midline of her body, the infant may accidently strike a mobile suspended above the crib. After several repetitions, each having the same result, she notices the effect of her action and attempts to repeat that effect. But repeating the specific arm movement that caused the mobile to move requires a more sophisticated schema than a primary circular reaction. The infant must accommodate the schema that merely swings her arm back and forth to one that directs that movement to a specific effect on the environment: hitting the mobile. This new schematic form is known as **secondary circular reactions** (SCRs).

Infants gradually develop a repertoire of secondary circular reactions that enables them to use parts of their body to create simple effects on their environment. They learn to shake a rattle and to squeeze bath toys in order to hear sounds, and they learn to knock objects off the highchair in order to make them disappear from view.

This is a momentous development! For the first time, the object has some value to the infant, so that the effect on the object—not the action itself—becomes the focus of the action pattern. The infant begins to sense the difference between means and ends and between causes and effects. Most important, the infant begins to sense that he can influence his environment—the primitive beginning of the infant's belief that "I can make this happen!" However, infants will only develop this belief with reactive environments and responsive caregivers. Consider Heather's and Carlos's contrasting experiences during this substage.

> *Four-and-a-half-month-old Heather has been lying in her crib unattended for almost two hours. She is hungry and irritated from a filthy diaper that has not been changed since her mother last looked in on her. She has cried repeatedly with no response, not just today but for many days with the same result. She cries less and moves less than she used to.*
>
> *Although she reaches out occasionally to touch the sides of her crib, the high white bumpers cannot be grasped or moved in any way. There are no toys to touch, nothing to look at other than the light fixture on the ceiling, and nothing to hear other than the faint sounds of traffic. When Barbara finally comes to change her daughter, she performs only those behaviors required for routine care. Barbara offers no emotion and does not respond in any way to her daughter's movements, gestures, or sounds.*

Heather's physical and human environment fails to react to her behavior. At a time in development when she should be reaching out to affect the world around her, she moves in stereotyped patterns with no apparent purpose. In contrast, consider Carlos's highly responsive environment at five months:

> *Carlos is on his stomach on the living room floor. As he pushes his body up from the rug, his hand presses down on one of several squeeze-toys that litter the area. The toy frog emits a "griiiibit" sound that immediately captures his attention. He presses down two more times, repeating the effect. Its novelty worn off, Carlos turns his head toward his father and smiles broadly. Emilio smiles back and offers a formidable "griiiibit" of his own. Carlos giggles, looks back at the toy frog, and tries to reproduce the "griiiibit" sound by pressing down on the toy. The game goes on for some time with several variations.*

Carlos lives in a very responsive world that he is rapidly learning to manipulate and affect. Toys react to his touch, and his father acts and reacts in harmony with his son's explorations.

A P P L I C A T I O N

Promoting Secondary Circular Reactions

Your four- to eight-month-old develops schemas most efficiently with reactive environments and with responsive caregiving. When you respond enthusiastically to your infant's spontaneous behaviors, you can expect optimal cognitive development during this substage. Unresponsive caregivers and unreactive environments place their infant's cognitive development at risk. Caregivers may follow these simple guidelines.

Provide toys that react easily to your infant's touch—such as mobiles, squeeze toys, and specially designed crib toys that react with multiple sounds and movements.

React to your baby's movements and facial expressions with sounds, smiles, and head and body movements. Timing is important; your baby should sense that she is the initiator, at least some of the time.

The Substage III infant begins to sense that objects exist even when they are not being acted upon. This awareness is called **object permanence**. Piaget (1936/1953) cites several types of evidence to support this notion. First, if you show a six-month-old infant a familiar object that is partially covered, she will reach for that object as if she knows that it is a whole object. Second, when the infant sees an object disappear — for example, when a rattle rolls off the edge of a table — she will continue to stare in the direction of the object for a brief time, suggesting that she has some inkling that the object still exists even though it is no longer in view. However, at this substage, she does not stare for long and she does not actively search for the object.

One of the sure signs of an infant's emerging sense of object permanence is her predictable reaction to playing peek-a-boo with her mother. This baby is not fooled when her mother partially hides her face. She knows that her mother exists even though she can see only part of her face. By late in the first year, out of sight is no longer out of mind.

Four- to eight-month-old infants can imitate modeled behavior, but only if they already have a reasonable facsimile of that behavior in their repertoire of schemas. For example, while the baby will imitate her mother waving her hand, she will be unable to imitate her mother pointing or snapping her fingers.

Substage IV: The Coordination of Secondary Schemas (8–12 Months)

In the infant's world, most problems cannot be solved by simply swinging an arm or kicking a leg. Solving problems typically requires the sequencing of behaviors. For example, an infant who wants an object that is beyond his reach may have to adjust his posture or creep toward the object before it can be grasped. Obstacles such as floor pillows and cabinet doors may impede getting at desired objects.

Piaget reasoned that infants can solve such problems only by using one schema as a means to performing a second schema as an end. He called this new form of schema a **coordinated secondary circular reaction** and suggested that it typically appears in two forms. First, crawling infants frequently encounter obstacles—such as floor pillows, cabinet doors—that bar their access to toys and other objects they wish to see or touch. To solve the problem, the infant must learn to *sequence* an obstacle-removing schema (a swiping motion of the arm) with the object-grasping schema. Second, infants may sometimes need an instrument to accomplish an otherwise unattainable goal. For example, infants frequently throw toys out of their playpens, beyond their reach. According to Piaget, the Substage IV infant may attempt to solve the problem by first finding an object in the playpen that can be used as an instrument to reach the toy outside the playpen. The infant takes the instrument, reaches through the bars of the playpen, nudges the object closer, then reaches out with his hand and grasps the toy. Nothing new is occurring here other than the infant's sequencing of schemas already in his repertoire. The infant's approach to problem solving remains rigid. Schemas are applied "as is" in an all-or-nothing fashion. If the initial schema fails to remove a particular obstacle, the entire sequence is aborted and the problem remains unsolved.

The Substage IV infant's ability to keep the toy he desires in mind while removing the obstacle suggests that the toy must be mentally represented in some form. If there were no mental representations of objects, infants would be unlikely to follow through with the full sequence of schemas needed to attain their original goal. Thus, Substage IV infants have developed a relatively permanent concept of objects; that is, they know that objects exist, even when they are not looking at or touching them.

According to Piaget, Substage IV marks the first time that infants are able to imitate *invisible gestures*—gestures or expressions that infants cannot see themselves perform, including facial expressions. However, these infants are still unable to imitate novel behaviors by the model, that is, behaviors that infants do not already have in their repertoire.

A P P L I C A T I O N

Facilitating Coordinated Behaviors

*T*oward the end of the first year, infants need to find problems that they cannot solve by single movements. Fortunately, the home environment is filled with obstacles that impede their movements as they creep through the house, searching and exploring. Although infants often encounter challenging problems, caregivers may undermine those challenges by solving problems for their babies: They remove obstacles to their baby's movement, fetch objects that are beyond their baby's reach, and

open boxes that their baby cannot easily open.

You can foster your almost one-year-old's cognitive development by allowing him time to solve problems for himself. While he is likely to become frustrated, that frustration—within limits—will motivate him to persist in his efforts to find solutions, typically by learning to sequence behaviors. If your baby persists with a problem that is clearly beyond his range, provide some assistance with appropriate modeling that may help him in future encounters.

Substage V: Tertiary Circular Reactions (12–18 Months)

Piaget described the infant's new capability as "the discovery of new means through active experimentation" (1951/1962). Whereas Substage IV infants are limited to sequencing familiar schemas, Substage V infants are capable of **tertiary circular reactions:** They can systematically vary existing schemas until they fit the requirements of a problem. In essence, the coordinated secondary circular reaction used in the previous substage is transformed by the infant's ability to *experiment*.

An example cited by Piaget (1936/1953) is the infant's ability to pull a stick through the bars of a playpen. The Substage IV infant will reach through the bars, pick up the stick, and attempt to pull it into the playpen. If the angle of the stick is not parallel to the bars, the infant will be defeated. However, the Substage V infant can systematically rotate the stick until it is approximately parallel to the bars and pull it through. Infants can now succeed with toys that require them to place shapes into similar-shaped holes or to fit cups of graduated size into one another—toys that are frequently given to much younger infants with disappointing results.

Substage V infants engage in what Piaget (1936/1953) called *experiments in order to see*: They become preoccupied with endless hours of grabbing, tearing, rubbing, squeezing, dropping, and throwing—discovering unique features and properties of objects and their relationship to other objects. They bang objects together, take them apart, and try to put them together again. They are particularly interested in the effects they have on objects as they vary their manipulations. For example, they may tap an object softly and, if nothing happens, systematically increase how hard they hit it until it breaks.

Infants now view objects as permanent parts of their world, regardless of whether they can see or touch the objects at any given moment. They will search for hidden or lost objects as if they know that objects do not simply disappear. This makes their world a more stable and predictable place than it had seemed during their first year.

For the first time, infants are able to imitate a model's novel behavior, even if that behavior is not already in their repertoire. They simply work with what they have, systematically varying their attempts until a good match is achieved. For instance, infants methodically attempt to use a spoon to match the way they see it used by their parents. These efforts take considerable time, but children persist until they master the new skill.

A P P L I C A T I O N

Facilitating Your Baby's Experimentation

As your baby enters her second year, she will be fascinated with objects and their function. She needs objects that come apart, can be put back together, and can be manipulated in a variety of ways to produce different effects. Toymakers have produced many challenging toys for this age: simple puzzles, dolls with moving parts, and blocks that stack and stick together easily.

Allow your baby the freedom and time to explore such toys and other safe household objects (pots and pans, shoes). There is no such thing as too much exploration and curiosity at this or any other age!

Substage VI: Inventing of New Means Through Mental Combinations (18 Months and Up)

During the first five substages, infants' problem solving is action based. They solve problems as they physically work through the solutions. They cannot simply look at a problem, think through the solution, and then implement it. In other words, young infants are unable to *premeditate*, or to think before they act. Piaget believed that this is due to the absence of *mental symbols* and *symbolic representation*.

A **symbol** is something that stands for something else, often bearing some physical similarity to the thing it stands for. For example, a child may symbolize his mother's car by creating a two-dimensional drawing of that car. Although he cannot drive the car, he can pretend to drive it by running around the house holding the drawing and making "vroom-vroom" noises.

Piaget believed that Substage VI infants develop the ability to construct *mental symbols* that represent objects in the real world. He labeled this process **symbolic representation**. The first symbols take the form of **images**, or "picture-like symbols in the head" (Flavell, 1963). Substage VI infants can use images to represent objects in the immediate environment, such as toys, utensils, clothing, or food—in other words, the stuff of everyday problems to be solved in the infants' world.

The power of images is that the infant can mentally manipulate them to solve problems. For example, when a Substage VI child encounters an obstacle, she imagines the actions necessary to remove the obstacle and then—and only then—implements the solution. Moreover, she can symbolize various solutions and choose the one that seems most likely to solve the problem. Thus, late in the second year, infants begin to solve problems "in their heads," dramatically increasing the efficiency of their problem solving.

The key to the infant's first attempts at symbolic reasoning is the ability to construct images that accurately represent objects. [Substage VI] infants are enthralled with the novelty of objects, using countless manual and visual scanning schemas to explore them. The movements of the child's hands and eyes literally trace the contours of the object over and over until the child can mentally reproduce or construct a mental image of the object. Thus, according to Piaget, the image is a mental drawing of the object, constructed by an internal tracing process.

A P P L I C A T I O N

Fostering Mental Combinations

*T*hose who care for Substage VI children should be aware of the gradual nature of their transition into the world of symbolic reasoning—a world where problem solving may be accomplished by *mental* action rather than *physical* action. The pace of this transition depends on the quality of children's experience in the world of objects; children cannot construct mental images of objects that they have not fully explored.

Caregivers may facilitate the development of symbolic reasoning by providing a rich object environment and by encouraging children's curiosity and active exploration. Even in the most enriched environment, the first images are rather primitive approximations of the objects they represent, and improvement in their quality requires continued exploratory experience.

The advent of mental imagery increases the child's sense of the world as made up of permanent objects. The image of an object in the child's mind is enduring proof of its existence, even when the object is not in view. If an adult places an object in view of the child and then secretly moves the object to another location, the child will search in all possible locations based on the knowledge that everything has to be someplace. Moreover, two-year-olds may accept an object's existence simply by seeing its picture. For example, a toddler who sees a toy advertised on TV has no doubt that it exists and usually insists upon having it.

The toddler's newfound command of images has important impact on his ability to imitate. For the first time, the child can observe a model, encode the model's behavior in images, and recall those images at a future time to guide his behavior. Piaget labeled this ability **deferred imitation**. Children use deferred imitation to learn from an expanding array of models—including those they see on TV—and transfer that what they learn to new situations. A summary of the development during the six substages of the sensori-motor period is presented in Table 7.1.

Although images are essential to the transition to symbolic reasoning, their value as mental symbols is extremely limited: They require considerable mental effort and prove cumbersome as tools of thought in the rapid flow of problem solving in children's daily experience. Images effectively represent physical objects, but they cannot be used to represent more abstract qualities of the child's experience, such as hot–cold, heavy–light, happy–sad, or nice and not-so-nice. Ultimately, a more efficient and flexible form of symbolism is needed to represent these and other qualitative aspects of children's experience. As we will see in the next section of this chapter, such symbols are provided by language. We turn now to the development of language in infancy.

TABLE 7.1

Summary of Piaget's Six Substages of Cognitive Development, Object Permanence, and Imitation in the Sensorimotor Period

	Schema Type	Object Permanence	Imitation
Substage I (birth–1 mo.)	Reflexes appear as the building blocks for schemas	No concept of the object as permanent	No imitative behavior
Substage II (1–4 mos.)	Primary circular reactions direct repetitive movement for the sake of movement	Objects of no special significance; no reaction to disappearance	Crude imitation of the model if the infant has a matching schema; no attempt to improve the match
Substage III (4–8 mos.)	Secondary circular reactions direct simple effects on the environment	First reactions to sudden disappear-ance of object but no search; infant reaches for partially hidden object	Imitation of modeled behaviors if they are in repertoire; no effort to improve match or to imitate novel behavior
Substage IV (8–12 mos.)	Coordinated secondary circular reac-tions direct first sequenced problem solving	First evidence of object permanence; infants search for fully hidden object; infants keep objects in mind as coor-dinated SCRs are performed	Imitation improves with some effort to match less familiar modeled be-havior, but model must still be pres-ent for imitation to occur
Substage V (12–18 mos.)	Tertiary circular reactions direct first experiments and systematic trial and error	Infants can now track visible dis-placements of objects from place to place; object is separate entity from the schema that represents it	First successful imitation of unfamil-iar modeled behavior; some effort to improve the match but model must still be present
Substage VI (18 mos. +)	Mental combinations enable the child to solve problems "in the head"	Images used to represent missing objects; "everything must be someplace!"	Deferred imitation enables imitation of previously modeled behavior with model not present

Language Development in Infancy

Somewhere between 10 and 14 months, infants will utter their first obviously intelligible **word**, a string of sounds that makes clear reference to a particular object in the real world. About one year later they will be speaking in two- to three-word sentences and engaging in simple but meaningful conversations. All those who care for children during this brief phase of their development cannot help but conclude that something truly extraordinary has taken place. The central question of interest to researchers is, How can so much developmental change occur in such a short period of time? To parents and caregivers, the central question is, What can they do to facilitate their child's language development?

The presentation in this chapter will seek a balance between what is presently known about the process of early language development and what is known about strategies for facilitating that development. We begin with a look at early language development.

The Study of Early Language Development

Developmentalists have organized the study of language development to simplify its enormous complexity. First, they make a distinction between comprehending and producing language. **Comprehension** is the child's ability to understand language input whereas **production** is the ability to generate output that others can comprehend. Although these functions are not independent, each involves distinct skills and underlying processes not contained in the other. Throughout development, babies generally comprehend language before they produce it. For example, children react meaningfully and appropriately to phrases such as "Pick up the spoon!" long before they are capable of saying such phrases themselves. Another example of considerable practical significance is the nine-month-old's meaningful response to the word *no*, long before she is capable of uttering that word.

Although in the everyday world we experience language as a totality, scientists have focused their research and theory on distinct components of language: phonology, morphology, semantics, syntax, and pragmatics. Brief definitions are presented below.

Phonology Humans are capable of producing a wide variety of different sounds and infinitely combining them, but each existing language makes use of only a particular selection of those sounds, known as phonemes. **Phonemes** are the smallest units of a language that cue changes in meaning to the listener. For example, we know that the sound of the letter "b" and the sound of the letter "p" are distinct phonemes in the English language because the word *bat* does not have the same meaning as the word *pat*. Each language permits only certain combinations and sequences of phonemes. The study of *phonology*, therefore, deals with how children come to attend to and produce only those sounds and sound sequences appropriate to their native language.

Morphology The smallest units of meaning in a language are **morphemes**. A morpheme is a set of phonemes combined in a specific order. Some morphemes, such as "girl" and "bird" can stand alone as words. Others, such as "ed" and "ing," must be attached to other morphemes to express their meaning. The system of rules governing the formation of the smallest meaningful units of the language is its *morphology*. Figure 7.1 illustrates phonemes and morphemes in one word.

Semantics When we say that a child has a certain word in his vocabulary, we are indicating that he knows what the word means and that he knows how to use the word

---

FIGURE 7.1

Phonemes and Morphemes in the Word **Selfishness**

Phonemes
(units of sound):

Morphemes
(units of meaning):

SELFISHNESS

---

in a sentence to convey that meaning. **Semantics** is the study of how words come to have meaning to the child.

Syntax   The average child has a 4–6 word vocabulary by 15 months and as many as 20 words by 17 months. Inevitably, the child will start stringing these words together. However, each language has its own system of rules that governs the way words can be sequenced in sentences. The arrangement of words into phrases and sentences is the **syntax** of the language.

Pragmatics   To have a conversation, children must learn how and when to take turns speaking, how to maintain a topic as they take turns, and how to elaborate meaning through gesture, intonation, and timing. Further, communication is a social act requiring an understanding of how a particular society expects language to be used. For example, in some cultures infants' vocalizations are responded to at any time, even if they interrupt adult conversation; in other cultures such interruption would be ignored or punished. **Pragmatics** refers to the function of language in communication.

It is important to note that the categories of language described above have been invented by scientists for their convenience. Only by isolating these components have scientists been able to comprehend the underlying complexity of the total language system. However, young children do not learn language through focused study of these individual language components; their early experience of spoken language does not provide isolated lessons in grammar or drill in new vocabulary. Infants experience language as a totality in social contexts, and all components of language emerge simultaneously. But how does this occur? We turn to this question next.

Theories of Language Development

A comprehensive theory of language development must somehow explain how this multifaceted system emerges in the natural ecology of early childhood. To do this, it must account for certain givens:

- Language is learned by all normal children.
- There are individual differences among children in language development (Nelson, 1981b; Rice, 1989).
- Language competency develops very rapidly as compared to other areas such as intellectual and social competency.
- Language is *generative*. That is, children don't simply repeat phrases that they have heard: They create unique sequences of words to express their meanings.

Attempts to explain these and other givens concerning the development of language can be broadly divided into two theoretical perspectives: learning theory and nativist theory.

The Learning Explanation of Language Acquisition

> *From the time Leshonda was just a few weeks old, she and her mother have played a game that has no beginning and no end; the only thing that changes is who starts the game. For instance, at 10 months, one brief episode of the game sounds like this:*
>
> LESHONDA: *Bababeeeeooo*
> KEISHA: *Beeoo, beeoo . . . . . beeoo to you too!*
> LESHONDA: *Beeoobebebebebe . . . . bebe*
> *Keisha smiles, touches Leshonda's nose, and says:*
> *Yes, you are a beautiful baby!*
> *Leshonda giggles, turns her head away, and babbles:*
> *babababababababababababababa . . .*

In this exchange, Leshonda's utterances get longer and Keisha's responses seem to reinforce them. Further, the similarity in sound sequences made by mother and daughter suggest that they are imitating each other. Do children acquire language by the same learning principles that have been used to explain other aspects of their behavior?

Reinforcement and Shaping   From the operant learning perspective, verbal behavior is no different from any other behavior. Caregivers and tutors take the cooing and babbling of the prelinguistic infant and shape it into words and sentences. In his classic book *Verbal Behavior* (1957), which applied learning theory to the acquisition of language, B. F. Skinner wrote, "A child acquires verbal behavior when relatively unpatterned vocalizations, selectively reinforced, assume forms which produce appropriate consequences in a given verbal community" (1957, p. 31). The acceptable sounds (or phonemes) of a particular language are reinforced so the child persists with them; irrelevant sounds are not reinforced so the child stops using them. Strings of sounds are shaped to approximate words and strings of words are shaped to approximate sentences.

However, language acquisition is far more complicated than Skinner's shaping explanation suggests. One flaw with the theory involves the vigilance that would be required of parents in doing all of that shaping. Although parents certainly respond to their children's vocalizations in a variety of ways, there is no evidence that they actually reinforce their children for the *form* of their language production. For example, parents, who eagerly anticipate their child's first "dada," are unlikely to reinforce the first utterances of "da." They typically withhold reinforcement of "da" until they hear the first "dada." More importantly, it has been estimated that by kindergarten age, the average child's vocabulary includes approximately 14,000 words (Templin, 1957). Shaping 14,000 words one at a time is a formidable task, even for the most dedicated parents.

Parents are more likely to reinforce their children for the accuracy of their messages than for proper syntax (Brown, 1973). For instance, if a child says "food allgone" when some food remains on his plate, reinforcement is unlikely since the statement is blatantly inaccurate. If, however, the child says "food allgone" after eating all of the food, this time the parents are likely to reinforce the child. The less-than-perfect syntax is not an issue in either case. Parents do, of course, occasionally correct their children's pronunciation, choice of words, and grammar. But such parental tutoring is infrequent and cannot possibly account for the speed at which babies learn all components of language.

Modeling and Imitation The role of imitation in language acquisition is far more complex than the role of reinforcement. Clearly, young children are incapable of imitating the long and complex sentences they hear adults speak. Even when adults simplify their sentences as they speak directly to children (Snow, 1972), the complexity is still well beyond what a young child can imitate. Further, children sequence words very differently than adults. With this in mind, we should consider whether imitation plays a role in the child's learning of language.

Albert Bandura (1989), the principal theorist of social learning theory, recognizes that language is generative—that children must learn a set of rules that allows them to produce novel yet syntactically correct phrases and sentences—but the source of the rules, he claims, is modeling:

> It is mainly through observational learning that children extract syntactic rules from the speech they hear around them. Once they acquire syntactic rules they can generate new sentences they have never heard. (p. 11)

According to Bandura, when parents speak in the presence of their child, they make considerable effort to design their speech to facilitate imitative learning. He points to parents' use of *expansion* and *recasting* of their child's utterances as variations on simple modeling. In **expansion**, parents restate their child's utterance with the addition of missing words and more complex linguistic elements. For example, when Leshonda babbles "dadadabeebee," Keisha might creatively expand the babble to "Yes, *daddy be* home soon!" One study (Penner, 1987) demonstrated that parents tend to follow their children's ungrammatical statements with expansions, suggesting that although parents do not reinforce their children's utterances for grammatical correctness, they do react in systematic ways that may improve language learning.

In **recasting**, parents restate the child's utterance into a new syntactic form without changing its meaning. For example, if the child says "I see cat o'dere," the parent might respond "Where do you see the cat?" Katherine Nelson (1977) demonstrated that this kind of exchange promotes children's mastery of advanced syntactic forms. Bandura believes that when parents use these techniques in the natural flow of conversation, they tend to capture their children's attention and encourage them to improve their linguistic competence (Bandura, 1989). Although the facilitative effects of such creative approaches to parental modeling have not been firmly established, their frequency in the natural speech of parents suggests that further study of their effects is warranted.

A P P L I C A T I O N

Expanding and Recasting Your Baby's Sentences

Most parents expand and recast their baby's speech naturally. There is no reason to believe that increasing the rate at which you perform these and other techniques (such as imitation) will promote more rapid or effective language learning.

The best way to promote early language development is to talk to your baby frequently, identifying objects and narrating your activities as if your baby were listening to every word. Respond to your baby's babble with similar sounding words and phrases; respond to her first meaningful words with short phrases and signal your understanding. Avoid correcting your baby's pronunciation or grammar.

The Nativist Explanation of Language Acquisition

In the same year that Skinner published *Verbal Behavior,* Noam Chomsky published *Syntactic Structures* (1957), a book that vigorously challenged Skinner's perspective and revolutionized our thinking about the development of language. Chomsky argued that all children master their native language in a virtually identical developmental sequence. He believed that we are biologically programmed to learn language; all children need is exposure to adult usage during childhood. Chomsky's theory is called the nativist explanation.

David McNeil (1970) elaborated Chomsky's ideas by describing an inborn faculty he called the **language acquisition device (LAD)**, the sole purpose of which is to discern a language's basic rules. For instance, a rule in standard English is that, in most instances, a verb can be changed from present tense to past tense by adding *ed* to the end (*call, called*). A rule of phonology indicates that the sound "p" cannot be followed by "z."

The child gathers samples of language simply by listening to what is said to him and from conversations overheard. The LAD, like a computer, studies the samples and forms hypotheses about the language's rule structure. The child tests these hypotheses by using them to generate novel utterances and then monitoring a listener's reactions. To the extent that the listener appears to understand the utterance, the child's hypothesis is confirmed. Over time, the child refines his hypotheses through continued testing and monitoring until he has mastered all of the rules.

The nativist perspective on language acquisition has been criticized for several alleged shortcomings. Michael Maratsos (1983) has argued that this perspective fails to recognize the active nature of children's efforts to master language. He believes that children, unlike computers, are *self-motivated* to acquire language to help them communicate their thoughts and ideas to others; they actively engage in conversation to improve their ability to communicate.

A more important criticism of the nativist perspective is its failure to recognize the effects of the environment on language acquisition. When information is fed into a computer, the input must be organized before the computer can process it. Similarly, one might expect that the quality of children's experience of language might affect the LAD's ability to study the language and discern its rule structure. For example, a father who consistently imitates, expands, and recasts his child's sentences may help the child to focus on specific phrases and their functions. Differences in the quality of language experienced by children might result in individual differences in language acquisition. The failure of nativists to specify the types of input required for optimal language development is a major limitation of this theory for those who deal with children.

A P P L I C A T I O N

Beyond the LAD

While nativists assume that infants have a built-in capability for learning a language, we do not know this as a fact. Even if we were certain that LAD exists, parents could not assume that it is automatic or infallible. The LAD is not an inborn knowledge of a language; it is a way of learning a language — any language — that it is exposed to. Like all computers, the output from the LAD can be no better than the input to the LAD. For optimal development, young children must be given extensive opportunities to hear their language spoken in its proper form and to experiment by producing their own utterances in conversation with competent speakers. This requires parents who are prepared to engage their children in spirited conversation — beginning with their infant's "ga ga goo goo" and continuing through their adolescent's irritating polemics.

The Course of Infant Language Development

Language develops in three phases during the first two years: prespeech (birth–10 months), the emergence of naming (10–18 months), and the emergence of the first sentences (18–24 months).

Prespeech (Birth–10 Months)

Although parents tend to date the origin of language from their child's first "mama" or "dada" late in the first year, critical developments from birth to 10 months prepare the child to understand and speak the language.

Perception of Speech Sounds Before a child can learn language, she must be able to perceive the differences among the speech sounds of her native language. As described in Chapter 6, the relatively advanced development of auditory perception in early infancy is fundamental to this process. More specifically, neonates are particularly sensitive to the sounds of the human voice and discriminate most and possibly all of the different sounds that occur in human languages (Aslin et al., 1983; Bates, O'Connell, & Shore, 1987).

Since every known language uses only a subset of all possible sounds, infants are required to learn only the subset of phonemes specific to their own language. Indeed, late in the first year infants gradually lose their ability to discriminate between sounds that do not signal changes of meaning in their native language (Werker, Gilbert, Humphrey, & Tees, 1981; Werker & Tees, 1984). Once they learn their native language's phonemes, they can begin to focus on identifying words and their meanings.

When a caregiver speaks to a young infant, the infant both hears the sounds of the words and sees the physical movements of the speaker's lips. There is evidence that young infants have some understanding of the relationship between the two: Studies of three- to five-month-old infants have shown that they practice a primitive form of lip-reading. Infants preferred to look at a film of a human mouth making an "ooo" or an "eee" sound as compared to a mouth making movements that did not match the sound produced (Kuhl & Meltzoff, 1982, 1984).

Production of Speech Sounds A child's first vocalizations take the form of crying, which effectively signals discomfort and pain. By six weeks infants begin to extend their repertoire by producing long vowel sounds, or **cooing**. By about five months cooing expands into a form of vocal play that becomes quite entertaining. Most important, around the middle of the first year babies begin to make sounds specific to the native language (Boysson-Bardies, Sagart, & Durand, 1984).

By five to six months infants start making consonant sounds, attempting to match many of the sounds they have been hearing adults make (Bates et al., 1987). An infant's early combinations of consonants and vowel sounds are referred to as **babbling**. Babbling typically begins between the sixth and tenth month and continues even after babies have begun to produce intelligible speech. Although developmentalists generally believe that the first appearance of babbling is genetically determined, its further development and differentiation is subject to environmental input. This conclusion is partially based on studies of deaf babies who receive little or no feedback for the sounds they produce. Deaf babies begin babbling at about the same time as hearing babies, but they don't continue—presumably because of the lack of auditory feedback (Stoel-Gammon & Otomo, 1986). In contrast, the quantity of hearing infants' babbling can be increased by modeling and reinforcement (Dodd, 1972; Todd & Palmer, 1968).

Infants suddenly begin repeating consonant–vowel sequences such as "mama" and "dada," called *canonical babbling*, somewhere between 6 and 10 months. Although parents welcome these consonant–vowel sequences as the long-anticipated first meaningful words, careful study of the context of their first occurrence suggests that these sounds do not refer to anyone and have no meaning (Bates et al., 1987).

The babbling of some babies comes to sound more and more like sentences from adult language (Dore, 1975), a phenomenon that has been described as "learning the tune before the words" (Bates et al., 1987). The relationship of this increasingly sophisticated babbling to the development of words and sentences is not clearly understood. Babbling is, therefore, best thought of as a warm-up or preparatory phase that provides some but not all of the elements necessary for language development.

Development of Gestures   Another important form of prelinguistic communication — gesturing — emerges around 9 to 10 months (Bates, Camaioni, & Volterra, 1975). The infant begins to gesture by using **performatives**, nonverbal signals that convey requests to adults and direct adult attention to objects and events. The infant's first performatives involve showing and giving objects to caregivers to elicit their attention. Some infants elaborate by fussing, looking back and forth between the adult and the desired object, and — in rare instances — by physically nudging the adult in the direction of the object. One study (Acredelo & Goodwyn, 1988) indicated that infants use performatives frequently in their interaction with caregivers to communicate a great variety of objects, desires, and states. Table 7.2 summarizes how some of these performatives are used and their age of appearance.

TABLE 7.2

Five Categories of Symbolic Gestures

Category and Examples	Mean Age of Onset*
Object "Flower": sniff "Dog": panting "Airplane": arms out	13.5
Request "Out": know-turn gesture "Nurse": pats mother's chest "Food": smacks lips	12.9
Attributes "Hot": blow or wave hand "Many": wave hand back and forth "Big": raise arms	12.4
Reply "I don't know": open palms	14.1
Event "Baseball game": clapping	13.0

SOURCE: *Adapted with permission from Acredelo & Goodwyn, "Symbolic Gesturing in Normal Human Infants,"* Child Development, *59, 1988. © The Society for Research in Child Development, Inc.*

Age rounded to nearest tenth of month

The first use of performatives precedes the first appearance of *pointing* at about 11 months (Bates et al., 1987). Pointing—the fundamental act of reference—emerges during the second year, improving the infant's ability to draw the parent's attention to desired objects (Desrochers, Ricard, & Décarie, 1993). Taken together, these prelinguistic gestures show the infant's newfound ability (and motivation) for intentional communication. Communication by gesture continues to develop after the onset of productive speech. Infants expand their use of gestures if their parents react as if their infants were speaking to them.

Conversing in Prespeech   As early as the third or fourth month, parents and their infants begin to engage in **pseudodialogues**, or mock conversations without words. Pseudodialogues are driven primarily by parents, who listen for pauses in the infant's cooing and/or babbling, elicit attention, talk to the baby, and patiently wait for or stimulate a vocal response. At first infants are passive partners in the conversation, but they gradually adopt a more active role as they discover the potential for parental reinforcement. In the second half of the first year this interaction often takes the form of *conventional infant games*, such as pat-a-cake and peek-a-boo. The infant's improvement with performatives, pointing, and imitation facilitates a more active infant role in this early conversation. None of this would happen without facilitating efforts of parents over a period of several months. Sensitive parental vocal stimulation early in infancy gradually seduces the infant into a more active role later in the first year. Parental responsiveness to the infant's prespeech behavior in the context of pseudodialogues allows the infant to feel that he can affect the behavior of the adult (Bruner, 1977).

Naming: The First Word and Beyond (10–18 Months)

Parents report their infant's first comprehensible spoken word anywhere between 8 and 18 months, but typically in the eleventh or twelfth month (Clarke, 1983). Many of these reports, however, merely indicate that parents have heard an approximation of a familiar word such as *mama*, with little concern about the symbolic value of that word. Infants begin using words to name objects by about 13 months (Bates et al., 1987).

Fast-Mapping and the Acquisition of New Words   The first use of words with symbolic reference marks an important step forward. After spending many months developing sensorimotor concepts of objects and actions, infants are now ready to associate particular sequences of sounds with these concepts. For example, the sequence of the "d," "o," and "g" sounds refers to the family pet. This process is known as **fast-mapping** and indicates that words, both heard and spoken, begin to have *referential meaning* for the infant. *Fast-mapping* is an appropriate term considering that the average child learns approximately nine new words per day in early childhood (Clarke, 1983).

Although the infant's first words tend to be names of manipulable objects that play a practical role in the infant's daily routine (for example, *doggie, cookie, spoon*), there appear to be stylistic differences in the development of the first vocabulary. Katherine Nelson (1973, 1981a) has described two distinctive approaches to fast-mapping in her study of children's first 50 words. Some children tended toward a **referential style**, emphasizing names of common objects, while others adopted a more **expressive style**, containing diverse instances of pronouns, adverbs, prepositions and even some phrases like "gimme dat," "stop it," and "I want it." The expressive style appears to focus more on engaging the parents in social interaction.

No matter which style is preferred, vocabulary develops quite slowly until the middle of the second year. Then comes a burst of new words for the next few weeks and months. This rapid expansion of vocabulary sets the stage for the first combinations of words into sentences.

The Holophrase A baby's single word may express a good deal more meaning than is normally attributed to just one word. This rich interpretation—favored by most parents—is particularly compelling when the single word is accompanied by gestures and performatives: "Dat!" for example, accompanied by pointing and gazing toward a rattle, suggests "Give that rattle to me now!" This phenomenon, the expression of a complete thought with a single word, has been termed the **holophrase**. Although it is not clear whether a child's first words actually represent more complete thoughts, parents who *believe* that their baby is speaking in holophrases are likely to respond with expansions and other conversation-provoking responses.

First Word Combinations (18–22 Months)

Children typically combine words for the first time at about 20 months (Bates et al., 1987). Regardless of their native language, children use these two-word combinations to express a highly similar core of meanings (Braine, 1976; Slobin, 1973). In English, for example, common two-word utterances express the following meanings:

Possession	"My toy."
Location	"Book up."
Existence	"Allgone milk."
Question	"Where mama?"
Agent-action	"Mommy go."
Action-direct object	"See doggie."

Although children of different cultures express common meanings in their first two-word combinations, there is little evidence of a universal structure in these utterances (Braine, 1976). One way to describe these patterns is by the term **telegraphic speech**. The term aptly describes the tendency of children between 18 months and 30 months to omit less important words (such as *the* and *a, in* and *on, am* and *will*) from their speech. A sample of Heather's utterances just after her second birthday illustrates the telegram-like nature of speech at this age:

"Mama me toy-toy."
"Doggie bite cookie."
"Put dolly potty."
"Baby go nite-nite."

The milestones in language development in the first two years are summarized in Table 7.3.

Facilitating Early Language Development

At 14 months, Leshonda has a vocabulary of 7 words: "da" (dog), "mama" (mother), "foos" (food), "mik" (milk), "wawa" (water), "ba" (bottle), and "ge" (get). A typical conversation with her mother goes as follows:

LESHONDA: ge . . . . ge

KEISHA: What you want baby? Get milk? Get bottle? What you want girl?

TABLE 7.3

Milestones in Early Language Development

Prespeech (birth–10 months)	
0–4 weeks	Neonates discriminate among all possible speech sounds
6 weeks	Cooing (long vowel sounds) begins
3–4 months	Babbling with consonants begins
6–10 months	Canonical babbling of "mama" and "dada," but without reference
9 months	Responds to the word *No!*
9–10 months	First use of gestures; performatives used as nonverbal signals to direct the attention of adults and to make requests

Naming (10–18 months)	
11–12 months	Parents report hearing first word
13 months	Developmentalists report first word with reference
15–18 months	Single words suggest holophrases, especially when accompanied by gestures
18 months	Fast-mapping begins and vocabulary expands rapidly
20 months	First two-word combinations; expressive vocabulary approaches 50–60 words

SOURCE: *Adapted from Rovee-Collier, 1987*

LESHONDA: mik, mik, mik . . .

KEISHA: Oh, you want some milk! Milk, milk, milk. That's what you want. Leshonda gonna get milk. Leshonda likes milk! Leshonda likes milk very much (*rising tone*).

We know that children develop prespeech and productive language at optimal rates only when a linguistically competent adult participates (Hoff-Ginsberg, 1986). Parents in all cultures have a special way of talking to babies and young children (Ferguson, 1977; Grieser & Kuhl, 1988; Snow, 1972): They use shorter sentences, higher pitch, exaggerated intonation (high to low), simplified syntax, more repetitions (including expansions and recastings), and a vocabulary that makes frequent reference to concrete objects. They also slow their speech and tranform many object names to end in the "y" sound, as when they change *Dad* to *Daddy* or *dog* to *doggie*. These speech modifications are collectively called **motherese** or baby talk. However, we now recognize that the term *motherese* is misleading in that virtually all adults—mothers and fathers, parents and nonparents— modify their use of language extensively with young children (Golinkoff & Ames, 1979; Jacobson, Boersma, Fields, & Olson, 1983).

Motherese appears to facilitate language development by drawing the infant's attention to the parent's voice (Fernald, 1985; Fernald & Kuhl, 1987) and by reducing adult speech to bite-sized pieces that the infant can assimilate. Compare the following two sentences from the point of view of an infant who is trying to learn the basic rules of language:

Typical adult speech "Here is the rattle that you like so much! Would you like to take it out of my hand?"

Motherese: "Baby want rattle? Here! Take it! Take it! That's my girl!"

Compared to the typical adult speech, the motherese provides bite-sized chunks, greater simplicity of ideas, redundancy, and critical pauses and uses of intonation to help the infant identify phrases—the basic units of grammar. In short, motherese seems tailor-made for the infant's limited capacity for information processing. But does motherese work?

Research suggests that motherese promotes the development of specific aspects of infants' language, including their ability to ask questions (Nelson, 1977), to take turns in conversation (Snow & Fergusen, 1977), and to use auxiliaries and new verb forms (Hoff-Ginsberg, 1985, 1986). We still don't know whether individual differences in parents' use of motherese result in differences in the rate of children's language development. However, we do know that depressed mothers are less likely to use motherese with their young infants, possibly placing them at greater risk of language and personality disturbance (Bettes, 1988).

Although we need to further research the function of motherese, it is clear that its structure is designed to promote the pattern of language interaction between parent and infant through the early months of prespeech and to maintain the parent's role in facilitating the development of conversational language in the second year. Remember that although motherese provides a simplified input, it is still up to the infant to process the input, develop hypotheses about the structure of the language, and produce intelligible speech as output.

Looking Back

We have traced the parallel emergence of cognitive and language development in infancy. Under optimal conditions, the infant progresses from no knowledge and simple reflex behaviors to mastery of action-oriented problem solving in the world of physical objects. The infant also evolves from communicating its needs solely through crying to conversing with comprehension and production of intelligible language. Although the foundation for these extraordinary changes appears to be inborn, we have noted the significant effects that parents and other caregivers may have on their infant's progress through the stages and phases of cognitive and language development.

C H A P T E R   R E V I E W

LEARNING   Learning refers to any relatively permanent change in behavior or knowledge resulting from experience or practice. Infants engage in several types of learning: They use habituation to adapt to the diversity and intensity of stimulation in natural settings and to "shut down" when they become overloaded. Higher rates of habituation in infancy are associated with higher intellectual performance later in childhood.

CLASSICAL CONDITIONING   In classical conditioning, infants learn to respond to different stimuli as if they were equivalent, engendering a sense of orderliness and sequence in their sensory experience. Newborns can be classically conditioned; conditionability increases rapidly in the first months of life.

OPERANT CONDITIONING   Although newborns can be operantly conditioned, parents shape infants' behaviors slowly over long periods of time. Infants who learn that they can affect their environment may develop a sense of mastery; those who do not may develop a sense of helplessness.

OBSERVATIONAL LEARNING Piaget believed that infants' imitation of modeled behavior develops gradually over the first two years, culminating in deferred imitation. Other researchers have shown that very young infants imitate simple gestures and expressions. While infants' imitation may be imprecise, it plays an important role in initiating and sustaining interactions between parents and their babies.

MEMORY Memory involves encoding (storing learned information) and retrieval (calling up stored information). We retrieve by recognition (responding to cues) and by recall (remembering without cues). While neonates show some short-term memory when they learn by habituating and by conditioning, longer-term memory does not emerge until the end of the first month and then develops more rapidly during the next few months.

PIAGET Piaget portrayed infants as active, requiring no stimulation to become active, nor reinforcement to stay active. He suggests that cognitive development is the process by which infants adapt to the world of physical objects, with each object perceived as a problem to be solved. Schemas organize infants' manipulations and explorations of objects during the sensorimotor period.

SUBSTAGES Infants' reflexes in the first month develop into primary circular reactions (1–4 months) that direct simple movements for the sake of movement. Primary circular reactions develop into secondary circular reactions (4–8 months) that direct simple movements to affect the environment. Toward the end of the first year, infants sequence schemas to solve means–ends problems. In the second year, they learn to experiment with their schemas to develop more flexible problem solving. By the end of the second year, mental symbols (images) enable them to solve problems by mental combinations. Infants develop a sense of object permanence and the ability to imitate in a stagelike progression during the first two years.

COMPONENTS Scientists have focused their research and theory on distinct components of language: phonology, morphology, semantics, syntax, and pragmatics. However, infants do not experience or learn language in components; they experience language as a totality in social contexts, and all components of language emerge simultaneously.

LEARNING EXPLANATION Skinner argued that children learn language by the same principles that govern the learning of other behaviors: Acceptable sounds and strings of sounds are reinforced; unacceptable utterances are not reinforced. However, research shows that parents more likely to reinforce their children for the accuracy of their messages than for proper syntax.

MODELING AND IMITATION Bandura argues that children learn language by observing their parents' use of language and deriving the rules for producing their own utterances. Parents use expansion and recasting to facilitate their children's imitation of their language.

NATIVIST EXPLANATION Chomsky argued that all children are biologically programmed to learn language; the only thing they need is exposure to adult usage during childhood. The child's language acquisition device studies the spoken language, derives its rules, and then generates unique utterances.

PHASES Language develops through a series of phases in infancy: *Prespeech* (birth–10 months) includes perceiving and producing phonemes and making gestures; *naming* (10–18 months) begins with the first meaningful word and expands to fast-mapping; *two-word combinations* (18–22 months) involves the child's efforts to string together words to express common meanings.

MOTHERESE Adults in all cultures have a special way of talking to babies and young children called motherese. Motherese appears to facilitate language development by drawing the infant's attention to the parent's voice and breaking down adult speech into bite-size pieces that the infant can process.

Key Terms

learning	adaptation	tertiary circular reactions
observational learning	sensorimotor stage	symbol
memory	schema	symbolic representation
encoding	primary circular reactions (PCRs)	image
retrieval	secondary circular reactions (SCRs)	deferred imitation
recognition	object permanence	word
recall	coordinated secondary circular reactions	comprehension

production	recasting	referential style
phonemes	language acquisition device (LAD)	expressive style
morphemes	cooing	holophrase
semantics	babbling	telegraphic speech
syntax	performatives	motherese
pragmatics	pseudodialogues	
expansion	fast-mapping	

8

Emotional and Social Development in Infancy

Looking Ahead

- From the first piercing cry, parents are convinced that they know what their infants are feeling. Do infants feel what we think they feel? When do infants begin to feel specific emotions, such as happiness, sadness, disgust, fear, and guilt?

- By the second half of the first year, infants can sense the differences among adults' emotions. How does this affect their mood and behavior?

- Societies have expectations about which emotions are appropriate in various contexts. How do infants learn which emotions should and should not be expressed?

- Parents are often at the mercy of their infant's mood. How can parents influence their infant's mood in routine care?

- From the day they are born, infants show differences in temperament. What are these differences and how do they affect interaction with caregivers?

- Relating to others requires knowing oneself. When do infants develop a sense of self?

- The first interactions of parents and newborns are charged with emotion. Does this have a lasting effect?

- Parents and their infants vary widely in the quality of their relationships. How do these differences evolve and what effects do they have on children's behavior?

- Many fathers seem to be as emotionally involved with their infants as are mothers. Do fathers achieve the same attachment with their babies?

- Many parents use day care for their infants. What effect does day care have on infant development?

hen we watch the first interactions of parents and their new-born baby, it is obvious that something of great significance is taking place. The parents are struggling to understand and interpret their baby's every sound and motion, and the baby seems to be trying to manage the overwhelming onslaught of stimulation. Although they are very differently prepared for what is going on, the parents and the infant are involved in an intensely emotional and distinctly social experience. In this chapter we will examine how infants develop emotionally and socially and the delicate balance of risk and opportunity in that development.

Emotional Development in Infancy

Emotions reflect the outcomes of our transactions with the environment: When our transactions are adaptive, we generally feel positive emotions; when our transactions are maladaptive, we feel negative emotions. These contrasts in adaptation and their emotional consequences are apparent in the early transactions of Leshonda and Heather with their mothers:

> *It is 6 A.M. and Keisha has to wake three-month-old Leshonda to get her to day care by 7:30. She enters the darkness of Leshonda's room, quietly turns on a soft light, leans over the crib, simultaneously caresses Leshonda's foot and the back of her head, and whispers "Leshonda, Sweetie. Time to get up, baby. Time to get up." She massages Leshonda's back until she feels her baby's first movement and responds to that first stir with a gentle caress. Leshonda relaxes and Keisha repeats the caress with a slight increase in rhythm and intensity. "Leshonda is a sleepy baby today," says Keisha in a soft sing-song synchronized to the gentle responsive caress.*
>
> *Leshonda slowly opens her eyes and smiles into the watchful gaze of her mother, who smiles in return. She fusses momentarily as Keisha lifts her smoothly into the familiar warm cuddle. Leshonda calms immediately as she molds against her mother's body. She comes alive on the dressing table—waving her arms and legs rhythmically and smiling frequently at her mother. Her mood stays consistently positive; Keisha seems to anticipate her baby's emotional responses with calming tones and soothing gestures that relieve distress, almost before it begins.*
>
> *Keisha plays with Leshonda at every traffic light on the drive to day care. She accepts the inevitability of day care for her infant, but carefully monitors her daughter's experience. When an unfamiliar caregiver reaches out to accept Leshonda, Keisha politely declines, walking instead toward Mrs. Jefferson, a familiar caregiver who has shown interest in Leshonda since her first day. Mrs. Jefferson smiles broadly as they approach. Although Keisha is late, she*

takes the time to alert the caregiver to Leshonda's present mood and slight sniffle. One last warm cuddle, and Keisha gives her baby to Mrs. Jefferson. Leshonda smiles at her mother, quickly turns and smiles at Mrs. Jefferson, and cuddles into her arms. Keisha leaves for work with an image that would carry her through the day, but this is never going to be easy.

It is 6:15 A.M., and Barbara has overslept again. She hurries into Heather's room, turns on the bright ceiling light, and wakes Heather with a shout and a shake. Heather startles and protests with a weak cry, but her mother's only response is to mutter "Oh, shut up," while digging a diaper out of the drawer. Working with a cool efficiency to get the job done quickly, she pulls off the old diaper and flips up Heather's legs to slip on the new diaper. Heather alternates between mild fussing and intense crying. Barbara's only response is to clench her teeth and work faster as the crying intensifies.

In less than 45 minutes, Heather is plopped and secured in her car seat in the backseat of the car on her way to the day-care center. There, they are met at the entrance by a stranger—the fifth different person in the last five days. Neither woman speaks or smiles as Barbara hands Heather over and they walk away from each other. Heather cries throughout the transition, but no one is listening.

Barbara cares *for* but does not care *about* her infant. There is no interaction, no reciprocity, no sharing of emotion. A precise sequence of physical manipulations prepares Heather to meet the daily minimum intake standards of the day-care center.

At three months of age, Heather and Leshonda have a few things in common. They were born just a few hours apart to working mothers who purchase substitute care in day-care centers. However, their experiences during their first three months have been very different. Leshonda spends most of her time smiling and taking in everything there is to see; Heather is typically scowling or crying. Leshonda and Heather also differ dramatically in their interactions with their mothers and other caregivers. Keisha interacts sensitively *with* Leshonda and actively monitors the quality of her substitute care; Barbara tends to Heather much the same way she washes and dries the dishes, with little emotional involvement or responsiveness and no interest in her daughter's emotional needs when not in her care.

These differences between Leshonda's and Heather's early experiences raise a number of interesting questions:

- Do infants feel what we think they feel? Do infants' outward facial expressions and behaviors tell us what they are feeling on the inside?
- When do infants begin to feel specific emotions such as distress, happiness, disgust, surprise, sadness, fear, guilt, or jealousy?
- Do infants and caregivers read each other's emotional signals and affect each other's emotions?
- Finally, and perhaps most important, does the quality of infants' early emotional experiences affect the development of their later relationships?

This chapter will attempt to answer these questions. We begin with a consideration of the major contemporary theories of emotional development in infancy.

Theories of Emotional Development

Most contemporary thinking and research in the area of emotional development is organized around one of two very different theories: *Discrete emotions theory* emphasizes the
forces of nature, while *cognitive emotions theory* emphasizes the effects of nurture. We will
consider these theories in some detail.

Discrete Emotions Theory

Charles Darwin, the father of the theory of evolution, proposed that certain basic emotions are innate and universal in both humans and animals (Darwin, 1872). Darwin
believed that emotions serve an adaptive purpose critical to the survival of the species:
Emotions allow infants to communicate their needs for nurturance and protection
to their caregivers. Darwin's early thinking on this subject has evolved into a highly
provocative theory known as the discrete emotions theory (Izard & Malatesta, 1987;
Malatesta, Culver, Tesman, & Shepard, 1989). **Discrete emotions theory** assumes that
human infants are innately preadapted to experience discrete emotions according to an
inborn, biologically determined timetable.

According to this theory each discrete emotion consists of three components:

1. A *neural* component, which includes a specific pathway and region in the autonomic nervous system associated with each discrete emotion.
2. A *motor-expressive* component, which includes patterns of observable facial, vocal, and bodily expressions that signal the quality and intensity of the emotion
   to others.
3. A *mental processes* component, which involves the conscious (and perhaps unconscious) subjective feelings of the emotion, that organizes and motivates
   behavior.

According to the discrete emotions theory, the experience of an emotion begins with
a biologically and psychologically meaningful stimulus such as a loud noise. The stimulus activates preadapted "wiring" in the autonomic nervous system specific to that emotion. The nervous system then sends signals to the muscles, resulting in the appropriate
facial expression. Contraction of the facial muscles produces its own stimulation of the
nervous system, generating the subjective feeling of the emotion. This sequence is illustrated in Figure 8.1.

In discrete emotions theory, infants' facial expressions reflect their subjective emotional experience, regardless of their age. Thus a smiling baby feels happy, a crying baby
feels distress. These cues allow caregivers to read the emotional state of infants and to
respond effectively to their needs. For example, facial expressions of distress or disgust
should alert caregivers to the presence of painful or unpleasant stimuli, which they can
then try to remove. Similarly, a look of interest and a smile should encourage caregivers
to stay close to and interact with the infant, thus promoting social bonding and
attachment.

Cognitive Emotions Theory

Proponents of the second theory of emotions, the **cognitive emotions theory**, assume
that infants are not preadapted for discrete emotions and that the capacity to experience
and express discrete emotions begins to emerge after two to three months of life (Lewis
& Michalson, 1982, 1983; Sroufe, 1979). These theorists maintain that the experience of

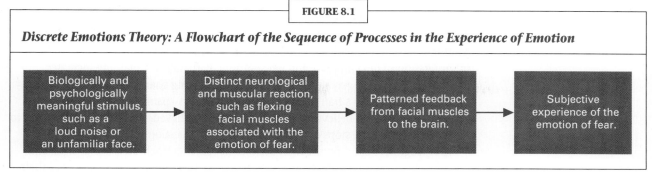

FIGURE 8.1

Discrete Emotions Theory: A Flowchart of the Sequence of Processes in the Experience of Emotion

SOURCE: *Adapted from Malatesta, Culver, Tesman, & Shepard, 1989*

discrete emotions is tied to the emergence of elementary forms of cognitive capability, including the ability to differentiate oneself from others, a development that doesn't occur until the second half of the first year.

In direct contrast to discrete emotions theory, cognitive emotions theory assumes there is no relationship between expressive behaviors and the subjective feeling of emotion in early infancy (Lewis & Michalson, 1982, 1983). Although newborns and young infants display primitive signs of distress or well-being, we have no way of knowing what they really feel subjectively.

But most parents interact with their infants as if they are discrete emotions theorists. They believe that they can interpret their baby's feelings by reading the newborn's facial expressions and behavior. Once parents have made their interpretation, they continue to act as if their interpretation is valid. For example, when a mother sees her newborn make what the mother believes to be a sad face, she imitates her baby by making an even sadder face and then soothes the baby's alleged sadness. By two to three months, the effects of parents' rich interpretations of their infants' expressions teach the baby what feelings are appropriate in particular situations. Consider the different responses of Keisha, Barbara, and Maria as each mother approaches her *mildly* distressed infant:

> *Keisha reads fear in three-week-old Leshonda's teary eyes and, in a soothing voice says, "Poor baby, you look so scared. Did you have a bad dream?" She rocks Leshonda for several minutes, asking her what has frightened her. "Did you wake up all alone and get scared? Poooor baby. Mama wasn't here and you got scared." After just a few seconds, Leshonda quiets and smiles up at her mother.*

> *Barbara, without looking at one-month-old Heather, sighs pathetically. "Are you pissed at me again? Can't you get off my back just for a minute?" As Heather continues to whimper, Barbara shouts, "Wipe that look off your face or I'll give you something to be mad about!"*

> *Carlos, at six weeks, whimpers softly as Maria takes him in her arms. She rocks him frantically and strokes his head to make the pain go away. "What's hurting you?" she says over and over. "Does your tummy hurt? Is your diaper too tight? Did I stick you with the pin?" After several minutes of stroking and questioning, Carlos takes a deep breath, stops crying, and falls asleep.*

Despite the ambiguous nature of each infant's behavior, each mother has her own notion of what her baby is trying to tell her and each behaves accordingly. Keisha's soothing calms Leshonda's alleged fear, and Leshonda's smile reinforces her mother's interpretation of her emotions and her soothing. Barbara's complaining increases Heather's supposed anger, and Heather's increased crying changes her mother's annoyance into anger. Maria's frantic rocking soothes Carlos's "pain," and Carlos's falling asleep causes Maria to believe that the pain has been relieved. Ironically, Carlos seems to have learned that if he stops crying, the stroking and questioning will go away.

Thus, cognitive emotion theorists believe that parents teach their babies what emotions to feel in various contexts, and their babies, in turn, inadvertently reinforce their parents' teachings. As infants' perceptual and cognitive abilities improve over the first few months of life, their ability to know the right emotion to feel in particular contexts improves rapidly. Discrete emotions theorists do not reject the nurturing effects of socialization on emotional development, but view these forces as superimposed on the preadapted discrete emotions supplied by nature.

Both discrete and cognitive emotions theories have stimulated research on emotional development in infancy. We turn now to the answers that this research has provided with respect to our questions about the nature of emotional development in infancy.

A   P   P   L   I   C   A   T   I   O   N

Approaching an Unfamiliar Baby

Approaching a baby with whom you have not previously interacted can be awkward, particularly after the baby is six months old when many show wariness to strangers. You may reduce stranger anxiety by allowing the baby to check you out before making your approach. If possible, engage in some positive conversation with the parent. Then, approach the baby slowly, avoiding intrusive behavior such as tickling. Don't try to hold the baby until he or she has had some time to adjust to your closeness and appearance. With older babies, you may increase your acceptance by playing with the infant's toys as the mother would (Gunnar, 1980).

Do Infants Feel What We Think They Feel?

According to discrete emotions theory, the ability to feel and express the discrete emotions of interest, distress, and disgust is present at birth: *Interest* can be elicited by novelty or movement, *distress* by painful stimulation, and *disgust* by offensive tastes or smells (Izard, Dougherty, & Hembree, 1980). Other emotions will appear (without learning) within a maturationally based timetable during the first months of life. The social smile (indicating joy) can be elicited from three to six weeks by a moving, vocalizing, human face. Anger can be observed at two months during painful medical procedures and by four months as a result of restrained physical movement. Sadness can be reliably identified by three to four months, and fear by seven months on the visual cliff (Gibson & Walk, 1960)(see Chapter 6).

As infants' cognitive abilities become more sophisticated in the second half of the first year, the way they express emotions becomes noticeably more complex. For example, eight-month-olds show different emotional reactions to routine inoculations than two-month-olds do (Izard, Hembree, Dougherty, & Spizzirri, 1983). Prior to six months, this presumably painful stimulus produces intense distress; after six months, it also produces anger. This developmental change is consistent with the concept that infant cogni-

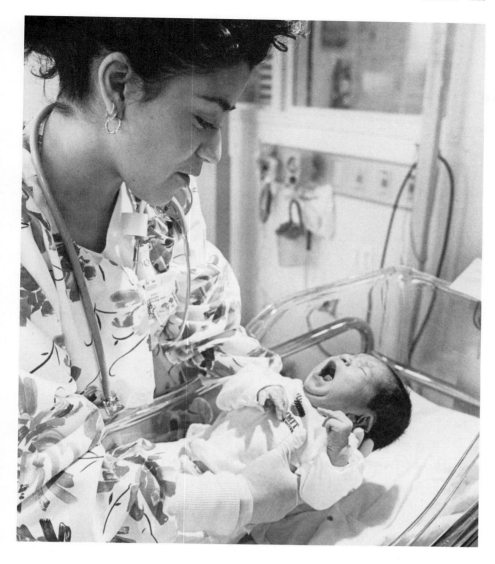

Although this infant's cries are easily identifiable as signs of distress, babies show other facial expressions that are much more ambiguous and difficult to interpret. When a baby smiles is it happy? When the baby is wide-eyed, is it showing interest?

tion has increasingly greater effects on emotions with age. Apparently, older infants have learned to identify the cause of their distress and to direct their emotions toward the source.

The increasing sophistication of the cognitive system late in the first year and into the second year results in the more complex emotions of anxiety, depression, hostility, contempt, love, jealousy, shame, and pride (Izard & Malatesta, 1987). For example, by seven to eight months, some infants display a distinct pattern of **stranger anxiety** by looking away, withdrawing physically, and crying when approached by unfamiliar adults (Emde, Gaensbauer, & Harmon, 1976). Consistent with the increasing influence of cognition late in the first year, stranger anxiety is highly dependent on the nature of the situation: Infants are less likely to react negatively to strangers if their mother is nearby (Clarke-Stewart, 1978; Ross & Goldman, 1977; Trause, 1977) or if they encounter the stranger in their own home (Sroufe, 1977).

Do infants feel what we think they feel? Research generally supports the conclusion that young infants feel a variety of discrete emotions (happiness, distress, and anger) and that the same stimuli that elicit those emotions in more mature children also elicit them

TABLE 8.1

Timetable for the Appearance of Discrete Emotions

Emotion Expressed	Approximate Timing
Interest Nonsocial reflex smile Distress Disgust	At birth
Social smile	4–6 weeks
Anger Surprise Sadness	3–4 months
Fear	5–7 months
Shame, shyness Awareness of self	6–8 months
Contempt Guilt Jealousy	Second year

SOURCE: *Izard & Malatesta, 1987; Malatesta et al., 1989.*

in infants (Izard et al., 1980). By the end of the second year, infants' emotions are highly differentiated and rapidly conforming to the socializing influence of parents and other caregivers. Table 8.1 presents the timetable for the appearance of discrete emotions.

Emotional Transactions Between Infants and Caregivers

The relationship between parents and infants emerges from an infinite series of transactions, most of which take place during routine caregiving. For example, Carlos and his father gradually learned about one another with each diaper change, bath, and middle-of-the-night feeding. These transactions are initiated by either the infant or the parents and are sustained by their respective abilities to read each other's emotional signals. Researchers have studied these respective abilities extensively. We will look first at what researchers have learned about caregivers' ability to read infants' emotions.

Do Caregivers Read Infants' Emotional Signals?   Evidence suggests that adults can reliably identify a range of emotional expressions in infants. Carroll Izard filmed one- to nine-month-old infants in a variety of natural situations and developed slides to illustrate the expressions of happiness, sadness, surprise, interest, fear, contempt, anger, and disgust. When adult subjects were asked to identify the emotion on each slide, they did so accurately. (See Figure 8.2.) They became more accurate after training that emphasized the facial expressions typically associated with particular emotions (Izard et al., 1980).

Unfortunately, the ability to read emotional signals is not universal. In one study, abusive and nonabusive mothers were compared on their ability to identify infants' emotional signals. Abusive mothers were less able than nonabusive mothers to distinguish among infants' emotional signals. Abusive mothers were also more likely to identify negative emotional signals as positive (Kropp & Haynes, 1987). Thus the inability to read emotional signals may be a significant risk factor in child abuse.

A P P L I C A T I O N

Dealing with Infants' Emotions

*I*nfants improve at communicating their feelings to their parents over the first few months, but their signals are often ambiguous. For example, your infant's way of showing pain and anger may be quite similar. Also, your infant's signals may be inconsistent with the physical situation. Suppose that your infant remains highly irritable even after eating and having her diaper changed. Such ambiguity can be frustrating to parents. These suggestions may help:

- Trust your judgment! If you think you know what your baby is telling you, act on it. Being right or wrong is less important than being responsive. You simply cannot be on target every time, and occasional misinterpretations will do no harm.

- Accept the fact that even when you know what your baby is feeling, you often won't know why. If you can't identify the cause, deal with the symptom. For example, if you don't know why your baby is crying, concentrate on soothing; if your baby seems frightened but the cause is unclear, concentrate on making her feel secure.

- Be sensitive to your baby's increasing ability to feel and express emotions. The changes in your baby's signals are often quite subtle, so you must pay close attention.

Do Infants Read Caregivers' Emotional Signals?   Considerable evidence supports the view that infants can read their caregiver's emotional signals—both facial and vocal. Several related studies (Caron, Caron, & MacLean, 1988; Walker-Andrews, 1986; Walker-Andrews & Grolnick, 1983) asked women to read scripted passages to five- and seven-month-old infants. The women were asked to read contrasting emotions (for instance, happy and sad), with and without appropriate facial expressions and tone of voice. As early as five months, the infants could discriminate these contrasting emotions from just the voice component. They could discriminate them by facial expressions at seven months. The investigators speculated that infants may initially discriminate emotional expressions strictly by the sound of the mother's voice, only gradually learning which vocal and facial expressions go together. This view was supported by a study in which seven-month-old infants looked more at a happy face accompanied by a happy voice and an angry face accompanied by an angry voice than presentations of mismatched vocal and facial expressions (Walker-Andrews, 1986).

FIGURE 8.2

Infant Expressions of Different Emotions

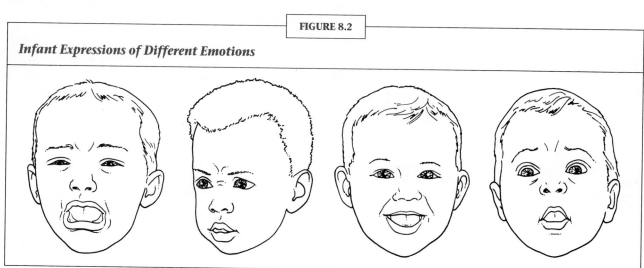

SOURCE: *Based on Izard et al., 1980.*

Although infants apparently can recognize differences in adult signals of emotion, do they respond emotionally to the caregiver's emotional signals? The evidence suggests that they do. In one study, researchers (Haviland & Lelwica, 1987) asked mothers of 10-week-old infants to interact with their babies by displaying a series of contrasting emotions — happiness, sadness, and anger — and in each case to match the emotion with the appropriate facial and vocal expression. The researchers then videotaped the infants' facial expressions. Infants reacted by smiling to their mothers' happiness, by looking angry or becoming immobile to their mothers' display of anger, and by oral behaviors such as thumbsucking to their mothers' sadness. Termine and Izard (1988) extended these findings with nine-month-old infants and happy and sad mothers. Not only did the infants respond in kind to their mothers' emotional displays, but the mood carried over into a subsequent period of play with toys. Infants whose mothers expressed happiness spent more time playing with the toys. Apparently, babies' readings of their mothers' emotions can affect both the quality of their mood and of their play.

In fact, infants appear to be very sensitive to their mothers' signals. Psychologist Tiffany Field (1977) found that when mothers imitated their 3½-month-old's behavior naturally — for instance, by smiling to smiles — the infants responded with increased attention and positive emotion. However, when mothers were instructed to be more intrusive in trying to get their infants' attention — for example, by making sounds and gestures — the infants tended to look away and become upset. The infants appeared to be overwhelmed by the mothers' overstimulating approach.

Interestingly, similar effects have been shown when mothers *fail* to react to their infants' emotional signals. When mothers were totally unresponsive to their six-month-olds' smiling and gazing at them, the infants significantly decreased their signaling (Gusella, Muir, & Tronick, 1988).

If maternal unresponsiveness has a sobering effect on infants, what might be the effect of the more extreme unresponsiveness of depressed mothers? Researchers (Cohn &

Infants not only recognize the differences among their parents' emotions, they also share in those emotions. The mother on the left is joyful and enthusiastic and her positive mood is likely to transfer to her baby. The mother on the right appears to be in a calm and positive mood that is likely to have a calming effect on her baby. Unfortunately, the mother's negative emotions are just as likely to pass to the baby as positive ones.

Tronick, 1983) compared the effects of mothers interacting with their infants in normal and depressed patterns. The infants' behavior varied significantly according to the mothers' expression of emotion. In the "depressed mother" condition infants spent nearly half of their time in protest or wary states; in the "normal mother" condition, infants rarely displayed either of these negative states.

The investigators were also interested in how these two conditions would affect changes of infant state—for instance, from protest to wariness or from playfulness to distraction. "Normal mother" infants typically cycled from brief episodes of positive behavior, to glancing at their mothers, to playfulness when they were engaged with their mothers. In contrast, "depressed mother" infants cycled from wariness, to protest, to looking away. This negative mood pattern tended to carry over into subsequent episodes of interaction with the mother, even though the mother's display of depression was limited to only three minutes. The investigators expressed concern that long-term exposure to depressed caregivers would place infants at risk.

A P P L I C A T I O N

Your Mood and Your Baby's Mood

Your baby becomes increasingly sensitive to his caregiver's moods. He knows what you are feeling by the sound of your voice, by the look on your face, and by the way you interact with him. Your moods are contagious: Your baby will often feel what you feel and carry that mood over into his play. If you tend to be happy and upbeat, your baby is likely to be predominantly happy. If you tend to be depressed, your baby is likely to be depressed.

Your baby will also pick up on other people's moods, including your spouse, siblings, other caregivers, and even strangers. Be particularly sensitive to the characteristic mood of those who help you care for your baby.

Bottom Line: You do not have to be interacting directly with your infant to affect his mood. Your positive or negative interactions with others, as well as your general mood while doing routine tasks, can be contagious. Keep this in mind the next time you lose your temper watching a football game or putting up wallpaper.

Do Caregivers Influence How Infants Express Emotions?   Every society has cultural expectations about which emotions are appropriate in which circumstances and how they should and should not be expressed. These expectations take the form of unwritten **display rules** that must be internalized to guide the socially acceptable expression of emotion (Ekman & Riesen, 1972). Display rules may be thought of as the etiquette of emotional expression. Different cultures prescribe display rules by gender, social class, age, and situation. Parents begin to encourage their children's learning of display rules early in infancy.

Carol Malatesta and her colleagues (Malatesta, Grigoryev, Lamb, Albin, & Culver, 1986; Malatesta & Haviland, 1982) studied how children learn display rules by observing how mothers reacted to the emotional expressions of their three- to six-month-old infants. They found that infants expressed a wide range of emotions, changing their expressions every seven to nine seconds. The mothers responded by attempting to shape the infants' emotional expression: They imitated and modeled positive emotions but actively avoided displaying negative emotions. The investigators interpreted their results as clear evidence of maternal instruction in the facial display of emotion.

In a longitudinal study of two- to seven-month-old infants, Malatesta and her colleagues (1986) showed that mothers were relatively more responsive when their infants showed expressions of interest and relatively less responsive to their infants' expressions of pain; preterm infants' mothers seemed particularly unresponsive to infants' expressions of pain. Not surprisingly, this maternal behavior appeared to influence the infants' behavior: It was associated with an increase in the expression of positive emotion and a decrease in the expression of negative emotion from two to seven months. Mothers of preterm infants engaged in less imitation of their infants' expressions, possibly due to the greater irritability of these infants.

The learning of display rules is complicated by the fact that these rules tend to be highly specific to the behavioral setting. For instance, the rules for displaying emotions at home may be very different from those at the day-care center. In general, however, children learn to deal with this complexity. Research suggests that even as young as two years children can be expected to demonstrate an organized understanding of display rules (Lewis & Michalson, 1983).

A P P L I C A T I O N

Helping Your Infant Learn Display Rules

You can promote your infant's learning of display rules by:

- Maintaining consistent expectations and responding consistently to your baby's emotional expressions within similar situations. For example, if you laugh at your infant giggling as she plays with her food one day, be prepared to do so the next day.

- Helping your infant to understand that the rules may differ from situation to situation. For example, while a clown falling down at the circus is funny, her brother falling down at home is not.

Do Caregivers and Infants Mutually Regulate One Another? You may recall from Chapter 2 that theorist Erik Erikson (1950/1963) described the emotional reciprocity between parent and child as **mutual regulation** (Erikson, 1951). Erikson implied that mutual regulation is essential for healthy personality development. Parents who achieve mutual regulation with their infant foster a **sense of trust** in their infant: a generalized belief that the world is a safe and satisfying place. Where mutual regulation fails, infants learn to **mistrust**.

Edward Tronick and his colleagues (1986) adopted the term and the concept of *mutual regulation* into a model to describe early emotional development. These theorists believe that parent and infant share the goal of achieving a mutually satisfying positive emotional state as a result of their continuous interaction. According to the mutual regulation model,

> . . . the infant, through active deployment of his emotional signals, attempts to control the social environment. When the infant succeeds, positive emotions are generated and the infant gains a sense of effectance. When the infant fails, negative emotions are generated and a sense of ineffectance or helplessness results. The infant's success to some extent depends on the sensitivity—cooperation—of the mother in responding reciprocally to him. Emotions are not magically transferred

from mother to infant but rather the infant generates his own emotions as he processes the emotional input provided by the mother in relation to his own interactive goal. (Tronick, Cohn, & Shea, 1986, p. 12)

The mutual regulation model recognizes the complexity of the task for both mother and infant. Although studies cited in this chapter clearly support the idea that young infants are capable of responding to the caregivers' emotions, the gradual development of this ability suggests that the mother must assume the major responsibility for creating mutual regulation (Field, 1987).

Tiffany Field (1987) says the mother must respond to her baby with *optimal stimulation* and with *arousal modulation*. **Optimal stimulation** is a relative term that recognizes individual differences in infants' thresholds and tolerance for stimulation and the fluctuations of these thresholds for any particular infant during the course of a day. Mothers must learn to read what their babies are trying to tell them about the level of stimulation they can tolerate (or enjoy) at any given time. **Arousal modulation** is a related process by which mothers influence their infants' emotional state to match the emotional requirements of a specific task, such as nursing or a diaper change. It takes just the right emotional touch to calm an agitated baby or arouse a sleepy baby in a particular caregiving context.

Thus competent mothers can learn to match their caregiving behaviors to the rhythm of their babies' emotions—a state referred to as **affective attunement** (Stern, Hofer, Haft, & Dore, 1985). Attunement and nonattunement are illustrated in Figure 8.3. Mother A in the upper graph looks at her infant (solid line) until the infant looks away (dotted line), whereupon she immediately withdraws her gaze. When the infant looks at her again, she looks back. Mother B, however, continues to gaze long after her infant has looked away, apparently causing the baby to minimize the stimulation by looking elsewhere for awhile.

Mothers and their infants generally achieve reliable levels of attunement (or synchrony) by about three months (Lester, Hoffman, & Brazelton, 1985). However, *preterm* babies and their mothers often do not attune. These findings suggest that mutual regulation and affective attunement can be elusive or improbable for mothers and high-risk infants—preterm, low birth weight, small-for-dates—as well as for infants born to

Mother A sensitively adjusts her looking to avoid overstimulating her infant. Mother B insensitively overstimulates her baby and her baby appears to avoid looking at her.
SOURCE: *Adapted from Brazelton, Koslowski, & Main, 1974. Reprinted by permission of Leonard A. Rosenblum and Michael Lewis.*

FIGURE 8.3

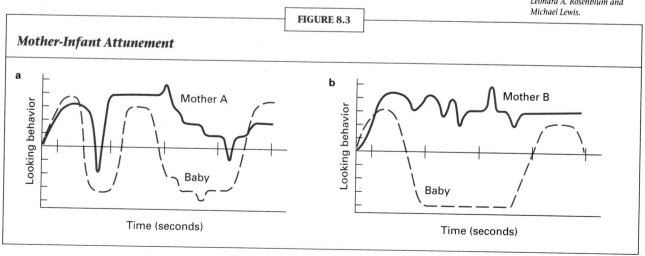

Mother-Infant Attunement

mothers categorized as "high risk" due to young age, poverty, or psychological maladjustment.

Summarizing an extensive body of research on this topic, Field (1987) suggests that high-risk infants display abnormally high or low thresholds for stimulation, with very limited ability to attend or respond to emotional signals from caregivers. In addition, the emotions of high-risk babies are difficult to read. Thus mothers of such infants face a formidable challenge. Mothers of high-risk babies—particularly high-risk mothers of high-risk babies—are likely to time their behaviors inappropriately and provide either too much or too little stimulation (Field, 1987). If the interaction of these mothers and these babies were likened to a dance, it could be said that they spend a lot of time stepping on each other's toes. Heather and her mother Barbara have the bruises to prove it. Field (1987) has argued such infants are predisposed to emotional disturbance.

A P P L I C A T I O N

Dancing with Your Baby

*I*nteracting with your baby is very much like dancing with a partner. While both dancers' movements must be synchronized, one of the partners must take the lead. Parents obviously lead during infancy, at least in most interactions. You lead by knowing how to stimulate your baby without overstimulating, and how to influence your baby's emotions to match a given task. For example, changing a diaper has a different rhythm and tempo than giving a bath. You will need to stimulate your baby for some tasks and calm him for others.

Perhaps most important, dancing successfully requires two motivated partners, both ready and willing to attune to one another. In some instances, this does not happen. For example, it is difficult for a parent to dance with an unresponsive infant or for an infant to dance with a depressed parent. While a parent can compensate by stimulating an unresponsive infant, an infant is clearly at risk with a depressed parent—a situation that calls for professional help.

Temperament

It is 6 A.M. on the maternity floor, and a nurse is taking three-day-old Leshonda to her mother for the first feeding of the day. Leshonda is alert, fussing, and obviously hungry. Keisha greets her baby with a smile and outstretched arms. While Keisha gently talks to Leshonda as she adjusts herself to begin the feeding, Leshonda calms quickly. Leshonda begins to suck rhythmically and enthusiastically. The nurse smiles and tiptoes out.

Six months later Keisha tells Marcus how lucky she is to have a baby who is so easy to care for. Leshonda is typically in a good mood, and she has already settled into a predictable pattern of sleep and activity that allows Keisha to anticipate most of her baby's needs. Knowing that Leshonda will be highly energetic and responsive at specific times of the day helps Keisha to pace herself and to conserve energy.

Although Leshonda is fussy occasionally, Keisha can easily relieve the distress by lifting Leshonda to her breast and whispering a few soothing words. Her ability to calm her baby reinforces her sense of competence as a mother.

The nurse unconsciously grits her teeth as she reluctantly takes three-day-old Heather to her mother. Heather is restless and fussy after a night of erratic sleep. Barbara takes the baby from the nurse as passively as if she has been handed a bag of groceries. As Heather cries more passionately, Barbara only continues to hold her, virtually motionless. Resisting sarcasm, the nurse suggests that Barbara might try to feed her baby to relieve her distress. Barbara offers the bottle, but her abrupt, awkward motion only intensifies Heather's crying. The nurse takes Heather from Barbara, soothes her, and gives her back. Barbara jabs the nipple into Heather's mouth, reactivating the intense cry. The nurse later asks the child life specialist, who has had some success facilitating the interaction of newborns with their mothers, to visit Barbara.

At six months Barbara continues to be overwhelmed and annoyed by Heather. Her baby's sleep is irregular, and she is extremely irritable throughout the day. The pediatrician calls it a touch of colic, but that is little consolation to Barbara. Heather is a grumpy baby who doesn't take well to handling, and her mother's infrequent and inadequate efforts to soothe her only make matters worse.

When the nurse brings Carlos to Maria for the first time, he sleeps right through the half-hour visit, never opening his eyes. On the second day, Carlos seems a little more lively, but he sleeps almost constantly. The only time that he seems alert is when he is crying. Maria and Emilio express their concern to the doctor, but he assures them that Carlos is in excellent health. "Just a quiet baby," he says. "Nothing to worry about."

At six months, Carlos continues to be in his own world. Maria often has to wake him intentionally, and he often does not fully wake up for a half-hour or more. He shows little interest in interacting with anyone, and he is easily overstimulated. Loud noises, the presence of a stranger, or more than two people in the room make him restless and irritable. If he cannot avoid the stimulation, he shuts down completely, resisting all efforts to elicit his attention.

These descriptions of Leshonda, Heather, and Carlos illustrate two important characteristics of their development: (1) All three infants have been remarkably consistent in their patterns of emotional expression, (2) each displays a unique pattern. Developmentalists call these individual patterns **temperament**, the characteristic behavioral and emotional style of the infant. *Temperament* is a descriptive term that refers to *how* infants behave over time, rather than *why* infants behave as they do (a question of motivation) or *what* specific behaviors are performed (Thomas & Chess, 1977).

An individual's temperamental style is deeply rooted in biological inheritance, and as such, temperament suggests considerable stability over time, at least through infancy. However, most developmental theorists accept the notion that temperament, although stable, is also subject to modification by experience, particularly over long periods of time (Bates, 1987). There is no "chicken and the egg" dilemma here, though: Temperament clearly precedes experience; it is an innate given, manifest soon after birth.

Dimensions of Temperament: The New York Longitudinal Study

Much of what we know about temperament comes from the New York Longitudinal Study (Thomas & Chess, 1977, 1984). Stella Chess and Alexander Thomas followed the behavior of 141 subjects from early infancy into young adulthood. To describe their

TABLE 8.2
Dimensions of Temperament

Activity Level	Frequency and tempo of bodily movement
Rhythmicity (regularity)	Regularity of bodily functioning (e.g., sleep, elimination, eating, and resting)
Adaptability	Modification of response to new situations and transitions
Approach–Withdrawal	First reactions to new situations and strangers
Threshold	Sensitivity or the level of a stimulus needed to elicit a response
Mood	Emotional state from happy and pleasant to sad and unfriendly
Intensity	Strength of response
Distractability	Tendency to have one's behavior disrupted by distracting stimuli
Persistence (attention span)	Tendency to remain engaged in a task, such as gazing at or exploring objects

SOURCE: *Thomas & Chess, 1984*

subjects' behavior and emotional expression, the researchers used nine distinct dimensions of temperament: activity level, rhythmicity, adaptability, approachability, threshold, mood, intensity, distractability, and persistence. These temperament dimensions are defined in Table 8.2. According to Thomas and Chess, each of these dimensions may be thought of as a measure of infant personality. Each dimension describes the range of individual differences for each quality of temperament. Presumably, a child's profile on these dimensions describes the pattern of this inborn template of early personality. Although the template resists change, it does alter somewhat over extended periods of time.

TABLE 8.3
Summary of Thomas and Chess's Temperament Types

Easy Child	Difficult Child	Slow-to-Warm-Up Child
Regular in body function Copes well with changes in routine Adapts well to new situations	Irregular in body function Reacts poorly to change Withdraws from the unfamiliar	Does not adapt well to changes in routine Tends to be inactive

SOURCE: *Adapted from Thomas & Chess, 1984*

Although the full set of temperament dimensions implies extensive variation among children, Thomas and Chess provide evidence that most children fall into one of three distinct temperamental types, each with its own profile on selected dimensions (Thomas & Chess, 1977).

About 10 percent of the children in Thomas and Chess's study were classified as "difficult" in temperament. The *difficult child* withdraws from the unfamiliar, adapts slowly to changes in routine, and is irregular in bodily function, negative in mood, and high in activity level. Difficult children are at risk for the development of behavior problems (Thomas & Chess, 1977). Heather could probably be described as fitting this temperament category.

Forty percent of the sample were classified as "easy" in temperament. The *easy child* is relaxed when approaching new situations, copes well with changes in routine, is regular in bodily function, and maintains a positive mood and low to moderate intensity. Leshonda would fit the "easy" temperament classification.

Fifteen percent of the children studied were described as "slow-to-warm-up." The *slow-to-warm-up child* is inactive, somewhat negative in mood, and does not do well in new situations or respond well to change of routine. These characteristics seem to describe Carlos fairly well.

The remaining 35 percent of children in Thomas and Chess's sample could not be classified into one of these three categories because they showed consistent or mixed profiles of traits. The three temperamental types are described in Table 8.3.

Temperament and Infant-Parent Relationships: Goodness-of-Fit

Temperament provides a preliminary outline of infant personality, an outline that parents must reconcile with their expectations and their own temperamental traits. The extent to which the temperaments of parents match the temperament of the infant is known as **goodness-of-fit**. An optimal goodness-of-fit exists where parents are suited to and accepting of the given temperament of their child. Such parents are likely to nurture and reinforce their child's emotional expression and behavior, thereby minimizing the potential for conflict. Keisha's sensitive interaction with Leshonda in the hospital is an excellent example.

Where the fit is less perfect, conflict is likely to arise. For instance, the mismatch between Heather's "difficult" temperament and her mother's pattern of low energy and depression is a formula for long-term conflict. When the goodness-of-fit is less than optimal, parents typically attempt to alter their child's temperament through socialization, often without much success.

The goodness-of-fit model cautions that there is no particular temperamental pattern that will prove universally adaptive. For example, the model suggests that a temperamentally "easy" baby in the care of highly irritable and impulsive parents might be at substantially greater risk than a "difficult" infant in the care of highly flexible and patient parents.

A P P L I C A T I O N

Improving Goodness-of-Fit

The notion of goodness-of-fit suggests that if you are sensitive to the nature of your baby's temperamental characteristics and if you attempt to adapt your caregiving to those idiosyncrasies, you can anticipate favorable long-term developmental outcomes. By adjusting your caregiving, you can improve goodness-of-fit. For instance, "slow-to-warm-up" infants require subtle transitions to new situations, gradual increases in the intensity of stimulation, and a great deal of personal encouragement and reinforcement for their spontaneous efforts. In contrast, "difficult" infants require patience and tolerance, highly flexible scheduling of events, and careful control of extraneous environmental stimulation.

Bottom Line: If you are prepared to make such adjustments, you can substantially improve your baby's "fit" and markedly reduce your baby's risk of maladjustment.

Culture and Temperament

A basic principle of ethological theory suggests that traits that improve the likelihood of survival will be selectively bred into the species. Is it possible that children with certain temperament types might enjoy a survival advantage over children with other temperaments within a given culture or ecology? This notion gets some support from a study of Kenya's Masai tribe. The researcher (deVries, 1984) found that "difficult" 4- to 5-month-old infants were more resilient, and that during a 10-year drought these infants were more likely to survive than were "easy" infants. The Masai culture has a high tolerance for fussiness in babies, and Masai mothers tend to respond to fussiness by feeding their infants. Thus, these "difficult" infants behaved in a way that maximized their chances of being fed under the extreme conditions of malnutrition. The "difficult" temperament established a more favorable goodness-of-fit than the "easy" temperament within that particular ecology. We might wonder whether the same thing happens among children growing up in the crime-ridden streets of America's inner cities.

The Development of the Concept of Self

Cognitive emotions theory (Sroufe, 1979) emphasizes that infants must ultimately learn to express themselves emotionally and temperamentally in social relationships. Forming and maintaining relationships implies two participating social partners. Thus Michael Lewis (1987) suggests that in order to participate in true relationships the infant must first develop some sense of self as distinct from others. The concept of self and other as separate is also necessary for the development of complex emotions such as love, hate, jealousy, or guilt. But at what point has the sense of self developed sufficiently to make relationships or complex emotions possible?

Based on extensive observation of infants and toddlers, Margaret Mahler and her colleagues (1975) theorized that the self gradually differentiates over the first two to three years of life in a process Mahler calls hatching. *Hatching* involves separating the self from the mother and developing an autonomous identity. In the first few months of life, the infant does not conceive of the self as separate from the mother. Separation begins around the sixth month when the infant shows his first interest in touching and visually exploring the mother's body and face. By seven or eight months, the infant displays a mixture of curiosity and anxiety as he visually compares the features of his mother with those of strangers. In the first half of the second year, walking enables the infant to separate from the mother and to deal with the environment autonomously. Finally, in the second half of the second year, the infant shows interest in developing a true relationship with his mother—a relationship between two independent selves.

One phenomenon that reveals the infant's sense of self is her reaction to her own reflection in a mirror. It is common knowledge that six- to nine-month-old infants show simple social responses to their reflected image: They point at and occasionally even kiss the image they see. However, these behaviors do not provide conclusive evidence of *self-recognition*, for they might respond in the same way to someone else's image. The problem is to identify and elicit behavior that would indicate recognition of the self.

To do this, Lewis and Brooks-Gunn (1979) devised two clever tasks. In one task, infants were individually videotaped and simultaneously exposed to their own moving images on a TV monitor; 9- to 12-month-olds moved parts of their body to cause the TV image to move. They also played peek-a-boo with the camera, causing their image to appear and disappear. When the infants were shown replays of earlier tapings, they tried the game again but lost interest when the image did not respond to their movement. This finding suggests that by the end of the first year, infants are beginning to understand that they affect the movement of the mirror image. However, this does not indicate that they know the image is their own.

So the researchers devised a second task. They placed each baby in front of a full-size mirror. While pretending to wipe her infant's nose, the mother applied a noticeable red spot of rouge to her baby's nose. Whereas young infants expressed some curiosity about the red spot only as it appeared in the mirror image, by 15 months infants began to reach toward their own nose — indicating that they understood the spot in the mirror was actually located on their own nose. By the end of the second year, infants labeled a picture of themselves with their own name and responded to the picture with a smile of recognition.

The emerging concept of self is evident in an infant's response to seeing its image in the mirror. While this baby is interested in the image in the mirror and may be curious about the spot on its nose, he will only reach toward the spot in the mirror. Toward the middle of the second year, he will reach toward his own nose to touch the spot, suggesting a more developed sense of self and an improved understanding of the image he sees in the mirror.

Taken together these studies indicate that the toddlers' concept of self has begun to take on the attributes of a true "self schema" and that the babies are developmentally prepared to form reciprocal relationships (Lewis, 1987). The sequential development of the self in infancy is summarized in Table 8.4.

Social Development

The preceding sections have traced the development of emotions, their elaboration and expression in temperament, and the emergence of a primitive sense of self in infancy. These interrelated developments can be thought of as preparation for the most significant developmental accomplishment of infancy: the development of relationships

<table>
<tr><td colspan="2">**TABLE 8.4**</td></tr>
<tr><td colspan="2">*Milestones in Developing a Sense of Self*</td></tr>
<tr><td>0–5 months</td><td>Infants have no sense of the separation of self from mother.</td></tr>
<tr><td>6 months</td><td>Infants show their first interest in touching and exploring the features of the mother.</td></tr>
<tr><td>7–8 months</td><td>Infants visually compare the features of mother and others.</td></tr>
<tr><td>6–9 months</td><td>Infants perform simple responses to image in mirror but no self-recognition.</td></tr>
<tr><td>9–12 months</td><td>Infants control own movements in mirror image; sense the self's effects.</td></tr>
<tr><td>12–18 months</td><td>Infants able to regulate their physical distance from mother through walking, facilitating sense of a separate self.</td></tr>
<tr><td>15 months</td><td>Infants reach toward the spot on their nose rather than the spot on the image in the mirror.</td></tr>
<tr><td>24 months</td><td>Infants identify their image in a photograph and label the image with their name.</td></tr>
<tr><td>24 + months</td><td>Infants' self schema is sufficiently formed to facilitate reciprocal relationships with caregivers and peers.</td></tr>
</table>

to caregivers. It is in the context of relationships to caregivers that temperament is socialized into personality. Under optimal conditions, relationships give the child the opportunity to develop adaptive and resilient patterns of personality. Thus Leshonda's relationship with her parents provides a positive context for Leshonda's social-emotional development. Maria and Emilio's relationship with Carlos will promote his optimal development. In contrast, Heather's less than optimal relationship with her mother will place her at continuing risk for maladaptive social and emotional development.

Parents and Newborns: The Bonding Controversy

From the day that pregnancy is confirmed, most parents begin to feel affection toward their unborn child. By the time the baby is born, this emotion may reach levels of intensity that even take the parents by surprise: Many rational adults are hard-pressed to explain the surge of love they feel for their newborns and are amazed at their own engrossment with them. Is this early emotional involvement by parents reciprocated by the newborn? That is, do the parents and their infant form an instantaneous bond? If such a bond does form within the first few hours or days, does it have long-term effects on the infant's personality development?

These questions have received a great deal of attention in recent years, stemming primarily from research published in the 1970s by Marshall Klaus and John Kennell (1976). These researchers hypothesized a so-called *sensitive period*—perhaps no longer than a few hours or minutes—immediately after birth during which affectionate **bonding** most likely takes place between the newborn and its mother. According to Kennell and Klaus, this early bonding does indeed have long-term effects:

> This original mother-infant bond is the wellspring for all the infant's subsequent attachments and is the formative relationship in the course of which the child develops a sense of himself. Throughout his lifetime the strength and character of

this attachment will influence the quality of all future bonds to other individuals. (1976, pp. 1–2)

Thus, according to Klaus and Kennell, separation from the mother or any disturbance in the normal mother-child relationship (as might result from anxiety, abuse, or neglect) can have disastrous consequences for the child's long-term social development.

Kennell and his colleagues (1974) reported the results of a test of their *bonding hypothesis* in a study of 14 poor, predominantly African American mothers who were given extended contact with their newborn babies (extended contact included one full hour with their nude baby in the first three hours after birth and five hours each of the first three days after birth). Another 14 control-group mothers and their newborns experienced routine hospital care (brief visits after birth and at 12 hours, followed by 20- to 30-minute feeding visits every 4 hours for the first 3 days).

At one month, both groups were observed. The extended-contact mothers were more likely to pick up, soothe, and fondle their infants when they cried. In addition, they stayed home more with their infants and spent more time looking into their babies' faces than the control mothers did. At one year, the extended-contact mothers seemed more preoccupied with their babies, devoting more time to soothing and caring for them.

This study and others conducted by Klaus and Kennell (Kennell et al., 1974; Klaus, Jeraud, Kreger, McAlpine, Steffa, & Kenneth, 1972) appeared to support the concept of a sensitive period for bonding in the hours following birth. However, all of these studies suffered from both conceptual and methodological shortcomings—confounding of treatment effects, small sample sizes, and overinterpretation of results—that have cast considerable doubt on the validity of the bonding hypothesis.

In a thorough review of studies of bonding, Michael Lamb (1982) concluded that there is no empirical support for the concept of a sensitive period in the early hours and days following the birth of the baby, nor is there support for any long-term effects on personality. Nonetheless, the medical community's extremely positive reaction to the early reports of the bonding effect resulted in pervasive changes in obstetric and newborn care, particularly for premature and sick babies. Whereas obstetricians had earlier insisted on strict isolation and only minimal handling of newborns to prevent infection, they now encourage parents to interact with their newborns in the nursery (Chess & Thomas, 1982).

A P P L I C A T I O N

Relating to Your Newborn

The lack of scientific evidence supporting an early sensitive period for bonding has several important practical implications. First, you should realize that although your newborn has many capabilities, he is simply incapable of holding up his end of the relationship. Newborns and young infants will respond indiscriminantly to caregivers for some months. Of course, that should not deter you from relating (or bonding) to your baby as if the baby were relating back. Babies learn to relate to others by having others relate to them.

For the parents who are unable to interact with their newborns—typically for health reasons—the lack of evidence regarding the sensitive period indicates that their newborns are *not* at risk of long-term maladjustment. However, these parents must take full advantage of the opportunity to interact with their babies when contact is finally established.

The Development of Attachment Relationships

Barbara checks her watch for the fifth time in three minutes. She needs to get to the grocery store before it closes, and she is waiting for Sharon, her upstairs neighbor, to come down to watch Heather so she can go. Heather is exactly 12 months old and, much to her mother's annoyance, she has been walking for almost 2 months. As she puts it, "I can't get away from her for a minute."

Sharon walks into the dimly lit apartment as Heather toddles down the hall. Knowing that Sharon's arrival means her mother is about to leave, Heather begins to cry uncontrollably and runs toward Barbara, who deftly slips through the door without a word. Heather's crying is so loud Sharon doesn't hear the door slam. Sharon, who has watched Heather two or three times before, tries to soothe her, but the harder she tries, the louder Heather cries.

After only 10 minutes, Barbara returns, cursing the grocer for closing before she could shop. Heather, still screaming, runs toward her, grabs her leg, and begins to alternately tear at her skirt and punch her. Barbara ignores Heather's behavior completely for a few minutes, but after she shows no sign of calming, Barbara abruptly picks Heather up and sits her in her lap, but with no eye contact or soothing remarks. When Heather continues to cry and clutch at her mother, Barbara simply stands up and pushes Heather away in a single motion.

The interaction between Heather and her mother has settled into a mutually frustrating and emotionally exhausting pattern, a pattern that places Heather at risk for less than optimal social-emotional development. Heather is also becoming overly demanding to other caregivers, compounding the risk.

Leshonda, at 20 months, peers out from behind her mother's leg with a shy but curious look on her face. Keisha gently lifts her daughter into her arms as she introduces Alisha, the new babysitter, by name. Keisha's friendly tone and broad smile directed to Alisha quickly eliminate Leshonda's shyness. She runs to her room, returns with her favorite doll, and hands it to Alisha assertively. Comforted by Leshonda's friendly gesture, Alisha smiles, thanks her for the doll, and begins to rock it in her arms. Leshonda laughs and jams herself up against Alisha's knees, obviously ready to play.

Keisha puts on her coat and walks toward the door. Leshonda stiffens just a bit, but turns back to the sitter. Keisha says goodbye and leaves. Leshonda looks briefly at the door with tears in the corners of her eyes, but she does not cry. Seconds later she runs to her bedroom and comes back carrying several dolls; she is obviously well in command of the situation. When her mother returns, she runs to her with a big smile but, after a hug and kiss, returns to Alisha to play some more.

While Leshonda and Keisha's relationship helps them to deal well with separation and reunion, Carlos and his mother exhibit a very different pattern on the occasion of Carlos's first day at a new day-care center.

> *Carlos, at age two, walks slowly into the toddler room of the new day-care center, four or five paces in front of his mother. Although Maria is obviously uneasy, Carlos shows no emotion. He looks around the room, notices that the block area is unoccupied, and heads straight for it without looking at his mother. Maria waits several minutes for him to look up, but he just keeps on playing. Uncomfortable leaving without saying goodbye, Maria goes to Carlos, leans over, and kisses his forehead. Carlos looks up momentarily but says nothing and exhibits no emotion. When Maria finally leaves the room, Carlos is unaware that she has left.*
>
> *Later that morning, Carlos asks a caregiver where his mother is. He shows no reaction when he is told that she is at work and will return later in the day. When Maria arrives, Carlos displays little interest, puts on his jacket, and walks out of the room. Maria, seemingly unaffected by Carlos's dispassion, follows him out of the building.*

Heather, Leshonda, and Carlos each react very differently when their mothers leave them with a stranger. Leshonda, clearly wary of the babysitter, copes with the situation through rituals that ease the stress of transition from mother to babysitter. She runs for her dolls, which is her way of testing the responsiveness and personality of the babysitter as a temporary source of security. Keisha smoothes the transition by taking her time, introducing the babysitter, and leaving in a natural manner. In sharp contrast, Heather reacts with uncontrollable distress to her mother's escape; and although Carlos is attending a day-care center for the first time, he pays no attention to his mother's departure or her return several hours later.

These natural interactions demonstrate individual differences among infants in their *attachment relationships* with their parents and other caregivers. **Attachment** refers to the enduring relationships that gradually emerge in infancy between caregivers and their infants. The quality of caregiving during the first year has great impact on the quality of the attachment, and the quality of the attachment has profound effects on the child's social adjustment.

Perspectives on Attachment

Although all children become attached to their parents, the brief descriptions of Leshonda, Heather, and Carlos show that attachment relationships vary considerably in quality. What accounts for the universal phenomenon of attachment? Are children and their parents predisposed to develop these relationships? And what might account for their variations in quality? Do the differences reflect variation in the quality of care or temperamental differences among children? For these answers, we will examine various theoretical perspectives on attachment.

The Behaviorist Perspective   The human infant is born without the ability to feed or protect itself, totally dependent on caregivers to provide nurturance and protection. Behaviorists call these basic needs *primary drives*. Because the mother is most often associated with satisfying the primary drive for food, the infant eventually develops a *secondary* *drive* for the mother's presence. With time, this secondary drive to be close to the mother evolves into an enduring, traitlike component of the child's personality known as dependency (Sears, 1963). For some behaviorists, dependency explains attachment.

Other behaviorists believe that attachment is understood more simply by operant conditioning principles. Every time infants approach their parents and reach out to them for food, parents reinforce these behaviors by offering food and other acts of caring. These behaviors develop into habits, which explain the tendency of young children to stay close to their parents.

There are a number of serious problems with the behaviorist explanations of attachment. First, infants require a great deal more from their mothers (and other caregivers) than a steady supply of food. In a classic series of studies by Harry Harlow and his colleagues (Harlow & Zimmerman, 1959; Suomi & Harlow, 1972), infant rhesus monkeys were raised in a laboratory with inanimate surrogate mothers substituting for real, flesh-and-blood monkey mothers. For some of these infants, the surrogate was made out of wire mesh and contained a baby bottle from which the infant could feed. Other infants were raised by a similar structure, this one covered with terry cloth and without the

This infant monkey was raised by terry-cloth mother. Even after one year of separation, the infant maintains contact with the terry-cloth mother—a sign of attachment—as it attempts to drink from the bottle in the wire-mesh mother. Despite this attachment, Harlow's monkeys were all disturbed at maturity, showing that it takes more than food and a soft touch to create a secure attachment relationship.

bottle. If the behaviorist explanations were correct, the infant monkeys would prefer the wire surrogate because it satisfied their hunger drive and provided the reinforcement of food.

Interestingly, just the opposite happened. When both groups of monkeys were exposed to both types of surrogates, they all showed a preference for the cloth mother, even though some had been exclusively fed by the wire mother. Then Harlow separated the monkeys from all surrogate mothers for a year. When he reunited them, infants raised by the terry-cloth mother displayed attachment behaviors to the cloth mother, whereas the wire-mother monkeys showed no interest in their surrogates.

It should be noted that none of Harlow's subjects grew up with normal monkey personalities. They showed severe disturbances in their play with objects and other monkeys. Moreover, when the females grew to maturity, they were incapable of mothering their offspring (Suomi & Harlow, 1972). Apparently, even relating to a mother who feels good to cling to is not enough for the development of normal personality.

Harlow's research casts considerable doubt on the behaviorist explanation of the attachment relationship. If the combination of the dependent's need for food and the mother's ability to provide that food is inadequate to explain attachment in infant monkeys, it is even less adequate to explain the complex relationship between human mothers and their infants.

The behaviorist explanation of dependency also fails to account for the fact that human infants develop *enduring* relationships with their caregivers, even when caregivers are abusive and neglectful. Heather and her mother have an enduring attachment relationship, even though Barbara tends to her daughter's needs inconsistently and ineffectively. Moreover, there is also evidence that attachment relationships persist through long periods of separation, when parents are not physically present to reinforce their children's dependent behaviors (Ainsworth, 1969).

The Psychoanalytic Perspective   Psychoanalytic theory has made an important contribution to our understanding of attachment relationships. Freud (1940/1964, p. 188) described the significance of the mother to the young infant as "unique, without parallel, established unalterably for a whole lifetime as the first and strongest love-object and as the prototype of all later love-relations." During the first two years (which Freud called the *oral stage*), infants derive their pleasure from sucking, and good mothering provides a plentiful source of oral pleasure at the breast. Disruption or termination of the mother's role in providing oral satisfaction generates intense anxiety, a condition Freud called *trauma*. Infants who are thus traumatized during the oral stage maintain a permanent residue of *oral dependency* in their adult personality: a predominance of timidity, gullibility, or insecurity.

The Freudian perspective was later expanded by Erik Erikson (1950/1963), who saw Freud's oral stage as a sensitive phase for the development of a *sense of trust* that establishes a foundation for all future social relationships. Erikson defined trust as an integrated set of beliefs, attitudes, and expectations that express a positive, confident, and optimistic view of the world as a potentially reinforcing place. Since trust can be derived only in the context of a mother-child relationship characterized by *mutual regulation*, Erikson transformed Freud's one-directional model (that the mother determines the quality of her infant's experience) to a bidirectional model (that personality emerges from the reciprocal relationship between mother and infant).

The Ethological Perspective   Integrating his psychoanalytic training and the ethological perspective, John Bowlby (1969) reasoned that, in the course of evolution, the best way for infants to survive predators was to stay as close as possible to adults. Thus infant and maternal behaviors that promoted proximity would have increased the likelihood of survival. The ethological perspective suggests that such adaptive behaviors become genetically "wired into" the behavioral dispositions of the species in much the same way as following behavior is imprinted into young goslings (Lorenz, 1971). Bowlby reasoned that the ability of infants and caregivers to signal one another and to read each other's signals would help to establish and maintain proximity. He identified the young infant's crying, sucking, clinging, grasping, smiling, and gazing into the mother's face as pre-adapted *signals* that attract the mother's attention and promote proximity. Older infants employ more sophisticated attachment behaviors—for instance, approaching the mother when afraid or anxious to elicit her protection. Bowlby believed that just as infants are prewired to send signals to their mothers, their caregivers are biologically predisposed to approach their infants in response to these signals.

Bowlby suggested that the attachment relationship emerges as a *motivational system* that regulates the child's ability to explore the environment. When children experience an unfamiliar stimulus such as a stranger, they become anxious. If the mother has proven to be a reliable source of care and protection, being close to her makes the child feel secure, which displaces the child's anxiety. Once fortified and reassured, the child may return to explorative play. Mary Ainsworth (Ainsworth, Blehar, Waters, & Wall, 1978) coined the term **secure base** to describe the adult who serves this adaptive function. In Ainsworth's view, the primary goal of the infant's attachment system is a healthy balance between security and exploration.

The term *attachment* refers not only to the actual relationship between the infant and the caregiver but also to the child's emerging conceptualization of that relationship (Main, Kaplan, & Cassidy, 1985). Bowlby believed that children develop **internal working models**—mental representations of the relationship between oneself and the caregiver. The internal working model includes the child's assessment of the caregiver's availability and responsiveness to the child's efforts to elicit protection and nurturance. The child constantly revises the internal working model to reflect his expanding cognitive and emotional capabilities and the changes in his ongoing relationship with the adult.

Phases in the Development of Attachment

Bowlby (1969) proposed a specific sequence of phases in the development of the attachment relationship:

Phase 1: Preattachment (birth through the first few weeks of life)   During the first few weeks of life infants display a repertoire of reflex behaviors such as crying, rooting, and smiling that tend to elicit caregiving. However, during this phase, infants do not direct signals toward any particular adult and no preference is shown for one caregiver over another. Thus there is no basis for an attachment relationship at this early stage.

Phase 2: Attachment-in-the-Making (2 to 7 months)   During this phase, the infant gradually develops a preference for familiar caregivers (usually the mother) as indicated by vocalizing and smiling more in their presence. Preferred caregivers are typically more successful than others in soothing the distressed baby. By five months many infants show the first signs of wariness to strangers: a sober look followed shortly by crying (Bronson & Pankey, 1977). However, no specific attachment has yet developed, as is demonstrated by the absence of distress when the infant is separated from the preferred caregiver.

Phase 3: Clear-Cut Attachment (8 months to 2 years)   Two major developmental
advances toward the end of the first year reveal the emergence of a clear-cut attachment
relationship. First, infants become increasingly aware that their primary caregivers continue to exist even when they cannot be seen. This is consistent with Piaget's concept of
object permanence. Second, as infants begin to crawl, then creep, and then walk, they
become able to control their proximity to caregivers; they can now distance themselves
from their mothers as they venture away to play, knowing that they can return quickly if
strangers or dangers appear. But separating from the caregiver is more than a cognitive
and physical act; it is a profoundly emotional experience for most infants.

Beginning at about seven to eight months, the infant shows varying degrees of **separation anxiety** to departure of the primary caregiver (Schaffer & Emerson, 1964). When
the caregiver leaves the room, the infant cries, protests, and tries to follow; the infant
does not, however, show separation anxiety when she ventures away from the caregiver.
As Figure 8.4 shows, there is some variation in the onset of separation anxiety in different cultures, but the pattern appears in 50 percent of babies by 9 months, peaks at about
15 months, and declines dramatically thereafter (Kagan, Kearsley, & Zelazo, 1978). From
the ethological perspective, separation anxiety protects the infant by maintaining close
proximity between infant and mother during this vulnerable period. Thus by 12 to
18 months, the attachment relationship is firmly established, both behaviorally and
psychologically.

Phase 4: Goal-Corrected Partnership (18 months and beyond)   Toward the end of
the second year, the attachment relationship begins to reflect the toddler's rapidly increasing cognitive, linguistic, and social skills. In particular, the child's internal working
model of the attachment relationship begins to include some awareness of the mother's
independent goals. The child must learn to modify his personal goals to accommodate
the adult's needs. On the other hand, the child will also begin to display more sophisticated strategies for eliciting adult attention and getting the adult to do what he wants.

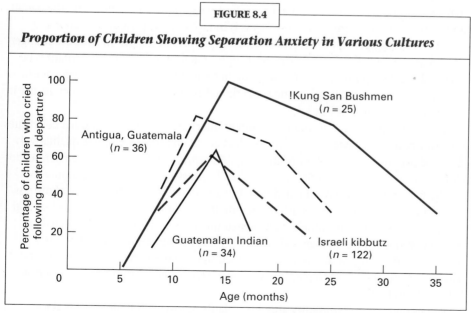

FIGURE 8.4

Proportion of Children Showing Separation Anxiety in Various Cultures

SOURCE: *Reprinted by permission of the publisher from* Infancy: Its Place in Human Development *by Jerome
Kagan, Richard B. Kearsley, and Philip R. Zelazo, Cambridge, Mass.: Harvard University Press. Copyright © 1978 by
the President and Fellows of Harvard College.*

The term *goal-corrected partnership* suggests alteration in the attachment relationship to allow both the child and the mother to pursue a measure of autonomy. Some of these changes are reflected in the child's increasing ability to deal with separation from the mother as he moves into the third year of life.

A P P L I C A T I O N

Dealing with Separation

You can substantially reduce your infant's separation anxiety by:

- Beginning brief separations early in infancy, before your infant experiences separation anxiety, and continuing brief, periodic separations throughout the first year.
- Providing your toddler with advance notice shortly before your departure, and recommending activities to fill the interim (Weinraub & Lewis, 1977). Brief explanations, adjusted to your child's level of understanding, are more effective than long, drawn out warnings provided far in advance of the scheduled departure (Adams & Passman, 1981).
- Leaving your child in the care of a familiar, competent babysitter.

Variations in Attachment Patterns

While the phases just described provide a general description of the development of attachment, there is a great deal of individual variation in the pattern of attachment behaviors among children and their parents. Psychologist Mary Ainsworth (Ainsworth et al., 1978), observing such variations in the home, created a laboratory analogue to more effectively study individual differences in the organization of attachment behavior. She devised what has come to be known as the **Strange Situation**, a laboratory procedure that exposes the infant to sequential episodes of separation and reunion with the parent under conditions of increasing stress. Stress is induced by the periodic entrance and presence of a stranger and the carefully timed departures of the parent with the stranger present and absent. The procedure is most appropriately applied when the infant is between 12 and 18 months, well into the phase of clear-cut attachment. The sequence of episodes of the Strange Situation and some thought-provoking questions about its use in research are presented in Box 8.1.

By studying the variations of mother-infant interaction, Ainsworth and her colleagues (Ainsworth, Bell, & Stayton, 1971; Ainsworth et al., 1978) formulated three qualitatively different patterns of attachment relationship. A fourth pattern has since been defined for children who do not fit the criteria established by Ainsworth (Main & Solomon, 1986).

The first group, **securely attached** infants, varied somewhat in the degree of distress experienced at the mother's departure. Despite this variation, however, it was clear that these infants were not just lonely; they missed their mothers and were unaffected or even relieved when the stranger departed. For these infants, reunion is a time for a much-needed pit stop at the secure base, which stopped their crying immediately and usually expedited a return to play. Approximately 65 percent of middle-class American babies fit this pattern.

The second group, **avoidantly attached** infants, showed either no distress at the mother's departure or equal distress at the departure of both the mother and the

BOX 8.1

The Strange Situation

The Strange Situation assessment is accomplished in just over 21 minutes, divided into 7 precisely timed, sequential episodes. Without the advantage of seeing the procedure live, the best way to understand it is to role-play through the episodes.

Imagine that you have a 12-month-old daughter and you have volunteered for a study on attachment at your local university. You bring her into a small laboratory room. You encourage her to play with the available toys and, just as she warms up to the situation and begins to play, a stranger en-

ters and tries to engage your daughter (by talking to her and playing with her). You then leave her with the stranger for three (very long) minutes. You return, replacing the stranger for three minutes, attempting to calm her and reinstate explorative play. You then leave your daughter alone for three minutes, if her distress is not too great. The stranger joins your daughter as you watch through the one-way mirror for three minutes. You then reenter for the last time, trading places again with the stranger.

The entire sequence of episodes is videotaped, and the reunion episodes are carefully studied for the following infant behaviors: proximity seeking, contact maintenance, avoidance of the mother, resistance to the mother's attempts to interact, and frequency of crying.

Now that you have finished role-playing, you might con-

sider whether (if the assessment has actually taken place) you believe that this sample of your interaction with your daughter has been representative of your attachment relationship. What if your daughter had a slight cold that day and her mood was off? Perhaps a business trip had separated the two of you in the days preceding the assessment, temporarily increasing your daughter's insecurity?

Comprehensive assessment of the attachment relationship should include naturalistic observation of parents and their infants under a variety of settings and under varying degrees of stress (Field, 1987). The almost exclusive use of the Strange Situation in assessing attachment relationships must be taken into account by those who wish to make practical use of the findings of these studies.

SOURCE:
Ainsworth et al., 1978

stranger. For these infants, the mother had no unique secure base function: They simply didn't like being left alone! Many of these infants, like Carlos in our earlier example, filled their time by playing quite intensely. Although some infants approached their mothers at reunion, most avoided their mothers or showed no special recognition of their return. In all, they showed a distinct absence of fear, anger, or distress in the Strange Situation. Approximately 20–25 percent of middle-class American infants display this pattern of attachment.

The third group, **ambivalently attached** infants, stayed close to mother before separation and were greatly distressed throughout the Strange Situation. The distinctive feature of these infants is their behavior at reunion: They approached their mothers in great distress but at the same time resisted their mothers' efforts to comfort them. These infants alternately clung to their mothers and pushed them away, often hitting their mothers as if to punish them for leaving. The mothers are incapable of functioning (or the infants do not accept the mothers) as the secure base, and the infants are unlikely to return to active play. Heather's behavior after her mother's brief shopping trip (described earlier) typifies the reunion behavior in ambivalent attachment. About 15 percent of American middle-class babies display this pattern.

Those infants who could be classified neatly into one of Ainsworth's three categories displayed "coherent" strategies for dealing with their mothers in mild stress situations: The secure infant used the mother as a secure base; the avoidant infant continued to play; and the ambivalent infant used extreme dependency and emotionality to command the mother's attention. Researchers sometimes reduce these three "coherent" classifications to two—distinguishing between securely attached and anxious-attached (avoidant plus ambivalent) children.

But not all infants display such coherent strategies. The infant who defies simple classification often combines contradictory attachment behaviors in a single interaction with the mother (Main & Solomon, 1986). The infant who exhibits this unusual pattern is known as **disorganized/disoriented attached**. A description of this strange behavior in the Strange Situation is provided in Box 8.2.

Explaining Differences in Attachment Patterns

The differences in attachment relationships are much easier to describe than to explain. If, as Mary Ainsworth claims, the set goal of the attachment system is to balance the infant's need for security and exploration, why do mothers and their infants approach this conflict in such radically different ways? We will examine several factors that affect the nature of the attachment relationship.

The Quality of Early Caregiving   According to Bowlby (1969), the quality of the attachment relationship at one year is dependent upon the quality of caregiving during the first year. In an attempt to verify Bowlby's hypothesis, Ainsworth and her colleagues (1978) observed how the mothers of securely attached infants interacted with them. Their findings confirmed Bowlby's hypothesis. Ainsworth found that mothers of securely attached infants were able to read their infants' signals of distress and discomfort, adjusting their behavior accordingly. They responded quickly and consistently to their infants' cries, handled them with tender loving care, and made special and consistent efforts to time their behaviors to suit their infants' tempo. Ainsworth described this pattern as **sensitive care**. A later study described these mothers as "synchronized" with their infants (Isabella, Belsky, & vonEye, 1989).

Mothers of securely attached infants also enjoyed close physical contact with their babies (Ainsworth et al., 1978)—an observation that fits nicely with the findings of Harlow's research with infant monkeys. The importance of close physical contact is supported by another study that demonstrated that mothers of more securely attached infants tended to carry their babies next to their bodies in soft infant pouches, rather than using babyseats for transport (Cunningham, Anisfeld, Casper, & Nozyce, 1987). Such behaviors seem likely to promote an internal working model of the mother as available, responsive, and trustworthy (Isabella et al., 1989).

In contrast, mothers of both avoidantly and ambivalently attached infants are less sensitive to and less synchronized with their infants' needs. They frequently read their infants' signals of distress inaccurately and respond to them inappropriately. Mothers of avoidantly attached infants tend to *overstimulate* their infants, generally in a highly intrusive and untimely manner, causing them to turn away to avoid becoming overaroused (Belsky, Rovine, & Taylor, 1984; Smith & Pederson, 1988). Earlier we described how Carlos withdrew when his mother overreacted to his mild distress, and how Carlos showed no reaction to his mother's departure and return on his first day in day care. Carlos and his mother are avoidantly attached. Although mothers like Maria often physically approach their babies, they fail to meet their infants' need for security by

BOX 8.2

Strange Behavior in the Strange Situation

Mary Main and Judith Solomon (1986) reviewed studies that used the Strange Situation and concluded that some children display a set of contradictory and unusual behavior patterns that do not fit into the traditional Ainsworth categories. They noted that many researchers had ignored the discrepancies by arbitrarily forcing unusual cases into one category or another. Main and Solomon studied 55 "unclassifiable" infants and discovered one common element among them: They lacked a coherent pattern of attachment behavior to their mothers.

These infants shared a tendency to display certain unusual behavior patterns, including behavior that violated common expectations of what should follow what. For instance, an infant might give his mother a broad smile (or display intense anger), then turn away abruptly and avoid her completely. Another infant might be calmed down by her mother, then suddenly burst out crying.

Some infants approached their mothers but simultaneously displayed signs of avoidance. A classic example was an abused infant crawling or creeping sideways or backward toward the parent with head averted, avoiding face-to-face gaze. Another infant reached assertively toward the parent, but with his eyes looking down at the floor, temporarily frozen, unable to finish the approach or initiate a withdrawal. Some infants appeared confused and frightened—hiding from the parents and sucking their fingers vigorously at reunion. Some locked into an unfocused "dead" stare, with the body and face still or frozen, sometimes in very unusual postures. Main and Solomon argued that lack of a coherent pattern of attachment in these babies required a separate attachment classification: the *disorganized/ disoriented pattern*.

The research available on disorganized/disoriented attachment has not been encouraging. One study (Carlson, Cicchetti, Barnett, & Bravonwald, 1989) compared the incidence of disorganized/ disoriented attachment in low-income mothers who had maltreated their infants and low-income mothers who had no history of maltreatment; 82 percent of the maltreated infants were classified disorganized/disoriented, compared to only 19 percent of the nonmaltreated infants. The re-sults suggested that children's vulnerability under conditions of maltreatment depended on the child's gender and family context; the risk was particularly severe for maltreated boys who had no fathers present in the home.

The disorganized/disoriented pattern is by no means exclusively associated with low-income families. One team of researchers (O'Connor, Sigman, & Brill, 1987) studied mother-infant attachment and alcohol consumption in a predominantly white, middle-class, highly educated sample. Thirty-five percent of the infants of mothers who either abstained or drank only lightly during pregnancy were classified as insecurely attached, compared to 70 percent for infants whose mothers drank more.

The disorganized/disoriented classification should be recognized as a red flag. Maltreatment and/or maternal alcoholism are likely background factors, and the prognosis is not good. When Main and her colleagues (1985) followed up disorganized/disoriented infants at six years, they found many of them "parentified": They had reversed roles with their mothers, often controlling their mothers by punitive means. Although we know little about the long-term outlook for such children, what we do know suggests increased risk for social-emotional maladjustment.

remaining emotionally unavailable. Many avoidantly attached infants prefer to be picked up by strangers than by their mothers (Harmon, Suwalsky, & Klein, 1979).

In contrast, mothers of ambivalently attached infants tend to *understimulate* their infants, attending superficially to their behavior while not being particularly responsive (Isabella et al., 1989). When their infants send a distress signal, these mothers may glance in their babies' direction, but then appear quite helpless and unable to respond (Smith & Pederson, 1988). Such unresponsiveness frustrates the infants to anger and eventually to negativity or passivity as the mothers prove consistently uninvolved (Belsky et al., 1984). Heather and her mother are ambivalently attached.

A P P L I C A T I O N

Providing Sensitive Care

Although some might assume that sensitive parents are "born, not made," sensitive care is probably more a function of the parents' willingness to learn about their baby than inborn ability. All parents — particularly first-time parents — must learn to read their infants' signals and to respond to them consistently and appropriately. Key aspects of that learning are as follows:

- Babies will tell you when they want more stimulation and when they have had enough. You have to trust your baby's judgment, learn his signals, and respond accordingly.

- Babies vary the tempo of their activity levels in different activities and at different times of the day. For example, a baby might be characteristically more active in the bath and less active while feeding, more active in the morning and less active in the afternoon. Learn to adjust your tempo to your baby's tempo, rather than expecting or demanding that your baby adjust to yours.

- Most babies enjoy your closeness and the feel of your body: Your arms are more comforting than a swing, your hands more soothing than a washcloth, and your smile and voice more consoling than a pacifier.

The Effects of Stress   Attachment relationships develop in a social context that includes family, friends, and neighbors, all of whom may provide support or perhaps stress to the developing relationship. In general, insecure attachment relationships are much more common in families living in very stressful conditions (Sroufe, 1985). Poverty, illness, crime, drugs, alcohol, divorce, and family conflict all take their toll, limiting the time and energy remaining for the formidable task of sensitive, 24-hour care.

Brian Vaughn and his colleagues (1979) studied attachment in low-income and middle-class mothers. Mothers of anxious-attached (avoidant and ambivalent) 18-month-olds reported significantly more stressful events in their lives than mothers of securely attached infants. Further, relationships that changed from secure at 12 months to anxious attachment at 18 months experienced relatively higher degrees of stress during those months than relationships that remained stable. One research team (Thompson, Lamb, & Estes, 1982) found that, from 12 to 19 months, nearly half of their middle-class sample changed their attachment status. These changes were associated with mothers' return to work and with the use of nonmaternal child care (both fathers and day care). Interestingly, in this middle-class sample, infants were as likely to change from anxious to secure attachment as they were from secure to anxious attachment. Apparently, in middle-class samples mothers "renegotiate" their relationship with their infants, and some of these relationships deal better with stress than others.

The effects of stress can be tempered by social support—from community, friendships, and other intimate relationships—that facilitates more sensitive and responsive care (Crnic et al., 1983; Crockenberg, 1981). In some instances, even minimal social support can go a long way. Radke-Yarrow and colleagues (1985) reported that, although children are much more likely to form insecure attachments with clinically depressed mothers, the probability of a secure relationship with a depressed mother is increased if the father is present in the home (even if the father is also depressed). This finding is consistent with Belsky's (1981) conclusion that a positive marital relationship is a critical element in competent parenting.

A P P L I C A T I O N

Stress and Caregiving

*H*igh levels of stress—regardless of their source—can undermine the quality of your caregiving and your relationship with your baby. There are three preventive strategies: plan your pregnancy for a time of low stress, arrange for multiple sources of social support, and learn to deal more effectively with unavoidable stress. All these strategies require good communication between the prospective parents, long-term planning, and a willingness to accept help and advice from others.

Infant Temperament and Attachment   Although we have presented attachment as a "relational" concept (Bowlby, 1969; Sroufe, 1985), there is considerable appeal to the notion that it just reflects the infant's temperament. Intuitively, it would seem that a temperamentally "easy" infant like Leshonda would be more likely to foster a secure attachment, and a "difficult" infant like Heather more likely to form an anxious attachment with its parent.

As appealing as this idea is, it raises an important question: If the infant's temperament alone determines the quality of attachment, then wouldn't *any* intimate caregiver become attached in the same qualitative way to any infant? Although this temperament-attachment proposition has been presented (Chess & Thomas, 1982; Kagan, 1984), it has received little empirical support (Belsky & Rovine, 1987; Sroufe, 1985; Vaughn, Bradley, Joffee, Seifer, & Barglow, 1987). The fact that individual infants form qualitatively different types of attachment to different caregivers (Main & Weston, 1981) argues against the *predominant* influence of temperament in determining the quality of attachment.

Current thinking assumes that temperament may affect the emotional flavor of the attachment relationship. For example, an easy infant in an avoidant relationship with her mother may appear more content than a difficult infant in an avoidant relationship with her mother, even though neither infant uses the mother as a secure base. Thus, infant temperament and attachment status must be simultaneously considered in a comprehensive assessment of an infant's social and psychological well-being.

The Consequences of Attachment Status

Consistent with both psychoanalytic and ethological theory, the quality of attachment at 12 to 18 months has proven to be a powerful predictor of later social-emotional functioning. Several researchers have compared preschool-age children who had been assessed as securely and insecurely attached between 12 and 18 months. Preschoolers who had been securely attached as infants were more sociable and more positively oriented to both their mothers and their peers (Pastor, 1981), were significantly more socially competent and self-assured (Waters, Wippman, & Sroufe, 1979), and were more curious, more resilient, and generally more effective in problem solving (Arend, Gove, & Sroufe, 1979) than insecurely attached preschoolers. Even at age five, children who had had secure attachments during infancy displayed more independence and less need for comfort, approval, and attention from adults than insecurely attached children (Sroufe, Fox, & Pancake, 1983).

Infants' attachment status has also been related to later behavior problems. In one study (Lewis, Feiring, McGuffog, & Jaskir, 1984), securely attached boys (but not girls) displayed fewer behavior problems at age six. In another study (Gotowiec, Goldberg, & Simmons, 1993), insecurely attached children were more than twice as likely to be classified as behaviorally disturbed. Collectively, these findings suggest that attachment status at 12 to 18 months offers an informative preview of the child's developmental trajectory, provided that the social context of the family does not undergo major changes in stress or support during the interim.

A P P L I C A T I O N

Attachment and Later Social Development

A secure attachment relationship can prepare your child to relate competently to peers during the preschool years. From this attachment, your child learns to take turns, rely on others, and give and take—socially and emo-tionally. Because your child feels secure when separated from you, he is free to explore relationships with peers, giving him a solid foundation for gaining social acceptance.

Attachment and Culture

It is important to recognize that the attachment research cited in previous sections have been conducted almost exclusively by U.S. scientists using American infants as subjects. Is it possible that our interpretation could be culturally biased? Cross-cultural studies have provided some answers.

For instance, when traditionally raised Japanese infants and their mothers were tested in the Strange Situation, no infants showed avoidant attachment, whereas a relatively high percentage showed ambivalent attachment (Miyake, Chen, & Campos, 1985). The researchers explained this finding as consistent with traditional Japanese cultural values. Japanese mothers encourage intense dependency in their infants and provide only occasional separation experience. Since Japanese babies spend so little time away from their mothers during the first months, separation is highly stressful when it does occur.

That explanation applies to babies raised in traditional Japanese families. But Japanese society is undergoing the same rapid change as the United States, with increasing numbers of mothers remaining in the work force. When Japanese infants and their nontraditional, career-oriented mothers were studied in the Strange Situation, the pattern of attachment classification was highly similar to that described in the United States (Durrett, Otaki, & Richards, 1984).

In contrast to traditionally raised Japanese infants, almost half of West German infants in one research study were classified as avoidant attached (Grossman, Grossman,

The quality of attachment relationships varies by culture. Compared to American mothers, Japanese mothers are highly protective of their babies, resulting in a disproportionate number of ambivalent-attachments. This is the norm in Japan and is not considered a risk factor for healthy social and emotional development of children.

Spangler, Suess, & Unzer, 1985). Again, these findings seem to reflect distinctive child-rearing practices. Traditional German mothers strongly discourage physical closeness once their infants become mobile. Picking up a crying baby is considered spoiling the infant and therefore inconsistent with good mothering. The researchers interpreted this high level of avoidant reactions to mothers as "a temporary disturbance of the relationship due to premature demands on self-reliance" (Grossman et al., 1985, p. 254). It is likely that these mothers expected to see avoidant-attachment behavior and would describe it as perfectly normal.

Such cross-cultural comparisons suggest that children's behavior must be evaluated in its sociocultural context. With respect to attachment, oversimplified generalities about what is normal or healthy can be highly misleading.

Attachment to the Father

To this point, our discussion of attachment has focused on the ties between mothers and infants, and indeed, this relationship has been the focus of the great preponderance of research, based on the biological realities of pregnancy and breastfeeding. Although fathers cannot become pregnant, give birth, or nurse babies, it is clear that they are most capable of feeding with bottles, changing diapers, bathing, making eye contact, talking motherese, and doing virtually every other known caregiving function—and of forming attachments with their infants. In terms of caregiving and nurturance after birth, there is no more evidence of a maternal instinct than of a paternal instinct.

Indeed, pervasive changes in the contemporary Western family have strongly challenged traditional gender roles governing who cares for and nurtures very young children. Dramatically higher rates of maternal employment—frequently associated with paternal unemployment and the unavailability or unaffordability of high-quality day care—have thrown many men into the role of part-time or full-time caregiver for young children. Some fathers have assumed increased or primary caregiving responsibility; in divorces, many fathers have demanded and been granted primary custody, primary residence, or liberal visitation.

In sum, more and more men are assuming greater responsibility for the care and nurturance of their young children. These increased caregiving roles for men raise a number of important questions:

At What Point Do Fathers Get Involved with Their Children? Many fathers get involved very early in development. In some cultures, fathers participate in the **couvade**, a set of rituals that signify the father's deep involvement in the birth process (Munroe, Munroe, & Whiting, 1981). In couvade, the father takes to his bed and simulates the birth process during the mother's labor.

Although contemporary American fathers do not practice the couvade, some experience the couvade syndrome: sympathetic symptoms of childbirth including abdominal pain, fatigue, backache, and nausea (Leibenberg, 1967; Trethowan & Conlon, 1965). Not surprisingly, both father and mother recover from their respective symptoms simultaneously when the baby is born. After the birth, the father may experience **engrossment**, a fascination with his newborn, which is manifested by kissing, talking, and touching the newborn as much as mothers (Greenberg & Morris, 1974).

Can Fathers Provide Sensitive Care and Nurturance? Research has shown that when fathers are given the opportunity to care for infants, they respond as sensitively as mothers (Parke & Sawin, 1980). However, there are several qualifications. First, although fathers and mothers may be equally capable, the father tends to defer routine caregiving to the mother when she is present. Second, fathers enact caregiving roles somewhat differently than mothers. While nonworking mothers spend the greater proportion of their time with infants in routine caregiving functions such as changing diapers and feeding, fathers tend to spend the greater proportion of their time playing with infants (Kotelchuk, 1976). Even when mothers play with their infants, their style of play is often different than fathers': The mother tends to stimulate her infant in social play with toys while the father is more likely to play rough-and-tumble physical games (Clarke-Stewart, 1978). Consequently, young children turn increasingly to their fathers, rather than their mothers, for playful stimulation (Clarke-Stewart, 1978; Lamb, 1976a, 1976b, 1976c, 1977a).

There is some evidence that the changing gender roles in families include important changes in parents' patterns of interaction with infants. Mothers who work outside the home spend proportionately more time playing with their infants than do nonworking mothers. They also spend more time playing with infants than do fathers, and still manage to spend more time than fathers in routine care of the baby (Pedersen, Cain, & Zaslow, 1982).

Further, it has been estimated that, despite some increases in the amount of time traditional breadwinner fathers spend with their infants and young children, fathers spend only 20–35 percent as much time as mothers interacting with their young children (Lamb & Bornstein, 1987). However, when the father willingly accepts the role of primary caregiver, he tends to behave more like the typical mother than the typical father (Field, 1978), except that he maintains higher levels of play with his infant than does the mother (Hwang, 1986; Palkovitz, 1984).

The remaining question is whether these stylistic differences in mothers' and fathers' interactions with their infants affect the quality of their attachment relationships.

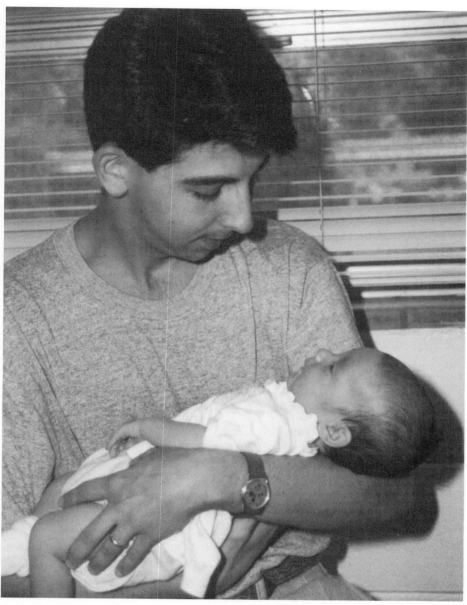

Fathers are just as capable as mothers at providing sensitive care to their infants. But is the father just as likely to change the baby's diaper or give the baby a bath as the mother? Research has shown that most fathers spend a disproportionate proportion of their time playing with their babies, deferring to the mother on routine caregiving tasks.

Do Fathers and Mothers Form Similar Attachment Relationships with Their Infants?   Early interview studies (Pedersen & Robson, 1969; Schaffer & Emerson, 1964) and later observational studies (Clarke-Stewart, 1978; Kotelchuk, 1976) have indicated that infants form stable attachment relationships with their fathers and that the proportion of secure versus anxious attachment is no different for fathers than it is for mothers (Clarke-Stewart, 1978). Home observations have demonstrated that mildly distressed infants showed the same attachment behaviors to whichever parent was present (Lamb, 1976a, 1977a, 1977b), although they preferred the mother as a secure base when both parents were present (Lamb, 1976a, 1976b). Thus, infants form attachment relationships with both parents despite the greater amount of time spent with mothers in most families.

Although fathers tend to behave more like mothers when they assume the primary caregiver role, mothers are unlikely to behave like fathers when they assume the primary breadwinner role. In essence, whether the mother does or does not work outside the home, she is most likely to maintain her routine caregiving responsibilities. Working mothers, with or without husbands, tend to play the role of "supermom" by trying to do it all.

A P P L I C A T I O N

Father Attachment

We now accept that fathers can provide adequate care and nurturance for their infants and that they form secure attachments with their infants as well. In addition, we must accept that:

■ Caregiving roles could be more equally distributed in two-parent American families

without negative consequences for the overall development of children.

■ In separation and divorce, the courts should consider fathers to be as capable of supporting their infants' emotional needs as mothers.

■ Boys and young men should gain experience caring for young children to prepare them for their caregiving role as fathers.

Day Care, Attachment, and Emotional Development

In 1987, for the first time more mothers of infants under one year were in the work force than were home with their babies (U.S. Bureau of the Census, 1987). And during the eighties, mothers of children under two joined the work force at several times the rate of mothers of children two and over (Klein, 1985).

Who is taking care of the children while these mothers work? Nonmaternal infant care is highly diverse: It is provided in a variety of settings including family day-care homes, infant day-care centers, professional and nonprofessional nannies and sitters, and fathers and other relatives. (Included in this last category are an unknown number of children who receive care from older siblings, many of whom are still children themselves.)

One extensive survey of working mothers found that less than 10 percent of infant day care was provided in a day-care center (Klein, 1985). The overwhelming majority of infants were cared for in private homes, primarily by relatives. The lower the income and the less educated the mothers, the more likely they were to rely on extended family for care. Interestingly, the predominant form of care used by full-time employed mothers was by a nonrelative in a private home, typically referred to as *family day care*. Part-time employed mothers tended to use fathers for child care. This diversity of nonmaternal care has important implications, not just for the families involved, but for society as a whole. Are there short- and long-term advantages and/or disadvantages for children and families who use nonmaternal infant care as compared to traditional mothering at home? There is both good news and bad news.

Beginning with the good news, studies in the 1970s indicated that infants in very high-quality, university-based day-care centers did not differ from home-reared infants in their reactions to separation and reunion with their mothers (Brookhart & Hock, 1976;

Doyle, 1975). A comprehensive review of more recent studies concluded that *high-quality* day care has no detrimental effects on infants (Hoffman, 1989). This conclusion assumes that the families are stable and that they try to minimize their use of substitute care and maximize the quality of their private time with their infants. We examine what it takes to operate a high-quality day-care center for infants in "Careers: The Infant Care Director."

On a less positive note, the United States has a severe shortage of high-quality infant day care, and many parents, particularly those with limited finances, do not have access to high-quality care. This reflects the cold, hard fact that quality day care is expensive to provide. For some insight into the business of infant day care and why business and quality often don't mix, see Box 8.3.

BOX 8.3

The Business of Infant Day Care

Weekly Income to the Center
3 infants × $50–$75/infant = $150–$225

Weekly Expenditures by the Center

Food, diapers, play materials, cleaning supplies, utilities, rent, liability insurance, etc.	$50–$100
1 caregiver/3 infants, 40 hours at $7–$10/hr	$280–$400
	Total = $330–$500

Why is high-quality day care not more readily available? The answer has to do with numbers, ratios, and dollars.

Ideally, high-quality infant day care should assign no more than three infants to one trained caregiver, who will remain with the infant throughout its stay in infant care. That sounds simple, but it is not. The business of day care, as it is presently constituted, works against this ideal.

An average family pays from $50 to $75 per week for 40 hours of infant day care. In order to attract a trained infant caregiver to long-term service, a day-care center would have to pay $7–$10 per hour. If the infant-to-caregiver ratio is set at 3 to 1, the calculations in the table above apply for any given week for three infants. Clearly, the center will lose money if the ideal ratio is maintained and high-quality staff is recruited.

How is the problem solved? Usually, by lowering the quality of the program. In the absence of state regulation, the ratio can be raised to 5 to 1, 6 to 1, 7 to 1, or higher while hourly staff wages can be pushed lower. At some point, the center will make a profit.

If the ratio is state regulated, the provider must get creative. For example, a not-uncommon practice is for a center to hire floating aides who are assigned on paper to the nursery and are thus factored into the ratio. However, these aides are merely being used in a shell game—moving back and forth between the nursery and rooms for older children—having no practical impact on the real nursery ratio. In such situations it is not unusual for a state inspector on an unannounced visit to find a single caregiver in the nursery with 10 or more infants.

Does this mean that day care for infants must be low quality if the center is to be profitable? No. It means that parents must be willing and able to pay higher fees, or that the care must be subsidized by government, employers, or others. Unfortunately, the availability of subsidized care has remained limited, forcing many parents—particularly those with difficult financial situations—to settle for lower quality care for their children.

Families with limited finances must take what they can get. Minimum quality standards for infant day care vary widely by state, and enforcement of standards is extremely lax in certain areas of the country (Young & Zigler, 1986). But even if standards were uniform and enforcement were more vigorous, they would have virtually no impact on the most pervasive day-care arrangement for infants: informal, unlicensed care in private homes.

This raises the question of the effects of low-quality infant day care. Low-income infants in poor-quality day care show a disproportionate tendency to develop avoidant attachments with their mothers, especially when they were enrolled prior to their first birthday (Vaughn, Gove, & Egeland, 1980). One study indicated that both parents and caregivers in low-quality day care place little value on children's compliance to adults, and that children in these settings demonstrate lower compliance and poorer self-regulation than children in higher quality day care (Howes & Olenick, 1986). Although Alison Clarke-Stewart, a recognized expert in this area, summarily dismissed the findings of lower compliance as a sign of maladjustment, her choice of words leaves some concern:

> Children who have spent time in day care, then, may be more demanding and independent, more disobedient and aggressive, more bossy and bratty than children who stay at home because they want their own way and do not have the skills to achieve it smoothly, rather than because they are maladjusted. (Clarke-Stewart, 1989, p. 269)

Although these children may not be maladjusted in a strictly clinical sense, Clarke-Stewart's characterization suggests that they present a formidable challenge to their parents and day-care providers.

Studies of the effects of day care on the attachment relationships of middle-class infants have provided conflicting findings. Barglow, Vaughn, and Molitor (1987) studied a "low-risk," middle-class sample and concluded that "repeated daily separations experienced by infants whose mothers are working full-time constitute a risk factor for the development of 'insecure-avoidant' attachments" (p. 945). Similarly, Belsky and Rovine (1988) found that 20 or more hours of nonparental care per week significantly increased the risk of insecure infant-mother attachment.

In the same study, sons with 20 or more hours of nonparental care were more likely to be insecurely attached to both parents. Chase-Lansdale and Owen (1987) found a similar result for boys, but not for girls. However, several other studies failed to show these effects for boys or girls (Easterbrooks & Goldberg, 1985; Hock, 1980; Owen, Easterbrooks, Chase-Lansdale, & Goldberg, 1984). Clarke-Stewart concludes:

> We know that there is a somewhat elevated likelihood that infants in day care will avoid their mothers after a brief separation and that children who were in day care as infants are more likely to disobey their mothers and bully their peers. We also know that infants and children in day care gain knowledge and self-confidence from their experience. We know less of whether these patterns have any short- or long-term benefits or disadvantages for individuals or society. (1989, p. 271)

In summary, the effects of nonmaternal care for infants remain highly controversial. It should be noted that there is no indication from the studies reviewed that even the best of infant day care offers any identifiable social-emotional *advantage* for infants. A

The Infant Care Director

Pamela C. Phelps is the director of the Creative Preschool and Infant and Toddler Child Care Center in Tallahassee, Florida. She has undergraduate, Master's, and doctoral degrees in early childhood education. Her sprawling center provides care for 8 infants, 36 toddlers, and over 90 preschoolers. Her center was one of the first to be accredited by the National Association for the Education of Young Children in Florida.

Pamela's 20 years of experience in infant day care and powerful personality provided a most interesting interview.

How did you become involved in the care of infants?

The rapid expansion of women in the work force in the 1970s created a great need for infant care. I knew that high-quality care for babies would be very expensive. So I began with a small number of babies, committed to the idea that if I couldn't provide high-quality care at a reasonable price, I wouldn't continue. That was 20 years ago and I am still caring for infants.

What does it take to provide high-quality care for infants?

The only way to provide high-quality care for babies is to resign yourself to not making a profit. In fact, you're very likely to lose money. High-quality care is very expensive and most parents cannot afford to pay for it! High quality means a ratio of one highly trained caregiver to every three infants. You also have to pay a high enough wage to prevent staff turnover — one of the worst possible things that can happen to a baby during the first year.

But high-quality infant care goes beyond finances. When you accept an infant for care, you enter into a partnership with the family to help raise their child. You must do everything to promote optimal development and to keep parents involved with their babies. We encourage parents to visit at any hour — particularly mothers who would like to continue nursing. We also train parents and counsel them when they have problems.

High quality also means recognizing babies' individual differences. All babies do not sleep or eat on the same schedule, and each baby has its own unique personality and temperament.

How can you run a program that loses money?

My solution has been to subsidize the infant program from other sources. I channel profits from my toddler and preschool programs to support the infant program. We also save by preparing our own infant food and by getting toys at garage sales. I also do consulting and training to bring in extra funds.

We do all this because we believe that offering a high-quality infant program is important to the families who use our center. These families get continuous high-quality care from birth to the time their children enter school. The children that stay with us for five years are our stars; they have turned out so well. We are now beginning to get our second generation of infants — that is, infants of adults who were infants in our program.

How would a student train to become a director of an infant care center?

Begin with a degree in child and family development, with an emphasis on infants and toddlers. Training should include lots of hands-on experience, including an internship with an experienced administrator in a high-quality infant-toddler program. The internship should involve direct contact with infants and their families and the study of infant care as a business and as a social service. Finally, you'll need some years of caregiving before directing. It takes awhile, but the rewards are enormous, both for you and the children and families you serve.

For more information on the standards for high-quality infant care, write to the National Association for the Education of Young Children, 1509 16th Street, N.W., Washington, D.C. 20036-1426.

cautious interpretation of the research suggests that, under less than optimal conditions, the relationships of *some* infants and their parents will be compromised by extended use of day care during the first year of life and that the social behavior of infants may be affected negatively.

Which families and which infants will be most vulnerable? Although there is no simple answer, the degree of risk for any individual infant can be approximated by adding up the known risk factors: disorganization and dysfunction in the infant's family, difficult infant temperament, and more than 20 hours per week of low-quality day care.

Unfortunately, these risk factors are pervasive in low-income families and not uncommon in middle-class families. In the absence of alternatives, many American families will continue to enroll their infants in day care with a reasonable prospect of unsatisfactory development of their children.

A P P L I C A T I O N

Selecting a Day-Care Center

When considering a day-care center for your infant or older child, observe the following precautions:

- Ask about the ratio of children to caregivers and meet each staff member assigned to the nursery. Count for yourself; a 3 to 1 ratio is considered standard.
- Ask staff members how long they have been with the center, how long they have been assigned to the infants, and what is the nature of their training.
- Ask if specific infants are assigned to specific caregivers.
- Visit the center several times before enrolling your infant and do not announce the timing of your visits. Attend at least two different times of the day and note the consistency of staff.

- Talk to other parents at pickup time to assess their satisfaction with the center.
- Make certain that the center is licensed by the state.
- Examine the center for cleanliness, safety devices on outlets and cabinets, and age-appropriate toys and equipment. Ask to see the plans for emergencies (accidents, fire, etc.).
- After enrolling your infant and allowing time for adjustment, monitor daily the physical and emotional condition of your infant. Some occasional fussiness is normal, but chronic upset, dirty or soiled clothes or diapers, and staff that fail to communicate openly about your baby's daily experience are signs that your infant may be at risk and that further actions may be necessary.

Looking Back

We have shown the delicate balance of risk and opportunity for healthy social and emotional development in infancy. Infants learn to express discrete emotions, and they and their parents learn to read each others' emotional signals. Some parents and their infants are more successful at dealing with emotions than others. Those families that do well set the stage for the development of secure attachment relationships that enable the children to learn about themselves and to explore their social world. Those families that do poorly must face less than optimal relationships; their children are at continuing risk of social and emotional maladjustment.

C H A P T E R   R E V I E W

EMOTIONS   Discrete emotions theory assumes that the infant is born with the innate capacity to experience and express discrete emotions, and that there is a biologically determined timetable for their expression. Thus, parents can interpret their newborns' expressions as reflecting their feelings. Cognitive emotions theory assumes that we don't know what newborns feel. Parents gradually socialize their infants to express their emotions as their cognitive abilities and concepts of self improve over the first months of life.

TRANSACTIONS   Parents and infants learn to read each other's emotional signals through the first year. Infants also learn to respond to their parents' changes in mood, becoming upset when their mothers are unresponsive to them. Depressed mothers tend to depress the mood of their infants, perhaps placing them at long-term risk.

DISPLAY RULES   Parents shape their children's expression of emotions according to display rules that define the situational appropriateness of emotional expression. There is evidence that by the end of the second year of life most children have begun to conform to these rules.

TRUST   Erikson suggested that parents who achieve mutual regulation with their infants foster a sense of trust — a belief that the world is a safe and satisfying place. Parents can achieve mutual regulation or affective attunement through optimal stimulation (recognizing the infant's tolerance for stimulation) and arousal modulation (influencing the infant's state to match a given task). Mothers of high-risk babies — particularly high-risk mothers — have difficulty achieving mutual regulation.

TEMPERAMENT   Infant temperament refers to the inborn behavioral and emotional style of the infant. About two-thirds of children can be classified into three temperament types: the "easy" child, the "difficult" child, and the "slow-to-warm-up" child. The stability of temperament pattern is affected by the goodness-of-fit between the infant's temperament and the context of caregiving.

SELF   In order to engage in relationships, the infant must first develop some sense of self as distinct from others. Research has shown that infants do not develop a "self schema" until late in their second year.

BONDING   Researchers have speculated that the first few hours and days after birth may be a sensitive period for bonding, with long-term effects on personality. Although little scientific support has been found for the bonding hypothesis, the notion of bonding instigated major improvements in newborn care, with parents now encouraged to immediately interact with their newborns.

ATTACHMENT   Attachment refers to the enduring relationships that gradually emerge in infancy between caregivers and infants. While behaviorist and psychoanalytic explanations of attachment are incomplete, Bowlby's ethological perspective has proven most useful. Bowlby argued that attachment ensures survival by keeping the baby close to its mother. Ainsworth expanded this concept, suggesting that the goal of attachment is to balance the infant's security and exploration.

PHASES   Attachment develops in four phases: preattachment, attachment-in-the-making, clear-cut attachment, and the goal-corrected partnership. Thus, by 12 to 18 months, the attachment relationship is firmly established.

VARIATIONS   Children assessed in the Strange Situation can be classified into three qualitatively different, coherent patterns of attachment. Securely attached infants use their mothers as a secure base; avoidantly attached infants do not use their mothers as a secure base; ambivalently attached infants seek security but are unable to get it from their mothers.

SENSITIVE CARE   Mothers of securely attached infants read their infants' signals and adjust their behavior accordingly.

They respond quickly and consistently to their infants and provide tender loving care in a pattern of sensitive care. Mothers of ambivalently attached and avoidantly attached infants are less sensitive to their infants' needs. Mothers of avoidantly attached infants tend to overstimulate their infants; mothers of ambivalently attached infants tend to understimulate their babies.

STRESS   Insecure attachments are more common in families who live with great stress. However, the effects of stress can be tempered by social support from community, friends, and family.

LONG-TERM EFFECTS   Secure attachment at 12 to 18 months is associated with better social-emotional adjustment in early childhood.

CULTURE   Cross-cultural studies have shown variations in patterns of attachment in different cultures. Traditionally raised Japanese babies show less and German babies show more avoidant attachment. Thus, children's attachment must be evaluated in its sociocultural context.

FATHERS   Many fathers become engrossed with their newborns and, when given the opportunity, provide sensitive care for their infants. Fathers spend a greater proportion of their time playing with rather than caring for their infants compared to nonworking mothers. Infants form stable attachments with fathers in the same proportion as with mothers.

DAY CARE   Nonmaternal infant care is highly diverse, including family day care, day-care centers, nannies, sitters, fathers, and other relatives. While high-quality infant day care has no detrimental effects on infants, low-quality care may have negative effects on attachment and children's behavior. Families with limited finances are typically relegated to lower quality care. The risk of maladjustment is greater for "difficult" infants in dysfunctional families who use more than 20 hours of care per week.

Key Terms

discrete emotions theory

cognitive emotions theory

stranger anxiety

display rules

mutual regulation

sense of trust

mistrust

optimal stimulation

arousal modulation

affective attunement

temperament

goodness-of-fit

bonding

attachment

secure base

internal working models

separation anxiety

Strange Situation

securely attached

avoidantly attached

ambivalently attached

disorganized/disoriented attached

sensitive care

couvade

engrossment

Early Childhood

9

Physical and Motor Development in Early Childhood

Looking Ahead

- During the preschool years, children's rate of growth slows, their muscular and skeletal systems strengthen, and their body proportions begin to approximate those of adults. What effects do these changes have on the development of motor skills?

- Preschool-age children make enormous progress in locomotion from ages three to six. What changes can parents expect to see in the development of walking, running, jumping, and hopping?

- By the third year of life, parents and other caregivers may be growing tired of tending to every physical need of their children. When can parents expect their children to develop self-help skills such as washing, brushing teeth,

and using the toilet? What can parents do to promote the development of self-help skills?

- Preschoolers are generally physically active, particularly in outdoor settings. Do these activities promote adequate levels of physical fitness? Is there a relationship between early fitness and cardiovascular disease in adulthood?

- On average, young children catch one cold every six weeks. What are the effects of minor illness on the children and on the families? Can minor illness have any positive effects on children's development?

- Accidental injury has replaced infectious disease as the major cause of death and disability among American children. Why are young children so vulnerable to injury and what can adults do to reduce the risk to their children?

- Contemporary families are under increasing stress. Does this stress affect young children? Can parents help their children to cope with stress?

- Millions of young children are maltreated every year by adults, with severe consequences to all aspects of their development. What are the causes of child maltreatment? What roles do parents, children, communities, and society play in maltreatment? Are parents who were maltreated as children destined to abuse their own children? What can we do to reduce the risk of maltreatment of children in our society?

Threee preschool years (ages three to six) are when children start making the transition from helplessness and dependence to mastery and independence. An essential aspect of this change is the development of new and more powerful ways of coping with the physical environment. Children learn to run and climb, dress themselves, feed themselves, and use a toilet. Their natural tendency to play helps keep them physically fit, unless it is derailed by passive pursuits such as watching too much television. Their optimal physical development can be marred by obesity, illness, injury, stress, and maltreatment; it can be helped along by plenty of exercise, active playmates, proper nutrition, and social support in coping with stress.

While there are predictable stages of children's physical development, each child has his or her own schedule for reaching each stage, as Leshonda and her friends demonstrate.

With her pigtails streaming behind her, three-year-old Leshonda runs the full length of the playground, easily eluding the two- and three-year-old boys who follow. She runs with a fluid, graceful motion: arms swinging rhythmically close to her body, perfectly synchronized with her legs. Her feet never seem to hit the ground.

The three-year-old boy's arms swing close to his body as he runs too, but they are out of synch with his legs, breaking the rhythm and sacrificing speed. The two-year-old boy's steps are heavy and flat-footed, and he has to hold his arms outward just to keep his balance.

Leshonda shouts at the boys, "Y'all gotta do like me!" then jumps forward four times with a two-legged broad jump. The three-year-old boy imitates without difficulty, but the two-year-old falls onto his stomach on the first jump. Uninjured and undaunted, he keeps trying, but with little success.

Hoping to keep the game alive, Leshonda climbs a ladder leading to a small treehouse, alternating her steps with her left and right legs. She teases the boys, "Y'all can't catch me!" Rising to the challenge, the three-year-old boy runs to the ladder and begins to climb. He progresses tentatively up the ladder, stepping with his right leg each time. The two-year-old, knowing that he cannot climb a single step, watches helplessly as the older boy disappears into the treehouse after Leshonda.

Leshonda and her friends' play illustrates several important aspects of gross motor behavior and development in the preschool years. First, a three-year-old's motor capabilities are strikingly better than a two-year-old's; children's bodies change dramatically in size, strength, and proportion after the second year. Second, physically healthy preschoolers tend to be in perpetual motion when they play outdoors, creating unlimited opportunities for motor learning. Much of this learning takes place in impromptu *play-games*, loosely organized escapades that get every part of their bodies learning and practicing new motor skills. Leshonda's "chase me/imitate me" play-game will end as spontaneously as it began, only to be followed by another.

Third, preschoolers engaged in gross motor play are expressing their emotions and interacting socially. Leshonda and her friends are not merely flexing their muscles to improve coordination, strength, and endurance; they are flexing their emerging personalities and temperaments. As preschool children play together, they learn to compete, cooperate, share, dominate, and empathize with each other. Thus, children's optimal development of motor skills requires both physically challenging environments and physically active playmates.

Finally, the playground episode illustrates that children of different ages have considerably different motor skills and that same-age children have more subtle, but readily observable, variations in motor skills. For example, Leshonda runs, jumps, and climbs more competently than her fellow three-year-old, but both three-year-olds are more competent than the two-year-old. Such individual differences in same-age children's physical abilities and physical fitness can be identified soon after children begin to walk independently.

Although a child's physical development may ultimately be subject to genetic limitations, caregivers can have a great impact—both positive and negative—on how closely each child comes to reaching his or her individual potential. While children can never be fully protected from illness and accidental injury, caregivers can take steps to minimize the risks. For example, allowing children to build a sedentary lifestyle around countless hours of television watching, inappropriate exercise, and poor eating habits puts their physical development at risk. Poorly designed playgrounds and play equipment increase the likelihood of injury; well-designed playgrounds and equipment and safeguards against injury help children reach their optimal physical and motor development. Although parents and other caregivers may jeopardize children's physical well-being through abuse and neglect, families and communities can work together to prevent these threats to development.

Therefore, for caregivers to promote physical fitness in young children they need to understand physical and motor development as well as the unique forms of risk and opportunity inherent in early childhood social and physical environments.

Physical Growth During the Preschool Years

During the preschool years, children's rate of growth slows, their muscular and skeletal systems strengthen, and their body proportions change significantly (Cratty, 1986). These skeletal-muscular changes can now support a vast expansion in the development of motor skills: Children learn to run without falling, jump for distance, throw and catch balls, climb stairs and trees, and manipulate objects and tools with increasing precision and efficiency.

The slowing of the growth rate in height and weight is illustrated in Table 9.1. Whereas children reach one-half of mature height by age two, they have reached only two-thirds of mature height by age six. The slower rate of growth in height remains stable from the preschool years through puberty, with children gaining approximately two to four inches per year. Similarly, whereas weight quadruples between birth and the end of the second year, the average child gains only four to five pounds per year from age two to puberty.

As the growth rate slows, the child's body proportions change significantly. The characteristic physique of the toddler—protruding stomach, curved legs, and disproportionately large head circumference—transforms into the taller, thinner, more adultlike physique of the six-year-old. With regular, vigorous exercise and proper nutrition, the child's "baby fat" will have largely disappeared by the first day of kindergarten. This

TABLE 9.1				
Height and Weight Change in the Preschool Years				
	Height (inches)		Weight (pounds)	
Age	Girls	Boys	Girls	Boys
3	37.2	38.0	31.2	32.2
4	40.5	40.1	36.2	36.5
5	43.0	43.2	41.0	41.5
6	46.0	46.0	47.0	48.0

SOURCE: _Adapted from Lowrey, 1978._

taller, thinner body is strengthened internally by **ossification** — the process by which the skeletal system converts from cartilage to bone. The brain grows from approximately 75 percent of its mature adult weight at age two-and-a-half to 90 percent of its mature weight at age five, increasing the child's ability to regulate body movements. The strengthening of the skeletal system and the growth and further differentiation of the brain provide the essential ingredients for the rapid development of motor skills during the preschool period.

The Development of Motor Skills

Toward the end of the first year, infants gain sufficient control over posture and locomotion to allow their first independent walking movements; as well, they've refined their grasp so that they can pick up and manipulate relatively small objects. By the end of the second year mastery of basic body movements — such as walking, reaching, and grasping — sets off an explosion in children's ability to control body movements to solve highly complex problems in the physical environment. On the playground, Leshonda and her friends not only run, jump, and climb in rapid sequence; by age three they can perform these skills on virtually any surface or structure. They are also developing an extensive repertoire of skills to move or manipulate objects: throwing, catching, kicking, striking, tugging, pulling, grasping, twisting, and lifting. At home, they are perfecting _self-help skills_ such as feeding and grooming themselves, which contribute to their growing independence from their parents' care. In the classroom, we see rapid development of _construction skills_ for completing puzzles, filling pegboards, and cutting and pasting. These skills evolve in gradual and orderly sequences during the preschool years (Cratty, 1986; Keogh & Sugden, 1985). Knowing these sequences will help you match physically challenging activities and play equipment to children's abilities at each developmental stage, facilitating their optimal skill development and markedly reducing their risk of injury during physical activity.

Walking, Stair Climbing, and Running

When toddlers walk on flat surfaces they have to extend their arms outward and separate their legs to keep their balance. Late in the second and into the third year, improvements in children's control of posture and leg movements allow them to lower their arms to their sides without loss of balance. They begin to swing their arms alternately forward and backward, synchronized with their leg movements to achieve an adultlike *walking* pattern. With practice, they learn to adjust their walk to cope with irregular surfaces and stairs.

Infants first attempt *stair climbing* late in the first year in a sitting or crawling position, with the center of gravity kept low to prevent falling. In the early stages of learning this skill, infants may crawl up a few steps, become frightened, and begin to cry when they sense their lack of a "reverse gear." The first true stair climbing without support involves **marking time**, using one preferred foot to raise the body to a higher step followed by bringing the other foot up to that same step. Children become able to mark time up and down steps without support in the second half of the third year; they can alternate their feet without support to *ascend* stairs by the end of the third year, and they can alternate their feet to *descend* stairs by the end of the fourth year (Keogh & Sugden, 1985).

Learning to climb up and down stairs entails considerable risk of serious injury. Parents should restrict young children's access to stairways and allow them to practice only under close supervision until they become competent sometime in the fourth or fifth year.

Children master *running* at about the same time. Although most children achieve a flat-footed running motion between 18 and 24 months, they will not achieve good running form—with leg thrusts that make the children momentarily airborne—until somewhere between four and six years (Fortney, 1983). Obesity and/or the lack of opportunity for outdoor gross motor exercise may delay the onset of skilled running.

Jumping and Hopping

Children incorporate a wide variety of jumping and hopping movements into their play-games, often with balls, ropes, and obstacles as props. *Jumping* develops in a fixed sequence in most children: While toddlers may make rudimentary attempts to jump off the ground during the second year, they have little control over the landing, particularly if they try several jumps in a row (Keogh & Sugden, 1985). They manage a simple, two-legged, vertical jump off the ground with a balanced landing somewhere around the end of the second year. They develop the forward long jump some months later as they gradually learn to crouch their legs, hold their arms back, and lean into the jump for extra distance. The forward long jump should traverse 20 inches by the fourth year, 27 inches by the fifth year, and 38 inches by the sixth year—a distance that would challenge many out-of-shape adults (Morris, Williams, Atwater, & Wilmore, 1982). The more that young children see how older children jump, the sooner they develop their own skill.

Hopping on one leg is more challenging. Children do not achieve competent hopping until the fourth year because it requires so much balance and coordination. By the fifth year, *skipping* and *galloping* emerge as elaborations of the basic hopping movement. Children work hopping and its variations into many children's play-games—such as hopscotch, jumping rope, and games of imitation (Simon Says)—so they are important additions to preschoolers' array of motor skills.

Although all children learn to walk and climb stairs, children's competency in running, jumping, and variations of hopping differ considerably. At one extreme, some children remain awkward and tentative in gross motor skills, shying away from physical games and competition. At the other extreme, some children like Leshonda show extraordinary levels of achievement that distinguish them from other less proficient children. They approach motor tasks with great confidence and consistently perform with efficiency, competence, and grace. Are these children our future athletes and ballet dancers? Although research has had little to say about the long-term effects, it seems likely that such children will maintain their advantage into later childhood and beyond if their skills are encouraged.

Self-Help: Grooming and Feeding

Parents and other caregivers tend dutifully to the grooming, feeding, and elimination needs of children through the first two years of life. The novelty of these caregiving tasks wears off quickly, and most parents look forward to the day when their children will be able to perform these tasks independently. Late in the second year, children's increasing strivings for autonomy and advances in fine and gross motor control allow the development of many self-help skills, including washing, brushing teeth, dressing, and self-feeding. To the frustration of parents, these skills emerge rather slowly. Consider Carlos at 30 months.

This child's fluid running motion on an irregular, declining surface shows the preschool child's potential for coordinated gross motor skill. Her expression suggests that she is not only skilled for her age, but that she has growing confidence in her ability. Each new level of sophistication in physical skills builds on skills mastered earlier.

> *Carlos decides that he is going to put his jeans on by himself for the first time. The jeans lie in a shapeless clump on the floor. As he lifts the jeans, he looks at them as if he were seeing them for the first time. He doesn't know the top from the bottom, the front from the back, or the inside from the outside. He remembers vaguely that his mother starts by putting his foot in a hole, but his first attempt only gets his foot stuck in a pocket. After some maneuvering, he gets his right leg into the left pant leg and falls over, twisting his body to get his left leg into the right leg of the pants.*
>
> *After several more tries, he runs triumphantly to his parents' room. Carlos stands proudly before Maria and Emilio with his jeans on backwards and inside out. As he turns to run back to his room, his bare bottom, protruding through the unzipped fly, signals that it will still be some time before he perfects the act of putting on jeans.*

Although Carlos is motivated to dress himself, he lacks the conceptual and motor skills to accomplish the task. In the next 12 to 18 months he will learn to dress by first reshaping the jeans into a recognizable form, orienting the jeans in space to match the orientation of his body, balancing his body to facilitate control of dressing movements, and zipping, snapping, or buckling to keep the jeans from falling down. Conceptually, Carlos must develop a schema of the relevant body parts and a matching schema of the garment that covers those body parts; then he must integrate those schemas to coordinate the relevant fine and gross motor skills involved in dressing. This should be accomplished for most garments—including putting on and lacing shoes—during the second half of the fourth year (Knobloch & Pasamanick, 1974).

Self-help skills at the dinner table also develop quite slowly. Although most children have learned to feed themselves with a cup and spoon by 24 months, some food continues to find its way to the floor well into the third year. With coaching from parents, competent handling of eating utensils improves significantly during the third and fourth years.

Self-Help: Toilet Training

Freud (1940/1964) believed that young children experience pleasure from the uninhibited elimination of waste products through the "eroticized" anus and the urethra. In this view, therefore, the toilet training efforts by parents counteract young children's instinct to eliminate whenever and wherever they choose. Overly abrupt and/or punitive approaches by parents would be expected to "traumatize" children with grave consequences for personality development. Erikson (1950/1963) interpreted Freud's anal stage as a "psychosocial crisis" between parents striving to socialize their children's self-help habits and children's striving for a "sense of autonomy."

Freud's trauma theory has yet to be substantiated, but Erikson's views have become widely accepted. Erikson believed that toilet training can be tumultuous for both parents and children. Under extreme circumstances, the crisis may not be completely resolved, resulting in children's enduring conflicts with respect to authority and compliance.

When should toilet training begin? The Digo of Africa believe that training can begin early in the first year (see Box 9.1). In Western society, there is some consensus among experts that most children are incapable of voluntarily control of *sphincters* (the circular muscles that control defecation) until the end of the second year of life. Children typically show readiness for training by signaling that they are aware that a bowel movement is about to occur. Even if children are physiologically ready and can anticipate the need to defecate, they also must be motivated to change. This motivation waxes and wanes, in many instances prolonging successful toilet training well beyond the age of physiological readiness.

Bowel training typically precedes daytime bladder training, which in turn precedes nighttime bladder training. The entire process can take from several weeks to several

---

Early Toilet Training: The Digo of East Africa

The Digo mother is not concerned with disturbing her child's sense of autonomy or traumatizing her child with early toilet training; she has a house to keep clean and diapers are not readily available in the bush. Using a mixed classical and operant conditioning approach, the mother begins training when her baby is two to three weeks old. When she senses that her baby is likely to urinate (for example, after feeding), she holds the baby in a spread-legged position, cues the baby with a distinctive "shuus" sound, and reinforces the baby with hugs, smiles, and/or food if urination occurs.

Thus, the baby learns that, if he or she urinates at the "shuus" sound (conditioned stimulus), rewards will be forthcoming. Night and day dryness is reported to be complete by five to six months of age (deVries & deVries, 1977).

The Digo baby has not been toilet trained in the sense of establishing *voluntary control* of elimination. It is likely that the Digo mother and baby have conditioned each other to various cues that, over time, become so reliable that accidents are avoided. The Digo mother's goal is to achieve a satisfactory level of hygiene in her home, and her intuitive understanding of the early learning capability of her baby is adapted to that purpose.

Although the Digo method is clearly not recommended for infants in our culture, the creative spirit of the Digo mother can serve as a model for solving some of the difficult problems we face with children at all ages.

Potty training can take anywhere from several days to many months, depending on the child's readiness and motivation to change and the approach taken by caregivers. This child's efforts to potty train her toy dog are a good sign, suggesting that she is well on her way to learning this self-help skill.

months, generally during the third year of life. Accidents will be common during the training period, and use of diapers at night may be necessary for several months after daytime dryness is achieved.

If the child has not learned to control the bladder by the end of the third year, we refer to the problem as **enuresis**. In one survey (Verhulst, Van der Lee, Akkerhuis, Sanders-Woudstra, Timmer, & Donkhorst, 1985), the percentage of girls who were enuretic dropped off rapidly from the fourth year (17 percent) to the sixth year (5 percent), but the rate decreased much more slowly for boys. At age 11, approximately 8 percent of boys were still enuretic compared to just over 1 percent of girls. Although nighttime enuretic children show no maladjustment (Kolvin, Taunch, Currah, Garside, Nolan, & Shaw, 1972), children who have both day and night accidents were reported to have lower self-esteem (Wagner, Smith, & Norris, 1988). The fear of public embarrassment is a persistent source of stress for older enuretic, children, which may contribute to maladjustment in peer and school settings. Enuresis is a treatable disorder that parents should bring to the attention of a pediatrician well before the child enters kindergarten.

A P P L I C A T I O N

Promoting Self-Help Skills

You can promote self-help behaviors — including toilet training — through modeling, verbal instruction, encouragement, and reinforcement. Your coaching at this level should be unobtrusive and highly supportive and should complement your child's spontaneous efforts to master these skills. Criticism, punishment, nagging, and rigid expectations for progress are likely to generate your child's resistance and resentment and to slow his progress.

You must remain sensitive to the physical and conceptual demands of particular self-help tasks. Be wary of published norms that prescribe precise ages at which children perform certain tasks. Adjust your expectations to your child's unique rate of physical and motor development.

You can facilitate training for self-help by providing equipment specifically for these purposes—potty seats, easy-grip fasteners, nonspilling cups, child-sized grooming tools—and by placing them where your child can watch and imitate you and others using adult versions.

Bottom Line: You can make this process less of a battle if you keep your expectations flexible and your persistence, patience, and emotional support high.

Construction Skills

Infants develop the pincer grasp at the end of the first year, which enables them to pick up relatively small objects, visually inspect them, and move them from place to place. During the second year toddlers develop the skills to open, tear, topple, bend, stack, and crumple materials, but these skills are rarely used to construct a specific product. However, during the preschool years they rapidly develop **construction skills**—skills such as building, stacking, molding, cutting, and pasting that manipulate and transform materials to produce specific states or products. Construction skills involve the first use of tools such as brushes, hammers, and scissors.

Even though most preschool programs offer fine motor experiences in the form of puzzles and pegboards as an interest or activity area, many children forgo these activities, leaving skills underdeveloped and talent undiscovered. One reason the programs don't emphasize these experiences more is the limited research available on the subject. We know little about how children learn fine motor skills or whether training can facilitate development of these skills. Although it seems reasonable that early training in fine motor skills might establish a foundation for children to develop manual or artistic competencies later in life, there are no studies of the long-term effects of construction skills training in early childhood. Future research will likely show a vast, untapped potential for the development of construction skills in young children. But even without such specific evidence we do know generally that skills don't improve much without practice. So greater emphasis on these skills in preschool programs seems warranted.

Not so long ago, children who, at an early age, acquired the manual control skills discussed in this section were highly regarded. Like the Digo families in Africa, parents ensured survival by early and intense training of their children in self-help and the skills required to make and use tools and utensils. Proficiency was expected and achieved in many areas during the preschool years. Although modern conveniences have all but eliminated the need for such training, our young children retain this potential for learning manual control skills and might profit from greater challenge in this area of development.

Physical Fitness

Physical fitness refers to a state of physical conditioning characterized by optimal development of strength, endurance, power, and flexibility. We generally accept that vigorous physical activity and proper nutrition are required, but, unfortunately, we know very little about the nature of physical fitness during the preschool years (Seefeldt, 1984). What we do know refers mostly to the medical risks associated with the *lack* of physical fitness.

Obesity in Preschool Children

At 3 years of age and a height of 39 inches, Carlos should weigh about 34 pounds. Instead, he weighs 44 pounds—more than 30 percent above the ideal weight-for-height ratio for his age. Children whose weight exceeds 120 percent of the ideal weight-for-height ratio are diagnosed as **obese** (Behrman & Kliegman, 1990). But for Carlos and other children like him, obesity is more than simply numbers.

> *Carlos stands out from his peers at day care not just because of his size but because of the effect of his size on his physical movement. He moves slowly and awkwardly, shifting his weight ponderously from leg to leg as he walks and runs. His occasional efforts to imitate the gross motor behaviors of his peers are largely unsuccessful. The strength of his arm and leg muscles is commensurate with his age, not his size, leaving him defeated by gravity in gross motor activities.*
>
> *Carlos's bluejeans tell the story: Sized for a child several inches taller, the cuffs are rolled up at the ankle. With his waist bigger than his hips, his jeans inch precariously downward every time he moves, causing him to tug repeatedly to keep them in place. A high center of gravity makes him lose his balance and fall with some regularity, leaving his jeans shredded at the knees.*
>
> *The difficulty of physical movement limits his exercise, further compounding his weight problem. Other children tease and call him names, which further isolates Carlos from group activities, particularly in outdoor play. His caregivers' assumption that he will eventually outgrow his obesity only adds to the problem. So far all he has outgrown in the last year are clothes.*

Carlos's weight problem is not unusual; obesity is widespread among young children in the United States and its incidence is increasing (Epstein, Wing, & Valoski, 1985). We have become aware in recent years that childhood obesity is a significant risk to children's physical health and psychological adjustment. We have also come to recognize that childhood obesity is a highly complex developmental problem that defies simple solutions.

Why do children become obese? For the same reasons that adults become obese: from a **positive energy balance**—taking in more calories than they expend through physical activity and exercise, with the excess calories stored as fat. However, it would be an oversimplification to conclude that children are obese because they eat too much and exercise too little, or conversely, that obese children can lose weight by eating less and exercising more. Clearly, it is not just a matter of choice. Most obese children would prefer not to be overweight but face enormous obstacles in overcoming their battle with positive energy balance. The critical question is *why* some children maintain a positive energy balance and others do not.

First, it is important to recognize that obesity tends to run in families. If one parent is obese, there is a 40 percent chance that the child will be obese; if both parents are obese, the probability doubles to 80 percent (Behrman & Kliegman, 1990). Both environmental and genetic factors seem to be involved: Parents model patterns of overeating and lack of exercise and their children imitate them. Moreover, parents of obese children are more likely than parents of thin children to encourage overeating at meals and less likely to encourage their children to get vigorous exercise (Klesges, 1986; Klesges, Malott, Boschee,

& Weber, 1986). These family behavior patterns tend to be stable over the course of childhood and are very resistant to intervention by professionals.

There is some evidence of a genetic predisposition to obesity (Epstein & Cluss, 1886; Stunkard, Harris, Pederson, & McClearn, 1990; Stunkard et al., 1986). Research has shown that, when comparing adults, the weight of infants adopted at birth is highly correlated with the weight of the *biological* parents and unrelated to the weight of the *adoptive* parents (Stunkard et al., 1986). There is also a strong correlation between the weight of identical twins reared apart (Stunkard et al., 1990). The genetic predisposition to obesity helps to explain why treatment of obesity at any age is extremely difficult (Epstein & Wing, 1987).

While some children are genetically predisposed to obesity, others maintain a positive energy balance simply by lack of exercise. Thus, two children who take in equal numbers of calories may differ markedly in weight gain or loss depending on the level of energy each child expends. Unfortunately, children's energy expenditure has become strongly affected by television viewing habits: Children who watch more television are more likely to be obese than children who watch less (Dietz & Gortmaker, 1985). Several factors contribute to a vicious cycle. The more time they spend watching television, the less time they spend in energy-intensive activities such as climbing, running, and bike riding (Dietz & Gortmaker, 1985). Less active children become progressively less physically competent, making them less likely to engage in physical activities and more likely to use leisure time watching TV. Moreover, television advertising prompts children to eat more high-calorie snack foods (Galst & White, 1976).

Should we be concerned about obesity in early childhood? Obese children are more likely to exhibit signs of high blood pressure and high cholesterol—important risk factors for cardiovascular disease in adults. Also, research has shown that obesity places children at increased risk for psychological difficulties and at significantly greater risk for social rejection by peers. These facts suggest the need for early intervention to prevent obesity in young children.

Contrary to popular belief, most children do *not* simply outgrow their weight problem. The longer children remain obese, the more likely they are to be obese as adults. Whereas 40 percent of obese seven-year-olds will become obese adults, 70 percent of obese adolescents will continue to be overweight in adulthood (Kolata, 1986).

A P P L I C A T I O N

Preventing Childhood Obesity

Although you cannot alter your child's genetic predisposition to obesity, you can prevent positive energy balance by modeling a physically active lifestyle, encouraging sound nutrition, and reinforcing your child's participation in physically challenging activities. Parents should regulate television viewing and resist children's requests for calorie-dense snack foods promoted in TV advertising.

Parents, and particularly if your child is at risk for obesity, should seek child-care programs with a structured approach to physical fitness and nutrition. You should not, however, attempt major changes of your obese child's exercise and/or diet without consulting your pediatrician. Adult weight control techniques are not appropriate for children.

Bottom Line: Genetic predispositions notwithstanding, childhood obesity is largely preventable. Intervention should begin early in development and should involve all members of the family.

Physical Fitness and Cardiovascular Disease

Among adults, it is well established that poor nutritional habits and physical inactivity throughout the early and middle adult years predispose individuals to cardiovascular disease. Is there a relationship between physical fitness during childhood and cardiovascular disease in adulthood? Although research has not identified a direct causal relationship between early risk factors and later heart disease, two types of evidence justify some concern.

First, recent studies have shown that the adult risk factors—that is, hypertension (high blood pressure), obesity, high cholesterol, and physical inactivity—are also present in preschool-age children (American Academy of Pediatrics, 1987). Preventative intervention to reduce or eliminate these risk factors in preschool-age children seems justified.

Second, there is disturbing evidence that a majority of older children have risk factors for heart disease: Only half of the children in grades 5–12 are sufficiently active to maintain efficient cardiorespiratory systems (U.S. Department of Health and Human Services, 1984) and 64 percent of 6- to 17-year-olds failed to meet minimum fitness requirements established by the President's Council on Physical Fitness and Sports (Thornberg, 1987). Moreover, there is direct evidence that even when young children have access to adequate equipment for gross motor exercise they do not *voluntarily* exercise enough to benefit their hearts (Gilliam, Freedson, Geenen, & Shahraray, 1981).

The presence of risk factors for heart disease—beginning in early childhood and extending through the middle childhood years—suggests that physical fitness programs for young children should be given high priority by parents and those institutions that serve young children, such as scouts, recreation centers, camps, and schools.

Physical Fitness in the Preschool

Vern Seefeldt, an expert in exercise science and physical education, argues that early childhood educators have failed to establish physical fitness as a priority in programs for young children (Seefeldt, 1984):

> Programs in early childhood, especially, have been governed by a prevailing philosophy that children should have ample opportunities to create and explore in a supportive environment, often in the absence of any specific, measurable objectives that relate to diet, motor skills, or physical fitness. This philosophy, which often borders on carefree indulgence, is likely to be at odds with the greater discipline demanded by a curriculum that advocates substituting vigorous activity for sedentary play, or the learning and assessment of specific gross motor skills . . . (p. 34).

Seefeldt has not overstated the case: Contemporary day-care centers and preschools have been guilty of blatant disregard for the physical fitness of preschool-age children (Javernik, 1988). Preschool teachers typically give children the option of *not* participating in gross motor activities and *not* eating certain foods essential to physical fitness. Given the probable connection between early risk factors and later disease, we may question whether this practice is wise. We do not let children choose whether or not to be immunized against disease; why, then, do we let them choose options that may increase their risk of cardiovascular disease?

In general, preschools and day-care centers have great potential for promoting physical fitness in young children. One very impressive demonstration of how it can be done

BOX 9.2

Promoting Motor Skill Development in Preschoolers

Susan Miller (1978) was interested in comparing structured and free play approaches to the learning of motor skills by preschool children. Her experimental design included four groups:

Group 1 Children were taught specific lessons by movement specialists using standard exercise equipment.

Group 2 Children were taught the same lessons with respect to the same equipment by parents who had been coached by physical education specialists on how to teach the lessons.

Group 3 Children were exposed to the same equipment and same facilities, but in a free-play format with no lessons.

Group 4 Children were included as a control group with no training and no special equipment.

All children were pretested for level of skill development and retested after a 27-week experimental period. The children taught by specialists and those taught by parents profited equally from the training, and both of the instructed groups were significantly more advanced than the free-play group and the control group.

The failure to improve motor skills in the free-play group appeared to result from the limited challenge of the equipment. After the initial novelty of the equipment wore off, the children rarely engaged in vigorous play with the equipment. Instead, they preferred to congregate in small, relatively inactive social groups, resulting in some regression from baseline levels on some skills.

Miller concluded that movement skills do not develop when children are left totally to their own resources with play equipment. Young children's motor learning requires some degree of structure, including instruction, organized activities, and encouragement.

Parents can be highly effective in promoting motor skill development when provided with appropriate curriculum and instructional skills. Parents' reaction to the program was highly positive.

is presented in Box 9.2. Free-play access to exercise equipment combined with more structured approaches would improve the physical fitness of *all* young children, even those who tend not to participate spontaneously in fitness-promoting activities. Children who show extreme fitness deficits can be helped through home-based, parent-implemented interventions (Taggart, Taggart, & Siedentop, 1986).

The contemporary emphasis on adult physical fitness in our society has apparently not generalized to the preschool years, and the lack of research on early fitness and the absence of fitness-promoting programs for young children are a cause for concern.

A P P L I C A T I O N

Promoting Physical Fitness in the Family

As a parent, you should recognize the critical role of your *family* in your child's fitness. Your family should take an active approach to fitness by promoting exercise, nutrition, and disease and accident prevention.

The strategy involves developing a family lifestyle built around active physical movement rather than passive entertainment: Take active rather than passive vacations, ones that promote lifetime fitness activities such as biking, running, and swimming. Participate with your child rather than just watching from the sidelines. Look for health facilities that let all members of the family exercise. Limit television watching for all family members.

Model healthy nutrition and encourage a low-fat, low-sodium diet, consistent with RDA requirements for the preschool-age child. Avoid junk foods and take-out foods. Also avoid using food as a reward or punishment: Forcing your child to eat foods she doesn't like, depriving her of food as punishment, and using food (particularly sweets) as a reinforcement defines some foods as good and some as bad. Your child will have a hard enough time learning good nutrition without conflicting messages.

Bottom Line: Surround your child with positive models of physical fitness. Make sure that you are one of those positive models.

Minor Childhood Illness

Carlos walks slowly toward the entrance to the day-care center where his dad is waiting for him. Emilio knows immediately that something is up; Carlos just doesn't look right. Even at a distance, he sees the telltale signs—flushed cheeks, droopy eyelids, and the "green drip"—indications of an illness that will last several days.

As Emilio lifts Carlos into his arms, he feels the heat coming from Carlos's body. He looks at the caregiver and sighs, "Here we go again!"

Emilio is not being insensitive when he vents his frustration at his son's illness. This is Carlos's seventh respiratory infection in the last year, and each illness has thrown the family into moderate chaos. Emilio knows that the day-care center makes no provision for illness, so he or his wife will have to take time off from work with considerable sacrifice of income. Even worse, the last time Carlos was ill, Emilio missed four days of work—two to care for Carlos and two to recuperate after he caught the virus.

This family's experience is not unusual. Children between the ages of one and three have an average of eight to nine colds in a given year, or approximately one cold every six weeks (Denny & Clyde, 1983). Since contagion is largely a function of how many infected people one is exposed to, larger families tend to have proportionately more illness (Loda, 1980), and children in group day care are at much greater risk for respiratory infections than children reared at home (Wald, Dashevsky, Byers, Guerra, & Taylor, 1988).

Negative Effects of Childhood Illness

Although most childhood illnesses are neither life threatening nor long lasting (2–14 days), they may have significant negative impact on family functioning. Few day-care centers can take care of sick children, and parents who cannot arrange for alternate care may send their symptomatic children to day care anyway, increasing the risk of infecting other children and staff. The risk of transmitting disease in day-care centers is very high, particularly in centers with children under two who are still in diapers (Marwick & Simmons, 1984).

Day-care centers can substantially reduce the risk of contagion (Marwick & Simmons, 1984) by implementing preventive measures: education of staff; separating toilet-trained and non-toilet-trained children; frequently washing and sanitizing hands, toys, and exposed surfaces used for diapering; and maintaining a mandatory policy for how to handle sick children (see Box 9.3). Parents should ask to see this policy and monitor the day-care provider's compliance.

Positive Effects of Childhood Illness

Although we usually think of it as a negative influence on children and their families, illness can promote child development in several ways (Parmelee, 1986). First, the experience of being sick can help children learn appropriate role expectations associated with illness. For example, when a child is ill, parents relax their expectations for performance—such as doing chores or taking a bath—but only with the understanding that the child must cooperate in all efforts to get better as soon as possible—such as staying in bed and taking medicine. Thus illness can provide unique opportunities to teach children about both illness and wellness.

There is another positive effect. Caregivers tend to use a rich descriptive language to characterize changes in inner states during the course of the illness:

> "You look so tired. Do you feel OK?"
> "Does your tummy still hurt?"
> "Did the medicine make you feel better?"
> "You are starting to act like yourself again!"

Such language helps preschooler's self-esteem emerge. They quickly adopt these terms to interpret and label the quality of their own inner mental states (Bretherton & Beeghly, 1982). For example,

Although minor illness is unpleasant for the child and inconvenient for parents, it does provide an excellent opportunity for a child to learn about illness and their role in recovery and to observe parents' empathy and caring.

BOX 9.3

Day Care and Infectious Disease

Estimates vary but as many as 10 million children are in some form of group day care on any given day in the United States. By definition, group care of young children involves close proximity of children in relatively small spaces—the perfect ecology for mixing children and germs. When some or all of these children are not yet toilet trained, the risk of contagion rises dramatically (Marwick & Simmons, 1984). The problem is exacerbated by caregivers who either don't know or who choose to ignore appropriate hygiene.

There are two important issues with respect to transmission:

1. The risk of infection—such as the common cold, diarrhea, and influenza—is much higher in children attending group day care than in children reared at home. The high rate of transmission stems from the close proximity of children, frequent physical contact among children, and young children's hand-to-mouth behavior. The unprecedented number of children in day care has affected the overall pattern of infectious disease in the United States (Marwick & Simmons, 1984).

2. Of equal concern is the transmission of disease from children in day care to adults. Although Hepatitis A has been largely brought under control in the United States, there has been some resurgence of the disease in adults exposed to children who attend day care. Adults are more susceptible to the disease and suffer more severe consequences than the children who infect them.

A similar problem has been identified with respect to cytomegalovirus (CMV), a known teratogen that may cause auditory, visual, and other neurological abnormalities to the fetus of an infected woman. In one study, 44 percent of the children in day care tested positive for the virus, which stays active in children for months and perhaps years (Hutto, as cited in Marwick & Simmons, 1984). Children show no symptoms. However, the disease can be transmitted from children to mothers and to the staff of the center.

The risk is greatest for women who contract the disease in the first half of pregnancy, with damage anticipated in approximately 15 percent of offspring (Stagno et al., 1986). Day-care workers should be tested for immunity and allowed not to work in the center during their pregnancy.

Children's primitive approach to hygiene helps infections to spread rapidly in day care centers. If the boy on the left has a cold, the other boy will probably become infected.

"I feel sick. I want aspirin."

"Stop, it doesn't feel good."

"Mommy, I feel better. Can I go outside?"

Unfortunately, some comments by parents suggest that children's behavior *causes* them to become ill. For example, a mother chides her son, "I told you you would get sick if you hit your brother!" The causal connection implied in the mother's comment contributes to what Piaget (1932/1965) referred to as the child's sense of **immanent justice**—the belief that bad behavior will be automatically punished. In one study immanent justice was the *predominant* explanation preschool children gave for the cause of illness and accidents (Kister & Patterson, 1980). However, children who showed a better understanding of the concept of contagion were less likely to resort to immanent justice explanations, suggesting that preschoolers may avoid misconceptions if their parents take the time to explain the real causes of illness.

Taking care of ill children also provides parents with an excellent opportunity to model empathic and prosocial helping behaviors (Parmelee, 1986). Children's relative immobility and heightened dependence combines with the parents' nurturing care to create an ideal modeling situation; children can observe and learn empathy, nurturance, caring, and helping in distress. This learning opportunity is also present when children are confined to hospitals for more serious illness or injury. We get an idea of the challenges and rewards for those who choose to work with hospitalized children in "Careers: The Child Life Specialist."

In conclusion, although childhood illness is a source of considerable stress for children and their families, it also provides a natural arena for the socialization of children's emotions and the development of self-concept. Parents should take the time—between wiping noses and spooning medicine into unwilling mouths—to promote the opportunity for learning and development associated with minor illness.

Accidental Injury

Accidental injury has replaced infectious disease as the major cause of death and disability among American children. Injuries account for half of the deaths of children under 15 and result in more deaths than the next 6 causes of death in children combined (cancer, congenital anomalies, pneumonia, heart disease, homicide, and stroke).

For every fatal injury there are 10 nonfatal serious injuries that result in the permanent disability of approximately 100,000 children per year. About 19 million children under age 15 receive medical treatment for injury each year, and 1 in 10 toddlers a year will visit a hospital emergency room for injuries (NICHHD, 1987). These statistics reveal the extreme vulnerability of young children to accidental injury and highlight the need for more proactive approaches to accident prevention.

Car Accidents and Restraints

The risk of transporting children by car derives as much from parental irresponsibility in the misuse or nonuse of restraints as it does from the inherent danger of collision. More than half of all children who die from injury do so in car crashes, and more than half of these deaths could be prevented by the use of child safety seats and seat belts (Highway

Safety Research Center, 1976). For example, when the state of Tennessee mandated child restraints, deaths among children declined 50 percent, despite only a 22 percent increase in the use of restraints (Decker, Dewey, Hutcheson, & Schaffner, 1984). In the Tennessee study, children who were not in restraints were 11 times more likely to die than children in restraints. Although all 50 states have mandated use of restraints, only 10 to 30 percent of parents comply (Roberts & Turner, 1984); educational programs and other promotional strategies have been largely ineffective in improving compliance (Geller, Casali, & Johnson, 1980). The problem may be poor design of the programs. As Box 9.4 shows, one multifaceted behavior modification training program for four- to seven-year-olds resulted in an extremely high compliance rate (Sowers-Hoag, Thyer, & Bailey, 1987).

Children's Psychological Characteristics and Injury

When parents hear that their child—particularly their boy—has been injured, they often respond by asking, "What did he get himself into this time?" They assume that the child behaved in a manner that predisposed himself or herself to the injury. Although some children do engage in high-risk behaviors that increase the likelihood of injury, other children seem to be prone to injury for different reasons.

One possibility is that children who are incompetent in motor skills are more likely to misuse exercise equipment and less likely to avoid injury during exercise. Another

---

BOX 9.4

Promoting the Use of Safety Belts by Young Children

Responding to the unimpressive results of prior attempts to increase children's compliance with safety belt laws, researchers at Florida State University designed a multifaceted approach to modify young children's buckling up behavior. The behavioral training program included four major components:

Education The researchers presented and discussed facts on the use of seat belts and famous role models—race car drivers, jet pilots, and selected TV stars—who used seat belts. They promoted use of seat belts as very adultlike behavior.

Assertiveness Training Children played roles asserting themselves to drivers when they were unable to find or successfully use the belts in a vehicle.

Behavioral Rehearsal Children practiced buckling up in cars in the school parking lot in a game format. They were praised for practicing buckling up within 10 seconds.

Lottery The researchers observed the children as they were driven home from school. Those who had used their seat belts became eligible to enter an easy-to-win lottery the following day. Inexpensive trinkets and safety award certificates were given as prizes.

The behavioral training program was highly successful in improving compliance. One of two experimental groups improved from 0 percent compliance before training to an average of 95.5 percent compliance after training; the second group improved from 6.4 percent compliance to an average of 81 percent compliance. Both groups were still using seat belts at nearly the same rate three months after the training ended.

The researchers reported that the program was relatively inexpensive in terms of time and resources and could be easily replicated by others.

SOURCE:
Sowers-Hoag, Thyer, & Bailey, 1987

The Child Life Specialist

Kristin Maier is a child life specialist at All Children's Hospital in St. Petersburg, Florida. *Child life specialists* are part of medical teams in pediatric hospitals. They deal with the psychosocial needs of children during hospitalization: They reduce children's fears and anxieties by providing emotional support, by taking the mystery out of hospital routines and medical treatments, and by giving children a sense of control over their life in the hospital environment.

The following episodes from one of Kristin's typical workdays illustrate what a child life specialist does:

■ It is just two days before seven-year-old Darryl's kidney operation. He is nervous as he responds to Kristin's invitation to meet her friend Doug — one of a set of specially designed puppets used to demonstrate the routine procedures associated with various forms of surgery. IVs can be inserted in Doug's arms, and a flap over his abdomen can be opened to reveal internal organs.

Kristin first uses Doug to assess Darryl's understanding of his medical problem and his concerns about surgery. He reluctantly shares that he really does not know much about it and that he is "just a little bit scared." She then uses the puppet to demonstrate the exact sequence of medical procedures that Darryl will experience, inviting him to participate at each step: taking Doug's blood pressure, sam-

pling his blood, and inserting an IV.

While demonstrating these procedures, Doug shares his feelings openly, pointing out how Darryl can help reduce pain and make things go faster by cooperating in specific ways. Kristin's facile use of the puppet helps Darryl relate to the experience, express his emotions, and understand the important role he can play in his recovery. Darryl's mother is grateful for the experience and says that it will help reduce both her son's anxiety and her own.

■ Later that day, Kristin prepares to visit twelve-year-old David, who has just been readmitted. She had developed a strong relationship with him during his previous hospital stays, and fears that his return means that cancer had reoccurred. As she approaches his room, a nurse stops her to tell her that the oncologist (cancer specialist) has just delivered some "very bad news."

Kristin enters the room slowly, trying not to draw attention to herself. David is sitting on his bed, crying. She smiles at him, but says nothing. After a few seconds, he looks up at her and makes a futile attempt to return her smile. He says that the doctor has just told him that the cancer is back and he will have to resume treatment immediately. She strokes his back and listens intently as he pours out his fears, frustra-

tion, and resentment. She feels herself slipping into his pain, but makes no effort to resist. She whispers a few carefully measured words of encouragement. They both know how serious the situation is and this is no time for a snow job.

After awhile he stops crying and says that he wants to sleep. She says she will leave, but encourages him to have her beeped if he needs anything.

I interviewed Kristin later in the day to learn more about her career.

How did you become interested in the field?

When I was 15 years old, my younger brother spent several weeks in a hospital, and I stayed with him night and day until he recovered. The child life specialist helped me to cope with his illness and was instrumental in his recovery. She inspired me to pursue child life as a career. I started by volunteering at a local hospital and eventually selected a college that offered a four-year degree in child development, with a specialization in child life. I interned at Cleveland Clinic Hospital in Ohio and was hired at All Children's Hospital in 1988.

What training is required to become a child life specialist?

Our training begins with an undergraduate major in child development (or a related field), which provides age-appropriate expectations for *healthy* children's behavior. We need this in order to maintain perspective when dealing with children under the stress of illness or disability. Our training includes extensive practicum experiences with children of all ages. It is also important to understand children's normal reactions to stress — how illness and hospitalization affect their ability to cope with everyday problems. Courses in death and dying, medical terminology, children and stress, family relationships, the hospitalized child, anatomy, and medical ethics are essential.

The most important and challenging aspect of our training is the internship. We intern in a pediatric hospital under the supervision of a certified child life specialist for a minimum of 440 hours, over a period of 3 to 4 months. Internship programs are available in pediatric hospitals throughout the United States and Canada.

The internship emerses us in every aspect of hospital life. At first it is overwhelming, but we soon learn to cope. We learn from everyone: child life supervisors, doctors, nurses, social workers, parents, and, most important, the children themselves. My most difficult intellectual challenge was learning the hundreds of different diseases and medical treatments and their effects on children of different ages. My most difficult emotional challenge was learning to cope with the constant exposure to children's suffering and the death of children I had come to know very well.

When we complete the internship, we apply for certification through the Child Life Certifying Commission.

What exactly does the child life specialist do in the hospital?
Our job is to deal with children's psychosocial needs — to help them cope with their pain, frustrations, anxieties, fears, and loneliness. We come to know each child individually, planning interventions tailored to a child's age, temperament, learning style, social skills, and cultural background. The doctors and nurses value our expertise and ask for our services by writing "consults" — specific requests for intervention. For example, a physician might ask the child life specialist to assess a child's ability to cooperate with a complex medical procedure. Specific interventions can then be applied to facilitate healthy coping.

We also build a social support system for each child by promoting relationships with doctors, nurses, parents, and other patients. Supportive relationships can play a significant role in speeding children's recovery.

What are the prospects for employment?
Child life is a rapidly expanding field. We have 12 full-time positions at All Children's Hospital, and many hospitals are initiating child life programs or expanding existing services. The future looks very bright.

How can a student learn more about a career in child life?
Write to the Child Life Council, 7910 Woodmont Avenue, Suite 300, Bethesda, MD 20814–3015.

possibility is that more competent children may increase risk of injury by participating more frequently in competitive physical activities. Although this important issue has not been adequately studied (Langley, 1984), parents and teachers should be aware that either extreme motor competency or incompetency may increase the injury risk during physical activity.

There is also the possibility that certain personality traits or temperaments predispose children to injury. Matheny and his colleagues (1971) found an association between frequent temperamental outbursts, irritability, inattentiveness, and activity level and the incidence of injury. This finding was confirmed in a later study of twins (Matheny, 1985), where the twin who was more negative in mood, less adaptable, and more withdrawn was injured more often.

However, other research suggests that many issues are involved, including children's temperament, age, and factors relating to parents and the home environment. One study (Matheny, 1987) found that active six- to nine-year-old boys—who had irregular patterns of sleeping and eating and were from homes with few rules—were more likely to have injuries that required medical attention. In contrast, injury in one- to three-year-olds was predicted more accurately by factors relating to the home environment and characteristics of the parents. The researcher recommended a parent-centered approach to injury prevention in younger children and a child-centered approach (involving the modification of attitudes and behavior) for older children.

Injuries on Playgrounds

Fitness-conscious parents tend to want physically challenging equipment and play partners for their children. This quest frequently leads them to public playgrounds. Unfortunately, playgrounds—both public and backyard versions—are not particularly safe places for children: Over 100,000 children are treated in emergency rooms for injuries sustained on playground equipment each year. Thus caregivers must be sensitive to the balance of risk and opportunity that children encounter on conventional playground equipment.

Why are playgrounds unsafe? One major problem is that designers of outdoor play equipment have consistently stressed durability over safety, resulting in equipment made of hard metal rather than softer materials, such as wood or plastic. A second problem is that the equipment in public playgrounds—particularly climbing equipment and swings—typically elevates children to a height of 8 to 10 feet above hard surfaces. By medical standards, a child's headfirst fall of *only one foot* onto a concrete or asphalt surface will result in serious injury (U.S. Consumer Product Safety Commission, 1981). It is not surprising, therefore, that 75 percent of playground injuries involve falls from swings and climbing apparatus onto concrete surfaces. Parents should be aware that conventional playground equipment places children at relatively high risk of serious injury, even with close adult supervision.

Fortunately, playgrounds have become somewhat safer for children. The publication of safety guidelines by the U.S. Consumer Product Safety Commission (1981) includes technical guidelines for equipment and surfacing materials. Compliance with these guidelines has been prompted by the success of lawsuits for injuries sustained on public playgrounds (Frost & Wortham, 1988). For a futuristic view of the potential of playgrounds for facilitating child development, see Box 9.5.

The statistics cited earlier suggest that serious injury is a highly probable event for children. While we cannot watch our children at all times, we can be aware of the risks of accidental injury in everyday activities, even those designed to promote children's

BOX 9.5

Building Developmentally Appropriate Playgrounds

Joe Frost and Sue Wortham (1988) have provocatively proposed how to build developmentally appropriate playgrounds for young children. The key elements include:

1. *Plan with the children.* Including children in the planning phase ensures that their physical and emotional needs are incorporated into the design.

2. *Establish guidelines for safety.* Follow the guidelines of the Consumer Product Safety Commission and consider the unique perspective of children at each stage of development.

3. *Enhance the natural features of the environment.* Make use of the natural landscape and add plants, trees, and grass.

4. *Survey the permanent features of the planned site.* Incorporate these features into the design. Be aware of the location of utilities and plan for proper drainage. Plan for future expansions.

5. *Consider the play and developmental needs of children.* Play equipment should facilitate every facet of development—motor, cognitive, social, and emotional—and it should stimulate creativity, problem solving, and just plain fun.

Frost and Wortham write,

The play environments we now envision are not mere collections of manufactured appliances, fantasy equipment, or concrete sculptures. . . . Americans must . . . involve children and adults in planning and participating in the evolution of play communities — total environments that integrate nature (plants, animals, streams, hills), technology (imaginative, flexible, safe, challenging play structures, knowledgeable, supportive adults), and raw materials (wood, tools, water, dirt, sand, scrap materials). Such playscapes must address the broad developmental needs of children and bring practice abreast of knowledge about play and its profound effects on child development. (1988, p. 26)

---

physical fitness. We can also recognize that children often contribute to their own risk of injury. Knowledge of the sources of risk can be readily translated into effective prevention.

Stress

People experience stress both physically and psychologically, with predictable effects on behavior. Physically, the symptoms may include loss of appetite, low energy, reduced drive, fever, sweating, headaches, and nausea. Psychologically, individuals may feel anxiety, guilt, depression, and a sense of helplessness. Although most adults think of early childhood as a time of innocence and tranquility, there is increasing evidence that young children are highly vulnerable to family stress and that stress has potent effects on young children's behavior (Brenner, 1984).

Family stressors, such as those listed in Table 9.2, may affect children directly or indirectly, as when parents react emotionally to stressful events and alter their behavior toward their children. The impact on preschool-age children can be quite serious. In one study, young children from families that experienced 12 or more common stressors over a 3-year period were 2 times as likely to require medical attention and 6 times as likely

TABLE 9.2

Common Sources of Family Stress

Moving to a new neighborhood

Parental job change

Conflict within the immediate family

Conflict with the extended family

Death of a close friend or relative

Death in the immediate family (father, mother, sibling)

Unemployment or underemployment

Financial problems

Separation/divorce

Serious illness/accident/death of family member

Family violence

Substance abuse

Pregnancy

Day care

Legal problems (being accused or convicted of a criminal offense)

SOURCE: *Adapted from Beautrais, Fergusson, & Shannon, 1982*

to require hospitalization for illnesses or accidents than children of families that experienced 3 or fewer stressors (Beautrais, Fergusson, & Shannon, 1982). The illnesses and accidents included respiratory infections, burns, and poisonings.

The researchers speculated that stress may have made mothers less vigilant, thereby increasing the risk of accidental injury. Stress may also have caused parents to neglect their children's health and nutrition and to ignore symptoms of minor illness, leading to more serious illness that required medical attention. Stress may also have reduced the immune response of family members, increasing children's vulnerability to infection. The relationship between family stress and childhood illness suggests that, in some instances, medical treatment may need to be supplemented with stress-reducing interventions geared toward the entire family, such as family therapy and social services.

In some extraordinary situations family stress may have even worse effects. If children perceive themselves to be the cause of parents' or siblings' stress, they may behave self-destructively to reduce their feelings of guilt, depression, or remorse. Researchers documented the experience of 16 *preschool-age* children who had seriously injured themselves or had attempted to do so (Rosenthal & Rosenthal, 1984); 13 of the 16 preschoolers had made repeated suicide attempts, including running into fast traffic, taking poison, stabbing themselves with knives, drowning, banging their heads with deadly intent, jumping off high places, and setting themselves on fire. These 13 children were reported to be unwanted by their parents and depressed. Most of the children had experienced severe neglect and/or abuse in the first years of their lives. The researchers suggested that suicide and suicide attempts by young children are often undetected or unreported (Rosenthal & Rosenthal, 1984).

Those who care for children should be aware that some accidents may not be entirely accidental and that some illnesses may involve more than mere exposure to infection. Children's reactions to stress are often quite subtle and delayed as compared to adults' reactions. Preventive interventions and/or therapies for high-risk families may be most successful if they include helping families *and* individual children cope with stress.

A P P L I C A T I O N

Helping Children Cope with Stress

Consider the following strategies to help your child cope with stress:

- *Prepare your child in advance.* When stressful events can be anticipated—such as divorce or separation—engage your child in discussion and planning for the event. Provide the child with meaningful roles with respect to the event where possible.

- *Remove at least one stressor.* Don't try to solve all of your child's problems simultaneously. Stress factors magnify each other's effects, and removing or reducing even one factor may offer great relief. Begin with the factor that your child identifies as the most troubling.

- *Teach new coping strategies.* Expand your child's repertoire of coping strategies to include relaxation, exercise, and positive imag-

ing. Story books that deal with common stressors such as hospitalization or divorce are most helpful.

- *Transfer coping strategies from other situations.* Remind your child of strategies that she has used successfully in similar stressful situations and encourage transfer. Subtle reference to strategies that have worked for other children—particularly children whom your child admires—may prove effective.

Bottom Line: Don't underestimate your young child's vulnerability to stress and don't overestimate her ability to cope. Take a pro-active approach, geared to the child's level of understanding of the problem.

SOURCE:
Adapted from Brenner, 1984

Maltreatment

In distinct contrast to virtually all other species, humans show a tendency to hurt children. These harmful acts take many forms.

- In Florida in 1989 a mother was convicted of drowning her three-year-old boy in a septic tank in the front yard of their home.

- In 1990, it was discovered that Nicolae Ceausescu, the deposed communist dictator of Romania, had implemented a policy of infant genocide, isolating hundreds and perhaps thousands of retarded infants in primitive institutions with no stimulation and only minimal custodial care. Half of the infants died.

- In several states, mothers are being convicted of prenatal child abuse for smoking crack during their pregnancies. If the baby dies, the charge is changed to manslaughter.

- In 1991, a three-year-old girl was arrested in Houston after she was videotaped selling two "dime" rocks of crack cocaine to an undercover police officer. The preschooler was apparently "dealing" under the supervision of her 22-year-old mother and 58-year-old grandmother.

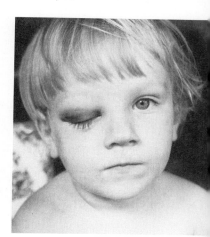

It is estimated that between 3 and 5 million children are maltreated each year. The perpetrators may be parents, caregivers, siblings, relatives or complete strangers. The physical and mental suffering is evident on this child's battered face.

- In Florida, the 20-year-old mother and 21-year-old father of a 2-year-old boy were charged with murder. They allegedly held their son upside down and dunked his head into a toilet until he drowned. The parents indicated to the sheriff's investigators that they had been having a difficult time trying to potty train the youngster.
- In 1986, a mother left her three- and four-year-old sons home alone after her child-care arrangements fell through. The boys tumbled and burned to death while playing in a clothes dryer.

And consider the all-too-familiar 3-year-old and her mother shopping for groceries:

> *Heather walks rigidly beside her mother down the aisle of the supermarket, trying desperately to keep pace with her mother's longer stride. When Barbara suddenly stops and reaches over her daughter's head toward a shelf, Heather recoils, instinctively covering her head with her hands. Barbara teases her daughter, "Thought that was for you, didn't you?"*
>
> *As they resume their rapid pace, Heather tries to resist the urge to reach for items on shelves or to make requests. When she slows to stare briefly at a brightly colored box of cereal, Barbara viciously smacks the back of her head, causing her to stumble forward into the cereal display. The "whaaackkk" can be heard the full length of the aisle; Heather's scream can be heard in the parking lot. As Barbara pulls Heather to a standing position, Heather again raises her arm to protect her face, anticipating the next assault. Barbara interprets this as hitting back and screams, "Hit your mother? Not while I have anything to say about it!" She smacks Heather repeatedly with both hands, clutches her hair, and drags her toward the checkout. Shoppers glance briefly but quickly turn to avoid Barbara's wrath. "Just wait till I get you home. You won't embarrass me again for a long time!"*

Each of the preceding descriptions represents an example of child **maltreatment**, adult behaviors that intentionally or unintentionally cause harm to children. *Maltreatment* is a general term that includes **child abuse** (*intentional* behaviors that cause physical injury to children) and **child sexual abuse** (sexual activities with children). Failure to provide for the care and protection of children is referred to as **neglect**. The number of Americans who maltreat children is staggering: There were 2.4 million reported instances of child abuse in 1989, and the frequency continues to increase (Children's Defense Fund, 1991). Many cases are never reported, however, because would-be reporters are afraid of reprisals from the perpetrators and are concerned for the welfare of all those involved. Thus the actual number of maltreated children may be as high as 3 to 5 million per year.

Young children are preferred targets for maltreatment; two out of every five victims of maltreatment are preschool-age (Children's Defense Fund, 1991). The extreme physical and psychological vulnerability of young children increases the likelihood of serious injury and long-term disability. A growing number of children do not survive maltreatment: There were more than 1,200 fatalities resulting from maltreatment in 1986, an increase of 23 percent over the previous year (Children's Defense Fund, 1991). Those children who do survive grow into adolescence and adulthood with physical and emotional scars that continue to influence their lives and the lives of others. In some (but not all) instances, maltreatment is passed down through generations of the same family, as abused children grow into abusive adults (Egeland, Jacobvitz, & Sroufe, 1988).

Causes of Maltreatment

Most people are shocked when they read the details of specific instances of child abuse such as those described earlier. How can human beings perpetrate acts of abuse on helpless children? Are these individuals mentally ill?

An early theoretical perspective assumed maltreatment to be symptomatic of mental illness, an expression of a severely disturbed personality. However, the search for a unique syndrome of mental illness associated with maltreatment—or an "abusive personality type"—has not been supported by research (Emery, 1989). It is currently estimated that perhaps no more that 5 percent of child abusers display symptomology consistent with mental illness (Parke & Collmer, 1975; Wolfe, 1985). If we can assume that the vast majority of perpetrators are not mentally ill, we must look to a broader theoretical model for explanation and prediction of maltreatment.

One promising alternative is to view maltreatment in Bronfenbrenner's (1979, 1986) ecosystem perspective (see Figure 1.1 in Chapter 1). Jay Belsky (1980) has described maltreatment in its *ecological context*, emphasizing influences on maltreatment at the microsystem, ecosystem, and macrosystem levels. At the level of the microsystem, researchers have examined the contributions of the developmental history and personality of the caregiver, the vulnerability and abuse-provoking potential of the child, and the history of child-caregiver transactions as they relate to maltreatment. At this level, maltreatment is seen as a bidirectional, gradually escalating pattern of negative interaction between a caregiver and a child. Risk factors for maltreatment in the context of the family begin to accumulate early in infancy. We know, for example, that premature infants and temperamentally difficult babies are at increased risk of maltreatment (Parke & Collmer, 1975). Mothers' low tolerance for infant crying has also been associated with abuse (Frodi & Lamb, 1980). The disturbed transactions between infants and parents promote insecure attachment relationships, which are believed to play a critical role in the emergence of maltreatment (Carlson et al., 1989; Egeland et al., 1988).

At the level of the ecosystem, we recognize that the community also has an important role. In communities that fail to respond to the needs of families—particularly families that are under high levels of stress—the risk of maltreatment can be greatly increased (Vondra, 1990). On the other hand, the presence of extended family, concerned and caring neighbors, religious and civic organizations, and social services provide opportunities for stressed families to overcome many of their difficulties and lower the risk of maltreatment.

At the level of the macrosystem, the ecological perspective emphasizes that individuals, families, and communities exist in a broader cultural context that organizes and influences our beliefs, values, and expectations. Some of our most cherished values and beliefs have been implicated in maltreatment. For example, it has been argued that the American emphasis on the right of privacy protects maltreating parents by severely limiting efforts at prevention, detection, and intervention with high-risk families (Melton & Davidson, 1987). When should the government intervene in cases of maltreatment? Should children at risk of maltreatment be removed from their families? There are no simple answers. Solutions to these problems can come only from a comprehensive analysis of the values and beliefs of the culture and its effects on the lives of children and their families.

The ecological perspective is helpful in establishing that maltreatment is not caused by any one factor; it is supported by a conspiracy of forces in the individual, the family, the community, and the society. This perspective suggests that, given a unique combination of unfortunate circumstances, *all* caregivers may be susceptible to the forces that promote maltreatment and *all* children are potentially at risk of abuse or neglect. This perspective also warns that prevention and intervention for maltreatment are more likely to succeed if they are designed to affect children, families, communities, and the society as a whole. We will now look more closely at the ecology of maltreatment.

Maltreated Children

Maltreated children show evidence of lasting effects in every aspect of physical, social, emotional, cognitive, and language development (Aber & Cicchetti, 1984). By far the most well-documented effect is a greater disposition to aggression in maltreated children as compared to children who have not been abused. This disposition to aggression has been identified in toddlers' and preschoolers' social play (George & Main, 1979; Hoffman-Plotkin & Twentyman, 1984) and in young children's story themes (Clyman, Buchsbaum, Emde, Toth, & Cicchetti, 1991). Even more disturbing is evidence of aggressive behavior in situations that would normally elicit *prosocial* behavior: Young maltreated children tend to respond with physical aggression both to the distress of their peers (Main & George, 1985) and to the friendly approach of caregivers in a day-care setting (George & Main, 1979; Howes & Eldridge, 1985).

Maltreated children's aggression carries over into middle childhood, resulting in more frequent discipline referrals in school settings (Eckenrode & Laird, 1991; Salzinger, Feldman, & Hammer, 1991). Maltreated children also show less prosocial behavior (Kaufman & Cicchetti, 1989) and less competent peer interactions (Howes & Espinosa, 1985). The disposition to aggression combined with deficits in prosocial behavior and social competence result in lower social status and higher risk of rejection among peers in day care (Salzinger et al., 1991) and in school settings (Price & Slyke, 1991).

Research has also shown that maltreatment significantly damages children's perception, cognition, and learning (Vondra, Barnett, & Cicchetti, 1990). Maltreated children showed less "secure readiness to learn" from unfamiliar adults (Aber & Allen, 1987) and impaired "cognitive control"—that is, less ability to regulate attention and memory in information processing tasks (Rieder & Cicchetti, 1989). There is also evidence that preschool- and school-age maltreated children have exaggerated perceptions of their own physical and social skills (Vondra, 1990). These deficiencies in motivation, cognitive skill, and self-perception greatly increase their risk of failing in school.

All forms of abuse are not equal in terms of their effects on children. The social and emotional consequences of *child sexual abuse* may be more severe than those associated with other forms of maltreatment. Short-term effects in young, sexually abused children include intense feelings of fear, anger, hostility, guilt, and shame. These are sometimes accompanied by inappropriate sexual behavior including open masturbation, excessive sexual curiosity, and frequent exposure of the genitals. These behaviors are even more frequent in older victims.

There is also considerable evidence of long-term effects of child sexual abuse. In one study of young boys who were exploited for pornography, a link was established between child sexual abuse and later drug abuse, juvenile delinquency, and criminal behavior (Burgess, Hartman, & McCormack, 1987). An extensive review of the clinical and research literature concluded that "a history of childhood sexual abuse is associated with greater risk for mental health and adjustment problems in adulthood'' (Browne & Finkelhor, 1986, p. 72).

Once maltreatment has established a disturbed behavior pattern in children, the disturbed behavior itself increases the risk of further abuse. Maltreated preschool-age children can be especially difficult to manage in the day-care environment. One study found that maltreated toddlers were more likely than non-maltreated children to rebuff friendly overtures from other children and caregivers, twice as likely to assault their peers, and four times as likely to assault and to harass caregivers (George & Main, 1979). Whereas non-maltreated, disadvantaged children responded to the distress of their day-care peers with concern, empathy, or sadness, abused toddlers in one study reacted *only* with physical attacks, fear, or anger (Main & George, 1985).

Thus, as their behavior becomes increasingly disturbed, maltreated children become their own worst enemies, increasing their potential for further abuse by parents, other caregivers, and peers.

Maltreating Parents

Although all parents may be susceptible to the forces that promote abuse, parents who maltreat children share certain characteristics. While most maltreating parents do not show specific symptoms of psychopathology, many experience stress-related symptoms of depression and other health problems (Wolfe, 1985). Maltreating mothers report lower self-esteem, more anxiety, more life stress, and greater family conflict (Perry, Wells, & Doran, 1983). These mothers also describe themselves as uninvolved in their

This father's physical abuse of his son is not difficult to understand. Like many abusive parents, he knows no other way to discipline and he believes that physical punishment is good for his son. He demands obedience and gets it in the only way he knows how. His approach is highly resistant to change.

Is this child more likely to be an abusive parent as an adult than a child who has not been physically abused? Although some abused children do abuse their own children, most do not. The abuse cycle can be broken when intervention comes early and focuses on strengthening the entire family.

communities, promoting an isolated lifestyle for themselves and their children (Trickett & Susman, 1988). In short, maltreating parents are not very happy people. Like their children, they are often victims — of abuse by their own parents, of dysfunctional relationships, and of uncaring communities.

Maltreating parents maintain negative attitudes toward their children and their role as parents. Compared to non-maltreating parents, they perceive childrearing to be more difficult, expect slower development of their children (Perry et al., 1983; Trickett & Susman, 1988), and have less knowledge of child care and development (Stainer & Thieman, 1991). One study showed that maltreating mothers harbored negative beliefs and expectations for their children's behavior (Larrance & Twentyman, 1983). For instance, when their children failed or disobeyed rules, maltreating mothers blamed their children and expected that the children would be likely to repeat the failure or transgression. When their children succeeded, they attributed the success to luck and believed that the success would be unlikely to recur. In contrast, non-maltreating mothers gave their children credit for successes and assumed the successes would recur over time. Although we can't know whether the children's behavior influenced the parents' expectations or the children were simply living up to their parents' expectations, we can see that parents' negative beliefs, attitudes, expectations, and attributions create a climate for dysfunctional parent-child relationships.

Not surprisingly, maltreating mothers are also distinguished by harsh approaches to discipline. They believe more in the effectiveness of spanking as compared to nonabusive parents and even to abusive fathers (Trickett & Susman, 1988). While abusive and nonabusive mothers report equal use of physical punishment, abusive mothers are more likely to use severe forms of punishment — hitting the face, hitting with an object, or pulling hair — and are less likely to use reasoning as a discipline technique (Trickett & Kuczynski, 1986). Overall, abusive and/or neglecting parents are highly stressed, harbor negative perceptions of their children, and are ill-prepared to cope with the responsibilities of childrearing.

One belief commonly held by professionals and laypeople is the concept of an **abuse cycle** — that is, all abused children are predisposed to become abusers themselves when they become parents. Most of the support for this concept comes from retrospective studies of agency and clinical records — a research approach that is subject to many sources of error. A review of the more methodologically sound studies (Kaufman & Zigler, 1987) found only qualified support for the hypothesis that child abuse is perpetuated from one generation to the next: Approximately one out of three adults who were physically and/or sexually abused or extremely neglected as children repeated the abuse on their own children.

However, it is perhaps more remarkable that two out of three maltreated children managed to transcend their unfortunate childhood experience and provide adequate care for their own children. Thus, an abusive childhood may predispose *some* individuals to abusive behavior toward their own children, but it may lead others to reject the harsh discipline their parents used (Main & Goldwyn, 1984).

What allows some maltreated children to break the cycle of abuse when they become parents? Byron Egeland and his colleagues (1988) found three factors that seem to make a difference: Mothers who had been maltreated as children but broke the cycle (1) had received emotional support from a *non*abusive adult during the period of childhood abuse, (2) had a supportive relationship with a nonabusive mate, and (3) had a successful experience in therapy at some point in their lives. In contrast, mothers who had been maltreated as children and who did repeat the abuse with their own children had experienced more life stress and were more anxious, dependent, immature, and depressed.

We may conclude that while *some* maltreated children are predisposed to maltreat their own children, this tendency may be overcome with high-quality social and professional support. Moreover, the concept of an abuse cycle is an oversimplified formula for identifying high-risk families. Social service agencies and professionals who rely on the cycle to identify potential abusers will be wrong twice as often as they will be right. When they are wrong, healthy parents may be subjected to suspicion and unfair treatment in their communities, their rights may be violated, and their family life may suffer. Relying on the abuse cycle to identify potential abusers also fails to consider that many adults who maltreat their children were not themselves maltreated as children (Belsky, 1980; Spinetta & Rigler, 1972).

While maltreating parents share some common characteristics, maltreatment cannot be explained or predicted by the study of individuals. Maltreatment is a social act that emerges in the context of the parent-child relationship. We turn now to a discussion of this issue.

A P P L I C A T I O N

Taking it Personally

If you were abused or neglected as a child, you are at some increased risk of maltreating your children. However, your risk is substantially reduced if you are aware of the problem and take precautions. A happy marriage, financial well-being, well-timed pregnancies, and reading parenting literature can significantly reduce your risk of repeating the sins of your parents.

If you already have children that you have abused or feel that you are likely to abuse them, seek professional help immediately. Social services can be most effective in relieving family stress, and family therapy can promote healthy relationships with your children and improve your parenting skills.

If you maltreated your children who are now parents themselves, recognize the risk you have created for them and seek family therapy that can deal specifically with the intergenerational issues involved.

Bottom Line: The cycle of abuse is not prophesy. It can be broken by anyone who is motivated to do so. Effective therapies are available for those with the courage and commitment to change.

The Parent-Child Relationship

The ecological perspective suggests that maltreatment is a function of the relationship between parent and child (Belsky, 1980), a view that has received considerable research support in the literature about parent-child attachment. Several studies have described an increased likelihood of anxious-attachment relationships—avoidant, ambivalent, and disorganized/disoriented patterns—between parents and children in maltreating families (Carlson et al., 1989; Egeland & Sroufe, 1981; Lyons-Ruth, Connell, Zoll, & Stahl, 1987). Disturbance or dysfunction in the attachment relationship may promote struggles over control and compliance between parents and children—fertile ground for escalation in the use of harsh discipline leading to maltreatment.

Apart from the attachment relationship, there is evidence that the interactions of maltreated children and their parents are decidedly negative (Bousha, Twentyman, & Craig, 1984; Burgess & Conger, 1978). Studies have shown that maltreating parents display lower rates of verbal and physical interaction with their children and tend to emphasize negative aspects of their children's behavior. Neglectful mothers stand out as the most negative of all mothers studied. The physical and psychological impact of disturbances in the mother-child relationship are described in Box 9.6.

BOX 9.6

The Maternal Deprivation Syndrome

Frederick II, king of Sicily, wanted to know which of the languages spoken in his time was the true natural language of mankind. He designed an experiment that assumed that if infants were not artificially stimulated by the language of their mothers, they would spontaneously emit the true language. He separated a group of newborns from their mothers and isolated them on an island in the care of wet nurses who were instructed not to speak to the babies.

The king never discovered the true language: All of the infant subjects in the experiment died. The king concluded "for they could not live without the petting and the joyful faces and loving words of their foster mothers" (Gardner, 1972, p. 76).

Is it possible that deprivation of maternal affection could affect the *physical* growth and development of the infant? Studies of the two types of growth retardation in infants and young children partially confirm this hypothesis.

In one pattern, known as **nonorganic failure to thrive** (NOFT), infants show growth retardation—low weight for height—with no identifiable organic disorder. The emaciated condition of NOFT ba-

bies makes them physically unattractive. They are emotionally flat, that is, they rarely smile or vocalize and are difficult to cuddle. The condition is usually diagnosed in the first two years of life, and early medical intervention results in rapid catch-up growth in the majority of cases (Oates, Peacock, & Forest, 1985). The absence of early intervention may result in long-term growth retardation and persistent cognitive and behavioral difficulties (Altemeier, O'Connor, Sherrod, & Vietz, 1985).

The mothers of failure to thrive babies are generally described as depressed or emotionally unresponsive (Field, 1987). They offer little stimulation and show minimal positive emotion toward their babies (Pollitt, Eichler, & Chan, 1975). A study of these mothers and their NOFT babies in the home environment indicated less maternal responsiveness to and acceptance of their babies and a more disorganized home environment as compared to mothers in a control sample (Casey, Bradley, & Wortham, 1984). Maternal stress associated with dysfunctional relationships to the infants' fathers, negative perception by the mothers of their own childhood experiences, and minor birth complications were associated with NOFT in a second study (Altemeier et al., 1985).

In general, failure to thrive emerges from a disturbance in the infant-mother relationship that disrupts the normal pattern of affection, nurturance, stimulation, and nutrition. This is a classic bidirectional problem, wherein the mother

does not nurture the infant adequately and the infant appears unable to elicit more responsive care (Casey et al., 1984). Treatment of NOFT, therefore, requires immediate medical intervention with the infant to restore normal weight, parental training in caregiving techniques, and family therapy to reduce disorganization and stress in the home environment.

The second pattern of growth retardation is referred to as **deprivation dwarfism**. This pattern is generally diagnosed after age two and is characterized by shortness of stature, with weight proportional to height. Malnutrition does not seem to be involved, but the children display bizarre eating-related behaviors such as stealing and hoarding food, gorging themselves, eating unusual substances, and eating from garbage cans. Some of the children display growth hormone deficiencies (Powell, Brasel, & Blizzard, 1967). When these children were removed from the disturbed home environment, they grew rapidly and growth hormone levels returned to normal.

Both failure to thrive and deprivation dwarfism evolve in a context of maternal deprivation and chaotic family lifestyle that disturbs the normal patterns of social interaction between infants and caregivers. These disturbed social patterns undermine the feeding/eating process, resulting in growth retardation. We do not yet know why some infants are affected early in development (failure to thrive) and others later in development (dwarfism).

The Maltreating Family in the Community

The status of the family in the community and the ability of the community to provide social support to the family have been related to the likelihood of maltreatment (Vondra, 1990). Research has shown that periods of unemployment are associated with episodes of child abuse (Steinberg, Catalano, & Dooley, 1981) and that maltreating families are more likely to have financial difficulties (Garbarino & Crouter, 1978). Further, isolation from social support systems—such as extended family, friends, and neighbors—also is associated with maltreatment (Garbarino, 1977). High-risk neighborhoods often lack the social support services that could relieve some of the stress that families experience in trying to raise young children (Garbarino & Sherman, 1980). Many distressed families—particularly maltreating parents—show great resistance and hostility toward social services, frustrating community efforts to intervene (Vondra, 1990).

Abusive parents perceive the world as a hostile place (Trickett & Susman, 1988) and have a strong tendency to isolate family members from outsiders. This isolation decreases children's exposure to more positive models and minimizes the family's access to social support. These studies suggest that interventions must be designed to break the pattern of isolation in maltreating families by encouraging parents to participate more actively in the community and by helping the community to better serve the needs of families under stress. Unfortunately, interventions with high-risk maltreating families have been successful only when community services have been coordinated and implemented at a very high level (Cicchetti & Toth, 1987).

Maltreatment and Culture

American society actively promotes, frequently rewards, and rarely punishes the display of aggression by adults. Our daily experience is saturated with images of violence on TV, in sports, and—with increasing frequency—in our homes and neighborhoods. In spite of this escalating pattern of violence and abuse, many American families adhere rigidly to a double standard with respect to violence. Parents defend their right to use physical punishment to discipline their children but argue against the use of any form of punishment to control their children in day-care centers and schools. Many Americans defend the right to own guns and to display them in their homes in full view of children, but react with righteous indignation when these same guns turn up at school.

It is difficult to imagine a climate more conducive to the maltreatment of children. I believe our children suffer, as do we, from our flagrant hypocrisy on the subject of violence in America. As long as our culture continues to maintain a double standard with respect to violence, we are doomed to reap what we sow in the minds of our children.

A P P L I C A T I O N

Preventing Maltreatment

Preventing maltreatment in your family begins with an honest appraisal of the potential for abuse by *all* family members, including children. Preventing maltreatment by nonfamily members involves three complementary strategies: (1) teach your children how to avoid and/ or to report abuse outside the home; (2) train your children to play an active role in the security of the home—for example, by locking doors and not admitting strangers; and (3) screen and monitor substitute caregivers such as neighbors, babysitters, day-care workers, and bus drivers. Watch your children for unusual changes in mood or behavior before and after episodes of substitute care. Communicate with other families that use these services.

For the community, the ultimate goal is to prevent maltreatment *before* children are victimized. However, identifying at-risk families is, at best, an inexact science, and the right of privacy must be respected. Preventive intervention must be aimed broadly at communities: supportive services to reduce family stress, family therapy to treat dysfunctional relationships, and education to improve parenting skills. Communities must work to provide opportunities for employment, housing, and health care services for all families.

The most effective way to prevent the *repetition* of maltreatment is to expose child abusers

to public scrutiny and legal sanctions. Reporting child abuse is now mandated in all states; failure to report abuse and neglect is considered a crime. Child abuse hot lines have been established in most areas of the country to respond to reports of abuse with information, advice, and referral to appropriate agencies (call Directory Assistance in your area). Confidentiality is assured.

Bottom Line: Prevent the abuse of your children with a *proactive* strategy, both inside and outside the home. Monitor and screen their social contacts and teach them to play an active role in protecting themselves.

Looking Back

We have illustrated the opportunities and risks associated with physical and motor development during the preschool years. Promoting optimal physical fitness and motor skills is a complex and challenging task for all who care for children at this early age. The danger lies in caregiver ignorance and complacency. The family's complacency with respect to physical development increases the risk of less than optimal physical fitness, obesity, illness, and accidental injury. Optimal physical development requires a proactive approach by parents and other caregivers that capitalizes on children's spontaneous physical activity, challenges them to participate in vigorous exercise, encourages their proper nutrition, and rewards them for physical and motor achievements.

Above all, we must be aware that we make daily choices that affect our children's physical development: When we sit passively watching sports on television rather than taking the children to a playground; when we buy children videogames rather than bicycles or sports equipment; and when we snack on chips and dip rather than fruit and vegetables, we are not giving our children the models they deserve. We must become sensitive to these choices and learn to consistently select those options that promote our children's physical well-being.

CHAPTER REVIEW

PHYSICAL GROWTH Although the rate of physical growth slows considerably in the preschool years as compared to the rapid growth of infancy, there are still impressive changes in weight, height, and body proportion from the beginning

of the third to the end of the sixth year. By kindergarten, most children have lost their baby fat and have begun to take on a more adultlike physique.

MOTOR DEVELOPMENT Under optimal conditions, preschool-age children make

enormous strides in gross motor and fine motor skills. Running, jumping, climbing, hopping, drawing, and construction skills develop in a maturationally defined sequence. The rate of development is influenced by the opportunity for practice and the availability of physically challenging and socially stimulating environments.

MANUAL CONTROL Preschool children make great strides in manual control, particularly in the area of self-help skills. Parents can facilitate this development by being sensitive to the complexity of these skills and by providing a supportive physical and emotional context for learning. The key elements are patience and persistence.

MINOR ILLNESS Infants and young children average eight to nine minor illnesses per year, with higher rates among children in day care. Childhood illness stresses the family, particularly when social support is lacking. Positive effects of minor illness include learning role expectations associated with illness, learning about inner states, and observing parents in helping and empathic roles.

ACCIDENTAL INJURY Injuries account for half of the deaths of children. Many of these deaths result from automobile accidents, and half of these could be prevented by the use of restraint devices. Compliance with seat-belt laws can be facilitated by well-designed community programs aimed at children and their parents.

CHILDHOOD INJURY Children with certain temperaments and disorganized home environments can promote childhood injury. Unsafe playground equipment is a major source of accidental injury in this age group.

PHYSICAL FITNESS Preschools and day-care centers have a great but largely untapped potential for promoting physical fitness in young children. They should integrate free-play activities and more structured approaches to maximize the potential of *all* children.

OBESITY Obesity in preschool children is now recognized as a risk factor for cardiovascular disease. Obesity results from a positive energy balance. Genetic factors predispose some children to obesity, but a family-based approach of exercise, proper nutrition, and limited TV-watching can be highly effective in controlling obesity.

STRESS Stress in the family life of preschool children is associated with elevated levels of illness and accidental injury. In extreme instances, children may show self-destructive behavior.

MALTREATMENT More than 2 million children are reportedly maltreated each year in the United States. Many more cases go unreported. Forty percent of these children are preschool-age.

ECOLOGY OF MALTREATMENT For the most part, adults who maltreat children are not mentally ill. Maltreatment is best understood in the ecological perspective as a conspiracy of negative influences on the individual parent, the family, the community, and the society. Prevention of maltreatment requires an integrated approach at all these levels.

CYCLE OF ABUSE The commonly held belief that maltreated children will eventually become abusers themselves is only partially supported by research. Two out of every three maltreated children show resilience in the face of their abuse and go on to become adequate parents who do not maltreat their children.

MALTREATING RELATIONSHIPS There is an association between maltreatment of children by parents and the emergence of anxious-attachment relationships.

FAILURE TO THRIVE Extreme forms of maternal deprivation can have devastating effects on the physical and emotional development of infants and young children. Disturbances in the mother-child relationship have been identified in cases of failure to thrive in infants and toddlers and deprivation dwarfism in older children.

Key Terms

ossification	obese	child sexual abuse
marking time	positive energy balance	neglect
enuresis	immanent justice	abuse cycle
construction skills	maltreatment	nonorganic failure to thrive (NOFT)
physical fitness	child abuse	deprivation dwarfism

10

Cognitive and Language Development in Early Childhood

Looking Ahead

- During the preschool years children increasingly use symbols to stand for perceived objects and events. How does this affect children's problem solving and behavior? What can caregivers do to promote symbolic reasoning?

- Preschoolers tend to perceive their world in piecemeal fashion, failing to grasp overall meaning. How does this affect their ability to form concepts?

- Preschoolers have difficulty adopting another individual's perspective and cannot mentally reverse their thought sequences. How do these limitations affect children's behavior? What can adults do to improve the quality of children's thinking?

- Preschoolers show the beginnings of a theory of mind: the ability to guess what others are thinking, feeling, and wanting. Do young children really know what adults are thinking? How does it affect their behavior?

- Preschoolers make substantial progress in their ability to process information. What specific changes can we expect in attention and memory? What limitations remain?

- Preschoolers make dramatic strides in language development, speaking in longer and more complex sentences. Can young children engage in conversations? Should we be concerned when children appear to be talking to themselves?

- Increasing numbers of preschoolers spend great proportions of their time in preschools and day care. What effects do these environments have on cognitive and language development? Can preschools compensate for lack of stimulation in the home environment?

T he preschool years mark a critical transition from the toddler's action-oriented problem solving and two-word utterances to the school-age child's logical thinking and adultlike use of language. During this transition children display a unique quality of thought and language that is captured in Keisha's observation of Leshonda at bedtime.

Keisha reads the last few lines of "Little Red Riding Hood" to four-year-old Leshonda, the fifth reading in as many days. She closes the book, kisses her daughter, turns out the light, and leaves the room. As she walks down the hall she hears the light click back on and decides to investigate. Listening through the partially open door, she overhears Leshonda "reading" her version of "Little Red Riding Hood" to her ragdoll, Bamunda.

"Now, Bamunda, there was this white girl, see, with this raggedy red hat and this wolf with this fine red hat, and they lived at Grandma's house in Brooklyn. See, this is Ridin' Hood and this is the wolf.

"Now you listen or I'll spank you!

"OK. So Ridin' Hood went to Grandma's house, but she was not home, so she called the wolf on the telephone and asked him where was her grandma, anyway! The wolf said, 'Behave yourself and come home!' So Ridin' Hood put on her raggedy hat and went to see the wolf. The wolf had long teeth and he was in bed 'cause he was sick.

"See, Bamunda? See that wolf's nose? He has a baaaad cold. I told you so! Why don't you listen to me when I tell you about this stuff? Now, you listen to the story and don't be bad like that wolf.

"Then Grandma and Grandpa came home and told Ridin' Hood the wolf was bein' bad and he was cussin' 'bout somethin' and she should spank him. Bad wolf, bad wolf, bad wolf, spank, spank, spank." Keisha hears Leshonda hitting the book repeatedly. "'You a bad wolf and I gonna take that fine red hat 'cause you be so bad.' And that is the end of the story.

"Now you go to sleep, Bamoooonda, like I told you."

Trying to keep from laughing out loud, Keisha tiptoes down the hallway, knowing that Leshonda and Bamunda would soon be fast asleep.

Just two years earlier Leshonda could not pay attention to or understand a story, much less narrate one. Now, at four, listening to stories and retelling them to her doll have become a daily ritual. Developmentalists would say that Leshonda's ability to tell a story to her doll—without prompting from her mother—reveals a great deal about her cognitive and language abilities. First, her ability to tell a story suggests that she has a **script** of the story—a mental representation of the story characters and the sequences of events involving those characters. Scripts help children to organize their behavior in everyday situations, increasing the efficiency and consistency of their responses (Nelson, 1981b). Second, Leshonda's ability to tell a story to her doll indicates that she can transform complex thought sequences into language to communicate meaning to others. Third, in this particular instance, she has chosen to communicate to a doll, suggesting that she has also developed the ability to *pretend*—a relatively sophisticated cognitive skill.

Although Leshonda's storytelling shows remarkable developmental progress, her rendition of the story also reveals significant limitations. Despite having heard the story over and over, her script for "Little Red Riding Hood" is largely inaccurate, departing substantially from the logic of the original story. Piaget believed that such inaccuracies and logical errors are typical of children's conceptual abilities at this age, reflecting the difficulties they experience in learning to think symbolically.

Although all children progress through similar sequences of cognitive and language development, their rate of progression varies substantially, resulting in wide-ranging individual differences in developmental outcome (McCall, 1981; Rutter, 1985). These differences reflect pervasive sources of risk and opportunity in the social context of development during this period. Variations in the quality of the home environment and day-care center, in the responsiveness of parents and other caregivers, and in access to early educational and social services have a predictable result: By the time children enter elementary school, some will be cognitively and linguistically competent and ready to cope with the challenges of middle childhood, while others will be developmentally delayed, incompetent, and maladaptive, particularly in learning situations.

The first sections of this chapter will describe the emergence of symbolic reasoning during the preschool years. Later sections will focus on language during the same period. Finally, we will examine risk and opportunity for cognitive and language development during the preschool years.

Cognitive Development in the Preschool Years

Our description of cognitive development during the preschool years emphasizes the extensive contributions of Jean Piaget (1962, 1970), his colleagues, and many researchers who have refined, elaborated, and reformulated his insights. Although specifics of Piaget's theory—such as the ages at which children develop certain abilities—have been revised by later research, his work continues to orient many researchers in their studies of child development.

Piaget refers to the period from three to six years as the **preoperational stage** of development. We will begin with a general description of children's thinking at this stage, followed by descriptions of the sequences of development in specific content domains such as causal reasoning and the concept of number.

Piaget's Preoperational Stage

Piaget uses the term **operational** to refer to the logical systems of thought that emerge in middle childhood. For example, by age seven or eight, most children understand that while all horses are animals, all animals are not necessarily horses. They also understand that addition is the reverse of subtraction. As implied in the term *preoperational*, Piaget describes preschoolers as incapable of these advanced forms of reasoning. His emphasis on children's limitations rather than their strengths has been somewhat frustrating for those seeking to apply the theory in practical settings (Hohmann, Banet, & Weikart, 1979). Nonetheless, Piaget and his colleagues (1945/1951) have presented a provocative description of the unique qualities of perceptual and cognitive development during the preschool years. We will begin with Piaget's concept of the *symbolic function*.

The Symbolic Function As indicated in Chapter 7, Piaget (1936/1953) identified the end of the second year of life as a major turning point in cognitive development, marked by the advent of the **symbolic function**: the ability to use *symbols* to represent or stand for perceived objects and events. The symbolic function takes several distinct forms as the child moves into the third year of life: deferred imitation, symbolic or pretend play, mental images, and language.

In *deferred imitation*, the child observes the behavior of a model and imitates that behavior when the model is no longer present. The child maintains modeled behavior in symbolic form over relatively long periods of time, imitating the behavior only when it becomes adaptive to do so. For example, after watching parents using eating utensils for several months, a toddler makes his first spontaneous attempts to use a spoon. Deferred imitation greatly expands children's capability for solving everyday problems.

In **symbolic** or **pretend play**, children pretend that an object is something other than what it really is. For instance, an 18-month-old lifts an empty cup to his face, tips it as if to drink, licks his lips, and looks at his mother with the telltale grin that indicates he knows he did not *really* drink. A somewhat older child transforms a doll into a "real" person or pretends that a wooden block is a boat, sailing the treacherous waters of the bathtub. For preschool children, symbolic play transforms virtally any situation into an unlimited world of make-believe, with pervasive effects on their social and emotional development.

Leshonda, Devon, and Tamara climb through the basement window into the open courtyard behind the Jackson family's 100-year-old 3-story brownstone apartment, now a wasteland of mounds of garbage, abandoned cars,

The advent of symbolic play late in the second year marks the child's entry into the world of make believe. These preschoolers have transformed everyday kitchen items into the props needed to support their pretense.

and discarded drug paraphernalia. Like other preschoolers, Leshonda and her friends are preparing to play house, but in Bed-Stuy there are no plastic eating utensils, rubber food, or simulated kitchen appliances — only the courtyard and its debris.

The children rummage through a nearby mound of trash, feverishly searching for props to support their pretend play. They quickly transform hubcaps, tin cans, and assorted sticks and scraps of metal into dinner ware; chips of concrete, chunks of wood, and rusty wire simulate food; the hulled-out interior of a 1973 Ford Mustang becomes a kitchen and dining area.

Although there are only three children, there are several imaginary guests — some friendly and others not so friendly. One reason the game is so much fun is that the children have much more control over this make-believe world than they do over their real world.

Although the ease with which Leshonda and her friends transform a pile of junk into a game suggests a simple underlying process, research has identified a number of distinct cognitive skills required to initiate and sustain pretend play (Rubin, Fein, & Vandenberg, 1983). Each of the pretend skills follows a unique course of development:

Shifting Context Two- and three-year-old children typically require support from the play setting to initiate and sustain their pretense. A toddler, for example, is more likely to pretend to eat in a setting like a kitchen than in a back yard. In contrast, an older child is capable of *shifting context*, performing routine behaviors outside her typical setting. Leshonda and her friends shifted context by transforming the abandoned car into a kitchen and dining room.

Substituting Objects Children often substitute one object for another in their pretend play. From 14–19 months toddlers act out pretense on realistic dolls, with little use of unrealistic or ambiguous substitute objects such as blocks or sticks (Watson & Fischer, 1977). During their third year, children become increasingly able to transform objects into the props needed for their pretend play episodes (Harris & Kavanaugh, 1993); during the preschool years, they become progressively less dependent on realistic props (Jackowitz & Watson, 1980; Ungerer, Zelazo, Kearsley, & O'Leary, 1981; Watson & Fischer, 1977). Leshonda and her friends easily substitute pieces of ambiguous junk for the utensils and food items necessary for their play. They also incorporate imaginary guests into their dinner, a capacity that typically appears by age three or four.

Substituting Other Agents for Oneself Researchers have observed a developmental progression in how children use *agents* in their pretense (Watson & Fischer, 1977). When pretense first appears early in the second year, toddlers are the agents of their own acts of pretense. For instance, a child may pretend to feed herself by bringing an empty spoon to her mouth, or pretend to go to sleep by putting her head down on a table. Later in the second year, children begin to use dolls in pretend play, but only as passive agents. For example, the child may talk to the doll, but she does not imagine the doll talking back to her or to other dolls. By the beginning of the third year most children use dolls as active agents; children pretend that dolls initiate and sustain their own behavior as in talking, running, or playing with other dolls. When the doll becomes its own agent, the child pulls the strings as the doll assumes a humanlike (or sometimes superhumanlike) role in the pretense.

Sequencing and Socialization of Pretend Episodes Although pretense begins with single acts, children coordinate the acts into sequences of increasing length and complexity through the preschool years (Nicolich, 1977; Piaget, 1962). A two-year-old's hair combing may expand into a four-year-old's sequenced grooming: washing, putting on makeup, combing hair, and dressing. Such sequences also begin to incorporate behavior patterns for agents who reflect conventional roles, that is, the police are expected to catch crooks but not to perform housecleaning tasks, and doctors give shots but do not milk cows (Flavell, 1985).

The symbolic function is also expressed in the ability to form *mental images*: internal representations of external objects or events. Mental images free children from the here and now, enabling them to think about objects when the objects are not physically present and to think about events before, during, and after their occurrence. For the first time, the child can integrate experiences from the past into the present to plan for the future.

The three forms of symbolic function mentioned thus far—deferred imitation, pretend play, and images—express private meanings derived from personal experience. For example, one child may pretend to eat with exaggerated motions of the arms and mouth while a less demonstrative child may simply move an empty spoon back and forth from her plate to her mouth. The idiosyncratic nature of the symbolic function in young children limits their ability to communicate their thoughts to others, challenging caregivers' interpretive skills and patience.

The Advent of Preconcepts

Piaget believed that preschool-age children tend to focus their attention on minute and often inconsequential aspects of their experience, a process he referred to as **centration**. For instance, a three-year-old may remember nothing about his babysitter other than her red hair. Centrated perception results in unsystematic samplings of isolated bits of information. Consider three-year-old Carlos's experience while visiting a zoo: Somewhat overwhelmed by the novelty and complexity of the day's events, Carlos's unsystematic sampling of centrated perceptions includes a lion's head, popcorn, cages, ice cream, throwing peanuts, raw meat, his father taking pictures, and his mother tearing her dress.

Piaget suggested that such collections of images, derived from centrated perception, merge into **preconcepts**: disorganized, illogical representations of the child's experiences. Carlos's representation of "zoo" is a prime example. Although his preconcept includes images relevant to the concept of "zoo," such as a lion and cages, it also includes irrelevant images of visitors and events unique to his family's experience. Similarly, Leshonda's preconcept of "Little Red Riding Hood" is a conglomeration of bits and pieces of the real story, extracted during her mother's many readings. These fragmentary images are integrated and elaborated to produce Leshonda's own, preconceptual rendition of the story. Although preconcepts provide a less than adequate representation of children's experiences, they do establish a foundation for the eventual emergence of logical concepts in the subsequent stage of cognitive development.

Transductive Reasoning: Thinking with Preconcepts

According to Piaget, the disorganized and illogical nature of preconcepts severely limits the quality of preschool-age children's reasoning and problem solving. We can understand the difficulty by comparing preoperational thought to the primary forms of logical thought in older children and adults: induction and deduction. In *induction*, we derive general principles from particular examples. An eight-year-old boy who observes that in each of his classes the teachers favor the girls might induce the general principle that girls are teachers' pets. Conversely, in *deduction*, we use general principles to predict particular outcomes: The same boy could use his general principle to deduce that when he enters his next grade, his new teacher will likely favor girls.

Piaget believed that preoperational children are incapable of thinking inductively or deductively. Instead, they think by **transduction**, reasoning within the unsystematic collections of images that constitute their preconcepts. Leshonda believes that Little Red Riding Hood took the fine red hat from the wolf because he had been "so bad." Her logic is transductive: private and meaningful only within her preconceptual understanding of the story.

Egocentrism   According to Piaget (1959; Piaget & Inhelder, 1967), one of the major limitations of preoperational thought is the child's inability to conceptualize the perspective of other individuals—a quality he called **egocentrism.** His use of the term did not imply that young children are selfish, merely that they have difficulty seeing the world as others see it.

The effects of egocentrism on perception and cognition are illustrated in Piaget's experiments with the three-mountain problem (Piaget & Inhelder, 1967). Children between 4 and 12 years of age were shown a 3-dimensional model of a mountain scene (see Figure 10.1). Each mountain had its own color, size, and shape and a unique object (a cross, a snowcap, or a tiny house) on its peak. Piaget asked each child to examine the model from different visual perspectives. He then moved a doll to various vantage points around the model and asked the child to select a picture that represented the doll's point of view at each location.

Piaget reported that children under eight consistently identified their own view as that of the doll—a clear demonstration of egocentrism. Later researchers have modified his experiment and have identified *non*egocentric responses from children as young as three years (see Box 10.1). Nevertheless, those who deal with preschoolers should not expect them to consistently recognize another individual's perspective.

Irreversibility   A second limitation of preoperational thought is **irreversibility**—the notion that preschoolers cannot mentally reverse their transductive sequences of

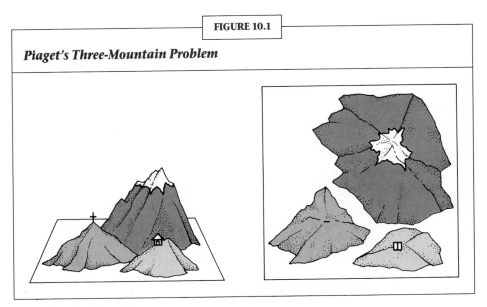

FIGURE 10.1

Piaget's Three-Mountain Problem

SOURCE: *Piaget & Inhelder, 1967*

thought. For instance, a three-year-old boy who is about to hit another boy has difficulty thinking about the fact that his behavior is likely to cause an act of retaliation by the other child. Similarly, the boy may not understand why saying he's sorry may compensate for some misbehavior. Irreversibility of thought can be a significant liability in problem solving; it explains why preschoolers can take things apart, but cannot put them back together; can find their way to distant locations, but cannot find their way home; and can climb to the top of structures but cannot climb down.

A P P L I C A T I O N

Dealing with Transductive Reasoning

Although your preschooler's thinking may frustrate you, forcing your logic on your child will prove even more frustrating. Rather than lecture, provide natural corrective experiences. For example, if your child is looking at an object that you cannot see and she insists that you can, don't argue. Simply ask her to join you and share your perspective. Then ask what she

BOX 10.1

Piaget's Egocentrism: An Opposing View

Are preschool children really as egocentric as Piaget's early findings indicated? Not according to a number of studies designed to replicate and extend Piaget's work (Borke, 1975; Gzesh & Surber, 1985; Huttenlocher & Pressen, 1979).

In one study, three- and four-year-olds were shown models of scenes that were more familiar to children than Piaget's three-mountain scene. One scene included a house, a lake and a sailboat, and miniature farm animals. Grover, a character from "Sesame Street," substituted for Piaget's doll, taking various positions around the model. The model was mounted on a revolving turntable to allow each child to turn it around to see how the scene looked to Grover at each position. The results showed consistent *nonegocentric* responses by the preschool-age subjects. This study casts considerable doubt on Piaget's description of the egocentricity of young children.

John Flavell and his colleagues (Flavell, Omanson, & Latham, 1978; Lempers, Flavell, & Flavell, 1977) challenged Piaget's notion of egocentrism in visual perception. Flavell devised a simple task using a card with different pictures — such as a dog and a cat — on each side. After the child was familiarized with both sides, the card was held up between the child and the researcher and the child was asked to describe what the researcher could see. The researcher placed a second picture on the table with a divider positioned so that only a portion of the picture was visible to the child and the other part was visible only to the researcher. Again, the child was asked to identify what the researcher could see.

The results suggested two developmental levels of visual perception. At level 1, three-year-olds showed the beginnings of nonegocentric response by identifying what the researcher could and could not see. At the developmentally more advanced level 2, four- and five-year-olds recognized that when an object is simultaneously visible to both themselves and another person from different vantage points, each individual receives a somewhat different impression of the object.

Thus, in contrast to Piaget's view, visual egocentrism appears to decline gradually through the preschool years.

sees and help her to compare her perceptions from the two vantage points. If your child confuses sequences of events, revisit the events with her, pointing out which comes first, second, and so on.

In general, parents can promote children's logical thinking by providing repetitive experiences with real objects and events, by reducing complexity to simple pieces, and by encouraging exploration.

Bottom Line: Be patient and tolerant of logical errors in your preschooler's thinking. Your child's thinking will become more logical as she discovers the natural order of objects and events in her environment through active explorative play.

Reasoning in Specific Content Domains

The centrated, egocentric, transductive, and irreversible qualities of preoperational thought profoundly affect children's reasoning in specific content domains: causal reasoning, classification, quantitative reasoning, and distinguishing between appearance and reality. In each domain, we will examine Piaget's views and the contributions of others who have extended or amended his work.

Causal Reasoning The concept of *physical causality*—knowledge of what makes various events and outcomes happen—is essential in developing an understanding of the world of objects. Piaget (1930) interviewed children to tap their understanding of the causes of natural phenomena, such as what makes clouds move and streams flow. Preschool children frequently gave magical explanations, as in the following interview (p. 62):

PIAGET: What makes clouds move?

CHILD: When we move along, they move along too.

PIAGET: Can you make them move?

CHILD: Yes.

PIAGET: When I walk and you are still, do they move?

CHILD: Yes.

PIAGET: And at night, when everyone is asleep, do they move?

CHILD: Yes.

PIAGET: But you tell me that they move when somebody walks.

CHILD: They always move. The cats, when they walk, and then the dogs, they make the clouds move.

Piaget believed that these explanations reflected the egocentric quality of the thought process during the preschool years. Egocentricity in this context may involve more than just the inability to take the perspective of another individual; it implies that preschool children tend to think of themselves as the center of the universe, with magical power to cause events to occur. Although Piaget suggested that egocentricity declines during the preschool years, even the seven-year-olds in his sample had progressed only to the point of explaining the movement of clouds as an act of God. Children did not attribute cloud movement to the effect of wind currents until age 10. Piaget did not discuss whether the children's responses may reflect what they had been taught rather than how they think.

Later research has suggested that causal reasoning is achieved somewhat earlier than Piaget had indicated. One study (Bullock & Gelman, 1979) examined whether young children understand that causes come before effects. The researchers designed an apparatus (see Figure 10.2) that contrasted two event sequences: In the first sequence the cause *preceded* the effect: A hand puppet dropped a steel ball into a visible runway on the left

FIGURE 10.2

Apparatus to Study Preschoolers' Understanding of Causality

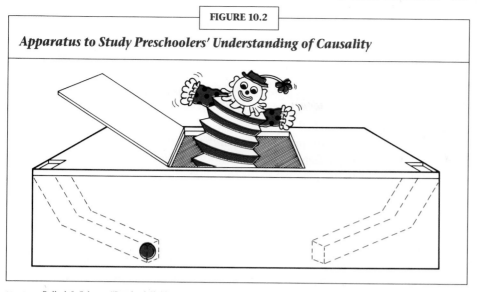

SOURCE: *Bullock & Gelman, "Preschool Children's Assumptions about Cause and Effect,"* Child Development,
50, 1979. © *The Society for Research in Child Development, Inc. Used by permission.*

side of the apparatus; when the ball reached the end of the runway, it disappeared momentarily, followed by the sudden appearance of a jack-in-the-box. In the second sequence the cause *followed* the effect: A different puppet placed a steel ball in an identical runway on the right side of the apparatus, just *after* the jack-in-the-box appeared.

When asked to choose the ball that "made jack come up," almost all of the three-, four-, and five-year-olds dropped the ball into the runway on the left side, indicating that they understood that causes precede effects. Thus preschoolers may show causal reasoning with respect to highly salient visual displays of cause and effect, presented in highly familiar settings.

Classification   **Classification** refers to the pervasive human tendency to group objects on the basis of particular sets of characteristics. For instance, adults maintain distinct categories for fruits and vegetables, indoor and outdoor sports, safe and unsafe sex, to name just a few. Adult classification systems are organized on the basis of *class inclusion*, that is, a class must be smaller than any more inclusive class in which it is contained (Bjorklund, 1989). For instance, while adults know that all dogs are animals, they also know that not all animals are dogs.

Do preschool children spontaneously group objects into inclusive classes? Maria inadvertently discovers the answer to this question a few days after Carlos's fourth birthday.

> *Cleaning Carlos's room is no picnic, but Maria is determined to get it over with as fast as possible. As she enters his room, she nearly faints: Carlos has removed every object from his shelves and drawers — toys, books, rocks, pencils, crayons, candy wrappers, socks, shoes, and various objects that defy description — and placed them on the floor. Maria yells "Caaaarrrllllos!" but Carlos is unavailable for comment.*
>
> *Sitting on the bed surveying the damage, she begins to notice some order to the chaos. Perhaps this is not the act of a madman (or madchild) after all. She first notices that everything is arranged in little piles of two or three objects,*

but none of the piles make any sense to her. For example, one pile has a huge lump of dried Play-Doh, a miniature soldier, and a shriveled apple core. A second pile has nearly every sock he owns, and a third pile has a fire engine, a valentine, and a red sock.

When Carlos appears sheepishly at the door, Maria surprises him by asking about the first pile. Without taking a breath he said, "The man climb-ded the mountain to get the apple."

"And what is this," his mother asks, pointing to the second pile.

"Thems're socks for feets."

"And what is that?" pointing to the third pile.

With a touch of arrogance, Carlos says, "Thems're all red stuffs, doncha know?"

Although Carlos shows a spontaneous tendency to classify, the principles that guide his sorting differ from those adults use. Piaget and Inhelder (1964) identified the principles that young children use for classification by asking them to sort geometric forms that varied on two or more dimensions, such as color and shape. The results suggested a three-stage developmental progression in classification:

Stage 1 Children (up to 5 years) produced *graphic collections*—pictures made with objects. For instance, a child might arrange several of the forms into a square and refer to it as a house or a barn. Children at this stage have no overall plan for their sorting, constantly shifting the basis for their collections.

Stage 2 Children (6 to 8 years) produced *nongraphic collections*—forms grouped by similarity on a single dimension at a time. For example, a child might first place all triangles in one pile and all squares in another, then switch to a new dimen-

The children's task is to choose the geometric shape that fits the empty matrix location. The matrix implies that the missing shape must be both round and small. Preschool-age children would generally not be able to solve this matrix problem without special training.

FIGURE 10.3

Two-Dimensional (Size and Shape) Matrix Sorting Task for the Study of Preschoolers' Classification

sion, placing all red forms in one pile and all blue forms in another. Children at this stage are incapable of classifying on two dimensions simultaneously.

Stage 3 Children (later childhood to early adolescence) understand the relationship between classes and subclasses. For example, viewing a display of four miniature horses and two cows, children will correctly answer the question—"Are there more horses or more animals?"—indicating that they understand that the larger class of animals includes the smaller subclass of horses. Children at this advanced stage can also use multiple dimensions to sort objects, for instance, grouping large triangles separately from small squares (see Figure 10.3).

Follow-up research has questioned Inhelder and Piaget's stage description of classification (Bjorklund, 1989). One study found few graphic collections in preschool children's sorting (Denny, 1972), and other studies showed that preschoolers spontaneously group play objects by similarities (Denny, 1972; Smith, 1979), perhaps as early as the second year of life (Gopnik & Meltzoff, 1987). Furthermore, there is evidence that language training—teaching preschoolers category labels, such as "furniture," "animals," or "clothing"—can promote their classification skills (Waxman & Gelman, 1986). These findings suggest that Piaget may have underestimated the classification ability of young children. Box 10.2 presents a more progressive view of the development of classification concepts.

Quantitative Reasoning **Quantitative reasoning** is the ability to estimate the amount of things in terms of number, size, weight, volume, speed, time, and distance. For instance, a three-year-old, attempting to serve herself from a serving dish, must

---

BOX 10.2

Phases of Classification

David Bjorklund (1989) describes the development of classification as a series of four phases:

In the *idiosyncratic phase*, two- and three-year-olds group objects in random pairs, justifying their pairings with the following type of comments:

"Horse and pants go together because that's a horse and those are pants."

"Boy and hammer go together because they're alike."

In the *perceptual phase*, three- and four-year-olds group objects by common perceptual characteristics, justifying their groupings with the following type of comments:

"Pie and hat go together because they're both round."

"Cat and squirrel go together because they both have long tails."

In the *complementary or thematic phase*, preschool- and kindergarten-age children group objects based on relationships that children observe in real life or in their play.

"Cat and milk go together because cats drink milk."

"Cowboy, horse, and pants go together because a cowboy needs pants to ride a horse."

In the final *conceptual phase*, school-age children group objects based by category (for instance, animals, vehicles, tools) or by similarity in function (birds, airplanes, and bumblebees).

Although preschool children have been shown to have the capacity for conceptual classification, they seem to prefer a complementary or thematic basis for classification. Carlos's groupings of objects on the floor (see page 298) are primarily of a thematic nature. If Maria asked him to, Carlos could probably reorganize the objects to produce conceptual groupings.

estimate how much to take in relation to the size of the space on her plate (and perhaps the size of her appetite). A four-year-old who has been asked to set the table for dinner faces an even more formidable task: He must count the number of individuals to be seated, group dissimilar objects (forks, knives, spoons, napkins) into settings, and distribute settings (or sets) in 1 to 1 correspondence to each place at the table. Are these concepts beyond the capability of preschoolers?

As in other domains, Piaget (1962) presented a more conservative view of children's development than other researchers. We will review these contrasting views with respect to the development of concepts of quantity, number, and counting.

Quantity   The development of quantitative reasoning begins with the notion that things in the natural environment exist in certain amounts, and that those amounts only change when actions—such as addition and subtraction—are carried out. For instance, a child must come to understand that the amount of a serving of mashed potatoes does not change when the mound of potatoes is squooshed into the shape a pancake. Piaget described this as an example of **conservation**—the notion that certain attributes of objects and events remain unchanged, despite transformations or changes in other attributes. The difficulty that preschool children experience with conservation of quantity is illustrated in Leshonda's interaction with her friend.

> *Keisha is in the kitchen preparing a snack for Leshonda and her friend Keta. Knowing the girls' sensitivity to "Who got more?" she painstakingly measures out exactly one-half the bottle of juice into each cup and tells the girls the snack is ready. Within a few moments the predictable squabbling has begun:*
> *"I want that glass."*
> *"No, I want that one."*
> *Although Keisha has taken care to pour equal amounts, she has made the mistake of selecting one glass that is tall and thin and another that is short and stout. Both girls want the tall and thin glass.*
> *When Keisha realizes the problem, she brings a second tall, thin glass to the table, pours the juice from the short, stout glass into it, and says, "You see, they both have the same amount. Now you can stop fighting." Although the girls are now satisfied, Keisha decides to try a little experiment: She pours the juice back into the short, stout glass. As she anticipates, the fight starts all over again, with both girls again wanting the taller, thinner glass.*

When Leshonda and Keta compare the two glasses as originally set out, both girls center on the higher level of the liquid in the taller, thinner glass as an indication of quantity. Neither child understands that the increase in the height of the liquid is compensated by a corresponding decrease in the diameter of the glass, leaving the quantity unchanged (see Figure 10.4). Despite Keisha's compelling visual demonstration of the equivalence of the two liquids, the girls revert to their original belief in nonequivalence when the juice is returned to the short, stout glass.

Number   Piaget (1962) adapted the conservation task to the study of children's understanding of number. In this study, the experimenter shows a container of white beans and a container of black beans. The experimenter forms an evenly spaced row of six black beans and asks a child to take an equal number of white beans and arrange them in a row parallel to the black beans. If the child selects the correct number, the experi-

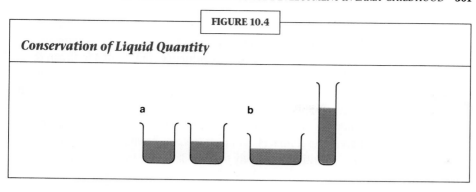

FIGURE 10.4

Conservation of Liquid Quantity

a. Identical beakers with equal amounts of liquid.
b. The original quantities in new containers.

menter spreads out the white beans to make their row longer than the row of black beans (see Figure 10.5) and asks the child if the two rows have the same amount. The experimenter varies the spacing of the beans to probe the child's understanding of 1 to 1 correspondence and the concept of number.

According to Piaget, children's responses show a consistent developmental trend: Young preoperational children show no understanding of 1 to 1 correspondence, responding only to the physical appearance of the rows: If one row is spread out, it is judged to have more beans; if compressed, it is judged to have fewer beans. Slightly older children show some understanding of 1 to 1 correspondence but continue to be confused by the superficial appearance of the rows. According to Piaget, conservation of number is not achieved until the stage of concrete operations, at seven to eight years of age.

As in other domains, there is convincing evidence that conservation of number may come much earlier than Piaget proposed. Rochel Gelman and her colleagues (Gelman, 1972; Gelman & Gallistel, 1978; Gelman, Meck, & Merkin, 1986) designed the "magic task"—a simplified conservation task in game format—to assess young children's number conservation. The task involves two sets of toy mice: a set of three mice called the winners and a set of two mice called the losers. After determining that the children distinguish between winners and losers, the experimenter secretly adds or subtracts a mouse from one of the sets while varying the distance between mice within the sets. Contrary to Piaget's findings, preschool-age children reacted consistently to any change in number and were unaffected by changes in the spacing between mice within a set. Apparently, preschoolers can conserve number, at least in very simple tasks.

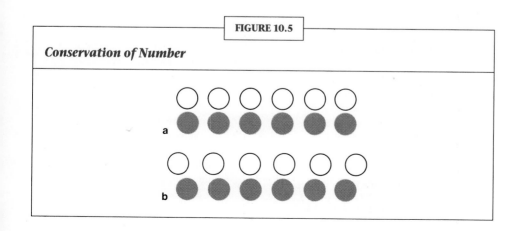

FIGURE 10.5

Conservation of Number

a. In 1 to 1 correspondence.
b. After one row is spread out by the experimenter.

Counting   If young children can conserve both quantity and number, can they count? For Gelman and her colleagues, **counting** implies the systematic assignment of numbers to items in an array, following the five principles in Box 10.3 (Gelman & Gallistel, 1978). Although many two-year-olds engage in countinglike behavior, they assign numbers to objects unsystematically—repeating and reversing number assignments and violating 1 to 1 correspondence. Three- and four-year-olds begin to incorporate all five principles when counting small numbers of objects. Children come to apply these principles to increasingly larger numbers of objects toward the end of the preschool years, with most children counting accurately to 20 or 30 by the time they enter first grade.

A P P L I C A T I O N

Promoting Quantitative Reasoning

From a practical perspective, parents and educators should be sensitive to the gradual nature of a child's development of number concepts and arithmetic skills during the preschool years. Young children may be predisposed to develop basic numerical skills without special

---

BOX 10.3

Five Principles of a Counting System

Gelman and Gallistel (1978) studied the counting behavior of young children and derived five principles that must be mastered for systematic, accurate counting of an array of items:

1. **The 1 to 1 Principle**   One and only one distinctive number name must be assigned to each item in the array. No item may be counted more than once and no number used more than once. Although preschoolers seem to understand the principle, they

tend to make more errors as the number of items grows.
2. **The Stable-Order Principle** Number names must be assigned in a stable, repeatable order. This principle is being followed as long as a sequence of number names is applied consistently across different arrays of items. While most preschoolers recognize this principle, some have idiosyncratic but stable order systems, such as a three-year-old's repetitive use of the sequence "one, two, three, five, eleben, forby-two."
3. **The Cardinal Principle** The final number in a counting sequence gives the total number of items in the array. Preschool children appear to follow this principle for arrays up to 19 items (Fuson, Pergament, Lyons, & Hall, 1985). Many young children show that they follow this principle by consistently offering the

last number name they assign when asked "How many are there?" This is true even when they count items incorrectly (Gelman et al., 1986).
4. **The Abstraction Principle** Virtually anything can be counted: tangibles such as objects and events and intangibles such as ideas, values, and emotions. This does not appear to be a problem for young children, at least with respect to tangible items. When children begin to play with number sequences, they count any set of objects they encounter.
5. **The Order-Irrelevance Principle**   The order in which objects are counted is irrelevant. For instance, if a child were counting the stuffed animals in her room, the bear could be counted first or second or third, as long as it is eventually assigned a number.

training or incentives (Gelman, 1980). Although some parents encourage their young children to count by rote to very high numbers—for example, from 1 to 100—it is unlikely that such training promotes the development of a *logical system* of counting.

Bottom Line: The natural environment provides unlimited opportunities for parents to introduce numbers to their preschoolers. Make counting fun and avoid drill. Unless children show specific signs of developmental delay, parents should make no special interventions to teach number concepts.

Distinguishing Between Appearance and Reality   Adults are aware that appearances do not always reflect reality: People do not necessarily mean what they say, intend what they do, or feel the emotions implied by their facial expressions. In contrast, young children are often confused by discrepancies between appearance and reality (Flavell, 1985). At three, Carlos is highly susceptible to illusion.

> *Carlos chases his cat Chico through the kitchen and into the pantry where the cat momentarily disappears. Carlos peers into the pantry and suddenly runs out screaming hysterically "monster, monster, monster, Daddy, monster, monster . . . ," his feet barely touching the floor as he runs. Emilio enters the kitchen and leans into the pantry tentatively to see what form this particular monster might have taken. Just beyond the pantry door sits Chico, covered from head to tail in flour, looking ghostly, terrifying, and slightly confused. Emilio tries to show his son what has happened, but Carlos will not accept the explanation. Even after some of the flour has been brushed off, Carlos keeps his distance from the monster, unable to recognize Chico's emerging identity.*

When Chico's fur changes suddenly from black to white, Carlos perceives a change in the animal's identity; that is, to Carlos, Chico is no longer Chico. Rheta DeVries (1969) explored children's ability to distinguish between appearance and reality with the help of an unusually cooperative cat named Maynard. She introduced three- to six-year-olds to Maynard and, after determining that each child could identify the cat as a cat, the experimenter hid the front of Maynard's body behind a screen with only its tail visible to the child. The experimenter then put a realistic mask of a dog's face on Maynard's face and brought him out from behind the screen.

Interviews with the children revealed a developmental progression: The youngest children were completely deceived, believing that the first animal had somehow disappeared or run away and the new animal was a real dog in every way. Although slightly older children believed that the animal was still Maynard, they speculated that he had been physically transformed. Most six-year-olds distinguished between appearance and reality, categorically denying the possibility that any change could have taken place in Maynard's identity. Further study of children's ability to distinguish between appearance and reality is presented in Box 10.4.

A P P L I C A T I O N

Appearances and Risk

The failure to distinguish between appearance and reality makes your preschooler vulnerable to deception and to other dangers disguised by benign appearance. For example, preschool-age children are highly susceptible to natural illusions such as the solid appearance of ice on the surface of a lake or the cool appearance of the metallic surface of a steam iron. You cannot ensure your child's safety with logical explanations. Not until first grade can your child understand both the appearance and the reality of common objects and events, reducing — but by no means eliminating — risks in natural settings.

Bottom Line: Be sensitive to situations and objects that can fool your child by their harmless appearance. Abstract explanations and warnings offer little protection. Direct intervention — for example, by removing dangerous objects — may be necessary throughout the preschool years.

Explaining Cognitive Development

So far in this chapter, we have described a series of stages (or substages) in children's cognitive development. We have not, however, explained what causes children to progress from one cognitive substage to another. People who work with children need to know those causes in order to know how to help children climb to each next stage.

BOX 10.4

Appearance and Reality

John Flavell and his colleagues extended the study of the *appearance-reality distinction* by exposing children to a variety of tasks. For instance, in one study (Flavell, Flavell, & Green, 1983a) they showed three- to five-year-old children a series of extremely realistic-looking fake objects. For example, one object was an egg that was really made of stone. The children were then asked "When you *look* at this with your *eyes* right now, what does it look like?" The experimenter then revealed the reality of the egg by squeezing it in front of the children and allowing the children to squeeze it.

The children were then asked "What is this *really*, *really*? Is it really, really an egg, or really, really a stone?" The experimenter also showed

them the fake egg through a magnifying glass that made it appear much larger and through a filter that made it appear blue rather than white. Each time the experimenter asked what the object really was.

Although some children as young as three showed a beginning understanding of the distinction between the object's appearance and its reality by answering both questions correctly, others tended to make one of two types of error. When describing the object's *properties*, such as its size and color, some children indicated that the fake egg both looked like an egg and really, really was an egg (which it was not) or that it looked blue and really and truly was blue (which it was not). In contrast, when they were asked about the *identity* of the object — that is, "what it really is" — they indicated not only that the fake egg is a stone but also that it looked like a stone (which it did not).

These errors suggest that the information processing ca-

pability of young children may be limited to thinking of objects in only one way at a time, thereby simplifying the way that objects and events are represented in the cognitive system. By focusing either on the object's appearance *or* on its reality, children maintain an artificial consistency between the perception of the object's appearance and the concept of its actual identity (Flavell, 1985). In contrast to the responses of preschoolers, older children are able to view the world of objects and events in more complex terms by simultaneously representing both the object's appearance and its identity (Flavell, 1985).

These findings were replicated with children in the People's Republic of China (Flavell, Zhang, Zou, Dong, & Qui, 1983b) and with tasks that were made easy (Flavell, Green, & Flavell, 1986). Even efforts to train young children to make the appearance-reality distinction have also been largely ineffective (Flavell et al., 1986; Taylor & Hart, 1990).

As we discussed in Chapter 2, Piaget explained cognitive development as a balance between what he called accommodation (adapting concepts to fit reality) and assimilation (applying concepts to interpret reality). As their physical and social environment becomes more and more complex, preschoolers adapt by gradually revising (accommodating) their preconcepts of how the world works. They can deal with only relatively small increases in the complexity of their environment by making correspondingly gradual increases in the complexity of their thinking.

For example, you will recall that in Gelman's (1972) study of number conservation, three-year-olds were able to recognize that two unevenly spaced rows of mice had the same number of mice (three) in them. Had Gelman increased the number of mice in each row to four, the children would have had to make a bite-size revision of their number concept. However, increasing each row to five or six mice would have been overwhelming, beyond the children's capacity to accommodate. Children consolidate their revised preconcepts by using them over and over to interpret (or assimilate) their environment, preparing to accommodate to even greater complexity.

Piaget suggested that such changes emerge quite naturally as children interact with their environment. But caregivers need to know what types of activities, materials, and adult input are most conducive to preschoolers' cognitive development. Those who have looked to Piaget for guidance on such matters have found him long on generalities and short on specifics (Hohmann et al., 1979).

More useful in this regard has been the independent work of James Hunt (1961) in the United States and Lev Vygotsky (1978) in the Soviet Union. Hunt (1961) conceptualized the *context* of cognitive developmental change as the **problem of the match**. By *match*, he meant the difference between the child's existing cognitive level in a given content area and the next level, that is, the level that can be achieved by accommodation of the relevant schema. You can think of the match as the next bite-size piece of new complexity in learning a concept. Children may find the match either in the course of explorative play — if the piece happens to be available — or more directly in the sequenced experiences of a preschool curriculum. Hunt suggested that regardless of the source, children are irresistibly drawn to complete the match. The task for those who deal with children is to create learning environments that consistently provide challenging experiences to all children at all levels in all content areas.

Lev Vygotsky (1978), a Soviet psychologist, said that cognitive development occurs within the **zone of proximal development**. The *zone* is the gap between what a child can accomplish independently and what the same child can accomplish when provided with optimal support from caregivers and challenging materials. Teaching and learning within the zone involve two related processes: *joint collaboration* and *transfer of responsibility* (Diaz, Neal, & Vachio, 1991). An adult and a child achieve **joint collaboration** when they share responsibility for solving some problem, such as a puzzle or learning to ride a bike. In the early stages of learning, the adult takes the primary role in guiding the learning process. As the child begins to grasp the nature of the problem, the adult **transfers responsibility** — that is, the adult decreases his or her role in guiding the child, giving the child greater opportunities to perform independently (Rogoff, 1986). Ideally, the adult provides the necessary support and assistance to enable a child to function at the upper limit of the zone of proximal development, then gradually withdraws that support as the child's ability to perform independently increases (Bruner, 1983). This process is called **scaffolding** (Diaz et al., 1991). If collaboration and transfer of responsibility are successful, the child solves the problem independently and is then ready to be challenged at a higher level of difficulty.

We can facilitate development through scaffolding — providing just enough support to help the child perform at his or her best. Here we see a preschooler scaffolding the early walking of her baby brother.

Together the concepts of the match and the zone of proximal development provide a theoretical base for those who seek to promote cognitive development in natural settings.

The Information Processing Perspective

Piaget's view of cognitive development as a discontinuous series of stages has been challenged by those who view the development as a more continuous process of change in children's information processing capabilities (Case, 1985; Fischer, 1980; Siegler, 1986). *Information processing* refers to children's use of attention and memory to gain and retain information about their environment and their use of that information to solve problems. Research in this area has attempted to show that these capabilities emerge gradually from infancy through the early and later childhood years.

Paying Attention   Heather's experience in day care at circle time—a structured group activity for storytelling, songs, and imitative games—illustrates the tenuous nature of information processing in preschool children.

> *A caregiver flicks the ceiling lights—the signal that circle time is about to begin. Heather and the other 19 children in her day-care class descend on the circle taped on the carpet and jockey for the best place to sit. The teacher says, "Quiet down now, children, and pay attention! I have a WONDERFUL book to read to you today." She repeats her request several times until all but one or two of the children are momentarily quiet and looking in her general direction.*
>
> *Before she reaches the third sentence of the book, however, Heather's eyes begin to dart around the circle, seduced by every child's movement and every toy within her view. Within seconds, several children follow Heather's lead, ignoring the story. The teacher pauses momentarily to recapture the children's attention, but succeeds only in losing others as a result of the disruption.*
>
> *Seeking to make an example of Heather, the teacher asks her to tell what the main character in the story has just done. Heather's mute response shows quite clearly that she remembers nothing of the story—a complete failure of information processing.*

This scene is not uncommon in groups of preschoolers. In many situations, the teacher spends more time trying to elicit and regain attention than in the activity itself. Similar problems in information processing can be observed when children are engaged in fine motor skill activities, such as coloring, pasting, or solving puzzles. Consistent with Piaget's notion of centration, young children have difficulty sustaining attention on play materials for long periods of time.

Moreover, their approach to gathering information tends to be unsystematic. This is illustrated in a classic study by Elaine Vurpillot (1968). Children from 3 to 10 years of age were shown paired line drawings of houses, as illustrated in Figure 10.6. Some of the paired houses were identical and others differed in one or more ways. She asked children to examine the pictures and identify which pairs were identical. Although even the youngest children had no difficulty when the drawings were identical, preschoolers had considerable difficulty when the drawings were not identical, especially when they differed in a single feature.

FIGURE 10.6

The Paired Drawings of Houses Used to Study Children's Attention

SOURCE: *Vurpillot, "The Development of Scanning Strategies and Their Relation to Visual Differentiation," Jour-*
nal of Experimental Child Psychology, 6, 1968. Used by permission of Academic Press Inc.

By studying the children's eye movements (which had been recorded on film) Vurpillot concluded that the children's errors were attributable to the unsystematic way that they visually scanned and compared the drawings. Preschoolers examined only some of the windows in each house and continued scanning even after they had noticed features that were obviously different. Older children deployed attention more strategically, working down rows or across columns of windows, systematically comparing features.

Remembering   Although the preschooler's unsystematic attention skills may limit the *quality* of input to the system, the *quantity* of available input is overwhelming. In any given situation, children are bombarded with far more information than they can possibly process. One problem lies in their limited memory capacity. Following the computer model for information processing systems (Atkinson & Shiffrin, 1968), the input to the system can be maintained only temporarily in *short-term memory*—a storage component capable of retaining information for up to 20 seconds. If the information is to be retained for longer periods of time, the child must employ strategies to move it to *long-term memory*, where large amounts of information can be maintained indefinitely.

Research has shown that preschool children have only limited capacity to process information for long-term memory. In general, young children are not very good at memorizing lists of meaningless and unrelated items, such as nonsense syllables or random sequences of digits presented in laboratory tasks. For example, the average four-year-old can recall only about four digits, the average six-year-old about five digits (Case, Kurland, & Goldberg, 1982; Chi, 1976). However, if the stimuli to be remembered are more meaningful and relevant to the children's life experiences—such as remembering cartoon characters or peers—preschoolers' memory approximates that of older children and adults (Chi & Ceci, 1987).

In contrast to their poor performance in laboratory tasks, young children remember a great deal of information about everyday events in which they have participated. One study (Fivush, 1984) examined kindergarten children's memory for activities experienced during a novel event: a trip to a museum. Six weeks after the event children had no difficulty reporting both general information about the type of event ("What happens when you go to *a* museum?") and specific details about the particular event ("What happened when you went to *the* museum?"). Even after one year, the children's recall of the event was extremely accurate. Similar results were demonstrated in a more recent study with three- and four-year-olds over an eight-week period (Jones, Swift, & Johnson, 1988).

Although preschoolers show considerable ability to remember novel events such as visiting a museum or a circus, their overall capacity for short- and long-term memory is much less sophisticated than older children's and adults'. How can we explain this deficiency in information processing? Several factors seem to be involved, but the most important one is that older children are more likely than younger children to use **strategies**, conscious activities that facilitate memory. For example, older children are more likely to use the strategies of *rehearsal* (repeating lists over and over) and *organization* (grouping items by category, such as all food items and all vehicles) when trying to memorize lists of items in a laboratory task (Flavell, 1985). Although some young children are capable of using such strategies when instructed to do so, they are unlikely to use these strategies spontaneously.

A second important factor is that older children are better able than preschoolers to conceptualize their own cognitive processes—an ability referred to as **metacognition**. Metacognition includes knowing how much you know about a given subject, knowing strategies for learning or remembering that subject, and knowing how and when to implement those strategies. In general, preschoolers show little understanding of why they have difficulty remembering or solving problems or what actions they might take to improve their performance. Preschoolers tend to overestimate their ability to remember (Flavell, Friedrichs, & Hoyt, 1970) and deny that they ever forget anything (Kreutzer, Leonard, & Flavell, 1975).

Can preschoolers' memory be improved through training? Garrett Lange and Sarah Pierce (1992) reasoned that young children's memory might be improved if instruction included several critical components: (1) demonstration and practice in using strategies; (2) encouragement to apply strategies in new tasks; (3) a rationale for strategy use; (4) feedback on strategy effectiveness; and (5) incentives for trying hard to use strategies. The results of their research showed that such training improved four- and five-year-olds' use of strategies and recall of study items. Thus, when instruction is designed to show children how, when, and where to use a memory strategy, and provides an incentive to perform well, preschoolers' limited capacity for information processing can be substantially improved.

A P P L I C A T I O N

Promoting Attention and Memory

An effective way to help your preschooler focus attention is to reduce distraction. In learning situations, eliminate extraneous visual exhibits (mobiles and posters), muffle background noises, provide succinct instructions, and display only those learning materials essential to learning. At home, provide a quiet play area, organize play materials, and eliminate background noise by turning off the TV. Elicit your child's attention directly by varying the level of your voice rather than shouting, by providing novel materials, and by reinforcing for sustained attention and task persistence.

Your child's memory can be enhanced in several ways: Provide repetitive experience with real objects and events, emphasize important things to remember, encourage rehearsal, and promote recall with incentives. If you engage your child in conversation about his experiences, his memory will be significantly improved.

Bottom Line: Be sensitive to your preschooler's limited capacity for processing information. Bombarding him with stimulation is just as destructive to learning as boring him with unchallenging materials.

The research on information processing supports the notion that some aspects of cognitive development emerge very gradually, without clearcut stages to define developmental change. Do these results refute Piaget's theory? Although some developmentalists argue that they do, others have accepted the challenge of reconciling the data on attention and memory with Piaget's observations, resulting in more sophisticated theories of cognitive development (Case, 1985; Fischer, 1980). We will consider these theories in Chapter 13.

Developing a Theory of Mind

As adults, we could not cope with our everyday social experience without the ability to guess what others are thinking, feeling, and wanting. The better we are at guessing what is going on in someone's head, the more adaptive we are likely to be. Psychologists have proposed that people develop a **theory of mind** that helps them explain and predict human behavior. The theory is based on the notion that people's *beliefs* and *desires* cause their behavior (Wellman, 1991).

For example, when strangers approach, we wonder what they might *want* and why they *think* that we might be of assistance. If we guess that they want to rob us because they think we have lots of money, we may adapt by avoiding their approach. When one child hits another child, we try to imagine what the child wanted from the victim and why the child believed that aggression was a good way to get it. **Mindreading**—not to be confused with supposed psychic abilities—is the term psychologists use to refer to the cognitive process by which individuals attribute desires and beliefs to other individuals in order to understand and predict their behavior. The competent mindreader assumes that different individuals may differ substantially in desires and beliefs in any given situation (Dunn, 1991). Thus, competent mindreading requires that the theory of mind be revised to predict the behavior of any given individual in any given setting. At what point in development do children become capable of mindreading?

Research in the 1980s indicated that children begin to develop a theory of mind in the early preschool years (Wellman, 1991). Researchers base this estimate on several sources of evidence. First, in the second and third year of life, there is considerable growth in children's use of terms that refer to their own and other's desires and beliefs. For example, desire is expressed in the following conversation (Wellman, 1991, p. 34):

DAD: What happened to your foot?

CHILD: It hurt.

DAD: Broken? Or cut?

CHILD: You *want* to see?

DAD: No, I'll see it later.

CHILD: I *want* to show you.

Belief is expressed in this exchange (p. 34):

CHILD: Which one you *think* could fit? This one?

MOTHER: I think that one's a little large. Oh. I guess it does fit.

CHILD: You were wrong.

In a study of young children's spontaneous utterances, the use of the term *want* was firmly established before the second birthday. Belief terms such as *think* and *know* did not appear until just before the third birthday (Wellman, 1991). Thus we may conclude that children's theory of mind—based on attributing both desires *and* beliefs—emerges at about three years of age (Wellman, 1991).

A second source of evidence on the development of theory of mind comes from the study of children's ability to distinguish between things in the real world and mental events. Piaget (1929) proposed that young children frequently confuse what is mental and what is real. For example, he argued that young children believe that the events in their dreams really happened. Recent research, however, suggests that young children can in fact distinguish between real and mental events (Wellman & Estes, 1986). Researchers read three-, four-, and five-year-old children a series of stories (with line drawings) that contrasted a child having a *mental* experience with another child having a *real* experience. For example: "See this boy. He likes cookies very much. Right now he is hungry, so he is *thinking* about a cookie. This other boy likes cookies too. Right now he

When preschoolers were asked to use a puppet to hide a treasure from an adult, children as young as 2½ were capable of deception; they erased potentially helpful cues (footprints) and added potentially misleading cues. Researchers concluded that young children are able to deceive, and thus have a beginning theory of mind.

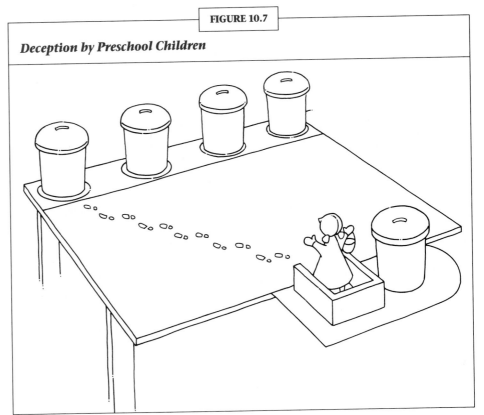

FIGURE 10.7

Deception by Preschool Children

SOURCE: *Chandler, Fritz, & Hala, "Small Scale Deceit: Deception as a Marker of 2-, 3-, and 4-Year-Olds' Early Theories of Mind,"* Child Development, *60, 1989. © The Society for Research in Child Development, Inc. Used by permission.*

is hungry, so his mother *gives* him a cookie." Subjects were asked to point to the boy who: (1) can see the cookie, (2) can *not* touch the cookie, and (3) can eat the cookie.

The results showed that even three-year-olds understood that you cannot see, touch, or eat something that another child *thinks, remembers, pretends,* or *dreams.* Thus, contrary to Piaget's theory, preschoolers can distinguish between mental and physical events.

A final source of evidence that preschoolers form a theory of mind comes from the study of their use of **deception** — that is, children's ability to create false beliefs in another individual. Michael Chandler and his colleagues (1989) developed a hide-and-seek game that required 2½- to 4-year-olds to use a puppet to hide a treasure in one of several differently colored containers. The puppet, called Tony, was designed to make ink footprints as it walked to a hiding place (see Figure 10.7). The children were shown that Tony made footprints but they could be wiped away with a sponge. Children were then taken from the room, and Tony hid the treasure while they were gone. When the children returned, they were able to follow the trail of footprints to find the treasure.

Then the children were told that it was their turn to "help Tony hide the treasure" so that the experimenter (who temporarily left the room) could not find it. Children's performances were scored on their use of deceptive strategies, including wiping out Tony's telltale tracks, lying to the experimenter about the location of the treasure, and laying false tracks to empty containers. Results showed that even the 2½-year-olds used a variety of deceptive strategies to create false beliefs.

All this evidence — that preschoolers use terms about desires and beliefs, that they can distinguish between mental events and actual events, and that they can deceive — provides strong support for the idea that preschoolers have a beginning theory of mind to help them explain and predict other people's behavior.

A P P L I C A T I O N

Theory of Mind

When your child makes a request and you respond, "Well, let me *think* about it," you are very likely promoting the development of your child's theory of mind. Comments like "You must be dreaming" or the classic teacher's command, "Let's put our thinking caps on" serve the same purpose. Be aware too that theory of mind may be expressed negatively, as in teasing and deception. You can help your child distinguish between socially acceptable applications of deception — in games and competitions — and less acceptable applications in personal relationships. Pointing out the natural consequences of deception will be far more effective than punishment, which is more likely to increase the deceptive behaviors.

Bottom Line: Parents beware! As your children progress through the preschool years, they will get better and better at "psyching you out," inferring your motives, anticipating your behavior, and catching you unaware.

Language Development in the Preschool Years

Toward the end of the second year of life, children have mastered many of the fundamental components of language: Their vocabulary is expanding rapidly, their pronunciation is improving, and they are forming two-word utterances for the first time. Their language development continues at a vigorous pace during the preschool years with continued expansion of vocabulary and syntax and dramatic progress in functional language use. Children begin to use language to regulate their own behavior. Carlos, for example, talks to himself while performing tasks that he doesn't like, as if giving himself instructions: "Bwush your teeths, bwush the back ones or you get cabities in your teeths." Most important, preschoolers begin to engage in conversation, exchanging ideas and points of view with adults and peers outside the family.

The Growth of Vocabulary

Young children live in a sea of language produced by adults, peers, and, in most homes, the endless drone of the TV. It is not surprising, therefore, that preschoolers learn up to nine new words per day (Clarke, 1983). Their vocabulary grows as they come to understand relationships among objects and events in their experience. For instance, children learn words that reflect their understanding of concepts of time, such as *before, now*, and *after*, and concepts of space, such as *under, over, far*, and *near*. The more complex the concept, the later in the developmental sequence children will learn the term for it. For instance, children learn *big-small* before learning *tall-short*, which in turn precedes the learning of *wide-narrow* (Clark, 1973; 1983). Similarly, while young preschoolers understand *top-bottom*, they typically do not master *front-back* until kindergarten age.

One other predictable sequence is the emergence of *wh-* words—*what, where, when, which*, and *why* (Bloom, Merkin, & Wooten, 1982; French, 1989). Although children begin to ask *wh-* questions in the third year, they show little interest in the answers they receive. However, older preschoolers employ these terms more appropriately—asking *wh-* questions and then waiting for answers and responding to the questions that are asked of them. One study showed, for example, that three- to five-year-olds responded meaningfully to *when* questions, if the questions were posed in meaningful contexts (French, 1989).

Learning the Rules of Grammar

To become competent speakers of a language, children must learn its **grammar**—the system of rules that structures how to combine words into meaningful sequences. John Flavell suggested that young children approach this learning as if they expect the language to be governed by rules. In Flavell's words, "They act as if they are constantly forming and testing hypotheses about the lawful and systematic properties of their language. They learn by rote when they must, but learn by rule when they can" (Flavell, 1985, p. 256).

One of the first rules learned by young children asserts that sentences are composed of noun phrases ("Little dolly") and verb phrases ("goes bye-bye"). They also learn that, in English, adjectives precede the nouns they modify. Thus while "big toy" is an acceptable utterance, "toy big" is not. Children growing up with Spanish learn just the opposite; "toy big" is correct in their language.

Roger Brown (1973) illustrated how children learn rules in his study of children's use of **grammatical morphemes**: inflections such as *-ing, -ed*, and *-s* that modify nouns, verbs, and adjectives. (Remember that a *morpheme* is the smallest unit of meaning in a language.) Brown showed that children learn grammatical morphemes in a fixed developmental sequence. For instance, English-speaking children learn to add *-ing* to verbs before learning to add *-s* to form plurals. Interestingly, children master the irregular form of the past tense of many verbs—such as *ran* and *broke*—before they learn the regular past tense form, *helped*.

Once they learn a rule, preschoolers tend to **overregularize** or overgeneralize its application. For instance, having first learned the *-ed* rule children may add *-ed* to all verbs—both regular and irregular forms—to indicate past occurrence: "The boy kicked the ball," "The boy ranned home," "She goed to the store." Much to the frustration of some parents, overregularization tends to be highly resistant to verbal correction and feedback.

Children first learn the grammatical morphemes that require the least information processing. For example, adding *-ed* to form a past tense requires only that children consider when the action took place. In contrast, learning the rule to form the past tense of the verb *to be*—that is, deciding whether to use *was* or *were*—requires that children simultaneously consider when the action took place and the number of subjects.

Communicating with Others

As important as vocabulary and grammar are, improved sentences alone do not ensure that meaning will be communicated from speaker to listener. Adequate communication requires that children master the *pragmatics* of language: the implicit rules, skills, and concepts that regulate the behavior of speakers and listeners in conversation. For example, young conversational partners must learn to take turns, alternating in the roles of speaker and listener. They need to be aware of each other's perspectives, adjusting and regulating their behavior accordingly. How well do preschool children cope with these requirements?

Piaget (1959) believed that egocentricity is a major impediment to mastering the pragmatics of conversation. He observed that preschool-age children frequently engage in **egocentric speech**: language that fails to consider the viewpoint of the listener. In **monologue**, children simply talk to themselves, seemingly oblivious to anyone around them. For example, Heather, all alone in her room, narrates a brief segment of her play with blocks: "Gonna put this here—oops, don't fit on top. But I can break it. No, no, it's too big and fat. Oops, I make it fall down."

At times, two or more children may engage in **collective monologue**: conversation-like turn-taking between egocentric speakers, with little or no transfer of meaning. Here is Carlos, at three, having a collective monologue with his friend Ramon:

CARLOS: Mine is gonna fall down.

RAMON: My mom gonna come pretty soon.

CARLOS: 'Cause its too big and too silly.

RAMON: She hafta go shopping with me.

CARLOS: What?

RAMON: We gonna get some pot pies for supper.

CARLOS: Watch out, it's gonna fall now!

RAMON: There she is! Mama, Mama!

Except for Carlos's fleeting interest in what Ramon said (when he asked for clarification), seven language turns resulted in no transfer of meaning.

It would be a mistake, however, to assume that collective monologue is the only kind of communication preschool children have with one another. Most preschoolers master the basic rules of conversation and use their scripts (knowledge of the routine sequences of behavior in common events) to extend conversations, particularly in sociodramatic play (Nelson & Gruendel, 1979). For example, children who have well-developed scripts for everyday activities—such as mealtime or getting ready for bed—can maintain the topic through multiple turns of a conversation. The type of toys that children are playing with also affects the length of conversation. In one study (Wanska, Pohlman, & Bedrosian, 1989) young children engaged in longer conversations when playing with Legos than when playing with a miniature hospital or with hospital props. Apparently, the less-structured toy caused the children to use language more productively to maintain the continuity of their play.

Egocentric speech has also been studied in the laboratory in the so-called *referential communication task* (Glucksberg & Krauss, 1967; Krauss & Glucksberg, 1969). In this task, two children—alternating in the roles of speaker and listener—communicate without being able to see what each other is doing (see Figure 10.8a). Both children have identical sets of blocks, with corresponding blocks in each set stamped with one of six novel designs (see Figure 10.8b). The speaker's task is to verbally direct the listener's stacking of the blocks in a preset order.

Kindergarten-age speakers were unable to provide the information the listeners needed to complete the task. They tended to point to the block in front of them and say "It goes like this," as though the listener could see what they were doing. The researchers concluded that competence with language—that is, the ability to utter grammatically correct sentences—does not necessarily imply competence with communication. In general, the results of the research on referential communication support Piaget's notion of egocentric speech.

However, there is considerable evidence that preschool children's speech may be less egocentric than Piaget claimed. In one study, three- to five-year-olds were paired with adults in a simplified referential communication task. The children communicated in greater detail to an adult whose vision was restricted than to an adult who could see the objects (Maratsos, 1973). In a second study, four-year-olds were observed to use simpler sentences and vocabulary when speaking to two-year-olds and more advanced levels of grammar and vocabulary when speaking to adults than when speaking to same-age peers (Shatz & Gelman, 1973). In a third study, four-year-olds were exposed to an adult who "accidentally" spilled a cup of liquid. When the children were brought back to the laboratory one week later and asked why the cup was on the floor, the children provided much more information about the spilling incident to an unfamiliar adult than to the adult who had caused the accident (Menig-Peterson, 1975).

The fact that children adjusted their speech complexity to the receptive capabilities of the listeners in each of the above studies suggests some appreciation of the listeners' perspective in a conversational context.

A P P L I C A T I O N

Dealing with Egocentric Speech

Although preschoolers may not be as egocentric as Piaget suggested, they will frequently misjudge the listener's perspective, providing less (or occasionally more) information than appropriate. They tend to be less egocentric if the information to be communicated is familiar and easy to describe, and if the plight of the listener is highly salient. You can help your child by alerting her to the differences that each individual can hear, see, and touch in a particular situation. For example, during a telephone conversation, you might say, "Remember, I can't see the toys you are playing with, so tell me *everything* that you see."

Bottom Line: Do not overestimate your preschooler's ability to understand and respond to the perspective of others. Tolerate your child's limitations, but also provide the cues that will help her move beyond egocentric responses.

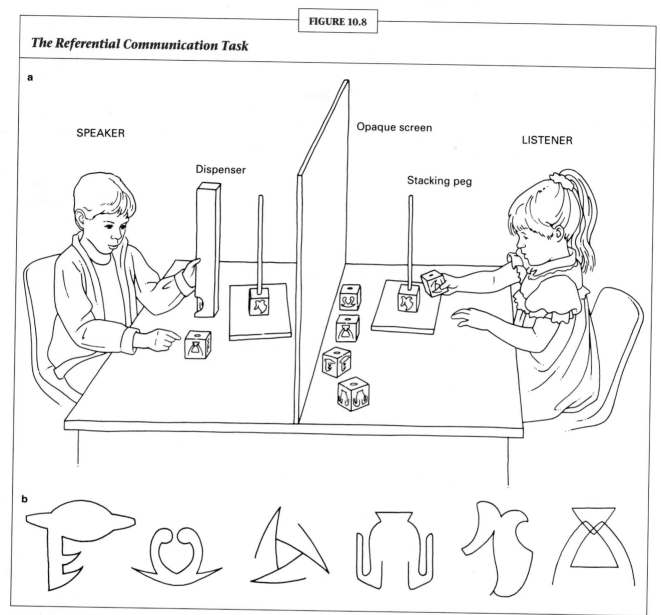

*a. Children participating in the task. **b.** The novel designs on the blocks used for this task.*

Private Speech

Leshonda at age three spends a great deal of time talking to herself, telling herself to do
things, narrating her own responses, and reinforcing or punishing herself for what she
has done: "Don't you take that cookie!" "Don't take it, now." "I told you." "Mmmmm,
mmmm, good cookies." "Oh oh, now you gonna get it. You bad, Leshonda!"

Most young children engage in some **private speech**, that is, speech with no apparent
communicative purpose. Research has shown that the form and function of private
speech vary widely during the preschool years. For example, some children characteristically mutter softly to themselves only in the privacy of their rooms, while others speak

audibly to themselves, even in the presence of others. Most private speech makes reference to children's ongoing activities: They narrate their behaviors and announce their next moves; they openly express emotion; they talk to and for dolls and create sound effects for solitary play; and they frequently repeat sounds and phrases over and over, just for the fun of it (Berk & Garvin, 1984).

Why do children engage in private speech? Developmentalists have varying views. Piaget (1959) viewed private speech as egocentric, serving no cognitive or communicative function. Vygotsky (1962) disagreed with Piaget, suggesting that private speech serves an important self-regulatory function; speech to the self organizes behavior by modifying its tempo or direction.

Vygotsky believed that children's use of private speech expands during the preschool years, increasing their behavioral self-control. He speculated that over time they gradually internalize private speech as **inner speech**, that is, thinking in words and sentences. Vygotsky's concept has received some support from studies of private speech, which have shown a developmental trend from talking out loud to muttering to oneself during the preschool years (Berk & Garvin, 1984; Frauenglass & Diaz, 1985). However, this trend may simply reflect children's growing awareness that talking out loud to oneself is socially unacceptable.

Cognitive and Language Development in Social Context

Although stage-by-stage descriptions provide useful perspectives on development, they tend to obscure the fact that children vary considerably in their rate and quality of cognitive and language development, particularly during the preschool years (Clarke, 1984, Rutter, 1985). As suggested in the introduction to this chapter, individual differences in intellectual development are a formidable challenge for those who deal with preschool children in practical settings: Parents must adjust their expectations to the differences in their offspring's rates of development; day-care workers must be flexible in their expectations for young children's mastery of self-help skills; and kindergarten and first-grade teachers must cope with the vast differences between high- and low-achieving students in a single classroom. How can we account for these individual differences?

Genetic factors account for some of the variation, but environmental experience also has a significant impact on the rate of cognitive and language development (Clarke, 1984; Hunt, 1961; Rutter, 1985). Dramatic evidence of environmental effects comes from several well-documented studies of children raised under extreme conditions of social isolation and physical deprivation (Clarke, 1984; Skuse, 1984).

For example, one study described the delicate balance between vulnerability and resilience in the development of a pair of twins, raised in a cellar from age 18 months to 7 years by an abusive stepmother (Koluchova, 1972, 1976). When discovered at age seven, the twins were mentally handicapped, emotionally disturbed, and unable to speak. However, years of rehabilitation and a favorable adoptive placement had a very positive impact on the children's intellectual and social development. The twins' IQ of 40 when first discovered at age 7, rose to 95 by age 11, and to 115 by age 20. Remarkably, both twins were eventually able to pursue professional careers in electronics (cited by Clarke, 1984, p. 143).

Further evidence of environmental effects comes from studies showing striking delays in cognitive and language development in children raised in some institutions (Dennis, 1973; Skeels & Dye, 1939). In one well-documented study, Wayne Dennis (1973) compared the experience of children raised in the Creche (an orphanage in Beirut, Lebanon) with children from the same institution placed in adoptive homes. The institution was staffed by unresponsive caregivers who provided minimal stimulation and no opportunity for explorative play. Among the children raised in the orphanage, Dennis found pervasive signs of retardation in infancy, with children averaging IQs of only 50 to 80 by their teenage years. Fortunately, some of the children at the Creche were adopted, with positive impact on their development. Despite the lack of stimulation in their first months of life, children adopted before their second birthday achieved normal intelligence later in childhood. However, resilience has its limits: Children adopted after two years of age regained only some of their intellectual potential, remaining several years below age level at later testing.

Similar evidence of young children's vulnerability and resilience came from observations of two severely neglected baby girls, ages 13 months and 16 months, placed in an overcrowded orphanage (Skeels, 1966; Skeels & Dye, 1939). Soon after their arrival, the babies were transferred to an institution for the retarded, where they were cared for, rather enthusiastically, by some of the older and less retarded institutionalized girls. Within just six months, the babies' intelligence reached normal levels.

This rapid gain prompted a broader study. Over the next several years, 13 additional retarded infants were removed from the orphanage and reared by retarded women in an institution. Researchers contrasted this experimental group with a comparison group of somewhat less retarded infants who remained at the orphanage. After 19 months, the infants in the experimental group were returned to the orphanage, tested, and compared to the children raised in the orphanage. The children in the experimental group had gained an average of 27 IQ points; the average IQ of the children in the comparison group had *declined* an average of 26 points over a similar period of time.

A follow-up study (Skeels, 1966) of the children in young adulthood showed that for the most part the experimental group children completed high school, married, and were employed in skilled or semiskilled jobs. Only one of the comparison group children became skilled, and several had never left the institution.

The studies of children raised in isolation or in institutions demonstrate that extreme changes in the environment can have dramatic negative and positive effects on cognitive and language development in early childhood (Rutter, 1985). However, these effects are not limited to the extreme environmental changes described in these studies. There is considerable evidence that typical variations in the caregiving environment have important impact on cognitive and language development (Clarke, 1984; Rutter, 1985).

More specifically, the quality of caregiving and stimulation in the home, nursery school, and day care has powerful effects on the rate and quality of cognitive and language development during the preschool years. Moreover, special educational interventions such as Project Head Start have been created to facilitate the cognitive and language development of disadvantaged children. The remainder of the chapter focuses on risk and opportunity for optimal cognitive and language development in these settings.

Risk and Opportunity in the Home Environment

Two longitudinal studies have provided insight into the effects of parents and the home environment on cognitive and language development in infancy and early childhood. The Harvard Preschool Project, conducted by Burton White and Jean Carew Watts (White & Watts, 1973), was initiated in 1965 to study the relationship between the quality of mothering during the second year of life and the development of children's competence during the preschool years. Detailed observations of mothers in direct interaction with their children in the home showed that mothers of more competent children

> . . . talk a great deal to their children. . . . They provide access to many objects and diverse situations. They lead the child to believe that he can expect help and encouragement most, but *not all* the time. They demonstrate and explain things to the child, but mostly on the child's instigation rather than their own. . . . They are imaginative, so that they make interesting associations and suggestions to the child when opportunities present themselves. They very skillfully and naturally strengthen the child's intrinsic motivation to learn. They also give him a sense of task orientation, a notion that it is desirable to do things well and completely. (p. 242)

Surprisingly, the more effective mothers made little effort to actively stimulate their children. Rather, they played the role of consultant, responding to questions and requests for help in relatively brief episodes of 30 seconds or less. While sharing their children's excitement and offering advice, they avoided solving problems for their children. These mothers created a home environment that recognized children's active role in cognitive development. They facilitated their children's exploration by providing a variety of interesting toys and by allowing the children access to most areas of the home. These mothers recognized that keeping their houses clean and neat was incompatible with their toddlers' curiosity and need to explore.

BOX 10.5

The HOME Scale

The HOME (home observation for measurement of the environment) scale provides a standard way to evaluate aspects of the home environment that are believed to promote young children's cognitive development. Trained observers visit the home for several hours, evaluating the family and physical environment on six subscales. Selected sample items included in each subscale are:

1. *Emotional and Verbal Responsivity of the Mother* Evaluates the mother's spontaneous vocalizations to her child, her verbal responsiveness to her child's vocalizations, and the mother's affection to her child during the home visit.
2. *Avoidance of Restriction and Punishment* Evaluates the mother's avoidance of shouting, spanking, and interference or restriction of her child's movements during the visit.
3. *Organization of the Physical and Temporal Environment* Evaluates the safety of the home environment and the family's access to substitute child care.
4. *Provision of Appropriate Play Materials* Evaluates whether the mother offers her child toys or interesting activities during the visit and whether the home contains age-appropriate toys and materials for the child's play.
5. *Maternal Involvement with the Child* Evaluates whether the mother talks to her child while doing her work, her surveillance of her child's activities, and her efforts to organize her child's activities.
6. *Opportunities for Variety in Daily Stimulation* Evaluates the father's involvement in care, the mother's story reading, the and the child's ownership of age-appropriate books.

Similar results were reported in a second longitudinal study of parent-child interaction and cognitive development (Bradley & Caldwell, 1976, 1980; Elardo, Bradley, & Caldwell, 1977). Using a new observational procedure called HOME they had developed for studying the quality of the home environment (Caldwell & Bradley, 1984; see Box 10.5), the researchers found significant relationships between selected aspects of the home environment and later intellectual development. In general, the children whose mothers were more verbally and emotionally responsive to them between 6 and 24 months of age had higher IQs (Bradley & Caldwell, 1976) and were more advanced in language development (Elardo et al., 1977) at 3 to 4 years of age.

While the results of these longitudinal studies support the *re*active or *re*sponsive role of parents, other studies point to a more *pro*active role for parents in promoting cognitive development (Brophy, 1970; Hess & Shipman, 1965). Jere Brophy compared middle-class and working-class mothers' approaches to teaching a sorting task to their four-year-old children. Middle-class mothers used a proactive approach that involved taking time to orient the children to the experimental task, focusing the children's attention on relevant aspects of the task, and providing appropriate labels. Working-class mothers gave brief and inadequate instructions and focused on their children's errors. The middle-class mothers' proactive approach was associated with greater success in the sorting task.

Highly effective parents do not constantly stimulate their children; they just provide an environment that encourages children's curiosity and facilitates their exploration. This mom is highly responsive to her son while continuing to do her own work at the computer.

These studies suggest that the opportunity for optimal cognitive and language development in the home is actively created by the enterprise of competent parents. Competent parents organize the home environment to encourage children to actively and safely explore and experiment (Wachs & Gruen, 1982). They are prepared to be responsive consultants and active teachers, flexibly adjusting their roles to their children's needs.

A P P L I C A T I O N

Promoting Cognitive Development at Home

The home environment offers excellent opportunities for young children's cognitive learning, but parents must be sensitive to what is enough and what is too much in promoting cognitive development at home. A noisy environment or an overstimulating regimen of planned activities can overwhelm your child's ability to process information, with much the same effect as an understimulating, restrictive environment. Try to achieve a balance. Provide both educational toys *and* safe access to the objects and events natural to the home. Common household events such as cooking, washing dishes, or fixing a faucet provide excellent opportunities for learning concepts—if your child is an active participant and if you engage in relevant conversation during the experience.

Most important, be a good consultant to your child. Respond to his interests and motivations. Answer his questions enthusiastically, add stimulating ideas where appropriate, and avoid abstract explanations. Don't solve problems for him that he is capable of solving by himself.

Bottom Line: Promote cognitive development at home by being a good consultant rather than a teacher and by providing a stimulating environment rather than implementing a curriculum.

The Influence of the Nursery School

The first nursery schools in the United States were established in the 1920s as university-based research and teacher-training centers. These early programs have been widely imitated over the years, with enrollment growing steadily to an estimated 1 million children each year in the United States (Peters, Neisworth, & Yawkey, 1985). Nursery schools have traditionally served the three- and four-year-old children of middle- and upper-class families; approximately two-thirds of the children enrolled in preschools in 1987 had annual family incomes over $35,000 (Children's Defense Fund, 1987). The part-time scheduling of most centers precludes their use as day care for many working parents.

Nursery school programs purport to enhance the development of normal children by providing a moderately stimulating socialization experience outside the home prior to entering elementary school. They typically claim to offer the "whole child" a well-balanced emphasis in all areas of development. They tend to expect cognitive and language abilities to develop as a natural product of spontaneous play, requiring little in the way of adult intervention. They make no pretense of serving the more demanding needs of handicapped, abused, or disadvantaged children.

Do nursery schools promote the cognitive and language development of the primarily middle-class children they serve? Very little research has been conducted on this subject. But a longitudinal study of low-risk children from educationally advantaged families indicated that boys (but not girls) who attended half-day preschool scored higher in reading and language in second and third grade than boys who had not attended preschool (Larsen & Robinson, 1989). In the absence of definitive research, middle-class parents of low-risk children may consider nursery school as an opportunity for subtle social and cognitive gains. Parents of children who show signs of developmental delay or learning disability are likely to find nursery schools unprepared to deal effectively with their children's special needs.

Risk and Opportunity in Day Care

The term *day care* refers to the provision of substitute care out of the family home for parents who cannot or choose not to provide that care themselves. Day care takes two distinct forms: *family day care* is provided in a private home, with a single caregiver for no more than five children; *center-based care* is provided for larger groups of children in a facility designed specifically for that purpose. Large day-care centers in urban areas may serve 100 to 200 children. Most centers operate on a 12- to 13-hour day, with some centers providing 24-hour service to accommodate the needs of parents on second and third shifts.

For the most part, day care in the United States is operated as a for-profit business within the private sector. As indicated in Chapter 8, the economics of day care often pits profit against program quality, resulting in wide variations in the quality of services in the community. While low-quality programs provide little more than custodial care, high-quality programs provide comprehensive services for the care and enrichment of young children. (For a career providing high-quality care, see p. 322.)

Does the quality of day care affect children's cognitive development? Despite a great deal of interest in this question, we can draw few conclusions from available research. There is evidence that middle-class children, cared for in high-quality centers, show no deficits in intellectual development (Clarke-Stewart, 1982; Clarke-Stewart & Fein, 1983) or in language development (Ackerman-Ross & Khanna, 1989), as compared to home-reared children. More positively, high-quality day care may slow the decline in test scores experienced by some disadvantaged children during the preschool years (Belsky & Steinberg, 1978), or temporarily increase cognitive performance in others (Clarke-Stewart, 1982).

For example, children in Bermuda who attended centers of uniformly high quality showed substantial gains in language and cognitive development (McCartney, 1984; McCartney, Scarr, Phillips, & Grajek, 1985). A longitudinal study conducted in Sweden indicated that children with early and extensive day-care experience—starting before the end of the first year—showed significantly higher cognitive test performance at age eight, as compared to children who began day care at later ages or who were raised at home (Andersson, 1989). The author attributed these positive findings to the very high quality of Swedish day care and to the fact that Swedish parents receive paid leave to care for their infants at home for the first six months, prior to placing them in day care.

Although research has demonstrated that *high*-quality day care may promote the development of children at risk, there has been little study of the short- or long-term effects of *low*-quality day care. One study of children's long-term experience in day care in the United States is a cause for serious concern (Vandell & Corasaniti, 1990). Researchers studied the effect of children's prior experience in day care on cognitive development. The subjects were eight-year-old middle-class children who had attended "minimal standard day care." The results: Children who had attended full-time day care from infancy through early childhood showed poorer academic performance and lower standardized test scores than children who had experienced part-time care or exclusive maternal care.

These results are not surprising. Children enrolled in full-time day care spend over

The Corporate Day Care Director

In 1984, Kay Moran was hired by the Publix Corporation — one of the largest grocery chains in the southeast — to develop a day-care center for its employees at its corporate headquarters in Lakeland, Florida. She began with nothing more than a concrete slab and a commitment from the corporate management to support her efforts to provide the highest quality care for children. The Publix Child Development Center is now in its eighth year, serving 160 children and their families. Kay and her staff have developed an extraordinary program that promotes the optimal development of every child in the center. Kay has begun her own effort to promote corporate child care, adapting the Lakeland model to the needs of other companies.

How did you first become interested in corporate day care?

When I finished my master's degree in child development and family relationships, I worked in preschools and then started my own cooperative preschool. When I heard that the Publix Corporation was interested in a day-care center for its employees, I recognized the opportunity to combine all my skills and interests. Publix already had a reputation as a progressive company, deeply committed to its employees and their families.

What is different about a corporate child-care center?

We do not have to depend completely on fees to fund our program. Our parents pay the going rate for day care, and the corporation subsidizes the program to ensure high quality. Everyone profits: The children get excellent care, the parents get peace of mind, and Publix gets a more stable and contented work force.

What is your formula for success?

First, Publix allowed us to take our time developing our program. We started with just 40 children and stopped enrollment when we reached the staff-to-child ratio that would ensure high quality. We trained extensively before seeing children for the first time, and we continue to train monthly. We made lots of changes, always using the children's responses as a guide. My staff and I work together as a team; we support each other emotionally and work toward common goals. Finally, we don't see ourselves as involved in just child care; we are involved in *families*. If a staff member or parent has a problem, it's our problem, and we do our best to solve it together.

What is the future of corporate child care?

Corporations and government agencies are beginning to see the value of providing high-quality child care for employees. It is cost-effective: Every dollar invested lowers the stress on families, reducing employee turnover and sick leave and increasing efficiency on the job. What we need are professionals — trained in child development *and* in business skills — who can consult with corporations to plan and develop high-quality child-care programs.

2,000 hours a year—approximately half of their waking hours—in the care and protection of individuals other than their parents. For some children this adds up to 10,000 hours over the first 5 years of their lives. When they spend these thousands of hours in the company of disinterested, unresponsive, and unaffectionate caregivers in uninteresting and unstimulating environments, damage to their cognitive and social-emotional development is inevitable. Even conservative estimates indicate that hundreds of thousands of American children share this fate each year (Children's Defense Fund, 1990).

Compensatory Preschools

Poverty, abuse, and neglect in the first two to three years of life often result in developmental delays in children's cognitive and language development. It is not unusual, for example, to find the cognitive and language development of 3-year-olds delayed by 6 to 18 months. To make matters worse, these children often are poorly behaved, making it even harder for caregivers to cope with them in group settings. Nursery school and day-care programs were never intended to deal with the special educational needs of such children.

In the 1960s, increasing concern over the plight of disadvantaged children led to the development of **compensatory preschools**—early childhood education programs designed to compensate for risks associated with growing up poor, neglected, or abused. The largest and most widely known of these efforts is Project Head Start, a federally funded program serving approximately 500,000 children annually, at a yearly cost of $500 million. The past, present, and future of Head Start is examined in Box 10.6, and we meet Katie Weatherspoon, a dedicated advocate of Head Start, in "Career: The Head Start Teacher." Although Head Start is the largest of these efforts, compensatory education programs have varied from relatively small, university-based research projects to extensive public school programs for three- and four-year-old children.

Developing compensatory preschool programs is enormously complex. Consider the challenge created by a three-year-old boy functioning at a two-year-old level who continually misbehaves and cannot sustain attention on a task beyond a few seconds. With no intervention, this child will be 18 to 24 months delayed by the time he enters kindergarten. If the goal of compensatory preschool is to bring the child to normal levels of functioning by that time, the child must make three years of developmental progress in just two years. Theoretically, the rate of development can be accelerated by teaching consistently within the *zone of proximal development*. From a practical perspective, however, the design of learning environments, teacher training, and the development of curriculum present problems of extraordinary proportions. Thirty years of research and development in search of the best approach has generated enormous controversy and very few clear-cut solutions. We will examine three major approaches.

The *cognitive stimulation approach* promotes cognitive development by challenging children within the zone of proximal development at every possible turn. One of the more popular variations—David Weikart's *Cognitively Oriented Curriculum* (Hohmann et al., 1979)—uses a curriculum based on Piaget's cognitive-developmental theory. Consistent with this theory, Weikart and his colleagues emphasize the child's active role in learning through direct experience with objects, people, and events. The teacher plays a supportive role as an "instigator of problem-solving activities" (1979, p. 6). The curriculum is organized around *key experiences*—activities that promote cognitive learning in specific areas such as number, time, space, and classification. For example, a key experience in the learning of number involves arranging two sets of objects in one-to-one

BOX 10.6

Project Head Start: Past, Present, and Future

In 1964, President Lyndon Johnson initiated the "war on poverty," a comprehensive approach to reducing poverty in the United States. One of the more creative programs, *Project Head Start*, was designed to break the cycle of poverty by focusing on the needs of preschool children and their families.

Head Start was initiated on a massive scale in 1965 as a short-term summer program but was soon expanded into a year-long program serving approximately 200,000 4-year-old children. The underlying assumption was that poor children were deprived of important cultural experiences, which placed them at a disadvantage in the public schools. The core of the approach was a multifaceted preschool program designed to facilitate children's physical, intellectual, and social-emotional development. Parents were involved in virtually every aspect of the program, and families were offered a variety of social services.

Although funding for the program has varied over the years, support has steadily grown to its present level of $500 million annually to provide services for almost 500,000 children in nearly 10,000 Head Start centers throughout the United States.

The massive investment in Head Start has prompted many to ask whether the program has lived up to its promises. A review of more than 1,500 studies evaluating the effectiveness of Head Start reported substantial short-term gains in participating children's cognitive and language development (Collins & Deloria, 1983). However, there are some important qualifications to these findings: The program is not equally effective for all children, and the short-term gains in cognitive and language skill may not hold up over time.

In one of the most well-controlled evaluation studies, researchers compared children in Head Start to disadvantaged children who had attended other preschools and to children who had had no preschool experience (Lee, Brooks-Gunn, & Schnur, 1988). At the beginning of the study the Head Start children were considerably more delayed on cognitive measures than the children in the comparison groups. After one year of exposure to the program, the Head Start children showed greater gains on the cognitive measures than children in either comparison group. Black children who had been at the greatest disadvantage at the start of the year had made the greatest gains by the end of the year. Although these gains were impressive, they did not completely eliminate the gap between the Head Start children and the other children.

Other effects of Head Start are less easy to document in research studies. Each locally run Head Start center has created a community of families who have learned to believe in their children and, by participating in an organized effort, to affect their children's futures. Many parents participate eagerly and tirelessly by volunteering in classrooms and serving on committees. In one study, mothers who spent more time as volunteers in the program reported greater life satisfaction, fewer psychological problems, and a greater sense of mastery in their lives (Parker, Piotrkowski, & Peay, 1987).

Although Head Start can be credited with gains in cognitive and language capability in children and reduction of helplessness and hopelessness in families, the experience only lasts one year and for many it is not long enough. Does that mean that Head Start is ineffective? No. It simply means that Head Start is not, by itself, able to ameliorate all of the negative effects of poverty on children and their families. The solution lies in further improving and expanding services and in developing programs that build upon the gains attributable to Head Start as the children move on to the public schools and beyond.

correspondence. Teachers provide children with pegs and pegboards, containers and lids, and nuts and bolts to promote the key experience; then they actively engage the children in relevant conversation as in the following exchange (Hohmann, 1979, p. 233):

CHILD: *(Alexis is putting one peg in each spool in each spool hole.)* Down the hole, down the hole. Another man down the hole.

TEACHER: What are the men doing down in the holes, Alexis?

CHILD: Fixing the water. Down the hole. Down the hole.

TEACHER: You mean for each hole you put one man down to fix the water?

CHILD: Yep, so it won't get out on the streets and all the people.

The Head Start Teacher

Katie Weatherspoon is a teacher in the Head Start Child Development Program in Tallahassee, Florida. She has been employed by Head Start for 14 years, first as a classroom aide, then as an assistant teacher, and presently as a head teacher and supervisor of the staff in her center. She is married, with four children and six grandchildren.

Katie has no illusions about the four-year-old children who come to her class. She watches as they walk toward the center each morning, passing the row of houses where crack cocaine is sold twenty-four hours a day. She knows the potentially devastating effects of living the first four years of life in poverty; and she is, therefore, not surprised when the children show cognitive and language deficits.

From the moment her children arrive each morning, Katie challenges them to learn. She uses her booming voice, broad smile, and powerful presence to engage every child in every activity; there are no "onlookers" in Katie's classroom. Each day is organized to bring some new experience to the children, to capture their imagination, and to advance their development in some significant way.

Katie's success comes both from her teaching skill and from her profound belief in her children's potential. She considers their so-called "disadvantage" as no more than a temporary setback that is totally reversible. In the true spirit of Head Start, she and her staff work with the parents and the community to help the children realize their full potential for learning and to fortify them for the challenges that await them in elementary school.

How did you first get involved in Head Start?

When I first heard about Head Start I knew that it was going to be special. It seemed like a chance to work with people who really cared about the children in my community. Head Start trained me for a *career*, rather than just a job. Teaching in Head Start requires more than the teaching skills you learn in college. You have to understand our children's problems and believe that those problems can be overcome. You have to respect your children's cultural backgrounds and their community and believe in every child's potential to learn. You also have to believe in yourself. Teaching in Head Start is a great challenge, and it takes someone very special to meet that challenge.

How can a student learn more about a career in Head Start?

Inquire at your Community Action Program, the local agency that administers the program in most communities.

Other early childhood educators argue that cognitive learning can be accomplished with considerably less structure. This approach assumes that the "match" is readily available in the traditional play materials of the nursery school such as blocks, dolls, and puzzles. The preschool teacher is available as a facilitator, capitalizing on teachable moments that occur regularly in the course of children's spontaneous play. Heather's experience with a water play activity at her day-care center is a good example.

> *Heather and Toby are splashing at the water table. Mrs. Simms—a paraprofessional aide with no formal training but 20 years of experience—slowly approaches the table. Although she has never heard of Piaget nor "zone of proximal development," she senses that if Heather and Toby enjoy dunking things they might be ready to learn something. Mrs. Simms watches as they put toys and twigs in and out of the water and argue over who has more "boats." When their attention begins to wane, she asks if they would like to play a game. She then holds a block under the water and asks the children to look at how the water level has risen above Heather's mark. Without further prompting, Heather and Toby invent a game to see who can make the water go higher.*

Still other early childhood educators have adopted more intrusive approaches to compensatory education. One of the most controversial is *Distar*, a model developed by Siegfried Engelmann, Carl Bereiter, and Wesley Becker (Bereiter & Engelmann, 1966). Distar integrates behavior modification strategies (to control classroom behavior) with highly structured, sequentially organized lessons (to promote the "match" in language, arithmetic, and reading). A brief segment of teacher-child interaction in an arithmetic lesson illustrates this approach:

TEACHER: Look up, look up. . . . Good looking! We're going to count from 5 to 12. What are we counting from?

CHILDREN: 5!

TEACHER: What are we counting to?

CHILDREN: 12!

TEACHER: OK. Count! (*with a standard hand gesture that cues children to respond*)

CHILDREN: 5, 6, 7, 8, 9, 10, 11, 12.

TEACHER: Very good! What did we count to?

CHILDREN: 12!

Which of these approaches offers the best program for compensatory education of preschool children? One longitudinal study compared the effects of three preschool curriculum models—a traditional nursery school program emphasizing play, the cognitively oriented curriculum, and the Distar model (Schweinhart, Weikart, & Larner, 1986). Sixty-eight economically disadvantaged children were randomly assigned to the three model programs. The average IQ of the children rose an astounding 27 points during their preschool experience, with few differences among the curriculum models. The success of *all* of the models strongly recommends continued diversity in research and development in this area.

Looking Back

The research and theory presented in this chapter suggests that children enter the preschool years with the potential to develop the ability to think and communicate symbolically. This potential appears to be fairly robust; that is, development emerges through a wide variety of experiences in highly diverse settings. As in infancy, there is no cookbook recipe for ideal sequences of environmental experience. Cognitive and language learning may take place at home, in preschool or day-care classrooms, on a subway, in a grocery store, in a zoo, in a sandpile, or on a mountain of junk in a vacant lot.

Moreover, normal rates of cognitive and language development do not necessarily require specially trained teachers, elaborate learning materials, expensive toys, gadgets, or computers. For example, a pile of leaves clogging the drain water on a city street may promote an understanding of the properties of liquids just as well or even better than an expensive water table in a preschool. Those who deal with young children should therefore maintain a broad perspective on where, when, and how cognitive and language learning may occur.

Although the potential for cognitive and language development is healthy in early childhood, this potential can easily be sacrificed. Extreme physical deprivation and social isolation, unstimulating or chaotic experiences in the home or in substitute care, and abuse and neglect may result in severe developmental delay. Without intervention, such delays are likely to predetermine failure in the early school grades and beyond.

Those who deal with children must recognize the sensitive nature of the preschool period and work toward fulfilling every child's potential for cognitive and language development.

CHAPTER REVIEW

PREOPERATIONAL STAGE Piaget refers to the period from three to six years as the preoperational stage of cognitive development. As suggested by the term, children at this stage are not yet able to think in logical systems.

SYMBOLIC FUNCTION The distinguishing feature of preoperational thinking is the symbolic function: the ability to use symbols to represent or stand for perceived objects and events. The symbolic function takes four forms: deferred imitation, pretend play, thinking in images, and language.

SYMBOLIC OR PRETEND PLAY In pretend play, children pretend that an object is something other than what it really is. Pretense is accomplished by shifting context, substituting objects, substituting

other agents for oneself, and sequencing and socializing of pretend episodes.

CENTRATION Piaget believed that preschoolers tend to focus their attention on minute and often inconsequential aspects of their experience, a process known as centration. Centration does not allow young children to perceive overall meaning, permitting only a piecemeal view of reality.

PRECONCEPTS Piaget suggested that collections of images, derived from centrated perception, merge into preconcepts: disorganized, illogical representations of the child's experiences.

TRANSDUCTIVE REASONING Young children think about their world transductively, reasoning within the unsystematic collections of images that

constitute their preconcepts. Transductive reasoning can be understood by comparison to induction and deduction—the logical forms of reasoning available to older children and adults.

REASONING IN CONTENT DOMAINS In contrast to Piaget's early findings, follow-up research indicates that preschoolers show some ability in causal reasoning, classification, quantitative reasoning, and distinguishing between appearance and reality.

COGNITIVE CHANGE Two important concepts help caregivers to promote cognitive change. The problem of the match—the difference between the child's existing cognitive level and the level the child can accommodate—helps to define how the mind and reality interact to promote cognitive development. The zone of proximal development—the gap between what a child can accomplish independently and what the same child can accomplish when provided with optimal support from caregivers and challenging materials—defines the process of scaffolding children's learning.

INFORMATION PROCESSING Children's attention and memory improve substantially during the preschool years, but important limitations remain. Children process information far more effectively in real life situations than in laboratory tasks with unfamiliar stimuli.

THEORY OF MIND Preschoolers develop a beginning theory of mind, an understanding of the psychological functioning of other individuals. Mindreading allows even young children to infer the desires and beliefs of others in order to understand and predict their behavior.

They also use their theory of mind to deceive.

LANGUAGE DEVELOPMENT Language develops rapidly during the preschool years, with major advances in vocabulary, grammar, and communication. Communication remains somewhat egocentric but gradually improves through the fourth and fifth years.

PRIVATE SPEECH Young children often talk to themselves, possibly helping them to regulate their own behavior. Vygotsky believed that private speech is eventually internalized as inner speech, or thinking in words or sentences.

COGNITIVE DEVELOPMENT AT RISK Studies of children raised in institutions and deprivation or isolation demonstrate how cognitive development can be delayed. However, even severely deprived children show resilience, reponding well to dramatic and early improvements in the environment.

THE HOME Studies have shown that parents may facilitate cognitive development as consultants, talking to and responding to their children's questions and initiatives. A more proactive role in teaching children can be effective in teaching specific concepts.

DAY CARE While high-quality day care has no negative effects on average children, disadvantaged children may actually profit from this experience. However, low-quality care is associated with poor academic performance and low test scores in school.

COMPENSATORY PRESCHOOL Compensatory education programs designed for disadvantaged children have positive effects on cognitive development. Programs that differ substantially in educational approach appear to have similar positive effects.

Key Terms

script	quantitative reasoning	strategies
preoperational stage	conservation	metacognition
operational	counting	grammar
symbolic function	problem of the match	grammatical morphemes
symbolic or pretend play	zone of proximal development	overregularize
centration	joint collaboration	egocentric speech
preconcepts	transfers responsibility	monologue
transduction	scaffolding	collective monologue
egocentrism	theory of mind	private speech
irreversibility	mindreading	inner speech
classification	deception	compensatory preschools

11

Social and Emotional Development in Early Childhood

Looking Ahead

- Preschoolers spend endless hours pretending that they are doctors, cowboys, astronauts, parents, and cartoon characters with superpowers. If adults did this, we would think they were mentally disturbed. Is this acceptable activity for young children? Does pretense serve some special purpose in development?

- Some children form friendships and others seem isolated from their peers. How do children form friendships and what purpose do they serve? Are preschoolers without friends at risk?

- When two or more preschoolers are together for any length of time, conflicts inevitably result. Are conflicts a sign of maladjustment?

- While most children resolve their conflicts peacefully, others resort to aggression. What causes some children to be more aggressive than others? What role do parents play in the development of aggression in their children? Can children's aggression be decreased?

- Parents often prompt their children to share toys and cooperate with other children. Do preschool children have difficulty sharing and cooperating with their peers?

- By the end of the preschool years, boys and girls engage in very different behaviors and play almost exclusively with children of the same sex. What causes these differences? Should parents help children to resist or change this pattern?

- As children progress through the preschool years, they become better at masking their emotions. Why would children want to hide their feelings? Is this a sign of emotional problems?

D uring the preschool years we see the emergence *personality*, a child's unique pattern of relating to other human beings. Some personalities seem to be far more successful than others in achieving personal and social goals. We can see these differences in the following episodes in the lives of Leshonda, Heather, and Carlos early in their preschool years.

Leshonda arrives late for day care, well after her class has begun their morning free-play activities. Three girls have taken over the dramatic play area where they are playing house. Denise, playing the role of mother, is cooking dinner for her two badly behaved children, Dinetta and Carmen. The girls are banging their utensils and yelling commands back and forth, creating a sense of urgency: "We want food!" "We hungry. Why you taking so long?" Denise, the "mother," chides, "You be quiet, children, or I'll put these foods on your heads!"

As Leshonda walks into the room, her eyes dart immediately to the three children in dramatic play—an area she has come to think of as her territory. Suppressing her anger and resisting an urge to just burst in, she approaches the group slowly and hovers at a distance, sizing up the situation before making her move. She thinks to herself that these girls are not "best" friends with each other; that should make it easier to join in. She also senses that she could boss these particular children; they would not put up much of a fight.

She carefully watches the interaction, studying who is playing which role and how the pretend play is unfolding. When the "mother" seems to be almost finished cooking dinner, Leshonda makes her move. She walks slowly into the play area and asks—in an undemanding voice—whether she can help by serving the dinner to the "sisters" at the table. Although the "mother" seems unsure, Dinetta and Carmen love being called "sisters" and, without hesitation, begin telling Leshonda how the dinner should be served. Leshonda assumes the role of servant and is quickly assimilated into the group play. Within 15 minutes she has subtly transformed the pretense from playing house to playing school and her role from servant to teacher—a role more consistent with Leshonda's view of herself and her status in the larger group.

As Heather, age four, comes out of her apartment building, she sees three slightly older girls playing jump rope. As one of the girls takes her turn jumping, Heather runs impulsively toward the girls and jumps into the swinging rope, completely disrupting the activity. Heather starts to laugh but the girls do not think her behavior is funny. They threaten Heather and chase her back into the building.

Excited by the attention, Heather reemerges from the building and charges recklessly toward the girls, again disrupting the activity. This time the girls grab her and hit her until she begins to scream. When they try to let her go, she goes into a tantrum—swinging, biting, and spitting. The girls seem overwhelmed by Heather's rage and, after a few minutes, offer to let her play if she will just quiet down.

Heather has gotten her way, but not without a price. The girls tease her mercilessly over the next several weeks and shun her attempts to join their play.

Carlos wanders through the three rooms of the day-care center, squeezing two Lego blocks together and occasionally observing the play of other children. After several minutes, he settles down in a corner of the block area, close to two other boys who are building a fort. Carlos quickly constructs a series of road-ways and, pretending that several blocks are trucks and motorcycles, races his vehicles with obvious enthusiasm. Although Carlos looks over at the boys occa-sionally, he looks away each time either of the boys returns his glance—a be-havior that encourages the boys to also look away when he looks at them.

Carlos continues to play by himself for over 20 minutes, without any effort to join other children's play. The boys make no overtures toward Carlos, play-ing as if he weren't there. Carlos does not appear to be unhappy playing alone, and his play is no less constructive or imaginative than that of the boys play-ing next to him.

Leshonda's success, Heather's failure, and Carlos's apparent disinterest in gaining en-try to the ongoing play of peers illustrate unique features of social and emotional devel-opment during the preschool years. First, preschool-age children show wide-ranging individual differences in **social competence**—the ability to establish and maintain satis-fying social interaction and relationships with peers and with adults. Leshonda's behav-ior epitomizes competent group entry: She studies the group's interaction, then enters the group slowly, without drawing attention to herself; with perfect timing, she suggests a nonthreatening but functional role for herself in the ongoing theme of the pretend play, eliciting instant social acceptance. In contrast, Heather's coercive approach to group entry is socially incompetent, generating retaliation from peers and long-term rejection. Carlos lives in a world apart from his peers, avoiding social interaction at every turn. Although less obviously than Heather, Carlos may also be at considerable risk for long-term social maladjustment.

Leshonda, Carlos, and Heather also show significant individual differences in emo-tional expression and control. Leshonda is her typical self: warm, friendly, and enthu-siastic, controlling her emotions and the tempo of her behavior to adapt to the situation.

Social pretend play enables a child to be anyone or anything he wants and to do it with a play partner who expects no less. The quality of social pretend play reflects the boundless imagination of the young participants. Here we have a young cowboy caring for a baby, with the obvious ap-proval of an older and wiser princess.

In contrast, Heather's loss of emotional control overwhelms the children on the street, greatly increasing the likelihood of rejection. Although Carlos expresses little overt emotion while he plays, he is a very sad and lonely young boy who is beginning to suffer dramatically from his social isolation.

These differences in social and emotional competence are enormously significant as children develop through the preschool years and approach the critical transition to middle childhood. The preschool years can be thought of as an opportunity to prepare for middle childhood, particularly the challenges of adjusting to life in elementary school. Schools are reasonably good at facilitating the development of socially competent and emotionally mature children, that is, children who relate effectively to peers and to adults in positions of authority. Children who vary significantly from this ideal are at risk of serious social maladjustment and school failure. Preschoolers must also prepare to deal with significant new challenges in relating to peers—particularly the emergence of sex-segregated peer groups.

We will begin by examining the unique opportunity that play with other children provides for social and emotional development during the preschool years.

The Development of Social Play

Play is one of the most distinguishing aspects of childhood and one of the most difficult to define. It is what children do when they are not responding to adult demands and not sick in bed. Play is a unique aspect of development that provides children with the opportunity to experiment with their own development—to practice and perfect what they have already become and to explore the cutting edge of their developmental potential. In play, children try out new roles and new ways of doing things and compare and contrast the new with the old.

Most importantly, play experiences do not have to be taken seriously. In play the emphasis is on *process* rather than on *product*. A child may build a tower of blocks just for the fun of doing it, not to reach a certain height or to outperform a peer. If the block tower falls over, the aim of the play can instantaneously change from constructing to destructing, with no loss in the potential for learning or fun. A child can pretend to be a monster just to see how it feels and how others react, without any permanent change in personality. Play is an ideal medium for social and emotional development.

Play provides a unique opportunity for the development of social competency by allowing children to regulate the degree to which they involve social partners in play episodes. In play, the social partners can be *real* or *pretend*. For example, a child can interact with a real friend or with an *imaginary companion*. What children do when they interact with real play partners can also be real or pretend. For example, two children can chase each other on their bicycles or they can pretend to be Batman and Robin chasing each other on pretend Batmobiles. We use the term **social play** to refer to playful interaction with real play partners and the term **social pretend play** to refer to playful interaction that involves pretense (Howes, Unger, & Seidner, 1989).

Social Play

More than 60 years ago Mildred Parten (1932) studied children's social play in the nursery school. Parten was interested in young children's **social participation**—that is, the degree to which children played with other children during free-play activities. Parten proposed a series of categories that she believed represented a dimension from the least to the greatest degree of social participation. Parten's scale includes six sequential categories:

Unoccupied behavior The child is not involved in play and does not interact with other children or teachers.

Onlooker behavior The child observes the play of other children with obvious interest but makes no effort to become involved in any way.

Solitary play The child plays independently with toys that are unlike those played with by other children. There is no social contact or apparent interest in what other children are doing.

Parallel play The child plays beside other children with toys that are similar to those used by those children. There is no social contact with other children nor any effort to coordinate play.

Associative play The child plays with other children, sharing materials and conversing, but there is no consistent theme to the play nor division of roles.

Cooperative play The child plays with other children in an organized manner, with roles differentiated to accomplish some goal or to act out some agreed-upon play theme.

Parten's observations of children in free play provided some support for her contention that the categories form a developmental progression: 24- to 30-month-olds were involved primarily in solitary play; 30- to 42-month-olds in parallel play; and 42- to 54-month-olds in associative play. However, more recent studies suggest that we revise Parten's age designations. One study using Parten's categories showed substantially higher percentages of unoccupied, solitary, and onlooker behaviors in four- and five-year-olds than reported by Parten, casting some doubt on Parten's categories as a "developmental" progression (Barnes, 1971).

Other studies (Howes, 1985; Howes et al., 1989) suggest that social play may develop more rapidly than described by Parten (1932). Carollee Howes's (1989) observations of the social play of well-acquainted toddlers at home showed parallel play by 12 to 15 months, associative play by 24 to 30 months, and cooperative play by 30 to 36 months (see Table 11.1). The earlier appearance of the mature forms of social play may reflect the more sophisticated observational techniques Howes and her colleagues used. It is also possible that today's toddlers and young preschoolers are more socially advanced than the children observed by Parten in the 1930s.

Social Pretend Play

According to Piaget (1951/1962), the advent of the symbolic function toward the end of the second year provides children with the initial ability to pretend. As indicated in Chapter 10, this early pretense is limited to behaving as if an object is something other than what it really is (making believe a stick is a gun) or pretending to do something that is not really being done (drinking from an imaginary cup). By the end of the third year, we begin to see the beginnings of *social pretend play*—that is, pretense episodes involving other children. These episodes typically involve two or more children acting out roles and themes associated with children's stories, television cartoon shows, or common family events (such as "supper time" or "bathing baby"). Social pretend play increases through the preoperational period (Rubin et al., 1983) and, according to Piaget (1962), declines at six or seven years, as games with rules begin to dominate children's social play.

Social pretend play—sometimes referred to as *sociodramatic play*—requires that children learn to negotiate and communicate about the roles, objects, settings, and actions that will be employed in any given "pretend engagement" (Garvey & Kramer, 1989). The failure to negotiate successfully can easily undermine the quality of social pretense. For example, if one player pretends that a stick is a gun and another player pretends that the same stick is a magic wand, conflict is inevitable. Such conflicts can be minimized by children's shared use of special language terms, which promotes a common understanding of what roles are being played, what real objects will substitute for pretend objects, and what will be left to the children's imagination. The following play sequence illustrates what Catherine Garvey refers to as the "language of social pretend play" (Garvey & Kramer, 1989).

CARLOS: Let's play "Space Invaders." I'll be the pilot.

ROBERTO: No, I don't like "Space Invaders." Let's play "Top Cops." I'll be the policeman in the police car and you be the bad guy. This can be your gun and this is mine (pointing to two blocks). I'll make the police car with these blocks.

CARLOS: OK, but I want to be a police too. We can both be police and we can pretend that the bad guys are in jail. These can be the bad guys (pointing to figurines) and we can hide them and find them and put them in jail.

ROBERTO: We don't have a jail! (*laughing hysterically*)

CARLOS: Yes, we do. Its right over here. (*Pointing to other blocks*)

ROBERTO: No, we don't want a jail. Let's just chase the bad guys and shoot them.

Howes and her colleagues (1989) have compared the early development of social play and social pretend play from 12 to 36 months. The developmental progressions are con-

---

TABLE 11.1

The Developmental Levels of Social Play and Social Pretend Play

Social Play	Social Pretend Play
12–15 Months Parallel play with eye contact, and/or exchanges of social behavior (A vocalizes, B smiles)	**12–15 Months** Pretend acts performed near other children with eye contact but no other response (A feeds self, B ignores)
15–20 Months Engagement in similar activities with turn-taking (while digging in sandbox, A smiles to B and B vocalizes back)	**15–20 Months** Similar/identical pretend acts performed with eye contact (both push dolls in carriages)
20–24 Months Social exchange marked by each partner taking turns at reversing actions of the other (run-chase game, roll ball back and forth)	**20–24 Months** Engagement in similar pretend activities accompanied by social exchanges (pushing dolls in carriages: A smiles at B, B offers doll to A)
24–30 Months Joint activity has a common plan, and the pair's actions are integrated (conversation during joint building of a block structure shows that both intend it for trucks to drive under)	**24–30 Months** Each child's pretense reflects the same theme but their actions show no within-pair integration (playing tea party, both pour tea, add sugar, and drink, smiling and talking)
30–36 Months Play activity shows differentiation of leader and follower roles (while jointly building a block structure, A directs building construction and B delivers the blocks)	**30–36 Months** Joint pretend activity involves complementary roles such as "mother-baby" or "doctor-patient" (A sets table, tells B where to sit, pours her tea, and feeds her; B emits babylike cries and says "More tea")

SOURCE: *Adapted from Howes, Unger, & Seidner, Child Development, 60, 77–84, 1989. © The Society for Research in Child Development, Inc. Reprinted by permission.*

trasted in Table 11.1. Early in the third year, playmates begin to share common themes in their pretense episodes—such as staging "rescue the baby from the monsters"—but they don't integrate their respective roles. For example, in "rescue the baby," both children may play the hero, ignoring each other's identity and the need for someone to play the baby. By the end of the third year, children can begin to enact complementary roles such as doctor and patient, where one child gives a shot and the partner submits to the treatment. By age six, dramatic play episodes are so well integrated that even interruptions— such as a prop falling over unexpectedly—can be readily integrated into the ongoing plot (DiLalla & Watson, 1988).

Social pretend play provides an invaluable opportunity for the development of social and emotional competence during the preschool years. Children can pretend to be anyone they choose, enact roles and behaviors they have only observed, and express their emotions freely and without penalty. Parents and other caregivers should provide the time, place, and materials to support children's social pretend play, particularly for children who show delays in social or emotional development.

Promoting Social Pretense

When adults observe the free play of young children, their attention is inevitably drawn to children's social pretend activities. There seems to be more action, more fun, more adventure, and more "development" going on in these activities.

Research has confirmed this impression. Children's interactions in social pretend play are more positive, sustained, enjoyable, and group oriented then in nonpretend play (Connolly & Doyle, 1984; Connolly, Doyle, & Reznick, 1988). Additionally, children who engaged frequently in social pretense and in complex dramatic episodes were more socially skilled, popular, and understanding of other children's emotions than children who participated less (Connolly & Doyle, 1984). Research has also shown that disadvantaged children show less social pretend play than more advantaged children (Rosen, 1974; Smilansky, 1968). These findings suggest that children who participate less in social pretend play, for whatever reason, may be at some disadvantage developmentally. Would specific training in dramatic play make up for this disadvantage?

There has been extensive research into the effects of training children in sociodramatic play skills. This research has typically involved organizing children into small groups for tutoring in acting out fantasy themes. In normal preschool children the studies demonstrated significant improvement in perspective-taking and language development (Burns & Brainerd, 1979; Levy, Schaefer, & Phelps, 1986). In disadvantaged preschool children studies showed enhanced cooperative problem solving, IQ, role-taking, and impulse control (Rosen, 1974; Saltz, Dixon, & Johnson, 1977). However, methodological problems in these studies suggest some caution in interpretating the results (Rubin et al., 1983).

A P P L I C A T I O N

Promoting Social Pretend Play

Parents can and should create opportunities for social pretend play by providing materials, props, and a physical location that offers some degree of privacy from adults. Providing

props consistent with children's favorite story themes can be most productive.

Preschool and day-care programs provide opportunities for social pretend play, typically by designating one part of the room as the dramatic play area. Since participation is almost always voluntary, some children will choose not to be involved. Preschool teachers should consider structuring the experience for children who show signs of developmental delay. They should make specific efforts to balance the materials available to encourage participation by both sexes: Props and materials in many programs are limited to "doll play" areas, which discourages the involvement of boys.

Bottom Line: Keep in mind that social pretend play comes naturally to children. You may do more harm than good by being intrusive. Pretend play should be encouraged wherever and whenever it occurs.

Relating to Peers

Four aspects of children's social relationships have profound impact on their social and emotional development during the preschool years:

- *Social preferences*   Wherever preschool children congregate in relatively stable groups, individual children develop both positive and negative **social preferences**—likes and dislikes for specific play partners. The fact that some children are more preferred than others means that they have widely different social experiences.

- *Friendships*   Social preferences by group members result in children developing **friendships**, relatively enduring, positive mutual relationships. Having friends offers unique opportunity for social development; not having friends places social and emotional development at some risk (Hartup, 1989).

- *Conflict*   Children's social interaction inevitably results in **conflict**, episodes in which children overtly oppose one another, typically expressed by one or both children protesting, denying, or in some way resisting the other's actions or statements (Shantz & Hobart, 1989). Resolving conflicts by nonaggressive means generally promotes social development; resolving conflicts by aggressive means creates serious problems for the children involved and for supervising adults.

- *Dominance*   When young children interact in groups, power and influence are unevenly distributed, making some children more dominant than others. **Dominance** is the system that defines who defers to whom in disputes over territory and possessions.

We will examine each of these four aspects in turn.

Social Preference

Young children tend to be uninhibited in their expression of social preferences for play partners. They typically express "likes" through behaviors that maximize closeness to the preferred partner (such as following, approaching, smiling) and by behaviors that increase the quality of interaction with the preferred partner (such as helping, cooperating, and suggesting play themes). They express "dislikes" by either avoiding or actively rejecting nonpreferred children's participation in group activities. The expressions of disappointment, sadness, and embarrassment on the faces of rejected children suggest that these experiences can be quite painful and may place chronically rejected children at risk for serious maladjustment.

Children's positive and negative social preferences are unevenly distributed among members of the peer group; that is, some children are more *popular* and others more *rejected*. Researchers have developed methods to quantify popularity and to classify children into qualitatively distinct social status groups. These methods and social status categories are described in Box 11.1.

Children in different status groups behave very differently toward peers and, in turn, are treated very differently by peers. The differences are well illustrated when popular preschool children try to enter the ongoing play of other children: They display better communication skills than rejected children (Black & Hazen, 1990; Hazen & Black, 1989), they direct their language to all members of the group rather than to a single child and are highly responsive to other children's communications (Hazen & Black, 1989), and they provide useful information and resist expressing negative emotions during entry attempts. All of these skills improve chances of acceptance by group members.

Social status differences become increasingly distinctive in middle childhood and adolescence, allowing more accurate prediction of long-term social maladjustment (Parker & Asher, 1987; Price & Dodge, 1989).

Friendships

When two children show positive preference for one another as play partners over time, a friendship is likely to result. A *friendship* is an enduring close, mutual relationship between two individuals, expressed by a tendency to spend a disproportionate amount of play time together. By this definition, preschool-age children form relatively stable friendships (Hartup, Laursen, Stewart, & Eastenson, 1988; Hinde, Titmus, Easton, &

BOX 11.1

Measuring Social Preferences and Social Status

Researchers have shown that children's social preferences for play partners can be assessed by simply asking children to express their preferences at a *sociometric interview*. In the standard procedure, individual children are asked to nominate three children they most like to play with and three they least like to play with. The nominations can be summarized in two ways: In the first approach, positive nominations are summed as an index of **popularity** and negative nominations are summed as an index of **rejection**. These measures have been used to identify the correlates of popularity and rejection. For example, research has shown that preschool children who are more popular tend to be more physically attractive (Dion, 1973; Dion & Berschied, 1974), more likely to reinforce and to be reinforced by their peers (Hartup, Glazer, & Charlesworth, 1967; Masters & Furman, 1981), and more active participants in group activities (Krantz, 1982).

In the second approach, positive and negative preferences have been used to classify children into social status subgroups (Coie, Dodge, & Coppotelli, 1982). Children who are clearly more liked than disliked are classified as "popular"; those who are clearly more disliked than liked are referred to as "rejected"; those who are neither liked nor disliked are called "neglected"; and children who are simultaneously liked by some children and disliked by others are referred to as "controversial." Children who do not fall neatly into one of these subgroups are referred to as "average." The development of this system for classifying children into social status groups was an important advance in social development research. Some of the differences among status groups at preschool-age are explored in this chapter and research on middle childhood and adolescence are described in later chapters.

Friends have a unique way of supporting and stimulating each other. Here, each girl intensifies the other's excitement while exploring art materials. Play between friends tends to continue over a longer period of time and is typically more constructive than play between nonfriends.

Tamplin, 1985). Approximately half of preschool children have mutual friends, and two-thirds of these friendships persist for six months or more (Gershman & Hayes, 1983). These friendships tend to be with children of the same sex (La Freniere, Strayer, & Gauthier, 1984) and of the same ethnic group (Howes & Wu, 1990). However, minority children are more likely than Caucasian children to form cross-ethnic friendships.

Note that the concepts of popularity and friendship, although related, are not identical. Whereas popularity is a one-way expression of preferences of the members of a group toward an individual, friendship is a two-way *relationship* between two individuals. Thus a child may be relatively popular among peers, but have no friends, or relatively unpopular among peers, with one or more friends. This implies that the skills that are necessary to simply get along successfully in the peer group may be different from those involved in initiating and maintaining friendships (Parker & Gottman, 1989).

What specific skills are involved in making friends? In one study, previously unacquainted children were paired in a series of play sessions to study the processes involved in forming friendships (Gottman, 1983). Analyses of the conversations of the children during the sessions showed that some pairs of children hit it off better than others, making more progress toward eventual friendship. The budding friendship pairs behaved differently than the pairs that made little or no progress toward friendship. Gottman described it this way:

> . . . when two strangers meet, they need to interact in a connected fashion, exchange information successfully, establish a common ground activity, and manage conflicts successfully. As the relationship proceeds, communication clarity becomes more important; so does information exchange, the establishment of common ground activity, the exploration of similarity and differences, the resolution of conflict, and self-disclosure. (1983, p. 44)

Interaction between friends offers unique opportunities for the development of social skills as compared to interaction between nonfriends or acquaintances. Friends are more likely to reinforce each other during play episodes (Masters & Furman, 1981) and to cooperate in the use of resources such as toys and props (La Freniere & Charlesworth, 1987). They are more likely than nonfriends to successfully resolve conflicts and to continue playing together after conflicts (Hartup et al., 1988). Friends develop a knack for initiating social interaction and extending that interaction over time (Howes, 1983). For example, when friends approach an activity area in a nursery school—such as block play—they waste little time generating fantasy themes to support extended play.

Jeff Parker and John Gottman, experts on the play of friends, have described the unique qualities of social pretend play between friends:

> Two friends do not simply *act* like tigers or dragons or ghosts—they *become* tigers or dragons or ghosts. Two friends pretending to drive their sick child to the hospital, simultaneously *pretend* to be frightened in this life-or-death situation and *are* frightened. If they were not frightened to some degree, it would hardly be an adventure. (Parker & Gottman, 1989, p. 105)

What can we conclude about the importance of friendship during the preschool years? Clearly, having friends provides an excellent opportunity for the development of social skills and contributes to long-term social adjustment (Hartup, 1989). However, the absence of friends may not necessarily place children at risk. Adequate social adjustment appears to be assured when children are well liked by peers, even if they do not have "best friends." However, at the other extreme, children who are consistently rejected by their peers or socially isolated may be at risk for maladjustment, particularly if the rejection carries over into the middle childhood years (Parker & Asher, 1987; Price & Dodge, 1989).

Conflicts

When two or more preschool children interact in situations where resources are limited, conflicts are inevitable. *Conflict* is defined as any situation in which children find themselves opposing one another: They want the same toy at the same time; they vie to be first in line at recess; they argue over who can do something better or who is smarter.

Conflicts are pervasive in the play of preschool-age children, with perhaps 10 to 20 conflict episodes generated per hour (Eisenberg & Garvey, 1981; O'Keefe & Benoit, 1982). Despite their frequent occurrence, most conflicts are short-lived, typically lasting less than one minute. The vast majority of conflicts at this age do not involve physical aggression—that is, the intentional effort of one child to hurt another child. The absence of aggression in most conflicts helps to explain their brief duration.

While children can argue over just about anything, research has shown that conflicts center on two issues: *control of objects* and *social influence* (Shantz, 1987). Quarrels over the control of objects focus on possession, access, and ownership:

HEATHER: Give me that block.

TASHA: No way girl, that's my block.

HEATHER: That's not yours. It's mine. I had it first.

TASHA: Nuh-uhh, I had it this morning when you wasn't here yet. You was home in your bed when I had it. So leave me be.

HEATHER: You have it too long. I'm gonna tell.

Disagreements over social influence may take the following form:

LESHONDA: Teacher, Denise is bossin' me around. Tell her to stop.

DENISE: I ain't bossin' her. She's bossin' me all day.

LESHONDA: Denise is too bossin' me. I told her to quit tellin' me what to do.

DENISE: You're a crybaby and I ain't playin' with you.

Conflicts that do not involve aggression are typically resolved without adult intervention; they end without a clear winner or loser, and children show very little negative emotion when the conflict is over (Dawe, 1934; Houseman, 1972). However, even though preschoolers do not seem to carry a grudge, the inevitable frustrations over territory and possessions keep the frequency of conflict high.

How well children resolve conflicts depends on the nature of the relationship between the children. In one study (Matsumoto, Haan, Yabrove, Theodorou, & Carney, 1986), researchers compared the behavior of pairs of friends and pairs of nonfriends in a competitive game called the Prisoner's Dilemma. The game created a moral conflict for the participants: Winning for one child meant losing for the other. However, the rules of the game allowed a third strategy that equalized the payoff, but at a lower level for each child compared to the payoff for winning. Friends were more likely than nonfriends to equalize the payoff. In general, while friends generated as much conflict in their interactions as nonfriends, friends showed greater ability to resolve conflicts by negotiation, with no clear winner or loser (Hartup et al., 1988).

Although conflicts may temporarily disrupt children's play, they have an important role in promoting social and cognitive development. Carolyn Shantz describes children's conflicts as "potent episodes for changing the behavior of individuals and their relationships" (Shantz & Hobart, 1989, p. 74). For example, a "potent episode" might involve two children trying to move a heavy box of toys from one location to another. Although the children's differing opinions on how to lift and carry the box might easily lead to disagreement, the conflict provides an opportunity for children to learn to discuss the problem, to share perspectives on the solution, and ultimately to solve the problem cooperatively.

Conflicts also provide children with opportunities to test the status of their relationships. Children who are just getting to know each other—that is, children in the early stages of friendship—may move closer to friendship by resolving conflicts successfully. Even relationships between best friends may profit from the opportunity to cope with occasional conflicts.

A   P   P   L   I   C   A   T   I   O   N

Resolving Conflicts

Your child's conflicts can be used as a barometer of the quality of her relationships with peers. When conflicts are infrequent and low in intensity, you should resist the urge to intervene. Your child and her peers will generally find solutions to their own disagreements if given sufficient time. More frequent or intense conflicts may signal a problem in the relationship that requires adult attention.

Your initial approach to intervention should be low key, designed to encourage the children to solve their own problems. In many instances this can be accomplished by suggesting alternative strategies for the children to consider, rather than imposing arbitrary solutions. For example, the conflict over how to move a heavy box might be facilitated by asking, "What do you think would happen if one of you pushes from the back, while the other pulls from the front?'' If the conflict persists, you might suggest that the children play apart for awhile, which can be highly effective.

Bottom Line: Lay back and give your child a chance to solve her own conflicts.

This discussion has shown that preschool children cope well with everyday conflicts that do not involve aggression. But what happens when children learn that aggression can be a most effective way to resolve conflicts in their favor? As we will see, aggression dramatically strains relations between children, and between children and caregivers.

Aggression

An inevitable consequence of preschool children's rapid growth in physical size and strength is an increased potential for children to hurt one another in the course of play. In some instances, children cause pain inadvertently through clumsiness or impulsiveness. Such events are typically of little consequence. But at other times, children hurt others by **aggression**—purposeful effort to inflict pain or injury on another child. As the following incident suggests, aggression can have devastating emotional consequences on its victims.

> *Carlos runs excitedly toward the block area, eagerly anticipating the opportunity to play with the large building blocks. As he approaches the blocks, he slows his pace noticeably, stopping just a few feet from his goal. He looks around, obviously wary of the situation. Seeing no one, he enters and begins to stack blocks enthusiastically.*
>
> *The sound of two boys approaching throws him into panic. Without turning to see who is coming, he drops the block he is holding and darts out of the area. The two boys respond immediately by chasing him. Within seconds the faster boy has grabbed Carlos's shirt, slowing him just enough for the second boy to circle in front. The second boy laughs as he punches Carlos in the stomach. As Carlos screams in pain, the two boys run in different directions. The one caregiver in the room does not respond, despite the intensity of Carlos's cries. This is the fifth time in two days that Carlos has been victimized by one or both of the boys.*
>
> *Carlos is terrified and confused. He does not understand why the boys are hitting him or why the caregivers either do not care or are unable to protect him. His stomach hurts—not so much from the most recent punch, but from a tightness inside that he has felt since the first attack. He wanders toward an isolated corner of the room, trying his best to be invisible. But Carlos does not feel invisible: He feels vulnerable and helpless, knowing that the boys will find him and hurt him again. He begins to cry.*

The Development of Aggression   Developmentalists have distinguished between instrumental and hostile aggression (Hartup, 1974). **Instrumental aggression** refers to *object-oriented* struggles between children over possession, territory, and privilege. This may involve grabbing a toy from another child, tugging for possession, chasing a child who has a desired object, or striking a child while fighting over a disputed object. **Hostile**

aggression refers to *person-oriented* acts aimed at gaining social control. This may involve threatening by gesture or word, or actually striking a child to persuade or intimidate.

For most children, instrumental aggression peaks during the second year of life, declines significantly during the preschool years (Cummings, Iannotti, & Zahn-Waxler, 1985), and continues to decline during middle childhood (Hartup, 1974). In contrast, hostile aggression is infrequent in toddlers and increases through the early and middle childhood years (Hartup, 1974). Individual differences in aggression are quite stable during the preschool years, children who are more aggressive at age two tend to be more aggressive at age five (Cummings, Iannotti, & Zahn-Waxler, 1989).

These findings suggest that while the targets of preschool children's aggression changes from objects to people, the aggressors remain the same. This implies that wherever older preschoolers congregate in significant numbers—such as kindergarten classrooms—we should expect to encounter some children who are well rehearsed in the use of aggression to gain social control. These children are a formidable challenge to those who deal with young children, sapping their time and energy and substantially reducing the quality of care for other children. Effective prevention or intervention with highly aggressive children requires that we have a theoretical understanding of the development of aggression and the ability to translate theory into practice. We will now examine various theoretical perspectives on the development of aggression.

Theories of Aggression   Although we are all aware of the pervasiveness of violence in our society, we are still shocked when we witness acts of hostile aggression between children.

> *As Keisha walks toward the playground gate to pick up Leshonda, she is horrified to see Charita—one of Leshonda's more aggressive friends—punch Leshonda in the back. Leshonda's scream sends Keisha rushing toward the gate to intervene. Before Keisha can open the gate to the playground, Leshonda turns and hits Charita squarely in the chest, knocking her to the ground. Keisha, appalled by the violence and her own feelings of rage, backs off and waits to see what will happen. Charita jumps to her feet and runs off, with Leshonda in hot pursuit. When Leshonda catches her, they wrestle momentarily, but the intensity is gone. Within minutes they are playing together as if nothing has happened.*
>
> *Keisha calls Leshonda to the fence and asks, "What started the fight?" Leshonda responds, "What fight?" Keisha shakes her head and wonders why two good friends would behave so violently toward each other. Where does the aggression come from?*

Keisha's question is shared by most parents and caregivers of preschool-age children. Psychoanalytic and social learning theories offer very different perspectives on the development of aggression, each with different practical implications.

Psychoanalytic Theory of Aggression   Sigmund Freud (1920) proposed that destructive impulses are *instinctive* in humans: biologically built into the individual from birth, highly pleasurable, and virtually irresistible. Children choose targets for satisfaction of hostile impulses in much the same way that sexual objects are selected. Infants feel aggressive pleasure for the first time when they bite down on their mother's nipple to relieve the pain of teething. Later in development children find aggressive pleasure in hurting others or, occasionally, in hurting themselves. Aggression can be acted out in reality (by hitting other children) or in fantasy (by imagining attack or retaliation). During the preschool period—Freud's *phallic stage*—children's destructive impulses are directed increasingly toward the same-sex parent, who is perceived as a rival for the affection of the opposite-sex parent.

Freud's theory implies that children's hostile impulses must be released for healthy psychological adjustment. They may channel their aggression into socially acceptable forms of expression (such as pounding clay or hammering pegs) but should not repress aggressive impulses for that will ultimately lead to psychological disorder. In practical terms, psychoanalytic theory implies that caregivers should tolerate children's aggression because these aggressive impulses need to be vented. However, since rolling with your child's punches is not a satisfactory solution for most parents, developmentalists have turned to social learning theory for explanation and practical solutions.

Social Learning Theory of Aggression   Social learning theory provides two complementary perspectives on children's aggression. The first perspective applies the principles of observational learning to the development of aggression: Children *acquire* aggressive responses by observing the aggressive behavior of models and *produce* aggressive responses when the situation suggests that such behavior will be reinforced (Bandura, 1977).

In a classic series of studies, Albert Bandura and his colleagues (Bandura, 1965; Bandura, Ross, & Ross, 1963) exposed preschool children to an adult who modeled—in person or on film—a variety of aggressive acts toward a "Bobo" doll in a laboratory setting (see Figure 11.1). When the children were subsequently left alone with the doll, they imitated the adult's aggressive behavior in great detail. Did the children learn to be aggressive by imitating the model's behavior? Perhaps, but it is also possible that the model's behavior merely *disinhibited* the children by suggesting that aggression was permissible in the laboratory situation.

The increasing levels of violence among young children, particularly the use of guns, is no mystery. This youngster is merely imitating a scenario that he has seen on TV thousands of times.

FIGURE 11.1

The Modeling and Imitation of Aggression

Observational learning of aggression. An adult's modeling of distinct aggressive acts on a bobo doll (top row) are imitated by a boy (middle row), and by a girl (bottom row). Although young children are not always motivated to imitate modeled behavior, they remember much of what they have observed and may imitate at a later time.

Note that the children behaved aggressively without seeing the model reinforced and without being reinforced themselves. Without reinforcement, how did the children learn to act aggressively? Social learning theorists suggest that reinforcement is not necessary for learning to occur; when children observe aggression, they learn specific aggressive acts and when and where they can get away with those acts. This learning is stored in memory. Whenever the children find themselves in a permissive situation, they are likely to imitate the aggressive behavior. This has ominous implications for a generation of children who, through the medium of television, are continually exposed to highly detailed portrayals of every known variety of human aggression.

A second social learning perspective on aggression is Gerald Patterson's **coercion theory** (Patterson, 1982). Patterson argues that aggressive interactions—whether among children or between children and parents—tend to escalate into chains of aversive events. In the simplest form of chaining, one child's aggression against another elicits retaliation by the victim. If the retaliation is successful in terminating the attack—and it often is (Patterson, Littman, & Bricker, 1967)—the *victim's* aggression is reinforced. If it is not successful, the original attacker (who is now the victim) retaliates for the retaliation, and so on (Patterson et al., 1967; Patterson, 1982). The exchange of retaliatory attacks continues until one child gives in, reinforcing the other child's aggression.

Patterson identified a second version of chaining in the interactions of mothers and their sons. He observed that mothers of highly aggressive boys fall prey to the **reinforcement trap**. The trap begins when the mother issues a command like, "Clean your room!'' The child responds with an aggressive behavior, such as throwing a tantrum or repeatedly hitting a sibling. The mother eventually gives in, saying, "OK, OK, forget about cleaning the room. Just cut that out." The child then stops the aggression. Patterson suggests that two critical behaviors have been reinforced in the trap. The boy's aggression is reinforced when the mother rescinds her command, and her submissive giving in is reinforced when it *temporarily* ends his aggression. Conversely, if she resorts to slapping him to stop the aggression, her aggression is reinforced when he temporarily stops, but her modeling of aggression encourages him to act aggressively in the future.

Patterson's main point is that coercive interaction has a life of its own. Once a chain begins, participating children and adults alternate in the roles of aggressor and victim in an escalating pattern of violence. Thus Patterson believes that parents who rely on physical punishment inadvertently train their children to be aggressive and are themselves trained by their children to use physical punishment. Not surprisingly, mothers of highly aggressive children feel they have failed as parents and experience low self-esteem. In most instances, they have little understanding of how they may have contributed to their children's problems.

A P P L I C A T I O N

Breaking the Chains

*I*n theory, the first step in helping parents to break chains of coercive interaction with their children is generating an awareness of how parental behavior contributes to children's inappropriate behavior and noncompliance. Such awareness should help parents avoid reliance on physical punishment and the tendency to give in. Parents can be encouraged to provide models of appropriate behavior and to reinforce their children's positive behavior.

In practice, however, coercive chains are often deeply embedded in the chronic frustrations, stress, and negative emotions that pervade dysfunctional families—particularly those who live in poverty. Chains feed on anger, jealousy, and resentment, creating formidable barriers to change. Intervention must be designed to deal with the root causes of these emotions and their effects on parent-child interaction. Social services, job training, and family therapy can successfully intervene with parents and children.

Bottom Line: Coercive chaining between parents and children is a symptom of family dysfunction; it is profoundly complex and highly resistant to change.

Dominance

As indicated earlier, when preschoolers gather, aggression is inevitable, particularly when adult monitoring of children's play is lax or inconsistent. Developmentalists have observed that aggressive behavior, or even the threat of aggression, has a powerful impact on the organization of children's groups. The interaction between Carlos and the other children at day care illustrates how *dominance relationships* evolve.

> *Carlos's class has just been let out for free play on the playground adjacent to the day-care center. Carlos, seemingly overwhelmed by the chaotic rush of children toward the play equipment, lumbers slowly toward a ladder leading to a treehouse about four feet off the ground. Roberto and Luis, who happen to be close friends, are already struggling to see who will go up the ladder first.*

When Carlos nears the ladder, the boys pause momentarily and look menacingly in his direction. Roberto makes a fist and shouts, "No way, fatty, you ain't goin' up in our treehouse."

Carlos cowers, turns, and slowly walks away. The two boys then quickly resolve their dispute — Luis deferring to the older and stronger Roberto's interest in going first. Carlos jealously watches the boys climb to the treehouse, making no further attempt to join the activity.

Although these three children may be peers, they are clearly not equals with respect to power and influence. In the competition for access to the treehouse, Luis defers to Roberto, but both boys dominate Carlos. Unfortunately for Carlos, this result has become routine: Carlos is dominated by *all* other children in his group in competitions for resources and in decision-making situations.

How can we explain these differences in the distribution of power among children? Primates in natural settings have provided some insight (Carpenter, 1942; Hinde, 1974; Jolly, 1972). Primates routinely threaten and enact aggression in conflicts over territory and resources. Over time, the aggressive interactions among members of the group establish a **dominance hierarchy**, a systematic ordering of power relationships from the most to the least powerful member. When firmly established, the dominance hierarchy minimizes aggression by allowing each member of the group to anticipate the outcome of potential aggressive interactions with other group members. For example, when one monkey encounters a higher ranked monkey, fighting is unnecessary since both already know the winner.

If the dominance hierarchy works for primates, could it also serve the same purpose for young children? In a classic study of dominance relationships, Fred Strayer and Janet Strayer (1976) observed the interactions of preschool children involving physical attack (biting, chasing, kicking, and hitting), threat gestures, or struggles over objects. In each instance, the researchers noted whether the aggressive act was followed by submission by the victim. They then analyzed the data for the entire group of children to see if the dominance relationships among all members of the group conformed to the *transitivity principle*, that is, the expectation that if child A dominates child B, and child B dominates child C, then child A will dominate child C. The researchers found that 92 percent of the aggressive interactions conformed to the transitivity principle.

They concluded that dominance hierarchies exist in groups of young children, just as they do in primates. A later study (Strayer & Trudel, 1984) showed that dominance hierarchies can be demonstrated in groups of children as early as the second year of life. A provocative alternative view of dominance relationships in human children is presented in Box 11.2.

Some researchers have argued that dominance relationships are much more complicated in humans than in primates (La Freniere & Charlesworth, 1987; Segal et al., 1987). One group of researchers asked how friendship might affect dominance relationships in the context of children's cooperative play (La Freniere & Charlesworth, 1987). They formed groups of four children each, some composed of nonfriends and others containing same-sex friendship pairs. Each group was placed in a room with a toy movie viewer that required the cooperation of two children — one to turn a crank and one to press a light switch — to enable a third child to view a movie. Although dominant children controlled the viewer more often by forcing more submissive children to cooperate, the effect was apparent only in groups composed of nonfriends. Groups that included *male* same-sex friends used the viewer more efficiently and more equitably than all other groups. The researchers speculated that male friends—but not female friends—used the competition to test their relationship: "Well, if you don't give me a turn, I'm not gonna be your friend anymore" (1987, p. 356). The researchers noted that friendly affiliative behaviors (such as asking for and offering assistance) were more frequent and at least as influential as aggressive behaviors in gaining control of resources.

Our review of research on the components of social competence suggests two distinct patterns: First, socially competent children are popular among peers, develop stable and intimate friendships, resolve conflicts without resorting to aggression, and are sufficiently assertive to avoid being dominated by others. Second, socially incompetent

BOX 11.2

The Medieval Kingdom Model of Dominance Relations

In one observational study (Adcock & Segal, 1983) children's social styles for resolving conflict and making decisions were likened to the roles played in a medieval kingdom. Five social styles were identified: three leader roles including *kings* (or *queens*), *lords*, and *bishops*, and two follower roles including *vassals* and *serfs*. The behavioral descriptions of these roles are presented below:

Kings or *queens* are identified as outgoing, fun-loving, independent, self-confident children who enjoy rough and tumble play fighting.

Lords (males or females) are described as bossy, assertive children devoted to controlling the pretend play of a small group of followers. Female lords tend to play mother in a pretend family.

Bishops are flexible, reasonable, verbal, nurturant, teacher-oriented children who engage in intimate dyadic play—mediating quarrels, creatively solving problems, playing the role of teacher.

Vassals are followers whose goal is to be the favored playmate of a king or lord. Once they gain this status they strive to preserve it, often by aggressive means. Although vassals tend to have good social skills, they have little social status.

Serfs follow their leader without protest. Serfs are at the bottom of the social ladder—rejected, socially isolated, and maladaptive, clinging to teachers and/or attacking innocent victims.

The medieval kingdom classification system was confirmed in a series of studies of young children's free-play activities (Segal, Peck, Vega-Lahr, & Field, 1987). For example, in one mixed-age group of preschoolers four lords, four bishops, eight vassals, and eight serfs were identified. There were no kings or queens. For the most part, the observed be-haviors of children classified into the five styles varied as predicted by the model.

Is the medieval kingdom concept of any practical use? Based on the assumption that vassals and serfs are at risk for social rejection and social isolation, the researchers identified three children—two vassals and one serf—who were highly aggressive and unsuccessful in fulfilling their roles. Each of the two unsuccessful vassals were paired with a successful lord, and the unsuccessful serf with a successful bishop. Teachers reinforced the positive interactions of each pair each time they played together over a period of 12 weeks. The intervention succeeded in reducing the vassals' and serf's aggression over the 12-week period, presumably making them more successful followers.

The success of the intervention suggests that longer-term intervention might aspire to go beyond changing unsuccessful serfs and vassals into successful serfs and vassals—that is, perhaps serfs may be transformed into vassals and vassals into one of the three leader styles. This is a very promising area for further research.

children are rejected or neglected by peers, have difficulty making friends, are in frequent conflict with peers, are frequent perpetrators or victims of aggression, and either dominate or are dominated by peers. These different patterns emerge in a social context that includes peers, families, and community influences such as day care and preschool. We will now consider the critical role of the family and other caregivers in promoting social competence in young children.

The Parents' Role in Promoting Social Competence

Developmentalists have distinguished between *indirect* and *direct* family influences on the development of social competence (Ladd & Golter, 1988; Parke & Bhavnagri, 1988). Indirect family influence refers to the general effects of the type of relationship that parents have with their children. Direct influences involve parents' specific efforts to promote social competence, such as planning a child's social calendar.

Indirect Influences on Social Competence

Parents *indirectly influence* the development of social competence by the quality of the interpersonal relationships they establish with their children. These influences take two forms: the quality of the attachment relationship and the family's approach to the children's socialization and discipline.

Attachment and Social Competence   Attachment theory proposes that children's social development depends on the quality of their relationships with their parents (Bowlby, 1988; Main et al., 1985). Early researchers confirmed that secure attachment to the mother *during the infant-toddler period* is associated with the child's development of social skills in the early preschool years (Pastor, 1981; Waters et al., 1979). More recently, researchers have asked whether the quality of the attachment relationship with parents *during the preschool years* continues to affect social competence (Cicchetti, Cummings, Greenberg, & Marvin, 1990).

As children develop during the preschool years their attachment relationship to their parents changes for two reasons: First, advances in language ability enable children and parents to communicate effectively at greater distances, decreasing the need for close proximity; second, mental representations of the attachment relationship (or *internal working models*) allow children to feel secure as they explore farther and farther from the attachment figure (see Chapter 8). The result is a new phase in the development of attachment known as the **goal-corrected partnership**—attachment based more on *emotional* closeness rather than *physical* closeness (Bowlby, 1969; Marvin, 1972, 1977). Secure parent-child "partners" can each pursue their own independent goals without threatening the relationship or generating anxiety—in the parent or child—over brief separation. Thus preschool children in goal-corrected partnerships feel secure as they increase their participation with peers (Cicchetti et al., 1990). Secure attachment with the mother, assessed at preschool age, has been positively related to measures of social competence (Silver, 1991) and to the quality of interaction between friends (Parke & Waters, 1989). We may conclude that secure attachment relationships, established in infancy *and* continuing through the preschool years, promote social competency with peers.

Childrearing and Social Competence   The second indirect family influence on the child's development of social competence is the parents' approach to socialization and

Parents frequently demand that their children conform to some standard or rule, but getting children to comply is not always so easy. Here, an authoritarian mother insists that her child put on his shoes, but the look on his face suggests that he has something else in mind.

discipline. Eleanor Maccoby and John Martin (1983) have identified two dimensions that describe the variation in socialization practices among parents: **Demandingness** refers to the degree to which parents maintain expectations for their children's behavior and attempt to control the outcome of their children's development; **responsiveness** refers to the degree to which parents accept or reject their children. When these dimensions are considered simultaneously, four distinct *styles of parenting* can be identified:

1. **Authoritarian** parents assert great power over their children, setting strict limits and standards on children's behavior. Rules are set by parental edict, with no room for negotiation or compromise. These parents interpret deviations from the rules as challenges to their authority, frequently responding with moderate to severe punishment.
2. **Indulgent-permissive** parents are very accepting of their children's impulses, avoid setting rules, and assert very little authority over their children's behavior. They defer to their children's inclinations with respect to time schedules (bedtime, mealtime) and avoid making demands for compliance.
3. **Authoritative** parents have expectations for their children's behavior, firmly enforce rules and standards, but allow children some say in the development of rules. Parents and children communicate openly, encouraging each to express their points of view and affirming the rights of both parents and children. While authoritative parents expect children to be responsive to their demands, they reciprocate by being responsive to their children's needs.
4. **Neglectful** parents are uninvolved in their children's lives and consider parenting a burden. They emotionally distance themselves from their children and minimize the time and effort devoted to child care.

Do these differences in parenting style make a difference in children's social competence? Several researchers (Baumrind, 1967, 1971, Baumrind & Black, 1967; Patterson,

1982) have described distinct patterns of children's social behavior associated with each style of parenting. Diana Baumrind found that the *authoritarian style* predicted different outcomes for boys and girls: Nursery school girls were more socially assertive and boys were more socially withdrawn than other children (Baumrind & Black, 1967). Gerald Patterson (1982) found that most parents of "out of control children" were authoritarian. When these parents used punishment to coerce their children to behave, the rate of children's aggressive behavior *increased* rather than decreased. Parents' coercive attempts to control their children's aggression were met by equally coercive efforts by the children to control their parents.

The *permissive style* has been related to aggressiveness (Olweus, 1980) and low levels of social responsibility in boys, and lack of self-reliance and lack of independence in girls (Baumrind & Black, 1967; Baumrind, 1971). Why would an approach based on unconditional positive regard for children be associated with such negative outcomes? It may be that some permissive parents find themselves in a catch-22: Unconditional acceptance of children's behavior encourages intolerably high levels of aggression, forcing parents to assert their authority. Imposing rules in midstream breeds resentment in children who have known no rules (Maccoby & Martin, 1983).

Authoritative parenting has been consistently associated with positive developmental outcomes, compared to other parenting styles. Children of authoritative parents were more friendly, cooperative, and independent than other children (Baumrind, 1971; Baumrind & Black, 1967). Baumrind found one sex-related difference: Daughters of authoritative parents were more socially assertive than other children. More recent studies have shown similar effects in older children: Adolescents and young adults raised by authoritative parents have higher self-esteem and perform more adequately in school than children raised by permissive or authoritarian parents (Buri, Louiselle, Misukanis, & Mueller, 1988; Dornbusch, Ritter, Liederman, Roberts, & Fraleigh, 1987). Some practical limitations of the concept of parenting styles are explored in Box 11.3.

The research reviewed in this section has shown that if children are securely attached to their parents and have been socialized in an authoritative parenting style—that is, rules are firmly enforced but children are given some say in what the rules are—they are likely to be socially competent in early childhood. Do parents have more direct effects on the social competence of their children?

Direct Influences on Social Competence

Parents who are concerned about their children's social development are unlikely to rely solely on secure attachment and authoritative parenting to promote social competence. Most parents make at least some effort to directly manage their children's social relationships by selecting, modifying, or structuring their children's social environment (Parke & Bhavnagri, 1988, p. 3). Several options are available, including choice of neighborhood, planning social contacts, and monitoring and supervising play.

Choosing a Neighborhood Middle- and upper-class families can choose to live in neighborhoods that afford their children access to other children whom parents consider acceptable social partners. Parents may also consider access to play areas, such as parks and playgrounds, and the availability of community activities for children, such as day camps and preschools. Unfortunately, poor families are often forced to live in communities that offer few of these opportunities for children. Consequently, middle-class parents are far more likely than less affluent parents to enroll their children in community activities and to participate in those activities with their children (O'Donnell & Stueve, 1983).

The Parent as Social Planner   Parents also manage their children's social lives by initiating and maintaining contacts with other children and their families (Parke & Bhavnagri, 1988). This includes inviting other children to the home, arranging visits to other families, and pairing their children with children of other families for community activities. Mothers are more likely than fathers to play the role of social planner, and social planning is carried out more often for younger preschool-age children (Bhavnagri, 1987; Ladd & Golter, 1988).

Do parents' efforts to manage their children's social lives promote social competence? In one study, preschoolers whose parents initiated a higher proportion of their peer contacts had more play partners and more consistent contact with those partners than other children (Ladd & Golter, 1988). Moreover, boys—but not girls—whose mothers actively initiated contacts were more socially accepted and less rejected in preschool.

BOX 11.3

A Closer Look at Parenting Styles

Separating parents into different styles and relating styles to child outcomes seems like a developmentalist's dream come true: Simply observe parents interacting with their children, classify them by style, and predict how the children will turn out. Unfortunately, it's not that simple.

First, classifying parents into styles has been problematic for researchers and poses significant problems for those who deal with children and their families in practical situations. For example, in Baumrind's research (1971), there was considerable variation among families within each parenting style, adding greatly to the complexity of interpreting results. Second, mothers and fathers within families may differ in parenting style, causing problems both for researchers and, in most instances, for the children who experience their parents' inconsistency. Third, it is likely that parents may not be completely consistent in their approach to their children across situations. For example, parents are probably more authoritarian in situations where their children are at risk and more authoritative or perhaps permissive when children are not at risk. Fourth, parents' style may drift with the developmental stage of their children. For example, it would not be surprising to find that parents are more demanding of their children during the second and third years of life—a period of intense socialization—than they are in the later preschool years. Finally, we must recognize that parenting style studies were conducted more than 20 years ago—a very different time in the history of the American family. We must consider whether a style implemented by parents in the late 1960s would have the same effect as the same style implemented in the 1990s. Unfortunately, research has not provided an answer.

Do these problems mean that the concept of parenting styles is invalid? No, but they do suggest that we use caution in interpreting and applying these concepts in practical situations. In general, predictions of a child's outcome are likely to be more accurate *if* the mother and father are similar in their approach, *if* they are consistent across situations and over time, and, most importantly, *if* their approach conforms precisely to one of the styles described in the literature. Even with all these conditions met, there will still be considerable variation in the child's outcome from Baumrind's predictions.

We also should not lose sight of the clear advantages inherent in the authoritative parenting style. Parents should be encouraged to approximate this as an ideal, adapting the style to the individuality of their children and life circumstances.

This mother is casually monitoring her children's play while continuing her household chores. This indirect approach is more likely to foster children's social competence than more intrusive approaches.

Similar results have been demonstrated in day care: Children whose parents provided regular opportunities for peer contact *outside* of the day-care center received more bids to play from other children *inside* the center (Kennedy, 1991).

Monitoring Social Activities   Parents also manage their children's social lives by **monitoring** children's social interaction with peers, that is, by observing interaction, supervising the choice of activities, and guiding the direction of play. For example, parents may attempt to mediate conflicts or to enhance the quality of play by suggesting play themes.

Does parental monitoring promote social competence? In one study (Ladd & Golter, 1988), children whose parents used intrusive forms of monitoring (direct intervention in children's play) were less socially accepted and more likely to be rejected in preschool. Moreover, teachers perceived these children as more hostile-aggressive than children who were less closely supervised by their parents. The children of parents who monitored their interactions more *in*directly (by observing at a distance) were more socially competent. It is unclear whether parental monitoring *caused* children to be more or less socially competent or whether socially incompetent children elicit more direct forms of monitoring from their parents. It is likely that the relationship between parental monitoring and children's social behavior is *bidirectional*, with parents influencing children as much as they are influenced by their children.

A P P L I C A T I O N

Managing Your Child's Social Life

*I*nitiating social contacts for your child can be an effective way of promoting social competence, particularly if your child has limited access to peers. The goal should be to establish a few good friendships through continuous contact with selected children. Be sensitive to his feelings about being paired with specific children and give him some control over the selection and the timing of social contacts. Always give your child the right to refuse.

There are some important cautions. If you compulsively book your child's social engagements, you are probably acting out your own social anxieties rather than tending to his social needs. If your child has limited social skills, you must be highly sensitive to the difficulties in finding appropriate social partners for your child. Monitor initial contacts closely, watching for signs of incompatibility.

You should also monitor your own *monitoring* of his social interaction with peers. Although monitoring your child may promote positive relationships with peers, if you hover over his activities you will take the spontaneity out of the play and reduce the chances for social learning.

Bottom Line: Observe your child's peer activities at a distance and be responsive to his requests. If your child wants or needs more parental involvement, the signs will be obvious.

The Development of Prosocial Behavior

The early appearance of aggression is balanced by the equally early appearance of **prosocial behavior**, behavior that shows concern for the welfare of others. Prosocial behaviors include helping, caring, sharing, rescuing, protecting, and donating. Researchers have shown that children respond to other people's distress before the end of the second year (Zahn-Waxler & Radke-Yarrow, 1982). The reactions of very young children are highly variable, including crying, laughing, seeking help, and even acting aggressively toward the distressed individual. From 2 to 2½ years children begin to respond with more direct efforts to reduce the suffering of others, such as these reported by researchers:

- At two years, a child responds to his mother's fatigue by saying, "I'll get you my teddy bear," and does.

- At 2½ years, a child responds to a playmate's crying by bringing him a toy, saying: "Here, Jimmy, here's a car; here's some coffee." Looking into his face, he says, "Jimmy, are you okay?"

- At 2½ years, a child responds to his mother's crying by saying, "What's the matter?" Asks to be picked up and says, "I'm kissing your eyes so they won't cry" (Zahn-Waxler & Radke-Yarrow, 1982, p. 124).

While some forms of prosocial behavior (such as helping and comforting) increase in frequency during the preschool years, other forms (such as sharing) may stay constant or even decrease (Bar-Tal, Ravin, & Goldberg, 1982; Grusec, 1991). Increases in prosocial behavior may depend in part on the development of children's ability to show **empathy**, the ability to understand and actually feel the emotions experienced by other individuals. Knowing that someone is in distress, for example, may help to elicit helping or rescue behaviors; knowing that someone is happy may elicit sharing of toys. In one study, preschoolers who were more understanding of other's emotions and displayed more positive emotions in free play exhibited more prosocial behaviors than children who displayed predominantly negative emotions such as anger (Denham, 1986). In general, children responded more prosocially to peer's displays of happy emotion than to displays of sadness or anger.

Children show stable individual differences in prosocial behavior during the preschool years; that is, children who are more prosocial at three to four years are likely to be more prosocial at five to six (Mussen & Eisenberg-Berg, 1977). How can we account for the differences among individuals? In one study, mothers of more prosocial children were more nurturant and emotionally responsive to their children than mothers of less

Children are more likely to develop prosocial behavior and moral reasoning when natural events in their lives pull for helping behaviors. Here a boy cares for his elderly grandmother.

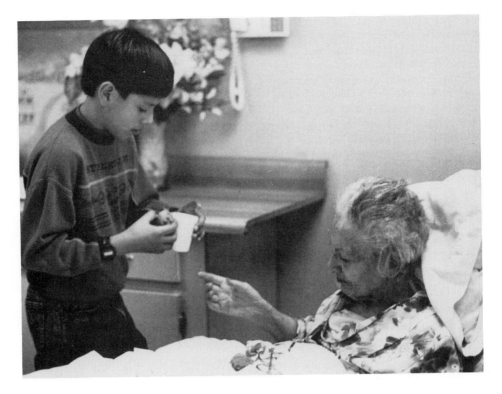

prosocial children (Zahn-Waxler, Radke-Yarrow, & King, 1979). When their children were the cause of distress in other children, these mothers tended to moralize in strong emotional tones: "Look what you did! Don't you see you hurt Amy? Don't ever pull hair" (1979, p. 327). Thus these mothers combined empathic caregiving and power-assertive moral communications to promote prosocial behavior in their children.

Joan Grusec (1991) observed mothers' responses to children's prosocial behavior at home. Mothers frequently used social praise rather than material reinforcements for children's prosocial behavior and infrequently punished them for failing to behave prosocially. Surprisingly, mothers *rarely* used "empathy training," that is, attempts to sensitize children to the impact of their behavior on others.

Did mothers' responses promote prosocial behavior? In Grusec's study, mothers' reinforcement had no effect on prosocial behavior. In fact, four-year-olds who typically received *no* response of any kind from their mothers for prosocial behavior were most likely to act prosocially. Operant principles obviously fail to explain differences in children's prosocial behavior in the home environment. Grusec concluded that parents may influence prosocial development by *modeling* prosocial behavior in their own lives and by assigning responsibilities to their children that encourage prosocial response, such as caring for younger siblings and assisting elderly grandparents or neighbors.

A P P L I C A T I O N

Promoting Prosocial Development

Promoting kind, caring, generous, helping, and cooperative behaviors in your preschooler is not simple. Your child's tenuous sense of self, concerns over territory and ownership, and lingering egocentrism may suppress her prosocial responses during the preschool years. These obstacles can be gradually over-come by combining *your* adult modeling of prosocial behavior, encouragement, and reinforcement of *her* prosocial behavior with empathy training—for example, by discussing people's feelings.

Consistency is essential. Your child is more likely to imitate salient displays of adult gener-osity, caring, and sharing toward less fortunate individuals if she and her models are consis-tently rewarded for behaving prosocially. Pro-vide consistent messages: Model the behavior you want your child to learn and reinforce what your child does.

Bottom Line: Be patient. Prosocial response does not come easy to your preschooler. With time, generous and caring parents are likely to have generous and caring children.

The Development of Gender Roles

Our society defines virtually all things, events, activities, and enterprises as more appro-priate for one gender than the other: Boys and men play baseball, curse, spit, and like the color blue; girls and women knit, gossip, care for babies, and like the color pink. All children are expected to learn these distinctions or suffer the consequences. Children who learn gender-appropriate behavior and attitudes are likely to be accepted by parents, peers, and teachers; those who do not risk rejection and prejudice. These distinctions by gender are, for the most part, arbitrary, but children are required to learn them as early in development as possible—certainly before the end of the preschool years.

Toddlers can barely tell the difference between boys and girls, or identify themselves as male or female. For most children, the first awareness of **gender identity**, the ability to classify oneself and others by gender, appears in the third year of life. Girls begin to identify with the label "girl" by their second birthday; boys identify with the label "boy" approximately a year later (Leinbach & Fagot, 1986). Children's understanding of gender identity develops gradually through the preschool years, eventually achieving **gender constancy**—the concept that gender does not change regardless of how one be-haves or what clothes one wears (Bem, 1989).

As gender identity improves, boys and girls learn their respective **gender roles**: the behaviors, attitudes, and beliefs that a particular culture considers appropriate for males and females. In our society, men are traditionally portrayed as strong, competent, inde-pendent, aggressive, and relatively unemotional. In contrast, women are expected to be nurturant, emotional, dependent, unassertive, and compliant.

There is good reason to believe that societal values have changed substantially in recent years, allowing males to be more nurturant and emotional and females to be more assertive and independent. As welcome as these changes may be for society, they create confusing and possibly inconsistent models for children learning gender roles. For example, televised images of women in combat positions and men as nurses in re-cent military actions challenge young children's thinking with respect to female and male gender roles.

The child's emerging concepts of gender identity, gender constancy, and gender role will have enormous impact on social adjustment. We will now look more closely at how children learn about gender.

Learning Gender Roles: Theoretical Approaches

The process by which children learn gender roles is referred to as **gender typing**. In general, we know more about the players in gender typing than we do about the process of how that learning takes place. We know that gender typing evolves through exposure to parents, siblings, peers, and portrayals of individuals in the media, particularly in children's books and on television. However, the process by which these exposures are incorporated into children's understanding of gender roles is less clear. We now consider the major theories of gender typing: psychoanalytic, social learning, cognitive-developmental, and gender schema theory.

The Psychoanalytic Perspective   Freud viewed the family as an emotionally charged system of intimate relationships. During the third stage of psychosexual development—the *phallic stage*—preschool-age children develop intense sexual love for the opposite-sex parent that can only be fulfilled by sexual intercourse with that parent. In the male this is referred to as the *Oedipal complex*; in the female, the **Electra complex.**

When children find their sexual aims blocked—due to the father's threats to castrate his son or the daughter's inconvenient lack of a penis—the children are overwhelmed by anxiety. Children unconsciously defend themselves against this anxiety through **identification**, by incorporating characteristics of the same-sex parent and to a lesser extent the opposite-sex parent into the personality as an **ego ideal**. The ego ideal becomes a permanent component of personality, providing a prescription for gender-appropriate role behavior (Freud, 1923/1960). Although Freud's theory has fallen into disfavor in recent years, many of his concepts deserve further study.

The Social Learning Perspective   Social learning theorists believe that children learn gender roles the same way they learn any other behavior: They observe how same-sex peers and adults behave, imitate what they see, and are reinforced or punished depending on whether their behaviors are gender appropriate. As we will see below, research has shown that social learning principles require some refinement and elaboration to explain variations in children's gender role learning in the natural environment. The theory has also been criticized for viewing children as *passive* recipients of environmental influences, ignoring the *active* role that children play in interpreting society's gender roles (Bem, 1983).

The Cognitive-Developmental Perspective   The cognitive-developmental perspective extends Piaget's theory to gender typing and gender role development. In direct contrast to the social learning perspective, this theory portrays children as active agents in the learning of gender roles. The process begins when children label themselves accurately as "boys" or "girls" during the second or third year of life. According to Maccoby (1988), the gender label works like a magnet, helping children to organize information about the world by sorting new experiences into gender-appropriate and gender-inappropriate categories. Children come to value only those new experiences that are perceived as gender appropriate, assimilating them to the concept of self. For example, repeated exposure to media portrayals of doctors and mechanics as males promotes assimilation of those occupations to a boy's preconcept of "things that are masculine."

Lawrence Kohlberg (1966) proposed that the limitations of preoperational thought prevent preschool-age children from "conserving" gender identity—that is, preschoolers believe that a boy dressed as a girl is not *really* a boy. Kohlberg argued that gender constancy is not achieved until children reach age six or seven.

However, a more recent study by Sandra Bem (1989) suggests that children conserve gender much earlier than proposed by Piaget and Kohlberg. She exposed three-, four-, and five-year-olds to two sequences of photographs: one sequence of a male toddler named Gaw; the second sequence of a female toddler named Kwann. The first photograph in each sequence showed the child fully nude, the second photograph showed

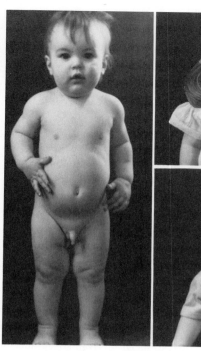

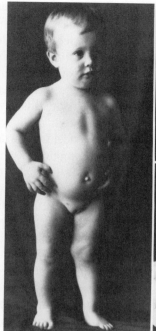

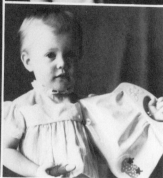

The two sets of photographs used in Bem's sex conservation test. On the left is Gaw (the boy); on the right Kwahn (the girl). Preschoolers who knew that genitalia are the defining attributes of females and males were able to conserve gender across the photographs.

Because of the sensitive nature of child nudity in our culture, each photograph used in the study was taken in the toddler's own home with at least one parent present. Parents provided written consent to use the photographs in the research, and parents of the two children pictured here also gave written consent to have their children's photographs published. Finally, parents of the children who served as subjects in the study gave written permission for their children to participate in a study in which they would be asked questions about pictures of nude toddlers.

the child in clothing and a hairstyle *inconsistent* with his or her gender, and the third showed the child in clothing and hairstyle *consistent* with his or her gender. The subjects were questioned to determine if they could identify the child's gender and if they could conserve gender through the changes of clothing and hairstyle.

The results showed that 40 percent of the preschoolers conserved Gaw's and Kwann's gender across the photographs. Importantly, only those children who were aware of the *genital* differences between males and females were able to conserve. Girls had significantly more genital knowledge than boys. This study suggests that Piaget's assumption that children are incapable of conservation until the concrete operational stage, particularly with respect to gender identity, requires some rethinking. However, the cognitive-developmental perspective continues to offer a valuable framework for research in this area.

The Gender Schema Theory   Gender schema theory (Bem, 1983, 1985) accounts for gender typing by combining the concepts of the child's active role from cognitive-developmental theory and environmental influence from social learning theory. The child's active role is incorporated into the concept of the **gender schema**: a cognitive structure with which the child actively searches for gender-related information from the environment. When a child enters a new experience, such as the first day in a new day-care center, the gender schema searches for information that helps the child define the situation in terms of femaleness or maleness.

For example, consider the situation of a boy checking out his new kindergarten classroom. Whereas familiar activities such as playing with balls, blocks, and climbing equipment are readily assimilated to the male gender schema, less familiar activities such as reading storybooks require that the gender schema search for gender-relevant information. If he perceives that the storybooks are being read primarily by boys and that the content is gender appropriate, he will assimilate the books to his male gender schema.

In our society, the gender schema does not have to strain to find gender-relevant information: Toy and clothing stores designate certain aisles for girls or boys, television commercials are geared for male or female consumption, and activity groups such as Scouts are conveniently gender segregated. The intensity of cultural programming of gender role assures that few children will have to think for themselves with respect to gender role.

As the gender schema develops, it becomes an essential component of the child's self-concept, prompting the child to perceive the world and the self through the framework of gender role. In Bem's words, "The gender schema becomes a prescriptive standard or guide, and self-esteem becomes its hostage" (Bem, 1983, p. 605). The gender schema builds upon itself, motivating the individual to conform to cultural definitions of femaleness and maleness. Bem speculates that parents and teachers can help children resist the learning of gender stereotypes (for example, that only males can be muscular and good at math and that only females can care for babies and use a sewing machine). Bem's controversial prescriptions for raising a nonsexist child in a predominantly sexist world are presented in Box 11.4.

Although the theories of gender typing differ on particulars, they all agree on the importance of learning during the preschool years. By first grade, children's understanding of gender-appropriate behavior has become essential to social survival. First graders must know which toilet facility to use, which line to join, which clothes to wear, and, most importantly, which behaviors are appropriate for boys and girls in various settings such as the playground, classroom, lunchroom, and school bus. The stakes are very high in gender role learning. Children who develop a clear sense of gender identity and gender role—consistent with a society's cultural values—are likely to be accepted by peers and adults. Children who develop cross-sex gender identity or gender role—particularly boys who adopt feminine traits—are likely to be rejected by peers and treated negatively by some adults, including parents and teachers. The risks are real and should not be taken lightly by those who dream of a nonsexist world, a dream that is far from reality in contemporary American society.

Parental Influence on Gender Role Learning

From a social learning perspective, parents are uniquely positioned to influence their children's gender role learning during infancy and early childhood. They monitor large segments of their children's behavior and can reinforce any behaviors they hope to increase and punish any behaviors they choose to decrease. They have virtually complete control over their children's access to resources. Most important, one parent happens to be a male and the other a female—a most convenient setup for the differential modeling of gender-appropriate behavior. Do parents influence the gender role learning of their children?

Research has consistently shown that while parents' behavior toward sons and daughters does not differ in most areas of socialization (such as in encouraging achievement or dependency), it does differ with respect to encouraging gender-typed behaviors (Lytton & Romney, 1991; Maccoby & Jacklin, 1974). These findings are illustrated in an early study by Beverly Fagot. Fagot's (1978) home observations of parent–child interaction showed parents reacting more positively to their children's same-sex behaviors and more negatively to cross-sex behaviors. For example, boys were reinforced more than girls for playing with blocks, and girls were reinforced more than boys for playing with dolls. Fathers were particularly negative when their sons played with dolls.

BOX 11.4

Raising Nonsexist Children in a Sexist Society

Sandra Bem (1983) argued that sexism in American society is deeply rooted in the early gender role learning of children. Exposure to gender stereotypes from parents, peers, and the media programs gender role learning. Bem warned that parents who simply ignore the problem leave their children vulnerable to the sexist views promulgated by the media. She believed that parents must actively "inoculate" their children against the tendency to see the world through gender-colored glasses. She recommended the following childrearing practices:

1. Parents should eliminate gender stereotyping from their own behavior by taking turns cooking dinner, changing diapers, driving the car, and mowing the lawn.
2. Parents should provide toys and other resources to their children without regard to gender. For example, both boys and girls should have equal access to dolls and trucks, male and female play partners, and pink and blue clothing.
3. Parents should actively censor children's books and television programs that promote gender stereotypes. Recognizing that this may eliminate most available materials, Bem recommended that parents create their own materials or doctor existing materials to eliminate stereotypes. For example, main characters in storybooks can be altered to counteract stereotyped portrayals of adult role models.
4. Parents should teach their children that males and females are defined *only* by differences in the genitalia and their function in reproduction.
5. Parents should draw their children's attention to overt stereotypes presented in cartoons and television programs. They might comment, for example, why the people who make cartoons always show men fighting and women running away screaming.
6. Parents can provide alternative schemas to substitute for traditional gender schemas. For example, parents can encourage their children to think in terms of individual differences rather than focusing on differences between men and women. Parents can also identify sexism directly as a form of discrimination. Situations where one gender has unfair advantage over the other or unequal access to resources are easily identified in the world of young children, for example, all-girl birthday parties, all-boy ball teams, Brownies, and Cub Scouts.

Bem's advice should not be accepted without careful consideration. There is no research on the effectiveness or long-term outcomes of raising children according to her recommendations. Even if the techniques are effective, one must consider the plight of a nonsexist child in a sexist society. While the child may represent the high moral purpose, the child's attitudes and behaviors may increase the risk of social rejection. Bem (1983) suggested that the benefits of raising nonsexist children are illustrated in her account of what happened to her four-year-old son Jeremy the day he decided to wear barrettes to nursery school.

Several times that day, another little boy told Jeremy that he, Jeremy, must be a girl because "only girls wear barrettes." After trying to explain that "being a boy means having a penis and testicles," Jeremy finally pulled down his pants as a way of making his point more convincingly. The other child was not impressed. He simply said, "Everybody has a penis; only girls wear barrettes." (Bem, 1983, p. 612)

We might ask whether the world is ready for Jeremy and whether Jeremy is ready to deal effectively with the reactions of other children and adults. His presentation of himself would presumably be at odds with the prevailing culture at the nursery school and might elicit some concern from teachers and parents. Clearly, societal change must start some place, but using one's children for such purposes without their consent raises some difficult moral questions.

Fagot's (1978) findings were confirmed in a laboratory study of preschool children's play with toys (Langlois & Downs, 1980). Fathers exhibited more positive reactions to the play of daughters and more negative reactions to the play of sons. Fathers also showed consistently greater pressure for gender-typed behaviors for both sons *and* daughters than mothers, often by ridiculing children for cross-sex play. Why do fathers bring more pressure to bear on gender-typed behaviors? Perhaps because they have benefited more from traditional family roles than mothers and hope to perpetuate the system. This explanation received some support in a study of fathers' personality traits, attitudes toward women, and gender-typed activities in the home in relation to their children's gender identity and gender-typed toy preferences (Weinraub, Clemens, Sockloff, Etheridge, Gracely, & Myers, 1984). Fathers who held more conservative attitudes toward women and who engaged less frequently in feminine role activities in the home had children who were more traditionally gender typed.

If the presence of fathers in the home has potent effects on gender role development, what are the effects of father absence? In particular, does the lack of an appropriate male role model negatively affect the gender typing of father-absent boys? An analysis of 67 studies (Stevenson & Black, 1988) showed no differences on gender role measures for girls from father-absent homes compared to girls from father-present homes. Whereas preschool-age boys from father-absent homes were less traditionally gender typed than father-present boys, the reverse was true for older boys. In general, the results do not suggest *consistent*, long-term effects of father absence on gender role development.

Learning Gender Roles in the Same-Sex Peer Group

Keisha is beside herself. After all her planning, nothing has gone right since Leshonda's fourth birthday party began. Marcus's buddy had a last-minute emergency with his car and Marcus just had "no choice" but to help him out. He said he would be back in time to help, but Keisha isn't holding her breath. "Just like a man!" she thinks. Marcus loves his daughter dearly but being a chaperone at a girl's birthday party makes him noticeably uncomfortable.

At Leshonda's insistence, Keisha has invited all of the girls in her day-care class and five girls from the neighborhood. Over Leshonda's objections, Keisha has purposely invited several boys from day care and two boys who live in the building. As the children arrive, they immediately separate into two groups by gender; the boys congregate in one corner of the room, and the girls wander everywhere except anywhere near the area occupied by the boys. The girls are obviously having a great deal of fun—giggling, telling secrets, and showing off their dresses; the boys look like they are attending a funeral.

Soon after the last child arrives, the oldest boy (a five-year-old) begins to tease the girls by imitating the way they walk and by mimicking their conversations in a high-pitched voice. Although the boys do not know each other well, they organize suddenly into a cohesive group aimed at making the girls miserable.

When the fun of teasing wears off, the boys begin to chase and wrestle with each other. When two boys crash into the dining room table, Leshonda's birthday cake lands on the floor. Keisha runs in, but it is too late. The boys look up from the floor with grins that simultaneously announce their guilt and their awareness that they are unlikely to get punished under the circumstances.

Leshonda is crying, the other boys are laughing hysterically, and Keisha is trying to quiet the children and salvage what she can of the cake.

Marcus chooses that moment to make a cameo appearance. One disapproving glance from him sends the boys running to their corner, trying their best to be invisible. The girls comfort Leshonda and whisper how they hate boys and why boys shouldn't be allowed at a girl's birthday party.

When young children are given free choice of play partners, particularly in unstructured settings such as Leshonda's party, there is a strong tendency to congregate in same-sex groups (Maccoby, 1988; Maccoby & Jacklin, 1987). The same-sex peer group is a training ground for the learning of gender roles—promoting dominance, aggression, and competitiveness for boys; nurturance, prosocial behavior, and compliance for girls. The children's interaction at Leshonda's party epitomizes the behaviors observed within and between segregated same-sex groups: rough and tumble behavior among the boys, highly verbal and polite behavior among the girls, and considerable antagonism between members of the respective groups.

Gender-segregrated groups begin to form very early in development: Girls prefer other girls as play partners by the end of the second year; boys prefer the company of other boys by the end of the third year (La Freniere et al., 1984). Gender segregation intensifies through the preschool years and dominates children's play in middle childhood. In one study (Maccoby & Jacklin, 1987), four-year-olds spent three times as much play time with same-sex partners as with opposite-sex partners; by first grade, the same children spent more than 90 percent of their time with same-sex play partners (see Figure 11.2). Similar behavior patterns have been identified in cultures throughout the world (Edwards & Whiting, 1988).

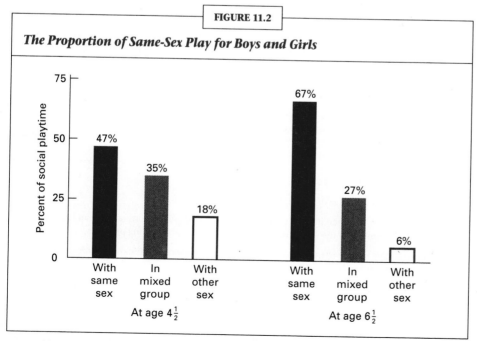

| FIGURE 11.2 |

The Proportion of Same-Sex Play for Boys and Girls

SOURCE: *Maccoby & Jacklin,* Advances in Child Behavior and Development, 20, *1987. Reprinted by permission of Academic Press and Eleanor E. Maccoby.*

Why Does Gender Segregation Occur?   Although some parents may encourage gender segregation in their role as gatekeepers of their children's social contacts, it is unlikely that this contributes to children's *preferences* for same-sex playmates. A more likely explanation is that something special happens when groups of boys and groups of girls gather that does not occur in mixed-sex groups (Maccoby & Jacklin, 1987). What could possibly be so special that it creates an irresistible and universal attraction to same-sex peers throughout the childhood years?

Eleanor Maccoby and Carol Jacklin, experts in gender development, believe that young children are attracted to the unique *subcultures* that emerge in all-girl and all-boy groups (Maccoby & Jacklin, 1987). The respective subcultures differ both in the children's styles of play and in the ways children influence one another (see Table 11.2). In the boys' subculture, the play style involves **rough and tumble play** — playful wrestling and chasing — and physical fighting. Boys influence each other by establishing dominance through physical force. The play style in the girls' subculture is friendly, with high rates of turn-taking and shared decisions. Girls influence each other by polite suggestion rather than by making demands.

Can the Tendency Toward Gender Segregation Be Reversed?   Research has shown mixed results in efforts to reduce gender segregation of young children's groups. Lisa Serbin and her colleagues (1977) trained teachers to reinforce preschool children's play with opposite-sex partners. Although reinforcement training significantly increased

---

TABLE 11.2
Male and Female Subcultures of Preschool Play Groups
Distinctive Features of Male Subculture
1. Boys tend to play in larger groups than girls.
2. Boys tend to play in more open spaces, as far as possible from adult monitoring and supervision.   3. Boys play rougher than girls, sometimes in rough and tumble play and sometimes in more aggressive forms of physical fighting, taunting, or teasing.
4. Boys establish dominance and a pecking order. Boys' groups are more likely to have a single leader who functions by issuing commands.
5. Boys use language to attract attention from others, to assert dominance by making threats, to boast, and to refuse to comply with requests.
Distinctive Features of Female Subculture
1. Girls play in small groups of 2–3 girls.
2. Girls play within the range of adult monitoring and supervision.
3. Girls tend to take turns and influence one another by making suggestions rather than issuing commands. All members of the group tend to participate in decision-making processes.
4. Girls make more intense friendships than boys, with more use of self-disclosure. Girls show more distress when friendships break up.
5. Girls tend to use language to create and maintain relationships and to criticize others in socially acceptable ways. They are less likely than boys to interrupt each other and more likely to agree with their play partners.

SOURCE: *Adapted from Maccoby & Jacklin, 1987, pp. 249–250*

cross-sex play, the children returned to their original low levels of cross-sex play as soon as the reinforcement was eliminated. There is some evidence of more cross-sex play in "open" nursery schools—that is, programs where children are given considerable choice of activities—than in traditional classrooms (Bianchi & Bakeman, 1978).

In general, preschool children have a strong tendency toward same-sex play. That tendency may be attenuated somewhat by the concerted efforts of caregivers and parents, but while the long-term effects of such efforts are unclear at this time, it is unlikely that high levels of cross-sex play can be sustained without continuing efforts by adults.

A P P L I C A T I O N

Dealing with Gender Segregation

Some argue that gender segregation should be promoted as an effective way of preparing children to live in largely gender-segregated society, while others argue that gender segregation is one of the causes of sexism in our culture and that it should be eliminated. Still others argue that there isn't much we can do about it, one way or another. So how should parents and other caregivers approach this issue?

Moderation seems to be the key. Gender segregation in children's play groups has a momentum of its own and requires no special assistance from adults. Subtle encouragement of cross-sex play may be effective in broadening your child's perspective, but don't expect radical changes in your child's choice of play partners. Keep in mind that your child is more likely to engage in cross-sex play if he believes his friends will not be aware of its occurrence.

Bottom Line: Think twice before programming your child to fight sexism in our society. He could pay a high price for your campaign.

Emotional Development During the Preschool Years

Preschoolers display a wide range of emotions and tend to have a short fuse for virtually every emotion in their repertoire: A broken toy generates instant sadness, a cartoon character falling into a hole releases gales of laughter, and someone sitting in his chair (invasion of territory) provokes intense anger. They display common emotions in very different proportions in natural settings (see Figure 11.3). Although neutral expressions predominate, the positive facial expressions of happiness, interest, and surprise far outweigh the negative expressions of sadness, anger, fear, and disgust (Field & Walden, 1982).

As preschoolers grow, they get more and more adept at sending emotional signals and reading the emotional signals of others.

Sending Masking Emotional Signals

Most young children wear their emotions on their sleeves. Young children's facial expressions of emotion are readily identified by adults and are identified with increasing accuracy by peers through the preschool years (Buck, 1975). They increasingly supplement their facial expressions with gestures (such as waving their arms and making fists) and with changes in posture and activity level. Parents develop the ability to read minute changes in their children's facial expressions, often anticipating their children's changes in mood. A father, for example, may sense his daughter's mounting sadness from a slight

FIGURE 11.3

Proportions of the Display of Emotions in Free Play

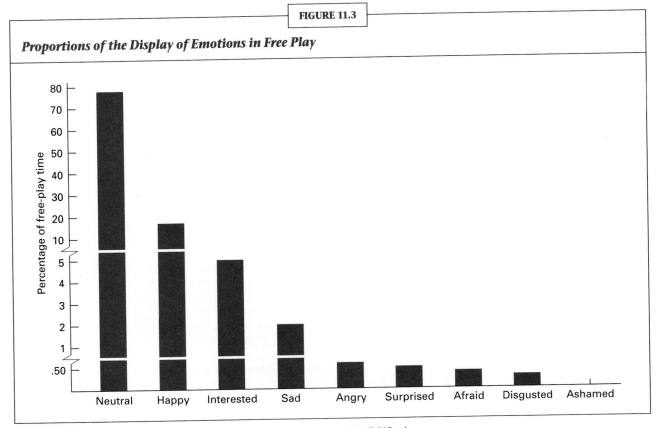

SOURCE: *Field & Walden*, Child Development 53, *1299–1311, 1982.* © *The Society for Research in Child Development, Inc. Reprinted by permission.*

reduction in the tempo of her play or a deepening of her tone of voice. In some instances, the parent's awareness precedes the child's awareness, setting off a heated discussion:

KEISHA: What's bothering you?

LESHONDA: Nothin'.

KEISHA: But you have an angry look on your face.

LESHONDA: No I don't.

KEISHA: Oh yes you do. I know when you are mad.

LESHONDA: (*now angry*) NO, NO, NO, NO, NO, NO, NO!

Children in our society are expected to learn that they cannot always express overtly what they feel (Saarni, 1979). As we indicated in Chapter 8, every culture has its own **display rules** or conventions for appropriate displays of emotion in particular situations. Learning display rules is complicated by the fact that the rules change from situation to situation. For example, crying in your room is appropriate, but crying while walking down the street is not; laughing in front of the TV is appropriate, but laughing at a funeral is not. Learning display rules is even more complicated because display rules in a given situation often change developmentally. For example, whereas silliness may be tolerated in three-year-olds at day care, it is considerably less appropriate for five-year-olds.

Difficulties arise when young children feel emotions—especially extreme intensities of emotion—that violate the display rules for a given situation. Although children have no control over what they feel, they can learn to control how they express their emotions to others. We refer to the process by which children alter the overt expression of emotions to conform to display rules as **masking**. In some instances, children simply put on a poker face to hide their feelings. A physically abused child, for example, may hide his pain to defy his abuser or out of a sense of guilt or fear of retribution.

In other instances, children learn to display an emotion opposite to the one they feel. For example, in laboratory studies children as young as four displayed positive rather than negative emotion in response to winning a disappointing prize (Cole, 1986; Morrongiello, Anderson, & Rocca, 1991). Girls showed greater masking of negative emotion than boys, smiling more broadly in response to a disappointing prize than to a desirable prize (Cole, 1986). Eleanor Maccoby (1980, p. 178) described an interesting variation of masking in this revealing anecdote: "When she noticed a cut on her 4-year-old son's hand, one mother said, 'Why honey, you've hurt yourself! I didn't hear you crying.' Said the boy, 'I didn't know you were home!'" It is not difficult to identify the seeds of more mature forms of deceit and hypocrisy in these early masking behaviors.

A P P L I C A T I O N

Reading Your Child's Emotions

As children mature through the preschool years, their facial expressions become progressively less reliable indicators of their true feelings. Attend closely to the situational context of your child's emotional displays, watching for discrepancies between her facial expressions and the expected emotion for that context. For example, when she smiles and cheers when a disliked peer is awarded a privilege, she may be masking her true feelings of anger or jealousy. Note that sexually abused children often mask their feelings about the perpetrator out of a sense of guilt or fear of retribution. Thus distinguishing between facial appearance and emotional reality requires careful attention to your child's behavior and to the context of that behavior. Wait until you are sure of the emotion, and approach the subject sensitively.

Bottom Line: Be sensitive to your child's emotions but recognize your child's right to private thoughts and feelings. Excessive probing is likely to provoke resentment and more effective masking.

Reading Emotional Signals

Successful social interaction often hinges on the ability to read emotional signals and to infer emotional states. For example, adults are generally aware that people are more approachable when they are in positive moods than in negative moods. We infer someone's emotional state by observing facial expression and context. For example, we infer that children feel happy when they smile persistently while playing with best friends and that they feel sad when more dominant children take away their toys. Research has shown that young children are fairly accurate in inferring one another's emotional states if the situation is familiar and the emotion is uncomplicated, such as happy, sad, or angry (Barden, Zelko, Duncan, & Masters, 1980; Borke, 1971). But what happens when the situation is more complex? For example, are preschool children aware that different people may feel different emotions in the same situation?

A recent study demonstrated that even two- and three-year-olds are aware that different people may have different feelings on a given issue and that feelings can change over time (Banerjee & Wellman, 1991). The following examples illustrate the first evidence of these abilities (p. 8):

MOTHER: Abe, Mommy and Daddy were just real cranky. We had an argument but we're OK now. We're happy.

ABE: I'm not!

ADAM: (*after tasting glue*) I don't like it.

MOTHER: Why would you put that in your mouth?

ADAM: I thought it was good.

While these examples show that young children are aware that emotional states can change and that different people can have different emotional reactions to the same event, a series of studies by Jackie Gnepp and her colleagues have shown that reasoning about emotions develops slowly during early and middle childhood (Gnepp, 1983; Gnepp & Gould, 1985; Gnepp, McKee, & Domanic; 1987). In one study Gnepp (1983) showed children pictures with conflicting facial and situational cues, for example, a child crying at a birthday party or a child happy in a dentist's office. Although preschoolers perceived both facial and situational cues, their inferences about the emotions were based solely on facial expressions. Older children tried to reconcile the discrepancies between facial expressions and situational cues, sometimes by suggesting that the children might be masking their true emotions.

Gnepp also studied whether young children recognize that emotional reactions may reflect people's prior experiences in a given situation (Gnepp & Gould, 1985). Children were read a series of stories consisting of two events, where the first event might be expected to influence the second event. For example, in one story the first event depicted a boy being bitten by the class gerbil. In the second event the teacher awarded the boy the privilege of feeding the gerbil—normally a fun experience, but not to a child who has been bitten. Kindergarten children were unable to consider the effect of the boy's prior experience of being bitten on his subsequent negative reaction to the award.

Children's ability to consider the effects of personal experiences on emotional reactions improves steadily through middle childhood. So does their ability to understand that different children may have different emotional reactions to the same situation (Gnepp et al., 1987). Overall, these studies show that while young children may use language that suggests emotional understanding, preschoolers are only beginning to integrate the complex sources of information required to infer emotions accurately. Preschoolers will be in error at least as often as they are correct, a ratio that will frequently prove maladaptive in relations with peers and adults.

Looking Back

In the introduction to this chapter we suggested that early childhood can be thought of as a time to prepare socially and emotionally for middle childhood, particularly the challenges of elementary school and expanded relationships with peers. The enormity of this task should now be apparent. Compared to infants and toddlers, preschoolers are increasingly challenged by peers and other caregivers, and they are often far removed from the protective care of parents. Unlike parents, peers do not provide unconditional positive regard. Children respond to each other based on what children bring with them to play settings: the ability to pretend, to enter groups unobtrusively, to share, to comply, to cooperate, to enact appropriate genders, and to adapt to the subculture of the same-sex peer group. Preschoolers begin to expect their peers to express emotions and to react to the emotional signals of others in predictable ways. Extremes of emotional response will not be tolerated. Children who fail to achieve social and emotional competence are at risk of social rejection, domination by others, and social isolation. Above all, they face an unpredictable future, entering middle childhood with social and emotional deficits that may prove impossible to overcome.

We have highlighted the opportunities for the development of healthy social and emotional development in early childhood. In general, social and emotional competence emerge from secure attachment relationships, authoritative parenting, and extended exposure to peers. Socially competent children leave the preschool years ready to hit the ground running in middle childhood—prepared to cope with the risks and opportunities in the family, in school, and with their peers.

CHAPTER REVIEW

SOCIAL PRETEND PLAY Social pretend play increases rapidly during the preschool years, providing an arena for experimenting with social roles and expressing emotion. Social pretense requires that children negotiate the roles, objects, settings, and actions for episodes of pretend play. While children can stage social pretense by age three, pretend episodes continue to develop in complexity into the kindergarten year.

SOCIAL STATUS The uneven distribution of likes and dislikes in children's groups results in differences in social status. Popular children, as compared to rejected children, enjoy considerable social advantage, particularly with respect to joining other children at play.

FRIENDSHIP Preschoolers are capable of forming friendships that endure over several months. Children show wide individual differences in the communication and conflict resolution skills required to initiate and sustain friendships. Having friends provides excellent opportunity for the development of social skills. Friends interact in a unique way as compared to acquaintances: They reinforce each other, resolve conflicts effectively, and are particularly adept at pretend play. Children

who do not have friends but who are well accepted by peers do not appear to be at risk of maladjustment.

CONFLICT Although preschool children are frequently in conflict, most conflicts are short-lived and do not involve aggression. Most conflict focuses on control of objects and social influence. Conflicts offer a unique opportunity to enhance social and cognitive development.

AGGRESSION While instrumental, object-oriented aggression decreases during the preschool years, hostile aggression directed at other individuals tends to increase. The Freudian instinctive view of aggression suggests that aggressive impulses can be channeled but should not be repressed. In contrast, the social learning perspective suggests that children's aggression is modifiable by social learning principles. Aggression in families often appears in the form of interactive chains, with children and parents alternating as aggressors and victims. These chains are highly resistant to change.

DOMINANCE Like primates, aggressive interactions among children in groups can be described by the dominance hierarchy—ordered power relationships from

the most to the least powerful member of the group. The hierarchy helps to reduce overt aggression by allowing each member to anticipate the outcome of potential aggressive interactions.

PARENTS AND SOCIAL COMPETENCE Parents have both indirect and direct influence on the development of children's social competence. Indirect influence includes the quality of the attachment relationship and the parents' approach to socialization and discipline. In general, secure attachment and authoritative parenting are associated with higher levels of social competence in children. Parents directly influence children's social competence through choice of neighborhood, social planning for their children, and direct monitoring of children's social activities.

PROSOCIAL BEHAVIOR Prosocial behavior develops slowly during the preschool years, limited by the preschooler's egocentricity and lack of empathy for the plight of peers. The parents' role in promoting prosocial development remains unclear.

GENDER Gender identity, gender constancy, and knowledge of gender roles develop rapidly during the preschool years. Psychoanalytic, social learning, cognitive-developmental, and gender schema theories offer contrasting accounts of gender role development.

GENDER ROLE LEARNING Parents play a major role in gender role development through modeling and selective reinforcement of children's gender-appropriate behaviors. Gender role learning is strongly influenced in the subcultures of gender-segregated peer groups that form early in the preschool period.

EMOTION EXPRESSION Preschoolers rapidly learn display rules for the appropriate expressions of emotion in particular situations. Children learn to mask their true feelings, often overtly expressing the opposite of what they feel.

READING EMOTIONS Preschoolers become quite adept at reading other children's emotional signals. By the end of the preschool years, most children are aware that different individuals may react to the same situation with differing emotions, and that an individual's emotions with respect to a given event may change with time and experience.

Key Terms

social competence
social play
social pretend play
social participation
social preference
friendship
conflict
dominance
popularity
rejection
aggression
instrumental aggression
hostile aggression

coercion theory
reinforcement trap
dominance hierarchy
goal-corrected partnership
demandingness
responsiveness
authoritarian
indulgent-permissive
authoritative
neglectful
monitoring
prosocial behavior
empathy

gender identity
gender constancy
gender roles
gender typing
Electra Complex
identification
ego ideal
gender schema
rough and tumble play
display rules
masking

Middle Childhood

Physical Development and Disability in Middle Childhood

Looking Ahead

- Although children's growth rate slows somewhat in middle childhood, their size and weight significantly increase, and their body proportions change noticeably. What is the magnitude of these changes and what effects do they have on development of motor skills?

- Many people—including most children—assume that boys' physical development and motor skills are far superior to those of girls during middle childhood. Are these differences real or simply another example of gender bias?

- As children grow through their middle childhood years, they show wide variation in physique: some fat, some skinny, and others muscular. How do these differences come about and what effects do they have on children's physical and social development?

- Many fitness-conscious adults are concerned about their school-age children's physical fitness. How physically fit are our children? Do children get enough vigorous exercise to ensure lifelong physical fitness?

- Some children participate in competitive athletics during middle childhood. Is this experience healthy? Do athletes have advantages over their less athletic peers? How well do team sports promote general fitness?

- About 1 percent of the population of children are mentally retarded. How does retardation affect their lives and what is their potential for learning and developing?

- Many children in our society are over-active and have severe problems paying attention to their parents and teachers. What causes these problems and how can these children be helped?

- From the moment of birth, children with multiple handicaps face enormous challenges in every aspect of their lives. How can we provide for these children's special needs and the challenges their caregivers face?

- The special needs of children with handicaps has become one of our most important national education priorities. Can these children be educated in regular classrooms? What effect does the presence of children with handicaps have on normally developing children?

- Parents of children with special needs face enormous challenges throughout their children's lives. What are the special needs of these parents?

Y ou will recall from Chapter 6 that although children's growth rate slows during the preschool years, significant changes in body size and proportion dramatically affect their motor skill development. For example, by age three changes in Leshonda's body proportions and the strengthening of her legs enable her to develop a smooth, graceful running motion, with her arms swinging rhythmically close to her body. Although the rate of children's growth slows even more after the preschool years, middle childhood is a time of extraordinary advances in children's physical and motor development. Physical changes in size, proportion, strength, and endurance provide the foundation for significant improvements in children's motor skills. Under optimal conditions the kindergartener's rudimentary jumping, climbing, throwing, and catching skills develop into the sixth grader's highly sophisticated athletic and artistic performance. Under less optimal conditions, however, school-age children risk developing inactive lifestyles that undermine physical fitness, promote obesity, and increase the likelihood of cardiovascular disease in adulthood.

Preschoolers' physical and motor development required little more than access to safe and physically challenging play areas and simple equipment, such as tricycles, balls, jungle gyms, seesaws, and swings. However, school-age children's competitive, organized games and athletics often require special facilities. For example, baseball requires balls, bats, gloves, and an appropriately sized outdoor play area. Baseball also requires sizable numbers of children and in some cases special training equipment and the active support of adults as coaches, sponsors, and team organizers.

Still, school-age children can find physically challenging activities without these conveniences. Leshonda and her classmates show what can be accomplished with minimal special equipment or facilities.

It is that chaotic free-play time before the bell rings at Public School 25 in Brooklyn. Some of the boys just hang out, some chase each other in endless circles, and some play basketball at one end of the schoolyard.

The basketball game begins each day, an hour or more before the bell rings, with the school's two best players—Derrick and Tyrone—choosing up players for their respective teams in descending order of skill. With only one rim and backboard that have not been vandalized and an overabundance of highly skilled players, only a handful of those who want to play are chosen on any given day. The less skilled boys are relegated to the less organized and considerably less physically challenging playground activities.

For the boys who do play basketball, the games are physically demanding and highly competitive. Derrick epitomizes the schoolyard athlete: He plays with complete intensity, he shows no pain, and he physically and verbally dominates his opponent at all times. While he plays unselfishly—passing off when it is in his team's best interest—he also makes certain that he outscores every other player every day. While other players vent their emotions with the highs and lows of the flow of the game, Derrick is always cool and in control.

At the other end of the playground, groups of girls play Double Dutch—a challenging variation of jump rope in which players jump two ropes turning in opposite directions. Each grade has its own ropes and its own group of dedicated girls lined up for a turn to jump. The lines along the schoolyard fence form a developmental progression of jump-rope skill, from the awkward and erratic attempts of the kindergarten girls to the gymnastic and artistic excellence of the sixth graders. The girls' intensity in jump rope is no less than the boys' intensity in basketball.

At the sixth-grade line, Leshonda and Sharonda turn the ropes rhythmically for Keta, who has been jumping flawlessly for nearly four minutes. As Keta begins to tire, she grins at Leshonda, a signal that challenges the rope turners to pump it up to top speed. After sustaining her jump for a few seconds at the new speed—just enough to protect her reputation—Keta jumps out without hitting the ropes. Although her performance has been good, the onlookers seem unimpressed. Their attention has already turned to the next girl in the rotation, the "baddest" jumper at P.S. 25, Leshonda Martin.

Leshonda gets into the jump position, rocks back and forth to get synchronized with the twirl of the ropes, and slips in between them effortlessly and gracefully. As the rope turners and onlookers chant a rap song to the sound of the ropes hitting the pavement, Leshonda begins the sequence of moves that has earned her reputation: She reels off a series of different jump steps with perfect timing and grace; she periodically closes her eyes and spins her body to reverse direction; when the rope turners slow the ropes, she dives to a handstand and back to her feet three times in succession, does two complete flips (front and back), and then jumps clear of the ropes, without ever breaking a sweat.

With the dignity of an Olympic gymnast who has just scored a perfect 10, Leshonda saunters to the end of the line to await her next turn. Several girls on line defer to her by letting her move up. But, despite her accomplishment and her peers' admiration, Leshonda is distracted. When she thinks no one is watching her, she glances toward the basketball court to catch sight of Derrick. He is the best among the boys, and she is the best among the girls. Occasionally, their eyes meet, but they quickly turn away.

Leshonda and her classmates' playground behavior shows the opportunities for physical and motor development during middle childhood. The most impressive feature is how much more fluidly the sixth graders integrate jumping, running, balancing, and ball skills than they could have in earlier grades. Jumping Double Dutch and playing basketball both require strength, endurance, timing, agility, and complex coordinations of body parts. These skilled performances require years of practice.

The children's play also reveals the problem of uneven participation: While some children actively participate in physically challenging activities, others passively watch them perform. While some children who are motivated to play are prevented by limited opportunity, others make no effort to play. Those who cannot or will not participate do not get the exercise and practice needed for optimal physical and motor development.

Finally, the children's play highlights the strict gender segregation in informal physical activities at the elementary school level. This segregation is also apparent in schools with more formal organized sports teams. Thus, while girls are given more opportunities to participate in sports—often equal to those traditionally given to boys—"separate but equal" is the prevailing rule. This segregation is supported by the attitudes and actions of many parents, teachers, and coaches. As we will see, the highly similar physical and motor development in boys and girls during middle childhood provides no sound *physical* basis for gender segregation during the elementary school years (American Academy of Pediatrics, 1981).

Physical Development in Middle Childhood

Although children's growth rate slows during middle childhood, their size, weight, and body proportions do change significantly. On average, children will grow about 1 foot in height, from just under 4 feet tall at age 6 to about 5 feet tall at age 12. Girls typically grow faster than boys in fifth and sixth grades, with girls achieving about 90 percent and boys achieving 80 percent of their adult height by age 10 or 11 (Tanner, 1978). On average, children also double their weight during this same period, from just over 40 pounds to about 80 pounds.

It is important to note that these averages obscure the wide individual differences in height, weight, and body type among children throughout the middle childhood years. A typical classroom of fifth graders shows great variation among children, with some children still looking much like children and others beginning to take on the more mature look of adolescents. The earlier maturing of many girls causes them to tower over some boys, giving the illusion that the girls are much older. Wide variation in nutrition and exercise habits among the children have already resulted in noticeable differences in their ease and grace of physical movement.

Changes in Body Proportion, Body Type, and Body Image

While dramatic changes in school-age children's height and weight affect their motor skill development, more subtle changes in body proportion and physique have powerful effects on their social and personality development. William Sheldon, an anthropologist, classified human physique by body type or **somatotype**—the degree of fatness (*endomorphy*), thinness (*ectomorphy*), and muscularity (*mesomorphy*) (Sheldon, 1940, 1942). Although Sheldon believed that individuals exhibit a certain measure of each of these traits, common usage refers to children who epitomize each somatotype as either rela-

These elementary school girls show the typical variation in physical attractiveness, physical size, and body type among children in their grade. These differences make a difference: Children whose physical features correspond more closely to society's ideals tend to be favored by adults and peers and feel more positively about themselves.

tively fat children (*endomorphs*), relatively thin, skinny children (*ectomorphs*), or well-built, muscular children (*mesomorphs*). The classification of children's somatotype remains stable through middle childhood, despite changes in their size and proportion (Hammond, 1953).

Richard Lerner and his colleagues (Lerner, 1969a, 1969b, 1971; Lerner & Korn, 1972; Lerner & Schroeder, 1971a, 1971b) demonstrated that children in Western society, regardless of age or gender, have highly specific opinions about somatotypes: They think positively toward muscular children, negatively toward chubby children, and negatively, but somewhat less so, toward skinny children. Lerner showed that these opinions translate into discriminatory behaviors toward children who differ in body type. By kindergarten, chubby and thin children are less liked by their peers (Lerner & Geller, 1969; Lerner & Schroeder, 1971b) and are considered less attractive by their peers (Lerner, 1969a; Staffieri, 1967, 1972), as compared to muscular children and children who do not fit neatly into one of the body types.

In one study (Staffieri, 1967) children's attitudes toward different somatotypes were studied by showing fat, thin, and muscular silhouettes to 6- to 10-year-old boys. While the children attached positive adjectives to the muscular figure, such as ''strong,'' ''best friend,'' ''clean,'' and ''healthy,'' the fat silhouette elicited negative descriptors such as ''fights,'' ''nervous,'' ''lies,'' ''stupid,'' and ''dirty.'' The thin silhouette elicited ''quiet,'' ''lonely,'' ''afraid,'' and ''sad.'' Moreover, the children's preference for the muscular body type and their accuracy at perceiving their own body type increased with age.

Do these discriminatory attitudes toward children with various body types affect those children's personalities? Lerner (Lerner & Jovanovic, 1990) argues that what a child brings to a given situation physically—that is, temperament, body type, physical attractiveness, and motor skills—has powerful effects on the child's self-concept. For example, in one study (Lerner & Korn, 1972), Lerner compared chubby and average-build children's **body image**—their qualitative appraisal of their own bodies; 5-, 15-, and 20-year-old chubby males were shown to have more negative body images than those with average builds. The results are even more impressive with respect to children's physical attractiveness. Physically unattractive male and female fourth and sixth graders were less liked by their classmates, interacted less well with their peers, and were less well adjusted than their more physically attractive peers (Lerner & Lerner, 1977).

In Lerner's words, this research suggests that, ''by 'bringing' different physical characteristics to a situation, children . . . may affect how others react and provide feedback to them. This feedback may be linked to differential body-image development and psychosocial functioning'' (1990, p. 120). If a child masters the demands of a given physical situation (such as trying out successfully for a ball team), this experience will have a favorable effect on his or her body image. A positive body image enables the child to approach new situations with confidence that he or she will be able to adapt by meeting the physical demands of the situation.

APPLICATION

Making the Most of Your Child's Body Type

Those who deal with children must be sensitive to the powerful effects of a child's body type on the behavior and attitudes of other children and adults, particularly those adults who coach or supervise children's physical activities. While children with muscular body types are given extensive opportunities to develop motor skills and physical fitness, children with other body types often receive very little. If *all* children are to achieve their potential for physical development and fitness, parents and teachers must ensure that they have equal opportunities for training and exercise, regardless of their body type. The following recommendations may be helpful to those parents whose children are not born athletes.

■ Encourage your child to participate in physical activities that fit his body type: Relatively thin children are more likely to succeed in activities that call for speed and agility, such as running or swimming; chubby children are typically more successful in activities that require strength, such as wrestling or certain positions in football (lineman) or baseball (catcher).

■ Let your child know that he can modify his body type within limits through diet and exercise. Thin children can become strong with proper nutrition and exercise; chubby children can become agile with practice.

■ Let your child's physical education teacher know that you expect your child to be physically challenged consistent with his size, strength, and skill. Ask the teacher to share his or her specific goals for your child. Visit the teacher periodically to monitor your child's progress.

Gender Differences in Play-Game Skills

Children's abilities to perform the skills required for organized sports—such as jumping, running, and throwing a ball—increase substantially through middle childhood (see Figure 12.1). The distance covered in the standing long jump increases about 3–5 inches per year, with boys jumping about 3–5 inches farther than girls at each age—a 45 percent improvement from ages 7 to 12 for both sexes (Keogh & Sugden, 1985). There is a similar linear increase in running speed through age 12 for both sexes, with boys running somewhat faster than girls. By age seven, boys are already throwing balls faster and farther than girls and their advantage continues to increase throughout the middle childhood years. As is evident in Figure 12.1, boys continue to increase their skill in jumping, running, and throwing through the adolescent years, while girls' performance levels off in all three skills.

Should we conclude from these results that boys have naturally superior physical abilities? Although the results clearly suggest moderate advantages in physical skills for boys during middle childhood, there is reason to believe that these differences have little to do with built-in biological differences (Hall & Lee, 1984; Thomas & French, 1985). An analysis of 64 studies on gender differences concluded that the physical characteristics of girls and boys are not significantly different before puberty (Thomas & French, 1985).

Moreover, the authors concluded that boys' moderate superiority in motor performance prior to puberty—for example, in balance, catching, long jump, and situps—is primarily induced by the environment. The authors pointed to the powerful influence of gender-stereotyped beliefs by parents, teachers, and coaches in giving greater opportunities for practice to boys than to girls throughout middle childhood. In their words, "If equal expectations, encouragement, and practice opportunities were provided by parents, teachers, and coaches, differences of this size could probably be eliminated (1985, p. 274).

One longitudinal study (Hall & Lee, 1984) showed how easily these modest gender differences can be eliminated. The researchers monitored the motor skill development of third-, fourth-, and fifth-grade males and females over three years in a *coeducational* physical education program. The program stressed vigorous exercises for cardiovascular fitness, muscular strength, and endurance. Children were tested on situps, shuttle run,

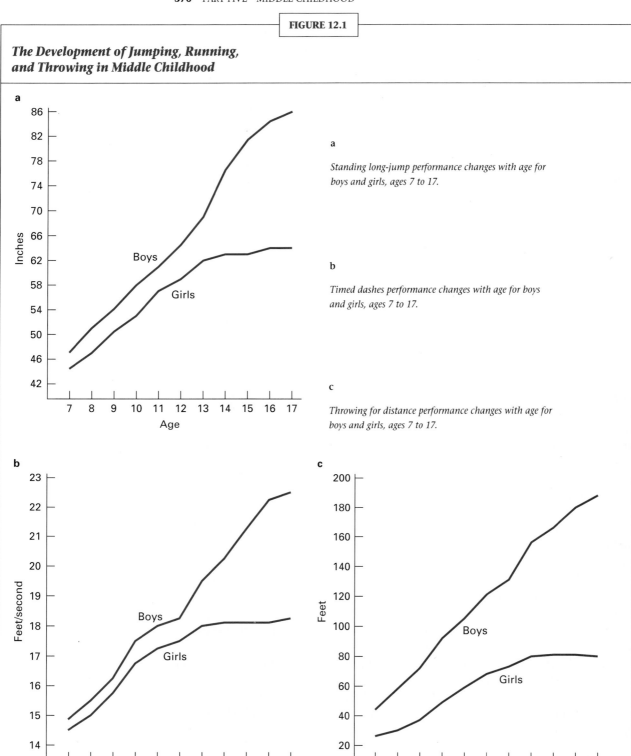

FIGURE 12.1

The Development of Jumping, Running, and Throwing in Middle Childhood

a

Standing long-jump performance changes with age for boys and girls, ages 7 to 17.

b

Timed dashes performance changes with age for boys and girls, ages 7 to 17.

c

Throwing for distance performance changes with age for boys and girls, ages 7 to 17.

SOURCE: *Jack Keogh and David Sugden.* Movement Skill Development. *Copyright © 1985 Macmillan Publishing Company. Reprinted by permission of the publisher.*

the 50-yard dash, broad jump, and the 600-yard walk/run. The training was highly successful in promoting both boys' and girls' motor skills through the three years of the study. More important, the equal opportunity for exercise and practice for *both* sexes virtually wiped out gender differences. Girls actually outperformed boys on selected skills!

Although we may conclude that gender differences before puberty are largely due to environmental factors, biologically based physical changes at puberty—particularly with respect to the ratio of muscle to fat—give adolescent boys a clear advantage over girls in motor skills involving size, strength, and power (Thomas & French, 1985). This advantage is reflected in the divergent paths of skill development for boys and girls in Figure 12.1. Although biological changes play a predominant role, opportunities for practice and gender-role stereotypes favoring males also contribute to the widening gender differences in motor skills through adolescence. Thus, while male adolescents' physical advantage enables them to outperform female adolescents, the differences in performance would be much smaller if females had equal opportunity and motivation for exercise and practice.

A P P L I C A T I O N

Minimizing Gender Differences in Play-Game Skills

Middle childhood is a period of great improvement in children's play-game skills, particularly for boys. The advantage for boys results primarily from people's discriminatory attitudes and behaviors. With equal encouragement and opportunities for training and practice, school-age girls can develop play-game skills equal to those of boys. You can help:

- Foster positive attitudes and expectations for play-game skill achievement in girls and acceptance of girls' participation in what have been considered boys' games and sports.
- Encourage your child's elementary school to develop coeducational physical education programs and to invest resources equally in programs for boys and girls.

Physical Fitness in Middle Childhood

American adults interested in their own physical fitness have become predictably concerned about the fitness of their children. Do children get enough exercise to ensure adequate levels of physical fitness? As we saw in Chapter 9, while hard data are not available, anecdotal reports from parents and other caregivers suggest that most *preschoolers* get reasonable amounts of physical exercise—at least enough to maintain sufficient strength, endurance, and flexibility to chase their friends, climb jungle gyms, and engage in rough and tumble play for hours at a time.

However, significant changes in lifestyle in middle childhood reduce children's opportunities to engage in physical activity. By age six, children begin to spend large portions of their waking hours in the relatively structured elementary school environment, substantially limiting their freedom of movement for many hours at a time. With the exception of brief periods in recess and physical education, the elementary school is a highly sedentary environment with uncompromising rules against vigorous movement of any kind. These constraints carry over into the home as children are required to devote increasing amounts of time to homework with each advancing grade. Thus, whatever its other benefits, the elementary school experience is not generally conducive to children's physical fitness.

For many schoolage children, the TV has become the centerpiece of leisure-time activity, significantly decreasing the amount of time they spend in moderate to vigorous physical activity. Over time these children are likely to become less physically fit and less physically skilled than children who find TV less addictive.

Unfortunately, many children do not compensate for their schooltime inactivity by pursuing fitness activities during their leisure time. Although some children do use their free time engaging in sports and improving athletic skills, others spend much of their time hanging out with their friends or watching TV. Most important, children spend very little of their in-school and out-of-school time engaging in **moderate to vigorous physical activity (MVPA)** — the kind of activity known to prevent cardiovascular disease in adults (Powell, Thompson, Caspersen, & Kendrick, 1987). In one study less than 50 percent of children engaged in MVPA on a daily basis (Baranowski, Tsong, Hooks, Cieslik, & Nader, 1987). Even those children who do exercise get less than one hour per day of MVPA (Gilliam, Freedson, Geenen, & Shahraray, 1981; MacConnie, Gilliam, Geenen, & Pels, 1982).

Surprisingly, despite their lack of physical activity and an increasing rate of childhood obesity (Ross & Gilbert, 1985), most school-age children do not show extreme *deficiencies* in physical fitness (Simons-Morton, O'Hara, Simons-Morton, & Parcel, 1987). However, as these habits are incorporated into sedentary lifestyles in adolescence and young adulthood, it is just a matter of time before deficiencies in fitness appear, increasing the risk of cardiovascular disease.

The Effects of Physical Education   As indicated earlier, virtually all school-age children attend physical education (PE) classes throughout their elementary school years. One might assume that participating in PE would improve children's physical fitness. Unfortunately, contemporary PE classes do not live up to their potential. Recent funding cuts have made quality PE classes less available to most children. Many children no longer attend on a daily basis, and their instructors are less likely to be trained specialists (Ross & Pate, 1987). Also, children's time in PE tends to be used inefficiently. In one study (Parcel, Simons-Morton, O'Hara, Baranowski, Kolbe, & Bee, 1987), upper elementary school children spent on average less than 2 minutes of a 30-minute class in MVPA — far less than required to have positive effects on fitness.

Despite the problems in practice, experts agree that PE offers great potential for promoting children's physical fitness. Some experts have suggested that dollars could be better spent by increasing the percentage of time children spend in MVPA and by making the experience more fulfilling to participants (Simons-Morton et al., 1987). This recommendation is supported by evidence that intense endurance training—for example, long-distance running—has significant positive effects on school-age children's cardiovascular fitness (Savage, Petratis, Thompson, Berg, Smith, & Sady, 1986; Tuckman & Hinkle, 1986). More rigorous training could easily be incorporated into existing PE programs.

Others have suggested that PE can have long-term effects only if what children learn *in school* affects what they do *out of school*. Thus, the goal of PE should be to promote the development of physically active lifestyles. For example, children can learn to enjoy fitness activities (such as jogging, swimming, and cycling) that can be practiced throughout their lives. This could be accomplished by making sure children understand fitness and by helping them set realistic goals for self-improvement both inside and outside of school (Lee, Carter, & Greenockle, 1987).

The Emphasis on Athletics   The PE curriculum for the first three grades in most elementary schools emphasizes movement skills (throwing, catching, jumping, running, and kicking) that can be easily transferred to out-of-school play-games (tag, catch, hopscotch, and jump rope). However, by third or fourth grade most school PE programs begin to emphasize the athletic skills needed for competitive team sports, such as basketball, baseball/softball, soccer, and volleyball (Ross & Pate, 1987).

Although the *fitness* benefits that young athletes derive from these opportunities have not been adequately researched, the *psychosocial* benefits of participating in team sports have been well documented. First, despite some public criticism of organized sports for school-age children, the children themselves report that they thoroughly enjoy their participation on sports teams (Harris, 1984; Wankel & Kreisel, 1985; Wankel & Sefton,

The increasing emphasis on competitive athletics during the middle childhood years—both in school and in the community—creates very uneven opportunities for children to participate in activities that promote physical fitness. These young baseball players are much more likely than nonparticipants to maintain high levels of fitness. Unfortunately, in most schools and communities only a small percentage of children have adequate opportunity to engage in organized athletics.

1989). When asked why they enjoy sports, participants emphasize the challenge of the game, their feelings of personal achievement, and the opportunity to improve their skills (Wankel & Kreisel, 1985; Wankel & Sefton, 1989). Very few children participate to earn extrinsic rewards, such as praise from adults, winning awards, or even winning games. There is also evidence that athletic prowess contributes to both boys' and girls' popularity among their peers (Gross & Johnson, 1984). Unfortunately, this change in emphasis benefits only a small percentage of school-age children.

One of the major problems is the limited opportunity for practice of athletic skills in after-school settings. Less than 20 percent of children—invariably those who are more proficient—qualify for extracurricular team sports programs at school. Less skilled children—precisely those who need fitness activities the most—are typically excluded. Furthermore, most communities offer limited opportunities for children to participate in organized sports teams, such as Little League baseball and soccer (Kleiber & Roberts, 1983; Ross, Dotson, Gilbert, & Katz, 1985). Participation usually requires considerable parental support, including money for uniforms, equipment, and transportation. Children whose families cannot meet these requirements are typically excluded. Opportunities for children to participate in organized athletics are particularly lacking in inner-city communities.

Thus, by the end of elementary school, the school's emphasis on organized sports creates a minority of haves and a majority of have-nots. The haves—selected for their superior skills in the early elementary grades—are exposed to exercise and training opportunities that are not available to the have-nots.

We may conclude that the change in the school's emphasis from movement education in the early grades to athletics and team sports in later grades profits only a small percentage of children. Children who have no access to community-based sports teams and those who fail to make the team derive little benefit from the school's emphasis on sports. Some experts have also expressed reservations about school-age children's readiness for competitive sports (Coleman & Skeen, 1985) and have expressed doubt that the emphasis on sports is likely to carry over into one's adult lifestyle (Sallis, 1987). The poorly defined roles and goals of the elementary school and the community in promoting children's physical and motor development is not in the best interests of the majority of our children.

A P P L I C A T I O N

Promoting Lifelong Physical Fitness

*I*n our sports-minded society, parents often dream of their children's potential for athletic excellence. The first time your son hits a ball farther than you thought possible for his age, you may be tempted to ask whether your child might be the next superstar. While the multimillion dollar contracts of professional athletes are tempting, the chance of attaining that goal is infinitely small. Long-term, consistent participation in vigorous physical activities is far more valuable for your child than a shelf of dusty trophies commemorating short-term involvement in sports.

Middle childhood offers an unprecedented opportunity for children to develop lifelong exercise habits that promote physical fitness. You can help:

■ Encourage realistic performance goals suited to your child's physical abilities. Physically challenging goals within your child's reach will sustain your child's motivation.

■ Emphasize your child's involvement, skill development, and enjoyment in sports programs. Physical activity can and should be fun. Deemphasize winning and striving for specific awards.

- Model a physically active lifestyle; emphasize activities that encourage your child to imitate you and join in.
- Encourage your child to participate in team sports only as long as she seems self-motivated and unstressed by competition. Beware of overzealous coaches and your own ego, neither of which is likely to have a favorable effect on your child's physical development.
- Help your child develop a conceptual understanding of the benefits of physical fitness and establish goals for physical fitness that extend beyond the ball field or gym.

Children with Special Needs

Thus far we have presented a positive image of physical and motor development in middle childhood. With access to physically challenging experiences and with the encouragement of parents, teachers, and coaches, normally developing schoolchildren learn to run, jump, climb, chase, throw, and catch, and to integrate these skills in play-games, dance, sports, and gymnastics. Under optimal conditions, children may achieve the high levels of competency required for competitive athletics and artistic performance. Learning these skills requires both physical capability and the mental capability to plan, guide, monitor, and evaluate the motor behaviors involved. However, many children are unable to develop these skills due to physical and/or psychological factors that limit their physical behavior and development. Children with such limitations have **handicaps** or **disabilities**.

Children can develop handicaps at any point during growth. Handicaps may be precipitated by a wide variety of causes and circumstances: chromosomal abnormalities, hereditary disorders, prenatal factors, difficult birth, accidental injury, physical abuse, malnutrition, and disease. Regardless of the cause, disabilities have significant negative effects on children's ability to adapt successfully to age-appropriate challenges in their family, school, and community. We will review three of the most frequent childhood handicaps here: mental retardation, hyperactivity, and physical disability. Specific forms of school-related learning disabilities and schooling for the gifted and talented are reviewed in the next chapter. For a closer look at a professional who works with children with special needs in the schools, see "Careers: The School Psychologist."

Mental Retardation

Mental retardation is defined as below average intellectual ability associated with impaired adaptive behavior that appears before the age of 18 (American Psychiatric Association, 1987). *Below average intellectual ability* refers to cognitive ability as measured by standardized tests of mental ability (the Stanford-Binet or Wechsler Intelligence Scale for Children), and *adaptive behavior* refers to age-appropriate self-help skills and social competencies needed in everyday life. For example, a seven-year-old would be expected to be able to use a telephone and engage in simple conversations.

Around 1 percent of the general population is classified "mentally retarded." The ratio is about three males for every two females. Two roughly comparable classification systems have evolved that describe the severity of retardation—both based on specific ranges of IQ points. The two classification systems are compared in Table 12.1. Children with mild retardation (85 percent of the total population with retardation) have IQs between 50 and 70. The majority of these children are termed "educable" because, with time and special educational services, they can be expected to learn the elementary

The School Psychologist

Renee Wolfman is a school psychologist in Broward County, Florida. She taught for several years while studying for her Master's degree in school psychology and has been in her present position for nine years. She is responsible for three schools: an elementary school, a middle school, and a high school.

What does a school psychologist do?

My primary role is to facilitate children's optimal learning and development in the school environment. Children typically come to my attention when a teacher and/or parent notices that a child is experiencing some difficulty in class — a learning problem, behavior problem, or difficulty relating to peers. If the problem is not too severe, I may recommend interventions that the teacher can implement in the classroom. For example, I might suggest strategies for a child who has fallen behind in reading, or adjusting an unmotivated child's curriculum to make the work more challenging. If the child's problems are more serious and the interventions are unsuccessful, a child study team — including the principal, teachers, guidance counselor, and social worker — may initiate a *formal referral*.

As the school psychologist, I respond to a referral by conducting a *psychoeducational evaluation* — a formal assessment of the child's intellectual abilities and disabilities, achievement motivation, social skills, family influences, and other factors relevant

to the problem. I use tests that are specifically designed to identify learning disabilities, cognitive deficits, and social-emotional problems, as well as a child's strengths. I report the results of the evaluation to a staffing committee to help determine the child's eligibility for placement in an exceptional education program or other appropriate interventions. My evaluation is just one piece of the puzzle; the committee uses every bit of information to make this important decision.

How did you become interested in school psychology?

When I was an undergraduate, I double-majored in special education and psychology. After I graduated, I taught emotionally handicapped and learning disabled children for 3½ years. When I began to consider graduate programs, I realized that school psychology would allow me to integrate my interests in psychology and education.

What do you find most challenging in your work?

Diagnosing a child's problem is like solving an enormously complicated puzzle. Each test, observation, parent report, and teacher comment provides a unique piece of the puzzle, and the challenge is to put the pieces together to provide an accurate picture of the child. Once the picture is complete, the challenge is to coordinate the efforts of school personnel, the child's family, and specialists to determine the best approach to the problem. Each

child's situation is unique, and finding an effective solution to a child's problems requires the collective effort and creativity of many people. This job never gets boring!

How would a student become a school psychologist?

Begin with an undergraduate degree in education leading to certification in your chosen area. Include as many courses in child development and psychology as possible. After graduation, teach for some time before going for your Master's degree. You may not have much credibility as a school psychologist if you haven't spent time in the classroom setting. Then look for a Master's program that offers the kind of emphasis you want; programs differ in how much they stress assessment, therapy, and early intervention.

You can find out more by writing to the National Association of School Psychologists, 8455 Colesville Rd., Suite 1000, Silver Springs, MD 20910.

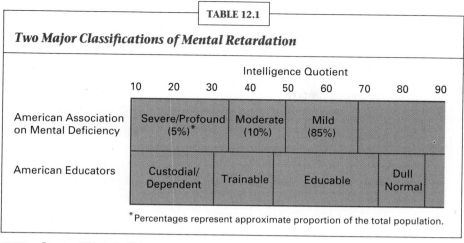

TABLE 12.1

Two Major Classifications of Mental Retardation

Intelligence Quotient

	10	20	30	40	50	60	70	80	90
American Association on Mental Deficiency	Severe/Profound (5%)[*]			Moderate (10%)		Mild (85%)			
American Educators	Custodial/ Dependent		Trainable		Educable			Dull Normal	

[*]Percentages represent approximate proportion of the total population.

SOURCES: *Grossman, 1983; Smith, 1971*

school curriculum up to fifth or sixth grade. They would, of course, be considerably older than children with normal abilities by the time they achieved this level. Educable individuals should be able to live independently as adults.

Children termed "moderately retarded" (10 percent of the population with retardation) have IQs between 35 and 49. The label "trainable" applied to most of these children suggests that while they will never progress beyond the second-grade level, they can be successfully trained in self-help and vocational skills. Those with severe and profound retardation (5 percent of the population with retardation) are incapable of learning academics or vocational skills, and are highly dependent on others for care throughout their lives.

The causes of mental retardation are not always known. Up to 50 percent of cases may be a direct result of chromosomal abnormalities—primarily Down syndrome and fragile X syndrome. Some 30–35 percent result from prenatal exposure to teratogens (such as drugs and pollutants) and diseases (such as rubella and herpes). There is also evidence that parents and other caregivers who are extremely unresponsive to their young children may induce mild forms of mental retardation (Bradley, Caldwell, & Rock, 1988). Thus, while most forms of mental retardation cannot be cured, they can be prevented through genetic counseling, high-quality prenatal care, fetal monitoring, and competent parenting.

Hyperactivity

Although she has just begun to read a story to the children, Ms. Goldman— Heather's second-grade teacher—is already reaching the limits of her patience. She has just lost her place for the third time, and she knows that her errors are taking their toll on the children's attention. The looks on their faces suggest that they will remember very little of the story. The problem is not with her teaching or the class's motivation to listen; the problem is the commotion coming from one child—Heather Allen.

Heather has been in perpetual motion ever since she arrived in class. She has not stayed in her seat more than a few minutes at a time all morning. She has repeatedly taken pencils, paper, crayons, and books from the desks of children around her and has dropped most of them on the floor beneath her desk. Heather is completely overwhelmed by the demands of sitting still and listening during story time.

Ms. Goldman quickly ends the story and passes out a study assignment. Despite Ms. Goldman's warnings to work quietly, Heather involuntarily taps her feet, bangs her arms on the desk, rustles paper, and talks incessantly to herself or others, even if they are not listening. Although she seems generally oriented to the study assignment in front of her, she does not answer a single question. Today, like most days, Heather is incapable of keeping pencil to paper long enough to write more than one word at a time.

Ms. Goldman marks time until the teacher's aide arrives. The aide, Ms. Fong, has been specially trained to work with hyperactive children. Ms. Fong brings Heather to an alcove, which reduces distraction and distances her from other children. She breaks the assignment down, and goes through the work with Heather in a rhythm timed just one beat slower than Heather's frantic pace. Ms. Fong maintains a cool, calm demeanor. Within a few minutes, Heather's pace has slowed slightly, allowing her to work independently on her assignment for the first time since she arrived.

Heather is very bright, but she can only be productive with one-to-one supervision.

Heather is a classic example of a child with **attention deficit/hyperactivity disorder (ADHD)** (American Psychiatric Association, 1987), commonly referred to as **hyperactivity**. She is very intelligent, extremely active, impulsive, inattentive, and highly disruptive to her classmates. Millions of American children—perhaps as many as 10 percent of the population—have been diagnosed with this disorder. Some of these children have serious attention deficits without high levels of activity, but these two symptoms are typically found together in children.

Although children diagnosed with ADHD or hyperactivity vary considerably in their symptoms (Jacobvitz, Sroufe, Stewart, & Leffert, 1990), they share difficulties attending to structured tasks and following instructions (Barkley, 1990; Pearson & Lane, 1991; Seidel & Joschko, 1990), with devastating effects on their learning and productivity in school. Their work tends to be sloppy and incomplete, often departing substantially from the teacher's instructions. Most ADHD children are impulsive, taking little or no time to plan what they do or to consider the consequences of their actions. Hyperactive children's impulsivity makes them prone to errors in problem solving and increases their risk of accidental injury.

ADHD children's distractibility, high activity level, and impulsivity makes them disruptive to their classmates and teachers. The presence of even one ADHD child in a regular classroom can markedly reduce the efficiency of learning for other children and create high levels of stress for the teacher. Heather's effect on her teacher's ability to read a story is a good example. Two or more ADHD children in a single classroom can overwhelm an otherwise competent teacher. Unfortunately, with 5–8 percent of the school-age population ADHD (August & Garfinkel, 1989; Safer & Krager, 1988; Szatmari, Offord, & Boyle, 1989), virtually all teachers and their non-ADHD children must cope with this problem daily.

What causes ADHD? Thus far, the search for neurological causes of ADHD has been unproductive (Jacobvitz et al., 1990). Many psychiatrists, physicians, and psychologists assume that hyperactivity and attention deficits are inborn temperamental traits that are largely unaffected by environmental influences (Wender, 1987). However, one study (Jacobvitz & Sroufe, 1987) provided intriguing evidence that parents may be a significant part of the problem. The researchers reasoned that children learn to regulate their own level of arousal — for example, the ability to intentionally stop crying — in emotional transactions with their parents. Parents who react inappropriately to their children's emotions (for example, by overstimulating them when they are upset) may disrupt their children's ability to regulate their own state of arousal. The results of the study confirmed their hypothesis: ADHD was accurately predicted from disturbed parent-infant interactions at six months.

We may tentatively conclude that, while ADHD may have many causes, it is likely to develop in children who are vulnerable by temperament and who interact with parents who have difficulty adjusting to their children's emotions. Unfortunately, once the child's symptoms become well established, they take on a life of their own. The ADHD child's behavior tends to bring out the worst in other children and adults, and these reactions further confuse and agitate the ADHD child. Therefore, it is unlikely that ADHD children will simply outgrow their symptoms. Improvement requires the coordinated efforts of parents, teachers, and professionals over extended periods of time.

Can the symptoms of ADHD be treated? Physicians have used the stimulant Ritalin (methylphenidate) to control hyperactivity in millions of American children. Why would a stimulant calm hyperactive children? Physicians believe — without scientific verification — that the drug compensates for a chemical deficiency in the brains of ADHD children. While Ritalin seems to have short-term positive effects on some children's attention, there is little evidence of long-term positive effects on their school performance or behavior problems (Jacobvitz et al., 1990; Weiss & Hechtman, 1986). In contrast, behavior modification strategies in the classroom have achieved some success (Kendall, 1990). Unfortunately, the number of ADHD children and the severity of their problems far outweigh the resources available to most elementary schools.

A P P L I C A T I O N

Dealing with Hyperactive Children

*P*arents and teachers face enormous challenges in coping with ADHD children at home and in the classroom. Dealing with the problem requires the joint efforts of professionals (physicians, psychologists, teachers, and social workers) and parents over extended periods of time. The following recommendations may be helpful.

Working with Professionals:

■ If your child shows symptoms of ADHD, seek professional advice from psychologists, physicians, and educators who are experienced with hyperactive children. ADHD is difficult to diagnose and even more difficult to treat. This is a job for experts. Even though your family physician may diagnose ADHD and prescribe medication, he or she is unlikely to have hands-on experience. This is not in your child's best interest.

■ Be skeptical if your physician prescribes drugs as the *sole* solution to the problem. Medication may prove effective for your child, but only as one part of a comprehensive approach to your child's behavior. Behavior modification techniques — the systematic and consistent use of rewards and punishments — can be most helpful.

■ If your physician prescribes medication, read up on the medication's effects and side effects. Ask the physician about how the effectiveness of the medication will be determined, and how your child's physical and behavioral response to the drug will be monitored. Always seek a second opinion.

Maintaining Your Own Well-Being:

■ Don't take your child's behavior too personally. Although you should avoid overstimulating your child, many other factors (which may be beyond your control) are involved.

Blaming yourself only makes you less capable of coping with the problem.

■ Get respite periodically. No one can deal with a child's hyperactivity without a break.

Bottom Line: With time and professional help, your child will very likely overcome the symptoms of ADHD. However, it takes years rather than days, weeks, or even months. Patience, tolerance, consistency, and persistence are your greatest assets in helping your child.

Children with Multiple Handicaps

The rapid growth and differentiation of nerve tissue before, during, and shortly after birth makes the immature central nervous system extremely vulnerable to damage by various environmental influences. Prenatal exposure to teratogens, deprivation of oxygen, and infection are likely to cause permanent, severe physical and mental disability. These children have **multiple handicaps.**

From birth, children with multiple handicaps face tremendous challenges in every aspect of their lives. They are typically nonverbal with profound retardation (IQ from 0 to 30). They also have extremely limited adaptive behavior—unable to feed or groom themselves, use the toilet, or move around independently. Self-abusive behaviors, such as biting themselves and head-banging, are common. Most of these children suffer from a wide array of severe medical problems, including respiratory difficulties, digestive problems, sensory impairments, seizures, and bowel and urinary dysfunction.

The severe impairment of the central nervous system usually affects all parts of the child's body, limiting motor capability. Brain damage may cause **hypotonia,** too little muscle tone (often found in Down syndrome), or **hypertonia,** too much muscle tone. Overly stiff or *spastic* muscles create unbalanced stress on bones and joints, often resulting in **skeletal deformity** (Fraser & Hensinger, 1983). Most children with multiple handicaps require extra support to sit up in a chair and only a small percentage are able to stand, even with assistance.

Historically, children with multiple handicaps have been denied appropriate medical and educational opportunities that could have significantly improved their quality of life (Fraser, Hensinger, & Phelps, 1987). However, dramatic changes in the law and public attitudes since the 1970s have substantially improved their care and education. Advances in special education, medical treatment, physical therapy, and the development of mechanical devices to facilitate transportation and communication have enabled many of these children to achieve a reasonable quality of life.

Educating Children with Special Needs

Thus far we have described three groups of children with special needs: retarded children, hyperactive children, and multiply handicapped children. Other groups of children with special needs include those who are *emotionally disturbed,* those who have *academic learning disabilities* (in reading, writing, or arithmetic), those who have *developmental disabilities* (specific problems in language, speech, perception, attention, memory, or problem solving), and those who are *visually or hearing impaired.* In total, these groups comprise approximately 10 percent of the school-age population. All of these groups of children require special educational services from the schools if they are to realize their potential for learning and development. The challenge for educators has been providing for their highly diverse physical, social, and educational needs.

One of the most controversial issues in special education has been whether special-needs children should be taught in separate classrooms (isolated from the mainstream of normally developing children) or integrated into regular classrooms for all or part of the school day. In the 1950s and 1960s a growing awareness of handicapped children's special educational needs led to the proliferation of self-contained special education classrooms. Although these classrooms were frequently located in the elementary school, the children in them were totally segregated from children in regular classrooms.

In the 1970s there was a growing belief that separate classrooms were not the best approach to educating children with handicaps. Educators argued—often without data to back up their claims—that separate education stigmatized handicapped children and relegated them to teachers who consistently maintained low expectations for their performance (Haderman, 1976, Leikowitz, 1972). Educators also claimed that separate classes isolated handicapped children from the positive modeling effects of the brighter, more socially competent children in regular classrooms. This thinking prompted the passage of Public Law 94-142, the Education for All Handicapped Children Act of 1975, which mandated a free appropriate education for all children with handicaps in the **least restrictive environment**. This law—with additional legislation in 1986 extending coverage to preschool-age children—remains the basis for providing services to those with handicaps throughout the United States.

One of the most significant aspects of PL 94-142 is the provision for educating those with handicaps in the *least restrictive environment*. This provision implies that handicapped children can be placed in separate classrooms only when the severity of their impairment precludes learning in regular classrooms. In practical terms, every effort

Advances in legislation and technology have created a permanent place for handicapped children in regular classrooms. While many mainstreamed children fare well, others have considerable difficulty adjusting. Handicapped children tend to be rejected by their nonhandicapped peers and find their teachers unprepared or unwilling to deal with their special educational needs and abilities.

has to be made to integrate handicapped children into regular classrooms for at least 50 percent of the school day, a process known as **mainstreaming** (Gresham, 1982). The learning of mainstreamed children in regular classrooms is to be facilitated by *individual education planning* for each child and a close working relationship between regular and special education teachers and administrators.

Unfortunately, mainstreaming has had more than its share of problems. First, in many schools — particularly those with limited finances — mainstreaming has amounted to little more than dumping children with handicaps into regular classrooms with little or no preparation or support for the regular classroom teachers (Zigler & Muenchow, 1980). Without training and support, many teachers have been unable to meet the special needs of mainstreamed children.

Second, many mainstreamed children have been unable to gain the social acceptance of their nonhandicapped peers (Gresham, 1982; Taylor, Asher, & Williams, 1986). One study (Taylor et al., 1986) compared the social adjustment of mildly retarded mainstreamed children and regular education students. The mildly retarded children were far more rejected by their peers and more anxious and dissatisfied about their social relations than their nonretarded peers. Of the mildly retarded children, 77 percent were categorized as "rejected," compared to only 15 percent of nonretarded children. Although data were not available on more severely handicapped children, it is likely that such children would experience even greater peer rejection.

How do we go about solving these problems? Some educators have argued that mainstreaming could be more effective if we trained handicapped children in social skills to improve their social acceptance (Gresham, 1982; Guralnick, 1990; Taylor et al., 1986). However, it is unclear how effective these efforts might be, particularly for children with severe handicaps.

Others have argued for a completely new perspective called the **Regular Education Initiative (REI)**, an approach that recommends that *all* special education classes be abandoned in favor of regular classrooms that are fully prepared to teach *all* children, regardless of their disability. The principle underlying REI is that the school should adjust to the needs of the child, rather than the reverse (Chalfant, 1989). Under REI, schools are expected to provide more intense, individualized instruction for children with handicaps, give more support to teachers, and offer principals more control over programs and resources (Will, 1986). Although the future of REI is uncertain, the approach has stimulated much-needed debate among educators on this difficult problem (Chalfant, 1989).

A P P L I C A T I O N

Providing Alternatives for Children with Handicaps

Although self-contained special classrooms, mainstreaming, and REI may each be helpful for specific subgroups of children, the overall problem requires a more balanced and varied strategy (Hallahan, Keller, McKinney, Lloyd, & Bryan, 1988). Clearly, severely handicapped children who are unable to profit from regular classroom experience must be placed in separate classrooms. For example, children with multiple handicaps require separate facilities where parents and teams of professionals — teachers, physical and occupational therapists, physicians, and social workers — can coordinate their efforts to provide individual education plans suited to each child's needs.

Children with milder handicaps are more likely to profit from mainstreaming, provided that both handicapped and nonhandicapped children are prepared for social interaction and teachers are trained and supported for the extraordinary challenge they face in integrated classrooms.

Finally, new approaches such as REI should be intensely studied for their potential contribu-

tion. In the long run the highly varied needs of children with handicaps will be best served by highly varied approaches to their education.

Parenting Children with Disabilities

Parenting normally developing children is a challenging and rewarding human endeavor. However, when children experience significant delays in development—for whatever reason—parenting often becomes less challenging and rewarding and more stressful and frustrating. By definition, children with disabilities reach some developmental milestones later than most children and never attain others. For example, while children with mild mental retardation due to Down syndrome may learn to read two to three years later than nonretarded children, it is unlikely that they will ever achieve the levels of comprehension required for the typical high school curriculum. More severe forms of retardation, particularly when combined with physical disabilities, further reduce children's potential for growth and development.

Not surprisingly, research has confirmed that parenting children with handicaps is far more stressful than parenting nonhandicapped children (Chetwynd, 1985). In one study (Weiss, 1991) parents were asked to describe the major sources of stress in dealing with their severely handicapped children. The six stressors most frequently cited were:

1. Arranging for professional services (such as medical care, psychiatric services, and special education) and support services (such as day care, babysitting, and respite for themselves—time completely away from children). Parents cited the difficulty in finding appropriate services and the misinformation that such services provided about their children's condition.
2. Interference with family life caused by the child's disability. Sibling rivalry and family conflict are major concerns.
3. The stigma of the child's condition: feeling embarrassed and ashamed by negative reactions of family members, neighbors, community members, and health professionals. Some parents reported that health professionals had blamed them for their child's disability.
4. Dealing with the child's extreme or bizarre behavior. Parents expressed anxiety over not being able to predict or control their child's behavior, particularly in public places.
5. Parents' concern over their own mental health. Many parents reported intense anger, guilt, depression, and anxiety associated with their child's disability; more than half reported that they had required psychotherapy to help them deal with their problems.
6. Fear about the child's future. Many parents expressed concern over the eventual need to institutionalize their child and over who might care for their child if they were no longer able to do it themselves.

While virtually all families of children with handicaps experience these and other stressors, some families cope with stress better than others. In one researcher's words, "It has become clear that increased stress does not necessarily lead to distress or dysfunction in families" (Beckman, 1991, p. 585). Thus, two families with identically handicapped children may show very different reactions to the same stressful event: While one family shows great resiliency and adapts successfully to their child's disability, another family becomes dysfunctional and fails to meet its child's needs.

Various factors influence the family's ability to cope with the stress of parenting a disabled child: family resources, parents' belief systems, the type and severity of the child's disability, the role played by fathers, personal factors between the child and the parents, and social support from the extended family, professionals, and community.

Severity of the Disability   It seems logical that parents should feel stress in direct proportion to the degree of their child's handicap or disability; a more disabled child simply requires more care. Several studies have confirmed that mothers' stress is directly proportional to their disabled children's caregiving demands (Beckman, 1983, 1991; Goldberg, Marcovitch, MacGregor, & Lojkasek, 1986a; Holroyd & MacArthur, 1976). One study (Goldberg et al., 1986a) compared families' responses to three different forms of disability: Down syndrome, neurological impairment (seizure disorder and cerebral palsy), and disabilities of unknown origin. Mothers of Down syndrome children reported more positive experiences with their children and more support from their family and community than parents in the other two groups.

Why would parents of Down syndrome children cope better than parents of other disabled children? The researchers speculated that these parents typically learn about their child's disability much earlier in development than most other parents. That enables them to begin dealing with the problem earlier, which gives them a feeling of efficacy—a sense of being able to do something to promote their child's development. Parents of Down syndrome children also have had greater success in accessing services from the community than have parents of children with less specific diagnoses. Finally, we also know more about the course of development in Down syndrome. This helps parents achieve realistic expectations for their child's development and prepare for their present and future caregiving roles.

In contrast, parents of neurologically impaired children or children with disabilities of unknown origin often wait years for a specific diagnosis, delaying appropriate intervention. These parents feel frustrated by professionals who can tell them little about their child's problem or how to cope with it. The uncertain diagnosis and prognosis generate helplessness and hopelessness in parents. Many parents do not know if or when their child will learn to walk or talk or achieve other milestones of normal development. While not knowing may offer hope to some parents, it can also create enormous confusion, anxiety, and helplessness.

Mothers, Fathers, and Stress   There is evidence that fathers and mothers of handicapped children have very different experiences of stress. In one study (Goldberg et al., 1986a) fathers, regardless of their child's disability, experienced less stress, greater self-esteem, more control of their lives, and more support than mothers (Goldberg et al., 1986a). In another study (Beckman, 1991) fathers of disabled children reported feeling less depressed, less restricted in the parental role, more competent, and having fewer problems with the marriage and better health than mothers. These differences are probably due to the greater responsibility that mothers bear in caring for their children (Goldberg et al., 1986a). These results suggest that, in times of limited community resources, intervention should emphasize support to mothers of children with handicaps.

Effects of Social Support   Many severely retarded and physically disabled children require virtually 24-hour care, severely taxing the parents' time and energy. As mentioned above, the burden is borne primarily by the mother in most families (Goldberg et

Children with disabilities can create considerable stress on their parents, particularly on their mothers. This couple's facial expressions show the mixed emotions of pride and frustration typical of parents of disabled children.

al., 1986a). Mothers who have access to informal support—such as babysitting, housework, and companionship from extended family, friends, and neighbors—report significantly less stress than mothers who have little support (Beckman, 1991).

While informal support may be helpful in reducing stress, parents of children with disabilities also require **respite**—temporary but total relief from the physical and emotional responsibility of caring for disabled children. Respite requires that parents be physically—and to some extent emotionally—separated from their children for brief periods of time. In one study (Botuck & Winsberg, 1991), mothers were given 10 days of overnight (out-of-home) respite from their severely retarded children. As expected, the mothers were happier and less depressed during respite than before or after. The mothers made good use of their respite time, resting and sleeping, engaging in personal care, and socializing with relatives and friends. Mothers continued to experience a heightened sense of well-being after returning to their children, compared to their feelings before the respite experience. Periodic respites should be considered an essential aspect of health care for families of disabled children (Beckman, 1983; Botuck & Winsberg, 1991).

A P P L I C A T I O N

Coping with the Stress of Parenting a Child with Handicaps

You can improve your ability to cope with the extraordinary stress of caring for your handicapped child:

- Seek the earliest possible diagnosis and prognosis of your child's condition and adjust

your expectations for development accordingly. Always seek second and third opinions.

- Become an expert on your child's condition and on the potential long-term effects on your family.

- Become an expert on the sources of professional services and support available in your community for your child and your family. Make respite for yourself and other family members a top priority.
- Seek professional and community services for your child *and* for the affected members of

your family. Avoid professionals and others who tend to blame you for your child's disability.

- Know the federal, state, and local laws that provide for your child's needs and the advocacy groups that can help you get your fair share.

Behavior Problems in Children with Disabilities

One of the most difficult aspects of caring for or teaching children with disabilities is their tendency to have behavior problems, such as aggressiveness or hyperactivity (Marcovitch, Krekewich, Campbell, Goldberg, & MacGregor, 1991; Quine, 1986; Wallender, Hubert, & Varni, 1988). While up to 20 percent of the nondisabled school-age population display serious behavior problems, as many as 50–60 percent of severely disabled children display highly aggressive, destructive, or overactive behavior (Marcovitch et al., 1991; Quine, 1986).

Many of their behavior problems are a direct result of their disability; they get very frustrated when they repeatedly try and fail to accomplish age-appropriate physical, cognitive, and social skills. Developmentally delayed children tend to have deficiencies in self-control, frustration tolerance, empathy, communication skills, and perspective taking. Also, some severely retarded children learn to get their way through tantrums and other forms of acting out. When these children come together in groups—for example, in classrooms or at sporting events—these problems aggravate one another and tend to result in social conflict. Their behavior problems undoubtedly contribute to their substantial risk of social rejection when they are mainstreamed into regular classrooms (Taylor et al., 1986). In a vicious cycle, that rejection only compounds the behavior problems.

Unfortunately, children with disabilities tend not to outgrow their behavior problems; there is longitudinal evidence that, for the most part, children who have difficulty during the preschool years are likely to continue having problems in middle childhood (Marcovitch et al., 1991). Likewise, as might be expected, their parents' stress and responsiveness to them are also highly stable across age periods. These results suggest that the behavior problems that many families experience with their handicapped children are chronic: The children's inappropriate behavior does not improve, and the parents' stress does not decrease. Stated more positively, the situation for these children and their families does not get any worse.

A P P L I C A T I O N

Dealing with Disabled Children's Behavior

*A*lthough there are so-called experts who would have you believe that dealing with disabled children's behavior problems is no different from dealing with other children's problems, this is unlikely to be true. What works for other children may or may not be effective for your child. Traditional behavior modification

principles are more difficult to apply with children who have cognitive and language impairments. The following recommendations may be helpful.

- Consult only professionals who have had hands-on experience with the behavior problems of children with your child's disability.

■ Develop a flexible, individualized approach to discipline, uniquely suited to your child's abilities and disabilities. Keep in mind that what is reinforcing or punishing for one disabled child may not have the same effects on your child. Also, what is reinforcing or punishing one day may not have the same effects over time.

Bottom Line: Effective discipline requires both consistency and flexibility. Make sure that everyone approaches your child in the same way and that everyone is prepared to change or abandon those techniques that prove ineffective.

Looking Back

Middle childhood is truly an extraordinary time for children's physical development. Children who have access to physically challenging environments, high-quality training and coaching, and parental encouragement and support will fulfill their developmental potential for physical and motor development. However, the uneven distribution of these resources in our communities and other negative influences place physical development at risk. These factors create the haves (children who have fulfilled their potential and will likely continue) and the have-nots (children who squander their potential for physical development by watching TV or hanging out on street corners). We have seen how the differences between the haves and have-nots could easily be reduced by more effective efforts by parents, physical educators, and concerned members of the community.

We have also seen how some children's potential for physical and mental development can be limited by genetic and environmental influences. Although handicapped children's potential for development may be delayed or severely limited, we must be committed to provide for their special needs. With special training, educational opportunities, and parental support, these children can fulfill their potential for physical and mental development and achieve a reasonable quality of life.

CHAPTER REVIEW

GROWTH Although the rate of children's growth slows even more after the preschool years, middle childhood is a time of extraordinary advancement in children's physical and motor development. Changes in size, proportion, strength, and endurance provide the foundation for significant improvement in children's motor skills. The quality of physical development depends on the opportunities children have for training and practice in their school, family, and community.

BODY TYPE AND BODY IMAGE Subtle changes in body proportion and physique have powerful effects on children's social and personality development. Children have highly specific opinions about body type: They think positively toward muscular children, negatively toward chubby children, and negatively, but somewhat less so, toward skinny children. These attitudes affect children's body image and their social status among peers.

GENDER DIFFERENCES Children's ability to perform play-game skills increases rapidly during middle childhood, with boys consistently performing better than girls. Boys' greater opportunities for training and practice account for much of the difference. Girls who are encouraged by parents and teachers and given the opportunity for practice perform as well as boys on most motor skills.

PHYSICAL FITNESS Significant changes in lifestyle in middle childhood—particularly attending elementary school—

reduce children's opportunities to engage in physical activity. Children spend very little time engaging in moderate to vigorous physical activity. Although lack of MVPA does not result in obvious fitness deficits during middle childhood, the level of fitness of those who remain inactive into adolescence will decline.

PHYSICAL EDUCATION While virtually all school-age children attend physical education classes, contemporary PE classes do not live up to their potential. Many children no longer attend on a daily basis, and instructors are less likely to be trained specialists. The potential of PE classes could be fulfilled by increases in funding and by making more efficient use of the time children spend in MVPA when in class.

ATHLETICS By third or fourth grade, most school PE programs begin to emphasize athletic skills needed for competitive team sports. Unfortunately, this change benefits only a small percentage of school-age children, resulting in a minority of haves and a majority of have-nots.

MENTAL RETARDATION Children who have below average intellectual ability and impaired adaptive functioning have

mental retardation. They make up 1 percent of the population, with a ratio of three boys to every two girls. The causes are not always known but about 50 percent of the cases result from Down syndrome and fragile X syndrome.

HYPERACTIVITY Children with normal intelligence but who are extremely active, impulsive, and inattentive are classified as having attention deficit/hyperactivity disorder (ADHD). While symptoms vary, most ADHD children have difficulty attending to structured tasks, following instructions, and behaving in classrooms. While ADHD may have many causes, it is likley to develop in children who are vulnerable by temperament and whose parents have difficulty adjusting to their children's emotions. Despite their widespread use, drugs have had mixed results in treating ADHD.

MULTIPLE HANDICAPS Chromosomal abnormalities, prenatal exposure to teratogens, and deprivation of oxygen and infection at birth are likely to cause permanent, severe physical and mental disability. These children have multiple handicaps. They are typically retarded and have severe limitations in adaptive behavior. Dramatic changes in the law

since the 1970s have substantially improved the care and education of these children, enabling many of them to achieve a reasonable quality of life.

MAINSTREAMING Educators have debated whether special-needs children should be educated in separate classrooms or integrated in classrooms with nonhandicapped children, a process known as mainstreaming. Mainstreaming has not always been successful, due to inadequate preparation of regular classroom teachers and peer rejection.

PARENTING THE DISABLED Parents of disabled children experience great stress and frustration. They have difficulty finding professional services and dealing with their children's needs and behaviors. Some families cope with these stressors better than others, depending on the severity of the child's disability and their access to services and support. Social support—particularly respite for the mother—is essential.

BEHAVIOR PROBLEMS Parents of disabled children often have to cope with serious behavior problems, including aggressive and impulsive behavior. These problems tend to be chronic and add significantly to the stress on caregivers.

Key Terms

somatotype

body image

moderate to vigorous physical activity (MVPA)

handicaps

disabilities

mental retardation

attention deficit/hyperactivity disorder (ADHD)

hyperactivity

multiple handicaps

hypotonia

hypertonia

skeletal deformity

least restrictive environment

mainstreaming

regular education initiative (REI)

respite

Cognitive Development and Schooling in Middle Childhood

Looking Ahead

- In kindergarten, first grade, and second grade, children go through a dramatic shift from unsystematic, illogical thinking to more organized and logical thought processes. What accounts for these changes and how can parents and teachers challenge children's thinking during this transition in cognitive ability?

- The advent of concrete operations is marked by reversible thinking, decentered perception, and reduced egocentrism. How do these changes appear in children's everyday behavior?

- According to one view of cognitive development, children learn to make more efficient and effective use of their limited capacity to process information during middle childhood. What are the implications of limited capacity and how do children overcome these limits?

- By late middle childhood, children become experts in areas of their special interest. What effect does expertise have on children's memory and problem solving?

- Children gradually become more aware of what they know and how to use what they know to solve problems during middle childhood. How can we facilitate this important new cognitive ability?

- Middle childhood coincides with the years that children spend in elementary school. What effects does schooling have on children's cognitive development? Why do low-income minority children not do as well in elementary school as other children?

- During middle childhood, schools become a dominant influence on children's cognitive development. Should parents simply defer to the school's influence in this area?

- Children show varying degrees of spontaneous interest in school-related tasks and activities. Can intrinsic motivation be stimulated? What are the effects of reinforcement on children's intrinsic motivation?

- Children learn to read during their elementary school years. Is there a best approach to teaching reading? Why do some children learn to read better than others?

- Children also make important strides in learning mathematics in middle childhood. How do children learn to add and subtract? Why do some children—particularly girls—have difficulty learning math?

- Some children are exceptionally bright and talented. How do schools approach the special needs of these children?

Cognitive Development in Middle Childhood

You may recall the unique way Carlos sorts his possessions when he is four (Chapter 10). He combines a lump of Play-Doh, a toy soldier, and a dried apple core for reasons that make sense only to him: "The man climb-ded the mountain to get the apple." Now, at age 10, his classification ability is comparably more sophisticated.

Carlos, a fifth grader, has become a collector. He collects insects, stamps, rocks, comic books, and model airplanes. Although he devotes some time to each collection, his predominant interest is his massive collection of baseball cards, which he started accumulating in second grade.

Although Carlos's card collection appears to be completely disorganized, with hundreds of cards stuffed haphazardly in a suitcase under his bed, the chaos is by design. Immediately after getting home from school, he begins his daily ritual of dumping the cards into a big pile in the middle of his room and, for the next hour or two, sorting and resorting the cards into a series of complex multidimensional categories. For example, one afternoon he begins by classifying players by their teams' division in the major leagues (1 of 4) and by their respective playing positions (1 of 9), for a total of 36 subcategories.

After mulling over the results of the first sort, he shuffles the cards and does a second sort, this time classifying players by division and by team, with players sequenced within teams in descending order of their previous season's batting average. His final sort is the most complex: Players are classified by their playing position, batting average (above .300, between .250 and .299, or below .250), then the year they entered the major leagues.

Carlos accomplishes each sort effortlessly, making only occasional reference to the backs of cards to check an individual player's statistics.

Carlos's involvement in his card collection illustrates several advances in children's cognitive abilities in middle childhood—the years from 6 through 10. First, he has memorized hundreds of statistical facts about dozens of baseball players, a feat far beyond the limits of his memory capacity in early childhood. Second, he can now classify objects by more than one dimension at a time, and his sorts show clear evidence of *class inclusion*, with superordinate categories, such as "all baseball players," and subordinate categories, such as pitchers, catchers, infielders, and outfielders. Third, his ability to rank players in order of their batting averages and year of entry to the major leagues suggests significant advances in quantitative reasoning.

But Carlos's newfound cognitive abilities go well beyond improved memory, classification, and quantitative reasoning; he can now integrate these skills into a *logical system of thought* that he uses to draw inferences. For example, Carlos knows that younger players are always competing for older players' jobs and that .250 is a mediocre showing. So he takes special interest in two subcategories that result from one of his many sorts: shortstops with lifetime batting averages below .250 who entered the majors before 1986, and shortstops batting over .250 who entered the majors during or after 1986. As he compares the two subcategories, he reasons that members of the former group are less likely than the latter group to still be active players. He further deduces that the likely-to-be inactive players' cards will soon become more valuable as they become increasingly hard to find.

Thus, Carlos's ability to categorize and recategorize facts has fostered new forms of reasoning and insight into his daily experience. He has come a long way from "The man climb-ded the mountain to get the apple."

One additional point should be emphasized. For his age, Carlos is an expert in the domain of baseball. His extensive store of baseball facts and his elaborate, well-practiced schemes for organizing those facts enable him to process information in a highly sophisticated manner, comparable to that of knowledgeable adults. When he encounters new baseball information—for instance, the details of a trade or an injury to a player—he can grasp its meaning far more rapidly than most children his age. However, while Carlos is an expert in baseball, he knows virtually nothing in many other domains of knowledge, such as chemistry, cooking, tools, basketball, mammals, or classical music, to name just a few. As a novice in these other domains, his ability to process information is severely limited.

The point is that children's knowledge of their world tends to be very uneven across domains (Fischer, 1980), and they enjoy highly efficient information processing only in those areas of their expertise (Bjorklund, 1987).

As with earlier periods of development, developmentalists disagree on the best way to describe and explain these dramatic advances in cognitive ability from early to middle childhood. Piaget proposed that cognitive development emerges in a stagelike progression, reflecting a fundamental reorganization of the way children think. He believed that the egocentric, centered, irreversible reasoning of the preschooler gives way to the more systematic, logical reasoning of middle childhood. Once the new stage is achieved, children should be able to think consistently at that level in all domains, such as conservation, classification, and moral reasoning.

In contrast, information processing theorists such as Robert Siegler (1986), Robbie Case (1985), and Kurt Fischer (1980) view cognitive development as more continuous and less stagelike, reflecting gradual increases in children's information processing capabilities from early to middle childhood. In contrast to Piaget's views, information processing theory suggests that children's knowledge in various domains is uneven, reflecting differential exposure of individual children to diverse learning experiences. In general, the information processing view is far more receptive than Piaget's view to the notion that cognitive development can be substantially influenced by training. We will discuss both.

Piaget's Concrete Operations

Piaget, while believing that cognitive development progresses in stages, recognized that the change from one stage to another is not abrupt. He suggested that between ages five and seven children go through a gradual period of transition from the illogical and unsystematic reasoning of the preoperational period to the more logical and systematic reasoning of middle childhood. We refer to this transition as the **5-to-7 shift**. This shift coincides with children's first two to three years in the elementary school. The timing is no accident. Educators have long recognized the opportunity for educational intervention that this period of significant cognitive change provides.

Piaget described children's reasoning during the 5-to-7 shift as **intuitive**, a term that implies noticeable improvement over preoperational thought, but with lingering lapses in logic. With intuitive reasoning, children often get the right solutions to problems but without understanding the underlying principles. For example, a six-year-old may recognize that the amount of liquid stays the same when it is poured from a tall, thin container to a short, stout container but not be able to express *why* changing the shape of the container is irrelevant to the amount of liquid inside.

Intuitive thinkers also show inconsistent reasoning across situations. For example, a child may conserve quantity when a liquid is poured from one container to another, but fail to conserve when the same liquid is subsequently divided among several smaller containers. Intuitive thinkers also seem tentative about their solutions to problems, even when those solutions are correct. You can test this by presenting the water glass problem to a five- to six-year-old who seems to be on the verge of understanding conservation. If the child manages to tell you that the two liquids remained the same, even when poured into dissimilar containers, ask, "Are you *really* sure that they are the same?" When challenged, the child is likely to regress to a less sophisticated, preoperational response, saying incorrectly that they are unequal.

Piaget believed that by age seven or eight, children advance to the next major stage of cognitive development, the *period of concrete operations*. The **concrete operation** is a new form of cognitive ability that enables children to adapt to their environment with systematic logic. For the first time, children begin to understand relationships among objects and events in their environment: Objects can be systematically related in classes; quantities can be added, subtracted, multiplied, and divided; rules can be systematically combined to organize games and other activities. According to Piaget, children reason and solve problems with concrete operations throughout the elementary school years.

Significant advances in cognitive abilities in middle childhood help children to better understand concepts such as cause and effect. However, this child is about to discover how much more he has to learn about inertia and the force of gravity in this popular magic trick.

How does concrete operational thought differ from preoperational thought? Concrete operational thought offers four significant advances in children's ability to reason. First, concrete operations enable children to reverse their thinking, that is, to mentally cancel out (or reverse) any mental action. For example, a 10-year-old who is tempted to disassemble his brother's bicycle is able to think about how he will put the bicycle back together *before* he takes it apart. Similarly, a concrete operational thinker can cancel out adding by subtracting, multiplying by dividing. Piaget referred to this quality of operational thinking as **reversibility**.

Second, while preschoolers often mistake appearances for reality, school-age children become progressively less influenced by how things *seem* and far more capable of inferring how they really are (Flavell, Miller, & Miller, 1993). For example, even though the ice on a lake appears solid to an eight-year-old girl, she is well aware that looks may be deceiving. When children come to know—or even just suspect—that superficial changes in the appearance of objects and events may have no effect on the way things really are, their physical and social world becomes more concrete, less subject to change, and far easier to understand and predict.

Third, while preschoolers perceive their world through *centered perception*, focusing their attention on isolated parts of their experience, older children are able to **decenter**, distributing their attention across multiple features of their experience. Decentered perception helps children to understand the notion of compensating changes. For example, children understand that when one side of a seesaw goes up, the other side must go down. They understand that when one part of a solid object moves in space, other parts of that object also move. In general, decentered perception helps children take a broader view of problems they encounter, to "see the forest for the trees." Decentered perception plays a critical role in children's ability to achieve conservation, one of the hallmarks of concrete operational thought.

A fourth significant advance that comes with concrete operational thought is the decline in *egocentrism*—that is, children begin to view the world more like adults, distinguishing other points of view from their own. Leshonda comes to understand, for example, that when she is watching TV and her father is in another room preparing dinner, he cannot possibly see what she is watching. She knows that she must take this into account when she talks to him about what she saw.

The decrease in egocentricity also helps children to understand that different people may interpret and react to the same situations differently. For instance, two nine-year-olds are not necessarily surprised when they have very different reactions to the same TV show. (Of course, that does not mean that they will be particularly tolerant of each other's positions. Knowing that other people think and feel differently than you does not mean you have to like it, even in middle childhood.

Thus, children's improving ability to reverse their thought, distinguish appearances from reality, decenter their perception, and be less egocentric has a profound effect on their ability to adapt to their physical and social environments. The effect of these new operational capabilities is apparent in three domains of children's thinking and problem solving: conservation, classification, and moral reasoning.

Conservation Preschool (preoperational) children do not spontaneously "conserve" matter—that is, they do not recognize that the amount of a substance remains unchanged despite changes in the shape of the container in which it is held. You will recall from Chapter 10 how Keisha inadvertently starts an argument between four-year-old Leshonda and her friend by pouring equal amounts of juice for each child into glasses

In contrast to the confused preschooler, the concrete operational child knows that the amount of a substance is conserved despite changes in the shape of the container in which it is held.

that are dissimilar in shape. When she tries to resolve the dispute by pouring the juice into identically shaped glasses to *prove* their equivalence, the girls are temporarily satisfied. However, when she pours the juice back into the original glasses, the girls revert to their original belief that one glass has more juice than the other. More generally, preschoolers do not spontaneously conserve number, matter, weight, volume, or length.

As children gradually develop concrete operations, they begin to show consistent conservation of matter, number, and length (Piaget & Inhelder, 1974). For example, in the conservation of length problem, a child is shown two sticks of equal length, laid side by side (see Figure 13.1). After the child confirms that the sticks are of equal length, the experimenter moves one of the sticks slightly to the right in full view of the child. While preschoolers center their attention on the endpoint of the stick, concluding that it is now longer, older children's decentered perception enables them to see that *both* ends of the stick have moved the same distance and direction, thereby conserving the stick's length.

Similarly, concrete operational thought convinces children that changing the shape of the container does not affect the amount of a liquid, and that changing the spacing between objects has no effect on number. These insights are followed by conservation of weight by age 10 or 11, and volume by age 11 or 12 (Gulko, Doyle, Serbin, & White, 1988; Piaget & Inhelder, 1974).

Two sticks of equal length are used in a conservation of length experiment. One of two equal-sized balls of clay is reshaped for use in an experiment on conservation of mass.

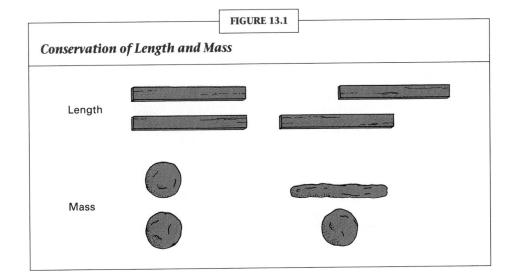

FIGURE 13.1

Conservation of Length and Mass

Length

Mass

Piaget's rigid position on the developmental timing of children's achievement of conservation has spurred numerous research attempts to elicit conservation responses at much younger ages by simplifying Piaget's instructions and tasks and by eliminating distractions. In a comprehensive review of conservation training studies, Dorothy Field (1987) concluded that, under highly controlled laboratory conditions, children as young as four can be trained to produce conservation responses. However, the research suggested that training does not hold up over time or transfer to natural settings. We may conclude that without long-term intervention, children do not achieve conservation until middle to late childhood. Further discussion of this issue is presented in Box 13.1.

Classification   The second ability Piaget regarded as a defining feature of concrete operational thought is the ability to classify objects *hierarchically* (Inhelder & Piaget, 1964). The term *hierarchy* refers to the fact that any given object can be classified in a series of increasingly inclusive levels. For example, apples are included in the class of fruits, which can be included in the class of foods. The logical rule of **class inclusion** states that any class of objects must be smaller than the inclusive class in which it is contained.

BOX 13.1

Training Conservation in Young Children

Researchers have demonstrated conclusively that children can be taught to conserve at much earlier ages than Piaget suggested, in most instances as early as age four or five. But does the ability to teach them conservation in the lab mean that we should attempt to teach conservation in preschool?

Unless one is driven by some compulsion to disprove or improve upon Piaget's theory, it is difficult to imagine what practical purpose would be served by training normally developing young children to conserve. Children who show obvious signs of cognitive delay, however, may benefit from these training procedures. Robert Pasnak and his colleagues (Pasnak, 1987; Pasnak, Brown, Kurkjian, Mattran, Triana, & Yammamoto, 1987) investigated this possibility with developmentally delayed kindergarten children. The children were trained in conventional classification, seriation, and conservation tasks. As expected, these children scored higher on a measure of general reasoning than children exposed only to a standard math curriculum (Pasnak, 1987). In a second study, Pasnak showed that these effects are still detectable after a delay of one year (Pasnak et al., 1987). Thus, while training seems unnecessary for normally developing children, it may be useful for children who show significant cognitive delay.

But what about parents at home with their children? Would it do any harm to give your children a little cognitive edge over their untrained peers? These lab training procedures are quite specialized, and most parents are unlikely to learn them. In any case, we recommend that parents avoid trying to apply these procedures at home. Training your preschoolers to do conservation party tricks for the entertainment of family and friends may be tempting but serves no useful developmental purpose. Children will learn to conserve soon enough if parents provide a reasonably stimulating home environment and encourage their children's curiosity and exploration.

Piaget studied children's understanding of the rule of class inclusion by testing them with objects (or pictures of objects) that could be classified separately into subclasses (for example, cats and dogs) or together into a more inclusive class (animals). The objects in the subclasses were purposely presented in unequal numbers—for example, seven dogs and three cats. After confirming that the children could group the dogs and cats into subclasses, they were questioned to tap their understanding of class inclusion:

RESEARCHER: Are there more dogs than cats?

CHILD: Yes. (*correct*)

RESEARCHER: Are there more animals than dogs?

CHILD: No. (*incorrect*)

According to Piaget, children do not consistently indicate that the class (animals) must be larger than the subclass (cats *or* dogs) until seven or eight years of age. While there is considerable evidence that simple forms of class inclusion can be demonstrated in preschoolers—for example, by providing them with category labels, such as "fruits" or "clothes" (Waxman & Gelman, 1986)—young children do not display the level of mastery of class inclusion shown by Carlos's understanding of baseball until 10 or 11 years of age (Winer, 1980).

Ann McCabe and her colleagues (1982) showed the complex nature of the development of class inclusion. McCabe tested three- to eight-year-olds on several class inclusion problems. As expected, the oldest children (seven- to eight-year-olds) applied the rule of class inclusion, solving most problems correctly. Preschoolers responded randomly, getting approximately 50 percent of the problems correct by chance. Interestingly, the middle group of children (the five- to six-year-olds) consistently performed worse than the preschoolers, well below chance levels.

Why would older children not do as well as younger children? Apparently, while the five- to six-year-olds had advanced to a level of applying a rule to solve the problems, their rule was oversimplified, interpreting every problem as a comparison of the relative size of the *subclasses*. Thus, in the above problem, when asked, "Are there more animals than dogs?" they answered "No," consistent with their rule.

Moral Reasoning   One of the more important responsibilities of parents is to ensure that their children learn to distinguish between right and wrong. Parents promote this learning in their toddlers by responding differently to appropriate behaviors than to inappropriate behaviors in various situations, that is, by reinforcing appropriate behaviors and by ignoring or punishing inappropriate behaviors. Most parents try to facilitate their children's learning by articulating rules that enable their children to anticipate the consequences of their actions in everyday situations.

But no two situations are completely alike, and parents cannot always be present to provide guidance and sanctions. If children are to be socialized to live independently in society, they must ultimately learn to reason about the situations in which they find themselves, to make judgments about what constitutes morally correct behavior in those situations, and to enact that behavior. We refer to these cognitive abilities as **moral reasoning**—our thinking about the rightness or wrongness of specific behaviors in everyday situations. While developmentalists have generally agreed that moral reasoning changes developmentally, there is far less agreement on the best way to characterize these changes.

Freud's View   Sigmund Freud, the famed psychoanalyst, believed that children develop moral concern late in the preschool years as a by-product of the resolution of the

Oedipus complex (in boys) or Electra complex (in girls). As we indicated in Chapter 2, toward the end of the Freud's phallic stage of psychosexual development, children are overwhelmed by anxiety caused by the impending loss of the opposite-sex parent as a love object. They defend themselves against the anxiety by identifying with the same-sex parent, and to a lesser extent with the *same-sex* parent — taking on their parents' morality as their own. Freud (1923/1960) believed that the child's morality takes the form of a **superego**, a mental structure that unconsciously guides a child's behavior. The superego contains both a *conscience* that prohibits certain behaviors and an *ego ideal* that provides the child with an internal image that the child strives to become. Violating the conscience or not living up to the ego ideal is punished by *unconscious guilt*, a debilitating psychological state that undermines the child's ability to think or behave rationally. Once formed at age five or six, the superego remains unchanged throughout life, unconsciously motivating the individual to moral behavior.

In Freud's view, children do not engage in moral reasoning. Rather, they are unconsciously motivated to avoid the experience of guilt by behaving in ways that are consistent with the prohibitions and ideals of the superego. Morality is a matter of internalized values and emotional responses. Even though these notions cannot be verified by research, we should not overlook Freud's ideas. First, we should keep in mind that children's moral judgments and behaviors may be significantly influenced by children's emotions, both at the time of initial learning and when their morality is tested in everyday situations. Second, we should recognize the powerful influence of the family in children's moral development, particularly the idea that children may learn morality by identifying with their parents.

While Freud provided an intriguing view of children's moral development, he failed to credit children with the ability to make rational moral choices and he failed to account for the fact that morality changes developmentally. Other theorists, such as Jean Piaget (1932/1965) and Lawrence Kohlberg (1969), have rejected the psychoanalytic view, describing morality as a cognitive developmental process.

Piaget's View As in other areas, Piaget is credited with the first effort to describe developmental changes in children's moral reasoning. Piaget's insights were derived from detailed observations of children's games and their understanding of rules that organize games. He also read stories to children and studied their reasoning about the moral issues implicit in the stories. For example, children were asked "Who was naughtier: the child who accidentally broke several teacups on a tray or the child who broke a single teacup while attempting to steal something from the dinner table?" He found that younger, preoperational level children were more likely than cognitively more advanced children to judge the breaking of multiple teacups as naughtier.

Piaget (1932/1965) proposed a stage progression in moral reasoning that reflects children's stage of cognitive development. He believed that preoperational children are essentially **amoral**, unable to reason logically about rules and concepts of right and wrong. They may, of course, *behave* morally but only in response to the rewards and punishments presented by adults. The cognitive changes during the concrete operational stage enable children to think about their behavior and its consequences, and about the logic of rules that govern their behavior. Piaget described this first logical reasoning as **moral realism**, an inflexible view that behaviors are either right or wrong, with no in-between. Laws are created by the absolute authority of adults, and that authority cannot be questioned. Children as moral realists decide the rightness and wrongness of behaviors — their own or those of others — strictly by their consequences, irrespective of the person's intentions. Thus, in the example cited above, the unintentional breaking of several teacups would be judged naughtier than purposeful breaking of only one.

Moral realists' view of right and wrong is epitomized in their belief in **immanent justice:** You *always* get punished for behaving inappropriately and rewarded for behaving appropriately; conversely, if you get punished, you must have done something bad, or if you get rewarded, you must have done something good. This belief causes some young children to blame themselves when something unfortunate happens to them or to members of their family. For example, a child may believe that her parents' divorce is punishment for her past misbehavior or that her illness is punishment for teasing her sister. Unfortunately, some parents reinforce this belief by using their children's painful experiences as opportunities to build moral character.

Piaget believed that late in the middle childhood years and in early adolescence children gradually come to realize that rules are not irrevocably set by external authorities, that rules can be changed through negotiation, and that an individual's intentions must be considered in judging whether a behavior is right or wrong. He described this more advanced thinking as **autonomous moral reasoning.**

Kohlberg's View Lawrence Kohlberg (1969) believed that Piaget had oversimplified the progression of children's moral reasoning. He studied children's reasoning by presenting them with moral dilemmas that challenged their ability to consider the many factors relevant to judgments of right and wrong. One of his dilemmas is the story of Heinz:

> In Europe, a woman was near death from cancer. One drug might save her, a form of radium that a druggist in the same town had recently discovered. The druggist was charging $2000, ten times what the drug cost him to make. The sick woman's husband, Heinz, went to everyone he knew to borrow the money, but he could get together only about half of what it cost. He told the druggist that his wife was dying and asked him to sell it cheaper or let him pay later. But the druggist said no. The husband got desperate and broke into the man's store to steal the drug for his wife. Should the husband have done that? Why? (Kohlberg, 1969, p. 379)

Like Piaget, Kohlberg (1969) described the children's responses to the dilemmas as a series of nonoverlapping, qualitatively distinct, sequential levels of moral reasoning: *preconventional morality, conventional morality,* and *postconventional (or principled) morality,* with each level subdivided into two stages.

At the first level (Stages 1 and 2), young children engage in **preconventional moral reasoning,** believing that the rightness or wrongness of a behavior is determined solely by its consequences. *Stage 1 children* believe that behaviors that avoid punishment must be good or right. Kohlberg referred to this as the *obedience and punishment orientation.* For example, some children insist that Heinz should not steal the drug because he would be put in jail. Others center more on the negative consequences to Heinz if he lets his wife die, that he would be sad and lonely.

Stage 2 children advance to a *hedonistic and instrumental orientation,* believing that behaviors are good if they meet one's personal needs. The emphasis is on behaving to gain rewards, rather than to avoid punishments. While children remain egocentrically involved in meeting their own needs, they begin to recognize that they may have to please others in order to please themselves, as in "I'll scratch your back if you scratch mine." Thus, they might suggest that Heinz should steal to help his wife get better—even though he may spend some time in jail—because he needs her to cook his dinner. Children typically engage in preconventional moral reasoning well into the concrete operational stage of cognitive development, until about age 9 or 10 (Kohlberg, 1976).

At the level of **conventional moral reasoning** (Stages 3 and 4), children develop internal standards that reflect *society's* values of what is right and wrong. *Stage 3 children* adopt the *good boy, good girl orientation*, engaging in good behavior to gain adult approval or to avoid disapproval. Heinz should steal the drugs and save his wife's life because everyone will admire him for doing the right thing. Conventional thinkers believe that they should "do unto others as they would have others do unto them."

Stage 4 adolescents embrace a *law and order orientation*, believing dogmatically that laws define what is right and wrong. Heinz should not steal because it is forbidden. Conventional moral reasoning predominates from late childhood, through adolescence, and into the young adult years (Colby, Kohlberg, Gibbs, & Lieberman, 1983). Kohlberg believed that this is likely to be the highest level of moral reasoning achieved by most people.

At the most advanced level (Stages 5 and 6), **postconventional moral reasoning** enables the individual to think beyond specific laws to abstract principles, such as justice, equality, and human rights. *Stage 5 individuals* adopt a *social contract orientation*, believing that laws should be respected as the best way to balance individual interests against the needs of the group. People should obey the law because it is the best way for everyone to live harmoniously. Heinz knows that society cannot survive if individuals can break the laws at their convenience. While Heinz will struggle with his decision, ultimately he must do what is right for the common good.

Those few individuals who manage to reach *Stage 6* embrace the *universal principles orientation*, believing that universal moral principles (justice, equality, human rights) transcend laws made by human beings. At this level Heinz must follow his own conscience, basing his decision on what he believes is just. In this situation he would reason that nothing is more important than a human life! Kohlberg maintained that very few adults achieve postconventional moral reasoning, particularly the Stage 6 principled orientation.

A P P L I C A T I O N

Promoting Children's Moral Development

Although parents are universally interested in promoting their children's moral development, the path to that goal remains elusive. Most parents guide their children's learning by rewarding good behaviors and punishing bad behaviors. Parents also model appropriate behaviors to facilitate their children's imitation. But if children are to learn to behave morally, they must do more than simply follow the precepts of their parents; they must develop the ability to think about the complex interplay of forces in novel situations. You can promote your child's moral reasoning:

- Encourage your child to understand people's needs and empathize with their feelings.
- Promote your child's participation in social situations with same-age peers, particularly those that involve both cooperative and competitive play experiences.
- Allow your child to deal with her own social dilemmas, rather than imposing your morality.
- Discuss complex moral issues with your child, pointing out differences in points of view, motivations, and feelings of the participants.
- Do not provide overly simplistic moral views of right and wrong. Make it clear that rules need to be flexible, depending on the situation.

Bottom Line: Moral reasoning is no different than other forms of reasoning: It develops only when it is exposed to increasingly complex problems in an atmosphere that encourages curiosity and exploration.

Kohlberg's stage description has come under intense criticism for possible bias in the criteria used to classify children's responses to the dilemmas. Some of this criticism stems from Kohlberg's decision to base the criteria for classification on the responses of an all-male sample. Carol Gilligan (1982) claimed that this approach biased the criteria for classification in favor of males. She argued that girls are socialized differently than boys in our society: girls to show more concern about feelings and personal relationships than boys, and boys to be less sensitive to people's needs and more concerned about justice and fairness. Since responses to Kohlberg's moral dilemmas that refer to caring or concern about relationships are scored Stage 3 (conventional) and responses that refer to concepts of abstract principles are scored Stage 5 or 6 (postconventional), boys would typically appear to be at a higher level of moral reasoning than girls. Gilligan argued that the differences between boys' and girls' responses to dilemmas have less to do with level of moral reasoning than with differences in interests and values.

Despite Gilligan's view that boys and girls follow different pathways to moral development, research has shown few differences in boys' and girls' level of moral reasoning (Friedman, Robinson, & Friedman, 1987; Snarey, 1985; Walker, 1984, 1986). However, Gilligan's analysis has succeeded in sensitizing developmentalists to subtle qualitative differences in the way boys and girls think about moral issues. The unanswered question is whether these differences can also be identified in the everyday moral behavior of males and females.

Despite these conceptual advances that come with concrete operations, one very important limitation remains. As the term *concrete* implies, children think operationally about objects and events in their everyday experience: They can think reversibly about the effects of their actions on the problems they attempt to solve, overcome appearances to perceive reality, and see others' points of view. However, they are incapable of developing hypotheses or theories concerning what might be possible, rather than what is. If they can't see, hear, touch, or smell something, they have difficulty thinking about it. They can imagine something they have once experienced, but not some hypothetical event. They are confused by questions in the form of "What if?" The ability to think about hypothetical events will not come until adolescence, during what Piaget called the period of *formal operations*.

A P P L I C A T I O N

Making the Most of Operational Thought

As intuitive thought gives way to operational thought by second or third grade, parents and teachers can begin to rely on and challenge children's intellect in ways that were not previously possible:

- For the first time, parents can urge children to consider whether they think they can put something back together—such as the kitchen clock or their bicycle—*before* they begin to take it apart. Reversibility of thought can be most practical!

- Parents may assume that children are considerably less vulnerable to illusion, less dependent on superficial appearances, and more likely to recognize how things really are. For example, children are more likely to understand that lake water may be deeper than it looks and that strangers may be more dangerous than their benign appearance suggests.

- Teachers can encourage children to simultaneously consider their own *and* others' points of view. They can do so by openly discussing controversial issues and by encouraging children to *role-play* each other's positions.

- Parents and teachers can expect children to attend to *all* relevant aspects of a problem, rather than allowing their perception to be seduced by the problem's most salient features.

The Information Processing View

Although Piaget has advanced our understanding of cognitive development in middle childhood, other developmentalists have had difficulty with Piaget's strict adherence to the notion of discontinuous, qualitatively distinct stages of development and his difficult to define concepts. Information processing theory offers a useful alternative by describing cognitive development as a more continuous process of increasing ability throughout development and by demanding far more precise definitions of terms.

According to John Flavell, a leading developmental psychologist, the information processing view focuses on exactly what a child's cognitive system actually *does* when solving problems (Flavell, 1985): What does the child do first, second, and so on? How does information flow in the system, and what happens to it at each successive step? In Flavell's words, this approach attempts to provide an "odyssey of information flow . . . a model of cognitive processing in real time that is so precisely specified, explicit, and detailed that it can actually be run successfully as a working program on the computer" (1985, p. 76). Although not all information processing researchers take the computer analogy quite so seriously, Flavell's description does convey the unique emphasis of this view of cognitive development.

One important assumption of this theory is the notion of **limited capacity**: Each individual is constrained by a finite pool of mental resources that can be allocated to various thought processes (Shiffrin & Schneider, 1977), and total mental capacity is a constant throughout development (Case, 1985). In practical terms, there is only so much mental resource to go around; investment in one mental activity means less is available

The information processing perspective sensitizes parents and teachers to the importance of sustained attention in school learning. Unfortunately, it is often difficult to tell what a child is thinking. Is this girl mulling over possible strategies to solve a problem, or is she simply distracted and unable to concentrate on the task before her?

for other activities. For example, a child may be unable to study effectively for an exam if she is preoccupied thinking about her friends.

A second important assumption is that some mental activities require more mental resources than others. Mental activities that require more resources are *effortful*; those that require less are *automatic*. While effortful mental activities drain the system, automatic mental activities are highly efficient, freeing up resources for other purposes. Robbie Case has proposed that, while an individual's total mental capacity does not change with age, thinking becomes less effortful and more automatic as a result of experience, practice, and neurological maturation (Bjorklund & Harnishfeger, 1990; Case, 1985; Case et al., 1982). The mental operations involved in learning to read provide a clear example: While first graders struggle to sound out every word as they read, older children and adults read whole words and phrases rapidly and effortlessly. This savings in effort allows older children and adults to comprehend and remember more of what they read than first or second graders.

These improvements in the efficiency and effectiveness of information processing are reflected in advances in three key aspects of children's cognitive functioning: (1) their increasing use of *strategies* to solve problems, (2) their expanding knowledge base or expertise in specific content areas, and (3) their increasing awareness and control of their mental abilities. We will examine each of these developmental changes more closely.

Becoming Strategic   **Strategies** are goal-directed mental operations that individuals use to deliberately facilitate their memory, attention, and problem solving (Harnishfeger & Bjorklund, 1990). For example, children can repeat a series of numbers over and over to facilitate memory, scan a visual display to systematically gather information, and count on their fingers to solve math problems.

The development of children's use of strategies has been studied most extensively in the area of memory. Three memory strategies become increasingly effective as children progress through the elementary school grades: *rehearsal*, *organization*, and *elaboration*.

Rehearsal is a relatively simple strategy that involves repeating items over and over — aloud or to oneself — to facilitate storage of information for later retrieval. For example, children learn that they are less likely to forget someone's phone number if they repeat it several times immediately after hearing it. Rehearsal is simple in the sense that it requires little thinking.

A more sophisticated strategy is **organization**, the purposeful attempt to identify conceptual relationships among items to be remembered. For example, if a child were asked to memorize the following items:

> potato, car, airplane, apple, spinach, bicycle

she could improve her recall by grouping the items into two exclusive categories: foods and vehicles. She could then organize the items into conceptually distinct groups for storage. The objects could be recalled at a later time by using the category labels to help locate the objects in memory.

When items cannot be easily grouped into familiar categories, children can use a third strategy called **elaboration** — relating objects to one another with absurd or fanciful visual images. For example, if a child were asked to memorize the following items:

> book, boy, horse, field, rain

she could elaborate by generating a visual image such as "A boy was riding his horse across a field, reading his book in the rain." Recalling the image should facilitate recall of the individual items. Of course, other sets of items may prove more difficult to elaborate.

Research has shown that children's use of strategies for attention, memory, and problem solving gradually improves from early to middle childhood. Preschoolers typically show very little spontaneous use of strategies, solving most problems by guessing or by applying rigid approaches that offer no advantage. For example, a preschooler may try to solve a puzzle by arbitrarily selecting puzzle pieces, then trying to force the pieces to fit by banging them against the board. If a child has no strategies and does not profit from training to promote the use of strategies, we say that the child has a **mediational deficiency** (Reese, 1962). Mediational deficiencies may persist beyond the preschool years if parents and teachers do not encourage the child to use strategies.

By kindergarten or first grade, children can be taught simple strategies to facilitate attention and memory, but they typically stop using the strategies shortly after training is terminated. That is, they know the strategy but they do not use it spontaneously, even when it would help them to solve problems. We refer to this failure to use a known strategy as a **production deficiency** (Flavell, 1970). We are not sure why children would fail to use a strategy that offers obvious advantage in a cognitive task. Perhaps the advantage is not as obvious to young children as it is to older children and adults. Children may need exposure to others' successful use of strategies before they become motivated to use it themselves (Bandura, 1977).

Although many children begin to use strategies spontaneously in second or third grade, their use of strategies often fails to improve their performance. We refer to this failure as a **utilization deficiency** (Miller 1990; Miller, Seier, Probert, & Aloise, 1991). Thus, while younger children may employ strategies just as spontaneously as older children, the older children profit more by using the strategies more effectively (Miller et al., 1991).

We may conclude that the development of children's use of strategies is quite gradual during middle childhood. Children must progressively overcome mediational deficiencies, production deficiencies, and utilization deficiencies before strategies can be used spontaneously *and* effectively. In general, it is unlikely that children will show spontaneous, consistent, efficient, and effective use of strategies for problem solving, memory, and attention until fifth or sixth grade.

A P P L I C A T I O N

Promoting Children's Use of Strategies

While young school-age children are capable of learning strategies for solving problems, they tend to not use them spontaneously. After teaching new strategies, encourage their use by prompting during problem-solving exercises.

- Help your child grasp the benefits of using strategies in concrete terms. For example, when he saves time by using a strategy appropriately, allow him to use that time in a preferred activity.

- Point out how other children have used strategies effectively, and the time and energy they have saved.

- Encourage your child to share successful strategies with other children.

- Encourage your child to use proven strategies, even when he fails to use them successfully. Practice will eventually make perfect.

  Bottom Line: Keep in mind that your child's use of strategies is far more important than getting the right answers. Reinforce for both.

Becoming Expert At the beginning of this chapter, we saw that Carlos, by age 10, has developed considerable expertise in the area of major league baseball, even by adult standards. His expertise has not come easily. He has devoted thousands of hours studying details of the sport printed on the backs of baseball cards, watching games on TV, reading magazines, and discussing baseball with his parents, who have been dedicated fans since their childhoods. Consistent with the concept of limited capacity, Carlos's investment of mental resources in baseball means less time and energy for other subjects, particularly school subjects that he finds less interesting. Variations in children's interests and in the quality of their training in different school subjects ensures that their knowledge across domains is uneven (Fischer, 1980).

Research has shown that becoming expert in a particular domain implies more than just knowing more; it also implies "thinking better" (Bjorklund, 1987). This notion is illustrated in a classic study by Micheline Chi (1978). Chi compared the performance of 10-year-old children and graduate students on 2 memory tasks: a task that requires recall of numbers and a second task that requires recall of the positions of chess pieces on a chess board. Although we would normally expect adults to fare better than children on any test of memory, Chi had purposely selected adults who had little knowledge of chess and children who were expert chess players.

As she expected, while adults outperformed the children on recall of numbers, the children outperformed the adults on recall of the positions of chess pieces. Thus, children were able to "think better" in their area of expertise than novice adults, but their advantage over adults in chess did not carry over into memory for numbers. Other studies by Chi and her colleagues have shown the same effect in other domains such as knowledge of physics (Chi & Glaser, 1980).

Why would knowledge of facts in a particular domain have such powerful effects on memory? David Bjorklund (1987) believes that the answer lies in the way facts are stored in memory. As children accumulate increasing numbers of facts in a given domain, they organize this knowledge in increasingly complex ways. For example, once a child has memorized the names of all of her classmates, she may organize the names by gender, where they sit in class, who is friends with whom, their respective reading groups, and so on. Bjorklund refers to this interconnected body of facts as an **elaborated knowledge base**. The elaborated knowledge base operates like a cross-referenced computer file. Strategies can be used to recall specific facts (the name of a particular child) or a whole categories of facts (the names of all children in the top reading group). Bjorklund argues that storing or recalling facts from the elaborated knowledge base is accomplished with great savings in mental effort, freeing up mental resources for other activities. Thus, experts—regardless of age—have a great advantage over novices, but only within their domain of expertise.

Becoming Metacognitive As children's reasoning becomes more strategic, they also become increasingly aware of their own cognitive abilities. We refer to children's emerging awareness and control of their cognitive abilities as **metacognition** (Cross & Paris, 1988). It includes knowing what you know, knowing what you do not know, and knowing what to do with what you know to solve problems. Leshonda's approach to a difficult homework assignment in fifth-grade mathematics represents an advanced level of metacognitive knowledge and skill, compared to other children her age.

On the way home from school, Leshonda begins to think about the killer homework assignment in math. Her teacher has introduced a new topic called long division, but had not adequately explained the new concept. Leshonda knew that she was confused when the class ended, and she anticipates difficulty with her homework. She likes math, and knows that she is good at it, but she also knows that this assignment will take more than a positive attitude. It is going to be a long afternoon!

When she gets home, she wastes no time getting into her pre-homework nesting ritual: books thrown on the living room floor, TV on, and the portable phone in the "fast draw" position. A quick reading of the first math problem confirms her fear: She does not know enough to get through the first problem. She declares a math emergency: She turns off the TV and the ringer on the telephone to reduce distraction and moves from the floor to her desk where the light is better.

She begins by reading several problems and writing down words she does not know. Two words ("divisor" and "dividend") come up repeatedly. She knows she has to understand these words, but the definitions had not been given in class. She tries the glossary, but reading the definitions out of context does not help.

She reluctantly concludes that she will have to teach herself the new material by reading the dreaded chapter introduction. She reads it several times, taking time to work through the sample problems. When she is able to solve them without looking at the explanation, she tackles the homework problems. She is surprised that she solves them easily, with only an occasional glance at the text. She confirms her answers to the odd-numbered problems by checking with the appendix.

Feeling relieved and ready for some reinforcement, she turns on the TV and telephone ringer. She knows that her classmates will not make the effort she has made to solve the problems and will soon be calling for consultation. Within seconds, the first of several children call for help. Leshonda doesn't mind. She enjoys the attention and knows that teaching the concepts to others improves her understanding of the material.

Leshonda's approach to her homework assignment illustrates the two major components of metacognition: *self-appraisal* and *self-management* (Paris & Winograd, 1990). She self-appraises by recognizing that she has not learned the concepts required to complete her assignment, by assessing what concepts she needs to know, and by sensing when her self-study has adequately prepared her to tackle the problems. She self-manages by altering her study environment to reduce distraction and by enacting specific information gathering strategies to compensate for her deficiencies: listing the words she does not know and using the text's glossary and the chapter introduction. She even knows that teaching her friends will provide rehearsal to consolidate what she has just learned.

Research has shown that children's metacognitive abilities improve dramatically from early to middle childhood in various cognitive domains, including memory (Flavell & Wellman, 1977), attention (Miller & Weiss, 1981), and reading (Paris & Oka, 1986). In reading, for example, children gradually learn that difficult passages must be read more than once, that skipping words is likely to distort sentence meaning, and that reading too fast sacrifices comprehension and memory for detail.

Unfortunately, many children fail to develop the metacognitive skills that are critical to achievement in the upper elementary grades. The reasons for this are not entirely clear, but a variety of factors in the home and school environments seem to be involved. Some parents make less effort than others to foster metacognitive skills. In one cross-cultural study, it was shown that German parents are more persistent and successful than American parents in fostering their children's metacognitive skills (Carr, Kurtz, Schneider, Turner, & Borkowski, 1989; Schneider, Borkowski, Kurtz, & Kerwin, 1986). It is not clear why American parents make less effort. It may be because they tend to believe that children develop metacognitive skills in the natural course of their daily experiences, rather than by direct parental instruction (Sonnenschein, Baker, & Lasaga, 1991).

Teachers can be highly effective in fostering children's metacognitive development (Cross & Paris, 1988; Kurtz & Borkowski, 1987; Moely, Hart, Leal, Johnson, Rao, & Burney, 1986), particularly in the context of teaching strategic approaches to classroom assignments (Ghatala, Levin, Pressley, & Godwin, 1986; Leal, Crays & Moely, 1985; Lodico, Ghatala, Levin, Pressley, & Bell, 1983). For example, in one study (Kurtz & Borkowski, 1987), children were trained to identify topic sentences and main ideas in paragraphs. The children's use of strategies improved when teachers encouraged them to work slowly, to monitor their own performance, and to periodically evaluate the effectiveness of each strategy employed. Thus, children's school performance can be improved by teaching them to monitor and control their use of strategies in problem solving, memory, and attention.

A P P L I C A T I O N

Promoting School-Age Information Processing

Parents and teachers can promote their children's information processing by working within the principle of limited capacity, by teaching strategies, by encouraging the development of expertise, and by fostering metacognitive skills.

- Accept the idea that your child has a limited capacity for processing information. Help him to make the most efficient and effective use of his current capacity. For example, encourage him to focus attention on one cognitive task at a time, particularly with respect to effortful mental activities. Keep in mind that thinking is always more effortful when a child is learning new skills, concepts, and strategies.
- Promote your child's development of expertise in areas of his own spontaneous interest.

Try not to influence his choices. The emphasis should be on helping your child to appreciate the advantages of an elaborated knowledge base. Achieving expertise in one area—any area—will likely lead to the desire to develop expertise in other areas. Above all, don't try to expand your child's first expertise into a lifelong career.

- Teachers should promote children's use of strategies by teaching strategies directly, rather than assuming that children will develop and apply them spontaneously. Show children *why* certain strategies work and others do not and how strategies improve accuracy and save time and energy. Make children aware that strategies are within their control and can be generalized across settings.

The Schooling of Our Children

We have described cognitive development during middle childhood as children's progressive integration of skills and abilities that should result in highly systematic, logical, and coherent thought processes by age 10 or 11. However, children need optimal learning environments if they are to fully realize their potential for optimal cognitive development. While natural environments may provide optimal experiences for children to learn certain skills—for instance, informal peer groups promote social competencies—modern societies create formal learning environments to ensure that children learn basic skills in reading, mathematics, science, and social studies. We refer to these efforts as the science and practice of **schooling** (Linney & Seidman, 1989). In North America, we have designed the first major component of schooling—kindergarten through sixth grade of the elementary school—to coincide precisely with the period of middle childhood. As we will see, schooling is far more successful for some children than for others.

What Makes a School Good?

Pretend that your family—including your five-year-old child—is about to move to a new city. Your top priority is choosing the best school for your child. Assuming you have time to visit every school in the city, what should you be looking for? Smiling teachers? Enthusiastic children? Clean restrooms?

Although a comprehensive discussion of the characteristics of effective schools is beyond the purposes of this text, we offer the following summary of what some experts consider the essential features of an effective school (Good & Weinstein, 1986; Linney & Seidman, 1989). An effective school must have:

1. Strong leadership provided by a principal who actively and energetically organizes the activities of the school. The principal's leadership style must engender the trust and respect of teachers, parents, children, and the community. (See "Careers: The Elementary School Principal.")
2. An orderly atmosphere that provides a sense of direction and momentum to the learning process, without being oppressive. There must be clear lines of authority and sanctions for dealing with those who choose to jeopardize the learning process.
3. Teachers who actively participate in the school's decision making processes, representing the best interests of the children.
4. A principal and teachers with consistently high expectations for the learning of *all* children, and a relentless commitment to academic excellence.
5. Consistent monitoring of children's performance, with strategies for dealing assertively with children who work below their potential.

Unfortunately, many schools—particularly those that serve low-income minority children—depart significantly from these ideals. We will examine the experience of low-income minority children in school in greater detail.

Schooling and Minorities

While most children and parents share the excitement and enthusiasm of the first day of school, these emotions are soon displaced by more realistic reactions to the day-to-day demands of the school environment. Many children—particularly children from middle- and upper-income families—react favorably to these demands, conforming to teachers' expectations for appropriate behavior and enthusiasm for learning. These children hit the ground running in first grade—cognitively, socially, and emotionally ready for the curriculum that teachers are ready to teach. These children are likely to maintain their momentum throughout their elementary school experience.

The Elementary School Principal

Jayne Hall has been the principal of Pasadena Lakes Elementary School in Broward County, Florida, for the last two and a half years. The students at her school are 80-percent middle-class children from the local neighborhood and 20-percent very low-income children who are bused in to achieve racial balance.

How did you first become interested in becoming a principal?

I'm not certain, but I think it was during the years I was a classroom teacher. Most administrators at that time ran their schools in a traditional manner, failing to bring out the best in their teachers and children. Parents were largely irrelevant to the daily functioning of the school. I wanted to see if I could make a difference.

What exactly does the principal of an elementary school do?

I think of myself as a coach whose job is to bring out the best in the teachers, parents, and children. My challenge is to facilitate the education of the children by coordinating the efforts of teachers, parents, and the community. All have a stake in the children's education and all have something important to contribute. I challenge my teachers to try new approaches and to not be threatened by change. We work together to achieve a balance between the old and the new.

I make certain that I don't get too isolated from the day-to-day activities of my school; I visit two classrooms each day and try to teach as often as I can. I focus on what my teachers and children are doing well, and I reward them for their efforts and achievements. I respect them for what they have become and challenge them to grow even more.

What is the most difficult challenge for a principal?

Each year we are asked to teach increasing numbers of children with no new funds or resources. We are also asked to keep up with complex changes in state and local curriculum requirements. It's difficult to be creative and to keep up your teachers' morale under these conditions. But over all, I think we cope quite well. I like to think that it has to do with the way we approach these problems. Teachers, parents, and other members of the community work together like a family to set and achieve the goals for our children. Our parents are actively involved in their children's education. I believe in my teachers and parents, and I think they believe in me.

How does one become an elementary school principal?

The career path to becoming a principal begins in the classroom—at least five years of full-time teaching. If you eventually hope to be an administrator, it is important to become active in your school and your community while teaching. Get involved in education organizations and take on leadership roles. You will also need a Master's degree in administration and supervision. After the Master's, you must compete for an administrative internship. If you are lucky enough to get one, you will intern while you teach—a very stressful and difficult challenge. Unfortunately, even after you complete your internship, you must compete for administrative positions—first as assistant principal (including a second internship) and then as principal. It can take many years.

How can students find out more about this career?

They can write to the National Association of Elementary School Principals, 1615 Duke Street, Alexandria, VA 22314.

Other children—particularly those from low-income minority families—respond poorly to their first experience in school (Comer, 1988). Before the end of first grade, many poor children have fallen well behind more privileged children in every subject, and the gap widens with each passing year. By the end of elementary school, they are likely to be from one to two years behind grade-level expectations. For these children, schooling is no more than an accumulation of experiences of academic failure, social rejection, and loss of self-esteem.

While the dismal failure of American schooling for poor minority children is one of the most serious problems facing our society, we are only beginning to understand the complexity of the issue. One significant part of the problem is the children themselves. The results of several studies suggested that many low-income African American children do not have the necessary cognitive, social, and emotional skills to meet the challenge of first grade. For example, one longitudinal study (Entwisle, Alexander, Pallas, & Cadigan, 1988; Entwisle & Hayduk, 1982) pointed to deficiencies in children's "classroom temperament." Compared to white children, poor African American first graders showed less concentration, more restlessness, and more frequent behavior problems—behaviors that are highly disruptive to classroom instruction. Not surprisingly, these behaviors were associated with less learning, lower marks, and decreased teacher expectations for children's performance throughout first grade. Other research (Reynolds, 1989) has shown that cognitive deficits, lack of motivation to learn, and lack of parent involvement also contribute to minority children's low achievement in first grade.

These results clearly suggest that what low-income minority children bring to school—cognitive readiness, temperament and personal maturity, and family support—may be at least as important as the quality of schooling itself in determining their early academic failure and maladjustment to the elementary school classroom. For a glimpse of what it is like to teach in the inner city, see "Careers: The Inner-City Teacher."

James Comer, a leading authority in minority education, argues that it is a mistake to blame poor children for the problems they face in school. He believes that the children's problems are symptomatic of the sense of alienation that poor families feel toward the mainstream culture. Poor African American parents in particular distrust the schools and their children's teachers (Comer, 1988). Poor children bring this distrust to school on the first day, with immediate effects on their attitude toward learning.

Comer describes a black first-grade teacher's experience with distrust on her first day in a black inner-city school. After she had explained the class rules, a six-year-old responded, "Teacher, my mama said I don't have to do anything you say" (1988, p. 46). Children's distrust undermines the teacher's authority and sets the stage for high levels of inappropriate classroom behavior. Comer recommends major restructuring of the relationship between the schools and minority communities to promote direct family involvement—and hopefully increased trust—in the process of schooling.

Parents and Schooling

When parents bring their children to school on the first day, they ceremoniously hand their children over to teachers to begin the process of schooling. For some parents, this is an act of deference and a transfer of responsibility. It is as if they are saying, "We have done our job; now it is time for you to do yours." But many parents—particularly those who are more educated—realize that they can and should continue to influence their children's learning and development by taking an active role in the process of schooling. More educated parents tend to be more informed about their children's school perfor-

The Inner-City Teacher

Cora Frost is a language arts teacher at Booker T. Washington Middle School in Baltimore City, Maryland. Cora is 21 years old and is finishing her first year of teaching. Virtually all of the students in her classes and in the school are African American and from lower socioeconomic families. Cora is a participant in the Teach for America Program — a program designed to attract highly motivated young people to teach in inner-city and rural school districts.

What attracted you to teaching in the inner city?

I'd like to say that this was my lifelong goal, but I really found my way to teaching by accident. I was working as an apprentice social worker in the county jail. I found that I was only helping people out of crisis situations but I wasn't giving them the skills that would empower them to improve their lives. I decided that teaching would be the best way to equip people to solve their own problems. When I heard about the opportunity to teach urban children immediately after college, I jumped at the chance. I was apprehensive, but I knew that this was what I was looking for.

What is Teach for America?

Teach for America is a nonprofit organization for college graduates who may not have majored in education. You are asked to make a two-year commitment to teach in school districts experiencing chronic teacher shortages. The program provides six weeks of summer training and two years of support both in and out of the classroom. In most locations, you are expected to work toward your certification by going to school at night. I will be certified at the end of this year. It is exhausting — physically, intellectually, and emotionally. It is the hardest thing I have ever done in my life and probably the hardest thing I will ever do.

mance, interact more with their children's teachers, and make more effort to manage their children's academic performance (Baker & Stevenson, 1986). Research has shown that children of involved parents achieve at higher levels than children of uninvolved parents (Stevenson & Baker, 1987).

However, the family's effects on schooling depend on more than the parents' level of education. Another very important factor is the family's cultural background. Different cultures maintain very different attitudes and beliefs about children's intelligence and set very different goals for their children's development (Hoffman, 1988; Stevenson & Stigler, 1992). In one study (Okagaki & Sternberg, 1991, 1993), parents of kindergarteners,

How have the children responded to you?

At first, I was totally overwhelmed. My first few weeks in the classroom were depressing. I had to convince myself that just getting the children to sit in their seats was a major accomplishment. And I felt like I wasn't teaching them anything. I made the mistake of trying to be their friend rather than their teacher. As one of my colleagues said, "Kindness is weakness at this school." My students were more in control of me than I was of them. They knew that they could reward or punish me by paying or not paying attention, but I didn't seem to have anything they wanted.

But things gradually changed as I learned to use discipline effectively and to consider the children's interests. I knew that although my students were way behind grade level, they were enormously clever and resourceful. They had learned to survive on the streets, and school was largely irrelevant to that process. I had to change that if I was going to succeed.

Most importantly, I came to understand that the children would not learn from me until I made my classroom into a place where they could feel safe. My initial approach was too permissive, and no one — including me — felt safe. As I began to assert myself and to organize my classroom, the children began to respect me more and to feel that my classroom was a safe place to learn.

Do you think you are being effective?

Yes, but I had to adjust my goals. My children come from the poorest and the toughest elementary schools in this city. Many had failed every grade prior to this school year. I can't compensate for all that failure. But when I see one of my children avoiding a fight or using words instead of fists to resolve a dispute, I know I am making progress. When a child shows spontaneous interest in a book for the first time, it's really inspiring. I am amazed by my children's energy and their cleverness and how much they have to teach me about myself and about life. My kids have enormous potential for learning; I'm just beginning to tap that potential.

Do you recommend this to other young people?

This is not for everyone. You have to be very dedicated and able to deal with frustration and failure. You have to be persistent and never give up on any of your students, even when they try hard to make you give up on them. You have to be able to laugh at yourself and to apply humor in your teaching. Most importantly, you have to believe in the children and believe in yourself, regardless of what happens from moment to moment in your class.

Are you going to keep teaching in the inner city after you are certified?

I am pretty sure I will. If I was offered a job at this school right now, I would definitely take it. I can't imagine finding a school and children that would be more fulfilling. I learn something new every day, and every day is a new challenge.

How can someone find out more about Teach for America?

You can learn more by calling the National Office for Teach for America at 1-800-TFA-1230.

first graders, and second graders were asked to indicate their beliefs about childrearing, their concept of children's intelligence, and the educational goals they set for their children. Parents were selected to represent a cross-section of different cultures (all residing in the United States), including Anglo-American, Cambodian, Filipino, Mexican immigrant, Mexican American, and Vietnamese.

The results showed that parents in different cultural groups differed significantly in their beliefs and goals for their children. Consistent with American values, Anglo- and Mexican American parents valued children's independence over conformity. The opposite was true for the immigrant parents.

Parents can positively influence their elementary school child's experience in school by taking an active role in the affairs of the school and by monitoring their child's progress. Here, both of this girl's parents have joined with a teacher to discuss her progress in a difficult subject.

Parents in different cultural groups also had very different views on what characterizes an intelligent child. While immigrant families emphasized noncognitive attributes, such as the drive to do well and work hard, Anglo-American parents emphasized cognitive (verbal and creative abilities) over noncognitive attributes. Hispanic parents gave roughly equal weight to cognitive and social skills.

With respect to schooling, parents of all cultures agreed that teachers should emphasize getting children to conform (follow directions and obey classroom rules), rather than helping them to make friends or make decisions. However, while American-born parents wanted teachers to emphasize thinking skills, immigrant parents held a broader view of intelligence that emphasized working hard and doing well in cognitive *and* social endeavors. The narrower cognitive emphasis of Anglo-American parents was associated with superior academic performance of their children.

Should we conclude, therefore, that the narrow view of intelligence is better for children? The researchers did not seem to think so. In their words, "Perhaps, the majority culture can benefit from the input of minority cultures in adopting a broader view of intellectual abilities that will enable all children to develop and capitalize on multiple abilities" (1991, p. 27). Differences in beliefs and attitudes toward schooling in people of different nations is explored in Box 13.2.

A P P L I C A T I O N

Parent Involvement in Children's Schooling

As a parent, you can expand your child's opportunities for learning and development in school, and you can increase the likelihood that your child will take advantage of those opportunities.

- Become an active member of your school's parent teacher organization (PTO). Groups of well-organized parents can influence school policy, increase community and government support for schools, and improve the quality of education in the classroom.

- Monitor your child's homework and provide consults, without actually doing assignments for your child.

- Model academic excellence for your child by practicing your own school-related skills— reading, writing, and arithmetic—in your child's presence. Demonstrate the practical value of school subjects in everyday living.

- Make a daily habit of asking your child about her experiences at school, watching for signs of learning or social problems. Discuss recurring problems with the teacher and participate actively in their solution.

- Get to know your child's teachers on a first-name basis. Parents and teachers who trust each other and communicate openly are in a unique position to improve the quality of children's school experience.

- Volunteer in your child's school. You can provide a valuable service to the school, help integrate your culture into the thinking and activities of the school, and get a first-hand view of the school's strengths and weaknesses.

BOX 13.2

The Learning Gap: A Cross-Cultural Comparison

As Americans observe the rapidly changing position of their country in the global marketplace, they have been forced to consider whether some of their problems in competitiveness internationally may be a result of problems in the competitiveness of our children. Perhaps the children of the 1950s and 1960s who are now working for and running our corporations do not have what it takes to compete on an international scale. Perhaps—as has been suggested by leaders of other countries—our workers are too lazy and too uneducated to keep our industry competitive. Perhaps our schools have failed us. Perhaps U.S. schools are continuing to fail us by producing new generations of lazy and uneducated young Americans who will cause even further decline as they move into our work force and unenthusiastically climb our corporate ladders.

A recent study by Harold Stevenson and James Stigler (1992) has provided important new insight into this most important subject. In their book *The Learning Gap* the authors have summarized their own and others' cross-cultural research on schooling in Japan, Taiwan, China, and the United States. The study involved matched, representative samples of children in each of the four cultures. The children were compared on tests that were judged to be "culture fair."

In general, the authors concluded that U.S. elementary school children lag far behind their Asian counterparts. The reasons for this lag can be found in significant cultural differences in family attitudes and values toward their children's schooling and in the children's approach to the learning process.

Asian parents consider academic learning to be their children's primary responsibility. They believe that successful achievement results from hard work and effort, rather than from innate influences. They maintain high expectations for their children's performance in school and interpret low marks as signs of insufficient effort on their children's part. They respond to underachievement by encouraging their children to try harder.

In contrast, American parents and teachers tend to believe that academic success is substantially influenced by innate factors—a notion that is frequently shared by their children. Parents and teachers who believe in innate influences are unlikely to respond to their children's underachievement by encouraging them to try harder. Why bother? American parents tend to be satisfied with their children's achievement and are very concerned about the negative psychological effects of raising expectations for their children's school performance.

Stevenson and Stigler believe that the situation is likely to get considerably worse before it gets better. They believe that the solution does not involve spending more money on our schools. They indicate that we already spend more per student than is spent in the Asian countries considered in their study. They believe, rather, that the answer lies in challenging our children in school, as we do in athletics. In the authors' words, "The belief in hard work is not alien to Americans."

Perhaps the decline in American competitiveness will encourage us to reexamine our approach to schooling our children, and we may instill in them an appropriate attitude toward the hard work necessary to succeed academically.

Asian parents tend to value their children's academic achievement and think that it is a product of hard work; American parents tend to think of academic ability as innate and make less effort to deal with their children's under-achievement.

The Motivation to Learn and Achieve

Elementary school children show wide variation in their motivation to learn and to achieve. While some children are deeply and spontaneously involved in virtually every school-related task, others show little enthusiasm for school activities. We say that children who are spontaneously involved in learning show **intrinsic motivation**—an urge to learn and to achieve that comes from within. Children who perform in school but with little spontaneous interest in learning show **extrinsic motivation**. Extrinsically oriented children (extrinsics) participate in school activities only to earn rewards or to avoid punishment. When teachers fail to use rewards and punishments effectively, extrinsics show little involvement in school activities and little learning.

The wide range of individual differences in children's motivation within classrooms creates an enormous problem for teachers. Intrinsically motivated children are relatively easy to teach. They are challenged by new tasks, persist until problems are solved or competency is achieved, and then seek tasks that provide even greater challenge. They have more favorable attitudes toward school, achieve at higher levels, perceive themselves as more competent, and have higher self-esteem and less school anxiety than extrinsically motivated children (Gottfried, 1982, 1985, 1990). (The special case of children who may be *too* motivated to achieve is explored in Box 13.3.)

In contrast, teachers must prod and prompt extrinsically motivated children to learn; they must sustain these students' tenuous involvement with bribes, threats of punishment, and constant surveillance. Although many teachers believe that power control techniques (rewards and punishments) are more effective than low control techniques (encouragement and reasoning) for promoting *intrinsic interest* in academic tasks (Boggiano, Barrett, Weiher, McClelland, & Lusk, 1987), research contradicts them. Research has shown that powerful control techniques *decrease* rather than increase children's intrinsic motivation (Deci & Ryan, 1980, 1985).

Moreover, these negative effects can come quickly. In one study, teachers' repeated use of highly controlling reinforcement early in the school year transformed children from intrinsic to extrinsic orientations in just six weeks (Deci, Nezlek, & Sheinman, 1981).

Why would the teacher's well-intentioned use of reinforcement undermine intrinsic motivation? One reason may be that external rewards are so stimulating that young children simply lose all sense of their own spontaneous interest in the task. Or children may *discount* their own interest as the real reason for engaging in the task. A child may reason, "If someone has to reward me to do this, I probably didn't really want to do it myself." It is also possible that children like to feel that they have control over their choices in a classroom. When children think they are being manipulated by their teacher's rewards (or bribes), they rebel by avoiding the activity (Deci & Ryan, 1985).

Does this mean that teachers should avoid use of reinforcement to promote intrinsic motivation? Not exactly. Research has shown that loss of intrinsic motivation is not the inevitable result of teachers' use of reinforcement. The problem exists only when teachers reinforce children simply for participating in or for completing tasks. When teachers reward children for competent performance, however, the reward tends to *enhance* children's intrinsic interest in the activity (Boggiano, Harackiewicz, & Main, 1985). For example, while a teacher's comment "If you finish your work, you can go outside" will *decrease* a child's interest (in the "work"), the comment "You are doing a fine job!" should *increase* interest (in the "job"). These effects are more apparent in middle than in early childhood (Boggiano & Ruble, 1979). Furthermore, children who perceive themselves to be both competent and in control of the outcomes of a challenging problem are not negatively affected by the teachers comments (Boggiano, Main, & Katz, 1988).

A P P L I C A T I O N

Promoting Intrinsic Motivation

*P*arents and teachers can promote children's intrinsic motivation:

- Provide an environment that stimulates children's natural curiosity, challenges their abilities, captures their imagination, promotes task persistence, and encourages creativity. Take care, however, not to overstimulate your children by providing too many choices.
- Reinforce children for competent performance rather than just for completing tasks.
- Help children to accurately perceive their own competence and to recognize improvements in their performance.

- Promote children's sense of control of their environment by encouraging them to take credit for both their successes and their failures.
- Expose children to models—particularly same-age peers—who feel pride and joy in their work and play, without expectations of external rewards.
- Recognize that inappropriate use of rewards by other people, such as substitute caregivers, can undermine your children's intrinsic motivation.

Learning to Read

While it may seem simple and automatic for the mature reader, learning to read is no simple task. It requires that children learn to integrate their cognitive, perceptual, and linguistic abilities in response to several years of sequenced instruction. In U.S. schools, formal reading instruction typically begins in first grade, when children are approximately six years old, and continues throughout the elementary school grades. The first three grades have been described as a time of learning to read, and the remaining grades as a time of reading to learn (Chall, 1983).

The Problem of Over-achieve-ment: Type A Behavior

Intuitively, we have all had the impression that adults who are extremely competitive, highly achievement oriented, easily angered, and aggressive are likely candidates for a stroke or heart attack. Research has confirmed that these behaviors—referred to as **Type A behaviors**—cluster together in certain individuals, making them more prone to coronary heart disease (Haynes, Feinlieb, & Kannel, 1980; Rosenman, Brand, Sholtz, & Friedman, 1976).

Type B individuals—those who are more easygoing, less competitive, less anxious, and more laid-back—are less prone to heart disease. The relationship of Type A behavior to heart disease in adulthood has prompted developmentalists to search for the pattern earlier in development.

Do children and adolescents show Type A behavior patterns? Karen Matthews and her colleagues (Matthews & Jennings, 1984; Matthews & Siegel, 1983) have identified a Type A behavior pattern in children analogous to the pattern in adults. Type A children are highly competitive in achievement situations, impatient, and easily aroused to anger and aggression. They set high standards for themselves and compete openly with others to be "best," even when faced with tasks that have little personal meaning to them or clear criteria for success (Corrigan & Moskowitz, 1983; Matthews & Angulo, 1980; Matthews & Volkin, 1981).

Type A behavior is made up of two separate components: The *prosocial* component involves striving for achievement, persevering, being self-motivated and competitive; the *antisocial* component involves being impatient and easily frustrated, angered, and annoyed (Steinberg, 1986b). The prosocial and antisocial components are fused in childhood and become increasingly differentiated with age: Whereas children who show powerful strivings to achieve are typically impatient and irritable, many adolescents learn that one can strive for achievement goals without being frustrated or annoyed by others (Steinberg, 1986b).

Why are some children Type A and others Type B? Although the antecedents are unclear, several studies have suggested that parents may have significant effects on the development of Type A behavior. In one recent study (Treiber et al., 1990), parental hostility was related to Type A

Two contrasting approaches have been used to teach reading: the **look-say** (or **whole-word**) approach and phonics. In look-say children memorize whole printed words as pictures, associating each picture with a word in their vocabulary. We see the primitive beginnings of whole-word reading when preschoolers surprise their parents by deciphering the name under the golden arches, or correctly identifying the word *stop* on the red sign at the end of the street. Thus, even very young children can form simple associations between printed and spoken words and can retain a small number of such associations in long-term memory.

Reading by Look-Say First-grade teachers begin whole-word instruction by showing children printed words (such as *cat* or *sit*) and pronouncing each word out loud. The children are then asked to look at the word and say it. Teachers make no effort to teach children to associate particular letters with individual sounds; in look-say, letters are merely elements of word-pictures.

By this method, reading ability improves steadily and quite rapidly through first grade, as children memorize increasing numbers of associations between printed and

behavior in children. Other research by Geri Weidener and her colleagues (Kliewer & Weidner, 1987; Weidner, Sexton, Matarazzo, Pereira, & Friend, 1988) has shown that the relationship between fathers and their sons may be of particular importance. In one study (Weidner et al., 1988) fathers' Type A behaviors (impatience and hard-driving competitiveness) were correlated with Type A behaviors in their sons. The parents' effects on daughters were less clear. In another study (Kliewer & Weidner, 1987), fathers — but not mothers — of Type A sons reported setting high goals for their sons that their sons were unable to accomplish. Again, no effects were found for daughters. This suggests that males may be at greater risk than females for Type A and its consequences.

What are the long-term consequences of being a Type A individual? Researchers have approached this as two related questions. First, how stable is Type A behavior from childhood to adolescence to adulthood? Research has shown that children who are classified as Type A in childhood are no more likely than other children to still be classified Type A in adulthood (Steinberg, 1986b). However, male adolescents — but not female adolescents — who are Type A are very likely to continue to be Type A as young adults. This may be due, at least in part, to the unique relationship between Type A behavior in fathers and their sons mentioned above.

The second question is whether Type A behavior in childhood or adolescence is a risk factor for coronary heart disease in adulthood. While research has shown that both preschool and older Type A children respond to stress with heightened physiological response (blood pressure, heart rate, and skin conductance) (Lawler, Allen, Critcher, & Standard, 1981; Lundberg, 1983), no longitudinal data are available that relate Type A behaviors in *childhood* to coronary heart disease in *adulthood*. The fact that Type A classifications are not stable from childhood to adulthood suggests that such a relationship is unlikely. However, because male Type A adolescents are likely to remain Type A as adults suggests that they are at increased risk of coronary heart disease — particularly those teenage boys who are high on the antisocial component of Type A.

What can we conclude at this point? Assuming that we still have a great deal more to learn about the development of Type A behavior, parents and practitioners should recognize early Type A behavior as a red flag that bears watching. While it is normal for young children to strive to achieve in and out of school, too much competition, frustration, and anxiety in the pursuit of perfection over too many years of development may be bad for your children's health.

spoken words. However, from an information processing perspective, look-say places increasingly heavy demands on children's limited memory capacity, slowing the rate of learning over time. Consequently, children taught *exclusively* by look-say typically progress more rapidly in first and second grade than in later grades (Freebody & Byrne, 1988).

Reading by Phonics   The second approach to reading instruction is known as **phonics**. Proponents of this approach conceptualize reading as an integration of *decoding* and *comprehension* (Gough & Tunmer, 1986). **Decoding** refers to the ability to interpret printed letters as a code for spoken words, and **comprehension** refers to the ability to understand words that have been decoded.

Phonics instruction requires that children develop **phonemic awareness**, an understanding that spoken words are composed of sequences of sounds (called phonemes). For example, the word *bat* has three identifiable sounds: "b" "a" "t." Kindergarten teachers promote phonemic awareness with simple games and activities that encourage children to break down spoken words into their constituent sounds, and to blend those sounds

Children who learn to read exclusively by the look-say method learn quickly at first, then slow down. Children who learn by phonics progress more slowly at first, but can decode unfamiliar words. Teachers are more effective when they avoid relying on any one method exclusively.

back together to reconstruct the original words. Rhyming and nursery rhymes enhance phonemic awareness by helping children recognize that certain sounds and combinations of sounds are common to many words. Research has shown that phonemic awareness is essential to the acquisition of reading skill (Juel, Griffith, & Gough 1986; Stanovich, 1988; Wagner & Torgesen, 1987), and that preschool children's sense of rhyme predicts later success in reading (Bryant, MacLean, Bradley, & Crossland, 1990; MacLean, Bryant, & Bradley, 1987).

Once phonemic awareness is firmly established, teachers introduce the alphabet. The emphasis should be on helping children to visually discriminate among the letters, rather than simply teaching them to say the alphabet from memory. The ultimate goal is to teach children to accurately and rapidly identify letters as they scan printed words from left to right. In one study, the speed of letter-naming in kindergarten was associated with successful reading in later grades (Walsh, Price, & Gillingham, 1988).

Finally, children are taught that the alphabet is a *code* for the sounds of the language, with letters—individually and in combination, such as *sh* and *ch*—representing each of the 45 phonemes that make up the English language. For example, children are taught that the printed letter *b* stands for the sound "b" as in *bat*. After learning the complete code, children can decode or sound out virtually any printed word in the language: They identify individual letters in sequence within a word, conjure up the sequence of sounds represented by those letters, and blend the sequence of sounds to form the word. In the early stages of reading by phonics, children comprehend the word by hearing their own pronunciation of the blended sounds. Comprehension, of course, is limited by the words available in the children's vocabulary.

In the early stages of phonics instruction, comprehension of word meaning is quite slow and effortful, as children methodically sound out every letter in every word. With time and practice, though, children's decoding strategies become more automatic, freeing up mental resources for improved comprehension. Most teachers supplement phonics instruction with storybooks that facilitate reading speed and comprehension.

Children trained in phonics have one very important advantage over children trained exclusively in look-say: They can decode unfamiliar words, a skill that becomes increasingly important as children encounter the explosion of new vocabulary in third grade and beyond. Although some children trained exclusively in look-say eventually deduce the code on their own, those who do not will continue to have difficulty with new words. The relative progress of children with and without decoding skills is explored in Box 13.4.

A P P L I C A T I O N

Choosing the Best Approach to Reading

Although the controversy has raged on for many years (Chall, 1967, 1989; Turner, 1989), the consensus of research suggests that phonemic awareness and decoding skills are essential elements in the early stages of learning to read (Wagner & Torgesen, 1987).

Phonemic awareness should be stressed in children's early experiences at home, in pre-school, and especially in kindergarten. Phonics training can begin when children demonstrate phonemic awareness, typically late in the kindergarten year or early in first grade. After decoding skills are well developed, whole-word recognition can be promoted with readers and storybooks that enhance comprehension.

Reading Disability   Unfortunately, despite years of compulsory reading instruction, millions of American children complete elementary school with deficiencies in their ability to read. The study of children's reading problems has become a distinct area of theory and research in child development.

Educators have traditionally divided children's reading problems into two categories: (1) garden variety reading problems associated with a general pattern of academic under-achievement, and (2) **dyslexia**, a more specific reading disability that is independent of aptitude or intelligence (Rutter & Yule, 1975). This distinction assumes that whereas some children have difficulty reading because they are less intelligent or less motivated to learn, dyslexics have cognitive deficits specific to reading. Thus, dyslexics should have little difficulty learning subjects that call for skills other than reading—such as mathematics and some aspects of science. This view of dyslexia as a specific form of disability has had pervasive influence on funding for remedial programs and on popular conceptions of children's reading problems in the media (Stanovich, 1988).

However, recent research has shown little support for the specific diagnosis of dyslexia. First, the problems that so-called dyslexics have in school are typically *not* limited just to reading (Stanovich, 1988). They differ from other children on a wide variety of cognitive and language abilities. Second, there is evidence that the diagnosis of dyslexia is not stable over time. In one study, only 28 percent of the children identified as dyslexic in first grade still tested dyslexic in third grade, and only 17 percent by sixth grade (Shaywitz, Escobar, Shaywitz, Fletcher, & Makuch, 1992). This suggests that reading problems are temporary for most children. Thus, while early identification of children with reading problems is still recommended, the use of the term *dyslexia* may be inappropriate.

Although a specific diagnosis of dyslexia may be unproductive, this does not alter the fact that many children show significant reading difficulties beginning in first grade and that these problems are likely to persist for many years. In one longitudinal study, 88 percent of children who were poor readers in first grade continued to be poor readers through fourth grade (Juel, 1988). Since reading problems can often be identified in first grade, we will consider children's experiences before, during, and after first grade as they relate to the development of reading skill.

Children's experience in the home and day-care center in the years *before* first grade may set the stage for the development of reading problems. Some parents and caregivers use language in a highly restricted manner, making verbal demands of their children, but rarely engaging them in conversation (Bernstein, 1961). These children fail to learn appropriate listening skills and show limited growth in vocabulary. Children whose parents encourage conversation, read them stories, and promote vocabulary are better prepared for language exchange with their teachers (Juel, 1988). These experiences also promote phonemic awareness, a critical preskill for learning to read.

Other reading problems may result from extreme approaches to reading instruction *during* first grade. Some children who receive an overemphasis on phonics drill, with little attention to listening skills and comprehension, fail to progress to the more automatic processing expected by second or third grade. Teachers refer to these children as

---

BOX 13.4

Early Reading Problems: Whole-Word Readers and Decoders

Peter Freebody and Brian Byrne (1988) were interested in the relationship between children's word-reading strategies and their reading comprehension. They studied second- and third-grade children's reading strategies by asking them to read lists of irregularly spelled words, such as *laugh*, and nonsense words, such as *lemat*. They expected that children who relied on a whole-word, sight-reading strategy would perform well reading irregularly spelled words but would have difficulty with nonsense words. Conversely, decoders would do well with nonsense words but have difficulty with irregularly spelled words.

Approximately half of the children at both grades performed above average on both types of words, and about one-eighth performed poorly on both tests. As expected, some children depended primarily on sight reading, while others plodded through each word by decoding.

The researchers compared performance of the whole-word readers and the decoders by grade. Although second-grade whole-word readers showed better comprehension than decoders, the opposite was true of third graders. Why? Decoders significantly improve reading comprehension from second to third grade while whole-word readers show little improvement.

The researchers concluded that while whole-word readers may hold their own through second grade, this strategy eventually falters in the face of the rapid increase in irregularly spelled words in the third-grade vocabulary. Whole-word readers are likely to continue to experience reading problems as the introduction of irregularly spelled words accelerates. In contrast, decoders should eventually gain speed and overcome their initial disadvantage.

plodders, alluding to their struggle to sound out every letter of every word at the expense of comprehension. Conversely, children who have been taught exclusively by look-say often lack the decoding skills needed to cope with new reading vocabulary.

Finally, children's early reading problems may be exacerbated *after* first grade by **Matthew effects**—named for the biblical passage that suggests that "the rich get richer and the poor get poorer" (Stanovich, 1986, 1988). Matthew effects refer to the long-term consequences of being a good or a bad reader. Children who learn to read early "get richer" in the elementary school's fast track, where their reading speed, comprehension, and general knowledge increase rapidly. As their reading becomes more automatic, their language and cognitive skills expand even more rapidly as a direct result of new concepts acquired through reading. In marked contrast, slow readers "get poorer" in the elementary school's slow track, where they fight a losing battle with the increasing demands for reading competence in each new grade.

Matthew effects create vastly different experiences for good and poor readers. This is illustrated in estimates of the differences in good and poor readers' exposure to print: competent, motivated readers in the middle grades read as many as 10 million words a year, average readers 1 million words, and poor readers as few as a hundred thousand words a year (Nagy & Anderson, 1984).

Matthew effects also affect children's self-concepts. In one study, researchers showed that poor readers do not expect to succeed when they approach a task that requires reading (Butkowsky & Willows, 1980). Moreover, when the experimenters increased the difficulty of the reading task, poor readers persisted an average of 40 percent less of the time than good readers.

Good and poor readers also had very different perspectives on their successes and failures in reading tasks (Butkowsky & Willows, 1980). Poor readers were less likely than good readers to take credit for their successes and more likely to blame themselves for their failures. Whereas poor readers believed that they had failed because of lack of *ability*, average and good readers blamed their failures on lack of *effort*. Since effort is much easier to change than ability, good readers are more likely to believe that they can overcome their failure by increasing effort and persistence. Thus, it may be that the rich get richer because they believe in themselves, and the poor get poorer because they feel helpless and hopeless in tasks that require reading.

A P P L I C A T I O N

The Importance of Early Identification

Research highlights the importance of identifying reading difficulties as early as possible in development, before Matthew effects add significantly to the problem. Thus, while interventions in the early elementary grades may focus exclusively on improving phonemic awareness and decoding skills (Stanovich, 1988), intervention in later grades must be designed to deal not only with problems of decoding and comprehension, but with children's self-doubt and helplessness brought on by years of low achievement and failure.

Learning Mathematics

While some American elementary schoolchildren achieve great competency in mathematics and are well prepared to move on to the study of algebra and geometry in high school, others—in increasing numbers—leave sixth grade overwhelmed by simple procedures such as multiplication and division. This will prove to be a lifelong disability for many individuals, severely limiting their access to higher education and opportunities for employment. As with reading, the first grades of elementary school provide a critical, one-time opportunity to learn the fundamentals of these essential skills. We will examine the normal progression of learning mathematics in the elementary school and why so many children — particularly girls — find this important subject so difficult to master.

By the time they enter kindergarten, most children have mastered the fundamentals of counting, including both the ability to accurately recite numbers in correct sequence and to count objects by systematically assigning number names. However, their assignment of numbers to objects may be somewhat unique (Gelman & Gallistel, 1978). For example, a five-year-old may count "one, two, three, five, twelveteen, fourteen," repeating this exact sequence of number names in all situations that call for counting. Children rapidly improve their counting during the kindergarten year, stimulated by the kindergarten curriculum, TV programs such as "Sesame Street," and the family's active encouragement of number concepts. These experiences are particularly effective if they stimulate extensive counting practice in children's play (Resnick, 1989).

Kindergarten children also develop intuitive notions of quantity: They can make rough comparisons of the absolute size or amount of objects or substances; they sense increasing or decreasing quantities and show some awareness of part-whole relationships (Resnick, 1989). However, these intuitions work best when they are supported by highly salient perceptual cues. For example, children are able to accurately compare quantities when substances are displayed in identically shaped containers, and they interpret part-whole relationships better with familiar objects (such as the slices of a birthday cake) than with abstract figures (such as triangles and squares).

As children's counting skills and quantitative reasoning improve, they gradually learn to integrate these abilities so they can compare relative quantity and estimate increasing and decreasing quantities more precisely. For example, first graders begin to use increasingly precise comparative terms, such as "more than," "a little bit more than," and "a lot more than." At some point children come to understand that even greater precision can be achieved by assigning numbers rather than adjectives to specify quantities and by using counting procedures to express changes in quantity. These emerging abilities accumulate in children learning to add and subtract in first and second grade.

Learning To Add and Subtract   The first challenge for first graders is learning to solve simple addition problems where one single-digit number (or addend) is added to a second number, as in 3 + 5 = ?. Some kindergarten and most first-grade children spontaneously discover the **counting-all** strategy (Fuson & Secada, 1986; Nesher, 1986). In counting-all, children use physical objects — such as pegs or small cubes — to stand for each of the addends in a simple addition problem. They begin by counting out objects to represent each of the addends. They then combine the two sets of objects into one set and *re*count all of the items to derive the total sum. Counting-all is an accurate but rather inefficient strategy, particularly when applied to bigger numbers, such as 15 + 17 = ?.

By second grade, many children discover **counting-on**, a more advanced addition strategy that eliminates the need to recount everything. They *begin* counting-on by saying the number of the first addend out loud, then counting from that number through the numbers of the second addend. They keep track of the count by raising one finger for each number named while counting through the second addend. For example, in the 3 + 5 = ? problem, a child would begin by saying "three" (pause), then "four, five, six, seven, eight" while successively raising each of five fingers. When the fifth finger is

Although some adults think of counting on one's fingers as ineffectual, this strategy plays a critical role in children's learning to add and subtract. Here, one child helps another child learn the min strategy.

raised, the procedure is complete, and the last number named ("eight") is the final sum. Children eventually learn to save more time by the **min** strategy—that is, by always beginning counting-on with the larger of the two addends. In our problem the child would say "five" (rather than "three"), then count "six, seven, eight." The efficiency of min is even more obvious when the addends are very different in size, as in $17 + 3 = ?$.

By fourth grade, most children learn that counting-on can be adapted to subtraction, by counting-*up* from the smaller number or by counting-*down* to the smaller number (Resnick, 1989). For example, a child could solve $7 - 2 = ?$ either by counting-down, "seven, (pause), six, five," or counting-*up* "two, (pause), three, four, five, six, seven," raising one finger for each number named to give the difference of five.

Karen Fuson and Walter Secada (1986; Secada, Fuson, & Hall, 1983) wanted to try speeding up this gradual process. They observed that not all children learn counting-on strategies spontaneously and that even those who do learn them typically take several years to master them in addition and subtraction. Why not give all children an advantage by systematically teaching counting-on in the early elementary grades? They adapted a one-handed technique to help first and second graders keep track of their counting. The training was highly successful. First and second graders easily learned to add and subtract by counting-on, even without objects present. Many children learned to extend the strategy to add 10-digit numbers. The researchers concluded that counting-on strategies could be used to teach addition and subtraction problems from one to four years earlier than is typical in U.S. classrooms.

The slow and effortful process of adding and subtracting by counting-on gradually gives way to more automatic, efficient strategies. After two to three years of practice and drill, most children have memorized all possible sums and differences among the single-digit numbers. With these sums and differences available as *facts*, children are able to add and subtract rapidly by **fact retrieval**, recalling facts such as $2 + 6 = 8$, or $9 - 3 = 6$ from memory (Ashcraft, 1982, 1990). By fourth or fifth grade, most children solve simple addition and subtraction problems automatically, freeing them to devote their mental capacity to more complex aspects of mathematical problems (Ashcraft & Fierman, 1982).

Mathematics Disability As in learning to read, learning mathematics is difficult for millions of American children. Severe disability in learning mathematics is often referred to as **dyscalcula**. As with the diagnosis of dyslexia, there is little evidence that children's problems in learning mathematics should be attributed to a specific form of cognitive dysfunction. Rather, children's risk of experiencing difficulties in math derives from several overlapping factors: psychological factors within the child, the school's approach to instruction, and family influences.

One important psychological factor is **math anxiety**, an extreme lack of confidence in one's ability to learn and to perform mathematics (Resnick, 1989). Research has indicated that children show increasing math anxiety as they get older, with predictable effects on their self-perception and achievement in math (Meece, Wigfield, & Eccles, 1990; Wigfield & Meece, 1988) . In one study, middle-school children who were anxious about math perceived themselves as less competent and expected to perform less well in math (Meece et al., 1990). However, the children's math anxiety by itself did not predict poor achievement in math. Only those children who felt anxious *and* perceived themselves as less competent were likely to earn poor math grades.

Math anxiety may be more of a problem for girls than for boys (LeFevre & Kulak, 1991; Wigfield & Meece, 1988). This difference reflects a widely held but largely unfounded belief in Western society that boys are naturally more capable in math than girls. Although there is no proven basis for male superiority in math, this belief may be self-fulfilling. One study showed that mothers believe that their sons are more likely to succeed in math than their daughters, and that mothers do more to promote math skills in their sons (Entwisle & Alexander, 1990). Not surprisingly, boys in this study had higher expectations for success in math than girls.

Many educators believe that the schools' approach to math instruction may be a major part of the problem for many children. American schools tend to place a heavy emphasis on teaching and drilling children in methods of calculation, with little emphasis on math concepts and reasoning (Resnick, 1989). With little understanding of underlying principles, children fail to discern the sources of their errors and persist in their inappropriate use of formulas despite corrective feedback from teachers. Schools also fail to teach the special language skills that upper elementary children need in order to understand and solve mathematical problems expressed verbally (Noonan, 1990). For example, common words with special mathematical meanings, such as *product*, *mean*, and *dividend* (not to mention mathematical symbols, such as $>$, $=$, and x), can be quite confusing to young children. Children also need special training in the unique syntax of verbally expressed problems, such as, "Is three plus four equal to or greater than five times two?"

A P P L I C A T I O N

Preventing Math Anxiety and Failure

Parents should be aware that their children — particularly their daughters — are at risk for negative attitudes toward math learning that are likely to affect their achievement. Some of the problems begin at home. If you are anxious about math, you are likely to transfer that anxiety to your daughter. If you believe females are less capable of learning math than males, your daughters are likely to absorb your expectations.

You can prevent problems by following these simple recommendations:

- Most important, believe in your child's ability to achieve competency in math. If you can express this belief in a credible manner, the belief may be self-fulfilling.

- Expose your child to *age-appropriate* mathematical terms and ideas early in the preschool years. Encourage counting through games, toys, and TV shows such as "Sesame Street." Engage your child in everyday activities that require quantitative reasoning—such as measuring during sewing, cooking, or carpentry.

- Show your child that numbers can be fun. Be enthusiastic and reinforce yourself when solving numerical problems. Displays of anger and frustration while doing your taxes or balancing your checkbook give the wrong message.

- Avoid drill and flashcards that teach facts that are meaningless to young children. Emphasize your child's understanding of concepts rather than dwelling on right answers.

- Talk to your child's teachers and elicit their biases about teaching math before the school year begins. A teacher who does not like teaching math, or one who has inappropriate expectations for *your* child's ability to learn math, puts your child at risk. Don't waste your time trying to change the teacher; request a new placement for your child.

Schooling the Intellectually Gifted and Talented

When Leshonda is in second grade, her parents are notified by school authorities that Leshonda has qualified for the gifted program and that she is expected to begin the program in third grade. Marcus and Keisha's initial delight at the news is moderated when they realize that they know nothing about giftedness. What does it mean to be gifted? How does the school know that Leshonda has a gift? What do children do in a gifted class, and is it really all that good for them? After all, Marcus does not want Leshonda to be pressured and turned off to school. Keisha wonders what effect the change will have on Leshonda's social relationships. Will she have to make new friends? Will her former friends reject her?

What does it mean to be gifted? While educators and psychologists agree that gifted children have an advantage in learning and problem solving compared to other children, they disagree on the precise nature of that advantage (Reis, 1989). One major source of debate has been whether **giftedness** is a general advantage in all aspects of a child's life or a more specific ability or talent in a particular area such as music, mathematics, or science.

Robert Sternberg and Janet Davidson (1985) viewed giftedness as a general ability to process information. They argued that giftedness involves making highly effective use of the components of one's information processing system: recognizing problems, perceiving relationships, selecting relevant information, and enacting strategies. Gifted children integrate these components more effectively than other children. They frequently show *insight* as they solve problems, deriving novel understandings and solutions (Davidson, 1986). Leshonda often finds unique solutions to everyday problems. For example, during a test in third grade, she is distracted by a classmate's persistent coughing. She reaches into her lunchbag, removes a slice of bread from her sandwich, kneads the bread into two small balls, and inserts one in each ear, effectively reducing the distracting sound. This creative adaptation to real life problems is a key feature of gifted children's thinking (Sternberg, 1986).

Howard Gardner (1983) rejected the notion of giftedness as a general ability. He suggested that giftedness and talent develop in distinct domains, each with its own specific form of intelligence. Development across domains tends to be uneven—for example, a child may be gifted in science but considerably less skilled in mathematics or interpersonal relationships. Gardner suggested that developing intelligence or talent in a particular domain requires *crystallized experiences*—special events that bring out latent abilities early in development. For example, parents who expose their young child to physical challenges may inspire interest and skill in athletics. Without such experiences, the child's potential would be sacrificed.

How do we identify gifted children? Identification of the gifted and talented remains "a relatively inexact science" (Feldhusen, 1989, p. 7). Most school systems use achievement tests and IQ scores of 130 or higher as criteria for selection (Horowitz & O'Brien, 1986). However, some educators argue that while IQ tests measure some aspects of information processing, they do not assess creative abilities or special talents. IQ test scores also fail to correlate with children's out-of-school achievements, such as sports and personal relationships (Wallach, 1985), and they may be biased against minorities (Baldwin, 1985). Despite the limitations, most school systems continue to use IQ scores as a major consideration in placement. This approach virtually eliminates special education opportunities for talented children of average intelligence and for many gifted minority children.

What is the best way to educate gifted and talented children? Educators have tried two different approaches, both of which emphasize intellectual development (Horowitz & O'Brien, 1986). In the *enrichment approach*, classroom teachers try to broaden the gifted children's learning with more challenging experiences than are provided to other children, but the gifted children remain at the grade level consistent with their chronological age. These enrichment experiences can be provided by the regular classroom teacher or by special education teachers in learning centers. Some schools segregate gifted children into special classes, completely isolating them from nongifted children. While gifted children in special classes achieve at a higher rate than gifted children in regular classes, they may develop less satisfactory social relationships (Goldring, 1990).

In the *acceleration approach*, gifted children are either grouped together is a special accelerated learning track—for example, completing three school years in two chronological years—or are "skipped" to a more advanced grade to study with older, nongifted children. Although some parents express concern that skipping places children at a social disadvantage with older classmates, research has shown that accelerated children exhibit equal social adjustment and better academic achievement than children who are not accelerated (Brody & Benbow, 1987; Janos & Robinson, 1985). Unfortunately, there are no studies that compare the effects of the enrichment and acceleration approaches over time. In the absence of definitive research on selection criteria and appropriate curriculum for gifted children, local schools often base program decisions more on practical considerations (such as budget and space limitations) than on what is best for the children.

Should Keisha and Marcus accept the school's offer to place Leshonda in a gifted program? After conferring with school personnel, they decide that the opportunities seem to outweigh the risks for their daughter. Leshonda will remain in her grade level and leave her regular class for three hours a day. The teacher of the gifted class is well trained and the small class size ensures individual attention. While Leshonda will profit from this limited experience, we can only speculate on how much more her school could do to bring out her intellectual potential and special talents.

Looking Back

We began this chapter by contrasting the Piagetian and information processing views of cognitive development in middle childhood. Although these views involve very different concepts and principles, both help us visualize and appreciate children's enormous potential for cognitive development during this period of growth. Under optimal conditions, children become masters of their concrete experience, far more knowledgeable, strategic and aware of their own cognitive abilities than they were as preschoolers. Cognitively advanced sixth graders will think very much like average adults with respect to their everyday experiences.

We have also described selected aspects of the relationship between elementary schooling and children's cognitive development. Under the best of conditions, schooling provides excellent opportunities for cognitive development. The "best of conditions" requires that children enter first grade cognitively, emotionally, and socially prepared for the curriculum that teachers are prepared to teach. Supportive parents and good schools add to the prospects of children's success.

Children who are well prepared for school enter the school's fast track and typically advance through the six grades with few difficulties. They learn to read and write and to solve word problems, and they graduate from elementary school with the skills required for successful achievement in middle or junior high school. Gifted and talented children are given special attention that maximizes their potential.

In stark contrast, those who enter first grade unprepared for the beginning instruction in reading and math proceed at great risk. These children learn, but less efficiently and effectively than other children. They tend to fail with ever-increasing frequency with each passing grade. They eventually come to think of themselves as failures. Their potential for cognitive development is sacrificed in classrooms that are unprepared for children who are unprepared to learn. It is difficult to understand how we can know so much about cognitive development in middle childhood and the kind of schooling that promotes it and yet be so ineffective in ensuring optimal cognitive development of so many children in our society.

CHAPTER REVIEW

THE 5-TO-7 SHIFT Between ages five and seven children go through a gradual transition from the illogical reasoning of the preoperational period to the more logical and systematic reasoning of concrete operations. During the shift, children think intuitively, solving conservation problems inconsistently and without being able to explain their reasoning.

CONCRETE OPERATIONS Concrete operational thought is an advanced form of thinking that enables children to think simultaneously about an action and its reverse. With reversible thought children can mentally cancel out any action. It enables children to overcome their egocentrism. They conserve mass, number, and length by age 7 to 8, weight by age 10, and volume by age 11, and they are

able to classify objects by the rule of class inclusion.

INFORMATION PROCESSING The information processing view of cognitive development assumes that each individual has limited capacity for processing information—a finite pool of mental resources that can be allocated to thought processes. Total capacity is constant throughout development. More effortful mental activities drain capacity; more automatic processes free up mental resources for other activities. Mental operations become less effortful and more automatic as a result of experience, practice, and neurological maturation.

STRATEGIES Strategies are goal-directed mental devices that individuals use to de-

liberately facilitate memory, attention, and problem solving. Three strategies account for the rapid increase in memory function during middle childhood: rehearsal, organization, and elaboration. Children use rehearsal to repeat the content to be remembered over and over; they use organization to identify conceptual relationships among items to be remembered; and they use elaboration to create associations among items.

MEMORY DEFICIENCIES Children must overcome three types of deficiencies that limit their ability to make optimal use of memory strategies: mediational deficiencies, production deficiencies, and utilization deficiencies. Mediational deficiency refers to having no strategies; production deficiency refers to not using strategies that one is capable of using; and utilization deficiency refers to using strategies without improvements in performance.

BECOMING EXPERT During middle childhood many children develop expertise in areas of their own special interest. Expertise requires an *elaborated knowledge base*, which operates like a cross-referenced computer file, saving great effort in storing and retrieving information. Children with an elaborated knowledge base do not just know more, they think better. However, the advantage is limited to their domain of expertise.

BECOMING METACOGNITIVE As children become more strategic in their thinking, they also become more metacognitive, that is, more aware and in control of their own cognitive abilities. It includes knowing what you know, knowing what you do not know, and knowing what to do with what you know to solve problems. Metacognition includes the ability to self-appraise what you know and the ability to self-manage your mental strategies to solve problems. Metacognitive abilities improve dramatically during middle childhood.

GOOD SCHOOLING Experts agree that good schools require strong leadership from the principal, an orderly atmosphere, clear lines of authority, active teachers with high expectations for the learning of *all* children, and consistent monitoring of children's performance.

SCHOOLING MINORITIES Children from low-income minority families tend to do less well in elementary school than other children. Research has shown that they are cognitively, emotionally, and socially less ready for the challenges of first grade. Low-income minority families' distrust of the schools may also be an important factor.

PARENTS AND SCHOOLING More educated parents tend to be more informed about their children's school experience, interact more with teachers, and make more effort to manage their children's ac-

ademic performance. Their children respond by achieving at higher levels than other children.

CULTURAL INFLUENCES ON SCHOOLING Different cultural groups maintain different beliefs about schooling and different goals for their children. While American-born parents tend to emphasize cognitive goals for their children, other groups take a broader view that emphasizes social goals at least as strongly as cognitive goals. The narrow emphasis of Anglo-American parents is associated with higher levels of achievement compared to children from other cultures.

MOTIVATION TO LEARN AND ACHIEVE Children who are spontaneously involved in learning show intrinsic motivation—an urge to learn and achieve that comes from within. Children with little spontaneous interest in learning show extrinsic motivation when they participate in school activities. Rewarding children merely for participating in a task or for completing a task undermines intrinsic motivation. However, rewarding children for competent performance enhances intrinsic motivation.

LEARNING TO READ Children have been traditionally taught to read by either the look-say method or by phonics. In look-say, children memorize whole words as pictures. In phonics, children learn to decode printed letters as a code. Phonics instruction is based on becoming aware of the sounds (phonemes) that make up words and learning the alphabet as a code for the sounds of the language.

READING DISABILITY Educators have traditionally divided children with reading problems into two categories: underachievers and *dyslexics*—children with cognitive deficits specific to reading. Although there remains some controversy, research has not supported a separate diagnosis of dyslexia. Children with reading problems also have problems in other areas of learning, and reading disability is not stable over time. Language deficien-

cies, rigid approaches to reading instruction, and Matthew effects all contribute to children's reading disabilities.

LEARNING MATHEMATICS Kindergarten children's intuitive notions of quantity and their ability to count establishes a foundation for learning to add and subtract in the early elementary grades. Learning to add typically begins with the counting-all strategy, followed by the more efficient counting-on and min strategies. Children learn to subtract by counting-down or counting-up. The slow and effortful use of counting for adding and subtracting gradually gives way to more automatic fact retrieval strategies for addition and subtraction.

MATHEMATICS DISABILITY Like dyslexia, children's problems in math (dyscalcula) are not associated with a specific form of cognitive dysfunction. Many children's problems seem to come from math anxiety—an extreme lack of confidence in one's ability to learn math. Girls seem to be more susceptible than boys, most likely a result of the unfounded belief that boys are naturally more adept at learning math than girls. Schools also contribute to the problem by emphasizing drill in calculation rather than teaching math concepts and reasoning.

SCHOOLING THE GIFTED AND TALENTED A small percentage of children have an intellectual advantage or special talent that distinguishes them from other children. Special education programs for gifted and talented children provide enrichment experiences or accelerated academic schedules. These efforts have been successful, but the school's selection criteria and curriculum remain problematic.

Key Terms

5-to-7 shift
intuitive
concrete operation
reversibility
decenter
class inclusion
moral reasoning
superego
amoral
moral realism
immanent justice
autonomous moral reasoning
preconventional moral reasoning
conventional moral reasoning
postconventional moral reasoning

limited capacity
strategies
rehearsal
organization
elaboration
mediational deficiency
production deficiency
utilization deficiency
elaborated knowledge base
metacognition
schooling
intrinsic motivation
extrinsic motivation
Type A behaviors
look-say

whole-word
phonics
decoding
comprehension
phonemic awareness
dyslexia
Matthew effects
counting-all
counting-on
min
fact retrieval
dyscalcula
math anxiety
giftedness

14

Social and Emotional Development in Middle Childhood

Looking Ahead

- In middle childhood, children become increasingly selective about what they look for in a friend. What specific personality traits are important to children of different ages?

- Children spend a great deal of time gossiping about their peers, comparing their physical features, and psychological attributes. What purpose does gossip serve in children's social lives?

- Over time, each child in a peer group earns a reputation among his or her peers. How does peer reputation affect a child's social adjustment?

- The interaction among school-age friends often gets highly emotional. How do children learn to manage their emotions in these intimate relationships?

- Children vary considerably in how much they are liked and disliked by their peers. Do children in various status groups differ in their behavior and

social adjustment? Do they earn their status by behaving in certain ways?

- During middle childhood children learn to process social information to solve increasingly complex social problems. How does a child process a social problem?

- Aggressive children tend to walk around with a chip on their shoulders, fighting with peers at the slightest provocation. Why do they do this and what effects does it have on their social acceptance among peers?

- While some children who are rejected by their peers suffer from feelings of loneliness, others do not. Why are some children more susceptible to loneliness than others?

- Neglected and rejected children live every day with little or no positive interaction with their peers. What are the short- and long-term effects of peer rejection?

- As children improve their social cognitive ability, they better understand the effects of their behaviors on their peers. Why do some children seem more masterful and others more helpless in controlling their social outcomes?

- School-age children are much more likely than younger children to help their peers. How do we account for these advances in prosocial behavior?

- More than half of the children born in the 1990s will see their parents divorce and remarry during their childhood or adolescent years. Why do some children cope better than others with these family transitions?

- Changes in the American family since the 1950s have dramatically increased the numbers of mothers who work outside the home. How does a mother's employment affect her child's development?

W e have seen in previous chapters how the social world of the child expands gradually from infancy through the preschool years. Infants relate intimately only with their parents or selected caregivers, with peers serving as little more than interesting playthings. Although peers become progressively more important as playmates during the preschool years, parents remain the center of their preschoolers' social and emotional lives. In middle childhood, children's social world expands significantly as friends become more and more important sources of stimulation and social support. We see in this chapter that school-age children need more and demand more from their relationships with peers; they learn to think and to behave to promote those relationships. We also see that children who fail to learn or to apply the required social skills are bypassed or discarded as their peers search for more intimate relationships that meet their increasingly complex social and emotional needs.

Leshonda and Heather at age nine have each formed friendships that meet their emotional needs, each in her own distinctive way.

Leshonda and Makesha have been best friends for nearly six months, since the beginning of the fourth grade. Makesha had just moved to Leshonda's neighborhood and knew no one at the school. Leshonda had noticed some things about the new girl that she liked: Makesha's meticulously braided hair, her poise walking through the madness of the morning schoolyard, and the faint smile she gave Leshonda when their eyes met.

On Friday of the first week of school, Leshonda watched as several girls picked a fight with Makesha. At first, Makesha tried to be cool, but when they began hitting her, she could defend herself only by falling to the ground and covering her head. Leshonda ran over and jumped into the circle, threatening the girl who led the attack. Leshonda's intensity surprised the attackers and they backed off. Makesha jumped up and ran to her classroom without looking back. Leshonda and Makesha met later in the lunchroom, and, without a word being said, both girls knew a friendship had begun.

From that day on, Makesha and Leshonda are inseparable in and out of school. It is not just that they enjoy playing together—something each girl experiences with other children—they enjoy simply being together, even when they are not interacting directly. Just being in the same classroom is satisfying. Their friendship makes each girl stronger, more secure, more confident, and more resilient. They share secrets and are completely loyal to one another. If one girl is invited to a party and the other is not, neither girl goes. When one of them is punished or rewarded, the other feels pain or pride. Although they occasionally disagree, they resolve their differences with little difficulty or lingering resentment.

The friendship between Heather and Amanda emerges quite slowly over several months. Both have been persistently rejected by their peers and share the resulting desperation and loneliness. Heather—feisty, aggressive, and hyperactive—intimidates virtually all of her peers. Even those children who like her avoid deeper friendship because she is so unpredictable and impulsive. Associating with Heather also means joining her in annoying the teacher and other children—and suffering the inevitable retribution.

Amanda, on the other hand, is completely nonaggressive but just as actively rejected by her peers as Heather. Amanda has no social skills. When she tries to join other children at play, she just stands mute and motionless in the midst of their ongoing play. At some point her nonfunctional presence becomes annoying to the other children, and they ridicule and yell at her until she leaves. Although she tries less and less often to join other children's play, she still manages to get actively rejected each day.

One day Heather picks up Amanda like a stray. It begins with Heather demanding that her classmates clean up a mess she has made. Amanda, knowing no better and grateful for the attention, is the only one to comply. Heather soon discovers that Amanda will put up with just about anything, just for the privilege of having someone to hang out with. Both seem fulfilled by the relationship, although Heather's rapid tempo constantly strains Amanda.

Like other friends, Heather and Amanda share secrets, and they are loyal to one another. But unlike other friends, the girls share very little emotionally, other than mutual silliness and the occasional angry outbursts Heather directs at Amanda. Although their friendship does not seem to make either child happy, it does fend off the loneliness that both children have experienced for as long as they can remember. The girls would probably not say that they like each other: They need each other and complement each other, no more and no less.

Although Leshonda's and Heather's friendships appear to be very different in many ways, both serve critical purposes in the rapidly expanding social world of the school-age child.

Friendship in Middle Childhood

During the *preschool* years, the young child's pool of potential friends is typically limited to siblings, children who live next door, preschool or day-care classmates, or the children of family friends and relatives. Although play partners may be limited at this age, exclusive relationships begin to emerge between children who prefer each other's company, play well together, and are reasonably good at resolving conflicts. While these relationships have an emotional component (that is, friends like each other more than they like nonfriends), preschool children continue to rely on their parents to meet their most important emotional needs. When a preschooler is injured or frightened, she is much more likely to seek comfort from her parent than from her best friend. But all of this is about to change.

In *middle childhood*, children's growing independence from their parents, their increasing mobility in their neighborhoods, and broader exposure to children at school greatly expand their pool of potential friends. Paradoxically, as the pool expands, children become increasingly selective, choosing their friends more and more on the basis of those children's personality characteristics that are likely to fulfill their emotional needs. This new emphasis on personality is apparent in the following conversation between Leshonda and Makesha as they consider who should be invited to Makesha's birthday party.

MAKESHA:　I was gonna invite Denise, but she's too uppity when she's with those girls from her street. That girl can be *mean* when she don't like what you do.

LESHONDA: I know, but she ain't like that when she's by herself. Maybe she would be allright.

MAKESHA: No. I better not. She's gonna come and be bossy and tell everybody what to do. I don't need to deal with that!

LESHONDA: Yeah. I guess you're right. We don't need to deal with her. We just want to hang with girls who do stuff like us. You know, nice girls like Dinetta, Carmen, and Shauna.

School-age children choose friends on the basis of personality characteristics, but the traits they value change over time. Children in the early grades select friends on the basis of self-serving needs: Who is a good, reliable play partner? Who is willing to share resources, such as toys and video games? (Bigelow & LaGaipa, 1975). By third or fourth grade, however, children begin to seek friends they can relate to more intimately and exclusively, emphasizing loyalty, common interests, attitudes, and values. Harry Stack Sullivan (1953), a renowned psychiatrist and keen observer of children, referred to this advanced form of friendship as *chumship*. Chums are sensitive to each other's needs and show concern about each other's well-being. They genuinely care about one another as individuals, they share secrets and resources, and they expect loyalty in good times and in bad. Leshonda and Makesha are chums, even though they would be unlikely to use that term.

School-age children select friends who share their race, age, social class, and social status (Clark & Drewry, 1985; Ramsey & Myers, 1990; Singleton & Asher, 1977). They almost always choose friends of the same sex, but boys and girls use different criteria: While boys tend to emphasize similarity in superficial behaviors, such as interest in comic books or sports, girls focus more on similarity in personality traits, such as kindness or friendliness (Erwin, 1985). Choosing friends on the basis of similarity lessens in importance toward the end of the elementary school years as children show increasing attraction to peers who complement rather than match their skills and interests (Clark & Drewry, 1985; Erwin, 1985). For example, a streetwise but physically weak fifth grader might befriend a stronger but less savvy child to improve his chances of survival on the streets. Heather's domination of Amanda provides another example of children who complement rather than match each other's characteristics.

Making Friends

Cultivating the more intimate, reciprocal, and exclusive friendships of middle childhood requires far more sophisticated social skills and social cognitive abilities than were needed in early childhood. Moreover, children must apply their social skills continually if friendships are to be maintained over time: Children use these skills to identify peers who are likely candidates for friendship, to initiate social contacts with them, and to be a good friend themselves. We will examine two important factors that begin to have significant impact on making friends during this period: *social comparison* and *peer reputation*.

Social Comparison and Friendship An important social cognitive skill is **social comparison**—the ability to describe, rate, and rank peers on various traits and attributes. School-age children spend extraordinary amounts of social time comparing their peers, using increasingly complex trait descriptions as they get older (Rogosch & Newcomb, 1989). While young children focus on observable features in their ratings and rankings, such as peers' physical appearance, older children emphasize more abstract qualities, such as peers' likes and dislikes, thoughts, and feelings (Diaz & Berndt, 1982).

Children's social comparisons affect the way they interact with peers and make friends in several important ways. First, individual children mentally compare and

Elementary school children make increasingly sophisticated use of gossip to vilify, sanctify, and modify the behavior of their peers. These two girls show the personal and private nature of the contents of gossip. What we do not see are the powerful effects such exchanges have on the lives of the children who are targets of these discussions.

evaluate their peers on dimensions relevant to their needs and motivations in everyday work and play, and they use these rankings to guide their social behavior. For example, a child searching for a partner for a skilled activity (such as playing ball) is likely to choose someone whose skills compare well with those of other children. Children also use social comparison to refine their perceptions of their own competencies, again with significant impact on their social behavior (Harter, 1983). For example, a child who thinks of herself as socially competent, compared to her peers, is likely to be more assertive and confident in her social initiatives.

Children seek validation of their social comparisons by sharing their perceptions and opinions of their peers with children they trust. School-age children, particularly those in the upper grades, exchange social comparisons through the medium of **gossip**, the informal sharing of information and opinion on peers' strengths and shortcomings. Gossip, by its nature, is a synthesis of truths and untruths, elaborated and distorted by the emotions and biases of the participating children. Regardless of the accuracy of its content, gossip can have powerful effects on children's peer relationships, particularly in the extensive social interaction within and across grades in the elementary school.

Friends use gossip to confirm and elaborate the basis of their relationship (Parker & Gottman, 1989). Gossiping about others enables friends to probe each other's values, interests, and feelings without risking rejection. For example, in the following conversation, two nine-year-olds gossip to establish common ground for friendship, without having to disclose information about themselves:

MELISSA: I hate Leshonda. She thinks she is better than anybody in the whole school.

SHARONDA: Yeah! She really is a showoff. She wears those tight clothes just to show off, but she has nothin' to show, if you ask me.

MELISSA: I know what you mean, girl. Her clothes make her look like a boy—an *uuuu*gly boy if you ask me. (*Both girls laugh loudly and share a high five.*)

SHARONDA: What are you going to wear to school tomorrow?

MELISSA: I don't know yet, but I'll call you later so we can talk about it. Maybe we can both wear some tight clothes and show off like Leshonda! (*Both girls again laugh hysterically.*)

Note that by gossiping about a third party, Melissa and Sharonda confirm their common values without disclosing much information about themselves. Once common ground is established—in this case, their mutual dislike of Leshonda—Sharonda ventures a more personal question that redirects the conversation to their own relationship. Melissa, in turn, reciprocates by suggesting that they might match what they will wear the next day. This suggestion has important symbolic value, in that matching clothing will create a salient public display of their emerging friendship. If their friendship continues to evolve, the girls will eventually mix gossip and self-disclosure in the safe haven of their mutual trust.

Peer Reputation and Friendship   As children exchange and elaborate gossip about their peers, their comments about each child eventually crystallize into **peer reputation**, the relatively stable characterization of a child shared by members of the peer group. As with adults, children's reputations tend to precede them in social settings, with powerful effects on their acceptance/rejection among their peers (Rogosch & Newcomb, 1989). Thus, reputation—whether deserved or not—can make or break a child in the pursuit of friends and social acceptance.

Children gradually learn that they can influence their own reputation by controlling the impression they make on other children (Aloise, 1991; Fine, 1981). For example, children may improve their reputation (and social acceptance) by dressing and grooming themselves as their peers do. They also learn to emphasize particular attributes that they believe would be attractive to others. For example, a boy who wants to make friends with an athletic peer may create opportunities to show off his own skills in the presence of that individual. Children can also reverse a negative reputation by consistently behaving in ways incompatible with their reputation, for example, by sharing with others to counter a reputation of being selfish. However, once reputations have been firmly established in a given peer group, particularly in groups of older children, they are highly resistant to change.

Keeping Friends

After initiating friendships, children must apply additional social skills to consolidate and maintain their new relationships. An important skill is learning to manage one's emotions in the context of increasingly intimate and reciprocal relationships (Parker & Gottman, 1989). Managing emotions takes many forms. Children must learn to inhibit powerful emotional outbursts that can overwhelm and intimidate other children, particularly when friendships are just getting off the ground. Children must also become sensitive to their friends' changing emotions and learn to respond accordingly (McGuire & Weisz, 1982). For example, a friend's sadness or despair creates an opportunity for a child to improve the relationship by showing empathy and providing emotional support. Both in-school and out-of-school friends begin to play a key role in providing emotional support to one another in times of stress, such as illness or family crisis (Berndt & Perry, 1986; East & Rook, 1992).

Another important challenge children face is learning to attune or to match their emotions and the tempo of their behavior to that of their friends (Field et al., 1992). For example, when a child comes to a friend's house in an excited and energetic mood, but finds the friend tired and inactive, the friends are challenged to attune their emotions and behavior to facilitate their interaction. Attunement would require the more energetic friend to chill out and the inactive friend to pump up. Friends who are unable to consistently attune their emotions and behavior will experience frequent conflict that may ultimately threaten the relationship. Friends must also learn to avoid persistent nagging or complaining that may annoy their partner (Parker & Gottman, 1989). For example, a child who chronically complains about losing in competitive games may place an emerging friendship at risk. As children often say, "No one wants to play with a sore loser."

A P P L I C A T I O N

Facilitating Friendships in Middle Childhood

*T*he school-age child's expanding social arena can be frustrating to parents. Whereas during the preschool years parents could screen their children's potential play partners and monitor their social play, school-age children have social contacts in the elementary school and in the neighborhood streets that are well beyond parents' direct influence. However, parents can extend their influence on their children's social development well into middle childhood and beyond by assuming the role of social consultant and confidante.

- Pairs of school-age friends will seek increasing amounts of privacy together and will be less and less receptive to your efforts to structure their activities. They thrive on secrets, gossip, humor, and loyalties, most of which cannot be shared comfortably in your presence. They will be more likely to spend time in your home if they have their space. Avoid snooping! Simply having your child and her friends in your home from time to time will keep you reasonably aware of her activities and make her more likely to consult you when problems arise.

- Your child will come to you for advice about some aspects of her friendships, but not

about others. You must adjust to knowing less and less about things that are more and more important in your child's social life. Consider yourself informed if you know enough to be useful when your child does seek your advice.

- *Listen* when your child spontaneously talks about her interactions with her friends and other children in her social network. Remember the names of children she mentions and her impressions of those children. This information can help you be insightful when she shares her experiences or seeks advice.

- When your child seeks consultation, suggest *age-appropriate* strategies for solving social problems, rather than pat solutions adults use. Encourage your child to think about her social problems and challenges and to anticipate possible consequences of various alternatives. Above all, avoid lecturing or moralizing, and maintain confidentiality. You won't be a consultant for long if everyone in the family is privy to your child's private disclosures.

Bottom Line: Being a good social consultant to your child requires more listening than lecturing, more empathy than sympathy, and more insight than hindsight.

Social Status and Behavior

As indicated earlier, the term *friendship* implies that two (or more) children have mutually chosen each other as preferred play partners. But as important as friendship is to social adjustment, having or not having a friend does not tell us whether a child is *generally* liked or disliked by his or her peers (Bukowski & Hoza, 1989). For example, consider two children with contrasting peer relationships: one who has one close friend but is actively disliked by all of her other classmates, and a second child who has no close friends but is liked by many of her peers. Which child would be at greater risk of social maladjustment? Are children who are actively rejected at greater risk than children who are simply neglected by their peers?

Developmentalists have attempted to answer such questions by studying *social status* differences among children that reflect the degree to which they are liked and disliked by their peers. In a typical elementary school classroom, most children are liked (or socially accepted) by at least *some* of their peers, and a small percentage of children are liked by *many* of their peers; however, a few children are liked by *none* of their peers. Moreover, some children are not just not liked — they are actively *disliked* by their peers, purposely avoided as play or work partners, and frequently subjected to various forms of degradation, including teasing, taunting, and scapegoating.

Researchers have developed schemes for classifying children into social status categories based on how much they are liked and disliked by their peers (Bukowski & Hoza, 1989; Coie et al., 1982). The researchers interviewed children and asked them to name classmates whom they like and dislike. The researchers summarized the children's ratings and classified them into the following categories: **popular children**, who are liked by most of their peers and disliked by no one; **rejected children**, who are disliked by most peers and liked by very few; **neglected children**, who are neither actively liked nor disliked by anyone; **controversial children**, who are liked by many of their peers *and* disliked by many others; and **average status children**, who are liked by a few peers and disliked by some others.

Research has shown that children in various status categories earn their status by behaving in ways that consistently please or displease their peers. In a classic study of social status, John Coie and his colleagues (1982) classified third, fifth, and eighth graders into social status groups, and asked the children to rate each other's behaviors. Peers

Children earn their status among peers: Positive social behaviors (sharing, helping, caring) help children to be accepted by their peers; negative behaviors (aggression, moodiness, selfishness) foster rejection.

rated popular children high on cooperation and leadership, and low on being highly disruptive, starting fights, and asking for help. Rejected children were rated exactly the opposite: They were perceived as being disruptive and uncooperative, starting fights, and frequently asking for help. Peers rated neglected children high on being shy and withdrawn, and low on cooperation, leadership, starting fights, and disrupting. Although these descriptions were fairly consistent for boys and girls, there were certain factors that were particularly important for each sex: Popular boys were less likely than rejected boys to be aggressive or to seek help; popular girls were more likely than rejected girls to be cooperative.

More recent studies, using a variety of different measures and informants, confirmed and elaborated these early findings (Coie & Dodge, 1988; French & Waas, 1985; Ladd, 1983). Teachers rated rejected children as having more "externalizing" behavior problems, such as hyperactivity, aggression, and delinquency than popular or neglected children. Teachers also described rejected children as less willing to conform to rules and less competent at gaining group entry than popular children (Coie & Dodge, 1988).

These behavioral descriptions of children in various status groups confirm the assumption that children earn their social status through positive and negative behaviors, that is, that children's behaviors cause the positive and negative reactions of peers, thereby determining their social status. However, it is also possible that children's social status (or reputation) determines how peers react to them, which in turn causes children to behave the way they do. For example, when a child from a tough neighborhood moves to a new school, the children already living there may presume that the newcomer will be highly aggressive and disruptive; they may then reject that child before they even get to know him, prompting the newcomer to behave aggressively and disruptively to get attention.

The problem with the studies cited earlier is that social status and the children's behavior were measured approximately at the same point in time, making it impossible to determine which comes first—status or behavior. One way to answer the question is to form groups of children who are unfamiliar with one another at the start of the study and then observe the emergence of social status over time. This strategy would allow researchers to observe the children's behavior before status differences evolve.

Two studies (Coie & Kupersmidt, 1983; Dodge, 1983) have employed this strategy. John Coie and Janis Kupersmidt assessed the social status of fourth-grade boys in their regular classrooms and then assigned each boy to one of two types of small play groups: groups composed of unfamiliar children from other schools, and groups composed of familiar peers from each boy's own school. Each group included one popular, one rejected, one neglected, and one average status boy. The groups convened once a week for six weeks at a location away from the children's schools. Each child was individually interviewed after each session.

The researchers found that in both familiar and unfamiliar groups, the boys' prior status in their classrooms was highly correlated with their emerging status in the newly formed play groups, particularly for popular and rejected children. This suggests that the social behaviors that children bring to the group largely predetermine their eventual social status. Thus, most children are likely to achieve the same status in virtually any group they enter. In this study (as in others), rejected boys earned their status by being more aggressive and hostile than most other children. A follow-up study of the unfamiliar groups (Coie & Benenson, 1983) showed that rejected boys reacted with anger and aggression to the slightest provocation by other children.

Coie and Kupersmidt also examined changes in children's behavior over the six sessions. While the rejected boys were initially quite active in the newly formed groups, they gradually decreased their participation in group activities following their initial rejection by other group members. In contrast, while neglected children were inactive when grouped with familiar boys, they were far more active when grouped with unfamiliar children. This suggests that neglected—but not rejected—children's social status may be improved by giving them a second chance to establish social status (Coie, Dodge, & Kupersmidt, 1990).

The second study of emerging social status (Dodge, 1983) confirmed many of Coie and Kupersmidt's findings. In this study, groups of unfamiliar, second-grade boys met for eight daily sessions. Boys who behaved appropriately throughout the sessions (approaching their peers positively and prosocially and eliciting positive reactions) became popular. Boys who behaved inappropriately (hitting other boys and making more hostile comments) were rejected by their peers. As in the study by Coie and Kupersmidt, the rejected children began by being socially active but gradually retreated into isolated play after being spurned.

A P P L I C A T I O N

Promoting Your Child's Social Status

You can help your child improve his social status by helping him understand the connection between the way he behaves and the way others react to him. A child who becomes convinced that his peers do not appreciate disruptive, silly, and impulsive behaviors will be more likely to behave appropriately. When your child is rejected by others, point out how his specific behaviors caused a peer to terminate play. Balance this with instances where more positive behaviors maintained engagement. Make your comments while the incidents are still fresh in your child's mind.

Even if you convince your child that certain behaviors are problematic, he may need some help in learning to behave more positively. Coach your child on specific behaviors that gain acceptance and point out how more popular children behave in various social situations.

Some children—particularly those who are neglected by their peers—may profit from new opportunities to earn social acceptance. This can be accomplished by encouraging your child to join a new social group, such as the Scouts or a ball team. In more extreme situations of neglect by peers, you may consider moving to a new neighborhood or changing your child's school.

An aggressive child is unlikely to be helped by joining a new group of peers unless he changes his behaviors prior to meeting the new children.

Bottom Line: Help your child to make good first impressions with new peers. Gaining initial acceptance is far easier than trying to reverse rejection.

Social Information Processing and Social Competence

Those who deal with children in practical settings know that different children often respond to the same social situation very differently. One possible explanation is that children interpret social cues in various ways. For example, when one second grader growls and waves his arms like a monster as he approaches another second grader, the child being approached may have several possible interpretations and reactions to the monster's behavior: If the child interprets the behavior as a benign invitation to rough and tumble play, he may welcome the initiative and immediately become a monster too; if he perceives the behavior as a real threat of physical attack, he may run or try to defend himself; if he perceives the behavior merely as a rejected child's desperate attempt to get attention, he may simply ignore it.

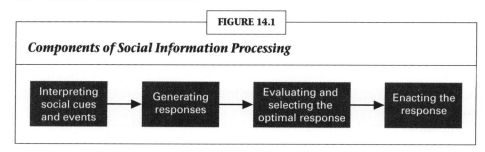

FIGURE 14.1

Components of Social Information Processing

Interpreting social cues and events → Generating responses → Evaluating and selecting the optimal response → Enacting the response

Children who accurately interpret their peers' social cues are likely to be adaptive in social settings; children who consistently misinterpret social cues are likely to be maladaptive and rejected. Thus, differences in the way children process information in social situations have significant effects on their social behavior and, consequently, on their social acceptance (Dodge & Feldman, 1990).

Developmentalists have proposed applying information processing theory to facilitate understanding of children's thinking and behavior in social situations. They have suggested models of **social information processing** (Dodge, 1986; Rubin & Krasnor, 1986) that include separate components for how children encode and interpret social events; how they generate, evaluate, and select responses to those events; and how they enact the responses they select (Dodge & Feldman, 1990; see Figure 14.1). Although this perspective has only recently been applied to the study of children's social behavior, it has already demonstrated its value in organizing our thinking and research in this complex area of children's development. We will review the components of children's social information processing and recent research that supports this view.

Interpreting Social Cues and Events

Humans interpret their circumstances at several different levels. At the simplest level, we examine the facial expressions of the participants to determine how they themselves feel about one another and the situation. We assume that people who are smiling are enjoying themselves and that those who are frowning are not. Individuals who cannot accurately read facial expressions risk behaving inappropriately. There is evidence that rejected children are less accurate than popular children in identifying emotions in photographs (Goldman, Corsini, & deUrioste, 1980), contributing to their poor social adjustment.

At a higher level, we observe social events and attempt to understand the ongoing interaction of the participants. For example, some children take time to observe their parents' interaction before asking for a privilege, assuming that their parents are more likely to grant a privilege if they are in a good mood. Children also observe their peers' interaction for indications of mood, attitude, intention, and motivation.

Developmentalists have identified particular social events that challenge children's social cognitive skills (Dodge, McClaskey, & Feldman, 1985). They have shown that girls have difficulty initiating entry into groups of their peers, but boys have difficulty knowing how to react to ambiguous provocations by their peers. Nearly all children struggle with being teased or laughed at by peers. Researchers have frequently used these situations to study how children interpret their peers' motives and intentions.

Kenneth Dodge and his colleagues have conducted a series of studies to understand how children interpret their peer's intentions in group entry, provocation, and teasing situations. In one study (Dodge, Murphy, & Buchsbaum, 1984), the researchers developed videotaped vignettes that showed two children playing. They portrayed three types of interaction: one child intentionally provoking the other, one child trying to help the other, and one child accidentally disrupting the other. Rejected and neglected children not only made more errors than popular children in identifying the child's intent, but they tended to presume *hostile* intent whenever the child's behavior resulted in negative consequences. For example, even if one child *accidentally* spilled paint on the other child, low-status children tended to assume that it had been done on purpose.

This tendency to misinterpret social cues may predispose rejected children to negative peer interaction. Heather and Amanda's experience in an after-school care program shows how a child's interpretation of ambiguous social cues can affect peer interaction.

> *It is nearly pick-up time at the after-school center, and the children are growing increasingly tired and restless. Several children crouch on the floor in the center of the classroom, hurrying to complete a picture puzzle before their parents arrive. Supervision is minimal as the caregivers rush to clean up the rooms before closing.*
>
> *Heather and Amanda, both age eight, have been aimlessly wandering through the room looking for something to do. Heather decides it might be fun to tease Amanda by threatening to take the bracelet she has just gotten as a birthday present. When Heather grabs for it, Amanda runs, and Heather chases her across the room. As Amanda runs toward the girls who are doing the puzzle on the floor, one of them shifts her position and inadvertently sticks her foot into Amanda's path. Amanda trips and falls flat on her stomach and immediately begins to cry. Heather stops just in time to avoid falling on top of her. Without even looking at Amanda, she spins around and lunges at the girl who has "tripped" Amanda. Heather curses the girl and smacks her before one of the teachers comes to the girl's rescue.*
>
> *The teacher drags Heather to a corner of the room and asks her why she hit the girl. She responds, "That brat hurt my friend, and she ain't never gonna do that again. Nobody hurts my friends." When the teacher suggests that it was an accident, Heather retorts, "That bitch hates me and Amanda and I knew she was gonna do us today. She's gonna get the same thing everytime she messes with us."*
>
> *The teacher just shakes his head and puts Heather into time out.*

Dodge's (1980) observations of children like Heather prompted him to ask whether aggressive children would be more likely than other children to attribute hostile intent to their peers. He asked children to imagine that they were the main character in stories that were read to them. In each story the main character was subjected to a negative outcome as a result of an ambiguous behavior by a peer. For example, the subject was hit in the back by a ball the peer had thrown. Dodge found that aggressive-rejected school-age boys were 50 percent more likely to attribute hostile intent than nonaggressive, popular boys. Dodge referred to the tendency to assume hostile intent as a **negative attributional bias**.

In a follow-up study (Dodge & Frame, 1982), the researchers asked whether aggressive boys' attributional bias represented a view that all peers are hostile to each other ("cyni-

Some children, particularly those who are aggressive and rejected, tend to attribute hostile intent to other children in ambiguous situations. This fight started when one boy inadvertently stepped on the other boy's foot.

cal") or a view that peers only show hostility toward the subject ("paranoid"). Aggressive boys were asked to respond to two types of stories: stories in which another child experiences negative outcomes, and stories in which the child in the story directs the negative behaviors at the subject himself. The results confirmed the "paranoid" view—that is, the subjects showed the negative attributional bias only when the negative outcome happened to them, not when it only happened to someone else. More recent evidence indicated that aggressive children remain negatively biased even when they interpret the behavior of a friend (Sancilio, Plumert, & Hartup, 1989), suggesting that the aggressive child's paranoia negatively affects *all* of their peer relationships.

Thus, there is considerable evidence that aggressive children are primed to retaliate with little or no provocation and without regard to their prior relationship with a particular peer. Amanda's accidental fall is a trip wire for Heather's biased interpretation of the event and an excuse for her to attack an innocent victim.

There is also evidence that even *non*-aggressive, rejected children maintain a negative attributional bias toward their peers and are more likely than nonrejected children to retaliate when provoked (Waas, 1988). Apparently, the experience of rejection causes both aggressive and otherwise nonaggressive children to adopt a defensive approach to their peers.

Generating Responses

The information processing view suggests that once children interpret the problem or challenge in a particular social dilemma, they must then consider possible solutions or courses of action to deal with the dilemma. Children search their repertoire of existing solutions—memories of how they or others have behaved in similar situations. Research has shown that children vary both in the quantity and quality of solutions available in their repertoire, and that unpopular or rejected children show a severely limited repertoire compared to their more popular peers (Asarnow & Callan, 1985; Dodge, 1986; Richard & Dodge, 1982; Spivack & Shure, 1974).

Researchers have studied school-age children's ability to generate responses to social problems presented to them in short stories or cartoons. The social problems involve everyday experiences of children, such as one child wanting to play with a toy that another child is already playing with. Research using these problems has shown that popular children generate more novel responses than rejected or neglected children (Asarnow & Callan, 1985; Richard & Dodge, 1982).

Not only do high-status children generate *more* responses to social problems than low-status children, they generate *better* responses. Popular children are more likely than low-status children to present solutions that are prosocial, assertive, mature, and relevant to the problem, and less likely to produce aggressive strategies (Asarnow & Callan, 1985; Dodge, 1986; Rubin & Daniels-Beirness, 1983). One study (Richard & Dodge, 1982) tested the depth of children's repertoire by asking them to give as many solutions as they could to social dilemmas. While the quality of *first* responses from popular, aggressive-rejected, and neglected children did not differ, the quality of *later* responses from rejected and neglected children was more aggressive and inappropriate to the problem than was the quality of responses of popular children. These studies suggest that low-status children have fewer and less appropriate solutions to social problems available to them. Unfortunately, research has not shown why these differences occur.

Evaluating and Selecting the Optimal Response

The next component of social information processing requires that the child evaluate the potential solutions he or she has generated and select one that is most likely to solve the problem. Although we know little about how children go about comparing and selecting strategies for solving social problems (Dodge & Feldman, 1990), some experts (Cooney & Selman, 1978; Rubin & Krasnor, 1986) have theorized that children approach the process of evaluation in two distinct ways: In **reflective reasoning**, children consciously and deliberately search their repertoire for the best solution; in **automatic reasoning**, children respond impulsively, selecting the first thing that comes to mind or the solution that requires the least mental effort.

To investigate children's evaluation style, researchers (Rabiner, Lenhart, & Lochman, 1990) asked aggressive-rejected, nonaggressive-rejected, and nonrejected children to solve social problems under conditions that promoted either reflective *or* automatic reasoning. They used three stories that involved interpersonal problems: a child provoked by a peer, a child frustrated by a peer, and a child trying to enter a group. To study automatic reasoning, the researchers instructed the children to respond as quickly as possible and reinforced them for prompt response. To study reflective reasoning, they encouraged the children to "think hard about the different ways the child in the story could solve his or her problem" (1990, p. 1012).

The results indicated that boys—but not girls—in the different status groups responded very differently in the two conditions. In the automatic or quick-response condition, aggressive- and nonaggressive-rejected boys were less likely than rejected boys to provide positive responses and more likely to produce solutions that would escalate conflict. However, in the reflective condition, while aggressive-rejected boys continued to provide fewer positive responses, *non*aggressive-rejected boys no longer differed from nonrejected boys.

This suggests that nonaggressive-rejected boys may have competent solutions to social problems in their repertoire but fail to access these solutions when they are under time pressure. This explains why these boys are unlikely to behave adaptively in emotionally charged real life social situations that require rapid response. In contrast, the quality of aggressive-rejected boys' responses did not improve when they were encouraged to take their time and think. Apparently, their repertoire of solutions to social problems is so deficient that no amount of time to reflect will improve their performance. Girls in different status groups did not respond differently to the two conditions.

Improving Information Processing in Rejected Children

Since rejected children process social information very differently than higher status peers, we may be able to improve their social acceptance by altering the way they interpret social cues and events and the way they generate and select solutions to social problems. The following suggestions may be helpful:

- If *all* rejected children—whether aggressive or non-aggressive—tend to attribute hostile intent to peers (even in ambiguous situations), these children should profit from training that helps them to make more accurate attributions. Begin by helping your child identify his peers' intentions in clear-cut social situations and work your way into more ambiguous situations. Ask him to identify facial expressions that signal hostile intent (such as teasing, taunting, and threatening), and facial expressions that signal benign intent (such as sympathy and interest). Help him understand that accidents do happen, that everybody is not out to get him, and that giving peers the benefit of the doubt can avoid conflict and improve his social acceptance.

- Keep in mind that aggressive- and nonaggressive-rejected children may need to be approached in different ways. Since many nonaggressive-rejected children possess po-

tential solutions to social problems but do not think of them in emotionally charged situations, they may profit from learning to be less impulsive and more reflective. Encourage your child to take time to think about *all* possible solutions or strategies rather than simply doing the first thing that comes to mind.

- Also keep in mind that the take-time-to-think approach may be less effective with *aggressive*-rejected children who have too few social strategies. These children will profit more from experiences that expand their repertoire of alternative solutions to social problems. Encourage your child to role-play prosocial skills, such as sharing, helping, and taking turns. Your child may also profit from direct coaching in specific social skills. For example, suggest that in group entry situations he avoid calling attention to himself, bossing his peers, or disrupting what they are doing. Suggest that he instead try to blend into his peers' ongoing activities.

Bottom Line: Remember that while all rejected children are at risk of maladjustment, they have not all been rejected for the same reasons. Suit your intervention to your child's unique strengths and deficiencies in information processing and social skill.

Enacting the Response

The final component in information processing is for the child to *enact* or perform the behaviors required by the strategy the child selected. Simply having the best solution to a social problem in one's repertoire and selecting it does not ensure that the child will enact it competently or effectively. For example, although a child may know that her rudeness in a certain situation calls for an apology, she may be unable to find the necessary words to frame the apology or fail to deliver the apology in time to do any good. Moreover, the child must do more than just go through the motions. Subtle differences in delivery style can affect the impact of a given social behavior. For example, an apology is likely to be more effective with eye contact than without, and with a smile rather than a frown. Unfortunately, we know very little about how children perform social behaviors effectively, and even less about the more subtle, stylistic aspects of enactment.

We do know, however, that situational factors may have great influence on children's social performance. In one study (Dodge et al., 1985), researchers asked children in various status groups to role-play (enact) responses to typical social problems, such as being teased or provoked, entering a group, and reacting to success. How competently children responded depended on the degree of stress involved in each social problem. While aggressive-rejected children responded less competently than average-status children did in the relatively stressful situations of being teased or provoked, they were not less competent in the less stressful situations of entering a group or responding to success. Although role-play may not fully represent how children would behave in real life settings, this study demonstrated the critical role of situational factors on the "output" of children's social information processing. Further research is sorely needed on the effects the social and emotional context on children's social behavior.

Integrating the Components of Information Processing

All of the studies cited in this section have focused on single components of social information processing. However, from a theoretical perspective, children's competent social behavior is the product of *all* information processing components: interpreting cues, generating responses, evaluating and selecting the optimal response, and enacting the response (Dodge, Pettit, McClaskey, & Brown, 1986; Rubin & Krasnor, 1986). Kenneth Dodge and his colleagues (Dodge et al., 1986; Feldman & Dodge, 1987) studied whether we could improve our ability to predict children's behavior in complex social situations by *simultaneously* considering multiple aspects of their social information processing.

The researchers showed school-age children videotapes of other children in two different situations: a child trying to enter a group and a child responding to provocation by a peer. The subjects were told to imagine that they were the child on the tape and were asked how they would interpret the social cues, generate responses, select and evaluate those responses, and enact the responses. Each subject was then observed in two *actual* situations: one in which the subject was asked to join the play of two unfamiliar same-age peers (group entry), and the second in which the subject had to respond to provocation by a peer.

The results showed that the components of the children's social information processing—separately and in combination—were related to the children's actual behavior in the two social situations. However, the relationships could be demonstrated *only* within each situation; that is, the children's ability to process information from the group entry videotape predicted their actual ability to enter a group but did not predict their response to actual provocation, and their ability to process videotaped provocation predicted their response to actual provocation but did not predict their actual entry behavior. Thus, the relationship between school-age children's social information processing and their social behavior appears to be specific to the social situation: Their social information processing does not generalize across situations. In practical terms, we can only predict children's behavior in a given social situation if we know the quality of their thinking in that situation; knowing how well they think in other, unrelated social situations is of no value.

In a related study, Esther Feldman and Kenneth Dodge (1987) compared the reactions of first, third, and fifth graders to three videotaped social situations: a child being teased, a child being provoked ambiguously, and a child trying to enter a group. They assessed four sequential components of the children's information processing: (1) *interpretations* of the children involved in the problem, (2) *response repertoire*, (3) *response evaluation*, and (4) role-play *enactment*.

The researchers found that popular and unpopular children responded differently only in the teasing situation. Unpopular children interpreted the teasing children as more hostile, they produced more aggressive and less competent responses, and they evaluated aggressive responses as more acceptable than average and popular children. Thus, the information processing of low-status children would be more likely to generate conflict.

Not surprisingly, the older the children were, the more competent they were at all information processing components. Popular children consistently generated a higher proportion of competent responses than neglected and rejected children. The researchers concluded that children vary greatly in how they process social information in different types of social problems, which suggests that there is no basis for assuming that low-status children are *generally* deficient in their ability to process information. The research suggests that adults hoping to facilitate children's competence should focus their interventions on particular children's difficulties in particular types of social problems.

To summarize, the studies that have related the sequential components of children's social information processing to social behavior have shown that the relationship only holds within particular types of situations. Children who process information well in one situation are likely to actually perform more competently in that situation. However, the relationship may or may not apply for the same children in different social situations.

A P P L I C A T I O N

Tuning the Information Processing System

*T*here are two important practical implications of referring to a child's information processing as a system:

First, the components of a child's social information processing system are not isolated units: They are parts of a system that can only work if all the parts are in working order and if the parts work in harmony. When we try to understand a child's social strengths and weaknesses from this perspective, we must first assess the individual components and then examine how they work as a system. For most children, a minor adjustment can be the difference between acceptance and rejection.

Second, we know that the effectiveness of the child's social information processing system is completely dependent on the *input* to the system. Children's experience in one social situation tells us little about their ability to process information in another situation. Thus, we should not expect children to be socially adaptive in a given situation unless we know that they have had extensive experience in that situation, regardless of how well they think and behave elsewhere. Children need broad social experience to be truly adaptive.

Rejection and Loneliness

> *Carlos enters the school yard and walks slowly to the place where his fourth-grade class will eventually line up at the bell. Of over 200 children in the yard, he is the only one standing in line. Children swarm around him in variously sized groups—chasing, teasing, and gossiping—but not one makes the slightest move to involve Carlos in their play.*

To pass the time and to appear preoccupied, Carlos begins his daily ritual: He looks around as if he has discovered that one of his possessions is missing. He searches through his jacket pockets, then deep into the recesses of his backpack, and finally among the many items in his lunchbag. Seemingly frustrated, he picks up his backpack and lunchbag and retraces the path he followed into the school yard, pretending to look for the elusive object. Failing in his search, he returns to his place in line and repeats the searching sequence until the bell rings.

When the bell rings, Carlos is terrified as the children in his class rush toward him in a frenzy. They crash into him, pushing and pulling until he is relegated to the end of the line, the only child without a partner for the slow procession to his classroom. As the line moves toward the school entrance, Carlos resumes looking for the phantom object, distracting himself from his loneliness.

Carlos's experience in the school yard is not unusual for him; he has no friends and his interaction with classmates is limited to very brief encounters, often involving blatant rejection. His rejection and isolation from other children has gone on for years and, like other rejected children, he pays a high emotional price for his low social status.

Compared to their more popular peers, rejected children interact more negatively with their classmates, do less well academically, and are perceived by their teachers as more deviant and depressed (Vosk, Forehand, Parker, & Richard, 1982). When they try to enter groups of children at play, they tend to be disruptive and are frequently rebuffed or ignored (Dodge, Schlundt, Schocken, & Delugach, 1983; Francis & Ollendick, 1987; Putallaz & Wasserman, 1989).

Children who are consistently rejected by their peers pay a high emotional price. The boy on the right in this photo has been unable to join the play of neighborhood children. Over time, this rejection causes deep feelings of loneliness and a sense of isolation that increase the risk of long-term maladjustment.

Not surprisingly, rejected children report dissatisfaction with their peer relationships and greater loneliness than children in other status groups (Asher, Parkhurst, Hymel, & Williams, 1990; Asher & Wheeler, 1985). The feeling of loneliness is particularly intense for rejected children who blame themselves for their social failures (Bukowski & Ferber, 1987). Rejected children report feeling lonely as early as age five or six, and the emotion appears to be very much like the feeling of loneliness reported by adults (Asher et al., 1990).

However, some rejected children may be less susceptible to loneliness than others: Aggressive-rejected children report feeling less lonely than nonaggressive-rejected children (Parkhurst & Asher, 1992). This difference should not be taken at face value, however: It may simply reflect aggressive children's tendency to deny their feelings. On the other hand, aggressive children often find companionship and security by hanging out with other aggressive peers (Cairns, Cairns, Neckerman, Gest, & Gariepy, 1988). Thus, although these children escape loneliness, they merely exchange one risk factor (loneliness) for another (negative peer influence).

Some children who are rejected by the overall peer group manage to avoid loneliness by having one mutual friend among their classmates. In one study (Bukowski & Newcomb, 1987) children who had at least one friend had higher feelings of self-worth, regardless of their overall level of social acceptance among their classmates. Other children fend off loneliness by seeking other sources of social support, such as out-of-school friends and siblings (East & Rook, 1992). In one study (East & Rook, 1992) researchers compared average status sixth graders with aggressive and socially isolated children. The isolated children reported less social support (companionship, emotional support, help, and intimacy) from their classmates than other children. They were also less well adjusted—more lonely, depressed, anxious, and immature and passive—than their more aggressive peers.

Interestingly, the isolated, aggressive, and average status children all reported about the same levels of social support from peers *outside* of school. In particular, isolated children received relatively high levels of social support from their siblings, with favorable effects on their overall adjustment. However, even with support from siblings, the loners remained less well-adjusted than children of average status. Thus, while support from siblings and out-of-school relationships may enhance isolated children's adjustment, it does not fully protect them from the feelings of loneliness, anxiety, and depression associated with rejection by school peers.

We may conclude that loneliness is a frequent but not inevitable emotional consequence of peer rejection in middle childhood. Submissive-rejected children are the most vulnerable to extreme feelings of loneliness. They are frequently victimized and bullied by their peers (Rubin, LeMare, & Lollis, 1990), and they tend to blame themselves for their social failures. Over time, submissive-rejected children's chronic feelings of loneliness and depression may cause them to withdraw even further from peer interaction.

A P P L I C A T I O N

The Rejected Child's Vulnerability to Loneliness

Many rejected children feel lonely and/or depressed, but there are some ways—both positive and negative—that help children to avoid these feelings. When rejected children seek out other rejected children for companionship, loneliness may be avoided but at the price of negative social support. These relationships must be watched closely for signs of delinquent behavior.

More positively, children who are rejected by most of their peers may avoid feelings of loneliness by having just one mutual friend. Thus, you may substantially reduce your child's vulnerability to serious long-term effects of rejection by promoting one positive relationship. It helps if this friendship is developed within the context in which rejection has taken place, particularly when the rejection takes place in school. When all else fails, positive relationships with siblings and children in other settings may be helpful.

Peer Rejection and Later Adjustment

Developmentalists have long maintained that children require extensive peer interaction for healthy social adjustment and personality development (Hartup, 1983; Sullivan, 1953). Harry Stack Sullivan (1953) argued that children who are deprived of social experience develop feelings of inferiority, low self-esteem, and disturbed self-concept. Willard Hartup (1977) expanded this view by suggesting that "without an opportunity to encounter individuals who are co-equals, children do not learn effective communication skills, do not acquire the competencies needed to modulate their aggressive actions, have difficulties with sexual socialization, and are disadvantaged with respect to the formation of moral values" (1977, p. 1).

The studies reviewed thus far in this chapter suggest that school-age children in different social status groups live in different social worlds. Popular, controversial, and average status children are, to varying degrees, involved in ongoing social interaction with their peer groups. For these children, each day is an opportunity to practice and perfect social skills and to improve their social cognitive abilities. In contrast, neglected and rejected children have little or no positive interaction with same-age peers. Their limited social experience teaches them to retreat, withdraw, and isolate themselves, or to offend, disrupt, tease, and hurt their peers—further decreasing the likelihood that their peers will accept them. If, as some experts have stated, extensive positive social experience plays an "indispensable role in the socialization of social competence" (Parker & Asher, 1987, p. 357), we would expect socially rejected and neglected children to be at risk of social maladjustment for both the short term (within the elementary school years) and the long term (from middle childhood to adulthood).

Short-Term Effects of Rejection

We have convincing evidence from short-term longitudinal studies that problems in peer relations in the early elementary grades place children at continuing risk for social problems in later elementary grades (Bierman, 1991; Burton & Krantz, 1990; Hymel, Rubin, Rowden, & LeMare, 1990; Kupersmidt & Coie, 1990; Kupersmidt & Patterson, 1991; Vitaro & Gagnon, 1991). In one longitudinal study (Burton & Krantz, 1990) children who were highly disliked by their peers in first and second grades were more likely than more popular children to exhibit disruptive and impulsive behavior in fourth and fifth grades. These disliked first and second graders were also less likely to take responsibility for the outcomes of their social acts in the later elementary grades.

In another study (Bierman, 1991) aggressive-rejected boys in the early elementary grades were shown to be at extremely high risk for continuing adjustment problems over a two-year period. In yet another study, children who were passive and isolated in second grade were predictably lonely and depressed in fifth grade (Rubin & Mills, 1988). One final study (Kupersmidt & Patterson, 1991) not only supported the concept of risk associated with low social acceptance, but emphasized that *neglected* girls are extremely vulnerable to depression. Girls who were neglected in second grade were twice as likely to be depressed in fourth grade as girls who had been rejected, and they were five times more likely to be depressed than girls who were in higher status groups.

Long-Term Effects of Rejection

It is not uncommon for parents and teachers to dismiss their children's short-term difficulties by suggesting that they will simply grow out of it. However, children do not appear to grow out of their experience of rejection. There is accumulating evidence that rejected children are at risk for adjustment problems later in life, such as juvenile delinquency, criminality, marital dysfunction, and mental illness (Cowen, Pederson, Babijian, Izzo, & Trost, 1973; Parker & Asher, 1987; Roff, 1961, 1990; Roff, Sells, & Golden, 1972).

A comprehensive review of the extensive research in this area (Parker & Asher, 1987) concluded that a significant proportion of maladjusted adults have a history of difficult peer relationships. This does not mean, however, that rejected children will necessarily become maladjusted adults. Parker and Asher summarized studies that started with maladjusted adults and looked backward for a history of childhood problems, which is not the same thing as starting with maladjusted children and predicting which ones will eventually show maladjustment problems as adults. Making such predictions is problematic because different measures of children's peer problems predict different adult outcomes. For example, while low peer acceptance predicts later dropping out of school, it does not predict adult criminality. Conversely, early aggression predicts criminality but does not predict dropping out. Parker and Asher's review of studies also found little support for predicting adult maladjustment from early measures of shyness and withdrawal.

Although the reviewers recognized the limitations of the existing research on long-term outcomes, they concluded that the literature provides general support for the notion that children who experience problems with their peers are at increased risk of later life difficulties. What remains unclear is why certain types of peer problems in childhood lead to certain types of difficulties in adulthood.

Social Cognition and Social Competence

We have described how children attribute motives—some positive and some negative—to understand their peers' behaviors. These attributions may be accurate or biased, depending at least in part on the children's experience in dealing with the social problem in question. However even a great deal of real life experience may not correct an attributional bias. For instance, as we have seen, aggressive children attribute hostile motivations to others even when the intentions are ambiguous.

Besides trying to understand their peers, children must try to understand their own behavior and its effects on others. For example, do children take credit and blame for their social successes and failures? If they do take credit, do they believe that they can purposely change their own social outcomes by changing their behavior?

To answer these questions, developmentalists (Earn & Sobol, 1990; Goetz & Dweck, 1980; Sobol & Earn, 1985a, 1985b) have studied how children explain their own social behavior. They suggest that children differ in **attributional style**—that is, in the characteristic way that they attribute intent to explain their own and other's social behavior.

This girl is the last to be chosen for one of two soccer teams. What effect does this have on her adjustment? If she believes that she is last because she is unskilled and that she can do nothing to improve her skill, she may come to feel helpless in such situations, with negative effects on her motivation and self-concept. This physical education teacher could have easily avoided placing this girl at risk by setting up teams on a chance basis.

Children's attributions vary on three important dimensions: locus, stability, and control. *Locus* is the degree to which children take credit (or blame) for their social outcomes. *Stability* refers to whether children view the causes of their behavior as consistent over time. *Control* refers to the degree to which they believe that they can change their behavior to alter their social outcomes. For example, when we ask a child why his peers refuse to include him in their baseball game, he may say, "It's because I always have bad luck," thus attributing his failure to an external, stable cause beyond his control. In contrast, another child says, "I didn't try hard enough," attributing his failure to an internal, unstable cause that he can alter by simply trying harder next time.

Developmentalists have reasoned that differences in children's social attributional style have significant effects on their social behavior. Therese Goetz and Carolyn Dweck (1980) studied the attributions that children make when they experience social failures. They reasoned that children who attribute their social failures to causes that are internal, stable, and difficult to control (such as their own incompetence) would be less able to cope with failure than children who attribute their difficulties to external, unstable, and controllable causes (such as a peer's mood or incompatibility with that peer). They called the tendency to attribute failures to internal, stable, and uncontrollable causes as **social learned helplessness**.

In the first part of their study, the researchers assessed children's attributional styles by asking them to attribute their failure in a series of social problems. For example, they asked the children, "Suppose someone stops telling you her secrets. Why would this happen to you?" In the second part of the study, they asked children to attempt to initiate a relationship with a pen pal by sending a message by one-way radio. All children were initially rejected by the pen pal (who wasn't quite certain he/she liked the child), and each child was encouraged to try again. The researchers observed the children's reactions to the mild rejection. Children who attributed their rejection to their own incompetence demonstrated social learned helplessness, failing to renew their effort to establish the pen pal relationship after the initial rejection. A more recent replication of the study (Lepore, Kiely, Bempechat, & London, 1989) showed that children who believed that their social skills were unchangeable and that their social outcomes were beyond their control were likely to show extreme helplessness after rejection. Many of these children actively resisted the experimenter's encouragement to make a second attempt to initiate a pen pal relationship.

These intriguing results of laboratory studies bring up the possibility that children's social attributional style might be related to their social adjustment. Recent research has demonstrated a relationship between children's attributional style and their social status (Earn & Sobol, 1990). Popular children were more likely than low-status children to attribute their failures to controllable causes. Popular children were less likely than low-status children to attribute their social successes and failures to luck, and more likely to attribute their outcomes to a peer's personality.

The researchers concluded that popular children employ a "more sophisticated social analysis" than other children, taking more credit for their social successes and attributing their failures to more sophisticated external causes, such as other people's motives. Thus, popular children display a "mastery" orientation, persisting in the face of social failure and seeking social challenges (Dweck & Leggett, 1988). The researchers also suggested that intervention with low-status children should be aimed at altering the way these children make attributions for social success and failure.

A P P L I C A T I O N

Changing Attributions of Learned Helpless Children

*I*t is not hard to see how social learned helplessness would place a child at serious risk of maladjustment. Blaming yourself for your rejections, not taking credit for your social successes, and believing that you have no control over the process would undermine all motivation to engage in social relationships. How can this be changed?

If your child's attributional style is to change, the child must experience social success—that is, opportunities to take credit for something other than failure—over considerable periods of time. You may have to set up such experiences, for example, by pairing your child with friendly but not overly popular children for brief play periods. The activities during these periods should encourage cooperative play. When your child experiences positive social outcomes, point out what she did that brought about the positive effect. For example, if the playmate laughs, point out to your child what she said that was funny. When a playmate cooperates in a task, point out what she did to promote that cooperation. Continue to program your child for positive experiences and provide feedback that promotes internal, stable, and controllable attributions for positive outcomes. Your child can also be helped to *not* take credit for negative outcomes that are beyond her control, for example, when a playmate is uncooperative because of a bad cold.

Bottom Line: It takes a long time and many failure experiences for your child to acquire social learned helplessness. It will take just as long for your child to become more masterful, even with favorable social experiences.

The Development of Prosocial Behavior

Children show the first signs of spontaneous *prosocial behavior*—the intentional helping or caring for others—during the *preschool* years (Iannotti, 1985). However, spontaneous prosocial behavior remains relatively infrequent. While children do occasionally share possessions with their peers, help peers and siblings when they are distressed, and cooperate with other children in play and work situations (Eisenberg-Berg & Hand, 1979; Mussen & Eisenberg-Berg, 1977), they lack the cognitive and emotional skills necessary to fully understand and empathize when others are in need. Important advances in children's cognitive and emotional abilities from early to middle childhood significantly increase their tendency to behave prosocially.

Cognitively, the decline in egocentricity from early to middle childhood improves children's ability to perceive when others are in need, when they are in distress, and when they are likely to cooperate. More important, children show significant improvements in **prosocial moral reasoning**—the ability to think about conflicts in which they must choose between satisfying their own needs or those of other persons (Eisenberg, Lennon, & Roth, 1983). These include situations in which helping or sharing with someone else means some sacrifice or loss for the helper. It seems likely that children who show more sophisticated moral reasoning about sharing and helping would be more likely than less sophisticated children to share and help others in real life situations.

Emotionally, as children grow into middle childhood they show increasing ability to empathize or sympathize with the emotional states of children in need or in distress. One might expect that children who are in touch with other children's emotions would be more likely to behave prosocially than children who lack empathy or sympathy. We first examine the evidence on the relationship between prosocial moral reasoning and prosocial behavior, followed by a review of research on empathy and prosocial behavior.

Prosocial Moral Reasoning and Prosocial Behavior

Nancy Eisenberg and her colleagues (Eisenberg et al., 1983; Eisenberg, Shell, Pasternack, Lennon, & Mathy, 1987; Eisenberg-Berg & Hand, 1979) have investigated the development of prosocial moral reasoning by studying children's responses to moral dilemmas, presented in story format. For example, one story describes a child (who has fallen down and hurt her leg) asking another child (who is on her way to a birthday party) to help her get medical attention. The story's wording makes it clear that if the child stops to help the injured child, she will be late for the party and miss the ice cream, cake, and games. Eisenberg asked her subjects to tell what the child should do in each dilemma and why. She classified the content of the children's responses by the different developmental levels of reasoning they used to justify their thinking (see Table 14.1).

Using the dilemmas, Eisenberg gathered longitudinal data on children's emerging prosocial moral reasoning from early childhood through middle childhood (Eisenberg-Berg & Hand, 1979; Eisenberg et al., 1983; Eisenberg et al., 1987). The results supported a developmental progression of prosocial moral reasoning. Many preschoolers responded *hedonistically*, motivated by selfish gain. In the above example, the subject might say, "She should go to the birthday party because she likes ice cream!" The more young children relied on hedonistic reasoning in the moral dilemmas, the less likely they were to share with other children in preschool (Eisenberg-Berg & Hand, 1979). Preschoolers also referred frequently to *needs-oriented* reasoning, recognizing the pain or suffering of individuals in the dilemmas. In the example above the subject might say, "She should stop to help the girl because she is hurt!" The more children referred to the persons' needs in the dilemmas, the more likely they were to share with other children in preschool.

In general, while children's reference to hedonistic reasoning decreased from early to middle childhood, references to needs-oriented ("She needs help"), *approval-oriented* ("She will like me if I help"), and *stereotyped* ("It's nice to help people") notions of good

TABLE 14.1

Developmental Levels of Prosocial Moral Reasoning

Level	Orientation	Description	Group
1	Hedonistic, self-focused	Child is concerned with self-oriented consequences, assists others for self-gain or future reciprocity.	Preschoolers and young elementary schoolchildren
2	Needs of others	Child expresses concern for the physical and psychological needs of others, even when they conflict with the child's own needs. No evidence of role-taking, sympathy, or guilt.	Preschoolers and elementary schoolchildren
3	Approval and stereotyped	Child has stereotypic images of good and bad persons and behaviors. Concerns about others' approval to justify prosocial or nonhelping behavior.	Elementary and high school students
4	Empathic	The child's judgments are based on sympathy, role-taking, and/or guilt related to the consequences of one's actions.	Elementary and high school students
5	Internalized	The child's justifications for helping are based on internalized values, norms, or responsibilities, and belief in human rights.	Only a minority of high school students and virtually no elementary school children

SOURCE: *Adapted from Eisenberg, Lennon, & Roth, 1983, p. 850*

or bad behavior increased with age (Eisenberg et al., 1983; Eisenberg et al., 1987). These results suggest a major shift from self-orientation to other-orientation during the elementary years.

By age 9 to 10, girls—but not boys—begin to show more sophisticated forms of reasoning involving empathy and a true understanding of the plight of those in need. This finding is consistent with other research that found girls more likely than boys to behave prosocially and that girls were more consistently prosocial than boys across varied situations (Larrieu & Mussen, 1986).

Empathy, Sympathy, and Prosocial Behavior

We would expect advances in emotional development from early to middle childhood to affect the development of prosocial behavior. Developmentalists have reasoned that we are more likely to help, care about, and share with others when we identify with their emotional state. We can identify with emotions by *empathizing* and by *sympathizing*. **Empathy** refers to an emotional state that results from vicariously experiencing the emotions of another individual: We feel what they feel. **Sympathy**, on the other hand, is an emotional response where one feels sorrow or concern for another's welfare. Thus, in both empathy and sympathy the focus is on the other person rather than on the self (Eisenberg & Miller, 1987).

Are children more likely to share with or help another child when they empathize or sympathize with the child's plight? When very young children are aroused by another person's strong emotions, they are likely to become distressed themselves, a response that is *not* conducive to acting prosocially (Hoffman, 1984). Children's empathy does not begin to result in prosocial behavior until late in the elementary school years, at about age eleven (Eisenberg & Miller, 1987; Eisenberg et al., 1987). However, even at that age the cause–effect relationship is not nearly as strong as it is in adults. It remains unclear why empathy translates so slowly into prosocial behavior.

A P P L I C A T I O N

Promoting Prosocial Moral Reasoning and Prosocial Behavior

*I*n theory, young children may learn to share and help their peers through modeling or because they expect a payoff—that is, when they share with others, others are likely to share back. But don't get your hopes up. Your child is unlikely to get the idea of behaving prosocially by watching his same-age peers. There is just not enough modeling to go around. You could promote your child's prosocial behavior by observing his every behavior and pouncing on him with reinforcement for every prosocial act. This might work, but it would also take more time than it is worth. When you stop reinforcing, your young child will probably revert to his more selfish, hedonistic ways.

If you would like to have a more lasting effect on your child's prosocial development, take a hint from researchers who use dilemmas to *test* children's prosocial moral reasoning. Moral dilemmas—in story form or in real life—challenge children's thinking. The more frequently they are challenged, the more they will learn. Fortunately, family life provides an endless sequence of such dilemmas—prime material for children's learning. Promote your child's empathy and sympathy by highlighting the emotional consequences of various courses of behavior. For example, when your child has a conflict about sharing, point out how the potential beneficiary's feelings will vary, depending on how your child chooses to behave.

Bottom Line: Your child will learn to behave prosocially when he learns to think and feel prosocially. This can only happen when he is challenged cognitively and emotionally in real life situations.

Divorce and Children's Social Adjustment

As recently as the 1960s, American children were very likely to be reared from infancy through adolescence by their biological mother and father living together in the family home. Now, by one estimate (Hetherington, Stanley-Hagan, & Anderson, 1989), half of the children born in the 1980s will experience their parents' divorce, and most of these children will experience one or both of their parents' remarriage during their childhood years.

After their parents divorce, 90 percent of children live with their unmarried mothers. Some 75 to 80 percent of divorced parents remarry an average of five years after the divorce. Since the divorce rate for remarriages is even higher than for first marriages, some children will experience a second divorce.

Thus, developmentalists have come to view divorce and remarriage not as isolated events but as a sequence of family transitions that punctuate children's development (Hetherington & Clingempeel, 1992; Hetherington et al., 1989). Each family transition—that is, from family of origin to single-parent family, from single-parent family to stepfamily, from stepfamily back to single-parent family—brings with it unique and pervasive changes in the context of children's development, with dramatic effects on their social adjustment.

Are all parents and their children devastated by divorce? No. While most parents and children find the first weeks and months following divorce traumatic, most manage to adapt to their new circumstances within two to three years (Hetherington, 1989). In the period immediately following dissolution of the household, many children do poorly in school and show a variety of emotional and behavioral problems both at home and at school that were not present prior to the divorce (Hetherington & Camara, 1984). Children who have just experienced divorce typically feel anger, resentment, and anxiety. Those children who blame themselves for the divorce or who feel relieved that the parents are no longer fighting may feel guilt and/or depression. Divorce often causes increased rivalry and conflict between siblings (MacKinnon, 1989).

Although virtually all children are initially overwhelmed by their parents' separation, children vary widely in their ability to adapt. While some children are deeply distressed and continue to react negatively for many years, others show great resiliency and go on with their lives. Others show very little response initially, but negative reactions appear eventually, although often not until adolescence (Hetherington, 1989). Some children actually benefit from the divorce experience by learning adaptive skills that can be applied in other settings, such as at school or in the peer group. We meet a professional who helps parents and children cope with divorce in ''Careers: The Marriage and Family Therapist.''

Why do some children do so much better than others? There is no simple answer to this question. Two longitudinal studies—one directed by Mavis Hetherington (Hetherington, 1989) and one by Judith Wallerstein (Wallerstein, Corbin, & Lewis, 1988)—have identified major influences on the outcome of divorce for children. Hetherington (1989) has focused on children's ''protective factors,'' which promote adequate family coping with their new circumstances, and ''vulnerability factors,'' which undermine their coping. Protective factors include positive personality dispositions in the children, supportive family relationships, and social support from family and friends. Vulnerability factors include continuing parental conflict after the divorce, personality disturbances in the parents, and decreased financial resources. The changing balance of protective and vulnerability factors over time ultimately determines children's long-term adjustment.

The complex interplay of protective and vulnerability factors is clearly illustrated in Hetherington's (1989) findings on how children's temperament (''easy'' or ''difficult'') affects their relationships with their parents after divorce. Hetherington reasoned that the effects of a child's temperament could be understood only by simultaneously considering the mother's personality, stress level, and access to social support. Hetherington's results showed that mothers with stable personalities *and* relatively little stress had no more problems dealing with ''difficult'' temperament children than with ''easy'' temperament children. However, mothers who were either unstable *or* greatly stressed were significantly more negative than stable or nonstressed mothers toward their ''difficult'' children, but were less negative when they had social support. Mothers who were unstable *and* stressed were even more negative to their ''difficult'' children, and were not helped by the availability of social support.

In general, these results suggest that vulnerability factors have a way of adding up; beyond a certain point, social support from family and friends do not make much difference.

Hetherington and her colleagues (1989) also showed that the child's gender has significant effects on the mother's ability to cope with postdivorce family life. Divorced, nonremarried mothers were particularly ineffectual in dealing with their sons. They made demands without following through with appropriate rewards or punishments. Their

The Marriage and Family Therapist

Sharon Cheatham-Krantz is a licensed marriage and family therapist in private practice in Tallahassee, Florida. Sharon's therapy focuses on problems that parents face in the course of their children's development. She also sees couples for premarital counseling and for marital therapy. She works extensively with the family court system providing assessments of parents and their children and making recommendations for primary physical residence and visitation in divorce cases.

What is a typical workday like for a family therapist?

My typical day includes a series of six to eight hour-long therapy sessions with families and their children, punctuated by phone conversations with clients, physicians, teachers, lawyers, and other therapists. Because I typically see families rather than individuals, I interact with as many as 20 to 30 people each day. I also observe children (at home, day care, or school), keep detailed case notes, write reports, and testify in court.

What is your approach to therapy with children?

I believe that children's problems can be understood and treated only in the context of their families. So after I see the child for the first time, I invite members of the family — parents, stepparents, siblings, and even grandparents — to the therapy sessions simultaneously. I observe the family's in-teraction over time and help them recognize the recurrent patterns in their behavior. I show them how certain patterns are dysfunctional, creating or reinforcing problem behavior in the child and making everyone in the family unhappy. For example, parents often use children as scapegoats for their own hostility toward each other.

To accommodate families and children in my practice, I have created a homelike environment for my therapy — including a large living area, a sunroom, an elaborate playroom, and a kitchen. Family members may move naturally from area to area during therapy sessions. This environment allows them to be themselves, exposing their strengths and weaknesses as a family. The environment is also an ideal context for change that transfers easily to the family home.

How did you become interested in family therapy?

My Master's-level training in counseling prepared me to work only with individuals. I soon found that many of my clients' problems are deeply rooted in their experiences in their family of origin. When they themselves become parents, they repeat many of the same behaviors their parents used with them. Many families pass their problems across several generations. I eventually chose a doctoral program that trained therapists to engage the family as a multigenerational system.

What training is required to become a family therapist?

Clinical training for marriage and family therapy is typically available at the postgraduate level at universities and training institutes throughout the country. Several doctoral programs also provide training, but with an emphasis on research. Look for programs that are accredited by the American Association for Marriage and Family Therapy.

For more information write to the American Association for Marriage and Family Therapy, 1100 17th Street, N.W., Washington, DC 20036.

interactions with their sons frequently got out of hand, with increasing cycles of anger and hostility. They were generally not in control of their sons. However, they related quite well to their daughters—about as well as mothers and daughters in intact families.

This is not to suggest that girls fare better than boys in divorced families, only that girls get along better than boys with their mothers. Girls miss their fathers and suffer as much as boys from the continuing conflict between their parents. Moreover, girls appear to do more poorly than boys in adjusting to their mothers' remarriage. This is not surprising, considering that girls' relatively good relations with their mothers after divorce may be threatened by the arrival of a stepfather. On the other hand, boys—many of whom already relate poorly to their mothers—are less affected by their mothers' remarriage, perhaps because they feel they have nothing to lose (Hetherington et al., 1989).

Children's age or stage of development at the time of divorce also has significant effects on their adjustment. Preschoolers suffer because they have great difficulty understanding why their parents are separating. They do not comprehend their parents' actions or emotions. Many fear abandonment, and others maintain naive expectations that their parents will reconcile their differences. But failing to process what is going on also has its advantages. Judith Wallerstein and her colleagues (1988) interviewed children 10 years after their parents' divorce and found that those who were relatively young at the time of divorce had few clear memories of their experience. In contrast, those who had been adolescents at the time of the divorce retained much more detail and were more troubled by those memories (Wallerstein et al., 1988).

What does the research tell us about facilitating children's long-term adjustment to divorce? Although there is a strong tendency for fathers without custody to decrease their contact with their children over time, those fathers who do maintain strong relationships with their children contribute positively to their development (Furstenberg & Nord, 1985). Well-negotiated divorce agreements that establish plentiful visitation for the noncustodial parent and equitable financial situations for both parents will help prevent continuing conflict. There is some evidence that school-age children fare better when custody is granted to the same-sex parent (Zill, 1988). Ultimately, the parents' mutual concern for their children's welfare and their ability to communicate and cooperate in the best interests of their children determine the quality of their children's adjustment (Camara & Resnick, 1988).

A P P L I C A T I O N

Helping Your Children Cope with Divorce

While every family's situation is unique, there are some do's and don'ts that can help your children cope.

- Agree to a custody arrangement that best meets your children's emotional needs. Joint custody—even when an option—is not for everyone. Although children may be better off with the same-sex parent, particularly when they are older, splitting up brothers and sisters is probably not in the children's best interests. Keep in mind that continuing to be a good parent after the divorce has little to do with custody!

- When your children are visiting with you, be a *parent*, not an entertainer. Avoid negative comments about your ex-spouse, and don't try to compete with the resources he or she provides. Help your children integrate their lives by showing genuine interest in their lives when they are with you *and* when they are with your ex-spouse. Call them or write to them *every day* they are not with you. If you are awarded sole custody, agree to generous visitation and try your best to make it work. Make transfers as smooth as possible.

- Agree to adequate child support and fulfill your obligations in full and always on time. Creating an inequitable distribution of resources for your children breeds resentment that will only get worse over time.
- Be a good parent, nothing more and nothing less!

Bottom Line: The challenge for parents is to be far more competent and creative in dealing with their divorce than they were in dealing with their marriage. Your children's well-being depends on your ability to reduce conflict with your ex-spouse and to meaningfully integrate your children into your new and separate lives.

Working, Parenting, and Children's Social Adjustment

In the 1950s and 1960s, TV shows frequently featured typical intact, nuclear American families. Fathers were portrayed as fulfilled in their role as breadwinners, and mothers were equally fulfilled as full-time housewives. There was a hint of something changing in the 1970s when Mike Brady came home to his blended family on "The Brady Bunch," but Mike was still the sole provider, and Carol Brady needed Alice (the live-in maid) to help her in the full-time care of the "bunch." This token recognition of change did not even begin to reflect the extraordinary transformation that was taking place in the American family during those years.

Structural changes in the American family since the 1960s have significantly altered the context of child development: In any given year only 60 percent of our children live with both biological parents, and 25 percent of children live with only one parent (U.S. Bureau of the Census, 1990). One in every four children is born to an unwed mother, typically a teenager. Many Americans—particularly those that have experienced divorce—have found it increasingly difficult to provide for their families, both financially and emotionally. These pressures have created a steady and unprecedented increase in the employment of mothers of children under 18. By one estimate (Hoffman, 1989), 71 percent of mothers in two-parent families are employed, and the rate continues to rise. How does maternal employment affect the social development of children?

There are a variety of possible positive and negative effects of mothers leaving the home for full- or part-time work. On the positive side, mothers' employment improves the family's financial situation, increasing resources to support children's needs. Women who find personal fulfillment in outside employment may improve their morale and self-esteem, fortifying them to cope with the stresses of caring for their children. Finally, mothers' employment may result in more equitable sharing of roles and responsibilities between mothers and fathers with respect to child care and household tasks. On the negative side, working mothers spend less time supervising their children, forcing them to rely on substitute care. (We take a closer look at children left home alone in Box 14.1.) Those mothers who find fulfillment and independence in their careers may be a threat to their husbands, particularly those men with more traditional values. Mothers may also have difficulty coping with the combined stress of their multiple roles.

A P P L I C A T I O N

Minimizing the Risk to Latchkey Children

Parents who have no alternative other than to leave their children undersupervised for extended periods may reduce the risk to their children by following these simple recommendations:

- Telephone your children at home regularly, and make certain that they know how to reach you and feel free to do so.
- Ask trusted neighbors to observe your residence and to check on your children

Latchkey Children

The increasing rates of teenage pregnancy, divorce, and maternal employment have caused millions of American families to seek substitute care for their children during working hours. While infants and preschoolers are likely to be cared for in day care or by extended family, elementary school-age children are increasingly left in the care of older siblings or are completely unsupervised.

We refer to children who are left to care for themselves for extended periods of time before or after school as **latchkey** or **self-care** children. (The term *latchkey* derives from many unsupervised children carrying a key to enter their homes after school.) By one estimate (U.S. Bureau of the Census, 1987), over 2 million American children (1 percent of 5-year-olds and 14 percent of 13-year-olds) may be classified as "latchkey," and approximately 60 percent of these children have no adult supervision after school on a regular basis. These estimates are undoubtedly conservative since few families would admit to neglect of their children.

Because families who leave their children unsupervised typically begin this practice by third or fourth grade (Messer, Wuensch, & Diamond, 1989), logic suggests that many latchkey children are at serious risk of accidental injury, loneliness, antisocial behavior, and poor school performance. Although the rationale for considering latchkey children at risk of these problems is clear, research has failed to show consistent differences between latchkey and nonlatchkey children on a variety of personality, cognitive, and academic measures (Galambos & Garbarino, 1985; Messer et al. 1989; Vandell & Corasaniti, 1988). In one study (Vandell & Corasaniti, 1988), third graders who attended after-school day care were less socially and academically well adjusted than latchkey children or than those cared for by their mothers.

The degree of risk associated with lack of direct supervision may depend on what the children are doing when they are home alone. One study (Steinberg, 1986a) of fifth through ninth graders showed that latchkey children who stayed home alone actually were less likely to engage in antisocial behavior than those who were routinely hanging out with their friends.

Moreover, parents who consistently knew where their children were and who used an authoritative approach to parenting had children who were less vulnerable to the negative influence of peers when unsupervised. Thus, the risk to latchkey children may be considerably lower for children who feel visible and responsible to their parents, even when their parents are not physically present. The phrase promoted on public service messages — "Parents, do you know where your children are?" — may hold the key to reducing children's risk whenever and wherever direct adult supervision is lacking.

We may conclude that latchkey children are not necessarily at greater risk of maladjustment than children who are more closely supervised. The potential risks encountered by latchkey children can be substantially reduced by thoughtful parents who structure and monitor their children's activities at a distance. Moreover, latchkey children have a unique opportunity to learn self-care, self-control, and survival skills that other children lack. This opportunity can be greatly facilitated by parents who remain responsible for and responsive to their children at all times.

occasionally. Make certain that neighbors know how to reach you in an emergency.

- Teach your children how to deal with security (locking doors and windows), emergencies (such as fires or storms), strangers at the door or on the phone, appliances, and safe and nutritious food preparation. Test your children's preparedness regularly.

- Establish specific rules for your child leaving the home, including places where children are and are not permitted to go, how long they may be gone, and how they are to inform you of their location and activities.

- Let your children know that you expect appropriate behavior, especially that they do their homework and chores. Monitor compliance daily.

Increasingly, working parents are forced to leave their children home alone without direct supervision. Parents can minimize the risks to their "latchkey" children by establishing rules and monitoring their children's compliance frequently by telephone and through the help of trusted neighbors. More positively, children can learn to be self-reliant and independent when forced to meet their own everyday needs.

Considering the balance of positive and negative factors, it is not surprising that research on the effects of maternal employment in two-parent families has failed to show negative effects on children's cognitive or social-emotional development (Gottfried, Gottfried, & Bathurst, 1988, 1991; Hoffman, 1989). Moreover, research has failed to uncover negative effects on family relationships (Hoffman, 1989) or on the quality of home environments for children (Gottfried et al., 1988). More positively, fathers with employed wives spend more time caring for their children than do fathers with unemployed wives (Gottfried et al., 1991).

Thus, we must look beyond the question of whether maternal employment is simply good or bad for families and their children. More important are the attitudes of various family members toward the mother's employment. Mothers who are more satisfied with their employment, compared to less satisfied mothers, have children who are better adjusted (Guidubaldi & Nastasi, 1987). Research has shown few positive or negative effects of maternal employment on fathers' morale (Hoffman, 1989). However, fathers with traditional gender role values may be threatened by their wives' growing independence and success in the workplace (Staines, Pottick, & Fudge, 1986).

One study (Greenberger & Goldberg, 1989) examined how parents' relative investments in their work and parenting affects their approach to socializing their children. Although the researchers assumed that a parent's strong commitment to work might be associated with less adequate parenting, the results showed that mothers who were highly committed to both work *and* parenting were most often authoritative (controlling, but flexible) with their children—the parenting style most likely to result in positive child outcomes (Baumrind, 1971). Thus, parents who invest a great deal of time and effort in their children need not worry about the negative effects of their career investments.

Looking Back

We have tried to convey that middle childhood is a critical time for the development of children's social skills and social cognitive abilities. The risks and opportunities for development center on children's interaction with their peers. Their success or failure at making and keeping friends may indicate how well they will relate to others throughout their lives. Children who are rejected by their peers are less happy, more lonely, and less successful in school than their more popular peers, and they are more likely than other children to continue to show social maladjustment into their adolescent and adult years. Those who deal with school-age children should consider rejected and neglected children at serious risk of maladjustment and should intervene vigorously to improve their social competencies.

Despite the many risks to development during middle childhood, we must be impressed by children's resiliency in the face of expanding social challenges, family dysfunction, and decreasing parental supervision. We are encouraged that most children leave middle childhood with the social and emotional competencies necessary to cope with adolescence. We now turn to this tumultuous last phase of development before adulthood.

CHAPTER REVIEW

FRIENDS Friendships become an increasingly important part of children's social lives in middle childhood. Although they choose friends from an expanding pool of children in their neighborhood and at school, they are increasingly selective, picking friends for particular personality characteristics. By the upper elementary grades, children seek friends who are loyal and who share common interests, values, and attitudes.

CRITERIA FOR FRIENDSHIP In the lower elementary grades children choose friends who are similar to themselves: Boys choose friends who are similar in superficial characteristics, such as interest in sports, and girls choose friends who have similar personalities, feelings, and interests. By the upper elementary grades, similarity becomes less important as children begin to choose friends who complement their personalities.

COMPARING PEERS School-age children spend extraordinary amounts of time socially comparing their peers, using increasingly complex traits (such as loyalty and aspects of personality) as they grow older. While young children focus on observable features, such as physical appearance, older children emphasize abstract qualities, such as likes and dislikes, attitudes, and interests.

GOSSIP Children share their social comparisons through gossip. Irrespective of its accuracy, gossip can have powerful effects on children's peer relationships. Children use gossip to confirm and elaborate the basis of their friendships. Gossip also contributes to individual children's reputation, which can make or break a child in the pursuit of friends and peer acceptance. Children gradually learn that they can improve their reputation by behaving in ways that please their peers.

MANAGING EMOTIONS Keeping friends requires that children learn to manage their emotions. They must learn to avoid emotional outbursts and to attune their emotions and the tempo of their behavior to that of their friends. Friends who fail to attune their emotions risk conflict, which may ultimately threaten the relationship.

EARNING SOCIAL STATUS Research has shown that children earn their social status by behaving in ways that consistently please or displease their peers. Popular children tend to be cooperative and rarely start fights. Rejected children are disruptive, uncooperative, and frequently ask others for help. Neglected children are typically shy and withdrawn.

SOCIAL INFORMATION PROCESSING Developmentalists have formulated models of social information processing to describe the way children solve social problems. The components of information processing include interpreting social cues, generating responses, evaluating and selecting the optimal response, and enacting the response.

AGGRESSIVE CHILDREN Aggressive children have a negative attributional bias that assumes hostile intent in their peers' behaviors. Thus, these children have a chip on their shoulder that makes them more likely to engage in physical conflict.

SELECTING SOLUTIONS According to the social information processing model, children must take the time to evaluate the potential solutions to a social problem in their repertoire in order to select the best response. Children who respond impulsively (automatic reasoning) select the first solution that comes to mind or the solution that requires the least effort. Children who use reflective reasoning consciously and deliberately search for the best solution to the problem.

LONELINESS   Rejected children report less satisfying peer relationships and greater feelings of loneliness than higher status children do. Feelings of loneliness can be particularly intense in children who blame themselves for their social failures. However, some rejected children avoid loneliness by hanging out with other rejected peers.

EFFECTS OF REJECTION   The opportunity for extensive peer interaction is essential to healthy social adjustment and personality development. Peer rejection places children at risk of both short- and long-term social-emotional maladjustment. Children who are rejected in the early elementary grades are likely to show adjustment problems in the upper grades. Moreover, children do not easily outgrow their problems with peers. Rejection in childhood has been associated with adolescent and adult social maladjustment.

TAKING RESPONSIBILITY   Children vary in the extent to which they take credit for their social successes and failures. Popular children tend to adopt a masterful style, taking credit for their successes and persisting in the face of social failures. Low-status children show a learned helpless style, attributing their failures to incompetence and bad luck, causes they consider beyond their control.

PROSOCIAL BEHAVIOR   School-age children are much more likely than younger children to behave prosocially with peers. This change is associated with significant advances in their prosocial moral reasoning and their ability to show empathy and sympathy. This reflects a major shift in children's orientation, from thinking only of their own needs to considering the needs of others.

COPING WITH DIVORCE   Children born in the 1980s are very likely to experience both the divorce and the remarriage of their parents during their childhood or adolescent years. Children vary greatly in their reactions to divorce, depending on protective and vulnerability factors. Protective factors (such as children's positive personality dispositions and social support) promote coping and vulnerability factors (such as continuing parental conflict after the divorce) undermine coping. Age and gender influence children's ability to cope. Mothers have more difficulty relating to their sons than to their daughters, but daughters have more difficulty than sons in dealing with their mothers' remarriage. Children who were quite young at the time of divorce seem to do better than children who were older, particularly adolescents.

WORKING MOTHERS   Numerous changes in U.S. society since the early 1960s have resulted in dramatic increases in maternal employment. Seventy-one percent of mothers in two-parent families are now employed. Research has failed to identify negative effects in children or in the family relationships where the mother is employed full- or part-time. Even latchkey children avoid negative effects when parents take appropriate precautions. In general, children of mothers who are satisfied with their employment are better adjusted than children of mothers who are less satisfied. Working mothers who remain committed to parenting their children are likely to experience few negative effects.

Key Terms

social comparison	average status children	social learned helplessness
gossip	social information processing	prosocial moral reasoning
peer reputation	negative attributional bias	empathy
popular children	reflective reasoning	sympathy
rejected children	automatic reasoning	latchkey
neglected children	attributional style	self-care
controversial children		

Adolescence

15

Physical and Cognitive Development in Adolescence

Looking Ahead

■ By middle adolescence, most teenagers have gone through a series of physical changes that result in sexual maturity. What processes are involved, and what specific effects do they have on the teenager's physical development and behavior?

■ Some adolescents reach sexual maturity much earlier or later than others, some as early as 10 (technically before becoming "teenagers") and others as late as 16. What are the effects of early versus later sexual maturation?

■ Extensive physical changes during adolescence offer a unique opportunity to enhance physical development through exercise and sports. Do teenagers take advantage of this opportunity? How should teenagers use their leisure time to maximize physical development?

■ Physical changes during adolescence often result in increased body fat, leading many teenage girls to attempt to lose weight. What approaches do teenagers take to lose weight?

■ A small percentage of teenagers develop eating disorders that can be life threatening. What causes these problems and how can they be treated?

■ AIDS is spreading in epidemic proportions among adolescents. Why are adolescents so vulnerable to infection, and what can be done to prevent the spread of the disease?

■ Adolescence provides new opportunities for advances in cognitive development. How do adolescents think differently than children? Why do some adolescents fail to develop these advanced cognitive abilities?

■ Cognitive changes during adolescence foster a new form of egocentrism that significantly affects adolescents' behavior and adjustment. What form does this egocentrism take, and what effects does it have on adolescent behavior?

■ Many U.S. high school students achieve well below their academic potential. What factors undermine academic achievement, and what can be done to improve it?

■ Advances in cognitive ability in adolescence allow potential improvements in moral reasoning. What is the nature of this new level of moral reasoning, and why do some adolescents fail to develop advanced capability?

Physical Development in Adolescence

This chapter describes the developmental changes in mind and body during **adolescence**, the period of development from age 11 through age 20. During this period the child's body transforms to the size and proportions of the young adult, and the child's mind transcends its focus on concrete reality and begins to apply itself to abstract reasoning. The potential physical and cognitive changes can be as dramatic and significant as those in the preceding developmental periods. If we photographed a group of children at the beginning and at the end of adolescence and asked a stranger to match each adolescent's photographs, the stranger would be no more accurate than he would be in matching photographs of newborns and toddlers. The cognitive changes during adolescence can be equally impressive.

As in earlier periods, optimal physical development in adolescence requires consistent opportunities—for proper nutrition, adequate exercise, and necessary medical care. Unfortunately, the typical American teenage lifestyle is less than conducive to optimal physical development. Too much TV, experimentation with drugs, exposure to disease, poor nutrition, and lack of exercise all take their toll. Cognitive development in adolescence requires educational and social opportunities that are increasingly difficult to find in our schools, our families, and our neighborhoods. Overcrowded classrooms, academically unmotivated peers, overburdened parents, and inadequately trained teachers eat away at the adolescent's potential for cognitive development. This chapter describes the major risks and opportunities for physical and cognitive development during the adolescent years.

The Experience of Puberty

The child's transformation from sexual immaturity to reproductive capability is known as **puberty**. The physical changes of puberty include accelerated gains in height and weight, salient changes in body proportion, maturing of the reproductive system, appearance of secondary sex characteristics, changes in the body's fat and muscle composition, and, for many teenagers, acne. Although puberty is defined by physical changes of the body, it is more broadly recognized as a rite of passage from childhood to adolescence, with profound effects on every aspect of adolescent development. Heather's experience of puberty illustrates the far-reaching effects of these changes.

In Heather's eleventh year, she begins to grow rapidly, becoming taller and heavier than most of the girls and almost all of the boys in her class. She has just turned 11 when she notices a slight increase in the size of her nipples. Over the next few months her breasts grow quite rapidly to the point that boys at school begin to tease her about her "big tits." She is embarrassed at first, but she realizes that her rapidly changing body is getting attention from several of the older boys at school and even from some men in her neighborhood. Hungry for the attention, she begins to wear clothing that accentuates her figure. By her twelfth birthday Heather has had her first period, and her physique looks like that of a much older adolescent. In seventh grade, Heather can easily pass for 16 or 17. A preadolescent's emotions in a woman's body and dress make a disastrous combination.

Flaunting her new physical endowments does not help Heather's already tenuous social relationships with the other girls her age. Although a few of her classmates are also beginning puberty, most are much more ambivalent about the changes in their bodies and unlikely to view them as assets. They tease Heather mercilessly, adding to her sense of rejection.

It does not take long for Heather to realize that her new physique will be more appreciated by the older boys and girls at her school. Although Heather is physically suited to this older group of peers, she is way over her head socially and emotionally. Keeping up with her new peers means conforming to their expectations. With little going for her beyond her curvaceous body, she earns her membership by doing virtually anything that is demanded of her, particularly by older, more dominant boys. Within months of her first contact with this older group, Heather has become sexually active. By her thirteenth birthday, she is having sexual intercourse regularly with several different boys. She uses her sexuality as a weapon to get what she wants and to gain some control over her life.

Some individuals pass through puberty uneventfully, taking the changes in stride and maintaining the developmental momentum they sustained through childhood. For other, less resilient individuals, puberty can be an overwhelming experience that results in significant social and emotional maladjustment. We examine the major physical changes during puberty and their effects on adolescent lifestyle and adjustment. We are concerned with four interrelated aspects of puberty: the changing balance of hormones that stimulate and regulate pubertal development, the changing physical structure of the body, achieving sexual maturity, and the timing of puberty for males and females.

The Surge of Hormones

Although we do not know exactly what biological and environmental events trigger the onset of puberty, we do know that puberty begins with a sudden surge of *hormones* that stimulate and regulate the complex biological changes required for sexual maturation. **Hormones** are complex chemical substances produced by endocrine glands and distributed throughout the body by the bloodstream. One part of the brain, the **hypothalamus**, stimulates the pituitary gland (located at the base of the brain) to produce a hormone that stimulates the testes or ovaries to increase their production of sex hormones, known as *androgens* and *estrogens*.

The male testes produce more androgens than estrogens, and the female ovaries produce more estrogens than androgens. Dramatic increases during puberty in the production of one particular androgen, **testosterone**, accounts for the biological changes in males: the size of the testes, the growth of pubic hair, and the deepening of the voice (Fregly & Luttge, 1982). One particular form of estrogen, **estradiol**, increases significantly in females, stimulating changes in their sex characteristics: breast development and changes in the uterus.

The Growth Spurt

The most noticeable change associated with puberty is a sudden increase in height and weight, commonly referred to as the **adolescent growth spurt**. The spurt begins at an average age of 10½ in girls and 12½ in boys, and lasts about two years for both sexes. Whereas girls typically enter puberty slightly taller than boys, boys grow more rapidly than girls during puberty and are taller than girls by the time they enter high school (Tanner, 1970). On average, girls gain just under 40 pounds and 10 inches in height between ages 10 and 14, and boys gain 42 pounds and 10 inches in height from 12 to 16 years. The changes in height during puberty are illustrated in Figure 15.1. These increases in height and weight are a considerable challenge to parents struggling to replace outgrown clothing and to feed their teenager's bottomless pit.

Most children begin the growth spurt by gaining weight rather than height. Much of this weight is fat. Soon after the initial weight gain, increases in height gradually stretch out children's bodies, slowly improving body proportion. As puberty progresses, girls tend to retain a higher percentage of body fat than boys, particularly in their hips and legs (Warren, 1983). Both sexes tend to gain muscle tissue later in puberty, but boys gain far more, especially in the upper body. This increase in upper body strength gives boys an advantage over girls in sports that require strength and endurance (Petersen & Taylor, 1980). Although much of this advantage in body strength in boys is genetically determined, some of the boys' advantage is a function of their greater participation than girls in vigorous exercise during the middle to late adolescent years.

The averages presented are somewhat misleading in that they do not reflect the extreme variability in children's growth during puberty. Also, different parts of the body grow at different times: The hands and feet tend to grow rapidly first, then the arms and legs, then the torso. Ears, nose, and lips may grow faster than the head. Some adolescents may also grow asymetrically, with one leg, arm, or breast growing faster than the other. Although these disproportions in growth even out with time, they do place the teenager's emerging sense of self at some risk. When a teenager's peers notice his or her lopsidedness in locker rooms, swimming pools, or during sleepovers, it can be terribly embarrassing.

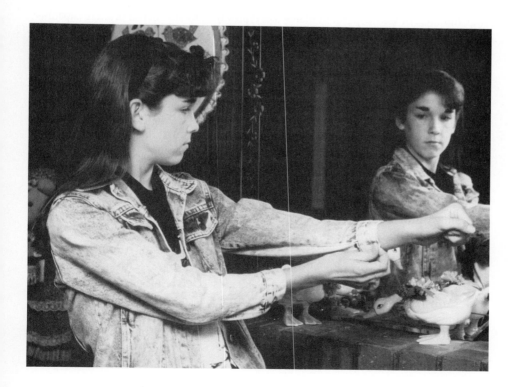

The adolescent growth spurt affects different individuals—and different parts of the same person's body—at different times. When it does hit, teenagers' physical movements may become temporarily awkward and uncoordinated, and they seem to outgrow their clothing overnight.

A P P L I C A T I O N

Coping with the Growth Spurt

Parents and teachers should not underestimate the psychological risks inherent in
their teenager's accelerated growth during puberty. Pants and sleeves that are too short, shoes
that are too tight, and clothing styles that are
too childish accentuate the disproportion of pubescent bodies and the awkwardness of their
physical movements. What can you do to help?

- Avoid drawing attention to your child's awkward appearance and occasional clumsiness,
particularly in public settings. Most of this is
beyond your child's control and putting her
on stage is likely to breed resentment and
encourage social withdrawal.

- Shopping for clothing provides an opportunity to help your teenager weather this awk-

ward period. Anticipate her rapid growth by
buying clothing a half-size bigger than required at the time. Be prepared to alter or
replace outgrown clothing regularly.

- Be aware that rapid bone growth can cause
considerable joint pain—sometimes referred
to as growing pains. If your child has persistent complaints, bring them to the attention
of a physician.

- Be particularly sensitive to your teenager's
struggle with acne. Recent advances in the
treatment of acne can significantly improve
her physical appearance, with equally positive
effects on her mood, peer acceptance, and
self-concept.

Achieving Sexual Maturity

Achieving sexual maturity—the ability to reproduce—is a truly momentous experience
in an individual's lifetime. The changes affect virtually every part of the body and have
significant impact on one's social and emotional development. We deal with the physical aspects of this process here and the psychosocial aspects in Chapter 16.

Sexual maturity is defined by the first ovulation in females and the production of
large numbers of viable sperm in males. We typically mark the arrival of these capabilities by **spermarche** (pronounced spermarkey), the first ejaculation in males, and by
menarche, the first menstrual period in females, although in fact ovulation typically
begins several months after the first period.

There are two types of biological changes associated with achieving sexual maturity:
changes in the *primary* and in the *secondary sex characteristics*. Changes in **primary sex
characteristics** involve the biological features that are directly involved in reproduction,
such as changes in the penis and testes in males and changes in the ovaries, vagina, and
uterus in females. **Secondary sex characteristics** are visible features that are not related
to reproduction, many of which differentiate males and females, such as growth of facial
hair and the development of breasts.

Boys' primary and secondary sex characteristics develop in a predictable sequence,
beginning with growth of the testicles and scrotum and the appearance of straight pubic
hair. As the growth spurt begins, the penis enlarges, the pubic hair becomes coarser and
kinked, the voice slowly deepens, and the skin on the face and back becomes more
prone to acne. In one study (Gaddis & Brooks-Gunn, 1985), the average age of spermarche—the first ejaculation—was just over 12, most often resulting from masturbation
or nocturnal emission (wet dream). Most boys experienced spermarche with mixed but
generally positive feelings. While most boys felt excited and proud, some less-informed
boys were surprised and a little scared. Most boys were highly secretive about their experience, not even telling their friends.

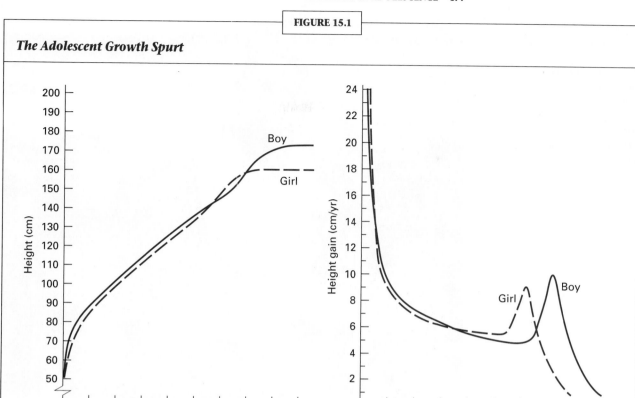

FIGURE 15.1

The Adolescent Growth Spurt

SOURCE: *Marshall, from* Puberty in Human Growth, *Vol. 2, F. Falkener and J. Tanner, eds., 1978, (New York: Plenum Publishing Corporation). First appeared in Tanner, Whitehouse, and Takaishi,* Archives of Diseases in Childhood, 41, *454–471, 1966. Reprinted by permission of the publishers.*

Girls' primary and secondary sex characteristics develop in a somewhat less predictable sequence. The first sign may be either the emergence of breast buds or the appearance of pubic hair. As the breasts continue to develop, pubic hair becomes coarser and more curled, and internal growth of the vagina, uterus, and ovaries culminates in menarche—the first menstrual period. Although some girls develop a negative perception of menarche based on myth and rumor, most girls adjust quite well after experiencing several periods (Brooks-Gunn & Ruble, 1982; McGrory, 1990). While many girls are just as secretive about menarche as boys are about spermarche, girls are generally more likely than boys to share their experience immediately with their mothers and eventually with their close friends (Brooks-Gunn & Ruble, 1982). Thus, with the exception of girls who may be intimidated and confused by misleading information, most girls deal well with the experience of menarche.

The Timing of Puberty

The timing and duration of puberty are highly variable. While some children begin puberty as early as 9 or 10 years of age, others may not begin until 15 or 16. Since the sequence of physical changes typically takes from one to two years, some adolescents will complete puberty well before others have even begun (Brooks-Gunn, 1988). Puberty

The biological changes at puberty have prepared these teenage girls for reproduction and have stimulated their interest in sexuality. Unfortunately, rapid physical changes come well before the social and emotional maturity needed to cope with sexuality and its consequences.

typically begins one to two years earlier in girls than in boys (Petersen & Taylor, 1980). Since pubertal changes are highly conspicuous symbols of sexual maturity, the timing of puberty is likely to have significant impact on a teenager's personality and social adjustment, particularly for those who mature much earlier or much later than the majority of their peers. Earlier in this section we described Heather's early experience of puberty and the effects on her social life. We now compare Heather's experience with Leshonda's.

> *Leshonda is what developmentalists call a late maturer. At 14, she has grown quite tall, but there are still no clear signs of pubertal change. Her legs are disproportionately long and slim, and there are no signs of the extra fat that has begun to round the bodies of her female peers. Her family physician has speculated to her mother that Leshonda's athletic lifestyle, particularly the long-distance running and weight training, may have delayed her sexual maturation. She assures Keisha that there is no cause for concern. However, by age 14, the absence of any breast development has become a sore subject and an occasional source of teasing from her friends. Her mother has reassured Leshonda that "everything will come in good time," but her mother's words wear thin when the last of her friends confide that she too has had her first period.*
>
> *But finally, a few weeks after her fifteenth birthday, Leshonda notices the first signs of pubic hair and breast development. She menstruates for the first time a few months later. It is a very special moment for Leshonda, but she tells no one, trying to avoid the notoriety of being the last in her group to reach*

puberty. She also begins to notice other subtle changes in her body that are less to her liking: Her hips seem wider and her shoulders narrower than they once were. Her legs, although still quite slender, seem more in proportion to the rest of her body. She begins to spend more time looking at herself in the mirror and liking what she sees. She has the distinct impression that some of the boys at school share her opinion.

At 16, Leshonda has grown to just over 5 feet 7 inches and weighs only 106 pounds. Her body is quite muscular, well proportioned, and very low in body fat. Her legs are particularly strong, making her one of the fastest runners in her high school and competitive with the best runners in New York City. Her athletic skills extend to all track and field events, and her coach believes that, barring injuries, she will be offered college scholarships in track.

Like Heather, girls who grow to sexual maturity earlier than the majority of their peers (that is, by sixth or seventh grade) enter a very different developmental pathway than girls who do not reach menarche until ninth or tenth grade. The pathway for early maturers begins on a positive note. They react to the first signs of puberty positively, showing more favorable adjustment, peer relations, and body image than their less mature peers (Brooks-Gunn & Warren, 1988). They are also more independent of their parents and more popular than late maturing girls (Simmons & Blythe, 1987).

However, early maturation also poses a number of risks. Early maturing girls are more likely than later maturing girls to start dating early (Simmons & Blythe, 1987), and early dating often leads to earlier sexual activity (Phinney, Jensen, Olsen, & Cundick, 1990) and a higher incidence of unwanted pregnancy (Stattin & Magnusson, 1990). Early maturers are also more likely to cut school, use hashish and alcohol, steal, ignore their parents' prohibitions (Magnusson, Stattin, & Allen, 1985), and associate with deviant peers (Silbereisen, Petersen, Albrecht, & Kracke, 1989).

While the developmental pathway for many early maturing girls becomes a fast track to adultlike behaviors and consequences, a longitudinal study conducted by David Magnusson and his colleagues in Sweden suggests that not all early maturing girls are at risk of social maladjustment (Magnusson et el., 1985; Magnusson, Stattin, & Allen, 1986; Stattin & Magnusson, 1990). Magnusson noted that 74 percent of early maturing girls in middle adolescence reported having older friends. These girls were significantly more likely to engage in inappropriate behaviors (such as smoking, drinking, and stealing) than the remaining 26 percent of early maturing girls who did not have older friends. Thus, not all early maturing girls are predisposed to the fast track. If Magnusson's data can be generalized to our culture, it would seem that the effects of early maturation depend, at least in part, on the company one keeps. Those early maturing girls who are rejected by their same-age peers and/or seek older friends are at greater risk of social maladjustment.

What are the *long-term* outcomes for early maturing girls? When Magnusson followed up his subjects as young adults, the early maturers were not very different from later maturers (Magnusson et al., 1985), suggesting that early maturation may not be a risk factor for *long-term* social maladjustment. However, early maturers did pay a price for their wilder lifestyle. They were significantly less likely than later maturers to attend school beyond ninth grade. Only 2.3 percent of the earliest maturing girls went on to college, compared to 12 to 15 percent of the other girls in the study. Thus, those early maturing girls who chose older friends, dated earlier, and engaged in earlier sexual relations were less involved in school than later maturing girls.

Another longitudinal study—the Berkeley Growth Study—followed development from birth through adulthood (Jones, 1957, 1965; Jones & Bayley, 1950; Livson & Peskin, 1980; Mussen & Jones, 1957). These researchers found that, while early maturing girls experience a good deal of stress during adolescence, most grow into self-directed, adaptive adults (Livson & Peskin, 1980). Late maturing girls—who faced less stress and turbulence in adolescence—were less able to cope with problems in their adult lives.

What is the effect of maturational timing in boys? We might expect that, unlike early maturing girls, early maturing boys would be well received by their same-age peers. Their greater size and strength and more mature physique should be admired and perhaps envied by their same-age peers, enabling them to take on leadership roles. Thus, it would seem likely that early maturation would have more favorable consequences for boys than for girls.

Unfortunately, there has been little research on the timing of sexual maturation in boys. What we do know comes primarily from the Berkeley Growth Study (Jones, 1957, 1965; Jones & Bayley, 1950; Livson & Peskin, 1980; Mussen & Jones, 1957), which showed that, in contrast to the results for girls, early maturing boys display more favorable short- and long-term adjustment than late maturing boys. During their high school years early maturers were more popular, more poised, less nervous, and more likely to be chosen as leaders than late maturers. However, those early maturers who reported hanging out with older friends were more likely to be truant and to have minor behavior problems in and out of school.

A follow-up study of the Berkeley boys in their thirties showed that early maturers turned out very differently from late maturers in certain areas (Livson & Peskin, 1980). As adults, they were more controlled, more responsible, and more likely to be leaders than the late maturers. However, the late maturing males had a better sense of humor and were more adaptive and more liberated from traditional gender roles than the early maturers.

What can we conclude about the effects of maturational timing in boys? First, we must recognize that the subjects in the Berkeley Growth Study reached puberty in the 1950s, which many would consider a less stressful time to grow up in than now. Thus, the timing of maturation may have very different effects today. With that said, we may tentatively conclude that while early maturing boys are at some advantage during adolescence, there are no clear *advantages* for either group in adulthood, only *differences*.

A P P L I C A T I O N

Helping Adolescents Cope with Puberty

All adolescents must cope with the surge in hormones, the awkward bodily changes, and the onset of sexual maturity. But the challenge and risk is more extreme for those who reach puberty noticeably earlier or later than their peers. In particular, early maturing girls and late maturing boys appear to be at increased risk of maladjustment. You may facilitate your child's coping in the following ways:

■ Be aware of your child's progress toward sexual maturity as compared to his or her

friends. Watch for obvious physical signs of puberty and the behavioral clues that typically accompany maturation, such as changes in your child's appetite, style of dress, and approach to grooming. Knowing your child's pubertal status gives you the opportunity to *anticipate* difficulties and crises and to be ready for them.

■ Maintain open lines of communication with your child, particularly with respect to providing information on the physical changes that are taking place. No child should be surprised, confused, or frightened by the first signs of puberty, particularly menarche and spermarche. There are excellent resources available from your physician and the library to help you prepare your child to cope with the physical and social-emotional changes at puberty.

■ Remember that early maturing girls—particularly those with older friends—are likely to date and to engage in sex earlier than other girls. These girls need to understand the choices available to them and the consequences associated with these choices. Most important, they need to know that they can *control* the outcome of their choices. Providing information on contraception and disease prevention is essential.

■ Late maturing boys—particularly those who are rejected by their peers—need understanding and encouragement that their turn will come. Help them to develop social skills that do not depend on physical size and strength, such as prosocial skills, verbal ability, and a sense of humor.

   Bottom Line: Regardless of the specific timing of your child's maturation, adjustment depends heavily on your understanding of what your child is going through and the information and emotional support that you can provide.

Wellness in Adolescence

An episode of a popular family sitcom portrayed a middle-age father's desperate attempts to compete with his teenage son in one-on-one basketball. After being overwhelmed by his son's agile movements and boundless energy, the father launched into nostalgic reminiscence of his own physical prowess during his teenage years. This popular stereotype is consistent with what we know about physical development during adolescence: increases in muscle mass, plentiful leisure time, and opportunities for exercise make the teenage years the ideal time to advance the athletic and artistic motor skills initiated in childhood.

   We might expect adolescents to recognize and take advantage of this unprecedented opportunity to perfect their physical development through exercise, nutrition, and doing everything possible to prevent disease. Unfortunately, adolescents seem to do very little to achieve optimal physical development. We will consider adolescents' use of leisure time, their approach to diet, and how they deal with the threat of AIDS.

Leisure Time and Sports

The slow and steady increases in height and weight during the middle childhood years allow children plenty of time to adapt their motor functions to their changing bodies. For example, a third grader who grows two inches and gains four pounds in a year may outgrow some of her clothes, but she is unlikely to appear more clumsy or uncoordinated as a result. However, many adolescents have great difficulty learning to adjust to the rapid changes in their bodies during puberty. The uneven growth of various parts of the body often results in an awkward appearance and characteristic clumsiness. Painfully aware of the risk of public embarrassment, many adolescents avoid active participation in sports and other outdoor activities. Carlos's experience in high school is not unusual.

> *At 15, Carlos stands five feet four inches tall and weighs 155 pounds. Although his obesity has not worsened through his first two years of high school, he remains well over the normal body weight for his height, and his continuing*

lack of physical fitness is beginning to take its toll. Every step he takes seems labored, and he loses his breath climbing a single flight of stairs. He catches colds frequently and suffers from allergies year-round. He shies away from virtually all physical activities and manages to get medical excuses to avoid mandatory physical education classes.

Although clumsy throughout childhood, the physical changes at puberty have made him even more uncoordinated. While other boys his age are rapidly gaining muscle mass, Carlos's lack of exercise and poor nutrition leave his body composition virtually unchanged. His shoulders are rounded, he has a "spare tire" around his waist, and he has no muscle tone in his upper arms and chest.

The increasing demands of school, social life, and part-time employment also reduce teenagers' participation in fitness activities. One study (Kleiber, Larson & Csikszentmihalyi, 1986) showed the following distribution of teenagers' time:

- 29 percent *productive activities* (school, studying, and jobs)
- 30 percent *maintenance activities* (eating, personal care, chores)
- 35 percent *relaxed leisure activities* (socializing, watching TV, nonschool reading, and thinking)
- 5 percent *sports, games, and hobbies*

Thus, while adolescents had plenty of leisure time, they devoted only a small percentage of that time to more effortful sports, games, and hobbies.

They did so despite having reported that they found these more effortful activities more intrinsically motivating, more free, more fun, and more challenging than time spent in relaxed leisure. The researchers concluded that sports, games, and hobbies may help adolescents to understand that highly effortful activities can be intrinsically interesting and enjoyable, an experience many adolescents do not derive from schoolwork or part-time jobs. Unfortunately, the researchers could not explain why teenagers avoid the very activities they say they value.

What about those teenagers who do participate in athletic activities? Do more physically active teenagers benefit from this investment of their time and energy? According to one study, the answer depends on *where* they choose to play and *what goals* they set for themselves. Lawrence Chalip and his colleagues (1984) compared the experiences of teenagers in different sports contexts: organized sports (league play), informal sports (playground pick-up games), and physical education classes. They found that while teenagers liked sports more than other aspects of their lives, their sports experiences varied across settings. In general, they were more comfortable with informal sports than with organized sports or gym class. They felt that it was easier to match their skills to the challenge of the sport in the informal setting. For example, in informal neighborhood pick-up games, a teenager who perceives himself less skilled in baseball than in football can easily choose to play only football. The teenagers reported that their skills often fell short of the challenges inherent in organized sports and gym class.

The types of goals that teenagers set for themselves in sports also affect the quality of their experience (Duda, 1987). Some teenagers select **task-involved goals** that focus on improving their own performance, irrespective of the performance of their peers. For example, Leshonda learns to set personal goals for her performance in various track events, ignoring other athletes' achievements. This approach helps keep her anxiety down and her motivation up at all times. Other teenagers select **ego-involved goals** that require that they continually outperform their peers. With task-involved goals you succeed whenever you improve your performance; with ego-involved goals you succeed only when you are the best. One study (Duda, 1986) showed that high school students tend to emphasize task-involved rather than ego-involved goals. For example, one student remarked, "Success was when I did the best I could in the game. Failure was when I didn't get any better in my shooting" (Duda, 1987, p. 138). There is evidence (Duda, 1986; Ewing, 1981) that adolescents who pursue ego-involved goals are more likely to drop out of sports than those who pursue task-involved goals.

Despite the small percentage of adolescents who engage in effortful leisure activities, those who do play benefit considerably. Those who select informal settings and focus on self-improvement appear to gain more than those who play organized, highly competitive sports. Perhaps if more teenagers were encouraged to pursue sports in informal settings emphasizing task-oriented goals more of them would take advantage of the opportunity.

Dieting and Eating Disorders

In any grade of any American junior high or high school we see enormous ranges in teenagers' weight status—from those who are exceptionally obese, to those who are within the normal range of weight for height, to those who are little more than skin and bones. Although some of this variation is due to genetic influences, cultural eating habits, and family economics, it is often a direct result of their *purposeful* eating, dieting, and compulsive exercising (Attie & Brooks-Gunn, 1989; Gralen, Levine, Smolak, & Murnen, 1990).

Like adults, female adolescents—and to a much lesser extent, male adolescents—diet and exercise to modify their bodies to conform to the extreme standard of thinness that has emerged in Western society (Attie & Brooks-Gunn, 1987). Adolescent girls in competitive social groups, such as cheerleaders and sororities, are particularly vulnerable to the pressure to conform to the thinness standard (Brooks-Gunn & Warren, 1985). Whereas occasional dieting has little effect on the adolescent's well-being, our concern here is with adolescents who take dieting to an extreme. Preoccupation with eating and/or dieting can become a central focus of the adolescent's lifestyle, and in extreme instances, lead to severe, life-threatening eating disorders (Wenar, 1990).

Adolescents engage in distinct patterns of eating/dieting behavior to control their weight to the thinness standard. These behaviors vary along a continuum: occasional dieting (engaged in by up to 60 percent of teenagers); more disturbed eating/dieting behaviors, such as self-induced vomiting (engaged in by up to 10 percent of teenagers); more serious eating disorders (engaged in by up to 4 percent of teenagers)(Hesse-Biber, 1989; Patton, 1988; Rosen & Gross, 1987). Thus, while many adolescents make some attempt to regulate their weight, a fraction of the adolescent population employs more drastic measures. Their numbers are comparatively small, but those with eating disorders are at serious medical and psychological risk.

We begin by examining the function of dieting in normal adolescent development, and follow with a discussion of severe eating disorders.

Normal Dieting and Weight Loss   Those who deal with teenagers on a daily basis are well aware of their preoccupation with their physical appearance. They spend inordinate amounts of time directly involved in physical grooming, and they seem spellbound by their reflection in a mirror. Unfortunately, they do not always like what they see. Facial blemishes, hair that refuses to curl, and the ever-so-slowly emerging signs of sexual maturity can be most distressing, particularly at an age when adolescents are convinced that they are the center of everyone else's attention (Elkind, 1967). As disturbing as these events may be, none surpass the frustrations teenagers experience with respect to the dramatic changes in weight and shape that come with puberty.

The female adolescent's first concerns about weight and dieting are triggered by significant increases in body fat in early puberty (Attie & Brooks-Gunn, 1989; Gralen et al., 1990). The normal increase in fat stimulated by hormonal changes is often exacerbated by the poor nutritional habits of American teenagers. As young adolescent girls sexually mature and begin to feel increasing pressure to date, they become frustrated with the excess fat accumulated during puberty. One study found that 78 percent of young adolescent girls would prefer to weigh less, and only 14 percent were satisfied with their present weight (Eisele, Hertsgaard, & Light, 1986). Girls who perceive themselves as overweight—irrespective of whether they are really overweight by medical standards—tend to be dissatisfied with their bodies and experience low self-esteem (Rosen & Gross, 1987).

The majority of adolescent girls turn to dieting and exercise to lose or to maintain weight (Kelley & Patten, 1985; Paxton, Wertheim, Gibbons, Szmukler, Hillier, & Pretrovich, 1991; Rosen & Gross, 1987). Most girls engage in relatively benign approaches to weight loss (skipping meals, exercise, and drinking large amounts of water), but girls with extremely poor body images are at great risk of resorting to more severe methods (Attie & Brooks-Gunn, 1989). In one study (Paxton et al., 1991), 13 percent of girls used at least one extreme approach to weight loss—including fasting, purging (self-induced vomiting), diet pills, and laxatives—at least once a week.

Developmentalists have shown that the causes of dieting change significantly from early to later adolescence (Attie & Brooks-Gunn, 1989; Gralen et al., 1990). Whereas dieting and eating disturbances in pubescent females are a direct response to increases in body fat and the pressures of early dating, older girls (ninth grade or beyond) diet primarily to achieve slender, ideal body proportions (Gralen et al., 1990). This highly elusive goal is likely to frustrate even the most dedicated efforts at dieting, increasing the tendency for some girls to resort to extreme dieting behaviors.

Severe Eating Disorders   Most teenagers who try to lose weight are in control of their weight-loss behaviors. They set reasonable goals for weight loss and diet or exercise until they achieve their goal. Those who fail to lose weight may try again or give up. Whether successful or not, these teenagers are in control of their own behavior.

However, as indicated earlier, approximately 4 percent of those who attempt to regulate their weight lose control of the process (Patton, 1988; Rosen & Gross, 1987). They set unreasonable goals, they resort to extreme measures to accomplish those goals, and they cannot stop even when they meet their goals. Their lives revolve around their attempts to regulate their weight; the extreme weight-loss strategies endanger their health and, in many instances, their lives. We say that such individuals suffer from **eating disorders**.

The most prevalent eating disorder is **anorexia nervosa**, the "voluntary pursuit of thinness to the point of extreme emaciation or even death" (Wenar, 1990, p. 164). Anorexia nervosa is diagnosed when an individual has lost 15 percent of normal body weight for height (or has failed to gain the same percentage of body weight during normal periods of growth) as a result of deliberate starvation. Two approaches to dieting occur: the *restricting type*, involving severe fasting, and the *bulimic type*, involving binge eating and self-induced vomiting, often combined with use of diet pills, laxatives, and diuretics. (Note that in anorexia, the use of the term *bulimic* refers only to one possible symptom that may or may not be present in an individual with extreme, deliberate weight loss.)

Anorectics typically have a severely distorted body image, perceiving themselves to be overweight regardless of how thin they become. Many anorectics exercise compulsively to burn additional calories. The dieting of anorectics is so severe and so prolonged that 1 in 10 succeeds in starving herself to death (Garfinkel, Garner, & Goldbloom, 1987).

Teenagers with eating disorders have a distorted view of their own body. Girls with anorexia tend to see themselves as overweight, regardless of how much they diet or how thin their bodies become.

> *Of Leshonda's many friends, she is especially fond of Shanice, a friend from her apartment house who is 16, 1 year older and 1 grade ahead of Leshonda. Shanice has been average in height and weight through junior high, but has lost considerable weight during her first year of high school. Although some of the girls tease Shanice about being so skinny, no one senses the seriousness of her problem.*
>
> *Leshonda has not seen Shanice for several weeks and decides to stop at her apartment after school. When she rings the doorbell, there is no answer. Leshonda hears noises coming from the apartment and decides to try the door. It is unlocked, so she walks in. "Shanice?" she calls out. "Shanice?" There is no response. As she walks into the living room she can't believe her eyes. The room is a total mess, with food scraps, candy wrappers, and dirty plates on all of the furniture and most of the floor. The smell of rotting food turns her stomach.*
>
> *Leshonda hears sounds coming from the bathroom and decides to investigate. She listens through the door and hears the water running and a retching sound. She knocks on the door several times. Shanice opens the door briefly, then slams it, screaming at Leshonda to get out of her house. Although she has only glimpsed Shanice for an instant, Leshonda notices that her face is puffy and she looks really sick.*
>
> *Before Leshonda has time to think, Shanice suddenly opens the door and runs toward her bedroom. Leshonda chases her, grabs her arm, and spins her around. Although Leshonda has heard about this kind of thing in health education class, she is not ready for what she sees. Shanice stands in front of her wearing only a bra and panties. Her stomach bulges out from her otherwise emaciated body. She smells from vomit, and her body and underwear are filthy. Her face is so swollen that Leshonda barely recognizes her. Shanice begins to cry and slumps to the floor.*
>
> *As Shanice cries, Leshonda takes a good look at her friend. Shanice's thinness is horrifying. Her skin is stretched over her bones, and her breasts have all but disappeared. She reminds Leshonda of a picture she has seen of people in a concentration camp. After some time, Shanice looks up at her friend and says, "I need help. I don't know what to do. I eat and I vomit. That's all I do. I steal the food, I eat it, then I go and steal some more. I can't stop." Leshonda asks how long this has been going on. "I'm not sure," Shanice says, "Two years, maybe three. I don't really know anymore."*

A second, closely related eating disorder is **bulimia**, which involves extended binge-eating episodes and the loss of self-control during such episodes. A bulimic may ingest as many as 20,000 calories in a single episode, approximately the number of calories an adult might consume in 10 days (Behrman & Kliegman, 1990). The bulimic's goal is to eat enormous amounts of forbidden foods (high caloric, high fat), but to do so without gaining weight. Weight gain is avoided through self-induced vomiting. Thus, adolescents who suffer from bulimia tend to be thin but still within the normal range of weight for height. Although bulimia often causes severe damage to the adolescent's

TABLE 15.1

Comparison of Anorexia Nervosa and Bulimia

Characteristics	Anorexia Nervosa	Bulimia
Intense preoccupation with food	Yes	Yes
Weight loss	Severe	Fluctuates
Typical age at onset	13–14 years, 17–18 years	17–25 years
Gender	90–95% female	90–95% female
Family history	Positive for anorexia	Positive for depression
Methods of weight control	Severe food restriction, possible binging and purging, and/or use of laxatives and diuretics	Binging and purging with use of laxatives and diuretics
Psychological features	Denial, withdrawal, depressed, asexual, suicidal	Guilt or shame, outgoing, heterosexual, impulsive, substance abuse, depressed, suicidal

SOURCES: *Adapted from Behrman & Kliegman, 1990; Wenar, 1990.*

teeth, stomach, and esophagus and is frequently associated with depression, the disorder is rarely life threatening. Bulimics tend to be both aware of and secretive about their disorder. The similarities and differences between anorexia and bulimia are highlighted in Table 15.1.

Not all adolescents are equally susceptible to developing severe eating disorders. Adolescent females—especially those who are both white and economically advantaged—are 20 times more likely than adolescent males to develop severe eating problems (Behrman & Kliegman, 1990; Johnson & Connors, 1987; Levine, 1987). Why would this relatively privileged group engage in such self-destructive behavior? Unfortunately, there are no simple answers.

Psychoanalytic explanations focus on disturbed relationships between infants and their mothers during the oral stage of development (Wenar, 1990). The problem allegedly begins when overprotective mothers generate hostile dependency in their infants. Fearful of abandonment, the infants repress their hostile feelings toward their mothers and any hope they may have of becoming autonomous. As they mature they succumb to their mothers' pressure to strive for perfection—including seeking the perfect body. In adolescence, these girls learn to control their mothers by engaging in self-destructive oral behaviors. As with other psychoanalytic notions, this intriguing explanation has had little scientific verification.

A second explanation has been offered by Salvadore Minuchin, a family systems theorist and therapist (1974). Minuchin speculates that anorexia nervosa is a product of family **enmeshment**, an exaggerated but superficial state of family togetherness that robs family members of a sense of individual identity. Family members are overprotective of one another, resistant to change, and unable to resolve conflict. The enmeshed family avoids dealing with conflict by focusing on their child's illnesses—real or imagined. The family becomes preoccupied with their child's eating behaviors and related bodily functions, promoting rigid approaches to eating and diet. Eventually, as the symptoms of anorexia emerge, the child's disorder provides an ideal focus for the family's enmeshment and a convenient distraction from other challenges.

In contrast to the psychoanalytic explanation of anorexia, Minuchin's ideas have found some empirical support (Rhodes & Kroger, 1991; Strober & Humphrey, 1987). Research has shown that families of anorectics and bulimics are indeed more enmeshed, intrusive, hostile, and unresponsive to their children's emotional needs than other families (Strober & Humphrey, 1987). Moreover, adolescent females with eating disorders, compared to those without disorders, report having overprotective mothers and less opportunity to develop autonomy (Rhodes & Kroger, 1991). Further study of Minuchin's ideas is sorely needed.

Anorectics are particularly challenging to both parents and therapists. As a parent, you can lead your daughter to the table, but you can't make her eat! Therapists often have no more success than parents. Several forms of therapy may be helpful: Behavioral therapies offer some short-term changes in eating behaviors (Geller, Kelley, Traxler, & Marone, 1978); cognitive behavior therapy may change distorted views and assumptions about food and weight loss (Ordman & Kirschenbaum, 1985; Thornton & DeBlassie, 1989); and family therapy may help families manage conflict and offer individual family members opportunities to gain autonomy (Minuchin, Rosman, & Baker, 1978).

A P P L I C A T I O N

Dealing with Adolescent Eating Disorders

*C*onsistent with the idea that eating disorders emerge in the context of dysfunctional families, particularly those who become preoccupied with food and eating, we recommend the following:

■ Make eating and nutrition a natural and positive component of family life. Avoid conflict at mealtimes by setting aside special times for discussion of family problems and disagreements. Also avoid promoting myths about eating and diet, and refrain from extreme dining rules, such as "You must clean your plate."

■ Avoid using food as a reward or punishment and ignore your child's efforts to punish you by refusing to eat or by engaging in extreme eating behaviors, such as self-induced vomiting and gorging.

■ Avoid overprotecting your child, and promote a healthy sense of autonomy at all stages of development. Keep in mind that encouraging overdependence through childhood and adolescence increases the risk of rebellion that may be expressed in extreme eating behaviors and dieting.

■ Promote physical fitness by planning nutritious meals with limits on fat content and by encouraging good exercise habits.

■ Do not miss the opportunity to prepare your child — particularly your daughter — for the physical changes that come with puberty. Teenagers who know that it is natural for their hips to widen and their bodies to accumulate some fat are less likely to resort to extreme efforts to fight these changes.

■ Watch your teenager for signs of eating disorders — persistent dieting, compulsive exercising, hoarding food, extreme variations in weight — and the more subtle signs of binging and purging — habitual use of the toilet after eating, puffy face, damaged teeth. If your suspicions are confirmed, consult with a physician and/or a family therapist who specializes in adolescent eating disorders.

Bottom Line: Teenage eating disorders must be recognized as serious, possibly life-theatening psychological disturbances that require professional intervention. Treatment is likely to be long and difficult, involving all members of the family.

Sexually Transmitted Diseases and the Risk of AIDS

One of the more prevalent health problems in adolescence is **sexually transmitted disease**, infections that are spread through sexual contact. Four of the most common forms are *syphilis, gonorrhea, chlamydia,* and *genital herpes.* All four diseases are highly infectious and spreading in epidemic proportions among adolescents. Syphilis, gonorrhea, and chlamydia can be treated successfully with antibiotics, but genital herpes cannot be cured; it can, however, be controlled by drugs. As we indicated in Chapter 4, women infected with herpes must take special precautions during pregnancy to prevent the spread of the disease to the fetus, particularly during childbirth. All four diseases can be prevented by the use of condoms during sexual intercourse.

In the early 1980s physicians in the United States and in several other countries began to identify seemingly isolated cases of a new disease characterized by the total breakdown of the immune system in otherwise healthy individuals. The deficiency of the immune system made the person susceptible to a host of opportunistic infections, several of which would prove fatal. We eventually came to know this disease by the virus that causes it, the human immunodeficiency virus (HIV), and by its full-blown form, acquired immune deficiency syndrome (AIDS).

As of 1990, approximately 140,000 Americans had died of the disease, and it is estimated that 1.5 million others are infected (AIDS Weekly Surveillance Report, 1990). The disease is transmitted by the exchange of body fluids through blood transfusion, the sharing of hypodermic needles among drug addicts, or through oral, anal, or genital sexual contact. While the length of survival after initial infection varies considerably, the disease is believed to always be fatal.

We don't know exactly when or how the first teenager was infected by HIV. However, we do know that the spread of the disease to adolescents was unavoidable and that the disease would eventually be epidemic in this age group. There are several reasons. First, today's adolescents are highly sexually active: 60 to 70 percent of high school students have had sexual intercourse (Keller, Bartlett, Schleifer, Johnson, Pinner, & Delaney, 1991; Strunin, 1991). Moreover, many teenagers who engage in sex live on the edge — tempting

Adolescents are prime candidates for HIV: They are sexually active, relatively indiscriminate in sex partners, think of themselves as invulnerable, and enjoy high-risk behaviors. This girl contracted HIV while engaging in typical adolescent social behaviors. It is unlikely that she will live long enough to be called an adult.

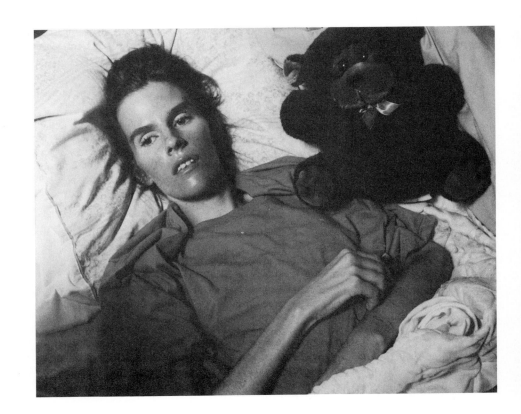

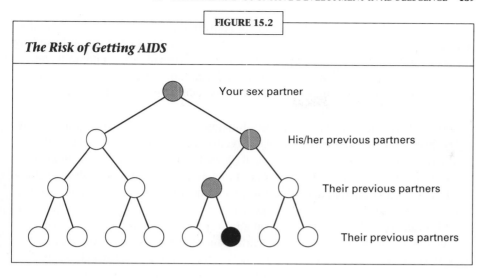

FIGURE 15.2

The Risk of Getting AIDS

Your sex partner

His/her previous partners

Their previous partners

Their previous partners

The chart represents all the partners whose sexually transmitted diseases you're sleeping with. Suppose that this is your first time and your partner has had un-protected sex with two other partners.

fate by having sex with multiple partners, using condoms irregularly (or not at all), and mixing sex with the disinhibiting effects of alcohol and drugs (Keller et al., 1991). Figure 15.2 illustrates the risk to teenagers of getting AIDS or any sexually transmitted disease.

Research has shown that the risks of HIV infection are pervasive in the lifestyle of many inner-city teenagers (Bowser, Fullilove, & Fullilove, 1990; Keller et al., 1991), particularly those who sell/use crack cocaine; the stimulating effect of crack promotes promiscuity, and the high cost of the severe dependency associated with crack addiction forces many addicts to trade sex for drugs (Bowser et al., 1990). The magnitude of the problem is enormous; one study (Bowser et al., 1990) estimated that there are more than 300,000 African American teenagers selling crack in the United States. Since this estimate does not count teenagers from other ethnic groups who engage in similar activities, this number must be considered quite conservative. It doesn't take an expert in public health to recognize this combination of behaviors as a disaster ready to explode. With the exception of the high-risk behaviors of some homosexuals in the early 1980s, it is hard to imagine a segment of the population more primed than teenagers—particularly those in our inner cities—to spread HIV in epidemic proportions.

Concern about the spread of AIDS among adolescents has led researchers to look more closely at the psychological factors involved. While studies conducted in the mid-1980s (DiClemente, Zorn, & Temoshok, 1986; Price, Desmond, & Kukulka, 1985) indicated that adolescents lacked knowledge about HIV and its transmission, more recent studies have shown them to be highly informed (Roscoe & Kruger, 1990; Strunin, 1991), including minority teenagers from the inner city (Keller et al., 1991). However, this knowledge has had little impact on their behavior (Keller et al., 1991; Roscoe & Kruger, 1990; Strunin, 1991). In one study (Roscoe & Kruger, 1990), only 33 percent of the girls and 37 percent of the boys indicated that they had changed their sexual behavior because of the threat of AIDS. Most of the change for both sexes consisted of being more selective in choosing sex partners. Since, however, there are rarely any visible signs of HIV infection—as opposed to full-blown AIDS—it is unlikely that becoming more selective would reduce the adolescents' risk of infection. If anything, it might increase risk by giving them a false sense of security.

Why would teenagers who know about the dangers of HIV and how it is transmitted continue to engage in high-risk sexual behaviors? One possible reason is that while adolescents believe that AIDS can happen to other people, they do not believe it can happen to them (Keeling, 1987). This notion would be consistent with the fact that many adolescents believe in the myth of their invulnerability (Elkind, 1967). Part of the problem may be that, while HIV-infected adolescents can be found in virtually any community, few have had the disease long enough to show visible symptoms. Thus, in the absence of visible effects of the disease in people their own age, adolescents see no reason for concern.

Adults can best understand adolescents' thinking on this by considering it from their perspective. Some developmentalists have suggested that adolescents' apparent lack of concern about HIV infection is not irrational (Bowser et al., 1990; Gardner & Herman, 1990). To the contrary, they argue that from the adolescent's viewpoint, high-risk behaviors may be quite rational in light of factors that influence their sexual decision making. Like adults, teenagers weigh the advantages and disadvantages associated with their decisions. For example, when faced with an opportunity to have sex with a new partner, teenagers must decide whether or not to participate and whether or not to use a condom. Most teenagers are smart enough to know that it is *unlikely* that any given sex partner is HIV infected. Some even know that avoiding high risk partners (those who sleep around and IV drug users) improves the odds and that safe sex is not really all that safe. Why pass up an opportunity for sex or reduce one's pleasure with a condom, they ask, when the chances of being infected are so slim?

Adolescents also weigh the promise of immediate gratification against the potential benefits of surviving to old age (Gardner & Herman, 1990). Unfortunately, many of today's teenagers—particularly those who live in poor, crime-ridden neighborhoods—discount the future, believing that they may not live that long anyway. Even if they do survive, many teens do not see the future as very promising. One group of researchers summarized the thinking of adolescents in poor communities this way:

> . . . What happens to adolescents in a community where parents and neighbors are cut off from—or are at best marginal to—the economy? If these young people see themselves through the eyes of their parents and neighbors, there is very little reason for them to see a different future for themselves. Very clearly there is less motivation to delay sexuality. . . . In communities where the "Crack Man" appears to have the only employment and the only source of income and mobility, what reason would a young person have for believing an anti-AIDS message? (Bowser et al., 1990, pp. 59–60, 64)

A P P L I C A T I O N

Preventing Adolescent HIV Infection

Although teenagers may not consider *all* relevant factors in making their decisions about sex and HIV, they are hardly behaving irrationally. We will be far more likely to succeed in our interventions to prevent HIV infection in teenagers if we respect their intelligence. They are unlikely to avoid high-risk sexual behavior until they are convinced that the benefits of caution truly outweigh the sacrifices. If they are not convinced, they will not protect themselves.

- Whether you are a parent dealing with your own teenager or a practitioner dealing with your clients, begin by making certain that everyone has accurate information on the nature of the disease, modes of transmission, and safer sex practices. To prevent redundancy, find out what your teenager or your audience knows before you begin. Provide information in a setting that allows for give and take and that ensures confidentiality. Keep in mind that information by itself will effect little change if you fail to deal with the major factors that keep teenagers from putting the HIV theory into safer sex practice.

- You must break the adolescent's myth of invulnerability. An effective way is to have teenagers come face to face with peers who have the disease, preferably those who have been infected long enough to show visible effects. Although this may sound insensitive, it may be your most effective means of changing high-risk behavior.

- You must also fight fatalism. As one adolescent put it, "Everybody is going to get AIDS anyway, so why bother? I probably already have it." Fatalistic teens must be convinced that what they do makes a difference. Those who believe they may already be infected may profit from a negative HIV test.

- Finally, you must give teenagers faith in their future. Expose them to models who have made it, particularly those who have transcended poverty and prejudice.

Bottom Line: To help teens fight HIV, don't underestimate their intelligence or the complexity of the decision they must make before they will commit to safer sex practices.

Cognitive Development in Adolescence

In Chapter 13 we described the elementary schoolchild's systematic, logical understanding of the world of real objects and events with Piaget's term, *concrete operational thought.* We illustrated operational reasoning by describing Carlos's complex sorting and resorting of his collection of baseball cards. His knowledge of baseball includes *classification concepts* (teams, leagues, good hitters), *spatial concepts* (the juxtaposition of players on the field), *temporal concepts* (batting orders, innings), and *numerical concepts* (batting averages, rankings of teams or players on various criteria). Importantly, all of Carlos's concepts refer to real people performing real physical movements, with real balls, bats, and gloves, in real ballparks. More generally, all concrete operational concepts, regardless of their complexity or content, are grounded in a child's concrete experience.

Although Carlos's concrete operational grasp of baseball is most impressive, his reasoning at age 10 has significant limitations. More specifically, if we asked him then to think about the game not as it *is*, but how it *might be*, he would have difficulty responding. For example, suppose we asked him to speculate on what baseball would be like if we changed the underlying principle of the game from competition to cooperation. That is, rather than trying to outscore one another, the teams would coordinate their efforts to score the most runs of any pair of teams playing on any given day. Carlos's concrete knowledge of the game would simply not allow him to deal effectively with this hypothetical question. For Carlos at age 10 baseball is what it is, and it cannot logically be anything else. His operational logic does not enable him to imagine what might be possible or to create new realities beyond his concrete experience.

In contrast, adolescents begin to think and solve problems at a more advanced level of reasoning: thinking in abstract terms that have little or no concrete reference, thinking about hypothetical consequences of hypothetical events, thinking about relationships among abstract concepts and propositions, and thinking in highly abstract terms about their own thinking. For example, Carlos's ability to think about baseball has changed dramatically in the last five years. At age 15, he still thinks about baseball in concrete terms, but he can also think about baseball as just one of the many games that people play. He frequently uses baseball as a metaphor to help him think about life. In a particularly solemn mood he says to his father, "Sometimes I think the world is really going down the tubes. It's like it's the ninth inning, two men are out, the bases are empty, and we are down by five runs. The situation is hopeless." Or, in a slightly more upbeat moment, "Y'know, Dad, it would be nice if life was like a baseball game. Y'know, like if you were kinda tired one day, someone could just come in and pinch hit for you. And when you didn't know if you were doing something right or wrong, you could just look up at the umpire and the mystery would be gone."

As with earlier phases of development, much of what we know about cognitive development in adolescence has been stimulated by the work of Piaget and his colleagues. We review Piaget's contribution to our understanding of cognitive development in adolescence, highlighting the distinctive characteristics of thought processes. Although not all of Piaget's ideas about development during this period have been confirmed, the concepts presented below are generally well accepted.

Formal Operational Thought

As children mature into adolescence they make significant advances in their ability to think and to solve problems. Piaget (1972) believed that these advances are highly integrated, representing an entirely new quality of reasoning that is fundamentally different from concrete operational thought. He referred to the adolescent's advanced cognitive ability as **formal operational reasoning** and to the period of time during which this thinking develops as the **period of formal operations**. As we see later, not all adolescents (or adults) develop formal operational reasoning.

According to Piaget, the centerpiece of *concrete operational reasoning* is the ability to think symbolically and systematically about real objects and events and about how those objects can be manipulated and changed. In contrast, the centerpiece of *formal operational thought* is the ability to reason about hypothetical events and hypothetical transformations of those events. Piaget called this **hypothetico-deductive reasoning**. To think hypothetically is to reason about phenomena that have no concrete reference (Piaget, 1972), including phenomena that do not or could not exist. For example, in mathematics, formal operational thinkers solve problems with unknowns, such as 4X or 5Y, and imaginary numbers, such as $3i + 4i$. They also reason about hypothetical transformations of those hypothetical phenomena, such as $3X + 4Y = ?$, or $3i + 4i = 7i$. In their social lives, adolescents reason about abstract qualities, such as loyalty, fairness, deceit, and immorality, and about how concepts such as loyalty and deceit are related to one another.

Formal operational thinkers are also distinguished by their approach to solving problems. When they encounter complex problems, they begin by developing a theory of what factors may be involved and how those factors—individually and in combination—determine the solution to the problem. They use the theory to deduce specific hypotheses to find the solution(s) to the problem. A typical hypothesis might take the form: "If we do X, then we can expect Y to occur." They then test the validity of the hypothesis by actually performing X and observing the result. For example, Leshonda develops a theory to determine how she might improve her distance in the long jump. Her theory includes timing, acceleration, body movements, and follow-through. She then tests the theory by making minor adjustments in each factor and systematically recording the results. Piaget observed this scientific approach in his laboratory experiments comparing children's and adolescents' problem-solving behaviors on a broad range of problems, including calculating the speed of a swinging pendulum, distinguishing between objects that float and those that sink, and other tests of scientific reasoning (Inhelder & Piaget, 1958).

In one test of scientific reasoning, Inhelder and Piaget (1958) presented subjects with four large flasks and one small jar, each of which contained a clear liquid. The researchers then showed each subject that a few drops from the small jar would turn the clear liquid in another "mystery" flask bright yellow. Finally, they challenged subjects to find all possible combinations of the liquids in the original containers that would reproduce the yellow color. The subjects did not know that there was only one three-liquid solution and only one four-liquid solution to the problem.

The school-age children and the teenagers approached the problem quite differently. The younger concrete thinkers began by adding drops from the jar to each of the four flasks and, failing to produce the yellow color, realized that producing the yellow color would require mixing at least three liquids. From that point they proceeded by trial and error, mixing liquids unsystematically, hoping to fall upon a solution. Their approach was highly inefficient: they often repeated mixtures that had already failed. When these children finally stumbled upon a solution, they stopped their search, not considering the possibility that other combinations might also produce the yellow color.

In contrast, the older formal operational thinkers approached the problem scientifically. They understood from the way the problem was presented that there might be more than one way to produce the desired result, and that the only way to discover *all* solutions was by systematically considering *all* possible two-, three-, four-, and five-liquid mixtures. By starting from what was possible and systematically eliminating non-solutions, the formal operational thinkers were certain to find *both* combinations that produced the yellow color.

Thus, we can see how formal operational thinkers go beyond their concrete experience, thinking about what is possible, rather than thinking only in terms of what is. They can mentally transform real and hypothetical events by asking "What if?" and they

Under optimal conditions, adolescents begin to show signs of formal operational thinking. Here, four teenagers engage in a lively discussion of a recent political event, one with complex philosophical and moral implications. Challenging teenagers to think at the formal operational level is one of the great challenges in our schools.

anticipate the results of those transformations by hypothesizing "If X, then Y." The only limits to their thinking are the boundaries of their own imagination and creativity. They can think about imaginary numbers; they can imagine a world without violence, disease, or prejudice; and they can logically create the means to those ends.

It is important to note, however, that logical solutions to problems are not always practical solutions, a distinction that adolescents often fail to recognize. Consequently, parents and adults often view adolescents as hopelessly naive.

Ideally, formal operational thought begins to emerge at age 11 or 12, and, with an appropriate level of environmental stimulation and challenge, should be well developed by age 15. However, Piaget suggested that the development of formal operations may proceed somewhat differently than cognitive development at earlier stages. First, the age at which children achieve this highest level of thought varies considerably, depending on each child's unique cultural, social, and educational experiences (Piaget, 1972). There is evidence that formal operational thinking appears only in individuals whose cultures offer opportunities for the development of technical skills through formal schooling and specialized training (Dasen & Heron, 1981).

Piaget (1972) also suggested that the development of formal operations is not automatic, even in Western society. The development of formal operational thinking may be delayed or even precluded in individuals who live in unstimulating environments. Studies of how pervasive formal operational thinking is among adolescents and adults have confirmed this notion (Capon & Kuhn, 1979; Keating, 1980; Kuhn, Langer, Kohlberg, & Haan, 1977). In one longitudinal study (Kuhn et al., 1977), Piagetian tests of adolescent and adult formal operational reasoning indicated that only 30 percent of the adult subjects were formal operational thinkers. Clearly, formal operational thinking evolves only in individuals who are provided specific learning opportunities.

Adolescent Egocentrism

While those adolescents who advance from concrete to formal operations greatly expand their cognitive abilities, the change has its downside as well. Piaget believed that formal operational thinking brings with it a new form of egocentrism, similar in some ways to the egocentrism that he described in preschoolers. Whereas preschoolers are egocentric in that they have difficulty imagining other people's perceptual and emotional perspectives, formal operational adolescents become so involved in their own perspectives that they have difficulty accepting the validity or legitimacy of anyone else's point of view. They may find it difficult to accept that anyone could possibly think differently than they do. Adolescents tend to be intolerant and disdainful of others' viewpoints and self-righteous about their own beliefs. Thus, **adolescent egocentrism** is a cognitive and emotional commitment to one's own beliefs and perspectives and a depreciation of the perspective of others.

David Elkind (1967, 1978) elaborated Piaget's concept of adolescent egocentrism. He included two distinct aspects of the adolescent's reaction to the advent of formal operational thinking: the *imaginary audience* and the *personal fable*. The concept of the **imaginary audience** refers to adolescents' exaggerated sense of self-importance: Their belief that they are the focus of attention for everyone around them, and that everyone in the imaginary audience shares the teenagers' views about themselves.

Why do teenagers feel that they are on stage, always under the watchful eye of others? Elkind speculated that it is a result of the rapid maturational changes in adolescence that make teenagers self-conscious and the fact that teenagers have some difficulty adjusting to their newfound mental capacities. The advent of formal operations is like getting a fascinating new toy—one that captivates and preoccupies the adolescent mind with new problems to be solved. They are so fascinated with the product of their new mental abilities they cannot imagine that others would not be equally enthralled. Formal operational ability takes some getting used to, both for the adolescents and for those who must deal with them.

Elkind's second concept, the **personal fable**, refers to adolescents' belief that they are both unique and invulnerable—legends in their own minds. When a teenager comes up with a new idea, she tends to believe that it is the first time the thought has ever occurred to anyone. This feature of the personal fable is illustrated in 16-year-old Leshonda's conversation with her mother.

KEISHA: (*peeking into Leshonda's room*) You can't keep moping around your room all day. Get out here and do your chores.

LESHONDA: But Mama, I'm waiting for my man Reggie to call.

KEISHA: Your what? Your man? Don't you be telling me about no man. You are 16 and he is 16 and you ain't no woman and he ain't no man!

LESHONDA: Mama, you don't know nothin' about it. You don't know how I feel. He is my man and I'm in love.

KEISHA: You don't think I know what love is? What do you think your daddy and I feel, chopped liver?

LESHONDA: Oh Mama. You just don't understand. Nobody could possibly feel what I feel right now. Nobody!

The personal fable fosters a sense that one can think and do no wrong, an attitude that easily wears thin on those who must deal with teenagers, including their own peers who also believe themselves to be unique and infallible. These feelings of invulnerability also promote high-risk behaviors such as drinking while driving, failing to practice safe sex, and abusing substances such as tobacco and drugs.

In Elkind's (1967) view, adolescent egocentrism is a direct expression of formal operational thinking. He proposed that the relationship between these factors should be strongest in early adolescence when formal operations are just beginning to form. By middle adolescence when formal operations are more firmly established, imaginary audience and personal fable thinking should decline.

Although there is some evidence that imaginary audience and personal fable thinking declines with age (Enright, Lapsley, & Shukla, 1979; Enright, Shukla, & Lapsley, 1980), the relationship between adolescent egocentrism and formal operations has not been supported (Lapsley, Milstead, Quintana, Flannery, & Bus, 1986; O'Connor & Nikolic, 1990). Other researchers (O'Connor & Nikolic, 1990) have argued that adolescent egocentrism is more likely an outgrowth of society's pressure on adolescents to develop a sense of identity. In this view, the imaginary audience is actually a reflection of (or reaction to) adult scrutiny and pressure, and the personal fable reflects an adolescent's evolving self-perceptions prior to feedback from others. The researchers found some limited support for the relationship between egocentrism and measures of self-concept (O'Connor & Nikolic, 1990).

In general, research has not supported Piaget's and Elkind's hypothesis of a relationship between adolescent egocentrism and formal operations. However, questions about that link do not detract from the usefulness of the concepts of imaginary audience and personal fable. Adolescents are certainly self-conscious, they often act as if they are on

Teenagers tend to see themselves in the spotlight—the focus of everyone's attention. They also believe that everything they do and think is unique and worthy. This egocentric perspective places them at some risk, particularly in social interactions with adults. Eventually, most teenagers learn to transcend their egocentrism, adopting a more realistic view of themselves and their effects on others. Those who do not may carry their unrealistic self-concept into adulthood.

stage, they often are overly sensitive to comments, and they have been known to think of themselves as more special and less vulnerable than their personal attributes would suggest. The contradictions implicit in these traits are frequently the basis for a teenager's personal conflict. For example, on certain days Leshonda dresses outlandishly—presumably to be the center of attention—but is outraged that everyone seems to be looking at her. Carlos often expresses personal opinions at the dinner table and is crushed when his parents either don't take him seriously or reject his logic. Parents and teachers who are sensitive to these contradictions may have some advantage in their everyday interactions with teenagers.

A P P L I C A T I O N

Dealing with Adolescent Egocentrism

*L*iving with a walking, talking personal fable who believes that he is always on stage can be quite a challenge, even for the most dedicated parent or teacher. Although teenagers tend to outgrow these notions as they get used to their new cognitive abilities, your relationship can go more smoothly if you follow a consistent strategy.

■ Consider your teenager's sense of invulnerability as a temporary condition that places him at greater than normal risk for accident and injury. Capitalize on real examples of those who have paid a price for high-risk be-

haviors, particularly friends, acquaintances, and celebrities. Above all, avoid nagging.

■ Although you may find your teenager's exaggerated sense of uniqueness annoying, it can be used to develop a realistic self-concept. Subtly reinforce and enhance the positive elements and ignore the negative.

■ Although imaginary audience behavior is normal, there is a fine line between your child thinking he is the center of attention and more serious delusional thinking and behavior. Bring your concerns to the attention of mental health professionals, particularly in situations that involve alcohol or drug abuse.

Achieving in School

Intuitively, we might think that the advanced cognitive skills that come with formal operations would prepare children for the increasingly complex subject matter of junior high and high school. High levels of academic achievement would seem to be ensured by hypothetical reasoning ability.

However, many American teenagers in junior high schools and high schools—including many with formal operational ability—perform well below their academic potential. Numerous surveys have shown that despite some increases in the late 1980s, our high school students are inadequately prepared in mathematics, science, and basic literacy (Carnegie Council on Adolescent Development, 1989; National Assessment of Educational Progress, 1986). One study (Mullis & Jenkins, 1988) concluded that more than half of U.S. high school seniors are unprepared for technical jobs or even job training, and that less than 1 in 10 is prepared to take college-level science courses. The situation is very similar in math, where most high school students are inadequately prepared to study introductory-level algebra and geometry (Dossey, Mullis, Lindquist, & Chambers, 1988). In reading and writing, one survey (National Assessment of Educational Progress, 1986) found that the *majority* of college-age individuals could not comprehend the text of a newspaper feature article or interpret a street map. For a closer look at the challenge faced by high school teachers, see "Careers: The High School Teacher."

How can we account for this apparent discrepancy between adolescents' advanced cognitive abilities and their poor academic performance? Part of the problem may be that many children have difficulty with the transitions from elementary to junior high school, and from junior high to high school (Entwisle, 1990; Petersen, 1986). The increase in average class size and the change from self-contained elementary classrooms to several subject-based junior high classrooms result in less personal relationships with teachers and less consistent contact with friends (Eccles, Midgley, & Adler, 1984). There is some evidence that these changes have more negative effects on girls than boys (Roberts, Sarigiani, Petersen, & Newman, 1990).

Peer pressure also takes its toll on many teenagers' academic performance, particularly when social and academic goals conflict. For example, if a student decides to do her homework rather than join her friends, she risks being called a nerd and possible peer rejection. Some developmentalists have proposed that these effects may intensify during puberty and may affect girls differently than boys. According to the **gender intensification hypothesis**, the demand for socializing with friends intensifies for girls (conflicting with their academic interests), while the demand for achievement intensifies for boys (Eder, 1985; Hill & Lynch, 1983). This notion implies that girls' self-image becomes *less* dependent—and boys' self-image *more* dependent—on successful academic performance during adolescence.

To investigate these relationships longitudinally, researchers followed a sample of teenagers from sixth through eighth grade (Roberts et al., 1990). The results supported the notion that social pressures for academic achievement increase for boys and decrease for girls, but only during *early* adolescence. By eighth grade, girls rebound, reinvesting more in academics. Thus, although the gender intensification hypothesis may not explain all that occurs to adolescents' commitments to academics and socializing, it does confirm the fact that young adolescents—particularly girls—may be torn by competing demands for their time and energy.

By far, the most powerful influence on adolescent academic achievement is the teenager's family. Middle- and upper-middle-class parents typically place high value on their children's achievement in high school and back up their values with supportive parent-

The High School Teacher

Larry Epstein is a teacher at Forest Hills High School in Queens, New York. He has been teaching English for 17 years, 15 at his present school. Like the city of New York, Forest Hills High School is a melting pot of ethnic minorities, with a large and increasing percentage of recent immigrants from Russia, Korea, China, and South America. I interviewed Larry at the end of a typical school day.

How did you first become interested in teaching high school?

I can't really say that I began with an interest in teaching high school. It was more of a deep passion for literature. I was an undergraduate English major and went on for my Master's degree in Literature. I thought I might teach college, but the opportunities were limited. One day I just knew I wanted to teach high school. I went back to school and earned my teacher certification.

What is a typical day like for a high school teacher?

In the New York City school system, a typical instructor teaches 5, 40-minute classes a day, with 34 students in each class, or 170 students a day. That's a lot of names to remember and an enormous number of papers to grade each week. My assignments are adjusted each year, and this term I am teaching both advanced and remedial classes.

What does it take to succeed as a high school teacher?

It's a combination of things, but the most important thing is having a deep passion for your subject. That has never been my problem. I love introducing my students to the great works: *Return of the Native*, *Hamlet*, *Pride and Prejudice*. I work hard to make my passion become their passion.

But passion, by itself, isn't enough. So many students come to school unmotivated and distracted. Many are very poor readers and few of them read for pleasure. When you give reading assignments, they may see them as punishments. Their disinterest often translates into behavior problems in class. When I began teaching, I was too concerned with winning student approval, which was interpreted as weakness. Eventually I learned that students are more comfortable if you assume authority, and classroom control is rarely a problem these days.

But even knowing how to control students is not enough. I slowly learned that I could succeed only by developing lessons that have power — lessons that break through my students' passivity and disinterest. The challenge is to show them that the great works of literature are relevant to their lives. *Hamlet* is a good example. My students can relate to Hamlet's cynicism and disillusionment and to his wit and imagination. I just have to show them the way by relating the concepts to their daily lives.

What keeps you going after all these years?

That's easy. When I see a student get turned on to a great book, that's all I need to keep me going. Just the other day, I was walking down the hallway behind two remedial students who didn't know I was there. They were arguing over the meaning of a poem I had read to them the day before. It doesn't get any better than that!

How would an undergraduate student pursue a career in high school teaching?

I think some educators might disagree, but I believe that you begin with an undergraduate degree that strongly emphasizes the subject area that you love. Your teacher training is important, of course, but it will be almost useless if you are not expert and passionately involved in your subject area. Ultimately, you are going to learn to teach after you begin to teach in your own classroom. It takes years to become truly effective, but it's a wonderful feeling when you get there.

ing (Dossey et al., 1988; Mullis & Jenkins, 1988). These parents communicate their expectations to their children, monitor homework and grades, provide resource materials, and actively participate in school functions. While lower-class families value their children's education, they are less likely than middle- and upper-class parents to provide emotional and behavioral support. However, many poor families strongly encourage their children to succeed in school and are highly effective in facilitating their children's schoolwork— more so than some more advantaged families who cannot or will not find the time to meet their children's academic needs.

Parenting style affects adolescent academic achievement. Several studies (Dornbusch et al., 1987; Lamborn, Mounts, Steinberg, & Dornbusch, 1991; Steinberg, Elman, & Mounts, 1989) have documented a modest relationship between parenting style as described by Diana Baumrind (1971) and teenagers' academic achievement. Overall, these studies have shown that an authoritative parenting style (see Chapter 11) is associated with higher levels of academic achievement. With few exceptions, the findings generalize across the students' gender, age, and ethnic background.

Why would authoritative parenting promote adolescents' academic performance? Perhaps because authoritative parents create expectations and standards for their teenagers' academic performance but remain flexible and willing to compromise on important issues. For example, an authoritative parent may grant an occasional request by their teenager to bend the rules about study time if the request seems justified. The teenager feels some degree of autonomy and is, therefore, willing to live by the study rules. In contrast, the authoritarian parent's inflexible demands encourage rebellion, and the permissive parent's lack of expectations undermines the teenager's motivation to achieve. In general, parents who convey expectations for academic excellence while interacting with their teenagers warmly, democratically, and firmly can expect positive effects on their teenagers' academic achievement (Steinberg et al., 1989).

Despite teenagers' difficulties in changing schools and friends, increasingly impersonal relationships with teachers in larger classes, advanced subject matter, and more intense peer pressure, parents have a continuing opportunity to positively affect their teenagers' academic performance through authoritative parenting and supporting their teenagers' school-related activities. However, the rather disappointing academic achievements of American high school students in science, mathematics, and reading and writing suggest that much more needs to be done by the schools, parents, and adolescents themselves to improve the overall level of academic achievement.

A P P L I C A T I O N

Promoting Academic Achievement

Regardless of how well your child performed academically in elementary school, her transition to high school entails considerable risk. You can make a difference by continuing to take a proactive approach to her school experience.

- An authoritative parenting style is the key to promoting your teenager's academic performance. Establish reasonable long-term goals for achievement, monitor homework and grades, and provide supportive materials required for classes. Give your teenager some autonomy with respect to study times and choice of elective courses.

- Maintain open dialogue with your teenager about school-related issues. Show interest in *all* aspects of her school life, not just her academic achievements.

- Keep in mind that emotional problems are often at the bottom of academic difficulties. Providing *consistent* emotional support is essential.

■ Stay active in your child's school by attending open school nights, joining parent organizations, and volunteering for school activities. Volunteering to chaperone a school dance can give you great insight into your teenager's high school experience.

Bottom Line: Parents can continue to positively influence their teenagers' academic achievement by being emotionally supportive, communicating reasonable expectations, and giving them some autonomy in study habits.

Moral Reasoning in Adolescence

You will recall from Chapter 13 that Lawrence Kohlberg and his colleagues (1976, 1984; Kohlberg & Gilligan, 1971) expanded Piaget's (1948) description of the development of moral reasoning to include three distinct levels: *preconventional*, *conventional*, and *postconventional* moral reasoning. To review briefly, preschoolers and young school-age children engage in preconventional moral reasoning, deferring to adult authority to determine whether a particular behavior is good or bad. Behaviors that are rewarded are good, and behaviors that are punished bad. Children obey in order to avoid punishment or for future rewards.

The decline in egocentricity and advances in logical reasoning late in the concrete operational period provide an opportunity for children to advance to the *conventional* level of moral reasoning. Those operational thinkers who are challenged by developmentally appropriate moral issues—for example, honesty versus dishonesty, cooperation versus competition, responsibility versus irresponsibility—develop an increasing respect for authority and a desire to obey the law and do one's duty. Those who are cognitively delayed or who do not have the required experiences will continue to struggle with conventional moral reasoning well into adolescence or beyond.

The advent of formal operational reasoning in adolescence provides an opportunity for the development of *postconventional* or *principled* moral reasoning. Achieving principled moral reasoning requires both formal operational ability and the challenge of more advanced moral issues, such as justice, equality, and human rights. Those who achieve principled moral reasoning recognize laws as necessary for everyone to live harmoniously, but believe that some laws are more just than others. At this most advanced level, one does not obey laws out of blind obedience, but because the principle underlying the law is consistent with fundamental human values. Kohlberg believed that very few adolescents (or even adults) progress to this highest level of moral reasoning.

While Piaget and Kohlberg described the ideal development of moral reasoning, they recognized that same-age adolescents may differ considerably in their level of moral reasoning, depending on their level of cognitive development and the extent to which they have been challenged by moral issues throughout their development. Most teenagers continue to struggle with conventional reasoning, but others show signs of postconventional reasoning. Moreover, since an individual has more experience in certain moral situations than others, he or she may use different levels of moral reasoning in different contexts. For example, a teenager who has lived on the streets may show signs of postconventional reasoning when discussing gang violence, but the same individual may think at the conventional level (or even at the preconventional level) on unfamiliar topics, such as the appropriate etiquette at a dinner party.

Just because teenagers appear to be at a particular level of moral reasoning that does not guarantee that their thinking or behavior will *consistently* reflect that level of moral development. Many factors cause adolescents to reason below their potential and/or to behave in a way that does not reflect their principles. In particular, an individual's level of moral reasoning can be negatively affected by intense emotions, peer pressure, and impulsive thinking. For example, a teenager who believes deeply in racial equality may

Although some teenagers begin to show evidence of postconventional moral reasoning, others may be slowed in their moral development by the powerful influence of adult authority figures. This child's experiences are likely to slow his moral development, making him more vulnerable than other children to blind obedience to authority.

occasionally make a prejudiced remark just to impress his friends. Similarly, the pressure of college admission may cause a principled teenager to cheat on an important examination. A discussion of adolescent moral reasoning with respect to cheating is presented in Box 15.1. We will explore the influence of peer pressure on adolescent social behavior in Chapter 16.

A P P L I C A T I O N

Preventing Cheating in High School

Adults and teenagers agree that cheating is a serious problem in American schools that begs for a solution (Evans & Craig, 1990b). However, cheating is so pervasive and so tolerated in our schools that it is difficult to know where to begin. Developmentalists (Calabrese & Cochran, 1990; Evans & Craig; 1990a, McLaughlin & Ross, 1989) have suggested the following:

■ Although we warn students not to cheat and punish them when they are caught, we rarely discuss cheating with them directly. Most students (and teachers) would benefit from clari-

fying definitions of cheating, particularly with respect to plagiarism. Include a frank discussion of the trade-offs of cheating for the individual versus society. Be prepared to deal assertively with fuzzy logic.

■ Because students are less motivated to cheat when they have learned the material to be tested, the best way to reduce cheating is to improve teaching. Teachers can also help by consistently testing only on material that has been taught.

BOX 15.1

To Cheat or Not to Cheat?

Kohlberg's (1976) description of moral reasoning in adolescence implies that those teenagers who consistently think on a conventional level would have a healthy respect for authority, would obey the law, and would be mindful of what is expected of them in social situations. Thus, we might expect at least some junior high school students and many high school students to be generally mindful of school rules and to defer to school authorities to determine the rightness and wrongness of school-related behaviors. Students' reactions to academic examinations provides a good test of this proposition. From a theoretical perspective, one might assume that since the rules for taking a test are explicitly stated by school authorities, students committed to a law-and-order orientation would be unlikely to break those rules.

Unfortunately, Kohlberg did not test his theory of moral development in typical American junior high schools and high schools where teenagers frequently cheat on exams and on homework assignments (Evans & Craig, 1990a, 1990b; McLaughlin & Ross, 1989). While it would be an overstatement to say that *every* student cheats, it is accurate to state that virtually everyone feels the pressure to cheat under certain circumstances and that most students are highly vulnerable to these pressures. In one laboratory study (Forsyth, Pope, & McMillan, 1985), college students and confederates (actors trained by the researchers to pose as subjects) were paired and asked to solve extremely difficult anagrams. When the experimenter left the room, the confederate "discovered" the answer sheet. When the experimenter returned, he told both students that they had done rather poorly, stressed that they both needed to do much better, and left a second time. The confederate then cheated and encouraged the subject to copy answers as well. Virtually all of the subjects cheated.

Why do teenagers cheat in school? Some see cheating as the only way to cope with their parents' pressure to achieve academically and their teachers' high standards. These pressures appear to be much greater for some teens than others. One study (Calabrese & Cochran, 1990) found that males are more likely to cheat than females and that students in affluent private schools are more likely to cheat than students in public high schools. This study also showed that students who were alienated from the school—that is, they disliked school and perceived school requirements to be unfair—were more likely to behave unethically than those who were not alienated. Cheating is the perfect solution for students who have rejected their parents' values. As long as their dishonest behavior goes undetected, cheating allows them to pacify both their teachers and their parents without disrupting their own lifestyles.

Although alienation may explain some aspects of cheating, not all students who cheat are alienated. How do these other teenagers reconcile their dishonest and unethical behavior with their conventional morality? Developmentalists (McLaughlin & Ross, 1989) have suggested that high school students manage this by engaging in **fuzzy logic**—by reinterpreting rules and rationalizing their behavior in self-serving ways. For example, some high school students reason that passive forms of cheating—for example, not covering your test answers to enable a friend to copy them—are not really dishonest: "I can't help it if somebody looks at my paper!"

Fuzzy logic also suggests that certain forms of cheating are not that bad because "everyone does it." One other variation proposes that copying someone else's homework is OK because teachers unfairly punish students when they "lose" their homework. Although some forms of fuzzy logic hint at more advanced principled moral reasoning, the lack of consistent logic argues against this interpretation. Fuzzy logic is a convenient way for teenagers to avoid guilt by rationalizing their dishonest behavior.

■ When teachers make it more difficult to cheat, there is less cheating (Leming, 1978). Teachers should monitor tests closely, use alternate test forms and homework assignments, sit students as far apart as possible, make clear the consequences for cheating, and punish consistently.

Bottom Line: Teenagers will be less likely to cheat when they believe it is in their best interest to be honest. Encouraging moral reasoning and rewarding honest behavior are two good places to start.

A P P L I C A T I O N

Fostering Teenagers' Moral Reasoning

Teenagers' moral reasoning is a function of their general level of cognitive development and their more specific experiences in dealing with complex moral issues. Thus, since both sources of influence are heavily dependent upon the individual's lifelong educational and social experiences, we can only expect to have limited effects. The following suggestions may prove helpful, particularly if they are applied over extended periods of time.

■ Because teenagers' level of moral reasoning reflects their level of cognitive development, any experience that promotes formal operational thinking should have positive effects on moral reasoning. Educational experiences that encourage abstract, hypothetico-deductive reasoning are beneficial.

■ But even formal operational thinking does not ensure postconventional reasoning. Teenagers must engage in real life experiences that challenge their perspectives in a wide variety of domains. Encourage them to travel and to meet people who differ from themselves in beliefs, values, and behaviors. Encourage them to volunteer in community activities, such as hospitals, retirement and nursing homes, and programs for the handicapped and poor.

■ Encourage your teenagers to engage in conversations that challenge their thinking on important moral issues, such as sex discrimination, human rights, abortion, and racial equality. Include many individuals with a variety of opinions whenever possible.

Bottom Line: Even under optimal conditions, postconventional reasoning develops very slowly, primarily during late adolescence. You are more likely to foster postconventional reasoning if you consistently think and model that behavior yourself.

Looking Back

We have shown how the delicate balance of risk and opportunity influences adolescents' physical and cognitive development. The dramatic physical changes during puberty introduce adolescents to the world of mature sexuality; the timing and social context of these changes ultimately determine how well each individual adjusts to them. While early maturing girls and late maturing boys are at relatively greater risk of maladjustment, these risks are substantially reduced with the social support of parents, peers, and teachers.

The physical changes during adolescence also provide opportunity for the development of a physically healthy lifestyle. Some adolescents realize the benefits of exercise and proper nutrition, but others succumb to sedentary habits, inappropriate eating/dieting behaviors, and high-risk sexual behaviors that sacrifice the potential for optimal physical development. Again, social support from family, peers, and teachers often make the difference between optimal development and the waste of their potential for growth.

Finally, teenagers' social and educational experiences during adolescence challenge their intellect to a more sophisticated understanding of the world. Some adolescents accept the challenge and engage in activities that promise to fulfill the full potential of human cognition. They achieve well in school and learn to reason about complex moral issues. But many adolescents—perhaps the majority—fail to fully meet the challenge. They make very little intellectual progress beyond the capabilities they had in childhood. These individuals achieve less and develop less, and are consequently less prepared intellectually and morally for the challenges of adult life. We have only begun to understand the balance of risk and opportunity during adolescence.

CHAPTER REVIEW

PUBERTY   Puberty is the period of development that spans the child's transformation from sexual immaturity to reproductive capability. Puberty includes accelerated gains in height and weight (the growth spurt), changes in body proportion, maturing of the reproductive system, and appearance of secondary sex characteristics.

HORMONES   Puberty begins with a sudden surge of hormones that stimulate and regulate maturational changes. Testosterone increases account for the changes in males, and estradiol increases for the changes in females.

VARIATIONS   The timing and duration of puberty varies considerably, with girls typically entering puberty earlier than boys. While some children go through puberty in less than a year, others take three years or more. Different parts of the body grow at different rates, creating body disproportions that even out over time.

SPERMARCHE AND MENARCHE   Sexual maturity is defined by the first ovulation in females and the production of large numbers of viable sperm in males. We typically mark the arrival of these abilities by spermarche (the first ejaculation in males) and menarche (the first menstruation in females). Changes in the primary and secondary sex characteristics also indicate sexual maturity.

TIMING OF PUBERTY   Early maturing girls enter a very different developmental pathway than girls who do not reach menarche until ninth or tenth grade. Early maturers tend to date earlier and

are at greater risk of unwanted pregnancy. In contrast, early maturing boys are at some developmental advantage over later maturing boys. They are more popular and better adjusted.

LEISURE TIME AND SPORTS   While adolescents spend considerable amounts of time in leisure activities, they devote only a small percentage of their time to more effortful sports, games, and hobbies. Those who do participate in sports find them highly challenging and motivating. Adolescents are more likely to enjoy sports in informal settings that encourage self-improvement rather than competition.

DIETING   Female adolescents try hard to lose weight through diet and exercise to conform to a standard of thinness. While most teenage girls use benign methods, some engage in extreme weight-loss behaviors, including purging and use of diet pills and laxatives.

EATING DISORDERS   A small percentage of female adolescents develop eating disorders. The most prevalent pattern is anorexia nervosa, or voluntary starvation. The disorder is extremely difficult to treat and can be life threatening. Bulimia is a disorder that involves alternating binging and purging, but with no effort to achieve extreme thinness.

HIV/AIDS   High rates of unprotected sex and risk taking make adolescents highly vulnerable to HIV/AIDS. This risk is aggravated by adolescents' feelings of invulnerability and by fatalism: the belief that they are likely to die young regardless of what they do.

FORMAL OPERATIONS   Piaget believed that some—but not all—adolescents progress to the fourth and most advanced period of cognitive development, the period of formal operations. Formal operational reasoning involves hypothetico-deductive reasoning: the ability to reason about hypothetical events and hypothetical transformations of those events. Formal operational thinkers approach problems by developing theories and by deducing testable hypotheses to solve the problems. Without the necessary experience, adolescents will never achieve formal operational ability.

ADOLESCENT EGOCENTRISM   Many adolescents become so involved in their own perspectives that they have trouble accepting the validity of anyone else's point of view. Adolescent egocentrism is a cognitive and emotional commitment to one's own beliefs and perspectives, often accompanied by a depreciation of the perspectives of others. Two components of adolescent egocentrism are the imaginary audience and the personal fable. The imaginary audience refers to a teenager's exaggerated sense of self-importance, a belief that he or she is the center of everyone's attention. The personal fable refers to the teenager's belief that he or she is both unique and invulnerable.

ACHIEVING IN SCHOOL   Many American high school students achieve well below their academic potential. Some of the problem may be the schools themselves, particularly the difficulties caused by transitions from one school to another.

Peer pressure may also have negative effects on interest in school, especially for girls at the beginning of high school. These negative influences can be reversed to some extent by supportive parents who use an authoritative parenting style.

MORAL DEVELOPMENT Adolescents who engage in conventional moral reasoning develop a healthy respect for authority and law and order. Adolescents who develop formal operational thinking and who acquire the necessary social experience may advance on to the postconventional level of moral reasoning, a level based on principles rather than blind obedience.

Key Terms

adolescence	primary sex characteristics	formal operational reasoning
puberty	secondary sex characteristics	period of formal operations
hormones	task-involved goals	hypothetico-deductive reasoning
hypothalamus	ego-involved goals	adolescent egocentrism
testosterone	eating disorders	imaginary audience
estradiol	anorexia nervosa	personal fable
adolescent growth spurt	bulimia	gender intensification hypothesis
spermarche	enmeshment	fuzzy logic
menarche	sexually transmitted disease	

16

Social and Emotional Development in Adolescence

Looking Ahead

- During the adolescent years, peers gain increasing influence over each other's decision making and lifestyle. Why do peers become so important and what are the effects of their influence?

- Teenagers gather and interact in organized groups that require new social skills. What form do these groups take and what does it take to be accepted?

- Many adults believe that teenagers are negatively influenced by peer pressure. How vulnerable are teenagers to peer pressure and are the effects always negative?

- The basis of friendship changes dramatically in adolescence. What does it take to be a good teenage friend? What effect does friendship have on the lives of teenagers?

- Adolescents must learn to deal with sexual impulses and the social and emotional consequences of their sexual behavior. What are the biological, social, and cultural influences on sexual development?

- Adolescents search for identity—the answer to the question, "Who am I?" What psychological processes are involved in this search, and do all adolescents succeed in answering the question?

- Most adolescents experiment with alcohol and drugs, but some are far more vulnerable than others to substance abuse. What are the risk factors for substance abuse?

- The stress and turmoil of adolescence leads some teenagers to consider suicide as a solution to their problems. Why do some consider suicide and others not?

- Juvenile delinquency has become a pervasive problem in our society, affecting the lives of all Americans. What are the causes of delinquency and how can it be prevented?

A t the beginning of this century, G. Stanley Hall, a pioneer in the study of adolescent development, described adolescence as a time of "storm and stress" (Hall, 1904, p. 6); for Hall the risks of adolescence far outweigh the opportunities for social and emotional development. Although his description adequately describes some teenagers' experience, this chapter shows that despite the risks, adolescence is a time of dramatic advances in the development of social skills and self-concept. We study how teenagers cope with increasingly complex social problems, the need to develop identity, and specific problems of adjustment during this final transition to adulthood.

Friendship and Peer Relations

The structure and function of peer relationships undergo rapid and significant change during adolescence. Making friends becomes enormously complex, peers gain unprecedented influence, and achieving peer acceptance while avoiding rejection requires new social skills and cognitive abilities. The risks and opportunities inherent in teenagers' social lives are particularly salient as they arrive for their first day of high school.

On his first day of high school, Carlos clutches his lunch bag under his arm and walks tentatively from the bus to the front steps of the school. The steps and the archway into the school are crowded with older students, laughing and catching up on what they have been doing all summer. Carlos tries to ignore the ache in his stomach as he climbs the steps and avoids looking anyone straight in the face. Just when he thinks he will make it through without incident, he hears a deep, condescending voice behind him yell, "Hey, where you goin', freshmeat? You scared the teachers are gonna start without you? Come over here and show us what you got under your arm."

Carlos quickens his pace but soon is blocked by a half dozen grinning, taunting seniors. He begins to tremble and perspire. Two of them lift him up in the air and shake him until he drops his lunch bag. One boy picks it up and throws it to another, who throws it to a third, and so on. Carlos falls to the pavement, tearing his pants and cutting his knee. Trying his best not to cry, he runs into the school and down a long corridor until the sound of the laughter has faded. Later in the day he searches for a side entrance to the school that will allow him to enter less conspicuously.

Although Carlos has a rough time during the first weeks of high school, he eventually associates with a small group of teenagers (two girls and three boys) known as the brains. Each of its members has a history of social isolation in elementary and junior high school. As the group's name implies, its members share an interest in learning and achievement. Although the group as a whole has little status compared to the other cliques and crowds in the school, it does provide its members opportunities for companionship, mutual understanding, and social support. The brains always sit together at lunch, call each other after school, and occasionally get together on weekends. Although they take a good bit of verbal abuse from other students, the teasing draws them closer together.

Leshonda knows that first impressions are important so she has psyched herself all summer to deal with the first day of high school. Some of her older street friends tell her what clothes to wear and how to fix her hair to fit in. They warn her not to do the things that freshmen do, like carry a lunch to school.

On the first day, Leshonda walks confidently up the front steps of the school, making sure to return every glance and to appear entirely unaffected by the chaos at the entrance. When an older girl purposely blocks her path, Leshonda surprises the girl by meeting her gaze straight on and staring her down. After a few uncomfortable seconds, the girl diverts her eyes and steps aside. Several girls who belong to the most popular group in the school watch the encounter and are impressed. One girl that the others seem to look up to says, "That's Leshonda Martin. Somebody said she can run faster than anyone in Brooklyn. We need to check her out."

Leshonda makes a lot of progress in her first week: She has entirely avoided getting teased by older students, she has met more new people than she can remember, and she is already sitting with the popular crowd at lunchtime—one of the few freshmen given that privilege. She is dressing like her new friends and using slang she had not even heard a week earlier. Although only a few days have gone by, she senses that with the support of her new friends she can cope with anything.

The Increasing Influence of Peers

One of the most distinctive aspects of adolescence is the increasing importance of peers. Adolescents become highly dependent upon one another for self-esteem (Brown & Lohr, 1987), companionship, and intimacy (Buhrmester, 1990). Peers influence adolescents' decision making at every level—from choosing what to wear to making complicated decisions about school, dating, sexuality, delinquency, and relationships with parents (Berndt, 1979).

As teenagers become more involved with peers, they become less emotionally attached to their families (Steinberg & Silverberg, 1986), and disclose less and less intimate information to their parents (Buhrmester & Furman, 1987). One recent study (Larsen & Richards, 1991) showed that teenagers spend progressively less time with their families from fifth to ninth grade. Boys and girls differ, however, in what they do with the time away from their families. Whereas junior high school girls use most of that time to be with their friends, junior high school boys spend the extra time alone. They spend no more time with friends than they used to. By high school, teenagers spend even less time with their families, and now both girls and boys devote that time to their peers. Moreover, the older adolescents reported that they enjoyed their time with friends even more than the younger adolescents did (Csikszentmihalyi & Larson, 1984).

Developmentalists warn that this trend sharply reduces the family's opportunities to promote adult values and family traditions with their teenagers and to fulfill other responsibilities, such as health care and protection (Larson & Richards, 1991).

But there is some evidence that parents continue to influence their teenagers, at least in certain areas of their lives. Research has shown that while many parents defer to peer influence on important personal issues, such as sexuality and dating, they maintain their influence in other domains, such as choice of college and career (Shah & Zelnik, 1981;

Zelnik & Kantner, 1977, 1980). Thus, although parents must learn to adjust to their teenagers' growing autonomy and reliance on peers, they can expect to consistently influence some important aspects of their teenagers' decision making throughout adolescence.

Cliques and Crowds

Although school-age children tend to relate to their close friends on a one-to-one basis or in small, loosely knit groups, teenagers relate to peers in larger, more well-defined groups, known as cliques or crowds. **Cliques** are close-knit, intimate groups of friends who prefer each other's company and exclude outsiders from their activities. Cliques are distinguishable from other groups by their clear boundaries and their explicit criteria for membership. For example, one clique might include several players on a sports team who hang out together on and off the field. Groups as diverse as fraternities and sororities, clubs, and street gangs all fit the definition.

Crowds are larger, more loosely defined groups of individuals who share common interests and social status. For example, high school lunchrooms frequently divide into tables for popular students and tables for others. We take a closer look at the emergence of popularity in crowds in Box 16.1.

Cliques and crowds offer their members power, prestige, status, and opportunities to identify with group values and beliefs. For example, group members frequently have

Hanging out with peers who look, dress, and think alike is one of the pervasive features of adolescent life. Shopping malls such as this offer a unique environment for hanging out—a place where teens can show off and be anonymous at the same time. But not everyone of the same age is included. One boy looks on with interest but with no obvious invitation from the others. Would a baseball cap help?

Hanging Out in Junior High School: The Development of Crowd Behavior

Donna Eder (1985) observed adolescent girls' social behavior at several times: lunch periods, the informal times before and after school, and special events such as picnics and school dances. The observers sat unobtrusively in the lunchroom — observing students' natural movements, recording conversations, and noting specific acts of social acceptance and rejection. For example, students frequently rejected others by saving seats for their friends.

Eder (1985) found substantial variation in peer relations from sixth to eighth grade. At sixth grade, most children paired off with their friends in groups of two or three. While these small groups of friends ate together at lunch, individual groups showed no consistency in where they sat for lunch. By seventh grade, the seating pattern had become more stable, with larger, more exclusive status groupings emerging for the first time. These larger groups "owned" their sections of the lunchroom. In seventh grade, the elite clique was composed of cheerleaders and student council members. By eighth grade the number of cliques had increased and the membership had become highly stable — once a student was included in a particular group, he or she tended to stay in it. The elite group had now expanded to include selected male athletes.

Eder's description of the "cycle of popularity" illustrates the delicate balance of risk and opportunity in social relationships in early adolescence. The cycle begins when a girl initially gains popularity by becoming a cheerleader or by becoming friends with one. Becoming popular means getting a lot of attention and social support both from other popular girls and from girls who believe they can gain social status by *associating* with a popular girl. However, popular girls who want to protect their newly acquired status have to reject the social initiatives of other, less popular girls. (After all, you can't be friends with everyone!) As they become less friendly, popular girls are known as snobs and many are *actively disliked* by girls who are not in the elite group. Thus, paradoxically, many girls who have been accepted into the most popular group actually have fewer rather than more social contacts.

reserved seating in the lunchroom and may control access to certain school resources, such as extracurricular activities. Cliques and crowds provide a sense of belongingness and identity that many teenagers no longer get — or want — from their families. Young adolescents prefer membership in crowds, where they find emotional support and the opportunity to make new friends (Brown, Eicher, & Petrie, 1986). However, older adolescents show declining interest in crowds as they grow dissatisfied with the crowd's demands for conformity and as their interest in dating increases.

Belonging to a clique or crowd offers many advantages, but membership is not without its risks. Although the group may provide perks (such as security and protection), it also typically restricts members' ability to associate with outsiders, narrowing their range of social experience and insulating them from new ideas. Rivalry and hostility between cliques can easily get out of hand, from skirmishes at school sporting events to gang violence in our cities.

One study (Brown & Lohr, 1987) examined high school students' perception of the crowds in their schools and the effects of crowd membership on self-esteem. Five distinct crowds were identified, each serving the social and emotional needs of very different groups of students and each occupying a distinct social status in the school. The groups included (in descending order of social status):

jocks (athletes)
populars (well known and socially active)
normals (average students)
druggies and toughs (delinquents)
nobodies (social and intellectual incompetents)

The remaining students were referred to as *outsiders*, students whom no one identified as members of a recognized crowd. The self-esteem of crowd members varied directly with the status of their crowd, students in higher status crowds had, on the average, higher self-esteem than students in lower status crowds.

While the researchers had assumed that outsiders would have lower self-esteem than crowd members (or insiders), they found that outsiders were not all alike. They identified three types of outsiders:

distorters (those who mistakenly believed they were part of a crowd)
envious (those who knew they were outsiders but wanted to belong)
independents (those who knew they were outsiders and did not want to belong)

This more fine-grained analysis showed that the envious had lower self-esteem than the insiders (jocks and populars) and other outsiders. The distorters also had less self-esteem than the insiders. However, independent outsiders had as much self-esteem as the insiders and more than the nobodies!

The results suggested that simply being included in a crowd is no guarantee of high self-esteem. An individual's self-esteem varies with the status of his or her crowd, but it also depends on the degree to which the individual identifies with the group's beliefs and values. A member of a high status crowd who does not fully accept the group's values may derive little self-esteem from membership. In contrast, a teenager who covets belonging to a group and identifies closely with its values is likely to gain considerable self-esteem from group membership, even from a group with relatively low status. Carlos's experience with the brains is a good example.

Why do peers become so important to teenagers? Lynne Zarbatany and her colleagues (1990) reasoned that the answer might lie in the unique activities in which teenagers engage. The researchers asked young adolescent girls to identify the activities they engaged in with peers and the functions those activities served in their relationships. For the most part, their everyday activities (watching TV, sports, games, shopping, telephone, eating, and schoolwork) were not very different from activities engaged in by other age groups. What was distinctive was the way young teenage girls *used* every activity as an opportunity to learn about themselves and to enhance their relationships. Although this study focused on girls, it is likely that boys too use their time together to enhance their sense of self and to solidify their relationships.

A P P L I C A T I O N

Dealing with Your Teenager's Hanging Out

You may consider many of your teenager's activities—such as hanging out and talking on the telephone—a waste of time, but you should recognize that these activities play an important role in the search for identity, developing social skills, and establishing new relationships. On the other hand, even a good thing can be overdone; encourage your teenager to distribute his time evenly between leisure activities, school, and work.

Bottom Line: Showing respect for your teenager's time with friends may help him strike a balance between peer activities and other important aspects of his life.

Peer Pressure and Conformity

One of the most striking features of adolescents' social behavior is the extreme conformity in actions and attitude among members of teenage crowds and cliques. Parents typically refer to this as **peer pressure**, a term that implies that peers force individuals to conform to group standards. Many parents see their children as highly vulnerable to peer pressure, blaming the peer group for their teenagers' inappropriate behaviors and negative moods—and thereby relieving themselves of any responsibility. Are teenagers as vulnerable to peer pressure as many parents believe?

There is little question that cliques and crowds influence their members' behavior. Peer groups often sanction particular styles of dress and activities that help define the group's identity. For example, gangs often encourage their members to wear certain colors and styles of dress and to engage in criminal behaviors to qualify for membership. However, while teenagers may behave in ways consistent with their friends' expectations, it is not clear whether their behavior results from the group's external pressure or from teenagers' own internal motivation to conform. That is, teenagers are not necessarily innocent victims of peer pressure. Teenagers in search of an identity may be predisposed to behave in outlandish ways to impress their friends or to gain status with the group. Gang members, for example, may attempt to establish dominance by engaging in extremely violent or daring behaviors. Thus, peer pressure and teenage conformity should be thought of as complementary but distinct forces that influence teenage attitudes and behavior.

Peer pressure and conformity increase rapidly during early adolescence—particularly in the junior high (middle) school years—and generally decline during the high school years (Coleman, 1980; Gavin & Furman, 1989; Steinberg & Silverberg, 1986). This intense phase of conformity to peers in early adolescence is not surprising. As adolescents begin to stake out their independence from their families, they need a convenient substitute arena that enables them to try out new roles and identities and provides emotional support. From the teenagers' perspective, conforming to group expectations is a small price to pay for group support and acceptance.

Unfortunately, behavior that pleases a peer group often offends parents and others. Loud, discordant sounds from boom boxes, prolific use of profanity, and bizarre forms of dress can be disturbing to adults, particularly adults who view such behaviors as immoral, threatening, or as signs of psychopathology. Even more disturbing is the tendency for peers to pressure each other to engage in high-risk behaviors (Csikszentmihalyi & Larson, 1984). Groups of adolescents, isolated from adult surveillance, often disinhibit one another, increasing the likelihood of illegal and destructive behaviors.

Fortunately, peer pressure and conformity do not always produce negative, socially unacceptable behaviors. In one study of junior high and high school students, researchers found that peers frequently pressured each other to engage in positive behaviors, such as studying hard and getting good grades, and actively discouraged negative behaviors, such as use of drugs (Brown, Clasen, & Eicher, 1986). Moreover, research has shown that peers influence each other more in some areas than in others (Clasen & Brown, 1985; Hartup, 1983). While peers tend to have greater influence in personal habits—such as style of dress, taste in music, and use of leisure time—parents continue to have greater influence in adolescents' choice of schools, courses, and careers (Wilks, 1986). Adolescents also report more peer pressure to socialize with friends than pressure to engage in misconduct (Brown et al., 1986b). It is also important to note that some adolescents—more often girls than boys—remain independent from peer influence throughout adolescence (Steinberg & Silverberg, 1986).

A P P L I C A T I O N

Dealing with Peer Pressure and Conformity

*P*arents may be increasingly challenged, offended, and intimidated by their teenagers' imitation of their peers. They argue with them over hairstyles, clothing, and taste in music, leaving little room for more positive interaction. The level of conflict often escalates over time, as both sides become increasingly rigid in their positions and more and more dedicated to winning. If left unchecked, these conflicts can eventually undermine the quality of their relationship and significantly reduce parents' influence in their children's lives. The following recommendations may be helpful:

■ Maintain perspective. Your teenager's outrageous behavior is probably no worse than many of the things you did when you were that age. He is declaring his identity as you once did, and you are reacting as your parents once did. You grew out of your outrageous behavior, and he is very likely to do the same.

■ If your teenager's conforming behavior is outrageous but essentially harmless, show a moderate amount of outrage (just enough to prove you are a parent) but avoid nagging and persistent attempts to change his behav-

ior. Nagging is likely to make matters worse, and prohibiting the behavior will encourage him to engage in the behavior covertly, far from your view and influence. Save your big guns for truly important situations.

■ If your teenager's conforming behavior is potentially harmful or dangerous, you must intervene. Grounding and tighter curfews may be effective, but don't overestimate your ability to coerce change. If you have avoided nagging and pestering your teenager on minor issues (such as hairstyle or clothes) in the past, he is much more likely to take you seriously on more important issues (such as sex and drugs). If you have managed to maintain a positive relationship with your teenager based on mutual love and respect, you may actually effect some change in his behavior — but it will take time and persistence.

Bottom Line: Given enough time, your teenager will eventually realize that giving in to peer pressure and conforming to group norms are incompatible with becoming an autonomous individual. Unfortunately, he will have to discover this for himself.

Adolescent Friendships

We noted in Chapter 14 that school-age children's peer relationships are based on mutual interests and activities, the ability to play well together, and the ability to resolve conflicts. Although these early friendships involve emotion, young children provide little emotional support. By early adolescence, friendship becomes an increasingly intimate relationship based on mutual understanding, mutual disclosure, empathy, trust, and loyalty (Berndt, 1982; Buhrmester, 1990; Buhrmester & Furman, 1987). Teenagers who fail to consistently maintain friendships must cope with the stresses of adolescence with no one — other than their parents — to share their feelings. Socially isolated, they are likely to feel lonely, alienated, and depressed (Sullivan, 1953).

What does it take to be a good friend during adolescence? According to Duane Buhrmester (1990), making and keeping friends during adolescence involves *close relationship competencies*, including conversational skills, the ability to share secrets and private feelings, and the ability to provide emotional support. Friends must be honest and open about their relationship and skilled at resolving conflicts. Buhrmester showed an increasingly strong relationship between close interpersonal relationship skills, social adjustment, and the intimacy of friendship from early adolescence (ages 10–13) to middle adolescence (ages 13–16). Adolescents in intimate relationships had higher self-esteem, were more socially competent, more sociable, less hostile, and less anxious/depressed than those in less intimate relationships.

Although there is some evidence that teenage girls' same-sex friendships are more intimate and more exclusive than those of boys (Berndt, 1982), at least some male friendships may be no less intimate than those of females (Eshel & Kurman, 1990; Jones & Dembo, 1989). One study (Jones & Dembo, 1989) confirmed that when all males are lumped together, they average less intimacy in their friendships than females. However, closer examination of the data shows that while the subgroup of "highly masculine" male friends is less intimate, friendships between "androgynous" males—that is, males who are high in both masculine and feminine traits—are just as intimate as those between females. These results suggest that personality factors may have more effect than gender on friendship intimacy. This would reinforce the popular notion that only certain types of individuals are capable of forming truly intimate relationships.

Social Acceptance and Rejection

Although school-age children who consistently avoid conflict and aggressive outbursts are virtually assured their peer acceptance, gaining social acceptance and avoiding rejection in junior high and high school require dramatic improvements in adolescents' social skills and social cognitive abilities (Elliott & Gresham, 1989). Leshonda's first-day success and Carlos's first-day failure on the front steps of their high schools poignantly illustrate the challenging social problems that teenagers face each day in their increasingly complicated social lives.

Compared to children's experience in elementary school, the complexity and diversity of interaction with peers in junior high and high school significantly increases the opportunities for social acceptance *and* the risks of peer rejection. The opportunities for social acceptance expand with the increasing numbers of students in junior high and high schools; that is, the mixing of more students from more neighborhoods produces a larger and more diverse pool of potential friends. Extensive extracurricular activities—such as team sports, clubs, and school dances—bring together students of common interests; free time both before and after school provides more time for social interaction.

However, middle schools and high schools also create new risks of peer rejection. Members of cliques and crowds jealously protect their boundaries with prohibitive criteria for membership, sometimes using cruel forms of rejection to keep outsiders at social distance. Some teenagers would rather be lonely than risk public humiliation. The increasing demand for intimacy in adolescent friendships intimidates many adolescents, particularly those with emotional problems or social skills deficits.

As adolescents juggle these risks and opportunities for social acceptance and rejection, they earn their way into social status groups similar to those found at earlier ages (Elliott & Gresham, 1989; Frentz, Gresham, & Elliott, 1991). One study (Frentz et al., 1991) classified sixth to tenth graders into social status categories as follows: 34 percent popular, 16 percent controversial (liked by some and disliked by others), 10 percent neglected, and 40 percent rejected. These results require replication, but the fact that half of the students in this sample were either neglected or actively rejected by their peers suggests that lack of social acceptance is a pervasive problem in middle school and the first two years of high school.

Why are teenagers so vulnerable to rejection? As in middle childhood, rejected teenagers behave very differently than those who are more accepted. Compared to more popular teenagers, rejected teenagers are less socially and academically skilled, less self-controlled, and more likely to show impulsive, aggressive, and disruptive behaviors (Elliott & Gresham, 1989; Frentz et al., 1991). One study (Bierman, Morrison, & Bitner, 1991) identified three distinct types of rejected boys: a *multiproblem type* with both con-

Cliques of like-minded teenagers are pervasive in the social life of a high school. Only members of this clique would consider sitting in the one empty place at this lunch table; anyone who breaks the pattern — purposely or accidentally — risks immediate rejection.

duct problems and delinquent behaviors, a *withdrawn type* with few conduct problems, and a *hyperactive-aggressive* (but nondelinquent) *type* — the most rejected of the three types. These findings suggest that there may be multiple pathways to rejection in adolescence and that teenagers may experience rejection in many different forms. This further suggests that we need to gear intervention to the specific behavioral and psychological problems associated with different forms of rejection.

A P P L I C A T I O N

Improving Your Teenager's Social Status

Social rejection in adolescence is a pervasive problem that is often associated with other serious adjustment problems, such as delinquency, eating disorders, suicide, and alcohol and drug abuse. Although the causes of peer rejection in adolescence are reasonably well understood, improving a teenager's peer acceptance is a formidable task. The following recommendations may prove helpful to parents and professionals who are in a position to intervene:

- Keep in mind that rejected teenagers are not all rejected for the same reasons: Some are overly aggressive, others are passive and withdrawn, and still others show attention deficits and hyperactivity. Gear your intervention to the specific behaviors, attitudes, and thinking that have led to rejection for your teenager.

- Recognize that, by adolescence, rejection has become a way of life for some teenagers, so it will be highly resistant to change. Parents, teachers, and therapists will need to coor-

dinate their efforts over extended periods of time.

- Teenagers — unlike younger children — are probably not rejected simply for inappropriate or annoying behaviors. Rejection is more likely due to complex combinations of social skill deficits, social cognition deficits, and underlying emotional problems.

- Design your intervention to promote positive social behaviors (cooperating, sharing, and helping), skills for initiating and maintaining relationships, and the ability to show loyalty and intimacy in existing relationships (Inderbitzen-Pisaruk & Foster, 1990). However, intervention is unlikely to succeed without addressing the underlying emotional problems.

  Bottom Line: Although brief periods of unpopularity or social withdrawal are not unusual during adolescence, chronic rejection is a sign of serious maladjustment that requires intervention by mental health professionals.

Dating and Sexual Relationships

In Chapter 15, we described how the physical changes at puberty equip young adolescents with the physical attributes necessary for sexual reproduction, and we discussed the effects of the timing of puberty on various aspects of development. We will now look more broadly at the emergence of **sexuality** during adolescence—that is, the development and integration of sexual interests, values, beliefs, attitudes, thinking, and behavior.

Learning to cope with sexuality is one of the most formidable developmental tasks of adolescence. While puberty provides the biological capacity to engage in mature sexual behaviors and to reproduce, the rather sudden onset of sexual feelings can overwhelm many teenagers, particularly those who are socially and emotionally unprepared to cope with the challenges, risks, and responsibilities associated with mature sexuality. At the risk of oversimplification, the problem for teenagers is that their hormones are pushing them to do things that they are socially and emotionally unprepared to do. After spending their childhood associating almost exclusively with same-sex peers, they are now expected to rapidly master the competencies required for intimate dealings with the opposite sex.

As they begin to experiment with sexual behavior, they find that most outlets are either forbidden or unavailable. Those who do find sexual outlets must face the risks of unwanted pregnancy and sexually transmitted disease. Those who either resist temptation or simply fail to find sexual outlets must endure the bragging, teasing, and possible rejection by their more sexually experienced peers. Although anthropologists are quick to point out that the challenge of sexual adjustment is far less complicated in other cultures (Barry & Schlegel, 1984, 1986), the fact remains that American teenagers find themselves between a rock and a hard place as they attempt to cope with their emerging sexuality.

Despite the conflicts and risks, many teenagers waste little time becoming sexually active. In one study (Scott-Jones & White, 1990), 28 percent of the 12- to 15-year-olds interviewed had already made their **sexual debut**—they had experienced their first sexual intercourse—at an average age of 12 years! Of those who had become active, 31 percent reported having sex "often" or "very often"; 60 percent of the females and 27 percent of the males who had not yet become active indicated—perhaps naively— that they expected to delay sexual intercourse until marriage.

Those teenagers who became sexually active usually did so in the context of a steady boyfriend/girlfriend relationship. Early sexual debut brought with it certain risks: Sexually active teenagers had lower educational expectations than those who were not sexually active. Whereas 50 percent of those who did not expect to attend college were sexually active, only 29 percent of those bound for college had had intercourse. The study also showed that those who were sexually active ran a high risk of becoming pregnant: Only 22 percent of the sexually active teenagers reported making "frequent" use of contraceptives. We take a closer look at teenagers' casual attitude toward contraception in Box 16.2.

Although many teenagers become sexually active, they differ in their approaches to sexual relationships. Robert Sorensen (1973) studied 13- to 19-year-olds and identified 2 distinct groups of sexually experienced teenagers, based on their approach to sexual relationships. One group, the **serial monogamists**, engaged in a series of relatively long-term, exclusive sexual relationships. Each successive relationship involved deep emo-

Raging hormones, increasingly adult-like bodies, and peer pressure encourage sexual behavior early in the teenage years. Unfortunately, the physical changes that encourage early sexual behavior come much earlier and much faster than the social and emotional maturity necessary to cope effectively with these changes.

BOX 16.2

Teenagers and Contraception

Although American teenagers' rate of sexual activity (including intercourse) is no greater than teenagers in other Western societies, teenage sexual intercourse is far more likely to result in pregnancy and childbirth in America than in other countries (Jones et al., 1985); 1 of every 3 American teenage girls will become pregnant before age 20 (Trussell, 1988).

An important part of this problem is the American teenagers' negative attitude toward the use of contraceptives, which reflects the broader confusion and ambivalence American adults have about it (Brooks-Gunn & Furstenberg, 1989). One study indicated that only 50 percent of teenagers use any form of birth control the first time they have intercourse (Zelnik & Shah, 1983). Unfortunately, most teenagers who fail to use contraception the first time continue to avoid it. In one study, half the teenage girls who were sexually active without contraception became pregnant within six months (Zabin, Kantner, & Zelnik, 1979).

Why do teenagers fail to use contraception? The teenagers in one study (Zelnik & Shah, 1983) gave the following reasons for not using contraception, in descending order:

- they hadn't planned to have sex.
- they didn't know about intercourse.
- they didn't want to use contraception.
- they didn't think about it.
- contraception wasn't available.
- they didn't think they could get pregnant.

Another study (Arnett, 1990) indicated that teenagers who were more egocentric (felt more invulnerable) and those who were highly concerned about the quality of sensation during sex were less likely to use contraception. Other risk factors associated with failure to use birth control include lower social class, low self-esteem, sense of powerlessness, lack of a steady partner, poor relationship with parents, and associating with peers who become parents (Chilman, 1986; Morrison, 1985).

Things may be improving. One indication comes from the National Survey of Adolescent Males conducted in 1988 (Pleck, Sonenstein, & Ku, 1990). The researchers found that males show some signs of becoming more responsible about using contraceptives: 60 percent of the 17- to 21-year-old males studied said they "almost certainly" would use a condom the first (or next) time they would have sex. Boys who were more likely to use condoms believed that males should be responsible for contraception, that their partners would be grateful, that condoms have little effect on sexual pleasure, and that condoms would prevent AIDS.

However, this study merely asked males to report on their intentions. Do good intentions translate into actual condom use? Another study (Adler, Kegeles, Irwin, & Wibbelsman, 1990) suggest that they do. Teenagers who indicated that they intended to use specific methods of contraception at the beginning of the study were shown to have actually used them one year later.

Unfortunately, the overall picture is discouraging. Those teenagers who are the least capable of managing the responsibilities of parenthood are also the least likely to use contraception consistently. Public policy about the school's responsibilities with respect to sex education and dissemination of condoms remains in turmoil. Thus, until an effective way is developed to increase teenagers' abstinence or use of birth control, the rate of unwanted pregnancies among teenagers will remain unacceptably high and our society will continue to bear the burden of caring for the offspring.

tional commitment, with sex as an important—but not the *most* important—aspect of the relationship. About 1 in every 5 of the teenagers studied was a serial monogamist, with girls outnumbering boys 2 to 1.

The second group, the **sexual adventurers**, engaged in multiple short-term, emotionally shallow relationships for sexual release. Adventurers made no emotional commitments to their partners and felt no responsibility for their welfare or happiness; 15 percent of the teenagers studied were sexual adventurers, with boys outnumbering girls 4 to 1. Although adventurers had many more partners than monogamists over time, they actually had sex less frequently and enjoyed it less than the monogamists.

Although Sorensen's distinction between adventurers and monogamists is informative, his descriptions are based on adolescent behavior in the early 1970s. These types most certainly still exist, but no follow-up study has been done. The percentages may have changed substantially over time, and additional types may have emerged that have not yet been described, such as those who persistently seek partners but rarely find one. It is also likely that some adolescents alternate between extended periods of monogamy and periods of adventuring, depending on their circumstances. A new study replicating and extending Sorensen's early work would add greatly to our understanding of the variation in adolescent sexual behavior.

We have reviewed research that has shown considerable variation in adolescent sexual attitude and behavior. How can we account for these differences? Developmentalists have considered three major sources of influence: biology, parents and peers, and culture (Brooks-Gunn & Furstenberg, 1989).

Biological Influences

We showed in Chapter 15 how specific hormonal changes stimulate the development of primary and secondary sex characteristics. But developmentalists have also considered the possibility that hormones also directly and indirectly affect sexual behavior (Udry, Billy, Morris, Groff, & Raj, 1985; Udry, Talbert, & Morris, 1986). *Direct effects* are hormonal influences on adolescents' level of arousal, their motivation to engage in sexual behavior, and their sensitivity to sexual stimulation. *Indirect effects* are the social impacts that secondary sex characteristics have when they appear—for example, the effects on boys when girls develop breasts.

J. Richard Udry and his colleagues have investigated the direct effects of hormone levels on teenagers' sexual behavior (Udry et al., 1985; Udry et al., 1986). They found different effects for males and females. Whereas testosterone levels in males were associated with their sexual interest *and* behavior (Udry et al., 1985), testosterone levels in females related only to their *interest* in sexual matters, not to their sexual *behavior* (Udry et al., 1986). Thus, social factors appear to moderate the effects of hormones in female arousal (Brooks-Gunn & Furstenberg, 1989). In general, while hormones play a direct role in adolescent sexuality, social and cultural influences account for much of the variation in adolescent sexual behavior.

Hormones also affect adolescent sexuality indirectly by influencing the timing of puberty. As we indicated in Chapter 15, early maturing girls date earlier, associate with older friends, and begin sexual intercourse earlier than late maturing girls (Brooks-Gunn, 1988; Magnusson et al., 1985). Although later maturing girls eventually catch up, the earlier sexual debut of early maturing girls substantially increases their risk of early pregnancy and disease.

Parent and Peer Influences

Parents vary considerably in their efforts to control or influence their teenagers' sexual behavior. Even those parents who try have limited options available to them. Many parents establish rules for dating. For example, they may set a minimum age for dating, insist on being introduced to dates, and enforce curfews. Of course, parents eventually realize that once they allow their teenager out the door, they relinquish direct control and must rely on their teenager's own sense of morality and self-control. Unfortunately, researchers know virtually nothing about teenagers' sexual self-control in dating.

Does it matter which approach parents take to their teenager's dating behavior? The results of research on parental effects are mixed. One study of African American adolescents (Hogan & Kitagawa, 1985) showed that parents who were lax in supervision had daughters who were 76 percent more sexually active and 64 percent more likely to get pregnant than daughters whose parents supervised more closely. A study of white and Hispanic adolescents ages 15 to 18 (Miller, McCoy, Olson, & Wallace, 1986) indicated that teenagers who perceived their parents as permissive in discipline and in setting rules for dating were more likely to have liberal sexual values and to have had intercourse than teenagers whose mothers were more strict. Teenagers whose parents used *moderate* discipline were the least likely to have liberal attitudes toward sex and to have had intercourse experience. However, other research (Moore, Peterson, & Furstenberg, 1986) found that parental monitoring and communication have little effect on teenagers' sexual behavior.

Although research suggests that parents may not have much direct control over their adolescents' sexual behavior, it is possible that other aspects of the parent–teenager relationship may have some effect. Daughters who relate more positively to their mothers

Teenage girls who are close to their mothers tend to be less sexually active and, consequently, are less likely to become pregnant or to contract a sexually transmitted disease. Open communication, particularly about sexuality and dating, is the key.

are likely to be less sexually experienced (Fox, 1981) and more likely to communicate successfully with their mothers about sex (Fox & Medlin, 1986). Thus, maintaining a generally positive relationship with their teenagers may be the best way for parents to exert continuing influence over their children's sexual attitudes and behavior. Teenagers who view their parents as reasonable and fair may be more likely to accept and conform to their parents' values.

Do peers influence each other's sexual behavior? Unfortunately, their direct influence has been inadequately studied (Brooks-Gunn & Furstenberg, 1989; Miller & Fox, 1987). For example, while we know that teenagers—particularly males—pressure one another through dares and bravado, it is not clear whether these behaviors have appreciable effects on actual sexual behavior. We do know that teenagers *believe* they are more influenced by their peers than by their parents with respect to sexual attitudes and behaviors (Shah & Zelnik, 1981; Zelnik & Kantner, 1977, 1980), but we do not understand how that influence is enacted or if it is truly effective. Do teenage boys believe everything they hear in locker rooms and set their sexual goals accordingly? Do teenage girls disinhibit one another by sharing their sexual exploits? We simply do not have answers to these questions. However, even without research, we should assume that teenagers have significant influence on one another's sexual behaviors, and that this influence is often at cross purposes to the influence of parents.

Cultural Influences

All cultures establish moral codes for sexual behavior; they teach their children those codes during development and establish sanctions to ensure that people behave accordingly. Not surprisingly, cultures differ significantly in this regard—from highly permissive societies that allow (or actively encourage) sexual behavior among children and adolescents to cultures that severely restrict sexual behavior until marriage (Barry & Schlegel, 1984; 1986; Ford & Beach, 1951).

The people of the Lepcha culture in India represent an extremely permissive approach. They believe sexual learning must begin in childhood and that heterosexual practice between children is a prerequisite to sexual maturation. Lepcha children as young as 11 engage in sexual intercourse without negative sanctions from adults (Ford & Beach, 1951). At the opposite extreme, the Cuna of Central America restrict all sexual exploration until marriage.

How permissive or restrictive is contemporary American culture about adolescent sexuality? It is difficult to say, for several reasons. First, our society is composed of many different ethnic/cultural groups who differ substantially in their sexual beliefs, values, and behavior. For example, African American and white teenagers vary significantly in their sexual attitudes and behaviors. African American teenagers begin sex earlier and engage in premarital intercourse more frequently than white teenagers (Hofferth, Kahn, & Baldwin, 1987).

Second, our cultural values have shifted over time. Substantial increases in sexual behavior among adolescents of all races during the 1970s moved our culture in the direction of greater permissiveness (Hofferth & Hayes, 1987; Zelnik & Kantner, 1980). The National Longitudinal Survey of Youth reported that by the early 1980s, 60 percent of all U.S. teenagers had engaged in intercourse (Hofferth & Hayes, 1987). Although this trend toward earlier sexual debut has leveled off for teenagers of all races, contemporary adolescents are far more sexually active and at earlier ages than any previous generation.

Finally, our culture is difficult to characterize because of frequent discrepancies between what we practice and what we preach. While many parents espouse conservative values for their children, they provide little or no supervision and deal ineffectively with their children's transgressions. Moreover, many parents fail to communicate with their children on sexual matters (Fox & Inazo, 1980) while opposing efforts by the schools to provide sex education. Sending mixed messages to our children about sex leads to their confusion and makes behavior less predictable.

Thus, our sexual values, beliefs, and behaviors are in a state of flux. Individual adolescents may engage in extreme sexual lifestyles of either promiscuity or abstinence, but the vast majority of adolescents—even those who debut early—manage to find a middle ground, balancing their sexual interests and behaviors with other important aspects of their lives.

A P P L I C A T I O N

Dealing with Your Teenager's Sexuality

*T*he literature on teenage sexuality is clear: It is *likely* that your teenager will become sexually active, and it is *unlikely* that she will consistently use contraception, placing her at risk of pregnancy and disease. What can you do to reduce the risks?

- Communicate openly with your child about sexuality. A continuing dialogue from childhood through adolescence enhances your influence on your teenager's decision making and behavior. Gear your advice to your teenager's approach to sexuality: While adventurers may need more persistent reminders than monogamists, both types are at high risk for pregnancy and disease.

- Avoid sending mixed messages about sex to your child. If you don't practice what you preach, she is unlikely to follow your advice.

- Take a *moderate* approach to discipline and to setting rules for dating. Since you cannot directly control your teenager's sexual behavior on a date, you must rely on her self-control. Self-control is more likely when teenagers know why it is necessary and the negative consequences of giving in.

  Bottom Line: Although your teenager is likely to become sexually active, your efforts can lessen the risks and enhance her sexual adjustment. Communication is the key.

Searching for Identity

Before the family sits down to dinner, Keisha notices that Leshonda is acting strangely. She has not even begun her homework, and she has been uncharacteristically rude and abrupt with her friends on the phone. Although Keisha knows something is wrong, she also knows that confronting her daughter would be a mistake. She decides to wait for Leshonda to make the first move. She doesn't have to wait long. Leshonda slams herself into her seat at the dinner table, interrupting her parents' conversation.

After a few uncomfortable moments of silence, Leshonda says, "I think I'm going crazy—schizo or psycho or something. I don't know. Just crazy I guess. I can't understand what is going on inside of me. This morning I told my teacher that Sharonda was late because her mother was sick. I lied! Then I told Sharonda that, even though she was my best friend, I would never lie for her again. That was a lie. Am I a liar? I hate liars! Does that mean I hate myself?

"Then I started thinking about all the things I do that don't make any sense. I like my friends, but I gossip about them. Sometimes I say some really nasty things. That's crazy! I think I'm tough, but coming home after dark scares me to death! I believe in God, but I only say my prayers when I think I'm in trouble. I know about eating right, but I eat all kinds of junk. I think I'm a smart person, but I'm always doing stupid things.

"Maybe I'm not as smart as I think I am, or as smart as I want to be, or something like that. It's like I'm a whole bunch of different people all at once, and they don't always get along with each other."

Leshonda finds the inconsistencies in her thinking and behavior disturbing, but her concerns are typical of adolescents searching for identity. According to Erik Erikson (1950/1963, 1968), adolescence is a critical time for developing of a **sense of identity**, an answer to the question, Who am I? He speculated that there are two fundamental aspects of identity: a *personal* aspect that involves making commitments to ideas, beliefs, and philosophical positions on politics, religion, and lifestyle; and a *social* aspect concerned with relating to others. Thus, developing an identity involves asking not only, Who am I? but also, How will I be accepted by and perceived by others? (Kamptner, 1988).

According to Erikson (1950/1963, 1968), the search for identity continues not just during adolescence but throughout the individual's lifetime. He argues that the ego gradually evolves through a series of *psychosocial crises* experienced during each of the *pre-adolescent* stages of development (1950/1963). Each crisis provides a unique opportunity to enhance the ego's ability to cope with social problems. In a supportive social and cultural context, the infant who learns to trust becomes the self-confident adolescent who is loyal and devoted to family and friends. The toddler with a healthy sense of autonomy becomes the adolescent who can compromise, resolve conflict, and show leadership among peers. The preschooler with initiative becomes the adolescent who can set goals and persist until they are accomplished. The school-age child with a sense of industry becomes the adolescent who is motivated to achieve and to pursue a vocation.

Erikson believed that successful resolutions of the preadolescent crises prepare the child for the ultimate crisis: the search for a *sense of identity* in adolescence. The identity crisis presents adolescents with an opportunity to integrate their childhood experiences with the rapid physical, social-emotional, and cognitive changes in adolescence to prepare for the challenges of adulthood. Erikson described the failure to resolve the identity crisis as **role confusion**. Thus, the identity crisis raises yet another set of risks and opportunities for the development of personality.

Leshonda, Heather, and Carlos have struggled with their identities in different ways, in different social contexts, with, of course, different results.

Leshonda tries to find out who she is at home with her family, in her gifted classes, on the track, with her new friends in the most popular crowd, and with several lifelong friends from her neighborhood. She feels proud to be good at so many things, but she often finds her assets are liabilities. Each day has only 24 hours and Leshonda has to learn to make choices. She has to accept that she cannot have it all or be it all. She has to learn to distinguish between being popular and being a good friend, between being competent and compulsively trying to be the best at everything, between being a caring person and trying to rescue every friend in every crisis.

By her senior year Leshonda has committed herself to a career in engineering, to liberal political values, to a private belief in God, and to a late marriage and children.

Heather's daily survival demands a precocious commitment to physical and mental toughness. Drugs and promiscuous sex are routine, and she is often hungry, hurting, sick, and exhausted. Although her lifestyle takes its toll, it convinces that she and her body can cope with just about any deprivation or assault.

She also thinks of herself as highly intelligent, particularly when dealing with people. She can scam just about anyone to get out of trouble or to get what she needs to survive. She is a model to other kids on the street, a role that she coveted and actively encouraged. By 16 she has come to think of herself as a leader. Many of her friends agree.

Although she consistently flunked her classes in junior high and high school, she occasionally applies herself just long enough to prove to herself that she is not stupid. For instance, while failing an English class in her sophomore year, she was briefly fascinated with several poems that her teacher read in class. To her teacher's astonishment, Heather memorized all of the poems in just a few days and earned an "A" on the poetry test. She then cut the next two weeks of school and failed every other exam that semester.

By her senior year, Heather thinks of herself as tough, resilient, intelligent, daring, and reckless. She has secretly decided on a career in law enforcement.

Since early childhood, Carlos has always thought of himself as clumsy, awkward, and physically unattractive. His elementary and junior high school peers have always rejected him, so he never gets to try out different social roles or develop any social skills. Despite his membership in the brains clique in high school, he thinks of himself as socially incompetent and unfriendly. His entire identity is wrapped up in school and academic achievement.

Emilio had always dreamed that his son would become a doctor. Carlos's frequent bouts of childhood illness provided many opportunities for Emilio to encourage his son toward a career in medicine. Carlos eventually conforms to his father's persistent hinting even though he has never made the effort to find out whether he has the talents and abilities to study and practice medicine. Although Emilio is delighted that his son will pursue a career in medicine, he secretly cringes at the thought of Carlos's clumsy hands holding a scalpel. He thinks to himself, "Maybe he will go into research!"

Forming an identity involves two processes: **exploration** and **commitment** (Grotevant, 1987). *Exploration* involves testing one's values and beliefs, trying out different roles, and experimenting with alternative lifestyles. Parents are often overwhelmed by their teenagers' explorations, as each new experience—joining a new crowd, making a new friend, or even hearing a new type of music—becomes an excuse (or opportunity) to try out another role or lifestyle. As one mother put it, "One day my daughter is

According to Erik Erikson, finding an identity requires a great deal of exploration. For many teenagers, the bathroom mirror becomes a safe place to explore the effects of different — often bizarre — hairstyles, makeup, and clothing on one's sense of self.

rebelling against our family traditions, and the next day she is talking about getting married and having children. She's driving me crazy!'' Although these rapid changes in adolescents' thinking and behavior may seem random and unproductive, they are natural and necessary expressions of their search for identity.

Successful exploration prepares adolescents for *commitment*, the process of dedicating themselves to goals, roles, values, and beliefs that provide meaning and direction to their lives (Erikson, 1968; Waterman, 1984). Commitments that integrate various aspects of a person's life are essential to establishing identity. For example, a teenager's experience with volunteering in a pediatric hospital may reveal how he could integrate a love for children into a professional career. Failure to explore and to commit leaves adolescents in a state of *role confusion*, with no future goals or ability to deal with the crises that they will encounter in adulthood, particularly the challenge of developing intimate relationships.

John Marcia (1966, 1980) adapted Erikson's notions of crisis, exploration, and commitment to describe the adolescent's search for identity. He suggested that at any given moment, a teenager exists in one of four *statuses*, with each status defined by a unique combination of exploration and commitment. Individuals who have experienced crisis and who have committed to an occupation and to an ''ideology'' or philosophy of life have reached **identity-achieved status**. Leshonda is well on her way to identity-achieved status. An individual who may or may not have experienced crisis but who has failed to make any commitments is in **identity-diffused status**. Such individuals may profess commitment to a career or to specific values, but their involvement is only superficial. Marcia considers this the most developmentally unsophisticated status (Archer & Waterman, 1983).

Adolescents experiencing crisis and actively exploring their way toward commitment by trying out different roles, lifestyles, and behaviors are in **moratorium**. Adolescents in moratorium often appear bewildered and disoriented, frustrated by trying to make decisions that integrate their personality, rather than pulling it apart. Heather's torturous fight to survive on the streets and to make sense of her life places her squarely in moratorium. Finally, adolescents who have not experienced crisis or exploration but who have made commitments anyway are in **foreclosure**. Such individuals have typically adopted their parents' values and career objectives without exploring their own life for a sense of identity. Carlos's premature choice of a career in medicine and acceptance of his parents' values with no exploration is the epitome of foreclosure. Marcia views foreclosure as another developmentally unsophisticated identity status.

Erikson (1968) pointed out that adolescents experience crises in various domains, such as religion, politics, friendships, dating, and sexuality. An individual's experience of crisis and commitment in one domain may have little or no effect on their experience in other domains. Thus, an adolescent is likely to be in different statuses in various domains at any given moment. For example, while a teenager may have foreclosed in choosing a career, she may have achieved identity in relationships with peers. However, a fully integrated sense of identity is not possible until an individual brings his or her experiences in *all* domains from crisis to achieved status. Research has shown that a majority of adolescents and adults remained diffused, having failed to do the necessary exploration and commitment to achieve identity (Archer & Waterman, 1990). The special challenge faced by minorities in their search for identity is examined in Box 16.3.

Research comparing adolescents in various identity statuses has generally shown that those in higher identity statuses (moratorium or achieved) are more advanced in cognitive and social-cognitive development than those in lower statuses (diffused or foreclosure) (Waterman, 1984). Consistent with Erikson's theory, one study (Adams, Abraham, & Markstrom, 1987) showed that identity-achieved teenagers were less self-conscious (or more self-assured) than those in other statuses.

A P P L I C A T I O N

Promoting Identity Exploration and Commitment

Supporting your teenager's search for identity can be one of the most difficult tasks you will face as a parent. If you try to intervene directly to promote your own values, you may inadvertently encourage your child to rebel. If you lay back too much, you may wind up blaming yourself after the fact for outcomes that are not to your liking. The following suggestions may help to define a middle ground that both you and your teenager can live with:

- Don't protect your teenager from crisis; crisis is essential to achieving identity. Encourage her to approach crisis constructively through exploration, trying alternatives, experimenting, and keeping track of the results of her experiments. But don't be surprised or

alarmed when she appears confused and aimless.

- As a parent, be sensitive to your potential for forcing your teenager into foreclosure. While there is nothing wrong with expressing your values or presenting yourself as a model, avoid manipulating your child's exploration—for example, by using guilt or intimidation. Commitment without crisis or exploration will leave your child vulnerable to another identity crisis later in life.

Bottom Line: Your teenager will have to find her identity by herself. Observe from a distance, provide emotional support, and set reasonable limits on her exploration. Above all, try to respect her commitments, particularly if they differ from your own.

BOX 16.3

The Search for Identity in Minority Teenagers

Although the search for identity is a formidable developmental task for virtually every adolescent, the task is considerably more difficult for members of minority groups (Spencer & Markstrom-Adams, 1990). According to Erikson (1968), members of "oppressed" minority groups struggle for their identity in the context of negative stereotypes and prejudice of the dominant society. He believed that many minority adolescents succumb to this pressure by developing a *negative identity*, that is, an identity that reflects the prejudiced views of the majority culture. Those who develop negative identity are prone to feelings of low self-esteem and self-hatred. We examine this view more closely in light of more recent research.

We begin by distinguishing between the concepts of identity and ethnic identity. While the term *identity* is used broadly to refer to an individual's integrated sense of self, *ethnic identity* refers more specifically to the degree to which an individual identifies with a particular culture and its traditions. Ethnic identity provides a framework for developing a view of oneself, a way of relating to others, and a way of looking at the future (Spencer & Markstrom-Adams, 1990).

When a person's ethnic identity is reasonably consistent with the values and beliefs of the dominant society, adjustment is enhanced. For example, Asian American children who internalize their families' cultural emphasis on academic achievement are likely to succeed in American schools. However, when the content of a person's ethnic identity is incompatible with the majority culture, that person has a hard time adjusting.

Minority families can help their children form their ethnic identity by exposing them to ethnic values, beliefs, and traditions during childhood and by more direct efforts to inculcate ethnic values. But parents face a difficult decision. While on the one hand they want their children to carry their culture's traditions and beliefs, they recognize that their children may pay a steep price for ethnic identity—their children's strong ethnic identity may elicit prejudice and discrimination. On the other hand, minority families may encourage their offspring to identify with the majority culture and to assimilate themselves into society.

Parents who feel strongly in either direction tend to pressure their children to adopt an identity consistent with their values, an approach that is likely to promote foreclosure. Research has shown that minority adolescents—including African American, Native American, Mexican American, and Asian American teenagers—are significantly more foreclosed than Anglo-American teenagers (Markstrom, 1987a; Streitmatter, 1988).

However, foreclosure is a status, not a permanent state of being. While their families may push many minority adolescents into foreclosure, social pressures that come with adolescence may force some foreclosed teenagers to reexamine their ethnic identity. Some will be thrown into identity crisis and explorations when they encounter direct prejudice and discrimination in school and in their community. For example, imagine the experience of a Hispanic child who has grown up and attended school in the barrio and is suddenly introduced to an integrated high school. Although the teenager may have internalized the ethnic identity of his parents, facing the power and privilege of white, middle-class adolescents could be overwhelming. The experience might sorely test the teenager's foreclosed commitments to his ethnic identity.

There has been some research on the development of ethnic identity in minority teenagers. Jean Phinney (1989) adapted Marcia's (1966) status categories to describe what she called the stages of development of ethnic identity in minority adolescents. The stage sequence and typical statements that Phinney used to classify her subjects are presented in Table 16.1.

The results showed that searching for ethnic identity is an important aspect of the lives of minority teenagers. Although more than half of the tenth graders (ages 15–17) she interviewed were in the first stage—they were either diffused or foreclosed—few showed the negative attitudes or self-hatred suggested by Erikson (1968). In fact, only a small percentage of subjects indicated that they would prefer to change their identity. More positively, approximately 25 percent of the subjects were in moratorium (exploring for identity), and an additional 25 percent were classified as identity-achieved. Thus, nearly half of the minority subjects were actively searching for or had achieved ethnic identity. The identity-achieved minority teenagers scored higher on measures of self-evaluation, sense of mastery, and peer and family relations than those who were diffused or foreclosed. These results suggested that ethnic identity may play a significant role in the social and emotional adjustment of minority teenagers.

TABLE 16.1

The Stages of Ethnic Identity Development

Diffusion

- "My past is back there; I have no reason to worry about it. I'm American now." (*Mexican American male*)

- "Why do I need to learn about who was the first black woman to do this or that? I'm just not too interested." (*black female*)

- "My parents tell me . . . about where they lived, but what do I care. I've never lived there." (*Mexican American male*)

Foreclosure

- "I don't go looking for my culture. I just go by what my parents say and do, and what they tell me to do, the way they are." (*Mexican American male*)

Foreclosure (Negative)

- "If I could have chosen, I would choose to be American white, because it's America and I would then be in my country." (*Asian American male*)

- "I would choose to be white. They have more job opportunities and are more accepted." (*Mexican American male*)

Moratorium

- "I want to know what we do and how our culture is different from others. Going to festivals and cultural events helps me to learn more about my own culture and about myself." (*Mexican American female*)

- "I think people should know what black people had to go through to get to where we are now." (*Black female*)

- "There are a lot of non-Japanese people around me, and it gets pretty confusing to try and decide who I am." (*Asian American male*)

Achieved

- "People put me down because I'm Mexican, but I don't care anymore. I can accept myself more." (*Mexican American female*)

- "I have been born Filipino and am born to be Filipino. . . . I'm here in America, and people of many different cultures are here too. So I don't consider myself only Filipino, but also American." (*Asian American male*)

- "I used to want to be white, because I wanted long flowing hair. And I wanted to be real light. I used to think being light was prettier, but now I think there are pretty dark-skinned girls and pretty light-skinned girls. I don't want to be white now. I'm happy being black." (*black female*)

SOURCE: *Adapted from Phinney, 1989.*

Adjustment Problems in Adolescence

Although adolescence is a time of challenge and opportunity, it is also a time of great turmoil, stress, and temptation that can overwhelm many teenagers.

The turmoil and temptations come in several forms.

> *Leshonda and two of her friends are invited to a party by girls from school that they hardly know. When they arrive, a thick, pungent smoke envelopes them, burning their eyes and noses. Within minutes they have been offered marijuana, hashish, beer, and their choice of pills. All three girls politely refuse, try to mingle, but soon find that their refusal to "use" is making others at the party uncomfortable. So they all accept a beer just to fit in.*
>
> *Although this is a first for Leshonda, she soon finds that drugs and alcohol are available at every party she goes to.*

> *When Heather is 12, she and one of her street friends steal nearly $500 worth of clothing from a department store over a three-day period. None of the clothes fit, and they give most of them to their friends at school. Although Heather often steals things that she needs, stealing is mostly a game. She masters it, gets away with it, and brags about it every chance she gets. For Heather, stealing is just as good as sex.*

Leshonda's and Heather's experiences have become quite common—perhaps pervasive—in the lives of contemporary U.S. teenagers. Virtually all teenagers are exposed to these and similar situations; most teenagers succumb in varying degrees, and all teenagers—those who succumb *and* those who resist—must learn to cope with the social and emotional consequences of their choices. While some adjust well, others show varying degrees of maladjustment, including the development of lifestyles built around delinquency and severe dependency on alcohol or drugs. We examine these subjects more closely, and we also consider the most extreme form of maladjustment during this period of development: adolescent suicide.

Adolescent Substance Abuse

Robert Newcomb and Peter Bentler (1989), researchers in adolescent substance abuse, have characterized the United States as a "drug culture." In their words,

> Drugs are used commonly and acceptably to wake up in the morning (coffee or tea), get through the stresses of the day (cigarettes), and relax in the evening (alcohol). The Marlboro Man and the Virgina Slims woman are widely seen models, and licit drugs are pushed to remedy all of the ills one may face—stress, headaches, depression, physical illness, and so on. (1989, p. 242)

We may add that children themselves are frequently dosed with various medications by well-intentioned parents, many of whom will go to any extreme to relieve their children's discomfort. Physicians who cater to such parents in this regard add significantly to the problem. Therefore, it should come as no surprise that our children start early looking to drugs to solve their problems. Just how early is indicated in a longitudinal

---

FIGURE 16.1

Junior High School Students' Acceptance/Rejection of Gateway Substances

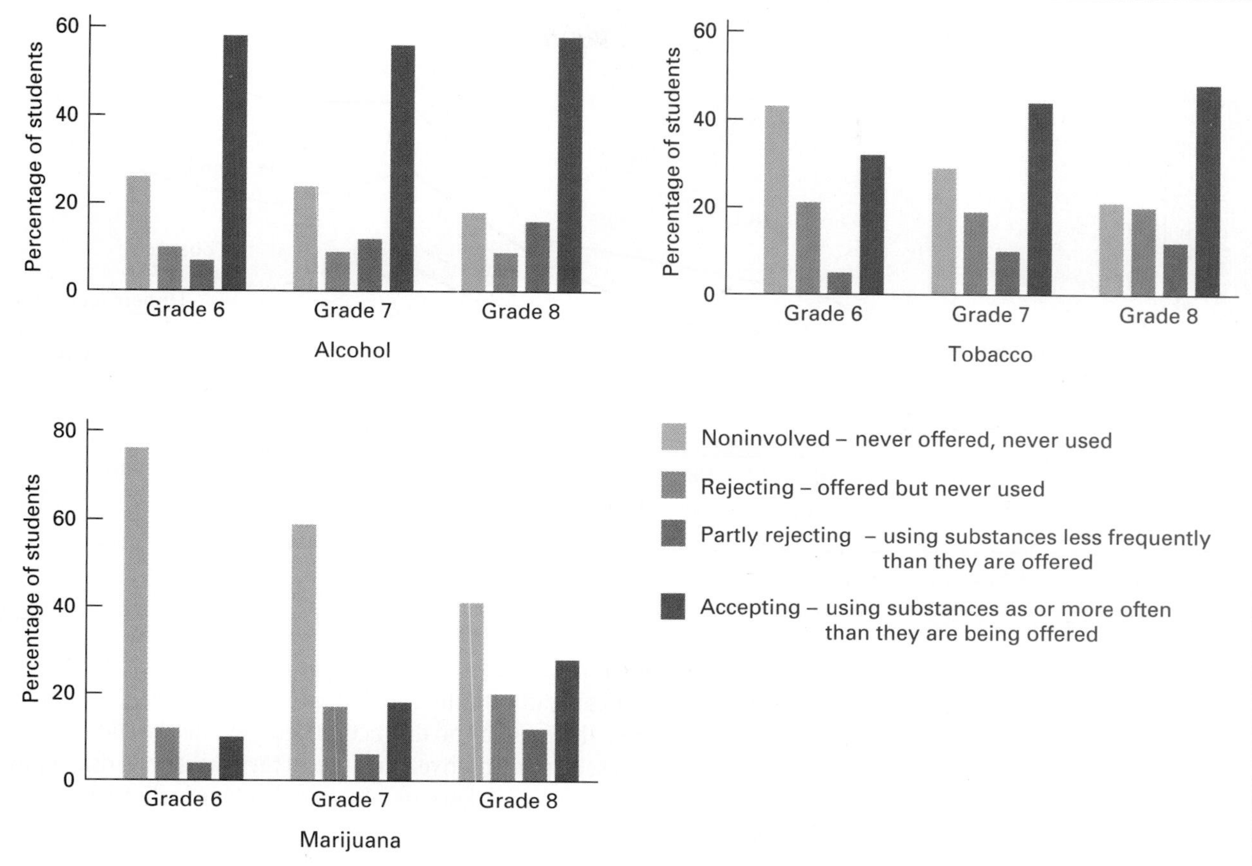

Noninvolved – never offered, never used

Rejecting – offered but never used

Partly rejecting – using substances less frequently than they are offered

Accepting – using substances as or more often than they are being offered

SOURCE: *Grady, Gersick, Snow, & Kessen, "The Emergence of Adolescent Substance Abuse,"* Journal of Drug Education, *16(3), 1986. Reprinted by permission of Baywood Publishing Co., Inc.*

---

study of the emergence of students' use of the **gateway substances** (alcohol, tobacco, and marijuana)—substances thought to be a gateway to the use of harder drugs (Grady, Gersick, & Snow, 1986). By sixth grade—the earliest grade studied—65 percent of children had already experimented with alcohol, 36 percent with tobacco, and 11 percent with marijuana. The increasing trend toward greater involvement in the gateway substances from sixth to eigth grade is illustrated in Figure 16.1.

Adolescents continue their use of gateway substances and proceed to other drugs during high school (Fournet, Estes, Martin, Robertson, & McCrary, 1990). The results of a survey of rural fifth to twelfth graders are presented in Figure 16.2. The results showed that by the senior year of high school, three of four students in this sample had used alcohol, more than half had used marijuana, and one in four had used stimulants, such as speed or cocaine; 35 percent admitted having using drugs before going to school, and 23 percent had driven while high on drugs or alcohol. If these statistics are not sufficiently discouraging, the study also revealed that 23 percent of twelfth graders who had *never* experimented with drugs admitted that they would like to give it a try!

FIGURE 16.2

The Percentage of Students Using Alcohol and Specific Drugs in Grades 5–12

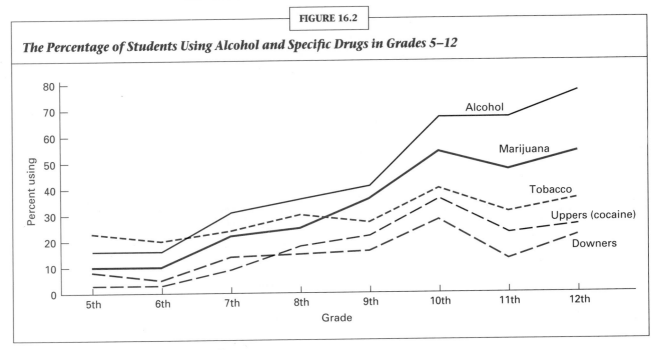

SOURCE: *Fournet, Estes, Martin, Robertson, & McCrary, 1990.*

Distinguishing Between Use and Abuse   Some developmentalists argue that the potential harmful effects of drugs varies with the child's age (Newcomb & Bentler, 1989). However, for young children, there can be no distinction between the use and abuse of drugs: Children's repetitive use of psychoactive drugs places them at serious risk of physical injury and social maladjustment. Adolescents who start drinking early are more likely to have serious alcohol problems in late adolescence (Newcomb, Maddahian, & Bentler, 1986), and the younger they are when they start the more serious their abuse is likely to be when they are older (Barnes & Welte, 1986). Put simply, children who use are at exceptionally high risk of becoming adolescents who abuse.

However, the distinction between use and abuse becomes less clear in middle and late adolescence. For example, by today's standards, 16- or 17-year-olds who *occasionally* drink beer or smoke marijuana at parties would probably not be considered abusers. However, the same behavior four or five nights a week would qualify as abuse. Even occasional use of a drug may constitute abuse if the adolescent indulges at very high doses or risks personal injury while under the influence of the drug—for example, by driving, swimming, or hanging off motel balconies. Abuse is also implied when teenagers require increasing amounts of drugs to get high, when they need drugs to get through the day, when they are unable to stop, or when they show signs of physical or psychological deterioration, such as severe weight loss, depression, or paranoia.

Risk Factors for Substance Abuse   A wide variety of factors contribute to teenagers' initial involvement with drugs. One of the most potent risk factors is how much an adolescent's parents, other significant adults, and peers use the drugs (McLaughlin, Baer, Burnside, & Pokorny, 1985; Newcomb et al., 1986). The risk is particularly high if these individuals model drug use openly and if they encourage the adolescent's involvement by providing access to drugs (Newcomb & Bentler, 1989).

One longitudinal study (Webb, Baer, McLaughlin, McKelvey, & Caid, 1991) compared various parental and peer risk factors associated with teenagers' use of alcohol. The researchers began by identifying a group of seventh graders who had not yet begun to use alcohol—"abstainers." The subjects were interviewed 15 months later and classified into 3 groups: those who were still abstainers, those who had begun experimenting with alcohol, and those who were beginning to drink more frequently. The results showed that those teenagers who had begun to use alcohol regularly were more likely than other teenagers to have rejected their parents' authority. Surprisingly, peer use of alcohol, peer approval of alcohol use, and parental use of alcohol did not discriminate among the three groups. Thus, this study suggested that teenagers' negative relationship with their parents may be more important than exposure to alcohol as a risk factor for teenagers' initiation of regular alcohol use.

Families also place their children at risk for later drug abuse by more subtle means. Follow-up data on the children in the New York Longitudinal Study (Thomas & Chess, 1977) showed that the quality of parent-child interaction in early childhood is related to substance abuse in late adolescence. More specifically, parental conflict in childrearing methods, inconsistent discipline, restrictive discipline, and maternal rejection predicted older adolescents' use of alcohol and marijuana (Vicary & Lerner, 1986).

Other possible risk factors include lower socioeconomic status, family dysfunction, academic failure, delinquent behavior, poor relationship with parents, and low self-esteem (Newcomb & Bentler, 1989; Newcomb et al., 1986). Not surprisingly, research has shown a direct relationship between the *number* of risk factors an individual experiences and how often he or she uses drugs in adolescence (Newcomb et al., 1986). We meet a professional who works to prevent drug abuse in "Careers: The Prevention Counselor."

A P P L I C A T I O N

Preventing Substance Abuse in Adolescence

*P*reventing your teenager's involvement with alcohol and drugs requires that you accept certain facts and then act accordingly:

- If your teenager wants alcohol or drugs, he will be able to get them without difficulty or detection. Where you live or which school you choose for your child will have little effect on access. By fourth or fifth grade, your child will have access.

- Your teenager *will* experiment with alcohol and cigarettes, and is likely to experiment with other drugs. Developing a strategy to delay your teenager's initiation is more likely to succeed and have long-term benefits than a strategy designed to preclude experimentation altogether.

- You probably will not know if or when your teenager first experiments with alcohol or drugs. Teenagers are adept at deception, and probing through their belongings or asking them questions will probably not provide much insight. On the other hand, there are obvious signs of substance abuse, including declining health and hygiene, weight loss, mental deterioration, mood swings, theft and other delinquent/criminal behaviors, sleep disturbance, and clear signs of intoxication. If you see these signs, particularly in combination, immediately intervene.

- Preventing your teenager's substance abuse begins when your child is very young. If you maintain open communication with him, provide emotional support, discipline him fairly and consistently, and avoid chronic conflict and family dysfunction, your teenager will be better prepared to deal with the challenge of alcohol and drugs.

- Before your child graduates from elementary school, see that he is well informed about the risks of drugs. Work with school and community programs where available, but be certain to discuss the issues with your child directly.

Bottom Line: While it is unlikely that you can prevent your teenager's experimentation with alcohol and drugs, you can do a great deal to keep it from getting out of hand and destroying his life. Families and communities that take a proactive approach to prevention can make a difference.

The Prevention Counselor

Ella Bryan is a prevention counselor at The House Next Door, a delinquency and drug abuse prevention program in the Volusia County Public Schools in Deland, Florida. This program — 1 of 75 throughout the state — is designed to identify fourth- and fifth-grade children who are at risk for drug abuse, delinquency, and school dropout and to intervene to improve their outcomes. Ella has been with the program since 1978, first as a counselor and, for the last eight years, as the director.

What does a prevention counselor do?

As a prevention counselor, I am a member of a team of professionals — including teachers, other counselors, and a social worker — who provide wraparound services for children and their families. We try to do it all: intense instructional and psychological services for the children and social support for the families. I observe children in class, counsel them individually and in groups, and do home visits. The home visits are critical if we are to engage families in support of their children.

How does your program work to prevent delinquency and drug abuse?

We identify children who are at risk through referrals from parents, school personnel, and professionals in the community. Fourth and fifth graders who are heading for trouble typically have problems in the classroom, at home, and in the community. So if we are going to turn a child's life around, we have to intervene in every aspect of their lives.

After referral, we approach the family and offer them an opportunity to be involved in our program. Participation is completely voluntary, but parents must commit themselves to actively participate in every aspect of the program through middle school and high school. If they accept, we place their child in one of our special learning environments — classrooms that are highly structured and highly supportive of individual learning and development. Each child gets six hours a week in individual counseling. Counselors do home visits, helping parents to deal more effectively with their children. The social worker helps the family to cope with other life problems. We monitor the children continually through middle school and high school and provide follow-up intervention at the first sign of trouble.

Is the program effective?

We have followed up all of our 1,400 children in their senior year of high school. We are proud to say that 86 percent of them are still in school, drug free, and not involved in the juvenile justice system. Is our program effective? I think our results speak for themselves. We have exceeded all of our original expectations.

We now know that with a great deal of effort and considerable expense, children who begin to get in trouble in elementary school do not have to move on to a delinquent lifestyle in high school. Prevention — at least the way we do it — is labor intensive and expensive, but it is also highly effective. We also know that we could not accomplish what we do without parents' total cooperation. Fortunately, we have had no difficulty finding highly motivated parents who want the best for their children.

What are the rewards for a prevention counselor?

There are lots of rewards. Watching our children get control of their lives is extremely satisfying. Every time I see one of our graduates productively involved in the community, I know the part that we played. When I get graduation announcements in the mail, I know that many of those kids never would have made it without us. This job is very fulfilling.

How would a student become a prevention counselor?

This work isn't for everyone. Begin by getting involved in your local community as a volunteer. If you enjoy the challenge, select undergraduate and graduate programs that integrate the study of child development, psychology, behavior modification, and family systems. Seek out specific training and certification in addiction. After graduation, look for programs that believe in the power of families and in the developmental potential of *all* children.

Adolescent Suicide

Teenagers must cope with a variety of stressors that severely challenge their ability to cope: The physical changes at puberty, relating to peers and parents, exposure to alcohol and drugs, sexuality and dating, and developing an identity can be overwhelming. However, we still are shocked that adolescents consider or attempt suicide as a solution to their problems. Upon hearing that a teenager has taken his own life, adults typically respond, "I can't believe it. He had so much to live for!"

But we can no longer afford to be surprised by adolescent suicide. The incidence of teenage suicide has grown rapidly and is now the second leading cause of death (after accidents) in the 10–24 age group (Maris, 1985). A study (Kandel, Raveis, & Davies, 1991) of urban adolescents has shown that **suicidal ideation**—thinking about taking one's life—is common among adolescents, particularly among teenage girls. Forty-two percent of the ninth- to eleventh-grade girls sampled (compared to 26 percent of the boys) reported having been bothered by suicidal thoughts within the preceding year; 12 percent of the girls and 6 percent of the boys reported having attempted suicide at least once. Even though only a small percentage of those who attempt suicide succeed, the problem of teenage suicide has reached epidemic proportions.

Why do teenagers consider taking their own lives? Are teenagers who think about and/or actually attempt suicide different from other teenagers? Psychologically healthy teenagers are highly unlikely to seriously consider taking their own lives, even when they are frustrated by some particularly troubling personal problems. Most teenagers have sufficient coping skills and access to social support to help them through even the most extreme personal or family problem.

However, while most adolescents manage to cope with their problems, others are overwhelmed to the point of despair. Those who are socially isolated from family and peers have no one to turn to for social support. In desperation, they turn to alcohol, illicit drugs, and delinquent behaviors to escape their problems, but find little relief from their suffering (Kandel et al., 1991). For some, suicide is the only escape.

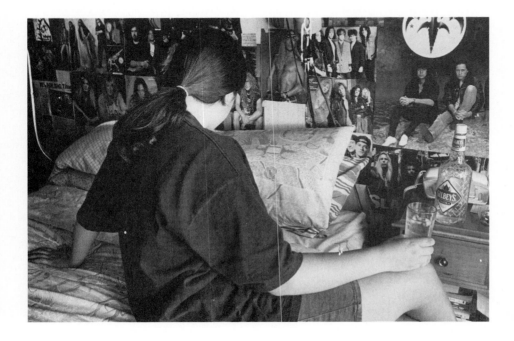

Suicidal ideation is not unusual among teenagers, particularly among those who drink heavily and even more particularly among those who drink alone in their room. This teenager's isolation and drinking should be seen as a "red flag" for the possibility of depression and suicide.

Several studies have examined differences between teenagers who engage in suicidal ideation and those who do not (Ball & Chandler, 1990; Kandel et al., 1991; Kashani, Goddard, & Reid, 1989; King, Raskin, Gdowski, Butku, & Opipari, 1990). These studies showed that teenagers who consider suicide have more serious identity problems (Ball & Chandler, 1990), are more depressed, poorly adjusted and delinquent (Brown, Overholser, Spirito, & Fritz, 1991; Kashani et al., 1989; King et al., 1990); more involved in drugs and alcohol (Windol, Miller-Tutzauer, & Baecher, 1991); and more isolated from and less valued by their families (Kandel et al., 1991; Woznica & Shapiro, 1990) than their nonsuicidal peers. Teenagers who drink alcohol heavily are at particularly high risk of suicidal ideation. In one study (Windol et al., 1991), 63 percent of female and 38 percent of male heavy drinkers had thought about committing suicide (half again more than the general adolescent population), and 39 percent of female drinkers and 22 percent of male drinkers had attempted suicide at least once (between three and four times more than the general adolescent population).

Teenagers who consider suicide tend to do so during periods of deep psychological disturbance and low social support (D'Attilio, Campbell, Lubold, Jacobson, & Richards, 1992; Renouf & Harter, 1991). The risk of suicide remains high as long as the adolescent remains seriously distressed (Garrison, Addy, Jackson, McKeown, & Walker, 1991). Intervention should be designed to provide *long-term* treatment of the adolescent's psychological disturbance and to ensure consistent access to social support from family, friends, and school personnel.

A P P L I C A T I O N

Identifying Teenagers at Risk of Suicide

Although we might be tempted to simply ask teenagers to help us identify those at risk of suicide, research has shown that most adolescents are unaware of the risk factors involved in suicide and are not very good at recognizing the warning signs in their peers (Norton, Durlak, & Richards, 1989). Nonetheless, when teenagers report having heard a peer's suicidal threats, such reports should be taken very seriously.

The most telling sign of risk is chronic depression, particularly when combined with stressful life events, such as social rejection, school failure, family conflict, or serious illness. Other warning signs include a decline in school attendance or performance (particularly in high-achieving students), social withdrawal by teenagers who are typically socially active, and increase in the use of alcohol or drugs. Teenagers who show these signs should be brought to the attention of mental health professionals without delay.

Parents and professionals should recognize that suicide can be contagious. When teenagers hear about the suicide of peers or celebrities, particularly those with whom they identify, they may be tempted to imitate their self-destructive behavior. When a suicide occurs, professionals should increase their vigilance, particularly toward teenagers who are considered at risk.

Teenagers who have previously attempted suicide or have considered it should be regarded at continuing risk, particularly if their coping skills have not improved and/or if their distress has not decreased since their attempt.

Bottom Line: Always take teenage depression seriously, provide persistent social and emotional support, and seek professional advice without delay.

Juvenile Delinquency

Delinquency refers to any illegal activity engaged in by a child or adolescent (Henggeler, 1989). By one estimate (Federal Bureau of Investigation, 1989), nearly 1 million juveniles are arrested each year in the United States for *index crimes* (serious offenses, such as rape,

The expression on this young victim's face tells of the pain caused by juvenile delinquents. How does a child become a delinquent? Research suggests that some parents inadvertently train their children to engage in violent behavior, and that this violence carries over into the teenage years. Once formed, delinquent behaviors are very difficult to extinguish or modify.

murder, and theft), and nearly 1.5 million more are arrested for *status offenses* (less serious activities that would not be illegal for adults, such as truancy, drinking, and running away). Teenage crime accounts for 1 of every 3 arrests in the United States (U.S. Department of Justice, 1991). If we assume that only a small percentage of teenagers get caught for their crimes, it is clear that juvenile delinquency is a staggering problem.

While most adolescents occasionally engage in some delinquent behaviors, particularly status offenses, the vast majority of serious juvenile crimes are committed by a relatively small percentage of teenagers (Henggeler, 1989). We generally refer to those teenagers who are chronically involved in criminal behavior as **juvenile delinquents**. How are delinquents different from other teenagers? Research has shown that they are much more likely to be male than female and from disadvantaged rather than advantaged families. They do less well than nondelinquents in school (Hawkins & Lishner, 1987) and are less competent with their peers (Kazdin, 1987). They are more egocentric and engage in lower levels of moral reasoning than nondelinquents (Lee & Prentice, 1988). They are more likely to be in conflict with their parents (Simons, Robertson, & Downs, 1989) and have less access to social support (Kashani & Sheppard, 1990). Contrary to a prevailing stereotype, delinquents are *not* more likely to come from "broken" homes (Farnworth, 1984).

Why do delinquents behave as they do? Gerald Patterson and his colleagues (1989) have described a step-by-step developmental pathway to juvenile delinquency (Figure 16.3). The first step begins in early childhood in families that use harsh and inconsistent discipline and that inadequately monitor and supervise their young children. Patterson argued that family members directly "train" their children to be coercive in an escalating pattern of physical violence. Their children learn to be highly aggressive and socially incompetent, primed to fail in school and to be rejected by their peers.

In junior high school and high school, these aggressive-rejected adolescents come together in groups that, in Patterson's words, provide a "major training ground for delinquent acts and substance use" (1989, p. 331). The groups encourage the attitudes, motivations, and rationalizations that support delinquent behavior and provide opportunities to engage in specific antisocial acts. More than half of the adolescents who go through this early family and peer training will eventually become adult offenders (Blumstein, Cohen, & Farrington, 1988; Farrington, 1987).

While Patterson's research suggested that *all* delinquency begins in early childhood as a result of inadequate parenting, Terrie Moffit (1990) argued that there may be more than one developmental pathway to delinquency. More specifically, Moffit proposed that the risk of juvenile delinquency may be greatest for children who behave aggressively and show symptoms of *attention deficit disorder* (ADD).

To support his argument, Moffit examined the developmental histories of 4 groups of 13-year-old boys: a group that diagnosed ADD but with no delinquency, a group both ADD and delinquent, a group with delinquency but without ADD, and a normal comparison group. Moffit found that, compared to the other groups, the ADD plus delinquent boys were troubled throughout their childhood. They were highly aggressive before entering school, and their antisocial behavior escalated significantly between ages five and seven and persisted into adolescence. They were significantly lower in verbal intelligence, had more difficulty learning to read, and had more conflict with their families than boys in the other groups.

In contrast, the ADD-only group showed no deficits in intelligence or reading, had relatively few conflicts with their families, and experienced only mild behavior problems in childhood. The delinquent but non-ADD boys also had a history of few family problems and showed no deficits in intelligence or reading; they simply began to show anti-

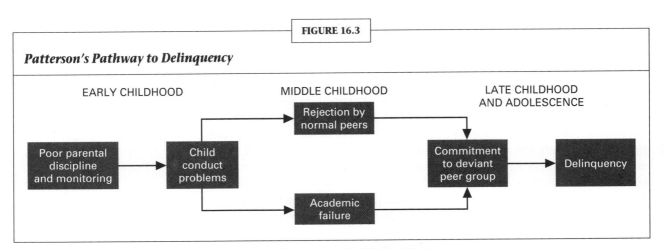

FIGURE 16.3

Patterson's Pathway to Delinquency

SOURCE: *G. R. Patterson, B. D. DeBaryshe, and E. Ramsey, "A Developmental Perspective on Antisocial Behavior."* American Psychologist, *44, 1989, p. 331. Copyright 1989 the American Psychological Association. Reprinted by permission of the publisher and Gerald Patterson.*

social behaviors at about age 11 and were just as aggressive as the ADD-delinquent group by age 13.

Moffit's results support the notion that there may be multiple pathways to juvenile delinquency that can be distinguished by the presence or absence of various risk factors, including symptoms of ADD and the degree of adversity that children experience in their families. Children who show early symptoms of attention deficit disorder but grow up in supportive family environments are *un*likely to develop delinquent lifestyles. In contrast, children who are both aggressive and ADD and experience conflict in their families are likely to show persistent problems of antisocial behavior from childhood through adolescence. Although Moffit suggested that the delinquents who had no history of antisocial behavior or family problems are probably going through a "transient" phase, he offers no evidence to support his contention. Further research is needed to see whether the prognosis is any better for this group than for the more disturbed delinquent plus ADD group.

Can juvenile delinquency be prevented? Most efforts to intervene during middle or late adolescence have shown few long-term benefits (see Kazdin, 1987, for a review). The poor results may reflect the fact that, with very few treatment programs available, only the most severely disturbed adolescents—those who are most resistant to change—find their way to treatment. There is some indication that intervention may be more successful with younger teenagers, particularly in comprehensive programs that combine academic and social skills training for children and behavior management training for parents (Patterson et al., 1989). Both Patterson's and Moffit's research strongly support the concept of early intervention for high-risk children.

APPLICATION

Dealing with Juvenile Delinquency

*I*f your child is preschool-age or school-age and you think you may be training him to engage in coercive patterns of violence with you and other family members, you need immediate professional help. If you don't change, it is only a matter of time until your child transfers these coercive behaviors to his peers and to innocent victims.

■ If your child has already begun to associate with others who engage in delinquent behaviors, recognize that membership will support and escalate the problem.

■ If your child shows symptoms consistent with attention deficit disorder *and* obvious behavior problems at home or in school, he may be at higher risk than other children of developing delinquent behaviors. A highly supportive home that is relatively free of conflict can make the difference.

■ If your teenager suddenly show signs of delinquency after an otherwise untroubled childhood, it is likely to be a passing phase.

■ If your teenager's delinquency becomes serious, seek professional help. Look for a *comprehensive* program that helps your teenager socially, emotionally, and academically and helps you to be a more effective parent.

Looking Back

This chapter has shown the challenges of social and emotional development during adolescence. Risk and opportunity hang in the balance as teenagers search, experiment, explore, and sometimes blunder their way through their daily lives, trying to cope with a host of extraordinarily difficult problems: relating to peers in cliques and crowds, dating and their first sexual experiences, searching for identity, and dealing with the temptations and risks of substance abuse and delinquency. Some teenagers build upon the solid foundation of social and emotional skills they learned in early and middle childhood. They are able to take advantage of the opportunities and avoid many of the risks. Others enter adolescence lacking the social and emotional skills required for optimal development.

Although childhood experiences may make a difference, all adolescents are severely challenged and tested as they struggle to cope with each new experience and progress slowly toward the responsibilities of adulthood. As we have seen, some come through far more socially and emotionally prepared for the challenges of adult life than others. The outcome is beyond any parent's or caregiver's direct control. But much of it remains susceptible to your influence. Exercising influence wisely is your most effective way to promote optimal outcomes during this difficult period of child development.

CHAPTER REVIEW

PEER INFLUENCE During adolescence, teenagers become less attached to their parents and increasingly influenced by their peers. However, parents continue to influence their teenagers in certain areas, such as choice of career and college.

THE PEER GROUP Teenagers relate to their peers in close-knit, intimate groups of friends called cliques, and in larger, loosely defined groups known as crowds. These groups offer their members security, prestige, status, and opportunities to learn about themselves and practice social skills. However, the groups tend to insulate their members from new friendships and new ideas.

PEER PRESSURE The tendency of members of cliques and crowds to imitate each other's behavior can be explained by *peer pressure*, force applied by the group to urge members' conformity to group standards or an expression of the members' internal motivation to conform. Peer pressure/conformity increases rapidly during early adolescence. Peer pressure may promote both negative and positive behaviors, depending upon the nature and context of the group.

FRIENDSHIP By early adolescence, friendship becomes an increasingly intimate relationship based on mutual understanding, trust, and loyalty. Friends become reliable sources of social support in times of crisis. Those who fail to make friends experience loneliness, alienation, and depression.

ACCEPTANCE/REJECTION Increasing complexity and diversity of peer relations among teenagers increase opportunities for social acceptance and risk of rejection. By one estimate, approximately half of all adolescents are neglected or rejected by their peers. Rejection may result from delinquent behavior, social withdrawal, or hyperactive-aggressive behavior.

SEXUAL RELATIONSHIPS Learning to cope with sexuality is one of the great challenges of adolescence. Many American teenagers become sexually active in early adolescence, but most have intercourse infrequently. Developmentalists have distinguished between serial monogamists (those who engage in relatively long-term, exclusive sexual relationships) and sexual adventurers (those who engage in short-term, emotionally shallow relationships just for sexual gratification).

INFLUENCES ON SEXUALITY Hormones affect sexuality directly (by regulating arousal) and indirectly (by the social impact of secondary sex characteristics). Hormones affect adolescent sexual behavior, but social and cultural factors also play important roles. Although parents may have little control over their teenager's sexual behavior, parents who use moderate discipline and relate well to their teenager may have greater influence than other parents.

IDENTITY Adolescence is a critical time for developing a sense of identity, an answer to the question, Who am I? Erik Erikson argued that, while identity evolves throughout the childhood years, adolescence is a time of identity crisis. Forming an identity involves exploration and commitment. Erikson refers to the failure to achieve identity as role confusion. The search for identity has been described in terms of statuses. Those who have experienced crisis and made commitments have identity-achieved status. Those who have failed to make commitments have identity-diffused status. Those who are actively exploring, but have not yet made commitments have moratorium status. Those who have made commitments, but without exploration, have foreclosure status.

SUBSTANCE ABUSE Substance abuse begins with gateway substances: alcohol, tobacco, and marijuana. Surveys suggest that most middle school students have experimented with gateway substances, particularly alcohol. Experimentation expands during the high school years, with the majority of students having tried alcohol and marijuana by their senior year. Adolescents who use drugs early are more likely to abuse drugs later in adolescence.

SUICIDE   The incidence of teenage suicide has grown rapidly in recent years and is now the second leading cause of death in the 10 to 24 age group. Many teenagers engage in suicidal ideation. These individuals tend to be more depressed, less well-adjusted, and more delinquent than other teenagers. Those who abuse alcohol are at particularly high risk of suicidal ideation.

DELINQUENCY   Juvenile delinquents are adolescents who engage in index crimes (serious offenses, such as murder, rape, and theft) or status offenses (truancy, drinking, and running away). Teenage crime accounts for 1 of every 3 arrests. The developmental pathway to delin-quency begins in early childhood in the family, where parents "train" their children to be disobedient and violent. The training for delinquency is passed on through the adolescent peer group. There is evidence that attention deficit disorder (ADD) may predispose some teenagers to delinquent behavior. While efforts to prevent delinquency have had disappointing results, intervention may be more successful with younger adolescents and in programs that work with teenagers and their parents.

Key Terms

cliques	sense of identity	moratorium
crowds	role confusion	foreclosure
peer pressure	exploration	gateway substances
sexuality	commitment	suicidal ideation
sexual debut	identity-achieved status	delinquency
serial monogamists	identity-diffused status	juvenile delinquents
sexual adventurers		

abuse cycle The notion that all abused children are predisposed to become abusers themselves when they become parents.

accommodation In Piaget's theory, adapting by modifying an existing cognitive structure to conform to some new aspect of the environment.

acuity Sharpness of vision.

adaptation In Piaget's theory, adjusting to the environment through a balance of assimilation and accommodation.

adolescence The period of development from age 11 through age 20.

adolescent egocentrism An adolescent's cognitive and emotional commitment to his or her own beliefs and perspectives and a depreciation of the perspective of others.

adolescent growth spurt The sudden increase in height and weight at puberty.

affective attunement The state achieved when caregivers match their caregiving behaviors to the rhythm of their babies' emotions; synchrony.

age of viability The age at which the fetus has some reasonable chance of survival if born prematurely, about the twenty-sixth week of gestation.

aggression Purposeful effort to inflict pain or injury on another child.

alleles The maternal gene and paternal gene for a particular trait existing side by side on their respective chromosomes.

alternative birthing center (ABC) A privately operated (or "freestanding") facility for childbirth that provides a simulated home environment with limited equipment for emergency care.

ambivalent attachment A form of insecure attachment in which the infant ignores the caregiver during episodes of anxiety.

amniocentesis A prenatal diagnostic procedure in which a hollow needle is used to obtain amniotic fluid to determine the presence of various genetic disorders.

amoral In Piaget's theory, a description of the young child's inability to reason logically about rules and concepts of right and wrong.

anal stage In Freud's theory, the second psychosexual stage during which the child experiences pleasure from anal activity.

anorexia nervosa An eating disorder in which an individual purposely pursues thinness to the point of extreme emaciation or even death.

anoxia Prolonged periods of oxygen deprivation of the fetus.

Apgar scale A technique for evaluating the state of the newborn at one and five minutes after birth.

arousal modulation Caregivers' ability to influence their infants' emotional state to match the emotional requirements of a given task.

artificial rupture of membranes (AROM) The process by which a physician induces labor by breaking the amniotic sac.

assimilation In Piaget's theory, adapting by using an existing cognitive structure to interpret some experience.

attachment The enduring relationship that gradually emerges between an infant and a caregiver.

attention deficit/hyperactivity disorder (ADHD); hyperactivity A behavior pattern characterized by normal intelligence, extreme activity, impulsivity, disruptive behavior, and an inability to sustain attention.

authoritarian The approach to discipline in which parents assert great power over their children, setting strict limits and standards, with no room for negotiation or compromise.

authoritative The approach to discipline in which parents have expectations for their children's behavior, firmly enforce rules and standards, but encourage independence by allowing children some say in the development of rules.

automatic reasoning In social problem solving, impulsively selecting the first thing that comes to mind or the solution that requires the least mental effort.

autonomous moral reasoning In Piaget's theory, the highest level of moral reasoning in which children realize that rules can be changed and that intentions must be considered in judging whether a behavior is right or wrong.

average status children Children who are liked by a few peers and disliked by some others.

avoidant attachment A form of insecure attachment in which the infant is drawn to the caregiver but the caregiver is unable to function as a secure base.

axon On a neuron, the single relatively long fiber that sends impulses to the next neuron.

babbling An infant's meaningless early combinations of consonants and vowel sounds.

behavior modification The system of applied operant techniques used to change behavior.

behaviorism The system of principles that explain behavior in terms of stimulus-response connections.

birth plan A way for a pregnant woman to express her wishes with respect to options for childbirth.

body image An individual's qualitative appraisal of his or her own body.

bonding The process by which the newborn develops a relationship with the caregiver.

Bradley method The approach to prepared childbirth that places the father in a central role directing the experience, rather than just supporting, as in Lamaze.

breech position General term for less than optimal positions of the fetus in the uterus.

bulimia An eating disorder that involves loss of self-control during extended binge eating episodes.

centration In Piaget's theory, the tendency of preschool-age children to focus attention on minute and often inconsequential aspects of their experience.

cephalocaudal principle Description of a growth trend in which growth of the head proceeds at a more rapid rate than the lower parts of the body.

cesarean delivery Birth of the baby through an incision through the abdomen and uterus.

child abuse A class of maltreatment that involves *intentional* behaviors that cause physical injury to children.

child sexual abuse A form of maltreatment that involves sexual activities with children.

chorionic villus sampling (CVS) A prenatal diagnostic procedure in which a hollow tube is used to extract fetal tissue to determine the presence of genetic disorders.

chromosomes Rodlike structures composed of genes that determine hereditary transmission.

circadian pattern A sleep-wake cycle based on a 24-hour clock.

class inclusion The logical rule that any class of objects must be smaller than the inclusive class in which it is contained.

classical conditioning A type of learning based on the association between paired stimuli.

classification The tendency to group objects on the basis of particular sets of characteristics.

cliques Close-knit, intimate groups of friends who prefer each other's company and exclude outsiders from their activities.

coercion theory The notion that simple aggressive acts tend to escalate into chains of aversive transactions.

cognitive emotions theory The theory of emotions that assumes that infants gradually learn to experience and express emotions throughout the first two years of life.

cognitive structures In Piaget's theory, the mental units that children use to represent reality; the strategies children use to solve problems.

collective monologue Conversation-like turn-taking between egocentric speakers, with little or no transfer of meaning.

commitment The process of dedicating oneself to goals, roles, values, and beliefs that provide meaning and direction to life.

compensatory preschools Early childhood education programs designed to compensate for risks associated with growing up poor, neglected, or abused.

comprehension In reading, the ability to understand words that have been decoded; more generally, the child's ability to understand language.

concrete operation In Piaget's theory, the cognitive structure used by the child during the concrete operations stage.

concrete operations stage In Piaget's theory, the third stage of cognitive development characterized by the first logical thinking using concrete operations.

conditioned response (CR) In classical conditioning, the response elicited by the conditioned stimulus.

conditioned stimulus (CS) In classical conditioning, the stimulus that comes to elicit the conditioned response.

conflict Episodes in which children overtly oppose one another, typically expressed by one or both children protesting, denying, or in some way resisting the other's actions or statements.

conservation In Piaget's theory, the notion that certain attributes of objects and events may remain unchanged, despite transformations or changes in other attributes.

construction skills Manual skills (building, stacking, molding, cutting, and pasting) that manipulate and transform materials to produce specific states or products.

continuous Term that describes theories that reject the concept of developmental stages.

contractions The flexing of the muscular walls of the uterus during childbirth.

controversial children Children who are liked by many of their peers *and* disliked by many others.

conventional level of moral reasoning In Kohlberg's theory, the second level of moral thinking in which children accept society's values of what is right and wrong.

cooing The infant's uttering of long vowel sounds.

coordinated secondary circular reaction The infant's first schema to solve problems by using one schema as a means of performing a second schema as an end.

correlational design The research strategy that demonstrates covariation among factors in natural settings.

counting The systematic assignment of numbers to items in an array.

counting-all A strategy in which children use physical objects to stand for each of the addends in a simple addition problem.

counting-on An addition strategy in which children count from one of two addends to the other.

couvade A set of rituals in which the father simulates the birth process during the mother's labor.

covariance The tendency of two factors to vary systematically with respect to each other.

creeping Forward locomotion by the infant with the stomach off the floor.

critical period The time during which an organ is developing most rapidly; the time during which an individual is particularly sensitive to certain forms of learning.

crossing over During meiosis, the random exchange of segments of genetic material between chromosomes.

cross-sectional design The research strategy in which various age groups of children are studied at a single point in time.

crowds Relatively large but loosely defined groups of individuals who share common interests and social status.

decenter The ability to distribute attention across multiple features of an event.

deception The process by which a child creates false beliefs in another individual.

decoding In reading, the ability to interpret printed letters as a code for spoken words.

defense mechanisms In psychoanalytic theory, unconscious mental strategies that provide *temporary* relief from anxiety and guilt.

deferred imitation The process by which a child observes a model, encodes the model's behavior in images, and recalls those images at a future time to guide his or her behavior.

delinquency Any illegal activity engaged in by a child or adolescent.

demandingness The degree to which the parents maintain expectations for their children's behavior and attempt to control the outcome of their development.

dendrites The short fibers on a neuron that receive impulses from neighboring neurons.

deoxyribonucleic acid (DNA) Long strands of genetic material wound in a double helix that carry hereditary messages.

dependent variable In an experimental study, the factor whose variation depends upon variation of the independent variable.

deprivation dwarfism An abnormal condition in children two years and older characterized by bizarre eating behaviors and shortness of stature, but with weight proportional to height.

design The researcher's strategy to demonstrate covariation between factors.

development The gradual accumulation of relatively permanent, age-related changes through transactions with the environment.

developmental stage The time elapsing between any two sequential developmental changes that reorganize the system.

developmentalists Researchers and practitioners who study the development process.

dexterity The coordinated manipulation of objects with the fingers.

dilation The process by which uterine contractions open the cervix to allow the fetus to pass through.

discontinuous A term that describes theories that explain development using the concept of qualitatively distinct developmental stages.

discrete emotions theory The theory that assumes that human newborns are innately preadapted to experience discrete emotions according to a prewired, biologically determined timetable.

discrimination The process by which individuals perceive two or more stimuli as different.

disorganized/disoriented attachment A noncoherent attachment pattern.

display rules A society's expectations for appropriate emotional expression; the etiquette of emotional expression.

dominance The system that defines who defers to whom in disputes over territory or possessions.

dominance hierarchy A systematic ordering of power relationships from the most to the least powerful member of a social group.

dominant gene The gene that wins the competition when paired with a recessive gene for a given trait.

dominant-recessive principle The rule that governs heredity when the child is heterozygous for a given trait.

Down syndrome A genetic disorder that results in a unique cluster of physical traits and varying degrees of mental retardation.

dyscalcula Severe disability in learning mathematics.

dyslexia A specific form of reading disability that is independent of aptitude or intelligence.

eating disorders Chronic preoccupation with eating and/or dieting that becomes a central focus of one's lifestyle.

ecosystem The nested levels of environmental influence on development, including the microsystem, mesosystem, exosystem, and macrosystem.

ego In psychoanalytic theory, the component of personality that uses conscious perception and intelligence to find pleasure.

ego ideal In Freud's theory, a component of the superego that provides a prescription for gender-appropriate role behavior.

egocentric speech Language that fails to consider the viewpoint of the listener.

egocentrism The child's inability to conceptualize the perspective of other individuals.

ego-involved goals Goals that are based on outperforming one's peers.

elaborated knowledge base An interconnected body of facts in memory.

elaboration Relating objects to one another with absurd or fanciful visual images to facilitate memory.

electronic fetal monitoring (EFM) The use of both external and internal devices to monitor the fetal heart rate.

empathy An emotional state that results from vicariously experiencing the emotions of another individual—feeling what he or she feels.

encoding The process by which individuals store learned information.

engrossment Fascination in the newborn.

enmeshment An exaggerated but superficial state of family togetherness that robs family members of a sense of individual identity.

enuresis A condition in which a child has not learned to control the bladder by the end of the third year.

episiotomy A surgical incision that widens the vaginal opening to allow the fetus to pass.

erogenous zone In psychoanalytic theory, a part of the body that is highly sensitive to sexual stimulation and a focus of pleasure.

estradiol A form of estrogen that stimulates changes in sex characteristics in females.

ethology The scientific study of behavior and development in evolutionary perspective.

evolution In Darwin's theory, the survival of the species.

expansion Restating a child's utterance by adding missing words and more complex linguistic elements.

experimental design The research strategy in which the investigator manipulates one factor (independent variable) in order to study its effect on the variation of a second factor (dependent variable).

exploration In adolescence, testing one's values and beliefs, trying out different roles, and experimenting with alternative lifestyles.

expressive style An approach to fast-mapping that emphasizes pronouns, adverbs, prepositions, and simple phrases.

extinction In learning, decreasing the frequency of a behavior simply by ignoring its occurrence.

extrinsic motivation Motivation based on seeking external rewards and avoiding punishments.

facilitate To foster development by minimizing risk and maximizing opportunity.

fact retrieval The automatic approach to adding by using memorized sums of numbers.

fast-mapping In early childhood, the process by which words rapidly come to have referential meaning.

fertilization The penetration of the egg by a sperm cell and the joining of genetic material.

fetal blood sampling Monitoring the state of the fetus by sampling blood from a small cut in the fetus's scalp.

fetal distress Prolonged deprivation of oxygen to the fetus.

5-to-7 shift The gradual period of transition from the illogical and unsystematic reasoning of the preschool period to the more logical and systematic reasoning of middle childhood.

fixates The process of attending to a particular stimulus.

fixed action patterns Complex behaviors that are necessary for survival, such as foraging for food, searching for a mate, and attacking or running.

fontanels Soft spots on the newborn's head where the bones of the skull have not yet fused.

forceps A tonglike instrument that may be used to assist the descent of the fetus through the birth canal.

foreclosure The status of an individual who prematurely commits to a particular set of values without sufficient exploration.

formal operational reasoning In Piaget's theory, the abstract reasoning ability that one achieves during the period of formal operations.

formal operations stage In Piaget's theory, the fourth stage of cognitive development, characterized by the ability to consider general propositions and principles and to think about hypothetical events.

fovea The densely packed set of highly sensitive cells at the center of the retina.

fragile X syndrome A genetic disorder in which breaks or tears on the X chromosome result in unique physical traits and mental retardation.

friendships Relatively enduring, positive mutual relationships.

fuzzy logic In moral development, reinterpreting rules and rationalizing behavior to reconcile dishonest or unethical behavior.

gametes The sex cells (sperm and ova).

gateway substances Substances thought to be a gateway to the use of harder drugs (alcohol, tobacco, and marijuana).

gender constancy The child's understanding that gender does not change regardless of how one behaves or what clothes one wears.

gender identity The ability to classify oneself and others by gender.

gender intensification hypothesis The notion that gender-related characteristics strengthen over time.

gender roles The behaviors, attitudes, and beliefs that a particular culture considers appropriate for males and females.

gender schema A cognitive structure that causes the child to actively search for gender-related information from the environment.

gender typing The process by which children learn gender roles.

genes The smallest units of heredity; located on chromosomes.

genetic counseling A vocation that provides counseling to parents on genetic transmission of traits to offspring.

genetic counselor A professional trained in genetics and counseling who advises on the probability of genetic disorders.

genital stage In Freud's theory, the fifth psychosexual stage — the period of mature sexuality beginning in adolescence and extending through adulthood.

giftedness A general advantage in all aspects of a child's life; a more specific ability or talent in a particular area such as music, mathematics, or science.

goal-corrected partnership An advanced form of attachment relationship in which child and parent can each pursue independent goals without threatening the relationship or generating anxiety.

goodness-of-fit The extent to which the parent's temperament and caregiving environment match the temperament of the child.

gossip The informal sharing of information and opinion on peers' strengths and shortcomings.

grammatical morphemes Inflections such as *-ing*, *-ed*, and *-s* that modify nouns, verbs, and adjectives.

handicapped; disabled A physical, cognitive, or emotional condition that interferes with one's functioning.

hemophilia A genetic disorder characterized by inability of the blood to clot.

heredity The genetic transmission of characteristics from parent to offspring.

heterozygous In genetics, when the maternal gene and the paternal gene for a particular trait are not identical.

holophrase The infant's expression of a complete thought with a single word.

homologous Pairs of chromosomes, matched according to size, shape, and the precise sequence of genes.

homozygous When the maternal gene and the paternal gene for a particular trait are of identical form.

hormones Complex chemical substances produced by endocrine glands and distributed throughout the body by the bloodstream.

hostile aggression Person-oriented acts aimed at gaining social control.

hypertonia Too much muscle tone.

hypothalamus The part of the brain that regulates metabolic processes and stimulates functioning of the testes and ovaries.

hypothesis A formal statement that alleges the possibility of a relationship between two factors.

hypothetico-deductive reasoning The ability to reason about hypothetical events and hypothetical transformations of those events.

hypotonia Too little muscle tone.

Id In psychoanalytic theory, the place in the mind/body where libido is stored.

identification In psychoanalytic theory, the defense mechanism by which the child incorporates traits of significant others into his or her personality.

identity-achieved status An individual who has experienced crisis, and who has committed to an occupation and a philosophy of life.

identity-diffused status An individual who may or may not have experienced identity crisis, but who has failed to make commitments.

image The first mental symbol; picture-like symbols in the child's mind.

imaginary audience Adolescents' belief that they are the focus of the attention of everyone around them and that everyone shares their self-perceptions.

immanent justice The young child's notion that you *always* get punished for behaving inappropriately and rewarded for behaving appropriately and, conversely, that if you get punished, you must have done something bad, or if you get rewarded, you must have done something good.

implantation The process by which the fertilized egg lodges itself in the wall of the uterus.

imprinting Lorenz's concept of biological readiness for certain forms of learning in particular species.

independent variable In an experimental study, the factor that is manipulated to study its effect on the dependent variable.

induction The process by which labor may be initiated artificially.

indulgent-permissive The approach to discipline in which parents accept their children's impulses, avoid setting rules, and assert very little authority.

infancy The period from birth to the end of the second year.

information processing system A model of the flow of information in human reasoning, attention, memory, and problem solving.

information processing theory A theory of cognitive functioning that describes the capacity to derive information from the environment, interpret that information, and organize behavior on the basis of such interpretation.

inner speech In Vygotsky's theory, the form of speech resulting from internalizing spoken words and sentences.

instrumental aggression Object-oriented struggles between children over possession, territory, or privilege.

internal working model An individual's mental representation of his or her attachment relationship with a particular caregiver.

intrinsic motivation An inner urge to learn and to achieve.

intuitive In Piaget's theory, the form of reasoning during the 5-to-7 shift.

irreversibility In Piaget's theory, the notion that preschoolers cannot mentally reverse their transductive sequences of thought.

joint collaboration The component of scaffolding in which the adult and child share responsibility for solving some problem.

juvenile delinquents Those teenagers who are chronically involved in criminal behavior.

Klinefelter's syndrome A genetic disorder in which males inherit an extra X chromosome (XXY) resulting in underdeveloped genitals and mental retardation.

labor The process by which a woman gives birth to her baby.

Lamaze method An approach to prepared childbirth in which the father (or an appropriate substitute) serves as a coach.

Language Acquisition Device (LAD) A hypothetical inborn faculty, the sole purpose of which is to discern a language's basic rules.

latchkey; self-care Children who are left to care for themselves for extended periods of time before or after school.

latency In Freud's theory, the fourth psychosexual stage, marked by massive repression of sexual and aggressive drives.

learning Any relatively permanent change in behavior or knowledge resulting from experience or practice.

least restrictive environment The concept that handicapped children may be placed in separate classrooms only when the severity of their impairment precludes learning in regular classrooms.

libido In psychoanalytic theory, the energy that drives all thinking and behavior.

limited capacity In information processing theory, the notion that each individual is constrained by a finite pool of mental resources that can be allocated to various thought processes.

locomotion The ability to move one's self from one place to another.

longitudinal design The research strategy in which the researcher observes the same group of children at predetermined intervals over time.

look-say (whole-word) An approach to reading instruction that asks children to memorize whole printed words as pictures.

mainstreaming The process by which handicapped children are integrated into regular classrooms.

maltreatment Adult behaviors that—intentionally or unintentionally—cause harm to children.

manual control The self-regulation of arm and hand movements to manipulate objects.

marking time Stair climbing using one preferred foot to raise the body to higher steps.

masking The process by which children alter the overt expression of emotions to conform to display rules.

maternal serum alpha-fetoprotein test (MSAFP) A prenatal screening procedure used to detect neural tube disorders.

math anxiety An extreme lack of confidence in one's ability to learn and to perform mathematics.

Matthew effects The notion that early readers "get richer" in the elementary school's fast track, whereas slow readers "get poorer" in the elementary school's slow track.

maturation Term used generally to refer to growth, or used more specifically with Gesell's proposition that development is predetermined by an inherited biological plan largely unaffected by nurture.

mediational deficiency A description of a child who has no strategies and does not profit from training to promote the use of strategies.

meiosis The process whereby sex cells are produced.

memory Recording the results of learning and storing it as knowledge.

memory stores In information processing theory, three sites for storing and processing information: the sensory register, short-term store (or working memory), and long-term store.

menarche The first menstrual period in females.

menstrual cycle The timing and sequence of biological events that constitute the female's reproductive capacity.

mental retardation Below average intellectual ability associated with impaired adaptive behavior.

metacognition Children's awareness and control of their cognitive abilities.

midwife A nonphysician who facilitates the birthing of babies, including lay midwives and certified nurse-midwives.

min A variation of the counting-on strategy for addition in which children begin counting-on with the larger of two addends.

mindreading The cognitive process by which individuals attribute desires and beliefs to other individuals in order to understand and predict their behavior.

minitheory A theoretical frame of reference composed of factors and their respective relationships to a target behavior.

mitosis The process whereby body cells duplicate themselves.

moderate to vigorous physical activity (MVPA) The kind of activity known to prevent cardiovascular disease in adults.

monitoring Managing children's social lives by observing interaction, supervising the choice of activities, and guiding the direction of play.

monologue The form of language in which children simply talk to themselves, seemingly oblivious to anyone around them.

moral realism In Piaget's theory, the second level of moral development in which children decide the rightness and wrongness of behaviors strictly by their consequences, irrespective of the person's intentions.

moral reasoning Thinking about the rightness or wrongness of specific behaviors in everyday situations.

moratorium The status of an individual who is experiencing crisis and actively exploring his or her way toward commitment.

morphemes The smallest units of meaning in a language.

motherese A special way of talking to babies and young children in which parents use shorter sentences, higher pitch, exaggerated intonation, simplified syntax, repetitions, and frequent reference to concrete objects.

multiply handicapped Classification of children who have severe impairment of the central nervous system that affects all parts of the children's body and motor ability.

mutual regulation In Erikson's theory, the sensitive, reciprocal caring, and emotional sharing between parent and child.

myelin sheath The fatty coating on the axon of nerve cells that facilitates the transmission of impulses.

natural selection In Darwin's theory, the notion that adaptive traits are selected into the species across generations.

negative attributional bias The child's tendency to assume hostile intent.

neglect A form of maltreatment that involves failure to provide for the care and protection of children.

neglected children Children who are neither actively liked nor disliked by any of their peers.

neglectful The approach to discipline in which parents are uninvolved in their children's lives and consider parenting a burden.

Neonatal Behavioral Assessment Scale Brazelton's technique for assessing the infant's ability to manage his or her physiological system.

neonate Term used for the infant during the first four weeks.

neurons Cells that pass electrical impulses through the nervous system.

nonorganic failure to thrive (NOFT) An abnormal condition in which infants show growth retardation — low weight for height — with no identifiable organic disorder.

nonrapid eye movement (NREM) sleep Regular (or quiet) sleep.

obese Children whose weight exceeds 120 percent of the ideal weight for height.

object permanence The infant's awareness that objects exist even when they are not being acted upon.

objectivity The characteristic of the scientific method that requires researchers to agree on what is observed or what is to be done or has been done in research.

observational learning A type of learning in which children observe the behavior of a model and the consequences of that behavior to the model.

obstetrician A physician who specializes in the safe and efficient delivery of babies, typically within the confines of a hospital.

Oedipal conflict In Freud's theory, the notion of the intense emotional experience of boys in the family during the phallic stage.

operant Any behavior that can be modified by reinforcement or punishment.

operant conditioning A form of learning in which spontaneous behaviors (*operants*), are altered by the consequences they yield.

operational In Piaget's theory, the term for the logical systems of thought that emerge in middle childhood.

operational definition A description of factors in ways that can be measured objectively.

opportunity Factors that support development and promote the realization of potential.

optimal stimulation The ability of the caregiver to adjust stimulation within a baby's varying levels of tolerance.

oral stage In Freud's theory, the first psychosexual stage in which the child experiences pleasure from sucking.

organization A strategy that involves purposeful attempts to identify conceptual relationships among items to facilitate memory.

ossification The process by which the skeletal system converts from cartilage to bone.

overregularize In language, the child's tendency to overgeneralize the application of a rule.

ovulation The release of a ripened egg through the wall of the ovary.

peer pressure The social forces to conformity among peers.

peer reputation The relatively stable characterization of a child shared by members of the peer group.

perception The processing of sensory information by the brain.

performatives Nonverbal signals (gestures) that convey requests to adults and direct adult attention to objects and events.

period of formal operations In Piaget's theory, the fourth and final stage of cognitive development, characterized by formal operational reasoning.

period of the embryo From the beginning of the third week to the end of the eighth week of pregnancy.

period of the fetus The final and longest stage of prenatal development, extending from the beginning of the ninth week to birth.

period of the zygote The first two weeks following fertilization.

personal fable Adolescents' belief that they are both unique and invulnerable — "legends in their own minds."

phallic stage In Freud's theory, the third psychosexual stage during which the child selects the opposite-sex parent as a love object.

phenotype The observable expression of hereditary traits.

phenylketonuria (PKU) A metabolic disorder in which the child fails to produce a certain enzyme needed to convert a potentially destructive amino acid into a harmless substance.

phonemes The smallest units of a language that cue changes in meaning to the listener.

phonemic awareness An understanding that spoken words are composed of sequences of sounds.

phonics An approach to reading instruction that focuses on integration of decoding and comprehension.

physical fitness A state of physical conditioning characterized by optimal development of strength, endurance, power, and flexibility.

placenta The organ that sustains the baby by allowing oxygen and nutrients from the mother's blood to cross to the baby, and waste products from the baby to return to the mother.

plasticity The ability of the brain to reprogram itself.

pleasure principle In psychoanalytic theory, the basis upon which infants invest libido — the demand for instant gratification.

popular children Children who are liked by most of their peers and disliked by no one.

popularity The degree to which children are selected as play partners by their peers.

positive energy balance Taking in more calories than one expends through physical activity and exercise, with the excess calories stored as fat.

postconventional moral reasoning In Kohlberg's theory, moral reasoning at its highest level; the ability to think beyond specific laws to abstract principles, such as justice, equality, and human rights.

pragmatics The function of language in communication.

preconcepts The disorganized, illogical representations of the preschool-age child's experiences; the products of centrated perception.

preconventional moral reasoning In Kohlberg's theory, the young child's belief that the rightness or wrongness of a behavior is determined solely by its consequences.

prenatal development Growth during the prenatal period.

prenatal stage of development The period from fertilization to birth.

preoperational stage In Piaget's theory, the second stage of cognitive development (three to six years of age), characterized by the first symbolic reasoning using preconcepts.

prepared childbirth General term for techniques for reducing the pain of childbirth by nonmedical means.

preterm; premature Term used for babies born prior to the thirty-eighth week.

primary circular reactions (PCRs) The infant's schema for repeating movements, just for the sake of movement.

primary sex characteristics The biological features directly involved in reproduction, such as changes in the penis and testes in males and changes in the ovaries, vagina, and uterus in females.

private speech Speech with no apparent communicative purpose.

problem of the match The difference between the child's existing cognitive level in a given content area and the next level; the next bite-sized piece of new complexity in learning a concept.

production In language, the child's ability to generate speech that others can comprehend.

production deficiency A description of a child who knows a strategy but who does not use it spontaneously, even when it would help the child to solve problems.

prosocial behavior Behavior that shows concern for the welfare of others, such as helping, caring, and rescuing.

proximodistal principle A growth trend in which development proceeds from the center (or proximal) regions of the body out toward the extremities (or distal parts).

pseudodialogues Mock conversations without words.

psychoanalytic theory The explanation of development proposed by Sigmund Freud and his followers.

psychosexual stages In Freud's theory, the periods that mark the development of personality.

psychosocial crisis In Erikson's theory, an intense conflict that must be successfully resolved if the ego is to develop.

psychosocial theory Erikson's variation of Freud's theory describing the development of the ego through eight psychosocial stages.

puberty The transformation from sexual immaturity to reproductive capability.

punishments Consequences that decrease the frequency of a behavior.

quantitative reasoning The ability to estimate the amount of things in terms of number, size, weight, volume, speed, time, and distance.

rapid eye movement (REM) sleep Irregular (or active) sleep.

reaction range The potential variation of phenotypic expressions for a given trait.

reality principle In psychoanalytic theory, the basis upon which the ego invests libido, recognizing the frustrations inherent in living in the real world.

recall The memory process by which the child retrieves stored information without cues.

recasting An adult's restatement of a child's utterance into a new syntactic form without changing its meaning.

recessive gene A gene that is expressed only when paired with a similar recessive gene.

recognition The memory process by which a child retrieves information in response to a cue.

referential style An approach to fast-mapping that emphasizes names of common objects.

reflective reasoning In social problem solving, conscious and deliberate searching of one's repertoire for the best solution.

reflex Involuntary stimulus-response circuit in the nervous system that provides for a specific behavioral response to a specific form of stimulation.

Regular Education Initiative (REI) An approach to special education in which children with special needs are educated exclusively in regular classrooms.

rehearsal A relatively simple strategy that involves repeating items over and over to facilitate storage of information for later retrieval.

reinforcement trap A pattern of interaction in which two or more individuals inadvertently reinforce each other's aggressive behavior.

reinforcements Consequences that increase the frequency of a behavior.

rejected children Children who are disliked by most peers and liked by very few.

rejection The process by which peers actively shun one another as play partners.

reliability The consistency of scientific observations.

research problem In research, specifying the behavior or development that the researcher seeks to explain, the theoretical perspective that will be applied in providing that explanation, and a formal statement of the relationships that the research seeks to confirm.

resilience Factors within the individual that help overcome risk.

respiratory distress syndrome (RDS) Condition in which the baby's lungs are too immature to sustain independent breathing.

respite Temporary but total relief for parents from the physical and emotional responsibility of caring for a disabled child.

responsiveness The degree to which parents accept or reject their children.

retrieval The process by which we call up memories for present use.

reversibility In Piaget's theory, the ability to cancel out one mental action with another.

Rh disease A form of blood incompatibility between mother and fetus that develops when an Rh-negative woman and an Rh-positive man conceive an Rh-positive fetus.

rhythmical movement stereotypies An infant's repetitious, patterned movements.

risk Factor that threatens to undermine development and sacrifice the child's potential.

role confusion In Erikson's theory, the failure to resolve the identity crisis in adolescence.

rough and tumble play Playful wrestling, chasing, and physical fighting.

scaffolding The process by which an adult provides the necessary support and assistance to enable a child to function at the upper limit of the zone of proximal development, then gradually withdraws that support as the child's ability to perform independently increases.

schemas In Piaget's theory, cognitive structures that regulate the infant's body movements and the effects of those movements on objects (sometimes a synonym for cognitive structure).

schooling Society's efforts to create formal learning environments to ensure that children learn basic skills.

scientific method A systematic approach to developing factual knowledge based on observation of phenomena in the real world.

script A mental representation of an everyday sequence of events that helps a child organize his or her behavior.

secondary circular reaction (SCR) The infant's schema that directs movement for a specific effect on the environment.

secondary sex characteristics Visible features that differentiate males and females but are not related to reproduction.

secure attachment The infant's relationship with a caregiver who functions as a secure base.

secure base The function of an attachment figure who makes an infant feel secure and able to explore.

semantics The study of how words come to have meaning.

sensation The ability to register information concerning internal and external events, and to transmit that information to the central nervous system.

sense of autonomy In Erikson's theory, the resolution of the second psychosocial crisis when the child learns to cope with power and decision making in relationships.

sense of identity In Erikson's theory, the satisfactory resolution of the adolescent's search for a sense of self.

sense of trust In Erikson's theory, a generalized belief that the world is a safe and satisfying place.

sensitive care Highly consistent, responsive infant care.

sensorimotor stage In Piaget's theory, the first stage in cognitive development, characterized by action-oriented problem solving.

sensory deprivation; sensory enrichment The effect of negative and positive experience, respectively, on the development of the brain.

separation anxiety An infant's fear of separation as shown by distress at the departure of a primary caregiver.

sex-linked inheritance The genetic transmission of traits and disease by the twenty-third pair of chromosomes, particularly the X chromosome in males.

sexual adventurers Individuals who engage in multiple, short-term, emotionally shallow relationships for sexual release.

sexual debut The first experience of sexual intercourse.

sexuality The development and integration of sexual interests, values, beliefs, attitudes, thinking, and behavior.

sexually transmitted disease An infection that is spread through sexual contact.

shaping In operant conditioning, the systematic reinforcement of successive approximations of a desired behavior.

sickle-cell anemia A genetic disorder that produces abnormal blood cells that harm internal organs.

skeletal deformity Distortions in the structure of the skeletal system.

small-for-date; small for gestational age Term used for low birthweight babies who weigh less than 90 percent of babies of a given gestational age.

smooth pursuit movements Scanning movements that track moving objects in space.

social cognitive theory An advanced theory of learning that accepts that cognitive factors influence the learning process.

social comparison Describing, rating, and ranking peers on various traits and attributes.

social competence The ability to establish and maintain satisfying social interaction and relationships with peers and adults.

social information processing Children's thought processes in social situations.

social learned helplessness The tendency to attribute failures to internal, stable, and uncontrollable causes.

social participation The child's degree of involvement with other children during play.

social play Playful interaction with real play partners.

social preferences Children's likes and dislikes for specific play partners.

social pretend play Playful interaction that involves pretense.

somatotype Classification of human physique by body type.

spermarche The first ejaculation in males.

Strange Situation A laboratory procedure that exposes the infant to sequential episodes of separation and reunion with the parent to assess the attachment relationship.

stranger anxiety A pattern of behavior shown by some infants at seven to eight months, including looking away, withdrawing physically, and crying when approached by unfamiliar adults.

strategies Goal-directed mental operations that individuals use to deliberately facilitate their memory, attention, and problem solving.

suicidal ideation Thinking about taking one's life.

superego In Freud's theory, the component of personality that unconsciously guides a child's behavior; the seat of morality.

symbol Something that stands for something else, often bearing some physical similarity to the thing it stands for.

symbolic function The ability to use symbols to represent or stand for perceived objects and events.

symbolic play; pretend play The child's ability to pretend that an object is something other than what it really is.

symbolic reasoning In Piaget's theory, thought that is mediated by words and images.

symbolic representation The ability to construct mental symbols that represent objects in the real world.

sympathy An emotional response in which one feels sorrow or concern for another's welfare.

syntax The system of language rules that governs the way words can be sequenced in sentences.

task-involved goals Goals that focus on improving one's own performance, irrespective of the performance of peers.

Tay-Sachs disease A genetic disorder in which the child is unable to produce a certain enzyme necessary for fat metabolism, causing fatty acids to build up in the brain, liver, and spleen.

telegraphic speech An early form of speech that omits less important words.

temperament An individual's characteristic behavioral and emotional style.

teratogens Agents that are known to enter into the biological system of the embryo and fetus and negatively influence development.

tertiary circular reaction In Piaget's theory, the infant's schema that can be systematically varied to fit the requirements of a problem.

testosterone The hormone responsible for the primary and secondary sex characteristics in males.

theory A set of interrelated ideas intended to explain the workings of highly complex events; it answers the how and why questions that people ask when trying to understand those events.

theory of mind An individual's concept of what others are thinking, feeling, and wanting.

transduction The preschool-age child's reasoning within the unsystematic collections of images that constitute their preconcepts.

transfers responsibility The component of scaffolding in which the adult delegates responsibility to a child to perform independently in problem solving.

trauma Extreme experiences of anxiety that have permanent effects on psychological adjustment.

triple X syndrome A genetic disorder in females resulting in deficits in verbal skills and memory.

Turner syndrome A genetic disorder in which all or part of one of the X chromosomes is missing in females, resulting in failure to develop secondary sex characteristics at puberty.

Type A behaviors Behaviors that predict the likelihood of stroke or heart attack.

ultrasound The use of very high frequency sound waves to form an electronic image of the fetus.

unconditioned response (UCR) In classical conditioning, the response that is elicited automatically by the unconditioned stimulus.

unconditioned stimulus (UCS) In classical conditioning, the stimulus that automatically elicits the unconditioned response.

utilization deficiency A description of a child who begins to use strategies spontaneously, but their use fails to improve performance.

vacuum extraction A technique to speed labor in which a suction cup is attached to the top of the fetus's head allowing the physician to pull with each contraction.

validity The quality of scientific data that demonstrates that observations are a true reflection of reality.

variance Term referring to the differences among children's scores on a given factor.

visual cliff An experimental device that provides kinetic depth cues to the infant.

visual preference method A laboratory method of determining infants' preference for visual stimuli.

visually directed reaching The infant's first accurate reaching for objects on the same side as the hand that does the reaching.

visually initiated reaching The newborn's primitive swiping in the general direction of objects.

vulnerability Factors within the individual that increase the tendency to succumb to risk.

word Any string of sounds that makes clear reference to a particular object in the real world.

zone of proximal development In Vygotsky's theory, the gap between what a child can accomplish independently and what the same child can accomplish when provided with optimal support from caregivers and challenging materials.

zygote The fertilized egg.

Aber, J. L., & Allen, J. P. (1987). The effects of maltreatment on young children's socioemotional development: An attachment theory perspective. *Developmental Psychology, 23,* 406–414.

Aber, J. L., & Cicchetti, D. (1984). The socioemotional development of maltreated children: An empirical and theoretical analysis. In H. Fitzgerald, B. Lester, & M. Yogman (Eds.), *Theory and research in behavioral pediatrics* (Vol. 2, pp. 147–205). New York: Plenum Press.

Ackerman-Ross, S., & Khanna, P. (1989). The relationship of high quality day care to middle-class 3-year-olds' language performance. *Early Childhood Research Quarterly, 4,* 97–116.

Acredelo, L. P., & Goodwyn, S. W. (1988). Symbolic gesturing in normal infants. *Child Development, 59,* 450–466.

Adams, G. R., Abraham, K. G., & Markstrom, C. A. (1987). The relations among identity development, self-consciousness, and self-focusing during middle and late adolescence. *Developmental Psychology, 23,* 292–297.

Adams, R. E., Jr., & Passman, R. H. (1981). The effects of preparing two-year-olds for brief separations from their mothers. *Child Development, 52,* 1068–1070.

Adcock, D., & Segal, M. (1983). *Making friends.* Englewood Cliffs, NJ: Prentice-Hall.

Adler, N. E., Kegeles, S. M., Irwin, C. E., & Wibbelsman, C. (1990). Adolescent contraceptive behavior: An assessment of decision processes. *Journal of Pediatrics, 116,* 463–471.

Ahl, V. (1993, March). *Classification by infants prenatally exposed to cocaine.* Paper presented at the biennial meeting of the Society for Research in Child Development, New Orleans.

AIDS weekly surveillance report. (1990, September). United States AIDS Program Center for Disease Control, Department of Health & Human Services.

Ainsworth, M. D. S. (1969). Object relations, dependency, and attachment: A theoretical review of the mother-infant relationship. *Child Development, 40,* 969–1025.

Ainsworth, M. D. S., Bell, S. M., & Stayton, D. J. (1971). Individual differences in strange situation behavior of one-year-olds. In H. R. Schaffer (Ed.), *The origins of human social relations.* New York: Academic Press.

Ainsworth, M. D. S., Blehar, M. C., Waters, E., & Wall, S. (1978). *Patterns of attachment. A psychological study of the strange situation.* Hillsdale, NJ: Erlbaum.

Aloise, P. A. (1991, April). *The development of self-presentation.* Paper presented at the biennial meeting of the Society for Research in Child Development, Seattle.

Altemeier, W. A., O'Connor, S. M., Sherrod, K. B., & Vietz, P. M. (1985). Prospective study of antecedents for nonorganic failure to thrive. *Journal of Pediatrics, 106,* 360–365.

American Academy of Pediatrics. (1987). Report on the second task force on blood pressure control in children — 1987. *Pediatrics, 79,* 1–25.

American Academy of Pediatrics, Committee on Pediatric Aspects of Physical Fitness, Recreation and Sports. (1981). Competitive athletics for children of elementary school age. *Pediatrics, 67* (6).

American Psychiatric Association. (1987). *Diagnostic and statistical manual of mental disorders* (3rd ed., rev.). Washington, DC: Author.

American Psychological Association. (1983). *Publication Manual.* Washington, DC: Author.

Ames, L. B., Gillespie, C., Haines, J., & Ilg, F. L. (1978). *The Gesell Institutes's childhood from one to six.* New York: Harper & Row.

Anders, T. F., & Chalemian, R. J. (1974). The effect of circumcision on sleep-wake stages in human neonates. *Psychosomatic Medicine, 36,* 174–179.

Anderson, C., & Sawin, D. B. (1983). Enhancing responsiveness in mother-infant interactions. *Infant Behavior and Development, 6,* 361–368.

Andersson, B. E. (1989). Effects of public day care: A longitudinal study. *Child Development, 60,* 857–866.

Apgar, V. (1953). A proposal for a new method of evaluation of the newborn infant. *Anesthesia & Analgesia, 52,* 260–267.

Archer, S. L., & Waterman, A. S. (1983). Identity in early adolescence: A developmental perspective. *Journal of Early Adolescence, 3,* 203–214.

———. (1990). Varieties of identity diffusions and foreclosures: An exploration of the subcategories of the identity statuses. *Journal of Adolescent Research, 5,* 96–111.

Arend, R., Gove, R., & Sroufe, A. (1979). Continuity of individual adaptation from infancy to kindergarten: A predictive study of ego resiliency and curiosity with preschoolers. *Child Development, 50,* 950–959.

Arnett, J. (1990). Contraceptive use, sensation seeking, and adolescent egocentrism. *Journal of Youth and Adolescence, 19,* 171–180.

Aronson, M., Kyllerman, M., Sabel, K.-G., Sandin, B., & Olegard, R. (1985). Children of alcoholic mothers. *Acta Paediatr Scand, 74,* 27–35.

Asarnow, J. R., & Callan, J. W. (1985). Boys with peer adjustment problems: Social cognitive processes. *Journal of Consulting and Clinical Psychology, 53,* 80–87.

Ashcraft, M. H. (1982). The development of mental arithmetic: A chronometric approach. *Developmental Review, 2,* 213–236.

———. (1990). Strategic processing in children's mental arithmetic: A review and proposal. In D. F. Bjorklund (Ed.), *Children's strategies: Contemporary views of cognitive development* (pp. 185–211). Hillsdale, NJ: Erlbaum.

Ashcraft, M. H., & Fierman, B. A. (1982). Mental addition in third, fourth, and sixth graders. *Journal of Experimental Child Psychology, 33,* 216–234.

Asher, S. R., Parkhurst, J. T., Hymel, S., & Williams, G. A. (1990). Peer rejection and loneliness in childhood. In S. R. Asher & J. D. Coie (Eds.), *Peer rejection in childhood* (pp. 253–273). New York: Cambridge University Press.

Asher, S. R., & Wheeler, V. A. (1985). Children's loneliness: A comparison of rejected and neglected peer status. *Journal of Counseling and Clinical Psychology, 53,* 500–505.

Aslin, R. N. (1987). Visual and auditory development in infancy. In J. D. Osofsky (Ed.), *Handbook of infant development* (pp. 5–97). New York: Wiley.

Aslin, R. N., & Dumais, S. T. (1980). Binocular vision in infants. In H. W. Reese & L. P. Lipsitt (Eds.), *Advances in child development and behavior* (Vol. 15). New York: Academic Press.

Aslin, R. N., Pisoni, D. B., & Jusczyk, P. W. (1983). Auditory development and speech perception in infancy. In M. M. Haith & J. J. Campos (Eds.), *Handbook of child psychology: Vol. 2 Infancy and developmental psychobiology* (4th ed., pp. 573–687). New York: Wiley.

Aslin, R. N., & Salapatek, P. (1975). Saccadic localization of peripheral targets by the very young human infant. *Perception and Psychophysics, 17,* 293–302.

Atkinson, R. C., & Shiffrin, R. M. (1968). Human memory: A proposed system and its control processes. In K. W. Spence & J. T. Spence (Eds.), *Advances in the psychology of learning and motivation* (Vol. 2, pp. 90–195). New York: Academic Press.

Attie, I., & Brooks-Gunn, J. (1987). Weight-related concerns in women: A response to or a cause of stress? In R. C. Barnett, L. Biener, & G. K. Baruch (Eds.), *Gender and stress* (pp. 218–254). New York: Free Press.

———. (1989). Development of eating problems in adolescent girls: A longitudinal study. *Developmental Psychology, 25,* 70–79.

August, G. J., & Garfinkel, B. D. (1989). Behavioral and cognitive subtypes of ADHD. *Journal of the American Academy of Child and Adolescent Psychiatry, 28,* 739–748.

Baker, D., & Stevenson, D. (1986). Mother's strategies for school achievement: Managing the transition to high school. *Sociology of Education, 59,* 156–167.

Baldwin, A. Y. (1985). Programs for the gifted and talented: Issues concerning minority populations. In F. D. Horowitz & M. O'Brien (Eds.), *The gifted and talented: Developmental perspectives* (pp. 223–249). Washington, DC: American Psychological Association.

Ball, L., & Chandler, M. (1990). Identity formation in suicidal and nonsuicidal youth: The role of self-continuity. *Developmental Psychopathology, 1,* 257–275.

Bandura, A. (1965). Influence of model's reinforcement contingencies on the acquisition of imitative responses. *Journal of Personality and Social Psychology, 1,* 589–595.

———. (1977). *Social learning theory.* Englewood Cliffs, NJ: Prentice-Hall.

———. (1989). Social cognitive theory. In R. Vasta (Ed.), *Annals of child development* (Vol. 6, pp. 1–60). Greenwich, CT: JAI Press.

Bandura, A., Ross, D., & Ross, S. A. (1963). Imitation of film-mediated aggressive models. *Journal of Abnormal and Social Psychology, 66,* 3–11.

Banerjee, M., & Wellman, H. M. (1991). *Preschoolers' use of emotion contrastives: Evidence for a mentalistic understanding of emotions.* Presented at the biennial meeting of the Society for Research in Child Development, Seattle.

Banks, M. S., & Salapatek, P. (1981). Infant pattern vision: A new approach based on the contrast sensitivity function. *Journal of Experimental Child Psychology, 31,* 1–45.

Baranowski, T., Tsong, Y., Hooks, P., Cieslik, C., & Nader, P. R. (1987). Aerobic physical activity among third to sixth grade children. *Journal of Development and Behavioral Pediatrics, 8,* 203–206.

Barden, R. C., Zelko, F. A., Duncan, S. W., & Masters, J. C. (1980). Children's consensual knowledge about the experimental determi-

nants of emotion. *Journal of Personality and Social Psychology, 39,* 968–976.

Barglow, P., Vaughn, B. E., & Molitor, N. (1987). Effects of maternal absence due to employment on the quality of infant-mother attachment on a low-risk sample. *Child Development, 58,* 945–954.

Barkley, R. A. (1990). Attention deficit disorders: History, definition, and diagnosis. In M. Lewis & S. M. Miller (Eds.), *Handbook of developmental psychopathology* (pp. 65–76). New York: Plenum Press.

Barnes, G. M., & Welte, J. W. (1986). Patterns and predictors of alcohol use among 7–12th grade students in New York State. *Journal for the Study of Alcohol, 47,* 53–62.

Barnes, K. E. (1971). Preschool play norms: A replication. *Developmental Psychology, 5,* 99–103.

Barrera, M. E., & Maurer, D. (1981). The perception of facial expressions by the 3-month-old. *Child Development, 52,* 203–206.

Barrera, M. E., Rosenblum, P. L., & Cunningham, C. E. (1986). Early home intervention with low birth-weight infants and their parents. *Child Development, 57,* 20–33.

Barry, H., III, & Schlegel, A. (1984). Measurements of adolescent sexual behavior in the standard sample of societies. *Ethnology, 23,* 315–329.

———. (1986). Cultural customs that influence sexual freedom in adolescence. *Ethology, 25,* 151–162.

Bar-Tal, D., Ravin, A., & Goldberg, M. (1982). Helping behavior among preschool children: An organizational study. *Child Development, 53,* 396–402.

Bates, E., Camaioni, L., & Volterra, V. (1975). The acquisition of performatives prior to speech. *Merrill-Palmer Quarterly, 21,* 205–226.

Bates, E., O'Connell, B., & Shire, C. (1987). Language and communication in infancy. In J. D. Osofsky (Ed.), *Handbook of infant development* (2nd ed., pp. 149–203). New York: Wiley.

Bates, J. E. (1975). Effects of a child's imitation versus non-imitation on adults' verbal and nonverbal positivity. *Journal of Personality and Social Psychology, 31,* 84–85.

———. (1987). Temperament in infancy. In J. D. Osofsky (Ed.), *Handbook of infant development* (2nd ed., pp. 1101–1149). New York: Wiley.

Baumrind, D. (1967). Child care practices anteceding three patterns of pre-school behavior. *Genetic Psychology Monographs, 75,* 43–88.

———. (1971). Current patterns of parental-authority. *Developmental Psychology Monographs, 4,* 1–103.

Baumrind, D., & Black, A. E. (1967). Socialization practices associated with dimensions of competence in preschool boys and girls. *Child Development, 38,* 291–327.

Bayley, N. (1969). *Bayley scales of infant development.* New York: Psychological Corporation.

Beauchamp, G. K., & Cowart, B. J. (1985). Congenital and experiential factors in the development of human food preferences. *Appetite, 6,* 357–372.

Beauchamp, G. K., & Moran, M. (1985). Acceptance of sweet and salty tastes in 2-year-old children. *Appetite, 5,* 291–305.

Beautrais, A. L., Fergusson, D. M., & Shannon, F. T. (1982). Life events and childhood morbidity. *Pediatrics, 70,* 935–940.

Beckman, P. J. (1983). Influence of selected child characteristics on stress in families of handicapped infants. *American Journal of Mental Deficiency, 88,* 150–156.

———. (1991). Comparisons of mothers' and fathers' perceptions of the effect of young children with and without disabilities. *American Journal on Mental Retardation, 95,* 585–595.

Behrman, R. E., & Kliegman, R. (1990). *Nelson essentials of pediatrics.* Philadelphia: W. B. Saunders.

Bell, R. Q. (1979). Parent, child, and reciprocal influences. *American Psychologist, 34,* 821–826.

Belsky, J. (1980). Child maltreatment: An ecological integration. *American Psychologist, 35,* 320–335.

———. (1981). Early human experience: A family perspective. *Developmental Psychology, 17,* 3–23.

Belsky, J., & Rovine, M. J. (1987). Temperament and attachment security in the strange situation: An empirical rapprochement. *Child Development, 58,* 787–795.

———. (1988). Nonmaternal care in the first year of life and the security of infant-parent attachment. *Child Development, 59,* 157–167.

Belsky, J., Rovine, M. J., & Taylor, D. G. (1984). The Pennsylvania Infant and Family Development Project III: The origins of individual differences in infant and mother attachment: maternal and infant contributions. *Child Development, 55,* 718–728.

Belsky, J., & Steinberg, L. D. (1978). The effects of day care: A critical review. *Child Development, 49,* 929–949.

Bem, S. L. (1983). Gender schema theory and its implications for child development: Raising gender-aschematic children in a gender-schematic society. *Signs, 8,* 598–616.

———. (1985). Androgny and gender schema theory: A conceptual and empirical integration. In T. B. Sondergger (Ed.), *Nebraska Symposium on Motivation: Psychology and Gender,* 179–226.

———. (1989). Genital knowledge and gender constancy in preschool children. *Child Development, 60,* 649–662.

Bereiter, C., & Engelmann, S. (1966). *Teaching the disadvantaged in the preschool.* Englewood Cliffs, NJ: Prentice-Hall.

Berg, W. K., & Berg, K. M. (1987). Psychophysiological development in infancy: State, startle, and attention. In J. Osofsky (Ed.), *Handbook of infant development* (2nd ed., pp. 238–317). New York: Wiley.

Bergsma, D. (1979). *Birth defects compendium.* New York: Alan Liss, Inc.

Berk, L. E., & Garvin, R. A. (1984). Development of private speech among low-income Appalachian children. *Developmental Psychology, 20,* 271–286.

Berndt, T. J. (1979). Developmental changes in conformity to peers and parents. *Developmental Psychology, 15,* 606–616.

———. (1982). The features and effects of friendship in early adolescence. *Child Development, 53,* 1447–1460.

Berndt, T. J., & Perry, T. B. (1986). Children's perceptions of friendships as supportive relationships. *Developmental Psychology, 22,* 640–648.

Bernstein, B. (1961). Language and social class. *British Journal of Sociology, 11,* 271–276.

Bertenthal, B. I., & Campos, J. J. (1987). New directions in the study of early experience. *Child Development, 58,* 560–567.

Bertenthal, B. I., Campos, J. J., & Barrett, K. C. (1984). A re-examination of fear and its determinants on the visual cliff. *Psychophysiology, 21,* 413–417.

Bettes, B. A. (1988). Maternal depression and motherese: Temporal and intonational features. *Child Development, 59,* 1089–1096.

Bhavnagri, N. (1987). *Parents as facilitators of preschool children's relationships.* Unpublished doctoral dissertation, University of Illinois at Champaign-Urbana.

Bianchi, B. D., & Bakeman, R. (1978). Sex-typed affiliation preferences observed in preschoolers: Traditional and open school differences. *Child Development, 49,* 910–912.

Bierman, K. L. (1991, April). *Social adjustment problems of aggressive-rejected, aggressive, and rejected boys: A longitudinal analysis.* Paper presented at the biennial meeting of the Society for Research in Child Development, Seattle.

Bierman, K. L., Morrison, D., & Bitner, B. (1991, April). *Conduct problems, depressed and withdrawn social behavior, and peer rejection in adolescence.* Paper presented at the biennial meeting of the Society for Research in Child Development, Seattle.

Bigelow, B. J., & LaGaipa, J. J. (1975). Children's written description of friendships: A multidimensional analysis. *Developmental Psychology, 11,* 857–858.

Bijou, S. W. (1989). Behavior analysis. In R. Vasta (Ed.), *Annals of child development* (Vol. 6, pp. 61–84). Greenwich, CT: JAI Press.

Bijou, S. W., & Baer, D. M. (1961). *Child development: A systematic and empirical theory* (Vol. 1). Englewood Cliffs, NJ: Prentice-Hall.

Bingol, N., Fuchs, M., Diaz, V., Stone, R. K., & Gromisch, D. S. (1987). Teratogenicity of cocaine in humans. *Journal of Pediatrics, 110,* 93–96.

Birnholz, J. C., & Benacerraf, B. R. (1983). The development of human fetal hearing. *Science, 222,* 516–518.

Bjorklund, D. F. (1987). How age changes in knowledge base contribute to the development of children's memory: An interpretive review. *Developmental Review, 7,* 93–130.

———. (1989). *Children's thinking: Developmental functions and individual differences.* Pacific Grove, CA: Brooks/Cole.

Bjorklund, D. F., & Harnishfeger, K. K. (1990). The resources construct in cognitive development: Diverse sources of evidence and a theory of inefficient inhibition. *Developmental Review, 10,* 48–71.

Black, B., & Hazen, N. L. (1990). Social status and patterns of communication in acquainted and unacquainted preschool children. *Developmental Psychology, 26,* 379–387.

Blass, E. M., Ganchrow, J. R., & Steiner, J. E. (1984). Classical conditioning in newborn humans 2–48 hours of age. *Infant Behavior and Development, 7,* 223–235.

Bloom, L., Merkin, S., & Wooten, J. (1982). Wh-questions: Linguistic factors that contribute to the sequence of acquisition. *Child Development, 53,* 1084–1092.

Blumstein, A., Cohen, J., & Farrington, D. P. (1988). Criminal career research: Its value for criminology. *Criminology, 26,* 1–35.

Bodner, B., Benjamin, A., McLean, F. H., & Usher, R. H. (1986). Has use of cesarean section reduced the risks of delivery with preterm breech presentation? *American Journal of Obstetrics and Gynecology, 154,* 244–249.

Boggiano, A. K., Barrett, M., Weiher, A. W., McClelland, G. H., & Luck, C. M. (1987). Use of maximal-operant principle to motivate children's intrinsic interest. *Journal of Personality and Social Psychology, 53,* 866–879.

Boggiano, A. K., Harackiewicz, J. M., & Main, D. S. (1985). Increasing children's interest through performance-contingent rewards. *Social Cognition, 3,* 400–411.

Boggiano, A. K., Main, D. S., & Katz, P. A. (1988). Children's preference for challenge: The role of perceived competence and control. *Journal of Personality and Social Psychology, 54,* 134–141.

Boggiano, A. K., & Ruble, D. N. (1979). Perception of competence and the overjustification effect: A developmental study. *Journal of Personality and Social Psychology, 37,* 1462–1468.

Borke, H. (1971). Interpersonal perception of young children: Egocentrism or empathy? *Developmental Psychology, 5,* 263–269.

———. (1975). Piaget's mountains revisited: Changes in the egocentric landscape. *Developmental Psychology, 11,* 240–243.

Bornstein, M. H. (1985). How infant and mother jointly contribute to developing cognitive competence in the child. *Proceedings of the National Academy of Science, 82,* 7470–7473.

Bornstein, M. H., & Benasich, A. A. (1986). Infant habituation: Assessments of individual differences and short term reliability at 5 months. *Child Development, 57,* 87–99.

Bornstein, M. H., & Sigman, M. D. (1986). Continuity in mental development from infancy. *Child Development, 57,* 251–274.

Boswell, A. E., Garner, E. E., & Berger, W. K. (1993, March). *Ontogeny of anticipation in infancy: Heart rate components.* Paper presented at the biennial meeting of the Society for Research in Child Development, New Orleans.

Botuck, S., & Winsberg, B. G. (1991). Effects of respite on mothers of school-age and adult children with severe disabilities. *Mental Retardation, 29,* 43–47.

Bousha, D. M., Twentyman, C. T., & Craig, T. (1984). Mother-child interactional style in abuse, neglect, and control groups: Naturalistic observations in the home. *Journal of Abnormal Psychology, 93*(1), 106–114.

Bowlby J. (1969). *Attachment & loss: Vol. I Attachment.* New York: Basic Books.

———. (1988). *A secure base: Parent-child attachment and healthy human development.* New York: Basic Books.

Bowser, B. P., Fullilove, M. T., & Fullilove, R. E. (1990). African-American youth and AIDS high-risk behavior: The social context and barriers to prevention. *Youth & Society, 22,* 54–66.

Boysson-Bardies, B., Sagart, C., & Durand, C. (1984). Discernible differences in the babbling of infants according to target language. *Journal of Child Language, 11,* 1–15.

Brackbill, Y. (1979). Obstetrical medication and infant behavior. In J. D. Osofsky (Ed.), *Handbook of infant development* (pp. 76–125). New York: Wiley.

Brackbill, Y., McManus, K., & Woodward, L. (1985). *Medication in maternity: Infant exposure and maternal information.* Ann Arbor: University of Michigan Press.

Bradley, R. H., & Caldwell, B. M. (1976). The relation of infants' home environments to mental test performance at fifty-four months: A follow-up study. *Child Development, 47,* 1172–1174.

———. (1980). The relation of home environment, cognitive competence, and IQ among males and females. *Child Development, 51,* 1140–1148.

Bradley, R. H., Caldwell, B. M., & Rock, S. L. (1988). Home environment and school performance: A ten-year followup and examination of three models of environmental action. *Child Development, 59,* 852–867.

Braine, M. (1976). Children's first word constructions. *Monographs of the Society for Research in Child Development, 41*(1, Serial No. 164).

Brazelton, T. B. (1984). *Neonatal Behavioral Assessment Scale* (2nd ed.). Philadelphia: J. B. Lippincott.

Brazelton, T. B., Koslowski, B., & Main, M. (1974). The origins of reciprocity: The early mother-infant interaction. In M. Lewis & L. Rosenblum (Eds.), *The effect of the infant on its caregivers* (pp. 49–76). New York: Wiley.

Brazelton, T. B., Nugent, K. J., & Lester, B. M. (1987). Neonatal Behavioral Assessment Scale. In J. D. Osofsky (Ed.), *Handbook of infant development* (pp. 780–817). New York: Wiley.

Brenner, A. (1984). *Helping children cope with stress.* Lexington, MA: Lexington Books.

Bretherton, I., & Beeghly, M. (1982). Talking about internal states: The acquisition of an explicit theory of mind. *Developmental Psychology, 18,* 906–921.

Breuer, J., & Freud, S. (1895). Studies on hysteria. In J. Strachey (Ed.), *Standard edition of the complete psychological works of Sigmund Freud.* London: Hogarth Press.

Brody, L. E., & Benbow, C. P. (1987). Accelerative strategies: How effective are they? *Gifted Child Quarterly, 3,* 105–110.

Bronfenbrenner, U. (1979). *The ecology of human development: Experiments by nature and design.* Cambridge, MA: Harvard University Press.

———. (1986). Ecology of the family as a context for human development research perspectives. *Developmental Psychology, 22,* 723–742.

Bronson, G., & Pankey, W. (1977). On the distinction between fear and wariness. *Child Development, 48,* 1167–1183.

Brookhart, J., & Hock, E. E. (1976). The effects of experimental context and experiential background on infants' behavior toward their mothers and a stranger. *Child Development, 47,* 333–340.

Brooks-Gunn, J. (1988). Antecedents and consequences of variations in girls' maturational timing. *Journal of Adolescent Health Care, 9,* 1–9.

Brooks-Gunn, J., & Furstenberg, F. F., Jr. (1989). Adolescent sexual behavior. *American Psychologist, 44,* 249–257.

Brooks-Gunn, J., & Ruble, D. N. (1982). The development of menstrual-related beliefs and behaviors during early adolescence. *Child Development, 53,* 1567–1577.

Brooks-Gunn, J., & Warren, M. P. (1985). The effects of delayed menarche in different contexts: Dance and nondance students. *Journal of Youth and Adolescence, 14,* 285–300.

———. (1988). The psychological significance of secondary sexual characteristics in 9- to 11-year-old girls. *Child Development, 59,* 1061–1069.

Brophy, J. E. (1970). Mothers as teachers of their own preschool children: The influence of socioeconomic status and task structure

on teaching specificity. *Child Development, 41,* 79–94.

Brown, B. B., Clasen, D. R., & Eicher, S. A. (1986). Perceptions of peer pressure, peer conformity dispositions, and self-reported behavior among adolescents. *Developmental Psychology, 22,* 520–530.

Brown, B. B., Eicher, S. A., & Petrie, S. (1986). The importance of peer group affiliation in adolescence. *Journal of Adolescence, 9,* 73–96.

Brown, B. B., & Lohr, M. J. (1987). Peer group affiliation and adolescent self-esteem: An integration of ego-identity and symbolic interaction theories. *Journal of Personality and Social Psychology, 52,* 47–55.

Brown, L. K., Overholser, J., Spirito, A., & Fritz, G. K. (1991). The correlates of planning in adolescent suicide attempts. *Journal of the American Academy of Child and Adolescent Psychiatry, 30,* 95–99.

Brown, R. W. (1973). *A first language: The early stages.* Cambridge, MA: Harvard University Press.

Brown, S. S. (1985). Can low birth weight be prevented? *Family Planning Perspectives, 3,* 112–118.

Browne, A., & Finkelhor, D. (1986). Impact of child sexual abuse: A review of the research. *Psychological Bulletin, 99,* 66–77.

Bruner, J. (1977). Early social interaction and language acquisition. In H. Schaffer (Ed.), *Studies in mother-infant interaction* (pp. 271–289). New York: Academic Press.

———. (1983). *Child's talk.* New York: Norton.

Bryant, P. E., MacLean, M., Bradley, L. L., & Crossland, J. (1990). Rhyme and alliteration, phoneme detection, and learning to read. *Developmental Psychology, 26,* 429–438.

Buck, R. (1975). Non-verbal communication of affect in children. *Journal of Personality and Social Psychology, 31,* 644–653.

Buckwald, S., Zorn, W. A., & Egan, E. A. (1984). Mortality and follow up data for neonates weighing 500 to 800 grams at birth. *American Journal of Diseases of Children, 138,* 779–792.

Buhrmester, D. (1990). Intimacy of friendship, interpersonal competence, and adjustment during

preadolescence and adolescence. *Child Development, 61,* 1101–1111.

Buhrmester, D., & Furman, W. (1987). The development of companionship and intimacy. *Child Development, 58,* 1101–1113.

Bukowski, W. M., & Ferber, J. S. (1987, April). *A study of peer relations, attributional style, and loneliness during adolescence.* Paper presented at the biennial meeting of the Society for Research in Child Development, Baltimore.

Bukowski, W. M., & Hoza, B. (1989). Popularity and friendship: Issues in theory, measurement and outcome. In T. J. Berndt & G. W. Ladd (Eds.), *Peer relationships in child development* (pp. 15–45). New York: Wiley.

Bukowski, W. M., & Newcomb, A. F. (1987, April). *Friendship quality and the "self" during early adolescence.* Paper presented at the biennial meeting of the Society for Research in Child Development, Baltimore.

Bullock, M., & Gelman, R. (1979). Preschool children's assumptions about cause and effect: Temporal ordering. *Child Development, 50,* 89–96.

Burgess, A. W., Hartman, C. R., & McCormack, A. (1987). Abused to abuser: Antecedents of socially deviant behaviors. *American Journal of Psychiatry, 144*(1), 1431–1436.

Burgess, R. L., & Conger, R. D. (1978). Family interaction in abusive, neglectful and normal families. *Child Development, 49,* 1163–1173.

Buri, J. R., Louiselle, P. A., Misukanis, T. M., & Mueller, R. A. (1988). Effects of authoritarianism and authoritativeness on self-esteem. *Personality and Social Psychology Bulletin, 14,* 271–282.

Burns, S. M., & Brainerd, C. (1979). Effects of constructive and dramatic play on perspective taking in very young children. *Developmental Psychology, 15,* 512–521.

Burton, C. B., & Krantz, M. (1990). Predicting adjustment in middle childhood from early peer status. *Early Child Development and Care, 60,* 89–100.

Bushnell, E. W. (1985). The decline of visually guided reaching during infancy. *Infant Birth and Development, 8,* 139–155.

Bushnell, I. W. R. (1979). Modification of the externality effect in young infants. *Journal of Exceptional Child Psychology, 28*, 211–229.

Butkowsky, S., & Willows, D. (1980). Cognitive-motivational characteristics of children varying in reading ability: Evidence for learned helplessness in poor readers. *Educational Psychology, 72*, 408–422.

Butler, N. R., Goldstein, H., & Ross, E. M. (1972). Cigarette smoking in pregnancy: Its influence on birth weight and perinatal mortality. *British Medical Journal, 2*, 127–130.

Cairns, R. B., Cairns, B. D., Neckerman, J. J., Gest, S. D., & Gariepy, J. L. (1988). Social networks and aggressive behavior: Peer support or peer rejection? *Developmental Psychology, 24*, 815–823.

Calabrese, R. L., & Cochran, J. T. (1990). The relationship of alienation to cheating among a sample of American adolescents. *Journal of Research and Development in Education, 23*, 66–72.

Caldwell, B. M., & Bradley, R. H. (1984). *Home observation for the measurement of the environment.* New York: Dorsey.

Camara, K. A., & Resnick, G. (1988). Interparental conflict and cooperation: Factors moderating children's post divorce adjustment. In E. M. Hetherington & J. D. Arasteh (Eds.), *Impact of divorce, single-parenting, and stepparenting on children* (pp. 169–195). Hillsdale, NJ: Erlbaum.

Campos, J. J., Langer, A., & Krowitz, A. (1970). Cardiac responses on the visual cliff in prelocomotor human infants. *Science, 70*, 196–197.

Capon, N., & Kuhn, D. (1979). Logical reasoning in the supermarket: Adult females' use of proportional reasoning strategy in an everyday context. *Developmental Psychology, 15*, 450–452.

Carlson, V., Cicchetti, D., Barnett, D., & Bravonwald, K. (1989). Disorganized/disoriented attachment relations on maltreated infants. *Developmenal Psychology, 25*, 525–531.

Carnegie Council on Adolescent Development, Task Force on Education of Young Adolescents. (1989). *Turning points: Preparing American youth for the 21st century.* New York: Carnegie Corporation of New York.

Caron, A. J., Caron, R. F., & MacLean, D. J. (1988). Infant discrimination of naturalistic emotional expressions: The role of face and voice. *Child Development, 59*, 606–616.

Carpenter, C. R. (1942). Sexual behavior of free ranging rhesus monkeys. Periodicity of estrus, homo- and auto-erotic and nonconformist behavior. *Journal of Comparative Psychology, 33*, 147–162.

Carpenter, M. W., Sady, S. P., Hoegsberg, B., Sady, M. A., Haydon, B., Cullinanse, E. M., Coustian, D. R., & Thompson, P. D. (1988). Fetal heart rate response to maternal exertion. *Journal of the American Medical Association, 259*, 3006–3009.

Carr, M., Kurtz, B. E., Schneider, W., Turner, L. A., & Borkowski, J. G. (1989). Strategy acquisition and transfer among American and German children: Environmental influences on metacognitive development. *Developmental Psychology, 25*(5), 765–771.

Case, R. (1985). *Intellectual development: Birth to adulthood.* New York: Academic Press.

Case, R., Kurland, D. M., & Goldberg, J. (1982). Operational efficiency and the growth of short-term memory span. *Journal of Experimental Child Psychology, 33*, 386–404.

Casey, P. H., Bradley, R., & Wortham, B. (1984). Social and nonsocial home environment of infants with nonorganic failure to thrive. *Pediatrics, 73*(3), 348–353.

Cernoch, J. M., & Porter, R. H. (1985). Recognition of maternal axillary odors by infants. *Child Development, 56*, 1593–1598.

Chalfant, J. C. (1989). Learning disabilities: Policy issues and promising approaches. *American Psychologist, 44*, 392–398.

Chalip, L., Csikszentmihalyi, M., Kleiber, D., & Larson, R. (1984). Variations of experience in formal and informal sport. *Research Quarterly for Exercise and Sport, 55*, 109–116.

Chall, J. S. (1967). *Learning to read: The great debate.* New York: McGraw-Hill.

———. (1983). *Stages of reading development.* New York: McGraw-Hill.

———. (1989). Learning to read: The great debate 20 years later: A response to "Debunking the great phonics myth." *Phi Delta Kappan, 70*, 521–538.

Chandler, M., Fritz, A. S., & Hala, S. (1989). Small scale deceit: Deception as a marker of two-, three-, and four-year-old's early theories of mind. *Child Development, 60*, 1236–1277.

Chase-Lansdale, P. L., & Owen, M. T. (1987). Maternal employment in a family context: Effects on infant-mother and infant-father attachments. *Child Development, 58*, 1505–1512.

Chasnoff, I. J., Burns, W. J., Schnorr, S. H., & Burns, K. A. (1985). Cocaine use in pregnancy. *New England Journal of Medicine, 313*, 666–669.

Chasnoff, I. J., Griffith, D. R., Freier, C., & Murray, J. (1992). Cocaine/polydrug use in pregnancy: Two-year follow-up. *Pediatrics, 89*, 284–289.

Chasnoff, I. J., Griffith, D. R., MacGregor, S., Dirkes, K., & Burns, K. A. (1989). Temporal patterns of cocaine use in pregnancy. *Journal of the American Medical Association, 261*, 1741–1744.

Chasnoff, I. J., Hunt, C. E., Kletter, R., & Kaplan, D. (1989). Prenatal cocaine exposure is associated with respiratory pattern abnormalities. *American Journal of Diseases of Children, 143*, 583–587.

Chen, Y., Yu, S., & Li, W. (1988). Artificial feeding and hospitalization in the first month of life. *Pediatrics, 81*, 58–62.

Chess, S., & Thomas, A. (1982). Infant bonding: Mystique and reality. *American Journal of Orthopsychiatry, 52*, 213–222.

Chetwynd, J. (1985). Factors contributing to stress on mothers caring for an intellectually handicapped child. *British Journal of Social Work, 15*, 295–305.

Chi, M. T. H. (1976). Short-term memory limitations in children's capacity or processing deficits? *Memory and Cognition, 4*, 559–572.

———. (1978). Knowledge structure and memory development. In R. Siegler (Ed.), *Children's thinking: What develops?* (pp. 73–96). Hillsdale, NJ: Erlbaum.

Chi, M. T. H., & Ceci, S. J. (1987). Content knowledge: Its role, representation, and restructuring in memory development. In H. W. Reese (Ed.), *Advances in child development and behavior* (Vol. 20, pp. 91–142). Orlando: Academic Press.

Chi, M. T. H., & Glaser, R. (1980). The measurement of expertise: Analysis of the development of knowledge and skill as a basis for assessing achievement. In E. L. Baker & E. S. Quellmalz (Eds.), *Educational testing and evaluation: Design, analysis and policy* (pp. 37–47). Beverly Hills: Sage Publications.

Children's Defense Fund. (1987). *A children's defense budget*. Washington, DC: Author.

———. (1990). *Who knows how safe? The status of state efforts to ensure quality care*. Washington, DC: Author.

———. (1991). *The state of America's children*. Washington, DC: Author.

Chilman, C. S. (1986). Some psychosocial aspects of adolescent sexual and contraceptive behaviors in a changing American society. In J. B. Lancaster & B. A. Hamberg (Eds.), *School-age pregnancy and parenthood: Biosocial dimensions* (pp. 191–217). New York: Aldine DeGruyter.

Chomsky, N. (1957). *Syntactic structures*. The Hague: Mouton.

Cicchetti, D., & Aber, J. L. (1986). Early precursors of later depression: An organizational perspective. In L. P. Lipsitt & C. Rovee-Collier (Eds.), *Advances in infancy research* (Vol. 4, pp. 87–137). Norwood, NJ: Ablex.

Cicchetti, D., Cummings, E. M., Greenberg, M. T., & Marvin, R. S. (1990). An organizational perspective on attachment beyond infancy in M. T. Greenberg, D. Cicchetti, & E. M. Cummings (Eds.), *Attachment in the preschool years* (pp. 3–49). Chicago: University of Chicago Press.

Cicchetti, D., & Toth, S. L. (1987). The application of a transactional risk model to intervention with multirisk maltreating families. *Zero to Three, 7*, 1–8.

Clapp, J. F., III. (1989). Oxygen consumption during treadmill exercise before, during, and after pregnancy. *American Journal of Obstetrics and Gynecology, 161*, 1458–1464.

Clark, M. L., & Drewry, D. L. (1985). Similarity and reciprocity in the friendships of elementary school children. *Child Study Journal, 15*, 251–264.

Clarke, A. M. (1984). Early experience and cognitive development. *Reviews of Research in Education, 11*, 125–156.

Clarke, E. V. (1973). What's in a word? On the child's acquisition of semantics in his first language. In T. E. Moore (Ed.), *Cognitive development and the acquisition of language* (pp. 65–110). New York: Academic Press.

———. (1983). Meanings and concepts. In J. H. Flavell & E. M. Markman (Eds.) & P. H. Mussen (Series Ed.), *Handbook of child psychology: Vol. III Cognitive development* (pp. 787–840). New York: Wiley.

Clarke-Stewart, A. (1978). And daddy makes three. *Child Development, 49*, 466–479.

———. (1982). *Daycare*. Cambridge, MA: Harvard University Press.

———. (1989). Infant daycare: Maligned or malignant? *American Psychologist, 44*, 266–273.

Clarke-Stewart, A., & Fein, G. G. (1983). Early childhood programs. In P. H. Mussen (Series Ed.) & M. Haith & J. Campos (Vol. Eds.), *Handbook of child psychology: Vol. II Infancy and developmental psychobiology* (pp. 917–1000). New York: Wiley.

Clasen, D. R., & Brown, B. B. (1985). The multidimensionality of peer pressure in adolescence. *Journal of Youth and Adolescence, 14*, 451–468.

Clyman, R. R., Buchsbaum, H. K., Emde, R. N., Toth, S. L., & Cicchetti, D. (1991, April). *Moral development in maltreated preschool children's narratives*. Paper presented at the biennial meeting of the Society for Research in Child Development, Seattle.

Cohn, J. F., & Tronick, E. Z. (1983). Three-month-old infant's reactions to simulated maternal depression. *Child Development, 54*, 185–193.

Coie, J. D., & Benenson, J. F. (1983). *A qualitative analysis of the relationship between peer rejection and physically aggressive behavior*. Unpublished manuscript, Duke University, Durham, NC. (As cited in J. D. Coie, K. A. Dodge, & J. B. Kupersmidt. (1990). *Peer rejection in childhood* (pp. 17–59). Cambridge, MA: Cambridge University Press).

Coie, J. D., & Dodge, K. A. (1988). Multiple sources of data on social behavior and social status in the school: A cross-age comparison. *Child Development, 59*, 815–829.

Coie, J. D., Dodge, K. A., & Coppotelli, H. (1982). Dimensions and types of social status: A cross-age perspective. *Developmental Psychology, 18*, 557–570.

Coie, J. D., Dodge, K. A., & Kupersmidt, J. B. (1990). Peer group behavior and social status. In S. R. Asher & J. D. Coie (Eds.), *Peer rejection in childhood* (pp. 17–59). Cambridge, MA: Cambridge University Press.

Coie, J. D., & Kupersmidt, J. B. (1983). A behavioral analysis of emerging, social status in boys' groups. *Child Development, 54*, 1400–1416.

Colby, A., Kohlberg, L., Gibbs, J., & Lieberman, M. (1983). A longitudinal study of moral development. *Monographs of the Society for Research in Child Development, 48*(1-2, Serial No. 200).

Cole, P. M. (1986). Children's spontaneous control of facial expression. *Child Development, 57*, 1309–1321.

Coleman, J. C. (1980). Friendship and the peer group in adolescence. In J. Adelson (Ed.), *The handbook of adolescent psychology* (pp. 408–431). New York: Wiley.

Coleman, M., & Skeen, P. (1985). Play games and sport: A developmental perspective. *Childhood Education, 61*, 192–198.

Collins, R. C., & Deloria, D. (1983). Head Start research: A new chapter. *Children Today, 12*, 15–19.

Comer, J. P. (1988). Educating poor minority children. *Scientific American, 259*, 42–48.

Connolly, J. A., & Doyle, A. (1984). Relation of social fantasy play to social composure in preschoolers. *Developmental Psychology, 20*, 797–806.

Connolly, J. A., Doyle, A. B., & Reznick, E. (1988). Social pretend play and social interaction in preschoolers. *Journal of Applied Developmental Psychology, 9*, 301–313.

Cooney, E., & Selman, R. (1978). Children's use of social conceptions: Towards a dynamic model of social cognition. In W. Damon (Ed.), *Social Cognition.* San Francisco: Jossey-Bass.

Coons, S., & Guilleminault, C. (1982). Development of sleep-wake patterns and non-rapid eye movement sleepstages during the first six months of life in normal infants. *Pediatrics, 69*, 793–798.

Corrigan, S. A., & Moskowitz, D. S. (1983). Type A behavior in preschool children. *Child Development, 54*, 1513–1521.

Corsaro, W. A. (1981). Friendship in the nursery school: Social organization in a peer environment. In S. R. Asher & J. M. Gottman (Eds.), *The development of children's friendship* (pp. 207–241). New York: Cambridge University Press.

Cowen, E. L., Pederson, A., Babijian, H., Izzo, L. D., & Trost, M. A. (1973). Long-term follow-up of early detected vulnerable children. *Journal of Consulting and Clinical Psychology, 41*, 438–446.

Cratty, B. J. (1986). *Perceptual and motor development in infants and children* (3rd ed.). Englewood Cliffs, NJ: Prentice-Hall.

Crnic, L., Ragozin, A., Greenberg, M., Robinson, N., & Basham, R. (1983). Social interaction and developmental competencies of preterm and fullterm infants during first year of life. *Child Development, 54*, 1199–1210.

Crockenberg, S. (1981). Infant irritability, mother responsiveness and social support influences on the security of mother-infant attachment. *Child Development, 52*, 857–865.

Crook, C. K. (1978). Taste perception in the newborn infant. *Infant Behavior and Development, 1*, 52–69.

Crook, C. K., & Lipsitt, L. P. (1976). Neonatal nutritive sucking: Effects of taste stimulation upon sucking rhythm and heart rate. *Child Development, 47*, 518–522.

Cross, D. R., & Paris, S. G. (1988). Developmental and instructional analysis of children's metacognition and reading comprehension. *Journal of Educational Psychology, 80*, 131–142.

Csikszentmihalyi, M., & Larson, R. (1984). *Being adolescent: Conflict and growth in the teenage years.* New York: Basic Books.

Cummings, E. M., Iannotti, R. J., & Zahn-Waxler, C. (1985). Influence of conflict between adults on the emotions and aggression of young children. *Developmental Psychology, 21*, 495–507.

———. (1989). Aggression between peers in early childhood: Individual continuity and developmental change. *Child Development, 60*, 887–895.

Cunningham, N., Anisfeld, E., Casper, V., & Nozyce, M. (1987). Infant crying, breast feeding, and mother–infant relations. *The Lancet, 8529*, 379.

Darwin, C. (1859). *The origin of species.* New York: Modern Library.

———. (1872). *Expressions of the emotions in man and animals.* London: John Murray.

Dasen, P. R., & Heron, A. (1981). Cross-cultural tests of Piaget's theory. In H. Triandis & A. Heron (Eds.), *Handbook psychology.* Boston: Allyn & Bacon.

D'Attilio, J. P., Campbell, B. M., Lubold, P., Jacobson, T., & Richards, J. A. (1992). Social support and suicide potential: Preliminary findings for adolescent populations. *Psychological Reports, 70*, 76–78.

Davidson, J. E. (1986). The role of insight in giftedness. In R. J. Sternberg & J. E. Davison (Eds.), *Conception of giftedness* (pp. 201–223). New York: Cambridge University Press.

Dawe, H. C. (1934). An analysis of two hundred quarrels of preschool children. *Child Development, 5*, 139–157.

DeCasper, A., & Fifer, N. (1980). Newborns prefer their mother's voices. *Science, 208*, 1174–1176.

DeCasper, A., & Prescott, P. (1984). Human newborns' perception of male voices: Preference discrimination & reinforcing value. *Developmental Psychobiology, 17*, 481–491.

DeCasper, A. J., & Sigafoos, A. D. (1983). The intrauterine heartbeat. A potent reinforcer for newborns. *Infant Behavior and Development, 6*, 19–25.

DeCasper, A. J., & Spence, M. J. (1986). Prenatal maternal speech influences newborn's perception of speech sounds. *Infant Behavior and Development, 9*, 133–150.

Deci, E. L., Nezlek, J., & Sheinman, L. (1981). Characteristics of the rewarder and intrinsic motivation of the rewardee. *Journal of Personality and Social Psychology, 40*, 1–10.

Deci, E. L., & Ryan, R. M. (1980). The empirical exploration of intrinsic motivational processes. In L. Berkowitz (Ed.), *Advances in experimental social psychology* (Vol. 13, pp. 39–80). New York: Academic Press.

———. (1985). *Intrinsic motivation and self-determination in human behavior.* New York: Plenum Press.

Decker, M. D., Dewey, M. J., Hutcheson, R. H., & Schaffner, W. (1984). The use and efficacy of child restraint devices. *Journal of the American Medical Association, 252*, 2571–2575.

de Lissovoy, V. (1979). Toward the definition of "Abuse provoking child." *Child Abuse and Neglect, 3*, 341–350.

Denham, S. (1986). Social cognition, prosocial behavior, and emotion in preschoolers: Contextual validation. *Child Development, 57*, 194–201.

Dennis, W. (1960). Causes of retardation among institutionalized children. *Journal of Genetic Psychology, 96*, 47–59.

———. (1973). *Children of the Creche.* New York: Appleton-Century-Crofts.

Denny, F. W., & Clyde, W. A., Jr. (1983). Acute respiratory tract infections: An overview. In W. A. Clyde, Jr., & F. W. Denny (Eds.), *Workshop on acute respiratory diseases among children of the world. Pediatric Research, 17*, 1026–1029.

Denny, N. W. (1972). Free classification in preschool children. *Child Development, 43*, 1161–1170.

Desrochers, S., Ricard, M., & Decarie, T. G. (1993, March). *Taking care of the mother's point of view in the production of pointing gestures.* Paper presented at the biennial meeting of the Society for Research in Child Development, New Orleans.

deVries, M. W. (1984). Temperament and infant mortality among the Masi of East Africa. *American Journal of Psychiatry, 141,* 1189–1194.

deVries, M. W., & deVries, M. R. (1977). The cultural relativity of toilet training readiness: A perspective from East Africa. *Pediatrics, 60,* 170–177.

DeVries, R. (1969). Constancy of genetic identity in the years three to six. *Monographs of the Society for Research in Child Development, 34* (Serial No. 127). Chicago: University of Chicago Press.

Diaz, R. M., & Berndt, T. J. (1982). Children's knowledge of a friend: Fact or fancy? *Developmental Psychology, 18,* 787–794.

Diaz, R. M., Neal, C. J., & Vachio, A. (1991). Maternal teaching in the zone of proximal development: A comparison of low- and high-risk dyads. *Merrill-Palmer Quarterly, 37,* 83–108.

DiClemente, R. J., Zorn, J., & Temoshok, L. (1986). Adolescents and AIDS: A survey of knowledge, beliefs and attitudes about AIDS in San Francisco. *American Journal of Public Health, 76,* 1443–1445.

Dietz, W. H., Jr., & Gortmaker, S. L. (1985). Do we fatten our children at the television set? Obesity and television viewing in children and adolescents. *Pediatrics, 75,* 807–812.

DiLalla, L. F., & Watson, M. W. (1988). Differentiation of fantasy and reality: Preschoolers' reactions to interruptions in their play. *Developmental Psychology, 24,* 286–291.

Dion, K. K. (1973). Young children's stereotyping of facial attractiveness. *Developmental Psychology, 9,* 183–189.

Dion, K. K., & Berscheid, E. (1974). Physical attractiveness and peer perception and children. *Sociometry, 37,* 1–12.

Dodd, B. J. (1972). Effects of social and vocal stimulation on infant babbling. *Developmental Psychology, 7,* 80–83.

Dodge, K. A. (1980). Social cognition and children's aggressive behavior. *Child Development, 51,* 162–170.

———. (1983). Behavioral antecedents of peer social status. *Child Development, 54,* 1386–1399.

———. (1986). A social information processing model of social competence in children. In M. Perlmutter (Ed.), *Minnesota symposium on child psychology* (Vol. 18, pp. 77–125). Hillsdale, NJ: Erlbaum.

Dodge, K. A., & Feldman, E. (1990). Issues in social status. In S. R. Asher & J. D. Coie (Eds.), *Peer rejection in childhood* (pp. 119–155). Cambridge: Cambridge University Press.

Dodge, K. A., & Frame, C. L. (1982). Social cognitive bias and deficits in aggressive boys. *Child Development, 53,* 620–635.

Dodge, K. A., McClaskey, C. L., & Feldman, E. (1985). A situational approach to the assessment of social competence in children. *Journal of Consulting and Clinical Psychology, 53,* 344–353.

Dodge, K. A., Murphy, R. R., & Buchsbaum, K. (1984). The assessment of intention-cue detection skills in children: Implications for developmental psychopathology. *Child Development, 55,* 163–173.

Dodge, K. A., Pettit, G. S., McClaskey, C. L., & Brown, M. M. (1986). Social competence in children. *Monographs of the Society for Research in Child Development, 51*(2, Serial No. 213).

Dodge, K. A., Schlundt, D. G., Schocken, I., & Delugach, J. D. (1983). Social competence and children's sociometric status: The role of group entry strategies. *Merrill-Palmer Quarterly, 29,* 309–336.

Doman, R. J., Spitz, E. R., & Zucman, E. (1960). Children with severe brain injuries: Neurological organization in terms of mobility. *Journal of the American Medical Association, 17,* 257–261.

Dooher, M. (1980, July/August). Lamaze method of childbirth. *Nursing Research, 29,* 220–224.

Dore, J. (1975). Holophrase, speech acts, and language universals. *Journal of Child Language, 2* 21–40.

Dornbusch, S. M., Ritter, P. L., Liederman, P. H., Roberts, D. F., & Fraleigh, M. J. (1987). The relation of parenting style to adolescent school performance. *Child Development, 58,* 1244–1257.

Dossey, J. A., Mullis, I. V. S., Lindquist, M. M., & Chambers, D. L. (1988). *The mathematics report card: Are we measuring up? Trends and achievement based on the 1986 national assessment.* Princeton, NJ: Educational Testing Service.

Doyle, A.-B. (1975). Infant development in day care. *Developmental Psychology, 11,* 655–656.

Dubowitz, L. M. S., & Dubowitz, V. (1981). *The neurological assessment of the preterm and full-term newborn infant.* London: Heineman.

Duda, J. L. (1986). Perceptions of sport success and failure among white, black, and Hispanic adolescents. In J. Watkins, T. Reilly, & L. Burwitz (Eds.), *Sports science* (pp. 214–222). London: E. & F. N. Sport.

———. (1987). Toward a developmental theory of children's motivation in sport. *Journal of Sport Psychology, 9,* 130–145.

Dunn, J. (1991). Understanding others: Evidence from naturalistic studies of children. In A. Whiten (Ed.), *Natural theories of mind* (pp. 51–62). Cambridge, MA: Basil Blackwell.

Durrett, M. E., Otaki, M., & Richards, P. (1984). Attachment and mothers' perception of support from the father. *Journal of the International Society for the Study of Behavioral Development, 7,* 167–176.

Dweck, C. S., & Leggett, E. L. (1988). A social-cognitive approach to motivation and personality. *Psychological Review, 95,* 256–273.

Earn, B. M., & Sobol, M. P. (1990). A categorical analysis of children's attributions for social success and failure. *Psychological Record, 40,* 173–185.

East, P. L., & Rook, K. S. (1992). Compensatory patterns of support among children's peer relationships: A test using school friends, nonschool friends, and siblings. *Developmental Psychology, 28,* 163–172.

Easterbrooks, M. A., & Goldberg, W. (1985). Effects of early maternal employment on toddlers, mothers and fathers. *Developmental Psychology, 21,* 774–783.

Eccles, J., Midgley, C., & Adler, T. F. (1984). Gender related changes in the school environment: Effects on achievement motivation. In J. G. Nicholls (Ed.), *The development of achievement motivation* (pp. 283–331). Greenwich, CT: JAI Press.

Eckenrode, J., & Laird, M. (1991, April). *Social adjustment of maltreated children in the school setting.* Paper presented at the biennial meeting of the Society for Research in Child Development, Seattle.

Eder, D. (1985). The cycles of popularity: Interpersonal relations among female adolescents. *Sociology of Education, 58,* 154–165.

Edwards, C. P., & Whiting, B. B. (1988). *Children of different worlds.* Cambridge, MA: Harvard University Press.

Egeland, B., Jacobvitz, D., & Sroufe, A. L. (1988). Breaking the cycle of abuse: The mother-child intervention project. *Child Development, 59,* 1066–1088.

Egeland, B., & Sroufe, A. (1981). Developmental sequence of maltreatment in infancy. In R. Rizley & D. Cicchetti (Eds.), *Developmental perspectives on child maltreatment* (pp. 77–93). San Francisco: Jossey-Bass.

Eimas, P. D. (1985). The perception of speech in early infancy. *Scientific American, 252,* 46–52.

Eimas, P., Siqueland, E., Jusczyk, P., & Vigorito, J. (1971). Speech perception in infants. *Science, 171,* 303–306.

Eisele, J., Hertsgaard, D., & Light, H. K. (1986). Factors related to eating disorders in young adolescent girls. *Adolescence, 21,* 283–300.

Eisenberg, A. R., & Garvey, C. (1981). Children's use of verbal strategies in resolving conflicts. *Discourse Processes, 4,* 149–170.

Eisenberg, N., Lennon, R., & Roth, K. (1983). Prosocial development: A longitudinal study. *Developmental Psychology, 19,* 846–855.

Eisenberg, N., & Miller, P. A. (1987). The relation of empathy to prosocial and related behavior. *Psychological Bulletin, 101,* 91–119.

Eisenberg, N., Shell, R., Pasternack, J., Lennon, R., & Mathy, R. M. (1987). Prosocial development in middle childhood: A longitudinal study. *Developmental Psychology, 23,* 712–718.

Eisenberg-Berg, N., & Hand, M. (1979). The relationship of preschoolers' reasoning about prosocial moral conflicts to prosocial behavior. *Child Development, 50,* 356–363.

Ekman, P., & Riesen, W. (1972). Constants across culture in the face and emotion. *Journal of Personality and Social Psychology, 17,* 124–129.

Elardo, R., Bradley, R. H., & Caldwell, R. M. (1977). A longitudinal study of the relation of infant's home environments to language development at age 3. *Child Development, 48,* 595–603.

Elkind, D. (1967). Egocentrism in adolescence. *Child Development, 38,* 1025–1034.

———. (1978). Understanding the young adolescent. *Child Development, 38,* 1025–1034.

———. (1981). *The hurried child.* Reading, MA: Addison-Wesley.

Elliot, J. (1979). Risk of cancer, dysplasia for DES daughters found very low. *Journal of the American Medical Association, 241,* 1555.

Elliott, S. N., & Gresham, F. M. (1989). Teacher and self-ratings of popular and rejected adolescent boys' behavior. *Journal of Psychoeducational Assessment, 7,* 323–334.

Emde, R., Gaensbauer, T., & Harmon, R. (1976). Emotional expression in infancy: A biobehavioral study. *Psychological Issues Monograph Series, 10*(Serial No. 37).

Enright, R., Lapsley, D., & Shukla, D. (1979). Adolescent egocentrism in early and late adolescence. *Adolescence, 14,* 687–695.

Enright, R., Shukla, D., & Lapsley, D. (1980). Adolescent egocentrism-sociocentrism and self-consciousness. *Journal of Youth and Adolescence, 9,* 101–116.

Entwisle, D. R. (1990). Schools and the adolescent. In S. Feldman & G. Elliot (Eds.), *At the threshold: The developing adolescent* (pp. 197–224). Cambridge, MA: Harvard University Press.

Entwisle, D. R., & Alexander, K. L. (1990). Beginning school math competence: Minority and majority comparisons. *Child Development, 61,* 454–471.

Entwisle, D. R., Alexander, K. L., Pallas, A. M., & Cadigan, D. (1988). A social psychological model of the schooling process over first grade. *Social Psychology Quarterly, 51,* 173–189.

Entwisle, D. R., & Doering, S. G. (1981). *The first birth: A family turning point.* Baltimore: Johns Hopkins University Press.

Entwisle, D. R., & Hayduk, L. (1982). *Early schooling.* Baltimore: Johns Hopkins University Press.

Epstein, L. H., & Cluss, P. A. (1986). Behavioral genetics of childhood obesity. *Behavior Therapy, 17,* 324–334.

Epstein, L. H., & Wing, R. R. (1987). Behavioral treatment of childhood obesity. *Psychological Bulletin, 101,* 331–342.

Epstein, L. H., Wing, R. R., & Valoski, A. (1985). Childhood obesity. *Pediatric Clinics of North America, 32,* 363–379.

Erikson, E. H. (1950/1963). *Childhood and society.* New York: Norton.

———. (1968). *Identity: Youth and crisis.* New York: Norton.

Erwin, P. G. (1985). Similarity of attitudes and constructs in children's friendships. *Journal of Experimental Child Psychology, 40,* 470–485.

Eshel, Y., & Kurman, J. (1990). Love is not enough: Determinants of adolescent preference for other-sex and same-sex peers. *British Journal of Developmental Psychology, 8,* 171–178.

Evans, E. D., & Craig, D. (1990a). Adolescent cognitions for academic cheating as a function of grade level and achievement status. *Journal of Adolescent Research, 5,* 325–345.

———. (1990b). Teacher and student perception of academic cheating in middle and senior high schools. *Journal of Educational Research, 84,* 44–52.

Ewing, M. E. (1981). *Achievement orientations and sport behavior of males and females.* Unpublished doctoral dissertation, University of Illinois.

Fagen, J. W. (1984). Infants' long-term memory for stimulus color. *Developmental Psychology, 20,* 435–440.

Fagen, J. W., Morrongiello, B. A., Rovee-Collier, C., & Gekoski, M. J. (1984). Expectancies and memory retrieval in three-month-old infants. *Child Development, 55,* 936–943.

Fagot, B. I. (1978). The influence of sex of child on parental reactions to toddler children. *Child Development, 49,* 459–465.

Fallot, M. E., Boyd, J. L., & Oski, F. A. (1980). Breastfeeding reduces incidence of hospital admissions for infection in infants. *Pediatrics, 65*(6), 1121–1124.

Fantz, R. L. (1963). Pattern vision in newborn infants. *Science, 140,* 296–297.

Farnworth, M. (1984). Family structure, family attributes, and delinquency in a sample of low-income, minority males. *Journal of Youth and Adolescence, 13,* 349–364.

Farrington, D. P. (1987). Epidemiology. In H. C. Quay (Ed.), *Handbook of juvenile delinquency* (pp. 33–61). New York: Wiley.

Federal Bureau of Investigation. (1989). *Crime in the United States: Uniform crime reports—1988.* Washington, DC: U.S. Government Printing Office.

Feinbloom, R. I., & Forman, B. Y. (1987). *Pregnancy, birth, and the early months.* Reading, MA: Addison-Wesley.

Feldhusen, J. F. (1989, March). Synthesis of research on gifted youth. *Educational Leadership,* 6–11.

Feldman, E., & Dodge, K. A. (1987). Social information processing and sociometric status: Sex, age, and situational effects. *Journal of Abnormal Child Psychology, 15,* 211–227.

Ferguson, C. A. (1977). Baby talk as a simplified register. In C. A. Snow & C. A. Ferguson (Eds.), *Talking to children: Language input and acquisition* (pp. 209–235). Cambridge: Cambridge University Press.

Fernald, A. (1985). Four month old infants prefer to listen to mothers. *Infant Behavior and Development, 8,* 181–195.

Fernald, A., & Kuhl, P. (1987). Acoustic determinants of infant preference for motherese speech. *Infant Behavior and Development, 10,* 279–293.

Field, D. (1987). A review of preschool conservation training: An analysis of analyses. *Developmental Review, 7,* 210–251.

Field, T. M. (1977). Effects of separation, interactive deficits, and experimental manipulations on infant-mother face-to-face interaction. *Child Development, 48,* 763–771.

———. (1978). Interaction behaviors of primary versus secondary caretaker fathers. *Developmental Psychology, 14,* 183–184.

———. (1979). Games parents play with normal and high-risk infants. *Child Development, 10,* 41–48.

———. (1986). Interactions for premature infants. *Journal of Pediatrics, 109,* 183–190.

———. (1987a). Affective and interactive disturbances in infants. In J. D. Osofsky (Ed.), *Handbook of infant development* (2nd ed., pp. 972–1005). New York: Wiley.

———. (1987b). Interaction and attachment in normal and atypical infants. *Journal of Consulting and Clinical Psychology, 55,* 853–859.

Field, T. M., Dempsey, J. R., Hatch, J., Ting, G., & Clifton, R. K. (1979). Cardiac and behavior responses to repeated tactile and auditory stimuli by preterm and term neonates. *Developmental Psychology, 15,* 406–416.

Field, T. M., Greenwald, P., Morrow, C., Healy, B., Foster, T., Guthertz, M., & Frost, P. (1992). Behavior state matching during interactions of preadolescent friends versus acquaintances. *Developmental Psychology, 28,* 242–250.

Field, T. M., Ignatoff, E., Stringer, S., Brennan, J., Greenberg, S., Widmayer, S., & Anderson, G. C. (1982). Non-nutritive sucking during tube feedings: Effects on preterm neonates in an intensive care unit. *Pediatrics, 70*(3), 381–384.

Field, T. M., & Walden, T. A. (1982). Production and discrimination of facial expressions by preschool children. *Child Development, 53,* 1299–1311.

Field, T. M., Widmayer, S. M., Stringer, S., & Ignatoff, E. (1980). Teenage, lower-class, black mothers and their preterm infants: An intervention and developmental follow-up. *Child Development, 51,* 426–436.

Fine, G. A. (1981). Friends, impression management, and preadolescent behavior. In S. R. Asher & J. M. Gottman (Eds.), *The development of children's friendships* (pp. 29–52), Cambridge: Cambridge University Press.

Fischer, K. W. (1980). A theory of cognitive development: The control and construction of hierarchies of skills. *Psychological Review, 87,* 477–531.

Fivush, R. (1984). Learning about school: The development of kindergarteners' school scripts. *Child Development, 55,* 1697–1709.

Flavell, J. H. (1963). *The developmental psychology of Jean Piaget.* Princeton, NJ: Van Nostrand.

———. (1970). Developmental studies of mediated memory. In H. W. Reese & L. P. Lipsitt (Eds.), *Advances in child development and child behavior* (Vol. 5). New York: Academic Press.

———. (1985). *Cognitive development* (2nd ed.), Englewood Cliffs, NJ: Prentice-Hall.

Flavell, J. H., Beach, D. R., & Chinsky, J. H. (1966). Spontaneous verbal rehearsal in a memory task as a function of age. *Child Development, 37,* 283–299.

Flavell, J. H., Flavell, E. R., & Green, F. L. (1983a). Development of the appearance-reality distinction. *Cognitive Psychology, 15,* 95–120.

Flavell, J. H., Friedrichs, A. G., & Hoyt, J. D. (1970). Developmental changes in memorization processes. *Cognitive Psychology, 1,* 324–340.

Flavell, J. H., Green, T. L., & Flavell, E. R. (1986). Development of knowledge about the appearance-reality distinction. *Monographs of the Society for Research in Child Development, 51*(1, Serial No. 212).

Flavell, J. H., Miller, P. H., & Miller, S. A. (1993). *Cognitive development* (3rd ed.). Englewood Cliffs, NJ: Prentice-Hall.

Flavell, J. H., Omanson, R. C., & Latham, C. (1978). Solving spatial perspective-taking problems by rule versus computation: A developmental study. *Developmental Psychology, 14,* 462–473.

Flavell, J. H., & Wellman, H. M. (1977). Metamemory. In R. V. Hail, Jr., & J. W. Hagan (Eds.), *Perspectives on the development of memory and cognition* (pp. 3–33). Hillsdale, NJ: Erlbaum.

Flavell, J. H., Zhang, X. D., Zou, H., Dong, Q., & Qui, S. (1983b). A comparison between the development of the appearance-reality distinction in the People's Republic of China and the United States. *Cognitive Psychology, 15,* 459–466.

Ford, C. S., & Beach, F. A. (1951). *Patterns of sexual behavior*. New York: Harper & Row.

Forsyth, D. R., Pope, W. R., & McMillan, J. H. (1985). Students' reactions after cheating: An attributional analysis. *Contemporary Educational Psychology, 10*, 72–82.

Fortney, V. L. (1983). Kinematics and kinetics of the running pattern of two-, four-, and six-year-old children. *Research Quarterly for Exercise and Sport, 54*, 126–135.

Fournet, G. P., Estes, R. E., Martin, G. L., Robertson, E. D., & McCrary, J. S. (1990). Drug and alcohol attitudes and usage among elementary and secondary students. *Journal of Alcohol and Drug Education, 35*, 81–92.

Fox, G. L. (1981). The family's role in adolescent sexual behavior. In T. Ooms (Ed.), *Teenage pregnancy in a family context: Implications for policy* (pp. 73–130). Philadelphia: Temple University Press.

Fox, G. L., & Inazo, J. K. (1980). Patterns and outcomes of mother-daughter communication about sexuality. *Journal of Social Issues, 36*, 7–29.

Fox, G. L., & Medlin, C. (1986). Accuracy in mothers' perceptions of daughters' level of sexual involvement: Black and white single mothers and their teenage daughters. *Family Perspectives, 20*, 267–286.

Fox, R., Aslin, R. N., Shea, S. L., & Dumais, S. T. (1980). Stereopsis in human infants. *Science, 207*, 323–324.

Fraiberg, S. (1977). *Insights from the blind*. New York: Basic Books.

Francis, G., & Ollendick, T. H. (1987). Peer group entry behavior. *Child and Family Behavior Therapy, 9*, 45–54.

Francis, P. I., Self, P. A., & Horowitz, F. D. (1987). The behavioral assessment of the neonate: An overview. In J. D. Osofsky (Ed.), *Handbook of infant development* (2nd ed., pp. 723–779). New York: Wiley.

Frank, D. A., Zuckerman, B. S., Amard, H., Aboagye, K., Bauchner, H., Cabral, H., Fried, L., Hingson, R., Kayne, H., Levenson, S. M., Parker, S., Reece, H., & Vinci, R. (1988). Cocaine use during pregnancy: Prevalence and correlates. *Pediatrics, 82*, 888–895.

Frankenberg, W. K., & Dodds, J. B. (1967). The Denver Developmental Screening Test. *Journal of Pediatrics, 71*, 181–191.

Fraser, B. A., & Hensinger, R. N. (1983). *Handicaps: A practical guide for parents, care providers and educators*. Baltimore: Paul Brookes.

Fraser, B. A., Hensinger, R. N., & Phelps, J. A. (1987). *Physical management of multiple handicaps*. Baltimore: Paul Brookes.

Frauenglass, M., & Diaz, R. (1985). Self-regulatory functions of children's private speech. *Developmental psychology, 21*, 357–364.

Freebody, P., & Byrne, B. (1988). Word-reading strategies in elementary school children: Relations to comprehension, reading time, and phonemic awareness. *Reading Research Quarterly, 23*, 441–453.

Freedman, D. G., & Freedman, N. (1969). Behavioral differences between Chinese-American and European-American newborns. *Nature, 224*, 1127.

Fregly, M. J., & Luttge, W. G. (1982). *Human endocrinology: An interactive text*. New York: Elsevier Science.

French, D. C., & Waas, G. A. (1985). Behavior problems of peer-neglected and peer-rejected elementary-aged children: Parent and teacher perspectives. *Child Development, 56*, 246–252.

French, L. A. (1989). Young children's response to "when" questions: Issues of directionality. *Child Development, 60*, 225–236.

Frentz, C., Gresham, F. M., & Elliott, S. N. (1991). Popular, controversial, neglected, and rejected adolescents: Contrasts of social competence and achievement differences. *Journal of School Psychology, 29*, 109–120.

Freud, S. (1920). *Beyond the pleasure principle*. In J. Strachey (Ed.), *The standard edition of the complete works of Sigmund Freud*. London: Hogarth Press and the Institute of Psychoanalysis, 1953–1966.

———. (1923/1960). *The ego and the id*. New York: W. W. Norton and Company, Inc.

———. (1940/1964). *An outline of psychoanalysis*. In J. Strachey (Ed.), *The standard edition of the complete works of Sigmund Freud* (Vol. 23). London: Hogarth Press.

Friedman, S., Jacobs, B., & Werthmann, M. (1982). Preterms of low medical risk: Spontaneous behaviors and soothing ability at expected date of birth. *Infant Behavior and Development, 5*, 3–10.

Friedman, W. J., Robinson, A. B., & Friedman, B. L. (1987). Sex differences in moral judgments? A test of Gilligan's theory. *Psychology of Women Quarterly, 11*, 37–46.

Frietas, B. (1984). The development of taste acceptance in human infants. *Dissertation Abstracts International, 44*(7–5), 2272 (University Microfilms No. DA 83226288).

Frisch, N. E. (1988, March). Fatness and fertility. *Scientific American*, 88–95.

Frodi, A. M., & Lamb, M. (1980). Child abusers' responses to infant smiles and cries. *Child Development, 51*, 28–241.

Frost, J. L., & Wortham, S. C. (1988, July). The evolution of American playgrounds. (*Young Children*, 19–28.

Furstenberg, F. F., Jr., & Nord, C. W. (1985). Parenting apart: Patterns of childrearing after marital disruption. *Journal of Marriage and the Family, 47*, 893–912.

Fuson, K. C., Pergament, G. G., Lyons, B. G., & Hall, J. W. (1985). Children's conformity to the cardinal rule as a function of set size and counting accuracy. *Child Development, 56*, 1429–1436.

Fuson, K. C., & Secada, W. G. (1986). Teaching children to add by counting-on with one-handed finger patterns. *Cognition and Instruction, 3*, 229–260.

Gaddis, A., & Brooks-Gunn, J. (1985). The male experience of pubertal change. *Journal of Youth and Adolescence, 14*, 61–69.

Galambos, N. L., & Garbarino, J. (1985). Adjustment of unsupervised children in a rural setting. *Journal of Genetic Psychology, 146*, 227–231.

Galst, J. P., & White, M. A. (1976). The unhealthy persuader: The reinforcing value of television and children's purchase influencing attempts at the supermarket. *Child Development, 47*, 1089–1096.

Ganon, E. C., & Swartz, K. B. (1980). Perception of internal elements of compound figures by one-month-olds. *Journal of Experimental Child Psychology, 30,* 159–170.

Garbarino, J. (1977). The price of privacy: An analysis of the social dynamics of child abuse. *Child Welfare, 56,* 565–575.

Garbarino, J., & Crouter, A. (1978). Defining the community context for parent-child relations: The correlates of child maltreatment. *Child Development, 49,* 604–616.

Garbarino, J., & Sherman, D. (1980). High-risk neighborhoods and high-risk families: The human ecology of child maltreatment. *Child Development, 51,* 188–198.

Gardner, H. (1983). *Frames of mind.* New York: Basic Books.

Gardner, L. I. (1972, July) Deprivation dwarfism. *Scientific American, 227,* 76–82.

Gardner, W., & Herman, J. (1990). Adolescents' AIDS risk taking: A rational choice perspective. *New Directions for Child Development, 50,* 17–34.

Garfinkel, P. E., Garner, D. M., & Goldbloom, D. S. (1987). Eating disorders: Implications for the 1990s. *Canadian Journal of Psychiatry, 32,* 624–631.

Garrison, C. Z., Addy, C. L., Jackson, K. L., McKeown, R. E., & Walker, J. L. (1991). A longitudinal study of suicidal ideation in young adolescents. *Journal of the American Academy of Child and Adolescent Psychiatry, 30,* 597–603.

Garvey, C., & Kramer, T. L. (1989). The language of social pretend play. *Developmental Psychology, 9,* 364–382.

Gavin, L., & Furman, W. (1989). Age differences in adolescents' perceptions of their peer groups. *Developmental Psychology, 25,* 827–834.

Geller, E. S., Casali, J., & Johnson, R. (1980). Seatbelt usage: A parenting target for applied behavioral analysis. *Journal of Applied Behavior Analysis, 13,* 669–675.

Geller, M., Kelley, J., Traxler, W., & Marone, F. (1978). Behavioral treatment of an adolescent female's bulimic anorexia. *Journal of Clinical Child Psychology, 7,* 138–142.

Gelman, R. (1972). The nature and development of early number concepts. In H. W. Reese (Ed.), *Advances in child development and behavior* (Vol. 7, pp. 116–167). New York: Academic Press.

———. (1980). What young children know about numbers. *Educational Psychologist, 15,* 54–68.

Gelman, R., & Gallistel, R. (1978). *The child's understanding of number.* Cambridge, MA: Harvard University Press.

Gelman, R., Meck, E., & Merkin, S. (1986). Young children's numerical composure. *Cognitive Development, 1,* 1–30.

George, C., & Main, M. (1979). Social interactions of young aged children: Approach, avoidance, and aggression. *Child Development, 50,* 306–318.

Gershman, E. S., & Hayes, D. S. (1983). Differential stability of reciprocal friendships and unilateral relationships among preschool children. *Merrill-Palmer Quarterly, 29,* 169–177.

Gesell, A. (1929). *Infancy and human growth.* New York: Macmillan.

Ghatala, E. S., Levin, J. R., Pressley, M., & Goodwin, D. (1986). A componential analysis of the effects of derived and supplied strategy-utility information on children's strategy selections. *Journal of Experimental Child Psychology, 20,* 105–118.

Gibson, E. J., & Walk, R. D. (1960). The "visual cliff." *Scientific American, 202,* 64–71.

Gilliam, T., Freedson, P., Geenen, D., & Shahraray, B. (1981). Physical activity patterns determined by heart rate monitoring in 6- to 7-year-old children. *Medicine and Science in Sports and Exercise, 13,* 65–67.

Gilligan, C. F. (1982). *In a different voice.* Cambridge, MA: Harvard University Press.

Glucksberg, S., & Krauss, R. (1967). What do people say after they have learned to talk? Studies of the development of referential communication. *Merrill-Palmer Quarterly, 13,* 309–316.

Gnepp, J. (1983). Inferring emotions from conflicting cues. *Developmental Psychology, 19,* 805–814.

Gnepp, J., & Gould, M. E. (1985). The development of personality inferences: Understanding other people's emotional reactions in light of their prior experience. *Child Development, 56,* 1455–1464.

Gnepp, J., McKee, E., & Domaniac, J. A. (1987). Children's use of situational information to infer emotion: Understanding emotionally equivalent situations. *Developmental Psychology, 23,* 114–123.

Goetz, T. E., & Dweck, C. S. (1980). Learned helplessness in social situations. *Journal of Personality and Social Psychology, 39,* 246–255.

Goldberg, S. (1979). Premature birth: Consequences for the parent-infant relationship. *American Scientist, 67,* 214–220.

Goldberg, S., Marcovitch, S., MacGregor, D., & Lojkasek, M. (1986). Family responses to a developmentally delayed preschooler: Etiology and the father's role. *American Journal of Mental Deficiency, 90,* 610–617.

Goldman, J. A., Corsini, D. A., & deUrioste, R. (1980). Implications of positive and negative sociometric status for assessing the social competence of young children. *Journal of Applied Developmental Psychology, 1,* 209–220.

Goldring, E. B. (1990). Assessing the status of information on classroom organizational frameworks for gifted students. *Journal of Educational Research, 83,* 313–326.

Golinkoff, R. M., & Ames, G. J. (1979). A comparison of fathers' and mothers' speech with their young children. *Child Development, 50,* 28–32.

Good, T. L., & Weinstein, R. S. (1986). Schools make a difference: Evidence, criticisms, and new directions. *American Psychologist, 41,* 1090–1097.

Gopnik, A., & Meltzoff, A. N. (1987). The development of categorization in the second year and its relation to other cognitive and linguistic developments. *Child Development, 58,* 1523–1531.

Gotowiec, A., Goldberg, S., & Simmons, R. (1993, March). *Quality of attachment and parent ratings of preschool behavior problems: Contributions of the "disorganized" classification.* Paper presented at the biennial meeting of the Society for Research in Child Development, New Orleans.

Gottfried, A. E. (1982). Relationships between academic intrinsic motivation and anxiety in children and young adolescents. *Journal of School Psychology, 20,* 205–215.

———. (1985). Academic intrinsic motivation in elementary and junior high school students. *Journal of Educational Psychology, 77,* 631–645.

———. (1990). Academic intrinsic motivation in young elementary school children. *Journal of Educational Psychology, 82,* 525–538.

Gottfried, A. E., Gottfried, A. W., & Bathurst, K. (1988). Maternal employment, family environment and children's development: Infancy through the school years. In A. E. Gottfried & A. W. Gottfried (Eds.), *Maternal employment and children's development: Longitudinal research* (pp. 11–58). New York: Plenum Press.

———. (1991). *Parental employment and children's development in dual-earner families: A longitudinal study.* Paper presented at the biennial meeting of the Society for Research in Child Development, Seattle.

Gottman, J. M. (1983). How children become friends. *Monographs of the Society for Research in Child Development, 48*(3, Serial No. 201).

Gough, P. B., & Tunmer, W. E. (1986). Decoding, reading, and reading disability. *Remedial and Special Education, 7,* 6–10.

Grady, K., Gersick, K. E., Snow, D. L., & Kessen, M. (1986). The emergence of adolescent substance abuse. *Journal of Drug Education, 16,* 203–220.

Gralen, S. J., Levine, M. P., Smolak, L., Murnen, S. K. (1990). Dieting and disordered eating during early and middle adolescence: Do the influences remain the same? *International Journal of Eating Disorders, 9,* 501–512.

Green, B. B., Weiss, N. S., & Darling, J. R. (1988). Risk of ovulatory infertility in relation to body weight. *Fertility & Sterility, 50,* 721–725.

Green, M. (1989). *Theories of human development.* Englewood Cliffs, NJ: Prentice-Hall.

Greenberg, M., & Morris, N. (1974). Engrossment: The newborn's impact upon the father. *American Journal of Orthopsychiatry, 44,* 520–571.

Greenberger, E., & Goldberg, W. A. (1989). Work, parenting, and the socialization of children. *Developmental Psychology, 25,* 22–35.

Greenough, W. T. (1976). Enduring brain effects of differential experience and training. In M. R. Rosenzweig, & E. L. Bennett (Eds.), *Neural mechanisms of learning and memory* (pp. 255–278). Cambridge, MA: MIT Press.

Greenough, W. T., Black, J. E., & Wallace, C. S. (1987). Experience and brain development. *Child Development, 58,* 539–559.

Gresham, I. J. (1982). Misguided mainstreaming: The case for social skills training with handicapped children. *Exceptional Children, 48,* 422–433.

Grieser, D. L., & Kuhl, P. K. (1988). Maternal speech to infants in a tonal language: Support for universal prosodic features in motherese. *Developmental Psychology, 24,* 14–20.

Gross, A. M., & Johnson, T. C. (1984). Athletic skill and social status in children. *Journal of Social and Clinical Psychology, 2,* 89–96.

Grossman, H. J. (Ed.) (1983). *Classification in mental retardation.* Washington, DC: American Association on Mental Deficiency.

Grossman, K., Grossman, K. E., Spangler, C., Suess, G., & Unzer, L. (1985). Maternal sensitivity and newborn orienting responses as related to quality of attachment in Northern Germany. In I. Bretherton & E. Waters (Eds.), *Growing points of attachment theory and research. Monograph of the Society for Research in Child Development, 50,* 233–256.

Grotevant, H. D. (1987). Toward a process model of identity formation. *Journal of Adolescent Research, 2,* 203–222.

Grusec, J. (1991). Socializing concern for others in the home. *Developmental Psychology, 27,* 338–342.

Guidubaldi, J., & Nastasi, B. K. (1987, April). *Home environment factors as predictors of child adjustment in mother-employed households: Results of a nationwide study.* Paper presented at the biennial meeting of the Society for Research in Child Development, Baltimore.

Gulko, S., Doyle, A., Serbin, L., & White, D. (1988). Conversation skills: A replicated study of order of acquisition across tasks. *Journal of Genetic Psychology, 149,* 425–439.

Gunnar, M. (1980). Contingent stimulation: A review of its role in early development. In S. Levine & H. Ursin (Eds.), *Coping and health.* New York: Plenum Press.

Guralnick, M. H. (1990). Major accomplishments and future directions in early childhood mainstreaming. *Topics in Early Childhood Special Education, 10,* 1–17.

Gusella, J. L., Muir, D., & Tronick, E. Z. (1988). The effect of manipulating maternal behavior during an interaction on three- and six-month-olds' affect and affection. *Child Development, 59,* 1111–1124.

Gzesh, S. M., & Surber, C. F. (1985). Visual perspective taking skills in children. *Child Development, 56,* 1204–1213.

Haderman, K. F. (1976). Ability grouping—its effect on language learners. *NASSP Bulletin, 60,* 85–89.

Haith, M. M. (1986). Sensory and perceptual processes in early infancy. *Journal of Pediatrics, 109,* 158–171.

Hall, E. G., & Lee, A. M. (1984). Sex differences in motor performance of young children: Fact or fiction? *Sex Roles, 10,* 217–230.

Hall, G. S. (1904). *Adolescence: Its psychology and its relations to physiology, anthropology, sociology, sex, crime, religion and education.* New York: Appleton.

Hallahan, D. P., Keller, C. E., McKinney, J. D., Lloyd, J. W., & Bryan, T. (1988). Examining the research base of the regular education initiative: Efficacy studies and the adaptive learning environments model. *Journal of Learning Disabilities, 2,* 29–35.

Hammond, W. H. (1953). The determination of physical type in children. *Human Biology, 25,* 65–70.

Hanson, F. W., Tennant, F., Hune, S., & Brookhyser, K. (1992). Early amniocentesis: Outcome, risks, and technical problems at ≤ 12.8 weeks. *American Journal of Obstetrics & Gynecology, 166,* 1707–1711.

Hanson, J. W., Streissguth, A. P., & Smith, D. W. (1978). The effects of moderate alcohol consumption during pregnancy on growth and morphogenesis. *The Journal of Pediatrics, 92,* 457–460.

Harlow, H. F., & Zimmerman, R. R. (1959). Affectional responses in the infant monkey. *Science, 130,* 421–432.

Harmon, R. J., Suwalsky, J., & Klein, R. (1979). Infant's preferential response for mother versus unfamiliar adult. *Journal of the American Academy of Child Psychiatry, 18,* 437–449.

Harnishfeger, K. K., & Bjorklund, D. F. (1990). Children's strategies: A brief history. In D. F. Bjorklund (Ed.), *Children's strategies: Contemporary views of cognitive development.* Hillsdale, NJ: Erlbaum.

Harris, J. C. (1984). Interpreting youth baseball: Players' understanding of fun and excitement, danger, and boredom. *Research Quarterly for Exercise and Sport, 55,* 379–382.

Harris, P. L., & Kavanaugh, R. D. (1993). Young children's understanding of pretense. *Monographs of the Society for Research in Child Development, 58*(Serial No. 231).

Harrison, H. (1983). *The premature baby book.* New York: St. Martins Press.

Harter, S. (1983). Developmental perspective in the self system. In E. M. Hetherington (Ed.) & P. H. Mussen (Series Ed.), *Handbook of child psychology: Vol. 4: Socialization, personality, and social development* (pp. 275–385). New York: Wiley.

Hartup, W. W. (1974). Aggression in childhood: Developmental perspectives. *American Psychologist, 29,* 336–341.

———. (1977, Fall). Peers, play, & pathology: A new look at the social behavior of children. *SRCD Newsletter,* pp. 1–3.

———. (1983). Peer relations. In E. M. Hetherington (Ed.) & P. H. Mussen (Series Ed.), *Handbook of child psychology, Vol. 4: Socialization, personality, and social development* (4th ed., pp. 103–196). New York: Wiley.

———. (1989). Social relationships and their developmental significance. *American Psychologist, 44,* 120–126.

Hartup, W. W., Glazer, J. A., & Charlesworth, R. (1967). Peer reinforcement and sociometric status. *Child Development, 38,* 1017–1024.

Hartup, W. W., Laursen, B., Stewart, M. A., & Eastenson, A. (1988). Conflict and the friendship relations of young children. *Child Development, 59,* 1590–1600.

Haviland, J. M., & Lelwica, M. (1987). The induced affect response: 10-week-old infant and responses to three emotional expressions. *Developmental Psychology, 23,* 17–104.

Hawkins, J. D., & Lishner, D. M. (1987). Schooling and delinquency. In E. H. Johnson (Ed.), *Handbook on crime and delinquency prevention* (pp. 179–221). New York: Greenwood Press.

Hawley, T. L. (1991). *Maternal cocaine addiction: Correlates and consequences.* Paper presented at the biennial meeting of the Society for Research in Child Development, New Orleans.

Haynes, S. G., Feinlieb, M., & Kannel, W. B. (1980). The relationship of psychological factors to coronary heart disease in Framingham: III. Eight year incidence of coronary heart disease. *American Journal of Epidemiology, 111,* 37–58.

Hazen, N. L., & Black, B. (1989). Preschool peer communication skills: The role of social status and interaction context. *Child Development, 60,* 867–876.

Henggeler, S. W. (1989). *Delinquency in adolescence.* Newbury Park, CA: Sage Publications.

Hess, R. D., & Shipman, V. C. (1965). Early experience and the socialization of cognitive modes in children. *Child Development, 36,* 869–886.

Hesse-Biber, S. (1989). Eating patterns and disorders in a college population: Are college women's eating problems a new phenomenon? *Sex Roles, 20,* 71–89.

Hetherington, E. M. (1989). Coping with family transitions: Winners, losers, and survivors. *Child Development, 60,* 1–14.

Hetherington, E. M., & Camara, K. A. (1984). Families in transition: The process of dissolution and reconstitution. In R. Parke (Ed.), *Review of child development research* (Vol. 3, pp. 398–439). Chicago: University of Chicago Press.

Hetherington, E. M., & Clingempeel, W. G. (1992). Coping with marital transitions. *Monographs of the Society for Research in Child Development, 57* (Nos. 2-3).

Hetherington, E. M., Stanley-Hagan, M., & Anderson, E. R. (1989). Marital transitions: A child's perspective. *American Psychologist, 44,* 303–312.

Hicks, L. E., Langham, R. A., & Takenaka, J. (1982). Cognitive and health measure following early nutritional supplementation: A sibling study. *American Journal of Public Health, 72,* 1110–1118.

Highway Safety Research Center. (1976). Belts—Questions and answers. *Highway Safety Highlights, 10,* 1.

Hill, J. P., & Lynch, M. E. (1983). The intensification of gender-related role expectations during early adolescence. In J. Brooks-Gunn & A. C. Petersen (Eds.), *Girls at puberty: Biological and psychological perspectives* (pp. 201–228). New York: Plenum Press.

Hinde, R. A. (1974). *Biological bases of human social behavior.* New York: McGraw-Hill.

Hinde, R. A., Titmus, G., Easton, D., & Tamplin, A. (1985). Incidence of "friendship" and behavior toward strange associates versus non-associates in preschoolers. *Child Development, 56,* 234–245.

Hirsch, H. V. B., & Spinelli, D. N. (1970). Visual experience modifies distribution of horizontally and vertically assisted receptive fields in cats. *Science, 168,* 869–871.

Hock, E. (1980). Working and non-working mothers and their infants: A comparative study of maternal caregiving characteristics and infant social behavior. *Merrill-Palmer Quarterly, 26,* 79–102.

Hofferth, S. L., & Hayes, C. D. (Eds.) (1987). *Risking the future: Adolescent sexuality, pregnancy, and childrearing: Vol. 2. Working papers and statistical reports.* Washington, DC: National Academy Press.

Hofferth, S. L., Kahn, J. R., & Baldwin, W. (1987). Pre-marital sexual activity among U.S. teenage women over the past three decades. *Family Planning Perspectives, 19,* 46–53.

Hoff-Ginsberg, E. (1985). Some contributions of mother's speech to their children's syntactic growth.

Journal of Child Language, 12, 367–385.

———. (1986). Function and structure in maternal speech: Their relation to the child's development of syntax. *Developmental Psychology, 22*(2), 155–163.

Hoffman, L. W. (1988). Cross cultural differences in childrearing goals. In R. A. LeVine, P. M. Miller, & M. M. West (Eds.), *Parental behavior in diverse society* (pp. 99–122). In W. Damon (Series Ed.), *New directions for child development* (No. 44, Summer 1988). San Francisco: Jossey-Bass.

———. (1989). Effects of maternal employment in two-parent family. *American Psychologist, 44*, 283–292.

Hoffman, M. L. (1984). Interaction of affect and cognition in empathy. In C. E. Izard, J. Kanag, & R. B. Zajonc (Eds.), *Emotions, cognition, and behavior* (pp. 103–131). Cambridge: Cambridge University Press.

Hoffman-Plotkin, D., & Twentyman, C. T. (1984). A multimodal assessment of behavior and cognitive deficits in abused and neglected preschoolers. *Child Development, 55*, 794–802.

Hogan, D. P., & Kitagawa, E. M. (1985). The impact of social status, family structure, and neighborhood on the fertility of black adolescents. *American Journal of Sociology, 90*, 825–855.

Hohmann, M., Banet, B., & Weikart, D. P. (1979). *Young children in action: A manual for preschool educators*. Ypsilanti, MI: High/Scope Press.

Hollenbeck, A. R., Gewirtz, J. L., & Sebris, S. L. (1984). Labor and delivery medication influences parent-infant interaction in the first post-partum month. *Infant Behavior and Development, 7*, 201–209.

Holroyd, J., & MacArthur, D. (1976). Mental retardation and stress on parents: A contrast between Down's syndrome and childhood autism. *American Journal of Mental Deficiency, 80*, 431–436.

Horowitz, F. D. (1987). *Exploring developmental theories: Toward a structural/behavioral model of child development*. Hillsdale, NJ: Erlbaum.

Horowitz, F. D., & O'Brien, M. (1986). Gifted and talented children: State of knowledge and directions for research. *American Psychologist, 41*, 1147–1152.

Hotchner, T. (1984). *Pregnancy and childbirth*. New York: Avon Books.

Houseman, J. (1972). *An ecological study of interpersonal conflicts among preschool children*. Unpublished doctoral dissertation, Wayne State University, Detroit.

Howard, J., Beckwith, L., Rodning, C., & Kropenske, V. (1989, June). The development of young children of substance-abusing parents: Insights from seven years of intervention and research. *Zero to Three: Bulletin of the National Center for Clinical Infant Programs, 9*.

Howes, C. (1983). Patterns of friendship. *Child Development, 54*, 1044–1053.

———. (1985). Sharing fantasy: Social pretend play in toddlers. *Child Development, 56*, 1253–1258.

Howes, C., & Eldridge, R. (1985). Responses of abused, neglected, and nonmaltreated children to the behavior of their peers. *Journal of Applied Developmental Psychology, 6*, 261–270.

Howes, C., & Espinosa, M. (1985). The consequences of child abuse for the formation of relationships with peers. *Child Abuse and Neglect, 9*, 397–404.

Howes, C., & Olenick, M. (1986). Family and child care influences on toddler's compliance. *Child Development, 57*, 202–216.

Howes, C., Unger, O., & Seidner, B. K. (1989). Social pretend play in toddlers: Parallels with social play and with solitary pretend. *Child Development, 60*, 77–84.

Howes, C., & Wu, F. (1990). Peer interactions and friendships in an ethnically diverse school setting. *Child Development, 61*, 537–541.

Hoyseth, K. S., & Jones, J. H. (1989). Minireview: Ethanol induced teratogenesis: Characterization, mechanisms, and diagnostic approaches. *Life Sciences, 44*, 643–649.

Hughey, M. J., McElin, T. W., & Young, T. (1978). Maternal and fetal outcome of Lamaze prepared patients. *Obstetrics and Gynecology, 51*, 643–647.

Hume, R. F., Jr., O'Donnell, K. J., Stanger, C. L., Killam, A. P., & Gingras, J. L. (1989). In utero cocaine exposure: Observations of fetal behavior state may predict neonatal outcome. *American Journal of Obstetrics and Gynecology, 161*, 685–690.

Hunt, J., McV. (1961). *Intelligence and experience*. New York: Ronald Press.

Huttenlocher, J., & Presson, C. C. (1979). The coding and transformation of spatial information. *Cognitive Psychology, 11*, 375–394.

Huttenlocher, P. R. (1984). Synapse elimination and plasticity in developing human cerebral cortex. *American Journal of Mental Deficiency, 88*, 488–496.

Hutto, C., Arvin, A., Jacobs, R., Steele, R., Stagno, S., Lyrene, R., Willett, L., Powell, D., Anderson, R., Werthammer J., Ratcliff, G., Nahmias, A., Christy, C., & Whitley R. (1987). Intrauterine herpes simplex virus infections. *Journal of Pediatrics, 110*, 97–101.

Hwang, C. P. (1986). Behavior of Swedish primary and secondary caretaking father in relation to mother's presence. *Developmental Psychology, 22*, 749–751.

Hymel, S., Rubin, K. H., Rowden, L., & LeMare, L. (1990). Children's peer relationships: Longitudinal prediction of internalizing and externalizing problems from middle to late childhood. *Child Development, 61*, 2004–2021.

Iannotti, R. J. (1985). Naturalistic and structured assessments of prosocial behavior in preschool children: The influence of empathy and perspective-taking. *Developmental Psychology, 21*, 46–55.

Inderbitzen-Pisaruk, H., & Foster, S. L. (1990). Adolescent friendships and peer acceptance: Implications for social skills training. *Clinical Psychology Review, 10*, 425–439.

Inhelder, B., & Piaget, J. (1958). *The growth of logical thinking from childhood to adolescence: An essay on the construction of formal operational structures*. New York: Basic Books.

———. (1964). *The early growth of logic in the child*. New York: Norton.

Isabella, R., Belsky, J., & Von Eye, A. (1989). Origins of infant-mother attachment: An examination of interactional synchrony during the infant's first year. *Developmental Psychology, 25*, 12–21.

Istvan, J. (1986). Stress, anxiety, and birth outcomes: A critical review of the evidence. *Psychological Bulletin, 100*, 331–348.

Izard, C. E., Dougherty, L. M., & Hembree, E. A. (1980). *A system for identifying affect expressions by holistic judgements* (Affex). Newark, DE: University of Delaware Instructional Resource Center.

Izard, C. E., Hembree, E. A., Dougherty, L. M., & Spizzirri, C. (1983). Changes in 2- to 19-month-old infants' responses to acute pain. *Developmental Psychology, 19*, 418–426.

Izard, C. E., & Malatesta, C. (1987). Perspectives on emotional development I: Differential emotions theory of early emotional development. In J. D. Osofsky (Ed.), *Handbook of infant development* (2nd ed., pp. 494–554). New York: Wiley.

Jackowitz, E. R., & Watson, M. W. (1980). Development of object transformation in early pretend play. *Developmental Psychology, 16*, 543–549.

Jacobson, J. L., Boersma, D. C., Fields, R. B., & Olson, K. L. (1983). Paralinguistic features of adult speech to infants and small children. *Child Development, 54*, 436–442.

Jacobvitz, D., & Sroufe, L. A. (1987). The early caregiver-child relationship and attention deficit disorder with hyperactivity in kindergarten. *Child Development, 58*, 1496–1504.

Jacobvitz, D., Sroufe, L. A., Stewart, M., & Leffert, N. (1990). Treatment of attentional and hyperactivity problems in children with sympathomimetic drugs: A comprehensive review. *Journal of the American Academy of Child Psychiatry, 29*, 677–688.

Janos, P. M., & Robinson, N. M. (1985). Psychosocial development in intellectually gifted children. In F. D. Horowitz & M. O'Brien (Eds.), *The gifted and talented: Developmental perspectives*. Washington, DC: American Psychological Association.

Janowsky, J. S., & Finlay, B. L. (1986). The outcome of perinatal brain damage: The role of normal neuron loss and axon retraction. *Developmental Medicine & Child Neurology, 28*, 375–389.

Janzen, L., & Nanson, J. (1993, March). *Neuropsychological evaluation of preschoolers with fetal alcohol syndrome*. Paper presented at the biennial meeting of the Society for Research in Child Development, New Orleans.

Javernik, E. (1988). Johnny's not jumping: Can we help obese children? *Young Children, 43*, 18–23.

Johnson, C., & Connors, M. E. (1987). *The etiology and treatment of bulimia nervosa: A biosocial perspective*. New York: Basic Books.

Johnson, L. D., Driscoll, S. G., Hertig, A. T., Cole, P. T., & Nickerson, R. J. (1979). Vaginal adenosis in stillborns and neonates exposed to diethylstilbestrol and steroidal estrogens and progestins. *Obstetrics & Gynecology, 53*, 671–679.

Jolly, A. (1972). *The evolution of primate behavior*. New York: MacMillan.

Jones, D. C., Swift, D. J., & Johnson, M. A. (1988). Nondeliberate memory for a novel event among preschoolers. *Developmental Psychology, 24*, 641–645.

Jones, E. F., Forrest, J. D., Goldman, N., Nenshaw, S. K., Lincoln, R., Rosoff, J. I., Westoff, C. F., & Sulf, D. (1985). Teenage pregnancy in developed countries: Determinants and policy implications. *Family Planning Perspectives, 17*, 53–63.

Jones, G. P., & Dembo, M. H. (1989). Age and sex role differences in intimate friendships during childhood and adolescence. *Merrill-Palmer Quarterly, 35*, 445–462.

Jones, M. C. (1957). The later careers of boys who were early- or late-maturing. *Child Development, 28*, 113–128.

———. (1965). Psychological correlates of somatic development. *Child Development, 36*, 899–911.

Jones, M. C., & Bayley, N. (1950). Physical maturing among boys as related to behavior. *Journal of Educational Psychology, 41*, 129–248.

Juel, C. (1988). Learning to read and write: A longitudinal study of 54 children from first through fourth grades. *Journal of Educational Psychology, 80*, 437–447.

Juel, C., Griffith, P., & Gough, P. (1986). The acquisition of literacy: A longitudinal study of children in first and second grades. *Journal of Educational Psychology, 78*, 243–255.

Kagan, J. (1984). *The nature of the child*. New York: Basic Books.

Kagan, J., Kearsley, R. B., & Zelazo, P. (1978). *Infancy: Its place in human development*. Cambridge, MA: Harvard University Press.

Kamptner, N. L. (1988). Identity development in late adolescence: Casual modeling of social and familial influences. *Journal of Youth and Adolescence, 17*, 493–514.

Kandel, D. B., Raveis, V. H., & Davies, M. (1991). Suicidal ideation in adolescence: Depression, substance use, and other risk factors. *Journal of Youth and Adolescence, 2*, 289–308.

Kashani, J. H., Goddard, P., & Reid, J. C. (1989). Correlates of suicidal ideation in a community sample of children and adolescents. *Journal of the American Academy of Child and Adolescent Psychiatry, 28*, 912–917.

Kashani, J. H., & Shepperd, J. A. (1990). Aggression in adolescents: The role of social support and personality. *Canadian Journal of Psychiatry, 35*, 311–315.

Kaufman, J., & Cicchetti, D. (1989). The effects of maltreatment on school-age children's socioemotional development. *Developmental Psychology, 25*, 516–524.

Kaufman, J., & Zigler, E. (1987). Do abused children become abusive parents? *American Journal of Orthopsychiatry, 57*, 186–192.

Kazdin, A. E. (1987). Treatment of antisocial behavior in children: Current status and future directions. *Psychological Bulletin, 102,* 187–203.

Keating, D. (1980). Thinking processes in adolescence. In J. Adelson (Ed.), *Handbook of adolescent psychology.* New York: Wiley.

Keeling, R. P. (1987). Effects of AIDS on young Americans. *Medical Aspects of Human Sexuality, 21,* 22–33.

Keeney, T. J., Cannizzo, S. R., & Flavell, J. H. (1967). Spontaneous and induced verbal rehearsal in a recall task. *Child Development, 38,* 953–966.

Keller, S. E., Bartlett, J. A., Schleifer, S. J., Johnson, R. L., Pinner, E., & Delaney, B. (1991). HIV-relevant sexual behavior among a healthy inner-city heterosexual adolescent population in an endemic area of HIV. *Journal of Adolescent Health, 12,* 44–48.

Kelley, J. T., & Patten, S. E. (1985). Adolescent behaviors and attitudes toward weight and eating. In J. Mitchell (Ed.), *Anorexia nervosa and bulimia: Diagnosis and treatment* (pp. 191–204). Minneapolis: University of Minnesota Press.

Kellman, P. J., & Spelke, E. S. (1983). Perception of partly occluded objects in infancy. *Cognitive Psychology, 15,* 483–524.

Kendall, P. (1990). *Advances in cognitive-behavioral research and therapy.* New York: Academic Press.

Kennedy, E. T., et al. (1982). Evaluation of the effect of WIC supplemental feeding on birthweight. *Journal of American Dietetic Association, 80,* 220–226.

Kennedy, J. H. (1991, April). *Relationship of maternal beliefs and childrearing strategies to social competence in preschool children.* Paper presented at the biennial meeting of the Society for Research in Child Development, Seattle.

Kennell, J. H., Jerauld, R., Wolfe, H., Chesler, D., Kreger, N. C., McAlpine, W., Steffa, M., & Klaus, M. H. (1974). Maternal behavior one year after early and extended post-partum contact. *Developmental Medicine & Child Neurology, 16,* 172–179.

Keogh, J., & Sugden, D. (1985). *Movement and skill development.* New York: Macmillan.

Kerlinger, F. N. (1979). *Behavioral research: A conceptual approach.* New York: Holt, Rinehart & Winston.

King, C. A., Raskin, A., Gdowski, C. L., Butku, M., & Opipari, L. (1990). Psychosocial factors associated with urban adolescent female suicide attempts. *Journal of the American Academy of Child and Adolescent Psychiatry, 29,* 289–294.

Kisilevsky, B. S., & Muir, D. W. (1984). Neonatal habituation and dishabituation to tactile stimulation during sleep. *Developmental Psychology, 20,* 367–373.

Kister, M. C., & Patterson, C. J. (1980). Children's conceptions of the causes of illness: Understanding contamination and use of immanent justice. *Child Development, 51,* 839–848.

Kitzinger, S. (1989). *The complete book of pregnancy and childbirth.* New York: Knopf.

Klahr, D. (1989). Information-processing approaches. In R. Vasta (Ed.), *Annals of child development* (Vol. 6, pp. 133–186). Greenwich, CT: JAI Press.

Klaus, M. H., Jerauld, R., Kreger, N. C., McAlpine, W., Steffa, M., & Kennell, J. H. (1972). Maternal attachment: Importance of the first postpartum days. *New England Journal of Medicine, 286,* 460–463.

Klaus, M. H., & Kennell, J. H. (1976). *Maternal-infant bonding.* St. Louis: Mosby.

Kleiber, D. A., Larson, R., & Csikszentmihalyi, M. (1986). The experience of leisure in adolescence. *Journal of Leisure Research, 18,* 169–176.

Kleiber, D. A., & Roberts, G. C. (1983). The relationship between fame and sport involvement in later childhood: A preliminary investigation. *Research Quarterly for Exercise and Sport, 54,* 200–203.

Klein, R. P. (1985). Caregiving arrangements by employing women with children under one year of age. *Developmental Psychology, 21,* 403–406.

Klesges, R. C. (1983). Parental influences on children's eating behavior and relative weight. *Journal of Applied Behavioral Analysis, 16*(4), 371–378.

Klesges, R. C., Malott, J. M., Boschee, P. F., & Weber, J. M. (1986). Parental influences on children's food intake, physical activity, and relative weight: An extension and replication. *International Journal of Eating Disorders, 5,* 335–346.

Kliewer, W., & Weidner, G. (1987). Type A behavior and aspirations: A study of parents' and children's goal setting. *Developmental Psychology, 23,* 204–209.

Knobloch, H., & Pasamanick, B. (Eds.) (1974). *Gesell and Amatruda's developmental diagnosis.* Hagerstown, MD: Harper & Row.

Kohlberg, L. (1966). A cognitive developmental analysis of children's sex-role concepts and attitudes. In E. E. Maccoby (Ed.), *The development of sex differences* (pp. 82–173). Stanford, CA: Stanford University Press.

———. (1969). Stage and sequence: The cognitive-developmental approach to socialization. In D. A. Goslin (Ed.), *Handbook of socialization theory and research* (pp. 347–480). Chicago: Rand McNally.

———. (1976). Moral stages and moralization: The cognitive-developmental approach. In T. Lickona (Ed.), *Moral development behavior: Theory, research and social issues.* New York: Holt, Rinehart & Winston.

———. (1984). *Essay on moral development, Vol. II: The psychology of moral development.* New York: Harper & Row.

Kohlberg, L., & Gilligan, C. (1971). The adolescent as a philosopher: The discovery of the self in a postconventional world. *Daedalus, 100,* 1051–1086.

Kolata, G. (1986). Obese children: A growing problem. *Science, 232,* 20–21.

Koluchova, J. (1972). Severe deprivation in twins: A case study. *Journal of Child Psychology and Psychiatry, 13,* 107–114.

———. (1976). A report on the further development of twins after severe and prolonged deprivation. In A. M. Clarke & A. D. B. Clarke (Eds.), *Early experience: Myth and evidence* (pp. 56–66). London: Open Books.

Kolvin, I., Taunch, J., Currah, J., Garside, R., Nolan, J., & Shaw, W. (1972). Enuresis: A descriptive analysis and controlled trial. *Developmental Psychology, 14,* 715–726.

Kopp, C. B. (1983). Risk factors in development. In P. S. Mussen, M. M. Haith, & J. J. Campos (Eds.), *Handbook of child psychology, Vol II: Infant and developmental psychobiology* (4th ed., pp. 1081–1088). New York: Wiley.

Korner, A. F. (1987). Preventive intervention with high-risk newborns: Theoretical, conceptual, and methodological perspectives. In J. D. Osofsky (Ed.), *Handbook of infant development* (pp. 1006–1036). New York: Wiley.

Kotelchuck, M. (1976). The infant's relationship to the father. In M. E. Lamb (Ed.), *The role of the father in child development*. New York: Wiley.

Krantz, M. (1982). Sociometric awareness, social participation, and perceived popularity in preschool children. *Child Development, 53,* 376–379.

Krauss, R. M., & Glucksberg, S. (1969). The development of communication: competence as a function of age. *Child Development, 42,* 255–266.

Kreutzer, M. A., Leonard, C., & Flavell, J. H. (1975). An interview study of children's knowledge about memory. *Monographs of the Society for Research in Child Development, 40*(1, Serial No. 159).

Kropp, J. P., & Haynes, O. M. (1987). Abusive and non-abusive mothers ability to identify general and specific emotional signals of infants. *Child Development, 58,* 187–190.

Kuhl, P., & Meltzoff, A. (1982). The bimodal perception of speech in infancy. *Science, 218,* 1138–1141.

———. (1984). The intermodal representation of speech in infants. *Infant Behavior and Development, 7,* 361–381.

Kuhn, D., Langer, J., Kohlberg, L., & Haan, N. (1977). The development of formal operations in logical and moral judgement. *Genetic Psychology Monographs, 95,* 97–188.

Kupersmidt, J. B., & Coie, J. D. (1990). Preadolescent peer status, aggression, and school adjustment as predictors of externalizing problems in adolescence. *Child Development, 61,* 1350–1362.

Kupersmidt, J. B., & Patterson, C. J. (1991). Childhood peer rejection, aggression, withdrawal, and perceived competence as predictors of self-reported behavior problems in adolescence. *Journal of Abnormal Child Psychology, 19,* 427–449.

Kurtz, B. E., & Borkowski, J. G. (1987). Development of strategic skills in impulsive/reflective children: A longitudinal study of metacognition. *Journal of Experimental Child Psychology, 43,* 129–148.

Kyllerman, M., Aronson, M., Sabel, K. G., Karlberg, E., Sandin, A., & Olegard, R. (1985). Children of alcoholic mothers. *ACTA, 74,* 20–26.

Ladd, G. W. (1983). Social networks of popular, average and rejected children in school settings. *Merrill-Palmer Quarterly, 29,* 283–308.

Ladd, G. W., & Golter, B. S. (1988). Parents' management of preschooler's peer relations: Is it related to children's social competence. *Developmental Psychology, 24,* 109–117.

La Freniere, P. J., & Charlesworth, W. R. (1987). Effects of friendship and dominance status on preschooler's resource utilization in a cooperative/competitive situation. *International Journal of Behavioral Development, 10,* 345–358.

La Freniere, P. J., Strayer, F. F., & Gauthier, R. (1984). The emergence of same-sex affiliative preferences among preschool peers: A developmental/ethological perspective. *Child Development, 55,* 1958–1965.

Lagercrantz, H., & Slotkin, T. A. (1986). The stress of being born. *Scientific American, 254*(4), 100–107.

Lamb, M. E. (1976a). Effects of stress and cohort on mother- and father-infant interaction. *Developmental Psychology, 12,* 435–444.

———. (1976b). Interactions between two-year-olds and their mothers and fathers. *Psychological Reports, 38,* 447–450.

———. (1976c). Twelve-month olds and their parents: Interaction in a laboratory playroom. *Developmental Psychology, 12,* 237–244.

———. (1977a). Father-infant and mother-infant interactions in the first year of life. *Child Development, 48,* 167–181.

———. (1977b). The development of mother-infant attachments in the second year of life. *Developmental Psychology, 13,* 637–648.

———. (1982). Early contact and maternal infant bonding: One decade later. *Pediatrics, 70,* 763–768.

Lamb, M. E., & Bronstein, M. H. (1987). *Development in infancy*. New York: Random House.

Lamborn, S. D., Mounts, N. S., Steinberg, L., & Dornbusch, S. M. (1991). Patterns of competence and adjustment among adolescents from authoritative, authoritarian, indulgent, and neglectful homes. *Child Development, 62,* 1049–1065.

Lampert, R. W., & Schochet, S. S. (1968). Demyelination and remyelination in lead neuropathy. *Journal of Neuropathology and Experimental Neurology, 27,* 527–545.

Lange, G., & Pierce, S. H. (1992). Memory-strategy learning and maintenance in preschool children. *Developmental Psychology, 28,* 453–462.

Langley, J. (1984). Injury control: Psychosocial considerations. *Journal of Child Psychology and Psychiatry, 25,* 349–356.

Langlois, J. H., & Downs, A. C. (1980). Mothers, fathers, and peers as socialization agents of sex-typed play behaviors in young children. *Child Development, 51,* 1237–1247.

Lapsley, D. K., Milstead, M., Quintana, S. M., Flannery, D., & Bus, R. R. (1986). Adolescent egocentrism and formal operations: Tests of a theoretical assumption. *Developmental Psychology, 22,* 800–807.

Larrance, D. T., & Twentymen, C. T. (1983). Maternal addictions and child abuse. *Journal of Abnormal Psychology, 92,* 449–457.

Larrieu, J., & Mussen, P. (1986). Some personality and motivational correlates of children's prosocial behavior. *Journal of Genetic Psychology, 147,* 529–542.

Larsen, J. M., & Robinson, C. C. (1989). Latter effects of preschool on low risk children. *Early Childhood Research, 4,* 133–144.

Larsen, R., & Richards, M. H. (1991). Daily companionship in late childhood and early adolescence: Changing developmental contexts. *Child Development, 62,* 284–300.

Lauersen, N. H. (1983). *Childbirth with love*. New York: Berkley Books.

——. (1987). *It's your pregnancy.* New York: Simon & Schuster.

Lawler, K. A., Allen, M. R., Critcher, E. C., & Standard, B. A. (1981). The relationship of physiological responses to the coronary-prone behavior pattern in children. *Journal of Behavioral Medicine, 4,* 203–216.

Leal, L., Crays, N., & Moely, A. E. (1985). Training children to use a self-monitoring study strategy and generalization effects. *Child Development, 56,* 643–653.

Leboyer, F. (1975). *Birth without violence.* New York: Random House.

Lee, A. M., Carter, J. A., & Greenockle, K. M. (1987). Children and fitness: A pedagogical perspective. *Research Quarterly for Exercise and Sports, 58,* 321–325.

Lee, M., & Prentice, N. (1988). Interrelations of empathy, cognition, and moral reasoning with dimensions of juvenile delinquency. *Journal of Abnormal Child Psychology, 16,* 127–139.

Lee, V. E., Brooks-Gunn, J., & Schnur, E. (1988). Does Head Start work? A 1-year follow-up comparison of disadvantaged children after Head Start, no pre-school and other pre-school programs. *Developmental Psychology, 24*(2), 210–222.

LeFevre, J., & Kulak, A. (1991, April). *Assessing the uniqueness of math anxiety in children.* Paper presented at the biennial meeting of the Society for Research in Child Development, Seattle.

Leibenberg, B. (1967). Expectant fathers. *American Journal of Orthopsychiatry, 37,* 358–359.

Leikowitz, L. J. (1972). Ability grouping: Defacto segregation in the classroom. *Clearing House, 46,* 293–297.

Leinbach, M. D., & Fagot, B. I. (1986). Acquisition of gender labelling: A test for toddlers. *Sex Roles, 15,* 655–666.

Leming, J. S. (1978). Cheating behavior, situational influence, and moral development. *Journal of Educational Research, 71,* 214–217.

Lempers, J. D., Flavell, E. R., & Flavell, J. H. (1977). The development in young children of tacit knowledge concerning visual perception. *Genetic Psychology Monographs, 95,* 3–53.

Lenneberg, E. H. (1967). *Biological foundations of language.* New York: Wiley.

Lenz, W. (1966). Malformations caused by drugs in pregnancy. *American Journal of Disorders of Children, 112,* 99–106.

Lepore, S. J., Kiely, M. C., Bempechat, J., & London, P. (1989). Children's perceptions of social ability: Social cognitions and behavioral outcomes in the face of social rejection. *Child Study Journal, 19,* 259–271.

Lerner, R. M. (1969a). The development of stereotyped expectancies of body build–behavior relations. *Child Development, 40,* 137–141.

——. (1969b). Some female stereotypes of male body build–behavior relations. *Perceptual & Motor Skills, 28,* 363–366.

——. (1971). "Richness" analyses of body build stereotype development. *Developmental Psychology, 7,* 219.

Lerner, R. M., & Busch-Rossnagel, N. A. (1981). Individuals as producers of their development: Conceptual and empirical bases. In R. M. Lerner & N. A. Busch-Rossnagel (Eds.), *Individuals as producers of their development: A life span perspective* (pp. 1–36). New York: Academic Press.

Lerner, R. M., & Gellert, E. (1969). Body build identification, preference, and aversion in children. *Developmental Psychology, 1,* 456–462.

Lerner, R. M., & Jovanovic, J. (1990). The role of body image in psychosocial development across the lifespan: A developmental contextual perspective. In T. F. Cash, & T. Pruzinsky (Eds.). *Body Images: Development, deviance, and change* (pp. 110–127). New York: Guilford.

Lerner, R. M., & Korn, S. J. (1972). The development of body build stereotypes in males. *Child Development, 43,* 912–920.

Lerner, R. M., & Lerner, J. V. (1977). Effects of age, sex, and physical attractiveness on child-peer relations, academic performance, and elementary school adjustment. *Developmental Psychology, 13,* 585–590.

Lerner, R. M., & Schroeder, C. (1971a). Kindergarten children's active vocabulary about body build. *Developmental Psychology, 5,* 179.

——. (1971b). Physique identification, preference, and aversion in kindergarten children. *Developmental Psychology, 5,* 538.

Lesko, W., & Lesko, M. (1984). *The maternity sourcebook.* New York: Warner Books.

Lester, B. M., Hoffman, J., & Brazelton, T. B. (1985). The rhythmic structure of mother-infant interactions in term and pre-term infants. *Child Development, 56,* 15–27.

Leventhal, A. S., & Lipsitt, L. P. (1964). Adaptation, pitch discrimination, and sound localization in the neonate. *Child Development, 35,* 759–767.

Levine, M. P. (1987). *Student eating disorders: Anorexia nervosa and bulimia.* Washington, DC: National Education Association.

Levy, A. K., Schaefer, L., & Phelps, P. C. (1986). Increasing preschool effectiveness: Enhancing the language abilities of 3- and 4-year-old children through planned sociodramatic play. *Early Childhood Research Quarterly, 1,* 133–140.

Levy, H. L., Kaplan, G. N., & Erickson, A. M. (1982). Comparison of treated and untreated pregnancies in a mother with phenylketonuria. *Journal of Pediatrics, 6,* 876–880.

Lewis, M. (1987). Social development in infancy and early childhood. In J. D. Osofsky (Ed.), *Handbook of infant development* (2nd ed., pp. 419–493. New York: Wiley.

Lewis, M., & Brooks-Gunn, J. (1979). *Social cognition and the acquisition of self.* New York: Plenum Press.

Lewis, M., Feiring, C., McGuffog, C., & Jaskir, J. (1984). Predicting psychopathology in six-year-olds from early social relations. *Child Development, 55,* 123–136.

Lewis, M., & Michalson, L. (1982). The socialization of emotions. In T. Field & A. Fogel (Eds.), *Emotion and early interaction* (pp. 189–212). Hillsdale, NJ: Erlbaum.

——. (1983). *Children's emotions and minds: Developmental theory and measurement.* New York: Plenum Press.

Lieberman, E., & Ryan, K. J. (1989). Birth-day choices. *New England Journal of Medicine, 321,* 1824–1825.

Lifshitz, G., Pugliese, M. T., Moses, N., & Weyman-Daum, M. (1987). Parental healthy beliefs and a cause of non-organic-failure-to-thrive. *Pediatrics, 80,* 175–182.

Linney, J. A., & Seidman, E. (1989). The future of schooling. *American Psychologist, 44*(2), 336–340.

Liptak, G. S., Keller, B. B., Feldman, A. W., & Chamberlain, R. W. (1983) Enhancing infant development and parent practitioner interaction with the Brazelton NBAS. *Pediatrics, 72,* 71–78.

Livson, N., & Peskin, H. (1980). Perspectives on adolescence from longitudinal research. In J. Adelson (Ed.), *Handbook of adolescent psychology,* New York: Wiley.

Loda, F. A. (1980). Daycare. *Pediatrics in Review, 1*(9), 277–281.

Lodico, M. G., Ghatala, E. S., Levin, J. R., Pressley, M., & Bell, J. A. (1983). The effects of strategy-monitoring on children's selection of effective memory strategies. *Journal of Experimental Child Psychology, 35,* 263–277.

Lorenz, K. Z.(1937). The companion in the bird's world. *Auk, 54,* 245–273.

———. (1952). *King Solomon's ring.* New York: Thomas Y. Crowell.

———. (1971). *Studies in animal and human behavior* (Vol. 2). Cambridge, MA: Harvard University Press.

Lowrey, G. H. (1978). *Growth and development of young children* (7th ed.). Chicago: Year Book Medical.

Lozoff, B. (1989). Nutrition and behavior. *American Psychologist, 44,* 231–236.

Lundberg, U. (1983). Note on Type-A behavior and cardiovascular responses to challenge in 3–6 year old children. *Journal of Psychosomatic Research, 27,* 39–42.

Lyons-Ruth, K., Connell, D., Zoll, D., & Stahl, J. (1987). Infants at social risk: Relationships among infant maltreatment, maternal behavior, and infant attachment behavior. *Developmental Psychology, 23,* 223–232.

Lytton, H., & Romney, D. M. (1991). Parents differential socialization of boys and girls: A meta-analysis. *Psychological Bulletin, 109,* 267–296.

Maccoby, E. E. (1980). *Social development.* New York: Harcourt Brace Jovanovich.

———. (1988). Gender as a social category. *Developmental Psychology, 24,* 755–765.

Maccoby, E. E., & Jacklin, C. N. (1974). *The psychology of sex differences.* Stanford, CA: Stanford University Press.

———. (1987). Gender segregation in childhood. In *Advances in child development and behavior, 20.* New York: Academic Press.

Maccoby, E. E., & Martin, J. A. (1983). Socialization in the context of the family: Parent-child interaction. In E. M. Hetherington (Ed.), *Handbook of child psychology. Vol. 4: Socialization, personality and social development.* (4th ed., pp. 1–101, New York: Wiley.

MacConnie, S. E., Gilliam, T. B., Geenen, D. L., & Pels, A. E., III. (1982). Daily physical activity patterns of prepubertal children involved in a vigorous exercise program. *International Journal of Sports Medicine, 32,* 202–207.

MacKinnon, C. E. (1989). An observational investigation of sibling interactions in married and divorced families. *Developmental Psychology, 25,* 36–44.

MacLean, M., Bryant, P., & Bradley, L. (1987). Rhymes, nursery rhymes, and reading in early childhood. *Merrill-Palmer Quarterly, 33,* 255–281.

Magnusson, D., Stattin, H., & Allen, V. L. (1985). Biological maturation and social development: A longitudinal study of some adjustment processes from mid-adolescence to adulthood. *Journal of Youth and Adolescence, 14,* 267–283.

———. (1986). Differential maturation among girls and its relation to social adjustment in a longitudinal perspective. In D. L. Featherman & R. M. Lerner (Eds.), *Life-span development* (Vol. 7). New York: Academic Press.

Mahler, M. S., Pine, F., & Bergman, A. (1975). *The psychological birth of the human infant.* New York: Basic Books.

Main, M., & George, C. (1985). Responses of abused and disadvantaged toddlers to distress in agemates: A study in the daycare setting. *Developmental Psychology, 21,* 407–412.

Main, M., & Goldwyn, R. (1984). Predicting rejection of her infant from mother's representation of her own experience: Implications for the abused-abusing intergenerational cycle. *Journal of Child Abuse & Neglect, 8,* 203–217.

Main, M., Kaplan, N., & Cassidy, J. (1985). Security in infancy, childhood and adulthood: A move to the level of representation. *Monographs of the Society for Research in Child Development, 50*(1-2, Serial No. 209).

Main, M., & Solomon, J. (1986). Discovery of an insecure disorganized/disoriented attachment pattern: Procedures, findings, and implications for the classification of behavior. In T. B. Brazelton & M. W. Yogman (Eds.), *Affective development in infancy* (pp. 95–124). Norwood, NJ: Ablex.

Main, M., & Weston, D. R. (1981). The quality of the toddler's relationship to mother and to father: Related to conflict behavior and the readiness to establish new relationships. *Child Development, 52,* 932–940.

Malatesta, C. Z., Culver, C., Tesman, J. R., & Shepard, B. (1989). The development of emotion expression during the first two years of life. *Monographs of the Society for Research in Child Development, 54*(1-2, Serial No. 219).

Malatesta, C. Z., Grigoryev, P., Lamb, C., Albin, M., & Culver, C. (1986). Emotion socialization and expressive development in preterm and full term infants. *Child Development, 57,* 316–330.

Malatesta, C. Z., & Haviland, J. M. (1982). Learning display rules: The socialization of emotion expression in infancy. *Child Development, 53,* 991–1003.

Maratsos, M. P. (1973). Nonegocentric communication abilities in preschool children. *Child Development, 44,* 697–700.

———. (1983). Some current issues in the study of the acquisition of grammar. In J. H. Flavell & E. M. Markman (Eds.), *Handbook of child psychology: Vol. 3.* Cognitive development (4th ed., pp. 707–786). New York: Wiley.

March of Dimes. (1986). Low birthweight. *Public Health Education Information Sheet #09-285-00.*

———. (1987). Congenital AIDS. *Public Health Education Information Sheet #09-360-00.*

———. (1989). Infections during pregnancy: Toxoplasmosis and chlamydia. *Public Health Education Information Sheet #09-408-00.*

Marcia, J. E. (1966). Development and validation of ego identity status. *Journal of Personality and Social Psychology, 3,* 551–558.

———. (1980). Identity in adolescence. In J. Adelson (Ed.), *Handbook of adolescent psychology.* New York: Wiley.

Marcovitch, S., Krekewich, K., Campbell, L., Goldberg, S., & MacGregor, D. (1991, April). *Predictors of behavior problems in developmentally disabled school age children.* Paper presented at the biennial meeting of the Society for Research in Child Development, Seattle.

Maris, R. (1985). The adolescent suicide problem. *Suicide Life-Threat Behavior, 15,* 91–109.

Markstrom, C. A. (1987, April). *A comparison of psychosocial maturity between four ethnic groups during middle adolescence.* Paper presented at the biennial meeting of the Society for Research in Child Development, Baltimore.

Marshall, W. (1978). Puberty. In F. Falkener & J. Tanner (Eds.), *Human growth* (Vol. 2). New York: Plenum Press.

Martin, R. J., Herrell, N., Rubin, D., & Farnoff, A. (1979). Effect of supine and prone positions on arterial oxygenation in the preterm infant. *Pediatrics, 63,* 528–531.

Marvin, R. S. (1972). Attachment and cooperative behavior in two-, three-, and four-year-olds. Unpublished doctoral dissertation, University of Chicago.

———. (1977). An ethnological cognitive model for the attenuation of mother-child attachment behavior. In T. M. Alloway, L. Krames, & P. Piner (Eds.), *Advances in the study of communication and affect. Vol. 3: The development of attachments* (pp. 25–60). New York: Plenum Press.

Marwick, C., & Simmons, K. (1984). Changing childhood disease patterns linked with day-care boom. *Journal of the American Medical Association, 215,* 1245–1251.

Mast, V. K., Fagen, J. W., Rovee-Collier, C. K., & Sullivan, M. W. (1980). Immediate and long-term memory for reinforcement context: The development of learned expectancies in early infancy. *Child Development, 51,* 196–202.

Masters, J. C., & Furman, W. (1981). Popularity, individual friendship selection, and specific peer interaction among children. *Developmental Psychology, 17,* 344–350.

Matheny, A. P., Jr. (1985, April). *Toddler temperament and accident liability within twinships.* Paper presented at the biennial meeting of the Society for Research in Child Development, Toronto.

———. (1987). Psychological characteristics of childhood accidents. *Journal of Social Issues, 43,* 45–60.

Matheny, A. P., Jr., Brown, A., & Wilson, R. S. (1971). Behavioral antecedents of accidental injuries in early childhood. *Journal of Pediatrics, 79,* 122–124.

Matsumoto, D., Haan, N., Yabrove, G., Theodorou, P., & Carney, C. C. (1986). Preschooler's moral actions and emotions in prisoner's dilemma. *Developmental Psychology, 22,* 663–670.

Matthews, K. A., & Angulo, J. (1980). Measurement of the Type A behavior pattern in children: Assessment of children's competitiveness, impatience-anger, and aggression. *Child Development, 51,* 466–475.

Matthews, K. A., & Jennings, R. J. (1984). Cardiovascular responses of boys exhibiting the Type A behavior pattern. *Psychosomatic Medicine, 46,* 484–497.

Matthews, K. A., & Siegel, J. (1983). Type A behaviors by children: Social comparisons and standards for self-evaluation. *Developmental Psychology, 19,* 135–140.

Matthews, K. A., & Volkin, J. (1981). Efforts to excel and Type A behavior. *Child Development, 52,* 1283–1289.

Maurer, D., & Barrera, M. (1981). Infants' perception of natural and distorted arrangements of a schematic face. *Child Development, 52,* 196–202.

Maurer, D., & Salapatek, P. (1976). Developmental changes in the scanning of faces by young infants. *Child Development, 47,* 523–527.

McCabe, A. E., Siegel, L. S., Spence, I., & Wilkerson, A. (1982). Class inclusion reasoning: Patterns of performance from three to eight years. *Child Development, 53,* 780–785.

McCartney, K. (1984). Effect of quality of day care environment on children's language development. *Developmental Psychology, 20,* 244–260.

McCartney, K., Scarr, S., Phillips, D., & Grajek, S. (1985). Day care as intervention: Comparison of varying quality programs. *Journal of Applied Developmental Psychology, 6,* 247–260.

McCauley, E., Ito, J., & Kay, T. (1986). Psychosocial functioning in girls with Turner Syndrome and short stature. *Journal of the Academy of Child Psychiatry, 25,* 105–112.

McCutcheon-Rosegg, S., & Rosegg, P. (1984). *Natural childbirth the Bradley way.* New York: Dutton.

McGraw, M. B. (1935/1975). *Growth: A study of Johnny and Jimmy.* New York: Arno Press.

———. (1977, March). *Theories and techniques of child development research during the 1930s.* Invited address at the biennial meeting of the Society for Research in Child Development, New Orleans.

McGrory, A. (1990). Menarche: Responses of early adolescent females. *Adolescence, 25,* 265–270.

McGuire, K. D., & Weisz, J. R. (1982). Social cognition and behavior of preadolescent chumship. *Child Development, 53,* 1478–1484.

McKusick, V. A. (1986). *Mendelian inheritance in man.* Baltimore: Johns Hopkins University Press.

McLaughlin, R. D., & Ross, S. M. (1989). Student cheating in high school: A case for moral reasoning vs. "fuzzy logic." *High School Journal, 72,* 97–104.

McLaughlin, R. J., Baer, P. E., Burnside, M. A., & Pokorny, A. D. (1985). Psychosocial correlates of alcohol use at two age levels during adolescence. *Journal of the Study of Alcohol, 46,* 212–218.

McNeill, D. (1970). The development of language. In P. H. Mussen (Ed.), *Carmichael's manual of child psychology* (3rd ed., Vol. 1, pp. 1061–1161). New York: Wiley.

McWilliams, M. (1986). *The parents' nutrition book*. New York: Wiley.

Meece, J. L., Wigfield, A., & Eccles, J. S. (1990). Predictors of math anxiety and its influence on young adolescents' course enrollment intentions and performance in mathematics. *Journal of Educational Psychology, 82*, 60–70.

Melton, G. B., & Davidson, H. A. (1987). Child protection and society: When should the state intervene?. *American Psychologist, 42*, 172–175.

Meltzoff, A. N., & Moore, M. K. (1977). Imitation of facial and manual gestures by human neonates. *Science, 198*, 75–78.

Menig-Peterson, C. L. (1975). The modification of communicative behavior of preschool-aged children as a function of the listener's perspective. *Child Development, 46*, 1015–1018.

Messer, S. C., Wuensch, K. L., & Diamond, J. M. (1989). Former latch-key children: Personality and academic correlates. *Journal of Genetic Psychology, 150*, 301–309.

Milewski, A. E. (1976). Infants' discrimination of internal and external pattern elements. *Journal of Experimental Child Psychology, 22*, 229–246.

Miller, B. C., & Fox, G. L. (1987). Theories of adolescent sexual behavior. *Journal of Adolescent Research, 2*, 269–282.

Miller, B. C., McCoy, J. K., Olson, T. D., & Wallace, C. M. (1986). Parental discipline and control attempts in relation to adolescent sexual behavior. *Journal of Marriage and the Family, 48*, 503–512.

Miller, C. L., O'Callaghan, M. F., Whitman, T. L., & White, R. (1993, March). *The effects of the NICU environment on infant behavior and development*. Paper presented at the biennial meeting of the Society for Research in Child Development, New Orleans.

Miller, P. H. (1990). The development of strategies of selective attention. In D. F. Bjorklund (Ed.), *Children's strategies: Contemporary views of cognitive development*. Hillsdale, NJ: Erlbaum.

Miller, P. H., Seier, W. L., Probert, J. S., & Aloise, P. A. (1991, April). *Age differences in capacity demands of a strategy among spontaneously strategic children*. Paper presented at the biennial meeting of the Society for Research in Child Development, Seattle.

Miller, P. H., & Weiss, M. G. (1981). Children's attention allocation, understanding of attention, and performance on the incidental learning task. *Child Development, 52*, 1183–1190.

Miller, S. (1978). The facilitation of fundamental motor skill learning in young children. Unpublished doctoral dissertation, Michigan State University, East Lansing.

Milunsky, A. (1989). *Choices, not chance*. Boston: Little, Brown.

Minde, K., Perrotta, M., & Hellmann, J. (1988). Impact of delayed development in premature infants on mother-infant interaction: A prospective investigation. *Journal of Pediatrics, 112*, 136–142.

Minuchin, S. (1974). *Families and family therapy*. Cambridge, MA: Harvard University Press.

Minuchin, S., Rosman, B., & Baker, L. (1978). *Psychosomatic anorexia nervosa in context*. Cambridge, MA: Harvard University Press.

Miyake, K., Chen, S.-J., & Campos, J. J. (1985). Infant temperament, mother's mode of interaction, and attachment in Japan: An interim report. In I. Bretherton & E. Waters (Eds.), Growing points of attachment theory and research. *Monographs of the Society for Research in Child Development, 50*(1-2, Serial No. 209).

Mize, J., & Ladd, G. W. (1990). A cognitive-social learning approach to social skill training with low-status preschool children. *Developmental Psychology, 26*, 388–397.

Moely, B. E., Hart, S. S., Leal, L., Johnson, T., Rao, N., & Burney, L. (1986). How do teachers teach memory skills? *Educational Psychologist, 21*, 55–71.

Moffit, T. E. (1990). Juvenile delinquency and attention deficit disorder: Boys' developmental trajectories from age 3 to 15. *Child Development, 61*, 893–910.

Moore, K. A., Peterson, J. L., & Furstenberg, F. F. (1986). Parental attitudes and the occurrence of early sexual activity. *Journal of Marriage and the Family, 48*, 772–782.

Moore, K. L. (1989). *Before we are born* (3rd ed.). Philadelphia: Saunders.

Moore, T. R., Origel, W., Key, T. C., & Resnik, R. (1986). The perinatal and economic impact of prenatal care in a low socio-economic population. *American Journal of Obstetrics and Gynecology, 154*, 29–33.

Morris, A. M., Williams, J. L., Atwater, A. E., & Wilmore, J. H. (1982). Age and sex differences in motor performance of 3- through 6-year-old children. *Research Quarterly for Exercise and Sport, 53*, 214–221.

Morrison, D. M. (1985). Adolescent contraceptive behavior: A review. *Psychological Bulletin, 88*, 538–568.

Morrongiello, B. A., Anderson, S., & Rocca, P. (1991, April). *Masking of negative emotion by blind and sighted children*. Paper presented at the biennial meeting of the Society for Research in Child Development, Seattle.

Muir, D., & Field, J. (1979). Newborn infants orient to sound. *Child Development, 50*, 431–436.

Mullis, V. S., & Jenkins, L. B. (1988). *The science report card: Elements of risk and recovery. Trends and achievement based on the 1986 National Assessment*. Princeton, NJ: Educational Testing Service.

Munroe, R., Munroe, R., & Whiting, J. (1981). Male sex-role resolutions. In *Handbook of cross-cultural human development* (pp. 611–632). New York: Garland.

Murray, A. D., Dolby, R. M., Nation, R. L., & Thomas, D. B. (1981). Effects of epidural anesthesia on newborns and their mothers. *Child Development, 52*, 71–82.

Mussen, P., & Eisenberg-Berg, N. (1977). *The roots of caring, sharing and helping*. San Francisco: W. H. Freeman.

Mussen, P. H., & Jones, M. C. (1957). Self-conceptions, motivations, and interpersonal attitudes of late- and early-maturing boys. *Child Development, 28*, 243–256.

Naeye, R. L. (1978). Relationship of cigarette smoking to congenital anomalies and perinatal death.

American Journal of Pathology, 90, 269–293.

Nagy, W. E., & Anderson, R. C. (1984). How many words are there in printed school English? *Reading Research Quarterly, 19,* 304–330.

National Assessment of Educational Progress. (1986). *The reading report card: Progress toward excellence in our schools. Trends in reading over four national assessments 1971–1984.* Princeton, NJ: (NAEP) Educational Testing Service.

National Institute of Child Health & Human Development. (1987). *Behavior mechanisms and causes of childhood injury.* RFA.

Nelson, C. A., & Horowitz, F. D. (1982). The short-term behavioral sequelae of neonatal jaundice treated with phototherapy. *Infant Behavior and Development, 5,* 289–299.

Nelson, K. (1973). Structure and strategy in learning to talk. *Monographs of the Society for Research in Child Development, 38*(1-2).

———. (1977). Facilitating children's syntax acquisition. *Developmental Psychology, 13,* 101–107.

———. (1981a). Individual differences in language development: Implications for development and language. *Developmental Psychology, 17,* 170–187.

———. (1981b). Social cognition in a script framework. In J. H. Flavell & L. Ross (Eds.), *Social cognitive development* (pp. 97–118). Cambridge: Cambridge University Press.

Nelson, K., & Gruendel, J. M. (1979). At morning it's lunchtime: A scriptal view of children's dialogues. *Discourse Processes, 2,* 73–94.

Nesher, P. (1986). Learning mathematics: A cognitive perspective. *American Psychologist, 41,* 1114–1122.

Neutra, R., et al. (1978). The effect of fetal monitoring on neonatal death rate. *New England Journal of Medicine, 299,* 324–326.

Newcomb, M. D., & Bentler, P. M. (1989). Substance use and abuse among children and teenagers. *American Psychologist, 44,* 242–248.

Newcomb, M. D., Maddahian, E., & Bentler, P. M. (1986). Risk factors for drug use among adolescents: Concurrent and longitudinal analyses. *American Journal of Public Health, 76,* 525–531.

Nicolich, L. (1977). Beyond sensorimotor intelligence: Assessment of symbolic maturity through analysis of pretend play. *Merrill-Palmer Quarterly, 23,* 89–99.

Nieberg, P., Marks, J. S., McLaren, N. M., & Remington, P. L. (1985). The fetal tobacco syndrome. *Journal of the American Medical Association, 253,* 2998–2999.

Noonan, J. (1990). Readability problems presented by mathematics text. *Early Child Development and Care, 54,* 57–81.

Norbeck, J. S., & Tilden, V. P. (1983). Life stress, social support, and emotional disequilibrium in complications of pregnancy. *Journal of Health and Social Behavior, 24,* 30–46.

Norton, E. M., Durlak, J. A., & Richards, M. H. (1989). Peer knowledge of and reactions to adolescent suicide. *Journal of Youth and Adolescence, 18,* 427–437.

Nowakowski, R. S. (1987). Basic concepts of CNS development. *Child Development, 58,* 568–595.

Oates, R. K., Peacock, A., & Forest, D. (1985). Long-term effects of nonorganic failure to thrive. *Pediatrics, 75,* 36–40.

O'Connor, B. P., & Nikolic, J. (1990). Identity development and formal operations as sources of adolescent egocentrism. *Journal of Youth and Adolescence, 19,* 149–158.

O'Connor, M. J., Sigman, M., & Brill, N. (1987). Disorganization of attachment in relation to maternal alcohol consumption. *Journal of Consulting and Clinical Psychology, 55,* 831–836.

O'Donnell, L., & Steuve, A. (1983). Mothers as social agents: Structuring the community activities of school aged children. In H. Lopata & J. H. Pleck (Eds.), *Research in the interweave of social roles: Jobs and families (Vol. 3), families and jobs.* Greenwich, CT: JAI Press.

Okagaki, L., & Sternberg, R. J. (1993). Parental beliefs and children's school performance. *Child Development, 64,* 36–56.

O'Keefe, B. J., & Benoit, P. J. (1982). Children's arguments. In J. R. Cox & C. A. Willard (Eds.), *Advances in argumentation theory and research* (pp. 154–183). Carbondale: Southern Illinois University Press.

Olweus, D. (1980). Familial and temperamental determinants of aggressive behavior in adolescent boys: A causal analysis. *Developmental Psychology, 16,* 644–660.

Ordman, A. M., & Kirschenbaum, D. S. (1985). Cognitive-behavioral therapy for bulimia: An initial outcome study. *Journal of Consulting and Clinical Psychology, 53,* 305–313.

Owen, M. T., Easterbrooks, M. A., Chase-Lansdale, P. L., & Goldberg, W. (1984). The relation between maternal employment and the stability of attachments to mother and father. *Child Development, 55,* 1894–1901.

Palkovitz, R. (1984). Parental attitudes and fathers' interactions with their 5-month-old infants. *Developmental Psychology, 20,* 1054–1060.

Paneth, N., Kiely, M. A., Wallenstein, S., Marcus, M., Pakter, J., & Susser, M. (1982). Newborn intensive care and neonatal mortality on low birthweight infants. *New England Journal of Medicine, 307,* 149–155.

Panneton, R. K. (1985). *Prenatal auditory experience with melodies: Effects on postnatal auditory preferences in human newborns.* Unpublished doctoral dissertation, University of North Caroline-Greensboro.

Papousek, H., & Papousek, M. (1975). Cognitive aspects of preverbal social interactions between human infants and adults. In *Parent-infant interaction. Ciba Foundation Symposium, 33,* (New Series), Amsterdam: Elsevier.

Parcel, G. S., Simons-Morton, B. G., O'Hara, N. M., Baranowski, T., Kolbe, L. J., & Bee, D. E. (1987). School promotion of healthful diet and exercise behavior: An integration of organizational change and social learning theory intervention. *Journal of School Health, 57,* 150–156.

Paris, S. G., & Oka, E. R. (1986). Children's reading strategies, metacognition, and motivation. *Developmental Review, 6,* 25–56.

Paris, S. G., & Winograd, P. (1990). How metacognition can promote children's academic learning. In B. Jones & L. Idol (Eds.), *Dimensions of thinking* (pp. 15–51). Hillsdale, NJ: Erlbaum.

Parke, K. A., & Waters, E. (1989). Security of attachment and preschool friendships. *Child Development, 60,* 1079–1081.

Parke, R. D., & Bhavnagri, N. P. (1989). Parents as managers of children's peer relationships. In D. Belle (Ed.), *Children's social networks and social supports* (pp. 241–259). New York: Wiley.

Parke, R. D., & Collmer, C. W. (1975). Child abuse: An interdisciplinary analysis. In E. M. Hetherington (Ed.), *Review of child development research* (Vol. 5, pp. 509–590). Chicago: University of Chicago Press.

Parke, R. D., & Deur, J. L. (1972). Schedule of punishment and inhibition of aggression in children. *Developmental Psychology, 7,* 266–269.

Parke, R. D., & Sawin, D. B. (1980). The family in early infancy. In F. Pederson (Ed.). *The father-infant relationship: Observational studies in the family setting* (pp. 44–70). New York: Praeger.

Parker, F. L., Piotrkowski, S. S., & Peay, L. (1987). Head Start as a social support for mothers. *American Journal of Orthopsychiatry, 57,* 220–233.

Parker, J. G., & Asher, S. R. (1987). Peer relations and later personal adjustment: Are low-accepted children "at-risk"? *Psychological Bulletin, 102,* 357–389.

Parker, J. G., & Gottman, J. M. (1989). Social and emotional development in a relational context: Friendship interaction from early childhood to adolescence. In T. J. Berndt & G. W. Ladd (Eds.), *Peer relationships in child development* (pp. 95–132). New York: Wiley.

Parkhurst, J. T., & Asher, S. R. (1992). Peer rejection in middle school: Subgroup differences in behavior, loneliness, and interpersonal concerns. *Developmental Psychology, 28,* 231–241.

Parmelee, A. H. (1986). Children's illnesses: Their beneficial effects on behavioral development. *Child Development, 57,* 1–10.

Parmelee, A. H., Wenner, W. H., & Schulz, H. R. (1964). From birth to 16 weeks of age. *Journal of Pediatrics, 65,* 576.

Parten, M. B. (1932). Social participation among preschool children.

Journal of Abnormal and Social Psychology, 27, 243–269.

Pasnak, R. (1987). Acceleration of cognitive development of kindergarteners. *Psychology in the Schools, 24,* 358–363.

Pasnak, R., Brown, K., Kurkjian, M., Mattran, K., Triana, E., & Yammamoto, N. (1987). Cognitive gains through training on classification, seriation, and conservation. *Genetic, Social and General Psychology Monographs, 113,* 293–321.

Pastor, D. (1981). The quality of mother-infant attachment and its relationship to toddlers' initial sociability with peers. *Developmental Psychology, 17,* 326–335.

Patterson, G. R. (1982). *Coercive family processes.* Eugene, OR: Castilia Press.

Patterson, G. R., DeBaryshe, B. D., & Ramsey, E. (1989). A developmental perspective on antisocial behavior. *American Psychologist, 44,* 329–335.

Patterson, G. R., Littman, R. A., & Bricker, W. (1967). Assertive behavior in children: A step toward a theory of aggression. *Monographs of the Society for Research in Child Development, 32*(5, Serial No. 113).

Patton, G. C. (1988). The spectrum of eating disorder in adolescence. *Journal of Psychosomatic Research, 32,* 579–584.

Paxton, S. J., Wertheim, E. H., Gibbons, K., Szmukler, G. I., Hillier, L., & Pretrovich, J. L. (1991). Body image satisfaction, dieting beliefs, and weight loss behaviors in adolescent girls. *Journal of Youth and Adolescence, 20,* 361–379.

Pearson, D. A., & Lane, D. M. (1991, April). *Cueing effects in covert visual attention of children with attention deficit hyperactivity disorder.* Paper presented at the biennial meeting of the Society for Research in Child Development, Seattle.

Pedersen, F. A., Cain, R., & Zaslow, M. (1982). Variation in infant experience associated with alternative family roles. In L. M. Laosa & I. E. Sigel (Eds.), *Families as learning environments for children.* New York: Plenum Press.

Pedersen, F. A., & Robson, K. S. (1969). Father participation in infancy. *American Journal of Orthopsychiatry, 39,* 466–472.

Pedersen, F. A., Zaslow, M. J., Cain, R. L., & Anderson, B. J. (1981). Cesarean childbirth: Psychological implications for mothers and fathers. *Infant Mental Health Journal, 2,* 257–263.

Penner, S. G. (1987). Parental responses to grammatical and ungrammatical child utterances. *Child Development, 58,* 376–384.

Pennington, B. F., Bender, B., Puck, M., Salbenblatt, J., & Borinson, A. (1982). Learning disabilities in children with sex chromosome anomalies. *Child Development, 53,* 1182–1192.

Perry, M. A., Wells, E. A., & Doran, L. D. (1983). Parent characteristics in abusing and nonabusing families. *Journal of Clinical Child Psychology, 12,* 329–336.

Peters, D. L., Neisworth, J. T., & Yawkey, T. D. (1985). *Early childhood education: From theory to practice.* Monterey, CA: Brooks/Cole.

Petersen, A. (1986, April). *Early adolescence: A critical development transition?* Paper presented at the biennial meeting of the Educational Research Association, San Francisco.

Petersen, A., & Taylor, B. (1980). The biological approach to adolescence: Biological change and psychological adaptation. In J. Adelson (Ed.), *Handbook of adolescent psychology* (pp. 117–155). New York: Wiley.

Petitti, D. B., & Coleman, C. (1990). Cocaine and the risk of low birth weight. *American Journal of Public Health, 80,* 25–28.

Phinney, J. S. (1989). Stages of ethnic identity development. *Journal of Early Adolescence, 9,* 34–49.

Phinney, V. G., Jensen, L. C., Olsen, J. A., & Cundick, B. (1990). The relationship between early development and psychosexual behaviors in adolescent females. *Adolescence, 25,* 321–332.

Piaget, J. (1926). *The language and thought of the child.* New York: Harcourt Brace & Company.

———. (1929). *The child's conception of the world.* New York: Harcourt & Brace.

———. (1930). *The child's conception of physical causality.* London: Kegan Paul.

———. (1932/1965). *The moral judgement of the child*. New York: Free Press.

———. (1936/1953). *The origins of intelligence in children*. London: Routledge & Kegan Paul.

———. (1945/1951/1962). *Play, dreams, and imitation*. New York: Norton.

———. (1948). *The moral reasoning of the child*. New York: Basic Books.

———. (1959). *The language and thought of the child*. (3rd ed.). London: Routledge & Kegan Paul.

———. (1962). *The child's conception of number*. New York: Norton.

———. (1970). Piaget's theory. In P. H. Mussen (Ed.), *Carmichael's manual of child psychology* (Vol. 1). New York: Wiley.

———. (1972). Intellectual evolution from adolescence to adulthood. *Human Development, 15*, 1–12.

———. (1983). Piaget's theory. In P. H. Mussen (Ed.), *Handbook of child psychology*. (4th ed.). Vol. 1. W. Kessen (Ed.), *History, theory and methods* (pp. 103–128). New York: Wiley.

Piaget, J., & Inhelder, B. (1956). *The child's conception of space*. London: Routledge & Kegan Paul.

———. (1964). *The early growth of logic in the child*. New York: Norton.

———. (1974). *The child's construction of quantities*. London: Routledge & Kegan Paul.

Placek, P. J. (1986). Commentary: Cesarean rates still rising. *Statistical Bulletin, 67*, 9.

Pleck, J. H., Sonenstein, F. L., & Ku, L. C. (1990). Contraceptive attitudes and intention to use condoms in sexually experienced and inexperienced adolescent males. *Journal of Family Issues, 11*, 294–312.

Pollitt, E., Eichler, A. W., & Chan, C. K. (1975). Psychosocial development and behavior of mothers of failure to thrive children. *American Journal of Orthopsychiatry, 45*, 525–537.

Poore, M., & Foster, J. C. (1985). Epidural and no epidural anesthesia: Differences between mothers and their experience of birth. *Birth, 12*, 4.

Porter, R. H., Cernoch, J. M., & McLaughlin, F. J. (1983). Maternal recognition of neonates through olfactory cues. *Physiology & Behavior, 30*, 151–154.

Powell, G. F., Brasel, J. A., & Blizzard, R. M. (1967). Emotional deprivation and growth retardation simulating idiopathic hypopituirism: II. Endocrinologic evaluation of the syndrome. *New England Journal of Medicine, 272*, 1279–1283.

Powell, G. F., Brasel, J. A., Raiti, S., & Blizzard, R. M. (1967). Emotional deprivation and growth retardation simulating idiopathic hypopituirism: I. Endocrinologic evaluation of the syndrome. *New England Journal of Medicine, 276*, 1271–1278.

Powell, K. E., Thompson, P. D., Casperson, C. J., & Kendrick, J. S. (1987). Physical activity and the incidence of coronary heart disease. *Annual Reviews of Public Health, 8*, 253–287.

Price, J. H., Desmond, S., & Kukulka, G. (1985). High school students' perceptions and misperceptions of AIDS. *Journal of School Health, 55*, 107–109.

Price, J. M., & Dodge, K. A. (1989). Peers contributions to children's social maladjustment: Description and intervention. In T. J. Berndt & G. W. Ladd (Eds.), *Peer relationships in child development* (pp. 341–370). New York: Wiley.

Price, J. M., & Slyke, D. V. (1991, April). *Social information processing patterns and social adjustment of maltreated children*. Paper presented at the biennial meeting of the Society for Research in Child Development, Seattle.

Putallaz, M., & Wasserman, A. (1989). Children's naturalistic entry behavior and sociometric status: A developmental perspective. *Developmental Psychology, 25*, 297–305.

Queen, S. A., & Habenstein, R. W. (1967). *The family in various cultures*. Philadelphia: J. B. Lippincott.

Queenan, J. T. (1979). *A new life: Pregnancy, birth, and your child's first year*. New York: Van Nostrand Reinhold.

Quigley, M. E., Sheehan, K. L., Wildes, M. M., & Yen, S. S. C. (1979). Effects of maternal smoking on circulating catecholamine levels and fetal heart rates. *American Journal of Obstetrics and Gynecology, 133*, 685–690.

Quine, L. (1986). Behaviour problems in severely mentally handicapped children. *Psychological Medicine, 16*, 895–907.

Rabiner, D. L., Lenhart, L., & Lochman, J. E. (1990). Automatic versus reflective social problem solving in relation to children's sociometric status. *Developmental Psychology, 26*, 1010–1016.

Radke-Yarrow, M., Cummings, E. M., Kuczynski, L., & Chapman, M. (1985). Patterns of attachment in two- and three-year-olds in normal families and families with maternal depression. *Child Development, 56*, 884–893.

Ramsey, P. G., & Myers, L. C. (1990). Salience of race in young children's cognitive, affective, and behavioral responses to social environments. *Journal of Applied Developmental Psychology, 11*, 49–67.

Reese, H. W. (1962). Verbal mediation as a function of age level. *Psychological Bulletin, 59*, 502–509.

Reis, S. M. (1989). Reflections on policy affecting the education of gifted and talented students. *American Psychologist, 44*, 399–408.

Renouf, A. G., & Harter, S. (1991, April). *Levels of social support for adolescents with depressed affect and suicidal ideation*. Paper presented at the biennial meeting of the Society for Research in Child Development, Seattle.

Resnick, L. B. (1989). Developing mathematical knowledge. *American Psychologist, 44*, 162–169.

Reynolds, A. J. (1989). A structural model of first-grade outcomes for an urban, low socioeconomic status, minority population. *Journal of Educational Psychology, 81*, 594–603.

Rhoads, G. G., Jackson, L. G., Schlesselman, S. E., et al. (1989). The safety and efficacy of chorionic villus sampling for early prenatal diagnosis of cytogenetic abnormalities. *New England Journal of Medicine, 320*, 609–617.

Rhodes, B., & Kroger, J. (1991, April). *Parental bonding and separation-individuation difficulties among late adolescent eating disordered women*. Paper presented at the biennial meeting of the Society for Research in Child Development, Seattle.

Rice, M. L. (1989). Children's language acquisition. *American Psychologist, 44,* 149–156.

Richard, B. A., & Dodge, K. A. (1982). Social maladjustment and problem solving in school-aged children. *Journal of Consulting and Clinical Psychology, 50,* 226–233.

Rieder, C., & Cicchetti, D. (1989). Organizational perspective on cognitive control functioning and cognitive-affective balance in maltreated children. *Developmental Psychology, 25,* 382–393.

Rieser, J., Yonas, A., & Wikner, K. (1976). Radial localization of odors by human newborns. *Child Development, 47,* 856–859.

Robbins, W. J., Brody, S., Hogan, A. G., Jackson, C. M., & Green, C. W. (Eds.). (1928). *Growth.* New Haven: Yale University Press.

Roberts, C. J., & Lowe, C. R. (1975). Where have all the conceptions gone? *Lancet, 1,* 498–499.

Roberts, L. R., Sarigiani, P. A., Petersen, A. C., & Newman, J. L. (1990). Gender differences in the relationship between achievement and self-image during early adolescence. *Journal of Early Adolescence, 10,* 159–175.

Roberts, M. C., & Turner, D. S. (1984). Preventing death and injury in childhood: A synthesis of child safety efforts. *Health Education Quarterly, 11,* 181–193.

Roff, J. D. (1990). Childhood peer rejection as a predictor of young adults' mental health. *Psychological Reports, 67,* 1263–1266.

Roff, M. (1961). Childhood social interacts and young adult bad conduct. *Journal of Abnormal and Social Psychology, 63,* 333–337.

Roff, M., Sells, S. B., & Golden, M. M. (1972). *Social adjustment and personality development in childhood.* Minneapolis: University of Minnesota Press.

Roffwarg, H., Muzio, J., & Dement, W. (1966). Ontogenetic development of the human sleep-dream cycle. *Science, 152,* 604–619.

Rogoff, B. (1986). Adult assistance of children's learning. In F. F. Raphael (Ed.), *The contexts of school-based literacy* (pp. 27–40). New York: Random House.

Rogosch, F. A., & Newcomb, A. F. (1989). Children's perceptions of peer reputations and their social reputations among peers. *Child Development, 60,* 597–610.

Rooks, J. P., Weatherby, N. L., Ernst, E. K. M., Stapleton, S., Rosen, D., & Rosenfeld, A. (1989). Outcome of care in birth centers. *New England Journal of Medicine, 321,* 1804–1811.

Roscoe, B., & Kruger, T. L. (1990). AIDS: Late adolescents' knowledge and its influence on sexual behavior. *Adolescence, 25,* 39–47.

Rose, S. A., & Ruff, H. A. (1987). Cross-modal abilities in human infants. In J. D. Osofsky (Ed.), *Handbook of infant development* (2nd ed., pp. 318–362). New York: Wiley.

Rosen, C. (1974). The effects of socio-dramatic play on problem-solving behavior among culturally disadvantaged children. *Child Development, 45,* 920–927.

Rosen, J. C., & Gross, J. (1987). Prevalence of weight reducing and weight gaining in adolescent girls and boys. *Health Psychology, 6,* 131–147.

Rosenblith, J. F. (1992). *In the beginning: Development from conception to age two.* (2nd ed.). Newbury Park, CA: Sage Publications.

Rosenman, R. H., Brand, R. J., Sholtz, R. I., Friedman, M. (1976). Multivariate prediction of coronary heart disease during 8.5 year followup in the Western Collaborative Group study. *American Journal of Cardiology, 37,* 903–910.

Rosenthal, P. A., & Rosenthal, S. (1984). Suicidal behavior by preschool children. *American Journal of Psychiatry, 141,* 520–525.

Rosenzweig, M. R. (1966). Environmental complexity, cerebral change, and behavior. *American Psychologist, 21,* 321–332.

Rosett, L. R., Weiner, L., Lee, A., Zuckerman, B., Dooling, E., & Oppenheimer, E. (1983). Patterns of alcohol consumption and fetal development. *Obstetrics and Gynecology, 61,* 539–546.

Ross, H. S., & Goldman, B. D. (1977). Infants' sociability toward strangers. *Child Development, 48,* 638–642.

Ross, J. G., Dotson, C. O., Gilbert, G. G., & Katz, S. J. (1985). What are kids doing in school physical education? *Journal of Physical Edu-*cation, *Recreation, and Dance, 56,* 31–34.

Ross, J. G., & Gilbert, G. G. (1985). The national children and youth fitness study: A summary of findings. *Journal of Physical Education, Recreation, and Dance, 56,* 45–50.

Ross, J. G., & Pate, R. R. (1987). The national children and youth fitness study II: A summary of findings. *Journal of Physical Education, Recreation, and Dance, 58,* 51–56.

Rovee-Collier, C. (1987). Learning and memory in infancy. In J. D. Osofsky (Ed.), *Handbook of infant development* (pp. 98–148). New York: Wiley.

Rovee-Collier, C. K., Sullivan, M. W., Enright, M., Lucas, D., & Fagan, J. W. (1980). Reactivation of infant memory. *Science, 208,* 1159–1161.

Rovet, J., & Netley, C. (1983). The triple X chromosome syndrome in childhood: Recent empirical findings. *Child Development, 54,* 831–845.

Rubin, K. H., & Daniels-Beirness, T. (1983). Concurrent and predictive correlates of sociometric status in kindergarten and grade one children. *Merrill-Palmer Quarterly, 29,* 337–352.

Rubin, K. H., Fein, G. G., & Vandenberg, B. (1983). Play. In E. M. Hetherington (Ed.), *Handbook of child psychology. Vol. 4: Socialization, personality, and social development* (pp. 693–774). New York: Wiley.

Rubin, K. H., & Krasnor, L. R. (1986). Social-cognitive and social behavioral perspectives on problem-solving. In M. Perlmutter (Ed.), *Minnesota symposium on child psychology* (Vol. 18, pp. 1–65). Hillsdale, NJ: Erlbaum.

Rubin, K. H., LeMare, L. J., & Lollis, S. (1990). Social withdrawal in childhood: Developmental pathways to peer rejection. In S. R. Asher & J. D. Coie (Eds.), *Peer rejection in childhood* (pp. 217–249). New York: Cambridge University Press.

Rubin, K. H., & Mills, R. (1988). The many faces of isolation. *Journal of Consulting and Clinical Psychology, 6,* 916–924.

Rutter, M. (1984). Resilient children. *Psychology Today, 18,* 57–65.

———. (1985). Family and school influences on cognitive development. *Journal of Child Psychology and Psychiatry, 26,* 687–704.

Rutter, M., & Yule, W. (1975). The concept of specific reading retardation. *Journal of Child Psychology and Psychiatry, 16,* 181–197.

Saarni, S. (1979). Children's understanding of display rules for expressive behavior. *Developmental Psychology, 15,* 424–429.

Safer, D. J., & Krager, J. M. (1988). A survey of medication treatment for hyperactive/inattentive students. *Journal of the American Medical Association, 260,* 2256–2258.

Salapatek, P. (1975). Pattern perception in early infancy. In L. B. Cohen & P. Salapatek (Eds.), *Infant perception: From sensation to cognition. Vol. 1: Basic visual processes* (pp. 133–148). New York: Academic Press.

Sallis, J. F. (1987). A commentary on children and fitness: A public health perspective. *Research Quarterly for Exercise and Sport, 58,* 326–330.

Saltz, E., Dixon, D., & Johnson, J. (1977). Training disadvantaged preschoolers on various fantasy activities: Effects on cognitive functioning and impulse control. *Child Development, 48,* 367–380.

Sameroff, A. J. (1968). The components of sucking in the human newborn. *Journal of Experimental Child Psychology, 6,* 607–623.

Sameroff, A. J., & Chandler, M. J. (1975). Reproductive risk and the continuum of caretaking casualty. In F. D. Horowitz, M. Hetherington, S. Scarr-Salapatek, & G. Siegel (Eds.), *Review of child development research* (Vol. 4). Chicago: University of Chicago Press.

Sancilio, F. M., Plumert, J. M., & Hartup, W. W. (1989). Friendship and aggressiveness as determinants of conflict outcomes in middle childhood. *Developmental Psychology, 25,* 812–819.

Savage, M. P., Petratis, M. M., Thompson, W. H., Berg, K., Smith, J. L., & Sady, S. P. (1986). Exercise training affects serum lipids of prepubescent boys and adult men. *Medicine and Science in Sports and Exercise, 18,* 197–204.

Scanlon, J. W., Brown, W. V., Weiss, J. B., & Alper, M. H. (1974). Neurobehavioral responses of newborn infants after maternal epidural anesthesia. *Anesthesiology, 40,* 121–128.

Schaffer, H. R., & Emerson, P. E. (1964). The development of social attachments in infancy. *Monographs of the Society for Research in Child Development, 29*(Serial No. 94).

Schanberg, S. M., & Field, T. M. (1987). Sensory deprivation stress in the ratpup and preterm human neonate. *Child Development, 58,* 1431–1447.

Schenk, V. M., & Grusec, J. E. (1987). A comparison of prosocial behavior of children with and without day care experience. *Merrill-Palmer Quarterly, 33,* 231–240.

Schneider, W., Borkowski, J. G., Kurtz, B. E., & Kerwin, K. (1986). Metamemory and motivation: A comparison of strategy use performance in German and American children. *Journal of Cross-Cultural Psychology, 17,* 315–336.

Schwartz, D., Mayaux, M.-J., Spira, A., Moscato, M.-L., Juannet, P., Czyglik, F., & Georges, D. (1983). Semen characteristics as a function of age in 833 fertile men. *Fertility & Sterility, 39,* 530–535.

Schweinhart, L. J., Weikart, D. P., & Larner, M. B. (1986). A report on High/Scope Preschool Curriculum Comparison Study: Consequences of three preschool curriculum models through age 15. *Early Childhood Research Quarterly, 1,* 15–45.

Scott, S., & Richards, M. (1979). Nursing low birthweight babies on lambs wool. *Lancet, 1,* 1028.

Scott-Jones, D., & White, A. B. (1990). Correlates of sexual activity in early adolescence. *Journal of Early Adolescence, 10,* 221–233.

Sears, R. R. (1963). Dependency motivation. In M. Jones (Ed.), *Nebraska Symposium on Motivation* (Vol. 11, pp. 25–64). Lincoln: University of Nebraska Press.

Secada, W. G., Fuson, K. C., & Hall, J. W. (1983). The transition from counting-all to counting-on in addition. *Journal of Research in Mathematics Education, 4,* 47–57.

Seefeldt, V. (1984). Physical fitness in preschool and elementary school-aged children. *Journal of Physical Education, Recreation, and Dance, 55,* 33–37.

Segal, M., Peck, J., Vega-Lahr, N., & Field, T. (1987). A medieval kingdom: Leader-follower styles of preschool play. *Journal of Applied Developmental Psychology, 8,* 79–95.

Seidel, W. T., & Joschko, M. (1990). Evidence of difficulties in sustained attention in children with attention deficit hyperactivity disorder. *Journal of Abnormal Child Psychology, 18,* 217–229.

Serbin, L. A., Tronick, I. J., & Sternglanz, S. H. (1977). Shaping cooperative cross-sex play. *Child Development, 48,* 924–929.

Shah, F., & Zelnik, M. (1981). Parent and peer influence on sexual behavior, contraceptive use, and pregnancy experience of young women. *Journal of Marriage and the Family, 43,* 339–348.

Shantz, C. U. (1987). Conflict between children. *Child Development, 58,* 283–305.

Shantz, C. U., & Hobart, C. J. (1989). Social conflict and development: Peers and siblings. In T. J. Berndt & G. W. Ladd (Eds.), *Peer relationships in child development* (pp. 71–94). New York: Wiley.

Shatz, M., & Gelman, R. (1973). The development of communication skills. *Monographs of the Society for Research in Child Development, 38*(Serial No. 152).

Shaywitz, S. E., Escobar, M. D., Shaywitz, B. A., Fletcher, J. M., & Makuch, R. (1992). Evidence that dyslexia may represent the lower tail of a normal distribution of reading disability. *New England Journal of Medicine, 326,* 145–150.

Sheldon, W. H. (1940). *The varieties of human physique.* New York: Harper.

———. (1942). *The varieties of temperament.* New York: Harper.

Shiffrin, R. M., & Atkinson, R. C. (1969). Storage and retrieval processes in long-term memory. *Psychological Review, 76,* 179–193.

Shiffrin, R. M., & Schneider, W. (1977). Controlled and automatic human information processing II: Perceptual learning, automatic attending, and a general theory. *Psychological Review, 84,* 127–190.

Siegler, R. S. (1983). Information processing approaches to development. In W. Kessen (Ed.), *Handbook of child psychology: Vol. 1. History, theory, and methods* (4th ed., pp. 129–212). New York: Wiley.

———. (1986). *Children's thinking* (2nd ed.). Englewood Cliffs, NJ: Prentice-Hall.

Silber, S. J. (1991). *How to get pregnant with the new technology*. New York: Warner Books.

Silbereisen, R. K., Petersen, A. C., Albrecht, H. T., & Kracke, B. (1989). Maturational timing and the development of problem behavior: Longitudinal studies in adolescence. *Journal of Early Adolescence, 9*, 247–268.

Silver, D. H. (1991, April). *Representation of attachment and social behavior in the preschool*. Paper presented at the biennial meeting of the Society for Research in Child Development, Seattle.

Simkin, P. (1989). *The birth partner*. Boston: Harvard Common Press.

Simmons, R., & Blythe, D. (1987). *Moving into adolescence*. New York: Aldine de Gruyter.

Simons, R. L., Robertson, J. F., & Downs, W. R. (1989). The nature of the association between parental rejection and delinquent behavior. *Journal of Youth and Adolescence, 18*, 297–309.

Simons-Morton, B., O'Hara, N. M., Simons-Morton, D. G., & Parcel, G. (1987). Children and fitness: A public health perspective. *Research Quarterly for Exercise & Sport, 58*, 295–302.

Singleton, L., & Asher, S. (1977). Peer preferences and social interaction among third-grade children in an integrated school district. *Journal of Educational Psychology, 69*, 330–336.

Siqueland, E. R. (1968). Reinforcement patterns and extinction in human newborns. *Journal of Experimental Child Psychology, 6*, 431–432.

Siqueland, E. R., & Delucia, C. A. (1969). Visual reinforcement of non-nutritive sucking in human infants. *Science, 165*, 1144–1146.

Skeels, H. M. (1966). Adult status of children with contrasting early life experience: A follow-up study. *Monographs of the Society for Re-

search in Child Development, 31*(3, Serial No. 105).

Skeels, H. M., & Dye, H. B. (1939). A study of the effects of differential stimulation on mentally retarded children. *Program of the American Association of Mental Deficiency, 44*, 114–136.

Skinner, B. F. (1953). *Science and human behavior*. New York: Free Press.

———. (1957). *Verbal behavior*. New York: Appleton-Century-Crofts.

Skuse, D. (1984). Extreme deprivation in early childhood—I. Diverse outcomes for three siblings from an extraordinary family. *Journal of Child Psychology and Psychiatry, 25*, 523–541.

Slater, A., Morison, V., & Rose, D. (1984). Habituation in the newborn. *Infant Behavior and Development, 7*, 183–200.

Slobin, D. (1973). Cognitive prerequisites for the acquisition of grammar. In C. Ferguson & D. Slobin (Eds.), *Studies of child language development* (pp. 175–208). New York: Holt, Rinehart & Winston.

Smilansky, S. (1968). *The effects of sociodramatic play on disadvantaged children: Preschool children*. New York: Wiley.

Smilkstein, G., Helspaer-Lucas, A., Ashworth, C., Montano, D., & Pagel, M. (1984). Prediction of pregnancy complications: An application of the biopsychosocial model. *Social Science & Medicine, 18*, 315–321.

Smith, C. L. (1979). Children's understanding of natural language categories. *Journal of Experimental Child Psychology, 30*, 191–205.

Smith, P. B., & Pederson, D. R. (1988). Maternal sensitivity and patterns of infant-mother attachment. *Child Development, 59*, 1087–1101.

Smith, R. (1971). *Introduction to mental retardation*. New York: McGraw-Hill.

Snarey, J. R. (1985). Cross-cultural universality of social-moral development: A critical review of Kohlbergian research. *Psychological Bulletin, 97*, 202–232.

Snow, C. E. (1972). Mother's speech to children learning language. *Child Development, 43*, 549–565.

Snow, C. W., & Fergusen, C. A. (Eds.). (1977). *Talking to children*. Cambridge: Cambridge University Press.

Sobol, M. P., & Earn, B. M. (1985a). Assessment of children's attributions for social experience: Implications for social skills training. In B. H. Schneider, K. H. Rubin, & J. E. Ledingham (Eds.), *Children's peer relations: Issues in assessment and intervention* (pp. 93–110). New York: Springer-Verlag.

———. (1985b). What causes mean: An analysis of children's interpretations of the causes of social experience. *Journal of Social and Personal Relationships, 2*, 137–149.

Society for Research in Child Development, Committee for Ethical Conduct in Child Development Research. (1990, Winter). SRCD ethical standards for research with children. *SRCD Newsletter*. Chicago: Author.

Sonnenschein, S., Baker, L., & Lasaga, M. (1991, April). *Mothers' views of their role in fostering metacognition*. Paper presented at the biennial meeting of the Society for Research in Child Development, Seattle.

Sorensen, R. C. (1973). *Adolescent sexuality in contemporary America*. New York: World.

Sowers-Hoag, K. W., Thyer, B. A., & Bailey, J. S. (1987). Promoting automobile safety belt use by young children. *Journal of Applied Behavior Analysis, 20*, 133–138.

Spelke, E. S. (1985). Perception of unity, persistence, and identity: Thoughts on infants' conceptions of objects. In J. Mehler & R. Fox, *Neonate cognition* (pp. 89–114). Hillsdale, NJ: Erlbaum.

Spencer, M. B., & Markstrom-Adams, C. (1990). Identity processes among racial and ethnic minority children in America. *Child Development, 61*, 290–310.

Spinetta, J. J., & Rigler, D. (1972). The child abusing parent: A psychological review. *Psychological Bulletin, 77*, 296–304.

Spitz, R. A. (1945). Hospitalism: An inquiry into the genesis of psychiatric conditions in early childhood. *Psychoanalytic Study of the Child, 1*, 113–117.

———. (1946). Anaclitic depression. *Psychoanalytic Study of the Child, 2*, 313–342.

Spivack, G., & Shure, M. B. (1974). *The problem solving approach to adjust-

ment. Washington, DC: Jossey-Bass.

Sroufe, L. A. (1977). Wariness of strangers and the study of infant development. *Child Development*, *48*, 731–746.

———. (1979). Socioemotional development. In J. D. Osofsky (Ed.), *Handbook of infant development* (pp. 462–516). New York: Wiley.

———. (1985). Attachment classification from the perspective of infant caregiver relationship and infant temperament. *Child Development*, *56*, 1–14.

Sroufe, L. A., Fox, N. E., & Pancake, V. R. (1983). Attachment and dependency in a developmental perspective. *Child Development*, *54*, 1615–1627.

Staffieri, J. R. (1967). A study of social stereotype of body image in children. *Journal of Personality and Social Psychology*, *7*, 101–104.

———. (1972). Body build and behavioral expectencies in young females. *Developmental Psychology*, *6*, 125–127.

Stagno, S., Pass, R. F., Cloud, G., et al. (1986). Primary cytomegalovirus infection in pregnancy: Incidence, transmission to fetus, and clinical outcome. *Journal of the American Medical Association*, *256*, 1904–1908.

Stainer, K. E., & Thieman, A. (1991, April). *The relations of child, parent, and family characteristics to the severity of child maltreatment*. Paper presented at the biennial meeting of the Society for Research in Child Development, Seattle.

Staines, G. L., Pottick, K. J., & Fudge, D. A. (1986). Wife's employment and husband's attitudes toward work and life. *Journal of Applied Psychology*, *71*, 118–128.

Stanbury, J. B., Wyngaarden, J. B., & Frederickson, D. S. (1983). *The metabolic basis of inherited disease*. New York: McGraw-Hill.

Stanovich, K. E. (1986). Matthew effects in reading: Some consequences of individual differences in the acquisition of literacy. *Reading Research Quarterly*, *21*, 306–406.

———. (1988). The right and wrong place to look for the cognitive locus of reading disability. *Annals of Dyslexia*, *38*, 154–177.

Stattin, H., & Magnusson, D. (1990). *Puberty maturation in female development*. Hillsdale, NJ: Erlbaum.

Steinberg, L. (1986a). Latchkey children and susceptibility to peer pressure: An ecological analysis. *Developmental Psychology*, *22*, 433–439.

———. (1986b). Stability (and instability) of Type A behavior from childhood to young adulthood. *Developmental Psychology*, *22*, 393–402.

Steinberg, L., Catalano, R., & Dooley, D. (1981). Economic antecedents of child abuse and neglect. *Child Development*, *52*, 975–985.

Steinberg, L., Elmen, J. D., & Mounts, N. S. (1989). Authoritative parenting, psycho-social maturity, and academic success among adolescents. *Child Development*, *60*, 1424–1436.

Steinberg, L., & Silverberg, S. B. (1986). The vicissitudes of autonomy in early adolescence. *Child Development*, *57*, 841–851.

Steiner, J. E. (1977). Facial expressions of the neonate infant indicating the hedonics of food-related chemical stimuli. In J. M. Weiffenbach (Ed.), *Taste and development: The genesis of sweet preference*. Washington, DC: U.S. Government Printing Office.

———. (1979). Human facial expression in response to taste and smell stimulation. In H. W. Reese & L. P. Lipsitt (Eds.), *Advances in child development and behavior* (Vol. 13, pp. 257–295). New York: Academic Press.

Stern, D. (1977). *The first relationship*. Cambridge: Cambridge University Press.

Stern, D., Hofer, L., Haft, W., & Dore, J. (1985). Affect attunement: A descriptive account of the intermodal communication of affective states between mothers and infants. In T. Field & N. Fox (Eds.), *Social perception in infants*. Norwood, NJ: Ablex.

Stern, M., & Hilderbrandt, K. A. (1986). Prematurity stereotyping: Effects on mother-infant interaction. *Child Development*, *57*, 308–315.

Sternberg, R. J. (1986). A triarchic theory of intellectual giftedness. In R. J. Sternberg & J. E. Davidson (Eds.), *Conceptions of giftedness* (pp. 223–247). New York: Cambridge University Press.

Sternberg, R. J., & Davidson, J. E. (1985). *Cognitive development in the gifted and talented: Developmental perspectives* (pp. 37–44). Washington, DC: American Psychological Association.

Stevenson, D. L., & Baker, D. P. (1987). The family-school relation and the child's school performance. *Child Development*, *58*, 1348–1357.

Stevenson, H. W., & Stigler, W. (1992). *The learning gap*. New York: Summit Books.

Stevenson, M. R., & Black, K. N. (1988). Paternal absence and sex-role development: A meta-analysis. *Child Development*, *59*, 793–814.

Stillman, A. J. (1982). In utero exposure to diethylstilbestrol: Adverse effects on the reproductive tract and reproductive performance in male and female offspring. *American Journal of Obstetrics and Gynecology*, *142*, 905–921.

Stoel-Gammon, C., & Otomo, K. (1986). Babbling development of hearing-impaired and normally hearing subjects. *Journal of Speech and Hearing Disorders*, *51*, 33–41.

Strayer, F. F., & Strayer, J. (1976). An ethological analysis of social agonism and dominance relations among preschool children. *Child Development*, *47*, 980–989.

Strayer, F. F., & Trudel, M. (1984). Developmental changes in the nature and function of social dominance among young children. *Ethology & Sociobiology*, *5*, 279–295.

Streissguth, A. P., Barr, H. M., Sampson, P. D., Darby, B. L., & Martin, D. C. (1989). IQ at age 4 in relation to maternal alcohol use and smoking during pregnancy. *Developmental Psychology*, *25*, 3–11.

Streitmatter, J. L. (1988). Ethnicity as a mediating variable of early adolescent identity development. *Journal of Adolescence*, *11*, 335–346.

Strober, M., & Humphrey, L. L. (1987). Family contributions to the etiology and course of anorexia and bulimia. *Journal of Consulting & Clinical Psychology*, *55*, 654–659.

Strunin, L. (1991). Adolescents' perceptions of risk for HIV infection: Implications for future research. *Social Science Medicine*, *32*, 221–228.

Stunkard, A. J., Harris, J. R., Pedersen, N. L., & McClearn, G. E. (1990). The body-mass index of twins who have been reared apart. *New England Journal of Medicine, 322,* 1483–1487.

Stunkard, A. J., Sorensen, T. I. A., Hanis, C., Teasdale, T. W., Chakraborty, R., Schull, W. J., & Schulsinger, F. (1986). An adoption study of human obesity. *New England Journal of Medicine, 314,* 193–198.

Sullivan, H. S. (1953). *The interpersonal theory of psychiatry.* New York: Norton.

Sullivan, M. W., Rovee-Collier, C. K., & Tynes, D. M. (1979). A conditioning analysis of infant long-term memory. *Child Development, 50,* 152–162.

Suomi, S. (1982). Biological foundations and developmental psychobiology. In C. B. Kopp & J. B. Krakow (Eds.), *The child: Development in a social context* (pp. 42–91). Reading, MA: Addison-Wesley.

Suomi, S. J., & Harlow, H. F. (1972). Social rehabilitation of isolate-reared monkeys. *Developmental Psychology, 6,* 487–496.

Super, C. M. (1976). Environmental effects on motor development. *Developmental Medicine and Child Neurology, 18,* 561–567.

Szatmari, P., Offord, D. R., & Boyle, M. H. (1989). Ontario Child Health Study: Prevalence of attention deficit disorder with hyperactivity. *Journal of Child Psychology & Psychiatry, 30,* 219–230.

Taggart, A. C., Taggart, J., & Siedentop, D. (1986). Effects of a home-based activity program: A study of low fitness in elementary school children. *Behavior Modification, 10,* 487–507.

Tanner, J. M. (1970). Physical growth. In P. H. Mussen (Ed.), *Carmichael's manual of child psychology Vol. I* (3rd ed., pp. 77–156). New York: Wiley.

———. (1978). *Fetus into man: Physical growth from conception to maturity.* Cambridge, MA: Harvard University Press.

Taylor, A. R., Asher, S. R., & Williams, G. A. (1986). The social adaptation of mainstreamed mildly retarded children. *Child Development, 58,* 1321–1334.

Taylor, M., & Hart, B. (1990). Can children be trained in making the distinction between appearance and reality? *Cognitive Development, 5,* 89–99.

Templin, M. C. (1957). Certain language skills in children. *Institute of Child Welfare Monographs* (Serial No. 26). Minneapolis: University of Minnesota Press.

Termine, N. T., & Izard, C. E. (1988). Infants' responses to their mothers' expressions of joy and sadness. *Developmental Psychology, 24,* 223–229.

Thelen, E. (1979). Rhythmical stereotypes in normal human infants. *Animal Behavior, 27,* 699–715.

———. (1986). Treadmill-elicited stepping in seven-month-old infants. *Child Development, 57,* 1498–1506.

Thelen, E., & Ulrich, B. D. (1991). Hidden skills. *Monographs of the Society for Research in Child Development, 56*(No. 1).

Thomas, A., & Chess, S. (1977). *Temperament and development.* New York: Brunner/Mazel.

———. (1984). Genesis and evolution of behavioral disorders: From infancy to early adult life. *American Journal of Psychiatry, 141,* 1–9.

Thomas, J. R., & French, K. E. (1985). Gender differences across age in motor performance: A meta-analysis. *Psychological Bulletin, 98,* 260–282.

Thompson, R. A., Lamb, M., & Estes, D. (1982). Stability of infant-mother attachment and its relationship to changing life circumstances in an unselected middle-class sample. *Child Development, 53,* 144–148.

Thompson, R. J., Cappelman, M. W., & Zeitschel, K. A. (1979). Neonatal behavior of infants of adolescent mothers. *Developmental Medicine and Child Neurology, 21,* 474–482.

Thornberg, M. (1987, March). Fit to achieve. *Alliance Update,* p. 7.

Thornton, L. P., & DeBlassie, R. R. (1989). Treating bulimia. *Adolescence, 24,* 631–637.

Todd, G., & Palmer, B. (1968). Social reinforcement of infant babbling. *Child Development, 39,* 591–596.

Trause, M. A. (1977). Stranger responses: Effects of familiarity, stranger's approach, and sex of infant. *Child Development, 48,* 1657–1661.

Treiber, F. A., Mabe, P. A., Riley, W. J., McDuffie, M., et al. (1990). Children's Type A behavior: The role of parental hostility and family history of cardiovascular disease. Special issue: Type A behavior. *Journal of Social Behavior and Personality, 5,* 183–199.

Trethowan, W. H., & Conlon, M. F. (1965). The couvade syndrome. *British Journal of Psychiatry, 111,* 57–66.

Trickett, P. K., & Kuczynski, L. (1986). Children's misbehaviors and parental discipline strategies in abusive and nonabusive families. *Developmental Psychology, 22,* 115–123.

Trickett, P. K., & Susman, E. J. (1988). Parental perceptions of child-rearing practices in physically abusive and nonabusive families. *Developmental Psychology, 24,* 270–276.

Tronick, E. Z., Cohn, J., & Shea, E. (1986). The transfer of affect between mothers and infants. In T. B. Brazelton & M. W. Yogman (Eds.), *Affective development in infancy* (pp. 11–25). Norwood, NJ: Ablex.

Trussell, J. (1988). Teenage pregnancy in the United States. *Family Planning Perspectives, 20,* 262–272.

Tuckman, B. W., & Hinkle, J. S. (1986). An experimental study of the physical and psychological effects of aerobic exercise on school children. *Health Psychology, 5,* 197–207.

Turner, R. L. (1989). The great debate—Can both Carbo and Chall be right? *Phi Delta Kappan, 71,* 276–283.

Udry, J. R., Billy, J. O. G., Morris, N. M., Groff, T. R., & Raj, M. H. (1985). Serum androgenic hormones motivate general behavior in adolescent boys. *Fertility & Sterility, 43,* 90–94.

Udry, J. R., Talbert, L., & Morris, N. M. (1986). Biosocial foundation for adolescent female sexuality. *Demography, 23,* 217–230.

Ungerer, J. A., Brody, L. R., & Zelazo, P. R. (1978). Long-term memory for speech in 2- to 4-year-old infants. *Infant Behavior and Development, 1,* 127.

Ungerer, J. A., Zelazo, P. R., Kearsley, R. B., & O'Leary, K. (1981). Developmental changes in the representation of objects in symbolic play from 18–34 months of age. *Child Development, 52,* 186–195.

U.S. Bureau of the Census. (1987). *After school care of the school-age child.* (Current Population Reports, Series P-23, No. 149). Washington, DC: U.S. Government Printing Office.

U.S. Bureau of the Census. (1990). *Statistical Abstract of the United States: 1990* (110th ed.). Washington, DC: U.S. Government Printing Office.

U.S. Department of Health and Human Services. (1984). *Summary of findings from the national children and youth fitness study.* Washington, DC: U.S. Government Printing Office.

U.S. Department of Health and Human Services (USDHHS). (1980). *Preterm babies* (DHAS Publication No. ADM 80–792). Washington, DC: U.S. Government Printing Office.

U.S. Department of Justice. (1989). *Uniform crime report for the United States.* Washington, DC: U.S. Government Printing Office.

U.S. Department of Justice. (1991). *Crime in the United States.* Washington, DC: U.S. Government Printing Office.

Vandell, D. L., & Corasaniti, M. A. (1988). The relation between third graders' after-school care and social, academic, and emotional functioning. *Child Development, 59,* 868–875.

———. (1990). Variations in early child care: Do they predict sequential social, emotional, and cognitive differences? *Early Childhood Research Quarterly, 5,* 555–572.

Vaughn, B. E., Bradley, C. F., Joffee, L. S., Seifer, R., & Barglow, P. (1987). Maternal characteristics measured prenatally are predictive of ratings of temperamental "difficulties" on the "Carey" infant temperament questionnaire. *Developmental Psychology, 23,* 152–161.

Vaughn, B. E., Egeland, B., Waters, S. E., & Sroufe, L. A. (1979). Individual differences in infant-mother attachment at 12 and 18 months: Stability and change in families under stress. *Child Development, 50,* 971–975.

Vaughn, B. E., Gove, F. L., & Egeland, B. (1980). The relationship between out-of-home care and the quality of infant-mother attachment in an economically disadvantaged population. *Child Development, 51,* 1203–1214.

Verhulst, F. C., Van der Lee, J. H., Akkerhuis, G. W., Sanders-Woudstra, J. A. R., Timmer, F. C., & Donkhorst, I. D. (1985). The prevalence of nocturnal enuresis: Do DSM II criteria need to be changed? A brief research report. *Journal of Child Psychology and Psychiatry, 26,* 989–993.

Vicary, J. R., & Lerner, J. V. (1986). Parental attributes and adolescent drug use. *Journal of Adolescence, 9,* 115–122.

Vitaro, F., & Gagnon, C. (1991, April). *Behavioral and academic outcomes associated with stable and unstable peer rejection.* Paper presented at the biennial meeting of the Society for Research in Child Development, Seattle.

Vondra, J. I. (1990). The community context of child abuse and neglect. *Marriage and Family Review, 15,* 19–38.

Vondra, J. I., Barnett, D., & Cicchetti, D. (1990). Self-concept, motivation, and competence among preschoolers from maltreating families. *Child Abuse & Neglect, 14,* 525–540.

von Hofsten, C. (1984). Developmental changes in the organization of prereaching movements. *Developmental Psychology, 20,* 369–382.

von Hofsten, C., & Spelke, E. S. (1985). Object perception and object-directed reaching in infancy. *Journal of Experimental Psychology: General, 114,* 198–212.

Vosk, B., Forehand, R., Parker, J. B., & Richard, K. (1982). A multimethod comparison of popular and unpopular children. *Developmental Psychology, 18,* 571–575.

Vurpillot, E. (1968). The development of scanning strategies and their relation to visual differentiation. *Journal of Experimental Child Psychology, 6,* 632–650.

Vygotsky, L. S. (1962). *Thought and language.* Boston: MIT Press.

———. (1978). *Mind and society.* Cambridge, MA: Harvard University Press.

Waas, G. A. (1988). Social attributional bases of peer-rejected and aggressive children's behavior. *Child Development, 59,* 969–975.

Wachs, T. D., & Gruen, G. (1982). *Early experience and human development.* New York: Plenum Press.

Wagner, R. C., & Torgesen, J. K. (1987). The nature of phonological processing and its causal role in the acquisition of reading skills. *Psychological Bulletin, 101,* 192–212.

Wagner, W. G., Smith, D., & Norris, W. R. (1988). The psychological adjustment of enuretic children: A comparison of two types. *Journal of Pediatric Psychology, 13,* 33–38.

Wald, E. R., Dashevsky, B., Byers, C., Guerra, N., & Taylor, F. (1988). Frequency and severity of infections in day care. *Journal of Pediatrics, 112,* 540–546.

Walk, R. D., & Gibson, E. J. (1961). A comparative and analytical study of visual depth perception. *Psychological Monographs, 75*(15, Whole No. 519).

Walker, L. J. (1984). Sex differences in the development of moral reasoning: A critical review. *Child Development, 55,* 677–691.

———. (1986). Sex differences in the development of moral reasoning: A rejoinder to Baumrind. *Child Development, 57,* 522–526.

Walker-Andrews, A. S. (1986). Intermodal perception of expressive behaviors: Relation of eye and voice? *Developmental Psychology, 22,* 373–377.

Walker-Andrews, A. S., & Grolnick, W. (1983). Discrimination of vocal expression by young infants. *Infant Behavior and Development, 6,* 491–498.

Wallach, M. A. (1985). Creativity testing and giftedness. In F. D. Horowitz & M. O'Brien (Eds.), *The gifted and talented: Developmental perspectives* (pp. 99–123). Washington, DC: American Psychological Association.

Wallender, J. L., Hubert, N. C., & Varni, J. W. (1988). Child and maternal temperament characteristics, goodness of fit, and adjustment in physically handicapped children. *Journal of Clinical Psychology, 17,* 336–344.

Wallerstein, J. S., Corbin, S. B., & Lewis, J. M. (1988). Children of divorce: A ten-year study, In E. M. Hetherington & J. Arastem (Eds.), *Impact of divorce, single-parenting, and stepparenting on children.* Hillsdale, NJ: Erlbaum.

Walsh, D. J., Price, G. G., & Gillingham, M. G. (1988). The critical but transitory importance of letter naming. *Reading Research Quarterly, 23,* 108–122.

Walters, C. E. (1965). Prediction of postnatal development from fetal activity. *Child Development, 36,* 801–808.

Wankel, L. M., & Kreisel, P. S. J. (1985). Factors underlying enjoyment of youth sports: Sport and age group comparisons. *Journal of Sport Psychology, 7,* 51–64.

Wankel, L. M., & Sefton, J. M. (1989). A season-long investigation of fun in youth sports. *Journal of Sport & Exercise Psychology, 11,* 355–366.

Wanska, S. K., Pohlman, J. C., & Bedrosian, J. L. (1989). Topic maintenance in preschoolers' conversation in three play situations. *Early Childhood Research Quarterly, 4,* 393–402.

Warren, M. P. (1983). Physical and biological aspects of puberty. In J. Brooks-Gunn & A. C. Petersen (Eds.), *Girls at puberty: Biological and psychological perspectives* (pp. 3–28). New York: Plenum Press.

Waterman, A. S. (1984). *The psychology of individualism.* New York: Praeger.

Waters, E., Wippman, J., & Sroufe, L. A. (1979). Attachment, positive affect, and competence in the peer group: Two studies in construct validation. *Child Development, 50,* 821–829.

Watson, J. B. (1928). *Psychological care of infant and child.* New York: W. W. Norton.

———. (1930). *Behaviorism.* New York: Norton.

Watson, J. B., & Rayner, R. (1920). Conditioned emotional reactions. *Journal of Experimental Psychology, 3,* 1–14.

Watson, M. W., & Fischer, K. W. (1977). Development of social roles in elicited and spontaneous behavior during the preschool years. *Developmental Psychology, 16,* 483–494.

Waxman, S., & Gelman, R. (1986). Preschoolers' use of superordinate relations in classification and language. *Cognitive Development, 1,* 139–156.

Webb, J. A., Baer, P. E., McLaughlin, R. J., McKelvey, R. S., & Caid, C. D. (1991). Risk factors and their relation to initiation of alcohol use among early adolescents. *Journal of the American Academy of Child and Adolescent Psychiatry, 30,* 563–568.

Wegman, M. E. (1987). Annual summary of vital statistics — 1986. *Pediatrics, 80,* 817–827.

Weidner, G., Sexton, G., Matarazzo, J. D., Pereira, C., & Friend, R. (1988). Type A behavior in children, adolescents, and their parents. *Developmental Psychology, 24,* 118–121.

Weinraub, M., Clemens, L. P., Sockloff, A., Etheridge, T., Gracely, E., & Myers, B. (1984). The development of sex role stereotypes in the third year: Relations to gender labelling, sex-typed toy preference, and family characteristics. *Child Development, 55,* 1493–1503.

Weinraub, M., & Lewis, M. (1977). The determinants of children's responses to separation. *Monographs of the Society for Research in Child Development, 42*(4, Serial No. 172).

Weiss, G., & Hechtman, L. (1986). *Hyperactive children grown up.* New York: Guilford.

Weiss, S. J. (1991). Stressors experienced by family caregivers of children with pervasive developmental disorders. *Child Psychiatry & Human Development, 23,* 203–216.

Wellman, H. M. (1991). From desires to beliefs: Acquisition of a theory of mind. In A. Whiten (Ed.), *Nature theories of mind* (pp. 19–38). Cambridge MA: Basic Blackwell.

Wellman, H. M., & Estes, D. (1986). Early understanding of mental entities: A reexamination of childhood realism. *Child Development, 57,* 910–923.

Wenar, C. (1990). *Developmental psychopathology.* New York: McGraw-Hill.

Wender, P. H. (1987). *The hyperactive child, adolescent, and adult: Attention deficit disorder through the lifespan.* New York: Oxford University Press.

Werker, J. S., Gilbert, J., Humphrey, K., & Tees, R. (1981). Developmental aspects of cross-language speech perception. *Child Development, 52,* 349–355.

Werker, J. S., & Tees, R. C. (1984). Cross language speech perception in human infants. *Infant Behavior and Development, 7,* 49–63.

Werner, E. E., Bierman, J. M., & French, F. E. (1971). *The children of Kauai: A longitudinal study from the prenatal period to age ten.* Honolulu: University of Hawaii Press.

Werner, E. E., & Smith, R. S. (1982). *Vulnerable but invincible: A longitudinal study of resilient children and youth.* New York: McGraw-Hill.

White, B., & Held, R. (1966). Plasticity of sensori-motor development in the human infant. In J. F. Rosenblith & W. Allinsmith (Eds.), *The causes of behavior* (pp. 60–70). Boston: Allyn & Bacon.

White, B. L., & Watts, J. C. (1973). *Experience and environment.* Englewood Cliffs, NJ: Prentice-Hall.

Wigfield, A., & Meece, J. L. (1988). Math anxiety in elementary and secondary school students. *Journal of Educational Psychology, 80,* 210–216.

Wilks, J. (1986). The relative importance of parents and friends in adolescent decision-making. *Journal of Youth and Adolescence, 15,* 323–324.

Will, M. (1986). Educating students with learning problems: A shared responsibility: Washington, DC: U.S. Department of Education, Office of Special Education and Rehabilitative Services.

Windol, M., Miller-Tutzauer, C., & Baecher, D. (1991, April). *Alcohol use, suicidal behavior, and risky ac-*

tivities among adolescents. Paper presented at the biennial meeting of the Society for Research in Child Development, Seattle.

Winer, G. A. (1980). Class inclusion reasoning in children: A review of the empirical literature. *Child Development, 51*, 309–328.

Wolfe, D. A. (1985). Child-abusive parents: An empirical review and analysis. *Psychological Bulletin, 97*, 462–482.

Wolff, P. H. (1966). The causes, controls and organization of behavior in the neonate. *Psychological Issues, 5*(1, Serial No. 17).

Worobey, J., & Belsky, J. (1982). Employing the Brazelton Scale to influence mothering: An experimental comparison of three strategies. *Developmental Psychology, 18*, 736–743.

Woznica, J. G., & Shapiro, J. R. (1990). An analysis of adolescent suicide attempts: The expendable child. *Journal of Pediatric Psychology, 15*, 789–796.

Yogman, M. W., Cole, P., Als, H., & Lester, B. M. (1982). Behavior of newborns of diabetic mothers. *Infant Behavior and Development, 5*, 331–340.

Yonas, A., & Owsley, C. (1987). Development of visual space perception. In P. Salapatek & L. B. Cohen (Eds.), *Handbook of infant perception* (Vol. 2, pp. 79–122). New York: Academic Press.

Yonas, A., Pettersen, L., & Granrud, C. E. (1982). Infants' sensitivity to familiar size as information for distance. *Child Development, 53*, 1285–1290.

Yonas, A., Tilton, M. M., & Arterberry, M. E. (1993, March). *Assessing pictorial depth sensitivity in individual infants*. Paper presented at the biennial meeting of the Society for Research in Child Development, New Orleans.

Young, K. T., & Zigler, E. (1986). Infant and toddler day care: Regulations and policy implications. *American Journal of Orthopsychiatry, 56*, 43–55.

Zabin, L. S., Kantner, J. F., & Zelnik, M. (1979). The risk of adolescent pregnancy in the first months of intercourse. *Family Planning Perspectives, 11*, 215–222.

Zahn-Waxler, C., & Radke-Yarrow, M. (1982). The development of altruism: Alternative research strategies. In N. Eisenberg (Ed.), *The development of prosocial behavior* (pp. 109–137). New York: Academic Press.

Zahn-Waxler, C., Radke-Yarrow, M., & King, R. A. (1979). Child-rearing and children's prosocial initiations toward victims in distress. *Child Development, 50*, 319–330.

Zahr, L. K. (1993, March). *The response of premature infants to routine nursing interventions and noise in the NICU*. Paper presented at the biennial meeting of the Society for Research in Child Development, New Orleans.

Zarbatany, L., Hartmann, D. P., & Rankin, D. B. (1990). The psychological functions of preadolescent peer activities. *Child Development, 61*, 1067–1080.

Zelazo, P. R., Weiss, M., Randolph, M. Swain, I., & Moore, D. (1987). The effects of delay on neonatal retention of habituated head-turning. *Infant Behavior and Development, 10*, 417–434.

Zelazo, P. R., Zelazo, N. A., & Kolb, S. (1972). ''Walking'' in the newborn. *Science, 176*, 314–315.

Zelnik, M., & Kantner, J. F. (1977). Sexual contraceptive experience of young unmarried women in the United States, 1971 and 1976. *Family Planning Perspectives, 9*, 55–71.

———. (1980). Sexual activity, contraceptive use, and pregnancy among metropolitan-area teenagers: 1971–1979. *Family Planning Perspectives, 12*, 230–237.

Zelnik, M., & Shah, F. K. (1983). First intercourse among young Americans. *Family Planning Perspectives, 15*, 64–70.

Zigler, E. (1981). A plea to end the use of the patterning treatment for retarded children. *American Journal of Orthopsychiatry, 51*, 388–390.

Zigler, E., & Muenchow, S. (1979). Mainstreaming: The proof is in the implementation. *American Psychologist, 34*, 993–996.

Zigler, E., & Seitz, V. (1975). On an ''experimental'' evaluation of sensorimotor patterning: A critique. *American Journal of Mental Retardation, 79*, 483–492.

Zill, N. (1988). Behavior, achievement, and health problems among children in stepfamilies: Findings from a national survey of child health. In E. M. Hetherington & A. Rasteh (Eds.), *Impact of divorce, single-parenting and stepparenting on children* (pp. 325–368). Hillsdale, NJ: Erlbaum.

Aber, J. L., 182, 280
Aboagye, K., 78
Abraham, K. G., 525
Ackerman-Ross, S., 321
Acredelo, L. P., 202
Adams, G. R., 525
Adams, R. E., Jr., 236
Adcock, D., 347
Addy, C. L., 534
Adler, N. E., 517
Adler, T. F., 497
Ahl, V., 79
Ainsworth, M. D. S., 233–238
Akkerhuis, G. W., 261
Albin, M., 219–220
Albrecht, H. T., 479
Alexander, K. L., 415, 430
Allen, J. P., 280
Allen, M. R., 423
Allen, V. L., 479, 518
Aloise, P. A., 409, 441
Alper, M. H., 115
Als, H., 124
Altemeier, W. A., 284
Amard, H., 78
Ames, G. J., 18, 205
Anders, T. F., 161
Anderson, B. J., 121
Anderson, C., 124
Anderson, E. R., 461–462, 464
Anderson, G. C., 128
Anderson, R., 80
Anderson, R. C., 427
Anderson, S., 365
Andersson, B. E., 321
Angulo, J., 422
Anisfeld, E., 238
Apgar, V., 123–124
Archer, S. L., 524–525
Arend, R., 242
Arnett, J., 517
Aronson, M., 78
Arterberry, M. E., 156
Arvin, A., 80
Asarnow, J. R., 448–449
Ashcraft, M. H., 429
Asher, S. R., 44, 337, 339, 388, 392, 439,
    454–556
Ashworth, C., 83
Aslin, R. N., 149, 152–153, 155–156,
    158–159, 201
Atkinson, R. C., 35, 307
Attie, I., 483–484
Atwater, A. E., 258
August, G. J., 384

Babijian, H., 456
Baecher, D., 534

Baer, D. M., 16
Baer, P. E., 530
Bailey, J. S., 25, 271
Bakeman, R., 363
Baker, D. P., 416
Baker, L., 412, 487
Baldwin, A. Y., 432
Baldwin, W., 520
Ball, L., 534
Bandura, A., 17, 27–29, 182, 199,
    343–344, 409
Banerjee, M., 366
Banet, B., 305, 323, 325
Banks, M. S., 152
Baranowski, T., 378
Barden, R. C., 365
Barglow, P., 241, 248
Barkley, R. A., 384
Barnes, G. M., 530
Barnes, K. E., 333
Barnett, D., 239, 279–280, 283
Barr, H. M., 78
Barrera, M. E., 130, 155
Barrett, K. C., 156–157
Barrett, M., 420
Barry, H., III, 516, 520
Bar-Tal, D., 353
Bartlett, J. A., 488–489
Basham, R., 129
Bates, E., 201–204
Bates, J. E., 184, 223
Bauchner, H., 78
Baumrind, D., 349–350, 467, 499
Bayley, N., 164, 166–167, 480
Beach, D. R., 36
Beach, F. A., 520
Beauchamp, G. K., 160
Beautrais, A. L., 276
Beckman, P. J., 389–391
Beckwith, L., 79
Bedrosian, J. L., 314
Bee, D. E., 378
Beeghly, M., 268
Behrman, R. E., 90, 263, 485–486
Bell, J. A., 412
Bell, R. Q., 4
Bell, S. M., 236
Belsky, J., 126, 238, 240–241, 248, 279,
    283, 321
Bem, S. L., 355–359
Bempechat, J., 458
Benacerraf, B. R., 158
Benasich, A. A., 179
Benbow, C. P., 432
Bender, B., 95
Benenson, J. F., 444
Benjamin, A., 121
Benoit, P. J., 339

Bentler, P. M., 528, 530–531
Bereiter, C., 326
Berg, K., 379
Berg, K. M., 134
Berg, W. K., 134
Berger, W. K., 180
Bergman, A., 226
Bergsma, D., 80
Berk, L. E., 316
Berndt, T. J., 439, 441, 508, 512, 514
Bernstein, B., 426
Berscheid, E., 337
Bertenthal, B. I., 156
Bettes, B. A., 206
Bhavnagri, N. P., 348, 350–351
Bianchi, B. D., 363
Bierman, J. M., 129
Bierman, K. L., 455, 514
Bigelow, B. J., 439
Bijou, S. W., 16
Billy, J. O. G., 518
Bingol, N., 78
Birnholz, J. C., 158
Bitner, B., 514
Bjorklund, D. F., 17, 297, 299, 397, 408, 410
Black, A. E., 349–350
Black, B., 337
Black, J. E., 141, 147
Black, K. N., 360
Blass, E. M., 180
Blehar, M. C., 234, 236–238
Blizzard, R. M., 284
Bloom, L., 312
Blumstein, A., 536
Blythe, D., 479
Bodner, B., 121
Boersma, C. C., 205
Boggiano, A. K., 420–421
Borinson, A., 95
Borke, H., 295, 365
Borkowski, J. G., 412
Bornstein, M. H., 179, 244
Boschee, P. F., 263
Boswell, A. E., 180
Botuck, S., 391
Bousha, D. M., 283
Bowlby, J., 17, 38–39, 233–235, 238,
    241, 348
Bowser, B. P., 489–490
Boyd, J. L., 142
Boyle, M. H., 384
Boysson-Bardies, B., 201
Brackbill, Y., 115–116
Bradley, C. F., 241
Bradley, L. L., 424
Bradley, R., 284
Bradley, R. H., 318–319, 383
Braine, M., 204

Brainerd, C., 335
Brand, R. J., 422
Brasel, J. A., 284
Bravonwald, K., 239, 283
Brazelton, T. B., 115, 124–126, 133, 161, 221
Brennan, J., 128
Brenner, A., 275, 277
Bretherton, I., 268
Breuer, J., 19
Bricker, W., 344
Brill, N., 239
Brody, L. E., 432
Brody, L. R., 185
Brody, S., 141
Bronfenbrenner, U., 5, 279
Bronson, G., 234
Brookhart, J., 246
Brookhyser, K., 99
Brooks-Gunn, J., 226–227, 324, 476–477, 479, 483–484, 517–518, 520
Brophy, J. E., 319
Brown, A., 274
Brown, B. B., 508, 510, 512
Brown, K., 401
Brown, L. K., 534
Brown, M. M., 451
Brown, R. W., 198, 312
Brown, S. S., 132–133
Brown, W. V., 115
Browne, A., 281
Bruner, J., 203, 305
Bryan, T., 388
Bryant, P. E., 424
Buchsbaum, H. K., 280
Buchsbaum, K., 447
Buck, R., 363
Buckwald, S., 126, 128
Buhrmester, D., 508, 513
Bukowski, W. M., 443, 454
Bullock, M., 296–297
Burgess, A. W., 280
Burgess, R. L., 283
Buri, J. R., 350
Burney, L., 412
Burns, K. A., 78
Burns, S. M., 335
Burns, W. J., 78
Burnside, M. A., 530
Burton, C. B., 455
Bus, R. R., 495
Busch-Rossnagel, N. A., 16
Bushnell, I. W. R., 153
Bushnell, W. W., 169
Butkowsky, S., 427
Butku, M., 534
Butler, N. R., 77
Byers, C., 267
Byrne, B., 423, 426

Cabral, H., 78
Cadigan, D., 415
Caid, C. D., 530

Cain, R., 121, 245
Cairns, B. D., 454
Cairns, R. B., 454
Calabrese, R. L., 501–502
Caldwell, B. M., 318–319, 383
Callan, J. W., 448–449
Camaioni, L., 202
Camara, K. A., 462, 464
Campbell, B. M., 534
Campbell, L., 392
Campos, J. J., 156–157, 242
Cannizzo, S. R., 36
Capon, N., 494
Cappelman, M. W., 124
Carlson, V., 239, 279, 283
Carney, C. C., 340
Caron, A. J., 217
Caron, R. F., 217
Carpenter, C. R., 346
Carpenter, M. W., 84
Carr, M., 412
Carter, J. A., 379
Casali, J., 271
Case, R., 34–35, 306–307, 309, 397, 407–408
Casey, P. H., 284
Casper, V., 238
Casperson, C. J., 378
Cassidy, J., 234, 239, 348
Catalano, R., 285
Ceci, S. J., 307
Cernoch, J. M., 161
Chakraborty, R., 264
Chalemian, R. J., 161
Chalfant, J. C., 388
Chall, J. S., 421, 425
Challip, L., 482
Chambers, D. L., 497, 499
Chan, C. K., 284
Chandler, M. J., 4, 18, 128–129, 139, 310–311, 534
Chapman, M., 241
Charlesworth, R., 337
Charlesworth, W. R., 346–347
Chase-Lansdale, P. L., 248
Chasnoff, I. J., 78
Chen, S. J., 142, 242
Chesler, D., 229
Chess, S., 223–225, 229, 241, 531
Chetwynd, J., 389
Chi, M. T. H., 307, 410
Chilman, C. S., 517
Chinsky, J. H., 36
Chomsky, N., 200
Christy, C., 80
Cicchetti, D., 182, 239, 279–280, 283, 285, 348
Cieslik, C., 378
Clapp, J. F., III, 84
Clark, M. L., 439
Clarke, A. M., 316–317
Clarke, E. V., 312
Clarke-Stewart, A., 215, 242, 245, 248, 321

Clasen, D. R., 512
Clemens, L. P., 360
Clifton, R. K., 178
Clingempeel, W. G., 461
Cloud, G., 269
Cluss, P. A., 264
Clyde, W. A., Jr., 267
Clyman, R. R., 280
Cochran, J. T., 501–502
Cohen, J., 536
Cohn, J. F., 219–221
Coie, J. D., 337, 443–445, 455
Colby, A., 405
Cole, P., 124
Cole, P. M., 365
Cole, P. T., 75
Coleman, C., 78
Coleman, J. C., 512
Coleman, M., 380
Collins, R. C., 324
Collmer, C. W., 279
Comer, J. P., 415
Conger, R. D., 283
Conlon, M. F., 242
Connell, D., 283
Connolly, J. A., 335
Connors, M. E., 486
Cooney, E., 449
Coons, S., 134
Coppotelli, H., 337, 443
Corasaniti, M. A., 321, 466
Corbin, S. B., 462, 464
Corrigan, S. A., 422
Corsaro, W. A., 44
Corsini, D. A., 446
Coustian, D. R., 84
Cowart, B. J., 160
Cowen, E. L., 456
Craig, D., 501–502
Craig, T., 283
Cratty, B. J., 257
Crays, N., 412
Critcher, E. C., 423
Crnic, L., 129, 241
Crockenberg, S., 241
Crook, C. K., 160
Cross, D. R., 410, 412
Crossland, J., 424
Crouter, A., 285
Csikszentmihalyi, M., 482, 508, 512
Cullinanse, E. M., 84
Culver, C., 212–213, 219–220
Cummings, E. M., 241, 342, 348
Cundick, B., 479
Cunningham, C. E., 130
Cunningham, N., 238
Currah, J., 261

Daniels-Beirness, T., 449
Darby, B. L., 78
Darling, J. R., 68
Darwin, C., 36–39, 212

Dasen, P. R., 494
Dashevsky, B., 267
D'Attilio, J. P., 534
Davidson, H. A., 279
Davidson, J. E., 430
Davies, M., 533–534
Dawe, H. C., 341
DeBaryshe, B. D., 536–537
DeBlassie, R. R., 487
Decarie, T. G., 203
DeCasper, A., 151, 159, 181
Deci, E. L., 420–421
Decker, M. D., 271
Delaney, B., 488–489
de Lissovoy, V., 5
Deloria, D., 324
Delucia, C. A., 151
Delugach, J. D., 453
Dembo, M. H., 514
Dement, W., 134
Dempsey, J. R., 178
Denham, S., 353
Dennis, W., 39, 170, 316–317
Denny, F. W., 267
Denny, N. W., 299
Desmond, S., 489
Desrochers, S., 203
Deur, J. L., 25
deUrioste, R., 446
deVries, M. R., 260
deVries, M. W., 226, 260
DeVries, R., 303
Dewey, M. J., 271
Diamond, J. M., 466
Diaz, R. M., 305, 317, 439
Diaz, V., 78
DiClemente, R. J., 489
Dietz, W. H., Jr., 264
DiLalla, L. F., 335
Dion, K. K., 337
Dirkes, K., 78
Dixon, D., 335
Dodd, B. J., 201
Dodds, J. B., 164
Dodge, K. A., 337, 339, 443–449, 451, 453
Doering, S. G., 105
Dolby, R. M., 116
Doman, R. J., 148
Domaniac, J. A., 366
Dong, Q., 304
Donkhorst, I. D., 261
Dooker, M., 111
Dooley, D., 285
Dooling, E., 78
Doran, L. D., 281–282
Dore, J., 202, 221
Dornbusch, S. M., 350, 499
Dossey, J. A., 497, 499
Dotson, C. O., 380
Dougherty, L. M., 214, 216–217
Downs, A. C., 360
Downs, W. R., 535
Doyle, A. B., 246, 335, 400

Drewry, D. L., 439
Driscoll, S. G., 75
Dubowitz, L. M. S., 164
Dubowitz, V., 164
Duda, J. L., 482–483
Dumais, S. T., 152, 156
Duncan, S. W., 365
Durand, C., 201
Durlak, J. A., 534
Durrett, M. E., 242
Dweck, C. S., 456–457
Dye, H. B., 316–317

Earn, B. M., 456, 458
East, P. L., 441, 454
Eastenson, A., 337, 340
Easterbrooks, M. A., 248
Easton, D., 337
Eccles, J. S., 430, 497
Eckenrode, J., 280
Edelman, T., 5
Eder, D., 497, 510
Edwards, C. P., 361
Egan, E. A., 126, 128
Egeland, B., 240, 248, 279, 282–283
Eicher, S. A., 510, 512
Eichler, A. W., 284
Eimas, P. D., 159
Eisele, J., 484
Eisenberg, A. R., 339
Eisenberg, N., 459–461
Eisenberg-Berg, N., 353, 459–460
Ekman, P., 219
Elardo, R., 319
Eldridge, R., 280
Elkind, D., 7, 490, 494–495
Elliot, J., 75
Elliott, S. N., 514
Elmen, J. D., 499
Emde, R. N., 215, 280
Emerson, P. E., 235, 245
Engelmann, S., 326
Enright, M., 185, 495
Entwisle, D. R., 105, 415, 430, 497
Epstein, L. H., 263–264
Erickson, A. M., 91
Erikson, E. H., 21–23, 220, 233, 260,
    522–523, 525–526
Ernst, E. K. M., 109
Erwin, P. G., 439
Escobar, M. D., 425
Eshel, Y., 514
Espinosa, M., 280
Estes, D., 240, 310
Estes, R. E., 529–530
Etheridge, T., 360
Evans, E. D., 501–502
Ewing, M. E., 482

Fagan, J. W., 185–186
Fagot, B. I., 355, 358, 360
Fallot, M. E., 142

Fantz, R. L., 150
Farnoff, A., 128
Farnsworth, M., 535
Farrington, B. P., 536
Farrington, D. P., 536
Fein, G. G., 292, 321, 333, 335
Feinbloom, R. I., 97, 99
Feinlieb, M., 422
Feiring, C., 242
Feldhusen, J. F., 432
Feldman, A. W., 126
Feldman, E., 446, 449, 451
Feldman, R. S., 280
Ferber, J. S., 454
Ferguson, C. A., 205–206
Fergusson, D. M., 276
Fernald, A., 205
Field, D., 401
Field, J., 158
Field, T. M., 128–130, 178, 218, 221–222,
    245, 284, 346–347, 363–364, 442
Fields, R. B., 205
Fierman, B. A., 429
Fifer, N., 151, 159
Fine, G. A., 441
Finkelhor, D., 281
Finlay, B. L., 146
Fischer, K. W., 34, 306, 309, 397, 410
Fivush, R., 308
Flannery, D., 495
Flavell, E. R., 295, 304
Flavell, J. H., 34, 36, 194, 292, 295, 303–304,
    308, 312, 399, 407, 409, 411
Fletcher, J. M., 425
Ford, C. S., 520
Forehand, R., 453
Forest, D., 284
Forman, B. Y., 97, 99
Forrest, J. D., 517
Forsyth, D. R., 502
Fortney, V. L., 258
Foster, J. C., 115
Foster, T., 442
Fournet, G. P., 529–530
Fox, G. L., 520–521
Fox, N. E., 242
Fox, R., 156
Fraiberg, S., 170
Fraleigh, M. J., 350, 499
Frame, C. L., 447
Francis, G., 453
Francis, P. I., 124
Frank, D. A., 78
Frankenberg, W. K., 164
Fraser, B. A., 386
Frauenglass, M., 316
Frederickson, D. S., 90
Freebody, P., 423, 426
Freedman, D. G., 124
Freedman, N., 124
Freedson, P., 265, 378
Fregly, M. J., 474

Freier, C., 78
French, D. C., 444
French, F. E., 129
French, K. E., 375, 377
French, L. A., 312
Frentz, C., 514
Freud, S., 17–23, 233, 260, 342–343, 356, 402–403
Fried, L., 78
Friedman, B. L., 406
Friedman, M., 422
Friedman, S., 129
Friedman, W. J., 406
Friedrichs, A. G., 308
Friend, R., 423
Frietas, B., 160
Frisch, N. E., 68
Fritz, A. S., 310–311
Fritz, G. K., 534
Frodi, A. M., 279
Frost, J. L., 274–275
Frost, P., 442
Fuchs, M., 78
Fudge, D. A., 467
Fullilove, M. T., 489–490
Fullilove, R. E., 489–490
Furman, W., 337–339, 508, 512–513
Furstenberg, F. F., Jr., 464, 517–520
Fuson, K. C., 302, 428–429

Gaddis, A., 476
Gaensbauer, T., 215
Gagnon, C., 455
Galambos, N. L., 466
Gallistel, R., 301–302, 428
Galst, J. P., 264
Ganchrow, J. R., 180
Ganon, E. C., 153
Garbarino, J., 285, 466
Gardner, H., 431
Gardner, L. I., 284
Gardner, W., 490
Garfinkel, B. D., 384
Garfinkel, P. E., 485
Gariepy, J. L., 454
Garner, D. M., 485
Garner, E. E., 180
Garrison, C. Z., 534
Garside, R., 261
Garvey, C., 334, 339
Garvin, R. A., 316
Gauthier, R., 338, 361
Gavin, L., 512
Gdowski, C. L., 534
Geenen, D., 265, 378
Gekoski, M. J., 186
Geller, E. S., 271
Geller, M., 487
Gellert, E., 374
Gelman, R., 296–297, 299, 301–303, 305, 314, 402, 428

George, C., 280–281
Gershman, E. S., 338
Gersick, K. E., 529
Gesell, A., 18
Gest, S. D., 454
Gewirtz, J. L., 116
Ghatala, E. S., 412
Gibbons, K., 484
Gibbs, J., 405
Gibson, E. J., 156–157, 214
Gilbert, G. G., 378, 380
Gilbert, J., 201
Gillespie, C., 18
Gilliam, T. B., 265, 378
Gilligan, C. F., 406, 500
Gillingham, M. G., 424
Gingras, J. L., 78
Glaser, R., 410
Glazer, J. A., 337
Glucksberg, S., 314–315
Gnepp, J., 366
Goddard, P., 534
Godwin, D., 412
Goetz, T. E., 456–457
Goldberg, J., 307, 408
Goldberg, M., 353
Goldberg, S., 129, 242, 390–392
Goldberg, W. A., 248, 467
Goldbloom, D. S., 485
Golden, M. M., 456
Goldman, B. D., 215
Goldman, J. A., 446
Goldman, N., 516
Goldring, E. B., 432
Goldstein, H., 77
Goldwyn, R., 282
Golinkoff, R. M., 205
Golter, B. S., 348, 351–352
Good, T. L., 413
Goodwyn, S. W., 202
Gopnik, A., 299
Gortmaker, S. L., 264
Gotowiec, A., 242
Gottfried, A. E., 420, 467
Gottfried, A. W., 467
Gottman, J. M., 338–339, 440–441
Gough, P. B., 423–424
Gould, M. E., 366
Gove, F. L., 248
Gove, R., 242
Gracely, E., 360
Grady, K., 529
Grajek, S., 321
Gralen, S. J., 483–484
Granrud, C. E., 156
Green, B. B., 68
Green, F. L., 304
Green, M., 17
Greenberg, M., 129, 241, 244, 348
Greenberg, S., 128
Greenberger, E., 467

Greenockle, K. M., 379
Greenough, W. T., 146–147
Greenwald, P., 442
Gresham, F. M., 514
Gresham, I. J., 388
Grieser, D. L., 205
Griffith, D. R., 78
Griffith, P., 424
Grigoryev, P., 219–220
Groff, T. R., 518
Grolnick, W., 217
Gromisch, D. S., 78
Gross, A. M., 380
Gross, J., 483–484
Grossman, H. J., 383
Grossman, K., 242–243
Grossman, K. E., 242–243
Grotevant, H. C., 523
Gruen, G., 320
Gruendel, J. M., 313
Grusec, J. E., 50, 353–354
Guerra, N., 267
Guidubaldi, J., 467
Guilleminault, C., 134
Gulko, S., 400
Gunnar, M., 214
Guralnick, M. H., 388
Gusella, J. L., 218
Guthertz, M., 442
Gzesh, S. M., 295

Haan, N., 340, 494
Habenstein, R. W., 104
Haderman, K. F., 387
Haft, W., 221
Haines, J., 18
Haith, M. M., 149, 160
Hala, S., 310–311
Hall, E. G., 375
Hall, G. S., 507
Hall, J. W., 429
Hallahan, D. P., 388
Hammer, M., 280
Hammond, W. H., 374
Hand, M., 459
Hanis, C., 264
Hanson, F. W., 99
Hanson, J. W., 77
Harackiewicz, J. M., 421
Harlow, H. F., 232–233
Harmon, R., 215
Harmon, R. J., 240
Harnishfeger, K. K., 408
Harris, J. C., 379
Harris, J. R., 264
Harris, P. L., 292
Harrison, H., 126–128
Hart, B., 304
Hart, S. S., 412
Harter, S., 440, 534
Hartman, C. R., 280

Hartmann, D. P., 511
Hartup, W. W., 336–337, 339–341, 448, 455, 512
Hatch, J., 178
Haviland, J. M., 218–219
Hawkins, J. D., 535
Hawley, T., 79
Haydon, B., 84
Hayduk, L., 415
Hayes, C. D., 520
Hayes, D. S., 338
Haynes, O. M., 216
Haynes, S. G., 422
Hazen, N. L., 337
Healy, B., 442
Hechtman, L., 385
Held, R., 171
Hellmann, J., 130
Helspaer-Lucas, A., 83
Hembree, E. A., 214, 216–217
Henggeler, S. W., 534–535
Hensinger, R. N., 386
Herman, J., 490
Heron, A., 494
Herrell, N., 128
Hertig, A. T., 75
Hertsgaard, D., 484
Hess, R. D., 319
Hesse-Biber, S., 483
Hetherington, E. M., 5, 9, 461–462, 464
Hicks, L. E., 84
Hilderbrandt, K. A., 130
Hill, J. P., 497
Hillier, L., 484
Hinde, R. A., 337, 346
Hingson, R., 78
Hinkle, J. S., 379
Hirsch, H. V. B., 147
Hobart, C. J., 336–340
Hock, E. E., 246, 248
Hoegsberg, B., 84
Hofer, L., 221
Hofferth, S. L., 520
Hoff-Ginsberg, E., 205–206
Hoffman, J., 221
Hoffman, L. W., 247, 416, 465, 467
Hoffman, M. L., 461
Hoffman-Plotkin, D., 280
Hogan, A. G., 141
Hogan, D. P., 519
Hohmann, M., 305, 323, 325
Hollenbeck, A. R., 116
Holroyd, J., 390
Hooks, P., 378
Horowitz, F. D., 9, 18, 124, 432
Hotchner, T., 68, 73
Housemen, J., 340
Howard, J., 79
Howes, C., 248, 280, 332–334, 338–339
Hoyseth, K. S., 77
Hoyt, J. D., 308

Hoza, B., 443
Hubert, N. C., 392
Hughey, M. J., 111
Hume, R. J., Jr., 78
Humphrey, K., 201, 487
Hune, S., 99
Hunt, C. E., 78
Hunt, J., 305, 316
Hutcheson, R. H., 271
Huttenlocher, P. R., 147, 295
Hutto, C., 80
Hwang, C. P., 245
Hymel, S., 454–455

Iannotti, R. J., 342, 458
Ignatoff, E., 128, 130
Ilg, F. L., 18
Inazo, J. K., 521
Inderbitzen-Pisaruk, H., 515
Inhelder, B., 294, 298, 400–401, 492–493
Irwin, C. E., 517
Isabella, R., 238, 240
Istvan, J., 83
Ito, J., 95
Izard, C. E., 212, 214–218
Izzo, L. D., 456

Jacklin, C. N., 361–362
Jackowitz, E. R., 292
Jackson, K. L., 534
Jackson, L. G., 99
Jacobs, B., 129
Jacobs, R., 80
Jacobson, J. L., 205
Jacobson, T., 534
Jacobvitz, D., 279, 282, 384–385
Janos, P. M., 432
Janowsky, J. S., 146
Janzen, L., 79
Jaskir, J., 242
Javernik, E., 265
Jenkins, L. B., 497, 499
Jennings, R. J., 422
Jensen, L. C., 479
Jerauld, R., 229
Joffee, L. S., 241
Johnson, C., 486
Johnson, J., 335
Johnson, L. D., 75
Johnson, M. A., 308
Johnson, R., 271
Johnson, R. L., 488–489
Johnson, T., 412
Johnson, T. C., 380
Jolly, A., 346
Jones, D. C., 308
Jones, E. F., 517
Jones, G. P., 514
Jones, J. H., 77
Jones, M. C., 480
Joschko, M., 384

Jovanovic, J., 374
Juel, C., 424, 426
Jusczyk, P. W., 158–159, 201

Kagan, J., 235, 241
Kahn, J. R., 520
Kamptner, N. L., 522
Kandel, D. B., 533–534
Kannel, W. B., 422
Kantner, J. F., 509, 517, 520
Kaplan, D., 78
Kaplan, G. N., 91
Kaplan, N., 234, 239, 348
Karlberg, E., 78
Kashani, J. H., 534–535
Katz, P. A., 421
Katz, S. J., 380
Kaufman, J., 280, 282
Kavanaugh, R. D., 292
Kay, T., 95
Kayne, H., 78
Kazdin, A. E., 535, 537
Kearsley, R. B., 235, 292
Keating, D., 494
Keeling, R. P., 490
Keeney, T. J., 36
Kegeles, S. M., 517
Keller, B. B., 126
Keller, C. E., 388
Keller, S. E., 488
Kelley, J., 484, 487
Kellman, P. J., 155
Kendall, P., 385
Kendrick, J. E., 378
Kennedy, E. T., 84
Kennedy, J. H., 352
Kennell, J. H., 228–229
Keogh, J., 139, 164–170, 257–258, 375–376
Kerlinger, F. N., 42, 48
Kerwin, K., 412
Kessen, M., 529
Key, T. C., 83–84
Khanna, P., 321
Kiely, M. A., 128
Kiely, M. C., 458
Killam, A. P., 78
King, C. A., 534
King, R. A., 354
Kirschenbaum, D. S., 487
Kisilevsky, B. S., 161, 178
Kister, M. C., 270
Kitagawa, E. M., 519
Kitzinger, S., 73
Klahr, D., 17, 35
Klaus, M. H., 228–229
Kleiber, D. A., 380, 482
Klein, R., 240, 246
Klesges, R. C., 263
Kletter, R., 78
Kliegman, R., 90, 263, 485–486
Kliewer, W., 423

Knobloch, H., 259
Kohlberg, L., 356, 403–406, 494, 500
Kolata, G., 264
Kolb, S., 162, 171
Kolbe, L. J., 378
Koluchova, J., 316
Kolvin, I., 261
Kopp, C. B., 94
Korn, S. J., 374
Korner, A. F., 127–128
Koslowski, B., 221
Kotelchuk, M., 244–245
Kracke, B., 479
Krager, J. M., 384
Kramer, T. L., 334
Krantz, M., 337, 455
Krasnor, L. R., 446, 449, 451
Krauss, R. M., 314–315
Kreger, N. C., 229
Kreisel, P. S. J., 379–380
Krekewich, K., 392
Kreutzer, M. A., 308
Kroger, J., 487
Kropenske, V., 79
Kropp, J. P., 216
Krowitz, A., 157
Kruger, T. L., 489
Ku, L. C., 517
Kuczynski, L., 241, 282
Kuhl, P. K., 201, 205
Kuhn, D., 494
Kukulka, G., 489
Kulak, A., 430
Kupersmidt, J. B., 444–445, 455
Kurkjian, M., 401
Kurland, D. M., 307, 409
Kurman, J., 514
Kurtz, B. E., 412
Kyllerman, M., 78

Ladd, G. W., 42–43, 348, 351–352, 444
La Freniere, P. J., 338, 346–347, 361
LaGaipa, J. J., 439
Lagercrantz, H., 121
Laird, M., 280
Lamb, C., 219–220
Lamb, M. E., 229, 240, 279, 244–245
Lamborn, S. D., 499
Lampert, R. W., 145
Lane, D. M., 384
Lange, G., 308
Langer, A., 157
Langer, J., 494
Langham, R. A., 84
Langley, J., 274
Langlois, J. H., 360
Lapsley, D. K., 495
Larner, M. B., 326
Larrance, D. T., 282
Larrieu, J., 460
Larsen, J. M., 320
Larson, R., 508, 512

Lasaga, M., 412
Latham, C., 295
Lauersen, N. H., 66, 68–69, 85, 88, 97–98, 110
Laursen, B., 337, 340
Lawler, K. A., 423
Leal, L., 412
Leboyer, F., 111
Lee, A. M., 78, 375, 379
Lee, M., 535
Lee, V. E., 324
LeFevre, J., 430
Leffert, N., 384
Leggett, E. L., 458
Leibenberg, B., 244
Leikowitz, L. J., 387
Leinbach, M. D., 355
Lelwica, M., 217
LeMare, L. J., 454–455
Leming, J. S., 503
Lempers, J. D., 295
Lenhart, L., 449
Lenneberg, E. H., 147
Lennon, R., 459–461
Lenz, W., 74
Leonard, C., 308
Lepore, S. J., 458
Lerner, J. V., 531
Lerner, R. M., 16, 374
Lesko, M., 109, 113
Lesko, W., 109, 113
Lester, B. M., 115, 121, 124–126, 133, 221
Levenson, S. M., 78
Leventhal, A. S., 158
Levin, J. R., 412
Levine, M. P., 483–484, 486
Levy, A. K., 335
Levy, H. L., 91
Lewis, J. M., 462, 464
Lewis, M., 212–213, 220, 226–227, 236, 242
Li, W., 142
Lieberman, E., 109
Lieberman, M., 405
Liederman, P. H., 350, 499
Lifshitz, G., 143
Light, H. K., 484
Lincoln, R., 517
Lindquist, M. M., 497, 499
Linney, J. A., 413
Lipsitt, L. P., 158, 160
Liptak, G. S., 126
Lishner, D. M., 535
Littman, R. A., 344
Livson, N., 480
Lloyd, J. W., 388
Lochman, J. E., 449
Lodico, M. G., 412
Lohr, M. J., 508, 510
Lojkasek, M., 390–391
Lollis, S., 454
London, P., 458
Lorenz, K. Z., 37–38, 234

Louiselle, P. A., 350
Lowe, C. R., 71
Lowrey, G. H., 257
Lozoff, B., 142
Lubold, P., 534
Lucas, D., 185
Luck, C. M., 420
Lundberg, U., 423
Luttge, W. G., 474
Lynch, M. E., 497
Lyons, B. G., 302
Lyons-Ruth, K., 283
Lyrene, R., 80
Lytton, H., 358

Mabe, P. A., 422
Macarthur, D., 390
Maccoby, E. E., 349–350, 361–362, 365
MacConnie, S. E., 378
MacGregor, D., 390–392
MacKinnon, C. E., 462
MacLean, D. J., 217
MacLean, M., 424
Maddahian, E., 530–531
Magnusson, D., 479, 518
Mahler, M. S., 226
Main, D. S., 421
Main, M., 221, 234, 236–239, 241, 280–282, 348
Makuch, R., 425
Malatesta, C. Z., 212–213, 215, 219–220
Malott, J. M., 263
Maratsos, M., 200, 314
Marcia, J. E., 524, 526
Marcovitch, S., 390–392
Marcus, M., 128
Maris, R., 533
Marks, J. S., 76
Markstrom, C. A., 525–526
Markstrom-Adams, C. A., 526
Marone, F., 487
Marshall, W., 477
Martin, D. C., 78
Martin, G. L., 529–530
Martin, J. A., 349–350
Martin, R. J., 128
Marvin, R. S., 348
Marwick, C., 267, 268
Mast, V. K., 186
Masters, J. C., 337, 339, 365
Matarazzo, J. D., 423
Matheny, A. P., Jr., 274
Mathy, R. M., 459–461
Matsumoto, D., 340
Matthews, D. A., 422
Mattran, K., 401
Maurer, D., 153, 155
Mayaux, M. J., 68
McAlpine, W., 229
McCabe, A. E., 402
McCartney, K., 321
McCauley, E., 95

McClaskey, C. L., 446, 451
McClearn, G. E., 264
McClelland, G. H., 420
McCormack, A., 280
McCoy, J. K., 519
McCrary, J. S., 529–530
McCutcheon-Rosegg, S., 114
McDuffie, M., 422
McElin, T. W., 111
McGraw, M. B., 171–172
McGrory, A., 477
McGuffog, C., 242
McGuire, K. D., 441
McKee, E., 366
McKelvey, R. S., 530
McKeown, R. E., 534
McKinney, J. D., 388
McKusick, V. A., 90
McLaren, N. M., 76
McLaughlin, F. J., 161
McLaughlin, R. J., 501–502, 530
McLean, F. H., 121
McManus, K., 116
McMillan, J. H., 502
McNeill, D., 200
McWilliams, M., 83, 142
Meck, E., 301
Medlin, C., 520
Meece, J. L., 430
Melton, G. B., 281
Meltzoff, A. N., 183, 201, 299
Menig-Peterson, C. L., 314
Merkin, S., 301, 312
Messer, S. C., 466
Michalson, L., 212–213, 220
Midgley, C., 497
Milewski, A. E., 151
Miller, B. C., 519–520
Miller, C. L., 128
Miller, P. A., 460–461
Miller, P. H., 399, 409, 411
Miller, S., 266
Miller, S. A., 399
Miller-Tutzauer, C., 534
Mills, R., 455
Milstead, M., 495
Milunsky, A., 76–77, 81–82, 92, 95, 100
Minde, K., 130
Minuchin, S., 486–487
Misukanis, T. M., 350
Miyake, K., 242
Mize, J., 42–43
Moely, B. E., 412
Moffit, T. E., 536
Molitor, N., 248
Montano, D., 83
Moore, D., 185
Moore, K. A., 519
Moore, K. L., 72
Moore, M. K., 183
Moore, T. R., 83–84
Moran, M., 160

Morison, V., 178
Morris, A. M., 258
Morris, N., 244
Morris, N. M., 518
Morrison, D., 514
Morrison, D. M., 517
Morrongiello, B. A., 186, 365
Morrow, C., 442
Moses, N., 143
Moskowitz, D. S., 422
Mounts, N. S., 499
Mueller, R. A., 350
Muenchow, S., 388
Muir, D., 158, 161, 178, 218
Mullis, I. V. S., 497, 499
Munroe, R., 244
Murnen, S. K., 483–484
Murphy, R. R., 447
Murray, A. D., 116
Murray, J., 78
Mussen, P., 353, 459–460, 480
Muzio, J., 134
Myers, B., 360
Myers, L. C., 439

Nader, P. R., 378
Naeye, R. L., 76–77
Nagy, W. E., 427
Nahmias, A., 80
Nanson, J., 78
Nastasi, B. K., 467
Nation, R. L., 116
Neal, C. J., 305
Neckerman, J. J., 454
Neisworth, J. T., 320
Nelson, C. A., 124
Nelson, K., 197, 203, 206, 313
Nenshaw, S. K., 517
Nesher, P., 428
Netley, C., 95
Neutra, R., 118
Newcomb, A. F., 439, 441, 454
Newcomb, M. D., 528, 530–531
Newman, J. L., 497
Nezlek, J., 420
Nickerson, R. J., 75
Nicolich, L., 293
Nieberg, P., 76
Nikolic, J., 495
Nolan, J., 261
Noonan, J., 430
Norbeck, J. S., 83
Nord, C. W., 464
Norris, W. R., 261
Norton, E. M., 534
Nowakowski, R. S., 143
Nozyce, M., 238
Nugent, K. J., 115, 124–126, 133

Oates, R. K., 284
O'Brien, M., 432
O'Callaghan, M. F., 128

O'Connell, B., 201–204
O'Connor, B. P., 494
O'Connor, M. J., 239
O'Connor, S. M., 284
O'Donnell, K. J., 78
O'Donnell, L., 350
Offord, D. R., 384
O'Hara, N. M., 378–379
Oka, E. R., 411
Okagaki, L., 416, 418
O'Keefe, B. J., 339
O'Leary, K., 292
Olegard, R., 78
Olenick, M., 248
Ollendick, T. H., 453
Olsen, J. A., 479
Olson, K. L., 205
Olson, T. D., 519
Olweus, D., 350
Omanson, R. C., 295
Opipari, L., 534
Oppenheimer, E., 78
Ordman, A. M., 487
Origel, W., 83–84
Oski, F. A., 142
Otaki, M., 242
Otomo, K., 201
Overholser, J., 534
Owen, M. T., 248
Owsley, C., 156

Pagel, M., 83
Pakter, J., 128
Palkovitz, R., 245
Pallas, A. M., 415
Palmer, B., 201
Pancake, V. R., 242
Paneth, N., 128
Pankey, W., 234
Panneton, R. K., 159
Papousek, H., 184
Papousek, M., 184
Parcel, G., 378–379
Paris, S. G., 410–412
Parke, K. A., 348
Parke, R. D., 25, 244, 279, 348, 350–351
Parker, F. L., 324
Parker, J. B., 453
Parker, J. G., 44, 337–339, 440–441, 455–456
Parker, S., 78
Parkhurst, J. T., 454
Parmelee, A. H., 134, 268, 270
Parten, M. B., 332–333
Pasamanick, B., 259
Pasnak, R., 401
Pass, R. F., 269
Passman, R. H., 236
Pasternack, J., 459–461
Pastor, D., 348
Pate, R. R., 378–379
Patten, S. E., 484

Patterson, C. J., 270, 455
Patterson, G. R., 344–345, 349–350, 536–537
Patton, G. C., 483–484
Pavlov, I., 23–24
Paxton, S. J., 484
Peacock, A., 284
Pearson, D. A., 384
Peay, L., 324
Peck, J., 346–347
Pedersen, F. A., 121, 245
Pedersen, N. L., 264
Pederson, A., 456
Pederson, D. R., 238
Pels, A. E., III, 378
Pennington, B. F., 95
Pereira, C., 423
Pergament, G. G., 302
Perrotta, M., 130
Perry, M. A., 281–282
Perry, T. B., 441
Peskin, H., 480
Peters, D. L., 320
Petersen, A. C., 475, 478–479, 497
Peterson, J. L., 519
Petitti, D. B., 78
Petratis, M. M., 379
Petrie, S., 510
Pettersen, L., 156
Pettit, G. S., 451
Phelps, J. A., 386
Phelps, P. C., 335
Phillips, D., 321
Phinney, J. S., 526–527
Phinney, V. G., 479
Piaget, J., 16–17, 29–34, 50, 164, 182–183, 186–195, 270, 290–291, 293–294, 296, 298, 300–301, 305, 313–314, 316, 333, 397–404, 407, 492–494, 500
Pierce, S. H., 308
Pine, F., 226
Pinner, E., 488–489
Piotrkowski, S. S., 324
Pisoni, D. B., 158–159, 201
Placek, P. J., 121
Pleck, J. H., 517
Plumert, J. M., 448
Pohlman, J. C., 313
Pokorny, A. D., 530
Pollitt, E., 284
Poore, M., 115
Pope, W. R., 502
Porter, R. H., 161
Pottick, K. J., 467
Powell, D., 80
Powell, G. F., 284
Powell, K. E., 378
Prentice, N., 535
Prescott, P., 159, 181
Pressley, M., 412
Presson, C. C., 295

Pretrovich, J. L., 484
Price, G. G., 424
Price, J. H., 489
Price, J. M., 337, 339
Probert, J. S., 409
Puck, M., 95
Pugliese, M. T., 143
Putallaz, M., 453

Queen, S. A., 104
Queenan, J. T., 70
Qui, S., 304
Quigley, M. E., 76
Quine, L., 392
Quintana, S. M., 495

Rabiner, D. L., 449
Radke-Yarrow, M., 241, 353–354
Ragozin, A., 129, 241
Raj, M. H., 518
Ramsey, E., 536–537
Ramsey, P. G., 439
Randolph, M., 185
Rankin, D. B., 511
Rao, N., 412
Raskin, A., 534
Ratcliff, G., 80
Raveis, V. H., 533–534
Ravin, A., 353
Read, G. D., 110
Reece, H., 78
Reese, H. W., 409
Reid, J. C., 534
Reis, S. M., 431
Remington, P. L., 76
Renouf, A. G., 534
Resnick, G., 464
Resnick, L. B., 428–430
Resnik, R., 83–84
Reynolds, A. J., 415
Reznick, E., 335
Rhoads, G. G., 99
Rhodes, B., 487
Ricard, M., 203
Rice, M. L., 197
Richard, B. A., 448–449
Richard, K., 453
Richards, J. A., 534
Richards, M., 128
Richards, M. H., 508, 534
Richards, P., 242
Rieder, C., 280
Riesen, W., 219
Rieser, J., 160
Rigler, D., 283
Riley, W. J., 422
Ritter, P. L., 350, 499
Robbins, W. J., 141
Roberts, C. J., 71
Roberts, D. F., 350, 499
Roberts, G. C., 380, 482

Roberts, L. R., 497
Roberts, M. C., 271
Robertson, E. D., 529–530
Robertson, J. F., 535
Robinson, A. B., 406
Robinson, C. C., 320
Robinson, N., 129
Robinson, N. M., 432
Robson, K. S., 245
Rocca, P., 365
Rock, S. L., 383
Rodning, C., 79
Roff, J. D., 456
Roff, M., 456
Roffwarg, H., 134
Rogoff, B., 305
Rogosch, F. A., 439, 441
Romney, D. M., 358
Rook, K. S., 441, 454
Rooks, J. P., 109
Roscoe, B., 489
Rose, D., 178
Rose, S. A., 152
Rosegg, P., 115
Rosen, C., 335
Rosen, D., 109
Rosen, J. C., 483–484
Rosenblith, J. F., 185
Rosenblum, P. L., 130
Rosenfeld, A., 109
Rosenman, R. H., 422
Rosenthal, P. A., 276
Rosenthal, S., 276
Rosenzweig, M. R., 147
Rosett, L. R., 78
Rosman, B., 487
Rosoff, J. I., 517
Ross, D., 343
Ross, E. M., 77
Ross, H. S., 215
Ross, J. G., 378–380
Ross, S. A., 343
Ross, S. M., 501–502
Roth, K., 459–460
Rovee-Collier, C., 178, 180, 185–186, 205
Rovet, J., 95
Rovine, M., 238, 240–241, 248
Rowden, L., 455
Rubin, D., 128
Rubin, K. H., 292, 333, 335, 446, 449, 451, 454–455
Ruble, D. N., 421, 477
Ruff, H. A., 152
Rutter, M., 8, 316–317, 425
Ryan, K. J., 109
Ryan, R. M., 420–421

Saarni, S., 364
Sabel, K. G, 78
Sady, M. A., 84
Sady, S. P., 84, 379

Safer, D. J., 384
Sagart, C., 201
Salapatek, P., 152–153
Salbenblatt, J., 95
Sallis, J. F., 380
Saltz, E., 335
Salzinger, S., 280
Sameroff, A. J., 4, 18, 128–129, 139, 185
Sampson, P. D., 78
Sancilio, F. M., 448
Sanders-Woudstra, J. A. R., 261
Sandin, A., 78
Sarigiani, P. A., 497
Savage, M. P., 379
Sawin, D. B., 126, 244
Scanlon, J. W., 115
Scarr, S., 321
Schaefer, L., 335
Schaffer, H. R., 235, 245
Schaffner, W., 271
Schanberg, S. M., 128
Schenk, V. M., 50
Schlegel, A., 516, 520
Schleifer, S. J., 488–489
Schlesselman, S. E., 99
Schlundt, D. G., 453
Schneider, W., 407, 412
Schnorr, S. H., 78
Schnur, E., 324
Schochet, S. S., 145
Schocken, I., 453
Schroeder, C., 374
Schull, W. J., 264
Schulsinger, F., 264
Schulz, H. R., 134
Schwartz, D., 68
Schweinhart, L. J., 326
Scott, S., 128
Scott-Jones, D., 516
Sears, R. R., 232
Sebris, S. L., 116
Secada, W. G., 426–429
Seefeldt, V., 265
Sefton, J. M., 379–380
Segal, M., 346–347
Seidel, W. T., 384
Seidman, E., 413
Seidner, B. K., 332–334
Seier, W. L., 409
Seifer, R., 241
Seitz, V., 148
Self, P. A., 124
Sells, S. B., 456
Selman, R., 449
Serbin, L. A., 362, 400
Sexton, G., 423
Shah, F. K., 508, 517, 520
Shahraray, B., 265, 378
Shannon, F. T., 276
Shantz, C. U., 336, 339–340
Shapiro, J. R., 534

Shatz, M., 314
Shaw, W., 261
Shaywitz, B. A., 425
Shaywitz, S. E., 425
Shea, E., 156, 220–221
Sheehan, K. L., 76
Sheinman, L., 420
Sheldon, W. H., 373
Shell, R., 459–461
Shepard, B., 212–213
Shepperd, J. A., 535
Sherman, D., 285
Sherrod, K. B., 284
Shiffrin, R. M., 35, 307, 407
Shipman, V. C., 319
Shore, C., 201–204
Sholtz, R. I., 422
Shukla, D., 495
Shure, M. B., 448
Siedentop, D., 266
Siegel, J., 422
Siegel, L. S., 402
Siegler, R. S., 35, 397
Sigafoos, A. D., 181
Sigman, M. D., 179, 239
Silber, S. J., 69
Silbereisen, R. K., 479
Silver, D. H., 348
Silverberg, S. B., 512
Simkin, P., 105–106, 119
Simmons, K., 267, 269
Simmons, R., 242, 479
Simons, R. L., 535
Simons-Morton, D. G., 378–379
Simons-Morton, R., 378–379
Singleton, L., 439
Siqueland, E. R., 25, 151, 159, 181
Skeels, H. M., 316–317
Skeen, P., 380
Skinner, B. F., 25, 198
Skuse, D., 316
Slater, A., 178
Slobin, D., 204
Slotkin, T. A., 121
Smilansky, S., 335
Smilkstein, G., 83
Smith, C. L., 299
Smith, D., 261
Smith, D. W., 77
Smith, J. L., 379
Smith, P. B., 238
Smith, R., 383
Smith, R. S., 129
Smolak, L., 483–484
Snarey, J. R., 406
Snow, C. E., 199, 205–206
Snow, D. L., 529
Sobol, M. P., 456, 458
Sockloff, A., 360
Solomon, J., 236, 238–239
Sonenstein, F. L., 517

Sonnenschein, S., 412
Sorensen, R. C., 516, 518
Sorensen, T. I. A., 264
Sowers-Hoag, K. W., 25, 271
Spangler, C., 242–243
Spelke, E. S., 153–155
Spence, I., 402
Spence, M. J., 159
Spencer, M. B., 526
Spinelli, D. N., 147
Spinetta, J., 283
Spira, A., 68
Spirito, A., 534
Spitz, E. R., 149
Spitz, R. A., 39
Spivack, G., 448
Spizzirri, C., 214
Sroufe, A., 212, 215, 226, 240–242, 279, 282–283, 348, 384–385
Staffieri, J. R., 374
Stagno, S., 80, 269
Stahl, J., 283
Stainer, K. E., 282
Staines, G. L., 466
Stanbury, J. B., 90
Standard, B. A., 423
Stanger, C. L., 78
Stanley-Hagan, M., 461–462, 464
Stanovich, K. E., 424–425, 427
Stapleton, S., 109
Stattin, H., 479, 518
Stayton, D. J., 236
Steele, R., 80
Steffa, M., 229
Steinberg, L., 285, 321, 422–423, 466, 499, 512
Steiner, J. E., 160, 180
Stern, D., 184, 221
Stern, M., 130
Sternberg, R. J., 416, 418, 431
Sternglanz, S. H., 362
Steuve, A., 350
Stevenson, D. L., 416
Stevenson, H. W., 416, 419
Stevenson, M. R., 360
Stewart, M. A., 337, 340, 384
Stigler, W., 416, 419
Stillman, A. J., 75
Stoel-Gammon, C., 201
Stone, R. K., 78
Strayer, F. F., 338, 346, 361
Strayer, J., 342
Streissguth, A. P., 77–78
Streitmatter, J. L., 526
Stringer, S., 128, 130
Strober, M., 487
Strunin, L., 488–489
Stunkard, A. J., 264
Suess, G., 242–243
Sugden, D., 139, 164–170, 257–258, 375–376
Sulf, D., 517

Sullivan, H. S., 439, 455, 513
Sullivan, M. W., 185–186
Suomi, S., 145–147, 162, 232–233
Super, C. M., 170–171
Surber, C. F., 295
Susman, E. J., 282, 285
Susser, M., 128
Suwalsky, J., 240
Swain, I., 185
Swartz, K. B., 153
Swift, D. J., 308
Szatmari, P., 384
Szmukler, G. I., 484

Taggart, A. C., 266
Taggart, J., 266
Takenaka, J., 84
Talbert, L., 518
Tamplin, A., 338
Tanner, J. M., 141, 145, 373, 475
Taunch, J., 261
Taylor, A. R., 388, 392
Taylor, B., 475, 478
Taylor, D. G., 238, 240
Taylor, F., 267
Taylor, M., 304
Teasdale, T. W., 264
Tees, R., 201
Temoshok, L., 489
Templin, M. C., 198
Tennant, F., 99
Termine, N. T., 218
Tesman, J. R., 212–213
Thelen, E., 164–165, 171–172
Theodorou, P., 340
Thieman, A., 282
Thomas, A., 223–225, 229, 241, 531
Thomas, D. B., 116
Thomas, J. R., 375, 377
Thompson, P. D., 84, 378
Thompson, R. A., 240
Thompson, R. J., 124
Thompson, W. H., 379
Thornberg, M., 265
Thornton, L. P., 487
Thyer, B. A., 25, 271
Tilden, V. P., 83
Tilton, M. M., 156
Timmer, F. C., 261
Tinbergen, N., 37
Ting, G., 178
Titmus, G., 337
Todd, G., 201
Torgesen, J. K., 424–425
Toth, S. L., 280, 285
Trause, M. A., 215
Traxler, W., 487
Treiber, F. A., 422
Trethowan, W. H., 244
Triana, E., 401
Trickett, P. K., 282, 285
Tronick, E. Z., 218–221

Tronick, I. J., 362
Trost, M. A., 456
Trudel, M., 346
Trussell, J., 517
Tsong, Y., 378
Tuckman, B. W., 379
Tunmer, W. E., 423
Turner, D. S., 271
Turner, L. A., 412
Turner, R. L., 425
Twentymen, C. T., 280, 282–283
Tynes, D. M., 186

Udry, J. R., 518
Unger, O., 332–334
Ungerer, J. A., 185, 292
Unzer, L., 242–243
Usher, R. H., 121

Vachio, A., 305
Valoski, A., 263
Vandell, D. L., 321, 466
Vandenberg, B., 292, 333, 335
Van der Lee, J. H., 261
Varni, J. W., 392
Vaughn, B. E., 240–241, 248
Vega-Lahr, N., 346–347
Verhulst, F. C., 261
Vicary, J. R., 531
Vietz, P. M., 284
Vigorito, J., 159
Vinci, R., 78
Vitaro, F., 455
Volkin, J., 422
Volterra, V., 202
Vondra, J. I., 279–280, 285
Von Eye, A., 238, 240
von Hofsten, C., 155, 169
Vosk, B., 453
Vurpillot, E., 307
Vygotsky, L. S., 305

Waas, G. A., 444, 448
Wachs, T. D., 320
Wagner, R. C., 424–425
Wagner, W. G., 261
Wald, E. R., 267
Walden, T. A., 363–364
Walk, R. D., 156–157, 214
Walker, J. L., 534
Walker, L. J., 406
Walker-Andrews, A. S., 217
Wall, S., 234, 236–238
Wallace, C. M., 519
Wallace, C. S., 146–147
Wallach, M. A., 432
Wallender, J. L., 392
Wallenstein, S., 128
Wallerstein, J. S., 462, 464
Walsh, D. J., 424
Walters, C. E., 161
Wankel, L. M., 379–380

Wanska, S. K., 314
Warren, M. P., 475, 479, 483
Wasserman, A., 453
Waterman, A. S., 524–525
Waters, E., 234, 236–238, 242, 348
Waters, S. E., 240
Watson, J. B., 18, 23
Watson, M. W., 292, 335
Watts, J. C., 317–318
Waxman, S., 299, 402
Weatherby, N. L., 109
Webb, J. A., 530
Weber, J. M., 264
Wegman, M. E., 107, 132
Weidner, G., 423
Weiher, A. W., 420
Weikart, D. P., 305, 323, 325–326
Weiner, L., 78
Weinraub, M., 236, 360
Weinstein, R. S., 413
Weiss, G., 385
Weiss, J. B., 115
Weiss, M., 185
Weiss, M. G., 411
Weiss, N. S., 68
Weiss, S. J., 389
Weisz, J. R., 441
Wellman, H. M., 309–310, 366, 411
Wells, E. A., 281–282
Welte, J. W., 530
Wenar, C., 483–484, 486
Wender, P. H., 385
Wenner, W. H., 134
Werker, J., 201
Werner, E. E., 129
Wertheim, E. H., 484
Werthhammer, J., 80
Werthmann, M., 129
Westoff, C. F., 517
Weston, D. R., 241
Weyman-Daum, M., 143
Wheeler, V. A., 454
White, A. B., 516
White, B. L., 173, 317–318
White, D., 400
White, M. A., 264
White, R., 128
Whiting, B. B., 361
Whiting, J., 242
Whitley, R., 80
Whitman, T. L., 128
Wibbelsman, C., 517
Widmayer, S., 128, 130
Wigfield, A., 430
Wikner, K., 160
Wildes, M. M., 76
Wilkerson, A., 402
Wilks, J., 512
Will, M., 388
Willett, L., 80
Williams, G. A., 388, 392, 454
Williams, J. L., 258

Willows, D., 427
Wilmore, J. H., 258
Wilson, R. S., 274
Windol, M., 534
Winer, G. A., 402
Wing, R. R., 263–264
Winograd, P., 411
Winsberg, B. G., 391
Wippman, J., 242, 348
Wolfe, D. A., 279, 281
Wolfe, H., 229
Wolff, P. H., 134
Woodward, L., 116
Wooten, J., 312
Worobey, J., 126
Wortham, B., 274–275, 284
Woznica, J. G., 534

Wu, F., 338
Wuensch, K. L., 466
Wyngaarden, J. B., 90

Yabrove, B., 340
Yammamoto, N., 401
Yawkey, T. D., 320
Yen, S. S. C., 76
Yogman, M. W., 124
Yonas, A., 156, 160
Young, K. T., 348
Young, T., 111
Yu, S., 142
Yule, W., 435

Zabin, L. S., 517
Zahn-Waxler, C., 342, 353–354

Zahr, L. K., 128
Zarbatany, L., 511
Zaslow, M. J., 121, 245
Zeitschel, K. A., 124
Zelazo, N. A., 162, 171
Zelazo, P. R., 162, 171, 185, 292
Zelko, F. A., 365
Zelnik, M., 508–509, 517, 520
Zhang, X. D., 304
Zigler, E., 148, 248, 282, 388
Zill, N., 464
Zimmerman, R. R., 232
Zoll, D., 283
Zorn, J., 489
Zorn, W. A., 126, 128
Zou, H., 304
Zuckerman, B. S., 78

Academic achievement
in adolescence, 497–500
in middle childhood, 411–433
and parenting style, 499
Accidental injury, 270–277
car accidents and restraints, 270–271
and hyperactivity, 384
and playgrounds, 274–275
psychological characteristics and, 271–274
and stress, 276
and temperament, 274
Accommodation, 31, 186–187, 305
Accutane, 75
Achievement motivation, 420–421
Acuity, 152
Adaptation, 31, 187
Adjustment problems, 528–537
juvenile delinquency, 534–537
substance abuse, 528–531
suicide, 533–534
Adolescent egocentrism, 494–496
and formal operations, 495–496
imaginary audience, 494–496
personal fable, 495–496
Adolescent growth spurt, 474–477
Affective attunement, 221, 442
Age of viability, 72
Aggression, 341–345, 350, 448–449, 455, 536–537
and psychoanalytic theory, 342–343
and social learning theory, 343–344
AIDS (acquired immune deficiency syndrome)
in adolescence, 488–491
and pregnancy, 81
prevention, 490–491
risk factors, 488–490
Alleles, 89
Alpha fetoprotein testing, 99
Alternative birthing centers, 109
Ambivalent attachment, 237
Amoral reasoning, 403
Anoxia, 123, 148
Appearance and reality, 303–304
Arousal modulation, 221
Artificial rupture of membranes, 119
Assimilation, 31, 186–187, 305
Athletics, 379–380, 481–483
and goal-setting, 482–483
risk and opportunity, 380
Attachment, 212, 230–250, 348
and attention deficit/hyperactivity disorder, 383–386
and caregiving, 238, 240
and culture, 242–243
and day care, 246–250

fathers and, 244–246
internal working model, 234
long-term consequences of, 241–242
and maltreatment, 239, 283
patterns of, 236–238
phases of, 234–236
secure base, 234
and social competence, 348
strange situation, 236–237, 239
and stress, 240–241
and temperament, 241
theoretical perspectives on, 231–234
Attention
in early childhood, 306–309
facilitation of, 308–309
Attributional style, 456–458
Auditory perception, 158–160, 201
location of sound sources, 158–159
of speech sounds, 159–160
Authoritarian parenting, 349–350
Authoritative parenting, 349–350, 466
Automatic reasoning, 449
Autonomous moral reasoning, 404
Autonomy, 22
Average status children, 443, 451
Avoidant attachment, 236–237
Axons, 143–145

Babbling, 201, 205
Babytalk, 205
Bayley Scales of Infant Development, 164
Behavior problems, 242, 248, 392, 444–445, 514–515, 537. See also Adjustment problems
Behavior theory, 231–233
and attachment, 231–233
Bidirectional effects, 233, 279, 352
Birth place, 107
alternative birthing center, 109
homebirth, 107–109
hospital birthing rooms, 109
Birth plan, 106
Birth process. See Labor
Bleeding, in the brain, 128
Blindness, 170
Body image, 374
Body proportion, in infancy, 141
Body type, 373–375
Bonding, 212, 228–229
Bottle feeding, 142
Bradley method, 110–111
Brain, 143–148
development and experience, 146–148
structures of, 145–146
Breastfeeding, 142–143, 161
and AIDS, 81

Canonical babbling, 202, 205
Cardiovascular disease, risk of, 264–265
Careers in child development
child life specialist, 272–273
corporate day-care director, 322
developmental specialist, 131
elementary school principal, 414
genetic counselor, 96
Head Start teacher, 325
high school teacher, 498
infant care director, 249
inner-city teacher, 416–417
marriage and family therapist, 463
prevention counselor, 532
research scientist, 45
school psychologist, 382
Catecholamines, 121
Causal reasoning, 296–297
Centration, 32, 293
Cephalocaudal principle, 71, 141
Cesarean delivery, 80, 111, 119–121
Cheating, 501–503
Child abuse, 216, 278. See also Maltreatment
Childbirth
certified nurse-midwife, 107–108
due date, 105
lay midwife, 107
preparing for, 104–113
without fear, 110
Chorionic villus sampling, 99
Chromosomal abnormalities, 93–95, 383
Down syndrome, 93–94, 383
Fragile X syndrome, 95, 383
Klinefelter's syndrome, 94–95
Triple X syndrome, 95
Turner syndrome, 95
Chromosomes, 85
Chunking, 36
Cigarette smoking, and the fetus, 76–77, 127
Circadian sleep pattern, 134
Circumcision, 161
Classical conditioning, 23–24, 180
Classification, 297–299, 401–402
Class inclusion, 401–402
Cliques, 509–511
Cocaine, 78
Coercion theory, 344–345
Cognitive development
in adolescence, 491–494
classification, 401–402
concrete operations, 397–399
day care and, 321
in early childhood, 290–311
explanations of, 304–306
facilitation at home, 320
5-to-7 shift, 397–398
in infancy, 184–195

in middle childhood, 396–412
moral reasoning and, 402–406
parents and, 318–319
Cognitive-developmental theory, 29–34. *See also* Piaget's theory
Cognitive emotions theory, 212–213
Cognitively Oriented Curriculum, 323, 325
Cognitive structures, 30
Colic, 39
Collective monologue, 313
Colostrum, 142
Compensatory preschools, 323–326
Comprehension (language), 196
Conception, 66–67
female reproductive system, 66–67
male reproductive sysetem, 67
Concrete operations, 33, 397–399
Conflict, 339–341
Conscience, 403
Conservation, 300–301, 399–401
training of, 401
Continuity/discontinuity, 17, 397
Contraception, 517
Contractions, 113
Controversial children, 443
Conventional moral reasoning, 405, 500
Conversation, 203, 206, 313–314
Cooing, 201, 205
Coordinated secondary circular reactions, 192, 195
Counting, 302–303
Counting-all strategy, 428
Counting-on strategy, 428
Couvade, 244
Covariance, 51
Critical periods, 17, 38, 71, 77, 228–229
Cross-cultural comparisons of infants, 124
Crossing over, 87–88
Crowds, 509–511
Cultural influences, 226, 242–243, 520–521
Cytomegalovirus (CMV), 81, 269

Data gathering methods, 49–50
analogues, 50
event sampling, 49
experimental tasks, 50
interviews, 50
time sampling, 49
Dating, 516–519
Day care, 246–250, 321–322
illness, 267–269
risk and opportunity, 321, 323
Deafness, 201
Decentering, 399
Deception, 311
Decoding, 423–425
Deferred imitation, 195, 291
Delinquency, 444, 534–537
and attention deficit disorder, 536–537
developmental pathway to, 536
prevention of, 537

Dendrites, 143–144
Denver Developmental Screening Test, 164
Deprivation dwarfism, 284
Depth perception, 156–158
DES (diethylstilbestrol), 75
Development, concept of, 3–6
Dexterity, 167
Dieting. *See* Eating disorders
Digo of East Africa, 260
Dilation, 113
Disability, 381–393
behavior problems and, 392–393
parenting and, 389–393
social support for, 390–391
See also Special needs
Discipline, 282
Discrete emotions theory, 212–214
Discrimination, 149, 158–160
Disorganized/disoriented attachment, 238–239
Display rules, 219–220, 364
Distar, 326
Distractability, 78
Divorce, 461
gender differences, 463–464
helping children cope, 464–465
DNA, 85–88
Dominance, 345–348
Dominance hierarchy, 346
Dominant-recessive diseases, 90–93
PKU (phenylketonuria), 90–91
sickle-cell anemia, 91–93
Tay-Sachs, 91
Dominant-recessive principle, 89–90
heterozygous condition, 89
homozygous condition, 89
Down syndrome, 77, 93–94
Dropping out, 456
Dyscalcula, 430–431
Dyslexia, 425–427

Early amniocentesis, 99
Eating disorders, 483–487
anorexia nervosa, 484–485
bulimia, 485–486
coping with, 487
Ecosystem, 5–6
abuse and, 279–280
Egocentric speech, 313–314
Egocentrism, 294–295, 399. *See also* adolescent egocentrism
Ego ideal, 356, 403
Elaboration, 408
Electra complex, 356
Electronic fetal monitoring, 118
Emotional development
in early childhood, 363–366
in infancy, 210–222
masking emotions, 363–365
reading emotions, 365–366
theories of, 212–214

Emotional signals, 216–219
Emotions, management of, 441
Empathy, 353
Engrossment, 244
Enmeshment, 486–487
Enrichment. *See* Sensory enrichment
Environmental influences, on prenatal development, 74–82
Epidural block, 115, 119
Estradiol, 474
Ethical issues, and prenatal development, 100–101
Ethological theory, 37–40
attachment and, 233–234
critical periods, 38
fixed action patterns, 38
imitation and, 184
imprinting, 38
reflexes, 37, 162
Evolution, 37
Exercise and pregnancy, 84–85
Expansion (language), 199
Expertise, 410
Extinction, 25
Extrinsic motivation, 420–421
Eye, structures of, 152

Facilitation, 9–10, 129, 170–173, 186, 188, 190, 192, 193, 194, 204–206, 308–309, 409, 421, 442
and attention, 308–309
and cognitive development, 320
and early language, 204–206
and friendship, 442
and intrinsic motivation, 421
and memory strategies, 409
and motor control, 170–173
Family
and eating disorders, 486–487
and maltreatment, 285
parenting styles, 349–351
Fast-mapping, 203, 205
expressive style, 203
referential style, 203
Fathering, 244–246, 467
Fetal alcohol effects, 77
Fetal alcohol syndrome (FAS), 77
Fetal blood sampling, 118–119
Fetal distress, 111, 117–119
causes of, 118
electronic fetal monitoring, 118
fetal blood sampling, 118–119
Fetal monitoring, 113
Figure-ground separation in infant object perception, 153–155
5-to-7 shift, 397–398
Fixation, 149–151
Fixed action patterns, 38
Fontanels, 122
Foreclosure, 525

Formal operations, 33, 492–494
    and moral reasoning, 500
Fragile X syndrome, 77, 95
Freud, Sigmund. *See* Psychoanalytic theory
Friendship
    in adolescence, 513–514
    in early childhood, 337–339
    facilitatiion of, 442
    in middle childhood, 439–442
    peer reputation and, 441
    social comparison and, 439–441
Fuzzy logic, 502

Gateway substances, 529–530
Gender constancy, 355
Gender identity, 355
Gender intensification hypothesis, 497
Gender roles, 355–363
    parental influences, 358, 360
    peer influences, 360–363
    theories of, 355–358
        cognitive-developmental, 356–357
        gender schema, 357–358
        psychoanalytic, 356
        social learning, 356
Gender segregation, 361–363
Genes, 85
Genetic counseling, 95–97
Genetic influences, 85–101, 224
Genetic screening, 95–100
Genetic therapy, 100
Genetic transmission, 89–95
    alleles, 89
    homologous pairs, 89
Genotype, 86–87
    reaction range, 87
Gestures, 202–203, 205
    performatives, 202
    pointing, 203
Gifted and talented children, schooling of,
    431–432
Goodness-of-fit, 225
Gossip, 440–441
Grammar, 312–313
Grammatical morphemes, 312
Growth, 256–257
Growth retardation, 76, 78–79, 127, 284

Habituation, 151, 178–179
    and intelligence, 178–179
Handicap. *See* Disability; Special needs
Harvard Preschool Project, 317–318
Hatching, 226
Head Start, 324
Height, 140–141
Helplessness, 182
Hemophilia, 93
Hereditary mechanisms, 85–89
    chromosomes, 85
    crossing over, 87–88
    meiosis, 87
    mitosis, 87

Heroin, 78
Herpes, and pregnancy, 80
Heterozygous, 89
High-amplitude sucking, 151
HIV. *See* AIDS
Holophrase, 204–205
Home birth, 107–109
HOME scale, 318–319
Homologous pairs of chromosomes, 89
Homozygous, 89
Hospital birthing rooms, 109
Hostile aggression, 341–342
Hyperactivity, 78, 383–386, 444
Hypertonia, 386
Hypothetico-deductive reasoning, 492
Hypotonia, 386

Identification, 356
Identity, 521–527
    commitment, 523–527
    exploration, 523–527
    minority teenagers, 526–527
    role confusion and, 522
    sense of, 522
    See also Identity status
Identity-achieved status, 524–525
Identity status
    achieved status, 524–525
    diffused status, 524–525
    foreclosure, 525
    moratorium, 525
Illness, 267–269
    negative effects of, 267
    positive effects of, 268, 270
Images, 194
Imaginary audience, 494–496
Imitation, 191, 199. *See also* Observational
    learning
Immanent justice, 270, 404
Imprinting, 38
Induction, 119
Indulgent-permissive parenting, 349–350
Infancy, definition of, 139
Infant mortality, 126
Infant sleep, 333
    circadian sleep pattern, 134
    nonrapid eye movement (NREM)
        sleep, 134
    rapid eye movement (REM) sleep, 134
Infant states, 124, 133
Infant stimulation, 133
Infertility, 68–69
    female, 68–69
    male, 69
    timing of intercourse, 169–170
Information processing theory, 34–37,
    306–309
    attention, 306–307
    memory, 35–36, 184–186, 307–309
Inner speech, 316
Institutions, effects of, 316–317

Instrumental aggression, 341–342
Internal working model, 234, 238
Intrinsic motivation, 420–421
    facilitation of, 421
Intuitive reasoning, 397–398
Invulnerability and AIDS, 490
Irreversibility, 294–296, 399

Juvenile delinquency. *See* Delinquency

Kipsigi, 170–171
Klinefelter's syndrome, 94–95

Labor, 113–122
    assisting of, 119–121
        cesarean delivery, 119–121
        forceps, 119–120
        vacuum extraction, 119–120
    complications of, 119–121
        artificial rupture of membranes, 119
        induction, 119
    fetal monitoring, 117–119
    medication, 115–117
    stages of, 113–115
Lamaze method, 110
Language acquisition device (LAD), 200
Language development
    comprehension, 196
    conversation, 313–314
    in early childhood, 311–316
    egocentric speech, 313
    facilitation of, 204–206
    first word combinations, 204–205
    grammar, 312–313
    holophrase, 204
    in infancy, 196–206
    modeling and imitation, 199
    morphology, 196
    naming, 203–204
    nativist explanation of, 200
    phonology, 196
    pragmatics, 197, 313
    prespeech, 201–203
    private speech, 315–316
    production, 196
    reinforcement and shaping, 198–199
    risk and opportunity, 317–319
    semantics, 196–197
    social context, 316–317
    social speech, 313–314
    stages of, 201–204
    syntax, 197
    telegraphic speech, 204
    theories of, 197–200
    vocabulary, 312
Latchkey (self-care) children, 465–466
Learning, in infancy, 178–184
    classical conditioning, 180
    habituation, 178
    observational learning, 182–184
    operant conditioning, 180–183

Learning theory, 23–27. *See also* Behavior theory
Least restrictive environment, 387
Leboyer technique, 11
Libido, 19
Limited capacity, 407–408
Locomotion, 166–167
Loneliness, 452–454
Looking chamber, 150
Look-say, 422–423
Low birth weight, 83, 126–133
    long-term effects, 128–130
    prenatal care and, 132–133
    preterm, 126, 221
    prevention of, 132–133
    respiratory distress syndrome, 127
    risk factors for, 132–133
    small-for-date, 126–127, 221
    survival, 127–128

Mainstreaming, 388
Maltreatment, 239, 277–286
    abuse cycle, 282–283
    and attachment, 283
    causes of, 279–280
    child characteristics, 280–281
    community and, 279, 282, 285
    culture and, 285
    and discipline, 282
    ecosystem perspective, 279–280, 283
    intergenerational effects, 281
    maternal deprivation syndrome, 284
    parent-child relationship, 283–284
    by parents, 281–284
    prevention, 285–286
Manual control, 167–169
Marking time, 258
Masking, 365
Mastery, 181–182, 189–190, 199
Maternal employment, 244–245, 465–467
Math anxiety, 430
    prevention of, 430–431
Mathematics, 427–431
Mathematics disability, 430–431
Mathematics strategies, 428–429
    counting-all, 428
    counting-on, 428
    fact retrieval, 429
Matthew effects, 427
Maturation, 18
Mediational deficiency, 409
Meiosis, 87, 93
Memory, 35–36, 184–186, 307–309
    in early childhood, 307–309
    encoding, 184
    facilitation of, 308
    in infancy, 184–186
    long-term memory, 185–186
    recall, 184
    retrieval, 184
Memory strategies, 308, 408–409
    facilitation of, 409

Menarche, 476
Mental retardation, 381, 383
Metacognition, 308, 410–412
Method of evoked potentials, 151
Methylphenidate, 385
Mindreading, 309
Min strategy, 429
Miscarriage, 81
Mitosis, 87
Modeling, 184, 199, 344. *See also* Observational learning
Moderate to vigorous physical activity (MVPA), 378–379
Monologue, 313
Moral realism, 403
Moral reasoning, 402–406
    in adolescence, 500–503
    facilitation of, 405, 503
    formal operations, 500
    theories of, 402–404
Moratorium, 525
Morphemes, 196
Morphology, 196
Motherese, 205
Motor control
    in early childhood, 257–262
        climbing, 258
        construction skills, 262
        hopping, 258
        jumping, 258
        running, 258
        self-help: grooming and feeding, 259
        self-help: toilet training, 260–261
        walking, 257–258
    in infancy, 160–172
        facilitating motor control, 170–172
        locomotion, 166–167
        manual control, 167–169
        posture, 165–166
        self-help skills, 169
        transactional perspective, 169–170
Multiple handicaps, 386
Mutual regulation, 22, 220–221
MVPA, 378–379
Myelin sheath, 144–145

Naming, 203–204
Natural selection, 37
Nature-nurture, 17–18
Neat pincer grasp, 167
Negative attributional bias, 447
Neglect, 278
Neglected children, 443–445, 454–455
Neonatal Behavioral Assessment Scale (NBAS), 124–126, 161
Neonate, 124–128
    assessment by the Brazelton scale (NBAS), 124–126
    intensive care, 128
Neural tube defects, 99–100
Neurons, 143–146

Neurotransmitters, 143
Newborn, 122–133
    evaluation of, Apgar scale, 123–124
    physical features, 122, 140–141
New York Longitudinal Study, 223–225
Nonorganic failure to thrive (NOFT), 284
Nonrapid eye movement (NREM) sleep, 134
Number, 300–301
Nursery school, 320–321
Nutrition
    during infancy, 142–143
    during pregnancy, 83–84

Obesity, 263
Object permanence, 191–195
Observational learning, 28, 182–184, 343–344
Obstetrician, 107
Oedipal conflict, 21
Operant conditioning, 25–27, 180–183
Optimal stimulation, 178, 205, 221
Organization, 408
Overachievement, 422–423
Overprotection, and eating disorders, 486
Overregularizing, 313

Pain, 161
Parent-infant transactions, 128–129, 216–222, 225
Parenting styles, 349–351
Patterning, 148
Peer pressure, 508–513
    coping with, 513
Peer relationships
    in adolescence, 507–513
    in early childhood, 336–348
        aggression, 341–345
        conflict, 339–341
        dominance, 345–348
        friendship, 337–339
        social preference, 336–337
    in middle childhood, 439–458
Peer reputation, 441
Perception
    in infancy, 149–161
        pain, 161
        smell, 160–161
        study of, 149–151
            habituation procedure, 151
            high-amplitude sucking, 151
            looking chamber, 150
            method of evoked potentials, 151
            visual preference method, 150
        taste, 160
        touch, 161
    See also Auditory perception
Personal fable, 495–496
Phallic stage, 356
Phenotype, 86–87, 89
Phonemic awareness, 423–427
Phonics, 423–425
Phonology, 196

Physical development
  in adolescence, 473–491
  in middle childhood, 373–375
Physical fitness, 262–267
  athletics, 379–380
  cardiovascular disease, 265
  in early childhood, 265–266
  facilitation of, 266–267
  in middle childhood, 377–381
  obesity, 263
  physical education, 378–379
Piaget's theory, 29–34
  accommodation, 31, 305
  adaptation, 31, 187
  assimilation, 31, 305
  causal reasoning, 296
  centration, 32, 293
  classification, 298–299
  cognitive structures, 30
  concrete operations, 33
  coordination of secondary schemas,
      192, 195
  egocentrism, 294–295
  experiments in order to see, 193
  formal operations, 33, 492–494
  images, 194–195
  imitation, 192, 193, 195
  irreversibility, 294–296
  object permanence, 191–195
  preconcepts, 293
  preoperational stage, 32–33, 290–296
  primary circular reactions, 189, 195
  quantitative reasoning, 300–301
  schemas, 31, 187–188
  secondary circular reactions, 189–190, 195
  sensorimotor stage, 31–32, 186–195
  symbolic reasoning, 32, 194–195, 291–292
  tertiary circular reactions, 193, 195
  transductive reasoning, 293–296
PKU (phenylketonuria), 90–91
Plasticity, 147, 148
Play-game skills, gender differences in,
    375–377
Playgrounds, 275
Pleasure principle, 19
Popular children, 443–444, 449, 458
Popularity, 338, 452, 455, 458, 480, 512
Positive energy balance, 263
Postconventional moral reasoning, 405, 500
Postmature, 126
Posture, 165–166, 187
Pragmatics, 197
Preconcepts, 293
Preconventional moral reasoning, 404, 500
Pre-eclampsia, 126
Prenatal care, 83–84, 132–133
Prenatal development, 70–74
  period of the embryo, 71
  period of the fetus, 72–74
  period of the zygote, 70–71
Prenatal diagnosis, 97–100
  alpha fetoprotein testing, 99

  amniocentesis, 99
  chorionic villus sampling, 99
  ultrasound, 97–98
Preoperational stage, 32–33, 290–296
Prepared childbirth, 110–112
  birth partner, 110
  Bradley method, 110–111
  childbirth without fear, 110
  Lamaze method, 110
Prepping, 109
Prespeech, 201–203
Preterm birth, 78, 83, 126
Primary circular reactions, 189, 195
Primary sex characteristics, 476–477
Private speech, 315–316
Problem of the match, 307, 326
Production, of language comprehension,
    196
Production deficiency, 409
Prosocial behavior
  in early childhood, 353–355
  empathy and, 460–461
  facilitation of, 354–355
  in middle childhood, 458–461
Prosocial moral reasoning, 459–461
  facilitation of, 461
Proximodistal principle, 71, 141
Pseudodialogues, 203
Psychoanaltyic theory, 18–23
  attachment, 233
  aggression, 342–343
  eating disorders, 487
  Erikson's, 21–23
  Freud's, 19–21
  gender roles, 356
  libido, 19
  oedipal conflict, 21
  pleasure principle, 19
  psychodynamics, 20
  psychosexual development, 20–22
  psychosocial development, 21–22
  reality principle, 20
Puberty, 473–481
  adolescent growth spurt, 474–477
  coping with, 480
  hormones, 474
  maturational timing, 476–481, 518
Punishment, 25, 345, 350, 354

Quantitative reasoning, 299–303
  facilitation of, 302–303

Rapid eye movement (REM) sleep, 134
Reaction range, 87
Reactivation procedure, 185
Reading, 421–427
  learning by look-say, 422–423
  learning by phonics, 423–425
  reading strategies, 426
Reading disability, 425–427
Recasting, 199
Reflective reasoning, 449

Reflexes, 37, 161–164, 188
  exercise and, 162
  neurological assessment, 162–164
Regular Education Initiative (REI), 388
Rehearsal, 36, 408
Reinforcement, 25, 180–181, 184, 185,
    198–199
Reinforcement trap, 344–345
Rejected children, 443–445, 447–456
Rejection
  in adolescence, 514–515
  later adjustment and, 455–456
  loneliness, 452–454
  long-term effects of, 456
  maturational timing and, 479
  short-term effects of, 455–456
  social learned helplessness and, 457–458
Research design, 51–54
  correlational, 51–52
  cross-sectional, 54
  cross-sequential, 54
  experimental, 53
  longitudinal, 54
Research process, 46–57
  accessing scholarly research, 57–58
  developing hypotheses, 48
  ethical considerations, 58
  minitheory, 46–47
  operational definitions, 48
  reporting results, 56–57
  research problem, the, 46
  target behavior, 46
Resilience, 8–9, 121, 129, 147, 462
Respiratory distress syndrome (RDS), 127
Respite, 391
Rhythmical movement stereotypies,
    164–165
Risk and opportunity, 6–9, 37, 317–319, 321,
    332, 380, 455, 514
Ritalin, 385
Rough-and-tumble play, 244, 362
Rubella, 80

Scaffolding, 306
Schemas, 31, 187–195
Schooling, 412–432
  of African American children, 415–417
  and culture, 416–419
  effective schools, 413
  of the gifted and talented, 432
  of minorities, 413, 415
  and parents, 415–419
Scientific method, 42–43
  objectivity, 42
  reliability, 43
  validity, 43
Scripts, 289, 313
Seatbelts, 270–271
Secondary circular reactions, 189–190, 195
Secondary sex characteristics, 476–477
Secure attachment, 236
Secure base, 234

Self, 226–228
Self-concept, 28, 358, 427, 455
Self-help skills, 169
Self-regulation, 124, 133
Semantics, 196–197
Sensitive care, 238, 240, 244
Sensitive periods, 228. *See also* Critical periods
Sensorimotor stage, 31–32, 188–195
Sensory deprivation, 147, 170, 173
Sensory enrichment, 147–148, 170, 172–173
Separation anxiety, 235
Serial monogamists, 516, 518
Sex chromosome, 88–89
Sex determination, 88–89
Sex-linked inheritance, 93
Sexual abuse, 278, 280–281. *See also* Maltreatment
Sexual adventurers, 518
Sexual debut, 516
Sexually transmitted diseases, 487–491
Sexual maturity, 476–477
Sexual relationships, 516–521
    biological influences, 518
    cultural influences, 520–521
Shaping, 25, 219
Sickle-cell anemia, 91–93, 99, 127
Skeletal deformity, 386
Small-for-date, 126–127
Smell, 160–161
Smooth pursuit movements, 153
Social cognition, 456–458
Social cognitive theory, 27–29, 199
    aggression and, 343–345
    gender roles and, 356
Social comparison, 439–441
Social competence, 242, 331, 347–353
    attachment and, 348
    and childrearing, 348–350
    direct influences on, 350–353
    indirect influences, 348–350
    neighborhoods and, 350
    and parents, 348–353
        parental monitoring, 352
        parental social planning, 351–352
Social development in infancy, 227–248
Social information processing, 445–452
    enacting the response, 450–451
    facilitation of, 450, 452
    generating responses, 448–449
    interpreting social cues, 446–448
    selecting optimal responses, 449–450
    social learned helplessness, 457–458
Social participation, 332–333
Social play, 332–334
Social preference, 336–337
    measurement of, 337

Social pretend play, 333–336, 339
    facilitation of, 335–336
Social speech, 313–314
Social status
    in adolescence, 514
    in early childhood, 337
    facilitation of, 445
    in middle childhood, 442–445
Sociodramatic play, 313
Somatotype, 373–375
Special education
    least restrictive environment, 387
    mainstreaming, 388
    Regular Education Initiative (REI), 388
Special needs, 380–393
    and education, 386–389
Spermarche, 476
Sports. *See* Athletics
State regulation, 133
Stepfamilies, 461, 464
Stillbirth, 81
Stranger anxiety, 215
Strange Situation, The, 236–237, 239
Stress
    coping with, 277
    and illness, 275–277
    and pregnancy, 82–83
    and suicide, 276–277
Substance abuse
    prevention, 531–532
    risk factors, 530–531
Suicidal ideation, 533–534
Suicide
    in adolescence, 533–534
    in preschoolers, 276–277
    risk factors, 534
Superego, 403
Surfactant, 121, 127
Symbolic function, 291–292
    mental images, 293
    pretend play, 291–292
    symbolic representation, 194
Symbolic reasoning, 32
Sympathy, 460–465
Synapse, 143, 146
Synchrony, 221, 238
Syntax, 197

Talented, 431–432
Taste, 160
Tay-Sachs disease, 91, 99
Telegraphic speech, 204
Television, 264
Temperament, 222–226
    attachment and, 241

culture and, 226
    dimensions of, 224–225
Teratogens, 74–82
    alcohol, 77–78
    cigarette smoking, 76–77
    maternal diseases, 80–82
    medications, 74–75
    narcotics, 78–79
Tertiary circular reactions, 189–190, 195
Testosterone, 474
Theory, role of, 14–16
Theory of mind, 309–311
    facilitation of, 311
Toilet training, 260–261
Touch, 161
Toxemia, 126
Toxoplasmosis, 81–82
Transactional perspective, 4–5, 28, 128–129, 139, 169–170, 216, 279, 385
Transductive reasoning, 293–296
Trauma, 21
Triple X syndrome, 95
Trust, 22
Turner syndrome, 95
Type A behavior, 422–423

Ultrasound, 97–98
Utilization deficiency, 409

Variance, 51
Visual cliff, 156–157
Visually directed reaching, 169
Visually initiated reaching, 169
Visual perception
    of depth, 156–158
    of faces, 155
    of objects, 153–155
    tracking objects, 153
Visual preference method, 150
Vocabulary, 203–204, 312
Vulnerability, 9, 77, 128, 317
Vygotsky's theory, 305–306
    inner speech, 316
    scaffolding, 305–306
    zone of proximal development, 305–306, 323

Walkers, 157–158
Weight, 140–141
Wellness, in adolescence, 481–491
WIC, 83–85

Zone of proximal development, 305–306, 323